Format for Bank Reconciliation:

Cash balance according to bank statement		$XXX
Add: Additions by company not on bank statement	$XXX	
Bank errors	XXX	XXX
		$XXX
Deduct: Deductions by company not on bank statement	$XXX	
Bank errors	XXX	XXX
Adjusted balance		$XXX

Cash balance according to company's records		$XXX
Add: Additions by bank not recorded by company	$XXX	
Company errors	XXX	XXX
		$XXX
Deduct: Deductions by bank not recorded by company	$XXX	
Company errors	XXX	XXX
Adjusted balance		$XXX

Inventory Costing Methods:

- First-in, First-out (FIFO)
- Last-in, First-out (LIFO)
- Average Cost

Interest Computations:

$$\text{Interest} = \text{Face Amount (or Principal)} \times \text{Rate} \times \text{Time}$$

Methods of Determining Annual Depreciation:

Straight-Line: $\dfrac{\text{Cost} - \text{Estimated Residual Value}}{\text{Estimated Life}}$

Double-Declining-Balance: Rate* × Book Value at Beginning of Period

*Rate is commonly twice the straight-line rate (1 ÷ Estimated Life).

Adjustments to Net Income (Loss) Using the Indirect Method:

	Increase (Decrease)
Net income (loss)	$ XXX
Adjustments to reconcile net income to net cash flow from operating activities:	
Depreciation of fixed assets	XXX
Amortization of intangible assets	XXX
Losses on disposal of assets	XXX
Gains on disposal of assets	(XXX)
Changes in current operating assets and liabilities:	
Increases in noncash current operating assets	(XXX)
Decreases in noncash current operating assets	XXX
Increases in current operating liabilities	XXX
Decreases in current operating liabilities	(XXX)
Net cash flow from operating activities	$ XXX
	or
	$(XXX)

Contribution Margin Ratio $= \dfrac{\text{Sales} - \text{Variable Costs}}{\text{Sales}}$

Break-Even Sales (Units) $= \dfrac{\text{Fixed Costs}}{\text{Unit Contribution Margin}}$

Sales (Units) $= \dfrac{\text{Fixed Costs} + \text{Target Profit}}{\text{Unit Contribution Margin}}$

Margin of Safety $= \dfrac{\text{Sales} - \text{Sales at Break-Even Point}}{\text{Sales}}$

Operating Leverage $= \dfrac{\text{Contribution Margin}}{\text{Income from Operations}}$

Variances:

$$\begin{array}{l}\text{Direct Materials} \\ \text{Price Variance}\end{array} = \left(\begin{array}{l}\text{Actual Price} - \\ \text{Standard Price}\end{array}\right) \times \text{Actual Quantity}$$

$$\begin{array}{l}\text{Direct Materials} \\ \text{Quantity Variance}\end{array} = \left(\begin{array}{l}\text{Actual Quantity} - \\ \text{Standard Quantity}\end{array}\right) \times \begin{array}{l}\text{Standard} \\ \text{Price}\end{array}$$

$$\begin{array}{l}\text{Direct Labor} \\ \text{Rate Variance}\end{array} = \left(\begin{array}{l}\text{Actual Rate per Hour} - \\ \text{Standard Rate per Hour}\end{array}\right) \times \text{Actual Hours}$$

$$\begin{array}{l}\text{Direct Labor} \\ \text{Time Variance}\end{array} = \left(\begin{array}{l}\text{Actual Direct Labor Hours} - \\ \text{Standard Direct Labor Hours}\end{array}\right) \times \begin{array}{l}\text{Standard Rate} \\ \text{per Hour}\end{array}$$

$$\begin{array}{l}\text{Variable Factory} \\ \text{Overhead Controllable} \\ \text{Variance}\end{array} = \begin{array}{l}\text{Actual Variable} \\ \text{Factory} \\ \text{Overhead}\end{array} - \begin{array}{l}\text{Budgeted Variable} \\ \text{Factory Overhead}\end{array}$$

$$\begin{array}{l}\text{Fixed Factory} \\ \text{Overhead} \\ \text{Volume} \\ \text{Variance}\end{array} = \left(\begin{array}{l}\text{Standard Hours for} \\ \text{100\% of Normal} \\ \text{Capacity}\end{array} - \begin{array}{l}\text{Standard} \\ \text{Hours for} \\ \text{Actual Units} \\ \text{Produced}\end{array}\right) \times \begin{array}{l}\text{Fixed Factory} \\ \text{Overhead} \\ \text{Rate}\end{array}$$

Return on Investment (ROI) $= \dfrac{\text{Income from Operations}}{\text{Invested Assets}}$

Alternative ROI Computation:

$$\text{ROI} = \dfrac{\text{Income from Operations}}{\text{Sales}} \times \dfrac{\text{Sales}}{\text{Invested Assets}}$$

Capital Investment Analysis Methods:

Methods That Ignore Present Values:

- Average Rate of Return Method
- Cash Payback Method

Methods That Use Present Values:

- Net Present Value Method
- Internal Rate of Return Method

Average Rate of Return $= \dfrac{\text{Estimated Average Annual Income}}{\text{Average Investment}}$

Present Value Index $= \dfrac{\text{Total Present Value of Net Cash Flow}}{\text{Amount to Be Invested}}$

Present Value Factor for an Annuity of $1 $= \dfrac{\text{Amount to Be Invested}}{\text{Equal Annual Net Cash Flows}}$

The Warren/Reeve/Duchac Family

The Warren/Reeve/Duchac Family of solutions provides a host of options to fit your exact teaching style—all with an integrated technology solution.

Sole Proprietorship Approach

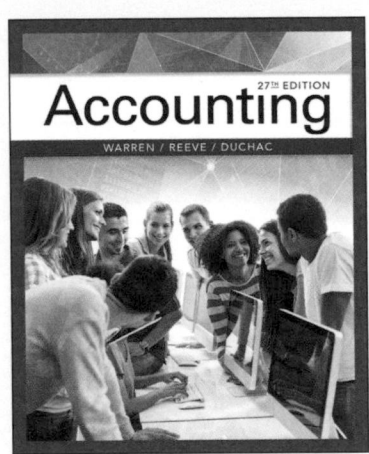

- 26 Chapters
- 65% Financial Accounting/
  35% Managerial Accounting

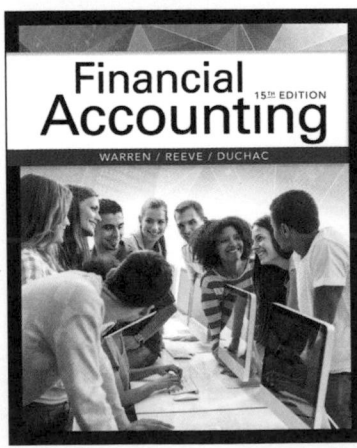

- Financial Chapters 1–17 from
  Accounting, 27e

Corporate Approach

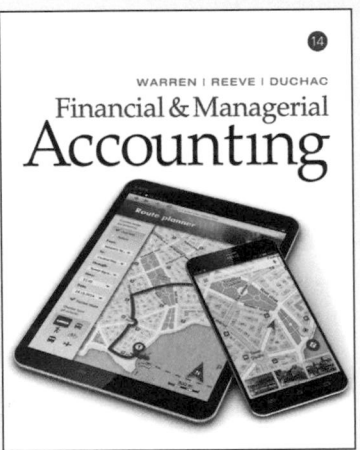

- 26 Chapters
- 50% Financial Accounting/
  50% Managerial Accounting

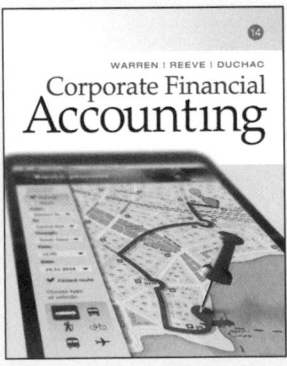

- Chapters 1–14
  from *Financial &
  Managerial
  Accounting, 14e*

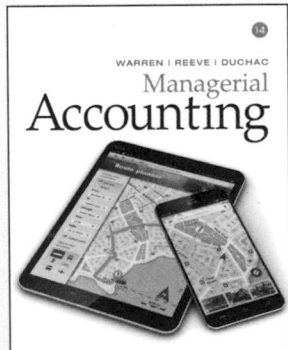

- Chapters 13–26
  from *Financial &
  Managerial
  Accounting, 14e*

Managerial
Accounting 14e

Carl S. Warren
Professor Emeritus of Accounting
University of Georgia, Athens

James M. Reeve
Professor Emeritus of Accounting
University of Tennessee, Knoxville

Jonathan E. Duchac
Professor of Accounting
Wake Forest University

CENGAGE
Learning®

Australia • Brazil • Japan • Korea • Mexico • Singapore • Spain • United Kingdom • United States

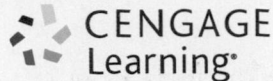

Managerial Accounting, 14e

Carl S. Warren
James M. Reeve
Jonathan E. Duchac

Senior Vice President, General Manager, Social Sciences, Humanities, and Business: Erin Joyner

Executive Product Director: Mike Schenk

Product Director: Jason Fremder

Senior Product Manager: Matt Filimonov

Content Development Manager: Daniel Celenza

Senior Content Developer: Diane Bowdler

Product Assistant: Audrey Jacobs

Executive Marketing Manager: Robin LeFevre

Marketing Program Manager: Eileen Corcoran

Senior Digital Production Project Manager: Jessica Robbe

Senior Digital Content Specialist: Tim Ross

Senior Content Project Manager: Tim Bailey

Manufacturing Planner: Doug Wilke

Production Service: Cenveo Publisher Services, Inc.

Senior Art Director: Michelle Kunkler

Cover Designer: cmillerdesign

Internal Designer: Ke Design

Intellectual Property
    Analyst: Brittani Morgan
    Project Manager: Betsy Hathaway

© 2018, 2016 Cengage Learning®

ALL RIGHTS RESERVED. No part of this work covered by the copyright herein may be reproduced or distributed in any form or by any means, except as permitted by U.S. copyright law, without the prior written permission of the copyright owner.

For product information and technology assistance, contact us at **Cengage Learning Customer & Sales Support, 1-800-354-9706**

For permission to use material from this text or product, submit all requests online at **www.cengage.com/permissions** Further permissions questions can be emailed to **permissionrequest@cengage.com**

Unless otherwise noted, all items are © Cengage Learning.

Microsoft Excel® is a registered trademark of Microsoft Corporation. © 2016 Microsoft.

Library of Congress Control Number: 2016949723

Student Edition ISBN: 978-1-337-27059-5
Loose-Leaf Edition ISBN: 978-1-337-27071-7

Cengage Learning
20 Channel Center Street
Boston, MA 02210
USA

Cengage Learning is a leading provider of customized learning solutions with employees residing in nearly 40 different countries and sales in more than 125 countries around the world. Find your local representative at **www.cengage.com**.

Cengage Learning products are represented in Canada by Nelson Education, Ltd.

To learn more about Cengage Learning Solutions, visit **www.cengage.com**

Purchase any of our products at your local college store or at our preferred online store **www.cengagebrain.com**

Printed in Canada
Print Number: 01   Print Year: 2016

Roadmap for Success

Warren/Reeve/Duchac *Managerial Accounting, 14e,* makes it easy for you to give students a solid foundation in managerial accounting. Warren/Reeve/Duchac covers the fundamentals AND motivates students to learn by showing how accounting is important to a business.

Warren/Reeve/Duchac is successful because it reaches students with a combination of new and tried-and-tested pedagogy.

This revision includes a range of exciting new and existing features that help Warren/Reeve/Duchac provide students with the context to see how accounting is valuable to business. These include:

- New! Schema
- New! Links to Business
- New! Why It Matters
- New! Analysis for Decision Making & Make a Decision
- New! Accounting Equation Impacts added beside journal entries

Warren/Reeve/Duchac also includes a thorough grounding in the fundamentals that any business student will need to be successful. These key features include:

- Presentation style designed around the way students learn
- New! Check Up Corner
- New! Let's Review

Hallmarks of the revision include:

- At the start of each chapter, **a schema, or roadmap, shows students what they are going to learn and how it is connected to the larger picture.** The schema illustrates how the chapter content lays the foundation with managerial concepts and principles. Then it moves students through developing the information and ultimately into evaluating and analyzing information in order to make decisions.

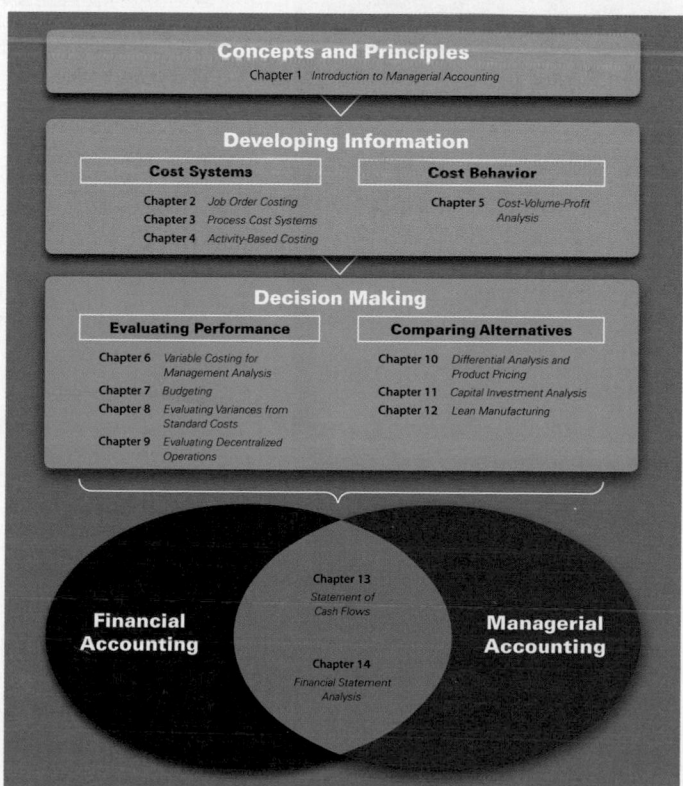

> "I do a similar thing in class mapping out where they are in the book. I generally use a balance sheet and mark it up like a 'map at the mall and you are here.' This does a similar thing."
>
> — Patricia Worsham, California State Polytechnic University, Pomona

> "The schema shows the 'big picture.' It connects all the chapters. Students need help seeing the big picture and the connection."
>
> — Gloria Sanchez, Mt. San Jacinto College

- **Link to the "opening company" of each chapter** calls out examples of how the concepts introduced in the chapter are connected. **This shows how accounting is used in the real world by real companies.**

Anyone can apply for and open a **Cold Stone Creamery** franchise. The company provides help in picking a location, constructing or leasing a building, and training employees. The initial franchise fee is $27,000, and it costs $250,000 to $400,000 to build and equip a store. The company receives a royalty fee of 6% and an advertising fee of 3% of gross sales.

Link to Cold Stone Creamery

Cold Stone Creamery

Have you ever had to request service repairs on an appliance at your home? The repair person may arrive and take five minutes to replace a part. Yet, the bill may indicate a minimum charge for more than five minutes of work.

Why might there be a minimum charge for a service call? The answer is that the service person must charge for the time and expense of coming to your house. In a sense, the bill reflects two elements of service: (1) the cost of coming to your house and (2) the cost of the repair. The first portion of the bill reflects the time required to "set up" the job. The second part of the bill reflects the cost of performing the repair. The setup charge will be the same, whether the repairs take five minutes or five hours. In contrast, the actual repair charge will vary with the time on the job.

Like the repair person, companies must be careful that the cost of their products and services accurately reflects the different activities involved in producing the product or service. Otherwise, the cost of products and services may be distorted and lead to improper management decisions.

To illustrate, **Cold Stone Creamery**, a chain of super premium ice cream shops, uses activity-based costing to determine the cost of its ice cream products, such as cones, mixings, cakes, frozen yogurt, smoothies, and sorbets. The costs of activities, such as scooping and mixing, are added to the cost of the ingredients to determine the total cost of each product. As stated by Cold Stone's president:

"...it only makes sense to have the price you pay for the product be reflective of the activities involved in making it for you."*

In this chapter, three different methods of allocating factory overhead to products are described and illustrated. In addition, product cost distortions resulting from improper factory overhead allocations are discussed. The chapter concludes by describing activity-based costing for selling and administrative expenses and its use in service businesses.

*Quote from "Experiencing Accounting Videos," Activity-Based Costing. © Cengage Learning, 2008.

Source: www.coldstonecreamery.com

149

■ NEW! Located early in each chapter, **Why It Matters** shows students how accounting is important to businesses with which they are familiar.

Why It Matters

Advanced Robotics

Boston Consulting Group (BCG) believes the use of advanced robotics in manufacturing is about to take off. It estimates that by 2025, 25% of all tasks will be automated through robotics, driving a 10–30% increase in productivity. China, the United States, Japan, Germany, and South Korea will be the primary drivers of this trend. BCG anticipates significant use of advanced robotics will have a number of important impacts on manufacturing:

■ Robotics reduces the need to move factories to low-labor cost countries to save costs.

■ Robotics will reduce the size of manufacturing facilities, allowing for greater flexibility and a more regional focus.

■ The economic costs of robotics will decline, opening up their broad use.

■ The workforce will require new skills, such as programming and technical maintenance, to support robotic manufacturing. For example, **Shenzhen Everwin Precision Technology** recently announced plans to replace 90% of its 1,800 employees with advanced robotics in the near future. The remaining employees will be retrained to work with the robots.

Increasing use of robots will cause direct labor to go down, while factory overhead will increase. As a result, accurate factory overhead allocation will become increasingly important in these advanced manufacturing environments.

Source: Boston Consulting Group, *"The Shifting Economics of Global Manufacturing: How a Takeoff in Advanced Robotics Will Power the Next Productivity Surge,"* February 2015.

"These features show students the relevance to the business world of what they are learning and so should help motivate them to learn."

— *Steven J. LaFave, Augsburg College*

"It does a good job of bringing the materials into a 'real world' environment."

— *Bob Urell, Irvine Valley College*

■ To aid comprehension and to demonstrate the impact of transactions, **journal entries include the net effect of the transaction on the accounting equation.**

A summary of the materials requisitions is used as a basis for the journal entry recording the materials used for the month. For direct materials, this entry increases (debits) Work in Process and decreases (credits) Materials as follows:

$A = L + E$
$+ \; -$

B.	Work in Process	13,000	
	Materials		13,000
	Materials requisitioned to jobs		
	($2,000 + $11,000).		

Many companies use computerized information processes to record the use of materials. In such cases, storeroom employees electronically record the release of materials, which automatically updates the materials ledger and job cost sheets.

■ To aid learning and problem solving, throughout each chapter new **Check Up Corners** provide students with step-by-step guidance on how to solve problems. Problem-solving tips help students avoid common errors.

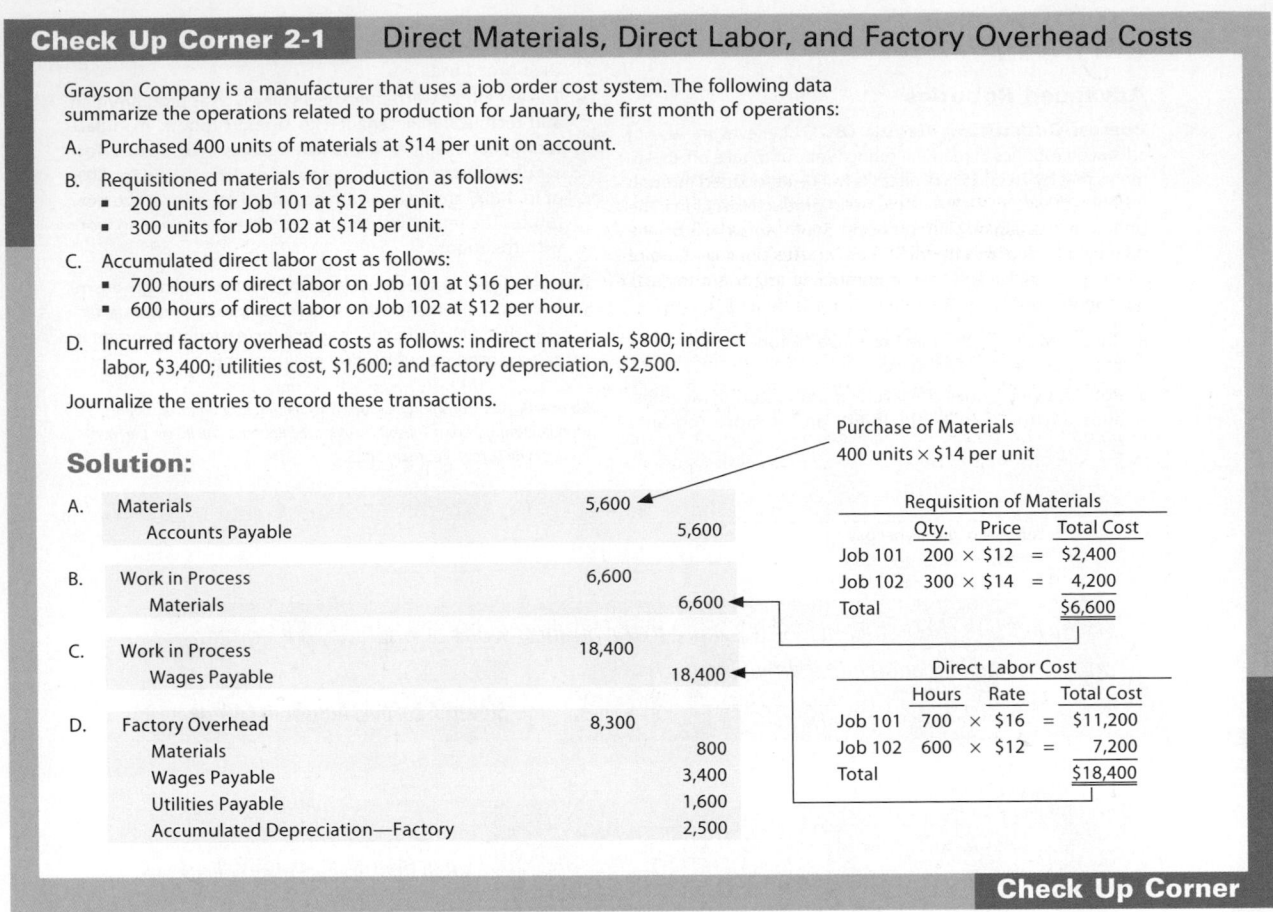

Check Up Corner 2-1   Direct Materials, Direct Labor, and Factory Overhead Costs

Grayson Company is a manufacturer that uses a job order cost system. The following data summarize the operations related to production for January, the first month of operations:

A. Purchased 400 units of materials at $14 per unit on account.

B. Requisitioned materials for production as follows:
   ■ 200 units for Job 101 at $12 per unit.
   ■ 300 units for Job 102 at $14 per unit.

C. Accumulated direct labor cost as follows:
   ■ 700 hours of direct labor on Job 101 at $16 per hour.
   ■ 600 hours of direct labor on Job 102 at $12 per hour.

D. Incurred factory overhead costs as follows: indirect materials, $800; indirect labor, $3,400; utilities cost, $1,600; and factory depreciation, $2,500.

Journalize the entries to record these transactions.

Solution:

Purchase of Materials
400 units × $14 per unit

A.	Materials	5,600	
	Accounts Payable		5,600

Requisition of Materials

	Qty.	Price	Total Cost
Job 101	200 × $12	=	$2,400
Job 102	300 × $14	=	4,200
Total			$6,600

B.	Work in Process	6,600	
	Materials		6,600

C.	Work in Process	18,400	
	Wages Payable		18,400

Direct Labor Cost

	Hours	Rate	Total Cost
Job 101	700 × $16	=	$11,200
Job 102	600 × $12	=	7,200
Total			$18,400

D.	Factory Overhead	8,300	
	Materials		800
	Wages Payable		3,400
	Utilities Payable		1,600
	Accumulated Depreciation—Factory		2,500

Check Up Corner

"These are good, I like the step-by-step approach. I also like it when it reinforces concepts before the solution begins."

— *Pam Neely, The College at Brockport, SUNY*

"I like giving students the opportunity to self-test themselves for mastery of this material …. I would use this tool for each major area in the chapter."

— *Lawrence A. Roman, Cuyahoga Community College*

- In each chapter, **Analysis for Decision Making** highlights how businesses use accounting information to make decisions and evaluate the health of a business. This provides students with context of why accounting is important to a business.

Analysis for Decision Making

Nonmanufacturing Staffing Levels

Objective

Describe and illustrate the use of staffing budgets for nonmanufacturing businesses.

The budgeting illustrated in this chapter is similar to budgeting used for nonmanufacturing businesses. However, many nonmanufacturing businesses often do not have direct materials purchases budgets, direct labor cost budgets, or factory overhead cost budgets. Thus, the budgeted income statement is simplified in many nonmanufacturing settings.

A primary budget in nonmanufacturing businesses is the labor, or staffing, budget. This budget, which is highly flexible to service demands, is used to manage staffing levels. For example, a theme park will have greater staffing in the summer vacation months than in the fall months. Likewise, a retailer will have greater staffing during the holidays than on typical weekdays.

To illustrate, Concord Hotel operates a hotel in a business district. The hotel has 150 rooms that average 120 guests per night during the weekdays and 50 guests per night during the weekend. The housekeeping staff is able to clean 10 rooms per employee. The number of housekeepers required for an average weekday and weekend is determined as follows:

	Weekday	Weekend
Number of guests per day	120	50
Rooms per housekeeper	÷ 10	÷ 10
Number of housekeepers per day	12	5

If each housekeeper is paid $15 per hour for an eight-hour shift per day, the annual budget for the staff is as follows.

	Weekday	Weekend	Total
Number of housekeepers per day	12	5	
Hours per shift	× 8	× 8	
Days per year	× 260*	× 104**	
Number of hours per year	24,960	4,160	
Rate per hour	× $15	× $15	
Housekeeping staff annual budget	$374,400	$62,400	$436,800

* 52 weeks × 5 days
** 52 weeks × 2 days

The budget can be used to plan and manage the staffing of the hotel. For example, if a wedding were booked for the weekend, the budgeted increase in staffing could be compared with the increased revenue from the wedding to verify the profit plan.

- Following the Analysis for Decision Making segment, students have an opportunity to apply their knowledge in making decisions.

Make a Decision   **Nonmanufacturing Staffing Levels**

Johnson Stores is planning its staffing for the upcoming holiday season. From past history, the store determines that it needs one additional sales clerk for each $12,000 in daily sales. The average daily sales is anticipated to increase by $96,000 from Black Friday until Christmas Eve, or 27 shopping days. Each additional sales clerk will work an eight-hour shift and will be paid $14 per hour.

A.   Determine the amount to budget for additional sales clerks for the holiday season.
B.   If Johnson Stores has an average 40% gross profit on sales, should it add the staff suggested by your answer in A? That is, is it profitable to staff for the increased sales in A?

Solution:

A.

Average daily revenue	$96,000
Revenue per clerk	÷12,000
Number of additional sales clerks	8
Hours per day per clerk	× 8
Number of hours per day	64
Number of shopping days	× 27
Number of hours	1,728
Rate per hour	× $14
Holiday staff budget for additional clerks	$24,192

B.

Johnson Stores should add the staff because it will be profitable.

Increase in daily revenue	$ 96,000
Gross profit percentage	× 40%
Increase in daily gross profit	$ 38,400
Number of shopping days	× 27
Additional gross profit	$1,036,800
Staff budget increase [from (A)]	(24,192)
Additional profit	$1,012,608

Make a Decision

"I like the explanation of how to calculate the ratio and the way it's demonstrated how to calculate McDonald's – the presentation is clear and concise. Then, I really like the clear and concise answer to 'Is 1.1 efficient?' Ex 14 is great. I like the Make a Decision feature so students get to practice right away. Overall, a great section."

– Barbara Muller, Arizona State University

"This encourages students to think about how the material relates to the real world and makes them realize that the information is being collected so decisions can be made."

– Sue Cunningham, Rowan Cabarrus Community College

■ At the end of each chapter, **Let's Review** is a new chapter summary and self-assessment feature that is designed to help busy students prepare for an exam. It includes a summary of each learning objective's key points, key terms, multiple-choice questions, exercises, and a sample problem that students may use to practice.

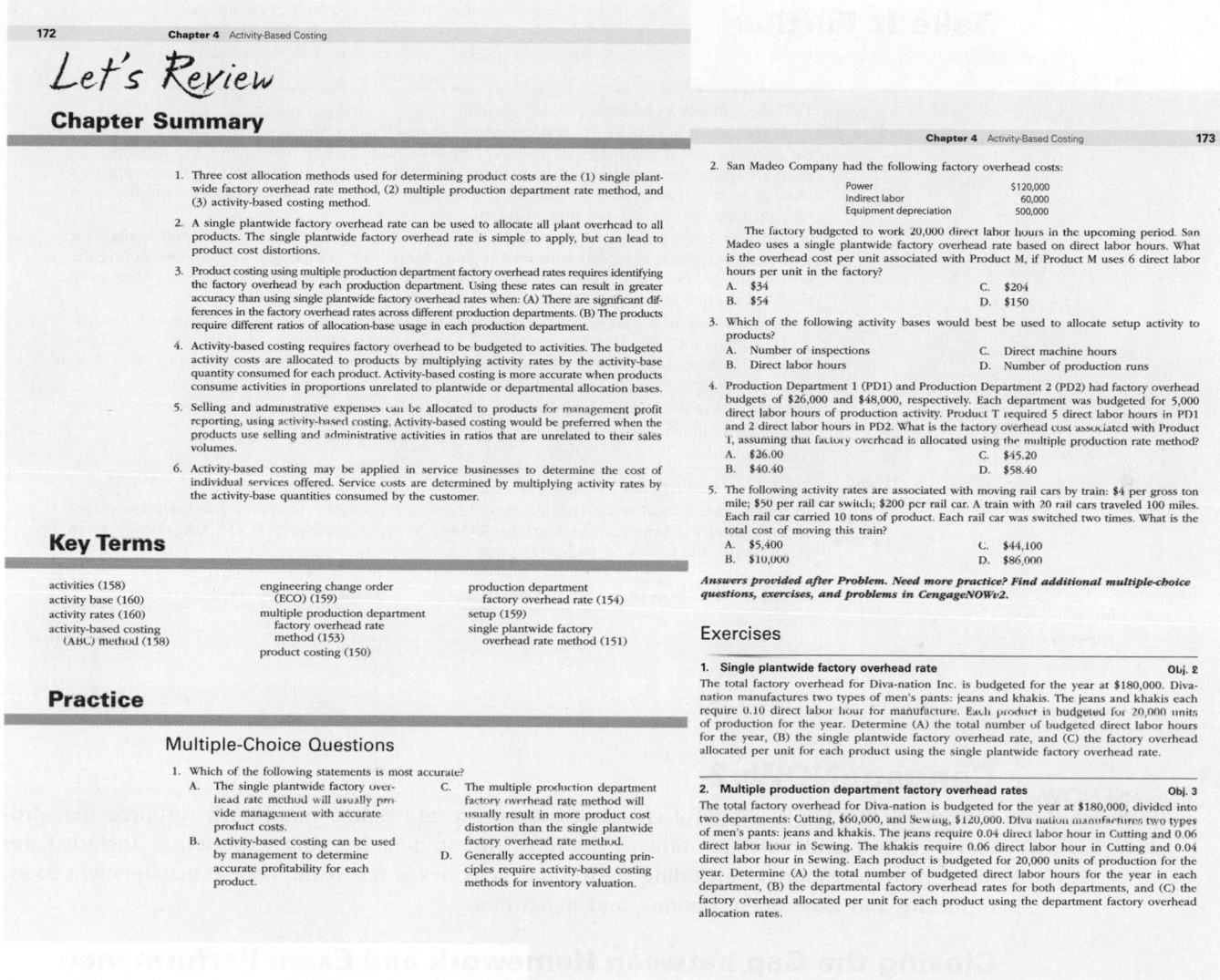

■ Sample multiple-choice questions allow students to practice with the type of assessments they are likely to see on an exam.
■ Short exercises and a longer problem allow students to apply their knowledge.
■ **Answers** provided at the end of the Let's Review section let students check their knowledge immediately.
■ Algorithmic practice activities in the accompanying CengageNOWv2 allow students to regenerate a practice activity at will.

"I like the idea that they're within the chapter and immediately after the specific chapter topic. Also, they're easy and promote a sense of accomplishment and understanding in the student."

— John Seilo, Irvine Valley College

■ **Take It Further** in the end-of-chapter activities allows instructors to assign other special activities related to ethics, communication, and teamwork.

Take It Further

TIF 1-1   Ethics in Action

Avett Manufacturing Company allows employees to purchase materials, such as metal and lumber, for personal use at a price equal to the company's cost. To purchase materials, an employee must complete a materials requisition form, which must then be approved by the employee's immediate supervisor. Brian Dadian, an assistant cost accountant, then charges the employee an amount based on Avett's net purchase cost.

Brian is in the process of replacing a deck on his home and has requisitioned lumber for personal use, which has been approved in accordance with company policy. In computing the cost of the lumber, Brian reviewed all the purchase invoices for the past year. He then used the lowest price to compute the amount due the company for the lumber.

The Institute of Management Accountants (IMA) is the professional organization for managerial accountants. The IMA has established four principles of ethical conduct for its members: honesty, fairness, objectivity, and responsibility. These principles are available at the IMA Web site: www.imanet.org.

➤ Using the IMA's four principles of ethical conduct, evaluate Brian's behavior. Has he acted in an ethical manner? Why?

TIF 1-2   Team Activity

In teams, visit a local restaurant. As you observe the operation, consider the costs associated with running the business. As a group, identify as many costs as you can and classify them according to the following table headings:

Cost	Direct Materials	Direct Labor	Overhead	Selling Expenses

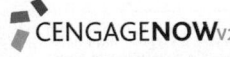

CengageNOWv2

CengageNOWv2 is a powerful course management and online homework resource that provides control and customization to optimize the student learning experience. Included are many proven resources, including algorithmic activities, a test bank, course management tools, reporting and assessment options, and much more.

Closing the Gap between Homework and Exam Performance

Many students perform well on homework but struggle when it comes to exams. Now, with the new Blank Sheet of Paper Experience, students must problem-solve on their own, just as they would if taking a test on a blank sheet of paper.

Blank Sheet of Paper Experience

A less-leading Blank Sheet of Paper Experience discourages overreliance on the system.

■ Instructors may choose between Learning Problems that guide student learning via drop-down menus, or they may use Blank Sheet of Paper problems.

■ In Blank Sheet of Paper items, students must refer to the Chart of Accounts and decide for themselves which account is impacted.

■ The number of accounts in each transaction is not given away.

■ Whether the account should be debited or credited is not given away.

■ Transactions may be entered in any order (as long as the entries are correct).

■ Check My Work feedback only reports on what students have actually attempted, which prevents students from "guessing" their way through the assignment.

Unprecedented Flexibility

In addition to Blank Sheet of Paper activities, instructors also have the option of assigning—or using in class for demonstration purposes—learning assignments that guide student learning via specially designed drop-down menus. Instructors can now carefully tailor their assignments to the needs of their students at that moment.

Multi-Panel View

The new Multi-Panel View in CengageNOWv2 enables students to see all the elements of a problem on one screen.

- Students make connections and see the tasks as connected components in the accounting process.
- Dramatically reduced scrolling eliminates student frustration.

With the ability to move and resize journals, ledgers, forms, and financial statements, it is easier to navigate the problem and understand the accounting system.

Adaptive Feedback

Adaptive Feedback in CengageNOWv2 responds to students based upon their unique answers and alerts them to the type of error they have made without giving away the answer.

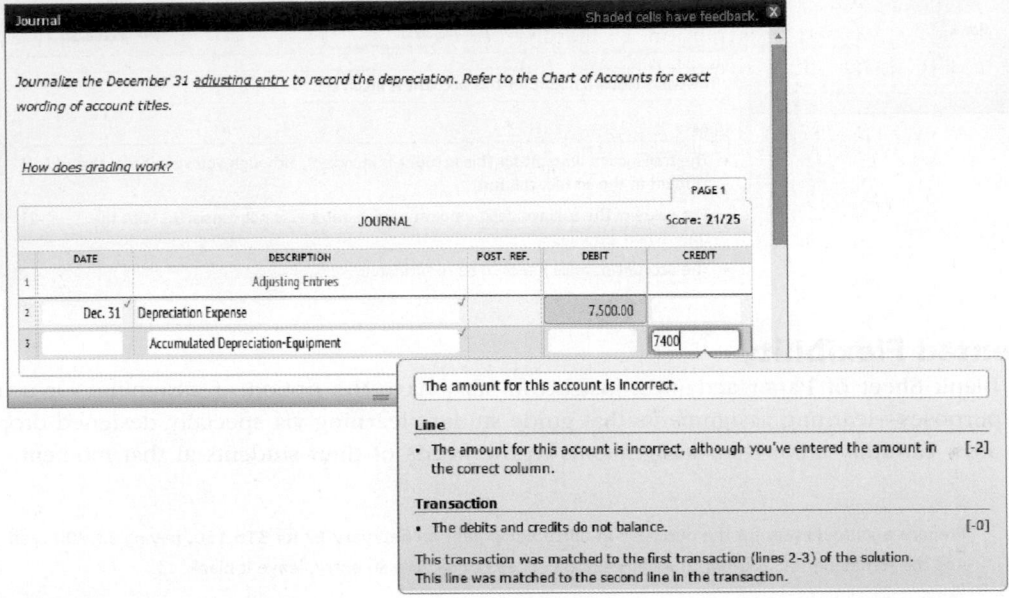

In addition to groundbreaking, adaptive feedback, CengageNOWv2 continues to provide multiple layers of guidance to keep students on track and progressing.

- **Check My Work Feedback** provides general guidance and hints as students work through homework assignments.
- **Check My Work Feedback** in CengageNOWv2 now only reports on what students have actually attempted, which prevents them from "guessing" their way through assignments.
- **Explanations** are available after the assignment has been submitted and provide a detailed description of how the student should have arrived at the solution.

Motivation: Set Expectations and Prepare Students for the Course

CengageNOWv2 helps motivate students and get them ready to learn by reshaping their misconceptions about the introductory accounting course and providing a powerful tool to engage students.

CengageNOWv2 Start-Up Center

Students are often surprised by the amount of time they need to spend outside of class working through homework assignments in order to succeed. The CengageNOWv2 Start-Up Center will help students identify what they need to do and where they need to focus in order to be successful with a variety of new resources.

- What Is Accounting? Module ensures students understand course expectations and how to be successful in the introductory accounting course. This module consists of two assignable videos: *Introduction to Accounting* and *Success Strategies*. The Student Advice Videos offer advice from real students about what it takes to do well in the course.
- Math Review Module, designed to help students get up to speed with necessary math skills, includes math review assignments and Show Me How math review videos to ensure that students have an understanding of basic math skills, including:
  - Whole number operations
  - Decimal operations and rounding
  - Percentage operations and conversion
  - Fraction operations
  - Converting numbers expressed in one form to a different form
  - Positive and negative numbers
  - Ratios and averages
- How to Use CengageNOWv2 Module focuses on learning accounting, not on a particular software system. Quickly familiarize your students with CengageNOWv2 and direct them to all of its built-in student resources.

Motivation: Prepare Them for Class

With all the outside obligations accounting students have, finding time to read the textbook before class can be a struggle. Point students to the key concepts they need to know before they attend class.

- **Video: Tell Me More.** Short Tell Me More lecture activities explain the core concepts of the chapter through an engaging auditory and visual presentation. Available either on a stand-alone basis or as an assignment, they are ideal for all class formats—flipped model, online, hybrid, or face-to-face.

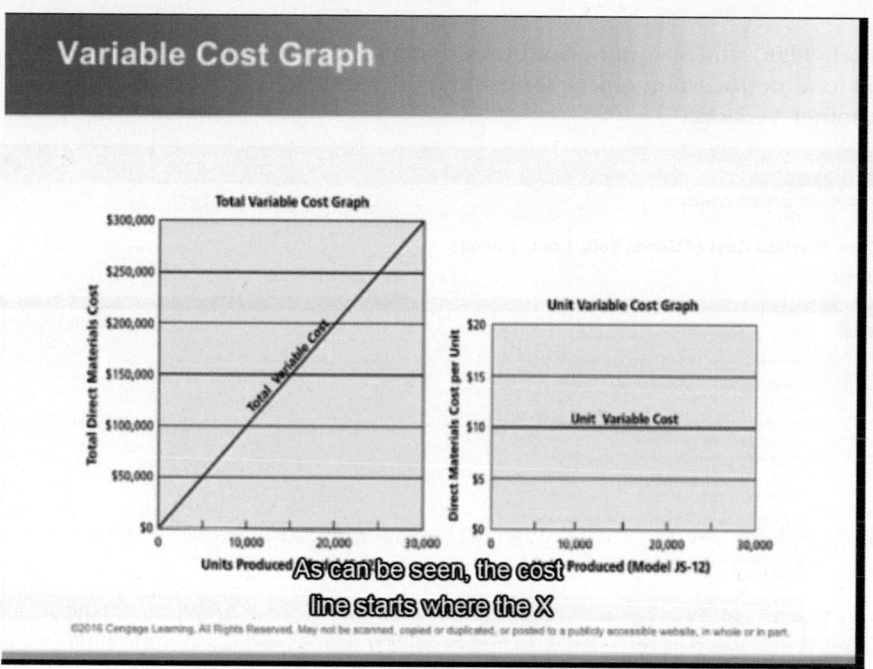

- **NEW Adaptive Study Plan** in CengageNOWv2 is an assignable/gradable study center that adapts to each student's unique needs and provides a remediation pathway to keep students progressing. With the NEW Adaptive Study Plan, they can focus on learning new topics and fully understanding difficult concepts.

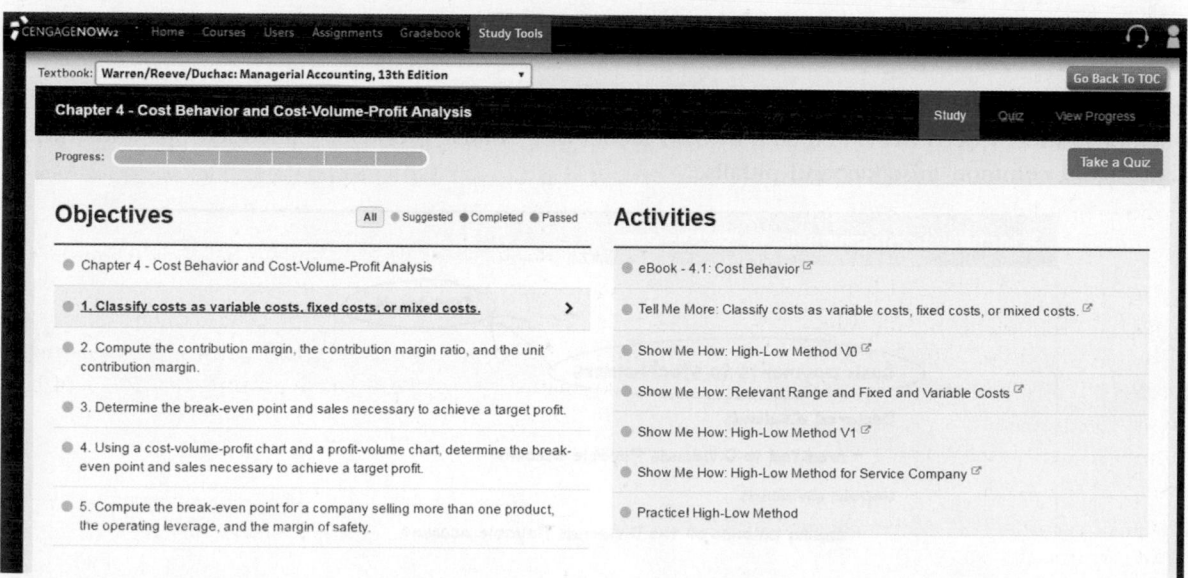

How Does It Work?

Step 1: Students take a chapter-level quiz consisting of random questions that cover both conceptual and procedural aspects of the chapter.

Step 2: Feedback is provided for each answer option explaining why the answer is right or wrong.

Step 3: Based on the quiz results, students are provided a remediation path that includes media assets and algorithmic practice problems to help them improve their understanding of the course material.

Instructors may use prerequisites that require students to achieve mastery in the Adaptive Study Plan before moving on to new material.

Using the Adaptive Study Plan, students may also review and check their knowledge with the new Practice! Activities. These items (generally one per learning objective) build application skills by allowing students to complete practice problems and "Try Another Version."

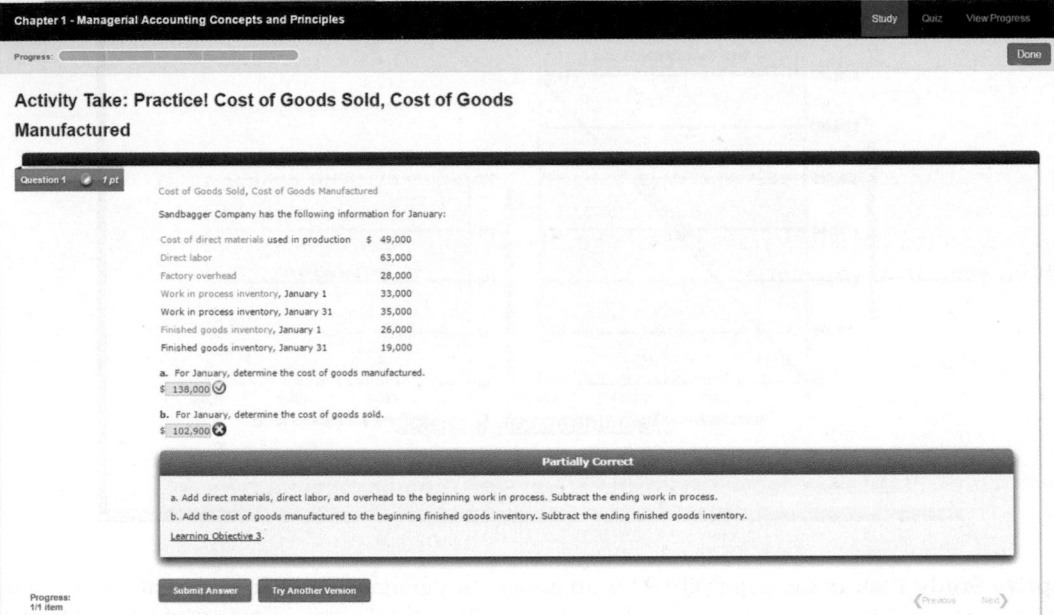

Provide Help Right When Students Need It

The best way to learn accounting is through practice, but students often get stuck when attempting homework assignments on their own.

■ **Video: Show Me How.** Created for the most frequently assigned end-of-chapter items, NEW Show Me How problem demonstration videos provide a step-by-step model of a similar problem. Embedded tips and warnings help students avoid common mistakes and pitfalls.

SHOW ME HOW

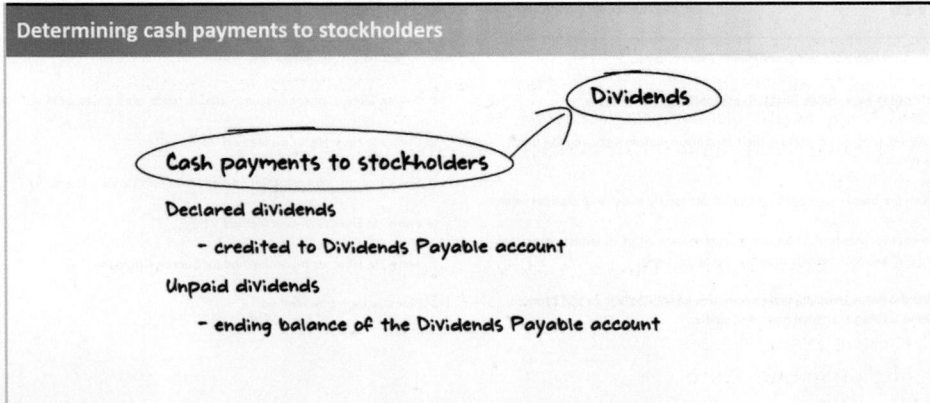

Help Students Go Beyond Memorization to True Understanding

Students often struggle to understand how concepts relate to one another. For most students, an introductory accounting course is their first exposure to both business transactions and the accounting system. While these concepts are already difficult to master individually, their combination and interdependency in the introductory accounting course often pose a challenge for students.

- **Mastery Problems.** New Mastery Problems enable you to assign problems and activities designed to test students' comprehension and mastery of difficult concepts.
- **Dynamic Exhibits.** To overcome this gap, the authors have created a series of interactive Dynamic Exhibits that allow students to change the variables in a scenario and see how a change ripples through the accounting system. Dynamic Exhibits allow students to see connections and relationships like never before.

DYNAMIC
EXHIBIT

Insight into Your Class Performance

With CengageNOWv2's new Gradebook Analytics, you have an unprecedented insight into your students' performance. You may view class results not only on an aggregate assignment or item basis, but also on the basis of a variety of criteria. These include book objectives, Bloom's Taxonomy, AICPA standards, and more!

Class Aggregate Report

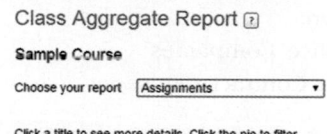

Sample Course

Choose your report   Assignments

Click a title to see more details. Click the pie to filter.

Assignment	Due Date	Class Average	# of Students Completed
Assignment 1	July 6, 2016, 12:00 AM	81%	11 / 13
Assignment 2	July 6, 2016, 12:00 AM	77%	11 / 13
Assignment 7	October 31, 2015, 12:00 AM	0%	1 / 13
Chapter 2 - ASP	September 11, 2017, 12:00 AM	0%	1 / 13
Exam	October 16, 2015, 12:00 AM	36%	1 / 13
test	October 29, 2017, 12:00 AM	25%	1 / 13

1 - 6 displayed, 6 in total

● 0% - 69.99%   ● 70% - 79.99%   ● 80% - 89.99%   ● 90% - 100%

Other features of Gradebook Analytics include:

- Ability to drill into both aggregate class performance and individual student performance.
- Preview items and view score distribution on that item.
- View at a glance summary information for a particular class, assignment, or item.

MindTap eReader

The MindTap eReader for Warren/Reeve/Duchac's *Managerial Accounting* is the most robust digital reading experience available. Hallmark features include:

- Fully optimized for the iPad.
- Note taking, highlighting, and more.
- Embedded digital media.
- The MindTap eReader also features ReadSpeaker®, an online text-to-speech application that vocalizes, or "speech-enables," online educational content. This feature is ideally suited for both instructors and learners who would like to listen to content instead of (or in addition to) reading it.

GENERAL LEDGER

Cengage Learning General Ledger Software (CLGL)

CLGL exposes students to computerized accounting software without teaching the specifics of a certain software system—preparing students for *any* software program they might encounter in the real world.

- Available in CengageNOWv2, CLGL allows students to work through end-of-chapter assignments and practice sets in a format that emulates commercial general ledger software, but in a manner that is more forgiving of errors.
- Assignments are automatically graded online.
- Selected problems that can be solved using CLGL are designated by an icon in the textbook and are listed in the assignment preparation grid in the Instructor's Manual.

New to This Edition

In this edition, we have reorganized the sequence of the chapters. Activity-Based Costing (Chapter 4) now follows Process Cost Systems (Chapter 3). Additionally, in all chapters, the following improvements have been made:

- Added schema at beginning of each chapter shows students how the chapter material fits within the overall textbook. Students follow the schema as they move through developing information and ultimately into evaluating and analyzing information in order to make decisions.
- Updated dates and real company information for currency
- Added "Link to" for the opening company to interweave real-world references throughout each chapter
- Added margin accounting equation impact for journal entries
- Refreshed end-of-chapter assignments with different numerical values and updated information
- Replaced the following:
  - "Financial Analysis and Interpretation" with "Analysis for Decision Making" followed by an exercise "Make a Decision"
  - "Business Connection" articles with "Why It Matters"
  - "Integrity, Objectivity, and Ethics in Business" articles with "Ethics: (Don't) Do It!"
  - "Example Exercises" with "Check Up Corner" boxes throughout chapter
  - "At a Glance" summaries with "Let's Review" while retaining key points
  - "Illustrative Problems" with "Practice" which includes multiple-choice questions, exercises, problems, and related answers
  - "Practice Exercises" with "Basic Exercises"
  - "Cases & Projects" with "Take It Further"

Chapter 1

- Revised chapter title
- New chapter opener on Gibson Guitars
- Added Links to Gibson Guitars throughout chapter
- Added new Learning Objective on Sustainability and Accounting Information
- Added "Why It Matters" on:
  - Line and Staff for Service Companies
  - Not According to Plan: Contract Clauses
  - Overhead Costs
  - Service Companies and Product Costs
- Added "Check Up Corner" boxes on:
  - Management Process
  - Manufacturing Operations
  - Manufacturing Financial Statements
- Added Analysis for Decision Making section on measuring utilization for a service company with related end-of-chapter assignments
- Added Take It Further section with assignments involving ethics, teams, and communication

Chapter 2

- New chapter opener on Gibson Guitars
- Added Links to Gibson Guitars throughout chapter
- Added in the margin the impact of each journal entry on the accounting equation
- Added "Why It Matters" on:
  - 3D Printing
  - Advanced Robotics
  - Job Order Costing in Hollywood
- Added "Check Up Corner" boxes on:
  - Direct Materials, Direct Labor, and Factory Overhead Costs
  - Applying Overhead and Determining Job Cost
  - Job Order Costing for a Service Business
- Added Analysis for Decision Making section on using job order costing information for decision making with related end-of-chapter assignments

- Added Take It Further section with assignments involving ethics, teams, and communication

Chapter 3

- Added Links to Dreyer's Ice Cream throughout chapter
- Added "Why It Matters" on:
  - Sustainable Papermaking
  - Cost of Gasoline
- Added "Check Up Corner" boxes on:
  - Equivalent Units
  - Cost per Equivalent Unit
  - Process Costing Journal Entries
- Added Analysis for Decision Making section on using cost of production reports with related end-of-chapter assignments
- Added Take It Further section with assignments involving ethics, teams, and communication

Chapter 4

- Chapter 11 in previous edition
- Revised chapter title
- Added Links to Cold Stone Creamery throughout chapter
- Added "Why It Matters" on:
  - Activity-Based Costing in the Public Sector
  - $600 Hammer (Cost Allocation Distortion)
- Added "Check Up Corner" boxes on:
  - Single Plantwide Factory Overhead Rate
  - Multiple Production Department Factory Overhead Rates
  - Activity-Based Costing: Factory Overhead Costs
  - Activity-Based Costing for a Service Business
- Added Analysis for Decision Making section on using ABC to reduce costs with related end-of-chapter assignments
- Added Take It Further section with assignments involving ethics, teams, and communication

Chapter 5

- Chapter 4 in previous edition
- Revised chapter title
- Added Links to Ford Motor Company throughout chapter
- Added "Why It Matters" on:
  - Variable Cost for Home and Business
  - Booking Fees
- Added "Check Up Corner" boxes on:
  - Cost Behavior
  - Contribution Margin
  - Break-Even Sales and Target Profit
  - Special Cost-Volume-Profit Relationships
- Added Analysis for Decision Making section on using cost-volume-profit analysis for service companies with related end-of-chapter assignments

- Removed the Variable Costing Appendix
- Added Take It Further section with assignments involving ethics, teams, and communication

Chapter 6

- Chapter 5 in the previous edition
- Added Links to Adobe Systems Incorporated throughout chapter
- Added "Why It Matters" on:
  - Business Segments
  - Eastman Revenue Price and Volume Effects
- Added "Check Up Corner" boxes on:
  - Absorption and Variable Costing Income Statements: Production Greater than Sales
  - Absorption and Variable Costing Income Statements: Different Levels of Production
  - Contribution Margin by Segment
  - Contribution Margin Analysis
- Added Analysis for Decision Making section on using segment analysis and EBITDA with related end-of-chapter assignments
- Added Take It Further section with assignments involving ethics, teams, and communication

Chapter 7

- Chapter 6 in previous edition
- Added Links to Hendrick Motorsports throughout chapter
- Added "Why It Matters" on Advertising Budget
- Added "Check Up Corner" boxes on:
  - Flexible Budget
  - Direct Materials, Direct Labor, and Cost of Goods Sold Budget
  - Cash Budget
- Added Analysis for Decision Making section on using staffing budgets for nonmanufacturing businesses with related end-of-chapter assignments
- Added Take It Further section with assignments involving ethics, teams, and communication

Chapter 8

- Chapter 7 in previous edition
- Revised chapter title
- Added Links to BMW Group throughout chapter
- Added "Why It Matters" on The Lesson of Moneyball
- Added "Check Up Corner" boxes on:
  - Direct Materials and Direct Labor Cost Variances
  - Factory Overhead Cost Variances
  - Income Statement with Variances
- Added Analysis for Decision Making section on using direct labor time variance in evaluating staff performance in a service business with related end-of-chapter assignments

- Added Take It Further section with assignments involving ethics, teams, and communication

Chapter 9

- Chapter 8 in previous edition
- Revised chapter title
- Added Links to Caterpillar Inc. throughout chapter
- Added "Why It Matters" on:
  - Dover Corporation: Many Pieces, One Picture
  - Coca-Cola Company Expansion
- Added "Check Up Corner" boxes on:
  - Cost Center Responsibility Measures
  - Profit Center Responsibility Reporting
  - Investment Center Performance Measures
  - Transfer Pricing
- Added Analysis for Decision Making section on whether a company should franchise its operations with related end-of-chapter assignments
- Added Take It Further section with assignments involving ethics, teams, and communication

Chapter 10

- Chapter 9 in previous edition
- Added Links to Facebook, Inc. throughout chapter
- Added a "Why It Matters" on Dynamic Pricing
- Added "Check Up Corner" boxes on:
  - Differential Analysis
  - Setting Product Selling Prices
- Added Analysis for Decision Making section on the use of yield pricing in service businesses with related end-of-chapter assignments
- Added Take It Further section with assignments involving ethics, teams, and communication

Chapter 11

- Chapter 10 in previous edition
- Added Links to Vail Resorts, Inc. throughout chapter
- Added "Check Up Corner" boxes on:
  - Capital Investment Analysis Not Using Present Value
  - Net Present Value and Internal Rate of Return Analyses
  - Net Present Value—Unequal Lives
- Added Analysis for Decision Making section on using capital investment analysis in evaluating a sustainability investment with related end-of-chapter assignments
- Added Take It Further section with assignments involving ethics, teams, and communication

Chapter 12

- Revised chapter title
- Added Links to Precor Incorporated throughout chapter

- Added a "Why It Matters" on External Failure Costs: Lululemon Stretched Thin
- Added "Check Up Corner" boxes on:
  - Lean Principles
  - Lean Accounting
  - Cost of Quality Report
- Added Analysis for Decision Making section on using lean principles in service or administrative settings with related end-of-chapter assignments
- Added Take It Further section with assignments involving ethics, teams, and communication

Chapter 13

- Chapter 14 in the previous edition
- Added "Check Up Corner" boxes on:
  - Cash Flows from Operating Activities
  - Cash Flows from Investing Activities
  - Classify Cash Flows
- Added "Why It Matters" on:
  - Growing Pains
  - Twenty Years After
- Refreshed exhibits on Statement of Cash Flows—Indirect Method and Statement of Cash Flows—Direct Method
- Moved the discussion of the direct method to Appendix 2

Chapter 14

- Chapter 15 in the previous edition
- Revamped sections on Analyzing Liquidity and Analyzing Solvency
- Name changes to several ratios:
  - "Number of Times Interest Charges Are Earned" to "Times Interest Earned"
  - "Ratio of Sales to Assets" to "Asset Turnover"
  - "Rate Earned on Total Assets" to "Return on Total Assets"
  - "Rate Earned on Stockholders' Equity" to "Return on Stockholders' Equity"
  - "Rate Earned on Common Stockholders' Equity" to "Return on Common Stockholders' Equity"
- Refreshed exhibit on Summary of Analytical Measures
- Added Appendix 2 on Fair Value and Comprehensive Income (from Chapter 13 in previous edition)
- Added "Check Up Corner" boxes on:
  - Horizontal and Vertical Analysis
  - Liquidity Analysis
  - Solvency Analysis
  - Profitability Analysis
- Added "Why It Matters" on:
  - Flying Off the Shelves
  - Economic Success
  - Investing for Yield

Instructor Resources

Solutions Manual

Author-written and carefully verified multiple times to ensure accuracy and consistency with the text, the Solutions Manual contains answers to the Discussion Questions, Basic Exercises, Exercises, Problems (Series A and Series B), Continuing Problems, Comprehensive Problems, Analysis for Decision Making, and Take It Further activities that appear in the text. These solutions help you easily plan, assign, and efficiently grade assignments.

Test Bank

Test Bank content is delivered via Cengage Learning Testing, powered by Cognero® a flexible, online system that allows you to:

- Author, edit, and manage test bank content from multiple Cengage Learning solutions
- Create multiple test versions in an instant
- Export tests as Word files
- Deliver tests from your LMS, your classroom, or through CengageNOWv2

Companion Web Site

This robust companion Web site provides immediate access to a rich array of teaching and learning resources—including the Instructor's Manual, PowerPoint slides, and Excel Template Solutions. Easily download the instructor resources you need from the password-protected, instructor-only section of the site.

Instructor's Manual Discover new ways to engage your students by utilizing the Instructor's Manual ideas for class discussion, group learning activities, writing exercises, and Internet activities. Moreover, simplify class preparation by reviewing a brief summary of each chapter, a detailed chapter synopsis, teaching tips regarding a suggested approach to the material, questions students frequently ask in the classroom, lecture aids, and demonstration problems in the Instructor's Manual. Transparency

Masters and Handouts (with solutions) are also included. Quickly identify the assignments that best align with your course with the assignment preparation grid that includes information about learning objective coverage, difficulty level and Bloom's taxonomy categorization, time estimates, and accrediting standard alignment for business programs, AICPA, ACBSP, and IMA.

PowerPoint Slides Bring your lectures to life with slides designed to clarify difficult concepts for your students. The lecture PowerPoints include key terms and definitions, equations, examples, and exhibits from the textbook. Descriptions for all graphics in the PowerPoints are included to enhance PowerPoint usability for students with disabilities.

A separate PowerPoint deck that includes just the Exhibits from the textbook is ideal for instructors who create their own PowerPoint decks and just want to refresh them.

Excel Template Solutions Excel Templates are provided for selected long or complicated end-of-chapter exercises and problems to assist students as they set up and work the problems. Certain cells are coded to display a red asterisk when an incorrect answer is entered, which helps students stay on track. Selected problems that can be solved using these templates are designated by an icon in the textbook and are listed in the assignment preparation grid in the Instructor's Manual. The Excel Template Solutions provide answers to these templates.

Practice Set Solutions Establish a fundamental understanding of the accounting cycle for your students with Practice Sets, which require students to complete one month of transactions for a fictional company. Brief descriptions of each Practice Set are provided in the Table of Contents. The Practice Set Solutions provide answers to these practice sets.

Student Resources

Study Guide

Now available free in CengageNOWv2, the Study Guide allows students to easily assess what they know with a "Do You Know" checklist covering the key points in each chapter. To further test their comprehension, students can work through Practice Exercises, which include a "strategy" hint and solution so they can continue to practice applying key accounting concepts.

Working Papers

Students will find the tools they need to help work through end-of-chapter assignments with the Working Papers. The preformatted templates provide a starting point by giving students a basic structure for problems and journal entries. Working Papers are available in a printed format as a bundle option.

Practice Sets

For more in-depth application of accounting practices, instructors may choose from among five different Practice Sets for long-term assignments. Each Practice Set requires students to complete one month of transactions for a fictional company. Practice Sets can be solved manually or with the Cengage Learning General Ledger software.

GENERAL LEDGER

Web Site

Designed specifically for your students' accounting needs, this Web site features student PowerPoint slides, Excel Templates, learning games, and flashcards.

- **PowerPoint Slides:** Students can easily take notes or review difficult concepts with the student version of this edition's PowerPoint slides.

- **Excel Templates:** These Excel Templates help students stay on track. If students enter an incorrect answer in certain cells, a red asterisk will appear to let them know something is wrong. Problems that can be solved using these templates are designated by an icon.

EXCEL TEMPLATE

- **Crossword Puzzles:** Students can focus on learning the key terms and definitions for each chapter in a different way by completing these crossword puzzles.

- **Flashcards:** Students can prepare with these flashcards, which cover the key terms and definitions they need to know for each chapter.

Acknowledgements

The many enhancements to this edition of *Managerial Accounting* are the direct result of one-on-one interviews, surveys, and focus groups with over 250 instructors at institutions across the country over the past year. We would like to take this opportunity to thank those who helped us better understand the challenges of the financial accounting course and provided valuable feedback on our content and digital assets.

Instructors:

Deborah S. Adkins, Remington Online

Deborah S. Adkins, University of Phoenix

Sol Ahiarah, SUNY Buffalo State

Dave Alldredge, Salt Lake Community College

Lynn Almond, Virginia Tech

Elizabeth Ammann, Lindenwood University

Sean Andre, York College of Pennsylvania

Rick Andrews, Sinclair Community College

Leah Arrington, Northwest Mississippi Community College

Christopher Ashley, Everest College

John Babich, Kankakee Community College

Benjamin Bae, California State University, Bakersfield

Felicia Baldwin, Richard J. Daley College

Laura K. Bantz, McHenry County College

Geoffrey Bartlett, Drake University

Elise Bartley, Westminster College

Jan Barton, Emory University

Progyan Basu, University of Maryland—College Park

Robert E. Bates, Glendale Community College

Jason Bergner, University of Nevada

Eric Blazer, Millersville University

Janell Blazovich, University of St. Thomas

Cindy Bleasdale, hilbert college

Cynthia E. Bolt-Lee, The Citadel

John Borke, University of Wisconsin—Platteville

Anna M. Boulware, St. Charles Community College

Amy Bourne, Oregon State University

Gary R. Bower, Community College of Rhode Island

Tom Branton, Alvin Community College

Robert L. Braun, Southeastern Louisiana University

Darryl L. Brown, Illinois Wesleyan University

Amy Browning, Monmouth College

Tracy L. Bundy, University of Louisiana at Lafayette

Esther Bunn, Stephen F. Austin State University

Lisa Busto, Harper College

Thane Butt, Champlain College

Marci L. Butterfield, University of Utah

Edward J. Bysiek, St. Bonaventure University

Magan Calhoun, Austin Peay State University

Julia Camp, Providence College

David Candelaria, Mt San Jacinto College

Brenda Canning, Springfield College

Kirk Canzano, Long Beach City College

Cassandra H. Catlett, Carson Newman University

David Centers, Grand Valley State University

Machiavelli Chao, University of California, Irvine

Bea Chiang, The College of New Jersey

C. Catherine Chiang, Elon University

Linda Christiansen, Indiana University Southeast

Lawrence Chui, University of St. Thomas

Bob Churchman, Harding University

Tony Cioffi, Lorain County Community College

George Cooper, Lakeland Community College

Sandra Copa, North Hennepin Community College

Leonard Cronin, Rochester Community and Technical College

Alyson Crow, Temple College

Louann Hofheins Cummings, The University of Findlay

Rick Cummings, University of Wisconsin—Whitewater

Sue Cunningham, Rowan-Cabarrus Community College

Dori Danko, Grand Valley State University

Bruce L. Darling, University of Oregon

Rebecca G. Davis, East Mississippi Community College

Julie Dawson, Carthage College

Laurence DeGaetano, Montclair State University

Peggy DeJong, Kirkwood Community College

Robert Derstine, West Chester University

Joel M. DiCicco, Florida Atlantic University

Carol Dickerson, Chaffey College

Julie Dilling, Moraine Park Technical College

Michael P. Dole, Marquette University

Patricia Dorris-Crenny, Villanova University

G. Seth Dunn, Tennessee Temple University

Gertrude A. Eguae-Obazee, Albright College

Karen C. Elsom, Fayetteville Technical Community College

James M. Emig, Villanova University

Sharif Erik-Soussi, Charter Oak State College

Mary Ewanechko, Monroe Community College

Farima Fakoor, Golden Gate University

Alan Falcon, Loyola Marymount University

Lucile Faurel, University of California, Irvine

Robert Foster, Pierce College

Corey Frad, Eastern Iowa Community Colleges

Kimberly Franklin, St. Louis Community College

Alan S. Fudge, Linn-Benton Community College

Michael J. Gallagher, DeSales University

Regan Garey, Lock Haven University

Alex Gialanella, Manhattanville College

John Giles, North Carolina State University

Michael Goeken, Northwest Vista College

Lynn P. Gonzalez, Concordia College

Saturnino (Nino) Gonzalez, Jr., El Paso Community College

Charles Goodman, University of Illinois at Chicago

Doug Gordon, University of California, Irvine

Carol Graham, The University of San Francisco

Thomas Grant, Kutztown University

Marina Grau, Houston Community College

Gloria Grayless, Sam Houston State University

Sheila Guillot, Lamar State College—Port Arthur

Hongtao Guo, Salem State University

Bob Gutschick, College of Southern Nevada

Joohyung Ha, University of San Francisco

Marcye S. Hampton, University of Central Florida

Becky Hancock, El Paso Community College

Martin Hart, Manchester Community College

Sueann Hely, West Kentucky Community & Technical College

Joshua Herbold, University of Montana

Len Heritage, Tacoma Community College

Katherine Sue Hewitt, Klamath Community College

Merrily Hoffman, San Jacinto College—Central

Jana Hosmer, Blue Ridge Community College

Jeff Hsu, St. Louis Community College at Meramec

Marianne James, California State University, Los Angeles

Ching-Lih Jan, California State University, East Bay

Cynthia Johnson, University of Arkansas, Little Rock

Lori Johnson, Minnesota State University, Moorhead

Jeffrey Jones, The College of Southern Nevada

Odessa Jordan, Calhoun Community College

Edward H. Julius, California Lutheran University

Brad Van Kalsbeek, University of Sioux Falls

Stani Kantcheva, Cincinnati State Technical and Community College

Stephen Keels, Everest University at Jacksonville

Taylor Klett, Sam Houston State University

Stacy Kline, Drexel University

William J. Knight, Flagler College

Satoshi Kojima, East Los Angeles College

Stephen Kolenda, Hartwick College

Lynn Krausse, Bakersfield College

Barbara Kren, Marquette University

Jeffrey T. Kunz, Carroll University

Steven J. LaFave, Augsburg College

Tara Laken, Joliet Junior College

Meg Costello Lambert, Oakland Community College—Auburn Hills Campus

Margie Ness LaShaw, Whitworth University

Richard Lau, California State University, Los Angeles

Greg Lauer, North Iowa Area Community College

David Laurel, South Texas College

G. Suzanne Lay, Colorado Mesa University

Rose Layton, University of Southern California

Charles J. F. Leflar, University of Arkansas

Annette M. Leps, Johns Hopkins University

Jennifer LeSure, Ivy Tech Community College

Erik H. Lindquist, Lansing Community College

Danny S. Litt, University of California, Los Angeles

Harold Little, Western Kentucky University

Katy Long, Hill College

Dawn Lopez, Johnson & Wales University

Ming Lu, Santa Monica College

Debra Luna, El Paso Community College

Jennifer A. Mack, Lindenwood University

Suneel Maheshwari, Indiana University of Pennsylvania

Lois S. Mahoney, Eastern Michigan University

Richard Mandau, Piedmont Technical College

Ken Marc, Johnson & Wales University

Michele Martinez, Hillsborough Community College

Anthony Masino, East Tennessee State University

Dawn L. Mason, Western Michigan University

Karen McDougal, St. Joseph's University

Robert W. McGee, Fayetteville State University

Noel McKeon, Florida State College Jacksonville

Allison McLeod, University of North Texas

Chris McNamara, Finger Lakes Community College

Glenn (Mel) McQueary, Houston Community College

Brenda J. McVey, University of Mississippi

Jean A. Meyer, Loyola University of New Orleans

Pam Meyer, University of Louisiana at Lafayette

Paul A. San Miguel, Western Michigan University

Linda Miller, Northeast Community College

Timothy Miller, El Camino College

Barbara J. Muller, Arizona State University

Johnna Murray, University of Missouri—St. Louis

Adam Myers, Texas A&M University

John Nader, Davenport University

Araks Navasartian, Everest University, Tampa Campus

Pam Neely, The College at Brockport, SUNY

Joseph Malino Nicassio, Westmoreland County Community College

Lisa Novak, Mott Community College

Christopher O'Byrne, Cuyamaca College

Joseph Onyeocha, South Carolina State University

Edwin Pagan, Passaic County Community College

Kalpana Pai, Texas Wesleyan University

Susanna Pendergast, Western Illinois University

Rachel Pernia, Essex County College

Dawn Peters, Southwestern Illinois College

Vickie Petritz, Highlands College of Montana Tech

Cynthia Phipps, Lake Land College

April Poe, University of the Incarnate Word

Sharon Price, Southwestern Assemblies of God University

Michael P. Prockton, Finger Lakes Community College

Craig Reeder, Florida A&M University

Barbara Rice, Gateway Community and Technical College

Renee Richard, Pima Community College

Laurie Hays Rivera, Western Michigan University

Cecile M. Roberti, Community College of Rhode Island

Shani N. Robinson, Sam Houston State University

Constance Rodriguez, SUNY Brockport

Patrick Rogan, Cosumnes River College

Lawrence A. Roman, Cuyahoga Community College

Debbie Rose, Northeast Wisconsin Technical College

Brent Russ, The University of Montana

Gloria Sanchez, Mt. San Jacinto College

Lynn K. Saubert, Radford University

Jennifer Schneider, University of North Georgia

Darlene Schnuck, Waukesha County Technical College

John Seilo, Irvine Valley College

Mon Sellers, Lone Star College—North Harris

Perry Sellers, Louisiana State University in Shreveport

Lewis Shaw, Suffolk University

James G. Shelton, Harding University

Eileen Shifflett, James Madison University

Ercan Sinmaz, Houston Community College

Lee G. Smart, Southwest Tennessee Community College

Gerald Smith, University of Northern Iowa

Nancy L. Snow, University of Toledo

Kristen Sohlberg, The University of Montana

Leslie "Andy" Speck, Embry-Riddle Aeronautical University

Marilyn Stansbury, Calvin College

Catherine L. Staples, Randolph-Macon College

Larry G. Stephens, Austin Community College District

Dawn W. Stevens, Northwest Mississippi Community College—Desoto Center

Jeff Strawser, Sam Houston State University

Ronald Strittmater, North Hennepin Community College

Joel Strong, St. Cloud State University

Gracelyn Stuart-Tuggle, Palm Beach State College—Boca

Mary Sykes, University of Houston

Linda H. Tarrago, Hillsborough Community College

Denise Teixeira, Chemeketa Community College

Theresa Tiggeman, University of the Incarnate Word

Patricia Hart Timm, Northwood University

Anthony L. Tocco, Rockhurst University

Lana Tuss, Chemeketa Community College

Mark M. Ulrich, St. John's University

Robert Urell, Irvine Valley College

Jeff Varblow, College of Lake County

Lynne Velie, College of Coastal Georgia

Drakopoulou Veliota, Ashford University

John Verani, White Mountains Community College

Marcia M. Vinci, Johnson & Wales University

Dale A. Walker, Arkansas State University

Robert J. Walsh, University of Dallas

Doris Warmflash, SUNY Westchester Community College

James Webb, University of the Pacific

Eric Weinstein, Suffolk County Community College

Robert J. Wesoloskie, Eastern University

Micheline West, Manchester Community College

Nancy L. Wilburn, Northern Arizona University

Patricia Worsham, California State Polytechnic University Pomona

Patricia Worsham, Norco College

Judith Zander, Grossmont College

Athena Zhang, Ithaca College

About the Authors

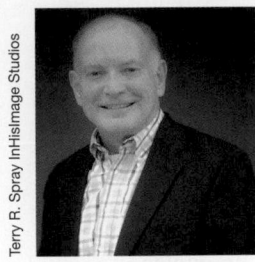

Terry R. Spray InHisImage Studios

Carl S. Warren

Dr. Carl S. Warren is Professor Emeritus of Accounting at the University of Georgia, Athens. Dr. Warren has taught classes at the University of Georgia, University of Iowa, Michigan State University, and University of Chicago. He focused his teaching efforts on principles of accounting and auditing. Dr. Warren received his PhD from Michigan State University and his BBA and MA from the University of Iowa. During his career, Dr. Warren published numerous articles in professional journals, including *The Accounting Review*, *Journal of Accounting Research*, *Journal of Accountancy*, *The CPA Journal*, and *Auditing: A Journal of Practice and Theory*. Dr. Warren has served on numerous committees of the American Accounting Association, the American Institute of Certified Public Accountants, and the Institute of Internal Auditors. He also has consulted with numerous companies and public accounting firms. His outside interests include handball, golfing, skiing, backpacking, motorcycling, and fly-fishing.

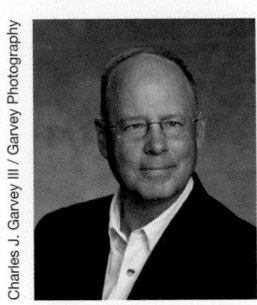

Charles J. Garvey III / Garvey Photography

James M. Reeve

Dr. James M. Reeve is Professor Emeritus of Accounting and Information Management at the University of Tennessee. Professor Reeve taught full time as part of the accounting faculty for twenty-five years after graduating with his PhD from Oklahoma State University. He presently teaches part time at UT. His teaching efforts focused on Senior Executive MBA programs. Beyond this, Professor Reeve is very active in the Supply Chain Certification program, which is a major executive education and research effort of the college. His research interests are varied and include work in managerial accounting, supply chain management, lean manufacturing, and information management. He has published over forty articles in academic and professional journals, including *Journal of Cost Management*, *Journal of Management Accounting Research*, *Accounting Review*, *Management Accounting Quarterly*, *Supply Chain Management Review*, and *Accounting Horizons*. He has consulted or provided training around the world for a variety of organizations, including Boeing, Procter & Gamble, Norfolk Southern, Hershey Foods, Coca-Cola, and Sony. When not writing books, Professor Reeve plays golf and is involved in faith-based activities.

© Ken Bennett

Jonathan Duchac

Dr. Jonathan Duchac is the Wayne Calloway Professor of Accounting and Acting Associate Dean of Accounting Programs at Wake Forest University. He earned his PhD in accounting from the University of Georgia and currently teaches introductory and advanced courses in financial accounting. Dr. Duchac has received a number of awards during his career, including the Wake Forest University Outstanding Graduate Professor Award, the T.B. Rose Award for Instructional Innovation, and the University of Georgia Outstanding Teaching Assistant Award. In addition to his teaching responsibilities, Dr. Duchac has served as Accounting Advisor to Merrill Lynch Equity Research, where he worked with research analysts in reviewing and evaluating the financial reporting practices of public companies. He has testified before the U.S. House of Representatives, the Financial Accounting Standards Board, and the Securities and Exchange Commission and has worked with a number of major public companies on financial reporting and accounting policy issues. In addition to his professional interests, Dr. Duchac is an avid runner, mountain biker, and snow skier.

Brief Contents

Contents

5 Cost-Volume-Profit Analysis 202

6 Variable Costing for Management Analysis 256

7 Budgeting 314

8 Evaluating Variances from Standard Costs 368

9 Evaluating Decentralized Operations 418

10 Differential Analysis and Product Pricing 470

Managerial
Accounting 14e

1 Introduction to Managerial Accounting

Concepts and Principles

Chapter 1 *Introduction to Managerial Accounting*

Developing Information

COST SYSTEMS

Chapter 2 *Job Order Costing*

Chapter 3 *Process Cost Systems*

Chapter 4 *Activity-Based Costing*

COST BEHAVIOR

Chapter 5 *Cost-Volume-Profit Analysis*

Decision Making

EVALUATING PERFORMANCE

Chapter 6 *Variable Costing for Management Analysis*

Chapter 7 *Budgeting*

Chapter 8 *Evaluating Variances from Standard Costs*

COMPARING ALTERNATIVES

Chapter 9 *Evaluating Decentralized Operations*

Chapter 10 *Differential Analysis and Product Pricing*

Chapter 11 *Capital Investment Analysis*

Chapter 12 *Lean Manufacturing*

Gibson Guitars

Gibson guitars have been used by musical legends over the years, including B.B. King, Chet Atkins, Brian Wilson (Beach Boys), Jimmy Page (Led Zeppelin), Jackson Browne, John Fogerty, Jose Feliciano, Miranda Lambert, and Wynonna Judd. Known for its quality, **Gibson Guitars** celebrated its 120th anniversary in 2014.

Staying in business for 120 years requires a thorough understanding of how to manufacture high-quality guitars. In addition, it requires knowledge of how to account for the costs of making guitars. For example, Gibson needs cost information to answer the following questions:

- What should be the selling price of its guitars?
- How many guitars does it have to sell in a year to cover its costs and earn a profit?

- How many employees should the company have working on each stage of the manufacturing process?
- How would purchasing automated equipment affect the costs of its guitars?

This chapter introduces managerial accounting concepts that are useful in addressing these questions. This chapter begins by describing managerial accounting and its relationship to financial accounting. Following this overview, the management process is described along with the role of managerial accounting. Finally, characteristics of managerial accounting reports, managerial accounting terms, and uses of managerial accounting information are described and illustrated.

Source: http://www.gibson.com/Gibson/History.aspx

What's Covered

Introduction to Managerial Accounting

Role of Managerial Accounting	**Manufacturing Operations**	**Sustainability and Accounting**	**Manufacturing Financial Statements**
■ Differences with Financial Accounting (Obj. 1) ■ Management Organization (Obj. 1) ■ Management Process (Obj. 1) ■ Uses of Managerial Accounting Information (Obj. 1)	■ Nature of Manufacturing (Obj. 2) ■ Direct and Indirect Costs (Obj. 2) ■ Manufacturing Costs (Obj. 2)	■ Sustainability (Obj. 3) ■ Eco-Efficiency Measures (Obj. 3)	■ Balance Sheet (Obj. 4) ■ Income Statement (Obj. 4)

Learning Objectives

Obj. 1 Describe managerial accounting, including its differences with financial accounting, its place in the organization, and its uses.

Obj. 2 Describe and illustrate the nature of manufacturing operations, including different types and classifications of costs.

Obj. 3 Describe sustainable business activities and eco-efficiency measures.

Obj. 4 Describe and illustrate financial statements for a manufacturing business, including the balance sheet, statement of cost of goods manufactured, and income statement.

Analysis for Decision Making

Describe and measure utilization in evaluating performance for a service company.

Objective 1

Describe managerial accounting, including its differences with financial accounting, its place in the organization, and its uses.

Managerial Accounting

Managers make numerous decisions during the day-to-day operations of a business and in planning for the future. Managerial accounting provides much of the information used for these decisions.

Some examples of managerial accounting information along with the chapter in which it is described and illustrated follow:

- Classifying manufacturing and other costs and reporting them in the financial statements (Chapter 1)
- Determining the cost of manufacturing a product or providing a service (Chapters 2 and 3)
- Evaluating the impact of cost allocation and activity-based costing (Chapter 4)
- Estimating the behavior of costs for various levels of activity and assessing cost-volume-profit relationships (Chapter 5)
- Evaluating operating performance using cost behavior relationships (Chapter 6)
- Planning for the future by preparing budgets (Chapter 7)
- Evaluating manufacturing costs by comparing actual with expected results (Chapter 8)
- Evaluating decentralized operations by comparing actual and budgeted costs as well as computing various measures of profitability (Chapter 9)
- Evaluating special decision-making situations by comparing differential revenues and costs, pricing products, and managing bottlenecks (Chapter 10)
- Evaluating alternative proposals for long-term investments in fixed assets (Chapter 11)
- Planning operations using principles of lean manufacturing and activity analysis (Chapter 12)

Link to Gibson Guitars

Orville Gibson started producing guitars in 1894 in Kalamazoo, Michigan. He produced guitars and mandolins based upon the arch-top design of violins.

Differences Between Managerial and Financial Accounting

Accounting information is often classified into two types: financial and managerial. Exhibit 1 shows the relationship between financial accounting and managerial accounting.

Exhibit 1 Financial Accounting and Managerial Accounting

Financial Statements

Managerial Accounting Reports

	Financial Statements	**Managerial Accounting Reports**
Users of Information	External users and company management	Management
Nature of Information	Objective	Objective and subjective
Guidelines for Preparation	Prepared according to GAAP	Prepared according to management needs
Timeliness of Reporting	Prepared at fixed intervals	Prepared at fixed intervals and on an as-needed basis
Focus of Reporting	Company as a whole	Company as a whole or segment

Financial accounting information is reported at fixed intervals (monthly, quarterly, yearly) in general-purpose financial statements. These financial statements—the income statement, retained earnings statement, balance sheet, and statement of cash flows—are prepared according to generally accepted accounting principles (GAAP). These statements are used by external users such as the following:

- Shareholders
- Creditors
- Government agencies
- The general public

Gibson Mandolin-Guitar Mfg. Co., Ltd. was formed in 1902 in Kalamazoo, Michigan, with the support of five investors.

Link to Gibson Guitars

Managers of a company also use general-purpose financial statements. For example, in planning future operations, managers often begin by evaluating the current income statement and statement of cash flows.

Managerial accounting information is designed to meet the specific needs of a company's management. This information includes the following:

- Historical data, which provide *objective measures* of past operations
- Estimated data, which provide *subjective estimates* about future decisions

Management uses both types of information in directing daily operations, planning future operations, and developing business strategies.

Unlike the financial statements prepared in financial accounting, managerial accounting reports do *not* always have to be:

- Prepared according to generally accepted accounting principles (GAAP). This is because *only* the company's management uses the information. Also, in many cases, GAAP are not relevant to the specific decision-making needs of management.
- Prepared at fixed intervals (monthly, quarterly, yearly). Although some management reports are prepared at fixed intervals, most reports are prepared as management needs the information.
- Prepared for the business as a whole. Most management reports are prepared for products, projects, sales territories, or other segments of the company.

Link to
Gibson Guitars

Chicago Musical Instrument Company purchased **Gibson** in 1944.

Managerial Accounting in the Organization

In most companies, departments or similar organizational units are assigned responsibilities for specific functions or activities. The operating structure of a company can be shown in an *organization chart*.

Exhibit 2 is a partial organization chart for **Callaway Golf Company**, the manufacturer and distributor of golf clubs, clothing, and other products.

Exhibit 2
Partial Organization
Chart for Callaway
Golf Company

The departments in a company can be viewed as having either of the following:

- Line responsibilities
- Staff responsibilities

A **line department** is directly involved in providing goods or services to the customers of the company. For Callaway Golf (shown in Exhibit 2), the following occupy line positions:

- Senior Vice President—Equipment
- Plant Manager—Chicopee, MA Plant
- Senior Vice President—Callaway Brand
- Managing Director, Callaway Golf Europe

Individuals in these positions are responsible for manufacturing and selling Callaway's products.

A **staff department** provides services, assistance, and advice to the departments with line or other staff responsibilities. A staff department has no direct authority over a line department. For Callaway Golf (Exhibit 2), the following are staff positions:

- Senior Vice President—Chief Administrative Officer
- Vice President, Human Resources
- Chief Financial Officer
- Controller

In most companies, the **controller** is the chief management accountant. The controller's staff consists of a variety of other accountants who are responsible for specialized accounting functions such as the following:

- Systems and procedures
- General accounting
- Budgets and budget analysis
- Special reports and analysis
- Taxes
- Cost accounting

Experience in managerial accounting is often an excellent training ground for senior management positions. This is not surprising because accounting touches all phases of a company's operations.

One of **Gibson**'s most influential managers was Ted McCarty, who was the company president from 1950–1966. During this period, Gibson was known for its innovations. For example, in 1954, McCarty invented the tune-o-matic bridge with adjustable saddles.

Link to Gibson Guitars

The Management Process

As a staff department, managerial accounting supports management and the management process. The **management process** has the following five basic phases, as shown in Exhibit 3:

- Planning
- Directing
- Controlling
- Improving
- Decision making

Why It Matters

Line and Staff for Service Companies

The terms *line* and *staff* may also be applied to service organizations. Some examples follow:

Service Industry	Line	Staff
Airline	Crew, baggage handling, and gate staff	Information systems, accounting, human resources
Hotel	Housekeeping and reception staff	Maintenance, hotel manager, grounds
Hospital	Doctors, nurses, other caregivers	Admissions, records, billing
Banking	Tellers, loan officers, trust officers, and brokers	Branch manager, information systems
Telecommunications	Sales, customer service, and customer installation staff	Information systems, regional management, and network maintenance

As Exhibit 3 illustrates, the five phases interact with one another.

Exhibit 3
The Management
Process

Planning Management uses **planning** in developing the company's **objectives (goals)** and translating these objectives into courses of action. For example, a company may set an objective to increase market share by 15% by introducing three new products. The actions to achieve this objective might be as follows:

- Increase the advertising budget
- Open a new sales territory
- Increase the research and development budget

Planning may be classified as follows:

- **Strategic planning**, which is developing long-term actions to achieve the company's objectives. These long-term actions are called **strategies**, which often involve periods of 5 to 10 years.
- **Operational planning**, which develops short-term actions for managing the day-to-day operations of the company.

Directing The process by which managers run day-to-day operations is called **directing**. An example of directing is a production supervisor's efforts to keep the production line moving without interruption (downtime). A credit manager's development of guidelines for assessing the ability of potential customers to pay their bills is also an example of directing.

Controlling Monitoring operating results and comparing actual results with the expected results is **controlling**. This **feedback** allows management to isolate areas for further investigation and possible remedial action. It may also lead to revising future plans. This philosophy of controlling by comparing actual and expected results is called **management by exception**.

Improving Feedback is also used by managers to support continuous process improvement. **Continuous process improvement** is the philosophy of continually improving employees, business processes, and products. The objective of continuous improvement is to eliminate the *source* of problems in a process. In this way, the right products (services) are delivered in the right quantities at the right time.

Decision Making Inherent in each of the preceding management processes is **decision making**. In managing a company, management must continually decide among alternative actions. For example, in directing operations, managers must decide on an operating structure, training procedures, and staffing of day-to-day operations.

Managerial accounting supports managers in all phases of the management process. For example, accounting reports comparing actual and expected operating results help managers plan and improve current operations. Such a report might compare the actual and expected costs of defective materials. If the cost of defective materials is unusually high, management might decide to change suppliers.

Gibson struggled financially from 1966–1986. The company was purchased and sold several times and experienced declining sales.

Link to Gibson Guitars

 Ethics: Do It!

Environmental Managerial Accounting

Throughout the last decade, environmental issues have become an increasingly important part of the business environment for most companies. Companies and managers must now consider the environmental impact of their business decisions in the same way that they would consider other operational issues. To help managers make sound business decisions, the emerging field of environmental management accounting focuses on calculating the environmental-related costs of business decisions. Environmental managerial accountants evaluate a variety of issues such as the volume and level of emissions, the estimated costs of different levels of emissions, and the impact that environmental costs have on product cost. Managers use these results to consider clearly the environmental effects of their business decisions.

Uses of Managerial Accounting Information

As mentioned earlier, managerial accounting provides information and reports for managers to use in operating a business. Some examples of how managerial accounting could be used by a guitar manufacturer include the following:

- The cost of manufacturing each guitar could be used to determine its selling price.
- Comparing the costs of guitars over time can be used to monitor and control costs.
- Performance reports could be used to identify any large amounts of scrap or employee downtime. For example, large amounts of unusable wood (scrap) after the cutting process should be investigated to determine the underlying cause. Such scrap may be caused by saws that have not been properly maintained.
- A report could analyze the potential efficiencies and savings of purchasing a new computerized saw to speed up the production process.
- A report could analyze how many guitars need to be sold to cover operating costs and expenses. Such information could be used to set monthly selling targets and bonuses for sales personnel.

Why It Matters

Not According to Plan

There are times even the best of plans go awry. Sometimes plans are impacted by events outside of management control. For example, Hurricane Sandy ruined the beach and resort businesses along the New Jersey shore. Few management plans would be able to provide for such an extreme contingency. Force majeure (meaning "superior force") clauses in contracts can be used to nullify contracts when such events occur. Such clauses are used when the normal operating plans are disrupted by events beyond management control or expectation. For example, a hotel damaged by Hurricane Sandy under a force majeure clause would not be required to fulfill a contract to supply rooms for a convention. In other cases, events may be dramatic, but can be anticipated. An example was the dramatic decline in oil prices during the middle 2010s that reduced the oil revenue earned by U.S. shale oil producers. Many of these producers planned and then executed financial contracts, termed hedges, that earned money from lower oil prices, to partially offset revenue losses.

As the prior examples illustrate, managerial accounting information can be used for a variety of purposes. In the remaining chapters of this text, we examine these and other areas of managerial accounting.

Check Up Corner 1-1   Management Process

1. Indicate whether the following statements are true or false:
   A. Managerial accounting information is designed primarily to meet the needs of external users such as shareholders, creditors, and the general public.
   B. Managerial accounting reports must be prepared for the business as a whole.
   C. The Senior Vice President—Manufacturing would be considered a line position in a line department.

2. Three phases of the management process are planning, controlling, and improving. Match the following descriptions to the proper phase:

Phase of Management Process	Description
Planning	A. Monitoring the operating results and comparing the actual results with expected results
Controlling	B. Rejects solving problems with temporary solutions that fail to address the root cause of the problem
Improving	C. Used by management to develop the company's objectives

Solution:

1. A. False. The primary focus and design of managerial accounting information is to meet the specific needs of a company's management.
   B. False. Managerial accounting reports do not have to be prepared for the business as a whole. Most management reports are prepared for products, projects, sales territories, or other segments of the company.
   C. True. A line department is directly involved in providing goods or services to the customers of the company. A staff department provides services, assistance, and advice to other departments.

2. Planning: **C.** Used by management to develop the company's objectives

   Controlling: **A.** Monitoring the operating results and comparing the actual results with expected results

   Improving: **B.** Rejects solving problems with temporary solutions that fail to address the root cause of the problem

Check Up Corner

Objective 2

Describe and illustrate the nature of manufacturing operations, including different types and classifications of costs.

Manufacturing Operations

The operations of a business can be classified as service, merchandising, or manufacturing. The chapters of this text focus primarily on manufacturing businesses. Most of the managerial accounting concepts discussed, however, also apply to service and merchandising businesses.

Nature of Manufacturing

As a basis for illustration of manufacturing operations, a guitar manufacturer, **Legend Guitars**, is used. Exhibit 4 is an overview of Legend's guitar manufacturing operations.

Exhibit 4 Guitar-Making Operations of Legend Guitars

Customer Places Order   Materials   Cutting   Assembly   Finished Guitar

Legend's guitar-making process begins when a customer places an order for a guitar. Once the order is accepted, the manufacturing process begins by obtaining the necessary materials. An employee then cuts the body and neck of the guitar out of raw lumber. Once the wood is cut, the body and neck of the guitar are assembled. When the assembly is complete, the guitar is painted and finished.

Gibson provides tours of its Memphis guitar factory located at 145 Lt. George W. Lee Avenue.

Link to Gibson Guitars

Direct and Indirect Costs

A **cost** is a payment of cash or the commitment to pay cash in the future for the purpose of generating revenues. For example, cash (or credit) used to purchase equipment is the cost of the equipment. If equipment is purchased by exchanging assets other than cash, the current market value of the assets given up is the cost of the equipment purchased.

In managerial accounting, costs are classified according to the decision-making needs of management. For example, costs are often classified by their relationship to a segment of operations, called a **cost object**. A cost object may be a product, a sales territory, a department, or an activity, such as research and development. Costs identified with cost objects are either direct costs or indirect costs.

Direct costs are identified with and can be traced to a cost object. For example, as shown in Exhibit 5, the cost of wood (materials) used by **Legend Guitars** in manufacturing a guitar is a direct cost of the guitar.

Materials   **Cost Object: Guitar**

Direct Cost

Exhibit 5
Direct Costs of
Legend Guitars

Indirect costs cannot be identified with or traced to a cost object. For example, as shown in Exhibit 6, the salaries of the **Legend Guitars** production supervisors are indirect costs of producing a guitar. Although the production supervisors contribute to the production of a guitar, their salaries cannot be identified with or traced to any individual guitar.

Exhibit 6
Indirect Costs of
Legend Guitars

Depending on the cost object, a cost may be either a direct or an indirect cost. For example, the salaries of production supervisors are indirect costs when the cost object is an individual guitar. If, however, the cost object is **Legend Guitars**' overall production process, then the salaries of production supervisors are direct costs.

This process of classifying a cost as direct or indirect is illustrated in Exhibit 7.

Exhibit 7
Classifying Direct
and Indirect Costs

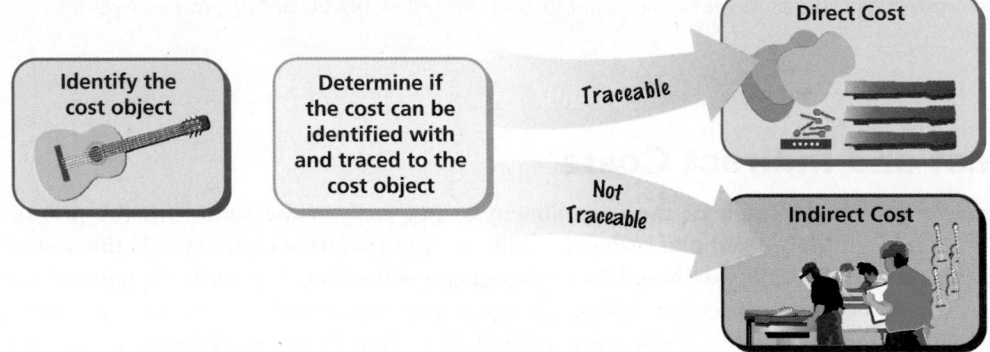

Manufacturing Costs

The cost of a manufactured product includes the cost of materials used in making the product. In addition, the cost of a manufactured product includes the cost of converting the materials into a finished product. For example, **Legend Guitars** uses employees and machines to convert wood (and other supplies) into finished guitars. Thus, as shown in Exhibit 8, the cost of a finished guitar (the cost object) includes the following:

- Direct materials cost
- Direct labor cost
- Factory overhead cost

Exhibit 8
Manufacturing
Costs of Legend
Guitars

Direct Materials Cost Manufactured products begin with raw materials that are converted into finished products. The cost of any material that is an integral part of the finished product is classified as a **direct materials cost**. For **Legend Guitars**, direct materials cost includes the cost of the wood used in producing each guitar. Other examples of direct materials costs include the cost of electronic components for a television, silicon wafers for microcomputer chips, and tires for an automobile.

To be classified as a direct materials cost, the cost must be *both* of the following:

- An integral part of the finished product
- A significant portion of the total cost of the product

For Legend, the cost of the guitar strings is not a direct materials cost. This is because the cost of guitar strings is an insignificant part of the total cost of each guitar. Instead, the cost of guitar strings is classified as a factory overhead cost, which is discussed later.

Direct Labor Cost Most manufacturing processes use employees to convert materials into finished products. The cost of employee wages that is an integral part of the finished product is classified as **direct labor cost**. For **Legend Guitars**, direct labor cost includes the wages of the employees who cut each guitar out of raw lumber and assemble it. Other examples of direct labor costs include mechanics' wages for repairing an automobile, machine operators' wages for manufacturing tools, and assemblers' wages for assembling a laptop computer.

Like a direct materials cost, a direct labor cost must meet *both* of the following criteria:

- An integral part of the finished product
- A significant portion of the total cost of the product

For Legend, the wages of the janitors who clean the factory are not a direct labor cost. This is because janitorial costs are not an integral part or a significant cost of each guitar. Instead, janitorial costs are classified as a factory overhead cost, which is discussed next.

Factory Overhead Cost Costs other than direct materials and direct labor that are incurred in the manufacturing process are combined and classified as **factory overhead cost**. Factory overhead is sometimes called **manufacturing overhead** or **factory burden**.

All factory overhead costs are indirect costs of the product. Some factory overhead costs include the following:

- Heating and lighting the factory
- Repairing and maintaining factory equipment
- Property taxes on factory buildings and land
- Insurance on factory buildings
- Depreciation on factory plant and equipment

Factory overhead cost also includes materials and labor costs that do not enter directly into the finished product. Examples include the cost of oil used to lubricate machinery and the wages of janitorial and supervisory employees. Also, if the costs of direct materials or direct labor are not a significant portion of the total product cost, these costs may be classified as factory overhead costs.

Why It Matters

Overhead Costs

Defense contractors such as **General Dynamics**, **Boeing**, and **Lockheed Martin** sell products such as airplanes, ships, and military equipment to the U.S. Department of Defense. Building large products such as these requires a significant investment in facilities and tools, all of which are classified as factory overhead costs. As a result, factory overhead costs are a much larger portion of the cost of goods sold for defense contractors than they are in other industries. For example, a U.S. General Accounting Office study of six defense contractors found that overhead costs were almost one-third of the price of the final product. This is more than three times greater than the factory overhead costs for a laptop computer, which are typically about 10% of the price of the final product.

For **Legend Guitars**, the costs of guitar strings and janitorial wages are factory overhead costs. Additional factory overhead costs of making guitars are as follows:

- Sandpaper
- Buffing compound
- Glue
- Power (electricity) to run the machines
- Depreciation of the machines and building
- Salaries of production supervisors

Prime Costs and Conversion Costs Direct materials, direct labor, and factory overhead costs may be grouped together for analysis and reporting. Two such common groupings are as follows:

- **Prime costs**, which consist of direct materials and direct labor costs
- **Conversion costs**, which consist of direct labor and factory overhead costs

Conversion costs are the costs of converting the materials into a finished product. Direct labor is both a prime cost and a conversion cost, as shown in Exhibit 9.

Exhibit 9
Prime Costs and
Conversion Costs

Product Costs and Period Costs** For financial reporting purposes, costs are classified as product costs or period costs.

- **Product costs** consist of manufacturing costs: direct materials, direct labor, and factory overhead.
- **Period costs** consist of selling and administrative expenses. *Selling expenses* are incurred in marketing the product and delivering the product to customers. *Administrative expenses* are incurred in managing the company and are not directly related to the manufacturing or selling functions.

Examples of product costs and period costs for **Legend Guitars** are presented in Exhibit 10.

To facilitate control, selling and administrative expenses may be reported by level of responsibility. For example, selling expenses may be reported by products, salespersons, departments, divisions, or territories. Likewise, administrative expenses may be reported by areas such as human resources, computer services, legal, accounting, or finance.

Why It Matters

Service Companies and Product Costs

Most service companies do not produce a product and, thus, do not have product costs. However, service companies may still have labor, materials, and overhead. Often, these costs are not associated with manufacturing product, but with serving customers. An example is a hospital. Caregivers provide care (similar to direct labor), drugs and health supplies are administered (similar to direct materials), and administrative salaries and utilities are paid (similar to factory overhead).

Exhibit 10 Examples of Product Costs and Period Costs—Legend Guitars

Product (Manufacturing) Costs

Direct Materials Cost
- Wood used in neck and body

Direct Labor Cost
- Wages of saw operator
- Wages of employees who assemble the guitar

Factory Overhead
- Guitar strings
- Wages of janitor
- Power to run the machines
- Depreciation expense—factory building
- Sandpaper and buffing materials
- Glue used in assembly of the guitar
- Salary of production supervisors

Period (Nonmanufacturing) Costs

Selling Expenses
- Advertising expenses
- Sales salaries expenses
- Commissions expenses

Administrative Expenses
- Office salaries expense
- Office supplies expense
- Depreciation expense—office building and equipment

The impact on the financial statements of product and period costs is summarized in Exhibit 11. As product costs are incurred, they are recorded and reported on the balance sheet as *inventory*. When the inventory is sold, the cost of the manufactured product sold is reported as *cost of goods sold* on the income statement. Period costs are reported as *expenses* on the income statement in the period in which they are incurred and, thus, never appear on the balance sheet.

Exhibit 11

Product Costs, Period Costs, and the Financial Statements

In January 1986, guitar enthusiasts Henry Juszkiewicz and David Berryman purchased **Gibson**. Together they restored Gibson's reputation for innovation and quality. Under their leadership, Gibson began generating profits.

Link to Gibson Guitars

Check Up Corner 1-2   Manufacturing Operations

A partial list of the costs for MLB Mitt Company, a baseball glove manufacturer, is as follows:

A. Ink used to print a player's autograph

B. Salesperson's salary and commission

C. Padding material

D. Coolants for machines that sew the baseball gloves

E. Wages of assembly line employees

F. Cost of endorsement from a professional baseball player

G. Salary of manufacturing plant supervisor

H. Leather used to make the gloves

I. Office supplies used at company headquarters

J. Wages of office administrative staff

Using the following headings, classify each cost as a product cost or a period cost. In addition, identify product costs as:

- Direct materials, direct labor, or factory overhead, and

- Prime cost, conversion cost, or both.

	Product Cost					Period Cost
Item	Direct Materials	Direct Labor	Factory Overhead	Prime Cost	Conversion Cost	

Solution:

	Product Cost					Period Cost
Item	Direct Materials	Direct Labor	Factory Overhead	Prime Cost	Conversion Cost	
A.			X		X	
B.						X
C.	X			X		
D.			X		X	
E.		X		X	X	
F.						X
G.			X		X	
H.	X			X		
I.						X
J.						X

Check Up Corner

Sustainability and Accounting

Managers must consider the social and environmental settings in which a business operates, in order to make sound strategic and operational decisions. Issues such as population growth, resource scarcity, declining ecosystems, increasing urbanization, and climate change all have a direct impact on a company's potential for success. As a result, managers are using new management techniques and tools that consider these issues.

Sustainability

Sustainability is the practice of operating a business to maximize profits while attempting to preserve the environment, economy, and needs of future generations. Sustainability practices acknowledge that a company's long-term success requires the continued availability of natural resources and a productive social environment. Examples of sustainable business activities are provided in Exhibit 12.

Exhibit 12 Sustainable Business Activities

Category	Description	Example
Agriculture	Farming and ranching techniques that do not damage or disrupt the environment	Mixed farming, crop rotation, multiple cropping
Energy	Generating energy with little or no pollution	Wind turbines, solar power
Engineering and Construction	Designing and constructing buildings that are highly efficient in using natural resources, while minimizing pollution	Recycled building materials, high-efficiency heating and cooling systems, renewable energy generation
Transportation	Using transportation methods that result in little pollution and have a minimal impact on the environment	Expanded public transportation systems, green vehicles, biofuel-powered vehicles
Waste Minimization	Recycling and reuse practices that reduce the amount of waste disposed in landfills	Curbside recycling collection, composting, reusable products (e.g. water bottles)

Eco-Efficiency Measures in Managerial Accounting

Sustainability information can provide important feedback to guide a company's strategic and operational decision making. Managers can use this information to increase revenue, control costs, and allocate resources efficiently. **Eco-efficiency measures** are a form of managerial accounting information that helps managers evaluate the savings generated by using fewer natural resources in a company's operations. Examples of eco-efficiency measures are provided in Exhibit 13.

Exhibit 13 Eco-Efficiency Measures

Energy Efficiency	Energy cost savings from replacing lighting fixtures in a production facility with energy-efficient lighting
Material Use Efficiency	Materials cost savings from reducing the amount of product packaging materials
Fuel Efficiency	Fuel cost savings from replacing gas-powered vehicles with hybrid or alternative energy-source vehicles
Waste Efficiency	Waste removal cost savings from recycling and reusing waste and by-product materials

Sustainability information can also benefit external financial statement users in their decision making. The risks and opportunities that a company faces are tied to the environment in which it operates and provide important insights into the potential for success. As such, external financial statement users may require sustainability information to evaluate investment and credit decisions. The **Sustainability Accounting Standards Board (SASB)** was organized in 2011 to develop accounting standards that help companies report decision-useful sustainability information to external financial statement users. While the SASB's standards are not required, they are designed to provide sustainability information that complements required financial statement information.

Financial Statements for a Manufacturing Business

Objective 4

Describe and illustrate financial statements for a manufacturing business, including the balance sheet, statement of cost of goods manufactured, and income statement.

The retained earnings and cash flow statements for a manufacturing business are similar to those for service and merchandising businesses. However, the balance sheet and income statement for a manufacturing business are more complex. This is because a manufacturer makes the products that it sells and, thus, must record and report product costs. The reporting of product costs primarily affects the balance sheet and the income statement.

Balance Sheet

A manufacturing business reports three types of inventory on its balance sheet as follows:

- **Materials inventory** (sometimes called raw materials inventory). This inventory consists of the costs of the direct and indirect materials that have not entered the manufacturing process.
  Examples for **Legend Guitars**: Wood, guitar strings, glue, sandpaper
- **Work in process inventory.** This inventory consists of the direct materials, direct labor, and factory overhead costs for products that have entered the manufacturing process, but are not yet completed (in process).
  Example for Legend: Unfinished (partially assembled) guitars
- **Finished goods inventory.** This inventory consists of completed (or finished) products that have not been sold.
  Example for Legend: Unsold guitars

Exhibit 14 illustrates the reporting of inventory on the balance sheet for a merchandising and a manufacturing business. MusicLand Stores, Inc., a retailer of musical instruments, reports only Inventory. In contrast, **Legend Guitars**, a manufacturer of guitars, reports Finished Goods, Work in Process, and Materials inventories. In both balance sheets, inventory is reported in the Current Assets section.

Exhibit 14
Balance Sheet Presentation of Inventory in Merchandising and Manufacturing Companies

MusicLand Stores, Inc.
Balance Sheet
December 31, 20Y8

Current assets:	
Cash..	$ 25,000
Accounts receivable (net)	85,000
Inventory	142,000
Supplies	10,000
Total current assets....................................	$262,000

Legend Guitars
Balance Sheet
December 31, 20Y8

Current assets:		
Cash...		$ 21,000
Accounts receivable (net)		120,000
Inventory:		
Direct materials...............................	$35,000	
Work in process................................	24,000	
Finished goods.................................	62,500	
Total inventory................................		121,500
Supplies...		2,000
Total current assets...........................		$264,500

Income Statement

The income statements for merchandising and manufacturing businesses differ primarily in the reporting of the cost of goods (merchandise) *available for sale* and *sold* during the period. These differences are shown in Exhibit 15.

Merchandising Business

Income Statement		
Sales		$XXX
Beginning inventory	$ XXX	
Net purchases	XXX	
Inventory available for sale	$ XXX	
Ending inventory	(XXX)	
Cost of goods sold		XXX
Gross profit		$XXX

Manufacturing Business

Income Statement		
Sales		$XXX
Beginning finished goods inventory	$ XXX	
Cost of goods manufactured	XXX	
Cost of finished goods available for sale	$ XXX	
Ending finished goods inventory	(XXX)	
Cost of goods sold		XXX
Gross profit		$XXX

As shown in Exhibit 15, a merchandising business determines its cost of goods sold by first adding its net purchases for the period to its beginning inventory. This determines inventory available for sale during the period. The ending inventory is then subtracted to determine the **cost of goods sold**.[1]

In contrast, a manufacturing business makes the products it sells using direct materials, direct labor, and factory overhead. As a result, a manufacturing business must determine its **cost of goods manufactured** during the period.

The cost of goods manufactured is determined by preparing a **statement of cost of goods manufactured**.[2] This statement summarizes the cost of goods manufactured during the period, as follows:

Statement of Cost of Goods Manufactured

Beginning work in process inventory..........		$ XXX
Direct materials:		
Beginning materials inventory..............	$ XXX	
Purchases.................................	XXX	
Cost of materials available for use..........	$ XXX	
Ending materials inventory................	(XXX)	
Cost of direct materials used	$XXX	
Direct labor	XXX	
Factory overhead...............................	XXX	
Total manufacturing costs incurred in period		XXX
Total manufacturing costs		$ XXX
Ending work in process inventory..............		(XXX)
Cost of goods manufactured		$ XXX

---

[1] To simplfy, we use the computation of cost of goods sold for periodic inventory systems.

[2] Chapters 2 and 3 describe and illustrate the use of job order and process cost systems. As will be illustrated, these systems do not require a statement of cost of goods manufactured.

To illustrate, the following data for **Legend Guitars** are used:

	Jan. 1, 20Y8	Dec. 31, 20Y8
Inventories:		
Materials..................................	$ 65,000	$ 35,000
Work in process	30,000	24,000
Finished goods............................	60,000	62,500
Total inventories..............................	$155,000	$121,500
Manufacturing costs incurred during 20Y8:		
Materials purchased.......................		$100,000
Direct labor...............................		110,000
Factory overhead:		
Indirect labor.........................	$ 24,000	
Depreciation on factory equipment	10,000	
Factory supplies and utility costs	10,000	
Total factory overhead.............		44,000
Total		$254,000
Sales...		$366,000
Selling expenses..............................		20,000
Administrative expenses.......................		15,000

The statement of cost of goods manufactured is prepared using the following three steps:

- Step 1. Determine the *cost of direct materials used* during the period.
- Step 2. Determine the *total manufacturing costs incurred* during the period.
- Step 3. Determine the *cost of goods manufactured* during the period.

Using the data for **Legend Guitars**, the cost of direct materials used, total manufacturing costs incurred, and cost of goods manufactured are computed as follows:

Step 1. The *cost of direct materials used* in production is determined as follows:

Materials inventory, January 1, 20Y8	$ 65,000
Purchases	100,000
Cost of materials available for use	$ 165,000
Materials inventory, December 31, 20Y8	(35,000)
Cost of direct materials used	$ 130,000

The January 1, 20Y8 (beginning), materials inventory of $65,000 is added to the cost of materials purchased of $100,000 to yield the $165,000 total cost of materials that are available for use during 20Y8. Deducting the December 31, 20Y8 (ending), materials inventory of $35,000 yields the $130,000 cost of direct materials used in production.

Step 2. The *total manufacturing costs incurred in 20Y8* are determined as follows:

Direct materials used in production (Step 1)	$130,000
Direct labor	110,000
Factory overhead	44,000
Total manufacturing costs incurred in 20Y8	$284,000

The total manufacturing costs incurred in 20Y8 of $284,000 are determined by adding the cost of direct materials used in production (Step 1), the direct labor cost, and the factory overhead costs.

Step 3. The *cost of goods manufactured* is determined as follows:

Work in process inventory, January 1, 20Y8	$ 30,000
Total manufacturing costs incurred (Step 2)	284,000
Total manufacturing costs incurred	$ 314,000
Work in process inventory, December 31, 20Y8	(24,000)
Cost of goods manufactured in 20Y8	$290,000

The cost of goods manufactured of $290,000 is determined by adding the total manufacturing costs incurred (Step 2) to the January 1, 20Y8 (beginning), work in process inventory of $30,000. This yields total manufacturing costs incurred of $314,000. The December 31, 20Y8 (ending), work in process inventory of $24,000 is then deducted to determine the cost of goods manufactured of $290,000.

The income statement and statement of cost of goods manufactured for **Legend Guitars** are shown in Exhibit 16.

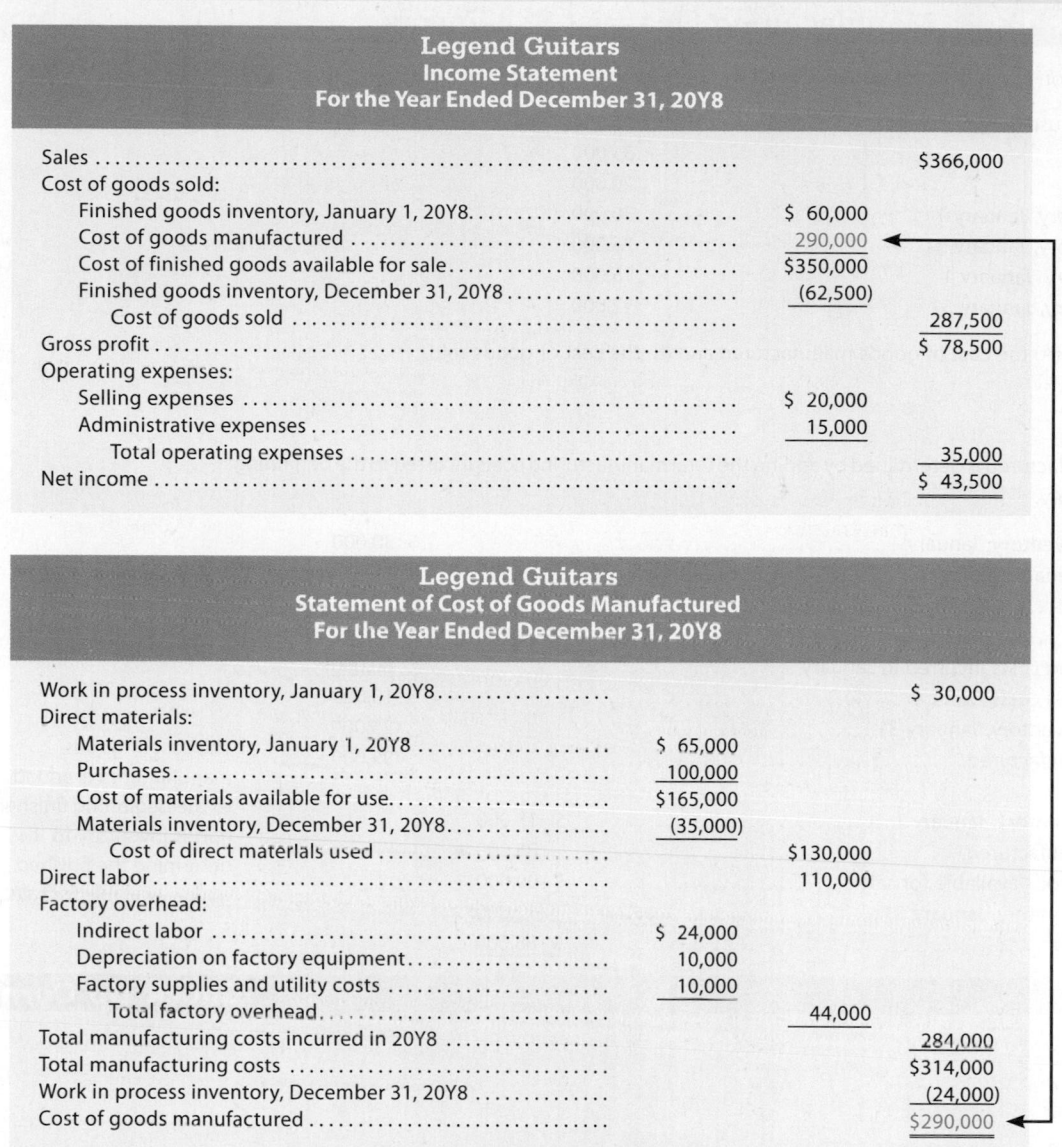

Legend Guitars
Income Statement
For the Year Ended December 31, 20Y8

Sales		$366,000
Cost of goods sold:		
Finished goods inventory, January 1, 20Y8.	$ 60,000	
Cost of goods manufactured	290,000	
Cost of finished goods available for sale	$350,000	
Finished goods inventory, December 31, 20Y8	(62,500)	
Cost of goods sold		287,500
Gross profit		$ 78,500
Operating expenses:		
Selling expenses	$ 20,000	
Administrative expenses	15,000	
Total operating expenses		35,000
Net income		$ 43,500

DYNAMIC
EXHIBIT

Legend Guitars
Statement of Cost of Goods Manufactured
For the Year Ended December 31, 20Y8

Work in process inventory, January 1, 20Y8			$ 30,000
Direct materials:			
Materials inventory, January 1, 20Y8	$ 65,000		
Purchases	100,000		
Cost of materials available for use	$165,000		
Materials inventory, December 31, 20Y8	(35,000)		
Cost of direct materials used		$130,000	
Direct labor		110,000	
Factory overhead:			
Indirect labor	$ 24,000		
Depreciation on factory equipment	10,000		
Factory supplies and utility costs	10,000		
Total factory overhead		44,000	
Total manufacturing costs incurred in 20Y8			284,000
Total manufacturing costs			$314,000
Work in process inventory, December 31, 20Y8			(24,000)
Cost of goods manufactured			$290,000

Exhibit 16
Manufacturing Company—Income Statement with Statement of Cost of Goods Manufactured

Exhibit 17 summarizes how manufacturing costs flow to the income statement and balance sheet of a manufacturing business.

Exhibit 17
Flow of Manufacturing Costs

Check Up Corner 1-3   Manufacturing Financial Statements

The following information is available for January for MLB Mitt Company, a baseball glove manufacturer:

Cost of direct materials used in production	$25,000
Direct labor	35,000
Factory overhead	20,000
Work in process inventory, January 1	30,000
Work in process inventory, January 31	25,000
Finished goods inventory, January 1	15,000
Finished goods inventory, January 31	12,000

For January, determine (A) the cost of goods manufactured and (B) the cost of goods sold.

Solution:

The cost of goods manufactured is determined by adding the total manufacturing costs incurred to the beginning work in process inventory.

A.	Work in process inventory, January 1		$ 30,000
	Cost of direct materials used	$ 25,000	
	Direct labor	35,000	
	Factory overhead	20,000	
	Total manufacturing costs incurred in January		80,000
	Total manufacturing costs		$110,000
	Work in process inventory, January 31		(25,000)
	Cost of goods manufactured		$ 85,000
B.	Finished goods inventory, January 1	$ 15,000	
	Cost of goods manufactured	85,000	
	Cost of finished goods available for sale	$100,000	
	Finished goods inventory, January 31	(12,000)	
	Cost of goods sold	$ 88,000	

The cost of goods manufactured is added to the beginning finished goods inventory to determine the finished goods available for sale.

Check Up Corner

Analysis for Decision Making

Objective
Describe and measure utilization in evaluating performance for a service company.

Service and Utilization

Nearly 80% of U.S. economic activity (gross domestic product) is represented by services. Services are activities that do not result in the transfer, possession, or ownership of goods. Services benefit a customer or an item under a customer's control. An example of the latter is an automobile that the owner brings in for maintenance by the dealer. Services cannot be stored and are often used instantly. For example, a hotel provides a room to a guest for a night. The guest does not own the room, but only receives the service for one night. Upon receiving the room, the service is used or completed by the next morning. Other examples of services are provided in Exhibit 18.

Service Industry	Service Example	Company Example
Utilities	Electric power generation	Consolidated Edison
Transportation	Overnight delivery	FedEx
Information	Social media	Facebook
Financial Services	Banking	Bank of America
Education	Higher education	University of Phoenix
Leisure and Hospitality	Entertainment	The Walt Disney Company
Health	General healthcare	Hospital Corporation of America
Personal Services	Fitness club	Life Time Fitness

Exhibit 18
Examples of Service Industries, Services, and Companies

Many of the principles discussed in this chapter for manufacturing companies can be applied to service companies. However, the unique characteristics of service companies also create some distinctions, as shown in Exhibit 19.

Manufacturing	Services
Uses materials, work in process, and finished goods inventory.	Inventory is often limited to supplies.
Uses both product and period costs.	Uses only period costs.
Uses cost of goods sold on the income statement.	May use cost of services on the income statement.
Manufacturing requires a physical production site.	Many services require a network that connects the service to the customer. Examples include telecommunications, banking, power distribution, distributed entertainment, and transportation.
Manufacturing overhead is an indirect cost in manufacturing products.	There is no manufacturing overhead; however, indirect costs are incurred in serving customers.
Labor is a direct cost to products.	Labor is not a direct cost to products, but may be a direct cost to customers. Examples are accountants in an accounting firm or doctors in a medical practice.
Materials are a direct cost to products.	Materials are often an indirect cost, but may be significant, such as fuel for transportation or utilities. In other cases, materials are not significant, such as financial, leisure, information, or education services.

Exhibit 19
Managerial Accounting Distinctions Between Manufacturing and Service Companies

Most of the distinctions in Exhibit 19 are caused by the nature of services. Service companies have no inventory or product costs. Managerial accounting in service companies is concerned with the economic use of people and fixed assets in serving customers.

The nature of services influences the performance measures used by management accountants. For example, the productive use of fixed assets is an important contributor to financial success for many service companies. This is because many service companies must build large networks or other fixed assets in order to deliver a service. For example, the cellular network of **Verizon Communications** is extremely costly and, thus, the use of the network is key to Verizon's financial success. Cruise lines (ships), utilities (power plants), railroads (track), hotels (buildings), hospitals (buildings), and educational services (buildings) also require costly fixed assets.

An important measure used in many service companies is utilization. **Utilization** measures the use of a fixed asset in serving customers relative to the asset's capacity. Higher utilization is considered favorable, while lower utilization is considered unfavorable. Different service industries will have different names and calculations used for measuring utilization. Some service industries, such as power generation, freight transportation, and telecommunications, measure utilization using complex formulas. However, other service industries use simpler methods to measure utilization. In the hotel industry, for example, utilization is measured by the *occupancy rate*, which is calculated as:

$$\text{Occupancy Rate} = \frac{\text{Guest Nights}}{\text{Available Room Nights}}$$

where,

Guest nights = number of guests × number of nights per visit (per time period)
Available room nights = number of available rooms × number of nights per time period

The number of guests is determined under single room occupancy, so that the number of guests is equal to the number of occupied rooms.

To illustrate, assume the EasyRest Hotel is a single hotel with 150 rooms. During the month of June, the hotel had 3,600 guests, each staying for a single night. The occupancy rate would be determined as follows:

$$\text{Occupancy Rate} = \frac{\text{Guest Nights}}{\text{Available Room Nights}}$$

$$= \frac{3{,}600 \text{ guest nights}}{150 \text{ rooms} \times 30 \text{ days}} = 80\%$$

The hotel was occupied to 80% of capacity, which would be considered favorable.

Make a Decision Utilization

Comfort Plus, Inc. has a hotel with 300 rooms in a metropolitan city. Its main competitor, Connors Hotel, has a hotel with 350 rooms in the same city. The following operating data are available for April for the two hotels:

Comfort Plus		Connors	
Number of Guests	**Nights per Visit**	**Number of Guests**	**Nights per Visit**
3,680	1	4,390	1
1,100	2	700	2
500	3	800	3

A. Determine the guest nights for each hotel in April.
B. Determine the available room nights for each hotel in April.
C. Determine the occupancy rate for each hotel in April.
D. Which hotel has the better utilization of capacity in April?

Solution:

A. Comfort Plus:

Number of Guests		Nights per Visit		Guest Nights
3,680	×	1	=	3,680
1,100	×	2	=	2,200
500	×	3	=	1,500
Total guest nights				7,380

Connors:

Number of Guests		Nights per Visit		Guest Nights
4,390	×	1	=	4,390
700	×	2	=	1,400
800	×	3	=	2,400
Total guest nights				8,190

B. Comfort Plus: 300 rooms × 30 days = 9,000 available room nights for April
Connors: 350 rooms × 30 days = 10,500 available room nights for April

C.

$$\text{Occupancy Rate} = \frac{\text{Guest Nights}}{\text{Available Room Nights}}$$

$$\text{Comfort Plus: } \frac{7,380 \text{ guest nights}}{9,000 \text{ available room nights}} = 82\%$$

$$\text{Connors: } \frac{8,190 \text{ guest nights}}{10,500 \text{ available room nights}} = 78\%$$

D. Comfort Plus has a better occupancy rate at 82% of capacity, compared to Connors' occupancy rate of 78%.

Make a Decision

Let's Review

Chapter Summary

1. Managerial accounting is a staff function that supports the management process by providing reports to aid management in planning, directing, controlling, improving, and decision making. This differs from financial accounting, which provides information to users outside of the organization. Managerial accounting reports are designed to meet the specific needs of management and aid management in planning long-term strategies and running the day-to-day operations. Managerial accounting provides a variety of information for decision making for use in operating a business.

2. Manufacturing companies use machinery and labor to convert materials into a finished product. A direct cost can be directly traced to a finished product, while an indirect cost cannot. The cost of a finished product is made up of three components: direct materials, direct labor, and factory overhead. These three manufacturing costs can be categorized into prime costs (direct materials and direct labor) or conversion costs (direct labor and factory overhead). Product costs consist of the elements of manufacturing cost—direct materials, direct labor, and factory overhead—while period costs consist of selling and administrative expenses.

3. To make sound strategic and operational decisions, managers must consider the social and environmental conditions in which their company operates. Sustainability is the practice of operating a business to maximize profits while attempting to preserve the environment, economy, and needs of future generations. Sustainability information provides important internal feedback that helps guide a company's strategic and operational decision making. This information also helps external financial statement users evaluate the risks and opportunities a company faces that are tied to the environment in which it operates.

4. The financial statements of manufacturing companies differ from those of merchandising companies. Manufacturing company balance sheets report three types of inventory: materials, work in process, and finished goods. The income statement of manufacturing companies reports the cost of goods sold, which is the total manufacturing cost of the goods sold. The income statement is supported by the statement of cost of goods manufactured, which provides the details of the cost of goods manufactured during the period.

Key Terms

continuous process improvement (8)
controller (7)
controlling (8)
conversion costs (14)
cost (11)
cost object (11)
cost of goods manufactured (19)
cost of goods sold (19)
decision making (8)
direct costs (11)
direct labor cost (13)
direct materials cost (13)
directing (8)
eco-efficiency measures (17)

factory burden (13)
factory overhead cost (13)
feedback (8)
financial accounting (5)
finished goods inventory (18)
indirect costs (11)
line department (6)
management by exception (8)
management process (7)
managerial accounting (5)
manufacturing overhead (13)
materials inventory (18)
objectives (goals) (8)
operational planning (8)

period costs (14)
planning (8)
prime costs (14)
product costs (14)
staff department (7)
statement of cost of goods manufactured (19)
strategic planning (8)
strategies (8)
sustainability (16)
Sustainability Accounting Standards Board (SASB) (17)
utilization (24)
work in process inventory (18)

Practice

Multiple-Choice Questions

1. Which of the following best describes the difference between financial and managerial accounting?
   A. Managerial accounting provides information to support decisions, while financial accounting does not.
   B. Managerial accounting is not restricted to generally accepted accounting principles, while financial accounting is restricted to GAAP.
   C. Managerial accounting does not result in financial reports, while financial accounting does result in financial reports.
   D. Managerial accounting is concerned solely with the future and does not record events from the past, while financial accounting records only events from past transactions.

2. Which of the following is *not* one of the five basic phases of the management process?
   A. Planning   C. Decision making
   B. Controlling   D. Operating

3. Which of the following is *not* considered a cost of manufacturing a product?
   A. Direct materials cost   C. Sales salaries
   B. Factory overhead cost   D. Direct labor cost

4. Which of the following costs would be included as part of the factory overhead costs of a microcomputer manufacturer?
   A. The cost of memory chips   C. Wages of microcomputer assemblers
   B. Depreciation of testing equipment   D. The cost of disk drives

5. For the month of May, Latter Company has beginning finished goods inventory of $50,000, ending finished goods inventory of $35,000, and cost of goods manufactured of $125,000. What is the cost of goods sold for May?
   A. $90,000   C. $140,000
   B. $110,000   D. $170,000

Answers provided after Problem. Need more practice? Find additional multiple-choice questions, exercises, and problems in CengageNOWv2.

Exercises

SHOW ME HOW

1. Management process   Obj. 1

Three phases of the management process are controlling, planning, and decision making. Match the following descriptions to the proper phase:

Phase of Management Process	Description
Controlling	A. Monitoring the operating results of implemented plans and comparing the actual results with expected results
Planning	
Decision making	B. Inherent in planning, directing, controlling, and improving
	C. Long-range courses of action

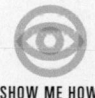
SHOW ME HOW

2. Direct materials, direct labor, and factory overhead   Obj. 2

Identify the following costs as direct materials (DM), direct labor (DL), or factory overhead (FO) for an automobile manufacturer:

A. Wages of employees that operate painting equipment

B. Wages of the plant manager

C. Steel

D. Oil used for assembly line machinery

SHOW ME HOW

3. Prime and conversion costs   Obj. 2

Identify the following costs as a prime cost (P), conversion cost (C), or both (B) for an automobile manufacturer:

A. Wages of employees that operate painting equipment

B. Wages of the plant manager

C. Steel

D. Oil used for assembly line machinery

SHOW ME HOW

4. Product and period costs   Obj. 2

Identify the following costs as a product cost or a period cost for an automobile manufacturer:

A. Steel

B. Wages of employees that operate painting equipment

C. Rent on office building

D. Sales staff salaries

SHOW ME HOW

5. Cost of goods sold, cost of goods manufactured   Obj. 4

Timbuk 3 Company has the following information for March:

Cost of direct materials used in production	$21,000
Direct labor	54,250
Factory overhead	35,000
Work in process inventory, March 1	87,500
Work in process inventory, March 31	92,750
Finished goods inventory, March 1	36,750
Finished goods inventory, March 31	42,000

For March, determine (A) the cost of goods manufactured and (B) the cost of goods sold.

Answers provided after Problem. Need more practice? Find additional multiple-choice questions, exercises, and problems in CengageNOWv2.

Problem

The following is a list of costs that were incurred in producing this textbook:

A. Insurance on the factory building and equipment

B. Salary of the vice president of finance

C. Hourly wages of printing press operators during production

D. Straight-line depreciation on the printing presses used to manufacture the text

E. Electricity used to run the presses during the printing of the text

F. Sales commissions paid to textbook representatives for each text sold

G. Paper on which the text is printed

H. Book covers used to bind the pages

I.   Straight-line depreciation on an office building

J. Salaries of staff used to develop artwork for the text

K. Glue used to bind pages to cover

Instructions

With respect to the manufacture and sale of this text, classify each cost as either a product cost or a period cost. Indicate whether each product cost is a direct materials cost, a direct labor cost, or a factory overhead cost. Indicate whether each period cost is a selling expense or an administrative expense.

Need more practice? Find additional multiple-choice questions, exercises, and problems in CengageNOWv2.

Answers

Multiple-Choice Questions

1. **B** Managerial accounting is not restricted to generally accepted accounting principles, as is financial accounting (answer B). Both financial and managerial accounting support decision making (answer A). Financial accounting is mostly concerned with the decision making of external users, while managerial accounting supports decision making of management. Both financial and managerial accounting can result in financial reports (answer C). Managerial accounting reports are developed for internal use by managers at various levels in the organization. Both managerial and financial accounting record events from the past (answer D); however, managerial accounting can also include information about the future in the form of budgets and cash flow projections.

2. **D** The five basic phases of the management process are planning (answer A), directing (not listed), controlling (answer B), improving (not listed), and decision making (answer C). Operating (answer D) is not one of the five basic phases, but operations are the object of managers' attention.

3. **C** Sales salaries (answer C) is a selling expense and is not considered a cost of manufacturing a product. Direct materials cost (answer A), factory overhead cost (answer B), and direct labor cost (answer D) are costs of manufacturing a product.

4. **B** Depreciation of testing equipment (answer B) is included as part of the factory overhead costs of the microcomputer manufacturer. The cost of memory chips (answer A) and the cost of disk drives (answer D) are both considered a part of direct materials cost. The wages of microcomputer assemblers (answer C) are part of direct labor costs.

5. **C** Cost of goods sold is calculated as follows:

Beginning finished goods inventory	$ 50,000
Cost of goods manufactured	125,000
Ending finished goods inventory	(35,000)
Cost of goods sold	$140,000

Exercises

1. Controlling (A)
   Planning (C)
   Decision making (B)
2. A. DL
   B. FO
   C. DM
   D. FO
3. A. B
   B. C
   C. P
   D. C
4. A. Product cost
   B. Product cost
   C. Period cost
   D. Period cost
5. A.

Work in process inventory, March 1		$ 87,500
Cost of direct materials used in production	$21,000	
Direct labor	54,250	
Factory overhead	35,000	
Total manufacturing costs incurred in March		110,250
Total manufacturing costs		$197,750
Work in process inventory, March 31		(92,750)
Cost of goods manufactured		$105,000

B.

Finished goods inventory, March 1	$ 36,750
Cost of goods manufactured	105,000
Cost of finished goods available for sale	$141,750
Finished goods inventory, March 31	(42,000)
Cost of goods sold	$ 99,750

Need more help? Watch step-by-step videos of how to compute answers to these Exercises in CengageNOWv2.

Problem

Cost	Product Cost			Period Cost	
	Direct Materials Cost	Direct Labor Cost	Factory Overhead Cost	Selling Expense	Administrative Expense
A.			X		
B.					X
C.		X			
D.			X		
E.			X		
F.				X	
G.	X				
H.	X				
I.					X
J.			X		
K.			X		

Discussion Questions

1. What are the major differences between managerial accounting and financial accounting?

2. A. Differentiate between a department with line responsibility and a department with staff responsibility.

   B. In an organization that has a Sales Department and a Personnel Department, among others, which of the two departments has (1) line responsibility and (2) staff responsibility?

3. What manufacturing cost term is used to describe the cost of materials that are an integral part of the manufactured end product?

4. Distinguish between prime costs and conversion costs.

5. What is the difference between a product cost and a period cost?

6. Name the three inventory accounts for a manufacturing business, and describe what each balance represents at the end of an accounting period.

7. In what order should the three inventories of a manufacturing business be presented on the balance sheet?

8. What are the three categories of manufacturing costs included in the cost of finished goods and the cost of work in process?

9. Describe sustainability and sustainable business practices.

10. How does the Cost of Goods Sold section of the income statement differ between merchandising and manufacturing companies?

Basic Exercises

SHOW ME HOW

BE 1-1   Management process   Obj. 1

Three phases of the management process are planning, directing, and controlling. Match the following descriptions to the proper phase:

Phase of Management Process	Description
Planning	A. Developing long-range courses of action to achieve goals
Directing	B. Isolating significant departures from plans for further investigation and possible remedial action; may lead to a revision of future plans
Controlling	C. Process by which managers, given their assigned levels of responsibilities, run day-to-day operations

SHOW ME HOW

BE 1-2   Direct materials, direct labor, and factory overhead   Obj. 2

Identify the following costs as direct materials (DM), direct labor (DL), or factory overhead (FO) for a magazine publisher:

A. Staples used to bind magazines

B. Wages of printing machine employees

C. Maintenance on printing machines

D. Paper used in the magazine

SHOW ME HOW

BE 1-3   Prime and conversion costs   Obj. 2

Identify the following costs as a prime cost (P), conversion cost (C), or both (B) for a magazine publisher:

A. Paper used for the magazine

B. Wages of printing machine employees

C. Glue used to bind magazine

D. Maintenance on printing machines

SHOW ME HOW

BE 1-4   Product and period costs   Obj. 2

Identify the following costs as a product cost or a period cost for a magazine publisher:

A. Sales salaries

B. Paper used for the magazine

C. Maintenance on printing machines

D. Depreciation expense—corporate headquarters

SHOW ME HOW

BE 1-5   Cost of goods sold, cost of goods manufactured   Obj. 4

Glenville Company has the following information for April:

Cost of direct materials used in production	$280,000
Direct labor	324,000
Factory overhead	188,900
Work in process inventory, April 1	72,300
Work in process inventory, April 30	76,600
Finished goods inventory, April 1	39,600
Finished goods inventory, April 30	41,200

For April, determine (A) the cost of goods manufactured and (B) the cost of goods sold.

Exercises

EX 1-1   Classifying costs as materials, labor, or factory overhead   Obj. 2

Indicate whether each of the following costs of an automobile manufacturer would be classified as direct materials cost, direct labor cost, or factory overhead cost:

A. Depreciation of robotic assembly line equipment

B. V8 automobile engine

C. Steering wheel

D. Wheels

E. Painting safety masks for employees working in the paint room

F. Salary of test driver

G. Glass used in the vehicle's windshield

H. Wages of assembly line worker

REAL WORLD

EX 1-2 Classifying costs as materials, labor, or factory overhead   Obj. 2

Indicate whether the following costs of **Procter & Gamble**, a maker of consumer products, would be classified as direct materials cost, direct labor cost, or factory overhead cost:

A. Plant manager salary for the Iowa City, Iowa, plant

B. Maintenance supplies

C. Salary of process engineers

D. Wages paid to Packaging Department employees in the Bear River City, Utah, paper products plant

E. Scents and fragrances used in making soaps and detergents

F. Wages of production line employees at the Pineville, Louisiana, soap and detergent plant

G. Depreciation on assembly line in the Mehoopany, Pennsylvania, paper products plant

H. Packaging materials

I. Resins for body wash products

J. Depreciation on the Auburn, Maine, manufacturing plant

REAL WORLD

EX 1-3 Classifying costs as factory overhead   Obj. 2

Which of the following items are properly classified as part of factory overhead for **Ford Motor Company**, a maker of heavy automobiles and trucks?

A. Plant manager's salary at Buffalo, New York, stamping plant, which manufactures auto and truck subassemblies

B. Depreciation on Flat Rock, Michigan, assembly plant

C. Dividends paid to shareholders

D. Machine lubricant used to maintain the assembly line at the Louisville, Kentucky, assembly plant

E. Leather to be used on vehicles that have leather interiors

F. Depreciation on mechanical robots used on the assembly line

G. Consultant fees for a study of production line efficiency

H. Dealership sales incentives

I. Vice president of human resources's salary

J. Property taxes on the Dearborn, Michigan, headquarters building

REAL WORLD

EX 1-4 Classifying costs as product or period costs   Obj. 2

For apparel manufacturer **Abercrombie & Fitch, Inc.,** classify each of the following costs as either a product cost or a period cost:

A. Research and development costs

B. Depreciation on sewing machines

C. Fabric used during production

D. Depreciation on office equipment

E. Advertising expenses

F. Repairs and maintenance costs for sewing machines

G. Salary of production quality control supervisor

H. Utility costs for office building

I. Sales commissions

J. Salaries of distribution center personnel

K. Wages of sewing machine operators

L. Factory janitorial supplies

M. Chief financial officer's salary

N. Travel costs of media relations employees

O. Factory supervisors' salaries

P. Oil used to lubricate sewing machines

Q. Property taxes on factory building and equipment

EX 1-5 Concepts and terminology
Obj. 1, 2, 4

From the choices presented in parentheses, choose the appropriate term for completing each of the following sentences:

A. Advertising costs are usually viewed as (period, product) costs.

B. Feedback is often used to (improve, direct) operations.

C. Payments of cash or the commitment to pay cash in the future for the purpose of generating revenues are (costs, expenses).

D. A product, sales territory, department, or activity to which costs are traced is called a (direct cost, cost object).

E. The balance sheet of a manufacturer would include an account for (cost of goods sold, work in process inventory).

F. Factory overhead costs combined with direct labor costs are called (prime, conversion) costs.

G. The implementation of automatic, robotic factory equipment normally (increases, decreases) the direct labor component of product costs.

EX 1-6 Concepts and terminology
Obj. 1, 2

From the choices presented in parentheses, choose the appropriate term for completing each of the following sentences:

A. The phase of the management process that uses process information to eliminate the source of problems in a process so that the process delivers the correct product in the correct quantities is called (directing, improving).

B. Direct labor costs combined with factory overhead costs are called (prime, conversion) costs.

C. The salaries of sales people are normally considered a (period, product) cost.

D. The plant manager's salary would be considered (direct, indirect) to the product.

E. Long-term plans are called (strategic, operational) plans.

F. Materials for use in production are called (supplies, materials inventory).

G. An example of factory overhead is (electricity used to run assembly line, CEO salary).

EX 1-7 Classifying costs in a service company
Obj. 2

A partial list of the costs for Wisconsin and Minnesota Railroad, a short hauler of freight, follows. Classify each cost as either indirect or direct. For purposes of classifying each cost, use the train as the cost object.

A. Cost to lease (rent) railroad cars

B. Cost of track and bed (ballast) replacement

C. Diesel fuel costs

D. Cost to lease (rent) train locomotives

E. Depreciation of terminal facilities

F. Maintenance costs of right of way, bridges, and buildings

G. Salaries of dispatching and communications personnel

H. Headquarters information technology support staff salaries

I. Safety training costs

J. Wages of train engineers

K. Wages of switch and classification yard personnel

L. Costs of accident cleanup

EX 1-8 Sustainability and Eco-Efficiency Measures
Obj. 3

Four types of eco-efficiency measures are identified below. Match the following descriptions to the proper eco-efficiency measures:

1. Energy Efficiency
2. Fuel Efficiency
3. Material Use Efficiency
4. Waste Efficiency

A. Cost savings from recycling and reusing waste and by-product materials

B. Cost savings from reducing the amount of product packaging materials

C. Cost savings from replacing lighting fixtures in a production facility with energy-efficient lighting

D. Cost savings from replacing gas-powered vehicles with hybrid or alternative energy-source vehicles

EX 1-9   Classifying costs   Obj. 2, 4

The following is a manufacturing cost report of Marching Ants Inc. Evaluate and correct this report.

Marching Ants Inc.
Manufacturing Costs
For the Quarter Ended June 30

Materials used in production (including $56,200 of indirect materials)	$ 607,500
Direct labor (including $84,400 maintenance salaries)	562,500
Factory overhead:	
Supervisor salaries—plant	517,500
Heat, light, and power—plant	140,650
Sales salaries	348,750
Promotional expenses	315,000
Insurance and property taxes—plant	151,900
Insurance and property taxes—corporate offices	219,400
Depreciation—plant and equipment	123,750
Depreciation—corporate offices	90,000
Total	$3,076,950

EX 1-10   Financial statements of a manufacturing firm   Obj. 4

✔ A. Net income, $145,000

SHOW ME HOW

The following events took place for Digital Vibe Manufacturing Company during March, the first month of its operations as a producer of digital video monitors:

A. Purchased $168,500 of materials.
B. Used $149,250 of direct materials in production.
C. Incurred $360,000 of direct labor wages.
D. Incurred $120,000 of factory overhead.
E. Transferred $600,000 of work in process to finished goods.
F. Sold goods for $875,000.
G. Sold goods with a cost of $525,000.
H. Incurred $125,000 of selling expense.
I. Incurred $80,000 of administrative expense.

Using the information given, complete the following:

A. Prepare the March income statement for Digital Vibe Manufacturing Company.
B. Determine the inventory balances at the end of the first month of operations.

EX 1-11   Manufacturing company balance sheet   Obj. 4

SHOW ME HOW

Partial balance sheet data for Diesel Additives Company at August 31 are as follows:

Finished goods inventory	$ 89,400	Supplies	$ 13,800
Prepaid insurance	9,000	Materials inventory	26,800
Accounts receivable	348,200	Cash	167,500
Work in process inventory	61,100		

Prepare the Current Assets section of Diesel Additives Company's balance sheet at August 31.

EX 1-12   Cost of direct materials used in production for a manufacturing company   Obj. 4

SHOW ME HOW

Okaboji Manufacturing Company reported the following materials data for the month ending November 30:

Materials purchased	$490,900
Materials inventory, November 1	64,900
Materials inventory, November 30	81,300

Determine the cost of direct materials used in production by Okaboji during the month ended November 30.

EX 1-13 Cost of goods manufactured for a manufacturing company
Obj. 4

✔ E. $165,000

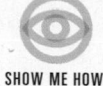

SHOW ME HOW

Two items are omitted from each of the following three lists of cost of goods manufactured statement data. Determine the amounts of the missing items, identifying them by letter.

Work in process inventory, August 1	$ 19,660	$ 41,650	(E)
Total manufacturing costs incurred during August	332,750	(C)	1,075,000
Total manufacturing costs	(A)	$515,770	$1,240,000
Work in process inventory, August 31	23,500	54,000	(F)
Cost of goods manufactured	(B)	(D)	$1,068,000

EX 1-14 Cost of goods manufactured for a manufacturing company
Obj. 4

SHOW ME HOW

The following information is available for Ethtridge Manufacturing Company for the month ending July 31:

Cost of direct materials used in production	$1,150,000
Direct labor	966,000
Work in process inventory, July 1	316,400
Work in process inventory, July 31	355,500
Total factory overhead	490,500

Determine Ethtridge's cost of goods manufactured for the month ended July 31.

EX 1-15 Income statement for a manufacturing company
Obj. 4

✔ D. $470,000

SHOW ME HOW

Two items are omitted from each of the following three lists of cost of goods sold data from a manufacturing company income statement. Determine the amounts of the missing items, identifying them by letter.

Finished goods Inventory, June 1	$116,600	$ 38,880	(E)
Cost of goods manufactured	825,900	(C)	180,000
Cost of finished goods available for sale	(A)	$540,000	$1,100,000
Finished goods inventory, June 30	130,000	70,000	(F)
Cost of goods sold	(B)	(D)	$ 945,000

EX 1-16 Statement of cost of goods manufactured for a manufacturing company
Obj. 4

✔ A. Cost of goods manufactured, $4,035,000

SHOW ME HOW   EXCEL TEMPLATE

Cost data for Sandusky Manufacturing Company for the month ended January 31 are as follows:

Inventories	January 1	January 31
Materials	$180,000	$145,500
Work in process	334,600	290,700
Finished goods	675,000	715,000

Direct labor	$2,260,000
Materials purchased during January	1,375,000
Factory overhead incurred during January:	
Indirect labor	115,000
Machinery depreciation	90,000
Heat, light, and power	55,000
Supplies	18,500
Property taxes	10,000
Miscellaneous costs	33,100

A. Prepare a cost of goods manufactured statement for January.

B. Determine the cost of goods sold for January.

| | **EX 1-17** | **Cost of goods sold, profit margin, and net income for a** | **Obj. 4** |

EX 1-17 Cost of goods sold, profit margin, and net income for a manufacturing company   Obj. 4

✔ A. Cost of goods sold, $4,595,000

SHOW ME HOW

The following information is available for Bandera Manufacturing Company for the month ending January 31:

Cost of goods manufactured	$4,490,000
Selling expenses	530,000
Administrative expenses	340,000
Sales	6,600,000
Finished goods inventory, January 1	880,000
Finished goods inventory, January 31	775,000

For the month ended January 31, determine Bandera Manufacturing's (A) cost of goods sold, (B) gross profit, and (C) net income.

EX 1-18 Cost flow relationships   Obj. 4

✔ A. $330,000

SHOW ME HOW

The following information is available for the first month of operations of Bahadir Company, a manufacturer of mechanical pencils:

Sales	$792,000
Gross profit	462,000
Cost of goods manufactured	396,000
Indirect labor	171,600
Factory depreciation	26,400
Materials purchased	244,200
Total manufacturing costs for the period	455,400
Materials inventory, ending	33,000

Using the information given, determine the following missing amounts:

A. Cost of goods sold

B. Finished goods inventory at the end of the month

C. Direct materials cost

D. Direct labor cost

E. Work in process inventory at the end of the month

Problems: Series A

PR 1-1A Classifying costs   Obj. 2

The following is a list of costs that were incurred in the production and sale of large commercial airplanes:

A. Salary of chief compliance officer of company

B. Power used by painting equipment

C. Instrument panel installed in the airplane cockpit

D. Annual bonus paid to the chief operating officer of the company

E. Turbo-charged airplane engine

F. Interior trim material used throughout the airplane cabin

G. Cost of normal scrap from production of airplane body

H. Hourly wages of employees that assemble the airplane

I. Salary of the Marketing Department personnel

J. Cost of paving the headquarters employee parking lot

K. Cost of electrical wiring throughout the airplane

L. Cost of electronic guidance system installed in the airplane cockpit

M. Salary of plant manager

N. Cost of miniature replicas of the airplane used to promote and market the airplane

O. Human Resources Department costs for the year

P. Metal used for producing the airplane body

Q. Annual fee to a celebrity to promote the aircraft

R. Hydraulic pumps used in the airplane's flight control system

S. Yearly cost of the maintenance contract for robotic equipment

T. Prebuilt leather seats installed in the first-class cabin

U. Depreciation on factory equipment

V. Special advertising campaign in *Aviation World* magazine

W. Oil to lubricate factory equipment

X. Masks for use by painters in painting the airplane body

Y. Decals for cockpit door, the cost of which is immaterial to the cost of the final product

Z. Salary of chief financial officer

Instructions

Classify each cost as either a product cost or a period cost. Indicate whether each product cost is a direct materials cost, a direct labor cost, or a factory overhead cost. Indicate whether each period cost is a selling expense or an administrative expense. Use the following tabular headings for your answer, placing an "X" in the appropriate column:

	Product Costs			Period Costs	
Cost	Direct Materials Cost	Direct Labor Cost	Factory Overhead Cost	Selling Expense	Administrative Expense

PR 1-2A   Classifying costs
Obj. 2

The following is a list of costs incurred by several businesses:

A. Cost of fabric used by clothing manufacturer

B. Maintenance and repair costs for factory equipment

C. Rent for a warehouse used to store work in process and finished products

D. Wages of production quality control personnel

E. Oil lubricants for factory plant and equipment

F. Depreciation of robot used to assemble a product

G. Travel costs of marketing executives to annual sales meeting

H. Depreciation of copying machines used by the Marketing Department

I. Fees charged by collection agency on past-due customer accounts

J. Electricity used to operate factory machinery

K. Maintenance costs for factory equipment

L. Pens, paper, and other supplies used by the Accounting Department in preparing various managerial reports

M. Charitable contribution to United Fund

N. Depreciation of microcomputers used in the factory to coordinate and monitor the production schedules

O. Fees paid to lawn service for office grounds upkeep

P. Cost of sewing machine needles used by a shirt manufacturer

Q. Cost of plastic for a telephone being manufactured

R. Telephone charges by president's office

S. Cost of 30-second television commercial

T. Surgeon's fee for heart bypass surgery

U. Depreciation of tools used in production

V. Wages of a machine operator on the production line

W. Salary of the vice president of manufacturing operations

X. Factory janitorial supplies

(Continued)

Instructions

Classify each of the preceding costs as a product cost or period cost. Indicate whether each product cost is a direct materials cost, a direct labor cost, or a factory overhead cost. Indicate whether each period cost is a selling expense or an administrative expense. Use the following tabular headings for preparing your answer, placing an "X" in the appropriate column:

	Product Costs			Period Costs	
Cost	Direct Materials Cost	Direct Labor Cost	Factory Overhead Cost	Selling Expense	Administrative Expense

PR 1-3A Cost classifications for a service company   Obj. 2

A partial list of Foothills Medical Center's costs follows:

A. Cost of patient meals
B. Nurses' salaries
C. Depreciation of X-ray equipment
D. Utility costs of the hospital
E. Salary of intensive care personnel
F. Cost of X-ray test
G. Operating room supplies used on patients (catheters, sutures, etc.)
H. Salary of the nutritionist
I. General maintenance of the hospital
J. Cost of new heart wing
K. Cost of drugs used for patients
L. Cost of advertising hospital services on television
M. Cost of improvements on the employee parking lot
N. Cost of intravenous solutions used for patients
O. Training costs for nurses
P. Cost of laundry services for operating room personnel
Q. Doctor's fee
R. Overtime incurred in the Patient Records Department due to a computer failure
S. Cost of blood tests
T. Cost of maintaining the staff and visitors' cafeteria
U. Depreciation on patient rooms

Instructions

1. What would be Foothills Medical Center's most logical definition for the final cost object?

2. Identify whether each of the costs is to be classified as direct or indirect. For purposes of classifying each cost as direct or indirect, use the patient as the cost object.

PR 1-4A Manufacturing income statement, statement of cost of goods manufactured   Obj. 4

✔ 1. B. Yakima Company, $1,330,000

EXCEL TEMPLATE

Several items are omitted from the income statement and cost of goods manufactured statement data for two different companies for the month of May:

	Rainier Company	Yakima Company
Materials inventory, May 1	$ 100,000	$ 48,200
Materials inventory, May 31	(A)	50,000
Materials purchased	950,000	710,000
Cost of direct materials used in production	938,500	(A)
Direct labor	2,860,000	(B)
Factory overhead	1,800,000	446,000
Total manufacturing costs incurred in May	(B)	2,484,200

	Rainier Company	Yakima Company
Total manufacturing costs	5,998,500	2,660,600
Work in process inventory, May 1	400,000	176,400
Work in process inventory, May 31	382,000	(C)
Cost of goods manufactured	(C)	2,491,500
Finished goods inventory, May 1	$ 615,000	$ 190,000
Finished goods inventory, May 31	596,500	(D)
Sales	9,220,000	4,550,000
Cost of goods sold	(D)	2,470,000
Gross profit	(E)	(E)
Operating expenses	1,000,000	(F)
Net income	(F)	1,500,000

Instructions

1. For both companies, determine the amounts of the missing items (A) through (F), identifying them by letter.
2. Prepare Yakima Company's statement of cost of goods manufactured for May.
3. Prepare Yakima Company's income statement for May.

PR 1-5A   Statement of cost of goods manufactured and income statement for a manufacturing company   Obj. 4

✔ 1. Cost of goods manufactured, $1,989,250

The following information is available for Robstown Corporation for 20Y8:

SHOW ME HOW   EXCEL TEMPLATE

Inventories	January 1	December 31
Materials	$ 44,250	$31,700
Work in process	63,900	80,000
Finished goods	101,200	99,800

Advertising expense	$ 400,000
Depreciation expense—office equipment	30,000
Depreciation expense—factory equipment	80,000
Direct labor	1,100,000
Heat, light, and power—factory	53,300
Indirect labor	115,000
Materials purchased	556,600
Office salaries expense	318,000
Property taxes—factory	40,000
Property taxes—office building	25,000
Rent expense—factory	27,000
Sales	3,850,000
Sales salaries expense	200,000
Supplies—factory	9,500
Miscellaneous costs—factory	11,400

Instructions

1. Prepare the 20Y8 statement of cost of goods manufactured.
2. Prepare the 20Y8 income statement.

Problems: Series B

PR 1-1B   Classifying costs   Obj. 2

The following is a list of costs that were incurred in the production and sale of lawn mowers:

A. Premiums on insurance policy for factory buildings

B. Tires for lawn mowers

C. Filter for spray gun used to paint the lawn mowers

D. Paint used to coat the lawn mowers, the cost of which is immaterial to the cost of the final product

E. Plastic for outside housing of lawn mowers

F. Salary of factory supervisor

G. Hourly wages of operators of robotic machinery used in production

H. Engine oil used in mower engines prior to shipment

I. Salary of vice president of marketing

J. Property taxes on the factory building and equipment

K. Cost of advertising in a national magazine

L. Gasoline engines used for lawn mowers

M. Electricity used to run the robotic machinery

N. Straight-line depreciation on the robotic machinery used to manufacture the lawn mowers

O. Salary of quality control supervisor who inspects each lawn mower before it is shipped

P. Attorney fees for drafting a new lease for headquarters offices

Q. Payroll taxes on hourly assembly line employees

R. Telephone charges for company controller's office

S. Steering wheels for lawn mowers

T. Factory cafeteria cashier's wages

U. Cash paid to outside firm for janitorial services for factory

V. Maintenance costs for new robotic factory equipment, based on hours of usage

W. Cost of boxes used in packaging lawn mowers

X. License fees for use of patent for lawn mower blade, based on the number of lawn mowers produced

Y. Steel used in producing the lawn mowers

Z. Commissions paid to sales representatives, based on the number of lawn mowers sold

Instructions

Classify each cost as either a product cost or a period cost. Indicate whether each product cost is a direct materials cost, a direct labor cost, or a factory overhead cost. Indicate whether each period cost is a selling expense or an administrative expense. Use the following tabular headings for your answer, placing an "X" in the appropriate column:

	Product Costs			Period Costs	
Cost	Direct Materials Cost	Direct Labor Cost	Factory Overhead Cost	Selling Expense	Administrative Expense

---

PR 1-2B   Classifying costs   Obj. 2

The following is a list of costs incurred by several businesses:

A. Salary of quality control supervisor

B. Packing supplies for products sold. These supplies are a very small portion of the total cost of the product.

C. Factory operating supplies

D. Depreciation of factory equipment

E. Hourly wages of warehouse laborers

F. Wages of company controller's secretary

G. Maintenance and repair costs for factory equipment

H. Paper used by commercial printer

I. Entertainment expenses for sales representatives

J. Protective glasses for factory machine operators

K. Sales commissions

L. Cost of hogs for meat processor

M. Cost of telephone operators for a toll-free hotline to help customers operate products

N. Hard drives for a microcomputer manufacturer

O. Lumber used by furniture manufacturer

P. Wages of a machine operator on the production line

Q. First-aid supplies for factory workers

R. Tires for an automobile manufacturer

S. Paper used by Computer Department in processing various managerial reports

T. Seed for grain farmer

U. Health insurance premiums paid for factory workers

V. Costs of operating a research laboratory

W. Costs for television advertisement

X. Executive bonus for vice president of marketing

Instructions

Classify each of the preceding costs as a product cost or period cost. Indicate whether each product cost is a direct materials cost, a direct labor cost, or a factory overhead cost. Indicate whether each period cost is a selling expense or an administrative expense. Use the following tabular headings for preparing your answer. Place an "X" in the appropriate column.

	Product Costs			Period Costs	
Cost	Direct Materials Cost	Direct Labor Cost	Factory Overhead Cost	Selling Expense	Administrative Expense

PR 1-3B Cost classifications for a service company

Obj. 2

A partial list of The Grand Hotel's costs follows:

A. Cost to mail a customer survey

B. Wages of convention setup employees

C. Pay-per-view movie rental costs (in rooms)

D. Cost of food

E. Cost of room mini-bar supplies

F. Training for hotel restaurant servers

G. Cost to paint lobby

H. Cost of laundering towels and bedding

I. Champagne for guests

J. Salary of the hotel manager

K. Depreciation of the hotel

L. Cost of valet parking

M. Wages of bellhops

N. Cost to replace lobby furniture

O. Cost of advertising in local newspaper

P. Wages of desk clerks

Q. Wages of maids

R. Cost of new carpeting

S. Guest room telephone costs for long-distance calls

T. Cost of soaps and shampoos for rooms

U. Utility cost

(Continued)

V. Wages of kitchen employees

W. General maintenance supplies

Instructions

1. What would be The Grand Hotel's most logical definition for the final cost object?

2. Identify whether each of the costs is to be classified as direct or indirect. For purposes of classifying each cost as direct or indirect, use the hotel guest as the cost object.

PR 1-4B   **Manufacturing income statement, statement of cost of goods manufactured**   Obj. 4

✔ 1. C. On Company, $800,800

EXCEL TEMPLATE

Several items are omitted from the income statement and cost of goods manufactured statement data for two different companies for the month of December:

	On Company	Off Company
Materials inventory, December 1	$ 65,800	$ 195,300
Materials inventory, December 31	(A)	91,140
Materials purchased	282,800	(A)
Cost of direct materials used in production	317,800	(B)
Direct labor	387,800	577,220
Factory overhead	148,400	256,060
Total manufacturing costs incurred in December	(B)	1,519,000
Total manufacturing costs	973,000	1,727,320
Work in process inventory, December 1	119,000	208,320
Work in process inventory, December 31	172,200	(C)
Cost of goods manufactured	(C)	1,532,020
Finished goods inventory, December 1	224,000	269,080
Finished goods inventory, December 31	197,400	(D)
Sales	1,127,000	1,944,320
Cost of goods sold	(D)	1,545,040
Gross profit	(E)	(E)
Operating expenses	117,600	(F)
Net income	(F)	164,920

Instructions

1. For both companies, determine the amounts of the missing items (A) through (F), identifying them by letter.

2. Prepare On Company's statement of cost of goods manufactured for December.

3. Prepare On Company's income statement for December.

PR 1-5B   **Statement of cost of goods manufactured and income statement for a manufacturing company**   Obj. 4

✔ 1. Cost of goods manufactured, $367,510

SHOW ME HOW   EXCEL TEMPLATE

The following information is available for Shanika Company for 20Y6:

Inventories	January 1	December 31
Materials	$ 77,350	$ 95,550
Work in process	109,200	96,200
Finished goods	113,750	100,100

Advertising expense	$ 68,250
Depreciation expense—office equipment	22,750
Depreciation expense—factory equipment	14,560
Direct labor	186,550
Heat, light, and power—factory	5,850
Indirect labor	23,660
Materials purchased	123,500

Inventories	January 1	December 31
Office salaries expense		77,350
Property taxes—factory		4,095
Property taxes—headquarters building		13,650
Rent expense—factory		6,825
Sales		864,500
Sales salaries expense		136,500
Supplies—factory		3,250
Miscellaneous costs—factory		4,420

Instructions

1. Prepare the 20Y6 statement of cost of goods manufactured.
2. Prepare the 20Y6 income statement.

Analysis for Decision Making

REAL WORLD

ADM-1　Hilton Hotels and Marriott International: Occupancy

A recent annual report of **Hilton Hotels** and **Marriott International** provided the following occupancy data for two recent years:

	Year 2	Year 1
Hilton Hotels	74.6%	72.2%
Marriott International	73.3%	71.3%

A. Is the occupancy trend favorable or unfavorable for Hilton Hotels?

B. Is the occupancy trend favorable or unfavorable for Marriott International?

C. Which company has the stronger occupancy?

D. ━━━━▶ What additional information would supplement occupancy in evaluating the performance of these two hotels?

ADM-2　Comparing occupancy for two hotels

Sunrise Suites and Nationwide Inns operate competing hotel chains across the region. Hotel capacity information for both hotels is as follows:

	Number of Hotels	Average Number of Rooms per Hotel
Sunrise Suites	120	90
Nationwide Inns	150	76

Information on the number of guests for each hotel and the average length of visit for June were as follows:

	Number of Guests	Average Length of Visit (in Nights)
Sunrise Suites	183,600	1.5
Nationwide Inns	228,000	1.2

A. Determine the guest nights for each hotel in June.

B. Determine the room nights for each hotel in June.

C. Determine the occupancy rate of each hotel in June.

D. ━━━━▶ Interpret the results in (C).

ADM-3   Occupancy for a hospital

The Valley Hospital measures the in-patient occupancy of the hospital by determining the number of patient days divided by the number of available bed days in the hospital for a time period. The following in-patient data are available for the months of April, May, and June:

	April	May	June
Admitted patients	1,440	1,860	2,250
Average length of stay per patient	4.0 days	3.5 days	3.0 days

The hospital has 200 rooms. One hundred rooms are private and have a single bed per room. The other hundred rooms are semi-private with two beds per room.

A. Determine the number of in-patient days for each month.

B. Determine the available bed days rate for each month.

C. Determine the occupancy rate for each month.

D. ▬▬▶ Interpret the results in (C).

ADM-4   Passenger load on a flight

Eastern Skies Airlines has three flights that depart from New York City and arrive in Chicago every day. The three flights are as follows:

Flight Number	Flight Departure Time	Flight Frequency
57	8:00 AM	7 days per week
85	10:00 AM	7 days per week
94	11:30 AM	7 days per week

Each flight uses a jet with a capacity of 180 seats. The airline measures the utilization of the aircraft by passenger load. Passenger load is the number of seats sold divided by the number of available seats on a flight for a time period. The following operating data are available for June:

Flight Number	Number of Seats Sold
57	5,130
85	2,592
94	2,376

A. Determine the available seat capacity for each flight number for June.

B. Determine the passenger load for each flight number for June.

C. ▬▬▶ What recommendations could you provide Eastern Skies based on the passenger load data?

Take It Further

TIF 1-1   Ethics in Action

ETHICS

Avett Manufacturing Company allows employees to purchase materials, such as metal and lumber, for personal use at a price equal to the company's cost. To purchase materials, an employee must complete a materials requisition form, which must then be approved by the employee's immediate supervisor. Brian Dadian, an assistant cost accountant, then charges the employee an amount based on Avett's net purchase cost.

Brian is in the process of replacing a deck on his home and has requisitioned lumber for personal use, which has been approved in accordance with company policy. In computing the cost of the lumber, Brian reviewed all the purchase invoices for the past year. He then used the lowest price to compute the amount due the company for the lumber.

The Institute of Management Accountants (IMA) is the professional organization for managerial accountants. The IMA has established four principles of ethical conduct for its members: honesty, fairness, objectivity, and responsibility. These principles are available at the IMA Web site: www.imanet.org.

➡ Using the IMA's four principles of ethical conduct, evaluate Brian's behavior. Has he acted in an ethical manner? Why?

REAL WORLD

TIF 1-2   Team Activity

In teams, visit a local restaurant. As you observe the operation, consider the costs associated with running the business. As a group, identify as many costs as you can and classify them according to the following table headings:

Cost	Direct Materials	Direct Labor	Overhead	Selling Expenses

TIF 1-3   Communication

Todd Johnson is the Vice President of Finance for Boz Zeppelin Industries Inc. At a recent finance meeting, Todd made the following statement: "The managers of a company should use the same information as the shareholders of the firm. When managers use the same information to guide their internal operations as shareholders use in evaluating their investments, the managers will be aligned with the stockholders' profit objectives."

➡ Prepare a one-half page memo to Todd discussing any concerns you might have with his statement.

Concepts and Principles

Chapter 1 *Introduction to Managerial Accounting*

Developing Information

COST SYSTEMS	COST BEHAVIOR
Chapter 2 *Job Order Costing* **Chapter 3** *Process Cost Systems* **Chapter 4** *Activity-Based Costing*	**Chapter 5** *Cost-Volume-Profit Analysis*

Decision Making

EVALUATING PERFORMANCE	COMPARING ALTERNATIVES
Chapter 6 *Variable Costing for Management Analysis* **Chapter 7** *Budgeting* **Chapter 8** *Evaluating Variances from Standard Costs* **Chapter 9** *Evaluating Decentralized Operations*	**Chapter 10** *Differential Analysis and Product Pricing* **Chapter 11** *Capital Investment Analysis* **Chapter 12** *Lean Manufacturing*

ANTONIODIAZ/SHUTTERSTOCK.COM

Gibson Guitars

The selling price of a Gibson guitar ranges from less than $500 to over $11,000 for a Gibson 2015 Wes Montgomery electric guitar. These differences in selling prices reflect the quality of the materials and the craftsmanship required in making a guitar. In all cases, however, the selling price of a guitar must be greater than the cost of producing it. So, how does **Gibson** determine the cost of producing a guitar?

Costs associated with creating a guitar include materials such as wood and strings, the wages of employees who build the guitar, and factory overhead. To determine the purchase price of a guitar, Gibson identifies and records the costs that go into the guitar during each step of the manufacturing process. As the guitar moves through the production process, the costs of direct materials, direct labor, and factory overhead are recorded. When the guitar is complete, the costs that have been recorded are added up to determine the cost of the guitar. The company then prices the guitar to achieve a level of profit (or revenue greater than the cost of the guitar).

This chapter describes a job order cost accounting system that illustrates how costs could be recorded and accumulated in manufacturing a guitar. The chapter also describes how a job order cost system could be used by service businesses.

Source: http://www.gibson.com/Gibson/History.aspx

What's Covered

Job Order Costing

Cost Accounting Systems Overview
- Job Order Cost Systems (Obj. 1)
- Process Cost Systems (Obj. 1)

Job Order Cost Systems for Manufacturing Businesses
- Materials (Obj. 2)
- Factory Labor (Obj. 2)
- Factory Overhead (Obj. 2)
- Work in Process (Obj. 2)
- Finished Goods (Obj. 2)
- Sales and Cost of Goods Sold (Obj. 2)
- Period Costs (Obj. 2)

Job Order Cost Systems for Service Businesses
- Job Order Service Businesses (Obj. 3)
- Flow of Costs (Obj. 3)

Learning Objectives

Obj. 1 Describe cost accounting systems used by manufacturing businesses.

Obj. 2 Describe and illustrate a job order cost accounting system for a manufacturing business.

Obj. 3 Describe job order cost accounting systems for service businesses.

Analysis for Decision Making

Describe the use of job order cost information for decision making.

Objective 1
Describe cost accounting systems used by manufacturing businesses.

Cost Accounting Systems Overview

Cost accounting systems measure, record, and report product costs. Managers use product costs for setting product prices, controlling operations, and developing financial statements.

The two main types of cost accounting systems for manufacturing operations are job order cost and process cost systems. Each system differs in how it accumulates and records costs.

Job Order Cost Systems

A **job order cost system** provides product costs for each quantity of product that is manufactured. Each quantity of product that is manufactured is called a *job*. Job order cost systems are often used by companies that manufacture custom products for customers or batches of similar products. For example, an apparel manufacturer, such as **Levi Strauss & Co.**, or a guitar manufacturer, such as **Gibson Guitars**, would use a job order cost system.

This chapter illustrates the job order cost system. As a basis for illustration, **Legend Guitars**, a manufacturer of guitars, is used. Exhibit 1 summarizes Legend Guitars' manufacturing operations.[1]

Process Cost Systems

A **process cost system** provides product costs for each manufacturing department or process. Process cost systems are often used by companies that manufacture units of a product that are indistinguishable from each other and are manufactured using a continuous production process. Examples would be oil refineries, paper producers, chemical processors, and food processors. The process cost system is illustrated in Chapter 3.

---

[1] Legend Guitars' manufacturing operation is described in more detail in Chapter 1.

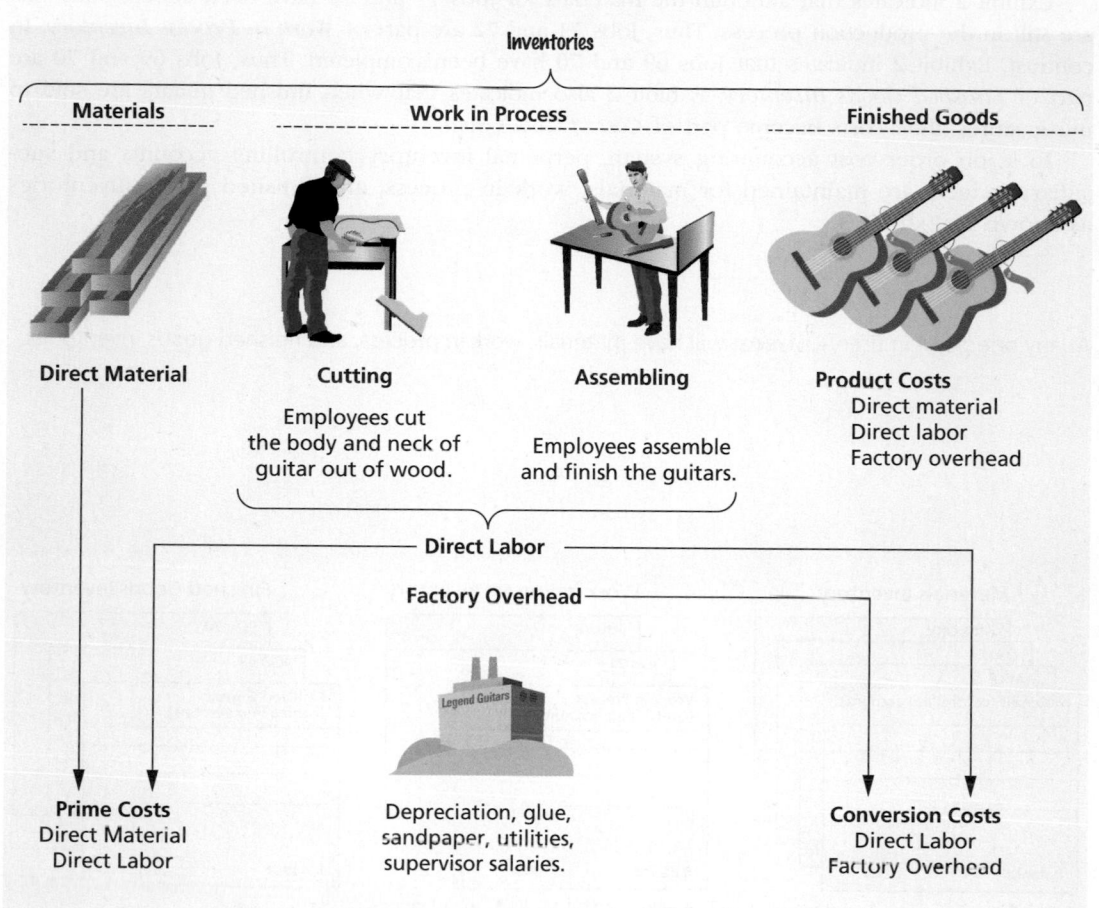

Exhibit 1
Summary of Legend Guitars' Manufacturing Operations

Job Order Cost Systems for Manufacturing Businesses

A job order cost system records and summarizes manufacturing costs by jobs. The flow of manufacturing costs in a job order system is illustrated in Exhibit 2.

Objective 2
Describe and illustrate a job order cost accounting system for a manufacturing business.

Exhibit 2
Flow of Manufacturing Costs

Exhibit 2 indicates that although the materials for Jobs 71 and 72 have been added, both jobs are still in the production process. Thus, Jobs 71 and 72 are part of *Work in Process Inventory*. In contrast, Exhibit 2 indicates that Jobs 69 and 70 have been completed. Thus, Jobs 69 and 70 are part of *Finished Goods Inventory*. Exhibit 2 also indicates that when finished guitars are sold to music stores, their costs become part of *Cost of Goods Sold*.

In a job order cost accounting system, perpetual inventory controlling accounts and subsidiary ledgers are maintained for materials, work in process, and finished goods inventories as shown in Exhibit 3.

Link to Gibson Guitars

At any one point in time, **Gibson** will have materials, work in process, and finished goods inventories.

Exhibit 3
Inventory Ledger Accounts

Materials Inventory

Work in Process Inventory

Finished Goods Inventory

Why It Matters

3D Printing

3D printing is a technology that creates a three-dimensional product from an "additive" process. "Additive" means the product is built from plastic, metal, or other material that is built layer by successive layer until the final object is complete. The layers are very thin, allowing for extremely precise final specifications. The process is like printing on a piece of paper (which adds a layer of ink), but in three dimensions, hence the term 3D printing. The machines that add the thin material layers are computer controlled, so that the layers are added in exactly the right way to create the final product. 3D printers can manufacture very complex final products. 3D printing fits well within a job shop environment because the technology provides an economical way to create custom products.

Materials

The materials account in the general ledger is a controlling account. A separate account for each type of material is maintained in a subsidiary **materials ledger**.

Exhibit 4 shows **Legend Guitars**' materials ledger account for maple. Increases (debits) and decreases (credits) to the account are as follows:

- Increases (debits) are based on *receiving reports* such as Receiving Report No. 196 for $10,500, which is supported by the supplier's invoice.
- Decreases (credits) are based on *materials requisitions* such as Requisition No. 672 for $2,000 for Job 71 and Requisition No. 704 for $11,000 for Job 72.

Exhibit 4
Materials
Information and
Cost Flows

Gibson uses a variety of woods (direct materials) in making guitars, including cedar.

Link to
Gibson Guitars

A **receiving report** is prepared when materials that have been ordered are received and inspected. The quantity received and the condition of the materials are entered on the receiving report. When the supplier's invoice is received, it is compared to the receiving report. If there are no discrepancies, a journal entry is made to record the purchase. The journal entry to record the supplier's invoice related to Receiving Report No. 196 in Exhibit 4 is as follows:

A.	Materials	10,500	
	Accounts Payable		10,500
	Materials purchased during December.		

A = L + E
+   +

The storeroom releases materials for use in manufacturing when a **materials requisition** is received. Examples of materials requisitions are shown in Exhibit 4.

The materials requisitions for each job serve as the basis for recording materials used. For direct materials, the quantities and amounts from the materials requisitions are posted to job cost sheets. **Job cost sheets**, which are also illustrated in Exhibit 4, make up the work in process subsidiary ledger.

Exhibit 4 shows the posting of $2,000 of direct materials to Job 71 and $11,000 of direct materials to Job 72.[2] Job 71 is an order for 20 units of Jazz Series guitars, while Job 72 is an order for 60 units of American Series guitars.

A summary of the materials requisitions is used as a basis for the journal entry recording the materials used for the month. For direct materials, this entry increases (debits) Work in Process and decreases (credits) Materials as follows:

A = L + E
+ −

B.	Work in Process	13,000	
	Materials		13,000
	Materials requisitioned to jobs		
	($2,000 + $11,000).		

Many companies use computerized information processes to record the use of materials. In such cases, storeroom employees electronically record the release of materials, which automatically updates the materials ledger and job cost sheets.

 Ethics: Do It!

Phony Invoice Scams

A popular method for defrauding a company is to issue a phony invoice. The scam begins by initially contacting the target firm to discover details of key business contacts, business operations, and products. The swindler then uses this information to create a fictitious invoice. The invoice will include names, figures, and other details to give it the appearance of legitimacy. This type of scam can be avoided if invoices are matched with receiving documents prior to issuing a check.

Factory Labor

When employees report for work, they may use *electronic badges, clock cards,* or *in-and-out cards* to clock in. When employees work on an individual job, they use **time tickets** to record the amount of time they have worked on a specific job. Exhibit 5 illustrates time tickets for Jobs 71 and 72 at **Legend Guitars**.

Exhibit 5 shows that on December 13, 20Y8, D. McInnis spent six hours working on Job 71 at an hourly rate of $10 for a cost of $60 (6 hrs. × $10). Exhibit 5 also indicates that a total of 350 hours was spent by employees on Job 71 during December for a total cost of $3,500. This total direct labor cost of $3,500 is posted to the job cost sheet for Job 71, as shown in Exhibit 5.

Likewise, Exhibit 5 shows that on December 26, 20Y8, S. Andrews spent eight hours on Job 72 at an hourly rate of $15 for a cost of $120 (8 hrs. × $15). A total of 500 hours was spent by employees on Job 72 during December for a total cost of $7,500. This total direct labor cost of $7,500 is posted to the job cost sheet for Job 72, as shown in Exhibit 5.

[2] To simplify, Exhibit 4 and this chapter use the first-in, first-out cost flow method.

Exhibit 5
Labor Information
and Cost Flows

DYNAMIC
EXHIBIT

A summary of the time tickets is used as the basis for the journal entry recording direct labor for the month. This entry increases (debits) Work in Process and increases (credits) Wages Payable, as follows:

C.	Work in Process	11,000	
	Wages Payable		11,000
	Factory labor used in production		
	of jobs ($3,500 + $7,500).		

A = L + E
+   +

As with direct materials, many businesses use computerized information processing to record direct labor. In such cases, employees may log their time directly into computer terminals at their workstations. In other cases, employees may be issued magnetic cards, much like credit cards, to log in and out of work assignments.

Link to Gibson Guitars

Gibson uses workers (factory labor) to perform a variety of tasks in making guitars, including cutting, matching wood grains, fitting braces, shaping and fitting necks, coloring, polishing, tuning, and inspecting.

Factory Overhead

Factory overhead includes all manufacturing costs except direct materials and direct labor. Factory overhead costs come from a variety of sources, including the following:

- *Indirect materials* comes from a summary of materials requisitions.
- *Indirect labor* comes from the salaries of production supervisors and the wages of other employees such as janitors.
- *Factory power* comes from utility bills.
- *Factory depreciation* comes from Accounting Department computations of depreciation.

To illustrate the recording of factory overhead, assume that **Legend Guitars** incurred $4,600 of overhead during December, which included $500 of indirect materials, $2,000 of indirect labor, $900 of utilities, and $1,200 of factory depreciation. The $500 of indirect materials consisted of $200 of glue and $300 of sandpaper. The entry to record the factory overhead is as follows:

A = L + E	D.	Factory Overhead	4,600	
+ − +		Materials		500
		Wages Payable		2,000
		Utilities Payable		900
		Accumulated Depreciation		1,200
		Factory overhead incurred in production.		

Check Up Corner 2-1   **Direct Materials, Direct Labor, and Factory Overhead Costs**

Grayson Company is a manufacturer that uses a job order cost system. The following data summarize the operations related to production for January, the first month of operations:

A. Purchased 400 units of materials at $14 per unit on account.

B. Requisitioned materials for production as follows:
- 200 units for Job 101 at $12 per unit.
- 300 units for Job 102 at $14 per unit.

C. Accumulated direct labor cost as follows:
- 700 hours of direct labor on Job 101 at $16 per hour.
- 600 hours of direct labor on Job 102 at $12 per hour.

D. Incurred factory overhead costs as follows: indirect materials, $800; indirect labor, $3,400; utilities cost, $1,600; and factory depreciation, $2,500.

Journalize the entries to record these transactions.

Solution:

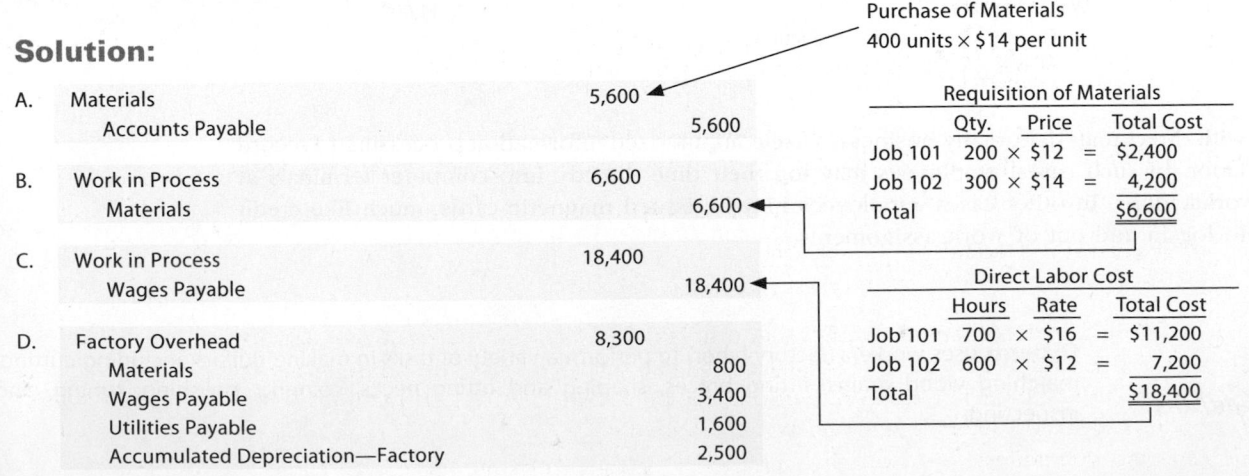

A.	Materials	5,600	
	Accounts Payable		5,600
B.	Work in Process	6,600	
	Materials		6,600
C.	Work in Process	18,400	
	Wages Payable		18,400
D.	Factory Overhead	8,300	
	Materials		800
	Wages Payable		3,400
	Utilities Payable		1,600
	Accumulated Depreciation—Factory		2,500

Purchase of Materials
400 units × $14 per unit

Requisition of Materials

	Qty.	Price		Total Cost
Job 101	200 × $12	=	$2,400
Job 102	300 × $14	=	4,200
Total			$6,600

Direct Labor Cost

	Hours	Rate		Total Cost
Job 101	700 × $16	=	$11,200
Job 102	600 × $12	=	7,200
Total			$18,400

Check Up Corner

Allocating Factory Overhead Factory overhead is different from direct labor and direct materials in that it is *indirectly* related to the jobs. That is, factory overhead costs cannot be identified with or traced to specific jobs. For this reason, factory overhead costs are allocated to jobs. The process by which factory overhead or other costs are assigned to a cost object, such as a job, is called **cost allocation**.

The factory overhead costs are *allocated* to jobs using a common measure related to each job. This measure is called an **activity base**, *allocation base*, or *activity driver*. The activity base used to allocate overhead should reflect the consumption or use of factory overhead costs. Three common activity bases used to allocate factory overhead costs are direct labor hours, direct labor cost, and machine hours.

Why It Matters

Advanced Robotics

Boston Consulting Group (BCG) believes the use of advanced robotics in manufacturing is about to take off. It estimates that by 2025, 25% of all tasks will be automated through robotics, driving a 10–30% increase in productivity. China, the United States, Japan, Germany, and South Korea will be the primary drivers of this trend. BCG anticipates significant use of advanced robotics will have a number of important impacts on manufacturing:

■ Robotics reduces the need to move factories to low-labor cost countries to save costs.

■ Robotics will reduce the size of manufacturing facilities, allowing for greater flexibility and a more regional focus.

■ The economic costs of robotics will decline, opening up their broad use.

■ The workforce will require new skills, such as programming and technical maintenance, to support robotic manufacturing. For example, **Shenzhen Everwin Precision Technology** recently announced plans to replace 90% of its 1,800 employees with advanced robotics in the near future. The remaining employees will be retrained to work with the robots.

Increasing use of robots will cause direct labor to go down, while factory overhead will increase. As a result, accurate factory overhead allocation will become increasingly important in these advanced manufacturing environments.

Source: Boston Consulting Group, *"The Shifting Economics of Global Manufacturing: How a Takeoff in Advanced Robotics Will Power the Next Productivity Surge,"* February 2015.

Predetermined Factory Overhead Rate Factory overhead costs are normally allocated or *applied* to jobs using a **predetermined factory overhead rate**. The predetermined factory overhead rate is computed as follows:

$$\text{Predetermined Factory Overhead Rate} = \frac{\text{Estimated Total Factory Overhead Costs}}{\text{Estimated Activity Base}}$$

To illustrate, assume that **Legend Guitars** estimates the total factory overhead cost as $50,000 for the year and the activity base as 10,000 direct labor hours. The predetermined factory overhead rate of $5 per direct labor hour is computed as follows:

$$\text{Predetermined Factory Overhead Rate} = \frac{\$50,000}{10,000 \text{ direct labor hours}} = \$5 \text{ per direct labor hour}$$

As illustrated, the predetermined overhead rate is computed using *estimated* amounts at the beginning of the period. This is because managers need timely information on the product costs of each job. If a company waited until all overhead costs were known at the end of the period, the allocated factory overhead would be accurate, but not timely. Only through timely reporting can managers adjust manufacturing methods or product pricing.

Many companies are using a method for accumulating and allocating factory overhead costs. This method, called **activity-based costing**, uses a different overhead rate for each type of factory overhead activity, such as inspecting, moving, and machining. Activity-based costing is discussed and illustrated in Chapter 4.

Applying Factory Overhead to Work in Process Legend Guitars applies factory overhead using a rate of $5 per direct labor hour. The factory overhead applied to each job is recorded in the job cost sheets, as shown in Exhibit 6.

Exhibit 6

Applying Factory Overhead to Jobs

Exhibit 6 shows that 850 direct labor hours were used in Legend Guitars' December operations. Based on the time tickets, 350 hours can be traced to Job 71, and 500 hours can be traced to Job 72.

Using a factory overhead rate of $5 per direct labor hour, $4,250 of factory overhead is applied as follows:

	Direct Labor Hours	**Factory Overhead Rate**	**Factory Overhead Applied**
Job 71	350	$5	$1,750 (350 hrs. × $5)
Job 72	500	$5	2,500 (500 hrs. × $5)
Total	850		$4,250

As shown in Exhibit 6, the applied overhead is posted to each job cost sheet. Factory overhead of $1,750 is posted to Job 71, which results in a total product cost on December 31, 20Y8, of $10,250. Factory overhead of $2,500 is posted to Job 72, which results in a total product cost on December 31, 20Y8, of $21,000.

The journal entry to apply factory overhead increases (debits) Work in Process and decreases (credits) Factory Overhead. This journal entry to apply overhead to Jobs 71 and 72 is as follows:

E.	Work in Process	4,250	
	Factory Overhead		4,250
	Factory overhead applied to jobs according to the predetermined overhead rate (850 hrs. × $5).		

$$A = L + E$$
$$+ \quad -$$

To summarize, the factory overhead account is:

- Increased (debited) for the *actual overhead* costs incurred, as shown for transaction (D).
- Decreased (credited) for the *applied overhead*, as shown for transaction (E).

The actual and applied overhead usually differ because the actual overhead costs are normally different from the estimated overhead costs. Depending on whether actual overhead is greater or less than applied overhead, the factory overhead account will either have a debit or credit ending balance as follows:

- If the applied overhead is *less than* the actual overhead incurred, the factory overhead account will have a debit balance. This debit balance is called **underapplied factory overhead** or *underabsorbed factory overhead*.
- If the applied overhead is *more than* the actual overhead incurred, the factory overhead account will have a credit balance. This credit balance is called **overapplied factory overhead** or *overabsorbed factory overhead*.

The factory overhead account for Legend Guitars, which follows, illustrates both underapplied and overapplied factory overhead. Specifically, the December 1, 20Y8, credit balance of $200 represents overapplied factory overhead. In contrast, the December 31, 20Y8, debit balance of $150 represents underapplied factory overhead.

Account Factory Overhead					Account No.	
					Balance	
Date	Item	Post. Ref.	Debit	Credit	Debit	Credit
20Y8						
Dec. 1	Balance					200
31	Factory overhead cost incurred		4,600		4,400	
31	Factory overhead cost applied			4,250	150	

Underapplied balance ────────
Overapplied balance ────────

If the balance of factory overhead (either underapplied or overapplied) becomes large, the balance and related overhead rate should be investigated. For example, a large balance could be caused by changes in manufacturing methods. In this case, the factory overhead rate should be revised.

Gibson incurs a variety of overhead costs in making guitars, including depreciation on buildings and equipment.

Link to Gibson Guitars

Check Up Corner 2-2 — Applying Overhead and Determining Job Cost

Grayson Company estimates that total factory overhead costs will be $100,000 for the year. Direct labor hours are estimated to be 25,000. The company had two completed jobs at the end of January, Jobs 101 and 102. Data on accumulated direct labor hours and units produced for these jobs are as follows:

	Direct Labor Hours	Units Produced
Job 101	700	500
Job 102	600	1,000

A. Using the information provided, determine:
   1. The predetermined factory overhead rate using direct labor hours as the activity base.
   2. The amount of factory overhead applied to Jobs 101 and 102 in January.

B. Prepare the journal entry to apply factory overhead to both jobs in January using the predetermined overhead rate from (A).

C. Using the information provided along with the job cost information from Check Up Corner 2-1, determine:
   1. The balance on the job cost sheets for Jobs 101 and 102 at the end of the month.
   2. The cost per unit for Jobs 101 and 102.

Solution:

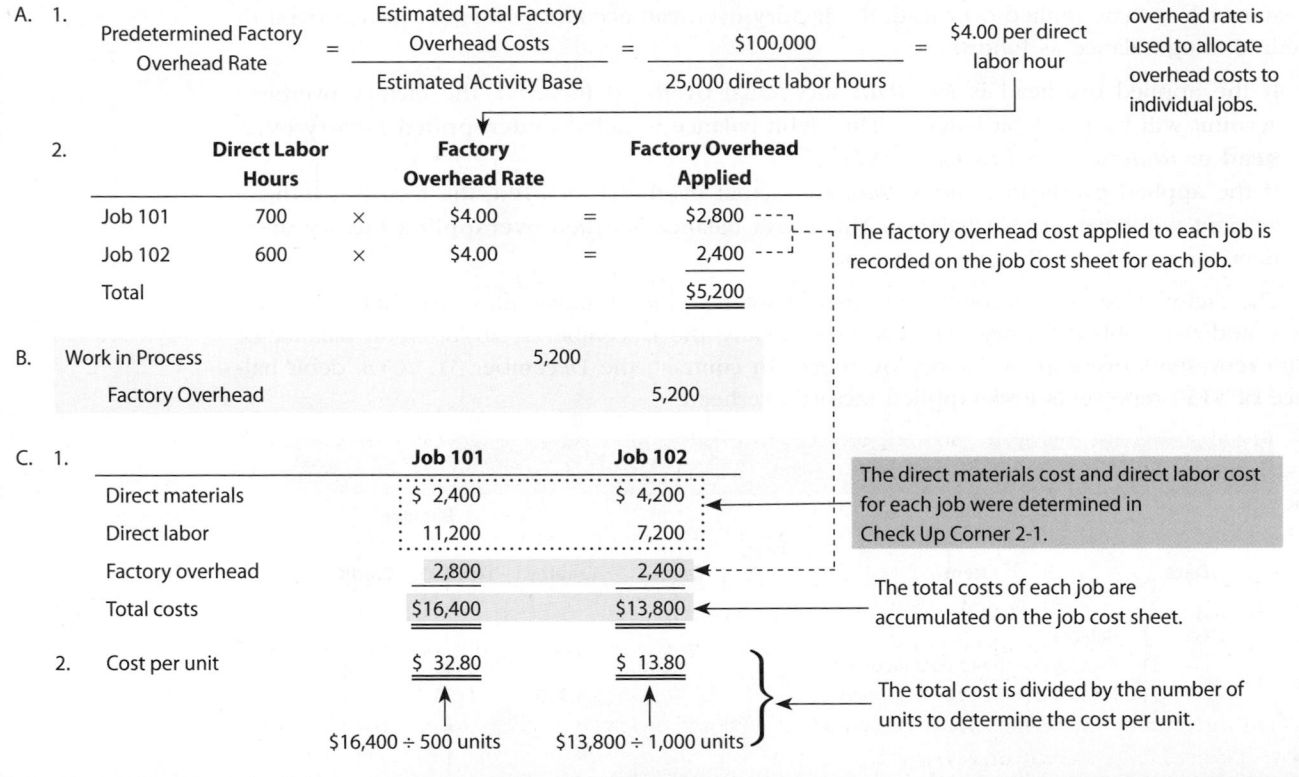

A. 1.
$$\text{Predetermined Factory Overhead Rate} = \frac{\text{Estimated Total Factory Overhead Costs}}{\text{Estimated Activity Base}} = \frac{\$100,000}{25,000 \text{ direct labor hours}} = \$4.00 \text{ per direct labor hour}$$

A predetermined overhead rate is used to allocate overhead costs to individual jobs.

2.

	Direct Labor Hours		Factory Overhead Rate		Factory Overhead Applied
Job 101	700	×	$4.00	=	$2,800
Job 102	600	×	$4.00	=	2,400
Total					$5,200

The factory overhead cost applied to each job is recorded on the job cost sheet for each job.

B.
| Work in Process | 5,200 | |
| Factory Overhead | | 5,200 |

C. 1.

	Job 101	Job 102
Direct materials	$ 2,400	$ 4,200
Direct labor	11,200	7,200
Factory overhead	2,800	2,400
Total costs	$16,400	$13,800

The direct materials cost and direct labor cost for each job were determined in Check Up Corner 2-1.

The total costs of each job are accumulated on the job cost sheet.

2. Cost per unit $ 32.80 $ 13.80

$16,400 ÷ 500 units $13,800 ÷ 1,000 units

The total cost is divided by the number of units to determine the cost per unit.

Check Up Corner

Disposal of Factory Overhead Balance During the year, the balance in the factory overhead account is carried forward and reported as a deferred debit or credit on the monthly (interim) balance sheets. However, any balance in the factory overhead account should not be carried over to the next year. This is because any such balance applies only to operations of the current year.

If the estimates for computing the predetermined overhead rate are reasonably accurate, the ending balance of Factory Overhead should be relatively small. For this reason, the balance of Factory Overhead at the end of the year is disposed of by transferring it to the cost of goods sold account as follows:[3]

[3] An ending balance in the factory overhead account may also be allocated among the work in process, finished goods, and cost of goods sold accounts. This brings these accounts into agreement with the actual costs incurred. This approach is rarely used and is only required for large ending balances in the factory overhead account. For this reason, it will not be used in this text.

■ If there is an ending debit balance (underapplied overhead) in the factory overhead account, it is disposed of by the entry that follows:

Cost of Goods Sold	XXX	
Factory Overhead		XXX
Transfer of underapplied		
overhead to cost of goods sold.		

■ If there is an ending credit balance (overapplied overhead) in the factory overhead account, it is disposed of by the entry that follows:

Factory Overhead	XXX	
Cost of Goods Sold		XXX
Transfer of overapplied		
overhead to cost of goods sold.		

To illustrate, the journal entry to dispose of **Legend Guitars**' December 31, 20Y8, underapplied overhead balance of $150 is as follows:

F.	Cost of Goods Sold	150	
	Factory Overhead		150
	Closed underapplied factory		
	overhead to cost of goods sold.		

$$A = L + E$$
$$- \qquad\qquad - \ \text{Exp}$$

Work in Process

During the period, Work in Process is increased (debited) for the following:

■ Direct materials cost
■ Direct labor cost
■ Applied factory overhead cost

To illustrate, the work in process account for **Legend Guitars** is shown in Exhibit 7. The balance of Work in Process on December 1, 20Y8 (beginning balance), was $3,000. As shown in Exhibit 7, this balance relates to Job 71, which was the only job in process on this date. During December, Work in Process was debited for the following:

■ Direct materials cost of $13,000 [transaction (B)], based on materials requisitions.
■ Direct labor cost of $11,000 [transaction (C)], based on time tickets.
■ Applied factory overhead of $4,250 [transaction (E)], based on the predetermined overhead rate of $5 per direct labor hour.

The preceding Work in Process debits are supported by the postings to job cost sheets for Jobs 71 and 72, as shown in Exhibit 7.

During December, Job 71 was completed. Upon completion, the product costs (direct materials, direct labor, factory overhead) are totaled. This total is divided by the number of units produced to determine the cost per unit. Thus, the 20 Jazz Series guitars produced as Job 71 cost $512.50 ($10,250 ÷ 20) per guitar.

After completion, Job 71 is transferred from Work in Process to Finished Goods by the following entry:

G.	Finished Goods	10,250	
	Work in Process		10,250
	Job 71 completed in December.		

$$A = L + E$$
$$+ \ -$$

Exhibit 7
Job Cost Sheets
and the Work in
Process Controlling
Account

Job Cost Sheets

Job 71
20 units of Jazz Series guitars

Balance	$ 3,000
Direct Materials	2,000
Direct Labor	3,500
Factory Overhead	1,750
Total Job Cost	$10,250
Unit Cost	$512.50

Job 72
60 units of American Series guitars

Direct Materials	$11,000
Direct Labor	7,500
Factory Overhead	2,500
Total Job Cost	$21,000

Account *Work in Process*   *Account No.*

G.

					Balance	
Date	Item	Post. Ref.	Debit	Credit	Debit	Credit
20Y8						
Dec. 1	Balance				3,000	
31	Direct materials		13,000		16,000	
31	Direct labor		11,000		27,000	
31	Factory overhead		4,250		31,250	
31	Jobs completed—Job 71			10,250	21,000	

Job 72 was started in December but was not completed by December 31, 20Y8. Thus, Job 72 is still part of work in process on December 31, 20Y8. As shown in Exhibit 7, the balance of the job cost sheet for Job 72 ($21,000) is also the December 31, 20Y8, balance of Work in Process.

Finished Goods

The finished goods account is a controlling account for the subsidiary **finished goods ledger** or *stock ledger*. Each account in the finished goods ledger contains cost data for the units manufactured, units sold, and units on hand.

Exhibit 8 illustrates the finished goods ledger account for **Legend Guitars**' Jazz Series guitars. The exhibit indicates that there were 40 Jazz Series guitars on hand on December 1, 20Y8. During the month, 20 additional Jazz guitars were completed and transferred to Finished Goods from the completion of Job 71. In addition, the beginning inventory of 40 Jazz guitars was sold during the month.

Exhibit 8
Finished Goods
Ledger Account

ITEM: *Jazz Series guitars*

Manufactured			Shipped			Balance			
Job Order No.	Quantity	Amount	Ship Order No.	Quantity	Amount	Date	Quantity	Amount	Unit Cost
						Dec. 1	40	$20,000	$500.00
			643	40	$20,000	9	—	—	—
71	20	$10,250				31	20	10,250	512.50

A virtual tour of **Gibson**'s Bozeman, Montana, manufacturing plant can be found at www2.gibson.com. The Bozeman plant makes acoustical guitars similar to those illustrated in this chapter. Acoustical guitars that do not require power or amps to produce sound are often used for folk and country music. Electric guitars are most often used for metal and rock music.

Link to Gibson Guitars

Sales and Cost of Goods Sold

During December, **Legend Guitars** sold 40 Jazz Series guitars for $850 each, generating total sales of $34,000 ($850 × 40 guitars). Exhibit 8 indicates that the cost of these guitars was $500 per guitar or a total cost of $20,000 ($500 × 40 guitars). The entries to record the sale and related cost of goods sold are as follows:

H.	Accounts Receivable	34,000	
	Sales		34,000
	Revenue received from guitars sold on account.		

$A = L + E$
$+$ $+ Rev$

I.	Cost of Goods Sold	20,000	
	Finished Goods		20,000
	Cost of 40 Jazz Series guitars sold.		

$A = L + E$
$-$ $- Exp$

In a job order cost accounting system, the preparation of a statement of cost of goods manufactured, which was discussed in Chapter 1 is not necessary. This is because job order costing uses the perpetual inventory system and, thus, the cost of goods sold can be directly determined from the finished goods ledger as illustrated in Exhibit 8.

Period Costs

Period costs are used in generating revenue during the current period but are not involved in the manufacturing process. As discussed in Chapter 1, *period costs* are recorded as expenses of the current period as either selling or administrative expenses.

Selling expenses are incurred in marketing the product and delivering sold products to customers. Administrative expenses are incurred in managing the company but are not related to the manufacturing or selling functions. During December, **Legend Guitars** recorded the following selling and administrative expenses:

J.	Sales Salaries Expense	2,000	
	Office Salaries Expense	1,500	
	Salaries Payable		3,500
	Recorded December period costs.		

$A = L + E$
$+$ $- Exp$

Why It Matters

Job Order Costing in Hollywood

A manufacturer uses a job order system to accumulate direct labor, direct material, and factory overhead costs by production job. In a similar way, Hollywood accumulates costs for a particular movie. However, rather than factory labor, a movie has the salaries of actors, directors, writers, and other creative and technical staff in making the movie. Rather than manufacturing materials, a movie will have scenery, costumes, props, and other materials in making the film. A movie will also have indirect costs associated with supervision, accounting, casting, and other costs that the studio shares with other movies. Such shared costs are allocated to each movie project using an overhead rate similar to that found in manufacturing. Work in process represents the costs accumulated while a movie is in production. A completed movie is treated similarly to finished goods inventory. Upon release, the accumulated costs will be expensed on the income statement as revenues from theatrical release, online streaming, cable, and DVDs are being earned.

Exhibit 9 Flow of Manufacturing Costs for Legend Guitars

Summary of Cost Flows for Legend Guitars

Exhibit 9 shows the cost flows through the manufacturing accounts of **Legend Guitars** for December. In addition, summary details of the following subsidiary ledgers are shown:

- *Materials Ledger*—the subsidiary ledger for Materials.
- *Job Cost Sheets*—the subsidiary ledger for Work in Process.
- *Finished Goods Ledger*—the subsidiary ledger for Finished Goods.

Entries in the accounts shown in Exhibit 9 are identified by letters. These letters refer to the journal entries described and illustrated in the chapter. Entries (H) and (J) are not shown because they do not involve a flow of manufacturing costs.

As shown in Exhibit 9, the balances of Materials, Work in Process, and Finished Goods are supported by their subsidiary ledgers. These balances are as follows:

Controlling Account	Balance and Total of Related Subsidiary Ledger
Materials	$ 3,500
Work in Process	21,000
Finished Goods	10,250

The income statement for **Legend Guitars** is shown in Exhibit 10.

Exhibit 10

Income Statement of Legend Guitars

Legend Guitars Income Statement For the Month Ended December 31, 20Y8		
Sales		$34,000
Cost of goods sold.		20,150*
Gross profit		$13,850
Selling and administrative expenses:		
Sales salaries expense	$2,000	
Office salaries expense	1,500	
Total selling and administrative expenses.		3,500
Income from operations		$10,350

*$20,150 = ($500 × 40 guitars) + $150 underapplied factory overhead

Job Order Cost Systems for Service Businesses

Objective 3

Describe job order cost accounting systems for service businesses.

A job order cost accounting system may be used by a service business. However, whether a service business uses a job order cost system depends upon the nature of the service provided to customers.

Types of Service Businesses

Hotels, taxis, newspapers, attorneys, accountants, and hospitals provide services to customers. All these businesses, however, would not use job order costing. For example, hotels, taxis, and newspapers would normally not use a job order cost system. In contrast, attorneys, accountants, and hospitals normally would use a job order system.

A service business using job order costing normally renders a service that is unique to each customer with related costs that vary significantly with each customer. For example, while hotels provide a service, the service is the same for each guest on any given night.

In contrast, an attorney or hospital provides a unique service for each client or patient. In addition, each client or patient incurs costs that are unique to them. For this reason, attorneys and hospitals normally use job order cost systems.[4] Other examples of service businesses using job order cost systems include advertising agencies, event planners, and car repair shops.

Flow of Costs in a Service Job Order Cost System

A service business using a job order cost system views each customer, client, or patient as a separate job for which costs are accumulated and reported.

Since a service is being provided, the primary product costs are normally direct labor and overhead. Any materials or supplies used in rendering services are usually insignificant. As a result, materials and supply costs are included as part of the overhead cost.

Like a manufacturing business, the direct labor and overhead costs of rendering services to clients are accumulated in a work in process account. Work in Process is supported by a cost ledger with a job cost sheet for each client.

When a job is completed and the client is billed, the costs are transferred to a cost of services account. Cost of Services is similar to the cost of goods sold account for a merchandising or manufacturing business. A finished goods account and related finished goods ledger are not necessary. This is because services cannot be inventoried and the revenues for the services are recorded upon completion.

In practice, other considerations unique to service businesses may need to be considered. For example, a service business may bill clients on a weekly or monthly basis rather than when a job is completed. In such cases, a portion of the costs related to each billing is transferred from the work in process account to the cost of services account. A service business may also bill clients for services in advance, which would be accounted for as deferred revenue until the services are completed.

The flow of costs through a service business using a job order cost accounting system is shown in Exhibit 11.

Exhibit 11 Flow of Costs Through a Service Business

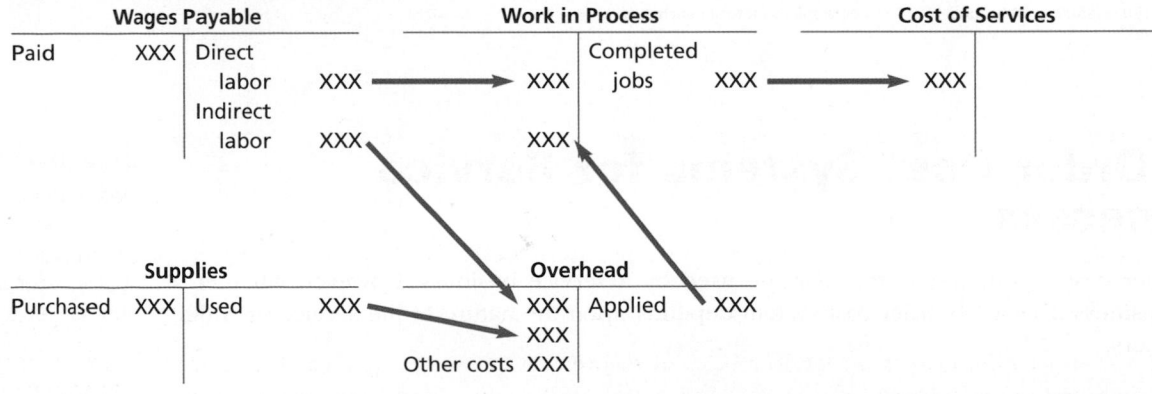

[4] Service businesses using job order cost systems normally require each customer, client, or patient to sign a contract that describes the nature of the service being rendered.

Check Up Corner 2-3   Job Order Costing for a Service Business

The Mad-Fly Agency provides consulting services to a variety of clients across the country. The agency accumulates costs for each consulting project on the basis of direct labor costs and allocated overhead costs. Mad-Fly's estimated direct labor and overhead costs for the year are as follows:

Direct labor hours (professional staff)	20,000 hours
Hourly rate for professional staff	$180 per hour
Estimated total overhead costs	$1,200,000

Mad-Fly allocates overhead costs to individual jobs based on the total estimated direct labor hours of its professional services staff.

A. Determine Mad-Fly's estimated predetermined overhead rate for the year.

B. Mad-Fly started and completed a consulting job for MT Industries during the year (Job 402). The job required 200 direct labor hours from the agency's professional services staff. Determine the cost of the MT Industries job (Job 402).

Solution:

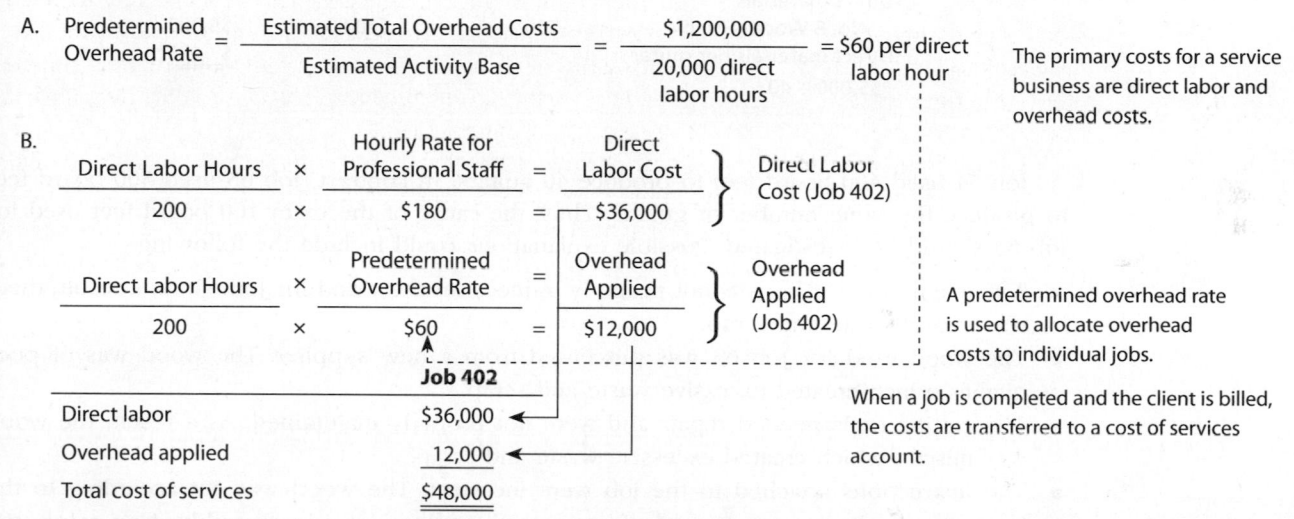

A. $$\text{Predetermined Overhead Rate} = \frac{\text{Estimated Total Overhead Costs}}{\text{Estimated Activity Base}} = \frac{\$1,200,000}{20,000 \text{ direct labor hours}} = \$60 \text{ per direct labor hour}$$

The primary costs for a service business are direct labor and overhead costs.

B.

Direct Labor Hours	×	Hourly Rate for Professional Staff	=	Direct Labor Cost	} Direct Labor Cost (Job 402)
200	×	$180	=	$36,000	

Direct Labor Hours	×	Predetermined Overhead Rate	=	Overhead Applied	} Overhead Applied (Job 402)
200	×	$60	=	$12,000	

A predetermined overhead rate is used to allocate overhead costs to individual jobs.

Job 402

Direct labor	$36,000
Overhead applied	12,000
Total cost of services	$48,000

When a job is completed and the client is billed, the costs are transferred to a cost of services account.

Check Up Corner

Analysis for Decision Making

Analyzing Job Costs

Objective
Describe the use of job order cost information for decision making.

A job order cost accounting system accumulates and records product costs by jobs. The resulting total and unit product costs can be compared to similar jobs, compared over time, or compared to expected costs. In this way, a job order cost system can be used by managers for cost evaluation and control.

To illustrate, Exhibit 12 shows the direct materials used for Jobs 54 and 63 for **Legend Guitars**. The wood used in manufacturing guitars is measured in board feet. Because Jobs 54 and 63 produced the same type and number of guitars, the direct materials cost per unit should be about the same. However, the materials cost per guitar for Job 54 is $100, while for Job 63 it is $125. Thus, the materials costs are significantly more for Job 63.

The job cost sheets shown in Exhibit 12 can be analyzed for possible reasons for the increased materials cost for Job 63. Because the materials price did not change ($10 per board foot), the increased materials cost must be related to wood consumption.

Exhibit 12
Comparing Data from Job Cost Sheets

Job 54
Item: 40 Jazz Series guitars

	Materials Quantity (board feet)	Materials Price	Materials Amount
Direct materials:			
No. 8 Wood—Maple	400	$10.00	$4,000
Direct materials per guitar			$ 100*
*$4,000 ÷ 40			

Job 63
Item: 40 Jazz Series guitars

	Materials Quantity (board feet)	Materials Price	Materials Amount
Direct materials:			
No. 8 Wood—Maple	500	$10.00	$5,000
Direct materials per guitar			$ 125*
*$5,000 ÷ 40			

Job 54 used 400 board feet to produce 40 guitars. In contrast, Job 63 used 500 board feet to produce the same number of guitars. Thus, the cause of the extra 100 board feet used for Job 63 should be investigated. Possible explanations could include the following:

- A new employee, who was not properly trained, cut the wood for Job 63. As a result, there was excess waste and scrap.
- The wood used for Job 63 was purchased from a new supplier. The wood was of poor quality, which created excessive waste and scrap.
- The cutting tools needed repair and were not properly maintained. As a result, the wood was miscut, which created excessive waste and scrap.
- The instructions attached to the job were incorrect. The wood was cut according to the instructions. The incorrect instructions were discovered later in assembly. As a result, the wood had to be recut and the initial cuttings scrapped.

Make a Decision   Analyzing Job Costs

Antolini Enterprises produces men's sports coats that are sold by popular department stores. Each retail order is treated as a job that accumulates materials, labor, and overhead costs for a batch of sports coats. Management has obtained data on the labor costs for four selected jobs over a six-month period. Each selected job represents a similar style and size of sports coat. The data are as follows:

	Count	Direct Labor Hours	Direct Labor Rate per Hour	Total Direct Labor Cost
Job 107	10	4.50	$14.00	$ 63.00
Job 125	14	7.00	14.00	98.00
Job 160	16	8.80	14.00	123.20
Job 192	8	3.20	16.00	51.20

A. Determine the direct labor cost per unit for each job.

B. Interpret the trend in per-unit labor cost.

C. Determine the direct labor hours per sports coat.

D. Interpret what may be happening with Job 192.

Solution:

A. Divide the total direct labor cost by the count to determine the direct labor cost per unit for each job:

	Total Direct Labor Cost	Count	Direct Labor Cost per Sports Coat
Job 107	$ 63.00	10	$6.30
Job 125	98.00	14	7.00
Job 160	123.20	16	7.70
Job 192	51.20	8	6.40

B. The direct labor cost per sports coat increased over the first three jobs, then declined with the last job. The increase for the first three jobs is not related to a change in the direct labor rate, which was the same for all three jobs. Thus, the increase in labor cost must be related to an increase in labor time to make the coats. This is confirmed in (C).

C. The direct labor hours per sports coat is determined by dividing the total direct labor hours by the count as follows:

	Direct Labor Hours	Count	Direct Labor Hours per Sports Coat
Job 107	4.50	10	0.45
Job 125	7.00	14	0.50
Job 160	8.80	16	0.55
Job 192	3.20	8	0.40

The direct labor hours per sports coat have increased over the first three jobs, which has led to the increased direct labor cost per coat noted in (B). Management would want to investigate why the direct labor hours per coat are increasing.

D. The direct labor rate for Job 192 increased from $14 to $16. This may be due to a raise in pay or the use of a more skilled and higher-paid employee. Regardless, the result was a significant drop in the direct labor hours per sports coat, down to 0.40 hours, which is the best of all the jobs. The net result of the higher efficiency, combined with the higher direct labor cost, was a direct labor cost per sports coat that was only ten cents higher than Job 107 and a significant improvement over Job 160.

Make a Decision

Let's Review

Chapter Summary

1. A cost accounting system accumulates product costs. The two primary cost accounting systems are the job order and the process cost systems. Job order cost systems accumulate costs for each quantity of product that passes through the factory. Process cost systems accumulate costs for each department or process within the factory.

2. A job order cost system accumulates costs for each quantity of product, or "job," that passes through the factory. Direct materials, direct labor, and factory overhead are accumulated on the job cost sheet, which is the subsidiary cost ledger for each job. Direct materials and direct labor are assigned to individual jobs, based on the quantity used. Factory overhead costs are assigned to each job, based on an activity base that reflects the use of factory overhead costs.

3. Job order cost accounting systems can be used by service businesses to plan and control operations. Because the product is a service, the focus is on direct labor and overhead costs. The costs of providing a service are accumulated in a work in process account and transferred to a cost of services account upon completion.

Key Terms

activity base (55)
activity-based costing (56)
cost accounting systems (48)
cost allocation (55)
finished goods ledger (60)
job cost sheets (52)

job order cost system (48)
materials ledger (50)
materials requisition (52)
overapplied factory overhead (57)
predetermined factory
   overhead rate (55)

process cost system (48)
receiving report (51)
time tickets (52)
underapplied factory
   overhead (57)

Practice

Multiple-Choice Questions

1. For which of the following would the job order cost system be appropriate?
   A. Antique furniture repair shop
   B. Rubber manufacturer
   C. Coal manufacturer
   D. Computer chip manufacturer

2. The journal entry to record the requisition of materials to the factory in a job order cost system is a debit to:
   A. Materials.
   B. Accounts Payable.
   C. Work in Process.
   D. Cost of Goods Sold.

3. Job order cost sheets accumulate all of the following costs except for:
   A. direct materials.
   B. indirect materials.
   C. direct labor.
   D. factory overhead applied.

4. A company estimated $420,000 of factory overhead cost and 16,000 direct labor hours for the period. During the period, a job was completed with $4,500 of direct materials and $3,000 of direct labor. The direct labor rate was $15 per hour. What is the factory overhead applied to this job?
   A. $2,100
   B. $5,250
   C. $78,750
   D. $420,000

5. If the factory overhead account has a credit balance, factory overhead is said to be:
   A. underapplied.
   B. overapplied.
   C. underabsorbed.
   D. in error.

Answers provided after Problem. Need more practice? Find additional multiple-choice questions, exercises, and problems in CengageNOWv2.

Exercises

SHOW ME HOW

1. Issuance of materials   Obj. 2

On April 6, Almerinda Company purchased on account 60,000 units of raw materials at $12 per unit. On April 21, raw materials were requisitioned for production as follows: 25,000 units for Job 50 at $10 per unit and 27,000 units for Job 51 at $12 per unit. Journalize the entry on April 6 to record the purchase and on April 21 to record the requisition from the materials storeroom.

SHOW ME HOW

2. Direct labor costs   Obj. 2

During April, Almerinda Company accumulated 20,000 hours of direct labor costs on Job 50 and 24,000 hours on Job 51. The total direct labor was incurred at a rate of $20 per direct labor hour for Job 50 and $22 per direct labor hour for Job 51. Journalize the entry to record the flow of labor costs into production during April.

SHOW ME HOW

3. Factory overhead costs   Obj. 2

During April, Almerinda Company incurred factory overhead costs as follows: indirect materials, $42,000; indirect labor, $90,000; utilities cost, $16,000; and factory depreciation, $54,000. Journalize the entry to record the factory overhead incurred during April.

SHOW ME HOW

4. Applying factory overhead   Obj. 2

Almerinda Company estimates that total factory overhead costs will be $1,750,000 for the year. Direct labor hours are estimated to be 500,000. For Almerinda Company, (A) determine the predetermined factory overhead rate using direct labor hours as the activity base, (B) determine the amount of factory overhead applied to Jobs 50 and 51 in April using the data on direct labor hours from Exercises 2 and 3, and (C) prepare the journal entry to apply factory overhead to both jobs in April according to the predetermined overhead rate.

SHOW ME HOW

5. Job costs   Obj. 2

At the end of April, Almerinda Company had completed Jobs 50 and 51. Job 50 is for 23,040 units, and Job 51 is for 26,000 units. Using the data from Exercises 1 through 4, determine (A) the balance on the job cost sheets for Jobs 50 and 51 at the end of April and (B) the cost per unit for Jobs 50 and 51 at the end of April.

SHOW ME HOW

6. Cost of goods sold   Obj. 2

Hosmer Company completed 312,000 units during the year at a cost of $7,800,000. The beginning finished goods inventory was 22,000 units at $440,000. Determine the cost of goods sold for 325,000 units, assuming a FIFO cost flow.

Answers provided after Problem. Need more practice? Find additional multiple-choice questions, exercises, and problems in CengageNOWv2.

Problem

Wildwing Entertainment Inc. is a manufacturer that uses a job order cost system. The following data summarize the operations related to production for March, the first month of operations:

A. Materials purchased on account, $15,500.

B. Materials requisitioned and labor used:

	Materials	Factory Labor
Job No. 100	$2,650	$1,770
Job No. 101	1,240	650
Job No. 102	980	420
Job No. 103	3,420	1,900
Job No. 104	1,000	500
Job No. 105	2,100	1,760
For general factory use	450	650

C. Factory overhead costs incurred on account, $2,700.

D. Depreciation of machinery, $1,750.

E. Factory overhead is applied at a rate of 70% of direct labor cost.

F. Jobs completed: Nos. 100, 101, 102, 104.

G. Jobs 100, 101, and 102 were shipped, and customers were billed for $8,100, $3,800, and $3,500, respectively.

Instructions

1. Journalize the entries to record these transactions.

2. Determine the account balances for Work in Process and Finished Goods.

3. Prepare a schedule of unfinished jobs to support the balance in the work in process account.

4. Prepare a schedule of completed jobs on hand to support the balance in the finished goods account.

Need more practice? Find additional multiple-choice questions, exercises, and problems in CengageNOWv2.

Answers

Multiple-Choice Questions

1. **A** Job order cost systems are best suited to businesses manufacturing special orders from customers, such as would be the case for a repair shop for antique furniture (answer A). A process cost system is best suited for manufacturers of similar units of products such as rubber manufacturers (answer B), coal manufacturers (answer C), and computer chip manufacturers (answer D).

2. **C** The journal entry to record the requisition of materials to the factory in a job order cost system is a debit to Work in Process and a credit to Materials.

3. **B** The job cost sheet accumulates the cost of direct materials (answer A), direct labor (answer C), and factory overhead applied (answer D). Indirect materials (answer B) are NOT accumulated on the job order cost sheets, but are included as part of factory overhead applied.

4. **B**

$$\text{Predetermined Factory Overhead Rate} = \frac{\text{Estimated Total Factory Overhead Costs}}{\text{Estimated Activity Base}}$$

$$\text{Predetermined Factory Overhead Rate} = \frac{\$420,000}{16,000 \text{ dlh}} = \$26.25$$

$$\text{Hours applied to the job:} = \frac{\$3,000}{\$15 \text{ per hour}} = 200 \text{ hours}$$

Factory overhead applied to the job: 200 hours × $26.25 = $5,250

5. **B** If the amount of factory overhead applied during a particular period exceeds the actual overhead costs, the factory overhead account will have a credit balance and is said to be overapplied (answer B) or overabsorbed. If the amount applied is less than the actual costs, the account will have a debit balance and is said to be underapplied (answer A) or underabsorbed (answer C). Since an "estimated" predetermined overhead rate is used to apply overhead, a credit balance does not necessarily represent an error (answer D).

Exercises

1.

Apr.	6	Materials	720,000	
		Accounts Payable		720,000
		$720,000 = 60,000 \times \$12.$		
	21	Work in Process*	574,000	
		Materials		574,000

* Job 50	$250,000 = 25,000 \times \$10$
Job 51	$324,000 = 27,000 \times \$12$
Total	$\$574,000$

2.

Work in Process*	928,000	
Wages Payable		928,000

* Job 50	$400,000 = 20,000$ hours $\times \$20$
Job 51	$528,000 = 24,000$ hours $\times \$22$
Total	$\$928,000$

3.

Factory Overhead	202,000	
Materials		42,000
Wages Payable		90,000
Utilities Payable		16,000
Accumulated Depreciation—Factory		54,000

4. A. $3.50 per direct labor hour = $1,750,000 ÷ 500,000 direct labor hours

   B. Job 50 $ 70,000 = 20,000 hours × $3.50 per hour

   Job 51   84,000 = 24,000 hours × $3.50 per hour

   $154,000

   C.

Work in Process	154,000	
Factory Overhead		154,000

5.

A.

	Job 50	Job 51
Direct materials	$250,000	$324,000
Direct labor	400,000	528,000
Factory overhead	70,000	84,000
Total costs	$720,000	$936,000

B. Job 50 $31.25 = \$720,000 \div 23,040$ units
    Job 51 $36.00 = \$936,000 \div 26,000$ units

6. $8,015,000 = \$440,000 + (303,000 \times \$25)^*$

    *Cost per unit of goods produced during the year = $25 = \$7,800,000 \div 312,000$ units

Need more help? Watch step-by-step videos of how to compute answers to these Exercises in CengageNOWv2.

Problem

1. A.

Materials	15,500	
Accounts Payable		15,500

B.

Work in Process	11,390	
Materials		11,390
Work in Process	7,000	
Wages Payable		7,000
Factory Overhead	1,100	
Materials		450
Wages Payable		650

C.

Factory Overhead	2,700	
Accounts Payable		2,700

D.

Factory Overhead	1,750	
Accumulated Depreciation—Machinery		1,750

E.

Work in Process	4,900	
Factory Overhead (70% of $7,000)		4,900

F.

Finished Goods	11,548	
Work in Process		11,548

Computation of the cost of jobs finished:

Job	Direct Materials	Direct Labor	Factory Overhead	Total
Job No. 100	$2,650	$1,770	$1,239	$ 5,659
Job No. 101	1,240	650	455	2,345
Job No. 102	980	420	294	1,694
Job No. 104	1,000	500	350	1,850
				$11,548

G.

Accounts Receivable	15,400	
Sales		15,400
Cost of Goods Sold	9,698	
Finished Goods		9,698

Cost of jobs sold computation:

Job No. 100	$5,659
Job No. 101	2,345
Job No. 102	1,694
	$9,698

2. Work in Process: $11,742 ($11,390 + $7,000 + $4,900 – $11,548)

Finished Goods: $1,850 ($11,548 – $9,698)

3.

Schedule of Unfinished Jobs

Job	Direct Materials	Direct Labor	Factory Overhead	Total
Job No. 103	$3,420	$1,900	$1,330	$ 6,650
Job No. 105	2,100	1,760	1,232	5,092
Balance of Work in Process, March 31				$11,742

4.

Schedule of Completed Jobs

Job No. 104:

Direct materials	$1,000
Direct labor	500
Factory overhead	350
Balance of Finished Goods, March 31	$1,850

Discussion Questions

1. A. Name two principal types of cost accounting systems.

   B. Which system provides for a separate record of each particular quantity of product that passes through the factory?

   C. Which system accumulates the costs for each department or process within the factory?

2. What kind of firm would use a job order cost system?

3. Which account is used in the job order cost system to accumulate direct materials, direct labor, and factory overhead applied to production costs for individual jobs?

4. What document is the source for (A) debiting the accounts in the materials ledger and (B) crediting the accounts in the materials ledger?

5. What is a job cost sheet?

6. What is the difference between a clock card and time ticket?

7. Discuss how the predetermined factory overhead rate can be used in job order cost accounting to assist management in pricing jobs.

8. A. How is a predetermined factory overhead rate calculated?

   B. Name three common bases used in calculating the rate.

9. A. What is (1) overapplied factory overhead and (2) underapplied factory overhead?

   B. If the factory overhead account has a debit balance, was factory overhead underapplied or overapplied?

   C. If the factory overhead account has a credit balance at the end of the first month of the fiscal year, where will the amount of this balance be reported on the interim balance sheet?

10. Describe how a job order cost system can be used for professional service businesses.

Basic Exercises

SHOW ME HOW

BE 2-1   Issuance of materials   Obj. 2
On May 7, Bergan Company purchased on account 10,000 units of raw materials at $8 per unit. During May, raw materials were requisitioned for production as follows: 7,500 units for Job 200 at $8 per unit and 1,480 units for Job 305 at $5 per unit. Journalize the entry on May 7 to record the purchase and on May 31 to record the requisition from the materials storeroom.

SHOW ME HOW

BE 2-2   Direct labor costs   Obj. 2
During May, Bergan Company accumulated 2,500 hours of direct labor costs on Job 200 and 3,000 hours on Job 305. The total direct labor was incurred at a rate of $28 per direct labor hour for Job 200 and $24 per direct labor hour for Job 305. Journalize the entry to record the flow of labor costs into production during May.

SHOW ME HOW

BE 2-3   Factory overhead costs   Obj. 2
During May, Bergan Company incurred factory overhead costs as follows: indirect materials, $8,800; indirect labor, $6,600; utilities cost, $4,800; and factory depreciation, $9,000. Journalize the entry to record the factory overhead incurred during May.

SHOW ME HOW

BE 2-4   Applying factory overhead   Obj. 2
Bergan Company estimates that total factory overhead costs will be $620,000 for the year. Direct labor hours are estimated to be 80,000. For Bergan Company, (A) determine the predetermined factory overhead rate using direct labor hours as the activity base, (B) determine the amount of factory overhead applied to Jobs 200 and 305 in May using the data on direct labor hours from BE 2-2, and (C) prepare the journal entry to apply factory overhead to both jobs in August according to the predetermined overhead rate.

SHOW ME HOW

BE 2-5   Job costs   Obj. 2
At the end of May, Bergan Company had completed Jobs 200 and 305. Job 200 is for 2,390 units, and Job 305 is for 2,053 units. Using the data from BE 2-1, BE 2-2, and BE 2-4, determine (A) the balance on the job cost sheets for Jobs 200 and 305 at the end of May, and (B) the cost per unit for Jobs 200 and 305 at the end of May.

SHOW ME HOW

BE 2-6   Cost of goods sold   Obj. 2
Pine Creek Company completed 200,000 units during the year at a cost of $3,000,000. The beginning finished goods inventory was 25,000 units at $310,000. Determine the cost of goods sold for 210,000 units, assuming a FIFO cost flow.

Exercises

EX 2-1   Transactions in a job order cost system   Obj. 2
Five selected transactions for the current month are indicated by letters in the following T accounts in a job order cost accounting system:

Materials		Work in Process	
(A)		(A)	(D)
		(B)	
		(C)	

Wages Payable		Finished Goods	
(B)		(D)	(E)

Factory Overhead		Cost of Goods Sold	
(A)	(C)	(E)	
(B)			

Describe each of the five transactions.

EX 2-2 Cost flow relationships   Obj. 2

✔ B. $4,425,000

SHOW ME HOW

The following information is available for the first year of operations of Engle Inc., a manu-facturer of fabricating equipment:

Sales	$7,270,000
Gross profit	1,450,000
Indirect labor	330,000
Indirect materials	195,000
Other factory overhead	90,000
Materials purchased	5,100,000
Total manufacturing costs for the period	6,170,000
Materials inventory, end of period	480,000

Determine the following amounts:

A. Cost of goods sold

B. Direct materials cost

C. Direct labor cost

EX 2-3 Cost of materials issuances under the FIFO method   Obj. 2

✔ B. $2,280

EXCEL TEMPLATE

An incomplete subsidiary ledger of materials inventory for May is as follows:

RECEIVED			ISSUED			BALANCE			
Receiving Report Number	Quantity	Unit Price	Materials Requisition Number	Quantity	Amount	Date	Quantity	Unit Price	Amount
						May 1	285	$30.00	$8,550
40	130	$32.00				May 4	___	___	___
			91	365		May 10	___	___	___
44	110	38.00				May 21	___	___	___
			97	100		May 27	___	___	___

A. Complete the materials issuances and balances for the materials subsidiary ledger under FIFO.

B. Determine the materials inventory balance at the end of May.

C. Journalize the summary entry to transfer materials to work in process.

D. ━━━▶ Explain how the materials ledger might be used as an aid in maintaining inventory quantities on hand.

SHOW ME HOW

EX 2-4   Entry for issuing materials   Obj. 2

Materials issued for the current month are as follows:

Requisition No.	Material	Job No.	Amount
201	Aluminum	500	$88,700
202	Plastic	503	27,600
203	Rubber	504	3,650
204	Glue	Indirect	2,250
205	Steel	510	38,750

Journalize the entry to record the issuance of materials.

EX 2-5   Entries for materials   Obj. 2

✔ C. fabric, $35,500   GenX Furnishings Company manufactures designer furniture. GenX Furnishings uses a job order cost system. Balances on June 1 from the materials ledger are as follows:

SHOW ME HOW

Fabric	$40,500
Polyester filling	28,600
Lumber	62,400
Glue	6,550

The materials purchased during June are summarized from the receiving reports as follows:

Fabric	$440,000
Polyester filling	180,000
Lumber	360,000
Glue	40,000

Materials were requisitioned to individual jobs as follows:

	Fabric	Polyester Filling	Lumber	Glue	Total
Job 601	$205,000	$ 75,000	$120,000		$400,000
Job 602	110,000	36,000	88,000		234,000
Job 603	130,000	55,000	125,000		310,000
Factory overhead—indirect materials				$34,800	34,800
Total	$445,000	$166,000	$333,000	$34,800	$978,800

The glue is not a significant cost, so it is treated as indirect materials (factory overhead).

A. Journalize the entry to record the purchase of materials in June.

B. Journalize the entry to record the requisition of materials in June.

C. Determine the June 30 balances that would be shown in the materials ledger accounts.

EX 2-6   Entry for factory labor costs   Obj. 2

A summary of the time tickets for the current month follows:

Job No.	Amount	Job No.	Amount
100	$ 3,500	Indirect	$ 9,100
101	6,650	111	8,620
104	21,900	115	2,760
108	14,440	117	18,550

Journalize the entry to record the factory labor costs.

EX 2-7 Entry for factory labor costs

Obj. 2

The weekly time tickets indicate the following distribution of labor hours for three direct labor employees:

	Job 301	Job 302	Job 303	Process Improvement
		Hours		
Tom Couro	10	15	13	2
David Clancy	12	12	14	2
Jose Cano	11	13	15	1

The direct labor rate earned per hour by the three employees is as follows:

Tom Couro	$32
David Clancy	36
Jose Cano	28

The process improvement category includes training, quality improvement, and other indirect tasks.

A. Journalize the entry to record the factory labor costs for the week.

B. Assume that Jobs 301 and 302 were completed but not sold during the week and that Job 303 remained incomplete at the end of the week. How would the direct labor costs for all three jobs be reflected on the financial statements at the end of the week?

SHOW ME HOW

EX 2-8 Entries for direct labor and factory overhead

Obj. 2

Townsend Industries Inc. manufactures recreational vehicles. Townsend uses a job order cost system. The time tickets from November jobs are summarized as follows:

Job 11-101	$6,240
Job 11-102	9,000
Job 11-103	7,210
Job 11-104	6,750
Factory supervision	4,000

Factory overhead is applied to jobs on the basis of a predetermined overhead rate of $18 per direct labor hour. The direct labor rate is $40 per hour.

A. Journalize the entry to record the factory labor costs.

B. Journalize the entry to apply factory overhead to production for November.

✔ B. $40.80 per direct labor hour

SHOW ME HOW

EX 2-9 Factory overhead rates, entries, and account balance

Obj. 2

Sundance Solar Company operates two factories. The company applies factory overhead to jobs on the basis of machine hours in Factory 1 and on the basis of direct labor hours in Factory 2. Estimated factory overhead costs, direct labor hours, and machine hours are as follows:

	Factory 1	Factory 2
Estimated factory overhead cost for fiscal year beginning March 1	$12,900,000	$10,200,000
Estimated direct labor hours for year		250,000
Estimated machine hours for year	600,000	
Actual factory overhead costs for March	$12,990,000	$10,090,000
Actual direct labor hours for March		245,000
Actual machine hours for March	610,000	

A. Determine the factory overhead rate for Factory 1.

B. Determine the factory overhead rate for Factory 2.

C. Journalize the entries to apply factory overhead to production in each factory for March.

D. Determine the balances of the factory overhead accounts for each factory as of March 31, and indicate whether the amounts represent over- or underapplied factory overhead.

SHOW ME HOW

EX 2-10   Predetermined factory overhead rate   Obj. 2

Spring Street Engine Shop uses a job order cost system to determine the cost of performing engine repair work. Estimated costs and expenses for the coming period are as follows:

Engine parts	$ 875,000
Shop direct labor	660,000
Shop and repair equipment depreciation	44,500
Shop supervisor salaries	138,000
Shop property taxes	27,500
Shop supplies	10,000
Advertising expense	22,100
Administrative office salaries	73,500
Administrative office depreciation expense	8,600
Total costs and expenses	$1,859,200

The average shop direct labor rate is $30 per hour.
Determine the predetermined shop overhead rate per direct labor hour.

✔ A. $290 per hour

SHOW ME HOW

EX 2-11   Predetermined factory overhead rate   Obj. 2

Poehling Medical Center has a single operating room that is used by local physicians to perform surgical procedures. The cost of using the operating room is accumulated by each patient procedure and includes the direct materials costs (drugs and medical devices), physician surgical time, and operating room overhead. On January 1 of the current year, the annual operating room overhead is estimated to be:

Disposable supplies	$299,600
Depreciation expense	75,000
Utilities	32,000
Nurse salaries	278,500
Technician wages	126,900
Total operating room overhead	$812,000

The overhead costs will be assigned to procedures, based on the number of surgical room hours. Poehling Medical Center expects to use the operating room an average of eight hours per day, seven days per week. In addition, the operating room will be shut down two weeks per year for general repairs.

A. Determine the predetermined operating room overhead rate for the year.

B. Bill Harris had a five-hour procedure on January 22. How much operating room overhead would be charged to his procedure, using the rate determined in part (A)?

C. During January, the operating room was used 240 hours. The actual overhead costs incurred for January were $67,250. Determine the overhead under- or overapplied for the period.

✔ B. $95,200

SHOW ME HOW

EX 2-12   Entry for jobs completed; cost of unfinished jobs   Obj. 2

The following account appears in the ledger prior to recognizing the jobs completed in August:

Work in Process	
Balance, August 1	$ 60,000
Direct materials	325,000
Direct labor	462,000
Factory overhead	210,000

Jobs finished during August are summarized as follows:

Job 210	$197,800	Job 224	$160,000
Job 216	240,000	Job 230	364,000

A. Journalize the entry to record the jobs completed.

B. Determine the cost of the unfinished jobs at August 31.

EX 2-13 Entries for factory costs and jobs completed   Obj. 2

✔ D. $73,750   Old School Publishing Inc. began printing operations on January 1. Jobs 301 and 302 were completed during the month, and all costs applicable to them were recorded on the related cost sheets. Jobs 303 and 304 are still in process at the end of the month, and all applicable costs except factory overhead have been recorded on the related cost sheets. In addition to the materials and labor charged directly to the jobs, $8,000 of indirect materials and $12,400 of indirect labor were used during the month. The cost sheets for the four jobs entering production during the month are as follows, in summary form:

Job 301		Job 302	
Direct materials	$10,000	Direct materials	$20,000
Direct labor	8,000	Direct labor	17,000
Factory overhead	6,000	Factory overhead	12,750
Total	$24,000	Total	$49,750

Job 303		Job 304	
Direct materials	$24,000	Direct materials	$14,000
Direct labor	18,000	Direct labor	12,000
Factory overhead	—	Factory overhead	—

Journalize the summary entry to record each of the following operations for January (one entry for each operation):

A. Direct and indirect materials used.

B. Direct and indirect labor used.

C. Factory overhead applied to all four jobs (a single overhead rate is used based on direct labor cost).

D. Completion of Jobs 301 and 302.

EX 2-14 Financial statements of a manufacturing firm   Obj. 2

✔ A. Income from operations, $170,000   The following events took place for Chi-Lite Inc. during June, the first month of operations as a producer of road bikes:

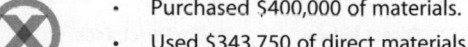

EXCEL TEMPLATE

- Purchased $400,000 of materials.
- Used $343,750 of direct materials in production.
- Incurred $295,000 of direct labor wages.
- Applied factory overhead at a rate of 75% of direct labor cost.
- Transferred $815,000 of work in process to finished goods.
- Sold goods with a cost of $789,000.
- Sold goods for $1,400,000.
- Incurred $316,000 of selling expenses.
- Incurred $125,000 of administrative expenses.

A. Prepare the June income statement for Chi-Lite. Assume that Chi-Lite uses the perpetual inventory method.

B. Determine the inventory balances at the end of the first month of operations.

EX 2-15   Job order cost accounting for a service company   Obj. 3

✔ B. Underapplied,
$5,530

The law firm of Furlan and Benson accumulates costs associated with individual cases, using a job order cost system. The following transactions occurred during July:

July   3.   Charged 175 hours of professional (lawyer) time to the Obsidian Co. breech of contract suit to prepare for the trial, at a rate of $150 per hour.

      10.   Reimbursed travel costs to employees for depositions related to the Obsidian case, $12,500.

      14.   Charged 260 hours of professional time for the Obsidian trial at a rate of $185 per hour.

      18.   Received invoice from consultants Wadsley and Harden for $30,000 for expert testimony related to the Obsidian trial.

      27.   Applied office overhead at a rate of $62 per professional hour charged to the Obsidian case.

      31.   Paid administrative and support salaries of $28,500 for the month.

      31.   Used office supplies for the month, $4,000.

      31.   Paid professional salaries of $74,350 for the month.

      31.   Billed Obsidian $172,500 for successful defense of the case.

A. Provide the journal entries for each of these transactions.

B. How much office overhead is over- or underapplied?

C. Determine the gross profit on the Obsidian case, assuming that over- or underapplied office overhead is closed monthly to cost of services.

EX 2-16   Job order cost accounting for a service company   Obj. 3

✔ D. Dr. Cost of
Services, $2,827,750

The Fly Company provides advertising services for clients across the nation. The Fly Company is presently working on four projects, each for a different client. The Fly Company accumulates costs for each account (client) on the basis of both direct costs and allocated indirect costs. The direct costs include the charged time of professional personnel and media purchases (air time and ad space). Overhead is allocated to each project as a percentage of media purchases. The predetermined overhead rate is 65% of media purchases.

On August 1, the four advertising projects had the following accumulated costs:

	August 1 Balances
Vault Bank	$270,000
Take Off Airlines	80,000
Sleepy Tired Hotels	210,000
Tastee Beverages	115,000
Total	$675,000

During August, The Fly Company incurred the following direct labor and media purchase costs related to preparing advertising for each of the four accounts:

	Direct Labor	**Media Purchases**
Vault Bank	$ 190,000	$ 710,000
Take Off Airlines	85,000	625,000
Sleepy Tired Hotels	372,000	455,000
Tastee Beverages	421,000	340,000
Total	$1,068,000	$2,130,000

At the end of August, both the Vault Bank and Take Off Airlines campaigns were completed. The costs of completed campaigns are debited to the cost of services account.

Journalize the summary entry to record each of the following for the month:

A. Direct labor costs

B. Media purchases

C. Overhead applied

D. Completion of Vault Bank and Take Off Airlines campaigns

Problems: Series A

SHOW ME HOW   GENERAL LEDGER

PR 2-1A   Entries for costs in a job order cost system   Obj. 2

Munson Co. uses a job order cost system. The following data summarize the operations related to production for July:

A. Materials purchased on account, $225,750.

B. Materials requisitioned, $217,600, of which $17,600 was for general factory use.

C. Factory labor used, $680,000, of which $72,300 was indirect.

D. Other costs incurred on account for factory overhead, $330,000; selling expenses, $180,000; and administrative expenses, $126,000.

E. Prepaid expenses expired for factory overhead were $27,500; for selling expenses, $8,100; and for administrative expenses, $5,250.

F. Depreciation of office building was $44,500; of office equipment, $16,800; and of factory equipment, $55,100.

G. Factory overhead costs applied to jobs, $548,000.

H. Jobs completed, $1,140,000.

I. Cost of goods sold, $1,128,000.

Instructions
Journalize the entries to record the summarized operations.

✔ 3. Work In Process
balance, $11,840

SHOW ME HOW   GENERAL LEDGER

PR 2-2A   Entries and schedules for unfinished jobs and completed jobs   Obj. 2

Kurtz Fencing Inc. uses a job order cost system. The following data summarize the operations related to production for March, the first month of operations:

A. Materials purchased on account, $45,000.

B. Materials requisitioned and factory labor used:

Job	Materials	Factory Labor
301	$1,850	$2,500
302	3,150	7,220
303	2,200	5,350
304	1,800	2,400
305	4,230	6,225
306	1,770	2,900
For general factory use	1,200	5,000

C. Factory overhead costs incurred on account, $1,800.

D. Depreciation of machinery and equipment, $2,500.

E. The factory overhead rate is $30 per machine hour. Machine hours used:

Job	Machine Hours
301	30
302	60
303	41
304	63
305	70
306	36
Total	300

(Continued)

F. Jobs completed: 301, 302, 303, and 305.

G. Jobs were shipped and customers were billed as follows: Job 301, $8,500; Job 302, $16,150; Job 303, $13,400.

Instructions

1. Journalize the entries to record the summarized operations.

2. Post the appropriate entries to T accounts for Work in Process and Finished Goods, using the identifying letters as transaction codes. Insert memo account balances as of the end of the month.

3. Prepare a schedule of unfinished jobs to support the balance in the work in process account.

4. Prepare a schedule of completed jobs on hand to support the balance in the finished goods account.

EXCEL TEMPLATE

PR 2-3A Job order cost sheet   Obj. 2

Remnant Carpet Company sells and installs commercial carpeting for office buildings. Remnant Carpet Company uses a job order cost system. When a prospective customer asks for a price quote on a job, the estimated cost data are inserted on an unnumbered job cost sheet. If the offer is accepted, a number is assigned to the job, and the costs incurred are recorded in the usual manner on the job cost sheet. After the job is completed, reasons for the variances between the estimated and actual costs are noted on the sheet. The data are then available to management in evaluating the efficiency of operations and in preparing quotes on future jobs. On October 1, Remnant Carpet Company gave Jackson Consulting an estimate of $9,450 to carpet the consulting firm's newly leased office. The estimate was based on the following data:

Estimated direct materials:	
200 meters at $35 per meter	$7,000
Estimated direct labor:	
16 hours at $20 per hour	320
Estimated factory overhead (75% of direct labor cost)	240
Total estimated costs	$7,560
Markup (25% of production costs)	1,890
Total estimate	$9,450

On October 3, Jackson Consulting signed a purchase contract, and the delivery and installation were completed on October 10.

The related materials requisitions and time tickets are summarized as follows:

Materials Requisition No.	Description	Amount
112	140 meters at $35	$4,900
114	68 meters at $35	2,380

Time Ticket No.	Description	Amount
H10	10 hours at $20	$200
H11	10 hours at $20	200

Instructions

1. Complete that portion of the job order cost sheet that would be prepared when the estimate is given to the customer.

2. ━━━▶ Record the costs incurred, and prepare a job order cost sheet. Comment on the reasons for the variances between actual costs and estimated costs. For this purpose, assume that the additional meters of material used in the job were spoiled, the factory overhead rate has proven to be satisfactory, and an inexperienced employee performed the work.

PR 2-4A   Analyzing manufacturing cost accounts

Obj. 2

✔ G. $751,870

EXCEL TEMPLATE

Fire Rock Company manufactures designer paddle boards in a wide variety of sizes and styles. The following incomplete ledger accounts refer to transactions that are summarized for June:

Materials

June	1	Balance	82,500	June 30	Requisitions	(A)
	30	Purchases	330,000			

Work in Process

June	1	Balance	(B)	June 30	Completed jobs	(F)
	30	Materials	(C)			
	30	Direct labor	(D)			
	30	Factory overhead applied	(E)			

Finished Goods

June	1	Balance	0	June 30	Cost of goods sold	(G)
	30	Completed jobs	(F)			

Wages Payable

		June 30	Wages incurred	330,000

Factory Overhead

June	1	Balance	33,000	June 30	Factory overhead applied	(E)
	30	Indirect labor	(H)			
	30	Indirect materials	44,000			
	30	Other overhead	237,500			

In addition, the following information is available:

A.   Materials and direct labor were applied to six jobs in June:

Job No.	Style	Quantity	Direct Materials	Direct Labor
201	T100	550	$ 55,000	$ 41,250
202	T200	1,100	93,500	71,500
203	T400	550	38,500	22,000
204	S200	660	82,500	69,300
205	T300	480	60,000	48,000
206	S100	380	22,000	12,400
Total		3,720	$351,500	$264,450

B.   Factory overhead is applied to each job at a rate of 140% of direct labor cost.

C.   The June 1 Work in Process balance consisted of two jobs, as follows:

Job No.	Style	Work in Process, June 1
201	T100	$16,500
202	T200	44,000
Total		$60,500

D.   Customer jobs completed and units sold in June were as follows:

Job No.	Style	Completed in June	Units Sold in June
201	T100	X	440
202	T200	X	880
203	T400		0
204	S200	X	570
205	T300	X	420
206	S100		0

(Continued)

Instructions

1. Determine the missing amounts associated with each letter. Provide supporting calculations by completing a table with the following headings:

Job No.	Quantity	June 1 Work in Process	Direct Materials	Direct Labor	Factory Overhead	Total Cost	Unit Cost	Units Sold	Cost of Goods Sold

2. Determine the June 30 balances for each of the inventory accounts and factory overhead.

PR 2-5A   Flow of costs and income statement   Obj. 2

✔ 1. Income from
operations, $432,000

EXCEL TEMPLATE

Ginocera Inc. is a designer, manufacturer, and distributor of custom gourment kitchen knives. A new kitchen knife series called the Kitchen Ninja was released for production in early 20Y8. In January, the company spent $600,000 to develop a late-night advertising infomercial for the new product. During 20Y8, the company spent an additional $1,400,000 promoting the product through these infomercials, and $800,000 in legal costs. The knives were ready for manufacture on January 1, 20Y8.

Ginocera uses a job order cost system to accumulate costs associated with the Kitchen Ninja Knife. The unit direct materials cost for the knife is:

Hardened steel blanks (used for knife shaft and blade)	$4.00
Wood (for handle)	1.50
Packaging	0.50

The production process is straightforward. First, the hardened steel blanks, which are purchased directly from a raw material supplier, are stamped into a single piece of metal that includes both the blade and the shaft. The stamping machine requires one hour per 250 knives.

After the knife shafts are stamped, they are brought to an assembly area where an employee attaches the handle to the shaft and packs the knife into a decorative box. The direct labor cost is $0.50 per unit.

The knives are sold to stores. Each store is given promotional materials, such as posters and aisle displays. Promotional materials cost $60 per store. In addition, shipping costs average $0.20 per knife.

Total completed production was 1,200,000 units during the year. Other information is as follows:

Number of customers (stores)	60,000
Number of knives sold	1,120,000
Wholesale price (to store) per knife	$16

Factory overhead cost is applied to jobs at the rate of $800 per stamping machine hour after the knife blanks are stamped. There were an additional 25,000 stamped knives, handles, and cases in process and waiting to be assembled on December 31, 20Y8.

Instructions

1. Prepare an annual income statement for the Kitchen Ninja knife series, including supporting calculations, from the information provided.

2. Determine the balances in the work in process and finished goods inventories for the Kitchen Ninja knife series on December 31, 20Y8.

Problems: Series B

PR 2-1B   Entries for costs in a job order cost system   Obj. 2

SHOW ME HOW   GENERAL LEDGER

Royal Technology Company uses a job order cost system. The following data summarize the operations related to production for March:

A. Materials purchased on account, $770,000.

B. Materials requisitioned, $680,000, of which $75,800 was for general factory use.

C. Factory labor used, $756,000, of which $182,000 was indirect.

D. Other costs incurred on account for factory overhead, $245,000; selling expenses, $171,500; and administrative expenses, $110,600.

E. Prepaid expenses expired for factory overhead were $24,500; for selling expenses, $28,420; and for administrative expenses, $16,660.

F. Depreciation of factory equipment was $49,500; of office equipment, $61,800; and of office building, $14,900.

G. Factory overhead costs applied to jobs, $568,500.

H. Jobs completed, $1,500,000.

I. Cost of goods sold, $1,375,000.

Instruction
Journalize the entries to record the summarized operations.

PR 2-2B Entries and schedules for unfinished jobs and completed jobs   Obj. 2

✔ 3. Work in Process balance, $127,880

SHOW ME HOW   GENERAL LEDGER

Hildreth Company uses a job order cost system. The following data summarize the operations related to production for April, the first month of operations:

A. Materials purchased on account, $147,000.

B. Materials requisitioned and factory labor used:

Job No.	Materials	Factory Labor
101	$19,320	$19,500
102	23,100	28,140
103	13,440	14,000
104	38,200	36,500
105	18,050	15,540
106	18,000	18,700
For general factory use	9,000	20,160

C. Factory overhead costs incurred on account, $6,000.

D. Depreciation of machinery and equipment, $4,100.

E. The factory overhead rate is $40 per machine hour. Machine hours used:

Job	Machine Hours
101	154
102	160
103	126
104	238
105	160
106	174
Total	1,012

F. Jobs completed: 101, 102, 103, and 105.

G. Jobs were shipped and customers were billed as follows: Job 101, $62,900; Job 102, $80,700; Job 105, $45,500.

Instructions
1. Journalize the entries to record the summarized operations.

2. Post the appropriate entries to T accounts for Work in Process and Finished Goods, using the identifying letters as transaction codes. Insert memo account balances as of the end of the month.

3. Prepare a schedule of unfinished jobs to support the balance in the work in process account.

4. Prepare a schedule of completed jobs on hand to support the balance in the finished goods account.

PR 2-3B Job order cost sheet   Obj. 2

EXCEL TEMPLATE

Stretch and Trim Carpet Company sells and installs commercial carpeting for office buildings. Stretch and Trim Carpet Company uses a job order cost system. When a prospective customer asks for a price quote on a job, the estimated cost data are inserted on an unnumbered job cost sheet. If the offer is accepted, a number is assigned to the job, and the costs incurred are recorded in the usual manner on the job cost sheet. After the job is completed, reasons for the variances between the estimated and actual costs are noted on the sheet. The data are then available to management in evaluating the efficiency of operations and in preparing quotes on future jobs. On May 9, Stretch and Trim gave Lunden Consulting an estimate

(Continued)

of $18,044 to carpet the consulting firm's newly leased office. The estimate was based on the following data:

Estimated direct materials:	
400 meters at $32 per meter	$12,800
Estimated direct labor:	
30 hours at $20 per hour......................................	600
Estimated factory overhead (80% of direct labor cost)...............	480
Total estimated costs	$13,880
Markup (30% of production costs)	4,164
Total estimate...	$18,044

On May 10, Lunden Consulting signed a purchase contract, and the carpet was delivered and installed on May 15.

The related materials requisitions and time tickets are summarized as follows:

Materials Requisition No.	Description	Amount
132	360 meters at $32	$11,520
134	50 meters at $32	1,600

Time Ticket No.	Description	Amount
H9	18 hours at $19	$342
H12	18 hours at $19	342

Instructions

1. Complete that portion of the job order cost sheet that would be prepared when the estimate is given to the customer. (Round factory overhead applied to the nearest dollar.)

2. ➡️Record the costs incurred, and prepare a job order cost sheet. Comment on the reasons for the variances between actual costs and estimated costs. For this purpose, assume that the additional meters of material used in the job were spoiled, the factory overhead rate has proven to be satisfactory, and an inexperienced employee performed the work.

PR 2-4B   Analyzing manufacturing cost accounts   Obj. 2

✔ G. $700,284

EXCEL TEMPLATE

Clapton Company manufactures custom guitars in a wide variety of styles. The following incomplete ledger accounts refer to transactions that are summarized for May:

Materials

May	1	Balance	105,600	May 31	Requisitions	(A)
	31	Purchases	500,000			

Work in Process

May	1	Balance	(B)	May 31	Completed jobs	(F)
	31	Materials	(C)			
	31	Direct labor	(D)			
	31	Factory overhead applied	(E)			

Finished Goods

May	1	Balance	0	May 31	Cost of goods sold	(G)
	31	Completed jobs	(F)			

Wages Payable

			May 31	Wages incurred	396,000

Factory Overhead

May	1	Balance	26,400	May 31	Factory overhead applied	(E)
	31	Indirect labor	(H)			
	31	Indirect materials	15,400			
	31	Other overhead	122,500			

In addition, the following information is available:

A. Materials and direct labor were applied to six jobs in May:

Job No.	Style	Quantity	Direct Materials	Direct Labor
101	AF1	330	$ 82,500	$ 59,400
102	AF3	380	105,400	72,600
103	AF2	500	132,000	110,000
104	VY1	400	66,000	39,600
105	VY2	660	118,800	66,000
106	AF4	330	66,000	30,800
	Total	2,600	$570,700	$378,400

B. Factory overhead is applied to each job at a rate of 50% of direct labor cost.

C. The May 1 Work in Process balance consisted of two jobs, as follows:

Job No.	Style	Work in Process, May 1
101	AF1	$26,400
102	AF3	46,000
	Total	$72,400

D. Customer jobs completed and units sold in May were as follows:

Job No.	Style	Completed in May	Units Sold in May
101	AF1	X	264
102	AF3	X	360
103	AF2		0
104	VY1	X	384
105	VY2	X	530
106	AF4		0

Instructions

1. Determine the missing amounts associated with each letter. Provide supporting calculations by completing a table with the following headings:

Job No.	Quantity	May 1 Work in Process	Direct Materials	Direct Labor	Factory Overhead	Total Cost	Unit Cost	Units Sold	Cost of Goods Sold

2. Determine the May 31 balances for each of the inventory accounts and factory overhead.

PR 2-5B Flow of costs and income statement

Obj. 2

✔ 1. Income from operations, $656,000

EXCEL TEMPLATE

Technology Accessories Inc. is a designer, manufacturer, and distributor of accessories for consumer electronic products. Early in 20Y3, the company began production of a leather cover for tablet computers, called the iLeather. The cover is made of stitched leather with a velvet interior and fits snugly around most tablet computers. In January, $750,000 was spent on developing marketing and advertising materials. For the first six months of 20Y3, the company spent an additional $1,400,000 promoting the iLeather. The product was ready for manufacture on January 21, 20Y3.

Technology Accessories Inc. uses a job order cost system to accumulate costs for the iLeather. Direct materials unit costs for the iLeather are as follows:

Leather	$10.00
Velvet	5.00
Packaging	0.40
Total	$15.40

The actual production process for the iLeather is fairly straightforward. First, leather is brought to a cutting and stitching machine. The machine cuts the leather and stitches an exterior edge into the product. The machine requires one hour per 125 iLeathers.

After the iLeather is cut and stitched, it is brought to assembly, where assembly personnel affix the velvet interior and pack the iLeather for shipping. The direct labor cost for this work is $0.50 per unit.

(Continued)

The completed packages are then sold to retail outlets through a sales force. The sales force is compensated by a 20% commission on the wholesale price for all sales.

Total completed production was 500,000 units during the year. Other information is as follows:

Number of iLeather units sold in 20Y3	460,000
Wholesale price per unit	$40

Factory overhead cost is applied to jobs at the rate of $1,250 per machine hour. There were an additional 22,000 cut and stitched iLeathers waiting to be assembled on December 31, 20Y3.

Instructions

1. Prepare an annual income statement for the iLeather product, including supporting calculations, from the information provided.

2. Determine the balances in the finished goods and work in process inventories for the iLeather product on December 31, 20Y3.

Analysis for Decision Making

ADM-1   Graph job order costs over time

Alvarez Manufacturing Inc. is a job shop. The management of Alvarez Manufacturing Inc. uses the cost information from the job sheets to assess cost performance. Information on the total cost, product type, and quantity of items produced is as follows:

Date	Job No.	Product	Quantity	Amount
Jan. 2	1	TT	520	$16,120
Jan. 15	22	SS	1,610	20,125
Feb. 3	30	SS	1,420	25,560
Mar. 7	41	TT	670	15,075
Mar. 24	49	SLK	2,210	22,100
May 19	58	SLK	2,550	31,875
June 12	65	TT	620	10,540
Aug. 18	78	SLK	3,110	48,205
Sept. 2	82	SS	1,210	16,940
Nov. 14	92	TT	750	8,250
Dec. 12	98	SLK	2,700	52,650

A. Develop a graph for *each* product (three graphs), with Job Number (in date order) on the horizontal axis and Unit Cost on the vertical axis. Use this information to determine Alvarez Manufacturing Inc.'s cost performance over time for the three products.

B. ➡ What additional information would you require in order to investigate Alvarez Manufacturing Inc.'s cost performance more precisely?

ADM-2   Analyzing increase in job order costs

Raneri Trophies Inc. uses a job order cost system for determining the cost to manufacture award products (plaques and trophies). Among the company's products is an engraved plaque that is awarded to participants who complete a training program at a local business. The company sells the plaques to the local business for $80 each.

Each plaque has a brass plate engraved with the name of the participant. Engraving requires approximately 30 minutes per name. Improperly engraved names must be redone. The plate is screwed to a walnut backboard. This assembly takes approximately 15 minutes per unit. Improper assembly must be redone using a new walnut backboard.

During the first half of the year, Raneri had two separate plaque orders. The job cost sheets for the two separate jobs indicated the following information:

Job 101	**May 4**		
	Cost per Unit	**Units**	**Job Cost**
Direct materials:			
Wood	$20/unit	40 units	$ 800
Brass	15/unit	40 units	600
Engraving labor	20/hr.	20 hrs.	400
Assembly labor	30/hr.	10 hrs.	300
Factory overhead	10/hr.	30 hrs.	300
			$2,400
Plaques shipped			÷ 40
Cost per plaque			$ 60

Job 105	**June 10**		
	Cost per Unit	**Units**	**Job Cost**
Direct materials:			
Wood	$20/unit	34 units	$ 680
Brass	15/unit	34 units	510
Engraving labor	20/hr.	17 hrs.	340
Assembly labor	30/hr.	8.5 hrs.	255
Factory overhead	10/hr.	25.5 hrs.	255
			$2,040
Plaques shipped			÷ 30
Cost per plaque			$ 68

A. ➤ Why did the cost per plaque increase from $60 to $68?

B. ➤ What improvements would you recommend for Raneri Trophies Inc.?

EXCEL TEMPLATE

ADM-3   Analyzing changes in job order direct material costs by product type

Brady Furniture Company manufactures wooden oak furniture. The company employs a job cost system to trace manufacturing costs to jobs. Each job represents a batch of furniture of the same type. Information regarding direct materials on selected jobs throughout the year is as follows:

Job No.	Date	Count	Style	Board Feet	Cost per Board Foot	Total Direct Materials Cost per Job
Job 102	Jan. 20	20	Dining tables	400	$5.00	$2,000
Job 106	Jan. 20	100	Coffee tables	1,000	5.00	5,000
Job 107	Jan. 20	50	Chairs	250	5.00	1,250
Job 203	Apr. 21	20	Dining tables	404	5.00	2,020
Job 205	Apr. 21	100	Coffee tables	990	5.00	4,950
Job 206	Apr. 21	52	Chairs	259	5.00	1,295
Job 289	July 20	20	Dining tables	448	6.00	2,688
Job 294	July 20	140	Coffee tables	1,414	6.00	8,484
Job 295	July 20	60	Chairs	312	6.00	1,872
Job 389	Oct. 18	22	Dining tables	517	6.00	3,102
Job 391	Oct. 18	160	Coffee tables	1,600	6.00	9,600
Job 392	Oct. 18	80	Chairs	400	6.00	2,400
Job 570	Dec. 11	25	Dining tables	615	6.00	3,690
Job 573	Dec. 11	180	Coffee tables	1,836	6.00	11,016
Job 574	Dec. 11	90	Chairs	450	6.00	2,700

(Continued)

Dining tables are the most difficult furniture item in Brady's catalog to manufacture. Thus, the most skilled employees are scheduled to make dining tables, unless they are required for other jobs.

A. Determine the material cost per unit for each job.

B. Use the January material cost per unit for each type of furniture as the base material cost. For each month and each type of furniture, determine the unit material cost as a percent of the base unit material cost. (Round percent to one decimal place.) Use the following table format:

	Jan.	Apr.	July	Oct.	Dec.
Dining tables	100%				
Coffee tables	100%				
Chairs	100%				

C. Develop a line chart of the percent of unit material cost to the base unit material cost. Place the months on the horizontal axis and use three lines for the three different types of furniture.

D. ━━━▶ Interpret the chart. What is happening to the dining tables?

Take It Further

ETHICS

TIF 2-1 Ethics in Action

TAC Industries Inc. sells heavy equipment to large corporations and federal, state, and local governments. Corporate sales are the result of a competitive bidding process, where TAC competes against other companies based on selling price. Sales to the government, however, are determined on a cost plus basis, where the selling price is determined by adding a fixed markup percentage to the total job cost.

Tandy Lane is the cost accountant for the Equipment Division of TAC Industries Inc. The division is under pressure from senior management to improve income from operations. As Tandy reviewed the division's job cost sheets, she realized that she could increase the division's income from operations by moving a portion of the direct labor hours that had been assigned to the job order cost sheets of corporate customers onto the job order costs sheets of government customers. She believed that this would create a "win–win" for the division by (1) reducing the cost of corporate jobs, and (2) increasing the cost of government jobs whose profit is based on a percentage of job cost. Tandy submitted this idea to her division manager, who was impressed by her creative solution for improving the division's profitability.

━━━▶ Is Tandy's plan ethical?

TIF 2-2 Team Activity

As an assistant cost accountant for Firewall Industries, you have been assigned to review the activity base for the predetermined factory overhead rate. The president, JoJo Gunn, is concerned about the wide fluctuation in the amount of over- or underapplied overhead in recent years.

An analysis of the company's operations and use of the current overhead rate (direct labor cost) has narrowed the possible alternative overhead bases to direct labor cost and machine hours. For the past five years, the following data have been gathered:

	Year 5	Year 4	Year 3	Year 2	Year 1
Actual overhead	$ 790,000	$ 870,000	$ 935,000	$ 845,000	$ 760,000
Applied overhead	777,000	882,000	924,000	840,000	777,000
(Over-) underapplied overhead	$ 13,000	$ (12,000)	$ 11,000	$ 5,000	$ (17,000)
Direct labor cost	$3,885,000	$4,410,000	$4,620,000	$4,200,000	$3,885,000
Machine hours	93,000	104,000	111,000	100,400	91,600

In teams:

A. Calculate a predetermined factory overhead rate for each alternative base, assuming that rates would have been determined using the total actual amount of factory overhead for the past five years to the total associated activity base for the same five-year period.

B. For each of the past five years, determine the over- or underapplied overhead, based on the two predetermined overhead rates developed in (A).

C. ➤ Select a predetermined overhead rate that the company should use, and discuss the basis for your recommendation.

TIF 2-3 Communication

Carol Creedence, the plant manager of the Clearwater Company's Revival plant, has prepared the following graph of the unit costs from the job cost reports for the plant's highest volume product, Product CCR.

➤ Carol is concerned about the erratic and increasing cost of Product CCR and has asked for your help. Prepare a one-half page memo to Carol, interpreting this graph and requesting any additional information that might be needed to explain this situation.

3 Process Cost Systems

Concepts and Principles

Chapter 1 *Introduction to Managerial Accounting*

Developing Information

COST SYSTEMS	COST BEHAVIOR
Chapter 2 *Job Order Costing*	**Chapter 5** *Cost-Volume-Profit Analysis*
Chapter 3 *Process Cost Systems*	
Chapter 4 *Activity-Based Costing*	

Decision Making

EVALUATING PERFORMANCE	COMPARING ALTERNATIVES
Chapter 6 *Variable Costing for Management Analysis*	**Chapter 9** *Evaluating Decentralized Operations*
Chapter 7 *Budgeting*	**Chapter 10** *Differential Analysis and Product Pricing*
Chapter 8 *Evaluating Variances from Standard Costs*	**Chapter 11** *Capital Investment Analysis*
	Chapter 12 *Lean Manufacturing*

THINKSTOCK/STOCKBYTE/GETTY IMAGES

Dreyer's Ice Cream

In making ice cream, an electric ice cream maker is used to mix ingredients, which include milk, cream, sugar, and flavoring. After the ingredients are added, the mixer is packed with ice and salt to cool the ingredients, and it is then turned on.

After mixing for half of the required time, would you have ice cream? Of course not, because the ice cream needs to mix longer to freeze. Now, assume that you ask the question:

What costs have I incurred so far in making ice cream?

The answer to this question requires knowing the cost of the ingredients and electricity. The ingredients are added at the beginning; thus, all the ingredient costs have been incurred. Because the mixing is only half complete, only 50% of the electricity cost has been incurred. Therefore, the answer to the preceding question is:

All the materials costs and half the electricity costs have been incurred.

These same cost concepts apply to larger ice cream processes like those of **Dreyer's Ice Cream** (a subsidiary of **Nestlé**), manufacturer of Dreyer's® and Edy's® ice cream. Dreyer's mixes ingredients in 3,000-gallon vats in much the same way you would with an electric ice cream maker. Dreyer's also records the costs of the ingredients, labor, and factory overhead used in making ice cream. These costs are used by managers for decisions such as setting prices and improving operations.

This chapter describes and illustrates process cost systems that are used by manufacturers such as Dreyer's. The principles of lean manufacturing are also described. Finally, the use of cost of production reports in decision making is discussed.

Source: www.dreyers.com

What's Covered

Process Cost Systems

Accounting for Process Manufacturers
- Compared to Job Order Cost Systems (Obj. 1)
- Cost Flows for Process Manufacturers (Obj. 1)

Cost of Production Report
- Units to Be Assigned Costs (Obj. 2)
- Equivalent Units (Obj. 2)
- Cost per Equivalent Unit (Obj. 2)
- Allocation of Costs (Obj. 2)
- Journalizing Costs (Obj. 3)
- Unit Cost Analysis (Obj. 4)

Lean Manufacturing
- Traditional Manufacturing Process (Obj. 5)
- Lean Manufacturing Process (Obj. 5)

Learning Objectives

Obj. 1 Describe process cost systems.

Obj. 2 Prepare a cost of production report.

Obj. 3 Journalize entries for transactions using a process cost system.

Obj. 4 Describe and illustrate the analysis of unit cost changes between periods.

Obj. 5 Compare lean manufacturing with traditional manufacturing processing.

Analysis for Decision Making

Describe and Illustrate the use of a cost of production report in evaluating a company's performance.

Objective 1
Describe process cost systems.

Accounting for Process Manufacturers

A **process manufacturer** produces products that are indistinguishable from each other using a continuous production process. For example, an oil refinery processes crude oil through a series of steps to produce a barrel of gasoline. One barrel of gasoline, the product, cannot be distinguished from another barrel. Other examples of process manufacturers include paper producers, chemical processors, aluminum smelters, and food processors.

The cost accounting system used by process manufacturers is called the **process cost system.** A process cost system records product costs for each manufacturing department or process.

In contrast, a job order manufacturer produces custom products for customers or batches of similar products. For example, a custom printer produces wedding invitations, graduation announcements, or other special print items that are tailored to the specifications of each customer. Each item manufactured is unique to itself. Other examples of job order manufacturers include furniture manufacturers, shipbuilders, and home builders.

As described and illustrated in Chapter 2, the cost accounting system used by job order manufacturers is called the *job order cost system*. A job order cost system records product costs for each job, using job cost sheets.

Ethics: Do It!

On Being Green

Process manufacturing often involves significant energy and material resources, which can be harmful to the environment. Thus, many process manufacturing companies, such as chemical, electronic, and metal processors, must address environmental issues. Companies such as **DuPont**, **Intel**, **Apple**, and **Alcoa** are at the forefront of providing environmental solutions for their products and processes.

For example, Apple provides free recycling programs for Macs®, iPhones®, and iPads®. Apple recovers more than 90% by weight of the original product in reusable components, glass, and plastic. You can even receive a free gift card for voluntarily recycling an older Apple product.

Source: www.apple.com.

Some examples of process and job order companies and their products are shown in Exhibit 1.

Process Manufacturing Companies		Job Order Companies	
Company	**Product**	**Company**	**Product**
PepsiCo	soft drinks	**Disney**	movies
Alcoa	aluminum	**Nike**	athletic shoes
Intel	computer chips	**Nicklaus Design**	golf courses
Apple	iPhone	**Tennessee Heritage**	log homes
Hershey	chocolate bars	**DDB Worldwide**	advertising

Exhibit 1
Examples of Process Cost and Job Order Companies

William Dreyer, an ice cream maker, and Joseph Edy, a candymaker, partnered to introduce **Dreyer's and Edy's Grand Ice Cream** in 1928. The ice cream was sold out of their ice cream parlor on Grand Avenue in Oakland, California.

Link to Dreyer's Ice Cream

Comparing Job Order and Process Cost Systems

Process and job order cost systems are similar in that each system:

- Records and summarizes product costs.
- Classifies product costs as direct materials, direct labor, and factory overhead.
- Allocates factory overhead costs to products.
- Uses a perpetual inventory system for materials, work in process, and finished goods.
- Provides useful product cost information for decision making.

Process and job costing systems are different in several ways. As a basis for illustrating these differences, the cost systems for **Frozen Delight** and **Legend Guitars** are used.

Exhibit 2 illustrates the process cost system for Frozen Delight, an ice cream manufacturer. As a basis for comparison, Exhibit 2 also illustrates the job order cost system for Legend Guitars, a custom guitar manufacturer. Legend Guitars was described and illustrated in Chapters 1 and 2.

Exhibit 2 indicates that Frozen Delight manufactures ice cream, using two departments:

- The Mixing Department mixes the ingredients, using large vats.
- The Packaging Department puts the ice cream into cartons for shipping to customers.

Because each gallon of ice cream is similar, product costs are recorded in each department's work in process account. As shown in Exhibit 2, Frozen Delight accumulates (records) the cost of making ice cream in *work in process accounts* for the Mixing and Packaging departments.

The product costs of making a gallon of ice cream include:

- *Direct materials costs,* which include milk, cream, sugar, and packing cartons. All materials costs are added at the beginning of the process for both the Mixing Department and the Packaging Department.
- *Direct labor costs*, which are incurred by employees in each department who run the equipment and load and unload product.
- *Factory overhead costs,* which include the utility costs (power) and depreciation on the equipment.

When the Mixing Department completes the mixing process, its product costs are transferred to the Packaging Department. When the Packaging Department completes its process, the product costs are transferred to Finished Goods. In this way, the cost of the product (a gallon of ice cream) accumulates across the entire production process.

Exhibit 2

Process Cost and
Job Order Cost
Systems

In contrast, Exhibit 2 shows that Legend Guitars accumulates (records) product costs by jobs, using a job cost sheet for each type of guitar. Thus, Legend Guitars uses just one work in process account. As each job is completed, its product costs are transferred to Finished Goods.

In a job order cost system, the work in process at the end of the period is the sum of the job cost sheets for partially completed jobs. In a process cost system, the work in process at the end of the period is the sum of the costs remaining in each department account at the end of the period.

Cost Flows for a Process Manufacturer

Exhibit 3 illustrates the *physical flow* of materials for **Frozen Delight**. Ice cream is made in a manufacturing plant in much the same way you would make it at home, except on a larger scale.

In the Mixing Department, direct materials in the form of milk, cream, and sugar are placed into a vat. An employee fills each vat, sets the cooling temperature, and sets the mix speed. The vat is cooled as the direct materials are being mixed by agitators (paddles). Factory overhead includes equipment depreciation and indirect materials.

Exhibit 3
Physical Flows
for a Process
Manufacturer

Dreyer's slow-churned ice cream uses a proprietary process that mixes nonfat milk slowly. This process, called low-temperature extrusion, allows ice cream to be made with one-third fewer calories and half the fat while tasting like normal ice cream.

Link to Dreyer's Ice Cream

In the Packaging Department, the ice cream is received from the Mixing Department in a form ready for packaging. The Packaging Department uses direct labor and factory overhead to package the ice cream into one-gallon containers. The ice cream is then transferred to finished goods, where it is frozen and stored in refrigerators prior to shipment to customers.

The *cost flows* in a process cost accounting system are similar to the *physical flow* of materials illustrated in Exhibit 3. The cost flows for **Frozen Delight** are illustrated in Exhibit 4 as follows:

A. The cost of materials purchased is recorded in the materials account.

B. The cost of direct materials used by the Mixing and Packaging departments is recorded in the work in process accounts for each department.

C. The cost of direct labor used by the Mixing and Packaging departments is recorded in work in process accounts for each department.

D. The cost of factory overhead incurred for indirect materials and other factory overhead such as depreciation is recorded in the factory overhead accounts for each department.

E. The factory overhead incurred in the Mixing and Packaging departments is applied to the work in process accounts for each department.

F. The cost of units completed in the Mixing Department is transferred to the Packaging Department.

G. The cost of units completed in the Packaging Department is transferred to Finished Goods.

H. The cost of units sold is transferred to Cost of Goods Sold.

As shown in Exhibit 4, the Mixing and Packaging departments have separate factory overhead accounts. The factory overhead costs incurred for indirect materials, depreciation, and other overhead are debited to each department's factory overhead account. The overhead is applied to work in process by debiting each department's work in process account and crediting the department's factory overhead account.

Exhibit 4 illustrates how the Mixing and Packaging departments have separate work in process accounts. Each work in process account is debited for direct materials, direct labor, and applied factory overhead. In addition, the work in process account for the Packaging Department is debited for the cost of the units transferred in from the Mixing Department. Each work in process account is credited for the cost of the units transferred to the next department.

Exhibit 4 shows that the finished goods account is debited for the cost of the units transferred from the Packaging Department. The finished goods account is credited for the cost of the units sold, which is debited to the cost of goods sold account.

Exhibit 4 Cost Flows for a Process Manufacturer—Frozen Delight

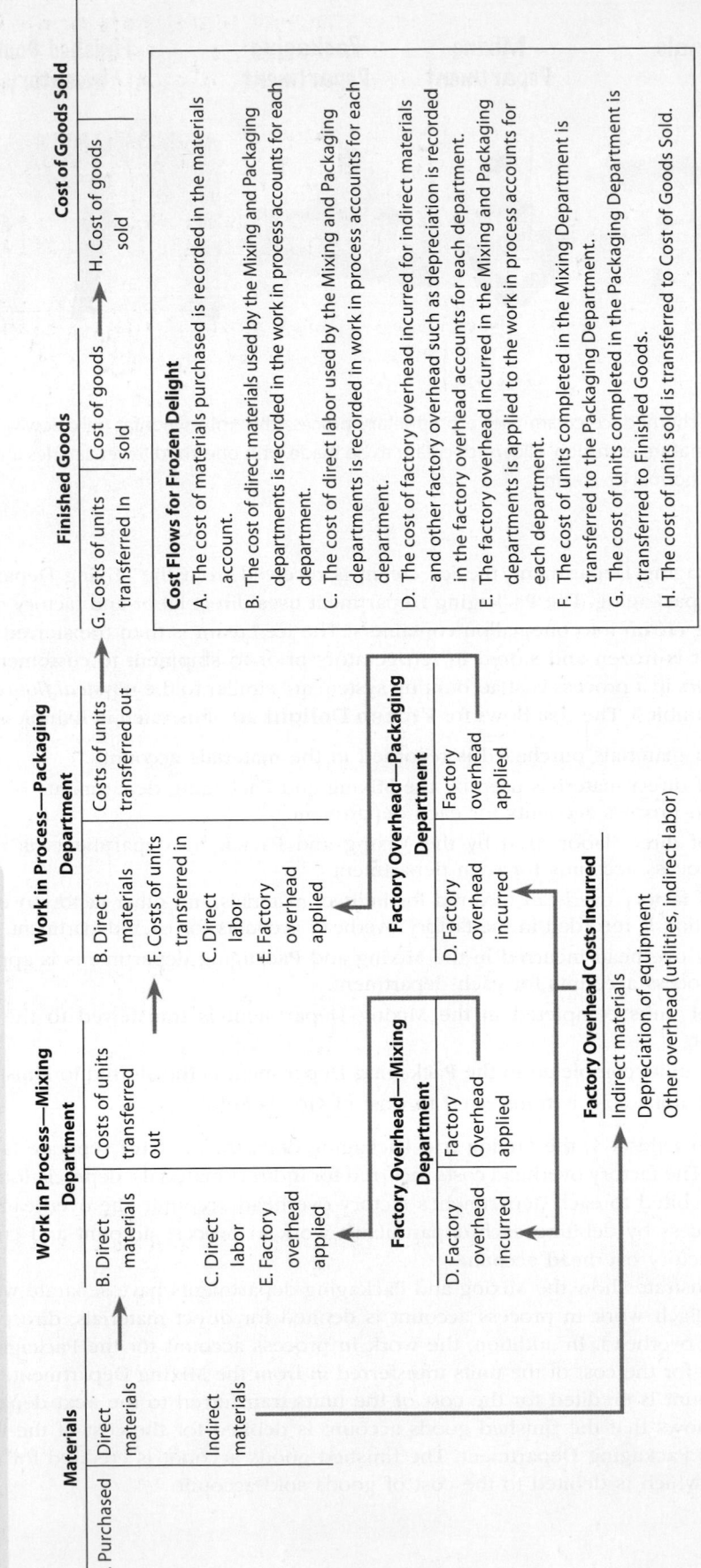

Cost Flows for Frozen Delight

A. The cost of materials purchased is recorded in the materials account.

B. The cost of direct materials used by the Mixing and Packaging departments is recorded in the work in process accounts for each department.

C. The cost of direct labor used by the Mixing and Packaging departments is recorded in work in process accounts for each department.

D. The cost of factory overhead incurred for indirect materials and other factory overhead such as depreciation is recorded in the factory overhead accounts for each department.

E. The factory overhead incurred in the Mixing and Packaging departments is applied to the work in process accounts for each department.

F. The cost of units completed in the Mixing Department is transferred to the Packaging Department.

G. The cost of units completed in the Packaging Department is transferred to Finished Goods.

H. The cost of units sold is transferred to Cost of Goods Sold.

Why It Matters

Sustainable Papermaking

We discussed social and environmental sustainability in the introductory managerial chapter. Processing companies involved with papermaking, refining, and chemical processing focus on sustainability because of their impact on the environment. For example, papermaking requires the use of large amounts of wood fiber (cellulous), energy, and water. Thus, papermakers are actively involved in sustainability efforts to reduce the negative environmental impacts from the use of these resources. To illustrate, **International Paper Company** provides an annual report to external stakeholders identifying its progress toward several sustainability objectives. A recent report identified six sustainability areas:

1. **Safety:** Improve worker health and safety, resulting in a 68% reduction in life-impacting injuries.
2. **Water use:** Identify and implement water conservation opportunities at each paper mill.
3. **Greenhouse gas emissions:** Reduce greenhouse gases by using renewable carbon-neutral biomass to meet over 70% of energy needs.
4. **Forest stewardship:** Implement sustainable forest management practices that provide a low-cost wood supply while simultaneously conserving primary forests.
5. **Ethics and compliance:** Train suppliers in the company's Supplier Code of Conduct.
6. **Stakeholder engagement:** Engage with communities, customers, and governments by participating in conferences, providing donations, and volunteering.

Source: *In Our Nature: Sustainability Year in Review 2014*, International Paper Company.

Dreyer's is currently a subsidiary of **Nestlé**, which produces Dreyer's ice cream at its Bakersfield, California plant.

Link to Dreyer's Ice Cream

Cost of Production Report

Objective 2
Prepare a cost of production report.

In a process cost system, the cost of units transferred out of each processing department must be determined along with the cost of any partially completed units remaining in the department. The report that summarizes these costs is a cost of production report.

The **cost of production report** summarizes the production and cost data for a department as follows:

- The units the department is accountable for and the disposition of those units.
- The product costs incurred by the department and the allocation of those costs between completed (transferred out) and partially completed units.

A cost of production report is prepared using the following four steps:

- Step 1. Determine the units to be assigned costs.
- Step 2. Compute equivalent units of production.
- Step 3. Determine the cost per equivalent unit.
- Step 4. Allocate costs to units transferred out and partially completed units.

Preparing a cost of production report requires making a cost flow assumption. Like merchandise inventory, costs can be assumed to flow through the manufacturing process, using the first-in, first-out (FIFO), last in, first-out (LIFO), or average cost methods. Because the **first-in, first-out (FIFO) method** is often the same as the physical flow of units, the FIFO method is used in this chapter.[1]

---

[1] The average cost method is illustrated in an appendix to this chapter.

To illustrate, a cost of production report for the Mixing Department of **Frozen Delight** for July is prepared. The July data for the Mixing Department are as follows:

Inventory in process, July 1, 5,000 gallons:
Direct materials cost, for 5,000 gallons	$5,000	
Conversion costs, for 5,000 gallons, 70% completed	1,225	
Total inventory in process, July 1		$ 6,225
Direct materials cost for July, 60,000 gallons		66,000
Direct labor cost for July		10,500
Factory overhead applied for July		7,275
Total production costs to account for		$90,000
Gallons transferred to Packaging in July (includes units in process on July 1), 62,000 gallons		?
Inventory in process, July 31, 3,000 gallons, 25% completed as to conversion costs		?

By preparing a cost of production report, the cost of the gallons transferred to the Packaging Department in July and the ending work in process inventory in the Mixing Department are determined. These amounts are indicated by question marks (?).

Step 1: Determine the Units to Be Assigned Costs

The first step is to determine the units to be assigned costs. A unit can be any measure of completed production, such as tons, gallons, pounds, barrels, or cases. For **Frozen Delight**, a unit is a gallon of ice cream.

The Mixing Department is accountable for 65,000 gallons of direct materials during July, computed as follows:

Total units (gallons) charged to production:
In process, July 1	5,000 gallons
Received from materials storage	60,000
Total units (gallons) accounted for	65,000 gallons

For July, the following three groups of units (gallons) are assigned costs:

- Group 1. Units (gallons) in beginning work in process inventory on July 1.
- Group 2. Units (gallons) started and completed during July.
- Group 3. Units (gallons) in ending work in process inventory on July 31.

Exhibit 5 illustrates these groups of units (gallons) in the Mixing Department for July. The 5,000 gallons of beginning inventory were completed and transferred to the Packaging Department. During July, 60,000 gallons of material were started (entered into mixing). Of the 60,000 gallons started in July, 3,000 gallons were incomplete on July 31. Thus, 57,000 gallons (60,000 − 3,000) were started and completed in July.

The total units (gallons) to be assigned costs for July are summarized as follows:

Group 1	Inventory in process, July 1, completed in July	5,000 gallons
Group 2	Started and completed in July	57,000
	Transferred out to the Packaging Department in July	62,000 gallons
Group 3	Inventory in process, July 31	3,000
	Total units (gallons) to be assigned costs	65,000 gallons

The total gallons to be assigned costs (65,000) equal the total gallons accounted for (65,000) by the Mixing Department.

Step 2: Compute Equivalent Units of Production

Whole units are the number of units in production during a period, whether completed or not. **Equivalent units of production** are the portion of whole units that are complete with respect to materials or conversion (direct labor and factory overhead) costs.

Exhibit 5
July Units to Be
Costed—Mixing
Department

To illustrate, assume that a 1,000-gallon batch (vat) of ice cream at **Frozen Delight** is only 40% complete in the mixing process on May 31. Thus, the batch is only 40% complete as to conversion costs such as power. In this case, the whole units and equivalent units of production are as follows:

	Whole Units	Equivalent Units
Materials costs	1,000 gallons	1,000 gallons
Conversion costs	1,000 gallons	400 gallons (1,000 × 40%)

Because the materials costs are all added at the beginning of the process, the materials costs are 100% complete for the 1,000-gallon batch of ice cream. Thus, the whole units and equivalent units for materials costs are 1,000 gallons. However, because the batch is only 40% complete as to conversion costs, the equivalent units for conversion costs are 400 gallons.

Equivalent units for materials and conversion costs are usually determined separately as shown earlier. This is because materials and conversion costs normally enter production at different times and rates. In contrast, direct labor and factory overhead normally enter production at the same time and rate. For this reason, direct labor and factory overhead are combined as conversion costs in computing equivalent units.

Materials Equivalent Units To compute equivalent units for materials, it is necessary to know how materials are added during the manufacturing process. In the case of **Frozen Delight**, all the materials are added at the beginning of the mixing process. Thus, the equivalent units for materials in July are computed as follows:

		Whole Units	Percent Materials Added in July	Equivalent Units for Direct Materials
Group 1	Inventory in process, July 1	5,000	0%	0
Group 2	Started and completed in July (62,000 − 5,000)	57,000	100%	57,000
	Transferred out to Packaging Department in July	62,000	—	57,000
Group 3	Inventory in process, July 31	3,000	100%	3,000
	Total gallons to be assigned costs	65,000		60,000

As shown, the whole units for the three groups of units determined in Step 1 are listed in the first column. The percent of materials added in July is then listed. The equivalent units are determined by multiplying the whole units by the percent of materials added.

To illustrate, the July 1 inventory (Group 1) has 5,000 gallons of whole units, which are complete as to materials. That is, all the direct materials for the 5,000 gallons in process on July 1 were added in June. Thus, the percent of materials added in July is zero, and the equivalent units added in July are zero.

The 57,000 gallons started and completed in July (Group 2) are 100% complete as to materials. Thus, the equivalent units for the gallons started and completed in July are 57,000 (57,000 × 100%) gallons. The 3,000 gallons in process on July 31 (Group 3) are also 100% complete as to materials because all materials are added at the beginning of the process. Therefore, the equivalent units for the inventory in process on July 31 are 3,000 (3,000 × 100%) gallons.

The equivalent units for direct materials for **Frozen Delight** are summarized in Exhibit 6.

Exhibit 6
Direct Materials Equivalent Units

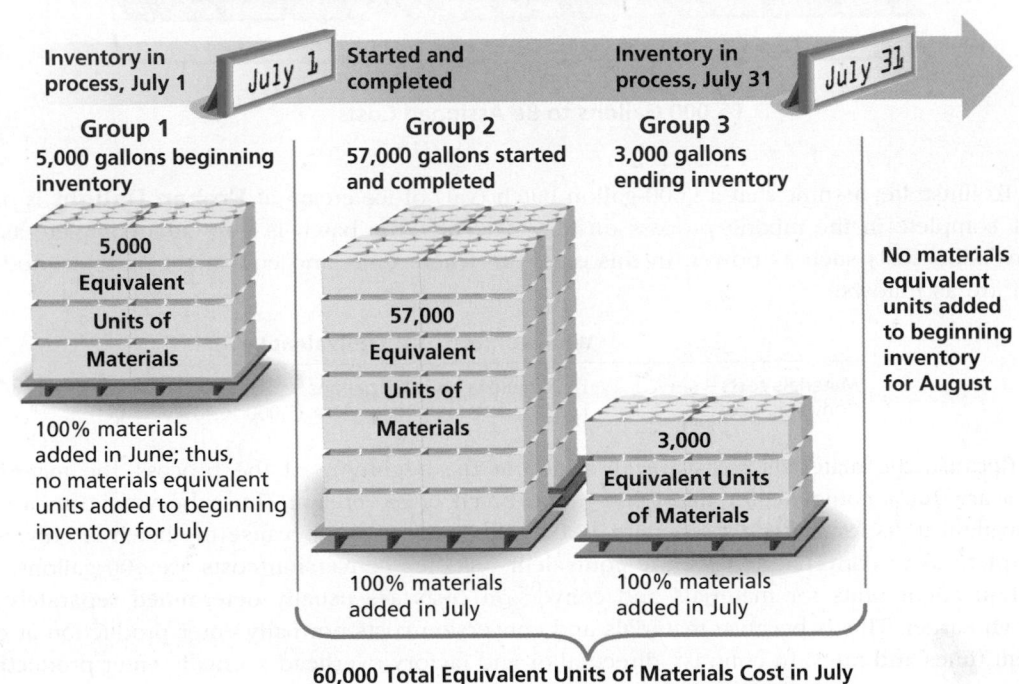

Conversion Equivalent Units To compute equivalent units for conversion costs, it is necessary to know how direct labor and factory overhead enter the manufacturing process. Direct labor, utilities, and equipment depreciation are often incurred uniformly during processing. For this reason, it is assumed that **Frozen Delight** incurs conversion costs evenly throughout its manufacturing process. Thus, the equivalent units for conversion costs in July are computed as follows:

		Whole Units	Percent Conversion Completed in July	Equivalent Units for Conversion
Group 1	Inventory in process, July 1 (70% completed)	5,000	30%	1,500
Group 2	Started and completed in July (62,000 − 5,000)	57,000	100%	57,000
	Transferred out to Packaging Department in July	62,000	—	58,500
Group 3	Inventory in process, July 31 (25% completed)	3,000	25%	750
	Total gallons to be assigned costs	65,000		59,250

As shown, the whole units for the three groups of units determined in Step 1 are listed in the first column. The percent of conversion costs added in July is then listed. The equivalent units are determined by multiplying the whole units by the percent of conversion costs added.

To illustrate, the July 1 inventory has 5,000 gallons of whole units (Group 1), which are 70% complete as to conversion costs. During July, the remaining 30% (100% − 70%) of conversion costs was added. Therefore, the equivalent units of conversion costs added in July are 1,500 (5,000 × 30%) gallons.

The 57,000 gallons started and completed in July (Group 2) are 100% complete as to conversion costs. Thus, the equivalent units of conversion costs for the gallons started and completed in July are 57,000 (57,000 × 100%) gallons.

The 3,000 gallons in process on July 31 (Group 3) are 25% complete as to conversion costs. Hence, the equivalent units for the inventory in process on July 31 are 750 (3,000 × 25%) gallons.

The equivalent units for conversion costs for **Frozen Delight** are summarized in Exhibit 7.

Exhibit 7
Conversion Equivalent Units

Check Up Corner 3-1 Equivalent Units

The Bottling Department of Rocky Springs Beverage Company had 2,000 liters in the beginning work in process (30% complete). During the month, 28,500 liters were started and 29,000 liters were completed. The ending work in process inventory was 1,500 liters (60% complete). Materials are added at the beginning of the process, while conversion costs are added evenly throughout the process.

A. How many units were started and completed during the month?

B. What are the total equivalent units for: (1) direct materials and (2) conversion costs?

Solution:

A. There are two ways to calculate the units started and completed.

	Units		Units
Completed (transferred out)	29,000	Started (during month)	28,500
Inventory in process, (beginning)	(2,000)	Inventory in process, (ending)	(1,500)
Started and completed	27,000	Started and completed	27,000

(Continued)

B. 1. Direct Materials

Whole units are the number of units in production.

	Whole Units	Percent Materials Added in Month	Equivalent Units for Direct Materials
Inventory in process, beginning of month	2,000	0%	0
Started and completed during the month	27,000	100%	27,000
Transferred out of Bottling (completed)	29,000	—	27,000
Inventory in process, end of month	1,500	100%	1,500
Total units to be assigned costs	30,500		28,500

Equivalent units are the portion of whole units that are complete for direct materials.

The equivalent units for beginning inventory is 0, because all (100%) of the materials were added at the beginning of the process, which occurred in the previous month.

Materials costs in ending inventory are 100% complete because all materials are added at the beginning of the process.

2. Conversion Costs

	Whole Units	Percent Conversion Completed in Month	Equivalent Units for Conversion
Inventory in process, beginning of month	2,000	70%	1,400
Started and completed during the month	27,000	100%	27,000
Transferred out of Bottling (completed)	29,000	—	28,400
Inventory in process, end of month	1,500	60%	900
Total units to be assigned costs	30,500		29,300

Equivalent units are the portion of whole units that are complete for conversion.

To complete the units in beginning inventory, an additional 70% of conversion costs (100% – 30% completed in prior month) must be added during the month.

Conversion costs in ending inventory are 60% complete because they are added evenly throughout the process during the current month.

Check Up Corner

Step 3: Determine the Cost per Equivalent Unit

The next step in preparing the cost of production report is to compute the cost per equivalent unit for direct materials and conversion costs. The **cost per equivalent unit** for direct materials and conversion costs is computed as follows:

$$\text{Direct Materials Cost per Equivalent Unit} = \frac{\text{Total Direct Materials Cost for the Period}}{\text{Total Equivalent Units of Direct Materials}}$$

$$\text{Conversion Cost per Equivalent Unit} = \frac{\text{Total Conversion Costs for the Period}}{\text{Total Equivalent Units of Conversion Costs}}$$

The July direct materials and conversion cost equivalent units for **Frozen Delight**'s Mixing Department from Step 2 are as follows:

		Equivalent Units	
		Direct Materials	Conversion
Group 1	Inventory in process, July 1	0	1,500
Group 2	Started and completed in July (62,000 – 5,000)	57,000	57,000
	Transferred out to Packaging Department in July	57,000	58,500
Group 3	Inventory in process, July 31	3,000	750
	Total gallons to be assigned costs	60,000	59,250

The direct materials and conversion costs incurred by Frozen Delight in July are as follows:

Direct materials		$66,000
Conversion costs:		
Direct labor	$10,500	
Factory overhead	7,275	17,775
Total product costs incurred in July		$83,775

The direct materials and conversion costs per equivalent unit are $1.10 and $0.30 per gallon, respectively, computed as follows:

$$\text{Direct Materials Cost per Equivalent Unit} = \frac{\text{Total Direct Materials Cost for the Period}}{\text{Total Equivalent Units of Direct Materials}}$$

$$\text{Direct Materials Cost per Equivalent Unit} = \frac{\$66,000}{60,000 \text{ gallons}} = \$1.10 \text{ per gallon}$$

$$\text{Conversion Cost per Equivalent Unit} = \frac{\text{Total Conversion Costs for the Period}}{\text{Total Equivalent Units of Conversion Costs}}$$

$$\text{Conversion Cost per Equivalent Unit} = \frac{\$17,775}{59,250 \text{ gallons}} = \$0.30 \text{ per gallon}$$

The preceding costs per equivalent unit are used in Step 4 to allocate the direct materials and conversion costs to the completed and partially completed units.

Step 4: Allocate Costs to Units Transferred Out and Partially Completed Units

Product costs must be allocated to the units transferred out and the partially completed units on hand at the end of the period. The product costs are allocated using the costs per equivalent unit for materials and conversion costs that were computed in Step 3.

The total production costs to be assigned for **Frozen Delight** in July are $90,000, computed as follows:

Inventory in process, July 1, 5,000 gallons:		
Direct materials cost, for 5,000 gallons	$ 5,000	
Conversion costs, for 5,000 gallons, 70% completed	1,225	
Total inventory in process, July 1		$ 6,225
Direct materials cost for July, 60,000 gallons	$66,000	
Direct labor cost for July	10,500	
Factory overhead applied for July	7,275	
Costs incurred in July		83,775
Total production costs to account for		$90,000

The units to be assigned these costs follow. The costs to be assigned these units are indicated by question marks (?).

		Whole Units	Total Cost
Group 1	Inventory in process, July 1, completed in July	5,000 gallons	?
Group 2	Started and completed in July	57,000	?
	Transferred out to the Packaging		
	Department in July	62,000 gallons	?
Group 3	Inventory in process, July 31	3,000	?
	Total	65,000 gallons	$90,000

Group 1: Inventory in Process on July 1 The 5,000 gallons of inventory in process on July 1 (Group 1) were completed and transferred out to the Packaging Department in July. The cost of these units of $6,675 is determined as follows:

	Direct Materials Costs	Conversion Costs	Total Costs
Inventory in process, July 1 balance			$6,225
Equivalent units for completing the July 1 in-process inventory	0	1,500	
Cost per equivalent unit	× $1.10	× $0.30	
Cost of completed July 1 in-process inventory	0	$450	450
Cost of July 1 in-process inventory transferred to Packaging Department			$6,675

As shown, $6,225 of the cost of the July 1 in-process inventory of 5,000 gallons was carried over from June. This cost plus the cost of completing the 5,000 gallons in July was transferred to the Packaging Department during July. The cost of completing the 5,000 gallons during July is $450. The $450 represents the conversion costs necessary to complete the remaining 30% of the processing. There were no direct materials costs added in July because all the materials costs had been added in June. Thus, the cost of the 5,000 gallons in process on July 1 (Group 1) transferred to the Packaging Department is $6,675.

Group 2: Started and Completed The 57,000 units started and completed in July (Group 2) incurred all (100%) of their direct materials and conversion costs in July. Thus, the cost of the 57,000 gallons started and completed is $79,800, computed by multiplying 57,000 gallons by the costs per equivalent unit for materials and conversion costs as follows:

	Direct Materials Costs	Conversion Costs	Total Costs
Units started and completed in July	57,000 gallons	57,000 gallons	
Cost per equivalent unit	× $1.10	× $0.30	
Cost of the units started and completed in July	$62,700	$17,100	$79,800

The total cost of $86,475 transferred to the Packaging Department in July is the sum of the beginning inventory cost and the costs of the units started and completed in July, computed as follows:

Group 1	Cost of July 1 in-process inventory	$ 6,675
Group 2	Cost of the units started and completed in July	79,800
	Total costs transferred to Packaging Department in July	$86,475

Why It Matters

Fill 'Er Up

A study of the cost per gallon of unleaded gasoline in various parts of the country revealed the following:

Los Angeles	$3.71	Cleveland	$2.65
Chicago	3.58	Atlanta	2.49
Seattle	3.11	Boston	2.49
New York	2.87	St. Louis	2.42
Detroit	2.84	Austin	2.36
Omaha	2.66		

The cost per gallon ranged from a high of $3.71 in Los Angeles to a low of $2.36 in Austin, or a 57% difference. The price per

barrel of oil was around $50 at the time of this study. Why would the price per gallon of gasoline be so different, when the price per barrel of oil, the basic material for making gasoline, is the same for everyone? Normally, the final price would be determined by the price of oil, the conversion cost of refining oil to gasoline, plus some additional amounts for distribution and profits. However, during this time period, refinery operations were shut down in parts of the country for repairs and overhauls. As a result, some regions were experiencing supply shortfalls that caused the price of gasoline to increase relative to those regions that remained well supplied. Refiners focus on minimizing downtime, so these types of disruptions do not occur.

Source: Alison Sider, "Refinery Woes Keep Pump Prices Up," *The Wall Street Journal,* August 24, 2015, p. A1.

Group 3: Inventory in Process on July 31 The 3,000 gallons in process on July 31 (Group 3) incurred all their direct materials costs and 25% of their conversion costs in July. The cost of these partially completed units of $3,525 is computed as follows:

	Direct Materials Costs	Conversion Costs	Total Costs
Equivalent units in ending inventory	3,000 gallons	750 gallons	
Cost per equivalent unit	× $1.10	× $0.30	
Cost of July 31 in-process inventory	$3,300	$225	$3,525

The 3,000 gallons in process on July 31 received all (100%) of their materials in July. Therefore, the direct materials cost incurred in July is $3,300 (3,000 × $1.10). The conversion costs of $225 represent the cost of the 750 (3,000 × 25%) equivalent gallons multiplied by the cost of $0.30 per equivalent unit for conversion costs. The sum of the direct materials cost ($3,300) and the conversion costs ($225) equals the total cost of the July 31 work in process inventory of $3,525 ($3,300 + $225).

To summarize, the total manufacturing costs for Frozen Delight in July were assigned as follows. In doing so, the question marks (?) for the costs to be assigned to units in Groups 1, 2, and 3 have been answered.

		Whole Units	Total Cost
Group 1	Inventory in process, July 1, completed in July	5,000 gallons	$ 6,675
Group 2	Started and completed in July	57,000	79,800
	Transferred out to the Packaging Department in July	62,000 gallons	$86,475
Group 3	Inventory in process, July 31	3,000	3,525
	Total..	65,000 gallons	$90,000

Dreyer's invented Rocky Road ice cream in 1929.

Link to Dreyer's Ice Cream

Preparing the Cost of Production Report

A cost of production report is prepared for each processing department at periodic intervals. The report summarizes the following production quantity and cost data:

■ The units for which the department is accountable and the disposition of those units
■ The production costs incurred by the department and the allocation of those costs between completed (transferred out) and partially completed units

Using Steps 1–4, the July cost of production report for **Frozen Delight**'s Mixing Department is shown in Exhibit 8. During July, the Mixing Department was accountable for 65,000 units (gallons). Of these units, 62,000 units were completed and transferred to the Packaging Department. The remaining 3,000 units are partially completed and are part of the in-process inventory as of July 31.

The Mixing Department was responsible for $90,000 of production costs during July. The cost of goods transferred to the Packaging Department in July was $86,475. The remaining cost of $3,525 is part of the in-process inventory as of July 31.

Exhibit 8 Cost of Production Report for Frozen Delight's Mixing Department—FIFO

	A	B	C	D	E	
1		Frozen Delight				
2		Cost of Production Report—Mixing Department				
3		For the Month Ended July 31				— Step 1
4						— Step 2
5			Whole Units	Equivalent Units		
6	**UNITS**			Direct Materials	Conversion	
7	Units charged to production:					
8	Inventory in process, July 1		5,000			
9	Received from materials storeroom		60,000			
10	Total units accounted for by the Mixing Department		65,000			
11						
12	Units to be assigned costs:					
13	Inventory in process, July 1 (70% completed)		5,000	0	1,500	
14	Started and completed in July		57,000	57,000	57,000	
15	Transferred to Packaging Department in July		62,000	57,000	58,500	
16	Inventory in process, July 31 (25% completed)		3,000	3,000	750	
17	Total units to be assigned costs		65,000	60,000	59,250	
18						
19					Costs	
20	**COSTS**			Direct Materials	Conversion	Total
21						
22	Cost per equivalent unit:					
23	Total costs for July in Mixing Department			$ 66,000	$ 17,775	
24	Total equivalent units (from Step 2)			÷60,000	÷59,250	
25	Cost per equivalent unit			$ 1.10	$ 0.30	— Step 3
26						
27	Costs assigned to production:					
28	Inventory in process, July 1					$ 6,225
29	Costs incurred in July					83,775ᵃ
30	Total costs accounted for by the Mixing Department					$90,000
31						
32						
33	Costs allocated to completed and partially					
34	completed units:					
35	Inventory in process, July 1—balance					$ 6,225
36	To complete inventory in process, July 1			$ 0	+ $ 450ᵇ	= 450
37	Cost of completed July 1 work in process					$ 6,675
38	Started and completed in July			$ 62,700ᶜ	+ $ 17,100ᵈ	= 79,800 — Step 4
39	Transferred to Packaging Department in July					$86,475
40	Inventory in process, July 31			$ 3,300ᵉ	+ $ 225ᶠ	= 3,525
41	Total costs assigned by the Mixing Department					$90,000
42						

ᵃ$66,000 + $10,500 + $7,275 = $83,775 ᵇ1,500 units × $0.30 = $450 ᶜ57,000 units × $1.10 = $62,700 ᵈ57,000 units × $0.30 = $17,100
ᵉ3,000 units × $1.10 = $3,300 ᶠ750 units × $0.30 = $225

Check Up Corner 3-2 | Cost per Equivalent Unit

The cost of direct materials transferred into the Bottling Department of Rocky Springs Beverage Company is $22,800. The conversion costs for the period in the Bottling Department are $8,790. The total equivalent units for direct materials and conversion costs are as follows:

	Equivalent Units (in liters)	
	Direct Materials	Conversion
Inventory in process, beginning of period	0	1,400
Started and completed during the period	27,000	27,000
Transferred out of Bottling (completed)	27,000	28,400
Inventory in process, end of period	1,500	900
Total units to be assigned costs	28,500	29,300

The beginning work in process inventory had a cost of $1,860.

A. Determine the cost per equivalent unit for: (1) direct materials and (2) conversion costs.

B. Determine the cost of units transferred out and the ending work in process inventory.

Note: The units transferred out and the equivalent units of production are computed in Check Up Corner 3-1.

Solution:

A. 1.

$$\frac{\text{Direct Materials Cost}}{\text{per Equivalent Unit}} = \frac{\text{Total Direct Materials Cost for the Period}}{\text{Total Equivalent Units of Direct Materials}}$$

$$\frac{\text{Direct Materials Cost}}{\text{per Equivalent Unit}} = \frac{\$22,800}{28,500 \text{ liters}} = \$0.80 \text{ per liter}$$

2.

$$\text{Conversion Cost per Equivalent Unit} = \frac{\text{Total Conversion Costs for the Period}}{\text{Total Equivalent Units of Conversion Costs}}$$

$$\text{Conversion Cost per Equivalent Unit} = \frac{\$8,790}{29,300 \text{ liters}} = \$0.30 \text{ per liter}$$

Costs per equivalent unit are used to allocate the direct materials and conversion costs to the completed and partially completed units in part B.

B.

Materials costs added during the current period →

Conversion costs added during the current period →

	Direct Materials Costs	Conversion Costs	Total Costs	
Inventory in process, beginning of period			$ 1,860	No materials cost is added during the current period for beginning inventory
To complete inventory in process, beginning of period	0	$ 420[a]	420	
Started and completed during the period	21,600[b]	$8,100[c]	29,700	
Transferred out of Bottling (completed)			$31,980	
Inventory in process, end of period	$ 1,200[d]	$ 270[e]	1,470	
Total costs assigned by the Bottling Department			$33,450	
Completed and transferred out of production			$31,980 ←	
Inventory in process, ending			$ 1,470 ←	

[a]$1,400 × $0.30 = $420 [b]$27,000 × $0.80 = $21,600 [c]$27,000 × $0.30 = $8,100 [d]$1,500 × $0.80 = $1,200
[e]$900 × $0.30 = $270

Check Up Corner

Objective 3
Journalize entries
for transactions
using a process cost
system.

Journal Entries for a Process Cost System

The journal entries to record the cost flows and transactions for a process cost system are illustrated in this section. As a basis for illustration, the July transactions for **Frozen Delight** are used. To simplify, the entries are shown in summary form, even though many of the transactions would be recorded daily.

A. Purchased materials, including milk, cream, sugar, packaging, and indirect materials on account, $88,000.

A = L + E
\+   +

| A. | Materials | 88,000 | |
| | Accounts Payable | | 88,000 |

B. The Mixing Department requisitioned milk, cream, and sugar, $66,000. This is the total amount from the original July data. Packaging materials of $8,000 were requisitioned by the Packaging Department. Indirect materials for the Mixing and Packaging departments were $4,125 and $3,000, respectively.

A = L + E
\+ −

B.	Work in Process—Mixing	66,000	
	Work in Process—Packaging	8,000	
	Factory Overhead—Mixing	4,125	
	Factory Overhead—Packaging	3,000	
	Materials		81,125

C. Incurred direct labor in the Mixing and Packaging departments of $10,500 and $12,000, respectively.

A = L + E
\+   +

C.	Work in Process—Mixing	10,500	
	Work in Process—Packaging	12,000	
	Wages Payable		22,500

D. Recognized equipment depreciation for the Mixing and Packaging departments of $3,350 and $1,000, respectively.

A = L + E
\+ −

D.	Factory Overhead—Mixing	3,350	
	Factory Overhead—Packaging	1,000	
	Accumulated Depreciation—Equipment		4,350

E. Applied factory overhead to Mixing and Packaging departments of $7,275 and $3,500, respectively.

A = L + E
\+ −

E.	Work in Process—Mixing	7,275	
	Work in Process—Packaging	3,500	
	Factory Overhead—Mixing		7,275
	Factory Overhead—Packaging		3,500

F. Transferred costs of $86,475 from the Mixing Department to the Packaging Department per the cost of production report in Exhibit 8.

F.	Work in Process—Packaging	86,475	
	Work in Process—Mixing		86,475

A = L + E
+ –

G. Transferred goods of $106,000 out of the Packaging Department to Finished Goods according to the Packaging Department cost of production report (not illustrated).

G.	Finished Goods—Ice Cream	106,000	
	Work in Process—Packaging		106,000

A = L + E
+ –

H. Recorded the cost of goods sold out of the finished goods inventory of $107,000.

H.	Cost of Goods Sold	107,000	
	Finished Goods—Ice Cream		107,000

A = L + E
–   – Exp

Exhibit 9 shows the flow of costs for each transaction. The highlighted amounts in Exhibit 9 were determined from assigning the costs in the Mixing Department. These amounts were computed and are shown at the bottom of the cost of production report for the Mixing Department in Exhibit 8. Likewise, the amount transferred out of the Packaging Department to Finished Goods would have also been determined from a cost of production report for the Packaging Department.

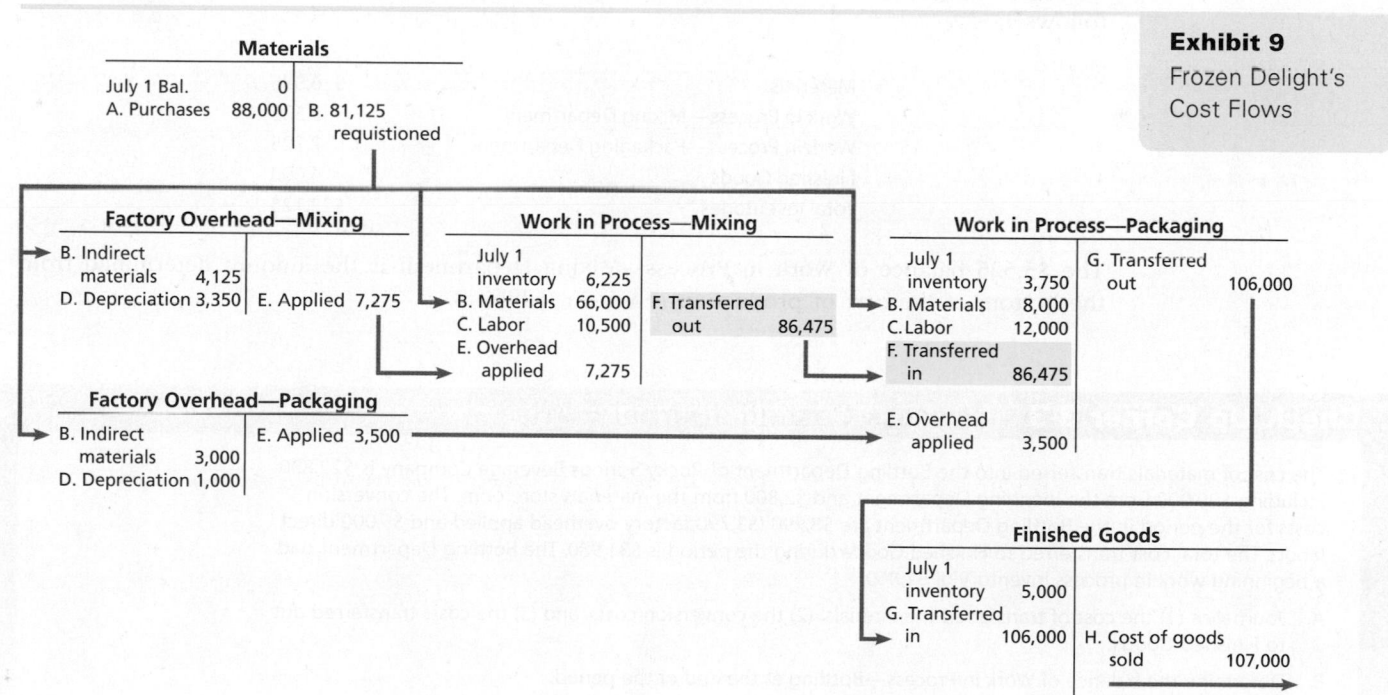

Exhibit 9

Frozen Delight's Cost Flows

Why It Matters

Process Costing for Services: Costing the Power Stack

Process costing can also be used in service businesses where the nature of the service is uniform across all units. Examples include electricity generation, wastewater treatment, and natural gas transmission. To illustrate, the unit of production in generating electricity is called a megawatt hour, where each megawatt hour is the same across all sources of generation.

Unlike product manufacturing, service companies often do not have inventory. For example, in generating electricity, the electricity cannot be stored. Thus, electric companies such as **Duke Energy Corporation** match the production of electricity to the demand in real time. Electric companies use what is termed the *power stack* to match power supply to demand by arranging generating facilities in order of cost per megawatt hour. The least-cost-per-megawatt-hour facilities satisfy initial demand at the bottom of the stack, while the highest-cost-per-megawatt-hour power sources are placed at

the top of the stack to satisfy peak loads, as illustrated in the following graph:

The cost per megawatt hour is determined using process costing by accumulating the conversion costs such as equipment depreciation, labor, and maintenance plus the cost of fuel for each facility. These costs are divided by the megawatt hours generated. Because there are no inventories, the additional complexity of equivalent units is avoided. The resulting cost per megawatt hour by facility is used to develop the power stack.

The ending inventories for Frozen Delight are reported on the July 31 balance sheet as follows:

Materials	$ 6,875
Work in Process—Mixing Department	3,525
Work in Process—Packaging Department	7,725
Finished Goods	4,000
Total inventories	$22,125

The $3,525 balance of Work in Process—Mixing Department is the amount determined from the bottom of the cost of production report in Exhibit 8.

Check Up Corner 3-3   Process Costing Journal Entries

The cost of materials transferred into the Bottling Department of Rocky Springs Beverage Company is $22,800, including $20,000 from the Blending Department and $2,800 from the materials storeroom. The conversion costs for the period in the Bottling Department are $8,790 ($3,790 factory overhead applied and $5,000 direct labor). The total cost transferred to Finished Goods during the period is $31,980. The Bottling Department had a beginning work in process inventory of $1,860.

A.   Journalize (1) the cost of transferred-in materials, (2) the conversion costs, and (3) the costs transferred out to Finished Goods.

B.   Determine the balance of Work in Process—Bottling at the end of the period.

Note: The costs transferred out of the Bottling Department and the cost of the Bottling Department's ending inventory are computed in Check Up Corner 3-2.

Solution:

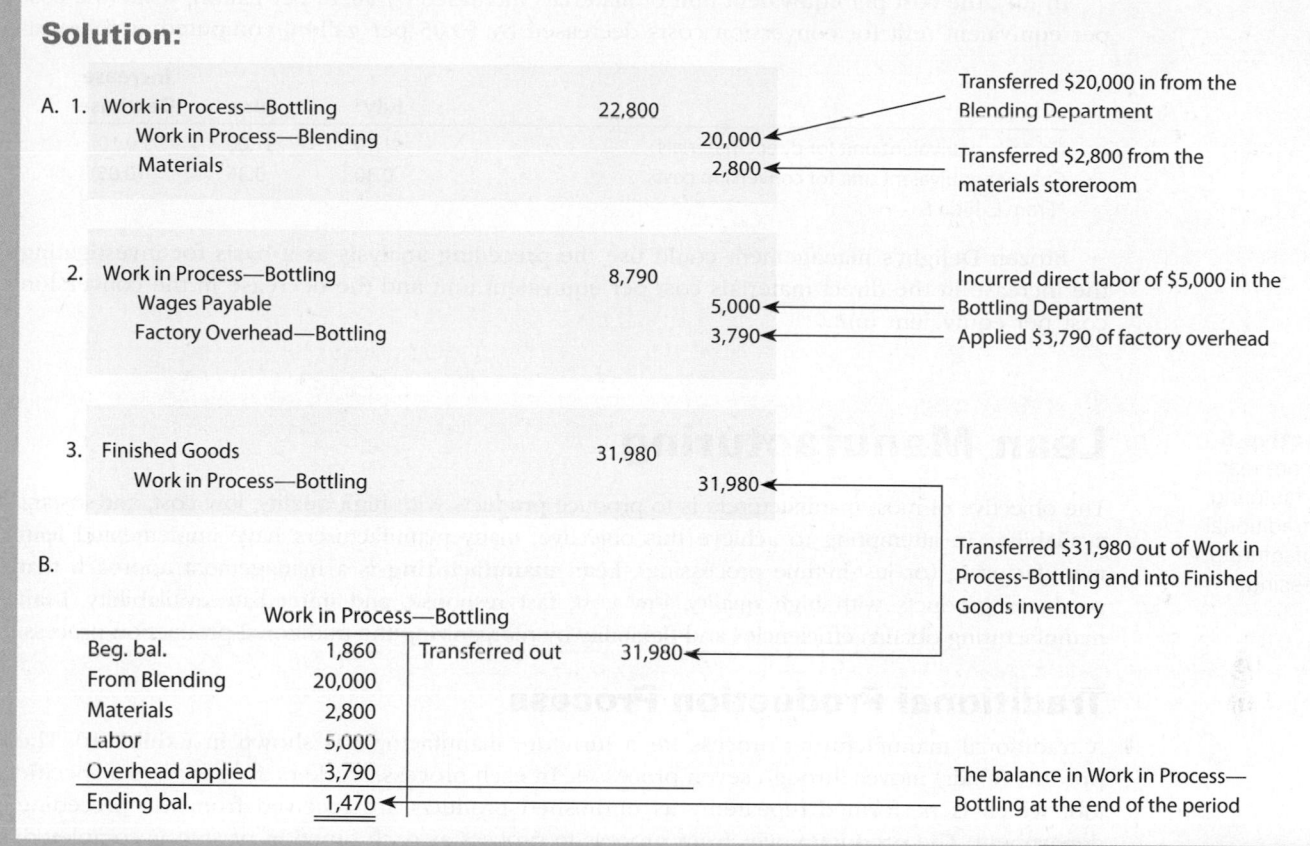

A. 1. Work in Process—Bottling   22,800

Transferred $20,000 in from the Blending Department

    Work in Process—Blending   20,000

    Materials   2,800

Transferred $2,800 from the materials storeroom

  2. Work in Process—Bottling   8,790

    Wages Payable   5,000

Incurred direct labor of $5,000 in the Bottling Department

    Factory Overhead—Bottling   3,790

Applied $3,790 of factory overhead

  3. Finished Goods   31,980

    Work in Process—Bottling   31,980

Transferred $31,980 out of Work in Process-Bottling and into Finished Goods inventory

B.

Work in Process—Bottling			
Beg. bal.	1,860	Transferred out	31,980
From Blending	20,000		
Materials	2,800		
Labor	5,000		
Overhead applied	3,790		
Ending bal.	1,470		

The balance in Work in Process—Bottling at the end of the period

Check Up Corner

Using the Cost of Production Report

Objective 4
Describe and illustrate the analysis of unit cost changes between periods.

The cost of production report is often used by managers for analyzing the change in the conversion and direct materials cost per equivalent unit between periods. To illustrate, the cost of production report for **Frozen Delight** is used.

The cost of production report for the Mixing Department is shown in Exhibit 8. The cost per equivalent unit for June can be determined from the beginning inventory. The original Frozen Delight data indicate that the July 1 inventory in process of $6,225 consists of the following costs:

Direct materials cost, 5,000 gallons	$5,000
Conversion costs, 5,000 gallons, 70% completed	1,225
Total inventory in process, July 1	$6,225

Using the preceding data, the June costs per equivalent unit of materials and conversion costs can be determined as follows:

$$\text{Direct Materials Cost per Equivalent Unit} = \frac{\text{Total Direct Materials Cost for the Period}}{\text{Total Equivalent Units of Direct Materials}}$$

$$\text{Direct Materials Cost per Equivalent Unit} = \frac{\$5,000}{5,000 \text{ gallons}} = \$1.00 \text{ per gallon}$$

$$\text{Conversion Cost per Equivalent Unit} = \frac{\text{Total Conversion Costs for the Period}}{\text{Total Equivalent Units of Conversion Costs}}$$

$$\text{Conversion Cost per Equivalent Unit} = \frac{\$1,225}{(5,000 \times 70\%) \text{ gallons}} = \$0.35 \text{ per gallon}$$

In July, the cost per equivalent unit of materials increased by $0.10 per gallon, while the cost per equivalent unit for conversion costs decreased by $0.05 per gallon, computed as follows:

	July*	June	Increase (Decrease)
Cost per equivalent unit for direct materials	$1.10	$1.00	$ 0.10
Cost per equivalent unit for conversion costs	0.30	0.35	(0.05)

*From Exhibit 8

Frozen Delight's management could use the preceding analysis as a basis for investigating the increase in the direct materials cost per equivalent unit and the decrease in the conversion cost per equivalent unit.

Objective 5
Compare lean manufacturing with traditional manufacturing processing.

Lean Manufacturing

The objective of most manufacturers is to produce products with high quality, low cost, and instant availability. In attempting to achieve this objective, many manufacturers have implemented lean manufacturing (or just-in-time processing). **Lean manufacturing** is a management approach that produces products with high quality, low cost, fast response, and immediate availabililty. Lean manufacturing obtains efficiencies and flexibility by reorganizing the traditional production process.

Traditional Production Process

A traditional manufacturing process for a furniture manufacturer is shown in Exhibit 10. The product (chair) moves through seven processes. In each process, workers are assigned a specific job, which is performed repeatedly as unfinished products are received from the preceding department. The product moves from process to process as each function or step is completed.

Exhibit 10
Traditional Production Line

Furniture Manufacturer

For the furniture maker in Exhibit 10, the product (chair) moves through the following processes:

1. In the Cutting Department, the wood is cut to design specifications.
2. In the Drilling Department, the wood is drilled to design specifications.
3. In the Sanding Department, the wood is sanded.
4. In the Staining Department, the wood is stained.
5. In the Varnishing Department, varnish and other protective coatings are applied.
6. In the Upholstery Department, fabric and other materials are added.
7. In the Assembly Department, the product (chair) is assembled.

In the traditional production process, supervisors enter materials into manufacturing so as to keep all the manufacturing departments (processes) operating. Some departments, however, may process materials more rapidly than others. In addition, if one department stops because of machine breakdowns, for example, the preceding departments usually continue production in order to avoid idle time. In such cases, a buildup of work in process inventories results in some departments.

Lean Manufacturing

In lean manufacturing, processing functions are combined into work centers, sometimes called **manufacturing cells**. For example, the seven departments illustrated in Exhibit 10 might be reorganized into the following three work centers:

1. Work Center 1 performs the cutting, drilling, and sanding functions.
2. Work Center 2 performs the staining and varnishing functions.
3. Work Center 3 performs the upholstery and assembly functions.

The preceding lean manufacturing process is illustrated in Exhibit 11.

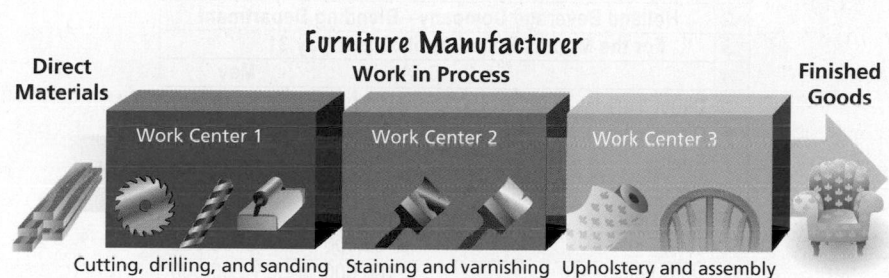

Furniture Manufacturer

Direct Materials — Work in Process — Finished Goods

Work Center 1: Cutting, drilling, and sanding
Work Center 2: Staining and varnishing
Work Center 3: Upholstery and assembly

Exhibit 11
Lean Production Line

In traditional manufacturing, a worker typically performs only one function. However, in lean manufacturing, work centers complete several functions. Thus, workers are often cross-trained to perform more than one function. Research has indicated that workers who perform several functions identify better with the end product. This creates pride in the product and improves quality and productivity.

The activities supporting the manufacturing process are called *service activities*. For example, repair and maintenance of manufacturing equipment are service activities. In lean manufacturing, service activities may be assigned to individual work centers, rather than to centralized service departments. For example, each work center may be assigned responsibility for the repair and maintenance of its machinery and equipment. This creates an environment in which workers gain a better understanding of the production process and their machinery. In turn, workers tend to take better care of the machinery, which decreases repairs and maintenance costs, reduces machine downtime, and improves product quality.

In lean manufacturing, the product is often placed on a movable carrier that is centrally located in the work center. After the workers in a work center have completed their activities with the product, the entire carrier and any additional materials are moved just in time to satisfy the demand or need of the next work center. In this sense, the product is said to be "pulled through." Each work center is connected to other work centers through information contained on a Kanban, which is a Japanese term for cards.

In summary, the primary objective of lean manufacturing is to increase the speed and quality, while reducing the cost of operations. This is achieved by eliminating waste and simplifying the production process. Lean manufacturing, including lean accounting and activity analysis, is further described and illustrated in Chapter 12.

Analysis for Decision Making

Objective

Describe and Illustrate the use of a cost of production report in evaluating a company's performance.

Analyzing Process Costs

Cost of production reports may be prepared showing more than direct materials and conversion costs. This greater detail can help managers isolate problems and seek opportunities for improvement.

To illustrate, the Blending Department of Holland Beverage Company prepared cost of production reports for April and May. Assume that the Blending Department had no beginning or ending work in process inventory in either month. That is, all units started were completed in each month. The cost of production reports showing multiple cost categories for April and May in the Blending Department are as follows:

	A	B	C
1	Cost of Production Reports		
2	Holland Beverage Company—Blending Department		
3	For the Months Ended April 30 and May 31		
4		April	May
5	Direct materials	$ 20,000	$ 40,600
6	Direct labor	15,000	29,400
7	Energy	8,000	20,000
8	Repairs	4,000	8,000
9	Tank cleaning	3,000	8,000
10	Total	$ 50,000	$106,000
11	Units completed	÷100,000	÷200,000
12	Cost per unit	$ 0.50	$ 0.53
13			

The reports indicate that total unit costs have increased in May from $0.50 to $0.53, or 6%. To determine the possible causes for this increase, the cost of production reports are restated in per-unit terms by dividing the costs by the number of units completed, as follows:

	A	B	C	D
1	Blending Department			
2	Per-Unit Expense Comparisons			
3		April	May	% Change
4	Direct materials	$0.200	$0.203	1.50%
5	Direct labor	0.150	0.147	−2.00%
6	Energy	0.080	0.100	25.00%
7	Repairs	0.040	0.040	0.00%
8	Tank cleaning	0.030	0.040	33.33%
9	Total	$0.500	$0.530	6.00%
10				

Both energy and tank cleaning per-unit costs have increased significantly in May. These increases should be further investigated. For example, the increase in energy may be due to the machines losing fuel efficiency. This could lead management to repair the machines. The tank cleaning costs could be investigated in a similar fashion.

Cost of production reports can also be used to compare the materials output quantity to the materials input quantity. Dividing the output quantities by the input quantities is termed the *yield* of a process. Often, there are materials losses from waste that will cause the materials output to be less than the materials input into the process. These materials losses can be investigated to improve the efficiency in using materials.

Make a Decision | Analyzing Process Costs

Dura-Conduit Corporation manufactures plastic conduit that is used in the cable industry. A conduit is a tube that encircles and protects the underground cable. In the process for making the plastic conduit, called *extrusion*, the melted plastic (*resin*) is pressed through a die to form a tube. Scrap is produced in this process.

Information from the cost of production reports for three months is as follows, assuming that inventory remains constant:

	May	June	July
Resin pounds input into the process	460,000	600,000	640,000
Price per pound	× $1.05	× $1.05	× $1.05
Plastic material costs	$483,000	$630,000	$672,000
Conversion costs	$ 90,000	$110,000	$112,000
Conduit output from the process (feet)	900,000	1,100,000	1,120,000

Assume that there is one-half pound of resin per foot of the finished product.

A. Determine the resin materials cost per foot of finished product for each month. (Round to the nearest whole cent.)

B. Determine the ratio of the number of resin pounds output in conduit by the number of pounds input into the process for each month. (Round percentages to one decimal place.)

C. Interpret the resin materials cost per foot for the three months. Use the information in (A.) and (B.) to explain what is happening.

D. Determine the conversion cost per foot of finished product for each month and interpret the result.

Solution:

A.

	May	June	July
Resin cost per foot	$0.54	$0.57	$0.60
	$483,000 ÷ 900,000 ft.	$630,000 ÷ 1,100,000 ft.	$672,000 ÷ 1,120,000 ft.

B. Pounds of resin:

	May	June	July
Conduit output (feet)	900,000	1,100,000	1,120,000
Pounds of resin per foot	× 0.5	× 0.5	× 0.5
Pounds of resin output	450,000	550,000	560,000

Ratio of output pounds to input pounds:

	May	June	July
Resin output pounds divided by input pounds	97.8%	91.7%	87.5%
	450,000 ÷ 460,000	550,000 ÷ 600,000	560,000 ÷ 640,000

C. The resin materials cost per foot of finished product is increasing over the three months, from $0.54 per foot in May to $0.60 per foot in July. This increased cost is not the result of a change in the price, which remained constant at $1.05 per pound. Rather, the increased cost is the result of the ratio of output pounds to input pounds deteriorating. Apparently, the level of scrap in the process is growing as fewer output pounds are being produced from input pounds.

D.

	May	June	July
Conversion cost per foot	$0.10	$0.10	$0.10
	$90,000 ÷ 900,000 ft.	$110,000 ÷ 1,100,000 ft.	$112,000 ÷ 1,120,000 ft.

The conversion cost per foot has remained constant and, thus, does not appear to need management attention.

Appendix Average Cost Method

A cost flow assumption must be used as product costs flow through manufacturing processes. In this chapter, the first-in, first-out cost flow method was used for the Mixing Department of Frozen Delight. In this appendix, the average cost flow method is illustrated for **S&W Ice Cream Company (S&W)**.

Determining Costs Using the Average Cost Method

S&W's operations are similar to those of Frozen Delight. Like Frozen Delight, S&W mixes direct materials (milk, cream, sugar) in refrigerated vats and has two manufacturing departments, Mixing and Packaging.

The manufacturing data for the Mixing Department for July are as follows:

Inventory in process, July 1, 5,000 gallons (70% completed)................	$ 6,200
Direct materials cost incurred in July, 60,000 gallons.......................	66,000
Direct labor cost incurred in July...	10,500
Factory overhead applied in July...	6,405
Total production costs to account for	$89,105
Cost of goods transferred to Packaging in July (includes units in process on July 1), 62,000 gallons	?
Cost of work in process inventory, July 31, 3,000 gallons, 25% completed as to conversion costs...	?

Using the average cost method, the objective is to allocate the total costs of production of $89,105 to the following:

- The 62,000 gallons completed and transferred to the Packaging Department
- The 3,000 gallons in the July 31 (ending) work in process inventory

The preceding costs show two question marks. These amounts are determined by preparing a cost of production report, using the following four steps:

- Step 1. Determine the units to be assigned costs.
- Step 2. Compute equivalent units of production.
- Step 3. Determine the cost per equivalent unit.
- Step 4. Allocate costs to transferred out and partially completed units.

Under the average cost method, all production costs (materials and conversion costs) are combined together for determining equivalent units and cost per equivalent unit.

Step 1: Determine the Units to Be Assigned Costs The first step is to determine the units to be assigned costs. A unit can be any measure of completed production, such as tons, gallons, pounds, barrels, or cases. For **S&W**, a unit is a gallon of ice cream.

S&W's Mixing Department had 65,000 gallons of direct materials to account for during July, as shown here.

Total gallons to account for:

Inventory in process, July 1	5,000 gallons
Received from materials storeroom	60,000
Total units to account for by the Packaging Department	65,000 gallons

There are two groups of units to be assigned costs for the period.

Group 1	Units completed and transferred out
Group 2	Units in the July 31 (ending) work in process inventory

During July, the Mixing Department completed and transferred 62,000 gallons to the Packaging Department. Of the 60,000 gallons started in July, 57,000 (60,000 − 3,000) gallons were completed and transferred to the Packaging Department. Thus, the ending work in process inventory consists of 3,000 gallons.

The total units (gallons) to be assigned costs for S&W can be summarized as follows:

Group 1	Units transferred out to the Packaging Department in July	62,000 gallons
Group 2	Inventory in process, July 31	3,000
	Total gallons to be assigned costs....................................	65,000 gallons

The total units (gallons) to be assigned costs (65,000 gallons) equal the total units to account for (65,000 gallons).

Step 2: Compute Equivalent Units of Production S&W has 3,000 gallons of whole units in the work in process inventory for the Mixing Department on July 31. Because these units are 25% complete, the number of equivalent units in process in the Mixing Department on July 31 is 750 gallons (3,000 gallons × 25%). Because the units transferred to the Packaging Department have been completed, the whole units (62,000 gallons) transferred are the same as the equivalent units transferred.

The total equivalent units of production for the Mixing Department are determined by adding the equivalent units in the ending work in process inventory to the units transferred and completed during the period, computed as follows:

Equivalent units completed and transferred to the Packaging Department during July	62,000 gallons
Equivalent units in ending work in process, July 31	750
Total equivalent units	62,750 gallons

Step 3: Determine the Cost per Equivalent Unit Because materials and conversion costs are combined under the average cost method, the cost per equivalent unit is determined by dividing the total production costs by the total equivalent units of production as follows:

$$\text{Cost per Equivalent Unit} = \frac{\text{Total Production Costs}}{\text{Total Equivalent Units}} = \frac{\$89,105}{62,750 \text{ gallons}} = \$1.42$$

The cost per equivalent unit is used in Step 4 to allocate the production costs to the completed and partially completed units.

Step 4: Allocate Costs to Transferred Out and Partially Completed Units

The cost of transferred and partially completed units is determined by multiplying the cost per equivalent unit times the equivalent units of production. For **S&W**'s Mixing Department, these costs are determined as follows:

Group 1	Transferred out to the Packaging Department (62,000 gallons × $1.42)	$88,040
Group 2	Inventory in process, July 31 (3,000 gallons × 25% × $1.42).................	1,065
	Total production costs assigned	$89,105

The Cost of Production Report

The July cost of production report for **S&W**'s Mixing Department is shown in Exhibit 12. This cost of production report summarizes the following:

- The units for which the department is accountable and the disposition of those units
- The production costs incurred by the department and the allocation of those costs between completed and partially completed units

Exhibit 12

Cost of Production Report for S&W's Mixing Department— Average Cost

	A	B	C
1	S&W Ice Cream Company		
2	Cost of Production Report—Mixing Department		
3	For the Month Ended July 31		
4	**UNITS**		
5		Whole Units	Equivalent Units
6			of Production
7	Units charged to production:		
8	Inventory in process, July 1	5,000	
9	Received from materials storeroom	60,000	
10	Total units accounted for by the Mixing Department	65,000	
11			
12	Units to be assigned costs:		
13	Transferred to Packaging Department in July	62,000	62,000
14	Inventory in process, July 31 (25% completed)	3,000	750
15	Total units to be assigned costs	65,000	62,750
16			
17	**COSTS**		Costs
18			
19	Cost per equivalent unit:		
20	Total production costs for July in Mixing Department		$89,105
21	Total equivalent units (from Step 2)		÷62,750
22	Cost per equivalent unit		$ 1.42
23			
24	Costs assigned to production:		
25	Inventory in process, July 1		$ 6,200
26	Direct materials, direct labor, and factory overhead incurred in July		82,905
27	Total costs accounted for by the Mixing Department		$89,105
28			
29			
30	Costs allocated to completed and partially completed units:		
31	Transferred to Packaging Department in July (62,000 gallons × $1.42)		$88,040
32	Inventory in process, July 31 (3,000 gallons × 25% × $1.42)		1,065
33	Total costs assigned by the Mixing Department		$89,105
34			

Step 1, Step 2, Step 3, Step 4

Let's Review

Chapter Summary

1. The process cost system is best suited for industries that mass produce identical units of a product. Costs are charged to processing departments, rather than to jobs as with the job order cost system. These costs are transferred from one department to the next until production is completed.

2. A cost of production report summarizes the production and cost data for each processing department. The cost of production report is prepared by (1) determining the units to be assigned costs, (2) computing equivalent units of production, (3) determining the cost per equivalent unit, and (4) allocating costs to units transferred out and partially completed units.

3. Journal entries to record the cost flows and transactions for a process cost system include those for the purchase of material, usage of materials and direct labor, incurrence of overhead, application of overhead to departments, and transferring costs among departments and to finished goods. When goods are sold, their costs are transferred from finished goods to cost of goods sold.

4. The cost of production report is used for decision making by providing information for controlling and improving operations. Comparisons of equivalent costs per unit over time can be used to isolate increases or decreases in costs for further investigation.

5. Lean manufacturing focuses on producing products with high quality, low cost, and instant availability. It does this by combining processing functions into manufacturing cells (work centers) where cross-trained workers perform more than one function.

Key Terms

cost of production report (99)
cost per equivalent unit (104)
equivalent units of production (100)

first-in, first-out (FIFO) method (99)
lean manufacturing (114)
manufacturing cells (115)

process cost system (94)
process manufacturer (94)
whole units (100)

Practice

Multiple-Choice Questions

1. For which of the following businesses would the process cost system be most appropriate?
   A. Custom furniture manufacturer
   B. Commercial building contractor
   C. Crude oil refinery
   D. Automobile repair shop

2. There were 2,000 pounds in process at the beginning of the period in the Packing Department. Packing received 24,000 pounds from the Blending Department during the month, of which 3,000 pounds were in process at the end of the month. How many pounds were completed and transferred to finished goods from the Packing Department?
   A. 23,000
   B. 21,000
   C. 26,000
   D. 29,000

3. Information relating to production in Department A for May is as follows:

May	1	Balance, 1,000 units, ¾ completed	$22,150
	31	Direct materials, 5,000 units	75,000
	31	Direct labor	32,500
	31	Factory overhead	16,250

If 500 units were one-fourth completed at May 31, 5,500 units were completed during May, and the first-in, first-out method is used, what was the number of equivalent units of production with respect to conversion costs for May?

A. 4,500   C. 5,500
B. 4,875   D. 6,000

4. Based on the data presented in Question 3, what is the conversion cost per equivalent unit?

A. $10   C. $25
B. $15   D. $32

5. Information from the accounting system revealed the following:

	Day 1	Day 2	Day 3	Day 4	Day 5
Materials	$20,000	$18,000	$22,000	$20,000	$20,000
Electricity	2,500	3,000	3,500	4,000	4,700
Maintenance	4,000	3,750	3,400	3,000	2,800
Total costs	$26,500	$24,750	$28,900	$27,000	$27,500
Pounds produced	÷10,000	÷ 9,000	÷11,000	÷10,000	÷10,000
Cost per unit	$ 2.65	$ 2.75	$ 2.63	$ 2.70	$ 2.75

Which of the following statements best interprets this information?

A. The total costs are out of control.
B. The product costs have steadily increased because of higher electricity costs.
C. Electricity costs have steadily increased because of lack of maintenance.
D. The unit costs reveal a significant operating problem.

Answers provided after Problem. Need more practice? Find additional multiple-choice questions, exercises, and problems in CengageNOWv2.

Exercises

SHOW ME HOW

1. Job order versus process costing   Obj. 1

Which of the following industries would typically use job order costing, and which would typically use process costing?

Dentist	Movie studio
Gasoline refining	Paper manufacturing
Flour mill	Custom printing

SHOW ME HOW

2. Units to be assigned costs   Obj. 2

Lilac Skin Care Company consists of two departments, Blending and Filling. The Filling Department received 45,000 ounces from the Blending Department. During the period, the Filling Department completed 42,800 ounces, including 4,000 ounces of work in process at the beginning of the period. The ending work in process inventory was 6,200 ounces. How many ounces were started and completed during the period?

SHOW ME HOW

3. Equivalent units of materials cost
Obj. 2

The Filling Department of Lilac Skin Care Company had 4,000 ounces in beginning work in process inventory (70% complete). During the period, 42,800 ounces were completed. The ending work in process inventory was 6,200 ounces (40% complete). What are the total equivalent units for direct materials if materials are added at the beginning of the process?

SHOW ME HOW

4. Equivalent units of conversion costs
Obj. 2

The Filling Department of Lilac Skin Care had 4,000 ounces in beginning work in process inventory (70% complete). During the period, 42,800 ounces were completed. The ending work in process inventory was 6,200 ounces (40% complete). What are the total equivalent units for conversion costs?

SHOW ME HOW

5. Cost per equivalent unit
Obj. 2

The cost of direct materials transferred into the Filling Department of Lilac Skin Care Company is $20,250. The conversion cost for the period in the Filling Department is $6,372. The total equivalent units for direct materials and conversion are 45,000 ounces and 42,480 ounces, respectively. Determine the direct materials and conversion costs per equivalent unit.

SHOW ME HOW

6. Cost of units transferred out and ending work in process
Obj. 2

The costs per equivalent unit of direct materials and conversion in the Filling Department of Lilac Skin Care Company are $0.45 and $0.15, respectively. The equivalent units to be assigned costs are as follows:

	Equivalent Units	
	Direct Materials	Conversion
Inventory in process, beginning of period	0	1,200
Started and completed during the period	38,800	38,800
Transferred out of Filling (completed)	38,800	40,000
Inventory in process, end of period	6,200	2,480
Total units to be assigned costs	45,000	42,480

The beginning work in process inventory had a cost of $2,200. Determine the cost of completed and transferred-out production, the ending work in process inventory, and the total costs assigned by the Filling Department.

SHOW ME HOW

7. Process cost journal entries
Obj. 3

The cost of materials transferred into the Filling Department of Lilac Skin Care Company is $20,250, including $6,000 from the Blending Department and $14,250 from the materials storeroom. The conversion cost for the period in the Filling Department is $6,372 ($1,600 factory overhead applied and $4,772 direct labor). The total cost transferred to Finished Goods for the period was $25,660. The Filling Department had a beginning inventory of $2,200.

A. Journalize (1) the cost of transferred-in materials, (2) the conversion costs, and (3) the costs transferred out to Finished Goods.

B. Determine the balance of Work in Process—Filling at the end of the period.

SHOW ME HOW

8. Analyzing changes in unit costs
Obj. 4

The costs of energy consumed in producing good units in the Baking Department of Pan Company were $14,875 and $14,615 for June and July, respectively. The number of equivalent units produced in June and July was 42,500 pounds and 39,500 pounds, respectively. Evaluate the change in the cost of energy between the two months.

Answers provided after Problem. Need more practice? Find additional multiple-choice questions, exercises, and problems in CengageNOWv2.

Problem

Southern Aggregate Company manufactures concrete by a series of four processes. All materials are introduced in Crushing. From Crushing, the materials pass through Sifting, Baking, and Mixing, emerging as finished concrete. All inventories are costed by the first-in, first-out method.

The balances in the accounts Work in Process—Mixing and Finished Goods were as follows on May 1:

Inventory in Process—Mixing (2,000 units, ¼ completed)	$13,700
Finished Goods (1,800 units at $8.00 a unit)	14,400

The following costs were charged to Work in Process—Mixing during May:

Direct materials transferred from Baking: 15,200 units at	
$6.50 a unit	$98,800
Direct labor	17,200
Factory overhead	11,780

During May, 16,000 units of concrete were completed, and 15,800 units were sold. Inventories on May 31 were as follows:

Inventory in Process—Mixing (1,200 units, ½ completed)
Finished Goods (2,000 units)

Instructions

1. Prepare a cost of production report for the Mixing Department for the month of May.

2. Determine the cost of goods sold (indicate number of units and unit costs).

3. Determine the finished goods inventory, May 31.

Need more practice? Find additional multiple-choice questions, exercises, and problems in CengageNOWv2.

Answers

Multiple-Choice Questions

1. **C** The process cost system is most appropriate for a business where manufacturing is conducted by continuous operations and involves a series of uniform production processes, such as the processing of crude oil (answer C). The job order cost system is most appropriate for a business where the product is made to customers' specifications, such as custom furniture manufacturing (answer A), commercial building construction (answer B), or automobile repair shop (answer D).

2. **A** The total pounds transferred to finished goods (23,000) are the 2,000 in-process pounds at the beginning of the period plus the number of pounds started and completed during the month, 21,000 (24,000 – 3,000). Answer B incorrectly assumes that the beginning inventory is not transferred during the month. Answer C assumes that all 24,000 pounds started during the month are transferred to finished goods, instead of only the portion started and completed. Answer D incorrectly adds all the numbers together.

3. **B** The number of units that could have been produced from start to finish during a period is termed *equivalent units*. The 4,875 equivalent units (answer B) is determined as follows:

To process units in inventory on May 1 (1,000 × ¼)	250
To process units started and completed in May (5,500 units – 1,000 units)	4,500
To process units in inventory on May 31 (500 units × ¼)	125
Equivalent units of production in May	4,875

4. **A** The conversion costs (direct labor and factory overhead) totaling $48,750 are divided by the number of equivalent units (4,875) to determine the unit conversion cost of $10 (answer A).

5. **C** The electricity costs have increased, and maintenance costs have decreased. Answer C would be a reasonable explanation for these results. The total costs, materials costs, and costs per unit do not reveal any type of pattern over the time period. In fact, the materials costs have stayed at exactly $2.00 per pound over the time period. This demonstrates that aggregated numbers can sometimes hide underlying information that can be used to improve the process.

Exercises

1.

Dentist	Job order	Movie studio	Job order
Gasoline refining	Process	Paper manufacturing	Process
Flour mill	Process	Custom printing	Job order

2. 38,800 ounces started and completed (42,800 ounces completed – 4,000 ounces beginning WIP), or (45,000 ounces started – 6,200 ounces ending WIP)

3.

	Whole Units	Percent Materials Added in Period	Equivalent Units for Materials
Inventory in process, beginning of period	4,000	0%	0
Started and completed during the period	38,800*	100%	38,800
Transferred out of Filling (completed)	42,800		38,800
Inventory in process, end of period	6,200	100%	6,200
Total units to be assigned costs	49,000		45,000

* 42,800 – 4,000

4.

	Whole Units	Percent Conversion Completed in Period	Equivalent Units for Conversion
Inventory in process, beginning of period	4,000	30%	1,200
Started and completed during the period	38,800*	100%	38,800
Transferred out of Filling (completed)	42,800		40,000
Inventory in process, end of period	6,200	40%	2,480
Total units to be assigned costs	49,000		42,480

* 42,800 – 4,000

5.

$$\text{Equivalent units of direct materials: } \frac{\$20{,}250}{45{,}000} = \$0.45 \text{ per ounce}$$

$$\text{Equivalent units of conversion: } \frac{\$6{,}372}{42{,}480} = \$0.15 \text{ per ounce}$$

6.

	Direct Materials Costs		Conversion Costs	Total Costs
Inventory in process, balance.....................				$ 2,200
Inventory in process, beginning of period.........	0	+	180[a]	180
Cost of completed beginning work in process.....				$ 2,380
Started and completed during the period.........	17,460[b]	+	5,820[c]	23,280
Transferred out of Filling (completed)............				$25,660
Inventory in process, end of period..............	2,790[d]	+	372[e]	3,162
Total costs assigned by the Filling Department....				$28,822
Completed and transferred-out production.......	$25,660			
Inventory in process, ending	$3,162			

[a]$1,200 × $0.15 = $180   [b]$38,800 × $0.45 = $17,460   [c]$38,800 × $0.15 = $5,820
[d]$6,200 × $0.45 = $2,790   [e]$2,480 × $0.15 = $372

7. A.

Work in Process—Filling	20,250	
Work in Process—Blending		6,000
Materials		14,250
Work in Process—Filling	6,372	
Factory Overhead—Filling		1,600
Wages Payable		4,772
Finished Goods	25,660	
Work in Process—Filling		25,660

B. $3,162 ($2,200 + $20,250 + $6,372 − $25,660)

8.

$$\text{Energy cost per pound, June: } \frac{\$14{,}875}{42{,}500} = \$0.35$$

$$\text{Energy cost per pound, July: } \frac{\$14{,}615}{39{,}500} = \$0.37$$

The cost of energy has increased by 2 cents per pound between June and July, indicating inefficiency in the use of energy.

Need more help? Watch step-by-step videos of how to compute answers to these Exercises in CengageNOWv2.

Problem

1.

	A	B	C	D	E
1	Southern Aggregate Company				
2	Cost of Production Report—Mixing Department				
3	For the Month Ended May 31				
4			Equivalent Units		
5	**UNITS**	Whole Units	Direct Materials	Conversion	
6	Units charged to production:				
7	Inventory in process, May 1	2,000			
8	Received from Baking	15,200			
9	Total units accounted for by the Mixing Department	17,200			
10					
11	Units to be assigned costs:				
12	Inventory in process, May 1 (25% completed)	2,000	0	1,500	
13	Started and completed in May	14,000	14,000	14,000	
14	Transferred to finished goods in May	16,000	14,000	15,500	
15	Inventory in process, May 31 (50% completed)	1,200	1,200	600	
16	Total units to be assigned costs	17,200	15,200	16,100	
17					
18			Costs		
19	**COSTS**		Direct Materials	Conversion	Total
20	Cost per equivalent unit:				
21	Total costs for May in Mixing Department		$ 98,800	$ 28,980	
22	Total equivalent units (row 16)		÷ 15,200	÷ 16,100	
23	Cost per equivalent unit		$ 6.50	$ 1.80	
24					
25	Costs assigned to production:				
26	Inventory in process, May 1				$ 13,700
27	Costs incurred in May				127,780
28	Total costs accounted for by the Mixing Department				$141,480
29					
30	Costs allocated to completed and partially				
31	completed units:				
32	Inventory in process, May 1—balance				$ 13,700
33	To complete inventory in process, May 1		$ 0	$ 2,700ᵃ	2,700
34	Cost of completed May 1 work in process				$ 16,400
35	Started and completed in May		91,000ᵇ	25,200ᶜ	116,200
36	Transferred to finished goods in May				$132,600
37	Inventory in process, May 31		7,800ᵈ	1,080ᵉ	8,880
38	Total costs assigned by the Mixing Department				$141,480
39					

ᵃ1,500 × $1.80 = $2,700   ᵇ14,000 × $6.50 = $91,000   ᶜ14,000 × $1.80 = $25,200   ᵈ1,200 × $6.50 = $7,800
ᵉ600 × $1.80 = $1,080

2. Cost of goods sold:

1,800 units at $8.00	$ 14,400	(from finished goods beginning inventory)
2,000 units at $8.20*	16,400	(from inventory in process beginning inventory)
12,000 units at $8.30**	99,600	(from May production started and completed)
15,800 units	$130,400	

*($13,700 + $2,700) ÷ 2,000
**$116,200 ÷ 14,000

3. Finished goods inventory, May 31:

2,000 units at $8.30 $16,600

Discussion Questions

1. Which type of cost system, process or job order, would be best suited for each of the following: (A) TV assembler, (B) building contractor, (C) automobile repair shop, (D) paper manufacturer, (E) custom jewelry manufacturer? Give reasons for your answers.

2. In job order cost accounting, the three elements of manufacturing cost are charged directly to job orders. Why is it not necessary to charge manufacturing costs in process cost accounting to job orders?

3. In a job order cost system, direct labor and factory overhead applied are debited to individual jobs. How are these items treated in a process cost system and why?

4. Why is the cost per equivalent unit often determined separately for direct materials and conversion costs?

5. What is the purpose for determining the cost per equivalent unit?

6. Rameriz Company is a process manufacturer with two production departments, Blending and Filling. All direct materials are introduced in Blending from the materials store area. What is included in the cost transferred to Filling?

7. What is the most important purpose of the cost of production report?

8. How are cost of production reports used for controlling and improving operations?

9. How does lean manufacturing differ from the conventional manufacturing process?

Basic Exercises

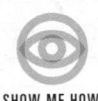

BE 3-1 Job order versus process costing   Obj. 1

Which of the following industries would typically use job order costing, and which would typically use process costing?

Steel manufactuirng	Computer chip manufacturing
Business consulting	Candy making
Web designer	Designer clothes manufacturing

BE 3-2 Units to be assigned costs   Obj. 2

Oak Ridge Steel Company has two departments, Casting and Rolling. In the Rolling Department, ingots from the Casting Department are rolled into steel sheet. The Rolling Department received 2,400 tons from the Casting Department. During July, the Rolling Department completed 2,200 tons, including 300 tons of work in process on July 1. The ending work in process inventory on July 31 was 500 tons. How many tons were started and completed during July?

BE 3-3 Equivalent units of materials cost   Obj. 2

The Rolling Department of Oak Ridge Steel Company had 300 tons in beginning work in process inventory (25% complete) on July 1. During July, 2,200 tons were completed. The ending work in process inventory on July 31 was 500 tons (40% complete). What are the total equivalent units for direct materials for July if materials are added at the beginning of the process?

BE 3-4 Equivalent units of conversion costs   Obj. 2

The Rolling Department of Oak Ridge Steel Company had 300 tons in beginning work in process inventory (25% complete) on July 1. During July, 2,200 tons were completed. The ending work in process inventory on July 31 was 500 tons (40% complete). What are the total equivalent units for conversion costs?

SHOW ME HOW

BE 3-5   Cost per equivalent unit

Obj. 2

The cost of direct materials transferred into the Rolling Department of Oak Ridge Steel Company is $432,000. The conversion cost for the period in the Rolling Department is $144,150. The total equivalent units for direct materials and conversion are 2,400 tons and 2,325 tons, respectively. Determine the direct materials and conversion costs per equivalent unit.

SHOW ME HOW

BE 3-6   Cost of units transferred out and ending work in process

Obj. 2

The costs per equivalent unit of direct materials and conversion in the Rolling Department of Oak Ridge Steel Company are $180 and $62, respectively. The equivalent units to be assigned costs are as follows:

	Equivalent Units	
	Direct Materials	Conversion
Inventory in process, July 1	0	225
Started and completed during July	1,900	1,900
Transferred out of Rolling (completed)	1,900	2,125
Inventory in process, July 31	500	200
Total units to be assigned costs	2,400	2,325

The beginning work in process inventory on July 1 had a cost of $80,000. Determine the cost of completed and transferred-out production, the ending work in process inventory , and the total costs assigned by the Rolling Department..

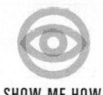
SHOW ME HOW

BE 3-7   Process cost journal entries

Obj. 3

In July, the cost of materials transferred into the Rolling Department from the Casting Department of Oak Ridge Steel Company is $432,000. The conversion cost for the period in the Rolling Department is $144,150 ($54,700 factory overhead applied and $89,450 direct labor). The total cost transferred to Finished Goods for the period was $553,750. The Rolling Department had a beginning inventory of $80,000.

A. Journalize (1) the cost of transferred-in materials, (2) the conversion costs, and (3) the costs transferred out to Finished Goods.

B. Determine the balance of Work in Process—Rolling at the end of the period.

SHOW ME HOW

BE 3-8   Analyzing changes in unit costs

Obj. 4

The costs of materials consumed in producing good units in the Forming Department of Thomas Company were $76,000 and $77,350 for September and October, respectively. The number of equivalent units produced in September and October was 800 tons and 850 tons, respectively. Evaluate the change in the cost of materials between the two months.

Exercises

REAL WORLD

EX 3-1   Entries for materials cost flows in a process cost system

Obj. 1, 3

The Hershey Company manufactures chocolate confectionery products. The three largest raw materials are cocoa, sugar, and dehydrated milk. These raw materials first go into the Blending Department. The blended product is then sent to the Molding Department, where the bars of candy are formed. The candy is then sent to the Packing Department, where the bars are wrapped and boxed. The boxed candy is then sent to the distribution center, where it is eventually sold to food brokers and retailers.

(Continued)

Show the accounts debited and credited for each of the following business events:

A. Materials used by the Blending Department

B. Transfer of blended product to the Molding Department

C. Transfer of chocolate to the Packing Department

D. Transfer of boxed chocolate to the distribution center

E. Sale of boxed chocolate

REAL WORLD

EX 3-2   Flowchart of accounts related to service and processing departments   Obj. 1

Alcoa Inc. is the world's largest producer of aluminum products. One product that Alcoa manufactures is aluminum sheet products for the aerospace industry. The entire output of the Smelting Department is transferred to the Rolling Department. Part of the fully processed goods from the Rolling Department are sold as rolled sheet, and the remainder of the goods are transferred to the Converting Department for further processing into sheared sheet.

Prepare a chart of the flow of costs from the processing department accounts into the finished goods accounts and then into the cost of goods sold account. The relevant accounts are as follows:

Cost of Goods Sold	Finished Goods—Rolled Sheet
Materials	Finished Goods—Sheared Sheet
Factory Overhead—Smelting Department	Work in Process—Smelting Department
Factory Overhead—Rolling Department	Work in Process—Rolling Department
Factory Overhead—Converting Department	Work in Process—Converting Department

---

SHOW ME HOW

REAL WORLD

EX 3-3   Entries for flow of factory costs for process cost system   Obj. 1, 3

Domino Foods, Inc., manufactures a sugar product by a continuous process, involving three production departments—Refining, Sifting, and Packing. Assume that records indicate that direct materials, direct labor, and applied factory overhead for the first department, Refining, were $400,000, $150,000, and $100,000, respectively. Also, work in process in the Refining Department at the beginning of the period totaled $40,000, and work in process at the end of the period totaled $35,000.

Journalize the entries to record (A) the flow of costs into the Refining Department during the period for (1) direct materials, (2) direct labor, and (3) factory overhead, and (B) the transfer of production costs to the second department, Sifting.

EX 3-4   Factory overhead rate, entry for applying factory overhead, and factory overhead account balance   Obj. 1, 3

✔ A. 125%

SHOW ME HOW

The cost accountant for Kenner Beverage Co. estimated that total factory overhead cost for the Blending Department for the coming fiscal year beginning May 1 would be $3,000,000, and total direct labor costs would be $2,400,000. During May, the actual direct labor cost totaled $198,400, and factory overhead cost incurred totaled $253,200.

A. What is the predetermined factory overhead rate based on direct labor cost?

B. Journalize the entry to apply factory overhead to production for May.

C. What is the May 31 balance of the account Factory Overhead—Blending Department?

D. Does the balance in part (C) represent over- or underapplied factory overhead?

EX 3-5   Equivalent units of production   Obj. 2

✔ Direct materials, 16,800 units

SHOW ME HOW

The Converting Department of Hopkinsville Company had 1,200 units in work in process at the beginning of the period, which were 25% complete. During the period, 16,000 units were completed and transferred to the Packing Department. There were 2,000 units in process at the end of the period, which were 40% complete. Direct materials are placed into the process at the beginning of production. Determine the number of equivalent units of production with respect to direct materials and conversion costs.

EX 3-6 Equivalent units of production

Obj. 2

✔ A. Conversion,
96,720 units

SHOW ME HOW

Units of production data for the two departments of Pacific Cable and Wire Company for November of the current fiscal year are as follows:

	Drawing Department	Winding Department
Work in process, November 1	5,000 units, 40% completed	3,200 units, 80% completed
Completed and transferred to next processing department during November	95,000 units	95,100 units
Work in process, November 30	6,200 units, 60% completed	3,100 units, 15% completed

If all direct materials are placed in process at the beginning of production, determine the direct materials and conversion equivalent units of production for November for (A) the Drawing Department and (B) the Winding Department.

EX 3-7 Equivalent units of production

Obj. 2

✔ B. Conversion,
335,100

SHOW ME HOW

The following information concerns production in the Baking Department for March. All direct materials are placed in process at the beginning of production.

ACCOUNT	Work in Process—Baking Department				ACCOUNT NO.	
					Balance	
Date		Item	Debit	Credit	Debit	Credit
Mar.	1	Bal., 18,000 units, ¼ completed			14,760	
	31	Direct materials, 336,000 units	252,000		266,760	
	31	Direct labor	40,000		306,760	
	31	Factory overhead	60,530		367,290	
	31	Goods finished, 330,000 units		346,410	20,880	
	31	Bal. ? units, ⅖ completed			20,880	

A. Determine the number of units in work in process inventory at March 31.

B. Determine the equivalent units of production for direct materials and conversion costs in March.

EX 3-8 Costs per equivalent unit

Obj. 2, 4

✔ A. 2. Conversion
cost per equivalent
unit, $0.30

SHOW ME HOW

A. Based upon the data in Exercise 3-7, determine the following for March::

1. Direct materials cost per equivalent unit
2. Conversion cost per equivalent unit
3. Cost of the beginning work in process completed during March
4. Cost of units started and completed during March
5. Cost of the ending work in process

B. Assuming that the direct materials cost is the same for February and March, did the conversion cost per equivalent unit increase, decrease, or remain the same in March?

EX 3-9 Equivalent units of production

Obj. 2

REAL WORLD

Kellogg Company manufactures cold cereal products, such as *Frosted Flakes*. Assume that the inventory in process on March 1 for the Packing Department included 1,200 pounds of cereal in the packing machine hopper (enough for 800 24-oz. boxes) and 800 empty 24-oz. boxes held in the package carousel of the packing machine. During March, 65,400 boxes of 24-oz. cereal were packaged. Conversion costs are incurred when a box is filled with cereal. On March 31, the packing machine hopper held 900 pounds of cereal, and the package carousel held 600 empty 24-oz. (1½-pound) boxes. Assume that once a box is filled with cereal, it is immediately transferred to the finished goods warehouse.

(Continued)

Determine the equivalent units of production for cereal, boxes, and conversion costs for March. An equivalent unit is defined as "pounds" for cereal and "24-oz. boxes" for boxes and conversion costs.

EX 3-10   Costs per equivalent unit   Obj. 2

✔ C. $2.40

SHOW ME HOW

Georgia Products Inc. completed and transferred 89,000 particle board units of production from the Pressing Department. There was no beginning inventory in process in the department. The ending in-process inventory was 2,400 units, which were $\frac{3}{5}$ complete as to conversion cost. All materials are added at the beginning of the process. Direct materials cost incurred was $219,360, direct labor cost incurred was $28,100, and factory overhead applied was $12,598.

Determine the following for the Pressing Department:

A. Total conversion cost

B. Conversion cost per equivalent unit

C. Direct materials cost per equivalent unit

EX 3-11   Equivalent units of production and related costs   Obj. 2

✔ A. 1,000 units

SHOW ME HOW   EXCEL TEMPLATE

The charges to Work in Process—Assembly Department for a period, together with information concerning production, are as follows. All direct materials are placed in process at the beginning of production.

Work in Process—Assembly Department			
Bal., 1,600 units, 35% completed	17,440	To Finished Goods, 29,600 units	?
Direct materials, 29,000 units @ $9.50	275,500		
Direct labor	84,600		
Factory overhead	39,258		
Bal. ? units, 45% completed	?		

Determine the following:

A. The number of units in work in process inventory at the end of the period

B. Equivalent units of production for direct materials and conversion

C. Costs per equivalent unit for direct materials and conversion

D. Cost of the units started and completed during the period

EX 3-12   Cost of units completed and in process   Obj. 2, 4

✔ A. 1. $21,808

A. Based on the data in Exercise 3-11, determine the following:

1. Cost of beginning work in process inventory completed this period

2. Cost of units transferred to finished goods during the period

3. Cost of ending work in process inventory

4. Cost per unit of the completed beginning work in process inventory, rounded to the nearest cent

B. ➤ Did the production costs change from the preceding period? Explain.

C. Assuming that the direct materials cost per unit did not change from the preceding period, did the conversion costs per equivalent unit increase, decrease, or remain the same for the current period?

EX 3-13   Errors in equivalent unit computation   Obj. 2

Napco Refining Company processes gasoline. On June 1 of the current year, 6,400 units were $\frac{3}{5}$ completed in the Blending Department. During June, 55,000 units entered the Blending Department from the Refining Department. During June, the units in process at the beginning of the month were completed. Of the 55,000 units entering the department, all were completed except 5,200 units that were ⅕ completed. The equivalent units for conversion costs for June for the Blending Department were computed as follows:

Equivalent units of production in June:	
To process units in inventory on June 1: 6,400 × ⅗	3,840
To process units started and completed in June: 55,000 – 6,400	48,600
To process units in inventory on June 30: 5,200 × ⅕	1,040
Equivalent units of production	53,480

List the errors in the computation of equivalent units for conversion costs for the Blending Department for June.

EX 3-14 Cost per equivalent unit   Obj. 2

✔ A. 12,400 units

SHOW ME HOW

The following information concerns production in the Forging Department for November. All direct materials are placed into the process at the beginning of production, and conversion costs are incurred evenly throughout the process. The beginning inventory consists of $9,000 of direct materials.

ACCOUNT *Work in Process—Forging Department*				ACCOUNT NO.	
				Balance	
Date	**Item**	**Debit**	**Credit**	**Debit**	**Credit**
Nov. 1	Bal., 900 units, 60% completed			10,566	
30	Direct materials, 12,900 units	123,840		134,406	
30	Direct labor	21,650		156,056	
30	Factory overhead	16,870		172,926	
30	Goods transferred, ? units		?	?	
30	Bal., 1,400 units, 70% completed			?	

A. Determine the number of units transferred to the next department.

B. Determine the costs per equivalent unit of direct materials and conversion.

C. Determine the cost of units started and completed in November.

EX 3-15 Costs per equivalent unit and production costs   Obj. 2, 4

✔ A. $11,646

Based on the data in Exercise 3-14, determine the following:

A. Cost of beginning work in process inventory completed in November

B. Cost of units transferred to the next department during November

C. Cost of ending work in process inventory on November 30

D. Costs per equivalent unit of direct materials and conversion included in the November 1 beginning work in process

E. The November increase or decrease in costs per equivalent unit for direct materials and conversion from the previous month

---

EX 3-16 Cost of production report   Obj. 2, 4

✔ A. 4. $2,092

EXCEL TEMPLATE

The debits to Work in Process—Roasting Department for Morning Brew Coffee Company for August, together with information concerning production, are as follows:

Work in process, August 1, 700 pounds, 20% completed		$ 3,479*
*Direct materials (700 × $4.70)	$3,290	
Conversion (700 × 20% × $1.35)	189	
	$3,479	
Coffee beans added during August, 14,300 pounds		65,780
Conversion costs during August		21,942
Work in process, August 31, 400 pounds, 42% completed		?
Goods finished during August, 14,600 pounds		?

(Continued)

All direct materials are placed in process at the beginning of production.

A. Prepare a cost of production report, presenting the following computations:

1. Direct materials and conversion equivalent units of production for August

2. Direct materials and conversion costs per equivalent unit for August

3. Cost of goods finished during August

4. Cost of work in process at August 31

B. Compute and evaluate the change in cost per equivalent unit for direct materials and conversion from the previous month (July).

EX 3-17   Cost of production report **Obj. 2, 4**

✔ Conversion cost per equivalent unit, $5.10

The Cutting Department of Karachi Carpet Company provides the following data for January. Assume that all materials are added at the beginning of the process.

Work in process, January 1, 1,400 units, 75% completed		$ 22,960*
*Direct materials (1,400 × $12.65)	$17,710	
Conversion (1,400 × 75% × $5.00)	5,250	
	$22,960	
Materials added during January from Weaving Department, 58,000 units		$742,400
Direct labor for January		134,550
Factory overhead for January		151,611
Goods finished during January (includes goods in process, January 1), 56,200 units		—
Work in process, January 31, 3,200 units, 30% completed		—

A. Prepare a cost of production report for the Cutting Department.

B. Compute and evaluate the change in the costs per equivalent unit for direct materials and conversion from the previous month (December).

EX 3-18   Cost of production and journal entries **Obj. 1, 2, 3, 4**

✔ B. $29,760

AccuBlade Castings Inc. casts blades for turbine engines. Within the Casting Department, alloy is first melted in a crucible, then poured into molds to produce the castings. On May 1, there were 230 pounds of alloy in process, which were 60% complete as to conversion. The Work in Process balance for these 230 pounds was $32,844, determined as follows:

Direct materials (230 × $132)	$30,360	
Conversion (230 × 60% × $18)	2,484	
	$32,844	

During May, the Casting Department was charged $350,000 for 2,500 pounds of alloy and $19,840 for direct labor. Factory overhead is applied to the department at a rate of 150% of direct labor. The department transferred out 2,530 pounds of finished castings to the Machining Department. The May 31 inventory in process was 44% complete as to conversion.

A. Prepare the following May journal entries for the Casting Department:

1. The materials charged to production

2. The conversion costs charged to production

3. The completed production transferred to the Machining Department

B. Determine the Work in Process—Casting Department May 31 balance.

C. Compute and evaluate the change in the costs per equivalent unit for direct materials and conversion from the previous month (April).

EX 3-19 Cost of production and journal entries

Obj. 1, 2, 3

✔ B. $14,319

Lighthouse Paper Company manufactures newsprint. The product is manufactured in two departments, Papermaking and Converting. Pulp is first placed into a vessel at the beginning of papermaking production. The following information concerns production in the Papermaking Department for March:

ACCOUNT *Work in Process—Papermaking Department*   ACCOUNT NO.

Date		Item	Debit	Credit	Balance Debit	Balance Credit
Mar.	1	Bal., 2,600 units, 35% completed			9,139	
	31	Direct materials, 105,000 units	330,750		339,889	
	31	Direct labor	40,560		380,449	
	31	Factory overhead	54,795		435,244	
	31	Goods transferred, 103,900 units		?	?	
	31	Bal., 3,700 units, 80% completed			?	

A. Prepare the following March journal entries for the Papermaking Department:

1. The materials charged to production

2. The conversion costs charged to production

3. The completed production transferred to the Converting Department

B. Determine the Work in Process—Papermaking Department March 31 balance.

EX 3-20 Process costing for a service company

Obj. 4

Madison Electric Company uses a fossil fuel (coal) plant for generating electricity. The facility can generate 900 megawatts (million watts) per hour. The plant operates 600 hours during March. Electricity is used as it is generated; thus, there are no inventories at the beginning or end of the period. The March conversion and fuel costs are as follows:

Conversion costs	$40,500,000
Fuel	10,800,000
Total	$51,300,000

Madison also has a wind farm that can generate 100 megawatts per hour. The wind farm receives sufficient wind to run 300 hours for March. The March conversion costs for the wind farm (mostly depreciation) are as follows:

Conversion costs	$2,700,000

A. Determine the cost per megawatt hour (MWh) for the fossil fuel plant and the wind farm to identify the lowest cost facility in March.

B. ➤ Why are equivalent units of production not needed in determining the cost per megawatt hour (MWh) for generating electricity?

C. ➤ What advantage does the fossil fuel plant have over the wind farm?

EX 3-21 Lean manufacturing

Obj. 5

The following are some quotes provided by a number of managers at Hawkeye Machining Company regarding the company's planned move toward a lean manufacturing system:

Director of Sales: I'm afraid we'll miss some sales if we don't keep a large stock of items on hand just in case demand increases. It only makes sense to me to keep large inventories in order to assure product availability for our customers.

Director of Purchasing: I'm very concerned about moving to a lean system for materials. What would happen if one of our suppliers were unable to make a shipment? A supplier could fall behind in production or have a quality problem. Without some safety stock in our materials, our whole plant would shut down.

(Continued)

Director of Manufacturing: If we go to lean manufacturing, I think our factory output will drop. We need in-process inventory in order to "smooth out" the inevitable problems that occur during manufacturing. For example, if a machine that is used to process a product breaks down, it would starve the next machine if I don't have in-process inventory between the two machines. If I have in-process inventory, then I can keep the next operation busy while I fix the broken machine. Thus, the in-process inventories give me a safety valve that I can use to keep things running when things go wrong.

→ How would you respond to these managers?

Appendix

EX 3-22   Equivalent units of production: average cost method

✔ A. 17,000

The Converting Department of Tender Soft Tissue Company uses the average cost method and had 1,900 units in work in process that were 60% complete at the beginning of the period. During the period, 15,800 units were completed and transferred to the Packing Department. There were 1,200 units in process that were 30% complete at the end of the period.

A. Determine the number of whole units to be accounted for and to be assigned costs for the period.

B. Determine the number of equivalent units of production for the period.

Appendix

EX 3-23   Equivalent units of production: average cost method

✔ A. 12,100 units to be accounted for

Units of production data for the two departments of Atlantic Cable and Wire Company for July of the current fiscal year are as follows:

	Drawing Department	Winding Department
Work in process, July 1	500 units, 50% completed	350 units, 30% completed
Completed and transferred to next processing department during July	11,400 units	10,950 units
Work in process, July 31	700 units, 55% completed	800 units, 25% completed

Each department uses the average cost method.

A. Determine the number of whole units to be accounted for and to be assigned costs and the equivalent units of production for the Drawing Department.

B. Determine the number of whole units to be accounted for and to be assigned costs and the equivalent units of production for the Winding Department.

Appendix

EX 3-24   Equivalent units of production: average cost method

✔ A. 3,100

The following information concerns production in the Finishing Department for May. The Finishing Department uses the average cost method.

ACCOUNT *Work in Process—Finishing Department*   **ACCOUNT NO.**

Date		Item	Debit	Credit	Balance Debit	Balance Credit
May	1	Bal., 4,200 units, 70% completed			36,500	
	31	Direct materials, 23,600 units	125,800		162,300	
	31	Direct labor	75,400		237,700	
	31	Factory overhead	82,675		320,375	
	31	Goods transferred, 24,700 units		308,750	11,625	
	31	Bal., ? units, 30% completed			11,625	

A. Determine the number of units in work in process inventory at the end of the month.

B. Determine the number of whole units to be accounted for and to be assigned costs and the equivalent units of production for May.

Appendix

EX 3-25 Equivalent units of production and related costs

✔ B. 8,820 units

EXCEL TEMPLATE

The charges to Work in Process—Baking Department for a period as well as information concerning production are as follows. The Baking Department uses the average cost method, and all direct materials are placed in process during production.

Work in Process—Baking Department			
Bal., 900 units, 40% completed	2,466	To Finished Goods, 8,100 units	?
Direct materials, 8,400 units	34,500		
Direct labor	16,200		
Factory overhead	8,574		
Bal., 1,200 units, 60% completed	?		

Determine the following:

A. The number of whole units to be accounted for and to be assigned costs

B. The number of equivalent units of production

C. The cost per equivalent unit

D. The cost of units transferred to Finished Goods

E. The cost of units in ending Work in Process

Appendix

EX 3-26 Cost per equivalent unit: average cost method

✔ A. $26.00

The following information concerns production in the Forging Department for June. The Forging Department uses the average cost method.

			ACCOUNT Work in Process—Forging Department			ACCOUNT NO.	
						Balance	
Date		Item	Debit	Credit	Debit	Credit	
June	1	Bal., 500 units, 40% completed			5,000		
	30	Direct materials, 3,700 units	49,200		54,200		
	30	Direct labor	25,200		79,400		
	30	Factory overhead	25,120		104,520		
	30	Goods transferred, 3,600 units		?	?		
	30	Bal., 600 units, 70% completed			?		

A. Determine the cost per equivalent unit.

B. Determine cost of units transferred to Finished Goods.

C. Determine the cost of units in ending Work in Process.

Appendix

EX 3-27 Cost of production report: average cost method

✔ Cost per equivalent unit, $3.60

The increases to Work in Process—Roasting Department for Highlands Coffee Company for May as well as information concerning production are as follows:

Work in process, May 1, 1,150 pounds, 40% completed	$ 1,700
Coffee beans added during May, 10,900 pounds	28,600
Conversion costs during May	12,504
Work in process, May 31, 800 pounds, 80% completed	—
Goods finished during May, 11,250 pounds	—

Prepare a cost of production report for May, using the average cost method.

Appendix

EX 3-28   Cost of production report: average cost method

✔ Cost per equivalent
unit, $9.00

EXCEL TEMPLATE

Prepare a cost of production report for the Cutting Department of Dalton Carpet Company for January. Use the average cost method with the following data:

Work in process, January 1, 3,400 units, 75% completed	$ 23,000
Materials added during January from Weaving Department, 64,000 units	366,200
Direct labor for January	105,100
Factory overhead for January	80,710
Goods finished during January (includes goods in process, January 1), 63,500 units	—
Work in process, January 31, 3,900 units, 10% completed	—

Problems: Series A

PR 3-1A   Entries for process cost system   **Obj. 1, 3**

✔ 2. Materials January
31 balance, $46,500

SHOW ME HOW   **GENERAL LEDGER**

Port Ormond Carpet Company manufactures carpets. Fiber is placed in process in the Spinning Department, where it is spun into yarn. The output of the Spinning Department is transferred to the Tufting Department, where carpet backing is added at the beginning of the process and the process is completed. On January 1, Port Ormond Carpet Company had the following inventories:

Finished Goods	$62,000
Work in Process—Spinning Department	35,000
Work in Process—Tufting Department	28,500
Materials	17,000

Departmental accounts are maintained for factory overhead, and both have zero balances on January 1.

Manufacturing operations for January are summarized as follows:

A. Materials purchased on account	$500,000
B. Materials requisitioned for use:	
Fiber—Spinning Department	$275,000
Carpet backing—Tufting Department	110,000
Indirect materials—Spinning Department	46,000
Indirect materials—Tufting Department	39,500
C. Labor used:	
Direct labor—Spinning Department	$185,000
Direct labor—Tufting Department	98,000
Indirect labor—Spinning Department	18,500
Indirect labor—Tufting Department	9,000
D. Depreciation charged on fixed assets:	
Spinning Department	$ 12,500
Tufting Department	8,500
E. Expired prepaid factory insurance:	
Spinning Department	$ 2,000
Tufting Department	1,000
F. Applied factory overhead:	
Spinning Department	$ 80,000
Tufting Department	55,000
G. Production costs transferred from Spinning Department to Tufting Department	$547,000
H. Production costs transferred from Tufting Department to Finished Goods	$807,200
I. Cost of goods sold during the period	$795,200

Instructions

1. Journalize the entries to record the operations, identifying each entry by letter.
2. Compute the January 31 balances of the inventory accounts.
3. Compute the January 31 balances of the factory overhead accounts.

PR 3-2A Cost of production report

Obj. 2, 4

✔ 1. Conversion cost per equivalent unit, $0.76

EXCEL TEMPLATE

Hana Coffee Company roasts and packs coffee beans. The process begins by placing coffee beans into the Roasting Department. From the Roasting Department, coffee beans are then transferred to the Packing Department. The following is a partial work in process account of the Roasting Department at July 31:

ACCOUNT *Work in Process—Roasting Department*				ACCOUNT NO.	
				Balance	
Date	Item	Debit	Credit	Debit	Credit
July 1	Bal., 30,000 units, 10% completed			121,800	
31	Direct materials, 155,000 units	620,000		741,800	
31	Direct labor	90,000		831,800	
31	Factory overhead	33,272		865,072	
31	Goods transferred, 149,000 units		?		
31	Bal., ? units, 45% completed			?	

Instructions

1. Prepare a cost of production report, and identify the missing amounts for Work in Process—Roasting Department.
2. Assuming that the July 1 work in process inventory includes $119,400 of direct materials, determine the increase or decrease in the cost per equivalent unit for direct materials and conversion between June and July.

PR 3-3A Equivalent units and related costs; cost of production report; entries

Obj. 2, 3, 4

✔ 2. Transferred to Packaging Dept., $40,183

EXCEL TEMPLATE

White Diamond Flour Company manufactures flour by a series of three processes, beginning with wheat grain being introduced in the Milling Department. From the Milling Department, the materials pass through the Sifting and Packaging departments, emerging as packaged refined flour.

The balance in the account Work in Process—Sifting Department was as follows on July 1:

Work in Process—Sifting Department (900 units, ⅗ completed):	
Direct materials (900 × $2.05)	$1,845
Conversion (900 × ⅗ × $0.40)	216
	$2,061

The following costs were charged to Work in Process—Sifting Department during July:

Direct materials transferred from Milling Department:	
15,700 units at $2.15 a unit	$33,755
Direct labor	4,420
Factory overhead	2,708

During July, 15,500 units of flour were completed. Work in Process—Sifting Department on July 31 was 1,100 units, ⅘ completed.

Instructions

1. Prepare a cost of production report for the Sifting Department for July.
2. Journalize the entries for costs transferred from Milling to Sifting and the costs transferred from Sifting to Packaging.
3. Determine the increase or decrease in the cost per equivalent unit from June to July for direct materials and conversion costs.
4. Discuss the uses of the cost of production report and the results of part (3).

PR 3-4A Work in process account data for two months; cost of production reports

Obj. 1, 2, 3, 4

✔ 1. C. Transferred to finished goods in April, $49,818

EXCEL TEMPLATE

Hearty Soup Co. uses a process cost system to record the costs of processing soup, which requires the cooking and filling processes. Materials are entered from the cooking process at the beginning of the filling process. The inventory of Work in Process—Filling on April 1 and debits to the account during April were as follows:

Bal., 800 units, 30% completed:		
Direct materials (800 × $4.30)	$ 3,440	
Conversion (800 × 30% × $1.75)	420	
	$ 3,860	
From Cooking Department, 7,800 units	$34,320	
Direct labor	8,562	
Factory overhead	6,387	

During April, 800 units in process on April 1 were completed, and of the 7,800 units entering the department, all were completed except 550 units that were 90% completed.

Charges to Work in Process—Filling for May were as follows:

From Cooking Department, 9,600 units	$44,160
Direct labor	12,042
Factory overhead	6,878

During May, the units in process at the beginning of the month were completed, and of the 9,600 units entering the department, all were completed except 300 units that were 35% completed.

Instructions

1. Enter the balance as of April 1, in a four-column account for Work in Process—Filling. Record the debits and the credits in the account for April. Construct a cost of production report, and present computations for determining (A) equivalent units of production for materials and conversion, (B) costs per equivalent unit, (C) cost of goods finished, differentiating between units started in the prior period and units started and finished in April, and (D) work in process inventory.

2. Provide the same information for May by recording the May transactions in the four-column work in process account. Construct a cost of production report, and present the May computations (A through D) listed in part (1).

3. ➡ Comment on the change in costs per equivalent unit for March through May for direct materials and conversion costs.

Appendix

PR 3-5A Cost of production report: average cost method

✔ Cost per equivalent unit, $2.70

EXCEL TEMPLATE

Sunrise Coffee Company roasts and packs coffee beans. The process begins in the Roasting Department. From the Roasting Department, the coffee beans are transferred to the Packing Department. The following is a partial work in process account of the Roasting Department at December 31:

ACCOUNT *Work in Process—Roasting Department*   ACCOUNT NO.

Date		Item	Debit	Credit	Balance Debit	Balance Credit
Dec.	1	Bal., 10,500 units, 75% completed			21,000	
	31	Direct materials, 210,400 units	246,800		267,800	
	31	Direct labor	135,700		403,500	
	31	Factory overhead	168,630		572,130	
	31	Goods transferred, 208,900 units		?	?	
	31	Bal., ? units, 25% completed			?	

Instructions

Prepare a cost of production report, using the average cost method, and identify the missing amounts for Work in Process—Roasting Department.

Problems: Series B

✔ 2. Materials
July 31 balance, $11,390

SHOW ME HOW   GENERAL LEDGER

PR 3-1B Entries for process cost system

Obj. 1, 3

Preston & Grover Soap Company manufactures powdered detergent. Phosphate is placed in process in the Making Department, where it is turned into granulars. The output of Making is transferred to the Packing Department, where packaging is added at the beginning of the process. On July 1, Preston & Grover Soap Company had the following inventories:

Finished Goods	$13,500
Work in Process—Making	6,790
Work in Process—Packing	7,350
Materials	5,100

Departmental accounts are maintained for factory overhead, which both have zero balances on July 1.

Manufacturing operations for July are summarized as follows:

A. Materials purchased on account...	$149,800
B. Materials requisitioned for use:	
Phosphate—Making Department	$105,700
Packaging—Packing Department	31,300
Indirect materials—Making Department.......................................	4,980
Indirect materials—Packing Department......................................	1,530
C. Labor used:	
Direct labor—Making Department	$ 32,400
Direct labor—Packing Department..	40,900
Indirect labor—Making Department...	15,400
Indirect labor—Packing Department	18,300
D. Depreciation charged on fixed assets:	
Making Department..	$ 10,700
Packing Department	7,900
E. Expired prepaid factory insurance:	
Making Department..	$ 2,000
Packing Department	1,500
F. Applied factory overhead:	
Making Department..	$ 32,570
Packing Department	30,050
G. Production costs transferred from Making Department to Packing Department.....	$166,790
H. Production costs transferred from Packing Department to Finished Goods	$263,400
I. Cost of goods sold during the period	$265,200

Instructions

1. Journalize the entries to record the operations, identifying each entry by letter.
2. Compute the July 31 balances of the inventory accounts.
3. Compute the July 31 balances of the factory overhead accounts.

✔ 1. Conversion cost per
equivalent unit, $6.00

EXCEL TEMPLATE

PR 3-2B   Cost of production report   Obj. 2, 4

Bavarian Chocolate Company processes chocolate into candy bars. The process begins by placing direct materials (raw chocolate, milk, and sugar) into the Blending Department. All materials are placed into production at the beginning of the blending process. After blending, the milk chocolate is then transferred to the Molding Department, where the milk chocolate is formed into candy bars. The following is a partial work in process account of the Blending Department at October 31:

ACCOUNT *Work in Process—Blending Department*				ACCOUNT NO.	
				Balance	
Date	Item	Debit	Credit	Debit	Credit
Oct. 1	Bal., 2,300 units, ⅗ completed			46,368	
31	Direct materials, 26,000 units	429,000		475,368	
31	Direct labor	100,560		575,928	
31	Factory overhead	48,480		624,408	
31	Goods transferred, 25,700 units		?		
31	Bal., ? units, ⅕ completed			?	

Instructions

1. Prepare a cost of production report, and identify the missing amounts for Work in Process—Blending Department.

2. Assuming that the October 1 work in process inventory includes direct materials of $38,295, determine the increase or decrease in the cost per equivalent unit for direct materials and conversion between September and October.

PR 3-3B   Equivalent units and related costs; cost of production report;   Obj. 2, 3, 4
entries

✔ 2. Transferred
to finished goods,
$705,376

EXCEL TEMPLATE

Dover Chemical Company manufactures specialty chemicals by a series of three processes, all materials being introduced in the Distilling Department. From the Distilling Department, the materials pass through the Reaction and Filling departments, emerging as finished chemicals.

The balance in the account Work in Process—Filling was as follows on January 1:

Work in Process—Filling Department
(3,400 units, 60% completed):

Direct materials (3,400 × $9.58)	$32,572
Conversion (3,400 × 60% × $3.90)	7,956
	$40,528

The following costs were charged to Work in Process—Filling during January:

Direct materials transferred from Reaction	
Department: 52,300 units at $9.50 a unit	$496,850
Direct labor	101,560
Factory overhead	95,166

During January, 53,000 units of specialty chemicals were completed. Work in Process—Filling Department on January 31 was 2,700 units, 30% completed.

Instructions

1. Prepare a cost of production report for the Filling Department for January.

2. Journalize the entries for costs transferred from Reaction to Filling and the costs transferred from Filling to Finished Goods.

3. Determine the increase or decrease in the cost per equivalent unit from December to January for direct materials and conversion costs.

4. ▬▬▶ Discuss the uses of the cost of production report and the results of part (3).

PR 3-4B   Work in process account data for two months;   Obj. 1, 2, 3, 4
cost of production reports

✔ 1. C. Transferred
to finished goods in
September, $702,195

EXCEL TEMPLATE

Pittsburgh Aluminum Company uses a process cost system to record the costs of manufacturing rolled aluminum, which consists of the smelting and rolling processes. Materials are entered from smelting at the beginning of the rolling process. The inventory of Work in Process—Rolling on September 1 and debits to the account during September were as follows:

Bal., 2,600 units, ¼ completed:	
Direct materials (2,600 × $15.50)	$40,300
Conversion (2,600 × ¼ × $8.50)	5,525
	$45,825
From Smelting Department, 28,900 units	$462,400
Direct labor	158,920
Factory overhead	101,402

During September, 2,600 units in process on September 1 were completed, and of the 28,900 units entering the department, all were completed except 2,900 units that were ⅕ completed. Charges to Work in Process—Rolling for October were as follows:

From Smelting Department, 31,000 units	$511,500
Direct labor	162,850
Factory overhead	104,494

During October, the units in process at the beginning of the month were completed, and of the 31,000 units entering the department, all were completed except 2,000 units that were ⅖ completed.

Instructions

1. Enter the balance as of September 1 in a four-column account for Work in Process—Rolling. Record the debits and the credits in the account for September. Construct a cost of production report and present computations for determining (A) equivalent units of production for materials and conversion, (B) costs per equivalent unit, (C) cost of goods finished, differentiating between units started in the prior period and units started and finished in September, and (D) work in process inventory.

2. Provide the same information for October by recording the October transactions in the four-column work in process account. Construct a cost of production report, and present the October computations (A through D) listed in part (1).

3. ━━━▶ Comment on the change in costs per equivalent unit for August through October for direct materials and conversion cost.

Appendix

PR 3-5B   Cost of production report: average cost method

✔ Transferred to
Packaging Dept.,
$54,000

EXCEL TEMPLATE

Blue Ribbon Flour Company manufactures flour by a series of three processes, beginning in the Milling Department. From the Milling Department, the materials pass through the Sifting and Packaging departments, emerging as packaged refined flour.

The balance in the account Work in Process—Sifting Department was as follows on May 1:

Work in Process—Sifting Department (1,500 units, 75% completed)	$3,400

The following costs were charged to Work in Process—Sifting Department during May:

Direct materials transferred from Milling Department: 18,300 units	$32,600
Direct labor	14,560
Factory overhead	7,490

During May, 18,000 units of flour were completed and transferred to finished goods. Work in Process—Sifting Department on May 31 was 1,800 units, 75% completed.

Instructions

Prepare a cost of production report for the Sifting Department for May, using the average cost method.

Analysis for Decision Making

EXCEL TEMPLATE

ADM-1   Analyzing process cost elements across product types

Mystic Bottling Company bottles popular beverages in the Bottling Department. The beverages are produced by blending concentrate with water and sugar. The concentrate is purchased from a concentrate producer. The concentrate producer sets higher prices for the more popular concentrate flavors. A simplified Bottling Department cost of production report separating the cost of bottling the four flavors follows:

	A	B	C	D	E
1		Orange	Cola	Lemon-Lime	Root Beer
2	Concentrate	$ 4,625	$129,000	$105,000	$ 7,600
3	Water	1,250	30,000	25,000	2,000
4	Sugar	3,000	72,000	60,000	4,800
5	Bottles	5,500	132,000	110,000	8,800
6	Flavor changeover	3,000	4,800	4,000	10,000
7	Conversion cost	1,750	24,000	20,000	2,800
8	Total cost transferred to finished goods	$19,125	$391,800	$324,000	$36,000
9	Number of cases	2,500	60,000	50,000	4,000
10					

Beginning and ending work in process inventories are negligible, so they are omitted from the cost of production report. The flavor changeover cost represents the cost of cleaning the bottling machines between production runs of different flavors. A production run of a new flavor is produced after a flavor changeover from the previous flavor. Higher-demand flavors are produced in larger production runs, while smaller-demand flavors are produced in smaller production runs.

> Prepare a memo to the production manager, analyzing this comparative cost information. In your memo, provide recommendations for further action, along with supporting schedules showing the total cost per case and cost per case by cost element. Round supporting calculations to the nearest cent.

ADM-2   Analyzing process cost elements over time

Pix Paper Inc. produces photographic paper for printing digital images. One of the processes for this operation is a coating (solvent spreading) operation, where chemicals are coated onto paper stock. There has been some concern about the cost performance of this operation. As a result, you have begun an investigation. You first discover that all materials and conversion prices have been stable for the last six months. Thus, increases in prices for inputs are not an explanation for increasing costs. However, you have discovered three possible problems from some of the operating personnel whose quotes follow:

Operator 1: "I've been keeping an eye on my operating room instruments. I feel as though our energy consumption is becoming less efficient."

Operator 2: "Every time the coating machine goes down, we produce waste on shutdown and subsequent startup. It seems like during the last half-year we have had more unscheduled machine shutdowns than in the past. Thus, I feel as though our yields must be dropping."

Operator 3: "My sense is that our coating costs are going up. It seems to me like we are spreading a thicker coating than we should. Perhaps the coating machine needs to be recalibrated."

The Coating Department had no beginning or ending inventories for any month during the study period. The following data from the cost of production report are made available:

	January	February	March	April	May	June
Paper stock	$67,200	$63,840	$60,480	$64,512	$57,120	$53,760
Coating	$11,520	$11,856	$12,960	$15,667	$16,320	$18,432
Conversion cost (incl. energy)	$38,400	$36,480	$34,560	$36,864	$32,640	$30,720
Pounds input to the process	100,000	95,000	90,000	96,000	85,000	80,000
Pounds transferred out	96,000	91,200	86,400	92,160	81,600	76,800

A. Prepare a table showing the paper cost per output pound, coating cost per output pound, conversion cost per output pound, and yield (pounds transferred out ÷ pounds input) for each month. Round costs to the nearest cent and yield to the nearest whole percent.

B. ━━━▶ Interpret your table results.

ADM-3 Determining cost relationships

Midstate Containers Inc. manufactures cans for the canned food industry. The operations manager of a can manufacturing operation wants to conduct a cost study investigating the relationship of tin content in the material (can stock) to the energy cost for enameling the cans. The enameling was necessary to prepare the cans for labeling. A higher percentage of tin content in the can stock increases the cost of material. The operations manager believed that a higher tin content in the can stock would reduce the amount of energy used in enameling. During the analysis period, the amount of tin content in the steel can stock was increased for every month, from April to September. The following operating reports were available from the controller:

	April	May	June	July	August	September
Materials	$ 14,000	$ 34,800	$ 33,000	$ 21,700	$ 28,800	$ 33,000
Energy	13,000	28,800	24,200	14,000	17,100	16,000
Total cost	$ 27,000	$ 63,600	$ 57,200	$ 35,700	$ 45,900	$ 49,000
Units produced	÷50,000	÷120,000	÷110,000	÷ 70,000	÷ 90,000	÷100,000
Cost per unit	$ 0.54	$ 0.53	$ 0.52	$ 0.51	$ 0.51	$ 0.49

Differences in materials unit costs were entirely related to the amount of tin content. In addition, inventory changes are negligible and are ignored in the analysis.

━━━▶ Interpret this information and report to the operations manager your recommendations with respect to tin content.

Take It Further

TIF 3-1 Ethics in Action

You are the Cookie division controller for Auntie M's Baked Goods Company. Auntie M recently introduced a new chocolate chip cookie brand called Full of Chips, which has more than twice as many chips as any other brand on the market. The brand has quickly become a huge market success, largely because of the number of chips in each cookie. As a result of the brand's success, the product manager who launched the Full of Chips brand has been promoted to division vice president. A new product manager, Brandon, has been brought in to replace the promoted manager.

At Auntie M's, product managers are evaluated on both the sales and profit margin of the products they manage. During his first week on the job, Brandon notices that the Full of Chips cookie uses a lot of chips, which increases the cost of the cookie. To improve the product's profitability, Brandon plans to reduce the amount of chips per cookie by 10%.

(Continued)

He believes that a 10% reduction in chips will not adversely affect sales, but will reduce cost and, hence, help him improve the profit margin. Brandon is focused on profit margins, because he knows that if he is able to increase the profitability of the Full of Chips brand, he will be in line for a big promotion.

To confirm this plan, Brandon has enlisted you to help evaluate it. After reviewing the cost of production reports segmented by cookie brand, you notice that there has been a continual drop in the materials costs for the Full of Chips brand since its launch. On further investigation, you discover that chip costs have declined because the previous product manager continually reduced the number of chips in each cookie. Both you and Brandon report to the division vice president, who was the original product manager for the Full of Chips brand who was responsible for reducing the chip count in prior periods.

1. ➤ Is this an ethical strategy for Brandon to pursue? What are the potential implications of this strategy?

2. ➤ What options might you, as the controller, consider taking in response to Brandon's plan?

REAL WORLD

TIF 3-2   Team Activity

The following categories represent typical process manufacturing industries:

- Beverages
- Chemicals
- Food
- Forest and paper products
- Metals
- Petroleum refining
- Pharmaceuticals
- Soap and cosmetics

In groups of two or three, identify one company for each category (following your instructor's specific instructions) and determine the following:

A. Typical products manufactured by the selected company, including brand names
B. Typical raw materials used by the selected company
C. Types of processes used by the selected company

Use annual reports, the Internet, or library resources in doing this activity.

TIF 3-3   Communication

Jamarcus Bradshaw, plant manager of Georgia Paper Company's papermaking mill, was looking over the cost of production reports for July and August for the Papermaking Department. The reports revealed the following:

	July	August
Pulp and chemicals	$295,600	$304,100
Conversion cost	146,000	149,600
Total cost	$441,600	$453,700
Number of tons	÷ 1,200	÷ 1,130
Cost per ton	$ 368	$ 401.50

Jamarcus was concerned about the increased cost per ton from the output of the department. As a result, he asked the plant controller to perform a study to help explain these results. The controller, Leann Brunswick, began the analysis by performing some interviews of key plant personnel in order to understand what the problem might be. Excerpts from an interview with Len Tyson, a paper machine operator, follow:

Len: We have two papermaking machines in the department. I have no data, but I think paper machine No. 1 is applying too much pulp and, thus, is wasting both conversion and materials resources. We haven't had repairs on paper machine No. 1 in a while. Maybe this is the problem.

Leann: How does too much pulp result in wasted resources?

Len: Well, you see, if too much pulp is applied, then we will waste pulp material. The customer will not pay for the extra product; we just use more material to make the product.. Also, when there is too much pulp, the machine must be slowed down in order to complete the drying process. This results in additional conversion costs.

Leann: Do you have any other suspicions?

Len: Well, as you know, we have two products—green paper and yellow paper. They are identical except for the color. The color is added to the papermaking process in the paper machine. I think that during August these two color papers have been behaving very differently. I don't have any data, but it just seems as though the amount of waste associated with the green paper has increased.

Leann: Why is this?

Len: I understand that there has been a change in specifications for the green paper, starting near the beginning of August. This change could be causing the machines to run poorly when making green paper. If this is the case, the cost per ton would increase for green paper.

Leann also asked for a database printout providing greater detail on August's operating results.

September 9   Requested by: Leann Brunswick
Papermaking Department—August detail

	A	B	C	D	E	F
1	Production					
2	Run	Paper		Material	Conversion	
3	Number	Machine	Color	Costs	Costs	Tons
4	1	1	Green	40,300	18,300	150
5	2	1	Yellow	41,700	21,200	140
6	3	1	Green	44,600	22,500	150
7	4	1	Yellow	36,100	18,100	120
8	5	2	Green	38,300	18,900	160
9	6	2	Yellow	33,900	15,200	140
10	7	2	Green	35,600	18,400	130
11	8	2	Yellow	33,600	17,000	140
12		Total		304,100	149,600	1,130
13						

Prior to preparing a report, Leann resigned from Georgia Paper Company to start her own business. You have been asked to take the data that Leann collected, and write a memo to Jamarcus Bradshaw with a recommendation to management. Your memo should include analysis of the August data to determine whether the paper machine or the paper color explains the increase in the unit cost from July. Include any supporting schedules that are appropriate. Round any calculations to the nearest cent.

4 Activity-Based Costing

Concepts and Principles

Chapter 1 *Introduction to Managerial Accounting*

Developing Information

COST SYSTEMS	COST BEHAVIOR
Chapter 2 *Job Order Costing*	**Chapter 5** *Cost-Volume-Profit Analysis*
Chapter 3 *Process Cost Systems*	
Chapter 4 *Activity-Based Costing*	

Decision Making

EVALUATING PERFORMANCE	COMPARING ALTERNATIVES
Chapter 6 *Variable Costing for Management Analysis*	**Chapter 9** *Evaluating Decentralized Operations*
Chapter 7 *Budgeting*	**Chapter 10** *Differential Analysis and Product Pricing*
Chapter 8 *Evaluating Variances from Standard Costs*	**Chapter 11** *Capital Investment Analysis*
	Chapter 12 *Lean Manufacturing*

Cold Stone Creamery

Have you ever had to request service repairs on an appliance at your home? The repair person may arrive and take five minutes to replace a part. Yet, the bill may indicate a minimum charge for more than five minutes of work.

Why might there be a minimum charge for a service call? The answer is that the service person must charge for the time and expense of coming to your house. In a sense, the bill reflects two elements of service: (1) the cost of coming to your house and (2) the cost of the repair. The first portion of the bill reflects the time required to "set up" the job. The second part of the bill reflects the cost of performing the repair. The setup charge will be the same, whether the repairs take five minutes or five hours. In contrast, the actual repair charge will vary with the time on the job.

Like the repair person, companies must be careful that the cost of their products and services accurately reflects the different activities involved in producing the product or service. Otherwise, the cost of products and services may be distorted and lead to improper management decisions.

To illustrate, **Cold Stone Creamery**, a chain of super premium ice cream shops, uses activity-based costing to determine the cost of its ice cream products, such as cones, mixings, cakes, frozen yogurt, smoothies, and sorbets. The costs of activities, such as scooping and mixing, are added to the cost of the ingredients to determine the total cost of each product. As stated by Cold Stone's president:

"...it only makes sense to have the price you pay for the product be reflective of the activities involved in making it for you."*

In this chapter, three different methods of allocating factory overhead to products are described and illustrated. In addition, product cost distortions resulting from improper factory overhead allocations are discussed. The chapter concludes by describing activity-based costing for selling and administrative expenses and its use in service businesses.

*Quote from "Experiencing Accounting Videos," Activity-Based Costing. © Cengage Learning, 2008.

Source: www.coldstonecreamery.com

What's Covered

Activity-Based Costing

Product Costing Allocation Methods	**Activity-Based Costing**	**Activity-Based Costing for Nonmanufacturing Uses**
■ Product Costing (Obj. 1) ■ Single Plantwide Rate (Obj. 2) ■ Multiple Department Rates (Obj. 3)	■ Activity Rates (Obj. 4) ■ Allocation (Obj. 4) ■ Distortion in Product Costs (Obj. 4) ■ Dangers of Product Cost Distortion (Obj. 4)	■ Selling and Administrative Expenses (Obj. 5) ■ Service Businesses (Obj. 6)

Learning Objectives

Obj. 1 Describe three methods used for allocating factory overhead costs to products.

Obj. 2 Illustrate the use of a single plantwide factory overhead rate for product costing.

Obj. 3 Use multiple production department factory overhead rates for product costing.

Obj. 4 Use activity-based costing for product costing.

Obj. 5 Use activity-based costing to allocate selling and administrative expenses to products.

Obj. 6 Use activity-based costing in a service business.

Analysis for Decision Making

Describe and illustrate the use of activity-based costing information in decision making.

Objective 1
Describe three methods used for allocating factory overhead costs to products.

Product Costing Allocation Methods

Determining the cost of a product is termed **product costing**. Product costs consist of direct materials, direct labor, and factory overhead. The direct materials and direct labor are direct costs that can be traced to the product. However, factory overhead includes indirect costs that must be allocated to the product as shown in Exhibit 1.

Exhibit 1
Allocation of Factory Overhead Costs

The factory overhead allocated to each product is $800. This is because each product uses the same number of direct labor hours.

The effects of Ruiz Company using the single plantwide factory overhead rate method are summarized in Exhibit 2.

Exhibit 2

Single Plantwide
Factory Overhead
Rate Method—
Ruiz Company

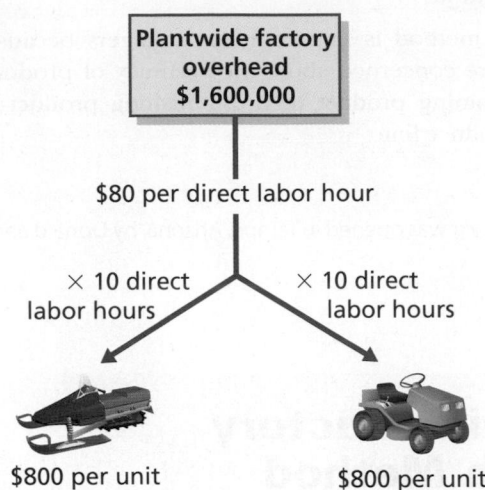

The primary advantage of using the single plantwide overhead rate method is that it is simple and inexpensive to use. However, the single plantwide rate assumes that the factory overhead costs are consumed in the same way by all products. For example, in the preceding illustration Ruiz assumes that factory overhead costs are consumed as each direct labor hour is incurred.

The preceding assumption may be valid for companies that manufacture one or a few products. However, if a company manufactures products that consume factory overhead costs in different ways, a single plantwide rate may not accurately allocate factory overhead costs to the products.

Link to Cold Stone Creamery   At **Cold Stone Creamery**, each serving of ice cream is blended on a frozen granite stone using a mixture of fruits, nuts, candy, cookies, and brownies. Each serving is unique to the customer and is called a "creation."

Check Up Corner 4-1   Single Plantwide Factory Overhead Rate

Lifestyle Furniture Company manufactures home furniture products. The total factory overhead for the company is budgeted at $600,000 for the year. The company manufactures two products: a computer desk and a designer table, each of which requires 4 direct labor hours (dlh) to make. Production for the year is budgeted for 5,000 units of each product.

Determine the:

A. Total number of budgeted direct labor hours for the year.

B. Single plantwide factory overhead rate.

C. Factory overhead allocated per unit for each product, using the single plantwide factory overhead rate.

Solution:

	Desks	Tables	Total
A. Planned production for the year....	5,000 units	5,000 units	
Direct labor hours per unit	× 4 hours	× 4 hours	
Budgeted direct labor hours	20,000 hours	20,000 hours	40,000 hours

Lifestyle allocates factory overhead using budgeted direct labor hours.

The budgeted allocation base is a measure of operating activity in the factory.

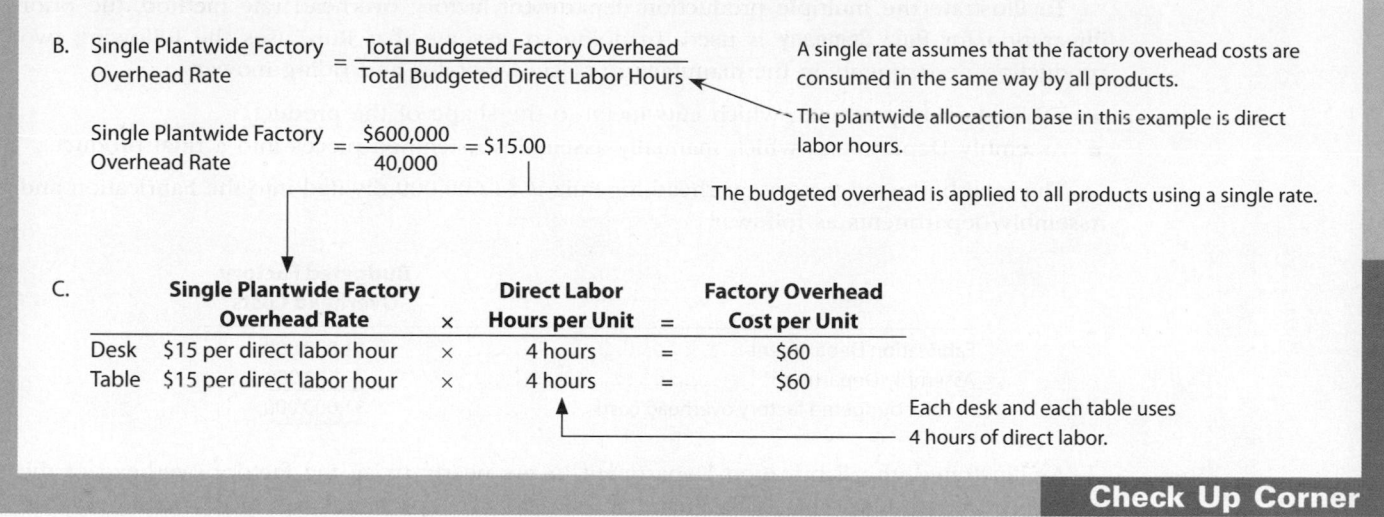

B. Single Plantwide Factory Overhead Rate $= \dfrac{\text{Total Budgeted Factory Overhead}}{\text{Total Budgeted Direct Labor Hours}}$

A single rate assumes that the factory overhead costs are consumed in the same way by all products.

Single Plantwide Factory Overhead Rate $= \dfrac{\$600,000}{40,000} = \$15.00$

The plantwide allocaction base in this example is direct labor hours.

The budgeted overhead is applied to all products using a single rate.

C.

	Single Plantwide Factory Overhead Rate	×	Direct Labor Hours per Unit	=	Factory Overhead Cost per Unit
Desk	\$15 per direct labor hour	×	4 hours	=	\$60
Table	\$15 per direct labor hour	×	4 hours	=	\$60

Each desk and each table uses 4 hours of direct labor.

Check Up Corner

Multiple Production Department Factory Overhead Rate Method

Objective 3
Use multiple production department factory overhead rates for product costing.

When production departments *differ significantly* in their manufacturing processes, factory overhead costs are normally incurred differently in each department. In such cases, factory overhead costs may be more accurately allocated using multiple production department factory overhead rates.

The **multiple production department factory overhead rate method** uses different rates for each production department to allocate factory overhead costs to products. In contrast, the single plantwide rate method uses only one rate to allocate factory overhead costs. Exhibit 3 illustrates how these two methods differ.

Single Plantwide Rate

Plantwide factory overhead

Plantwide rate

Products

Multiple Production Department Rate

Fabrication Department factory overhead

Assembly Department factory overhead

Fabrication Department factory overhead rate

Assembly Department factory overhead rate

Products

Exhibit 3
Comparison of Single Plantwide Rate and Multiple Production Department Rate Methods

To illustrate the multiple production department factory overhead rate method, the prior illustration for **Ruiz Company** is used. In doing so, assume that Ruiz uses the following two production departments in the manufacture of snowmobiles and riding mowers:

- Fabrication Department, which cuts metal to the shape of the product.
- Assembly Department, which manually assembles machined pieces into a final product.

The total budgeted factory overhead for Ruiz is $1,600,000 divided into the Fabrication and Assembly departments as follows:[1]

	Budgeted Factory Overhead Costs
Fabrication Department.............................	$1,030,000
Assembly Department	570,000
Total budgeted factory overhead costs	$1,600,000

As illustrated, the Fabrication Department incurs nearly twice the factory overhead of the Assembly Department. This is because the Fabrication Department has more machinery and equipment that uses more power, incurs more equipment depreciation, and uses more factory supplies.

Department Overhead Rates and Allocation

Each **production department factory overhead rate** is computed as follows:

$$\frac{\text{Production Department}}{\text{Factory Overhead Rate}} = \frac{\text{Budgeted Department Factory Overhead}}{\text{Budgeted Department Allocation Base}}$$

To illustrate, assume that **Ruiz Company** uses direct labor hours as the allocation base for the Fabrication and Assembly departments.[2] Each department uses 10,000 direct labor hours. Thus, the factory overhead rates are as follows:

$$\frac{\text{Fabrication Department}}{\text{Factory Overhead Rate}} = \frac{\$1,030,000}{10,000 \text{ direct labor hours}} = \$103 \text{ per direct labor hour}$$

$$\frac{\text{Assembly Department}}{\text{Factory Overhead Rate}} = \frac{\$570,000}{10,000 \text{ direct labor hours}} = \$57 \text{ per direct labor hour}$$

Ten direct labor hours are required for the manufacture of each snowmobile and riding mower. These 10 hours are consumed in the Fabrication and Assembly departments as follows:

	Snowmobile	**Riding Mower**
Fabrication Department	8 hours	2 hours
Assembly Department...................	2	8
Direct labor hours per unit............	10 hours	10 hours

The factory overhead allocated to each snowmobile and riding mower is shown in Exhibit 4. As shown in Exhibit 4, each snowmobile is allocated $938 of total factory overhead costs. In contrast, each riding mower is allocated $662 of factory overhead costs.

---

[1] Factory overhead costs are assigned to production departments using methods discussed in advanced cost accounting textbooks.
[2] Departments need not use the same allocation base. The allocation base should be associated with the operating activity of the department.

Exhibit 4 Allocating Factory Overhead to Products—Ruiz Company

	Allocation Base Usage per Unit	×	Production Department Factory Overhead Rate	=	Allocated Factory Overhead per Unit of Product
Snowmobile					
Fabrication Department	8 direct labor hours	×	$103 per dlh	=	$824
Assembly Department	2 direct labor hours	×	$ 57 per dlh	=	114
Total factory overhead cost per snowmobile					$938
Riding mower					
Fabrication Department	2 direct labor hours	×	$103 per dlh	=	$206
Assembly Department	8 direct labor hours	×	$ 57 per dlh	=	456
Total factory overhead cost per riding mower					$662

Exhibit 5 summarizes the multiple production department rate allocation method for Ruiz. Exhibit 5 indicates that the Fabrication Department factory overhead rate is $103 per direct labor hour, while the Assembly Department rate is $57 per direct labor hour. Since the snowmobile uses more Fabrication Department direct labor hours than does the riding mower, the total overhead allocated to each snowmobile is $276 greater ($938–$662) than the amount allocated to each riding mower.

Exhibit 5
Multiple Production Department Rate Method—Ruiz Company

Distortion of Product Costs

The differences in **Ruiz Company**'s factory overhead for each snowmobile and riding mower using the single plantwide and the multiple production department factory overhead rate methods are as follows:

	Factory Overhead Cost per Unit		
	Single Plantwide Method	Multiple Production Department Method	Difference
Snowmobile..............	$800	$938	$(138)
Riding mower	800	662	138

note:

The single plantwide factory overhead rate distorts product cost by averaging high and low factory overhead costs.

The single plantwide factory overhead rate distorts the product cost of both the snowmobile and riding mower. That is, the snowmobile is not allocated enough cost and, thus, is under-costed by $138. In contrast, the riding mower is allocated too much cost and is overcosted by $138 ($800 – $662).

The preceding cost distortions are caused by averaging the differences between the high factory overhead costs in the Fabrication Department and the low factory overhead costs in the Assembly Department. Using the single plantwide rate, it is assumed that all factory overhead is directly related to a single allocation base for the entire plant. This assumption is not real-istic for Ruiz. Thus, using a single plantwide rate distorted the product costs of snowmobiles and riding mowers.

The following conditions indicate that a single plantwide factory overhead rate may cause product cost distortions:

- **Condition 1:** *Differences in production department factory overhead rates.* Some departments have high rates, whereas others have low rates.
- **Condition 2:** *Differences among products in the ratios of allocation base usage within a department and across departments.* Some products have a high ratio of allo-cation base usage within departments, whereas other products have a low ratio of allocation base usage within the same departments.

To illustrate, Condition 1 exists for Ruiz because the factory overhead rate for the Fabrica-tion Department is $103 per direct labor hour, whereas the rate for the Assembly Department is only $57 per direct labor hour. However, this condition by itself will not cause product cost distortions.

Condition 2 also exists for Ruiz. The snowmobile consumes 8 direct labor hours in the Fabrication Department, whereas the riding mower consumes only 2 direct labor hours. Thus, the ratio of allocation base usage is 4:1 in the Fabrication Department, computed as follows:[3]

$$\frac{\text{Ratio of Allocation Base Usage}}{\text{in the Fabrication Department}} = \frac{\text{Direct Labor Hours for snowmobiles}}{\text{Direct Labor Hours for riding mowers}} = \frac{8 \text{ hours}}{2 \text{ hours}} = 4{:}1$$

In contrast, the ratio of allocation base usage is 1:4 in the Assembly Department, computed as follows:

$$\frac{\text{Ratio of Allocation Base Usage}}{\text{in the Assembly Department}} = \frac{\text{Direct Labor Hours for snowmobiles}}{\text{Direct Labor Hours for riding mowers}} = \frac{2 \text{ hours}}{8 \text{ hours}} = 1{:}4$$

Because both conditions exist for Ruiz, the product costs from using the single plantwide factory overhead rate are distorted. The preceding conditions and the resulting product cost distortions are summarized in Exhibit 6.

[3] The numerator and denominator could be switched as long as the ratio is computed the same for each department. This is because the objective is to compare whether differences exist in the ratio of allocation base usage across products and departments.

Exhibit 6 Conditions for Product Cost Distortion—Ruiz Company

	Fabrication Department		Assembly Department

Condition 1: Differences in production department factory overhead rates

$103 per direct labor hour

$57 per direct labor hour

Condition 2: Differences in the ratios of allocation base usage

8 direct labor hours

2 direct labor hours

2 direct labor hours

8 direct labor hours

Ratio of Allocation Base Usage = 4:1

Ratio of Allocation Base Usage = 1:4

Check Up Corner 4-2 Multiple Production Department Factory Overhead Rates

The total factory overhead for Lifestyle Furniture Company is budgeted at $600,000 for the year, divided between two departments: Fabrication, $420,000, and Assembly, $180,000. Lifestyle manufactures two products: a computer desk and a designer table. Each desk requires 1 direct labor hour (dlh) in Fabrication and 3 direct labor hours in Assembly. Each table requires 3 direct labor hours in Fabrication and 1 direct labor hour in Assembly. Production for the year is budgeted for 5,000 units of each product.

Determine the:

A   Total number of budgeted direct labor hours for the year in each department.

B.   Departmental factory overhead rate for each department.

C.   Factory overhead allocated per unit for each product, using the departmental factory overhead rates.

Solution:

A.

	Direct Labor Hours per Unit	×	Number of Units	=	Toal Direct Labor Hours
Fabrication Department					
Desks	1 dlh	×	5,000	=	5,000
Tables	3 dlh	×	5,000	=	15,000
Total budgeted direct labor hours					20,000
Assembly Department					
Desks	3 dlh	×	5,000	=	15,000
Tables	1 dlh	×	5,000	=	5,000
Total budgeted direct labor hours					20,000

The budgeted allocation base is a measure of operating activity in each department.

(Continued)

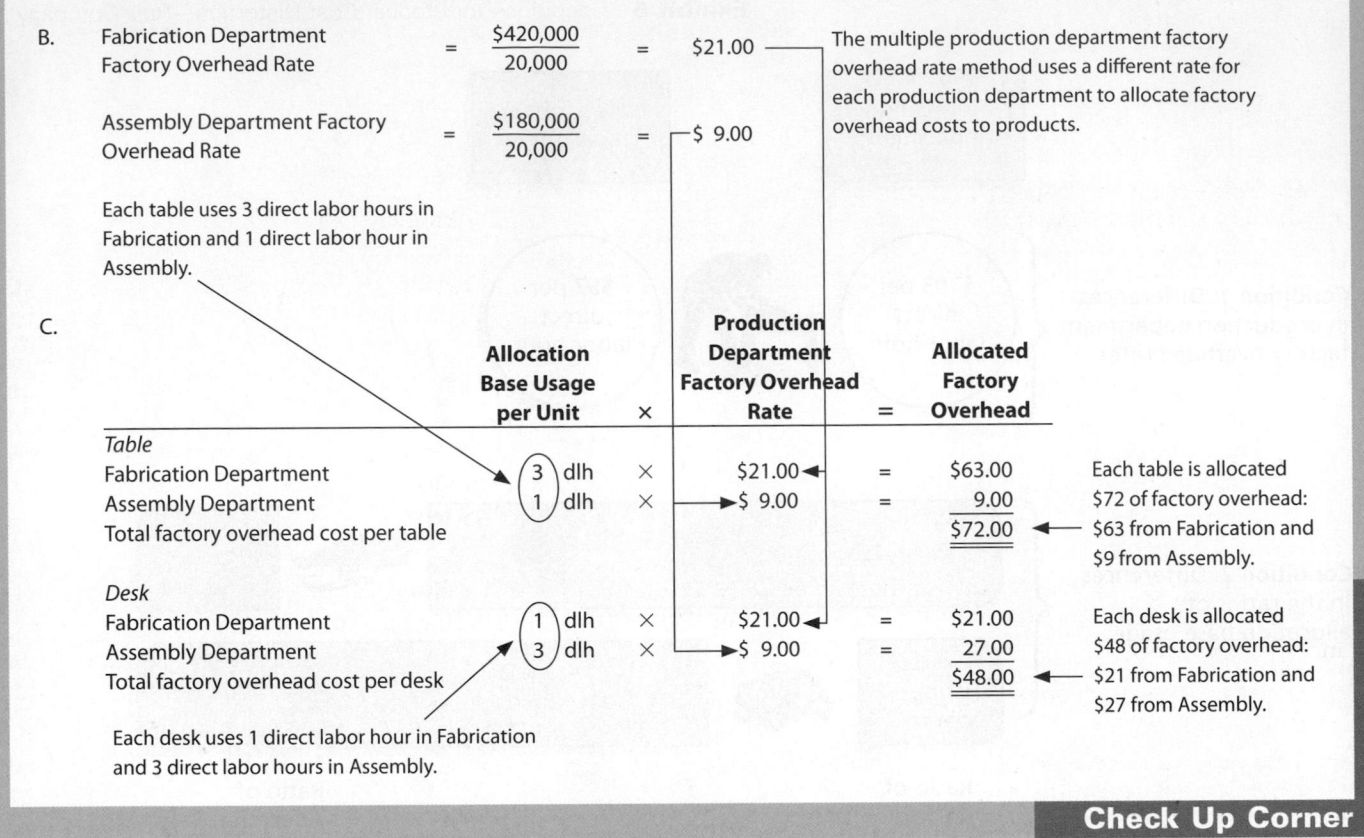

B.

Fabrication Department Factory Overhead Rate	=	$\dfrac{\$420,000}{20,000}$	=	$21.00	
Assembly Department Factory Overhead Rate	=	$\dfrac{\$180,000}{20,000}$	=	$ 9.00	

The multiple production department factory overhead rate method uses a different rate for each production department to allocate factory overhead costs to products.

Each table uses 3 direct labor hours in Fabrication and 1 direct labor hour in Assembly.

C.

	Allocation Base Usage per Unit	×	Production Department Factory Overhead Rate	=	Allocated Factory Overhead	
Table						
Fabrication Department	3 dlh	×	$21.00	=	$63.00	Each table is allocated
Assembly Department	1 dlh	×	$ 9.00	=	9.00	$72 of factory overhead:
Total factory overhead cost per table					$72.00	$63 from Fabrication and $9 from Assembly.
Desk						
Fabrication Department	1 dlh	×	$21.00	=	$21.00	Each desk is allocated
Assembly Department	3 dlh	×	$ 9.00	=	27.00	$48 of factory overhead:
Total factory overhead cost per desk					$48.00	$21 from Fabrication and $27 from Assembly.

Each desk uses 1 direct labor hour in Fabrication and 3 direct labor hours in Assembly.

Check Up Corner

Objective 4
Use activity-based costing for product costing.

Activity-Based Costing Method

As illustrated in the preceding section, product costs may be distorted when a single plantwide factory overhead rate is used. However, product costs may also be distorted when multiple production department factory overhead rates are used. Activity-based costing further reduces the possibility of product cost distortions.

The **activity-based costing (ABC) method** provides an alternative approach for allocating factory overhead that uses multiple factory overhead rates based on different activities. **Activities** are the types of work, or actions, involved in a manufacturing or service process. For example, the assembly, inspection, and engineering design functions are activities that might be used to allocate overhead.

Link to Cold Stone Creamery **Cold Stone Creamery** uses the principles of activity-based costing.

Under activity-based costing, factory overhead costs are initially budgeted for activities, sometimes called *activity cost pools*, such as machine usage, inspections, moving, production setups, and engineering activities.[4] In contrast, when multiple production department factory overhead rates are used, factory overhead costs are first accounted for in production departments.

---

[4] The activity rate is based on budgeted activity costs. Activity-based budgeting and the reconciliation of budgeted activity costs to actual costs are topics covered in advanced texts.

Exhibit 7 illustrates how activity-based costing differs from the multiple production department method.

Exhibit 7 Multiple Production Department Factory Overhead Rate Method vs. Activity-Based Costing

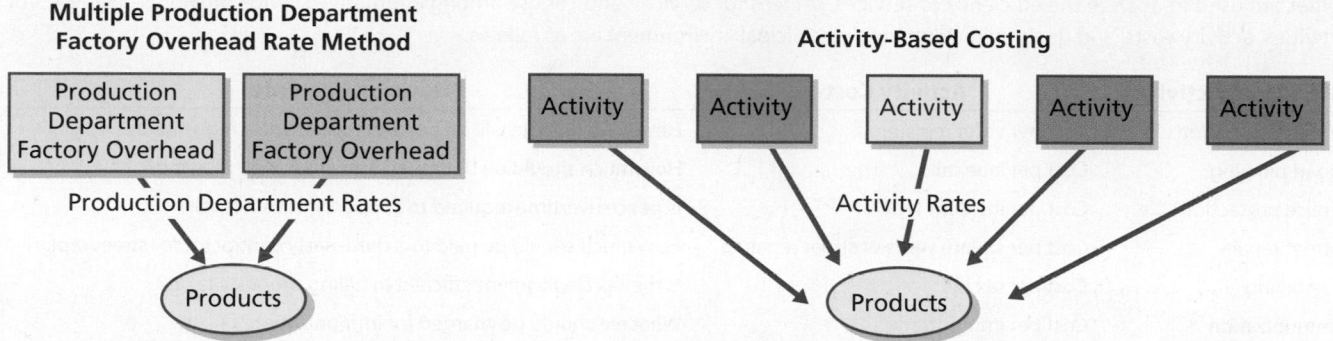

Exhibit 7 Multiple Production Department Factory Overhead Rate Method vs. Activity-Based Costing

To illustrate the activity-based costing method, the prior illustration for **Ruiz Company** is used. Assume that the following activities have been identified for producing snowmobiles and riding mowers:

- *Fabrication*, which consists of cutting metal to shape the product. This activity is machine-intensive.
- *Assembly*, which consists of manually assembling machined pieces into a final product. This activity is labor-intensive.
- *Setup*, which consists of changing tooling in machines in preparation for making a new product. Each production run requires a **setup**.
- *Quality-control inspections*, which consist of inspecting the product for conformance to specifications. Inspection requires product tear down and reassembly.
- *Engineering changes*, which consist of processing changes in design or process specifications for a product. The document that initiates changing a product or process is called an **engineering change order (ECO)**.

Fabrication and assembly are now identified as *activities* rather than *departments*. As a result, the setup, quality-control inspections, and engineering change functions that were previously allocated to the Fabrication and Assembly departments are now classified as separate activities. The budgeted cost for each activity is as follows:

Activity	Budgeted Activity Cost
Fabrication	$ 530,000
Assembly...	70,000
Setup...	480,000
Quality-control inspections	312,000
Engineering changes	208,000
Total budgeted activity costs.....................................	$1,600,000

The costs for the fabrication and assembly activities are less than the costs shown in the preceding section where these activities were identified as production departments. This is because the costs of setup, quality-control inspections, and engineering changes, which total $1,000,000 ($480,000 + $312,000 + $208,000), have now been separated into their own activity cost pools.

Why It Matters

Activity-Based Costing in the Public Sector

Activity-based costing is used by some municipal, state, and federal entities to guide decision making. In these cases, the cost of activities are used to analyze the efficiency of services, set fees for services, and choose among alternative service providers. Examples of activities, activity costs, and decision making in the municipal environment are as follows:

Municipal Activity	Activity Cost	Decision Example
Voter registration	Cost per voter registered	How many people will be needed to staff voter registration?
Road plowing	Cost per lane mile	How much should be budgeted for winter road plowing?
Police protection	Cost per incident type	Is police overtime required to support incident levels?
Street repair	Cost per square yards of street repaired	How much should be paid to a third-party contractor for street repair?
Tax billing	Cost per tax bill	Is the Tax Department efficient in billing property taxes?
Immunization	Cost per immunization	What fee should be charged for immunization?

Source: *Costing Municipal Services*, Massachusetts Department of Revenue, Division of Local Services, March 2005.

Activity Rates

The budgeted activity costs are assigned to products using factory overhead rates for each activity. These rates are called **activity rates** because they are related to activities. Activity rates are computed as follows:

$$\text{Activity Rate} = \frac{\text{Budgeted Activity Cost}}{\text{Total Activity-Base Usage}}$$

note:

Activity rates are computed by dividing the budgeted activity cost pool by the total estimated activity-base usage.

The term **activity base**, rather than *allocation base*, is used because the base is related to an activity.

To illustrate, assume that snowmobiles are a new product for **Ruiz Company**, and engineers are still making minor design changes. Ruiz has produced riding mowers for many years. Activity-base usage for the two products is as follows:

	Snowmobile	Riding Mower
Estimated units of total production	1,000 units	1,000 units
Estimated setups	100 setups	20 setups
Quality-control inspections	100 inspections (10%)	4 inspections (0.4%)
Estimated engineering change orders...................	12 change orders	4 change orders

The number of direct labor hours used by each product is 10,000 hours, computed as follows:

	Direct Labor Hours per Unit	Number of Units of Production	Total Direct Labor Hours
Snowmobile:			
Fabrication Department..............	8 hours	1,000 units	8,000 hours
Assembly Department	2 hours	1,000 units	2,000 hours
Total...............................			10,000 hours
Riding Mower:			
Fabrication Department..............	2 hours	1,000 units	2,000 hours
Assembly Department	8 hours	1,000 units	8,000 hours
Total...............................			10,000 hours

Exhibit 8 summarizes the activity-base usage quantities for each product.

Exhibit 8 Activity Bases—Ruiz Company

Products	Activity-Base Usage				
	Fabrication	Assembly	Setup	Quality-Control Inspections	Engineering Changes
Snowmobile	8,000 dlh	2,000 dlh	100 setups	100 inspections	12 ECOs
Riding mower..................	2,000	8,000	20	4	4
Total activity-base usage	10,000 dlh	10,000 dlh	120 setups	104 inspections	16 ECOs

The activity rates for Ruiz are shown in Exhibit 9.

Exhibit 9 Activity Rates—Ruiz Company

Activity	Budgeted Activity Cost	÷	Total Activity-Base Usage	=	Activity Rate
Fabrication	$530,000	÷	10,000 direct labor hours	=	$ 53 per direct labor hour
Assembly	$ 70,000	÷	10,000 direct labor hours	=	$ 7 per direct labor hour
Setup	$480,000	÷	120 setups	=	$ 4,000 per setup
Quality-control inspections	$312,000	÷	104 inspections	=	$ 3,000 per inspection
Engineering changes	$208,000	÷	16 engineering changes	=	$13,000 per engineering change order

Allocating Costs

Overhead costs of each activity are allocated to a product by multiplying the product's activity-base usage by the activity rate, as follows:

$$\text{Activity Overhead Allocated} = \text{Activity-Base Usage} \times \text{Activity Rate}$$

The estimated total factory overhead cost for a product is the sum of the product's individual activity allocations. The factory overhead cost per unit is computed by dividing the product's total factory overhead cost by the total units of estimated production, as follows:

$$\text{Factory Overhead Cost per Unit} = \frac{\text{Total Factory Overhead Cost}}{\text{Total Units of Estimated Production}}$$

These computations for Ruiz's snowmobile and riding mower are shown in Exhibit 10.

Exhibit 10   Activity-Based Product Cost Calculations

	A	B	C	D	E	F	G	H	I	J	K	L
1				Snowmobile						Riding Mower		
2		Activity-Base	×	Activity		Activity		Activity-Base	×	Activity		Activity
3	Activity	Usage	×	Rate	=	Cost		Usage	×	Rate	=	Cost
4												
5	Fabrication	8,000 dlh		$ 53 per dlh		$ 424,000		2,000 dlh		$ 53 per dlh		$106,000
6	Assembly	2,000 dlh		$ 7 per dlh		14,000		8,000 dlh		$ 7 per dlh		56,000
7	Setup	100 setups		$ 4,000 per setup		400,000		20 setups		$ 4,000 per setup		80,000
8	Quality-control											
9	inspections	100 inspections		$ 3,000 per insp.		300,000		4 inspections		$ 3,000 per insp.		12,000
10	Engineering											
11	changes	12 ECOs		$13,000 per ECO		156,000		4 ECOs		$13,000 per ECO		52,000
12	Total factory											
13	overhead cost					$1,294,000						$306,000
14	Estimated units											
15	of production					÷ 1,000						÷ 1,000
16	Factory overhead											
17	cost per unit					$ 1,294						$ 306
18												

The activity-based costing method for Ruiz is summarized in Exhibit 11.

Exhibit 11   Activity Bases—Ruiz Company

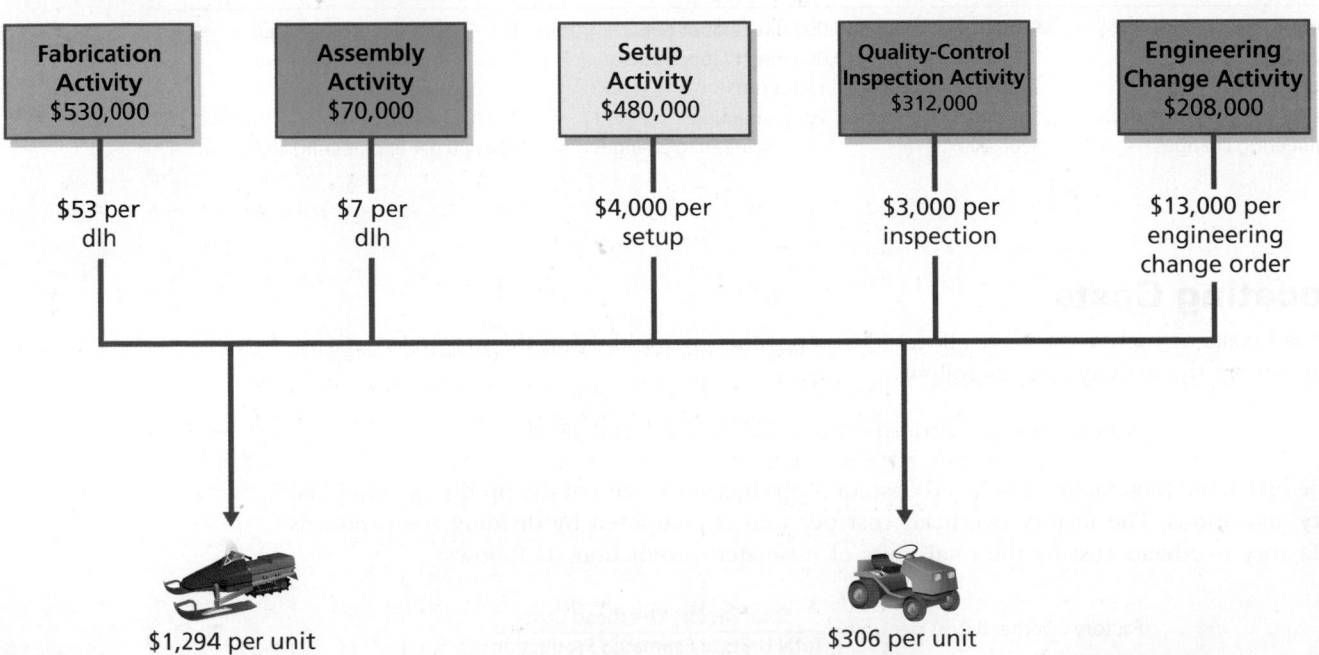

Fabrication Activity $530,000	Assembly Activity $70,000	Setup Activity $480,000	Quality-Control Inspection Activity $312,000	Engineering Change Activity $208,000
$53 per dlh	$7 per dlh	$4,000 per setup	$3,000 per inspection	$13,000 per engineering change order

$1,294 per unit $306 per unit

Why It Matters

$600 Hammer

An old story is one of an ordinary hammer purchased under a government contract costing the government $600. This is actually not a story about waste, but a story about cost allocation distortion. The actual story involves a hammer procured as part of a bundle of many different spare parts. When the engineering costs were allocated among the individual spare parts, every part was treated the same. Thus, a $15 hammer was allocated the same amount of relative engineering cost as were highly technical components. Thus, the hammer received as much relative overhead as did an engine. The allocation method did not trace engineering cost on the basis of engineering effort required by the product, but rather the cost was spread proportionally across all the products. In this way, the engine would end up under-allocated and the hammer over-allocated engineering cost. Today, this type of distortion is minimized through better cost allocation practices. This is accomplished through the Office of Federal Procurement Policy Cost Accounting Standards Board, which operates as part of the U.S. government for purposes of prescribing standard cost accounting practices for U.S. government contracts.

Source: Sydney J. Freedberg, "The Myth of the $600 Hammer," *Government Executive*, December 7, 1998.

Distortion in Product Costs

The factory overhead costs per unit for **Ruiz Company** using the three allocation methods are shown in Exhibit 12.

Exhibit 12 Overhead Cost Allocation Methods: Ruiz Company

	Factory Overhead Cost per Unit—Three Cost Allocation Methods		
	Single Plantwide Rate	Multiple Production Department Rates	Activity-Based Costing
Snowmobile	$800	$938	$1,294
Riding mower	800	662	306

The activity-based costing method produces different factory overhead costs per unit (product costs) than the multiple department factory overhead rate method. This difference is caused by how the $1,000,000 of setup, quality control, and engineering change activities are allocated.

Under the multiple production department factory overhead rate method, setup, quality control, and engineering change costs were allocated using departmental rates based on direct labor hours. However, snowmobiles and riding mowers did *not* consume these *activities* in proportion to direct labor hours. That is, each snowmobile consumed a larger portion of the setup, quality-control inspection, and engineering change activities. This was true even though each product consumed 10,000 direct labor hours. As a result, activity-based costing allocated more of the cost of these activities to the snowmobile. Only under the activity-based approach were these differences reflected in the factory overhead cost allocations and thus in the product costs.

Dangers of Product Cost Distortion

If **Ruiz Company** used the $800 factory overhead cost allocation (single plantwide rate) instead of activity-based costing for pricing snowmobiles and riding mowers, the following would likely result:

■ The snowmobile would be *underpriced* because its factory overhead cost would be understated by $494 ($1,294 − $800).

■ The riding mower would be *overpriced* because its factory overhead cost would be overstated by $494 ($800 − $306).

As a result, Ruiz would likely lose sales of riding mowers because they are overpriced. In contrast, sales of snowmobiles would increase because they are underpriced. Due to these pricing errors, Ruiz might incorrectly decide to expand production of snowmobiles and discontinue making riding mowers.

If Ruiz uses the activity-based costing method, its product costs would be more accurate. Thus, Ruiz would have a better starting point for making proper pricing decisions. Although the product cost distortions are not as great, similar results would occur if Ruiz had used the multiple production department rate method.

Check Up Corner 4-3   Activity-Based Costing

The total factory overhead for Lifestyle Furniture Company is budgeted at $600,000 for the year, divided among four activities: fabrication, $300,000; assembly, $120,000; setup, $100,000; and materials handling, $80,000. Lifestyle manufactures two designer furniture products: a wingback chair (chair) and a computer desk (desk). The activity-base usage quantities for each product by each activity are estimated as follows:

	Fabrication	Assembly	Setup	Materials Handling
Chair	5,000 dlh	15,000 dlh	30 setups	50 moves
Desk	15,000	5,000	220	350
Total activity-base usage	20,000 dlh	20,000 dlh	250 setups	400 moves

Production for the year is budgeted for 5,000 chairs and 5,000 desks.

Determine the:

A. Activity rate for each activity.

B. Activity-based factory overhead per unit for each product.

Solution:

A.

Fabrication	Assembly	Setup	Materials Handling
$300,000	$120,000	$100,000	$80,000
÷20,000 dlh	÷ 20,000 dlh	÷ 250 setups	÷ 400 moves
$ 15 per dlh	$ 6 per dlh	$ 400 per setup	$ 200 per move

The budgeted activity costs are assigned to products using a different rate for each activity.

$$\text{Activity Rate} = \frac{\text{Budgeted Activity Cost}}{\text{Total Activity-Base Usage}}$$

The activity rate for each department is multiplied by the department's activity-base usage for each product.

B.

	A	B	C	D	E	F	G	H	I	J	K	L
1				Chair						Desk		
2		Activity-Base		Activity		Activity		Activity-Base		Activity		Activity
3	Activity	Usage	×	Rate	=	Cost		Usage	×	Rate	=	Cost
4												
5	Fabrication	5,000 dlh		$ 15 per dlh		$ 75,000		15,000 dlh		$ 15 per dlh		$225,000
6	Assembly	15,000 dlh		$ 6 per dlh		90,000		5,000 dlh		$ 6 per dlh		30,000
7	Setup	30 setups		$400 per setup		12,000		220 setups		$400 per setup		88,000
8	Materials handling	50 moves		$200 per move		10,000		350 moves		$200 per move		70,000
9	Total factory overhead cost					$187,000						$413,000
10	Estimated units of											
11	production					÷ 5,000						÷ 5,000
12	Factory overhead											
13	cost per unit					$ 37.40						$ 82.60
14												

The factory overhead cost per unit is determined by dividing the factory overhead assigned to each product by the estimated number of units.

Check Up Corner

 Ethics: Do It!

Fraud Against You and Me

The U.S. government makes a wide variety of purchases. Two of the largest are health care purchases under Medicare and military equipment. The purchase price for these and other items is often determined by the cost plus some profit. The cost is often the sum of direct costs plus allocated overhead. Due to the complexity of determining cost, government agencies review the amount charged for products and services. In the event of disagreement between the contractor and the government, the U.S.

government may sue the contractor under the False Claims Act, which provides for three times the government's damages plus civil penalties. The U.S. Department of Justice has recovered billions from the False Claims Act.

Most of the cases were the result of allegations by private citizens under the act's whistleblower provision.

Source: The False Claims Act Legal Center of the TAF Education Fund, www.taf.org.

Anyone can apply for and open a **Cold Stone Creamery** franchise. The company provides help in picking a location, constructing or leasing a building, and training employees. The initial franchise fee is $27,000, and it costs $250,000 to $400,000 to build and equip a store. The company receives a royalty fee of 6% and an advertising fee of 3% of gross sales.

Link to Cold Stone Creamery

Activity-Based Costing for Selling and Administrative Expenses

Objective 5
Use activity-based costing to allocate selling and administrative expenses to products.

Generally accepted accounting principles (GAAP) require that selling and administrative expenses be reported as period expenses on the income statement. However, selling and administrative expenses may be allocated to products for managerial decision making. For example, selling and administrative expenses may be allocated for analyzing product profitability.

One method of allocating selling and administrative expenses to the products is based on sales volumes. However, products may consume activities in ways that are unrelated to their sales volumes. When this occurs, activity-based costing may be a more accurate method of allocation.

To illustrate, assume that Abacus Company has two products, Ipso and Facto. Both products have the same total sales volume. However, Ipso and Facto consume selling and administrative activities differently, as shown in Exhibit 13.

Exhibit 13 Selling and Administrative Activity Product Differences

Selling and Administrative Activities	Ipso	Facto
Post-sale technical support	Product is easy for the customer to use.	Product requires specialized training in order for the customer to use it.
Order writing	Product requires no technical information from the customer.	Product requires detailed technical information from the customer.
Promotional support	Product requires no promotional effort.	Product requires extensive promotional effort.
Order entry	Product is purchased in large volumes per order.	Product is purchased in small volumes per order.
Customer return processing	Product has few customer returns.	Product has many customer returns.
Shipping document preparation	Product is shipped domestically.	Product is shipped internationally, requiring customs and export documents.
Shipping and handling	Product is not hazardous.	Product is hazardous, requiring specialized shipping and handling.
Field service	Product has few warranty claims.	Product has many warranty claims.

If Abacus's selling and administrative expenses are allocated on the basis of sales volumes, the same amount of expense would be allocated to Ipso and Facto. This is because Ipso and Facto have the same sales volume. However, as Exhibit 13 implies, such an allocation would be misleading.

The activity-based costing method can be used to allocate the selling and administrative activities to Ipso and Facto. Activity-based costing allocates selling and administrative expenses based on how each product consumes activities.

To illustrate, assume that Abacus's field warranty service activity has a budgeted cost of $150,000. Additionally, assume that 100 warranty claims are estimated for the period. Using warranty claims as an activity base, the warranty claim activity rate is $1,500, computed as follows:

$$\text{Activity Rate} = \frac{\text{Budgeted Activity Cost}}{\text{Total Activity-Base Usage}}$$

$$\text{Warranty Claim Activity Rate} = \frac{\text{Budgeted Warranty Claim Expenses}}{\text{Total Estimated Warranty Claims}}$$

$$= \frac{\$150,000}{100 \text{ claims}} = \$1,500 \text{ per warranty claim}$$

Assuming that Ipso had 10 warranty claims and Facto had 90 warranty claims, the field service activity expenses would be allocated to each product as follows:

Ipso: 10 warranty claims × $1,500 per warranty claim = $ 15,000
Facto: 90 warranty claims × $1,500 per warranty claim = $135,000

The remaining selling and administrative activities could be allocated to Ipso and Facto in a similar manner.

In some cases, selling and administrative expenses may be more related to *customer* behaviors than to differences in products. That is, some customers may demand more service and selling activities than other customers. In such cases, activity-based costing would allocate selling and administrative expenses to customers.

Objective 6
Use activity-based costing in a service business.

Activity-Based Costing in Service Businesses

Service companies need to determine the cost of their services so that they can make pricing, promoting, and other decisions. The use of single and multiple department overhead rate methods may lead to distortions similar to those of manufacturing firms. Thus, many service companies use activity-based costing for determining the cost of services.

To illustrate, assume that Hopewell Hospital uses activity-based costing to allocate hospital overhead to patients. Hopewell applies activity-based costing as follows:

- Step 1. Identifying activities.
- Step 2. Determining activity rates for each activity.
- Step 3. Allocating overhead costs to patients based upon activity-base usage.

Hopewell has identified the following activities:

- Admission
- Radiological testing
- Operating room
- Pathological testing
- Dietary and laundry

Each activity has an estimated patient activity-base usage. Based on the budgeted costs for each activity and related estimated activity-base usage, the activity rates shown in Exhibit 14 were developed.

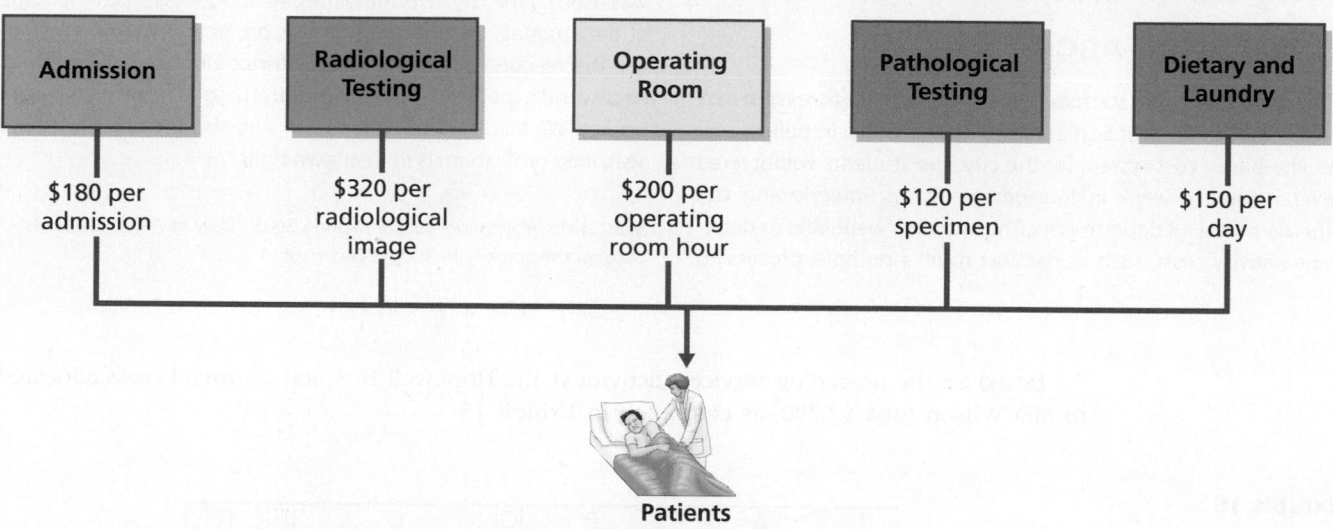

Exhibit 14 Activity-Based Costing Method—Hopewell Hospital

To illustrate, assume the following data for radiological testing:

Budgeted costs..................................... $960,000
Total estimated activity-base usage .... 3,000 images

The activity rate of $320 per radiological image is computed as follows:

$$\text{Activity Rate} = \frac{\text{Budgeted Activity Cost}}{\text{Total Activity-Base Usage}}$$

$$\text{Radiological Testing Activity Rate} = \frac{\text{Budgeted Radiological Testing Costs}}{\text{Total Estimated Images}}$$

$$= \frac{\$960,000}{3,000 \text{ images}} = \$320 \text{ per image}$$

The activity rates for the other activities are determined in a similar manner. These activity rates along with the patient activity-base usage are used to allocate costs to patients as follows:

$$\text{Activity Cost Allocated to Patient} = \text{Patient Activity-Base Usage} \times \text{Activity Rate}$$

To illustrate, assume that Mia Wilson was a patient of the hospital. The hospital overhead services (activities) performed for Mia Wilson were as follows:

	Patient (Mia Wilson) Activity-Base Usage
Admission	1 admission
Radiological testing...........................	2 images
Operating room..............................	4 hours
Pathological testing...........................	1 specimen
Dietary and laundry...........................	7 days

Why It Matters

Learning Your ABCs

Students at Harvard's **Kennedy School of Government** joined with the city of Somerville, Massachusetts, in building an activity-based cost system for the city. The students volunteered several hours a week in four-person teams, interviewing city officials within 18 departments. The students were able to determine activity costs, such as the cost to fill a pothole, processing a building permit, or responding to a four-alarm fire. Their study was used by the city in forming the city budget. As stated by some of the students participating on this project: "It makes sense to use the resources of the university for community building. . . . Real-world experience is a tremendous thing to have in your back pocket. We learned from the mayor and the fire chief, who are seasoned professionals in their own right."

Source: *Kennedy School Bulletin*, Spring 2005, "Easy as A-B-C: Students Take on the Somerville Budget Overhaul."

Based on the preceding services (activities), the Hopewell Hospital overhead costs allocated to Mia Wilson total $2,790, as computed in Exhibit 15.

Exhibit 15

Hopewell Hospital Overhead Costs Allocated to Mia Wilson

	A	B	C	D	E	F
1	Patient Name: Mia Wilson					
2		Activity-Base		Activity		Activity
3	Activity	Usage	×	Rate	=	Cost
4						
5	Admission	1 admission		$180 per admission		$ 180
6	Radiological testing	2 images		$320 per image		640
7	Operating room	4 hours		$200 per hour		800
8	Pathological testing	1 specimen		$120 per specimen		120
9	Dietary and laundry	7 days		$150 per day		1,050
10	Total					$2,790
11						

The patient activity costs can be combined with the direct costs, such as drugs and supplies. These costs and the related revenues can be reported for each patient in a patient (customer) profitability report. A partial patient profitability report for Hopewell is shown in Exhibit 16.

Exhibit 16

Customer Profitability Report—Hopewell Hospital

Hopewell Hospital
Patient (Customer) Profitability Report
For the Period Ending December 31

	Adcock, Aesha	Birini, Sergey	Diaz, Mateo	Wilson, Mia
Revenues	$9,500	$21,400	$5,050	$3,300
Patient costs:				
Drugs and supplies	$ 400	$ 1,000	$ 300	$ 200
Admission	180	180	180	180
Radiological testing	1,280	2,560	1,280	640
Operating room	2,400	6,400	1,600	800
Pathological testing	240	600	120	120
Dietary and laundry	4,200	14,700	1,050	1,050
Total patient costs	$8,700	$25,440	$4,530	$2,990
Income from operations	$ 800	$ (4,040)	$ 520	$ 310

Exhibit 16 can be used by hospital administrators for decisions on pricing or services. For example, there was a large loss on services provided to Sergey Birini. Investigation might reveal that some of the services provided to Birini were not reimbursed by insurance. As a result, Hopewell might lobby the insurance company to reimburse these services or request higher insurance reimbursement on other services.

Check Up Corner 4-4 | Activity-Based Costing for a Service Business

Metro University uses activity-based costing to assign indirect costs to academic departments, using four activities. The activity base, budgeted activity cost, and estimated activity-base usage for each activity are identified below.

Activity	Activity Base	Budgeted Activity Cost	Activity-Base Usage
Academic support	Number of departments	$ 400,000	40 departments (dept.)
Facilities	Square feet	1,800,000	200,000 square feet (sq. ft.)
Instruction	Number of course sections	2,000,000	1,000 sections (sec.)
Student services	Number of students	360,000	4,500 students (stdt.)

The activity-base usage associated with the Chemistry Department and History Department is as follows:

	Academic Support	Facilities	Instruction	Student Services
Chemistry	1 department	9,000 square feet	15 sections	80 students
History	1 department	3,200 square feet	30 sections	175 students

Determine the:

A. Activity rate for each activity.

B. Total activity cost for the Chemistry Department and the History Department.

Solution:

A.

Academic Support	Facilities	Instruction	Student Services
$400,000	$1,800,000	$2,000,000	$360,000
÷ 40 dept.	÷ 200,000 sq. ft.	÷ 1,000 sec.	÷ 4,500 stdt.
$ 10,000 per dept.	$ 9 per sq. ft.	$ 2,000 per sec.	$ 80 per stdt.

The budgeted activity costs are assigned to departments using a different rate for each activity. These rates are called activity rates.

$$\text{Activity Rate} = \frac{\text{Budgeted Activity Cost}}{\text{Total Activity-Base Usage}}$$

Activity rates for each activity are multiplied by the activity-base usage in each department.

B.

	Chemistry Department			History Department		
Activity	Activity-Base Usage ×	Activity Rate =	Activity Cost	Activity-Base Usage ×	Activity Rate =	Activity Cost
Academic support	1 dept. ×	$10,000 per dept. =	$ 10,000	1 dept. ×	$10,000 per dept. =	$ 10,000
Facilities	9,000 sq. ft. ×	$9 per sq. ft. =	81,000	3,200 sq. ft. ×	$9 per sq. ft. =	28,800
Instruction	15 sec. ×	$2,000 per sec. =	30,000	30 sec. ×	$2,000 per sec. =	60,000
Student services	80 stdt. ×	$80 per stdt. =	6,400	175 stdt. ×	$80 per stdt. =	14,000
Total activity cost			$127,400			$112,800

The total activity cost assigned to each department

Check Up Corner

Analysis for Decision Making

Objective

Describe and illustrate the use of activity-based costing information in decision making.

Using ABC Product Cost Information to Reduce Costs

Activity-based costing (ABC) can be used to improve the cost of a product. For example, Lee Corporation assembles LCD monitors. The following activity information is available for its 40-inch monitor:

Activity	Activity-Base Usage (hrs. per unit)	×	Activity Rate per Hour	=	Activity Cost
Assembly	0.80		$14		$11.20
Setup	0.30		20		6.00
Production control	0.15		32		4.80
Materials control	0.10		32		3.20
Moving	0.40		12		4.80
Testing	0.25		24		6.00
Activity cost per unit					$36.00

All of the activity cost is related to labor. The activity information can be used to isolate cost improvement opportunities. Management is seeking to remove $3.00 of activity cost from the product in order to remain price competitive. The activity cost reduction can be accomplished in two basic ways:

1. Improve operations so that the activity-base usage per unit is either reduced or eliminated.
2. Change the classification of employees doing an activity and thereby decrease the activity rate. Higher-classified employees are more expensive but more skilled than lower-classified employees.

Assume the process was improved so that the setup activity required one-third less time to complete per unit. In addition, the moving distance was cut in half. Would these improvements be sufficient to remove $3.00 of activity cost from the product? The activity information under the improvements would be as follows:

Activity	Activity-Base Usage (hrs. per unit)	×	Activity Rate per Hour	=	Activity Cost
Assembly	0.80		$14		$11.20
Setup	0.20		20		4.00
Production control	0.15		32		4.80
Materials control	0.10		32		3.20
Moving	0.20		12		2.40
Testing	0.25		24		6.00
Activity cost per unit					$31.60

The shaded areas show the improvements. Setup was reduced from 0.3 hours to 0.2 hours. The moving distance was cut from 0.4 hours to 0.2 hours. These changes reduced the activity cost of each monitor from $36.00 to $31.60, or $4.40, thus exceeding the $3.00 target.

Using ABC Product Cost Information to Reduce Costs

Life Force Fitness, Inc. assembles and sells treadmills. Activity-based product information for each treadmill is as follows:

Activity	Activity-Base Usage (hrs. per unit)	×	Activity Rate per Hour	=	Activity Cost
Motor assembly	1.50		$20		$30.00
Final assembly	1.00		18		18.00
Testing	0.25		22		5.50
Rework	0.40		22		8.80
Moving	0.20		15		3.00
Activity cost per unit					$65.30

All of the activity costs are related to labor. Management must remove $2.00 of activity cost from the product in order to remain competitive.

Rework involves disassembling and repairing a unit that fails testing. Not all units require rework, but the average is 0.40 hours per unit. Presently, the testing is done on the completed assembly; but much of the rework has been related to motors to test the motor independently, prior to assembling it into the final treadmill. Thus, motor assembly issues can be diagnosed and solved without having to disassemble the complete treadmill. This change will reduce the average rework per unit by one-quarter.

A. Determine the new activity cost per unit under the rework improvement scenario.

B. If management had the choice of doing the rework improvement in (A) or cutting the moving activity in half by improving the product flow, which decision should be implemented? Why?

Solution:

A. The average rework per unit will be improved by one-quarter, or 25%. Thus, the new average rework time will be reduced from 0.40 to 0.30 hours [0.40 × (1 − 0.25)].

Activity	Activity-Base Usage (hrs. per unit)	×	Activity Rate per Hour	=	Activity Cost
Motor assembly	1.50		$20		$30.00
Final assembly	1.00		18		18.00
Testing	0.25		22		5.50
Rework	0.30		22		6.60
Moving	0.20		15		3.00
Activity cost per unit					$63.10

B. The rework improvement reduces the cost per unit by $2.20 ($65.30 − $63.10), which meets management's $2.00 per unit cost improvement objective. Halving the moving activity would reduce the moving activity cost by $1.50 per unit (0.10 hours × $15 per hour), which is $0.70 less than the rework improvement ($2.20 − $1.50). Thus, management should select the rework improvement project.

Let's Review

Chapter Summary

1. Three cost allocation methods used for determining product costs are the (1) single plant-wide factory overhead rate method, (2) multiple production department rate method, and (3) activity-based costing method.

2. A single plantwide factory overhead rate can be used to allocate all plant overhead to all products. The single plantwide factory overhead rate is simple to apply, but can lead to product cost distortions.

3. Product costing using multiple production department factory overhead rates requires identifying the factory overhead by each production department. Using these rates can result in greater accuracy than using single plantwide factory overhead rates when: (A) There are significant differences in the factory overhead rates across different production departments. (B) The products require different ratios of allocation-base usage in each production department.

4. Activity-based costing requires factory overhead to be budgeted to activities. The budgeted activity costs are allocated to products by multiplying activity rates by the activity-base quantity consumed for each product. Activity-based costing is more accurate when products consume activities in proportions unrelated to plantwide or departmental allocation bases.

5. Selling and administrative expenses can be allocated to products for management profit reporting, using activity-based costing. Activity-based costing would be preferred when the products use selling and administrative activities in ratios that are unrelated to their sales volumes.

6. Activity-based costing may be applied in service businesses to determine the cost of individual services offered. Service costs are determined by multiplying activity rates by the activity-base quantities consumed by the customer.

Key Terms

activities (158)
activity base (160)
activity rates (160)
activity-based costing
    (ABC) method (158)

engineering change order
    (ECO) (159)
multiple production department
    factory overhead rate
    method (153)
product costing (150)

production department
    factory overhead rate (154)
setup (159)
single plantwide factory
    overhead rate method (151)

Practice

Multiple-Choice Questions

1. Which of the following statements is most accurate?
   A. The single plantwide factory overhead rate method will usually provide management with accurate product costs.
   B. Activity-based costing can be used by management to determine accurate profitability for each product.
   C. The multiple production department factory overhead rate method will usually result in more product cost distortion than the single plantwide factory overhead rate method.
   D. Generally accepted accounting principles require activity-based costing methods for inventory valuation.

2. San Madeo Company had the following factory overhead costs:

Power	$120,000
Indirect labor	60,000
Equipment depreciation	500,000

The factory budgeted to work 20,000 direct labor hours in the upcoming period. San Madeo uses a single plantwide factory overhead rate based on direct labor hours. What is the overhead cost per unit associated with Product M, if Product M uses 6 direct labor hours per unit in the factory?

A. $34
B. $54
C. $204
D. $150

3. Which of the following activity bases would best be used to allocate setup activity to products?

A. Number of inspections
B. Direct labor hours
C. Direct machine hours
D. Number of production runs

4. Production Department 1 (PD1) and Production Department 2 (PD2) had factory overhead budgets of $26,000 and $48,000, respectively. Each department was budgeted for 5,000 direct labor hours of production activity. Product T required 5 direct labor hours in PD1 and 2 direct labor hours in PD2. What is the factory overhead cost associated with Product T, assuming that factory overhead is allocated using the multiple production rate method?

A. $26.00
B. $40.40
C. $45.20
D. $58.40

5. The following activity rates are associated with moving rail cars by train: $4 per gross ton mile; $50 per rail car switch; $200 per rail car. A train with 20 rail cars traveled 100 miles. Each rail car carried 10 tons of product. Each rail car was switched two times. What is the total cost of moving this train?

A. $5,400
B. $10,000
C. $44,100
D. $86,000

Answers provided after Problem. Need more practice? Find additional multiple-choice questions, exercises, and problems in CengageNOWv2.

Exercises

SHOW ME HOW

1. Single plantwide factory overhead rate
Obj. 2

The total factory overhead for Diva-nation Inc. is budgeted for the year at $180,000. Diva-nation manufactures two types of men's pants: jeans and khakis. The jeans and khakis each require 0.10 direct labor hour for manufacture. Each product is budgeted for 20,000 units of production for the year. Determine (A) the total number of budgeted direct labor hours for the year, (B) the single plantwide factory overhead rate, and (C) the factory overhead allocated per unit for each product using the single plantwide factory overhead rate.

SHOW ME HOW

2. Multiple production department factory overhead rates
Obj. 3

The total factory overhead for Diva-nation is budgeted for the year at $180,000, divided into two departments: Cutting, $60,000, and Sewing, $120,000. Diva-nation manufactures two types of men's pants: jeans and khakis. The jeans require 0.04 direct labor hour in Cutting and 0.06 direct labor hour in Sewing. The khakis require 0.06 direct labor hour in Cutting and 0.04 direct labor hour in Sewing. Each product is budgeted for 20,000 units of production for the year. Determine (A) the total number of budgeted direct labor hours for the year in each department, (B) the departmental factory overhead rates for both departments, and (C) the factory overhead allocated per unit for each product using the department factory overhead allocation rates.

SHOW ME HOW

3. Activity-based costing: factory overhead costs   Obj. 4

The total factory overhead for Diva-nation is budgeted for the year at $180,000, divided into four activities: cutting, $18,000; sewing, $36,000; setup, $96,000; and inspection, $30,000. Diva-nation manufactures two types of men's pants: jeans and khakis. The activity-base usage quantities for each product by each activity are as follows:

	Cutting	Sewing	Setup	Inspection
Jeans	800 dlh	1,200 dlh	1,400 setups	3,000 inspections
Khakis	1,200	800	1,000	2,000
	2,000 dlh	2,000 dlh	2,400 setups	5,000 inspections

Each product is budgeted for 20,000 units of production for the year. Determine (A) the activity rates for each activity and (B) the activity-based factory overhead per unit for each product.

SHOW ME HOW

4. Activity-based costing: selling and administrative expenses   Obj. 5

Fancy Feet Company manufactures and sells shoes. Fancy Feet uses activity-based costing to determine the cost of the sales order processing and the shipping activity. The sales order processing activity has an activity rate of $12 per sales order, and the shipping activity has an activity rate of $20 per shipment. Fancy Feet sold 27,500 units of walking shoes, which consisted of 5,000 orders and 1,400 shipments. Determine (A) the total activity cost and (B) the per-unit sales order processing and shipping activity cost for walking shoes.

SHOW ME HOW

5. Activity-based costing for a service business   Obj. 6

Draper Bank uses activity-based costing to determine the cost of servicing customers. There are three activity pools: teller transaction processing, check processing, and ATM transaction processing. The activity rates associated with each activity pool are $3.50 per teller transaction, $0.12 per canceled check, and $0.10 per ATM transaction. Draper Bank had 12 teller transactions, 100 canceled checks, and 20 ATM transactions during the month. Determine the total monthly activity-based cost for Draper Bank during the month.

Answers provided after Problem. Need more practice? Find additional multiple-choice questions, exercises, and problems in CengageNOWv2.

Problem

Hammer Company plans to use activity-based costing to determine its product costs. It presently uses a single plantwide factory overhead rate for allocating factory overhead to products, based on direct labor hours. The total factory overhead cost is as follows:

Department	Factory Overhead
Production Support	$1,225,000
Production (factory overhead only)	175,000
Total cost	$1,400,000

The company determined that it performed four major activities in the Production Support Department. These activities, along with their budgeted activity costs, are as follows:

Production Support Activities	Budgeted Activity Cost
Setup	$ 428,750
Production control	245,000
Quality control	183,750
Materials management	367,500
Total	$1,225,000

Hammer estimated the following activity-base usage and units produced for each of its three products:

Products	Number of Units	Direct Labor Hrs.	Setups	Production Orders	Inspections	Material Requisitions
LCD TV...................	10,000	25,000	80	80	35	320
Tablet....................	2,000	10,000	40	40	40	400
Smartphone.............	50,000	140,000	5	5	0	30
Total cost	62,000	175,000	125	125	75	750

Instructions

1. Determine the factory overhead cost per unit for the LCD TV, tablet, and smartphone under the single plantwide factory overhead rate method. Use direct labor hours as the activity base.

2. Determine the factory overhead cost per unit for the LCD TV, tablet, and smartphone under activity-based costing. (Round to two decimal places.)

3. Which method provides more accurate product costing? Why?

Need more practice? Find additional multiple-choice questions, exercises, and problems in CengageNOWv2.

Answers

Multiple-Choice Questions

1. **B** Activity-based costing provides accurate product costs, which can be used for strategic product profitability analysis. The single plantwide factory overhead rate method (answer A) can distort the individual product costs under a variety of reasonable conditions. The multiple production department factory overhead rate method will lead to less (not more) distortion than the single plantwide factory overhead rate method (answer C). Generally accepted accounting principles do not require activity-based costing methods for inventory valuation (answer D).

2. **C** The single plantwide factory overhead rate is $34 per hour (answer A), determined as $680,000 ÷ 20,000 hours. This rate is multiplied by 6 direct labor hours per unit of Product M to determine the correct overhead per unit of $204 (answer C). The total overhead should be used in the numerator in determining the overhead rate, not just power and indirect labor (answer B) or equipment depreciation (answer D).

3. **D** The number of production runs best relates the activity cost of setup to the products. Number of inspections (answer A), direct labor hours (answer B), and direct machine hours (answer C) will likely have very little logical association with the costs incurred in setting up production runs.

4. **C** PD1 rate: $26,000 ÷ 5,000 dlh = $5.20 per dlh
   PD2 rate: $48,000 ÷ 5,000 dlh = $9.60 per dlh
   Product T: (5 dlh × $5.20) + (2 dlh × $9.60) = $45.20

5. **D** (100 miles × 20 cars × 10 tons × $4) + ($200 × 20 cars) + (20 cars × 2 switches × $50)
   = $80,000 + $4,000 + $2,000 = $86,000

Exercises

1.

A. Jeans: 20,000 units × 0.10 direct labor hour = 2,000 direct labor hours
   Khakis: 20,000 units × 0.10 direct labor hour = 2,000
                                                    4,000 direct labor hours

B. Single plantwide factory overhead rate: $180,000 ÷ 4,000 dlh = $45 per dlh

C. Jeans: $45 per direct labor hour × 0.10 dlh per unit = $4.50 per unit
   Khakis: $45 per direct labor hour × 0.10 dlh per unit = $4.50 per unit

2.

A. Cutting: (20,000 jeans × 0.04 dlh) + (20,000 khakis × 0.06 dlh)
            = 2,000 direct labor hours
   Sewing: (20,000 jeans × 0.06 dlh) + (20,000 khakis × 0.04 dlh)
            = 2,000 direct labor hours

B. Cutting Department rate: $60,000 ÷ 2,000 dlh = $30 per dlh
   Sewing Department rate: $120,000 ÷ 2,000 dlh = $60 per dlh

C. Jeans: Cutting Department 0.04 dlh × $30 = $1.20
           Sewing Department 0.06 dlh × $60 =   3.60
           Total factory overhead per pair of jeans $4.80

   Khakis: Cutting Department 0.06 dlh × $30 = $1.80
           Sewing Department 0.04 dlh × $60 =   2.40
           Total factory overhead per pair of khakis $4.20

3.

A. Cutting: $18,000 ÷ 2,000 direct labor hours = $9.00 per dlh
   Sewing: $36,000 ÷ 2,000 direct labor hours = $18.00 per dlh
   Setup: $96,000 ÷ 2,400 setups = $40.00 per setup
   Inspection: $30,000 ÷ 5,000 inspections = $6.00 per inspection

B.

| | Jeans | | | Khakis | | |
Activity	Activity-Base Usage	× Activity Rate =	Activity Cost	Activity-Base Usage	× Activity Rate =	Activity Cost
Cutting	800 dlh	$ 9.00 per dlh	$ 7,200	1,200 dlh	$ 9.00 per dlh	$10,800
Sewing	1,200 dlh	$18.00 per dlh	21,600	800 dlh	$18.00 per dlh	14,400
Setup	1,400 setups	$40.00 per setup	56,000	1,000 setups	$40.00 per setup	40,000
Inspections	3,000 insp.	$ 6.00 per insp.	18,000	2,000 insp.	$ 6.00 per insp.	12,000
Total			$102,800			$77,200
÷ Budgeted items			÷ 20,000			÷20,000
Factory overhead per unit			$ 5.14			$ 3.86

4.

A. Sales order processing activity: 5,000 orders × $12 per order = $60,000
   Shipping activity: 1,400 shipments × $20 per shipment =   28,000
   Total activity cost $88,000

B. $3.20 per unit ($88,000 ÷ 27,500 units)

5.

Teller transaction processing	$42.00	(12 transactions × $3.50)
Check processing	12.00	(100 checks × $0.12)
ATM transaction processing	2.00	(20 transactions × $0.10)
Total activity cost	$56.00	

Need more help? Watch step-by-step videos of how to compute answers to these Exercises in CengageNOWv2.

Problem

1. Single Plantwide Factory Overhead Rate $= \dfrac{\$1,400,000}{175,000 \text{ direct labor hours}}$

$= \$8$ per direct labor hour

Factory overhead cost per unit:

	LCD TV	Tablet	Smartphone
Number of direct labor hours....................	25,000	10,000	140,000
Single plantwide factory overhead rate..........	× $8 per dlh	× $8 per dlh	× $ 8 per dlh
Total factory overhead	$ 200,000	$ 80,000	$ 1,120,000
Number of units	÷ 10,000	÷ 2,000	÷ 50,000
Factory overhead cost per unit	$ 20.00	$ 40.00	$ 22.40

2. Under activity-based costing, an activity rate must be determined for each activity pool:

Activity	Budgeted Activity Cost	÷	Total Activity-Base Usage	=	Activity Rate
Setup......................	$428,750	÷	125 setups	=	$3,430 per setup
Production control.........	$245,000	÷	125 production orders	=	$1,960 per production order
Quality control.............	$183,750	÷	75 inspections	=	$2,450 per inspection
Materials management	$367,500	÷	750 requisitions	=	$ 490 per requisition
Production	$175,000	÷	175,000 direct labor hours	=	$ 1 per direct labor hour

These activity rates can be used to determine the activity-based factory overhead cost per unit as follows:

LCD TV

Activity	Activity-Base Usage	×	Activity Rate	=	Activity Cost
Setup	80 setups	×	$3,430	=	$274,400
Production control...........	80 production orders	×	1,960	=	156,800
Quality control..............	35 inspections	×	2,450	=	85,750
Materials management	320 requisitions	×	490	=	156,800
Production	25,000 direct labor hrs.	×	1	=	25,000
Total factory overhead					$698,750
Unit volume					÷ 10,000
Factory overhead cost per unit..............					$ 69.88

Tablet

Activity	Activity-Base Usage	×	Activity Rate	=	Activity Cost
Setup	40 setups	×	$3,430	=	$137,200
Production control...........	40 production orders	×	1,960	=	78,400
Quality control..............	40 inspections	×	2,450	=	98,000
Materials management	400 requisitions	×	490	=	196,000
Production	10,000 direct labor hrs.	×	1	=	10,000
Total factory overhead					$519,600
Unit volume					÷ 2,000
Factory overhead cost per unit..............					$ 259.80

Smartphone

Activity	Activity-Base Usage	×	Activity Rate	=	Activity Cost
Setup	5 setups	×	$3,430	=	$ 17,150
Production control..........	5 production orders	×	1,960	=	9,800
Quality control..............	0 inspections	×	2,450	=	0
Materials management	30 requisitions	×	490	=	14,700
Production	140,000 direct labor hrs.	×	1	=	140,000
Total factory overhead					$181,650
Unit volume					÷ 50,000
Factory overhead cost per unit..............					$ 3.63

3. Activity-based costing is more accurate, compared to the single plantwide factory overhead rate method. Activity-based costing properly shows that the smartphone is actually less expensive to make, while the other two products are more expensive to make. The reason is that the single plantwide factory overhead rate method fails to account for activity costs correctly. The setup, production control, quality control, and materials management activities are all performed on products in amounts that are proportionately different than their volumes. For example, the tablet requires many of these activities relative to its actual unit volume. The tablet requires 40 setups over a volume of 2,000 units (average production run size = 50 units), while the smartphone has only 5 setups over 50,000 units (average production run size = 10,000 units). Thus, the tablet requires greater support costs relative to the smartphone.

The smartphone requires minimum activity support because it is scheduled in large batches and requires no inspections (has high quality) and few requisitions. The other two products exhibit the opposite characteristics.

Discussion Questions

1. Why would management be concerned about the accuracy of product costs?

2. Why would a manufacturing company with multiple production departments still prefer to use a single plantwide overhead rate?

3. How do the multiple production department and the single plantwide factory overhead rate methods differ?

4. Under what two conditions would the multiple production department factory overhead rate method provide more accurate product costs than the single plantwide factory overhead rate method?

5. How does activity-based costing differ from the multiple production department factory overhead rate method?

6. Shipping, selling, marketing, sales order processing, return processing, and advertising activities can be related to products by using activity-based costing. Would allocating these activities to products for financial statement reporting be acceptable according to GAAP?

7. What would happen to net income if the activities noted in Discussion Question 6 were allocated to products for financial statement reporting and the inventory increased?

8. Under what circumstances might the activity-based costing method provide more accurate product costs than the multiple production department factory overhead rate method?

9. When might activity-based costing be preferred over using a relative amount of product sales in allocating selling and administrative expenses to products?

10. How can activity-based costing be used in service companies?

Basic Exercises

SHOW ME HOW

BE 4-1 Single plantwide factory overhead rate   Obj. 2

The total factory overhead for Bardot Marine Company is budgeted for the year at $600,000. Bardot Marine manufactures two types of boats: speedboats and bass boats. The speedboat and bass boat each require 12 direct labor hours for manufacture. Each product is budgeted for 250 units of production for the year. Determine (A) the total number of budgeted direct labor hours for the year, (B) the single plantwide factory overhead rate, and (C) the factory overhead allocated per unit for each product using the single plantwide factory overhead rate.

SHOW ME HOW

BE 4-2 Multiple production department factory overhead rates   Obj. 3

The total factory overhead for Bardot Marine Company is budgeted for the year at $600,000 divided into two departments: Fabrication, $420,000, and Assembly, $180,000. Bardot Marine manufactures two types of boats: speedboats and bass boats. The speedboats require 8 direct labor hours in Fabrication and 4 direct labor hours in Assembly. The bass boats require 4 direct labor hours in Fabrication and 8 direct labor hours in Assembly. Each product is budgeted for 250 units of production for the year. Determine (A) the total number of budgeted direct labor hours for the year in each department, (B) the departmental factory overhead rates for both departments, and (C) the factory overhead allocated per unit for each product using the department factory overhead allocation rates.

SHOW ME HOW

BE 4-3 Activity-based costing: factory overhead costs   Obj. 4

The total factory overhead for Bardot Marine Company is budgeted for the year at $600,000, divided into four activities: fabrication, $204,000; assembly, $105,000; setup, $156,000; and inspection, $135,000. Bardot Marine manufactures two types of boats: speedboats and bass boats. The activity-base usage quantities for each product by each activity are as follows:

	Fabrication	Assembly	Setup	Inspection
Speedboat	2,000 dlh	1,000 dlh	300 setups	1,100 inspections
Bass boat	1,000	2,000	100	400
	3,000 dlh	3,000 dlh	400 setups	1,500 inspections

Each product is budgeted for 250 units of production for the year. Determine (A) the activity rates for each activity and (B) the activity-based factory overhead per unit for each product.

SHOW ME HOW

BE 4-4 Activity-based costing: selling and administrative expenses   Obj. 5

Jungle Junior Company manufactures and sells outdoor play equipment. Jungle Junior uses activity-based costing to determine the cost of the sales order processing and the customer return activity. The sales order processing activity has an activity rate of $20 per sales order, and the customer return activity has an activity rate of $100 per return. Jungle Junior sold 2,500 swing sets, which consisted of 750 orders and 80 returns. Determine (A) the total and (B) the per-unit sales order processing and customer return activity cost for swing sets.

SHOW ME HOW

BE 4-5 Activity-based costing for a service business   Obj. 6

Sterling Hotel uses activity-based costing to determine the cost of servicing customers. There are three activity pools: guest check-in, room cleaning, and meal service. The activity rates associated with each activity pool are $8 per guest check-in, $25 per room cleaning, and $4 per served meal (not including food). Ginny Campbell visited the hotel for a three-night stay. Campbell had three meals in the hotel during her visit. Determine the total activity-based cost for Campbell's visit.

Exercises

EX 4-1   Single plantwide factory overhead rate
Obj. 2

Nixon Machine Parts Inc.'s Fabrication Department incurred $560,000 of factory overhead cost in producing gears and sprockets. The two products consumed a total of 8,000 direct machine hours. Of that amount, sprockets consumed 5,150 direct machine hours.

Determine the total amount of factory overhead that should be allocated to sprockets using machine hours as the allocation base.

EX 4-2   Single plantwide factory overhead rate
Obj. 2

✔ A. $380 per direct labor hour

Mozart Music Inc. makes three musical instruments: trumpets, tubas, and trombones. The budgeted factory overhead cost is $3,469,400. Factory overhead is allocated to the three products on the basis of direct labor hours. The products have the following budgeted production volume and direct labor hours per unit:

	Budgeted Production Volume	Direct Labor Hours per Unit
Trumpets	4,000 units	1.2
Tubas	1,200	0.9
Trombones	2,500	1.3

A.   Determine the single plantwide factory overhead rate.

B.   Use the factory overhead rate in (A) to determine the amount of total and per-unit factory overhead allocated to each of the three products.

EX 4-3   Single plantwide factory overhead rate
Obj. 2

✔ A. $60 per processing hour

Salty Sensations Snacks Company manufactures three types of snack foods: tortilla chips, potato chips, and pretzels. The company has budgeted the following costs for the upcoming period:

Factory depreciation	$ 31,360
Indirect labor	78,400
Factory electricity	7,840
Indirect materials	35,400
Selling expenses	25,000
Administrative expenses	18,000
Total costs	$196,000

Factory overhead is allocated to the three products on the basis of processing hours. The products had the following production budget and processing hours per case:

	Budgeted Volume (Cases)	Processing Hours per Case
Tortilla chips	4,000	0.20
Potato chips	5,000	0.15
Pretzels	2,500	0.40
Total	11,500	

A.   Determine the single plantwide factory overhead rate.

B.   Use the factory overhead rate in (A) to determine the amount of total and per-case factory overhead allocated to each of the three products under generally accepted accounting principles.

EX 4-4 Product costs and product profitability reports, using a single plantwide factory overhead rate

Obj. 2

✔ C. Pistons gross profit, $47,500

SHOW ME HOW

EXCEL TEMPLATE

Elliott Engines Inc. produces three products—pistons, valves, and cams—for the heavy equipment industry. Elliott Engines has a very simple production process and product line and uses a single plantwide factory overhead rate to allocate overhead to the three products. The factory overhead rate is based on direct labor hours. Information about the three products for 20Y2 is as follows:

	Budgeted Volume (Units)	Direct Labor Hours per Unit	Price per Unit	Direct Materials per Unit
Pistons	5,000	0.50	$45	$ 8
Valves	12,500	0.30	17	3
Cams	1,500	0.20	60	40

The estimated direct labor rate is $30 per direct labor hour. Beginning and ending inventories are negligible and are, thus, assumed to be zero. The budgeted factory overhead for Elliott Engines is $163,750.

A. Determine the plantwide factory overhead rate.

B. Determine the factory overhead and direct labor cost per unit for each product.

C. Use the information provided to construct a budgeted gross profit report by product line for the year ended December 31, 20Y2. Include the gross profit as a percent of sales in the last line of your report, rounded to one decimal place.

D. ━━━▶ What does the report in (C) indicate to you?

EX 4-5 Multiple production department factory overhead rate method

Obj. 3

✔ B. Small glove, $9.20 per unit

SHOW ME HOW

EXCEL TEMPLATE

Performance Gloves, Inc. produces three sizes of sports gloves: small, medium, and large. A glove pattern is first stenciled onto leather in the Pattern Department. The stenciled patterns are then sent to the Cut and Sew Department, where the glove is cut and sewed together. Performance Gloves uses the multiple production department factory overhead rate method of allocating factory overhead costs. Its factory overhead costs were budgeted as follows:

Pattern Department overhead	$ 216,000
Cut and Sew Department overhead	960,000
Total	$1,176,000

The direct labor estimated for each production department was as follows:

Pattern Department	36,000 direct labor hours
Cut and Sew Department	60,000
Total	96,000 direct labor hours

Direct labor hours are used to allocate the production department overhead to the products. The direct labor hours per unit for each product for each production department were obtained from the engineering records as follows:

Production Departments	Small Glove	Medium Glove	Large Glove
Pattern Department	0.20	0.24	0.30
Cut and Sew Department	0.50	0.60	0.72
Direct labor hours per unit	0.70	0.84	1.02

A. Determine the two production department factory overhead rates.

B. Use the two production department factory overhead rates to determine the factory overhead per unit for each product.

EX 4-6 Single plantwide and multiple production department factory overhead rate methods and product cost distortion

Obj. 2, 3

✔ B. Residential motor, $330 per unit

Pineapple Motor Company manufactures two types of specialty electric motors, a commercial motor and a residential motor, through two production departments, Assembly and Testing. Presently, the company uses a single plantwide factory overhead rate for allocating factory overhead to the two products. However, management is considering using the multiple production department factory overhead rate method. The following factory overhead was budgeted for Pineapple:

Assembly Department	$240,000
Testing Department	750,000
Total	$990,000

Direct machine hours were estimated as follows:

Assembly Department	3,000 hours
Testing Department	6,000
Total	9,000 hours

In addition, the direct machine hours (dmh) used to produce a unit of each product in each department were determined from engineering records, as follows:

	Commercial	Residential
Assembly Department	1.5 dmh	1.0 dmh
Testing Department	3.0	2.0
Total machine hours per unit	4.5 dmh	3.0 dmh

A. Determine the per-unit factory overhead allocated to the commercial and residential motors under the single plantwide factory overhead rate method, using direct machine hours as the allocation base.

B. Determine the per-unit factory overhead allocated to the commercial and residential motors under the multiple production department factory overhead rate method, using direct machine hours as the allocation base for each department.

C. ━━━▶ Recommend to management a product costing approach, based on your analyses in (A) and (B). Support your recommendation.

EX 4-7 Single plantwide and multiple production department factory overhead rate methods and product cost distortion

Obj. 2, 3

✔ B. Diesel engine, $370 per unit

The management of Firebolt Industries Inc. manufactures gasoline and diesel engines through two production departments, Fabrication and Assembly. Management needs accurate product cost information in order to guide product strategy. Presently, the company uses a single plantwide factory overhead rate for allocating factory overhead to the two products. However, management is considering the multiple production department factory overhead rate method. The following factory overhead was budgeted for Firebolt:

Fabrication Department factory overhead	$550,000
Assembly Department factory overhead	250,000
Total	$800,000

Direct labor hours were estimated as follows:

Fabrication Department	5,000 hours
Assembly Department	5,000
Total	10,000 hours

In addition, the direct labor hours (dlh) used to produce a unit of each product in each department were determined from engineering records, as follows:

Production Departments	Gasoline Engine	Diesel Engine
Fabrication Department	3.0 dlh	2.0 dlh
Assembly Department	2.0	3.0
Direct labor hours per unit	5.0 dlh	5.0 dlh

A. Determine the per-unit factory overhead allocated to the gasoline and diesel engines under the single plantwide factory overhead rate method, using direct labor hours as the activity base.

B. Determine the per-unit factory overhead allocated to the gasoline and diesel engines under the multiple production department factory overhead rate method, using direct labor hours as the activity base for each department.

C. ➤ Recommend to management a product costing approach, based on your analyses in (A) and (B). Support your recommendation.

EX 4-8 Identifying activity bases in an activity-based cost system   Obj. 4

Select Foods Inc. uses activity-based costing to determine product costs. For each activity listed in the left column, match an appropriate activity base from the right column. You may use items in the activity-base list more than once or not at all.

Activity	Activity Base
Accounting reports	Engineering change orders
Customer return processing	Kilowatt hours used
Electric power	Number of accounting reports
Human resources	Number of customers
Inventory control	Number of customer orders
Invoice and collecting	Number of customer returns
Machine depreciation	Number of employees
Materials handling	Number of inspections
Order shipping	Number of inventory transactions
Payroll	Number of machine hours
Production control	Number of material moves
Production setup	Number of payroll checks processed
Purchasing	Number of production orders
Quality control	Number of purchase orders
Sales order processing	Number of sales orders
	Number of setups

EX 4-9 Product costs using activity rates   Obj. 4

✔ B. $405,000

Nozama.com Inc. sells consumer electronics over the Internet. For the next period, the budgeted cost of the sales order processing activity is $540,000 and 60,000 sales orders are estimated to be processed.

A. Determine the activity rate of the sales order processing activity.

B. Determine the amount of sales order processing cost that Nozama.com would receive if it had 45,000 sales orders.

EX 4-10 Product costs using activity rates   Obj. 4

✔ Treadmill activity cost per unit, $82.10

Atlas Enterprises Inc. manufactures elliptical exercise machines and treadmills. The products are produced in its Fabrication and Assembly production departments. In addition to production activities, several other activities are required to produce the two products. These activities and their associated activity rates are as follows:

EXCEL TEMPLATE

Activity	Activity Rate
Fabrication	$28 per machine hour
Assembly	$20 per direct labor hour
Setup	$75 per setup
Inspecting	$30 per inspection
Production scheduling	$12 per production order
Purchasing	$ 8 per purchase order

(Continued)

The activity-base usage quantities and units produced for each product were as follows:

Activity Base	Elliptical Machines	Treadmill
Machine hours	700	600
Direct labor hours	182	64
Setups	20	15
Inspections	10	16
Production orders	30	20
Purchase orders	56	75
Units produced	400	250

Use the activity rate and usage information to calculate the total activity cost and activity cost per unit for each product.

EX 4-11   Activity rates and product costs using activity-based costing   Obj. 4

✔ B. Dining room lighting fixtures, $167.40 per unit

EXCEL TEMPLATE

Garfield Inc. manufactures entry and dining room lighting fixtures. Five activities are used in manufacturing the fixtures. These activities and their associated budgeted activity costs and activity bases are as follows:

Activity	Budgeted Activity Cost	Activity Base
Casting	$560,000	Machine hours
Assembly	75,000	Direct labor hours
Inspecting	30,000	Number of inspections
Setup	18,750	Number of setups
Materials handling	14,000	Number of loads

Corporate records were obtained to estimate the amount of activity to be used by the two products. The estimated activity-base usage quantities and units produced follow:

Activity Base	Entry	Dining	Total
Machine hours	7,500	12,500	20,000
Direct labor hours	2,000	3,000	5,000
Number of inspections	500	250	750
Number of setups	150	100	250
Number of loads	400	300	700
Units produced	5,000	2,500	7,500

A. Determine the activity rate for each activity.
B. Use the activity rates in (A) to determine the total and per-unit activity costs associated with each product.

EX 4-12   Activity cost pools, activity rates, and product costs using   Obj. 4
activity-based costing

✔ B. Ovens, $93.80 per unit

EXCEL TEMPLATE

Caldwell Home Appliances Inc. is estimating the activity cost associated with producing ovens and refrigerators. The indirect labor can be traced into four separate activity pools, based on time records provided by the employees. The budgeted activity cost and activity-base information are provided as follows:

Activity	Activity Pool Cost	Activity Base
Procurement	$ 12,600	Number of purchase orders
Scheduling	90,000	Number of production orders
Materials handling	11,000	Number of moves
Product development	50,000	Number of engineering changes
Total cost	$163,600	

The estimated activity-base usage and unit information for two product lines was determined as follows:

	Number of Purchase Orders	Number of Production Orders	Number of Moves	Number of Engineering Change Orders	Units
Ovens	400	800	300	80	1,000
Refrigerators	300	400	200	120	500
Totals	700	1,200	500	200	1,500

A. Determine the activity rate for each activity cost pool.

B. Determine the activity-based cost per unit of each product.

EX 4-13 Activity-based costing and product cost distortion

Obj. 2, 4

✔ C. Cell phones, $1.68 per unit

EXCEL TEMPLATE

Digital Storage Concept Inc. is considering a change to activity-based product costing. The company produces two products, cell phones and tablet PCs, in a single production department. The production department is estimated to require 3,750 direct labor hours. The total indirect labor is budgeted to be $375,000.

Time records from indirect labor employees revealed that they spent 40% of their time setting up production runs and 60% of their time supporting actual production.

The following information about cell phones and tablet PCs was determined from the corporate records:

	Number of Setups	Direct Labor Hours	Units
Cell phones	600	1,875	93,750
Tablet PCs	1,400	1,875	93,750
Total	2,000	3,750	187,500

A. Determine the indirect labor cost per unit allocated to cell phones and tablet PCs under a single plantwide factory overhead rate system using the direct labor hours as the allocation base.

B. Determine the budgeted activity costs and activity rates for the indirect labor under activity-based costing. Assume two activities—one for setup and the other for production support.

C. Determine the activity cost per unit for indirect labor allocated to each product under activity-based costing.

D. ▬▬▬▬▶ Why are the per-unit allocated costs in (A) different from the per-unit activity cost assigned to the products in (C)?

EX 4-14 Multiple production department factory overhead rate method

Obj. 3

✔ B. Blender, $18.20 per unit

EXCEL TEMPLATE

Four Finger Appliance Company manufactures small kitchen appliances. The product line consists of blenders and toaster ovens. Four Finger Appliance presently uses the multiple production department factory overhead rate method. The factory overhead is as follows:

Assembly Department	$186,000
Test and Pack Department	120,000
Total	$306,000

The direct labor information for the production of 7,500 units of each product is as follows:

	Assembly Department	Test and Pack Department
Blender	750 dlh	2,250 dlh
Toaster oven	2,250	750
Total	3,000 dlh	3,000 dlh

(Continued)

Four Finger Appliance used direct labor hours to allocate production department factory overhead to products.

A. Determine the two production department factory overhead rates.

B. Determine the total factory overhead and the factory overhead per unit allocated to each product.

EX 4-15 Activity-based costing and product cost distortion   Obj. 4

✔ B. Blender, $23.60
per unit

EXCEL TEMPLATE

The management of Four Finger Appliance Company in Exercise 14 has asked you to use activity-based costing instead of direct labor hours to allocate factory overhead costs to the two products. You have determined that $81,000 of factory overhead from each of the production departments can be associated with setup activity ($162,000 in total). Company records indicate that blenders required 135 setups, while the toaster ovens required only 45 setups. Each product has a production volume of 7,500 units.

A. Determine the three activity rates (assembly, test and pack, and setup).

B. Determine the total factory overhead and factory overhead per unit allocated to each product using the activity rates in (A).

EX 4-16 Single plantwide rate and activity-based costing   Obj. 2, 4

✔ A. Low, Col. C,
93.5%

EXCEL TEMPLATE   REAL WORLD

Whirlpool Corporation conducted an activity-based costing study of its Evansville, Indiana, plant in order to identify its most profitable products. Assume that we select three representative refrigerators (out of 333): one low-, one medium-, and one high-volume refrigerator. Additionally, we assume the following activity-base information for each of the three refrigerators:

Three Representative Refrigerators	Number of Machine Hours	Number of Setups	Number of Sales Orders	Number of Units
Refrigerator—Low Volume	24	14	38	160
Refrigerator—Medium Volume	225	13	88	1,500
Refrigerator—High Volume	900	9	120	6,000

Prior to conducting the study, the factory overhead allocation was based on a single machine hour rate. The machine hour rate was $200 per hour. After conducting the activity-based costing study, assume that three activities were used to allocate the factory overhead. The new activity rate information is assumed to be as follows:

	Machining Activity	Setup Activity	Sales Order Processing Activity
Activity rate	$160	$240	$55

A. Complete the following table, using the single machine hour rate to determine the per-unit factory overhead for each refrigerator (Column A) and the three activity-based rates to determine the activity-based factory overhead per unit (Column B). Finally, compute the percent change in per-unit allocation from the single to activity-based rate methods (Column C). (Round per-unit overhead to two decimal places and percents to one decimal place.)

Product Volume Class	Column A Single Rate Overhead Allocation per Unit	Column B ABC Overhead Allocation per Unit	Column C Percent Change in Allocation (Col. B – Col. A)/Col. A
Low			
Medium			
High			

B. Why is the traditional overhead rate per machine hour greater under the single rate method than under the activity-based method?

C. ▬▬▬▶ Interpret Column C in your table from part (A).

EX 4-17 Evaluating selling and administrative cost allocations   Obj. 5

Gordon Gecco Furniture Company has two major product lines with the following characteristics:

- Commercial office furniture: Few large orders, little advertising support, shipments in full truckloads, and low handling complexity
- Home office furniture: Many small orders, large advertising support, shipments in partial truckloads, and high handling complexity

The company produced the following profitability report for management:

Gordon Gecco Furniture Company
Product Profitability Report
For the Year Ended December 31

	Commercial Office Furniture	Home Office Furniture	Total
Revenue	$5,600,000	$2,800,000	$8,400,000
Cost of goods sold	2,100,000	980,000	3,080,000
Gross profit	$3,500,000	$1,820,000	$5,320,000
Selling and administrative expenses	1,680,000	840,000	2,520,000
Income from operations	$1,820,000	$ 980,000	$2,800,000

The selling and administrative expenses are allocated to the products on the basis of relative sales dollars.

➤ Evaluate the accuracy of this report and recommend an alternative approach.

EX 4-18 Construct and interpret a product profitability report, allocating selling and administrative expenses   Obj. 5

✔ B. Generators operating profit-to-sales, 24.29%

SHOW ME HOW

Naper Inc. manufactures power equipment. Naper has two primary products—generators and air compressors. The following report was prepared by the controller for Naper's senior marketing management for the year ended December 31:

	Generators	Air Compressors	Total
Revenue	$4,200,000	$3,000,000	$7,200,000
Cost of goods sold	2,940,000	2,100,000	5,040,000
Gross profit	$1,260,000	$ 900,000	$2,160,000
Selling and administrative expenses			610,000
Income from operations			$1,550,000

The marketing management team was concerned that the selling and administrative expenses were not traced to the products. Marketing management believed that some products consumed larger amounts of selling and administrative expense than did other products. To verify this, the controller was asked to prepare a complete product profitability report, using activity-based costing.

The controller determined that selling and administrative expenses consisted of two activities: sales order processing and post-sale customer service. The controller was able to determine the activity base and activity rate for each activity, as follows:

Activity	Activity Base	Activity Rate
Sales order processing	Sales orders	$ 65 per sales order
Post-sale customer service	Service requests	$200 per customer service request

The controller determined the following activity-base usage information about each product:

	Generators	Air Compressors
Number of sales orders	3,000	4,000
Number of service requests	225	550

(Continued)

A. Determine the activity cost of each product for sales order processing and post-sale customer service activities.

B. Use the information in (A) to prepare a complete product profitability report dated for the year ended December 31. Compute the gross profit to sales and the income from operations to sales percentages for each product. (Round to two decimal places.)

C. ━━━▶ Interpret the product profitability report. How should management respond to the report?

EX 4-19 Activity-based costing and customer profitability   Obj. 5

✔ A. Customer 1,
Income from
operations after
customer service
activities, $34,075

SHOW ME HOW

Schneider Electric manufactures power distribution equipment for commercial customers, such as hospitals and manufacturers. Activity-based costing was used to determine customer profitability. Customer service activities were assigned to individual customers, using the following assumed customer service activities, activity base, and activity rate:

Customer Service Activity	Activity Base	Activity Rate
Bid preparation	Number of bid requests	$400 per request
Shipment	Number of shipments	$ 80 per shipment
Support standard items	Number of standard items ordered	$ 25 per std. item
Support nonstandard items	Number of nonstandard items ordered	$150 per nonstd. item

Assume that the company had the following gross profit information for three representative customers:

	Customer 1	Customer 2	Customer 3
Revenue	$120,000	$200,000	$160,000
Cost of goods sold	76,800	110,000	83,200
Gross profit	$ 43,200	$ 90,000	$ 76,800
Gross profit as a percent of sales	36%	45%	48%

The administrative records indicated that the activity-base usage quantities for each customer were as follows:

Activity Base	Customer 1	Customer 2	Customer 3
Number of bid requests	14	38	55
Number of shipments	30	60	48
Number of standard items ordered	15	30	50
Number of nonstandard items ordered	5	70	80

A. Prepare a customer profitability report dated for the year ended December 31, 20Y8, showing (1) the income from operations after customer service activities, (2) the gross profit as a percent of sales, and (3) the income from operations after customer service activities as a percent of sales. Prepare the report with a column for each customer. Round percentages to the nearest whole percent.

B. ━━━▶ Interpret the report in part (A).

EX 4-20 Activity-based costing for a service company   Obj. 6

✔ A. Patient Umit,
$6,025

EXCEL TEMPLATE

Crosswinds Hospital plans to use activity-based costing to assign hospital indirect costs to the care of patients. The hospital has identified the following activities and activity rates for the hospital indirect costs:

Activity	Activity Rate
Room and meals	$ 240 per day
Radiology	$ 215 per image
Pharmacy	$ 50 per physician order
Chemistry lab	$ 80 per test
Operating room	$1,000 per operating room hour

The activity usage information associated with the two patients is as follows:

	Abel Putin	Cheryl Umit
Number of days	6 days	4 days
Number of images	4 images	3 images
Number of physician orders	6 orders	2 orders
Number of tests	5 tests	4 tests
Number of operating room hours	8 hours	4 hours

A. Determine the activity cost associated with each patient.

B. ➤ Why is the total activity cost different for the two patients?

EX 4-21 Activity-based costing for a service company   Obj. 5, 6

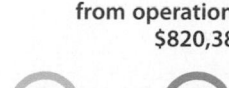

✔ A. Auto, Income
from operations,
$820,380

SHOW ME HOW   EXCEL TEMPLATE

Safety First Insurance Company carries three major lines of insurance: auto, workers' compensation, and homeowners. The company has prepared the following report:

Safety First Insurance Company
Product Profitability Report
For the Year Ended December 31

	Auto	Workers' Compensation	Homeowners
Premium revenue	$5,750,000	$6,240,000	$8,160,000
Estimated claims	4,312,500	4,680,000	6,120,000
Underwriting income	$1,437,500	$1,560,000	$2,040,000
Underwriting income as a percent of premium revenue	25%	25%	25%

Management is concerned that the administrative expenses may make some of the insurance lines unprofitable. However, the administrative expenses have not been allocated to the insurance lines. The controller has suggested that the administrative expenses could be assigned to the insurance lines using activity-based costing. The administrative expenses are comprised of five activities. The activities and their rates are as follows:

Activity	Activity Rates
New policy processing	$120 per new policy
Cancellation processing	$175 per cancellation
Claim audits	$320 per claim audit
Claim disbursements processing	$104 per disbursement
Premium collection processing	$ 24 per premium collected

Activity-base usage data for each line of insurance were retrieved from the corporate records as follows:

	Auto	Workers' Compensation	Homeowners
Number of new policies	1,320	1,500	4,080
Number of canceled policies	480	240	2,160
Number of audited claims	385	120	960
Number of claim disbursements	480	216	840
Number of premiums collected	8,400	1,800	15,000

A. Complete the product profitability report through the administrative activities. Determine the income from operations as a percent of premium revenue, rounded to the nearest whole percent.

B. ➤ Interpret the report.

Problems: Series A

PR 4-1A   Single plantwide factory overhead rate

Obj. 2

✔ 1. B. $48 per
machine hour

Orange County Chrome Company manufactures three chrome-plated products—automobile bumpers, valve covers, and wheels. These products are manufactured in two production departments (Stamping and Plating). The factory overhead for Orange County Chrome is $220,800.

The three products consume both machine hours and direct labor hours in the two production departments as follows:

	Direct Labor Hours	Machine Hours
Stamping Department		
Automobile bumpers	560	800
Valve covers	300	560
Wheels	340	600
	1,200	1,960
Plating Department		
Automobile bumpers	170	1,170
Valve covers	180	710
Wheels	175	760
	525	2,640
Total	1,725	4,600

Instructions

1. Determine the single plantwide factory overhead rate, using each of the following allocation bases: (A) direct labor hours and (B) machine hours.

2. Determine the product factory overhead costs, using (A) the direct labor hour plantwide factory overhead rate and (B) the machine hour plantwide factory overhead rate.

PR 4-2A   Multiple production department factory overhead rates

Obj. 3

✔ 2. Wheels,
$63,040

The management of Orange County Chrome Company, described in Problem 1A, now plans to use the multiple production department factory overhead rate method. The total factory overhead associated with each department is as follows:

Stamping Department	$115,200
Plating Department	105,600
Total	$220,800

Instructions

1. Determine the multiple production department factory overhead rates, using direct labor hours for the Stamping Department and machine hours for the Plating Department.

2. Determine the product factory overhead costs, using the multiple production department rates in (1).

PR 4-3A   Activity-based and department rate product costing and product cost distortions

Obj. 3, 4

✔ 2. Snowboards,
$390,000 and $65

EXCEL TEMPLATE

Black and Blue Sports Inc. manufactures two products: snowboards and skis. The factory overhead incurred is as follows:

Indirect labor	$507,000
Cutting Department	156,000
Finishing Department	192,000
Total	$855,000

The activity base associated with the two production departments is direct labor hours. The indirect labor can be assigned to two different activities as follows:

Activity	Budgeted Activity Cost	Activity Base
Production control	$237,000	Number of production runs
Materials handling	270,000	Number of moves
Total	$507,000	

The activity-base usage quantities and units produced for the two products follow:

	Number of Production Runs	Number of Moves	Direct Labor Hours—Cutting	Direct Labor Hours—Finishing	Units Produced
Snowboards	430	5,000	4,000	2,000	6,000
Skis	70	2,500	2,000	4,000	6,000
Total	500	7,500	6,000	6,000	12,000

Instructions

1. Determine the factory overhead rates under the multiple production department rate method. Assume that indirect labor is associated with the production departments, so that the total factory overhead is $315,000 and $540,000 for the Cutting and Finishing departments, respectively.

2. Determine the total and per-unit factory overhead costs allocated to each product, using the multiple production department overhead rates in (1).

3. Determine the activity rates, assuming that the indirect labor is associated with activities rather than with the production departments.

4. Determine the total and per-unit cost assigned to each product under activity-based costing.

5. ➡ Explain the difference in the per-unit overhead allocated to each product under the multiple production department factory overhead rate and activity-based costing methods.

PП 4-4A Activity-based product costing Obj. 4

✔ 2. Alpha total activity cost, $160,450

EXCEL TEMPLATE

Mello Manufacturing Company is a diversified manufacturer that manufactures three products (Alpha, Beta, and Omega) in a continuous production process. Senior management has asked the controller to conduct an activity-based costing study. The controller identified the amount of factory overhead required by the critical activities of the organization as follows:

Activity	Activity Cost Pool
Production	$259,200
Setup	55,000
Material handling	9,750
Inspection	60,000
Product engineering	123,200
Total	$507,150

The activity bases identified for each activity are as follows:

Activity	Activity Base
Production	Machine hours
Setup	Number of setups
Material handling	Number of parts
Inspection	Number of inspection hours
Product engineering	Number of engineering hours

(Continued)

The activity-base usage quantities and units produced for the three products were determined from corporate records and are as follows:

	Machine Hours	Number of Setups	Number of Parts	Number of Inspection Hours	Number of Engineering Hours	Units
Alpha	1,440	75	65	400	125	1,800
Beta	1,080	165	80	300	175	1,350
Omega	720	310	180	500	140	900
Total	3,240	550	325	1,200	440	4,050

Each product requires 40 minutes per unit of machine time.

Instructions

1. Determine the activity rate for each activity.

2. Determine the total and per-unit activity cost for all three products. Round to nearest cent.

3. ➤ Why aren't the activity unit costs equal across all three products since they require the same machine time per unit?

PR 4-5A   Allocating selling and administrative expenses using activity-based costing

Obj. 5

✔ 3. The Martin Group loss from operations, ($11,300)

SHOW ME HOW   EXCEL TEMPLATE

Arctic Air Inc. manufactures cooling units for commercial buildings. The price and cost of goods sold for each unit are as follows:

Price	$60,000 per unit
Cost of goods sold	28,000
Gross profit	$32,000 per unit

In addition, the company incurs selling and administrative expenses of $226,250. The company wishes to assign these costs to its three major customers, Gough Industries, Breen Inc., and The Martin Group. These expenses are related to three major nonmanufacturing activities: customer service, project bidding, and engineering support. The engineering support is in the form of engineering changes that are placed by the customer to change the design of a product. The budgeted activity costs and activity bases associated with these activities are:

Activity	Budgeted Activity Cost	Activity Base
Customer service	$ 31,500	Number of service requests
Project bidding	74,000	Number of bids
Engineering support	120,750	Number of customer design changes
Total costs	$226,250	

Activity-base usage and unit volume information for the three customers is as follows:

	Gough Industries	Breen Inc.	The Martin Group	Total
Number of service requests	36	28	116	180
Number of bids	50	40	95	185
Number of customer design changes	18	35	108	161
Unit volume	30	16	4	50

Instructions

1. Determine the activity rates for each of the three nonmanufacturing activity pools.

2. Determine the activity costs allocated to the three customers, using the activity rates in (1).

3. Construct customer profitability reports for the three customers, dated for the year ended December 31, using the activity costs in (2). The reports should disclose the gross profit and income from operations associated with each customer.

4. ➤ Provide recommendations to management, based on the profitability reports in (3).

PR 4-6A   Product costing and decision analysis for a service company   Obj. 6

✔ 3. Procedure B
excess, $597,700

EXCEL TEMPLATE

Pleasant Stay Medical Inc. wishes to determine its product costs. Pleasant Stay offers a variety of medical procedures (operations) that are considered its "products." The overhead has been separated into three major activities. The annual estimated activity costs and activity bases follow:

Activity	Budgeted Activity Cost	Activity Base
Scheduling and admitting	$ 432,000	Number of patients
Housekeeping	4,212,000	Number of patient days
Nursing	5,376,000	Weighted care unit
Total costs	$10,020,000	

Total "patient days" are determined by multiplying the number of patients by the average length of stay in the hospital. A weighted care unit (wcu) is a measure of nursing effort used to care for patients. There were 192,000 weighted care units estimated for the year. In addition, Pleasant Stay estimated 6,000 patients and 27,000 patient days for the year. (The average patient is expected to have a a little more than a four-day stay in the hospital.)

During a portion of the year, Pleasant Stay collected patient information for three selected procedures, as follows:

	Activity-Base Usage
Procedure A	
Number of patients	280
Average length of stay	× 6 days
Patient days	1,680
Weighted care units	19,200
Procedure B	
Number of patients	650
Average length of stay	× 5 days
Patient days	3,250
Weighted care units	6,000
Procedure C	
Number of patients	1,200
Average length of stay	× 4 days
Patient days	4,800
Weighted care units	24,000

Private insurance reimburses the hospital for these activities at a fixed daily rate of $406 per patient day for all three procedures.

Instructions

1. Determine the activity rates.

2. Determine the activity cost for each procedure.

3. Determine the excess or deficiency of reimbursements to activity cost.

4. ▬▬▶ Interpret your results.

Problems: Series B

PR 4-1B Single plantwide factory overhead rate
Obj. 2

✔ 1. B. $111 per machine hour

Spotted Cow Dairy Company manufactures three products—whole milk, skim milk, and cream—in two production departments, Blending and Packing. The factory overhead for Spotted Cow Dairy is $299,700.

The three products consume both machine hours and direct labor hours in the two production departments as follows:

	Direct Labor Hours	Machine Hours
Blending Department		
Whole milk	260	650
Skim milk	245	710
Cream	215	260
	720	1,620
Packing Department		
Whole milk	470	500
Skim milk	300	415
Cream	130	165
	900	1,080
Total	1,620	2,700

Instructions

1. Determine the single plantwide factory overhead rate, using each of the following allocation bases: (A) direct labor hours and (B) machine hours.

2. Determine the product factory overhead costs, using (A) the direct labor hour plantwide factory overhead rate and (B) the machine hour plantwide factory overhead rate.

PR 4-2B Multiple production department factory overhead rates
Obj. 3

✔ 2. Cream, $46,150

The management of Spotted Cow Dairy Company, described in Problem 1B, now plans to use the multiple production department factory overhead rate method. The total factory overhead associated with each department is as follows:

Blending Department	$178,200
Packing Department	121,500
Total	$299,700

Instructions

1. Determine the multiple production department factory overhead rates, using machine hours for the Blending Department and direct labor hours for the Packing Department.

2. Determine the product factory overhead costs, using the multiple production department rates in (1).

PR 4-3B Activity-based department rate product costing and product cost distortions
Obj. 3, 4

✔ 4. Loudspeakers, $465,430 and $66.49

EXCEL TEMPLATE

Big Sound Inc. manufactures two products: receivers and loudspeakers. The factory overhead incurred is as follows:

Indirect labor	$400,400
Subassembly Department	198,800
Final Assembly Department	114,800
Total	$714,000

The activity base associated with the two production departments is direct labor hours. The indirect labor can be assigned to two different activities as follows:

Activity	Budgeted Activity Cost	Activity Base
Setup	$138,600	Number of setups
Quality control	261,800	Number of inspections
Total	$400,400	

The activity-base usage quantities and units produced for the two products follow:

	Number of Setups	Number of Inspections	Direct Labor Hours— Subassembly	Direct Labor Hours— Final Assembly	Units Produced
Receivers	80	450	875	525	7,000
Loudspeakers	320	1,750	525	875	7,000
Total	400	2,200	1,400	1,400	14,000

Instructions

1. Determine the factory overhead rates under the multiple production department rate method. Assume that indirect labor is associated with the production departments, so that the total factory overhead is $420,000 and $294,000 for the Subassembly and Final Assembly departments, respectively.

2. Determine the total and per-unit factory overhead costs allocated to each product, using the multiple production department overhead rates in (1).

3. Determine the activity rates, assuming that the indirect labor is associated with activities rather than with the production departments.

4. Determine the total and per-unit cost assigned to each product under activity-based costing.

5. ⬤➤ Explain the difference in the per-unit overhead allocated to each product under the multiple production department factory overhead rate and activity-based costing methods.

PR 4-4B Activity-based product costing

Obj. 4

✔ 2. Brown sugar total activity cost, $293,600

EXCEL TEMPLATE

Sweet Sugar Company manufactures three products (white sugar, brown sugar, and powdered sugar) in a continuous production process. Senior management has asked the controller to conduct an activity-based costing study. The controller identified the amount of factory overhead required by the critical activities of the organization as follows:

Activity	Budgeted Activity Cost
Production	$500,000
Setup	144,000
Inspection	44,000
Shipping	115,000
Customer service	84,000
Total	$887,000

The activity bases identified for each activity are as follows:

Activity	Activity Base
Production	Machine hours
Setup	Number of setups
Inspection	Number of inspections
Shipping	Number of customer orders
Customer service	Number of customer service requests

(Continued)

The activity-base usage quantities and units produced for the three products were determined from corporate records and are as follows:

	Machine Hours	Number of Setups	Number of Inspections	Number of Customer Orders	Customer Service Requests	Units
White sugar	5,000	85	220	1,150	60	10,000
Brown sugar	2,500	170	330	2,600	350	5,000
Powdered sugar	2,500	195	550	2,000	190	5,000
Total	10,000	450	1,100	5,750	600	20,000

Each product requires 0.5 machine hour per unit.

Instructions

1. Determine the activity rate for each activity.

2. Determine the total and per-unit activity cost for all three products. (Round to nearest cent.)

3. ➤ Why aren't the activity unit costs equal across all three products since they require the same machine time per unit?

PR 4-5B   Allocating selling and administrative expenses using activity-based costing
Obj. 5

✔ 3. Supply Universe, income from operations, $283,820

SHOW ME HOW

EXCEL TEMPLATE

Shrute Inc. manufactures office copiers, which are sold to retailers. The price and cost of goods sold for each copier are as follows:

Price	$1,110 per unit
Cost of goods sold	682
Gross profit	$ 428 per unit

In addition, the company incurs selling and administrative expenses of $414,030. The company wishes to assign these costs to its three major retail customers, The Warehouse, Kosmo Co., and Supply Universe. These expenses are related to its three major nonmanufacturing activities: customer service, sales order processing, and advertising support. The advertising support is in the form of advertisements that are placed by Shrute Inc. to support the retailer's sale of Shrute copiers to consumers. The budgeted activity costs and activity bases associated with these activities are:

Activity	Budgeted Activity Cost	Activity Base
Customer service	$ 76,860	Number of service requests
Sales order processing	25,920	Number of sales orders
Advertising support	311,250	Number of ads placed
Total activity cost	$414,030	

Activity-base usage and unit volume information for the three customers is as follows:

	The Warehouse	Kosmo Co.	Supply Universe	Total
Number of service requests	62	340	25	427
Number of sales orders	300	640	140	1,080
Number of ads placed	25	180	44	249
Unit volume	810	810	810	2,430

Instructions

1. Determine the activity rates for each of the three nonmanufacturing activities.

2. Determine the activity costs allocated to the three customers, using the activity rates in (1).

3. Construct customer profitability reports for the three customers, dated for the year ended December 31, using the activity costs in (2). The reports should disclose the gross profit and income from operations associated with each customer.

4. ➤ Provide recommendations to management, based on the profitability reports in (3).

PR 4-6B Product costing and decision analysis for a service company   Obj. 6

✔ 3. Flight 102 income from operations, $4,415

EXCEL TEMPLATE

Blue Star Airline provides passenger airline service, using small jets. The airline connects four major cities: Charlotte, Pittsburgh, Detroit, and San Francisco. The company expects to fly 170,000 miles during a month. The following costs are budgeted for a month:

Fuel	$2,120,000
Ground personnel	788,500
Crew salaries	850,000
Depreciation	430,000
Total costs	$4,188,500

Blue Star management wishes to assign these costs to individual flights in order to gauge the profitability of its service offerings. The following activity bases were identified with the budgeted costs:

Airline Cost	Activity Base
Fuel, crew, and depreciation costs	Number of miles flown
Ground personnel	Number of arrivals and departures at an airport

The size of the company's ground operation in each city is determined by the size of the workforce. The following monthly data are available from corporate records for each terminal operation:

Terminal City	Ground Personnel Cost	Number of Arrivals/Departures
Charlotte	$256,000	320
Pittsburgh	97,500	130
Detroit	129,000	150
San Francisco	306,000	340
Total	$788,500	940

Three recent representative flights have been selected for the profitability study. Their characteristics are as follows:

	Description	Miles Flown	Number of Passengers	Ticket Price per Passenger
Flight 101	Charlotte to San Francisco	2,000	80	$695.00
Flight 102	Detroit to Charlotte	800	50	441.50
Flight 103	Charlotte to Pittsburgh	400	20	382.00

Instructions

1. Determine the fuel, crew, and depreciation cost per mile flown.

2. Determine the cost per arrival or departure by terminal city.

3. Use the information in (1) and (2) to construct a profitability report for the three flights. Each flight has a single arrival and departure to its origin and destination city pairs.

Analysis for Decision Making

ADM-1   Activity-based product cost improvement

Gourmet Master, Inc. uses activity-based costing to determine the cost of its stainless steel ovens. Activity-based product cost information is as follows:

Activity	Activity-Base Usage (hrs. per unit)	×	Activity Rate per Hour	=	Activity Cost
Fabrication	0.75		$24.00		$18.00
Assembly	1.50		20.00		30.00
Inspection	0.30		25.00		7.50
Moving	0.25		12.00		3.00
Total activity cost per unit					$58.50

These activities only include the labor portion of the cost. Fabrication is the cutting and shaping of metal to be used in the assembly of the ovens. If the metal is not fabricated properly, additional time is required during final assembly to trim and adjust the metal pieces to fit properly. This has been a problem in Assembly. Management proposes improvements in Fabrication requiring the fabrication work to be done slower, but more accurately. As a result, the time in fabrication will increase to an hour per unit. However, because of the additional care, the parts are expected to fit better during assembly, thus reducing assembly time to 1.10 hours per unit.

A. Determine the revised activity-based cost per unit under the new fabrication plan.
B. Does this plan reduce the activity cost per unit of the oven?

ADM-2   Labor classification trade-off

Skidmore Electronics manufactures consumer electronic products. The company has three assembly labor classifications, S-1, S-2, and S-3. The three classifications are paid $15, $18, and $22 per hour, respectively. The assembly activity for a new smartphone is as follows:

Activity	Activity-Base Usage (hrs. per unit)	×	Activity Rate per Hour (S-2)	=	Activity Cost
Assembly	0.40		$18.00		$7.20

A product engineer proposes using a higher-rated employee to perform the assembly on the new phone. His analysis has shown that an S-3 employee can perform the assembly in 0.35 hour per unit.

A. Determine the Assembly activity cost using the S-3 labor classification.
B. ➤ Is the product engineer's proposal supported?

ADM-3   Production run size and activity improvement

Littlejohn, Inc. manufactures machined parts for the automotive industry. The activity cost associated with Part XX-10 is as follows:

Activity	Activity-Base Usage	×	Activity Rate	=	Activity Cost
Fabrication	250 dlh		$80 per dlh		$20,000
Setup	10 setups		$80 per setup		800
Production control	10 prod. runs		$30 per prod. run		300
Moving	10 moves		$25 per move		250
Total activity cost per unit					$21,350
Estimated units of production					÷ 500
Activity cost per unit					$ 42.70

Each unit requires 30 minutes of fabrication direct labor. Moreover, Part XX-10 is manufactured in production run sizes of 50 units. Each production run is set up, scheduled (production control), and moved as a batch of 50 units. Management is considering improvements in the setup, production control, and moving activities in order to cut the production run sizes by half. As a result, the number of setups, production runs, and moves will double from 10 to 20. Such improvements are expected to speed the company's ability to respond to customer orders.

- Setup is reengineered so that it takes 60% of the original cost per setup.
- Production control software will allow production control effort and cost per production run to decline by 60%.
- Moving distance was reduced by 40%, thus reducing the cost per move by the same amount.

A. Determine the revised activity cost per unit under the proposed changes.
B. Did these improvements reduce the activity cost per unit?
C. What cost per unit for setup would be required for the solution in (A) to equal the base solution?

ADM-4   Hospital activity-based costing analysis

Lancaster County Hospital uses activity-based costing to determine the cost of serving patients. The hospital identified common treatments and developed the activity-based cost per patient by treatment. The activities and activity rates for a patient receiving coronary bypass surgery are as follows:

Activity	Activity Rate
Admission	$ 150 per admission
Operating room	$3,000 per hour
Nursing	$ 50 per nursing care unit
Discharge	$ 100 per discharge

Nursing care units are measures of time and effort to perform nursing duties, such as providing IV care, checking vital signs, and administering drugs. It is determined that there are an average of 10 nursing care units per patient-day in the hospital for a coronary bypass. The average bypass patient is in the hospital for 6 days. The bypass procedure requires an average of 3 hours of operating room time.

A. Determine the activity cost per patient for the coronary bypass treatment.
B. Assume the hospital was able to make improvements such that the average length of stay in the hospital for the bypass was reduced from 6 days to 5 days. Further assume that additional improvements in medical technology reduced the operating room time for a bypass to 2½ hours. Determine the activity cost per patient for the coronary bypass treatment under these revised conditions. What is the cost improvement?

Take It Further

ETHICS

TIF 4-1   Ethics in Action

The controller of Tri Con Global Systems Inc. has developed a new costing system that traces the cost of activities to products. The new system is able to measure post-manufacturing activities, such as selling, promotional, and distribution activities, and allocate these activities to products in a manner that provides a more complete view of the company's product costs. This system produces better strategic information about the relative profitability of product lines.

In the course of implementing the new costing system, the controller realized that the company's current period GAAP net income would increase significantly if the new product cost information were used for inventory valuation on the financial statements. The controller

(Continued)

has been under intense pressure to improve the company's net income, and this would be an easy and effective way for her to help meet the company's short-term net income goals. As a result, she has decided to use the new costing system to determine GAAP net income.

1. ➤ Why does the company's net income increase when the new costing system is applied?

2. ➤ Is the controller acting ethically by using the new costing system for GAAP net income? Explain your answer.

REAL WORLD

TIF 4-2 Team Activity

In teams, select a company from one of the following industries: banking, food service, manufacturing, or retail. For this company:

A. Identify the primary activities that the company must perform to provide its product or service.

B. Identify an activity base for each of these activities.

TIF 4-3 Communication

The controller of New Wave Sounds Inc. prepared the following product profitability report for management, using activity-based costing methods for allocating both the factory overhead and the marketing expenses. As such, the controller has confidence in the accuracy of this report.

	Home Theater Speakers	Wireless Speakers	Wireless Headphones	Total
Sales	$ 1,500,000	$1,200,000	$900,000	$3,600,000
Cost of goods sold	1,050,000	720,000	810,000	2,580,000
Gross profit	$ 450,000	$ 480,000	$ 90,000	$1,020,000
Marketing expenses	600,000	120,000	72,000	792,000
Income from operations	$ (150,000)	$ 360,000	$ 18,000	$ 228,000

In addition, the controller interviewed the vice president of marketing, who provided the following insight into the company's three products:

- The home theater speakers are an older product that is highly recognized in the marketplace.
- The wireless speakers are a new product that was just recently launched.
- The wireless headphones are a new technology that has no competition in the marketplace, and it is hoped that they will become an important future addition to the company's product portfolio. Initial indications are that the product is well received by customers.

The controller believes that the manufacturing costs for all three products are in line with expectations.

Based on the information provided:

1. Calculate the ratio of gross profit to sales and the ratio of income from operations to sales for each product.

2. ➤ Write a brief (one page) memo using the product profitability report and the calculations in (1) to make recommendations to management with respect to strategies for the three products.

Concepts and Principles

Chapter 1 *Introduction to Managerial Accounting*

Developing Information

COST SYSTEMS	COST BEHAVIOR
Chapter 2 *Job Order Costing* **Chapter 3** *Process Cost Systems* **Chapter 4** *Activity-Based Costing*	**Chapter 5** *Cost-Volume-Profit Analysis*

Decision Making

EVALUATING PERFORMANCE	COMPARING ALTERNATIVES
Chapter 6 *Variable Costing for Management Analysis* **Chapter 7** *Budgeting* **Chapter 8** *Evaluating Variances from Standard Costs*	**Chapter 9** *Evaluating Decentralized Operations* **Chapter 10** *Differential Analysis and Product Pricing* **Chapter 11** *Capital Investment Analysis* **Chapter 12** *Lean Manufacturing*

Ford Motor Company

Making a profit isn't easy for U.S. auto manufacturers like **Ford Motor Company.** The cost of materials, labor, equipment, and advertising makes it very expensive to produce cars and trucks.

How many cars does Ford need to produce and sell to break even? The answer depends on the relationship between Ford's sales revenue and costs. Some of Ford's costs, like direct labor and materials, will change in direct proportion to the number of vehicles that are built. Other costs, such as the costs of manufacturing equipment, are fixed and do not change with the number of vehicles that are produced. Ford will break even when it generates enough sales revenue to cover both its fixed and variable costs.

During the depths of the 2009 recession, Ford renegotiated labor contracts with its employees. These renegotiations reduced the direct labor cost incurred to build each car, which lowered the number of cars that the company needed to sell to break even by 45%.

As with Ford, understanding how costs behave, and the relationship between costs, profits, and volume, is important for all businesses. This chapter discusses commonly used methods for classifying costs according to how they change and techniques for determining how many units must be sold for a company to break even. Techniques that management can use to evaluate costs in order to make sound business decisions are also discussed.

Source: J. Booton, "Moody's Upgrades Ford's Credit Rating, Returns Blue Oval Trademark," *Fox Business*, May 22, 2012.

What's Covered

Cost-Volume-Profit Analysis

Cost Behavior	**Cost-Volume-Profit Relationships**	**Cost-Volume-Profit Analysis**	**Special Relationships and Analyses**
■ Variable Costs (Obj. 1)	■ Contribution Margin (Obj. 2)	■ Break-Even Point (Obj. 3)	■ Sales Mix (Obj. 5)
■ Fixed Costs (Obj. 1)	■ Contribution Margin Ratio (Obj. 2)	■ Target Profit (Obj. 3)	■ Operating Leverage (Obj. 5)
■ Mixed Costs (Obj. 1)	■ Unit Contribution Margin (Obj. 2)	■ Cost-Volume-Profit Chart (Obj. 4)	■ Margin of Safety (Obj. 5)
		■ Profit-Volume Chart (Obj. 4)	
		■ Assumptions (Obj. 4)	

Learning Objectives

Obj. 1 Classify costs as variable costs, fixed costs, or mixed costs.

Obj. 2 Compute the contribution margin, the contribution margin ratio, and the unit contribution margin.

Obj. 3 Determine the break-even point and sales necessary to achieve a target profit.

Obj. 4 Using a cost-volume-profit chart and a profit-volume chart, determine the break-even point and sales necessary to achieve a target profit.

Obj. 5 Compute the break-even point for a company selling more than one product, the operating leverage, and the margin of safety.

Analysis for Decision Making

Describe and Illustrate the use of cost-volume-profit analysis for decision making in a service business.

Objective 1
Classify costs as variable costs, fixed costs, or mixed costs.

Cost Behavior

Cost behavior is the manner in which a cost changes as a related activity changes. The behavior of costs is useful to managers for a variety of reasons. For example, knowing how costs behave allows managers to predict profits as sales and production volumes change. Knowing how costs behave is also useful for estimating costs, which affects a variety of decisions such as whether to replace a machine.

Understanding the behavior of a cost depends on the following:

■ Identifying the activities that cause the cost to change. These activities are called **activity bases** (or *activity drivers*).

■ Specifying the range of activity over which the changes in the cost are of interest. This range of activity is called the **relevant range**.

To illustrate, assume that a hospital is concerned about planning and controlling patient food costs. A good activity base is the number of patients who *stay* overnight in the hospital. The number of patients who are *treated* is not as good an activity base because some patients are outpatients and, thus, do not consume food. Once an activity base is identified, food costs can then be analyzed over the range of the number of patients who normally stay in the hospital (the relevant range).

Costs are normally classified as variable costs, fixed costs, or mixed costs.

Link to Ford Motor Company

The first vehicle built by Henry Ford in 1896 was a Quadricycle that consisted of four bicycle wheels powered by a four-horsepower engine. The first Ford Model A was sold by **Ford Motor Company** in 1903. In 1908, the Ford Model T was introduced, which had sales of 15 million before its production was halted in 1927.

Source: www.corporate.ford.com

Variable Costs

Variable costs are costs that vary in proportion to changes in the activity base. When the activity base is units produced, direct materials and direct labor costs are normally classified as variable costs.

To illustrate, assume that Jason Sound Inc. produces stereo systems. The parts for the stereo systems are purchased from suppliers for $10 per unit and are assembled by Jason Sound. For Model JS-12, the direct materials costs for the relevant range of 5,000 to 30,000 units of production are as follows:

Number of Units of Model JS-12 Produced	Direct Materials Cost per Unit	Total Direct Materials Cost
5,000 units	$10	$ 50,000
10,000	10	100,000
15,000	10	150,000
20,000	10	200,000
25,000	10	250,000
30,000	10	300,000

As shown, variable costs have the following characteristics:

- *Cost per unit* remains the same regardless of changes in the activity base. For Jason Sound, units produced is the activity base. For Model JS-12, the cost per unit is $10.
- *Total cost* changes in proportion to changes in the activity base. For Model JS-12, the direct materials cost for 10,000 units ($100,000) is twice the direct materials cost for 5,000 units ($50,000).

Exhibit 1 illustrates how the variable costs for direct materials for Model JS-12 behave in total and on a per-unit basis as production changes.

Exhibit 1 Variable Cost Graphs

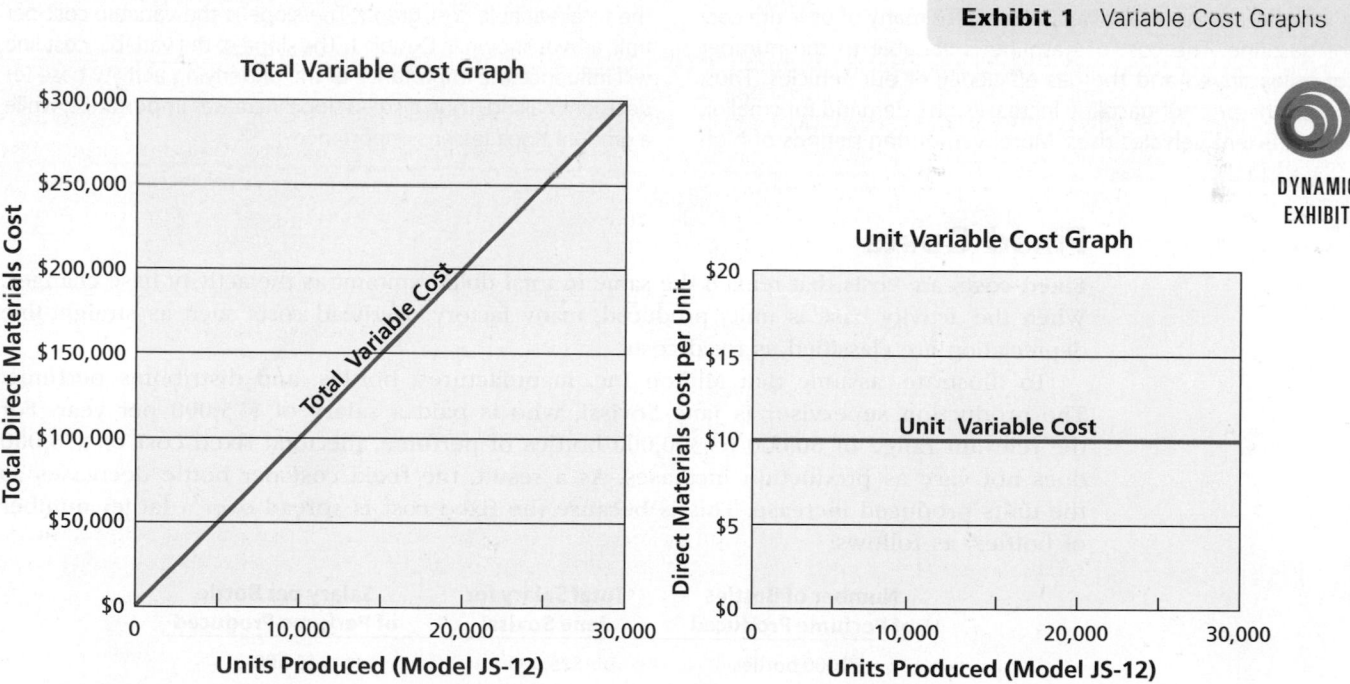

DYNAMIC EXHIBIT

Some examples of variable costs and their related activity bases for various types of businesses are shown in Exhibit 2.

Exhibit 2

Variable Costs and Their Activity Bases

Type of Business	Cost	Activity Base
University	Instructor salaries	Number of classes
Passenger airline	Fuel	Number of miles flown
Manufacturing	Direct materials	Number of units produced
Hospital	Nurse wages	Number of patients
Hotel	Housekeeping wages	Number of guests
Bank	Teller wages	Number of banking transactions

Link to Ford Motor Company   Changing emission, fuel economy, and safety standards increase the variable cost of each vehicle manufactured by **Ford Motor Company**.

Why It Matters

Variable Cost for Home and Business

Variable costs are important to our individual lives. For example, an important variable cost for many of us is the cost of gasoline. The cost of gasoline is variable to the number of miles driven and the gas efficiency of our vehicles. Thus, when the price of gasoline increases, the demand for smaller, fuel-efficient vehicles rises. Moreover, during periods of high gasoline prices, there is an incentive to drive less, even to the point of living closer to work or school. When the cost of gasoline falls, fuel efficiency and driving preferences become less important. This is seen with the slope of the variable cost line on the total variable cost graph. The slope is the variable cost per unit, as was shown in Exhibit 1. The slope of the variable cost line will influence the importance of the underlying activity base for decision making. Thus, a steep slope increases importance, while a gradual slope lessens importance.

Fixed Costs

Fixed costs are costs that remain the same in total dollar amount as the activity base changes. When the activity base is units produced, many factory overhead costs such as straight-line depreciation are classified as fixed costs.

To illustrate, assume that Minton Inc. manufactures, bottles, and distributes perfume. The production supervisor is Jane Sovissi, who is paid a salary of $75,000 per year. For the relevant range of 50,000 to 300,000 bottles of perfume, the total fixed cost of $75,000 does not vary as production increases. As a result, the fixed cost per bottle decreases as the units produced increase. This is because the fixed cost is spread over a larger number of bottles, as follows:

Number of Bottles of Perfume Produced	Total Salary for Jane Sovissi	Salary per Bottle of Perfume Produced
50,000 bottles	$75,000	$1.500
100,000	75,000	0.750
150,000	75,000	0.500
200,000	75,000	0.375
250,000	75,000	0.300
300,000	75,000	0.250

As shown, fixed costs have the following characteristics:

- *Cost per unit* decreases as the activity level increases and increases as the activity level decreases. For Jane Sovissi's salary, the cost per unit decreased from $1.50 for 50,000 bottles produced to $0.25 for 300,000 bottles produced.
- *Total cost* remains the same regardless of changes in the activity base. Jane Sovissi's salary of $75,000 remained the same regardless of whether 50,000 bottles or 300,000 bottles were produced.

Exhibit 3 illustrates how Jane Sovissi's salary (fixed cost) behaves in total and on a per-unit basis as production changes.

A high proportion of **Ford Motor Company**'s costs are fixed in nature.
Source: Ford Motor Company, Form 10-K for Year Ended December 31, 2014.

Link to Ford Motor Company

Exhibit 3   Fixed Cost Graphs

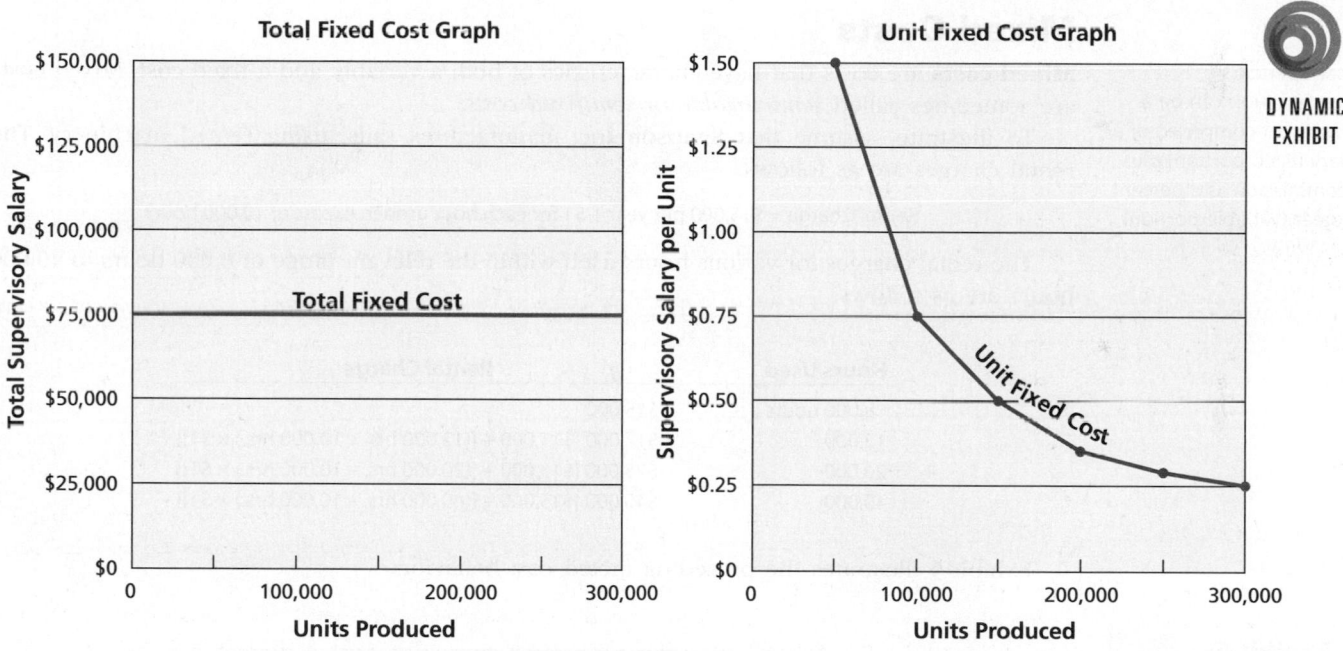

DYNAMIC EXHIBIT

Some examples of fixed costs and their related activity bases for various types of businesses are shown in Exhibit 4.

Type of Business	Fixed Cost	Activity Base
University	Building (straight-line) depreciation	Number of students
Passenger airline	Airplane (straight-line) depreciation	Number of miles flown
Manufacturing	Plant manager salary	Number of units produced
Hospital	Property insurance	Number of patients
Hotel	Property taxes	Number of guests
Bank	Branch manager salary	Number of customer accounts

Exhibit 4
Fixed Costs and Their Activity Bases

Why It Matters

Booking Fees

A major fixed cost for a concert promoter is the booking fee for the act. The booking fee is the amount to be paid to the act for a single show at a venue. **Degy Entertainment**, a booking agency, provided a list of asking prices for several popular acts. The following is a sampling from the list.

Taylor Swift	$1,000,000+
Justin Timberlake	$1,000,000+
Rihanna	$500K–$750K
Katy Perry	$500K
Keith Urban	$400K–$600K
Maroon 5	$400K–$600K

Kanye West	$400K–$600K
Carrie Underwood	$400K–$500K
Alicia Keys	$350k–$500K
Bruno Mars	$200K–$400K
Pitbull	$200K–$300K
Ke$ha	$150K–$200K
The Script	$125K–$175K

The promoter must cover these fixed costs with ticket revenues; thus, the size of the booking fee is necessarily related to the popularity of the act represented by the number of potential tickets sold and the ticket price.

Source: Zachery Crockett, "How Much Does It Cost to Book Your Favorite Band?" *Priceconomics.com*, May 16, 2014.

Mixed Costs

note:

A salesperson's compensation can be a mixed cost comprised of a salary (fixed portion) plus a commission as a percent of sales (variable portion).

Mixed costs are costs that have characteristics of both a variable and a fixed cost. Mixed costs are sometimes called *semivariable* or *semifixed costs*.

To illustrate, assume that Simpson Inc. manufactures sails, using rented machinery. The rental charges are as follows:

Rental Charge = $15,000 per year + $1 for each hour used in excess of 10,000 hours

The rental charges for various hours used within the relevant range of 8,000 hours to 40,000 hours are as follows:

Hours Used	Rental Charge
8,000 hours	$15,000
12,000	$17,000 {$15,000 + [(12,000 hrs. – 10,000 hrs.) × $1]}
20,000	$25,000 {$15,000 + [(20,000 hrs. – 10,000 hrs.) × $1]}
40,000	$45,000 {$15,000 + [(40,000 hrs. – 10,000 hrs.) × $1]}

Exhibit 5 illustrates the preceding mixed cost behavior.

Exhibit 5

Mixed Costs

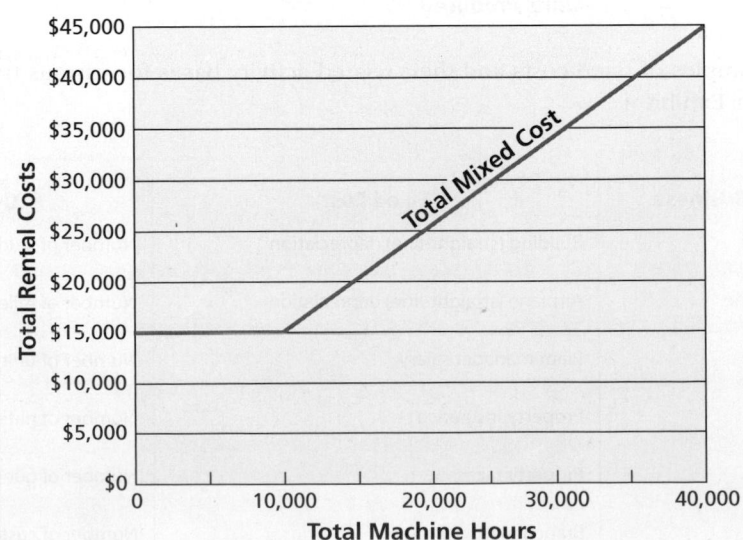

For purposes of analysis, mixed costs are usually separated into their fixed and variable components. The **high-low method** is a cost estimation method that may be used for this purpose.[1] The high-low method uses the highest and lowest activity levels and their related costs to estimate the variable cost per unit and the fixed cost.

To illustrate, assume that the Equipment Maintenance Department of Kason Inc. incurred the following costs during the past five months:

	Units Produced	Total Cost
June	1,000 units	$45,550
July	1,500	52,000
August	2,100	61,500
September	1,800	57,500
October	750	41,250

The number of units produced is the activity base, and the relevant range is the units produced between June and October. For Kason, the difference between the units produced and the total costs at the highest and lowest levels of production are as follows:

	Units Produced	Total Cost
Highest level	2,100 units	$61,500
Lowest level	750	41,250
Difference	1,350 units	$20,250

The total fixed cost does not change with changes in production. Thus, the $20,250 difference in the total cost is the change in the total variable cost. Dividing this difference of $20,250 by the difference in production is an estimate of the variable cost per unit. For Kason, this estimate is $15, computed as follows:

$$\text{Variable Cost per Unit} = \frac{\text{Difference in Total Cost}}{\text{Difference in Units Produced}}$$

$$= \frac{\$20,250}{1,350 \text{ units}} = \$15 \text{ per unit}$$

The fixed cost is estimated by subtracting the total variable costs from the total costs for the units produced, as follows:

$$\text{Fixed Cost} = \text{Total Costs} - (\text{Variable Cost per Unit} \times \text{Units Produced})$$

The fixed cost is the same at the highest and the lowest levels of production, as follows for Kason:

Highest level (2,100 units):

$$\begin{aligned} \text{Fixed Cost} &= \text{Total Costs} - (\text{Variable Cost per Unit} \times \text{Units Produced}) \\ &= \$61,500 - (\$15 \times 2,100 \text{ units}) \\ &= \$61,500 - \$31,500 \\ &= \$30,000 \end{aligned}$$

Lowest level (750 units):

$$\begin{aligned} \text{Fixed Cost} &= \text{Total Costs} - (\text{Variable Cost per Unit} \times \text{Units Produced}) \\ &= \$41,250 - (\$15 \times 750 \text{ units}) \\ &= \$41,250 - \$11,250 \\ &= \$30,000 \end{aligned}$$

[1] Other methods of estimating costs, such as the scattergraph method and the least squares method, are discussed in cost accounting textbooks.

Using the variable cost per unit and the fixed cost, the total equipment maintenance cost for Kason can be computed for various levels of production as follows:

$$\text{Total Cost} = (\text{Variable Cost per Unit} \times \text{Units Produced}) + \text{Fixed Costs}$$
$$= (\$15 \times \text{Units Produced}) + \$30,000$$

To illustrate, the estimated total cost of 2,000 units of production is $60,000, computed as follows:

$$\text{Total Cost} = (\$15 \times \text{Units Produced}) + \$30,000$$
$$= (\$15 \times 2,000 \text{ units}) + \$30,000$$
$$= \$30,000 + \$30,000$$
$$= \$60,000$$

Link to Ford Motor Company   **Ford Motor Company** entered into a collective bargaining agreement with the United Auto Workers union that provides for lump-sum payments in lieu of general wage increases. This has the effect of making wages more like a mixed cost.

Summary of Cost Behavior Concepts

The cost behavior of variable costs and fixed costs is summarized in Exhibit 6.

Exhibit 6
Variable and Fixed Cost Behavior

	EFFECT OF CHANGING ACTIVITY LEVEL	
Cost	**Total Amount**	**Per-Unit Amount**
Variable	Increases and decreases proportionately with activity level.	Remains the same regardless of activity level.
Fixed	Remains the same regardless of activity level.	Increases and decreases inversely with activity level.

Mixed costs contain a fixed cost component that is incurred even if nothing is produced. For analysis, the fixed and variable cost components of mixed costs are separated using the high-low method.

Exhibit 7 provides some examples of variable, fixed, and mixed costs for the activity base of *units produced*.

Exhibit 7
Variable, Fixed, and Mixed Costs

Variable Costs	**Fixed Costs**	**Mixed Costs**
■ Direct materials	■ Straight-line depreciation	■ Quality Control Department salaries
■ Direct labor	■ Property taxes	■ Purchasing Department salaries
■ Electricity expense	■ Production supervisor salaries	■ Maintenance expenses
■ Supplies	■ Insurance expense	■ Warehouse expenses

One method of reporting variable and fixed costs is called **variable costing** or *direct costing*. Under variable costing, only the variable manufacturing costs (direct materials, direct labor, and variable factory overhead) are included in the product cost. The fixed factory overhead is treated as an expense of the period in which it is incurred. Variable costing is described and illustrated in the appendix to this chapter.

Check Up Corner 5-1 Cost Behavior

O&W Metal Company makes designer emblems for luxury vehicles. Each emblem is handcrafted out of titanium to the customer's design specifications. O&W's artisans are paid an hourly wage and work between 30 and 60 hours a week. O&W uses the straight-line method of depreciation. To ensure that each emblem conforms to the customer's specifications, O&W has each emblem inspected by an independent company. The inspection company charges a set price per month, plus an additional amount for each item inspected. After inspection, each emblem is shipped in a crush-resistant shipping container.

A. Which of O&W's costs (titanium, artisan wages, equipment depreciation, inspection, shipping containers) is a mixed cost?

B. Data on total mixed costs and total production for O&W's last five months of operations follow:

	Units Produced	Total Cost
August	1,000 units	$ 80,000
September	1,200	86,000
October	1,600	98,000
November	2,500	125,000
December	2,200	116,000

Using the high-low method, determine the (1) variable cost per unit and (2) total fixed costs.

C. O&W estimates that it will produce 2,000 units during January. Using your answer to (B), estimate the (1) total variable costs and (2) fixed cost per unit for January.

Solution:

A. The inspection cost is a mixed cost because it includes a fixed cost (the set price per month) and a variable cost (an amount based on the number of items inspected).

B. 1.

	Total Cost	Units Produced
Highest level (November)	$125,000	2,500
Lowest level (August)	80,000	1,000
Difference	$ 45,000	1,500

Mixed costs have characteristics of both variable and fixed costs.

The high-low method separates mixed costs into their fixed and variable components.

$$\text{Variable Cost per Unit} = \frac{\text{Difference in Total Cost}}{\text{Difference in Units Produced}}$$

$$\frac{\$45,000}{1,500} = \$30.00 \text{ per unit}$$

The variable cost per unit is determined by dividing the difference between the highest and lowest cost by the difference between the highest and lowest activity level.

2. Fixed Costs = Total Costs − (Variable Cost per Unit × Units Produced)

Highest level (2,500 units):

Fixed Costs = $125,000 − ($30 × 2,500 units)
= $125,000 − $75,000
= $50,000

The variable cost per unit is constant at all activity levels.

Lowest level (1,000 units):

Fixed Costs = $80,000 − ($30 × 1,000 units)
= $80,000 − $30,000
= $50,000

The total fixed costs calculated are the same, using either the high or low activity level.

C. 1. Total Variable Costs = $30 per unit × 2,000 units = $60,000
2. Fixed Cost per Unit = Total Fixed Costs ÷ Units Produced
= $50,000 ÷ 2,000 units
= $25.00

Total variable costs increase as the activity level increases.

The fixed cost per unit decreases as the activity level increases.

Check Up Corner

Objective 2

Compute the contribution margin, the contribution margin ratio, and the unit contribution margin.

Cost-Volume-Profit Relationships

Cost-volume-profit analysis is the examination of the relationships among selling prices, sales and production volume, costs, expenses, and profits. Cost-volume-profit analysis is useful for managerial decision making. Some of the ways cost-volume-profit analysis may be used include the following:

- Analyzing the effects of changes in selling prices on profits
- Analyzing the effects of changes in costs on profits
- Analyzing the effects of changes in volume on profits
- Setting selling prices
- Selecting the mix of products to sell
- Choosing among marketing strategies

Contribution Margin

Contribution margin is especially useful because it provides insight into the profit potential of a company. **Contribution margin** is the excess of sales over variable costs, computed as follows:

$$\text{Contribution Margin} = \text{Sales} - \text{Variable Costs}$$

To illustrate, assume the following data for Lambert Inc.:

Sales	50,000 units
Sales price per unit	$20 per unit
Variable cost per unit	$12 per unit
Fixed costs	$300,000

Exhibit 8 illustrates an income statement for Lambert prepared in a contribution margin format.

Exhibit 8

Contribution Margin Income Statement Format

Sales (50,000 units × $20)	$1,000,000
Variable costs (50,000 units × $12)	600,000
Contribution margin (50,000 units × $8)	$ 400,000
Fixed costs	300,000
Income from operations	$ 100,000

Lambert's contribution margin of $400,000 is available to cover the fixed costs of $300,000. Once the fixed costs are covered, any additional contribution margin increases income from operations.

Contribution Margin Ratio

Contribution margin can also be expressed as a percentage. The **contribution margin ratio**, sometimes called the *profit-volume ratio*, indicates the percentage of each sales dollar available to cover fixed costs and to provide income from operations. The contribution margin ratio is computed as follows:

$$\text{Contribution Margin Ratio} = \frac{\text{Contribution Margin}}{\text{Sales}}$$

The contribution margin ratio is 40% for Lambert Inc., computed as follows:

$$\text{Contribution Margin Ratio} = \frac{\$400,000}{\$1,000,000} = 40\%$$

The contribution margin ratio is most useful when the increase or decrease in sales volume is measured in sales *dollars*. In this case, the change in sales dollars multiplied by the contribution margin ratio equals the change in income from operations, computed as follows:

Change in Income from Operations = Change in Sales Dollars × Contribution Margin Ratio

To illustrate, if Lambert adds $80,000 in sales from the sale of an additional 4,000 units, its income from operations will increase by $32,000, computed as follows:

Change in Income from Operations = Change in Sales Dollars × Contribution Margin Ratio
Change in Income from Operations = $80,000 × 40% = $32,000

The preceding analysis is confirmed by Lambert's contribution margin income statement that follows:

Sales (54,000 units × $20)	$1,080,000
Variable costs (54,000 units × $12)	648,000*
Contribution margin (54,000 units × $8)	$ 432,000**
Fixed costs	300,000
Income from operations	$ 132,000

*$1,080,000 × 60%
**$1,080,000 × 40%

Income from operations increased from $100,000 to $132,000 when sales increased from $1,000,000 to $1,080,000. Variable costs as a percentage of sales are equal to 100% minus the contribution margin ratio. Thus, in the preceding income statement, the variable costs are 60% (100% – 40%) of sales, or $648,000 ($1,080,000 × 60%). The total contribution margin, $432,000, can also be computed directly by multiplying the total sales by the contribution margin ratio ($1,080,000 × 40%).

In the preceding analysis, factors other than sales volume, such as variable cost per unit and sales price, are assumed to remain constant. If such factors change, their effect must also be considered.

The contribution margin ratio is also useful in developing business strategies. For example, assume that a company has a high contribution margin ratio and is producing below 100% of capacity. In this case, a large increase in income from operations can be expected from an increase in sales volume. Therefore, the company might consider implementing a special sales campaign to increase sales. In contrast, a company with a small contribution margin ratio will probably want to give more attention to reducing costs before attempting to promote sales.

Unit Contribution Margin

The unit contribution margin is also useful for analyzing the profit potential of proposed decisions. The **unit contribution margin** is computed as follows:

Unit Contribution Margin = Sales Price per Unit – Variable Cost per Unit

To illustrate, if Lambert Inc.'s unit selling price is $20 and its variable cost per unit is $12, the unit contribution margin is $8, computed as follows:

Unit Contribution Margin = Sales Price per Unit – Variable Cost per Unit
Unit Contribution Margin = $20 – $12 = $8

The unit contribution margin is most useful when the increase or decrease in sales volume is measured in sales *units* (quantities). In this case, the change in sales volume (units) multiplied by the unit contribution margin equals the change in income from operations, computed as follows:

Change in Income from Operations = Change in Sales Units × Unit Contribution Margin

To illustrate, assume that Lambert's sales could be increased by 15,000 units, from 50,000 units to 65,000 units. Lambert's income from operations would increase by $120,000 (15,000 units × $8), computed as follows:

Change in Income from Operations = Change in Sales Units × Unit Contribution Margin
Change in Income from Operations = 15,000 units × $8 = $120,000

The preceding analysis is confirmed by Lambert's contribution margin income statement that follows, which shows that income increased to $220,000 when 65,000 units are sold. The income statement in Exhibit 8 indicates income of $100,000 when 50,000 units are sold. Thus, selling an additional 15,000 units increases income by $120,000 ($220,000 – $100,000).

Sales (65,000 units × $20)	$1,300,000
Variable costs (65,000 units × $12)	780,000
Contribution margin (65,000 units × $8)	$ 520,000
Fixed costs	300,000
Income from operations	$ 220,000

Unit contribution margin analysis is useful information for managers. For example, in the preceding illustration, Lambert could spend up to $120,000 for special advertising or other product promotions to increase sales by 15,000 units and still increase income by $100,000, the $220,000 increase in sales minus the $120,000 cost of special advertising.

Check Up Corner 5-2   Contribution Margin

Toussant Company sells 20,000 units at $120 per unit. Variable costs are $90 per unit, and fixed costs are $250,000.

A. Prepare an income statement for Toussant in contribution margin format.

B. Determine Toussant's (1) contribution margin ratio and (2) unit contribution margin.

C. How much would income from operations change if Toussant's sales increased by 3,000 units?

Solution:

A.

Sales	$2,400,000	← 20,000 units × $120 sales price per unit
Variable costs	1,800,000	← 20,000 units × $90 variable cost per unit
Contribution margin	$ 600,000	← Contribution margin is the excess of sales over variable costs.
Fixed costs	250,000	← Toussant's contribution margin is available to cover its fixed costs of $250,000.
Income from operations	$ 350,000

Once fixed costs are covered, increases in contribution margin directly increase income from operations.

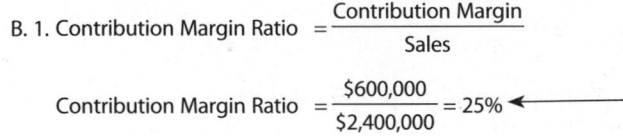

B. 1. Contribution Margin Ratio $= \dfrac{\text{Contribution Margin}}{\text{Sales}}$

Contribution Margin Ratio $= \dfrac{\$600,000}{\$2,400,000} = 25\%$ ← The contribution margin ratio indicates the percentage of each sales dollar available to cover fixed costs and provide income from operations.

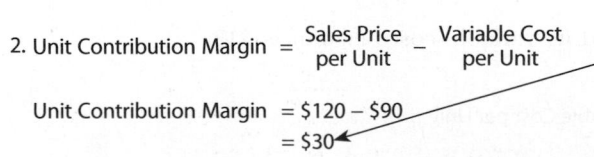

2. Unit Contribution Margin $= \dfrac{\text{Sales Price}}{\text{per Unit}} - \dfrac{\text{Variable Cost}}{\text{per Unit}}$

Unit Contribution Margin $= \$120 - \$90$
$= \$30$

The unit contribution margin measures the dollar amount of contribution margin generated from each unit sold.

Both the contribution margin ratio and unit contribution margin can be used to determine how changes in sales volume (units) impact income from operations.

C. *Using Contribution Margin Ratio:*

Change in sales dollars	$360,000	← 3,000 unit increase × $120 selling price per unit
Contribution margin ratio	× 25%
Change in income from operations	$ 90,000

Using Unit Contribution Margin:

Change in sales units	3,000
Unit contribution margin	× $30
Change in income from operations	$ 90,000

Both methods yield the same result.

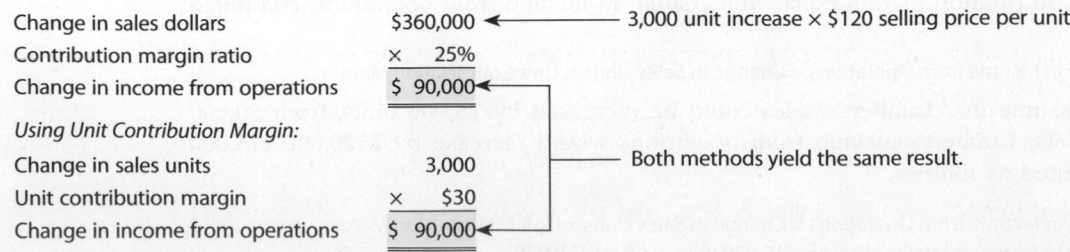

Check Up Corner

Mathematical Approach to Cost-Volume-Profit Analysis

Objective 3
Determine the break-even point and sales necessary to achieve a target profit.

The mathematical approach to cost-volume-profit analysis uses equations to determine the following:

- Sales necessary to break even
- Sales necessary to make a target or desired profit

Break-Even Point

The **break-even point** is the level of operations at which a company's revenues and expenses are equal, as shown in Exhibit 9. At break-even, a company reports neither income nor a loss from operations.

Revenues = **Costs**

Break-Even Point

Exhibit 9
Break-Even Point

The break-even point in *sales units* is computed as follows:

$$\text{Break-Even Sales (units)} = \frac{\text{Fixed Costs}}{\text{Unit Contribution Margin}}$$

To illustrate, assume the following data for Baker Corporation:

Fixed costs	$90,000
Unit selling price	$25
Unit variable cost	15
Unit contribution margin	$10

The break-even point for Baker is 9,000 units, computed as follows:

$$\text{Break-Even Sales (units)} = \frac{\text{Fixed Costs}}{\text{Unit Contribution Margin}} = \frac{\$90,000}{\$10} = 9,000 \text{ units}$$

The following income statement for Baker verifies the break-even point of 9,000 units:

Sales (9,000 units × $25)	$225,000
Variable costs (9,000 units × $15)	135,000
Contribution margin	$ 90,000
Fixed costs	90,000
Income from operations	$ 0

As shown in Baker's income statement, the break-even point is $225,000 (9,000 units × $25) of sales. The break-even point in *sales dollars* can be determined directly as follows:

$$\text{Break-Even Sales (dollars)} = \frac{\text{Fixed Costs}}{\text{Contribution Margin Ratio}}$$

The contribution margin ratio can be computed using the unit contribution margin and unit selling price as follows:

$$\text{Contribution Margin Ratio} = \frac{\text{Unit Contribution Margin}}{\text{Unit Selling Price}}$$

The contribution margin ratio for Baker is 40%, computed as follows:

$$\text{Contribution Margin Ratio} = \frac{\text{Unit Contribution Margin}}{\text{Unit Selling Price}} = \frac{\$10}{\$25} = 40\%$$

Thus, the break-even sales dollars for Baker of $225,000 can be computed directly as follows:

$$\text{Break-Even Sales (dollars)} = \frac{\text{Fixed Costs}}{\text{Contribution Margin Ratio}} = \frac{\$90,000}{40\%} = \$225,000$$

The break-even point is affected by changes in the fixed costs, unit variable costs, and unit selling price.

Link to Ford Motor Company

Ford Motor Company reported that its 2014 operations in the Middle East and Africa were at break-even.

Source: Ford Motor Company, Form 10-K for Year Ended December 31, 2014.

Effect of Changes in Fixed Costs Fixed costs do not change in total with changes in the level of activity. However, fixed costs may change because of other factors such as advertising campaigns, changes in property tax rates, or changes in factory supervisors' salaries.

Changes in fixed costs affect the break-even point as follows:

- Increases in fixed costs increase the break-even point.
- Decreases in fixed costs decrease the break-even point.

This relationship is illustrated in Exhibit 10.

Exhibit 10

Effect of Change in Fixed Costs on Break-Even Point

To illustrate, assume that Bishop Co. is evaluating a proposal to budget an additional $100,000 for advertising. The data for Bishop follow:

	Current	Proposed
Unit selling price	$90	$90
Unit variable cost	70	70
Unit contribution margin	$20	$20
Fixed costs	$600,000	$700,000

Bishop's break-even point *before* the additional advertising expense of $100,000 is 30,000 units, computed as follows:

$$\text{Break-Even Sales (units)} = \frac{\text{Fixed Costs}}{\text{Unit Contribution Margin}} = \frac{\$600,000}{\$20} = 30,000 \text{ units}$$

Bishop's break-even point *after* the additional advertising expense of $100,000 is 35,000 units, computed as follows:

$$\text{Break-Even Sales (units)} = \frac{\text{Fixed Costs}}{\text{Unit Contribution Margin}} = \frac{\$700,000}{\$20} = 35,000 \text{ units}$$

As shown for Bishop, the $100,000 increase in advertising (fixed costs) requires an additional 5,000 units (35,000 − 30,000) of sales to break even.[2] In other words, an increase in sales of

---

[2] The increase of 5,000 units can also be computed by dividing the increase in fixed costs of $100,000 by the unit contribution margin, $20, as follows: 5,000 units = $100,000 ÷ $20.

Why It Matters

Airline Industry Break-Even

Airlines measure revenues and costs by available seat miles. An available seat mile is one seat (empty or filled) flying one mile. Thus, the average revenue earned per available seat mile is termed the RASM, and the average cost per available seat mile is termed the CASM. The operating break-even occurs when the RASM equals the CASM. Since airlines have high aircraft fixed costs, filling passenger seats is an important contributor to exceeding break-even. This is measured by the average proportion of seats filled across all flights, which is termed the load factor. In addition, important variable costs such as labor and fuel impact the break-even performance. Thus, airlines monitor employee productivity and fuel costs to maintain

profitability. The RASM, CASM, and load factor for a recent year for major airlines are as follows:

	American Airlines	United Airlines	Delta Air Lines	Southwest Airlines	US Airways
RASM	$0.129	$0.124	$0.132	$0.135	$0.125
CASM	0.082	0.079	0.089	0.075	0.077
RASM – CASM	$0.047	$0.045	$0.043	$0.060	$0.048
Load factor	82%	84%	85%	82%	83%

As can be seen, all the major airlines are operating above their break-even points, with Southwest Airlines demonstrating the best profit performance by these metrics. The load factors are all more than 80%, indicating that the airlines are using their aircraft efficiently.

Source: MIT Airline Data Project.

5,000 units is required in order to generate an additional $100,000 of total contribution margin (5,000 units × $20) to cover the increased fixed costs.

Effect of Changes in Unit Variable Costs Unit variable costs do not change with changes in the level of activity. However, unit variable costs may be affected by other factors such as changes in the cost per unit of direct materials, changes in the wage rate for direct labor, or changes in the sales commission paid to salespeople.

Changes in unit variable costs affect the break-even point as follows:

■ Increases in unit variable costs increase the break-even point.
■ Decreases in unit variable costs decrease the break-even point.

This relationship is illustrated in Exhibit 11.

Exhibit 11
Effect of Change in Unit Variable Cost on Break-Even Point

To illustrate, assume that Park Co. is evaluating a proposal to pay an additional 2% commission on sales to its salespeople as an incentive to increase sales. The data for Park follow:

	Current	Proposed
Unit selling price	$250	$250
Unit variable cost	145	150*
Unit contribution margin	$105	$100
Fixed costs	$840,000	$840,000

*$150 = $145 + (2% × $250 unit selling price)

Park's break-even point *before* the additional 2% commission is 8,000 units, computed as follows:

$$\text{Break-Even Sales (units)} = \frac{\text{Fixed Costs}}{\text{Unit Contribution Margin}} = \frac{\$840,000}{\$105} = 8,000 \text{ units}$$

If the 2% sales commission proposal is adopted, unit variable costs will increase by $5 ($250 × 2%), from $145 to $150 per unit. This increase in unit variable costs will decrease the unit contribution margin from $105 to $100 ($250 − $150). Thus, Park's break-even point *after* the additional 2% commission is 8,400 units, computed as follows:

$$\text{Break-Even Sales (units)} = \frac{\text{Fixed Costs}}{\text{Unit Contribution Margin}} = \frac{\$840,000}{\$100} = 8,400 \text{ units}$$

As shown for Park, an additional 400 units of sales will be required in order to break even. This is because if 8,000 units are sold, the new unit contribution margin of $100 provides only $800,000 (8,000 units × $100) of contribution margin. Thus, $40,000 more contribution margin is necessary to cover the total fixed costs of $840,000. This additional $40,000 of contribution margin is provided by selling 400 more units (400 units × $100).

Effect of Changes in Unit Selling Price   Changes in the unit selling price affect the unit contribution margin and, thus, the break-even point. Specifically, changes in the unit selling price affect the break-even point as follows:

- Increases in the unit selling price decrease the break-even point.
- Decreases in the unit selling price increase the break-even point.

This relationship is illustrated in Exhibit 12.

Exhibit 12

Effect of Change in Unit Selling Price on Break-Even Point

To illustrate, assume that Graham Co. is evaluating a proposal to increase the unit selling price of its product from $50 to $60. The data for Graham follow:

	Current	Proposed
Unit selling price	$50	$60
Unit variable cost	30	30
Unit contribution margin	$20	$30
Fixed costs	$600,000	$600,000

Graham's break-even point *before* the price increase is 30,000 units, computed as follows:

$$\text{Break-Even Sales (units)} = \frac{\text{Fixed Costs}}{\text{Unit Contribution Margin}} = \frac{\$600,000}{\$20} = 30,000 \text{ units}$$

The increase of $10 per unit in the selling price increases the unit contribution margin by $10. Thus, Graham's break-even point *after* the price increase is 20,000 units, computed as follows:

$$\text{Break-Even Sales (units)} = \frac{\text{Fixed Costs}}{\text{Unit Contribution Margin}} = \frac{\$600,000}{\$30} = 20,000 \text{ units}$$

As shown for Graham, the price increase of $10 increased the unit contribution margin by $10, which decreased the break-even point by 10,000 units (30,000 units – 20,000 units).

Summary of Effects of Changes on Break-Even Point The break-even point in sales changes in the same direction as changes in the variable cost per unit and fixed costs. In contrast, the break-even point in sales changes in the opposite direction as changes in the unit selling price. These changes on the break-even point in sales are summarized in Exhibit 13.

Type of Change	Direction of Change	Effect of Change on Break-Even Sales
Fixed cost	↑ ↓	↑ ↓
Unit variable cost	↑ ↓	↑ ↓
Unit selling price	↑ ↓	↓ ↑

Exhibit 13
Effects of Changes in Selling Price and Costs on Break-Even Point

Target Profit

At the break-even point, sales and costs are exactly equal. However, the goal of most companies is to make a profit.

By modifying the break-even equation, the sales required to earn a target or desired amount of profit may be computed. For this purpose, target profit is added to the break-even equation, as follows:

$$\text{Sales (units)} = \frac{\text{Fixed Costs} + \text{Target Profit}}{\text{Unit Contribution Margin}}$$

To illustrate, assume the following data for Waltham Co.:

Fixed costs	$200,000
Target profit	100,000
Unit selling price	$75
Unit variable cost	45
Unit contribution margin	$30

The sales necessary for Waltham to earn the target profit of $100,000 would be 10,000 units, computed as follows:

$$\text{Sales (units)} = \frac{\text{Fixed Costs} + \text{Target Profit}}{\text{Unit Contribution Margin}} = \frac{\$200,000 + \$100,000}{\$30} = 10,000 \text{ units}$$

The following income statement for Waltham verifies this computation:

Sales (10,000 units × $75)	$750,000
Variable costs (10,000 units × $45)	450,000
Contribution margin (10,000 units × $30)	$300,000
Fixed costs	200,000
Income from operations	$100,000 ← Target profit

As shown in the income statement for Waltham, sales of $750,000 (10,000 units × $75) are necessary to earn the target profit of $100,000. The sales of $750,000 needed to earn the target profit of $100,000 can be computed directly using the contribution margin ratio as follows:

$$\text{Contribution Margin Ratio} = \frac{\text{Unit Contribution Margin}}{\text{Unit Selling Price}} = \frac{\$30}{\$75} = 40\%$$

$$\text{Sales (dollars)} = \frac{\text{Fixed Costs} + \text{Target Profit}}{\text{Contribution Margin Ratio}}$$

$$= \frac{\$200,000 + \$100,000}{40\%} = \frac{\$300,000}{40\%} = \$750,000$$

 Ethics: Do It!

Orphan Drugs

Each year, pharmaceutical companies develop new drugs that cure a variety of physical conditions. In order to be profitable, drug companies must sell enough of a product at a reasonable price to exceed break-even. Break-even points, however, create a problem for drugs, called "orphan drugs," targeted at rare diseases. These drugs are typically expensive to develop and have low sales volumes, making it impossible to achieve break-even. To ensure that orphan drugs are not overlooked, Congress passed the Orphan Drug Act, which provides incentives for pharmaceutical companies to develop drugs for rare diseases that might not generate enough sales to reach break-even. The program has been a great success. Since 1982, more than 200 orphan drugs have come to market, including **Jacobus Pharmaceutical Company Inc.**'s drug for the treatment of tuberculosis and **Novartis International AG**'s drug for the treatment of Paget's disease.

Objective 4

Using a cost-volume-profit chart and a profit-volume chart, determine the break-even point and sales necessary to achieve a target profit.

Graphic Approach to Cost-Volume-Profit Analysis

Cost-volume-profit analysis can be presented graphically as well as in equation form. Many managers prefer the graphic form because the operating profit or loss for different levels can be easily seen.

Cost-Volume-Profit (Break-Even) Chart

A **cost-volume-profit chart**, sometimes called a *break-even chart*, graphically shows sales, costs, and the related profit or loss for various levels of units sold. It assists in understanding the relationship among sales, costs, and operating profit or loss.

To illustrate, the cost-volume-profit chart in Exhibit 14 is based on the following data for Munoz Co.:

Total fixed costs	$100,000
Unit selling price	$50
Unit variable cost	30
Unit contribution margin	$20

The cost-volume-profit chart in Exhibit 14 is constructed using the following steps:

- Step 1. Volume in units of sales is indicated along the horizontal axis. The range of volume shown is the relevant range in which the company expects to operate. Dollar amounts of total sales and total costs are indicated along the vertical axis.
- Step 2. A total sales line is plotted by connecting the point at zero on the left corner of the graph to a second point on the chart. The second point is determined by multiplying

the maximum number of units in the relevant range, which is found on the far right of the horizontal axis, by the unit sales price. A line is then drawn through both of these points. This is the total sales line. For Munoz, the maximum number of units in the relevant range is 10,000. The second point on the line is determined by multiplying the 10,000 units by the $50 unit selling price to get the second point for the total sales line of $500,000 (10,000 units × $50). The sales line is drawn upward to the right from zero through the $500,000 point at the end of the relevant range.

- Step 3. A total cost line is plotted by beginning with total fixed costs on the vertical axis. A second point is determined by multiplying the maximum number of units in the relevant range, which is found on the far right of the horizontal axis, by the unit variable costs and adding the total fixed costs. A line is then drawn through both of these points. This is the total cost line. For Munoz, the maximum number of units in the relevant range is 10,000. The second point on the line is determined by multiplying the 10,000 units by the $30 unit variable cost and then adding the $100,000 total fixed costs to get the second point for the total estimated costs of $400,000 [(10,000 units × $30) + $100,000]. The cost line is drawn upward to the right from $100,000 on the vertical axis through the $400,000 point at the end of the relevant range.

- Step 4. The break-even point is the intersection point of the total sales and total cost lines. A vertical dotted line drawn downward at the intersection point indicates the units of sales at the break-even point. A horizontal dotted line drawn to the left at the intersection point indicates the sales dollars and costs at the break-even point.

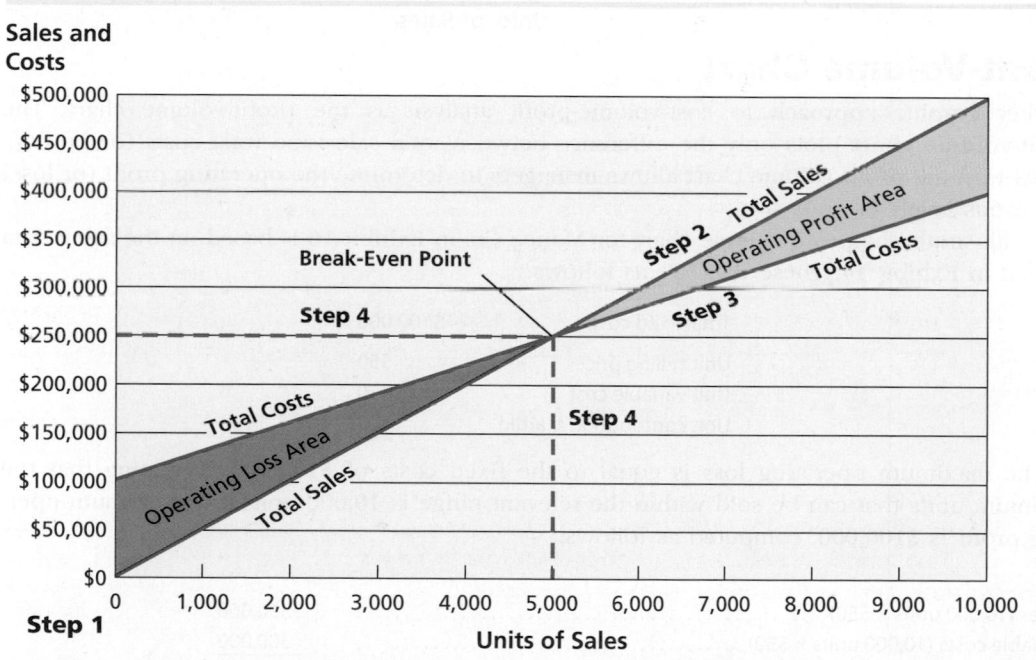

Sales and Costs

Exhibit 14

Cost-Volume-Profit Chart

In Exhibit 14, the break-even point for Munoz is $250,000 of sales, which represents sales of 5,000 units. Operating profits will be earned when sales levels are to the right of the break-even point (*operating profit area*). Operating losses will be incurred when sales levels are to the left of the break-even point (*operating loss area*).

Changes in the unit selling price, total fixed costs, and unit variable costs can be analyzed by using a cost-volume-profit chart. Using the data in Exhibit 14, assume that Munoz is evaluating a proposal to reduce fixed costs by $20,000. In this case, the total fixed costs would be $80,000 ($100,000 − $20,000).

Under this scenario, the total sales line is not changed, but the total cost line will change. As shown in Exhibit 15, the total cost line is redrawn, starting at the $80,000 point (total fixed costs) on the vertical axis. The second point is determined by multiplying the maximum number of units in the relevant range, which is found on the far right of the horizontal axis, by the unit variable costs and adding the fixed costs. For Munoz, this is the total estimated cost for 10,000 units, which is $380,000 [(10,000 units × $30) + $80,000]. The cost line is drawn upward to the right from $80,000 on the vertical axis through the $380,000 point. The revised cost-volume-profit chart in Exhibit 15 indicates that the break-even point for Munoz decreases to $200,000 and 4,000 units of sales.

Exhibit 15

Revised Cost-Volume-Profit Chart

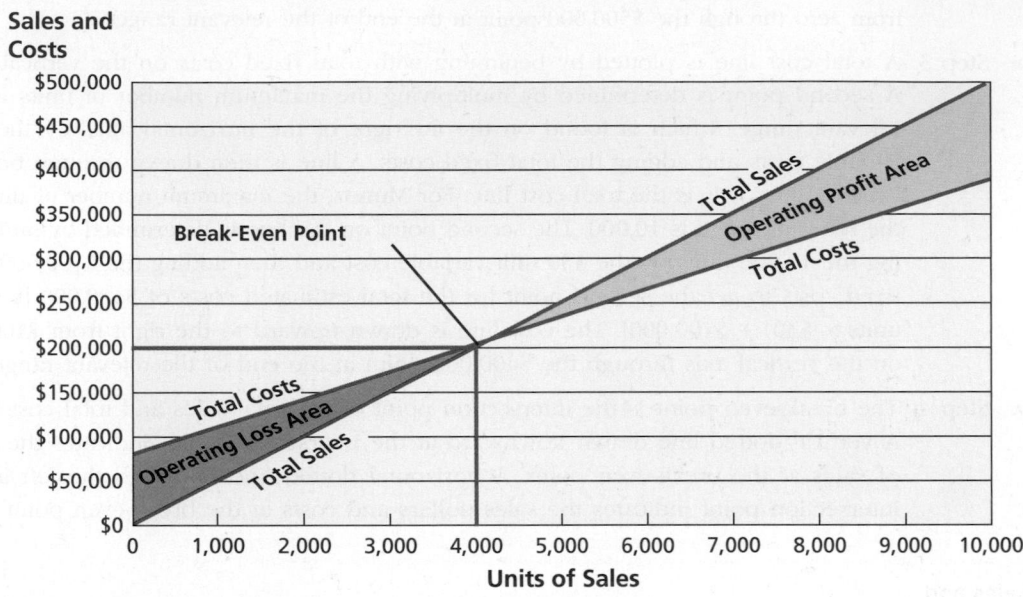

Profit-Volume Chart

Another graphic approach to cost-volume-profit analysis is the profit-volume chart. The **profit-volume chart** plots only the difference between total sales and total costs (or profits). In this way, the profit-volume chart allows managers to determine the operating profit (or loss) for various levels of units sold.

To illustrate, the profit-volume chart for Munoz Co. in Exhibit 16 is based on the same data as used in Exhibit 14. These data are as follows:

Total fixed costs	$100,000
Unit selling price	$50
Unit variable cost	30
Unit contribution margin	$20

The maximum operating loss is equal to the fixed costs of $100,000. Assuming that the maximum units that can be sold within the relevant range is 10,000 units, the maximum operating profit is $100,000, computed as follows:

Sales (10,000 units × $50)	$500,000
Variable costs (10,000 units × $30)	300,000
Contribution margin (10,000 units × $20)	$200,000
Fixed costs	100,000
Operating profit	$100,000 ◄—— Maximum profit

The profit-volume chart in Exhibit 16 is constructed using the following steps:

- Step 1. Volume in units of sales is indicated along the horizontal axis. The range of volume shown is the relevant range in which the company expects to operate. In Exhibit 16, the maximum units of sales is 10,000 units. Dollar amounts indicating operating profits and losses are shown along the vertical axis.
- Step 2. A point representing the maximum operating loss is plotted on the vertical axis at the left. This loss is equal to the total fixed costs at the zero level of sales. Thus, the maximum operating loss is equal to the fixed costs of $100,000.

- Step 3. A point representing the maximum operating profit within the relevant range is plotted on the right. Assuming that the maximum unit sales within the relevant range is 10,000 units, the maximum operating profit is $100,000.

- Step 4. A diagonal profit line is drawn connecting the maximum operating loss point with the maximum operating profit point.

- Step 5. The profit line intersects the horizontal zero operating profit line at the break-even point in units of sales. The area indicating an operating profit is identified to the right of the intersection, and the area indicating an operating loss is identified to the left of the intersection.

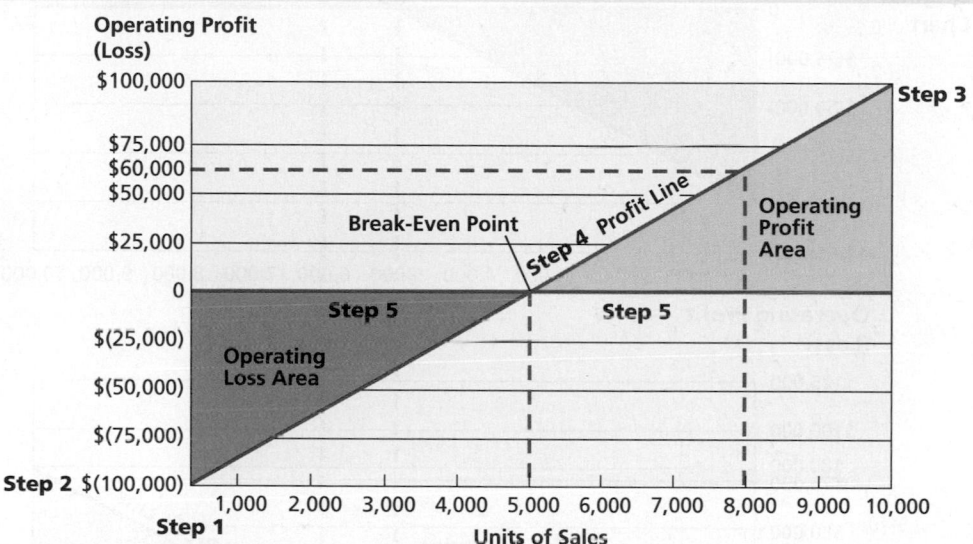

Exhibit 16
Profit-Volume Chart

In Exhibit 16, the break-even point for Munoz is 5,000 units of sales, which is equal to total sales of $250,000 (5,000 units × $50). Operating profit will be earned when sales levels are to the right of the break-even point (*operating profit area*). Operating losses will be incurred when sales levels are to the left of the break-even point (*operating loss area*). For example, at sales of 8,000 units, an operating profit of $60,000 will be earned, as shown in Exhibit 16.

The effect of changes in the unit selling price, total fixed costs, and unit variable costs on profit can be analyzed using a profit-volume chart. Using the data in Exhibit 16, consider the effect that a $20,000 increase in fixed costs will have on profit. In this case, the total fixed costs will increase to $120,000 ($100,000 + $20,000), and the maximum operating loss will also increase to $120,000. At the maximum sales of 10,000 units, the maximum operating profit would be $80,000, computed as follows:

Sales (10,000 units × $50).....................................	$500,000
Variable costs (10,000 units × $30)	300,000
Contribution margin (10,000 units × $20).....................	$200,000
Fixed costs	120,000
Operating profit...	$ 80,000 ← Revised maximum profit

A revised profit-volume chart is constructed by plotting the maximum operating loss and maximum operating profit points and drawing the revised profit line. The original and the revised profit-volume charts for Munoz are shown in Exhibit 17.

The revised profit-volume chart indicates that the break-even point for Munoz is 6,000 units of sales. This is equal to total sales of $300,000 (6,000 units × $50). The operating loss area of the chart has increased, while the operating profit area has decreased.

Use of Computers in Cost-Volume-Profit Analysis

With computers, the graphic approach and the mathematical approach to cost-volume-profit analysis are easy to use. Managers can vary assumptions regarding selling prices, costs, and

Exhibit 17

Original Profit-Volume Chart and Revised Profit-Volume Chart

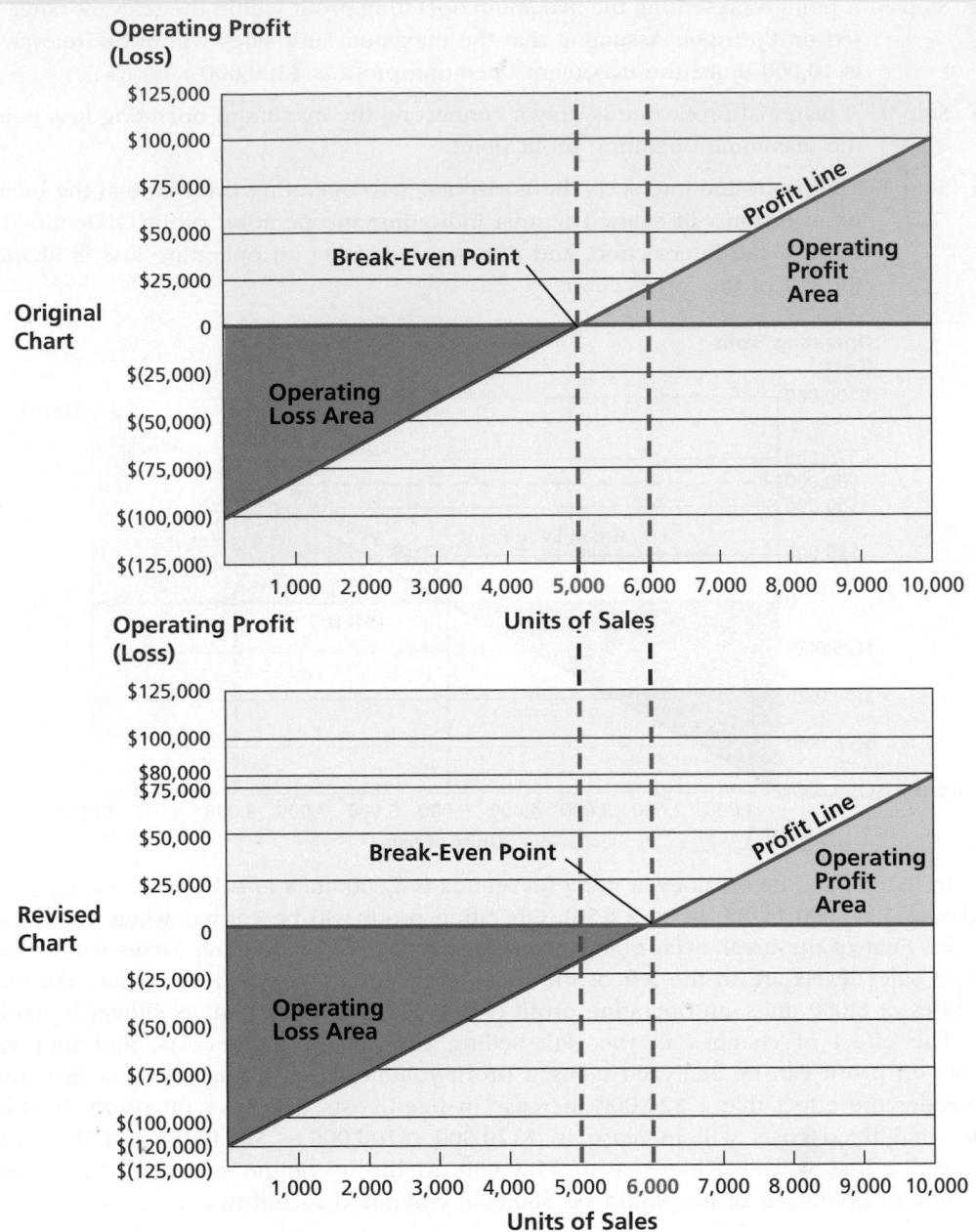

volume and can observe the effects of each change on the break-even point and profit. Such an analysis is called a *"what if"* analysis or *sensitivity* analysis.

Assumptions of Cost-Volume-Profit Analysis

Cost-volume-profit analysis depends on several assumptions. The primary assumptions are as follows:

- Total sales and total costs can be represented by straight lines.
- Within the relevant range of operating activity, the efficiency of operations does not change.
- Costs can be divided into fixed and variable components.
- The sales mix is constant.
- There is no change in the inventory quantities during the period.

These assumptions simplify cost-volume-profit analysis. Because they are often valid for the relevant range of operations, cost-volume-profit analysis is useful for decision making.[3]

---

[3] The impact of violating these assumptions is discussed in advanced accounting texts.

Check Up Corner 5-3 Break-Even Sales and Target Profit

DeHan Company, a sporting goods manufacturer, sells binoculars for $140 per unit. The variable cost is $100 per unit, while the fixed costs are $1,200,000.

A. Compute:
1. The anticipated break-even sales (units) for binoculars.
2. The sales (units) for binoculars required to realize target income from operations of $400,000.
B. Construct a cost-volume-profit chart for the anticipated break-even sales for binoculars.

Solution:

A. 1.

$$\text{Break-Even Sales (units)} = \frac{\text{Fixed Costs}}{\text{Unit Contribution Margin}}$$

Unit selling price	$140
Unit variable cost	100
Unit contribution margin	$ 40

$$\text{Break-Even Sales (units)} = \frac{\$1,200,000}{\$40}$$

$$= 30,000 \text{ units}$$

The break-even point is the level of operations at which a company's revenues and expenses are equal.

A company's revenues will equal costs when:
(Unit contribution margin × Units sold) = Fixed costs

Sales (30,000 units × $140)	$4,200,000
Variable costs (30,000 units × $100)	3,000,000
Contribution margin (30,000 units × $40)	$1,200,000
Fixed costs	1,200,000
Income from operations	$ 0

2.

$$\text{Sales (units)} = \frac{\text{Fixed Costs} + \text{Target Profit}}{\text{Unit Contribution Margin}}$$

$$\text{Sales (units)} = \frac{\$1,200,000 + \$400,000}{\$40}$$

$$= 40,000 \text{ units}$$

The sales required to earn a target or desired amount of profit may be computed by adding the amount of the target profit to fixed costs in the numerator of the break-even equation.

Sales (40,000 units × $140)	$5,600,000
Variable costs (40,000 units × $100)	4,000,000
Contribution margin (40,000 units × $40)	$1,600,000
Fixed costs	1,200,000
Income from operations	$ 400,000

B.

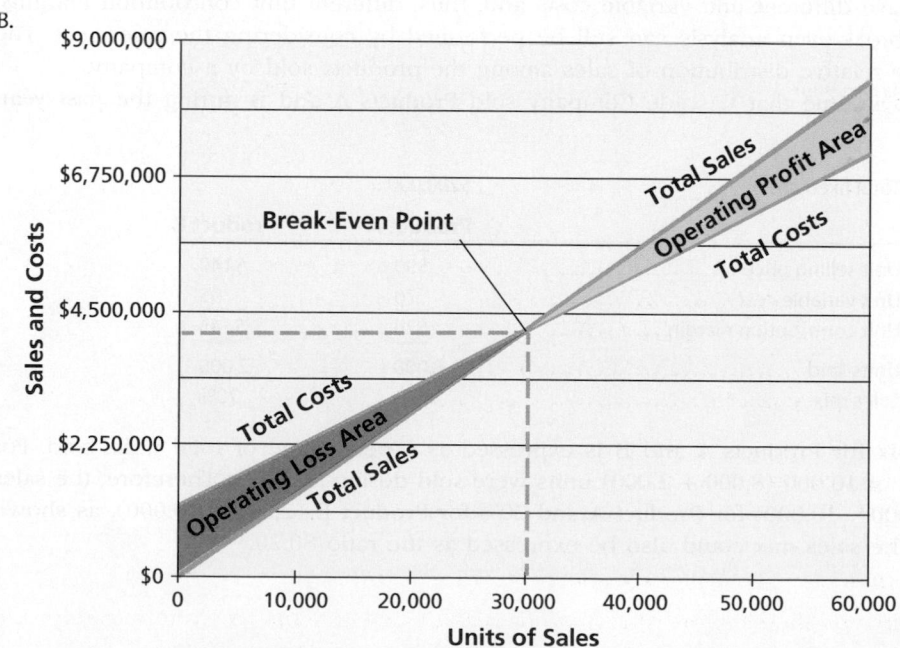

Why It Matters

Profit, Loss, and Break-Even in Major League Baseball

Major League Baseball is a tough game and a tough business. Ticket prices (unit selling price), player salaries and stadium fees (fixed costs), game day personnel (variable costs), and attendance (volume) converge to make it difficult for teams to make a profit, or at least break even. So, which major league baseball team was the most profitable in 2013? Well, it wasn't the World Champion Boston Red Sox. Nor was it the star-studded New York Yankees. Then, it had to be the recently turned around Los Angeles Angels, right? Not even close. It was actually the worst team in baseball—the Houston Astros.

Just how profitable were the Astros? They earned $99 million in 2013, which was more than the combined 2013 profits of the six most recent World Series champions. How could the team with the worst record in baseball since 2005 have one of the most

profitable years in baseball history? By paying careful attention to costs and volume. Between 2011 and 2013, the Astros cut their player payroll from $56 million to less than $13 million. That's right, all of the players on the Houston Astros baseball team, combined, made less in 2013 than Alex Rodriguez (New York Yankees), Cliff Lee (Philadelphia Phillies), Prince Fielder (Detroit Tigers), and Tim Lincecum (San Francisco Giants) made individually. While attendance at Astros games has dropped by around 20% since 2011, the cost reductions from reduced player salaries have far outpaced the drop in attendance, making the 2013 Astros the most profitable team in baseball history. While no one likes losing baseball games, the Houston Astros have shown that focusing on the relationship between cost and volume can yield a hefty profit, even when they aren't winning.

Source: D. Alexander, "2013 Houston Astros: Baseball's Worst Team Is the Most Profitable in History," *Forbes*, August 26, 2013.

Objective 5

Compute the break-even point for a company selling more than one product, the operating leverage, and the margin of safety.

Special Cost-Volume-Profit Relationships

Cost-volume-profit analysis can also be used when a company sells several products with different costs and prices. In addition, operating leverage and the margin of safety are useful in analyzing cost-volume-profit relationships.

Sales Mix Considerations

Many companies sell more than one product at different selling prices. In addition, the products normally have different unit variable costs and, thus, different unit contribution margins. In such cases, break-even analysis can still be performed by considering the sales mix. The **sales mix** is the relative distribution of sales among the products sold by a company.

To illustrate, assume that Cascade Company sold Products A and B during the past year, as follows:

Total fixed costs	$200,000	
	Product A	**Product B**
Unit selling price	$90	$140
Unit variable cost....................	70	95
Unit contribution margin	$20	$ 45
Units sold	8,000	2,000
Sales mix...........................	80%	20%

The sales mix for Products A and B is expressed as a percentage of total units sold. For Cascade, a total of 10,000 (8,000 + 2,000) units were sold during the year. Therefore, the sales mix is 80% (8,000 ÷ 10,000) for Product A and 20% for Product B (2,000 ÷ 10,000), as shown in Exhibit 18. The sales mix could also be expressed as the ratio 80:20.

Exhibit 18
Multiple Product
Sales Mix

Sales Mix

For break-even analysis, it is useful to think of Products A and B as components of one overall enterprise product called E. The unit selling price of E equals the sum of the unit selling prices of each product multiplied by its sales mix percentage. Likewise, the unit variable cost and unit contribution margin of E equal the sum of the unit variable costs and unit contribution margins of each product multiplied by its sales mix percentage.

For Cascade, the unit selling price, unit variable cost, and unit contribution margin for E are computed as follows:

Product E	Product A	Product B
Unit selling price of E	$100 = ($90 × 0.8)	+ ($140 × 0.2)
Unit variable cost of E	75 = ($70 × 0.8)	+ ($95 × 0.2)
Unit contribution margin of E	$ 25 = ($20 × 0.8)	+ ($45 × 0.2)

Cascade has total fixed costs of $200,000. The break-even point of 8,000 units of E can be determined as follows using the unit selling price, unit variable cost, and unit contribution margin of E:

$$\text{Break-Even Sales (units) for E} = \frac{\text{Fixed Costs}}{\text{Unit Contribution Margin}} = \frac{\$200,000}{\$25} = 8,000 \text{ units}$$

Because the sales mix for Products A and B is 80% and 20% respectively, the break-even quantity of A is 6,400 units (8,000 units × 80%) and B is 1,600 units (8,000 units × 20%) which is verified in Exhibit 19.

	Product A	Product B	Total
Sales:			
6,400 units × $90	$576,000		$576,000
1,600 units × $140		$224,000	224,000
Total sales	$576,000	$224,000	$800,000
Variable costs:			
6,400 units × $70	$448,000		$448,000
1,600 units × $95		$152,000	152,000
Total variable costs	$448,000	$152,000	$600,000
Contribution margin	$128,000	$ 72,000	$200,000
Fixed costs			200,000
Income from operations			$ 0

Exhibit 19
Break-Even Sales:
Multiple Products

← Break-even point

The effects of changes in the sales mix on the break-even point can be determined by assuming a different sales mix. The break-even point of E can then be recomputed.

The sales mix of Ford and Lincoln vehicles sold has a major impact on **Ford Motor Company**'s overall profitability.

*Link to Ford
Motor Company*

Operating Leverage

The relationship between a company's contribution margin and income from operations is measured by **operating leverage**. A company's operating leverage is computed as follows:

$$\text{Operating Leverage} = \frac{\text{Contribution Margin}}{\text{Income from Operations}}$$

The difference between contribution margin and income from operations is fixed costs. Thus, companies with high fixed costs will normally have high operating leverage. Examples of such companies include airline and automotive companies, like **Ford Motor Company**. Low operating leverage is normal for companies that are labor intensive, such as professional service companies, which have low fixed costs.

To illustrate operating leverage, assume the following data for Jones Inc. and Wilson Inc.:

	Jones Inc.	Wilson Inc.
Sales	$400,000	$400,000
Variable costs	300,000	300,000
Contribution margin	$100,000	$100,000
Fixed costs	80,000	50,000
Income from operations	$ 20,000	$ 50,000

As shown, Jones and Wilson have the same sales, the same variable costs, and the same contribution margin. However, Jones has larger fixed costs than Wilson and, thus, a higher operating leverage. The operating leverage for each company is computed as follows:

Jones Inc.

$$\text{Operating Leverage} = \frac{\text{Contribution Margin}}{\text{Income from Operations}} = \frac{\$100,000}{\$20,000} = 5$$

Wilson Inc.

$$\text{Operating Leverage} = \frac{\text{Contribution Margin}}{\text{Income from Operations}} = \frac{\$100,000}{\$50,000} = 2$$

Operating leverage can be used to measure the impact of changes in sales on income from operations. Using operating leverage, the effect of changes in sales on income from operations is computed as follows:

$$\frac{\text{Percent Change in}}{\text{Income from Operations}} = \frac{\text{Percent Change in}}{\text{Sales}} \times \frac{\text{Operating}}{\text{Leverage}}$$

To illustrate, assume that sales increased by 10%, or $40,000 ($400,000 × 10%), for Jones and Wilson. The percent increase in income from operations for Jones and Wilson is computed as follows:

Jones Inc.

$$\frac{\text{Percent Change in}}{\text{Income from Operations}} = \frac{\text{Percent Change in}}{\text{Sales}} \times \frac{\text{Operating}}{\text{Leverage}}$$

$$= 10\% \times 5 = 50\%$$

Wilson Inc.

$$\frac{\text{Percent Change in}}{\text{Income from Operations}} = \frac{\text{Percent Change in}}{\text{Sales}} \times \frac{\text{Operating}}{\text{Leverage}}$$

$$= 10\% \times 2 = 20\%$$

As shown, Jones's income from operations increases by 50%, while Wilson's income from operations increases by only 20%. The validity of this analysis is shown in the following income statements for Jones and Wilson based on the 10% increase in sales:

	Jones Inc.	Wilson Inc.
Sales	$440,000	$440,000
Variable costs	330,000	330,000
Contribution margin	$110,000	$110,000
Fixed costs	80,000	50,000
Income from operations	$ 30,000	$ 60,000

The preceding income statements indicate that Jones's income from operations increased from $20,000 to $30,000, a 50% increase ($10,000 ÷ $20,000). In contrast, Wilson's income from operations increased from $50,000 to $60,000, a 20% increase ($10,000 ÷ $50,000).

Because even a small increase in sales will generate a large percentage increase in income from operations, Jones might consider ways to increase sales. Such actions could include special advertising or sales promotions. In contrast, Wilson might consider ways to increase operating leverage by reducing variable costs.

The impact of a change in sales on income from operations for companies with high and low operating leverage is summarized in Exhibit 20.

Operating Leverage	Percentage Impact on Income from Operations from a Change in Sales
High	Large
Low	Small

Exhibit 20
Effect of Operating Leverage on Income from Operations

Ford Motor Company has a high proportion of fixed costs with the result that small changes in units sold can significantly affect its overall profitability.
Source: Ford Motor Company, Form 10-K for Year Ended December 31, 2014.

Link to Ford Motor Company

Margin of Safety

The **margin of safety** indicates the possible decrease in sales that may occur before an operating loss results. Thus, if the margin of safety is low, even a small decline in sales revenue may result in an operating loss.

The margin of safety may be expressed in the following ways:

- Dollars of sales
- Units of sales
- Percent of current sales

To illustrate, assume the following data:

Sales	$250,000
Sales at the break-even point	200,000
Unit selling price	25

The margin of safety in dollars of sales is $50,000 ($250,000 – $200,000). The margin of safety in units is 2,000 units ($50,000 ÷ $25). The margin of safety expressed as a percent of current sales is 20%, computed as follows:

$$\text{Margin of Safety} = \frac{\text{Sales} - \text{Sales at Break-Even Point}}{\text{Sales}}$$

$$= \frac{\$250,000 - \$200,000}{\$250,000} = \frac{\$50,000}{\$250,000} = 20\%$$

Therefore, the current sales may decline $50,000, 2,000 units, or 20% before an operating loss occurs.

Check Up Corner 5-4   Special Cost-Volume-Profit Relationships

Blueberry Inc., a consumer electronics company, manufactures and sells two products, smartphones and tablet computers. The unit selling price, unit variable cost, and sales mix for each product are as follows:

Products	Unit Selling Price	Unit Variable Cost	Sales Mix
Smartphone	$650	$560	60%
Tablet	550	475	40%

The company's fixed costs are $4,200,000.

A. How many units of each product would be sold at the break-even point?

B. Assume Blueberry sells 37,500 smartphones and 25,000 tablets during a recent year. Compute the company's (1) operating leverage and (2) margin of safety.

In break-even analysis for multiple products, it is useful to think of the individual product as components of one overall product called product E.

Solution:

A.

Product E		Smartphone	Tablet
Unit selling price of E	$610 =	($650 × 0.6) +	($550 × 0.4)
Unit variable cost of E	526 =	($560 × 0.6) +	($475 × 0.4)
Unit contribution margin of E	$ 84 =	($90 × 0.6) +	($75 × 0.4)

The unit selling price of E equals the sum of the unit selling price of each product multiplied by its sales mix percentage.

The unit variable cost of E equals the sum of the unit variable cost of each product multiplied by its sales mix percentage.

$$\text{Break-Even Sales of E (units)} = \frac{\text{Fixed Costs}}{\text{Unit Contribution Margin}}$$

$$\text{Break-Even Sales of E (units)} = \frac{\$4,200,000}{\$84}$$

$$= 50,000 \text{ units}$$

The break-even number of units of E is determined by dividing the company's total fixed costs by the unit contribution margin of E.

	Smartphones	Tablets
Break-even sales of E (units)	50,000	50,000
Sales mix	× 60%	× 40%
Break-even sales of product	30,000	20,000

The break-even quantity of each product is determined by multiplying the sales mix percentage of each product by the break-even units of product E.

B. 1.

	Smartphones	Tablets	Total
Sales	$24,375,000	$13,750,000	$38,125,000
Variable costs	21,000,000	11,875,000	32,875,000
Contribution margin	$ 3,375,000	$ 1,875,000	$ 5,250,000
Fixed costs			4,200,000
Income from operations			$ 1,050,000

37,500 units × $650 per unit

25,000 units × $550 per unit

37,500 units × $560 per unit

25,000 units × $475 per unit

$$\text{Operating Leverage} = \frac{\text{Contribution Margin}}{\text{Income from Operations}}$$

$$\text{Operating Leverage} = \frac{\$5,250,000}{\$1,050,000}$$

$$= 5.0$$

The relationship between a company's contribution margin and income from operations is called operating leverage.

2.

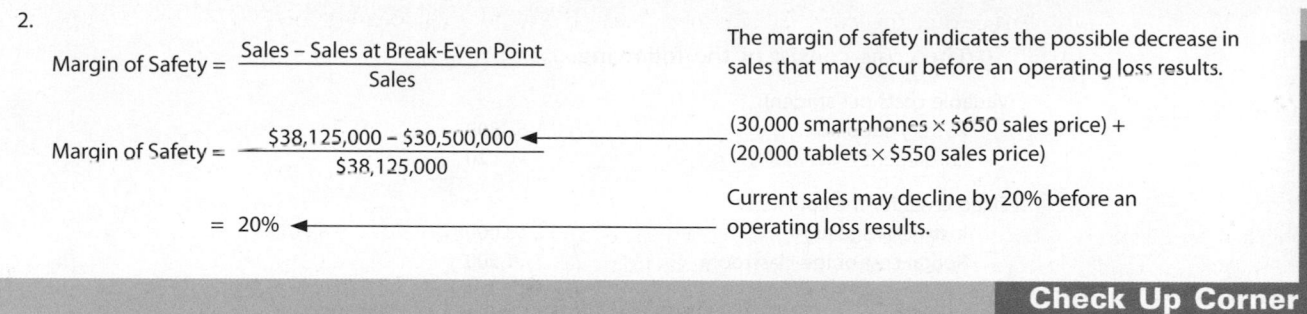

Margin of Safety $= \dfrac{\text{Sales} - \text{Sales at Break-Even Point}}{\text{Sales}}$

Margin of Safety $= \dfrac{\$38{,}125{,}000 - \$30{,}500{,}000}{\$38{,}125{,}000} \longleftarrow$

$= 20\% \longleftarrow$

The margin of safety indicates the possible decrease in sales that may occur before an operating loss results.

(30,000 smartphones $\times$ \$650 sales price) + (20,000 tablets $\times$ \$550 sales price)

Current sales may decline by 20% before an operating loss results.

Check Up Corner

Analysis for Decision Making

Cost-Volume-Profit Analysis for Service Companies

The break-even point is as relevant in a service company as it is in a manufacturing company. Services are delivered to customers, such as patients, or to other items, such as invested funds. Thus, cost-volume-profit relationships in a service company are measured with respect to customers and activities, rather than units of product. Examples are as follows:

Service	Break-Even Analysis
Education	Break-even number of students per course
Air transportation	Break-even number of passengers per flight
Health care	Break-even number of patients per outpatient facility
Hotel	Break-even number of guests per time period (day, month, etc.)
Freight transportation	Break-even number of tons per train
Theme park	Break-even number of guests per time period (day, month, etc.)
Financial services	Break-even number of invested funds (dollars) under management
Subscription services	Break-even number of subscribers

Break-even analysis for a service company involves identifying the correct unit of analysis and the correct measure of activity for that unit. For example, the unit of analysis for an educational institution could be a course, a major, a college, or the university as a whole. For a specific course, the measure of activity would be the number of students enrolled in the course. Each student is the same in his or her demand for course-level services. Thus, a break-even analysis would discover the number of students required for the course to break even.

At other units of analysis, the measure of activity may change. For example, the break-even for a college would likely be measured in number of student credit hours, not number of students. Not all students are equal in their demand for college services, because some students are part-time and some are full-time. However, each student credit hour is nearly the same.

Moreover, the unit of analysis can influence whether costs are defined as fixed or variable. For example, the instructor's salary is a fixed cost for a specific course, but can be a variable cost to the number of sections taught at the college level.

To illustrate, consider the break-even number of students for a noncredit course in pottery. The course tuition is $500.

Objective
Describe and illustrate the use of cost-volume-profit analysis for decision making in a service business.

The costs consist of the following:

Variable costs per student:

Pottery supplies	$ 300
Enrollment costs	20

Fixed costs for the course:

Instructor's salary	$3,000
Rental cost of the classroom	1,500

The break-even point is computed as follows:

$$\text{Break-Even Sales (units)} = \frac{\text{Fixed Costs}}{\text{Unit Contribution Margin}}$$

$$\text{Break-Even Sales (units)} = \frac{\$4,500}{\$500 - \$320} = 25 \text{ students}$$

Thus, the course would need to enroll 25 students to break even.

Make a Decision   Cost-Volume-Profit Analysis for Service Companies

An airline is considering a new flight between Atlanta and Los Angeles. The average fare per seat for the flight is $760. The costs associated with the flight are as follows:

Fixed costs for the flight:

Crew salaries.........................	$ 5,000
Operating costs.......................	50,000
Aircraft depreciation	25,000
Total...............................	$80,000

Variable costs per passenger:

Passenger check-in....................	$ 20
Operating costs.......................	100
Total...............................	$120

The airline estimates that the flight will sell 175 seats.

A. Determine the break-even number of passengers per flight.
B. Based on your answer in (A), should the airline add this flight to its schedule?
C. How much profit should each flight produce?
D. What additional issues might the airline consider in this decision?

Solution:

A.

$$\text{Break-Even Sales (units)} = \frac{\text{Fixed Costs}}{\text{Unit Contribution Margin}}$$

$$\text{Break-Even Sales (units)} = \frac{\$80,000}{\$760 - \$120} = 125 \text{ passengers}$$

B. The airline should consider adding the flight. The number of passengers (175) is well above the break-even number of passengers for the flight (125).

C. Each flight should cover fixed costs and produce a contribution margin for 50 additional passengers above break-even. Thus, the profit for the flight would be computed as:

$$(175 \text{ passengers} - 125 \text{ passengers}) \times (\$760 - \$120) = \$32,000$$

D. First, the airline should consider the impact of the new flight on other flights to Los Angeles. That is, the airline should determine whether the seats sold on the new flight are truly incremental seats for the airline, or whether passengers are shifting from one of the airline's other flights to this new flight. Second, the airline should consider the impact of the new flight on system load. For example, is there sufficient gate, runway, maintenance, and baggage handling capacity to support the additional flight? If not, the fixed costs of adding the flight could be much higher than $80,000.

Make a Decision

Let's Review

Chapter Summary

1. Variable costs vary in proportion to changes in the level of activity. Fixed costs remain the same in total dollar amount as the level of activity changes. Mixed costs are comprised of both fixed and variable costs.

2. Contribution margin is the excess of sales revenue over variable costs and can be expressed as a ratio (contribution margin ratio) or a dollar amount (unit contribution margin).

3. The break-even point is the point at which a business's revenues exactly equal costs. The mathematical approach to cost-volume-profit analysis uses the unit contribution margin concept and mathematical equations to determine the break-even point and the volume necessary to achieve a target profit.

4. Graphical methods can be used to determine the break-even point and the volume necessary to achieve a target profit. A cost-volume-profit chart focuses on the relationship among costs, sales, and operating profit or loss. The profit-volume chart focuses on profits rather than on revenues and costs.

5. Cost-volume-profit relationships can be used for analyzing the effects of sales mix on the break-even point and profits. Operating leverage can be used to analyze the effects of changes in sales on income from operations. The margin of safety indicates how much sales must decrease before an operating loss occurs.

Key Terms

activity bases (drivers) (204)
break-even point (215)
contribution margin (212)
contribution margin ratio (212)
cost behavior (204)
cost-volume-profit
   analysis (212)

cost-volume-profit chart (220)
fixed costs (206)
high-low method (209)
margin of safety (229)
mixed costs (208)
operating leverage (228)

profit-volume chart (222)
relevant range (204)
sales mix (226)
unit contribution margin (213)
variable costing (210)
variable costs (205)

Practice

Multiple-Choice Questions

1. Which of the following statements describes variable costs?
   A. Costs that vary on a per-unit basis as the level of activity changes
   B. Costs that vary in total in direct proportion to changes in the level of activity
   C. Costs that remain the same in total dollar amount as the level of activity changes
   D. Costs that vary on a per-unit basis, but remain the same in total as the level of activity changes

2. If sales are $500,000, variable costs are $200,000, and fixed costs are $240,000, what is the contribution margin ratio?
   A. 40%
   B. 48%
   C. 52%
   D. 60%

3. If the unit selling price is $16, the unit variable cost is $12, and fixed costs are $160,000, what is the break-even sales (units)?
   A. 5,714 units
   B. 10,000 units
   C. 13,333 units
   D. 40,000 units

4. Based on the data presented in Question 3, how many units of sales would be required to realize income from operations of $20,000?
   A. 11,250 units
   B. 5,000 units
   C. 40,000 units
   D. 45,000 units

5. Based on the following operating data, what is the operating leverage?

Sales	$600,000
Variable costs	240,000
Contribution margin	$360,000
Fixed costs	160,000
Income from operations	$200,000

   A. 0.8
   B. 1.2
   C. 1.8
   D. 4.0

Answers provided after Problem. Need more practice? Find additional multiple-choice questions, exercises, and problems in CengageNOWv2.

Exercises

SHOW ME HOW

1. High-low method   Obj. 1

The manufacturing costs of Lightfoot Industries for three months of the year follow:

	Total Costs	Units Produced
January	$640,000	30,000 units
February	900,000	40,000
March	350,000	12,500

Using the high-low method, determine (A) the variable cost per unit and (B) the total fixed cost.

SHOW ME HOW

2. Contribution margin   Obj. 2

Michigan Company sells 10,000 units at $100 per unit. Variable costs are $75 per unit, and fixed costs are $125,000. Determine (A) the contribution margin ratio, (B) the unit contribution margin, and (C) income from operations.

SHOW ME HOW

3. Break-even point   Obj. 3

Santana sells a product for $115 per unit. The variable cost is $75 per unit, while fixed costs are $65,000. Determine (A) the break-even point in sales units and (B) the break-even point if the selling price were increased to $125 per unit.

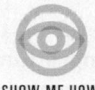
SHOW ME HOW

4. Target profit   Obj. 3

Versa Inc. sells a product for $100 per unit. The variable cost is $75 per unit, and fixed costs are $45,000. Determine (A) the break-even point in sales units and (B) the sales units required for the company to achieve a target profit of $25,000.

SHOW ME HOW

5. Sales mix and break-even analysis   Obj. 5

Wide Open Industries Inc. has fixed costs of $475,000. The unit selling price, variable cost per unit, and contribution margin per unit for the company's two products follow:

Product	Selling Price	Variable Cost per Unit	Contribution Margin per Unit
AA	$145	$105	$40
BB	110	75	35

The sales mix for products AA and BB is 60% and 40%, respectively. Determine the break-even point in units of AA and BB.

SHOW ME HOW

6. Operating leverage   Obj. 5

SungSam Enterprises reports the following data:

Sales	$340,000
Variable costs	180,000
Contribution margin	$160,000
Fixed costs	80,000
Income from operations	$ 80,000

Determine SungSam Enterprises's operating leverage.

SHOW ME HOW

7. Margin of safety   Obj. 5

Melton Inc. has sales of $1,750,000, and the break-even point in sales dollars is $875,000. Determine the company's margin of safety as a percent of current sales.

Answers provided after Problem. Need more practice? Find additional multiple-choice questions, exercises, and problems in CengageNOWv2.

Problem

Wyatt Inc. expects to maintain the same inventories at the end of the year as at the beginning of the year. The estimated fixed costs for the year are $288,000, and the estimated variable costs per unit are $14. It is expected that 60,000 units will be sold at a price of $20 per unit. Maximum sales within the relevant range are 70,000 units.

Instructions

1. What is (A) the contribution margin ratio and (B) the unit contribution margin?

2. Determine the break-even point in units.

3. Construct a cost-volume-profit chart, indicating the break-even point.

4. Construct a profit-volume chart, indicating the break-even point.

5. What is the margin of safety?

Need more practice? Find additional multiple-choice questions, exercises, and problems in CengageNOWv2.

Answers

Multiple-Choice Questions

1. **B** Variable costs vary in total in direct proportion to changes in the level of activity (answer B). Costs that vary on a per-unit basis as the level of activity changes (answer A) or remain constant in total dollar amount as the level of activity changes (answer C), or both (answer D), are fixed costs.

2. **D** The contribution margin ratio indicates the percentage of each sales dollar available to cover the fixed costs and provide income from operations and is determined as follows:

$$\text{Contribution Margin Ratio} = \frac{\text{Sales} - \text{Variable Costs}}{\text{Sales}}$$

$$\text{Contribution Margin Ratio} = \frac{\$500,000 - \$200,000}{\$500,000}$$

$$= 60\%$$

3. **D** The break-even sales of 40,000 units (answer D) is computed as follows:

$$\text{Break-Even Sales (units)} = \frac{\text{Fixed Costs}}{\text{Unit Contribution Margin}}$$

$$\text{Break-Even Sales (units)} = \frac{\$160,000}{\$4} = 40,000 \text{ units}$$

4. **D** Sales of 45,000 (answer D) units are required to realize income from operations of $20,000, computed as follows:

$$\text{Sales (units)} = \frac{\text{Fixed Costs} + \text{Target Profit}}{\text{Unit Contribution Margin}}$$

$$\text{Sales (units)} = \frac{\$160,000 + \$20,000}{\$4} = 45,000 \text{ units}$$

5. **C** The operating leverage is 1.8 (answer C), computed as follows:

$$\text{Operating Leverage} = \frac{\text{Contribution Margin}}{\text{Income from Operations}}$$

$$\text{Operating Leverage} = \frac{\$360,000}{\$200,000} = 1.8$$

Exercises

1.
    A. $20 per unit = ($900,000 − $350,000) ÷ (40,000 units − 12,500 units)

    B. $100,000 = $900,000 − ($20 × 40,000 units), or $350,000 − ($20 × 12,500 units)

2.
    A. 25.0% = ($100 − $75) ÷ $100, or ($1,000,000 − $750,000) ÷ $1,000,000

    B. $25 per unit = $100 − $75

    C.

Sales............................	$1,000,000	(10,000 units × $100 per unit)
Variable costs	750,000	(10,000 units × $75 per unit)
Contribution margin.............	$ 250,000	(10,000 units × $25 per unit)
Fixed costs	125,000	
Income from operations	$ 125,000	

3.
    A. 1,625 units = $65,000 ÷ ($115 − $75)

    B. 1,300 units = $65,000 ÷ ($125 − $75)

4.
    A. 1,800 units = $45,000 ÷ ($100 − $75)

    B. 2,800 units = ($45,000 + $25,000) ÷ ($100 − $75)

5.

Unit selling price of E: [($145 × 0.60) + ($110 × 0.40)] = $131.00

Unit variable cost of E: [($105 × 0.60) + ($75 × 0.40)] = $93.00

Unit contribution margin of E $ 38.00

Break-Even Sales (units) = $475,000 ÷ $38.00 = 12,500 units

Break-Even Sales (units) for AA = 12,500 units of E × 60% = 7,500 units of Product AA

Break-Even Sales (units) for BB = 12,500 units of E × 40% = 5,000 units of Product BB

6.
$$\text{Operating Leverage} = \frac{\text{Contribution Margin}}{\text{Income from Operations}} = \frac{\$160,000}{\$80,000} = 2$$

7.
$$\text{Margin of Safety} = \frac{\text{Sales − Sales at Break-Even Point}}{\text{Sales}}$$
$$= (\$1,750,000 − \$875,000) ÷ \$1,750,000 = 50\%$$

Need more help? Watch step-by-step videos of how to compute answers to these Exercises in CengageNOWv2.

Problem

1. A. $\text{Contribution Margin Ratio} = \dfrac{\text{Sales − Variable Costs}}{\text{Sales}}$

$$= \frac{(60,000 \text{ units} × \$20) − (60,000 \text{ units} × \$14)}{(60,000 \text{ units} × \$20)}$$

$$= \frac{\$1,200,000 − \$840,000}{\$1,200,000} = \frac{\$360,000}{\$1,200,000}$$

$$= 30\%$$

    B. Unit Contribution Margin = Unit Selling Price − Unit Variable Costs
$$= \$20 − \$14 = \$6$$

2.   Break-Even Sales (units) = $\dfrac{\text{Fixed Costs}}{\text{Unit Contribution Margin}}$

$$= \dfrac{\$288,000}{\$6} = 48,000 \text{ units}$$

3.   **Sales and Costs**

4.   **Operating Profit (Loss)**

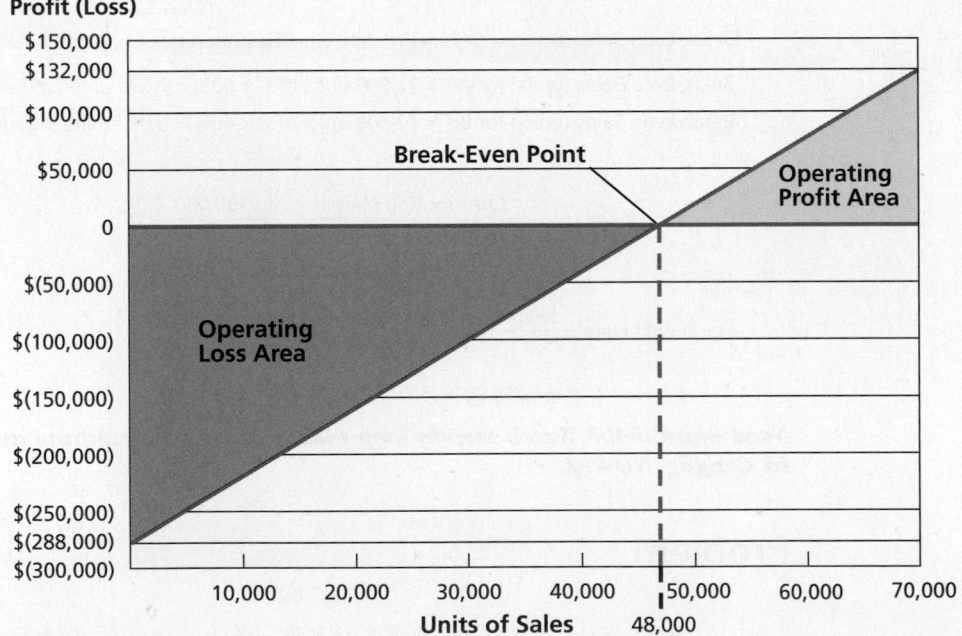

5.   Margin of safety:

Expected sales (60,000 units × $20)	$1,200,000
Break-even point (48,000 units × $20)	960,000
Margin of safety	$ 240,000

or

Margin of Safety (units) = $\dfrac{\text{Margin of Safety (dollars)}}{\text{Unit Selling Price}}$

$$= \dfrac{\$240,000}{\$20} = 12,000 \text{ units}$$

or

$$\text{Margin of Safety} = \frac{\text{Sales} - \text{Sales at Break-Even Point}}{\text{Sales}}$$

$$= \frac{\$240,000}{\$1,200,000} = 20\%$$

Discussion Questions

1. Describe how total variable costs and unit variable costs behave with changes in the level of activity.

2. Which of the following costs would be classified as variable and which would be classified as fixed, if units produced is the activity base?

   A. Direct materials costs
   B. Electricity costs of $0.35 per kilowatt-hour

3. Describe how total fixed costs and unit fixed costs behave with changes in the level of activity.

4. In applying the high-low method of cost estimation to mixed costs, how is the total fixed cost estimated?

5. If fixed costs increase, what would be the impact on the (A) contribution margin? (B) income from operations?

6. An examination of the accounting records of Clowney

Company disclosed a high contribution margin ratio and production at a level below maximum capacity. Based on this information, suggest a likely means of improving income from operations. Explain.

7. If the unit cost of direct materials is decreased, what effect will this change have on the break-even point?

8. Both Austin Company and Hill Company had the same unit sales, total costs, and income from operations for the current fiscal year; yet, Austin Company had a lower break-even point than Hill Company. Explain the reason for this difference in break-even points.

9. How does the sales mix affect the calculation of the break-even point?

10. What does operating leverage measure, and how is it computed?

Basic Exercises

SHOW ME HOW

BE 5-1 High-low method   Obj. 1

The manufacturing costs of Ackerman Industries for the first three months of the year follow:

	Total Costs	Units Produced
January	$1,900,000	20,000 units
February	2,250,000	27,000
March	2,400,000	30,000

Using the high-low method, determine (A) the variable cost per unit and (B) the total fixed cost.

SHOW ME HOW

BE 5-2 Contribution margin   Obj. 2

Lanning Company sells 160,000 units at $45 per unit. Variable costs are $27 per unit, and fixed costs are $975,000. Determine (A) the contribution margin ratio, (B) the unit contribution margin, and (C) income from operations.

SHOW ME HOW

BE 5-3 Break-even point   Obj. 3

Bigelow Inc. sells a product for $1,200 per unit. The variable cost is $816 per unit, while fixed costs are $3,120,000. Determine (A) the break-even point in sales units and (B) the break-even point if the selling price were increased to $1,232 per unit.

SHOW ME HOW

BE 5-4   Target profit   Obj. 3

Ramirez Company sells a product for $80 per unit. The variable cost is $60 per unit, and fixed costs are $4,850,000. Determine (A) the break-even point in sales units and (B) the sales units required for the company to achieve a target profit of $500,000.

SHOW ME HOW

BE 5-5   Sales mix and break-even analysis   Obj. 5

Hughes Company has fixed costs of $3,565,000. The unit selling price, variable cost per unit, and contribution margin per unit for the company's two products follow:

Product	Selling Price	Variable Cost per Unit	Contribution Margin per Unit
Model 94	$1,600	$960	$640
Model 81	1,000	800	200

The sales mix for products Model 94 and Model 81 is 25% and 75%, respectively. Determine the break-even point in units of Model 94 and Model 81.

SHOW ME HOW

BE 5-6   Operating leverage   Obj. 5

Taft Co. reports the following data:

Sales	$875,000
Variable costs	425,000
Contribution margin	$450,000
Fixed costs	150,000
Income from operations	$300,000

Determine Taft Co.'s operating leverage.

SHOW ME HOW

BE 5-7   Margin of safety   Obj. 5

Liu Company has sales of $48,500,000, and the break-even point in sales dollars is $31,040,000. Determine the company's margin of safety as a percent of current sales.

Exercises

EX 5-1   Classify costs   Obj. 1

Following is a list of various costs incurred in producing replacement automobile parts. With respect to the production and sale of these auto parts, classify each cost as either variable, fixed, or mixed.

1. Oil used in manufacturing equipment
2. Plastic
3. Property taxes, $165,000 per year on factory building and equipment
4. Salary of plant manager
5. Cost of labor for hourly workers
6. Packaging
7. Factory cleaning costs, $6,000 per month
8. Metal
9. Rent on warehouse, $10,000 per month plus $25 per square foot of storage used
10. Property insurance premiums, $3,600 per month plus $0.01 for each dollar of property over $1,200,000
11. Straight-line depreciation on the production equipment
12. Hourly wages of machine operators
13. Electricity costs, $0.20 per kilowatt-hour
14. Computer chip (purchased from a vendor)
15. Pension cost, $1.00 per employee hour on the job

EX 5-2 Identify cost graphs

Obj. 1

The following cost graphs illustrate various types of cost behavior:

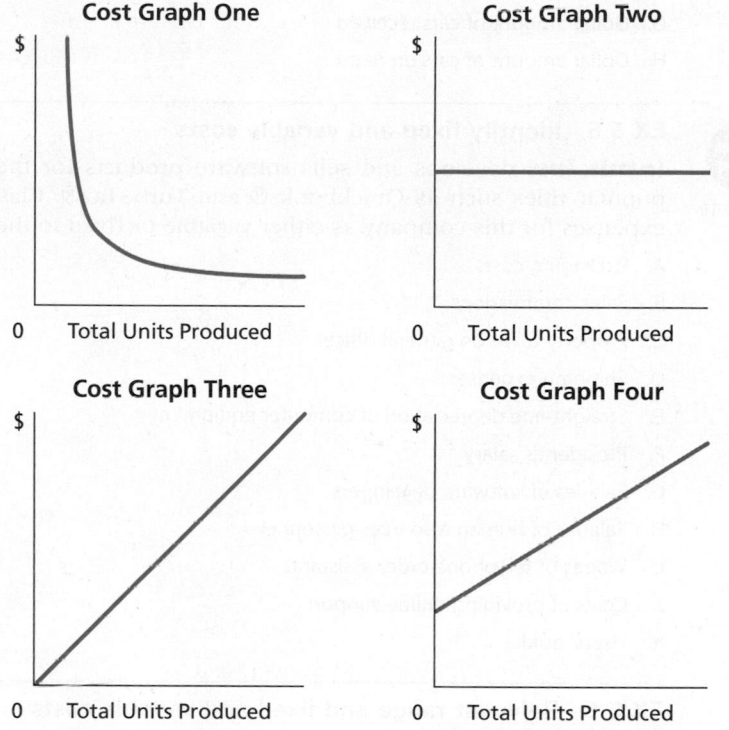

For each of the following costs, identify the cost graph that best illustrates its cost behavior as the number of units produced increases:

A. Total direct materials cost

B. Electricity costs of $1,000 per month plus $0.10 per kilowatt-hour

C. Per-unit cost of straight-line depreciation on factory equipment

D. Salary of quality control supervisor, $20,000 per month

E. Per-unit direct labor cost

EX 5-3 Identify activity bases

Obj. 1

For a major university, match each cost in the following table with the activity base most appropriate to it. An activity base may be used more than once or not used at all.

Cost:
1. Financial aid office salaries
2. Office supplies
3. Instructor salaries
4. Housing personnel wages
5. Employee wages for maintaining student records
6. Admissions office salaries

Activity Base:
A. Number of enrollment applications
B. Number of students
C. Student credit hours
D. Number of enrolled students and alumni
E. Number of financial aid applications
F. Number of students living on campus

EX 5-4 Identify activity bases

Obj. 1

From the following list of activity bases for an automobile dealership, select the base that would be most appropriate for each of these costs: (1) preparation costs (cleaning, oil, and gasoline costs) for each car received, (2) salespersons' commission of 5% of the sales price for each car sold, and (3) administrative costs for ordering cars.

A. Number of cars sold

B. Dollar amount of cars ordered

C. Number of cars ordered

(Continued)

D. Number of cars on hand

E. Number of cars received

F. Dollar amount of cars sold

G. Dollar amount of cars received

H. Dollar amount of cars on hand

REAL WORLD

EX 5-5 Identify fixed and variable costs
Obj. 1

Intuit Inc. develops and sells software products for the personal finance market, including popular titles such as Quickbooks® and TurboTax®. Classify each of the following costs and expenses for this company as either variable or fixed to the number of units produced and sold:

A. Packaging costs

B. Sales commissions

C. Property taxes on general offices

D. Shipping expenses

E. Straight-line depreciation of computer equipment

F. President's salary

G. Salaries of software developers

H. Salaries of human resources personnel

I. Wages of telephone order assistants

J. Costs of providing online support

K. Users' guides

EX 5-6 Relevant range and fixed and variable costs
Obj. 1

✔ A. $30.00

SHOW ME HOW

Vogel Inc. manufactures memory chips for electronic toys within a relevant range of 25,000 to 100,000 memory chips per year. Within this range, the following partially completed manufacturing cost schedule has been prepared:

Memory chips produced	45,000	60,000	75,000
Total costs:			
Total variable costs	$ 1,350,000	(D)	(J)
Total fixed costs	810,000	(E)	(K)
Total costs	$2,160,000	(F)	(L)
Cost per unit:			
Variable cost per unit	(A)	(G)	(M)
Fixed cost per unit	(B)	(H)	(N)
Total cost per unit	(C)	(I)	(O)

Complete the cost schedule, identifying each cost by the appropriate letter (A) through (O).

EX 5-7 High-low method
Obj. 1

✔ A. $175.50 per unit variable cost

SHOW ME HOW

EXCEL TEMPLATE

Ziegler Inc. has decided to use the high-low method to estimate the total cost and the fixed and variable cost components of the total cost. The data for various levels of production are as follows:

Units Produced	Total Costs
80,000	$25,100,000
92,000	27,206,000
120,000	32,120,000

A. Determine the variable cost per unit and the total fixed cost.

B. Based on part (A), estimate the total cost for 115,000 units of production.

EX 5-8 High-low method for a service company

Obj. 1

✔ Fixed cost, $600,000

SHOW ME HOW

Boston Railroad decided to use the high-low method and operating data from the past six months to estimate the fixed and variable components of transportation costs. The activity base used by Boston Railroad is a measure of railroad operating activity, termed "gross-ton miles," which is the total number of tons multiplied by the miles moved.

	Transportation Costs	Gross-Ton Miles
January	$1,776,000	560,000
February	2,700,000	1,000,000
March	1,650,000	500,000
April	1,860,000	600,000
May	1,440,000	400,000
June	1,566,000	460,000

Determine the variable cost per gross-ton mile and the total fixed cost.

EX 5-9 Contribution margin ratio

Obj. 2

✔ A. 41%

SHOW ME HOW

A. Young Company budgets sales of $112,900,000, fixed costs of $25,000,000, and variable costs of $66,611,000. What is the contribution margin ratio for Young Company?

B. If the contribution margin ratio for Martinez Company is 40%, sales were $34,800,000, and fixed costs were $1,500,000, what was the income from operations?

EX 5-10 Contribution margin and contribution margin ratio

Obj. 2

✔ B. 34.6%

SHOW ME HOW   REAL WORLD

For a recent year, **McDonald's** company-owned restaurants had the following sales and expenses (in millions):

Sales	$18,169.3
Food and packaging	$ 6,129.7
Payroll	4,756.0
Occupancy (rent, depreciation, etc.)	4,402.6
General, selling, and administrative expenses	2,487.9
	$17,776.2
Income from operations	$ 393.1

Assume that the variable costs consist of food and packaging, payroll, and 40% of the general, selling, and administrative expenses.

A. What is McDonald's contribution margin? Round to the nearest tenth of a million (one decimal place).

B. What is McDonald's contribution margin ratio? Round to one decimal place.

C. How much would income from operations increase if same-store sales increased by $500 million for the coming year, with no change in the contribution margin ratio or fixed costs? Round your answer to the nearest tenth of a million (one decimal place).

EX 5-11 Break-even sales and sales to realize income from operations

Obj. 3

✔ B. 128,500 units

SHOW ME HOW

For the current year ended October 31, Friedman Company expects fixed costs of $14,300,000, a unit variable cost of $250, and a unit selling price of $380.

A. Compute the anticipated break-even sales (units).

B. Compute the sales (units) required to realize income from operations of $2,405,000.

EX 5-12 Break-even sales

Obj. 3

✔ A. 168.9 million barrels

REAL WORLD

Anheuser-Busch InBev Companies, Inc., reported the following operating information for a recent year (in millions):

Sales	$47,063
Cost of goods sold	$18,756
Selling, general, and administration	12,999
	$31,755
Income from operations	$15,308*
*Before special items	

In addition, assume that Anheuser-Busch InBev sold 400 million barrels of beer during the year. Assume that variable costs were 75% of the cost of goods sold and 50% of selling, general, and administration expenses. Assume that the remaining costs are fixed. For the following year, assume that Anheuser-Busch InBev expects pricing, variable costs per barrel, and fixed costs to remain constant, except that new distribution and general office facilities are expected to increase fixed costs by $300 million.

A. Compute the break-even number of barrels for the current year. (*Note:* For the selling price per barrel and variable costs per barrel, round to the nearest cent. Round to one decimal place in millions of barrels.)

B. Compute the anticipated break-even number of barrels for the following year. (Round to one decimal place in millions of barrels.)

EX 5-13 Break-even sales

Obj. 3

✔ A. 15,000 units

SHOW ME HOW

Currently, the unit selling price of a product is $1,500, the unit variable cost is $1,200, and the total fixed costs are $4,500,000. A proposal is being evaluated to increase the unit selling price to $1,600.

A. Compute the current break-even sales (units).

B. Compute the anticipated break-even sales (units), assuming that the unit selling price is increased and all costs remain constant.

EX 5-14 Break-even analysis

Obj. 3

The Junior League of Yadkinville, California, collected recipes from members and published a cookbook entitled *Food for Everyone*. The book will sell for $18 per copy. The chairwoman of the cookbook development committee estimated that the club needed to sell 2,000 books to break even on its $4,000 investment. What is the variable cost per unit assumed in the Junior League's analysis?

EX 5-15 Break-even analysis

Obj. 3

REAL WORLD

Media outlets such as **ESPN** and **FOX Sports** often have Web sites that provide in-depth coverage of news and events. Portions of these Web sites are restricted to members who pay a monthly subscription to gain access to exclusive news and commentary. These Web sites typically offer a free trial period to introduce viewers to the Web site. Assume that during a recent fiscal year, ESPN.com spent $4,200,000 on a promotional campaign for the ESPN.com Web site that offered two free months of service for new subscribers. In addition, assume the following information:

Number of months an average new customer stays with the service (including the two free months)	14 months
Revenue per month per customer subscription	$10.00
Variable cost per month per customer subscription	$5.00

Determine the number of new customer accounts needed to break even on the cost of the promotional campaign. In forming your answer, (1) treat the cost of the promotional campaign as a fixed cost, and (2) treat the revenue less variable cost per account for the subscription period as the unit contribution margin.

EXCEL TEMPLATE   REAL WORLD

EX 5-16 Break-even analysis for a service company
Obj. 3

Sprint Nextel is one of the largest digital wireless service providers in the United States. In a recent year, it had approximately 32.5 million direct subscribers (accounts) that generated revenue of $35,345 million. Costs and expenses for the year were as follows (in millions):

Cost of revenue	$20,841
Selling, general, and administrative expenses	9,765
Depreciation	2,239

Assume that 70% of the cost of revenue and 30% of the selling, general, and administrative expenses are variable to the number of direct subscribers (accounts).

A. What is Sprint Nextel's break-even number of accounts, using the data and assumptions given? Round units (accounts) and per-account amounts to one decimal place.

B. How much revenue per account would be sufficient for Sprint Nextel to break even if the number of accounts remained constant?

EX 5-17 Cost-volume-profit chart
Obj. 4

✔ B. $1,500,000

For the coming year, Loudermilk Inc. anticipates fixed costs of $600,000, a unit variable cost of $75, and a unit selling price of $125. The maximum sales within the relevant range are $2,500,000.

A. Construct a cost-volume-profit chart.

B. Estimate the break-even sales (dollars) by using the cost-volume-profit chart constructed in part (A).

C. ➤What is the main advantage of presenting the cost-volume-profit analysis in graphic form rather than equation form?

EX 5-18 Profit-volume chart
Obj. 4

✔ B. $400,000

Using the data for Loudermilk Inc. in Exercise 17, (A) determine the maximum possible operating loss, (B) compute the maximum possible operating profit, (C) construct a profit-volume chart, and (D) estimate the break-even sales (units) by using the profit-volume chart constructed in part (C).

EX 5-19 Break-even chart
Obj. 4

Name the following chart, and identify the items represented by the letters (A) through (F):

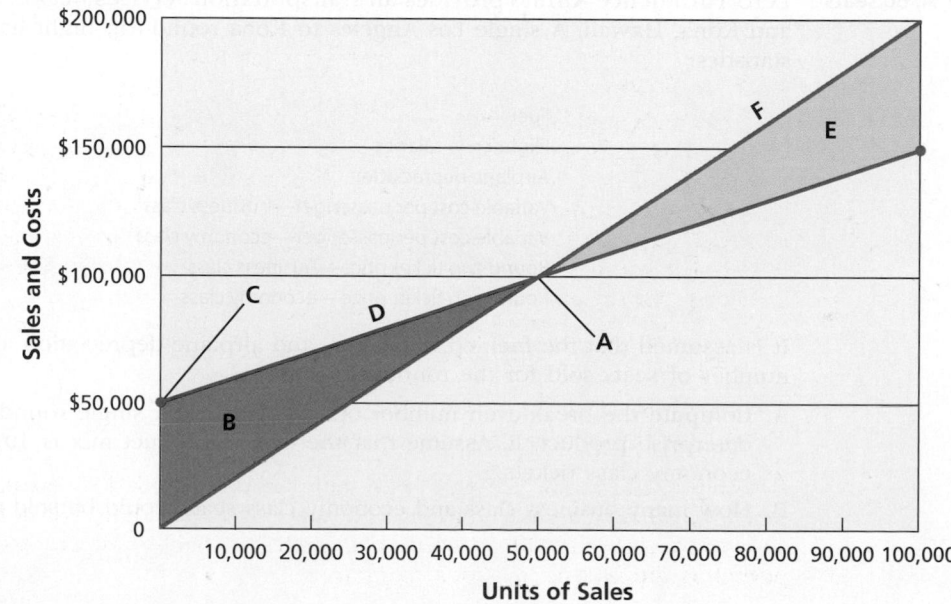

EX 5-20 Break-even chart

Obj. 4

Name the following chart, and identify the items represented by the letters (A) through (F):

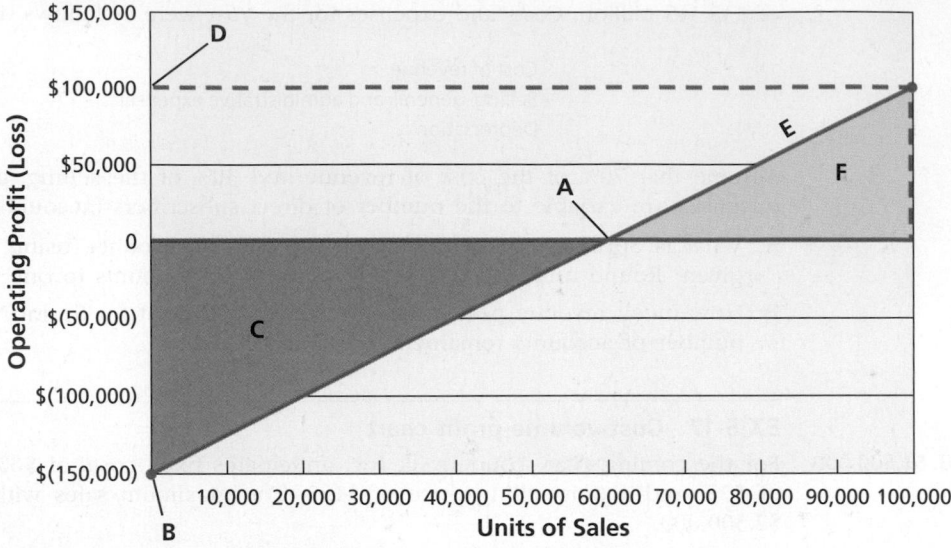

EX 5-21 Sales mix and break-even sales

Obj. 5

✔ A. 15,500 units

SHOW ME HOW

Dragon Sports Inc. manufactures and sells two products, baseball bats and baseball gloves. The fixed costs are $620,000, and the sales mix is 40% bats and 60% gloves. The unit selling price and the unit variable cost for each product are as follows:

Products	Unit Selling Price	Unit Variable Cost
Bats	$ 90	$50
Gloves	105	65

A. Compute the break-even sales (units) for the overall enterprise product, E.

B. How many units of each product, baseball bats and baseball gloves, would be sold at the break-even point?

EX 5-22 Break-even sales and sales mix for a service company

Obj. 5

✔ A. 60 seats

Zero Turbulence Airline provides air transportation services between Los Angeles, California, and Kona, Hawaii. A single Los Angeles to Kona round-trip flight has the following operating statistics:

Fuel	$7,000
Flight crew salaries	3,200
Airplane depreciation	3,480
Variable cost per passenger—business class	140
Variable cost per passenger—economy class	120
Round-trip ticket price—business class	800
Round-trip ticket price—economy class	300

It is assumed that the fuel, crew salaries, and airplane depreciation are fixed, regardless of the number of seats sold for the round-trip flight.

A. Compute the break-even number of seats sold on a single round-trip flight for the overall enterprise product, E. Assume that the overall product mix is 10% business class and 90% economy class tickets.

B. How many business class and economy class seats would be sold at the break-even point?

EX 5-23   Margin of safety   Obj. 5

✔ A. (2) 20%

SHOW ME HOW

A. If Canace Company, with a break-even point at $960,000 of sales, has actual sales of $1,200,000, what is the margin of safety expressed (1) in dollars and (2) as a percentage of sales?

B. If the margin of safety for Canace Company was 20%, fixed costs were $1,875,000, and variable costs were 80% of sales, what was the amount of actual sales (dollars)? (*Hint:* Determine the break-even in sales dollars first.)

EX 5-24   Break-even and margin of safety relationships   Obj. 5

At a recent staff meeting, the management of Boost Technologies Inc. was considering discontinuing the Rocket Man line of electronic games from the product line. The chief financial analyst reported the following current monthly data for the Rocket Man:

Units of sales	420,000
Break-even units	472,500
Margin of safety in units	29,400

➤ For what reason would you question the validity of these data?

EX 5-25   Operating leverage   Obj. 5

✔ A. Beck, 5.0

Beck Inc. and Bryant Inc. have the following operating data:

	Beck Inc.	Bryant Inc.
Sales	$1,250,000	$2,000,000
Variable costs	750,000	1,250,000
Contribution margin	$ 500,000	$ 750,000
Fixed costs	400,000	450,000
Income from operations	$ 100,000	$ 300,000

A. Compute the operating leverage for Beck Inc. and Bryant Inc.

B. How much would income from operations increase for each company if the sales of each increased by 20%?

C. ➤ Why is there a difference in the increase in income from operations for the two companies? Explain.

Problems: Series A

PR 5-1A   Classify costs   Obj. 1

Seymour Clothing Co. manufactures a variety of clothing types for distribution to several major retail chains. The following costs are incurred in the production and sale of blue jeans:

A. Shipping boxes used to ship orders

B. Consulting fee of $200,000 paid to industry specialist for marketing advice

C. Straight-line depreciation on sewing machines

D. Salesperson's salary, $10,000 plus 2% of the total sales

E. Fabric

F. Dye

G. Thread

H. Salary of designers

I. Brass buttons

J. Legal fees paid to attorneys in defense of the company in a patent infringement suit, $50,000 plus $87 per hour

K. Insurance premiums on property, plant, and equipment, $70,000 per year plus $5 per $30,000 of insured value over $8,000,000

(Continued)

L.   Rental costs of warehouse, $5,000 per month plus $4 per square foot of storage used

M.   Supplies

N.   Leather for patches identifying the brand on individual pieces of apparel

O.   Rent on plant equipment, $50,000 per year

P.   Salary of production vice president

Q.   Janitorial services, $2,200 per month

R.   Wages of machine operators

S.   Electricity costs of $0.10 per kilowatt-hour

T.   Property taxes on property, plant, and equipment

Instructions

Classify the preceding costs as either fixed, variable, or mixed. Use the following tabular headings and place an X in the appropriate column. Identify each cost by letter in the cost column.

Cost	Fixed Cost	Variable Cost	Mixed Cost

PR 5-2A   Break-even sales under present and proposed conditions   Obj. 2, 3

✔ 2. B. $50

SHOW ME HOW

Darby Company, operating at full capacity, sold 500,000 units at a price of $94 per unit during the current year. Its income statement is as follows:

Sales	$ 47,000,000
Cost of goods sold	25,000,000
Gross profit	$ 22,000,000
Expenses:	
Selling expenses.............. $4,000,000	
Administrative expenses...... 3,000,000	
Total expenses	7,000,000
Income from operations.........	$15,000,000

The division of costs between variable and fixed is as follows:

	Variable	Fixed
Cost of goods sold	70%	30%
Selling expenses	75%	25%
Administrative expenses	50%	50%

Management is considering a plant expansion program for the following year that will permit an increase of $3,760,000 in yearly sales. The expansion will increase fixed costs by $1,800,000 but will not affect the relationship between sales and variable costs.

Instructions

1.   Determine the total variable costs and the total fixed costs for the current year.

2.   Determine (A) the unit variable cost and (B) the unit contribution margin for the current year.

3.   Compute the break-even sales (units) for the current year.

4.   Compute the break-even sales (units) under the proposed program for the following year.

5.   Determine the amount of sales (units) that would be necessary under the proposed program to realize the $15,000,000 of income from operations that was earned in the current year.

6.   Determine the maximum income from operations possible with the expanded plant.

7.   If the proposal is accepted and sales remain at the current level, what will the income or loss from operations be for the following year?

8.   ━━━▶ Based on the data given, would you recommend accepting the proposal? Explain.

PR 5-3A Break-even sales and cost-volume-profit chart   Obj. 3, 4

✔ 1. 12,000 units For the coming year, Cleves Company anticipates a unit selling price of $100, a unit variable cost of $60, and fixed costs of $480,000.

Instructions

1. Compute the anticipated break-even sales (units).

2. Compute the sales (units) required to realize a target profit of $240,000.

3. Construct a cost-volume-profit chart, assuming maximum sales of 20,000 units within the relevant range.

4. Determine the probable income (loss) from operations if sales total 16,000 units.

PR 5-4A Break-even sales and cost-volume-profit chart   Obj. 3, 4

✔ 1. 1,000 units Last year, Hever Inc. had sales of $500,000, based on a unit selling price of $250. The variable cost per unit was $175, and fixed costs were $75,000. The maximum sales within Hever Inc.'s relevant range are 2,500 units. Hever Inc. is considering a proposal to spend an additional $33,750 on billboard advertising during the current year in an attempt to increase sales and utilize unused capacity.

Instructions

1. Construct a cost-volume-profit chart indicating the break-even sales for last year. Verify your answer, using the break-even equation.

2. Using the cost-volume-profit chart prepared in part (1), determine (A) the income from operations for last year and (B) the maximum income from operations that could have been realized during the year. Verify your answers using the mathematical approach to cost-volume-profit analysis.

3. Construct a cost-volume-profit chart indicating the break-even sales for the current year, assuming that a noncancellable contract is signed for the additional billboard advertising. No changes are expected in the unit selling price or other costs. Verify your answer, using the break-even equation.

4. Using the cost-volume-profit chart prepared in part (3), determine (A) the income from operations if sales total 2,000 units and (B) the maximum income from operations that could be realized during the year. Verify your answers using the mathematical approach to cost-volume-profit analysis.

PR 5-5A Sales mix and break-even sales   Obj. 5

✔ 1. 4,030 units Data related to the expected sales of laptops and tablets for Tech Products Inc. for the current year, which is typical of recent years, are as follows:

Products	Unit Selling Price	Unit Variable Cost	Sales Mix
Laptops	$1,600	$800	40%
Tablets	850	350	60%

The estimated fixed costs for the current year are $2,498,600.

Instructions

1. Determine the estimated units of sales of the overall (total) product, E, necessary to reach the break-even point for the current year.

2. Based on the break-even sales (units) in part (1), determine the unit sales of both laptops and tablets for the current year.

3. ▬▬▶ Assume that the sales mix was 50% laptops and 50% tablets. Compare the break-even point with that in part (1). Why is it so different?

PR 5-6A   Contribution margin, break-even sales, cost-volume-profit chart, margin of safety, and operating leverage   Obj. 2, 3, 4, 5

✔ 2. 25%

EXCEL TEMPLATE

Wolsey Industries Inc. expects to maintain the same inventories at the end of 20Y3 as at the beginning of the year. The total of all production costs for the year is therefore assumed to be equal to the cost of goods sold. With this in mind, the various department heads were asked to submit estimates of the costs for their departments during the year. A summary report of these estimates is as follows:

	Estimated Fixed Cost	Estimated Variable Cost (per unit sold)
Production costs:		
Direct materials..........................	—	$ 46
Direct labor	—	40
Factory overhead..........................	$200,000	20
Selling expenses:		
Sales salaries and commissions..............	110,000	8
Advertising................................	40,000	—
Travel	12,000	—
Miscellaneous selling expense	7,600	1
Administrative expenses:		
Office and officers' salaries	132,000	—
Supplies...................................	10,000	4
Miscellaneous administrative expense	13,400	1
Total.......................................	$525,000	$120

It is expected that 21,875 units will be sold at a price of $160 a unit. Maximum sales within the relevant range are 27,000 units.

Instructions

1. Prepare an estimated income statement for 20Y3.
2. What is the expected contribution margin ratio?
3. Determine the break-even sales in units and dollars.
4. Construct a cost-volume-profit chart indicating the break-even sales.
5. What is the expected margin of safety in dollars and as a percentage of sales?
6. Determine the operating leverage.

Problems: Series B

PR 5-1B   Classify costs   Obj. 1

Cromwell Furniture Company manufactures sofas for distribution to several major retail chains. The following costs are incurred in the production and sale of sofas:

A. Fabric for sofa coverings

B. Wood for framing the sofas

C. Legal fees paid to attorneys in defense of the company in a patent infringement suit, $25,000 plus $160 per hour

D. Salary of production supervisor

E. Cartons used to ship sofas

F. Rent on experimental equipment, $50 for every sofa produced

G. Straight-line depreciation on factory equipment

H. Rental costs of warehouse, $30,000 per month

I. Property taxes on property, plant, and equipment

J. Insurance premiums on property, plant, and equipment, $25,000 per year plus $25 per $25,000 of insured value over $16,000,000

K. Springs for seat cushions

L. Consulting fee of $120,000 paid to efficiency specialists

M. Electricity costs of $0.13 per kilowatt-hour

N. Salesperson's salary, $80,000 plus 4% of the selling price of each sofa sold

O. Foam rubber for cushion fillings

P. Janitorial supplies, $2,500 per month

Q. Employer's FICA taxes on controller's salary of $180,000

R. Salary of designers

S. Wages of sewing machine operators

T. Sewing supplies

Instructions

Classify the preceding costs as either fixed, variable, or mixed. Use the following tabular headings and place an X in the appropriate column. Identify each cost by letter in the cost column.

Cost	Fixed Cost	Variable Cost	Mixed Cost

PR 5-2B Break-even sales under present and proposed conditions   Obj. 2, 3

✔ 3. 29,375 units

SHOW ME HOW

Howard Industries Inc., operating at full capacity, sold 64,000 units at a price of $45 per unit during the current year. Its income statement is as follows:

Sales	$2,880,000
Cost of goods sold	1,400,000
Gross profit	$1,480,000
Expenses:	
Selling expenses $400,000	
Administrative expenses............ 387,500	
Total expenses....................	787,500
Income from operations	$ 692,500

The division of costs between variable and fixed is as follows:

	Variable	Fixed
Cost of goods sold	75%	25%
Selling expenses	60%	40%
Administrative expenses	80%	20%

Management is considering a plant expansion program for the following year that will permit an increase of $900,000 in yearly sales. The expansion will increase fixed costs by $212,500 but will not affect the relationship between sales and variable costs.

Instructions

1. Determine the total fixed costs and the total variable costs for the current year.

2. Determine (A) the unit variable cost and (B) the unit contribution margin for the current year.

3. Compute the break-even sales (units) for the current year.

4. Compute the break-even sales (units) under the proposed program for the following year.

5. Determine the amount of sales (units) that would be necessary under the proposed program to realize the $692,500 of income from operations that was earned in the current year.

6. Determine the maximum income from operations possible with the expanded plant.

7. If the proposal is accepted and sales remain at the current level, what will the income or loss from operations be for the following year?

8. ⟶ Based on the data given, would you recommend accepting the proposal? Explain.

PR 5-3B Break-even sales and cost-volume-profit chart   Obj. 3, 4

✔ 1. 20,000 units For the coming year, Culpeper Products Inc. anticipates a unit selling price of $150, a unit variable cost of $110, and fixed costs of $800,000.

Instructions

1. Compute the anticipated break-even sales (units).

2. Compute the sales (units) required to realize income from operations of $300,000.

3. Construct a cost-volume-profit chart, assuming maximum sales of 40,000 units within the relevant range.

4. Determine the probable income (loss) from operations if sales total 32,000 units.

PR 5-4B Break-even sales and cost-volume-profit chart   Obj. 3, 4

✔ 1. 3,000 units Last year, Parr Co. had sales of $900,000, based on a unit selling price of $200. The variable cost per unit was $125, and fixed costs were $225,000. The maximum sales within Parr Co.'s relevant range are 7,500 units. Parr Co. is considering a proposal to spend an additional $112,500 on billboard advertising during the current year in an attempt to increase sales and utilize unused capacity.

Instructions

1. Construct a cost-volume-profit chart indicating the break-even sales for last year. Verify your answer, using the break-even equation.

2. Using the cost-volume-profit chart prepared in part (1), determine (A) the income from operations for last year and (B) the maximum income from operations that could have been realized during the year. Verify your answers using the mathematical approach to cost-volume-profit analysis.

3. Construct a cost-volume-profit chart indicating the break-even sales for the current year, assuming that a noncancellable contract is signed for the additional billboard advertising. No changes are expected in the selling price or other costs. Verify your answer, using the break-even equation.

4. Using the cost-volume-profit chart prepared in part (3), determine (A) the income from operations if sales total 6,000 units and (B) the maximum income from operations that could be realized during the year. Verify your answers using the mathematical approach to cost-volume-profit analysis.

PR 5-5B Sales mix and break-even sales   Obj. 5

✔ 1. 4,500 units Data related to the expected sales of two types of frozen pizzas for Norfolk Frozen Foods Inc. for the current year, which is typical of recent years, are as follows:

Products	Unit Selling Price	Unit Variable Cost	Sales Mix
12" Pizza	$12	$3	30%
16" Pizza	15	4	70%

The estimated fixed costs for the current year are $46,800.

Instructions

1. Determine the estimated units of sales of the overall enterprise product, E, necessary to reach the break-even point for the current year.

2. Based on the break-even sales (units) in part (1), determine the unit sales of both the 12" pizza and 16" pizza for the current year.

3. ➤ Assume that the sales mix was 50% 12" pizza and 50% 16" pizza. Compare the break-even point with that in part (1). Why is it so different?

PR 5-6B **Contribution margin, break-even sales, cost-volume-profit chart, margin of safety, and operating leverage**   Obj. 2, 3, 4, 5

✔ 3. 8,000 units

EXCEL TEMPLATE

Belmain Co. expects to maintain the same inventories at the end of 20Y7 as at the beginning of the year. The total of all production costs for the year is therefore assumed to be equal to the cost of goods sold. With this in mind, the various department heads were asked to submit estimates of the costs for their departments during the year. A summary report of these estimates is as follows:

	Estimated Fixed Cost	Estimated Variable Cost (per unit sold)
Production costs:		
Direct materials.........................	—	$50.00
Direct labor............................	—	30.00
Factory overhead	$ 350,000	6.00
Selling expenses:		
Sales salaries and commissions........	340,000	4.00
Advertising............................	116,000	—
Travel	4,000	—
Miscellaneous selling expense	2,300	1.00
Administrative expenses:		
Office and officers' salaries............	325,000	—
Supplies...............................	6,000	4.00
Miscellaneous administrative expense ...	8,700	1.00
Total	$1,152,000	$96.00

It is expected that 12,000 units will be sold at a price of $240 a unit. Maximum sales within the relevant range are 18,000 units.

Instructions

1. Prepare an estimated income statement for 20Y7.
2. What is the expected contribution margin ratio?
3. Determine the break-even sales in units and dollars.
4. Construct a cost-volume-profit chart indicating the break-even sales.
5. What is the expected margin of safety in dollars and as a percentage of sales? (Round to one decimal place.)
6. Determine the operating leverage.

Analysis for Decision Making

ADM-1   Break-even number of passengers for a cruise

Ocean Escape Cruise Lines has a boat with a capacity of 1,200 passengers. An eight-day ocean cruise involves the following costs:

Crew	$240,000
Fuel	60,000
Fixed operating costs	800,000

The variable costs per passenger for the eight-day cruise include the following:

Meals	$900
Variable operating costs	400

(Continued)

The price of the cruise is $2,400 per passenger.

A. Determine the break-even number of passengers for the eight-day cruise.

B. Assume 900 passengers booked the cruise. What would be the profit or loss for the cruise?

C. Assume the cruise was booked to capacity. What would be the profit or loss for the cruise?

D. ➤ If the cruise cannot book enough passengers to break even, how might the cruise line respond?

ADM-2 Break-even subscribers for a video service

Star Stream is a subscription-based video streaming service. Subscribers pay $120 per year for the service. Star Stream licenses and develops content for its subscribers. In addition, Star Stream leases servers to hold this content. These costs are not variable to the number of subscribers, but must be incurred regardless of the subscriber base. In addition, Star Stream compensates telecommunication companies for bandwidth so that Star Stream customers receive fast streaming services. These costs are variable to the number of subscribers. These and other costs are as follows:

Server lease costs per year	$ 100,000,000
Content costs per year	2,000,000,000
Fixed operating costs per year	900,000,000
Bandwidth costs per subscriber per year	15
Variable operating costs per subscriber per year	25

A. Determine the break-even number of subscribers.

B. Assume Star Stream planned to increase available programming and thus increase the annual content costs to $2,600,000,000. What impact would this change have on the break-even number of subscribers?

C. Assume the same content cost scenario in (B). How much would the annual subscription need to change in order to maintain the same break-even as in (A)?

ADM-3 Break-even number of guests for a theme park

MusicLand Theme Park has an average daily admission price of $60 per guest. The following financial data are available for analysis:

Daily operating fixed costs	$750,000
Variable daily operating cost per guest	24
Average daily concession revenue per guest	30
Average daily variable cost of concession items per guest	16

Additional operating data indicate that the park averages 24,000 daily guests during the weekdays and 40,000 average daily guests on Saturdays and Sundays.

A. Determine the break-even number of guests per day at the theme park.

B. How much profit does MusicLand earn on an average weekday?

C. How much profit does MusicLand earn on an average weekend day?

D. Determine the revised break-even if the daily fixed costs increased to $1,000,000.

E. Would the theme park still remain profitable for an average weekday under the scenario in (D)?

Take It Further

ETHICS

TIF 5-1   Ethics in Action

Edward Seymour is a financial consultant to Cornish Inc., a real estate syndicate. Cornish finances and develops commercial real estate (office buildings) projects. The completed projects are then sold as limited partnership interests to individual investors. The syndicate makes a profit on the sale of these partnership interests. Edward provides financial information for prospective investors in a document called the offering "prospectus." This document discusses the financial and legal details of the limited partnership investment.

One of the company's current projects is called JEDI 2, and has the syndicate borrowing money from a local bank to build a commercial office building. The interest rate on the loan is 6.5% for the first four years. After four years, the interest rate jumps to 15% for the remaining 20 years of the loan. The interest expense is one of the major costs of this project and significantly affects the number of renters needed for the project to break even. In the prospectus, Edward has prominently reported that the break-even occupancy for the first four years is 65%. This is the amount of office space that must be leased to cover the interest and general upkeep costs during the first four years. The 65% break-even point is very low compared to similar projects and thus communicates a low risk to potential investors. Edward uses the 65% break-even rate as a major marketing tool in selling the limited partnership interests. Buried in the fine print of the prospectus is additional information that would allow an astute investor to determine that the break-even occupancy jumps to 95% after the fourth year when the interest rate on the loan increases to 15%. Edward believes prospective investors are adequately informed of the investment's risk.

➤ Is Edward behaving ethically? Explain your answer.

REAL WORLD

TIF 5-2   Team Activity

Break-even analysis is an important tool for managing any business, including colleges and universities. In a group, identify three areas where break-even analysis might be used at your college or university. For each area, identify the revenues, variable costs, and fixed costs.

TIF 5-3   Communication

Sun Airlines is a commercial airline that targets business and non-business travelers. In recent months, the airline has been unprofitable. The company has break-even sales volume of 75% of capacity, which is significantly higher than the industry average of 65%. Sun's CEO, Neil Armstrong, is concerned about the recent string of losses and is considering a strategic plan that could reduce the break-even sales volume by increasing ticket prices. He has asked for your help in evaluating this plan.

➤ Write a brief memo to Neil Armstrong evaluating this strategy.

Chapter 6

Variable Costing for Management Analysis

Concepts and Principles

Chapter 1 *Introduction to Managerial Accounting*

Developing Information

COST SYSTEMS	COST BEHAVIOR
Chapter 2 *Job Order Costing*	**Chapter 5** *Cost-Volume-Profit Analysis*
Chapter 3 *Process Cost Systems*	
Chapter 4 *Activity-Based Costing*	

Decision Making

EVALUATING PERFORMANCE	COMPARING ALTERNATIVES
Chapter 6 *Variable Costing for Management Analysis*	**Chapter 9** *Evaluating Decentralized Operations*
Chapter 7 *Budgeting*	**Chapter 10** *Differential Analysis and Product Pricing*
Chapter 8 *Evaluating Variances from Standard Costs*	**Chapter 11** *Capital Investment Analysis*
	Chapter 12 *Lean Manufacturing*

COMPUTER ARTS MAGAZINE/FUTURE/GETTY IMAGES

Adobe Systems Incorporated

Assume that you have three different options for a summer job. How would you evaluate these options? Naturally there are many things to consider, including how much you could earn from each job.

Determining how much you could earn from each job may not be as simple as comparing the wage rate per hour. For example, a job as an office clerk at a local company pays $8 per hour. A job delivering pizza pays $10 per hour (including estimated tips), although you must use your own transportation. Another job working in a beach resort over 500 miles away from your home pays $8 per hour. All three jobs offer 40 hours per week for the whole summer. If these options were ranked according to their pay per hour, the pizza delivery job would be the most attractive. However, the costs associated with each job must also be evaluated. For example, the office job may require that you pay for downtown parking and purchase office clothes. The pizza delivery job will require you to pay for gas and maintenance for your car. The resort job will require you to move to the resort city and incur additional living costs. Only by considering the costs for each job will you be able to determine which job will provide you with the most income.

Just as you should evaluate the relative income of various choices, a business also evaluates the income earned from its choices. Important choices include the products offered and the geographical regions to be served.

A company will often evaluate the profitability of products and regions. For example, **Adobe Systems Incorporated**, one of the largest software companies in the world, determines the income earned from its various product lines, such as Acrobat®, Photoshop®, Premiere®, and Dreamweaver® software. Adobe uses this information to establish product line pricing, as well as sales, support, and development effort. Likewise, Adobe evaluates the income earned in the geographic regions it serves, such as the United States, Europe, and Asia. Again, such information aids management in managing revenue and expenses within the regions.

In this chapter, how businesses measure profitability using absorption costing and variable costing is discussed. After illustrating and comparing these concepts, how businesses use them for controlling costs, pricing products, planning production, analyzing market segments, and analyzing contribution margins is described and illustrated.

Variable Costing for Management Analysis

Income Under Absorption and Variable Costing
- Absorption Costing (Obj. 1)
- Variable Costing (Obj. 1)
- Effects of Inventory (Obj. 1)
- Analyzing Income (Obj. 2)

Using Absorption and Variable Costing
- Controlling Costs (Obj. 3)
- Pricing Products (Obj. 3)
- Planning Production (Obj. 3)
- Analyzing Market Segments (Obj. 4)
- Contribution Margin Analysis (Obj. 5)

Variable Costing for Service Businesses
- Reporting Income (Obj. 6)
- Analyzing Segments (Obj. 6)
- Analyzing Contribution Margin (Obj. 6)

Learning Objectives

Obj. 1 Describe and illustrate reporting income from operations under absorption and variable costing.

Obj. 2 Describe and illustrate the effects of absorption and variable costing on analyzing income from operations.

Obj. 3 Describe management's use of absorption and variable costing.

Obj. 4 Use variable costing for analyzing market segments, including product, territories, and salespersons segments.

Obj. 5 Use variable costing for analyzing and explaining changes in contribution margin as a result of quantity and price factors.

Obj. 6 Describe and illustrate contribution margin analysis for service businesses.

Analysis for Decision Making

Describe and illustrate the use of segment analysis and earnings before interest, taxes, depreciation, and amortization (EBITDA) in evaluating a company's performance.

Objective 1

Describe and illustrate reporting income from operations under absorption and variable costing.

Income from Operations: Absorption and Variable Costing

Income from operations is one of the most important items reported by a company. Depending on the decision-making needs of management, income from operations can be determined using absorption or variable costing.

Absorption Costing

Absorption costing is required under generally accepted accounting principles for financial statements distributed to external users. Under absorption costing, the cost of goods manufactured includes direct materials, direct labor, and factory overhead costs. Both fixed and variable factory costs are included as part of factory overhead. In the financial statements, these costs are included in the cost of goods sold (income statement) and inventory (balance sheet).

The reporting of income from operations under absorption costing is as follows:

Sales	$XXX
Cost of goods sold	XXX
Gross profit	$XXX
Selling and administrative expenses	XXX
Income from operations	$XXX

The income statements illustrated in the preceding chapters of this text have used absorption costing.

Adobe Systems uses absorption costing for its annual financial statements filed with the Securities and Exchange Commission.

Link to Adobe Systems

Variable Costing

For internal use in decision making, managers often use variable costing. Under **variable costing**, sometimes called *direct costing*, the cost of goods manufactured includes only variable manufacturing costs. Thus, the cost of goods manufactured consists of the following:

- Direct materials
- Direct labor
- *Variable* factory overhead

Under variable costing, *fixed* factory overhead costs are not a part of the cost of goods manufactured. Instead, fixed factory overhead costs are treated as a period expense. Exhibit 1 illustrates the differences between absorption costing and variable costing.

Exhibit 1

Absorption Costing Versus Variable Costing

The reporting of income from operations under variable costing is as follows:

Sales...		$XXX
Variable cost of goods sold		XXX
Manufacturing margin		$XXX
Variable selling and administrative expenses		XXX
Contribution margin..		$XXX
Fixed costs:		
Fixed manufacturing costs.............................	$XXX	
Fixed selling and administrative expenses	XXX	
Total fixed costs......................................		XXX
Income from operations		$XXX

Manufacturing margin is the excess of sales over variable cost of goods sold:

Manufacturing Margin = Sales − Variable Cost of Goods Sold

Variable cost of goods sold consists of direct materials, direct labor, and variable factory overhead for the units sold. **Contribution margin** is the excess of manufacturing margin over variable selling and administrative expenses:

Contribution Margin = Manufacturing Margin − Variable Selling and Administrative Expenses

Subtracting fixed costs from contribution margin yields *income from operations*:

Income from Operations = Contribution Margin − Fixed Costs

To illustrate variable costing and absorption costing, assume that Martinez Co. manufactures 15,000 units, which are sold at a price of $50. The related costs and expenses for Martinez are as follows:

	Total Cost	Number of Units	Unit Cost
Manufacturing costs:			
Variable..	$375,000	15,000	$25
Fixed	150,000	15,000	10
Total	$525,000		$35
Selling and administrative expenses:			
Variable..	$ 75,000	15,000	$ 5
Fixed	50,000		
Total	$125,000		

Exhibit 2 shows the absorption costing income statement prepared for Martinez. The computations are shown in parentheses.

Exhibit 2
Absorption
Costing Income
Statement

Sales (15,000 × $50)...	$750,000
Cost of goods sold (15,000 × $35)..	525,000
Gross profit..	$225,000
Selling and administrative expenses ($75,000 + $50,000)......................	125,000
Income from operations	$100,000

Absorption costing does not distinguish between variable and fixed costs. All manufacturing costs are included in the cost of goods sold. Deducting the cost of goods sold of $525,000 from sales of $750,000 yields gross profit of $225,000. Deducting selling and administrative expenses of $125,000 from gross profit yields income from operations of $100,000.

Exhibit 3 shows the variable costing income statement prepared for Martinez. The computations are shown in parentheses.

Exhibit 3
Variable Costing
Income Statement

Sales (15,000 × $50)		$750,000
Variable cost of goods sold (15,000 × $25)................................		375,000
Manufacturing margin...		$375,000
Variable selling and administrative expenses (15,000 × $5)................		75,000
Contribution margin..		$300,000
Fixed costs:		
Fixed manufacturing costs	$150,000	
Fixed selling and administrative expenses	50,000	
Total fixed costs		200,000
Income from operations		$100,000

note:

The variable costing income statement includes only variable manufacturing costs in the cost of goods sold.

Variable costing income reports variable costs separately from fixed costs. Deducting the variable cost of goods sold of $375,000 from sales of $750,000 yields the manufacturing margin of $375,000. Deducting variable selling and administrative expenses of $75,000 from the manufacturing margin yields the contribution margin of $300,000. Deducting fixed costs of $200,000 from the contribution margin yields income from operations of $100,000.

The contribution margin reported in Exhibit 3 is the same as that used in Chapter 5. That is, the contribution margin is sales less variable costs and expenses. The only difference is that Exhibit 3 reports manufacturing margin before deducting variable selling and administrative expenses.

Effects of Inventory

Income from operations will vary between absorption and variable costing, depending upon whether there is any change in inventory. The effects of inventory on income from operations are illustrated for the following:

- Units manufactured equal units sold, resulting in no change in inventory.
- Units manufactured exceed units sold, resulting in an increase in inventory.
- Units manufactured are less than units sold, resulting in a decrease in inventory.

Units Manufactured Equal Units Sold In Exhibits 2 and 3, Martinez manufactured and sold 15,000 units. Thus, the variable and absorption costing income statements reported the same income from operations of $100,000. When the number of units manufactured equals the number of units sold, income from operations will be the same under both methods.

Units Manufactured Exceed Units Sold When units manufactured exceed the units sold, the variable costing income from operations will be *less* than it is for absorption costing. To illustrate, assume that only 12,000 units of the 15,000 units Martinez manufactured were sold.

Exhibit 4 shows the absorption and variable costing income statements when units manufactured exceed units sold.

Variable Costing Income Statement		
Sales (12,000 × $50)		$600,000
Variable cost of goods sold:		
Variable cost of goods manufactured (15,000 × $25)	$ 375,000	
Ending inventory (3,000 × $25)	(75,000)	
Total variable cost of goods sold		300,000
Manufacturing margin		$300,000
Variable selling and administrative expenses (12,000 × $5)		60,000
Contribution margin		$240,000
Fixed costs:		
Fixed manufacturing costs	$ 150,000	
Fixed selling and administrative expenses	50,000	
Total fixed costs		200,000
Income from operations		$ 40,000
Absorption Costing Income Statement		
Sales (12,000 × $50)		$600,000
Cost of goods sold:		
Cost of goods manufactured (15,000 × $35)	$ 525,000	
Ending inventory (3,000 × $35)	(105,000)	
Total cost of goods sold		420,000
Gross profit		$180,000
Selling and administrative expenses [(12,000 × $5) + $50,000]		110,000
Income from operations		$ 70,000

Exhibit 4

Units Manufactured Exceed Units Sold

Exhibit 4 shows a $30,000 ($70,000 − $40,000) difference in income from operations. This difference is due to the fixed manufacturing costs. All of the $150,000 of fixed manufacturing costs is included as a period expense in the variable costing statement. However, the 3,000 units of ending inventory in the absorption costing statement include $30,000 (3,000 units × $10) of fixed manufacturing costs. By being included in inventory, this $30,000 is thus excluded from the cost of goods sold. Thus, the absorption costing income from operations is $30,000 higher than the income from operations for variable costing.

Units Manufactured Less Than Units Sold When the units manufactured are less than the number of units sold, the variable costing income from operations will be *greater* than that of absorption costing. To illustrate, assume that beginning inventory, units manufactured, and units sold for Martinez were as follows:

Beginning inventory...	5,000 units
Units manufactured during current period	10,000 units
Units sold during current period at $50 per unit	15,000 units

Martinez's manufacturing costs and selling and administrative expenses are as follows:

	Total Cost	Number of Units	Unit Cost
Beginning inventory (5,000 units):			
Manufacturing costs:			
Variable	$125,000	5,000	$25
Fixed..	50,000	5,000	10
Total	$175,000		$35
Current period (10,000 units):			
Manufacturing costs:			
Variable	$250,000	10,000	$25
Fixed..	150,000	10,000	15
Total	$400,000		$40
Selling and administrative expenses:			
Variable	$ 75,000	15,000	$ 5
Fixed..	50,000		
Total	$125,000		

Exhibit 5 shows the absorption and variable costing income statements for Martinez when units manufactured are less than units sold.

Exhibit 5 Units Manufactured Are Less Than Units Sold	

Absorption Costing Income Statement

Sales (15,000 × $50)		$750,000
Cost of goods sold:		
Beginning inventory (5,000 × $35)...............................	$175,000	
Cost of goods manufactured (10,000 × $40).....................	400,000	
Total cost of goods sold		575,000
Gross profit..		$175,000
Selling and administrative expenses ($75,000 + $50,000)		125,000
Income from operations		$ 50,000

Variable Costing Income Statement

Sales (15,000 × $50)		$750,000
Variable cost of goods sold:		
Beginning inventory (5,000 × $25)...............................	$125,000	
Variable cost of goods manufactured (10,000 × $25).............	250,000	
Total variable cost of goods sold.............................		375,000
Manufacturing margin..		$375,000
Variable selling and administrative expenses (15,000 × $5)......................		75,000
Contribution margin..		$300,000
Fixed costs:		
Fixed manufacturing costs	$150,000	
Fixed selling and administrative expenses......................	50,000	
Total fixed costs..		200,000
Income from operations		$100,000

Exhibit 5 shows a $50,000 ($100,000 – $50,000) difference in income from operations. This difference is due to the fixed manufacturing costs. The beginning inventory under absorption costing includes $50,000 (5,000 units × $10) of fixed manufacturing costs incurred in the preceding period. By being included in the beginning inventory, this $50,000 is included in the cost of goods sold for the current period. Under variable costing, this $50,000 was included as an expense in an income statement of a prior period. Thus, the variable costing income from operations is $50,000 higher than the income from operations for absorption costing.

The preceding effects of inventory on income from operations reported under absorption and variable costing are summarized in Exhibit 6.

Exhibit 6

Effects of Inventory on Absorption and Variable Costing

IF Units Manufactured	=	Units Sold
THEN Absorption Costing Income from Operations	=	Variable Costing Income from Operations

IF Units Manufactured	>	Units Sold
THEN Absorption Costing Income from Operations	>	Variable Costing Income from Operations

IF Units Manufactured	<	Units Sold
THEN Absorption Costing Income from Operations	<	Variable Costing Income from Operations

Adobe Systems outsources its purchasing, production, inventory, and fulfillment activities to third parties in the United States. *Link to Adobe Systems*

Source: Adobe Systems Incorporated, Form 10-K for the Fiscal Year Ended November 27, 2015.

Check Up Corner 6-1   Absorption and Variable Costing Income Statements

Walsh Company manufactured 30,000 units during July. There were no units in inventory on July 1. Information on costs and expenses for July is as follows:

	Total Cost	Number of Units	Unit Cost
Manufacturing costs:			
Variable	$660,000	30,000	$22.00
Fixed	300,000	30,000	10.00
Total..	$960,000		
Selling and administrative expenses:			
Variable	$200,000		
Fixed	160,000		
Total..	$360,000		

If the company sells 25,000 units at $75 (units manufactured exceed units sold), prepare an income statement for July using:

A. Absorption costing
B. Variable costing

Solution:

A.

Under absorption costing, both fixed and variable manufacturing costs are included in cost of goods sold and in inventory.

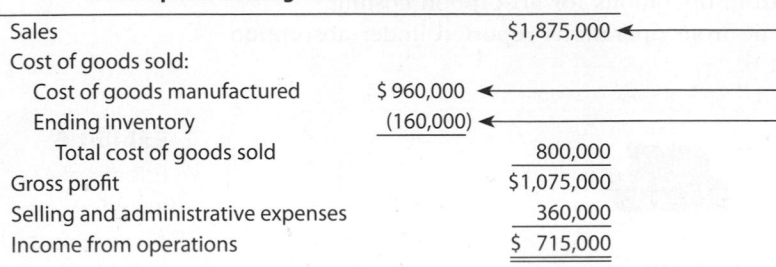

Absorption Costing Income Statement

Sales		$1,875,000	← 25,000 units sold × $75 selling price per unit
Cost of goods sold:			
Cost of goods manufactured	$ 960,000		← $660,000 variable manufacturing cost + $300,000 fixed manufacturing costs for 30,000 units
Ending inventory	(160,000)		← 5,000 units (30,000 units manufactured −25,000 units sold) × $32 manufacturing cost per unit ($960,000 total manufacturing cost ÷ 30,000 units manufactured)
Total cost of goods sold		800,000	
Gross profit		$1,075,000	
Selling and administrative expenses		360,000	
Income from operations		$ 715,000	

B.

Under variable costing, only variable manufacturing costs are included in cost of goods sold and inventory.

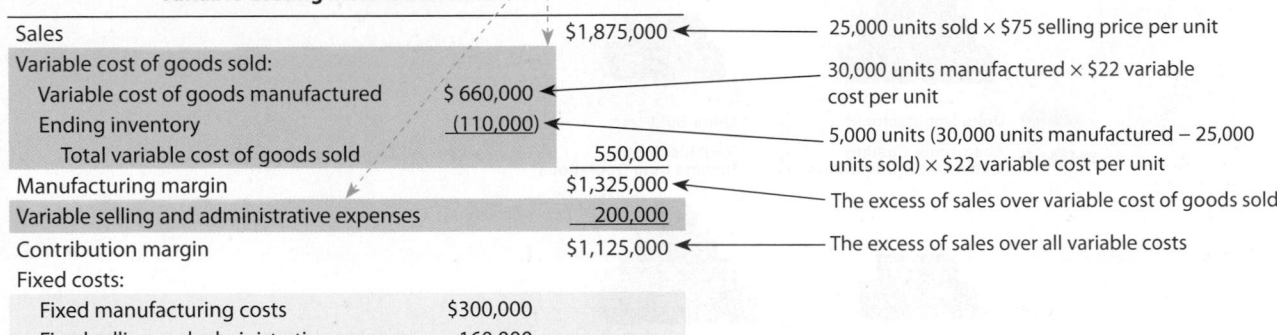

Variable Costing Income Statement

Variable Costs

Sales		$1,875,000	← 25,000 units sold × $75 selling price per unit
Variable cost of goods sold:			
Variable cost of goods manufactured	$ 660,000		← 30,000 units manufactured × $22 variable cost per unit
Ending inventory	(110,000)		← 5,000 units (30,000 units manufactured − 25,000 units sold) × $22 variable cost per unit
Total variable cost of goods sold		550,000	
Manufacturing margin		$1,325,000	← The excess of sales over variable cost of goods sold
Variable selling and administrative expenses		200,000	
Contribution margin		$1,125,000	← The excess of sales over all variable costs
Fixed costs:			
Fixed manufacturing costs	$300,000		
Fixed selling and administrative expenses	160,000		
Total fixed costs		460,000	←----------- Fixed Costs
Income from operations		$ 665,000	

Check Up Corner

Objective 2
Describe and illustrate the effects of absorption and variable costing on analyzing income from operations.

Analyzing Income Using Absorption and Variable Costing

Whenever the units manufactured differ from the units sold, finished goods inventory is affected. When the units manufactured are greater than the units sold, finished goods inventory increases. Under absorption costing, a portion of this increase is related to the allocation of fixed manufacturing overhead to ending inventory. As a result, increases or decreases in income from operations can be due to changes in inventory levels. In analyzing income from operations, such increases and decreases could be misinterpreted as operating efficiencies or inefficiencies.

To illustrate, assume that Frand Manufacturing Company has no beginning inventory and sales are estimated to be 20,000 units at $75 per unit. Also, assume that sales will not change if more than 20,000 units are manufactured.

Frand's management is evaluating whether to manufacture 20,000 units (Proposal 1) or 25,000 units (Proposal 2). The costs and expenses related to each proposal follow.

Proposal 1: 20,000 Units to Be Manufactured and Sold

	Total Cost	Number of Units	Unit Cost
Manufacturing costs:			
Variable..	$ 700,000	20,000	$35
Fixed	400,000	20,000	20*
Total	$1,100,000		$55
Selling and administrative expenses:			
Variable..	$ 100,000	20,000	$ 5
Fixed	100,000		
Total	$ 200,000		

*$400,000 ÷ 20,000 units

Proposal 2: 25,000 Units to Be Manufactured and 20,000 Units to Be Sold

	Total Cost	Number of Units	Unit Cost
Manufacturing costs:			
Variable..	$ 875,000	25,000	$35
Fixed	400,000	25,000	16*
Total	$1,275,000		$51
Selling and administrative expenses:			
Variable..	$ 100,000	20,000	$ 5
Fixed	100,000		
Total	$ 200,000		

*$400,000 ÷ 25,000 units

The absorption costing income statements for each proposal are shown in Exhibit 7.

Frand Manufacturing Company Absorption Costing Income Statements		
	Proposal 1 20,000 Units Manufactured	Proposal 2 25,000 Units Manufactured
Sales (20,000 units × $75)..	$1,500,000	$1,500,000
Cost of goods sold:		
Cost of goods manufactured:		
(20,000 units × $55)	$1,100,000	
(25,000 units × $51)		$1,275,000
Ending inventory:		
(5,000 units × $51)...		(255,000)
Total cost of goods sold	$1,100,000	$1,020,000
Gross profit...	$ 400,000	$ 480,000
Selling and administrative expenses:		
($100,000 + $100,000)...	200,000	200,000
Income from operations	$ 200,000	$ 280,000

Exhibit 7

Absorption Costing Income Statements for Two Production Levels

Exhibit 7 shows that if Frand manufactures 25,000 units, sells 20,000 units, and adds the 5,000 units to finished goods inventory (Proposal 2), income from operations will be $280,000. In contrast, if Frand manufactures and sells 20,000 units (Proposal 1), income from operations will be $200,000. In other words, Frand can increase income from operations by $80,000 ($280,000 − $200,000) by simply increasing finished goods inventory by 5,000 units.

The $80,000 increase in income from operations under Proposal 2 is caused by the allocation of the fixed manufacturing costs of $400,000 over a greater number of units manufactured. Specifically, an increase in production from 20,000 units to 25,000 units means that the fixed manufacturing cost per unit decreases from $20 ($400,000 ÷ 20,000 units) to $16 ($400,000 ÷ 25,000 units). Thus, the cost of goods sold when 25,000 units are manufactured is $4 per unit less, or $80,000 less in total (20,000 units sold × $4). Since the cost of goods sold is less, income from operations is $80,000 more when 25,000 units rather than 20,000 units are manufactured.

Managers should be careful in analyzing income from operations under absorption costing when finished goods inventory changes. Increases in income from operations may be created by simply increasing finished goods inventory. Thus, managers could misinterpret such increases (or decreases) in income from operations as due to changes in sales volume, prices, or costs.

Link to
Adobe Systems

In a recent absorption costing income statement, **Adobe Systems** reported (in millions) total revenue of $4,147, cost of revenue of $622, gross revenue of $3,525, operating expenses of $3,112, and operating income of $413.

Under variable costing, income from operations is $200,000, regardless of whether 20,000 units or 25,000 units are manufactured. This is because no fixed manufacturing costs are allocated to the units manufactured. Instead, all fixed manufacturing costs are treated as a period expense.

To illustrate, Exhibit 8 shows the variable costing income statements for Frand for the production of 20,000 units, 25,000 units, and 30,000 units. In each case, the income from operations is $200,000.

Exhibit 8

Variable Costing Income Statements for Three Production Levels

Frand Manufacturing Company **Variable Costing Income Statements**			
	20,000 Units Manufactured	**25,000 Units Manufactured**	**30,000 Units Manufactured**
Sales (20,000 units × $75)	$1,500,000	$1,500,000	$1,500,000
Variable cost of goods sold:			
Variable cost of goods manufactured:			
(20,000 units × $35)	$ 700,000		
(25,000 units × $35)		$ 875,000	
(30,000 units × $35)			$1,050,000
Ending inventory:			
(0 units × $35).......................	0		
(5,000 units × $35)..................		(175,000)	
(10,000 units × $35)			(350,000)
Total variable cost of goods sold.........	$ 700,000	$ 700,000	$ 700,000
Manufacturing margin....................	$ 800,000	$ 800,000	$ 800,000
Variable selling and administrative			
expenses	100,000	100,000	100,000
Contribution margin......................	$ 700,000	$ 700,000	$ 700,000
Fixed costs:			
Fixed manufacturing costs	$ 400,000	$ 400,000	$ 400,000
Fixed selling and administrative			
expenses	100,000	100,000	100,000
Total fixed costs........................	$ 500,000	$ 500,000	$ 500,000
Income from operations	$ 200,000	$ 200,000	$ 200,000

Ethics: Do It!

Taking an "Absorption Hit"

Aligning production to demand is a critical decision in business. Managers must not allow the temporary benefits of excess production through higher absorption of fixed costs to guide their decisions. Likewise, if demand falls, production should be dropped and inventory liquidated to match the new demand level, even though earnings will be penalized. The following interchange provides an example of an appropriate response to lowered demand for **H.J. Heinz Company**:

Analyst's question: *It seems....that you're guiding to a little bit of a drop in performance between 3Q (third Quarter) and 4Q (fourth Quarter)....if so, maybe you could walk us through some of the drivers of that relative softness.*

Heinz executive's response: *No, I think, frankly, we're really pleased with the performance in the business....We're*

also aggressively taking out inventory in the fourth quarter. And as you know, as you reduce inventory, you take an absorption hit. You're pulling basically fixed costs off the balance sheet into the P&L and there's a hit associated with that, but we think that's the right thing to do, to pull inventory out and to drive cash flow. So now, we feel very good about the business and feel very good about the fact that we're taking it to the middle of the range and taking up the bottom end of our guidance.

Management operating with integrity will seek the tangible benefits of reducing inventory, even though there may be an adverse impact on published financial statements caused by absorption costing.

Source of question and response from http://seekingalpha.com/article/375151-h-j-heinz-management-discusses-q3-2012-results-earnings-call-transcript?page=6&p=qanda. Accessed February 2012.

As shown, absorption costing may encourage managers to produce inventory. This is because producing inventory absorbs fixed manufacturing costs, which increases income from operations. However, producing inventory leads to higher handling, storage, financing, and obsolescence costs. For this reason, many accountants believe that variable costing should be used by management for evaluating operating performance.

Check Up Corner 6-2 | Absorption and Variable Costing with Different Levels of Production

Third Street Manufacturing Company has no beginning inventory, and sales are estimated to be 30,000 units at $100 per unit. Third Street's management is evaluating whether to manufacture 30,000 units (Proposal 1) or 40,000 units (Proposal 2). Sales will not change if more than 30,000 units are manufactured. The costs and expenses for each proposal follow:

	Proposal 1: 30,000 Units Manufactured			Proposal 2: 40,000 Units Manufactured		
	Total Cost	Number of Units	Unit Cost	Total Cost	Number of Units	Unit Cost
Manufacturing costs:						
Variable	$1,200,000	30,000	$40	$1,600,000	40,000	$40
Fixed	600,000	30,000	$20	600,000	40,000	$15
Total	$1,800,000			$2,200,000		
Selling and administrative expenses:						
Variable	$ 210,000	30,000	$ 7	$ 210,000	30,000	$ 7
Fixed	140,000			140,000		
Total	$ 350,000			$ 350,000		

A. Prepare an estimated income statement, comparing operating results if 30,000 and 40,000 units are manufactured in (1) the absorption costing format and (2) the variable costing format.
B. What is the reason for the difference in income from operations reported for the two levels of production by the absorption costing income statement?

Solution:

A. (1)

Absorption Costing Income Statements

	Proposal 1: 30,000 Units Manufactured	Proposal 2: 40,000 Units Manufactured
Sales (30,000 units × $100)	$3,000,000	$3,000,000
Cost of goods sold:		
Cost of goods manufactured	$1,800,000	$2,200,000
Ending inventory	—	(550,000)
Total cost of goods sold	$1,800,000	$1,650,000
Gross profit	$1,200,000	$1,350,000
Selling and administrative expenses	350,000	350,000
Income from operations	$ 850,000	$1,000,000

(30,000 units produced × $40 variable manufacturing cost per unit) + $600,000 fixed cost

(40,000 units produced × $40 variable manufacturing cost per unit) + $600,000 fixed cost

10,000 units (40,000 produced − 30,000 sold) × $55 per unit ($2,200,000 ÷ 40,000 units)

(30,000 units sold × $7 variable selling cost per unit) + $140,000

(2)

Variable Costing Income Statements

	Proposal 1: 30,000 Units Manufactured	Proposal 2: 40,000 Units Manufactured
Sales (30,000 units × $100)	$3,000,000	$3,000,000
Variable cost of goods sold:		
Variable cost of goods manufactured	$1,200,000	$1,600,000
Ending inventory	—	(400,000)
Total variable cost of goods sold	$1,200,000	$1,200,000
Manufacturing margin	$1,800,000	$1,800,000
Variable selling and administrative expenses	210,000	210,000
Contribution margin	$1,590,000	$1,590,000
Fixed costs:		
Fixed manufacturing costs	$ 600,000	$ 600,000
Fixed selling and administrative expenses	140,000	140,000
Total fixed costs	$ 740,000	$ 740,000
Income from operations	$ 850,000	$ 850,000

Variable Costs

30,000 units produced × $40 variable manufacturing cost per unit

40,000 units produced × $40 variable manufacturing cost per unit

10,000 units (40,000 produced − 30,000 sold) × $40 variable cost per unit

30,000 units sold × $7 variable selling cost per unit

◀---- Fixed Costs

B. The difference (in A.) is caused by including $150,000 fixed manufacturing costs (10,000 units × $15 fixed manufacturing cost per unit) in the ending inventory, which decreases the cost of goods sold and increases the income from operations by $150,000.

Check Up Corner

Using Absorption and Variable Costing

Objective 3

Describe management's use of absorption and variable costing.

Each decision-making situation should be carefully analyzed in deciding whether absorption or variable costing reporting would be more useful. As a basis for discussion, the use of absorption and variable costing in the following decision-making situations is described:

- Controlling costs
- Pricing products
- Planning production
- Analyzing contribution margins
- Analyzing market segments

The role of accounting reports in these decision-making situations is shown in Exhibit 9.

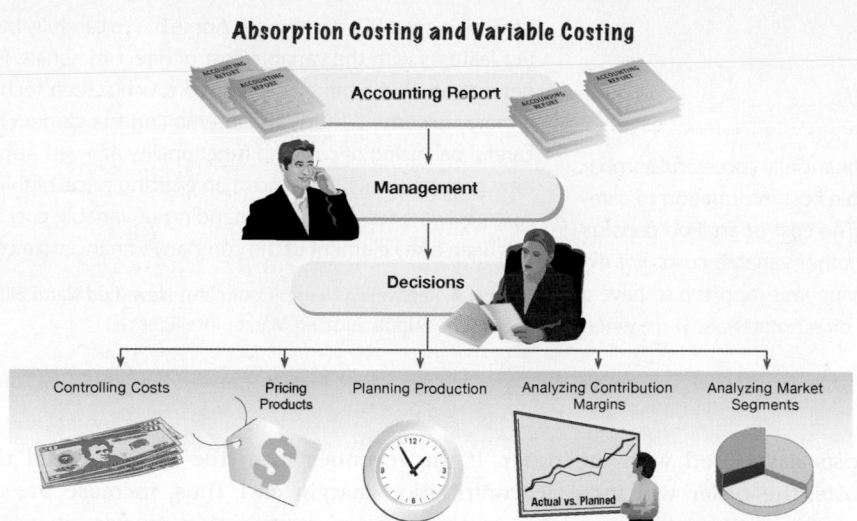

Exhibit 9
Accounting
Reports and
Management
Decisions

Controlling Costs

All costs are controllable in the long run by someone within a business. However, not all costs are controllable at the same level of management. For example, plant supervisors control the use of direct materials in their departments. They have no control, though, over insurance costs related to the property, plant, and equipment.

For a level of management, **controllable costs** are costs that can be influenced (increased or decreased) by management at that level. **Noncontrollable costs** are costs that another level of management controls. This distinction is useful for reporting costs to those responsible for their control.

Variable manufacturing costs are controlled by operating management. In contrast, fixed manufacturing overhead costs such as the salaries of production supervisors are normally controlled at a higher level of management. Likewise, control of the variable and fixed operating expenses usually involves different levels of management. Since fixed costs and expenses are reported separately under variable costing, variable costing reports are normally more useful than absorption costing reports for controlling costs.

Pricing Products

Many factors enter into determining the selling price of a product. However, the cost of making the product is significant in all pricing decisions.

In the short run, fixed costs cannot be avoided. Thus, the selling price of a product should at least be equal to the variable costs of making and selling it. Any price above this minimum selling price contributes to covering fixed costs and generating income. Since variable costing reports variable and fixed costs and expenses separately, it is often more useful than absorption costing for setting short-run prices.

In the long run, a company must set its selling price high enough to cover all costs and expenses (variable and fixed) and generate income. Since absorption costing includes fixed and variable costs in the cost of manufacturing a product, absorption costing is often more useful than variable costing for setting long-term prices.

Planning Production

In the short run, planning production is limited to existing capacity. In many cases, operating decisions must be made quickly before opportunities are lost.

To illustrate, a company with seasonal demand for its products may have an opportunity to obtain an off-season order that will not interfere with its current production schedule. The relevant factors for such a short-run decision are the additional revenues and the additional

Why It Matters

Direct Materials Cost

Apple has become one of the most financially successful companies of the past decade by using variable cost information to carefully price its iPod family of products. The cost of an iPod consists almost entirely of direct materials and other variable costs. For example, Apple's sixth generation iPod nano was reported to have a total cost of $45.10, of which $43.73 is direct materials. Thus, when designing a new iPod or iPhone, Apple has to carefully balance product features with the variable cost of direct materials. For the sixth generation iPod nano, Apple added touch screen technology and a more powerful battery, while removing the camera feature. This careful balancing of cost and functionality allowed Apple to offer a new generation of iPod nano at an enticing price, highlighting how Apple's awareness and understanding of variable cost information has been a key element of the company's financial success.

Source: A. Rassweiler, "ISuppli Estimates New iPod Nano Bill of Materials at $43.73," iSuppli, Applied Market Intelligence.

variable costs associated with the order. If the revenues from the order exceed the related variable costs, the order will increase contribution margin and, thus, increase the company's income from operations. Since variable costing reports contribution margin, it is often more useful than absorption costing in such cases.

In the long run, planning production can include expanding existing capacity. Thus, when analyzing and evaluating long-run sales and operating decisions, absorption costing, which considers fixed and variable costs, is often more useful.

Analyzing Contribution Margins

For planning and control purposes, managers often compare planned and actual contribution margins. For example, an increase in the price of fuel could have a significant impact on the planned contribution margins of an airline. The use of variable costing as a basis for such analyses is described and illustrated later in this chapter.

Analyzing Market Segments

Market analysis determines the profit contributed by the market segments of a company. A **market segment** is a portion of a company that can be analyzed using sales, costs, and expenses to determine its profitability. Examples of market segments include sales territories, products, salespersons, and customers. Variable costing as an aid in decision making regarding market segments is discussed next.

Link to Adobe Systems

Adobe Systems organizes its operations into three segments: Digital Marketing, Digital Media, and Print and Publishing.

Objective 4
Use variable costing for analyzing market segments, including product, territories, and salespersons segments.

Analyzing Market Segments

Companies can report income for internal decision making using either absorption or variable costing. Absorption costing is often used for long-term analysis of market segments. Variable costing is often used for short-term analysis of market segments. In this section, segment profitability reporting using variable costing is described and illustrated.

Most companies prepare variable costing reports for each product. These reports are often used for product pricing and deciding whether to discontinue a product. In addition, variable costing reports may be prepared for geographic areas, customers, distribution channels, or salespersons. A distribution channel is the method for selling a product to a customer.

To illustrate analysis of market segments using variable costing, the following data for the month ending March 31 for Camelot Fragrance Company are used:

Camelot Fragrance Company
Sales and Production Data
For the Month Ended March 31

	Northern Territory	Southern Territory	Total
Sales:			
Gwenevere	$60,000	$30,000	$ 90,000
Lancelot	20,000	50,000	70,000
Total territory sales	$80,000	$80,000	$160,000
Variable production costs:			
Gwenevere (12% of sales)	$ 7,200	$ 3,600	$ 10,800
Lancelot (12% of sales)	2,400	6,000	8,400
Total variable production cost by territory	$ 9,600	$ 9,600	$ 19,200
Promotion costs:			
Gwenevere (variable at 30% of sales)	$18,000	$ 9,000	$ 27,000
Lancelot (variable at 20% of sales)	4,000	10,000	14,000
Total promotion cost by territory	$22,000	$19,000	$ 41,000
Sales commissions:			
Gwenevere (variable at 20% of sales)	$12,000	$ 6,000	$ 18,000
Lancelot (variable at 10% of sales)	2,000	5,000	7,000
Total sales commissions by territory	$14,000	$11,000	$ 25,000

Camelot Fragrance manufactures and sells the Gwenevere perfume for women and the Lancelot cologne for men. To simplify, no inventories are assumed to exist at the beginning or end of March.

Why It Matters

Business Segments

A business segment represents a component of business that earns revenues and incurs expenses and whose performance is evaluated by management. Business segments can be determined along different dimensions, such as the nature of products and services, geographic region, class of customer, or methods for distributing products or providing services. Examples from a sampling of companies follow:

Company	Segment Type	Segments
Amazon	Geographic	North America, Germany, Japan, UK, Other International
Apple	Product	iPhone, iPad, Mac, Services, Other Products
Boeing	Product	Commercial Airplanes, Military Aircraft, Network and Space Systems, Global Services and Support, Boeing Capital
Comcast	Distribution channel	Cable Communications, Cable Networks, Broadcast TV, Filmed Entertainment, Theme Parks
Deere and Co.	Customer application	Agriculture and Turf, Construction and Forestry
Intel	Customer	Hewlett-Packard, Dell Inc., Lenovo Group Limited
McDonald's	Geographic	United States, Europe, APMEA (Asia-Pacific, Middle East, and Africa), Other Countries
Procter & Gamble	Product	Beauty, Grooming, Health Care, Fabric and Home Care
Skechers	Distribution channel	Domestic Wholesale, International Wholesale, Retail, E-commerce

Sales Territory Profitability Analysis

An income statement presenting the contribution margin by sales territories is often used in evaluating past performance and in directing future sales efforts. Sales territory profitability analysis may lead management to do the following:

- Reduce costs in lower-profit sales territories
- Increase sales efforts in higher-profit territories

To illustrate sales territory profitability analysis, Exhibit 10 shows the contribution margin for the Northern and Southern territories of Camelot Fragrance Company. As Exhibit 10 indicates, the Northern Territory is generating $34,400 of contribution margin, while the Southern Territory is generating $40,400 of contribution margin.

Exhibit 10

Contribution Margin by Sales Territory Report

Camelot Fragrance Company Contribution Margin by Sales Territory For the Month Ended March 31		
	Northern Territory	**Southern Territory**
Sales	$80,000	$80,000
Variable cost of goods sold	9,600	9,600
Manufacturing margin	$70,400	$70,400
Variable selling expenses:		
Promotion costs $22,000	$19,000	
Sales commissions 14,000	11,000	
Total variable selling expenses	36,000	30,000
Contribution margin	$34,400	$40,400
Contribution margin ratio..........................	43%	50.5%

In addition to the contribution margin, the contribution margin ratio for each territory is shown in Exhibit 10. The contribution margin ratio is computed as follows:

$$\text{Contribution Margin Ratio} = \frac{\text{Contribution Margin}}{\text{Sales}}$$

Exhibit 10 indicates that the Northern Territory has a contribution margin ratio of 43% ($34,400 ÷ $80,000). In contrast, the Southern Territory has a contribution margin ratio of 50.5% ($40,400 ÷ $80,000).

The difference in profit of the Northern and Southern territories is due to the difference in sales mix between the territories. **Sales mix**, sometimes referred to as *product mix*, is the relative amount of sales among the various products. The sales mix is computed by dividing the sales of each product by the total sales of each territory. Sales mix of the Northern and Southern territories is as follows:

	Northern Territory		**Southern Territory**	
Product	**Sales**	**Sales Mix**	**Sales**	**Sales Mix**
Gwenevere	$60,000	75%	$30,000	37.5%
Lancelot	20,000	25	50,000	62.5
Total	$80,000	100%	$80,000	100.0%

As shown, 62.5% of the Southern Territory's sales are sales of Lancelot. Since the Southern Territory's contribution margin ($40,400) is higher (as shown in Exhibit 10) than that of the Northern Territory ($34,400), Lancelot must be more profitable than Gwenevere. To verify this, product profitability analysis is performed.

Product Profitability Analysis

A company should focus its sales efforts on products that will provide the maximum total contribution margin. In doing so, product profitability analysis is often used by management in making decisions regarding product sales and promotional efforts.

To illustrate product profitability analysis, Exhibit 11 shows the contribution margin by product for Camelot Fragrance Company.

Camelot Fragrance Company
Contribution Margin by Product Line
For the Month Ended March 31

	Gwenevere		Lancelot	
Sales		$90,000		$70,000
Variable cost of goods sold		10,800		8,400
Manufacturing margin		$79,200		$61,600
Variable selling expenses:				
Promotion costs	$27,000		$14,000	
Sales commissions	18,000		7,000	
Total variable selling expenses		45,000		21,000
Contribution margin		$34,200		$40,600
Contribution margin ratio		38%		58%

Exhibit 11
Contribution Margin by Product Line Report

Exhibit 11 indicates that Lancelot's contribution margin ratio (58%) is greater than Gwenevere's (38%). Lancelot's higher contribution margin ratio is a result of its lower promotion and sales commissions costs. Thus, management should consider the following:

- Emphasizing Lancelot in its marketing plans
- Reducing Gwenevere's promotion and sales commissions costs
- Increasing the price of Gwenevere

Adobe Systems recently reported the following data (in millions) for its three segments:

	Digital Media	Digital Marketing	Print and Publishing
Revenue	$2,603	$1,355	$188
Cost of revenue	149	464	9
Gross profit	$2,454	$ 891	$179

Link to Adobe Systems

Source: Adobe Systems Incorporated, Form 10-K for the Fiscal Year Ended November 27, 2015.

Salesperson Profitability Analysis

A salesperson profitability report is useful in evaluating sales performance. Such a report normally includes total sales, variable cost of goods sold, variable selling expenses, contribution margin, and contribution margin ratio for each salesperson.

Exhibit 12 illustrates such a salesperson profitability report for three salespersons in the Northern Territory of Camelot Fragrance Company. The exhibit indicates that Beth Williams produced the greatest contribution margin ($15,200), but had the lowest contribution margin ratio (38%). Beth sold $40,000 of product, which is twice as much product as the other two salespersons. However, Beth sold only Gwenevere, which has the lowest contribution margin ratio (from Exhibit 11). The other two salespersons sold equal amounts of Gwenevere and Lancelot. As a result, Inez Rodriguez and Deshawn Thomas had higher contribution margin ratios because they sold more Lancelot. The Northern Territory manager could use this report to encourage Inez and Deshawn to sell more total product, while encouraging Beth to sell more Lancelot.

Exhibit 12

Contribution Margin by Salesperson Report

	Camelot Fragrance Company Contribution Margin by Salesperson—Northern Territory For the Month Ended March 31			
	Inez Rodriguez	Deshawn Thomas	Beth Williams	Northern Territory— Total
Sales	$20,000	$20,000	$40,000	$80,000
Variable cost of goods sold	2,400	2,400	4,800	9,600
Manufacturing margin	$17,600	$17,600	$35,200	$70,400
Variable selling expenses:				
Promotion costs	$ 5,000	$ 5,000	$12,000	$22,000
Sales commissions	3,000	3,000	8,000	14,000
Total variable selling expenses	$ 8,000	$ 8,000	$20,000	$36,000
Contribution margin	$ 9,600	$ 9,600	$15,200	$34,400
Contribution margin ratio	48%	48%	38%	43%
Sales mix (% Lancelot sales)	50%	50%	0%	25%

Other factors should also be considered in evaluating salespersons' performance. For example, sales growth rates, years of experience, customer service, territory size, and actual performance compared to budgeted performance may also be important.

Why It Matters

Chipotle Contribution Margin per Restaurant

Chipotle Mexican Grill's annual report identifies revenues and costs for its company-owned stores. We assume that food, beverage, packaging, and labor are variable and that occupancy (rent expense) and other expenses are fixed. By dividing the totals provided in the annual report by the number of stores (1,783), a contribution margin and income from operations can be constructed for an average restaurant as follows (in thousands):

Sales		$2,304
Variable restaurant expenses:		
Food, beverage, and packaging	$797	
Labor	507	
Total variable restaurant operating costs		1,304
Contribution margin		$ 1,000
Occupancy and other expenses		373
Income from operations		$ 627

As can be seen, the average Chipotle restaurant is very profitable. Chipotle can use this information for pricing products; evaluating the sensitivity of store profitability to changes in sales volume, prices, and costs; and analyzing profitability by geographic segment by aggregating individual store data.

Source: Chipotle 10-K Annual Report to the SEC, February 2015.

Check Up Corner 6-3 | Contribution Margin by Segment

Vintage Apparel Company manufactures and sells two styles of baseball jerseys, the Retro and the New Age. These jerseys are sold in two regions, East and West. Information about the two jerseys and sales in the two regions is as follows:

	Retro	New Age
Sales price	$100	$120
Variable cost of goods sold per unit	75	90
Manufacturing margin per unit	$ 25	$ 30
Variable selling expense per unit	17	18
Contribution margin per unit	$ 8	$ 12

	Units Sold	
	East Region	West Region
Retro	10,000	6,000
New Age	0	5,000

Prepare a contribution margin by sales territory report. Calculate the contribution margin ratio for each territory.

Solution:

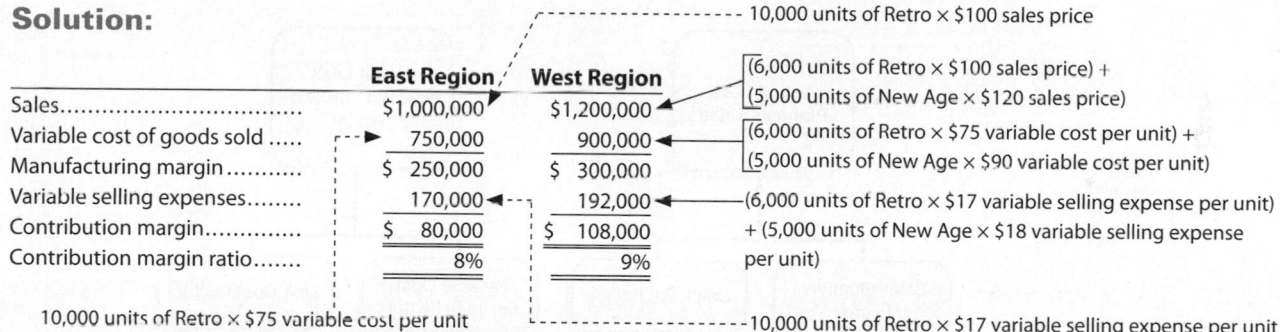

	East Region	West Region
Sales	$1,000,000	$1,200,000
Variable cost of goods sold	750,000	900,000
Manufacturing margin	$ 250,000	$ 300,000
Variable selling expenses	170,000	192,000
Contribution margin	$ 80,000	$ 108,000
Contribution margin ratio	8%	9%

- 10,000 units of Retro × $100 sales price
- (6,000 units of Retro × $100 sales price) + (5,000 units of New Age × $120 sales price)
- (6,000 units of Retro × $75 variable cost per unit) + (5,000 units of New Age × $90 variable cost per unit)
- (6,000 units of Retro × $17 variable selling expense per unit) + (5,000 units of New Age × $18 variable selling expense per unit)
- 10,000 units of Retro × $75 variable cost per unit
- 10,000 units of Retro × $17 variable selling expense per unit

Check Up Corner

Contribution Margin Analysis

Objective 5

Use variable costing for analyzing and explaining changes in contribution margin as a result of quantity and price factors.

Managers often use contribution margin in planning and controlling operations. In doing so, managers use contribution margin analysis. **Contribution margin analysis** focuses on explaining the differences between planned and actual contribution margins.

Contribution margin is defined as sales less variable costs. Thus, a difference between the planned and actual contribution margin may be caused by an increase or a decrease in:

- Sales
- Variable costs

An increase or a decrease in sales or variable costs may in turn be due to an increase or a decrease in the:

- Number of units sold
- Unit sales price or unit cost

The effects of the preceding factors on sales or variable costs may be stated as follows:

- **Quantity factor:** The effect of a difference in the number of units sold, assuming no change in unit sales price or unit cost. The *sales quantity factor* and the *variable cost quantity factor* are computed as follows:

  Sales Quantity Factor = (Actual Units Sold – Planned Units of Sales) × Planned Sales Price

  Variable Cost Quantity Factor = (Planned Units of Sales – Actual Units Sold) × Planned Unit Cost

The preceding factors are computed so that a positive amount increases contribution margin and a negative amount decreases contribution margin.

■ **Unit price factor** or *unit cost factor*: The effect of a difference in unit sales price or unit cost on the number of units sold. The unit price factor and unit cost factor are computed as follows:

Unit Price Factor = (Actual Selling Price per Unit – Planned Selling Price per Unit) × Actual Units Sold

Unit Cost Factor = (Planned Cost per Unit – Actual Cost per Unit) × Actual Units Sold

The preceding factors are computed so that a positive amount increases contribution margin and a negative amount decreases contribution margin.

The effects of the preceding factors on contribution margin are summarized in Exhibit 13.

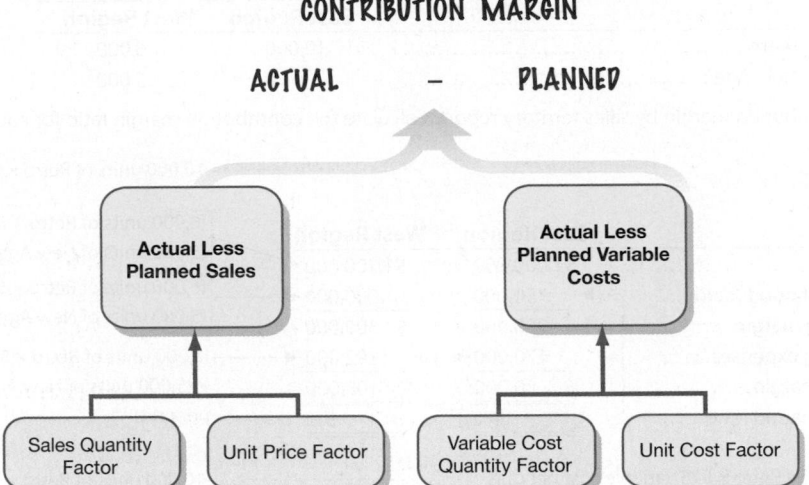

Exhibit 13
Contribution
Margin Analysis

To illustrate, the following data for the year ended December 31, for Noble Inc., which sells a single product, are used:[1]

	Actual	Planned
Sales	$937,500	$800,000
Variable cost of goods sold	$425,000	$350,000
Variable selling and administrative expenses	162,500	125,000
Total	$587,500	$475,000
Contribution margin	$350,000	$325,000
Number of units sold	125,000	100,000
Per unit:		
Sales price	$7.50	$8.00
Variable cost of goods sold	3.40	3.50
Variable selling and administrative expenses	1.30	1.25

Exhibit 14 shows the contribution margin analysis report for Noble Inc. for the year ended December 31. The exhibit indicates that the favorable difference of $25,000 ($350,000 – $325,000) between the actual and planned contribution margins was due in large part to an increase in the quantity sold (sales quantity factor) of $200,000. This $200,000 increase was partially offset by a decrease in the unit sales price (unit price factor) of $62,500 and an increase in the amount of variable costs of $112,500 ($75,000 + $37,500).

---

[1] To simplify, it is assumed that Noble Inc. sells a single product. The analysis would be more complex, but the principles would be the same, if more than one product were sold.

Exhibit 14
Contribution
Margin Analysis
Report

Noble Inc. Contribution Margin Analysis For the Year Ended December 31		
Planned contribution margin		$325,000
Effect of changes in sales:		
Sales quantity factor [(125,000 units – 100,000 units) × $8.00]	$200,000	
Unit price factor [($7.50 – $8.00) × 125,000 units]	(62,500)	
Total effect of changes in sales		137,500
Effect of changes in variable cost of goods sold:		
Variable cost quantity factor [(100,000 units – 125,000 units) × $3.50]	$ (87,500)	
Unit cost factor [($3.50 – $3.40) × 125,000 units]	12,500	
Total effect of changes in variable cost of goods sold		(75,000)
Effect of changes in selling and administrative expenses:		
Variable cost quantity factor [(100,000 units – 125,000 units) × $1.25]..............	$ (31,250)	
Unit cost factor [($1.25 – $1.30) × 125,000 units]................................	(6,250)	
Total effect of changes in selling and administrative expenses................		(37,500)
Actual contribution margin		$350,000

The contribution margin analysis reports are useful to management in evaluating past performance and in planning future operations. For example, the impact of the $0.50 reduction in the unit sales price by Noble Inc. on the number of units sold and on the total sales for the year is useful information in determining whether further price reductions might be desirable.

The contribution margin analysis report also highlights the impact of changes in unit variable costs and expenses. For example, the $0.05 increase in the unit variable selling and administrative expenses might be a result of increased advertising expenditures. If so, the increase in the number of units sold could be attributed to both the $0.50 price reduction and the increased advertising.

Check Up Corner 6-4   Contribution Margin Analysis

H-TECH Industries Inc. manufactures only one product. In an attempt to increase sales and improve the contribution margin, the company decreased the sales price of the product and pursued an aggressive marketing campaign. The marketing campaign increased variable selling and administrative expenses.

The following data have been gathered from the accounting records for the year ended December 31:

	Actual	Planned
Sales..	$3,360,000	$2,100,000
Variable cost of goods sold	$1,776,000	$1,050,000
Variable selling and administrative expenses........	552,000	280,000
Total variable costs.......................................	$2,328,000	$1,330,000
Contribution margin..	$1,032,000	$ 770,000
Number of units sold	24,000	14,000
Per unit:		
Sales price..	$140	$150
Variable cost of goods sold	74	75
Variable selling and administrative expenses.....	23	20

Prepare a contribution margin analysis report for the year ended December 31.

Solution:

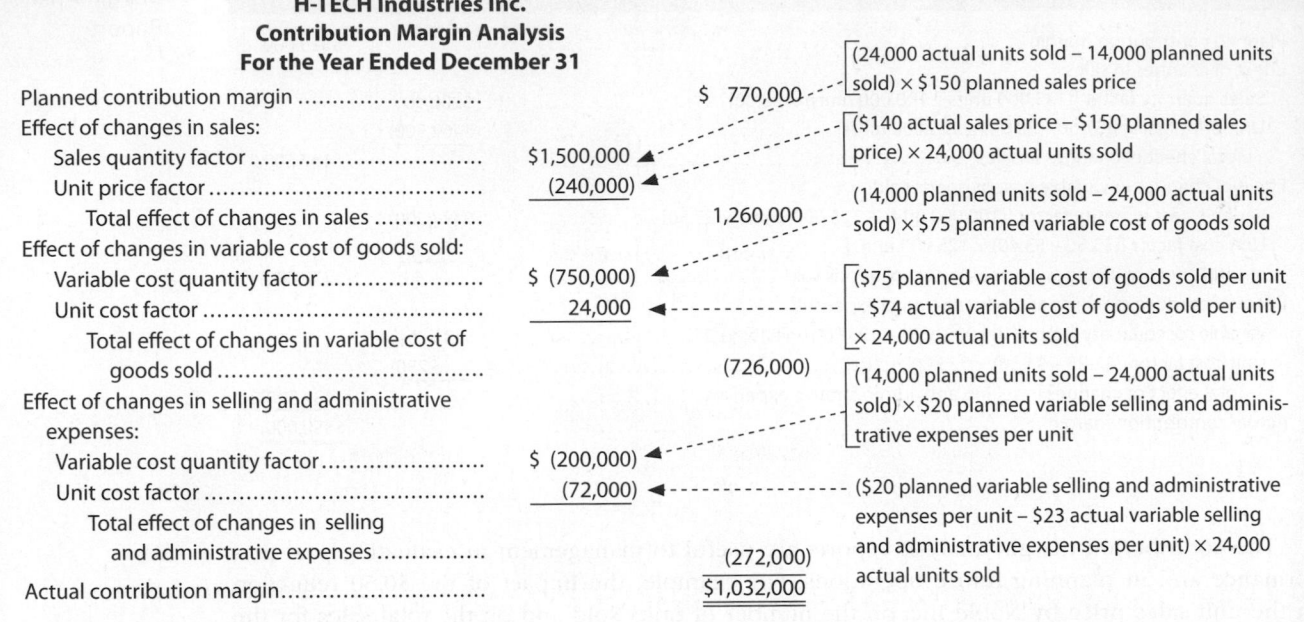

H-TECH Industries Inc.
Contribution Margin Analysis
For the Year Ended December 31

Planned contribution margin		$ 770,000
Effect of changes in sales:		
Sales quantity factor	$1,500,000	
Unit price factor	(240,000)	
Total effect of changes in sales		1,260,000
Effect of changes in variable cost of goods sold:		
Variable cost quantity factor......................	$ (750,000)	
Unit cost factor	24,000	
Total effect of changes in variable cost of goods sold		(726,000)
Effect of changes in selling and administrative expenses:		
Variable cost quantity factor......................	$ (200,000)	
Unit cost factor	(72,000)	
Total effect of changes in selling and administrative expenses		(272,000)
Actual contribution margin.............................		$1,032,000

(24,000 actual units sold – 14,000 planned units sold) × $150 planned sales price

($140 actual sales price – $150 planned sales price) × 24,000 actual units sold

(14,000 planned units sold – 24,000 actual units sold) × $75 planned variable cost of goods sold

($75 planned variable cost of goods sold per unit – $74 actual variable cost of goods sold per unit) × 24,000 actual units sold

(14,000 planned units sold – 24,000 actual units sold) × $20 planned variable selling and administrative expenses per unit

($20 planned variable selling and administrative expenses per unit – $23 actual variable selling and administrative expenses per unit) × 24,000 actual units sold

Check Up Corner

Why It Matters

Eastman Revenue Price and Volume Effects

Eastman Chemical Company is a global specialty chemical company. Eastman began as a division of Eastman Kodak, producing chemicals for Kodak's photographic processes. Eastman explains the changes in its revenues for each of its major segments by providing information on volume (quantity) and price effects. The disclosure for the Additives and Function Products Segment is as follows (in millions):

	2014	2013	Amount Change	% Change
Sales	$1,821	$1,719	$102	6%
Volume effect			82	5%
Price effect			20	1%

This analysis shows that the sales increase (6%) between 2013 and 2014 was mostly caused by increasing sales volume (5%), rather than increasing price (1%). Thus, Eastman is growing its business in this segment without sacrificing price.

Source: Eastman Chemical Company 10-K Annual Report to the SEC, February 2015.

Objective 6
Describe and illustrate contribution margin analysis for service businesses.

Variable Costing for Service Businesses

Variable costing and the use of variable costing for manufacturing firms have been discussed earlier in this chapter. Service companies also use variable costing, contribution margin analysis, and segment analysis.

Reporting Income

Unlike a manufacturing company, a service company does not make or sell a product. Thus, service companies do not have inventory. Since service companies have no inventory, they do not use absorption costing to allocate fixed costs. In addition, variable costing reports of service companies do not report a manufacturing margin.

To illustrate variable costing for a service company, Blue Skies Airlines Inc., which operates as a small commercial airline, is used. The variable and fixed costs of Blue Skies are shown in Exhibit 15.

Cost	Amount	Cost Behavior	Activity Base
Depreciation expense	$3,600,000	Fixed	
Food and beverage service expense..............	444,000	Variable	Number of passengers
Fuel expense.....................................	4,080,000	Variable	Number of miles flown
Rental expense...................................	800,000	Fixed	
Selling expense	3,256,000	Variable	Number of passengers
Wages expense...................................	6,120,000	Variable	Number of miles flown

Exhibit 15
Costs of Blue Skies Airlines Inc.

As discussed in Chapter 5, a cost is classified as a fixed or variable cost according to how it changes relative to an activity base. A common activity for a manufacturing firm is the number of units produced. In contrast, most service companies use several activity bases.

To illustrate, Blue Skies uses the activity base *number of passengers* for food and beverage service and selling expenses. Blue Skies uses *number of miles flown* for fuel and wage expenses.

The variable costing income statement for Blue Skies, assuming revenue of $19,238,000, is shown in Exhibit 16.

Blue Skies Airlines Inc. Variable Costing Income Statement For the Month Ended April 30		
Revenue		$19,238,000
Variable costs:		
Fuel expense	$4,080,000	
Wages expense	6,120,000	
Food and beverage service expense.........................	444,000	
Selling expense..	3,256,000	
Total variable costs		13,900,000
Contribution margin...		$ 5,338,000
Fixed costs:		
Depreciation expense.......................................	$3,600,000	
Rental expense	800,000	
Total fixed costs		4,400,000
Income from operations		$ 938,000

Exhibit 16
Variable Costing Income Statement for a Service Company

Unlike a manufacturing company, Exhibit 16 does not report cost of goods sold, inventory, or manufacturing margin. However, as shown in Exhibit 16, contribution margin is reported separately from income from operations.

Analyzing Segments

A contribution margin report for service companies can be used to analyze and evaluate market segments. Typical segments for various service companies are shown in Exhibit 17.

Exhibit 17   Service Industry Market Segments

Service Industry	Market Segments
Electric power	Regions, customer types (industrial, consumer)
Banking	Customer types (commercial, retail), products (loans, savings accounts)
Airlines	Products (passengers, cargo), routes
Railroads	Products (commodity type), routes
Hotels	Hotel properties
Telecommunications	Customer type (commercial, retail), service type (voice, data)
Health care	Procedure, payment type (Medicare, insured)

To illustrate, a contribution margin report segmented by route is used for Blue Skies Airlines Inc. In preparing the report, the following data for April are used:

	Chicago/Atlanta	Atlanta/LA	LA/Chicago
Average ticket price per passenger	$400	$1,075	$805
Total passengers served................................	16,000	7,000	6,600
Total miles flown...	56,000	88,000	60,000

The variable costs per unit are as follows:

Fuel	$ 20 per mile
Wages	30 per mile
Food and beverage service	15 per passenger
Selling	110 per passenger

A contribution margin report for Blue Skies is shown in Exhibit 18. The report is segmented by the routes (city pairs) flown.

Exhibit 18

Contribution Margin by Segment Report for a Service Company

Blue Skies Airlines Inc.
Contribution Margin by Route
For the Month Ended April 30

	Chicago/ Atlanta	Atlanta/ Los Angeles	Los Angeles/ Chicago	Total
Revenue				
(Ticket price × No. of passengers)	$ 6,400,000	$ 7,525,000	$ 5,313,000	$19,238,000
Aircraft fuel				
($20 × No. of miles flown)	(1,120,000)	(1,760,000)	(1,200,000)	(4,080,000)
Wages and benefits				
($30 × No. of miles flown)	(1,680,000)	(2,640,000)	(1,800,000)	(6,120,000)
Food and beverage service				
($15 × No. of passengers)	(240,000)	(105,000)	(99,000)	(444,000)
Selling expenses				
($110 × No. of passengers)	(1,760,000)	(770,000)	(726,000)	(3,256,000)
Contribution margin......................	$ 1,600,000	$ 2,250,000	$ 1,488,000	$ 5,338,000
Contribution margin ratio* (rounded)	25%	30%	28%	28%

*Contribution Margin/Revenue

Exhibit 18 indicates that the Chicago/Atlanta route has the lowest contribution margin ratio of 25%. In contrast, the Atlanta/Los Angeles route has the highest contribution margin ratio of 30%.

Analyzing Contribution Margin

Blue Skies Airlines Inc. is also used to illustrate contribution margin analysis. Specifically, assume that Blue Skies decides to try to improve the contribution margin of its Chicago/Atlanta route during May by decreasing ticket prices. Thus, Blue Skies decreases the ticket price from $400 to $380 beginning May 1. As a result, the number of tickets sold (passengers) increased from 16,000 to 20,000. However, the cost per mile also increased during May from $20 to $22 due to increasing fuel prices.

The actual and planned results for the Chicago/Atlanta route during May follow. The planned amounts are based on the April results without considering the price change or cost per mile increase. The highlighted numbers indicate changes during May.

	Chicago/Atlanta Route	
	Actual, May	Planned, May
Revenue	$7,600,000	$6,400,000
Variable expenses:		
Aircraft fuel	$1,232,000	$1,120,000
Wages	1,680,000	1,680,000
Food and beverage service	300,000	240,000
Selling expenses	2,200,000	1,760,000
Total variable expenses	$5,412,000	$4,800,000
Contribution margin	$2,188,000	$1,600,000
Contribution margin ratio	29%	25%
Number of miles flown	56,000	56,000
Number of passengers flown	20,000	16,000
Per unit:		
Ticket price	$380	$400
Aircraft fuel expense	22	20
Wages expense	30	30
Food and beverage service expense	15	15
Selling expense	110	110

Using the preceding data, a contribution margin analysis report can be prepared for the Chicago/Atlanta route for May as shown in Exhibit 19. Since the planned and actual wages and benefits expense are the same ($1,680,000), its quantity and unit cost factors are not included in Exhibit 19.

Exhibit 19

Contribution Margin Analysis Report—Service Company

Blue Skies Airlines Inc. Contribution Margin Analysis Chicago/Atlanta Route For the Month Ended May 31		
Planned contribution margin		$1,600,000
Effect of changes in revenue:		
Revenue quantity factor [(20,000 pass. – 16,000 pass.) × $400]	$1,600,000	
Unit price factor [($380 – $400) × 20,000 passengers]	(400,000)	
Total effect of changes in revenue		1,200,000
Effect of changes in fuel cost:		
Variable cost quantity factor [(56,000 miles – 56,000 miles) × $20]	$ 0	
Unit cost factor [($20 – $22) × 56,000 miles]	(112,000)	
Total effect of changes in fuel costs		(112,000)
Effect of changes in food and beverage expenses:		
Variable cost quantity factor [(16,000 pass. – 20,000 pass.) × $15]	$ (60,000)	
Unit cost factor [($15 – $15) × 20,000 passengers]	0	
Total effect of changes in food and beverage expenses		(60,000)
Effect of changes in selling expenses:		
Variable cost quantity factor [(16,000 pass. – 20,000 pass.) × $110]	$ (440,000)	
Unit cost factor [($110 – $110) × 20,000 passengers]	0	
Total effect of changes in selling expenses		(440,000)
Actual contribution margin		$2,188,000

Exhibit 19 indicates that the price decrease generated an additional $1,200,000 in revenue. This consists of $1,600,000 from an increased number of passengers (revenue quantity factor) and a $400,000 revenue reduction from the decrease in ticket price (unit price factor).

The increased fuel costs (by $2 per mile) reduced the contribution margin by $112,000 (unit cost factor). The increased number of passengers also increased the food and beverage service expenses by $60,000 and the selling expenses by $440,000 (variable cost quantity factors). The net increase in contribution margin is $588,000 ($2,188,000 – $1,600,000).

Analysis for Decision Making

Objective

Describe and illustrate the use of segment analysis and Earnings Before Interest, Taxes, Depreciation, and Amortization (EBITDA) in evaluating a company's performance.

Segment Analysis and Earnings Before Interest, Taxes, Depreciation, and Amortization (EBITDA)

The financial statements of public companies include footnote disclosure of selected segment information. This information can be used to identify strengths and weaknesses among segments.

To illustrate, **Amazon.com, Inc.** reports two Web site segments, North America and International. The sales, operating income, and depreciation expense are segment disclosures in Amazon's financial statement footnotes and are shown as follows for a recent year (in millions):

	North America	International
Sales	$55,469	$33,519
Segment operating income	2,105	(297)
Depreciation and amortization expense	2,701	915

North American sales are approximately 62% [$55,469 ÷ ($55,469 + $33,519)] of the total sales, and International sales are 38% of total sales. Thus, the International segment, while smaller than North America, is still significant.

Operating income is often expressed by adding back depreciation and amortization expense. This amount is termed earnings before interest, taxes, depreciation, and amortization, or **EBITDA**.[2] EBITDA removes a significant fixed and noncash cost from the operating income number and may approximate the contribution margin. As a result, EBITDA may be used by managers for decision making, either in addition to contribution margin or as a substitute.

The EBITDA as a percent of sales, termed EBITDA margin, can be compared between Amazon's two segments as follows:

	North America	International
Segment operating income (EBIT)	$2,105	$ (297)
Depreciation and amortization expense	2,701	915
Operating income before depreciation and amortization expense (EBITDA)	$4,806	$ 618
EBITDA as a percent of sales	8.7%	1.8%
	($4,806 ÷ $55,469)	($618 ÷ $33,519)

North America has an EBITDA of 8.7% of sales, while the International segment has an EBITDA of only 1.8% of sales. This performance difference is likely the result of more established recognition in North America. There also may be greater competition in international markets, such as from **Alibaba** in China. As Amazon grows its international business, these margins may improve.

[2] Recall that operating income is already determined prior to deducting interest and tax expense, and is often termed earnings before interest and taxes (EBIT).

Make a Decision | Segment Analysis and EBITDA

Comcast Corporation is a global media and entertainment company with operations divided into five major segments:

- Cable Communications (XFINITY)
- Cable Networks (USA Network, Syfy, E!, CNBC, others)
- Broadcast Television (NBC)
- Filmed Entertainment (Universal Pictures)
- Theme Parks (Universal)

Revenue, operating income, and depreciation and amortization information for these segments for a recent year are as follows (in millions):

	Revenue	Operating Income	Depreciation and Amortization
Cable Communications	$44,140	$18,112	$6,422
Cable Networks	9,563	3,589	748
Broadcast Television	8,542	734	127
Filmed Entertainment	5,008	711	21
Theme Parks	2,623	1,168	273
Total	$69,876	$24,314	$7,591

A. Prepare a vertical analysis of the segment revenues to total revenues. (Round to nearest whole percent.)
B. Which segment contributes most to total revenues?
C. Compute (1) EBITDA and (2) EBITDA as a percent of revenue for each segment. (Round to nearest whole percent.)
D. Evaluate segment EBITDA as a percent of revenue.
E. What might management do to increase performance in the segments with the lowest EBITDA?

Solution:

A.

	Revenue	Revenue as a Percent of Total Revenues
Cable Communications	$44,140	63%
Cable Networks	9,563	14%
Broadcast Television	8,542	12%
Filmed Entertainment	5,008	7%
Theme Parks	2,623	4%
Total	$69,876	100%

B. The Cable Communications segment has the largest revenue as a percent (63%) of total revenues. This segment provides more revenue than do all the other remaining segments combined.

C. 1. and 2.

	Revenue	Operating Income	Depreciation and Amortization	(1) EBITDA*	(2) EBITDA as a Percent of Revenue
Cable Communications	$44,140	$18,112	$6,422	$24,534	56%
Cable Networks	9,563	3,589	748	4,337	45%
Broadcast Television	8,542	734	127	861	10%
Filmed Entertainment	5,008	711	21	732	15%
Theme Parks	2,623	1,168	273	1,441	55%
Total	$69,876	$24,314	$7,591	$31,905	

*EBITDA = Operating Income + Deprecation and Amortization

D. The Cable Communications segment provides the greatest EBITDA as a percent of revenues (56%). Both the Cable Networks and Theme Parks segments are close behind at 45% and 55%, respectively. All three segments appear very profitable. The remaining two segments, Broadcast Television and Filmed Entertainment, are less profitable but acceptable.

E. Broadcast Television and Filmed Entertainment performance is highly contingent upon audience responses to TV shows and films. Management needs to build content development processes that maximize the audience appeal of TV shows and films.

Make a Decision

Let's Review

Chapter Summary

1. Under absorption costing, the cost of goods manufactured is comprised of all direct materials, direct labor, and factory overhead costs (both fixed and variable). Under variable costing, the cost of goods manufactured is composed of only variable costs: direct materials, direct labor, and variable factory overhead costs. Fixed factory overhead costs are considered a period expense.

   The variable costing income statement is structured differently than a traditional absorption costing income statement. Sales less variable cost of goods sold is presented as manufacturing margin. Manufacturing margin less variable selling and administrative expenses is presented as contribution margin. Contribution margin less fixed costs is presented as income from operations.

2. Management should be aware of the effects of changes in inventory levels on income from operations reported under variable costing and absorption costing. If absorption costing is used, managers could misinterpret increases or decreases in income from operations due to changes in inventory levels to be the result of operating efficiencies or inefficiencies.

3. Variable costing is especially useful at the operating level of management because the amount of variable manufacturing costs is controllable at this level. The fixed factory overhead costs are ordinarily controllable by a higher level of management.

   In the short run, variable costing may be useful in establishing the selling price of a product. This price should be at least equal to the variable costs of making and selling the product. In the long run, however, absorption costing is useful in establishing selling prices because all costs must be covered and a reasonable amount of operating income earned.

4. Variable costing can support management decision making in analyzing and evaluating market segments, such as territories, products, salespersons, and customers. Contribution margin reports by segment can be used by managers to support price decisions, evaluate cost changes, and plan volume changes.

5. Contribution margin analysis is the systematic examination of differences between planned and actual contribution margins. These differences can be caused by an increase/decrease in the amount of sales or variable costs, which can be caused by changes in the amount of units sold, unit sales price, or unit cost.

6. Service businesses will not have inventories, manufacturing margin, or cost of goods sold. Service firms can prepare variable costing income statements and contribution margin reports for market segments. In addition, service firms can use contribution margin analysis to plan and control operations.

Key Terms

absorption costing (258)
contribution margin (259)
contribution margin analysis (275)
controllable costs (269)
EBITDA (283)

manufacturing margin (259)
market segment (270)
noncontrollable costs (269)
quantity factor (275)
sales mix (272)

unit price (cost) factor (276)
variable cost of goods sold (259)
variable costing (259)

Practice

Multiple-Choice Questions

1. Sales were $750,000, the variable cost of goods sold was $400,000, the variable selling and administrative expenses were $90,000, and fixed costs were $200,000. The contribution margin was:
   A. $60,000.
   B. $260,000.
   C. $350,000.
   D. none of the above.

2. During the year in which the number of units manufactured exceeded the number of units sold, the income from operations reported under the absorption costing concept would be:
   A. larger than the income from operations reported under the variable costing concept.
   B. smaller than the income from operations reported under the variable costing concept.
   C. the same as the income from operations reported under the variable costing concept.
   D. none of the above.

3. The beginning inventory consists of 6,000 units, all of which are sold during the period. The beginning inventory fixed costs are $20 per unit, and the variable costs per unit are $90 per unit. What is the difference in income from operations between variable and absorption costing?
   A. Variable costing income from operations is $540,000 less than under absorption costing.
   B. Variable costing income from operations is $600,000 greater than under absorption costing.
   C. Variable costing income from operations is $120,000 less than under absorption costing.
   D. Variable costing income from operations is $120,000 greater than under absorption costing.

4. Variable costs are $70 per unit and fixed costs are $150,000. Sales are estimated to be 10,000 units. How much would absorption costing income from operations differ between a plan to produce 10,000 units and 12,000 units?
   A. $150,000 greater for 12,000 units
   B. $150,000 less for 12,000 units
   C. $25,000 greater for 12,000 units
   D. $25,000 less for 12,000 units

5. If actual sales totaled $800,000 for the current year (80,000 units at $10 each) and planned sales were $765,000 (85,000 units at $9 each), the difference between actual and planned sales due to the quantity factor is:
   A. a $50,000 increase.
   B. a $325,000 increase.
   C. a $45,000 decrease.
   D. none of the above.

Answers provided after Problem. Need more practice? Find additional multiple-choice questions, exercises, and problems in CengageNOWv2.

Exercises

SHOW ME HOW

1. Variable costing
Obj. 1

Light Company has the following information for January:

Sales	$648,000
Variable cost of goods sold	233,200
Fixed manufacturing costs	155,500
Variable selling and administrative expenses	51,800
Fixed selling and administrative expenses	36,800

Determine (A) the manufacturing margin, (B) the contribution margin, and (C) income from operations for Light Company for the month of January.

SHOW ME HOW

2. Variable costing—production exceeds sales

Obj. 1

Fixed manufacturing costs are $60 per unit, and variable manufacturing costs are $150 per unit. Production was 453,000 units, while sales were 426,000 units. Determine (A) whether variable costing income from operations is less than or greater than absorption costing income from operations, and (B) the difference in variable costing and absorption costing income from operations.

SHOW ME HOW

3. Variable costing—sales exceed production

Obj. 1

The beginning inventory is 11,600 units. All of the units that were manufactured during the period and 11,600 units of the beginning inventory were sold. The beginning inventory fixed manufacturing costs are $32 per unit, and variable manufacturing costs are $72 per unit. Determine (A) whether variable costing income from operations is less than or greater than absorption costing income from operations, and (B) the difference in variable costing and absorption costing income from operations.

SHOW ME HOW

4. Analyzing income under absorption and variable costing

Obj. 2

Variable manufacturing costs are $13 per unit, and fixed manufacturing costs are $75,000. Sales are estimated to be 12,000 units.

A. How much would absorption costing income from operations differ between a plan to produce 12,000 units and a plan to produce 15,000 units?

B. How much would variable costing income from operations differ between the two production plans?

SHOW ME HOW

5. Contribution margin by segment

Obj. 4

The following information is for Olivio Coaster Bikes Inc.:

	North	South
Sales volume (units):		
Red Dream	50,000	66,000
Blue Marauder	112,000	140,000
Sales price:		
Red Dream	$480	$500
Blue Marauder	$560	$600
Variable cost per unit:		
Red Dream	$248	$248
Blue Marauder	$260	$260

Determine the contribution margin for (A) Red Dream and (B) North Region.

SHOW ME HOW

6. Contribution margin analysis

Obj. 5

The actual price for a product was $28 per unit, while the planned price was $25 per unit. The volume decreased by 20,000 units to 410,000 actual total units. Determine (A) the sales quantity factor and (B) the unit price factor for sales.

Answers provided after Problem. Need more practice? Find additional multiple-choice questions, exercises, and problems in CengageNOWv2.

Problem

During the current period, McLaughlin Company sold 60,000 units of product at $30 per unit. At the beginning of the period, there were 10,000 units in inventory and McLaughlin Company manufactured 50,000 units during the period. The manufacturing costs and selling and administrative expenses were as follows:

	Total Cost	Number of Units	Unit Cost
Beginning inventory:			
Direct materials	$ 67,000	10,000	$ 6.70
Direct labor	155,000	10,000	15.50
Variable factory overhead	18,000	10,000	1.80
Fixed factory overhead	20,000	10,000	2.00
Total	$ 260,000		$26.00
Current period costs:			
Direct materials	$ 350,000	50,000	$ 7.00
Direct labor	810,000	50,000	16.20
Variable factory overhead	90,000	50,000	1.80
Fixed factory overhead	100,000	50,000	2.00
Total	$1,350,000		$27.00
Selling and administrative expenses:			
Variable	$ 65,000		
Fixed	45,000		
Total	$ 110,000		

Instructions

1. Prepare an income statement based on the absorption costing concept.

2. Prepare an income statement based on the variable costing concept.

3. Give the reason for the difference in the amount of income from operations in parts (1) and (2).

Need more practice? Find additional multiple-choice questions, exercises, and problems in CengageNOWv2.

Answers

Multiple-Choice Questions

1. **B** The contribution margin of $260,000 (answer B) is determined by deducting all the variable costs ($400,000 + $90,000) from sales ($750,000).

2. **A** In a period in which the number of units manufactured exceeds the number of units sold, the income from operations under the absorption costing concept is larger than the income from operations reported under the variable costing concept (answer A). This is because a proportion of the fixed manufacturing costs are deferred when the absorption costing concept is used. This deferment has the effect of excluding a portion of the fixed manufacturing costs from the current cost of goods sold.

3. **D** (6,000 units × $20 per unit) Answer A incorrectly computes the difference in income from operations using the variable cost per unit. Answer B incorrectly computes the difference in income from operations using the total cost per unit. Answer C is incorrect because variable costing income from operations will be greater than absorption costing income from operations when units manufactured is less than units sold.

4. **C** [2,000 units × ($150,000 ÷ 12,000)] Answers A and B incorrectly compute the difference in income from operations using variable cost per unit. When production exceeds sales, absorption costing will include fixed costs in the ending inventory, which causes costs of goods sold to decline and income from operations to increase. Thus, income from operations would not decline (answer D) for a production level of 12,000 units.

5. **C** The $45,000 decrease (answer C) attributed to the quantity factor is determined as follows:

Decrease in number of units sold.............................	5,000
Planned unit sales price...	× $9
Quantity factor decrease	$45,000

The difference between planned and actual sales can be attributed to a unit price factor. The unit price factor can be determined as follows:

Actual number of units sold.....................................	80,000
Increase in unit sales price	× $1
Price factor increase	$80,000

The increase of $80,000 attributed to the price factor less the decrease of $45,000 attributed to the quantity factor accounts for the $35,000 increase in total sales.

Exercises

1.
    A. $414,800 = $648,000 − $233,200
    B. $363,000 = $414,800 − $51,800
    C. $170,700 = $363,000 − $155,500 − $36,800

2.
    A.   Variable costing income from operations is less than absorption costing income from operations because the units manufactured are greater than the units sold.
    B. $1,620,000 ($60 per unit × 27,000 units)

3.
    A.   Variable costing income from operations is greater than absorption costing income from operations because the units manufactured are less than the units sold.
    B. $371,200 ($32 per unit × 11,600 units)

4.
    A. $15,000 greater in producing 15,000 units. 12,000 units × ($6.25* − $5.00**), or [3,000 units × ($75,000 ÷ 15,000 units)].
        * $75,000 ÷ 12,000 units
        ** $75,000 ÷ 15,000 units
    B.   There would be no difference in variable costing income from operations.

5.
    A. $28,232,000 = [50,000 units × ($480 − $248)] + [66,000 units × ($500 − $248)]
    B. $45,200,000 = [50,000 units × ($480 − $248)] + [112,000 units × ($560 − $260)]

6.
    A. $500,000 decrease in sales = 20,000 units × $25 per unit
    B. $1,230,000 increase in sales = ($28 − $25) × 410,000 units

Need more help? Watch step-by-step videos of how to compute answers to these Exercises in CengageNOWv2.

Problem

1.

Absorption Costing Income Statement		
Sales (60,000 × $30)		$1,800,000
Cost of goods sold:		
Beginning inventory (10,000 × $26)	$ 260,000	
Cost of goods manufactured (50,000 × $27)	1,350,000	
Total cost of goods sold		1,610,000
Gross profit..		$ 190,000
Selling and administrative expenses ($65,000 + $45,000)		110,000
Income from operations		$ 80,000

2.

Variable Costing Income Statement		
Sales (60,000 × $30)		$1,800,000
Variable cost of goods sold:		
Beginning inventory (10,000 × $24)	$ 240,000	
Variable cost of goods manufactured (50,000 × $25)	1,250,000	
Total variable cost of goods sold		1,490,000
Manufacturing margin...		$ 310,000
Variable selling and administrative expenses		65,000
Contribution margin...		$ 245,000
Fixed costs:		
Fixed manufacturing costs..	$ 100,000	
Fixed selling and administrative expenses...........................	45,000	
Total fixed costs...		145,000
Income from operations		$ 100,000

3. The difference of $20,000 ($100,000 – $80,000) in the amount of income from operations is attributable to the different treatment of the fixed manufacturing costs. The beginning inventory in the absorption costing income statement includes $20,000 (10,000 units × $2) of fixed manufacturing costs incurred in the preceding period. This $20,000 was included as an expense in a variable costing income statement of a prior period. Therefore, none of it is included as an expense in the current period variable costing income statement.

Discussion Questions

1. What types of costs are customarily included in the cost of manufactured products under (A) the absorption costing concept and (B) the variable costing concept?

2. Which type of manufacturing cost (direct materials, direct labor, variable factory overhead, fixed factory overhead) is included in the cost of goods manufactured under the absorption costing concept but is excluded from the cost of goods manufactured under the variable costing concept?

3. Which of the following costs would be included in the cost of a manufactured product according to the variable costing concept: (A) rent on factory building, (B) direct materials, (C) property taxes on factory building, (D) electricity purchased to operate factory equipment, (E) salary of factory supervisor, (F) depreciation on factory building, (G) direct labor?

4. In the variable costing income statement, how are the fixed manufacturing costs reported, and how are the fixed selling and administrative expenses reported?

5. Since all costs of operating a business are controllable, what is the significance of the term *noncontrollable cost?*

6. Discuss how financial data prepared on the basis of variable costing can assist management in the development of short-run pricing policies.

7. Why might management analyze product profitability?

8. Explain why rewarding sales personnel on the basis of total sales might not be in the best interests of a business whose goal is to maximize profits.

9. Discuss the two factors affecting both sales and variable costs to which a change in contribution margin can be attributed.

10. How is the quantity factor for an increase or a decrease in the amount of sales computed in using contribution margin analysis?

11. Explain why service companies use different activity bases than manufacturing companies to classify costs as fixed or variable.

Basic Exercises

SHOW ME HOW

BE 6-1 Variable costing

Obj. 1

Marley Company has the following information for March:

Sales	$912,000
Variable cost of goods sold	474,000
Fixed manufacturing costs	82,000
Variable selling and administrative expenses	238,100
Fixed selling and administrative expenses	54,700

Determine (A) the manufacturing margin, (B) the contribution margin, and (C) income from operations for Marley Company for the month of March.

SHOW ME HOW

BE 6-2 Variable costing—production exceeds sales

Obj. 1

Fixed manufacturing costs are $44 per unit, and variable manufacturing costs are $100 per unit. Production was 67,200 units, while sales were 50,400 units. Determine (A) whether variable costing income from operations is less than or greater than absorption costing income from operations, and (B) the difference in variable costing and absorption costing income from operations.

SHOW ME HOW

BE 6-3 Variable costing—sales exceed production

Obj. 1

The beginning inventory is 52,800 units. All of the units that were manufactured during the period and 52,800 units of the beginning inventory were sold. The beginning inventory fixed manufacturing costs are $14.70 per unit, and variable manufacturing costs are $30 per unit. Determine (A) whether variable costing income from operations is less than or greater than absorption costing income from operations, and (B) the difference in variable costing and absorption costing income from operations.

SHOW ME HOW

BE 6-4 Analyzing income under absorption and variable costing

Obj. 2

Variable manufacturing costs are $126 per unit, and fixed manufacturing costs are $157,500. Sales are estimated to be 10,000 units.

A. How much would absorption costing income from operations differ between a plan to produce 10,000 units and a plan to produce 15,000 units?

B. How much would variable costing income from operations differ between the two production plans?

SHOW ME HOW

BE 6-5   Contribution margin by segment   Obj. 4

The following information is for LaPlanche Industries Inc.:

	East	West
Sales volume (units):		
Product XX	45,000	38,000
Product YY	60,000	50,000
Sales price:		
Product XX	$700	$660
Product YY	$728	$720
Variable cost per unit:		
Product XX	$336	$336
Product YY	$360	$360

Determine the contribution margin for (A) Product YY and (B) West Region.

SHOW ME HOW

BE 6-6   Contribution margin analysis   Obj. 5

The actual variable cost of goods sold for a product was $140 per unit, while the planned variable cost of goods sold was $136 per unit. The volume increased by 2,400 units to 14,000 actual total units. Determine (A) the variable cost quantity factor and (B) the unit cost factor for variable cost of goods sold.

Exercises

EX 6-1   Inventory valuation under absorption costing and variable costing   Obj. 1

✔ B. Inventory, $780,800

At the end of the first year of operations, 6,400 units remained in the finished goods inventory. The unit manufacturing costs during the year were as follows:

Direct materials	$75
Direct labor	35
Fixed factory overhead	15
Variable factory overhead	12

Determine the cost of the finished goods inventory reported on the balance sheet under (A) the absorption costing concept and (B) the variable costing concept.

EX 6-2   Income statements under absorption costing and variable costing   Obj. 1

✔ A. Income from operations, $128,000

Shawnee Motors Inc. assembles and sells snowmobile engines. The company began operations on August 1 and operated at 100% of capacity during the first month. The following data summarize the results for August:

SHOW ME HOW

Sales (2,000 units)		$600,000
Production costs (2,400 units):		
Direct materials	$300,000	
Direct labor	115,200	
Variable factory overhead	43,200	
Fixed factory overhead	21,600	480,000
Selling and administrative expenses:		
Variable selling and administrative expenses	$ 50,000	
Fixed selling and administrative expenses	22,000	72,000

A. Prepare an income statement according to the absorption costing concept.

B. Prepare an income statement according to the variable costing concept.

C. ━━━▶ What is the reason for the difference in the amount of income from operations reported in (A) and (B)?

EX 6-3   Income statements under absorption costing and variable costing   Obj. 1

✔ B. Income
from operations,
$18,522,000

SHOW ME HOW

Joplin Industries Inc. manufactures and sells high-quality sporting goods equipment under its highly recognizable J-Sports logo. The company began operations on May 1 and operated at 100% of capacity (270,000 units) during the first month, creating an ending inventory of 24,000 units. During June, the company produced 246,000 garments during the month but sold 270,000 units at $300 per unit. The June manufacturing costs and selling and administrative expenses were as follows:

	Number of Units	Unit Cost	Total Cost
Manufacturing costs in June 1 beginning inventory:			
Variable...	24,000	$150.00	$ 3,600,000
Fixed	24,000	32.80	787,200
Total		$182.80	$ 4,387,200
Manufacturing costs in June:			
Variable...	246,000	$150.00	$36,900,000
Fixed	246,000	36.00	8,856,000
Total		$186.00	$45,756,000
Selling and administrative expenses in June:			
Variable	270,000	$ 45.00	$12,150,000
Fixed	270,000	3.60	972,000
Total		$ 48.60	$13,122,000

A. Prepare an income statement according to the absorption costing concept for June.

B. Prepare an income statement according to the variable costing concept for June.

C. ━━━━▶ What is the reason for the difference in the amount of income from operations reported in (A) and (B)?

EX 6-4   Cost of goods manufactured, using variable costing and absorption costing   Obj. 1

✔ B. Unit cost of
goods manufactured,
$275

On December 31, the end of the first year of operations, Frankenreiter Inc. manufactured 25,600 units and sold 24,000 units. The following income statement was prepared, based on the variable costing concept:

Frankenreiter Inc.
Variable Costing Income Statement
For the Year Ended December 31, 20Y1

Sales...		$9,600,000
Variable cost of goods sold:		
Variable cost of goods manufactured	$5,376,000	
Inventory, December 31.......................................	(336,000)	
Total variable cost of goods sold.............................		5,040,000
Manufacturing margin.......................................		$4,560,000
Total variable selling and administrative expenses.................		1,150,000
Contribution margin...		$3,410,000
Fixed costs:		
Fixed manufacturing costs	$1,664,000	
Fixed selling and administrative expenses......................	890,000	
Total fixed costs...		2,554,000
Income from operations		$ 856,000

Determine the unit cost of goods manufactured, based on (A) the variable costing concept and (B) the absorption costing concept.

EX 6-5   Variable costing income statement

Obj. 1

✔ Income from
operations, $720,000

SHOW ME HOW

On November 30, the end of the first month of operations, Weatherford Company prepared the following income statement, based on the absorption costing concept:

Weatherford Company
Absorption Costing Income Statement
For the Month Ended November 30

Sales (104,000 units)		$5,200,000
Cost of goods sold:		
Cost of goods manufactured (120,000 units)	$4,560,000	
Inventory, November 30 (16,000 units)	(608,000)	
Total cost of goods sold		3,952,000
Gross profit		$1,248,000
Selling and administrative expenses		400,000
Income from operations		$ 848,000

If the fixed manufacturing costs were $960,000 and the fixed selling and administrative expenses were $280,000, prepare an income statement according to the variable costing concept.

EX 6-6   Absorption costing income statement

Obj. 1

✔ Income from
operations,
$17,025,000

SHOW ME HOW

On March 31, the end of the first month of operations, Sullivan Equipment Company prepared the following income statement, based on the variable costing concept:

Sullivan Equipment Company
Variable Costing Income Statement
For the Month Ended March 31

Sales (264,000 units)		$66,000,000
Variable cost of goods sold:		
Variable cost of goods manufactured	$45,000,000	
Inventory, March 31 (36,000 units)	(5,400,000)	
Total variable cost of goods sold		39,600,000
Manufacturing margin		$26,400,000
Variable selling and administrative expenses		2,400,000
Contribution margin		$24,000,000
Fixed costs:		
Fixed manufacturing costs	$ 7,500,000	
Fixed selling and administrative expenses	375,000	
Total fixed costs		7,875,000
Income from operations		$16,125,000

Prepare an income statement under absorption costing.

EX 6-7   Variable costing income statement

Obj. 1

✔ A. Income from
operations,
$15,288

REAL WORLD

The following data were adapted from a recent income statement of **Procter & Gamble Company**:

	(in millions)
Sales	$83,062
Operating costs:	
Cost of products sold	$42,460
Marketing, administrative, and other expenses	25,314
Total operating costs	$67,774
Income from operations	$15,288

Assume that the variable amount of each category of operating costs is as follows:

	(in millions)
Cost of products sold	$23,778
Marketing, administrative, and other expenses	10,125

A. Based on the data given, prepare a variable costing income statement for Procter & Gamble Company, assuming that the company maintained constant inventory levels during the period.

B. 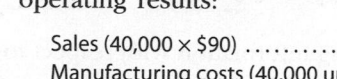 If Procter & Gamble reduced its inventories during the period, what impact would that have on the income from operations determined under absorption costing?

EX 6-8   Estimated income statements, using absorption and variable costing   Obj. 1, 2

✔ A. 1. Income from operations, $1,069,000 (50,000 units)

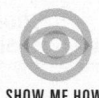

SHOW ME HOW

Prior to the first month of operations ending October 31, Marshall Inc. estimated the following operating results:

Sales (40,000 × $90)	$3,600,000
Manufacturing costs (40,000 units):	
Direct materials	1,440,000
Direct labor	480,000
Variable factory overhead	240,000
Fixed factory overhead	120,000
Fixed selling and administrative expenses	75,000
Variable selling and administrative expenses	200,000

The company is evaluating a proposal to manufacture 50,000 units instead of 40,000 units, thus creating an ending inventory of 10,000 units. Manufacturing the additional units will not change sales, unit variable factory overhead costs, total fixed factory overhead cost, or total selling and administrative expenses.

A. Prepare an estimated income statement, comparing operating results if 40,000 and 50,000 units are manufactured in (1) the absorption costing format and (2) the variable costing format.

B. ━━━ What is the reason for the difference in income from operations reported for the two levels of production by the absorption costing income statement?

EX 6-9   Variable and absorption costing   Obj. 1

✔ A. Contribution margin, $6,263

Ansara Company had the following abbreviated income statement for the year ended December 31, 20Y2:

	(in millions)
Sales	$18,769
Cost of goods sold	$15,471
Selling, administrative, and other expenses	2,049
Total expenses	$17,520
Income from operations	$ 1,249

Assume that there were $3,860 million fixed manufacturing costs and $1,170 million fixed selling, administrative, and other costs for the year.

The finished goods inventories at the beginning and end of the year from the balance sheet were as follows:

January 1	$2,354 million
December 31	$2,408 million

Assume that 30% of the beginning and ending inventory consists of fixed costs. Assume work in process and materials inventory were unchanged during the period.

A. Prepare an income statement according to the variable costing concept for Ansara Company for 20Y2. (Round numbers to nearest million.)

B. ━━━ Explain the difference between the amount of income from operations reported under the absorption costing and variable costing concepts. (Round numbers to nearest million.)

EX 6-10   Variable and absorption costing—three products   Obj. 2, 3

✔ B. Cross Training
Shoes, income
from operations,
$348,000

Winslow Inc. manufactures and sells three types of shoes. The income statements prepared under the absorption costing method for the three shoes are as follows:

Winslow Inc.
Product Income Statements—Absorption Costing
For the Year Ended December 31, 20Y1

	Cross Training Shoes	Golf Shoes	Running Shoes
Revenues	$5,800,000	$6,900,000	$4,200,000
Cost of goods sold	3,016,000	3,381,000	2,814,000
Gross profit	$2,784,000	$3,519,000	$1,386,000
Selling and administrative expenses	2,436,000	2,484,000	2,142,000
Income from operations	$ 348,000	$1,035,000	$ (756,000)

In addition, you have determined the following information with respect to allocated fixed costs:

	Cross Training Shoes	Golf Shoes	Running Shoes
Fixed costs:			
Cost of goods sold	$928,000	$897,000	$798,000
Selling and administrative expenses	696,000	828,000	588,000

These fixed costs are used to support all three product lines and will not change with the elimination of any one product. In addition, you have determined that the effects of inventory may be ignored.

The management of the company has deemed the profit performance of the running shoe line as unacceptable. As a result, it has decided to eliminate the running shoe line. Management does not expect to be able to increase sales in the other two lines. However, as a result of eliminating the running shoe line, management expects the profits of the company to increase by $756,000.

A. ━━━▶ Do you agree with management's decision and conclusions? Explain your answer.

B. Prepare a variable costing income statement for the three products.

C. ━━━▶ Use the report in (B) to determine the profit impact of eliminating the running shoe line, assuming no other changes.

EX 6-11   Change in sales mix and contribution margin   Obj. 4

Head Pops Inc. manufactures two models of solar-powered, noise-canceling headphones: Sun Sound and Ear Bling models. The company is operating at less than full capacity. Market research indicates that 28,000 additional Sun Sound and 30,000 additional Ear Bling headphones could be sold. The income from operations by unit of product is as follows:

	Sun Sound Headphones	Ear Bling Headphones
Sales price	$140.00	$125.00
Variable cost of goods sold	78.40	70.00
Manufacturing margin	$ 61.60	$ 55.00
Variable selling and administrative expenses	28.00	25.00
Contribution margin	$ 33.60	$ 30.00
Fixed manufacturing costs	14.00	12.50
Income from operations	$ 19.60	$ 17.50

Prepare an analysis indicating the increase or decrease in total profitability if 28,000 additional Sun Sound and 30,000 additional Ear Bling headphones are produced and sold, assuming that there is sufficient capacity for the additional production.

EX 6-12 Product profitability analysis

Obj. 4

✔ A. Desert Dragon
contribution margin,
$4,583,250

PowerTrain Sports Inc. manufactures and sells two styles of All Terrain Vehicles (ATVs), the Mountain Monster and Desert Dragon, from a single manufacturing facility. The manufacturing facility operates at 100% of capacity. The following per-unit information is available for the two products:

	Mountain Monster	Desert Dragon
Sales price	$5,400	$5,250
Variable cost of goods sold	3,285	3,400
Manufacturing margin	$2,115	$1,850
Variable selling expenses	1,035	905
Contribution margin.................	$1,080	$ 945
Fixed expenses.......................	485	310
Income from operations	$ 595	$ 635

In addition, the following sales unit volume information for the period is as follows:

	Mountain Monster	Desert Dragon
Sales unit volume	5,000	4,850

A. Prepare a contribution margin by product report. Calculate the contribution margin ratio for each.

B. ➡ What advice would you give to the management of PowerTrain Sports Inc. regarding the relative profitability of the two products?

EX 6-13 Territory and product profitability analysis

Obj. 4

✔ A. East Coast
contribution margin,
$640,000

Coast to Coast Surfboards Inc. manufactures and sells two styles of surfboards, Atlantic Wave and Pacific Pounder. These surfboards are sold in two regions, East Coast and West Coast. Information about the two surfboards is as follows:

	Atlantic Wave	Pacific Pounder
Sales price	$200	$120
Variable cost of goods sold per unit........	150	90
Manufacturing margin per unit	$ 50	$ 30
Variable selling expense per unit...........	34	16
Contribution margin per unit..............	$ 16	$ 14

The sales unit volume for the sales territories and products for the period is as follows:

	East Coast	West Coast
Atlantic Wave	40,000	25,000
Pacific Pounder	0	25,000

A. Prepare a contribution margin by sales territory report. Calculate the contribution margin ratio for each territory as a whole percent, rounded to two decimal places.

B. ➡ What advice would you give to the management of Coast to Coast Surfboards regarding the relative profitability of the two territories?

EX 6-14 Sales territory and salesperson profitability analysis Obj. 4

✔ A. Steve
contribution
margin, $145,920

SHOW ME HOW

Havasu Off-Road Inc. manufactures and sells a variety of commercial vehicles in the Northeast and Southwest regions. There are two salespersons assigned to each territory. Higher commission rates go to the most experienced salespersons. The following sales statistics are available for each salesperson:

| | Northeast | | Southwest | |
	Rene	Steve	Colleen	Paul
Average per unit:				
Sales price	$15,500	$16,000	$14,000	$18,000
Variable cost of goods sold	$9,300	$8,000	$8,400	$9,000
Commission rate	8%	12%	10%	8%
Units sold	36	24	40	60
Manufacturing margin ratio	40%	50%	40%	50%

A. 1. Prepare a contribution margin by salesperson report. Calculate the contribution margin ratio for each salesperson.

   2. ━━▶ Interpret the report.

B. 1. Prepare a contribution margin by territory report. Calculate the contribution margin for each territory as a percent, rounded to one decimal place.

   2. ━━▶ Interpret the report.

EX 6-15 Segment profitability analysis Obj. 4

✔ A. Electric Power,
$824.92

REAL WORLD

The marketing segment sales for **Caterpillar, Inc.**, for a year follow:

Caterpillar, Inc.
Machinery and Engines Marketing Segment Sales
(in millions)

	Building Construction Products	Cat Japan	Core Components	Earth-moving	Electric Power	Excavation	Large Power Systems	Logistics	Marine & Petroleum Power	Mining	Turbines
Sales	$2,217	$1,225	$1,234	$5,045	$2,847	$4,562	$2,885	$659	$2,132	$3,975	$3,321

In addition, assume the following information:

	Building Construction Products	Cat Japan	Core Components	Earth-moving	Electric Power	Excavation	Large Power Systems	Logistics	Marine & Petroleum Power	Mining	Turbines
Variable cost of goods sold as a percent of sales	45%	55%	49%	51%	54%	52%	53%	50%	50%	52%	48%
Dealer commissions as a percent of sales	9%	11%	8%	8%	10%	6%	5%	10%	9%	7%	9%
Variable promotion expenses (in millions)	310	120	150	600	200	600	300	75	270	480	400

A. Use the sales information and the additional assumed information to prepare a contribution margin by segment report. Round to two decimal places. In addition, calculate the contribution margin ratio for each segment as a percentage, rounded to one decimal place.

B. Prepare a table showing the manufacturing margin, dealer commissions, and variable promotion expenses as a percent of sales for each segment. (Round whole percents to one decimal place.)

C. ━━▶ Use the information in (A) and (B) to interpret the segment performance.

EX 6-16 Segment contribution margin analysis
Obj. 4, 6

✔ A. Turner, 60%

REAL WORLD

The operating revenues of the three largest business segments for **Time Warner, Inc.,** for a recent year follow. Each segment includes a number of businesses, examples of which are indicated in parentheses.

Time Warner, Inc.
Segment Revenues
(in millions)

Turner (cable networks and digital media)	$10,596
Home Box Office (pay television)	5,615
Warner Bros. (films, television, and videos)	12,993

Assume that the variable costs as a percent of sales for each segment are as follows:

Turner	40%
Home Box Office	35%
Warner Bros.	25%

A. Determine the contribution margin (round to whole millions) and contribution margin ratio (round to whole percents) for each segment from the information given.

B. Does the segment with the highest contribution margin in (A) mean that it is the most profitable segment with the highest operating income?

EX 6-17 Contribution margin analysis—sales
Obj. 5

✔ A. Sales quantity factor, $121,875

EXCEL TEMPLATE

Select Audio Inc. sells electronic equipment. Management decided early in the year to reduce the price of the speakers in order to increase sales volume. As a result, for the year ended December 31, the sales increased by $31,875 from the planned level of $1,048,125. The following information is available from the accounting records for the year ended December 31.

	Actual	Planned	Increase or (Decrease)
Sales	$1,080,000	$1,048,125	$31,875
Number of units sold	36,000	32,250	3,750
Sales price	$30.00	$32.50	$(2.50)
Variable cost per unit	$10.00	$10.00	$0

A. Prepare an analysis of the sales quantity and unit price factors.

B. Did the price decrease generate sufficient volume to result in a net increase in contribution margin if the actual variable cost per unit was $10, as planned?

EX 6-18 Contribution margin analysis—sales
Obj. 5

✔ Sales quantity factor, $(600,000)

EXCEL TEMPLATE

The following data for Romero Products Inc. are available:

For the Year Ended December 31	Actual	Planned	Difference— Increase or (Decrease)
Sales	$8,360,000	$8,200,000	$ 160,000
Variable costs:			
Variable cost of goods sold	$3,496,000	$3,280,000	$ 216,000
Variable selling and administrative expenses	760,000	902,000	(142,000)
Total variable costs	$4,256,000	$4,182,000	$ 74,000
Contribution margin	$4,104,000	$4,018,000	$ 86,000
Number of units sold	38,000	41,000	
Per unit:			
Sales price	$220	$200	
Variable cost of goods sold	92	80	
Variable selling and administrative expenses	20	22	

Prepare an analysis of the sales quantity and unit price factors.

✔ Variable
cost of goods
sold quantity
factor, EXCEL TEMPLATE
$240,000

EX 6-19 Contribution margin analysis—variable costs
Obj. 5

Based on the data in Exercise 18 prepare a contribution margin analysis of the variable costs for Romero Products Inc. for the year ended December 31.

✔ A. Contribution
margin, Atlanta/
Baltimore, $(29,291)

EX 6-20 Variable costing income statement for a service company
Obj. 4, 6

East Coast Railroad Company transports commodities among three routes (city-pairs): Atlanta/Baltimore, Baltimore/Pittsburgh, and Pittsburgh/Atlanta. Significant costs, their cost behavior, and activity rates for April are as follows:

Cost	Amount	Cost Behavior	Activity Rate	
Labor costs for loading and unloading railcars	$ 175,582	Variable	$46.00	per railcar
Fuel costs	460,226	Variable	12.40	per train-mile
Train crew labor costs	267,228	Variable	7.20	per train-mile
Switchyard labor costs	118,327	Variable	31.00	per railcar
Track and equipment depreciation	194,400	Fixed		
Maintenance	129,600	Fixed		
	$1,345,363			

Operating statistics from the management information system reveal the following for April:

	Atlanta/ Baltimore	Baltimore/ Pittsburgh	Pittsburgh/ Atlanta	Total
Number of train-miles	12,835	10,200	14,080	37,115
Number of railcars	425	2,160	1,232	3,817
Revenue per railcar	$600	$275	$440	

A. Prepare a contribution margin by route report for East Coast Railroad Company for the month of April. Calculate the contribution margin ratio in whole percents, rounded to one decimal place.

B. ➤ Evaluate the route performance of the railroad using the report in (A).

✔ A. East Coast
contribution
margin, $44,534

EXCEL TEMPLATE

EX 6-21 Contribution margin reporting and analysis for a service company
Obj. 5, 6

The management of East Coast Railroad Company introduced in Exercise 20 improved the profitability of the Atlanta/Baltimore route in May by reducing the price of a railcar from $600 to $500. This price reduction increased the demand for rail services. Thus, the number of railcars increased by 275 railcars to a total of 700 railcars. This was accomplished by increasing the size of each train but not the number of trains. Thus, the number of train-miles was unchanged. All the activity rates remained unchanged.

A. Prepare a contribution margin report for the Atlanta/Baltimore route for May. Calculate the contribution margin ratio in percentage terms to one decimal place.

B. Prepare a contribution margin analysis to evaluate management's actions in May. Assume that the May planned quantity, price, and unit cost were the same as April.

✔ A. Contribution
margin, $2,147,700

EXCEL TEMPLATE

EX 6-22 Variable costing income statement and contribution margin analysis for a service company
Obj. 5, 6

The actual and planned data for Underwater University for the Fall term were as follows:

	Actual	Planned
Enrollment	4,500	4,125
Tuition per credit hour	$120	$135
Credit hours	60,450	43,200
Registration, records, and marketing cost per enrolled student	$275	$275
Instructional costs per credit hour	$64	$60
Depreciation on classrooms and equipment	$825,600	$825,600

Registration, records, and marketing costs vary by the number of enrolled students, while instructional costs vary by the number of credit hours. Depreciation is a fixed cost.

A. Prepare a variable costing income statement showing the contribution margin and income from operations for the Fall term.

B. Prepare a contribution margin analysis report comparing planned with actual performance for the Fall term.

Problems: Series A

PR 6-1A   Absorption and variable costing income statements

Obj. 1, 2

✔ 2. Income from operations, $868,000

SHOW ME HOW

During the first month of operations ended August 31, Kodiak Fridgeration Company manufactured 80,000 mini refrigerators, of which 72,000 were sold. Operating data for the month are summarized as follows:

Sales		$10,800,000
Manufacturing costs:		
Direct materials	$ 6,400,000	
Direct labor	1,600,000	
Variable manufacturing cost	1,280,000	
Fixed manufacturing cost	320,000	9,600,000
Selling and administrative expenses:		
Variable	$1,080,000	
Fixed	180,000	1,260,000

Instructions

1. Prepare an income statement based on the absorption costing concept.

2. Prepare an income statement based on the variable costing concept.

3. ▬▬▬▶ Explain the reason for the difference in the amount of income from operations reported in (1) and (2).

PR 6-2A   Income statements under absorption costing and variable costing

Obj. 1, 2

✔ 2. Contribution margin, $92,800

The demand for solvent, one of numerous products manufactured by RZM Industries Inc., has dropped sharply because of recent competition from a similar product. The company's chemists are currently completing tests of various new formulas, and it is anticipated that the manufacture of a superior product can be started on June 1, one month in the future. No changes will be needed in the present production facilities to manufacture the new product because only the mixture of the various materials will be changed.

The controller has been asked by the president of the company for advice on whether to continue production during May or to suspend the manufacture of solvent until June 1. The controller has assembled the following pertinent data:

RZM Industries Inc.
Income Statement—Solvent
For the Month Ended April 30

Sales (4,000 units)	$500,000
Cost of goods sold	424,000
Gross profit	$ 76,000
Selling and administrative expenses	102,000
Loss from operations	$ (26,000)

(Continued)

The production costs and selling and administrative expenses, based on production of 4,000 units in April, are as follows:

Direct materials	$45 per unit
Direct labor	20 per unit
Variable manufacturing cost	16 per unit
Variable selling and administrative expenses	15 per unit
Fixed manufacturing cost	$100,000 for April
Fixed selling and administrative expenses	42,000 for April

Sales for May are expected to drop about 20% below those of the preceding month. No significant changes are anticipated in the fixed costs or variable costs per unit. No extra costs will be incurred in discontinuing operations in the portion of the plant associated with solvent. The inventory of solvent at the beginning and end of May is expected to be inconsequential.

Instructions

1. Prepare an estimated income statement in absorption costing form for May for solvent, assuming that production continues during the month.

2. Prepare an estimated income statement in variable costing form for May for solvent, assuming that production continues during the month.

3. What would be the estimated loss in income from operations if the solvent production were temporarily suspended for May?

4. ══════▶ What advice should the controller give to management?

PR 6-3A Absorption and variable costing income statements for two months and analysis   Obj. 1, 2

✔ 1. B. Income from operations, $847,000

SHOW ME HOW

During the first month of operations ended July 31, Western Creations Company produced 80,000 designer cowboy hats, of which 72,000 were sold. Operating data for the month are summarized as follows:

Sales		$4,320,000
Manufacturing costs:		
Direct materials	$1,600,000	
Direct labor	1,440,000	
Variable manufacturing cost	240,000	
Fixed manufacturing cost	320,000	3,600,000
Selling and administrative expenses:		
Variable	$ 144,000	
Fixed	25,000	169,000

During August, Western Creations produced 64,000 designer cowboy hats and sold 72,000 cowboy hats. Operating data for August are summarized as follows:

Sales		$4,320,000
Manufacturing costs:		
Direct materials	$1,280,000	
Direct labor	1,152,000	
Variable manufacturing cost	192,000	
Fixed manufacturing cost	320,000	2,944,000
Selling and administrative expenses:		
Variable	$ 144,000	
Fixed	25,000	169,000

Instructions

1. Using the absorption costing concept, prepare income statements for (A) July and (B) August.

2. Using the variable costing concept, prepare income statements for (A) July and (B) August.

3. A. ▬▬▬▬▶ Explain the reason for the differences in the amount of income from operations in (1) and (2) for July.

   B. ▬▬▬▬▶ Explain the reason for the differences in the amount of income from operations in (1) and (2) for August.

4. ▬▬▬▬▶ Based on your answers to (1) and (2), did Western Creations Company operate more profitably in July or in August? Explain.

PR 6-4A Salespersons' report and analysis   **Obj. 4**

✔ 1. Dix contribution margin ratio, 44.0%

Walthman Industries Inc. employs seven salespersons to sell and distribute its product throughout the state. Data taken from reports received from the salespersons during the year ended December 31 are as follows:

Salesperson	Total Sales	Variable Cost of Goods Sold	Variable Selling Expenses
Case	$610,000	$268,400	$109,800
Dix	603,000	241,200	96,480
Johnson	588,000	305,760	105,840
LaFave	586,000	281,280	123,060
Orcas	616,000	221,760	86,240
Sussman	620,000	310,000	124,000
Willbond	592,000	272,320	88,800

Instructions

1. Prepare a table indicating contribution margin, variable cost of goods sold as a percent of sales, variable selling expenses as a percent of sales, and contribution margin ratio by salesperson. (Round whole percent to one digit after decimal point.)

2. ▬▬▬▬▶ Which salesperson generated the highest contribution margin ratio for the year and why?

3. ▬▬▬▬▶ Briefly list factors other than contribution margin that should be considered in evaluating the performance of salespersons.

**PR 6-5A   Segment variable costing income statement and effect on income of   Obj. 4
change in operations**

✔ 1. Contribution margin, Size S, $235,520

EXCEL TEMPLATE

Valdespin Company manufactures three sizes of camping tents—small (S), medium (M), and large (L). The income statement has consistently indicated a net loss for the M size, and management is considering three proposals: (1) continue Size M, (2) discontinue Size M and reduce total output accordingly, or (3) discontinue Size M and conduct an advertising campaign to expand the sales of Size S so that the entire plant capacity can continue to be used.

If Proposal 2 is selected and Size M is discontinued and production curtailed, the annual fixed production costs and fixed operating expenses could be reduced by $46,080 and $32,240, respectively. If Proposal 3 is selected, it is anticipated that an additional annual expenditure of $34,560 for the rental of additional warehouse space would yield an additional 130% in Size S sales volume. It is also assumed that the increased production of Size S would utilize the plant facilities released by the discontinuance of Size M.

(Continued)

The sales and costs have been relatively stable over the past few years, and they are expected to remain so for the foreseeable future. The income statement for the past year ended June 30, 20Y9, is as follows:

	Size			
	S	M	L	Total
Sales	$668,000	$737,300	$ 956,160	$2,361,460
Cost of goods sold:				
Variable costs	$300,000	$357,120	$437,760	$1,094,880
Fixed costs	74,880	138,250	172,800	385,930
Total cost of goods sold	$374,880	$495,370	$ 610,560	$1,480,810
Gross profit	$293,120	$241,930	$ 345,600	$ 880,650
Operating expenses:				
Variable expenses	$132,480	$155,500	$ 195,840	$ 483,820
Fixed expenses	92,160	103,680	115,200	311,040
Total operating expenses	$224,640	$ 259,180	$ 311,040	$ 794,860
Income from operations	$ 68,480	$ (17,250)	$ 34,560	$ 85,790

Instructions

1. Prepare an income statement for the past year in the variable costing format. Use the following headings:

	Size	
S	M	L	Total

   Data for each style should be reported through contribution margin. The fixed costs should be deducted from the total contribution margin, as reported in the "Total" column, to determine income from operations.

2. Based on the income statement prepared in (1) and the other data presented, determine the amount by which total annual income from operations would be reduced below its present level if Proposal 2 is accepted.

3. Prepare an income statement in the variable costing format, indicating the projected annual income from operations if Proposal 3 is accepted. Use the following headings:

	Size	
S	L	Total

   Data for each style should be reported through contribution margin. The fixed costs should be deducted from the total contribution margin as reported in the "Total" column. For purposes of this problem, the expenditure of $34,560 for the rental of additional warehouse space can be added to the fixed operating expenses.

4. ━━━▶ By how much would total annual income increase above its present level if Proposal 3 is accepted? Explain.

PR 6-6A   Contribution margin analysis

Obj. 5

1. Sales quantity factor, $(2,200,000)

EXCEL TEMPLATE

Farr Industries Inc. manufactures only one product. For the year ended December 31, the contribution margin increased by $560,000 from the planned level of $5,200,000. The president of Farr Industries Inc. has expressed concern about such a small increase in contribution margin and has requested a follow-up report.

The following data have been gathered from the accounting records for the year ended December 31:

	Actual	Planned	Difference—Increase (Decrease)
Sales	$30,000,000	$28,600,000	$1,400,000
Variable costs:			
Variable cost of goods sold	$21,600,000	$21,450,000	$ 150,000
Variable selling and administrative expenses	2,640,000	1,950,000	690,000
Total variable costs	$24,240,000	$23,400,000	$ 840,000
Contribution margin	$ 5,760,000	$ 5,200,000	$ 560,000
Number of units sold	120,000	130,000	
Per unit:			
Sales price	$250	$220	
Variable cost of goods sold	180	165	
Variable selling and administrative expenses	22	15	

Instructions

1. Prepare a contribution margin analysis report for the year ended December 31.

2. ▬▬➤ At a meeting of the board of directors on January 30, the president, after reviewing the contribution margin analysis report, made the following comment:

It looks as if the price increase of $30 had the effect of increasing sales. However, this was a trade-off since sales volume decreased. Also, variable cost of goods sold per unit increased by $15 more than planned. The variable selling and administrative expenses appear out of control. They increased by $7 per unit more than was planned, which is an increase of over 47% more than was planned. Let's look into these expenses and get them under control! Also, let's consider increasing the sales price to $275 and continue this favorable trade-off between higher price and lower volume.

Do you agree with the president's comment? Explain.

Problems: Series B

PR 6-1B   Absorption and variable costing income statements   Obj. 1, 2

✔ 2. Contribution margin, $666,000

SHOW ME HOW

During the first month of operations ended July 31, YoSan Inc. manufactured 2,400 flat panel televisions, of which 2,000 were sold. Operating data for the month are summarized as follows:

Sales		$2,150,000
Manufacturing costs:		
Direct materials	$960,000	
Direct labor	420,000	
Variable manufacturing cost	156,000	
Fixed manufacturing cost	288,000	1,824,000
Selling and administrative expenses:		
Variable	$204,000	
Fixed	96,000	300,000

Instructions

1. Prepare an income statement based on the absorption costing concept.

2. Prepare an income statement based on the variable costing concept.

3. ▬▬➤ Explain the reason for the difference in the amount of income from operations reported in (1) and (2).

PR 6-2B **Income statements under absorption costing and variable costing**   Obj. 1, 2

✔ 2. Contribution
margin, $960,000

The demand for aloe vera hand lotion, one of numerous products manufactured by Smooth Skin Care Products Inc., has dropped sharply because of recent competition from a similar product. The company's chemists are currently completing tests of various new formulas, and it is anticipated that the manufacture of a superior product can be started on December 1, one month in the future. No changes will be needed in the present production facilities to manufacture the new product because only the mixture of the various materials will be changed.

The controller has been asked by the president of the company for advice on whether to continue production during November or to suspend the manufacture of aloe vera hand lotion until December 1. The controller has assembled the following pertinent data:

Smooth Skin Care Products Inc.
Income Statement—Aloe Vera Hand Lotion
For the Month Ended October 31

Sales (400,000 units)	$32,000,000
Cost of goods sold	28,330,000
Gross profit	$ 3,670,000
Selling and administrative expenses	4,270,000
Loss from operations	$ (600,000)

The production costs and selling and administrative expenses, based on production of 400,000 units in October, are as follows:

Direct materials	$15 per unit
Direct labor	17 per unit
Variable manufacturing cost	35 per unit
Variable selling and administrative expenses	10 per unit
Fixed manufacturing cost	$1,530,000 for October
Fixed selling and administrative expenses	270,000 for October

Sales for November are expected to drop about 20% below those of the preceding month. No significant changes are anticipated in the fixed costs or variable costs per unit. No extra costs will be incurred in discontinuing operations in the portion of the plant associated with aloe vera hand lotion. The inventory of aloe vera hand lotion at the beginning and end of November is expected to be inconsequential.

Instructions

1. Prepare an estimated income statement in absorption costing form for November for aloe vera hand lotion, assuming that production continues during the month.

2. Prepare an estimated income statement in variable costing form for November for aloe vera hand lotion, assuming that production continues during the month.

3. What would be the estimated loss in income from operations if the aloe vera hand lotion production were temporarily suspended for November?

4. ➤ What advice should the controller give to management?

PR 6-3B **Absorption and variable costing income statements for**   Obj. 1, 2
two months and analysis

✔ 2. A.
Manufacturing
margin, $37,440

SHOW ME HOW

During the first month of operations ended July 31, Head Gear Inc. manufactured 6,400 hats, of which 5,200 were sold. Operating data for the month are summarized as follows:

Sales		$104,000
Manufacturing costs:		
Direct materials	$47,360	
Direct labor	22,400	
Variable manufacturing cost	12,160	
Fixed manufacturing cost	15,360	97,280
Selling and administrative expenses:		
Variable	$10,920	
Fixed	5,200	16,120

During August, Head Gear Inc. manufactured 4,000 hats and sold 5,200 hats. Operating data for August are summarized as follows:

Sales		$104,000
Manufacturing costs:		
Direct materials	$29,600	
Direct labor	14,000	
Variable manufacturing cost	7,600	
Fixed manufacturing cost	15,360	66,560
Selling and administrative expenses:		
Variable	$10,920	
Fixed	5,200	16,120

Instructions

1. Using the absorption costing concept, prepare income statements for (A) July and (B) August.

2. Using the variable costing concept, prepare income statements for (A) July and (B) August.

3. A. ➤ Explain the reason for the differences in the amount of income from operations in (1) and (2) for July.

   B. ➤ Explain the reason for the differences in the amount of income from operations in (1) and (2) for August.

4. ➤ Based on your answers to (1) and (2), did Head Gear Inc. operate more profitably in July or in August? Explain.

PR 6-4B Salespersons' report and analysis
Obj. 4

✔ 1. Crowell contribution margin ratio, 44.0%

Pachec Inc. employs seven salespersons to sell and distribute its product throughout the state. Data taken from reports received from the salespersons during the year ended June 30 are as follows:

Salesperson	Total Sales	Variable Cost of Goods Sold	Variable Selling Expenses
Asarenka	$437,500	$196,875	$ 83,125
Crowell	570,000	228,000	91,200
Dempster	675,000	310,500	141,750
MacLean	587,500	246,750	123,375
Ortiz	525,000	215,250	126,000
Sullivan	587,500	246,750	99,875
Williams	575,000	253,000	115,000

Instructions

1. Prepare a table indicating contribution margin, variable cost of goods sold as a percent of sales, variable selling expenses as a percent of sales, and contribution margin ratio by salesperson.

2. ➤ Which salesperson generated the highest contribution margin ratio for the year and why?

3. ➤ Briefly list factors other than contribution margin that should be considered in evaluating the performance of salespersons.

PR 6-5B Variable costing income statement and effect on income of change in operations
Obj. 4

✔ 3. Income from operations, $106,820

EXCEL TEMPLATE

Kimbrell Inc. manufactures three sizes of utility tables—small (S), medium (M), and large (L). The income statement has consistently indicated a net loss for the M size, and management is considering three proposals: (1) continue Size M, (2) discontinue Size M and reduce total output accordingly, or (3) discontinue Size M and conduct an advertising campaign to expand the sales of Size S so that the entire plant capacity can continue to be used.

(Continued)

If Proposal 2 is selected and Size M is discontinued and production curtailed, the annual fixed production costs and fixed operating expenses could be reduced by $142,500 and $28,350, respectively. If Proposal 3 is selected, it is anticipated that an additional annual expenditure of $85,050 for the salary of an assistant brand manager (classified as a fixed operating expense) would yield an additional 130% in Size S sales volume. It is also assumed that the increased production of Size S would utilize the plant facilities released by the discontinuance of Size M.

The sales and costs have been relatively stable over the past few years, and they are expected to remain so for the foreseeable future. The income statement for the past year ended December 31, 20Y8, is as follows:

	Size			
	S	M	L	Total
Sales	$990,000	$1,087,500	$945,000	$3,022,500
Cost of goods sold:				
Variable costs	$538,500	$ 718,500	$567,000	$1,824,000
Fixed costs	241,000	288,000	250,000	779,000
Total cost of goods sold	$779,500	$1,006,500	$817,000	$2,603,000
Gross profit	$210,500	$ 81,000	$128,000	$ 419,500
Less operating expenses:				
Variable expenses	$118,100	$ 108,750	$ 85,050	$ 311,900
Fixed expenses	32,125	42,525	14,250	88,900
Total operating expenses	$150,225	$ 151,275	$ 99,300	$ 400,800
Income from operations	$ 60,275	$ (70,275)	$ 28,700	$ 18,700

Instructions

1. Prepare an income statement for the past year in the variable costing format. Use the following headings:

	Size		
S	M	L	Total

   Data for each style should be reported through contribution margin. The fixed costs should be deducted from the total contribution margin, as reported in the "Total" column, to determine income from operations.

2. Based on the income statement prepared in (1) and the other data presented above, determine the amount by which total annual income from operations would be reduced below its present level if Proposal 2 is accepted.

3. Prepare an income statement in the variable costing format, indicating the projected annual income from operations if Proposal 3 is accepted. Use the following headings:

	Size	
S	L	Total

   Data for each style should be reported through contribution margin. The fixed costs should be deducted from the total contribution margin as reported in the "Total" column. For purposes of this problem, the additional expenditure of $85,050 for the assistant brand manager's salary can be added to the fixed operating expenses.

4. ▬▶ By how much would total annual income increase above its present level if Proposal 3 is accepted? Explain.

PR 6-6B   Contribution margin analysis   Obj. 5

✔ 1. Sales quantity factor, $310,500

Mathews Company manufactures only one product. For the year ended December 31, the contribution margin decreased by $126,000 from the planned level of $540,000. The president of Mathews Company has expressed some concern about this decrease and has requested a follow-up report.

EXCEL TEMPLATE

The following data have been gathered from the accounting records for the year ended December 31:

	Actual	Planned	Difference—Increase or (Decrease)
Sales	$2,277,000	$2,070,000	$ 207,000
Variable costs:			
Variable cost of goods sold	$1,035,000	$ 990,000	$ 45,000
Variable selling and administrative expenses	828,000	540,000	288,000
Total variable costs	$1,863,000	$1,530,000	$ 333,000
Contribution margin	$ 414,000	$ 540,000	$(126,000)
Number of units sold	34,500	30,000	
Per unit:			
Sales price	$66	$69	
Variable cost of goods sold	30	33	
Variable selling and administrative expenses	24	18	

Instructions

1. Prepare a contribution margin analysis report for the year ended December 31.

2. At a meeting of the board of directors on January 30, the president, after reviewing the contribution margin analysis report, made the following comment:

   It looks as if the price decrease of $3.00 had the effect of increasing sales. However, we lost control over the variable cost of goods sold and variable selling and administrative expenses. Let's look into these expenses and get them under control! Also, let's consider decreasing the sales price to $60 to increase sales further.

   Do you agree with the president's comment? Explain.

Analysis for Decision Making

ADM-1   Yum! Brands: Segment sales and EBITDA analysis

REAL WORLD

Yum! Brands, Inc. is a worldwide operator and franchisor of fast food restaurants, under the familiar brands of KFC, Pizza Hut, and Taco Bell. Segment revenues, operating income, and depreciation and amortization expense for Yum!'s operating segments are provided for a recent year as follows (in millions):

	Sales	Operating Income	Depreciation and Amortization Expense
China	$6,934	$713	$411
KFC	3,193	708	187
Pizza Hut	1,148	295	39
Taco Bell	1,863	480	83
India	141	(9)	10

Yum!'s segments include the three restaurant brands plus two emerging regional segments, China and India. In China and India, all three restaurant brands are combined into the regional reporting.

A. Prepare a vertical analysis of the sales as a percent of total sales for the five segments. (Round percentages to the nearest whole percent.) Which segment has the greatest percentage of total sales?

B. Determine the earnings before interest, taxes, depreciation, and amortization (EBITDA) for the five segments.

(Continued)

C. Determine the EBITDA as a percent of sales (EBITDA margin) for the five segments. (Round percentages to the nearest whole percent.)

D. ━━━━► Interpret the analysis in (C).

REAL WORLD

ADM-2 Walt Disney: Segment revenue analysis

The Walt Disney Company is a leading worldwide entertainment company. Disney operates five business segments. These segments and some of their larger businesses are:

- Media Networks: ABC Network, ESPN, Disney Channel, and A&E
- Parks and Resorts: Walt Disney World Resort, Disneyland, and International Disney Resorts
- Studio Entertainment: Walt Disney Pictures, Pixar, Marvel, and Lucasfilm
- Consumer Products: licensing of Disney characters, publishing, and retail stores
- Interactive: video games

Recent comparative revenues for the five segments are as follows (in millions):

	Year 3	Year 1
Media Networks	$21,152	$19,436
Parks and Resorts	15,099	12,920
Studio Entertainment	7,278	5,825
Consumer Products	3,985	3,252
Interactive	1,299	845
Total	$48,813	$42,278

A. Prepare a vertical analysis of the segment sales to total sales for Year 1 and Year 3. (Round percentages to nearest whole percent.)

B. Using the analysis in (A), has the relative segment sales changed between Year 1 and Year 3?

C. Prepare a horizontal analysis of the segment sales between Year 1 and Year 3. (Round percentages to nearest whole percent.)

D. ━━━━► Interpret the horizontal segment sales analysis in (C).

REAL WORLD

ADM-3 Apple Inc.: Segment revenue analysis

Segment disclosure by **Apple Inc.** provides sales information for its major product lines for three recent years as follows (in millions):

	Year 3	Year 2	Year 1
iPhone	$101,991	$ 91,279	$ 78,692
iPad	30,283	31,980	30,945
Mac	24,079	21,483	23,221
iPod	2,286	4,411	5,615
iTunes, Software, and Services	18,063	16,051	12,890
Accessories	6,093	5,706	5,145
Total sales	$182,795	$170,910	$156,508

A. Which product had the greatest percentage of Year 3 sales? Which product had the least percentage of Year 3 sales? (Round to nearest whole percent.)

B. Which product grew the most in sales, in percentage terms, using Year 1 as the base year? (Round to nearest whole percent.)

REAL WORLD

ADM-4 LVMH: Group segment sales and EBITDA analysis

LVMH Group is a French domiciled company known for Dior, Givenchy, Louis Vuitton, and many other fashion brands. LVMH's operating segment revenues, operating income, and depreciation and amortization expenses for a recent year are as follows (in millions of euros):

	Wine and Spirits	Fashion and Leather Goods	Perfumes and Cosmetics	Watches and Jewelry	Selective Retailing
Sales	€3,973	€10,828	€3,916	€2,782	€ 312
Operating income	1,147	3,189	415	283	(162)
Depreciation and amortization expense	119	555	149	171	41

A. Prepare a vertical analysis of the segment sales to total sales. (Round to nearest whole percent.)

B. Interpret the vertical analysis in (A).

C. Compute (1) EBITDA and (2) EBITDA as a percent of sales (EBITDA margin) for each segment. (Round to nearest whole percent.)

D. Prepare a column bar chart of the EBITDA as a percent of sales for the segments in descending order.

E. ━━━━▶ Interpret the chart in (D).

Take It Further

ETHICS

TIF 6-1 Ethics in Action

The Southern Division manager of Texcaliber Inc. is growing concerned that the division will not be able to meet its current period income objectives. The division uses absorption costing for internal profit reporting and had an appropriate level of inventory at the beginning of the period. The division manager knows that he can boost profits by increasing production at the end of the period. The increased production will allocate fixed costs over a greater number of units, reducing cost of goods sold and increasing earnings. Unfortunately, it is unlikely that additional production will be sold, resulting in a large ending inventory balance.

The division manager has come to Aston Melon, the divisional controller, to determine exactly how much additional production is needed to increase net income enough to meet the division's profit objectives. Aston analyzes the data and determines that the division will need to increase inventory by 30% in order to absorb enough fixed costs to meet the division's income objective. Aston reports this information to the division manager.

━━━━▶ Is Aston acting ethically?

TIF 6-2 Team Activity

BendOR, Inc. manufactures control panels for the electronics industry and has just completed its first year of operations. The following discussion took place between the controller, Gordon Merrick, and the company president, Matt McCray:

Matt: I've been looking over our first year's performance by quarters. Our earnings have been increasing each quarter, even though our sales have been flat and our prices and costs have not changed. Why is this?

(Continued)

Gordon: Our actual sales have stayed even throughout the year, but we've been increasing the utilization of our factory every quarter. By keeping our factory utilization high, we will keep our costs down by allocating the fixed plant costs over a greater number of units. Naturally, this causes our cost per unit to be lower than it would be otherwise.

Matt: Yes, but what good is this if we are unable to sell everything that we make? Our inventory is also increasing.

Gordon: This is true. However, our unit costs are lower because of the additional production. When these lower costs are matched against sales, it has a positive impact on our earnings.

Matt: Are you saying that we are able to create additional earnings merely by building inventory? Can this be true?

Gordon: Well, I've never thought about it quite that way. . . but I guess so.

Matt: And another thing. What will happen if we begin to reduce our production in order to liquidate the inventory? Don't tell me our earnings will go down even though our production effort drops!

Gordon: Well. . .

Matt: There must be a better way. I'd like our quarterly income statements to reflect what's really going on. I don't want our income reports to reward building inventory and penalize reducing inventory.

Gordon: I'm not sure what I can do—we have to follow generally accepted accounting principles.

In teams:

A. Discuss why reporting income under generally accepted accounting principles "rewards" building inventory and "penalizes" reducing inventory.

B. Discuss what advice you would give to Gordon in responding to Matt's concern about the present method of accounting.

Be prepared to discuss your answers in class.

TIF 6-3 Communication

Bon Jager Inc. manufactures and sells medical devices used in cardiovascular surgery. The sales team consists of two salespeople, Dean and Martin. A contribution margin report by salesperson was prepared as follows:

Bon Jager Inc. Contribution Margin by Salesperson		
	Dean	**Martin**
Sales...	$400,000	$480,000
Variable cost of goods sold..	184,000	264,000
Manufacturing margin	$216,000	$216,000
Variable selling expenses:		
Variable promotion expenses..	$ 72,000	$ 43,200
Variable sales commission expenses	56,000	67,200
Total variable selling expenses	$128,000	$110,400
Contribution margin..	$ 88,000	$105,600
Manufacturing margin as a percent of sales		
(manufacturing margin ratio)..	54%	45%
Contribution margin ratio...	22%	22%

Write a brief memo to Anna Berenson, the Vice President of Marketing, evaluating the performance of the company's salespeople and providing recommendations on how the salespeople could improve profitability.

Concepts and Principles

Chapter 1 *Introduction to Managerial Accounting*

Developing Information

COST SYSTEMS	COST BEHAVIOR
Chapter 2 *Job Order Costing*	**Chapter 5** *Cost-Volume-Profit Analysis*
Chapter 3 *Process Cost Systems*	
Chapter 4 *Activity-Based Costing*	

Decision Making

EVALUATING PERFORMANCE	COMPARING ALTERNATIVES
Chapter 6 *Variable Costing for Management Analysis*	**Chapter 9** *Evaluating Decentralized Operations*
Chapter 7 *Budgeting*	**Chapter 10** *Differential Analysis and Product Pricing*
Chapter 8 *Evaluating Variances from Standard Costs*	**Chapter 11** *Capital Investment Analysis*
	Chapter 12 *Lean Manufacturing*

Hendrick Motorsports

You may have financial goals for your life. To achieve these goals, it is necessary to plan for future expenses. For example, you may consider taking a part-time job to save money for school expenses for the coming school year. How much money would you need to earn and save in order to pay these expenses? One way to find an answer to this question would be to prepare a budget. A budget would show an estimate of your expenses associated with school, such as tuition, fees, and books. In addition, you would have expenses for day-to-day living, such as rent, food, and clothing. You might also have expenses for travel and entertainment. Once the school year begins, you can use the budget as a tool for guiding your spending priorities during the year.

The budget is used in businesses in much the same way it can be used in personal life. For example, **Hendrick Motorsports**, featuring drivers Dale Earnhardt, Jr., Jeff Gordon, and Jimmie Johnson, uses budget information to remain one of the most valuable racing teams in NASCAR. Hendrick uses

budgets to keep revenues greater than expenses. For example, Hendrick plans revenues from car sponsorships and winnings. Primary and secondary sponsorships (car decals) can provide as much as 70% of the revenues for a typical race team. Costs include salaries, engines, tires, cars, travel, and research and development. In addition, star drivers such as Dale Earnhardt, Jr. can earn as much as $28 million in salary, winnings, and endorsements. Overall, Hendrick is estimated to earn $179 million in revenues and $16.6 million in operating income from its four race teams. The budget provides the company with a "game plan" for the year. In this chapter, you will see how budgets can be used for financial planning and control.

Sources: Kurt Badenhausen, "Hendrick Motorsports Tops List of Nascar's Most Valuable Teams," *Forbes*, March 13, 2013. Bob Pockrass, "NASCAR's highest-paid drivers make their money from a variety of sources," *Sporting News*, December 4, 2012. Ed Hilton, "Under the Hood at Hendrick Motorsports," *Chicago Tribune*, July 13, 2007. www.hendrickmotorsports.com.

What's Covered

Budgeting

Nature and Objectives of Budgeting
- Objectives (Obj. 1)
- Human Behavior (Obj. 1)

Budgeting Systems
- Static Budget (Obj. 2)
- Flexible Budget (Obj. 2)

Master Budget
- Operating and Financial Components (Obj. 3)
- Sales Budget (Obj. 4)
- Production Budget (Obj. 4)
- Direct Materials Purchases Budget (Obj. 4)
- Direct Labor Cost Budget (Obj. 4)
- Factory Overhead Cost Budget (Obj. 4)
- Cost of Goods Sold Budget (Obj. 4)
- Selling and Administrative Expenses Budget (Obj. 4)
- Budgeted Income Statement (Obj. 4)
- Cash Budget (Obj. 5)
- Capital Expenditures Budget (Obj. 5)

Learning Objectives

Obj. 1 Describe budgeting, its objectives, and its impact on human behavior.

Obj. 2 Describe the basic elements of the budget process, the two major types of budgeting, and the use of computers in budgeting.

Obj. 3 Describe the master budget for a manufacturing company.

Obj. 4 Prepare the basic operating budgets for a manufacturing company.

Obj. 5 Prepare financial budgets for a manufacturing company.

Analysis for Decision Making

Describe and Illustrate the use of staffing budgets for nonmanufacturing businesses.

Objective 1
Describe budgeting, its objectives, and its impact on human behavior.

Nature and Objectives of Budgeting

Budgets play an important role for organizations of all sizes and forms. For example, budgets are used in managing the operations of government agencies, churches, hospitals, and other nonprofit organizations. Individuals and families also use budgeting in managing their financial affairs. This chapter describes and illustrates budgeting for a manufacturing company.

Link to Hendrick Motorsports

Hendrick Motorsports holds a record of 11 NASCAR Sprint Cup Series Championships won by the following drivers: 6 by Jimmie Johnson, 4 by Jeff Gordon, and 1 by Terry Labonte.

Objectives of Budgeting

Budgeting involves (1) establishing specific goals, (2) executing plans to achieve the goals, and (3) periodically comparing actual results with the goals. In doing so, budgeting affects the following managerial functions:

- Planning
- Directing
- Controlling

The relationships of these activities are illustrated in Exhibit 1.

Planning involves setting goals to guide decisions and help motivate employees. The planning process often identifies where operations can be improved.

Directing involves decisions and actions to achieve budgeted goals. A budgetary unit of a company is called a **responsibility center**. Each responsibility center is led by a manager who has the authority and responsibility for achieving the center's budgeted goals.

Exhibit 1 Planning, Directing, and Controlling

Controlling involves comparing actual performance against the budgeted goals. Such comparisons provide feedback to managers and employees about their performance. If necessary, responsibility centers can use such feedback to adjust their activities in the future.

Human Behavior and Budgeting

Human behavior problems can arise in the budgeting process in the following situations:

- Budgeted goals are set too tight, which are very hard or impossible to achieve.
- Budgeted goals are set too loose, which are very easy to achieve.
- Budgeted goals conflict with the objectives of the company and employees.

These behavior problems are illustrated in Exhibit 2.

Budget Goals Too Tight   Budget Goals Too Loose   Conflicting Budget Goals

Exhibit 2
Human Behavior
Problems in
Budgeting

Setting Budget Goals Too Tightly Employees and managers may become discouraged if budgeted goals are set too high. That is, if budgeted goals are viewed as unrealistic or unachievable, the budget may have a negative effect on the ability of the company to achieve its goals.

Reasonable, attainable goals are more likely to motivate employees and managers. For this reason, it is important for employees and managers to be involved in the budgeting process. Involving employees in the budgeting process provides them with a sense of control and, thus, more of a commitment in meeting budgeted goals.

Setting Budget Goals Too Loosely Although it is desirable to establish attainable goals, it is undesirable to plan budget goals that are too easy. Such budget "padding" is termed **budgetary slack**. Managers may plan slack in their budgets to provide a "cushion" for unexpected events. However, slack budgets may create inefficiency by reducing the budgetary incentive to trim spending.

Setting Conflicting Budget Goals Goal conflict occurs when the employees' or managers' self-interest differs from the company's objectives or goals. To illustrate, assume that the sales department manager is given an increased sales goal and as a result accepts customers who are poor credit risks. Thus, while the sales department might meet sales goals, the overall firm may suffer reduced profitability from bad debts.

Ethics: Don't Do It!

Budget Games

The budgeting system is designed to plan and control a business. However, it is common for the budget to be "gamed" by its participants. For example, managers may pad their budgets with excess resources. In this way, the managers have additional resources for unexpected events during the period. If the budget is being used to establish the incentive plan, then sales managers have incentives to understate the sales potential of a territory to ensure hitting their quotas. Other times, managers engage in "land

grabbing," which occurs when they overstate the sales potential of a territory to guarantee access to resources. If managers believe that unspent resources will not roll over to future periods, then they may be encouraged to "spend it or lose it," causing wasteful expenditures. These types of problems can be partially overcome by separating the budget into planning and incentive components. This is why many organizations have two budget processes, one for resource planning and another, more challenging budget for motivating managers.

Objective 2

Describe the basic elements of the budget process, the two major types of budgeting, and the use of computers in budgeting.

Budgeting Systems

Budgeting systems vary among companies and industries. For example, the budget system used by **Ford Motor Company** differs from that used by **Delta Air Lines**. However, the basic budgeting concepts discussed in this section apply to all types of businesses and organizations.

The budgetary period for operating activities normally includes the fiscal year of a company. A year is short enough that future operations can be estimated fairly accurately, yet long enough that the future can be viewed in a broad context. However, for control purposes, annual budgets are usually subdivided into shorter time periods, such as quarters of the year, months, or weeks.

Link to Hendrick Motorsports

Rick Hendrick uses budgeting in **Hendrick Motorsports** as well as the **Hendrick Automotive Group**. The Hendrick Automotive Group is the largest privately held dealership group in the United States with 120 retail franchises.

A variation of fiscal-year budgeting, called **continuous budgeting**, maintains a 12-month projection into the future. The 12-month budget is continually revised by replacing the data for the month just ended with the budget data for the same month in the next year. A continuous budget is illustrated in Exhibit 3.

Exhibit 3   Continuous Budgeting

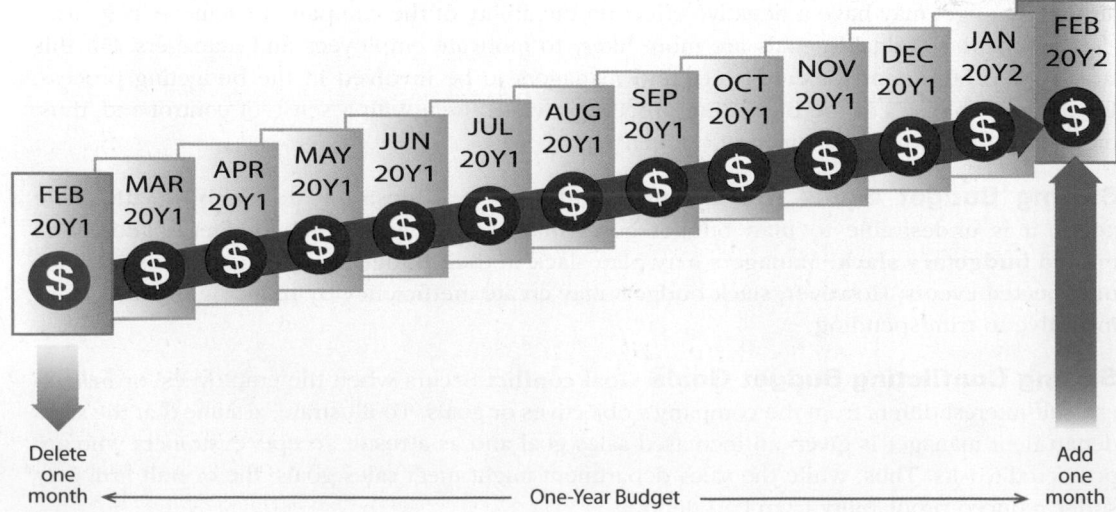

Developing an annual budget usually begins several months prior to the end of the current year. This responsibility is normally assigned to a budget committee. Such a committee often consists of the budget director, the controller, the treasurer, the production manager, and the sales manager. The budget process is monitored and summarized by the Accounting Department, which reports to the committee.

There are several methods of developing budget estimates. One method, called **zero-based budgeting**, requires managers to estimate sales, production, and other operating data as though operations are being started for the first time. This approach has the benefit of taking a fresh view of operations each year. A more common approach is to start with last year's budget and revise it for actual results and expected changes for the coming year. Two major budgets using this approach are the static budget and the flexible budget.

Static Budget

A **static budget** shows the expected results of a responsibility center for only one activity level. Once the budget has been determined, it is not changed, even if the activity changes. Static budgeting is used by many service companies and governmental entities and for some functions of manufacturing companies, such as purchasing, engineering, and accounting.

To illustrate, the static budget for the Assembly Department of Colter Manufacturing Company is shown in Exhibit 4.

	A	B
1	Colter Manufacturing Company	
2	Assembly Department Budget	
3	For the Year Ending July 31, 20Y8	
4	Direct labor	$40,000
5	Electric power	5,000
6	Supervisor salaries	15,000
7	Total department costs	$60,000
8		

Exhibit 4
Static Budget

A disadvantage of static budgets is that they do not adjust for changes in activity levels. For example, assume that the Assembly Department of Colter Manufacturing spent $70,800 for the year ended July 31, 20Y8. Thus, the Assembly Department spent $10,800 ($70,800 − $60,000), or 18% ($10,800 ÷ $60,000) more than budgeted. Is this good news or bad news?

The first reaction is that this is bad news and the Assembly Department was inefficient in spending more than budgeted. However, assume that the Assembly Department's budget was based on plans to assemble 8,000 units during the year. If 10,000 units were actually assembled, the additional $10,800 spent in excess of budget might be good news. That is, the Assembly Department assembled 25% (2,000 units ÷ 8,000 units) more than planned for only 18% more cost. In this case, a static budget may not be useful for controlling costs.

Why It Matters

Film Budgeting

Service businesses, like film and entertainment, use budgets as a roadmap to control expenses. In film production, the budget is a valuable tool to manage the tension between creative expression and cost.

The film budget is a static budget that can be divided into three major categories:

- above the line
- below the line
- post-production costs

The *above the line* costs include costs attributed to creative talent, such as the lead cast's and director's salaries and script fees. The *below the line* costs include the remaining costs to create the film, including location, costume, and prop rentals; permits; and other production costs. The *post-production costs* include the costs to complete the film, including editing, sound, and special effects. Marketing has a separate budget.

The total cost of the film is influenced by many decisions, including the cost of story rights, location, star quality of creative talent, union representation of the production crew, music, and special effects. Even a low-budget indie (independent) documentary could easily have a budget of more than $1 million. In contrast, a special effect-laden Hollywood film could have a budget in excess of $200 million.

Link to Hendrick Motorsports   Rick Hendrick started by selling used cars. At age 26, he invested all of his assets in a struggling Chevrolet dealership, becoming the youngest Chevrolet dealer in the United States. This dealership was the predecessor of the **Hendrick Automotive Group**.

Flexible Budget

note:
Flexible budgets show expected results for several activity levels.

Unlike static budgets, **flexible budgets** show the expected results of a responsibility center for several activity levels. A flexible budget is, in effect, a series of static budgets for different levels of activity.

To illustrate, a flexible budget for the Assembly Department of Colter Manufacturing Company is shown in Exhibit 5.

Exhibit 5
Flexible Budget

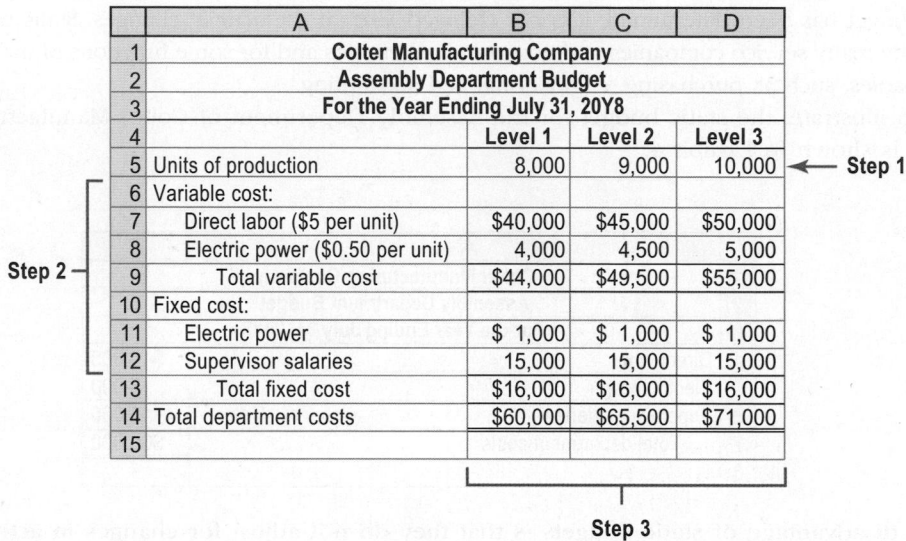

	A	B	C	D
1	Colter Manufacturing Company			
2	Assembly Department Budget			
3	For the Year Ending July 31, 20Y8			
4		Level 1	Level 2	Level 3
5	Units of production	8,000	9,000	10,000	← Step 1
6	Variable cost:			
7	Direct labor ($5 per unit)	$40,000	$45,000	$50,000
8	Electric power ($0.50 per unit)	4,000	4,500	5,000
9	Total variable cost	$44,000	$49,500	$55,000
10	Fixed cost:			
11	Electric power	$ 1,000	$ 1,000	$ 1,000
12	Supervisor salaries	15,000	15,000	15,000
13	Total fixed cost	$16,000	$16,000	$16,000
14	Total department costs	$60,000	$65,500	$71,000
15				

Step 2 (rows 6–12), Step 3 (columns B–D)

A flexible budget is constructed as follows:

- Step 1. Identify the relevant activity levels. The relevant levels of activity could be expressed in units, machine hours, direct labor hours, or some other activity base. In Exhibit 5, the levels of activity are 8,000, 9,000, and 10,000 units of production.
- Step 2. Identify the fixed and variable cost components of the costs being budgeted. In Exhibit 5, the electric power cost is separated into its fixed cost ($1,000 per year) and variable cost ($0.50 per unit). The direct labor is a variable cost, and the supervisor salaries are all fixed costs.
- Step 3. Prepare the budget for each activity level by multiplying the variable cost per unit by the activity level and then adding the monthly fixed cost.

With a flexible budget, actual costs can be compared to the budgeted costs for actual activity. To illustrate, assume that the Assembly Department spent $70,800 to produce 10,000 units. Exhibit 5 indicates that the Assembly Department was *under* budget by $200 ($71,000 − $70,800).

Under the static budget in Exhibit 4, the Assembly Department was $10,800 *over* budget. This comparison is illustrated in Exhibit 6.

The flexible budget for the Assembly Department is much more accurate and useful than the static budget. This is because the flexible budget adjusts for changes in the level of activity. Flexible budgets can be used in service businesses when the variable costs can be associated to an activity. For example, hospital room expenses are related to number of patients, or transportation fuel costs are related to number of miles.

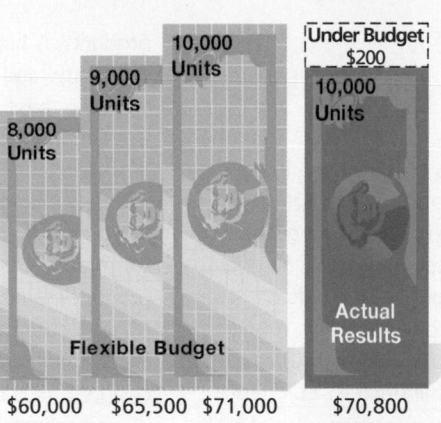

Exhibit 6
Static and Flexible
Budgets

Check Up Corner 7-1 Flexible Budget

O-wen Snowboard Company designs and manufactures snowboards. The boards are assembled in the company's Assembly Department in Colorado. Information for the Assembly Department is as follows:

Depreciation	$4,500 per month
Direct labor hours per unit produced	0.5 hours per board
Supervisor salaries	$22,000 per month
Utilities	$1 per direct labor hour plus $1,500 per month
Wages	$20 per hour

Prepare a flexible budget for the Assembly Department for 3,000, 4,000, and 5,000 boards in August 20Y1.

Solution:

Variable costs change with the level of activity

**O-wen Snowboard Company
Assembly Department Budget
For the Month Ending August 31, 20Y1**

Units of production	3,000	4,000	5,000
Variable costs:			
Direct labor	$30,000	$40,000	$50,000
Utilities	1,500	2,000	2,500
Total variable costs	$31,500	$42,000	$52,500
Fixed costs:			
Depreciation	$ 4,500	$ 4,500	$ 4,500
Supervisor salaries	22,000	22,000	22,000
Utilities	1,500	1,500	1,500
Total fixed costs	$28,000	$28,000	$28,000
Total department costs	$59,500	$70,000	$80,500

Flexible budgets show the expected results of a responsibility center for several activity levels.

3,000 units × 0.5 hour per unit × $20 per hour
4,000 units × 0.5 hour per unit × $20 per hour
5,000 units × 0.5 hour per unit × $20 per hour

The variable utility cost is equal to the activity level (# of units) × 0.5 direct labor hour × $1 per direct labor hour

Fixed costs remain constant across all activity levels.

Total estimated costs change with the level of activity.

Check Up Corner

Computerized Budgeting Systems

In developing budgets, companies use a variety of computerized approaches. Two of the most popular computerized approaches use:

- Spreadsheet software such as Microsoft Excel
- Integrated budget and planning (B&P) software systems

Why It Matters

Build Versus Harvest

Budgeting systems are not "one size fits all" solutions but must adapt to the underlying business conditions. For example, a business can adopt either a build strategy or a harvest strategy. A *build* strategy is one where the business is designing, launching, and growing new products and markets. **Apple Inc.**'s iPad® is an example of a product managed under a build strategy. A *harvest* strategy is often employed for business units with mature products enjoying high market share in low-growth industries. **H.J. Heinz Company**'s ketchup and **P&G**'s *Ivory* soap are examples of such products. A build strategy often has greater uncertainty, unpredictability, and change than a harvest strategy. The difference between these strategies implies different budgeting approaches.

The build strategy should employ a budget approach that is flexible to the uncertainty of the business. Thus, budgets should adapt to changing conditions by allowing periodic revisions and flexible targets. The budget serves as a short-term planning tool to guide management in executing an uncertain and evolving product market strategy.

In a harvest strategy, the business is often much more stable and is managed to maximize profitability and cash flow. Because cost control is much more important in this strategy, the budget is used to restrict the actions of managers.

Spreadsheets ease budget preparation by summarizing budget information in linked spreadsheets across the organization. In addition, the impact of proposed changes in various assumptions or operating alternatives can be analyzed on a spreadsheet.

B&P software systems use the Web (Intranet) to link thousands of employees together during the budget process. Employees can input budget data onto Web pages that are integrated and summarized throughout the company. In this way, a company can quickly and consistently integrate top-level strategies and goals to lower-level operational goals.

Objective 3

Describe the master budget for a manufacturing company.

Master Budget

The **master budget** is an integrated set of operating and financial budgets for a period of time. Most companies prepare a master budget on a yearly basis. Exhibit 7 shows that the operating budgets can be used to prepare a budgeted income statement, while the financial budgets provide information for a budgeted balance sheet.

Exhibit 7

Master Budget for a Manufacturing Company

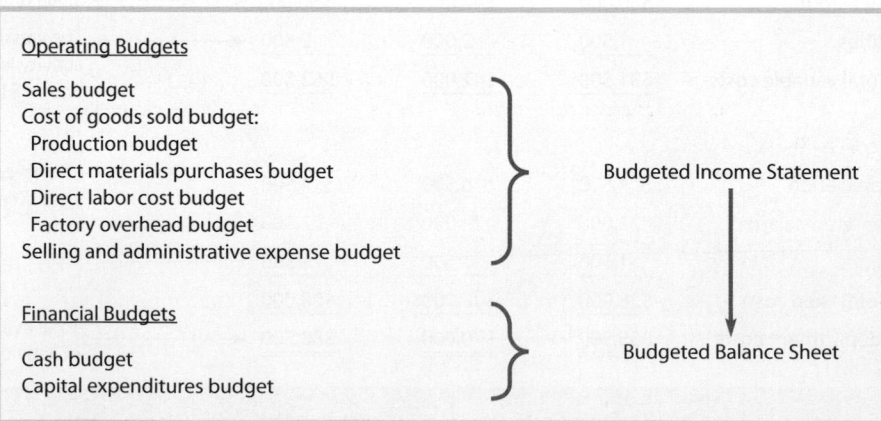

Operating Budgets

Sales budget
Cost of goods sold budget:
  Production budget
  Direct materials purchases budget
  Direct labor cost budget
  Factory overhead budget
Selling and administrative expense budget

} Budgeted Income Statement

Financial Budgets

Cash budget
Capital expenditures budget

} Budgeted Balance Sheet

The master budget begins with preparing the operating budgets, which form the budgeted income statement. Exhibit 8 shows the relationships among the operating budgets leading to an income statement budget.

Exhibit 8
Operating Budgets

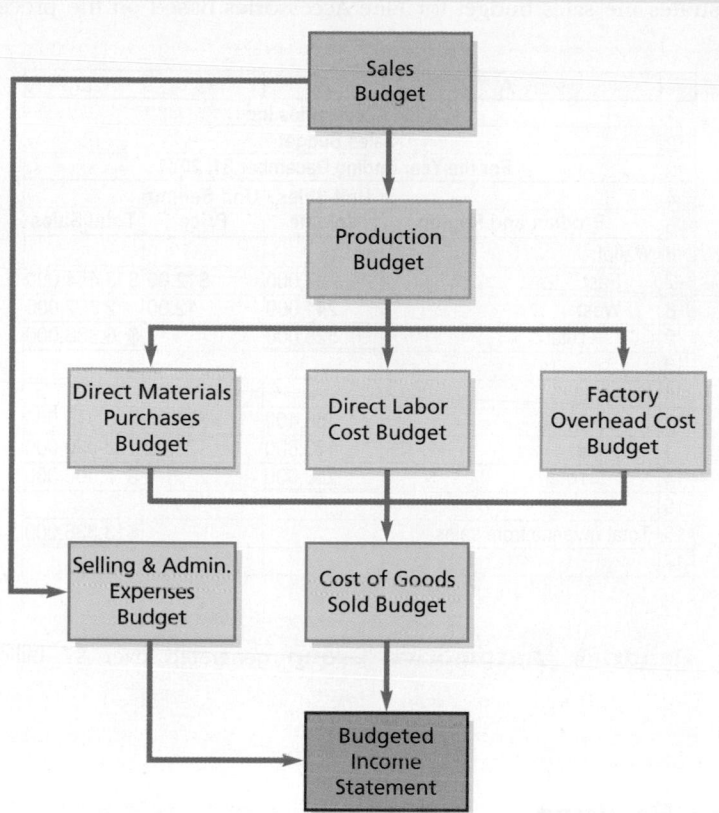

Operating Budgets

Objective 4
Prepare the basic
operating budgets
for a manufacturing
company.

The integrated operating budgets that support the income statement budget are illustrated for **Elite Accessories Inc.**, a small manufacturing company of personal accessories.

Sales Budget

The **sales budget** begins by estimating the quantity of sales. The prior year's sales are often used as a starting point. These sales quantities are then revised for such factors as planned advertising and promotion, projected pricing changes, and expected industry and general economic conditions.

Once sales quantities are estimated, the budgeted sales revenue can be determined as follows:

Budgeted Revenue = Expected Sales Volume × Expected Unit Sales Price

To illustrate, **Elite Accessories Inc.** manufactures wallets and handbags that are sold in two regions, the East and West regions. Elite Accessories estimates the following sales volumes and prices for 20Y1:

	East Region Sales Volume	West Region Sales Volume	Unit Selling Price
Wallets	287,000	241,000	$12
Handbags	156,400	123,600	25

Exhibit 9 illustrates the sales budget for Elite Accessories based on the preceding data.

Exhibit 9
Sales Budget

	A	B	C	D
1	Elite Accessories Inc.			
2	Sales Budget			
3	For the Year Ending December 31, 20Y1			
4		Unit Sales	Unit Selling	
5	Product and Region	Volume	Price	Total Sales
6	Wallet:			
7	East	287,000	$12.00	$ 3,444,000
8	West	241,000	12.00	2,892,000
9	Total	528,000		$ 6,336,000
10				
11	Handbag:			
12	East	156,400	$25.00	$ 3,910,000
13	West	123,600	25.00	3,090,000
14	Total	280,000		$ 7,000,000
15				
16	Total revenue from sales			$13,336,000
17				

Link to Hendrick Motorsports In a recent year, **Hendrick Automotive Group** generated over $7 billion of revenue across 13 states.

Production Budget

The production budget should be integrated with the sales budget to ensure that production and sales are kept in balance during the year. The **production budget** estimates the number of units to be manufactured to meet budgeted sales and desired inventory levels.

The budgeted units to be produced are determined as follows:

Expected units to be sold	XXX units
Desired units in ending inventory	XXX
Estimated units in beginning inventory	(XXX)
Total units to be produced	XXX units

Elite Accessories Inc. expects the following inventories of wallets and handbags:

	Estimated Inventory, January 1, 20Y1	Desired Inventory, December 31, 20Y1
Wallets	88,000	80,000
Handbags	48,000	60,000

Exhibit 10 illustrates the production budget for Elite Accessories.

Exhibit 10
Production Budget

	A	B	C
1	Elite Accessories Inc.		
2	Production Budget		
3	For the Year Ending December 31, 20Y1		
4		Units	
5		Wallet	Handbag
6	Expected units to be sold (from Exhibit 9)	528,000	280,000
7	Desired ending inventory, December 31, 20Y1	80,000	60,000
8	Total units available	608,000	340,000
9	Estimated beginning inventory, January 1, 20Y1	(88,000)	(48,000)
10	Total units to be produced	520,000	292,000
11			

Direct Materials Purchases Budget

The direct materials purchases budget should be integrated with the production budget to ensure that production is not interrupted during the year. The **direct materials purchases budget** estimates the quantities of direct materials to be purchased to support budgeted production and desired inventory levels and can be developed in three steps.

Step 1 Determine the budgeted direct material required for production, which is computed as follows:

$$\begin{array}{ll} \text{Budgeted Direct Material} & = \text{ Budgeted Production Volume } \times \text{ Direct Material Quantity} \\ \text{Required for Production} & \quad\text{(from Exhibit 10)} \qquad\qquad\qquad \text{Expected per Unit} \end{array}$$

To illustrate, **Elite Accessories Inc.** uses leather and lining in producing wallets and handbags. The quantity of direct materials expected to be used for each unit of product is as follows:

	Wallet	**Handbag**
Leather	0.30 sq. yd. per unit	1.25 sq. yds. per unit
Lining	0.10 sq. yd. per unit	0.50 sq. yd. per unit

For the wallet, the direct material required for production is computed as follows:

Leather: 520,000 units × 0.30 sq. yd. per unit = 156,000 sq. yds.
Lining: 520,000 units × 0.10 sq. yd. per unit = 52,000 sq. yds.

For the handbag, the direct material required for production is computed as follows:

Leather: 292,000 units × 1.25 sq. yds. per unit = 365,000 sq. yds.
Lining: 292,000 units × 0.50 sq. yd. per unit = 146,000 sq. yds.

Step 2 The budgeted material required for production is adjusted for beginning and ending inventories to determine the direct materials to be purchased for each material, as follows:

Materials required for production (Step 1)	XXX
Desired ending materials inventory	XXX
Estimated beginning materials inventory	(XXX)
Direct material quantity to be purchased	XXX

Step 3 The budgeted direct materials to be purchased is computed as follows:

$$\begin{array}{ll} \text{Budgeted Direct Material} & = \text{Direct Material Quantity to Be Purchased} \times \text{Unit Price} \\ \text{to Be Purchased} & \quad\text{(Step 2)} \end{array}$$

Complete Direct Materials Purchases Budget The following inventory and unit price information for **Elite Accessories Inc.** is expected:

	Estimated Direct Materials Inventory, January 1, 20Y1	**Desired Direct Materials Inventory, December 31, 20Y1**
Leather	18,000 sq. yds.	20,000 sq. yds.
Lining	15,000 sq. yds.	12,000 sq. yds.

The estimated price per square yard of leather and lining during 20Y1 follows:

	Price per Square Yard
Leather	$4.50
Lining	1.20

Exhibit 11 illustrates the complete direct materials purchases budget for Elite Accessories by combining all three steps into a single schedule.

Exhibit 11
Direct Materials
Purchases Budget

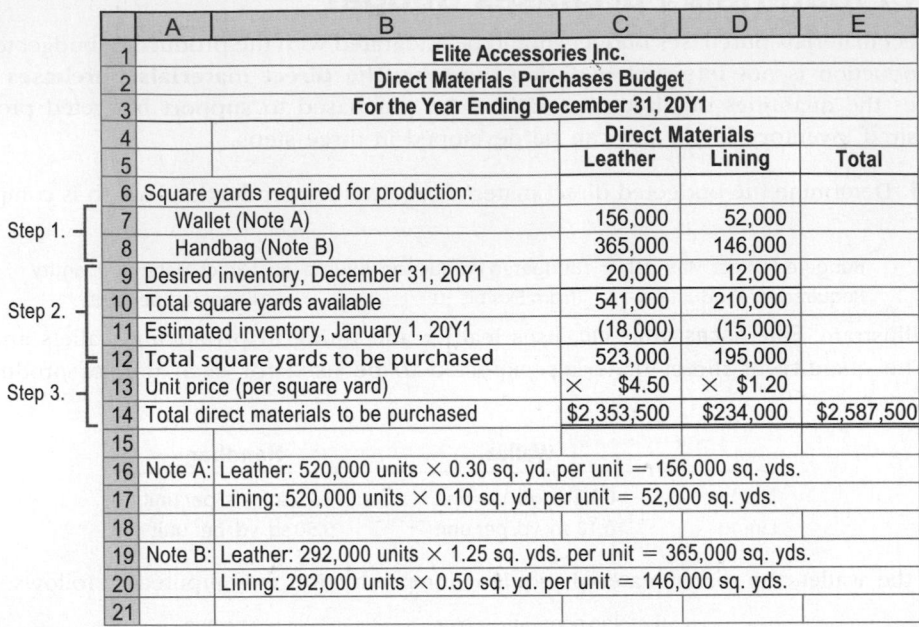

	A	B	C	D	E
1		Elite Accessories Inc.			
2		Direct Materials Purchases Budget			
3		For the Year Ending December 31, 20Y1			
4			Direct Materials		
5			Leather	Lining	Total
6	Square yards required for production:				
7		Wallet (Note A)	156,000	52,000	
8		Handbag (Note B)	365,000	146,000	
9	Desired inventory, December 31, 20Y1		20,000	12,000	
10	Total square yards available		541,000	210,000	
11	Estimated inventory, January 1, 20Y1		(18,000)	(15,000)	
12	Total square yards to be purchased		523,000	195,000	
13	Unit price (per square yard)		× $4.50	× $1.20	
14	Total direct materials to be purchased		$2,353,500	$234,000	$2,587,500
15					
16	Note A:	Leather: 520,000 units × 0.30 sq. yd. per unit = 156,000 sq. yds.			
17		Lining: 520,000 units × 0.10 sq. yd. per unit = 52,000 sq. yds.			
18					
19	Note B:	Leather: 292,000 units × 1.25 sq. yds. per unit = 365,000 sq. yds.			
20		Lining: 292,000 units × 0.50 sq. yd. per unit = 146,000 sq. yds.			
21					

Step 1. (rows 7–8)
Step 2. (rows 9–12)
Step 3. (rows 13–14)

The timing of the direct materials purchases should be coordinated between the purchasing and production departments so that production is not interrupted.

Link to Hendrick Motorsports

Hendrick Motorsports uses sheet metal in building its race cars. "Used" sections of sheet metal (from crashed cars) can be purchased from its online store.

Direct Labor Cost Budget

The **direct labor cost budget** estimates the direct labor hours and related cost needed to support budgeted production. Production managers study work methods to provide estimates used in preparing the direct labor cost budget.

The direct labor cost budget for each department is determined in two steps, as follows.

Step 1 Determine the budgeted direct labor hours required for production, which is computed as follows:

Budgeted Direct Labor = Budgeted Production Volume × Direct Labor Hours Expected
Hours Required for   (from Exhibit 10)   per Unit
Production

To illustrate, **Elite Accessories Inc.**'s production managers estimate the following direct labor hours are needed to produce a wallet and handbag:

	Wallet	Handbag
Cutting Department	0.10 hr. per unit	0.15 hr. per unit
Sewing Department	0.25 hr. per unit	0.40 hr. per unit

Thus, for the wallet, the budgeted direct labor hours required for production is computed as follows:

Cutting: 520,000 units × 0.10 hr. per unit = 52,000 direct labor hours
Sewing: 520,000 units × 0.25 hr. per unit – 130,000 direct labor hours

For the handbag, the budgeted direct labor hours required for production is computed as follows:

Cutting: 292,000 units × 0.15 hr. per unit = 43,800 direct labor hours
Sewing: 292,000 units × 0.40 hr. per unit = 116,800 direct labor hours

Step 2 Determine the total direct labor cost as follows:

Direct Labor Cost = Direct Labor Required for Production (Step 1) × Hourly Rate

The estimated direct labor hourly rates for the Cutting and Sewing departments for **Elite Accessories Inc.** during 20Y1 follow:

	Hourly Rate
Cutting Department	$12
Sewing Department	15

Complete Direct Labor Cost Budget Exhibit 12 illustrates the direct labor cost budget by combining both steps for **Elite Accessories Inc.**

	A	B	C	D	E
1		Elite Accessories Inc.			
2		Direct Labor Cost Budget			
3		For the Year Ending December 31, 20Y1			
4			Cutting	Sewing	Total
5	Hours required for production:				
6	Wallet (Note A)		52,000	130,000	
7	Handbag (Note B)		43,800	116,800	
8	Total		95,800	246,800	
9	Hourly rate		× $12	× $15	
10	Total direct labor cost		$1,149,600	$3,702,000	$4,851,600
11					
12	Note A:	Cutting Department: 520,000 units × 0.10 hr. per unit = 52,000 hrs.			
13		Sewing Department: 520,000 units × 0.25 hr. per unit = 130,000 hrs.			
14					
15	Note B:	Cutting Department: 292,000 units × 0.15 hr. per unit = 43,800 hrs.			
16		Sewing Department: 292,000 units × 0.40 hr. per unit = 116,800 hrs.			
17					

Step 1. → rows 6, 7
Step 2. → rows 9, 10

Exhibit 12
Direct Labor
Cost Budget

The direct labor needs should be coordinated between the production and personnel departments so that there will be enough labor available for production.

Hendrick Motorports offers an internship program for college students who want to experience and learn the operations of a NASCAR team.

Link to Hendrick Motorsports

Factory Overhead Cost Budget

The **factory overhead cost budget** estimates the cost for each item of factory overhead needed to support budgeted production.

Exhibit 13 illustrates the factory overhead cost budget for **Elite Accessories Inc.**

Exhibit 13

Factory Overhead Cost Budget

	A	B
1	Elite Accessories Inc.	
2	Factory Overhead Cost Budget	
3	For the Year Ending December 31, 20Y1	
4	Indirect factory wages	$ 732,800
5	Supervisor salaries	360,000
6	Power and light	306,000
7	Depreciation of plant and equipment	288,000
8	Indirect materials	182,800
9	Maintenance	140,280
10	Insurance and property taxes	79,200
11	Total factory overhead cost	$2,089,080
12		

The factory overhead cost budget shown in Exhibit 13 may be supported by departmental schedules. Such schedules normally separate factory overhead costs into fixed and variable costs to better enable department managers to monitor and evaluate costs during the year.

The factory overhead cost budget should be integrated with the production budget to ensure that production is not interrupted during the year.

Cost of Goods Sold Budget

The **cost of goods sold budget** is prepared by integrating the following budgets:

- Direct materials purchases budget (Exhibit 11)
- Direct labor cost budget (Exhibit 12)
- Factory overhead cost budget (Exhibit 13)

In addition, the estimated and desired inventories for direct materials, work in process, and finished goods must be integrated into the cost of goods sold budget.

Elite Accessories Inc. expects the following direct materials, work in process, and finished goods inventories:

	Estimated Inventory, January 1, 20Y1	Desired Inventory, December 31, 20Y1
Direct materials:		
Leather	$ 81,000 (18,000 sq. yds. × $4.50)	$ 90,000 (20,000 sq. yds. × $4.50)
Lining	18,000 (15,000 sq. yds. × $1.20)	14,400 (12,000 sq. yds. × $1.20)
Total direct materials	$ 99,000	$ 104,400
Work in process	$ 214,400	$ 220,000
Finished goods	$1,095,600	$1,565,000

The cost of goods sold budget for Elite Accessories in Exhibit 14 indicates that total manufacturing costs of $9,522,780 are budgeted to be incurred in 20Y1. Of this total, $2,582,100 is budgeted for direct materials, $4,851,600 is budgeted for direct labor, and $2,089,080 is budgeted for factory overhead. After considering work in process inventories, the total budgeted cost of goods manufactured and transferred to finished goods during 20Y1 is $9,517,180. Based on expected sales, the budgeted cost of goods sold is $9,047,780.

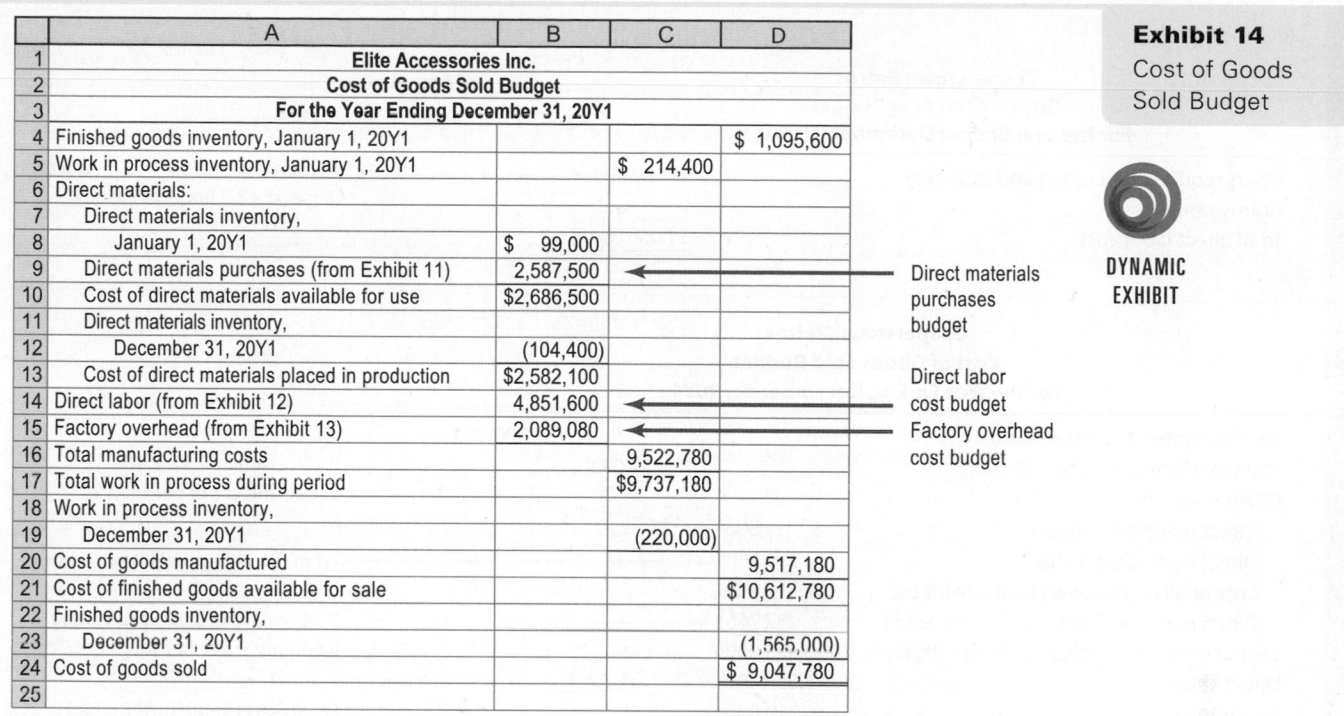

Exhibit 14
Cost of Goods Sold Budget

	A	B	C	D
1	Elite Accessories Inc.			
2	Cost of Goods Sold Budget			
3	For the Year Ending December 31, 20Y1			
4	Finished goods inventory, January 1, 20Y1			$ 1,095,600
5	Work in process inventory, January 1, 20Y1		$ 214,400	
6	Direct materials:			
7	Direct materials inventory,			
8	January 1, 20Y1	$ 99,000		
9	Direct materials purchases (from Exhibit 11)	2,587,500		
10	Cost of direct materials available for use	$2,686,500		
11	Direct materials inventory,			
12	December 31, 20Y1	(104,400)		
13	Cost of direct materials placed in production	$2,582,100		
14	Direct labor (from Exhibit 12)	4,851,600		
15	Factory overhead (from Exhibit 13)	2,089,080		
16	Total manufacturing costs		9,522,780	
17	Total work in process during period		$9,737,180	
18	Work in process inventory,			
19	December 31, 20Y1		(220,000)	
20	Cost of goods manufactured			9,517,180
21	Cost of finished goods available for sale			$10,612,780
22	Finished goods inventory,			
23	December 31, 20Y1			(1,565,000)
24	Cost of goods sold			$ 9,047,780
25				

Direct materials purchases budget

Direct labor cost budget

Factory overhead cost budget

DYNAMIC EXHIBIT

Check Up Corner 7-2   **Direct Materials, Direct Labor, and Cost of Goods Sold Budget**

Cooperstown Retros makes replica major league baseball jerseys that match those worn in the 1950s. The company budgeted production of 15,000 jerseys in 20Y1. Each jersey requires 1.5 square yards of wool fabric. Wool fabric costs $14 per square yard. Each jersey requires cutting and assembly. Assume that 3.5 hours are required to cut and assemble each jersey. Labor costs are estimated at $20 per hour. Factory overhead was budgeted for $210,000.

Estimated January 1 and desired December 31 inventories are as follows:

	Direct Materials: Wool Fabric	Work-In-Process	Finished Goods
Estimated inventory, January 1, 20Y1	2,250 sq. yds.	$20,000	$200,000
Desired inventory, December 31, 20Y1	2,340 sq. yds.	$24,500	$230,000

Prepare (A) a direct materials purchases budget, (B) a direct labor cost budget, and (C) a cost of goods sold budget for Cooperstown for the year ending December 31, 20Y1.

Solution:

A.

Cooperstown Retros
Direct Materials Purchases Budget
For the Year Ending December 31, 20Y1

Square yards of material required for production	22,500
Desired ending inventory, December 31	2,340
Total square yards available	24,840
Estimated beginning inventory, January 1	(2,250)
Total square yards to be purchased	22,590
Unit price (per square yard)	× $14
Total direct materials to be purchased	$316,260

15,000 expected units of production (jerseys) × 1.5 square yards per jersey

Estimated quantity of direct materials to be purchased to support budgeted production and meet desired inventory levels

B.

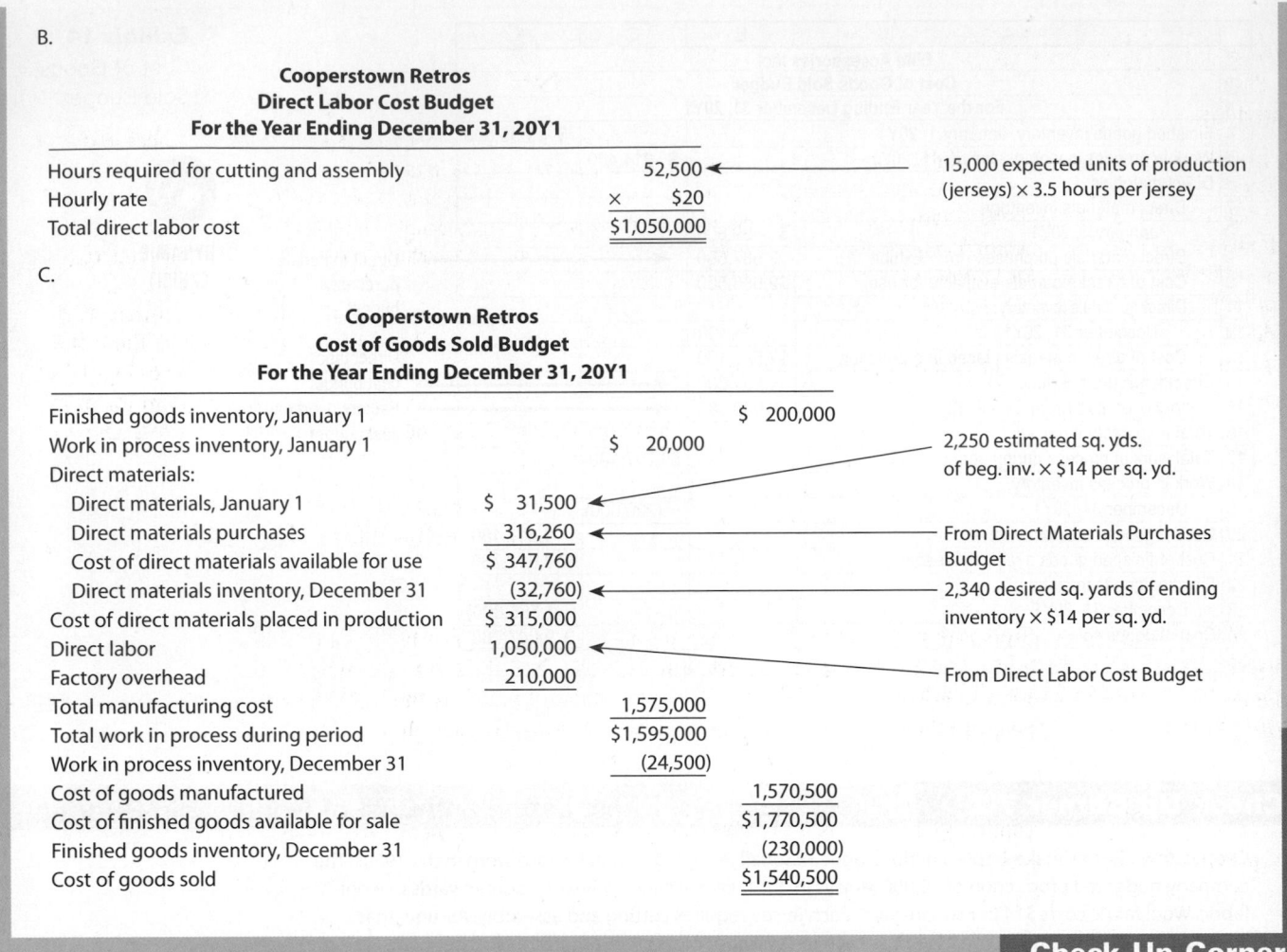

Cooperstown Retros
Direct Labor Cost Budget
For the Year Ending December 31, 20Y1

Hours required for cutting and assembly	52,500	15,000 expected units of production (jerseys) × 3.5 hours per jersey
Hourly rate	× $20	
Total direct labor cost	$1,050,000	

C.

Cooperstown Retros
Cost of Goods Sold Budget
For the Year Ending December 31, 20Y1

Finished goods inventory, January 1			$ 200,000
Work in process inventory, January 1		$ 20,000	
Direct materials:			
Direct materials, January 1	$ 31,500		2,250 estimated sq. yds. of beg. inv. × $14 per sq. yd.
Direct materials purchases	316,260		From Direct Materials Purchases Budget
Cost of direct materials available for use	$ 347,760		
Direct materials inventory, December 31	(32,760)		2,340 desired sq. yards of ending inventory × $14 per sq. yd.
Cost of direct materials placed in production	$ 315,000		
Direct labor	1,050,000		
Factory overhead	210,000		From Direct Labor Cost Budget
Total manufacturing cost		1,575,000	
Total work in process during period		$1,595,000	
Work in process inventory, December 31		(24,500)	
Cost of goods manufactured			1,570,500
Cost of finished goods available for sale			$1,770,500
Finished goods inventory, December 31			(230,000)
Cost of goods sold			$1,540,500

Check Up Corner

Selling and Administrative Expenses Budget

The sales budget is often used as the starting point for the selling and administrative expenses budget. For example, a budgeted increase in sales may require more advertising expenses.

Exhibit 15 illustrates the selling and administrative expenses budget for **Elite Accessories Inc.**

Exhibit 15

Selling and Administrative Expenses Budget

	A	B	C
1	Elite Accessories Inc.		
2	Selling and Administrative Expenses Budget		
3	For the Year Ending December 31, 20Y1		
4	Selling expenses:		
5	Sales salaries expense	$715,000	
6	Advertising expense	360,000	
7	Travel expense	115,000	
8	Total selling expenses		$1,190,000
9	Administrative expenses:		
10	Officers' salaries expense	$360,000	
11	Office salaries expense	258,000	
12	Office rent expense	34,500	
13	Office supplies expense	17,500	
14	Miscellaneous administrative expenses	25,000	
15	Total administrative expenses		695,000
16	Total selling and administrative expenses		$1,885,000
17			

Why It Matters

Mad Men

The advertising budget can be one of the largest selling and administrative expenses for a business. The top 200 leading national advertisers accounted for 51% of all advertising dollars for all businesses combined. Of this amount, 68.5% went toward video broadcast advertising, 7.2% for Internet display ads, and 24.3% for print and radio. The top five spenders according to *Advertising Age* were:

Company	U.S. Advertising Spending
Procter & Gamble	$4.6 billion
AT&T	3.3 billion
General Motors	3.1 billion
Comcast	3.0 billion
Verizon	2.5 billion

The advertising budget is segmented between "measured" and "unmeasured" media. Measured media are tracked to determine the number of impressions an ad is receiving due to audience, viewership, or readership counts. Unmeasured media are not counted for impressions, and include promotions, direct marketing, and coupons.

A major trend is allocating ad budget dollars toward digital strategies, such as search, social, video, and mobile. These strategies are believed to be more efficient and effective than TV or print. For **Colgate-Palmolive**, digital went from 2% of the advertising budget in 2006 to 13% in 2014, with expectations of growing to 25%.

Source: Bradley Johnson, "Big Spenders on a Budget: What the Top 200 U.S. Advertisers Are Doing to Spend Smarter," *Advertising Age*, July 5, 2015.

The selling and administrative expenses budget shown in Exhibit 15 is normally supported by departmental schedules. For example, an advertising expense schedule for the Marketing Department could include the advertising media to be used (newspaper, direct mail, television), quantities (column inches, number of pieces, minutes), and related costs per unit.

Budgeted Income Statement

The budgeted income statement for **Elite Accessories Inc.** in Exhibit 16 is prepared by integrating the following budgets:

- Sales budget (Exhibit 9)
- Cost of goods sold budget (Exhibit 14)
- Selling and administrative expenses budget (Exhibit 15)

In addition, estimates of other income, other expense, and income tax are also integrated into the budgeted income statement.

This budget summarizes the budgeted operating activities of the company. In doing so, the budgeted income statement allows management to assess the effects of estimated sales, costs, and expenses on profits for the year.

Exhibit 16

Budgeted Income Statement

	A	B	C
1	Elite Accessories Inc.		
2	Budgeted Income Statement		
3	For the Year Ending December 31, 20Y1		
4	Revenue from sales (from Exhibit 9)		$13,336,000	← Sales budget
5	Cost of goods sold (from Exhibit 14)		9,047,780	← Cost of goods sold budget
6			
7	Gross profit		$ 4,288,220
8	Selling and administrative expenses:		
9	Selling expenses (from Exhibit 15)	$1,190,000	
10	Administrative expenses (from Exhibit 15)	695,000	
11	Total selling and administrative expenses		1,885,000
12	Income from operations		$ 2,403,220
13	Other revenue and expense:		
14	Interest revenue	$ 98,000	
15	Interest expense	90,000	8,000
16	Income before income tax		$ 2,411,220
17	Income tax		600,000
18	Net income		$ 1,811,220
19			

Link to Hendrick Motorsports   **Hendrick Motorsports** is located in Concord, North Carolina, one mile from the Charlotte Motor Speedway. Visitors are welcome, and tours are provided at no charge during the week.

Objective 5

Prepare financial budgets for a manufacturing company.

Financial Budgets

While the operating budgets reflect the operating activities of the company, the financial budgets reflect the financing and investing activities. In this section, the following financial budgets are described and illustrated:

- Cash budget
- Capital expenditures budget

Cash Budget

note:

The cash budget presents the expected receipts and payments of cash for a period of time.

The **cash budget** estimates the expected receipts (inflows) and payments (outflows) of cash for a period of time. The cash budget is integrated with the various operating budgets. In addition, the capital expenditures budget, dividends, and equity or long-term debt financing plans of the company affect the cash budget.

To illustrate, a monthly cash budget for January, February, and March 20Y1 for **Elite Accessories Inc.** is prepared. The preparation of the cash budget begins by estimating cash receipts.

Estimated Cash Receipts The primary source of estimated cash receipts is from cash sales and collections on account. In addition, cash receipts may be obtained from plans to issue equity or debt financing as well as other sources such as interest revenue.

To estimate cash receipts from cash sales and collections on account, a *schedule of collections from sales* is prepared. To illustrate, the following data for **Elite Accessories Inc.** are used:

	January	February	March
Sales:			
Budgeted sales.....................................	$1,080,000	$1,240,000	$970,000
Accounts receivable:			
Accounts receivable January 1, 20Y1	$480,000		
Receipts from sales on account:			
From prior month's sales on account	40%		
From current month's sales on account	60		
	100%		

The budgeted cash collected for any month is the sum of the cash collected from previous month's sales and the cash collected from current month's sales. To illustrate, the cash collected in February is 40% of cash collected on sales in January ($1,080,000 × 40%) added to 60% of cash collected on sales in February ($1,240,000 × 60%), shown as follows:

	January	February
Budgeted sales..	$1,080,000	$1,240,000
	× 40%	× 60%
Cash collected from prior month's sales		$ 432,000
Cash collected from current month's sales..............		744,000
Total receipts from sales on account...................		$1,176,000

Using the preceding data, Exhibit 17 shows the schedule of collections from sales for Elite Accessories for all three months. To simplify, it is assumed that all accounts receivable are collected and there are no cash sales.

	A	B	C	D	E
1		Elite Accessories Inc.			
2		Schedule of Collections from Sales			
3		For the Three Months Ending March 31, 20Y1			
4			January	February	March
5	Cash collected from prior month's sales—Note A		$ 480,000	$ 432,000	$ 496,000
6	Cash collected from current month's sales—Note B		648,000	744,000	582,000
7	Total receipts from sales on account		$1,128,000	$1,176,000	$1,078,000
8					
9	Note A: $480,000, given as January 1, 20Y1, Accounts Receivable balance				
10		$432,000 = $1,080,000 × 40%			
11		$496,000 = $1,240,000 × 40%			
12					
13	Note B: $648,000 = $1,080,000 × 60%				
14		$744,000 = $1,240,000 × 60%			
15		$582,000 = $970,000 × 60%			
16					

Exhibit 17

Schedule of Collections from Sales

Estimated Cash Payments Estimated cash payments must be budgeted for operating costs and expenses such as manufacturing costs, selling expenses, and administrative expenses. In addition, estimated cash payments may be planned for capital expenditures, dividends, interest payments, or long-term debt payments.

To estimate cash payments for manufacturing costs, a *schedule of payments for manufacturing costs* is prepared. To illustrate, the following data for **Elite Accessories Inc.** are used:

	January	February	March
Manufacturing costs:			
Budgeted manufacturing costs	$840,000	$780,000	$812,000
Depreciation on machines included			
in manufacturing costs	24,000	24,000	24,000
Accounts payable:			
Accounts payable, January 1, 20Y1	$190,000		
Payments of manufacturing costs on account:			
From prior month's manufacturing costs	25%		
From current month's manufacturing costs..................	75		
	100%		

Depreciation on machines is included in budgeted manufacturing costs but does not require a cash outlay. Thus, depreciation is deducted (not included) in determining monthly budgeted cash payments. In addition, manufacturing costs incurred in one month may be paid in the following month. To illustrate, the cash paid in February is 25% of manufacturing costs (less depreciation) in January [($840,000 − $24,000) × 25%] added to 75% of cash paid on manufacturing costs (less depreciation) in February [($780,000 − $24,000) × 75%], computed as follows:

	January	February
Budgeted manufacturing costs	$840,000	$780,000
Depreciation on machines	(24,000)	(24,000)
Manufacturing costs (less depreciation)	$816,000	$756,000
× 25%		
Payments of prior month's manufacturing		
costs (less depreciation)		$204,000
× 75%		
Payments of current month's manufacturing		
costs (less depreciation)		567,000
Total payments		$771,000

Using the preceding data, Exhibit 18 shows the schedule of payments for manufacturing costs for Elite Accessories for all three months.

Exhibit 18
Schedule of
Payments for
Manufacturing
Costs

	A	B	C	D	E
1		Elite Accessories Inc.			
2		Schedule of Payments for Manufacturing Costs			
3		For the Three Months Ending March 31, 20Y1			
4			January	February	March
5	Payments of prior month's manufacturing costs				
6	{[25% × previous month's manufacturing costs				
7	(less depreciation)]—Note A}		$190,000	$204,000	$189,000
8	Payments of current month's manufacturing costs				
9	{[75% × current month's manufacturing costs				
10	(less depreciation)]—Note B}		612,000	567,000	591,000
11	Total payments		$802,000	$771,000	$780,000
12					
13	Note A:	$190,000, given as January 1, 20Y1, Accounts Payable balance			
14		$204,000 = ($840,000 − $24,000) × 25%			
15		$189,000 = ($780,000 − $24,000) × 25%			
16					
17	Note B:	$612,000 = ($840,000 − $24,000) × 75%			
18		$567,000 = ($780,000 − $24,000) × 75%			
19		$591,000 = ($812,000 − $24,000) × 75%			
20					

Completing the Cash Budget The cash budget is structured for a budget period as follows:

Budget Period:

Estimated cash receipts
Less estimated cash payments
_____
Cash increase (decrease)
Plus cash balance at the beginning of the month
Cash balance at the end of the month ⟶ Becomes the beginning balance for the next period
Less minimum cash balance
_____
Excess (deficiency)

The budgeted balance at the end of the period is determined by adding the net increase (decrease) for the period to the beginning cash balance. The ending balance is compared to a minimum cash balance to support operations as determined by management. Any difference between the ending balance and the minimum cash balance represents an excess or deficiency that may require management action.

To illustrate, assume the following additional data for **Elite Accessories Inc.**:

Cash balance on January 1, 20Y1	$225,000
Quarterly taxes paid on March 31, 20Y1	150,000
Quarterly interest expense paid on January 10, 20Y1	22,500
Quarterly interest revenue received on March 21, 20Y1	24,500
Sewing equipment purchased in February 20Y1	274,000
Selling and administrative expenses (paid in month incurred):	

January	February	March
$160,000	$165,000	$145,000

The cash budget for Elite Accessories is shown in Exhibit 19.

The estimated cash receipts include the total receipts from sales on account (Exhibit 17). The estimated cash payments include the cash payments from manufacturing costs (Exhibit 18). Other receipts and payments are provided by the additional information. Additionally, assume the minimum cash balance is $340,000.

Exhibit 19

Cash Budget

	A	B	C	D
1	Elite Accessories Inc.			
2	Cash Budget			
3	For the Three Months Ending March 31,20Y1			
4		January	February	March
5	Estimated cash receipts from:			
6	Collections of accounts receivable			
7	(from Exhibit 17)	$1,128,000	$1,176,000	$1,078,000
8	Interest revenue			24,500
9	Total cash receipts	$1,128,000	$1,176,000	$1,102,500
10	Less estimated cash payments for:			
11	Manufacturing costs (from Exhibit 18)	$ 802,000	$ 771,000	$ 780,000
12	Selling and administrative expenses	160,000	165,000	145,000
13	Capital additions (sewing equipment)		274,000	
14	Interest expense	22,500		
15	Income taxes			150,000
16	Total cash payments	$ 984,500	$1,210,000	$1,075,000
17	Cash increase (decrease)	$ 143,500	$ (34,000)	$ 27,500
18	Cash balance at beginning of month	225,000	368,500	334,500
19	Plus cash balance at end of month	$ 368,500	$ 334,500	$ 362,000
20	Less minimum cash balance	340,000	340,000	340,000
21	Excess (deficiency)	$ 28,500	$ (5,500)	$ 22,000
22				

Schedule of collections from sales ← (row 7)

Schedule of payments for manufacturing costs ← (row 11)

Exhibit 19 indicates that Elite Accessories expects a cash excess at the end of January of $28,500. This excess could be invested in temporary income-producing securities such as U.S. Treasury bills or notes. In contrast, the estimated cash deficiency at the end of February of $5,500 might require Elite Accessories to borrow cash from its bank.

Check Up Corner 7-3   Cash Budget

Quincy Company has both cash and credit customers. The company expects that 40% of total monthly sales will be collected in cash in the month of sale, and the remaining 60% will be collected in the month following the month of sale. The Accounts Receivable balance on January 1 is $97,500, all of which is expected to be collected during January. Projected sales for the first three months of the year are as follows:

January	$190,000
February	200,000
March	210,000

Projected manufacturing costs and selling and administrative expenses for the first three months of the year are as follows:

	Manufacturing Costs	Selling & Administrative Expenses
January	$110,000	$72,000
February	134,000	70,000
March	160,000	75,000

Manufacturing costs include depreciation, insurance, and property taxes, which represent $18,000 of the estimated monthly manufacturing costs. The annual insurance premium was paid on December 31 of the prior year, and property taxes for the year will be paid in June. Sixty percent of the remainder of manufacturing costs are expected to be paid in the month in which they are incurred, with the balance to be paid in the following month. The Accounts Payable balance on January 1, which consisted entirely of unpaid manufacturing costs from December, is $36,700. All selling and administrative expenses are paid in cash in the period in which they are incurred. The cash balance on January 1 was $26,000, and management desires to maintain a minimum cash balance of $20,000.

Prepare:

A. A schedule of collections from sales.
B. A schedule of cash payments for manufacturing costs.
C. A cash budget.

Solution:

A.

Quincy Company
Schedule of Collections from Sales
For the Three Months Ending March 31

	January	February	March
Cash collections from prior month's sales	$ 97,500	$114,000	$120,000
Cash collections from current month's sales	76,000	80,000	84,000
Total cash collections from sales	$173,500	$194,000	$204,000

January 1 accounts receivable balance

60% × January sales

40% × March sales

B.

Quincy Company
Schedule of Payments for Manufacturing Costs
For the Three Months Ending March 31

	January	February	March
Payment of prior month's costs	$36,700	$ 36,800	$ 46,400
Payment of current month's costs	55,200	69,600	85,200
Total manufacturing cost cash payments	$91,900	$106,400	$131,600

January 1 accounts payable balance

40% × January manufacturing costs excluding depreciation, insurance, and property taxes ($100,000 – $18,000)

60% × March manufacturing costs excluding depreciation, insurance, and property taxes ($142,000 – $18,000)

60% × February manufacturing costs excluding depreciation, insurance, and property taxes ($134,000 – $18,000)

C.

Quincy Company
Cash Budget
For the Three Months Ending March 31

	January	February	March
Estimated cash receipts	$173,500	$194,000	$204,000
Less estimated cash payments for:			
Manufacturing costs	$ 91,900	$106,400	$131,600
Selling and administrative expenses	72,000	70,000	75,000
Total cash payments	$163,900	$176,400	$206,600
Cash increase (decrease)	$ 9,600	$ 17,600	$ (2,600)
Plus cash balance at beginning of month	26,000	35,600	53,200
Cash balance at end of month	$ 35,600	$ 53,200	$ 50,600
Less minimum cash balance	20,000	20,000	20,000
Excess (deficiency)	$ 15,600	$ 33,200	$ 30,600

From Schedule of Cash Collections in Part A

From Schedule of Cash Payments in Part B

Check Up Corner

Capital Expenditures Budget

The **capital expenditures budget** summarizes plans for acquiring fixed assets. Such expenditures are necessary as machinery and other fixed assets wear out or become obsolete. In addition, purchasing additional fixed assets may be necessary to meet increasing demand for the company's product.

To illustrate, a five-year capital expenditures budget for **Elite Accessories Inc.** is shown in Exhibit 20.

Exhibit 20

Capital Expenditures Budget

	A	B	C	D	E	F
1	Elite Accessories Inc.					
2	Capital Expenditures Budget					
3	For the Five Years Ending December 31, 20Y5					
4	Item	20Y1	20Y2	20Y3	20Y4	20Y5
5	Machinery—Cutting Department	$400,000			$280,000	$360,000
6	Machinery—Sewing Department	274,000	$260,000	$560,000	200,000	
7	Office equipment		90,000			60,000
8	Total	$674,000	$350,000	$560,000	$480,000	$420,000
9						

As shown in Exhibit 20, capital expenditures budgets are often prepared for five to ten years into the future. This is necessary because fixed assets often must be ordered years in advance. Likewise, it could take years to construct new buildings or other production facilities.

The capital expenditures budget should be integrated with the operating and financing budgets. For example, depreciation of new manufacturing equipment affects the factory overhead cost budget. The plans for financing the capital expenditures also affect the cash budget.

Budgeted Balance Sheet

The budgeted balance sheet is prepared based on the operating and financial budgets of the master budget. The budgeted balance sheet is dated as of the end of the budget period and is similar to a normal balance sheet except that estimated amounts are used. For this reason, a budgeted balance sheet for Elite Accessories Inc. is not illustrated.

Analysis for Decision Making

Nonmanufacturing Staffing Levels

Objective

Describe and illustrate the use of staffing budgets for nonmanufacturing businesses.

The budgeting illustrated in this chapter is similar to budgeting used for nonmanufacturing businesses. However, many nonmanufacturing businesses often do not have direct materials purchases budgets, direct labor cost budgets, or factory overhead cost budgets. Thus, the budgeted income statement is simplified in many nonmanufacturing settings.

A primary budget in nonmanufacturing businesses is the labor, or staffing, budget. This budget, which is highly flexible to service demands, is used to manage staffing levels. For example, a theme park will have greater staffing in the summer vacation months than in the fall months. Likewise, a retailer will have greater staffing during the holidays than on typical weekdays.

To illustrate, Concord Hotel operates a hotel in a business district. The hotel has 150 rooms that average 120 guests per night during the weekdays and 50 guests per night during the weekend. The housekeeping staff is able to clean 10 rooms per employee. The number of housekeepers required for an average weekday and weekend is determined as follows:

	Weekday	Weekend
Number of guests per day	120	50
Rooms per housekeeper	÷ 10	÷ 10
Number of housekeepers per day	12	5

If each housekeeper is paid $15 per hour for an eight-hour shift per day, the annual budget for the staff is as follows:

	Weekday	Weekend	Total
Number of housekeepers per day	12	5	
Hours per shift	× 8	× 8	
Days per year	× 260*	× 104**	
Number of hours per year	24,960	4,160	
Rate per hour	× $15	× $15	
Housekeeping staff annual budget	$374,400	$62,400	$436,800

* 52 weeks × 5 days

** 52 weeks × 2 days

The budget can be used to plan and manage the staffing of the hotel. For example, if a wedding were booked for the weekend, the budgeted increase in staffing could be compared with the increased revenue from the wedding to verify the profit plan.

Make a Decision   Nonmanufacturing Staffing Levels

Johnson Stores is planning its staffing for the upcoming holiday season. From past history, the store determines that it needs one additional sales clerk for each $12,000 in daily sales. The average daily sales is anticipated to increase by $96,000 from Black Friday until Christmas Eve, or 27 shopping days. Each additional sales clerk will work an eight-hour shift and will be paid $14 per hour.

A.   Determine the amount to budget for additional sales clerks for the holiday season.
B.   If Johnson Stores has an average 40% gross profit on sales, should it add the staff suggested by your answer in A? That is, is it profitable to staff for the increased sales in A?

Solution:

A.

Average daily revenue	$96,000
Revenue per clerk	÷12,000
Number of additional sales clerks	8
Hours per day per clerk	× 8
Number of hours per day	64
Number of shopping days	× 27
Number of hours	1,728
Rate per hour	× $14
Holiday staff budget for additional clerks	$24,192

B.

Johnson Stores should add the staff because it will be profitable.

Increase in daily revenue	$ 96,000
Gross profit percentage	× 40%
Increase in daily gross profit	$ 38,400
Number of shopping days	× 27
Additional gross profit	$1,036,800
Staff budget increase [from (A)]	(24,192)
Additional profit	$1,012,608

Make a Decision

Let's Review

Chapter Summary

1. Budgeting involves (1) establishing plans (planning), (2) directing operations (directing), and (3) evaluating performance (controlling). In addition, budgets should be established to avoid human behavior problems.

2. The budget estimates received by the budget committee should be carefully studied, analyzed, revised, and integrated. The static and flexible budgets are two major budgeting approaches. Computers can be used to make the budget process more efficient and organizationally integrated.

3. The master budget is an integrated set of operating and financial budgets for a period of time. The operating budgets are prepared and integrated into a budgeted income statement. The financial budgets are prepared and integrated into a budgeted balance sheet.

4. The basic operating budgets are the sales budget, production budget, direct materials purchases budget, direct labor cost budget, factory overhead cost budget, cost of goods sold budget, and selling and administrative expenses budget. These budgets are the basis for preparing a budgeted income statement.

5. The cash budget and capital expenditures budget are financial budgets showing the investing and financing activities of the firm. These budgets are the basis for preparing a budgeted balance sheet.

Key Terms

budgetary slack (317)
budgets (316)
capital expenditures budget (336)
cash budget (332)
continuous budgeting (318)
cost of goods sold budget (328)

direct labor cost budget (326)
direct materials purchases
   budget (325)
factory overhead cost budget (328)
flexible budgets (320)
goal conflict (317)

master budget (322)
production budget (324)
responsibility center (316)
sales budget (323)
static budget (319)
zero-based budgeting (319)

Practice

Multiple-Choice Questions

1. A tight budget may create:
   A. budgetary slack.
   B. discouragement.
   C. a flexible budget.
   D. a "spend it or lose it" mentality.

2. The first step of the budget process is to:
   A. plan.
   B. direct.
   C. control.
   D. analyze feedback.

3. Static budgets are often used by:
   A. production departments.
   B. administrative departments.
   C. responsibility centers.
   D. capital projects.

4. The total estimated sales for the coming year is 250,000 units. The estimated inventory at the beginning of the year is 22,500 units, and the desired inventory at the end of the year is 30,000 units. The total production indicated in the production budget is:

    A. 242,500 units.   C. 280,000 units.
    B. 257,500 units.   D. 302,500 units.

5. Dixon Company expects $650,000 of credit sales in March and $800,000 of credit sales in April. Dixon historically collects 70% of its sales in the month of sale and 30% in the following month. How much cash does Dixon expect to collect in April?

    A. $800,000   C. $755,000
    B. $560,000   D. $1,015,000

Answers provided after Problem. Need more practice? Find additional multiple-choice questions, exercises, and problems in CengageNOWv2.

Exercises

SHOW ME HOW

1. Flexible budgeting   Obj. 2

At the beginning of the period, the Assembly Department budgeted direct labor of $112,000 and property tax of $12,000 for 7,000 hours of production. The department actually completed 7,500 hours of production. Determine the budget for the department, assuming that it uses flexible budgeting.

SHOW ME HOW

2. Production budget   Obj. 4

MyLife Chronicles Inc. projected sales of 240,000 diaries for the year. The estimated January 1 inventory is 19,900 units, and the desired December 31 inventory is 18,800 units. What is the budgeted production (in units) for the year?

SHOW ME HOW

3. Direct materials purchases budget   Obj. 4

MyLife Chronicles Inc. budgeted production of 238,900 diaries for the year. Paper is required to produce a diary. Assume five square yards of paper are required for each diary. The estimated January 1 paper inventory is 32,400 square yards. The desired December 31 paper inventory is 30,800 square yards. If paper costs $0.30 per square yard, determine the direct materials purchases budget for the year.

SHOW ME HOW

4. Direct labor cost budget   Obj. 4

MyLife Chronicles Inc. budgeted production of 238,900 diaries for the year. Each diary requires assembly. Assume that six minutes are required to assemble each diary. If assembly labor costs $12 per hour, determine the direct labor cost budget for the year.

SHOW ME HOW

5. Cost of goods sold budget   Obj. 4

Prepare a cost of goods sold budget for MyLife Chronicles Inc. using the information in Exercises 3 and 4. Assume the estimated inventories on January 1 for finished goods and work in process were $25,000 and $19,000, respectively. Also assume the desired inventories on December 31 for finished goods and work in process were $31,500 and $16,700, respectively. Factory overhead was budgeted at $197,100.

SHOW ME HOW

6. Cash budget   Obj. 5

MyLife Chronicles Inc. collects 30% of its sales on account in the month of the sale and 70% in the month following the sale. If sales on account are budgeted to be $170,000 for June and $200,000 for July, what are the budgeted cash receipts from sales on account for July?

Answers provided after Problem. Need more practice? Find additional multiple-choice questions, exercises, and problems in CengageNOWv2.

Problem

Selected information concerning sales and production for Cabot Co. for July are summarized as follows:

A. Estimated sales:

Product K: 40,000 units at $30 per unit
Product L: 20,000 units at $65 per unit

B. Estimated inventories, July 1:

Material A:	4,000 lbs.	Product K:	3,000 units at $17 per unit	$ 51,000
Material B:	3,500 lbs.	Product L:	2,700 units at $35 per unit	94,500
		Total		$145,500

There were no work in process inventories estimated for July.

C. Desired inventories at July 31:

Material A:	3,000 lbs.	Product K:	2,500 units at $17 per unit	$ 42,500
Material B:	2,500 lbs.	Product L:	2,000 units at $35 per unit	70,000
		Total		$112,500

There were no work in process inventories desired for July 31.

D. Direct materials used in production:

	Product K	Product L
Material A:	0.7 lb. per unit	3.5 lbs. per unit
Material B:	1.2 lbs. per unit	1.8 lbs. per unit

E. Unit costs for direct materials:

Material A: $4.00 per lb.
Material B: $2.00 per lb.

F. Direct labor requirements:

	Department 1	Department 2
Product K	0.4 hr. per unit	0.15 hr. per unit
Product L	0.6 hr. per unit	0.25 hr. per unit

G.

	Department 1	Department 2
Direct labor rate	$12 per hr.	$16 per hr.

H. Estimated factory overhead costs for July:

Indirect factory wages	$200,000
Depreciation of plant and equipment	40,000
Power and light	25,000
Indirect materials	34,000
Total	$299,000

Instructions

1. Prepare a sales budget for July.
2. Prepare a production budget for July.
3. Prepare a direct materials purchases budget for July.
4. Prepare a direct labor cost budget for July.
5. Prepare a cost of goods sold budget for July.

Need more practice? Find additional multiple-choice questions, exercises, and problems in CengageNOWv2.

Answers

Multiple-Choice Questions

1. **B** Individuals can be discouraged with budgets that appear too tight or unobtainable. Flexible budgeting (answer C) provides a series of budgets for varying rates of activity and thereby builds into the budgeting system the effect of fluctuations in the level of activity. Budgetary slack (answer A) comes from a loose budget, not a tight budget. A "spend it or lose it" mentality (answer D) is often associated with loose budgets.

2. **A** The first step of the budget process is to develop a plan. Once plans are established, management may direct actions (answer B). The results of actions can be controlled (answer C) by comparing them to the plan. This feedback (answer D) can be used by management to change plans or redirect actions.

3. **B** Administrative departments (answer B), such as Purchasing or Human Resources, will often use static budgeting. Production departments (answer A) frequently use flexible budgets. Responsibility centers (answer C) can use either static or flexible budgeting. Capital expenditures budgets are used to plan capital projects (answer D).

4. **B** The total production indicated in the production budget is 257,500 units (answer B), which is computed as follows:

Sales	250,000 units
Desired ending inventory	30,000 units
Total	280,000 units
Estimated beginning inventory	(22,500) units
Total production	257,500 units

5. **C** Dixon expects to collect 70% of April sales ($560,000) plus 30% of the March sales ($195,000) in April, for a total of $755,000 (answer C). Answer A is 100% of April sales. Answer B is 70% of April sales. Answer D adds 70% of both March and April sales.

Exercises

1. Variable cost:

Direct labor (7,500 hours × $16* per hour)	$120,000
Fixed cost:	
Property tax	12,000
Total department costs	$132,000

* $112,000 ÷ 7,000 hours

2.

MyLife Chronicles Inc.
Production Budget
For the Year Ending December 31

Expected units to be sold	240,000
Desired ending inventory, December 31	18,800
Total units available	258,800
Estimated beginning inventory, January 1	(19,900)
Total units to be produced	238,900

3.

MyLife Chronicles Inc.
Direct Materials Purchases Budget
For the Year Ending December 31

Square yards required for production:	
Diaries (238,900 × 5 sq. yds.)	1,194,500
Desired ending inventory, December 31	30,800
Total square yards available	1,225,300
Estimated beginning inventory, January 1	(32,400)
Total square yards to be purchased	1,192,900
Unit price (per sq. yd.)	× $0.30
Total direct materials to be purchased	$ 357,870

4.

MyLife Chronicles Inc.
Direct Labor Cost Budget
For the Year Ending December 31

Hours required for assembly:	
Diaries (238,900 × 6 min.).....................................	1,433,400 min.
Convert minutes to hours....................................	÷ 60 min.
Assembly hours	23,890 hrs.
Hourly rate..	× $12
Total direct labor cost	$ 286,680

5.

MyLife Chronicles Inc.
Cost of Goods Sold Budget
For the Year Ending December 31

Finished goods inventory, January 1.........................			$ 25,000
Work in process inventory, January 1		$ 19,000	
Direct materials:			
Direct materials inventory, January 1 (32,400 × $0.30).	$ 9,720		
Direct materials purchases	357,870		
Cost of direct materials available for use	$367,590		
Less direct materials inventory, December 31			
(30,800 × $0.30)	(9,240)		
Cost of direct materials placed in production	$358,350		
Direct labor	286,680		
Factory overhead	197,100		
Total manufacturing costs.....................................		842,130	
Total work in process during period..........................		$861,130	
Work in process inventory, December 31.....................		(16,700)	
Cost of goods manufactured...................................			844,430
Cost of finished goods available for sale			$869,430
Finished goods inventory, December 31			(31,500)
Cost of goods sold...			$837,930

6.

	July
Collections from June sales (70% × $170,000).................	$119,000
Collections from July sales (30% × $200,000)	60,000
Total receipts from sales on account.........................	$179,000

Need more help? Watch step-by-step videos of how to compute answers to these Exercises in CengageNOWv2.

Problem

1.

	A	B	C	D
1		Cabot Co.		
2		Sales Budget		
3		For the Month Ending July 31		
4	Product	Unit Sales Volume	Unit Selling Price	Total Sales
5	Product K	40,000	$30.00	$1,200,000
6	Product L	20,000	65.00	1,300,000
7	Total revenue from sales			$2,500,000
8				

2.

	A	B	C
1	Cabot Co.		
2	Production Budget		
3	For the Month Ending July 31		
4		Units	
5		Product K	Product L
6	Sales	40,000	20,000
7	Desired inventories at July 31	2,500	2,000
8	Total units available	42,500	22,000
9	Estimated inventories, July 1	(3,000)	(2,700)
10	Total units to be produced	39,500	19,300
11			

3.

	A	B	C	D	E	F	G
1	Cabot Co.						
2	Direct Materials Purchases Budget						
3	For the Month Ending July 31						
4			Direct Materials				
5			Material A		Material B		Total
6	Units required for production:						
7	Product K (39,500 × lbs. per unit)		27,650	lbs.*	47,400	lbs.*	
8	Product L (19,300 × lbs. per unit)		67,550	**	34,740	**	
9	Desired units of inventory, July 31		3,000		2,500		
10	Total		98,200	lbs.	84,640	lbs.	
11	Estimated units of inventory, July 1		(4,000)		(3,500)		
12	Total units to be purchased		94,200	lbs.	81,140	lbs.	
13	Unit price		× $4.00		× $2.00		
14	Total direct materials to be purchased		$376,800		$162,280		$539,080
15							
16	*27,650 = 39,500 × 0.7 47,400 = 39,500 × 1.2						
17	**67,550 = 19,300 × 3.5 34,740 = 19,300 × 1.8						
18							

4.

	A	B	C	D	E	F	G
1	Cabot Co.						
2	Direct Labor Cost Budget						
3	For the Month Ending July 31						
4			Department 1		Department 2		Total
5	Hours required for production:						
6	Product K (39,500 × hrs. per unit)		15,800	*	5,925	*	
7	Product L (19,300 × hrs. per unit)		11,580	**	4,825	**	
8	Total		27,380		10,750		
9	Hourly rate		× $12		× $16		
10	Total direct labor cost		$328,560		$172,000		$500,560
11							
12	*15,800 = 39,500 × 0.4 5,925 = 39,500 × 0.15						
13	**11,580 = 19,300 × 0.6 4,825 = 19,300 × 0.25						
14							

5.

	A	B	C	D
1	Cabot Co.			
2	Cost of Goods Sold Budget			
3	For the Month Ending July 31			
4	Finished goods inventory, July 1			$ 145,500
5	Direct materials:			
6	Direct materials inventory, July 1 (Note A)		$ 23,000	
7	Direct materials purchases		539,080	
8	Cost of direct materials available for use		$562,080	
9	Direct materials inventory, July 31 (Note B)		(17,000)	
10	Cost of direct materials placed in production		$545,080	
11	Direct labor		500,560	
12	Factory overhead		299,000	
13	Cost of goods manufactured			1,344,640
14	Cost of finished goods available for sale			$1,490,140
15	Finished goods Inventory, July 31			(112,500)
16	Cost of goods sold			$1,377,640
17				
18	Note A:			
19	Material A 4,000 lbs. at $4.00 per lb.	$16,000		
20	Material B 3,500 lbs. at $2.00 per lb.	7,000		
21	Direct materials inventory, July 1	$23,000		
22				
23	Note B:			
24	Material A 3,000 lbs. at $4.00 per lb.	$12,000		
25	Material B 2,500 lbs. at $2.00 per lb.	5,000		
26	Direct materials inventory, July 31	$17,000		
27				

Discussion Questions

1. What are the three major objectives of budgeting?

2. Briefly describe the type of human behavior problems that might arise if budget goals are set too tightly.

3. What behavioral problems are associated with setting a budget too loosely?

4. What behavioral problems are associated with establishing conflicting goals within the budget?

5. Under what circumstances would a static budget be appropriate?

6. How do computerized budgeting systems aid firms in the budgeting process?

7. Why should the production requirements set forth in the production budget be carefully coordinated with the sales budget?

8. Why should the timing of direct materials purchases be closely coordinated with the production budget?

9. A. Discuss the purpose of the cash budget.
   B. If the cash for the first quarter of the fiscal year indicates excess cash at the end of each of the first two months, how might the excess cash be used?

10. Give an example of how the capital expenditures budget affects other operating budgets.

Basic Exercises

SHOW ME HOW

BE 7-1   Flexible budgeting   Obj. 2

At the beginning of the period, the Fabricating Department budgeted direct labor of $33,600 and equipment depreciation of $5,000 for 1,200 hours of production. The department actually completed 1,300 hours of production. Determine the budget for the department, assuming that it uses flexible budgeting.

SHOW ME HOW

BE 7-2   Production budget   Obj. 4

Pasadena Candle Inc. projected sales of 800,000 candles for the year. The estimated January 1 inventory is 35,000 units, and the desired December 31 inventory is 20,000 units. What is the budgeted production (in units) for the year?

SHOW ME HOW

BE 7-3   Direct materials purchases budget   Obj. 4

Pasadena Candle Inc. budgeted production of 785,000 candles for the year. Wax is required to produce a candle. Assume 10 ounces of wax is required for each candle. The estimated January 1 wax inventory is 16,000 pounds. The desired December 31 wax inventory is 12,500 pounds. If candle wax costs $1.24 per pound, determine the direct materials purchases budget for the year.

SHOW ME HOW

BE 7-4   Direct labor cost budget   Obj. 4

Pasadena Candle Inc. budgeted production of 785,000 candles for the year. Each candle requires molding. Assume that six minutes are required to mold each candle. If molding labor costs $18 per hour, determine the direct labor cost budget for the year.

SHOW ME HOW

BE 7-5   Cost of goods sold budget   Obj. 4

Prepare a cost of goods sold budget for Pasadena Candle Inc. using the information in Basic Exercises 3 and 4. Assume the estimated inventories on January 1 for finished goods and work in process were $200,000 and $41,250, respectively. Also assume the desired inventories on December 31 for finished goods and work in process were $120,000 and $28,500, respectively. Factory overhead was budgeted at $300,000.

SHOW ME HOW

BE 7-6   Cash budget   Obj. 5

Pasadena Candle Inc. pays 40% of its purchases on account in the month of the purchase and 60% in the month following the purchase. If purchases are budgeted to be $40,000 for August and $36,000 for September, what are the budgeted cash payments for purchases on account for September?

Exercises

✔ A. December 31 cash
balance, $3,150

SHOW ME HOW

EXCEL TEMPLATE

EX 7-1   Personal budget   Obj. 2, 5

At the beginning of the school year, Priscilla Wescott decided to prepare a cash budget for the months of September, October, November, and December. The budget must plan for enough cash on December 31 to pay the spring semester tuition, which is the same as the fall tuition. The following information relates to the budget:

Cash balance, September 1 (from a summer job)	$6,000
Purchase season football tickets in September	150
Additional entertainment for each month	250
Pay fall semester tuition in September	3,500
Pay rent at the beginning of each month	450
Pay for food each month	400
Pay apartment deposit on September 2 (to be returned December 15)	450
Part-time job earnings each month (net of taxes)	1,300

A. Prepare a cash budget for September, October, November, and December.

B. Are the four monthly budgets that are presented prepared as static budgets or flexible budgets?

C. ➤ What are the budget implications for Priscilla Wescott?

EX 7-2 Flexible budget for selling and administrative expenses for a service company

Obj. 2, 4

✔ Total selling and administrative expenses at $400,000 sales, $332,500

SHOW ME HOW

EXCEL TEMPLATE

Cloud Productivity Inc. uses flexible budgets that are based on the following data:

Sales commissions	14% of sales
Advertising expense	18% of sales
Miscellaneous administrative expense	$6,500 per month plus 12% of sales
Office salaries expense	$28,000 per month
Customer support expenses	$12,000 per month plus 20% of sales
Research and development expense	$30,000 per month

Prepare a flexible selling and administrative expenses budget for March for sales volumes of $400,000, $500,000, and $600,000.

EX 7-3 Static budget versus flexible budget

Obj. 2, 4

✔ B. Excess of actual cost over budget for March, $45,750

SHOW ME HOW

EXCEL TEMPLATE

The production supervisor of the Machining Department for Niland Company agreed to the following monthly static budget for the upcoming year:

Niland Company
Machining Department
Monthly Production Budget

Wages	$1,125,000
Utilities	90,000
Depreciation	50,000
Total	$1,265,000

The actual amount spent and the actual units produced in the first three months in the Machining Department were as follows:

	Amount Spent	Units Produced
January	$1,100,000	80,000
February	1,200,000	90,000
March	1,250,000	95,000

The Machining Department supervisor has been very pleased with this performance because actual expenditures for January–March have been significantly less than the monthly static budget of $1,265,000. However, the plant manager believes that the budget should not remain fixed for every month but should "flex" or adjust to the volume of work that is produced

(Continued)

in the Machining Department. Additional budget information for the Machining Department is as follows:

Wages per hour	$15.00
Utility cost per direct labor hour	$1.20
Direct labor hours per unit	0.75
Planned monthly unit production	100,000

A. Prepare a flexible budget for the actual units produced for January, February, and March in the Machining Department. Assume depreciation is a fixed cost.

B. ━━━▶ Compare the flexible budget with the actual expenditures for the first three months. What does this comparison suggest?

EX 7-4 Flexible budget for Assembly Department

Obj. 2

✔ Total department cost at 25,000 units, $386,250

 SHOW ME HOW

 EXCEL TEMPLATE

 REAL WORLD

Steelcase Inc. is one of the largest manufacturers of office furniture in the United States. In Grand Rapids, Michigan, it assembles filing cabinets in an Assembly Department. Assume the following information for the Assembly Department:

Direct labor per filing cabinet	15 minutes
Supervisor salaries	$200,000 per month
Depreciation.	$30,000 per month
Direct labor rate.	$25 per hour

Prepare a flexible budget for 25,000, 40,000, and 55,000 filing cabinets for the month of March in the Assembly Department, similar to Exhibit 5.

EX 7-5 Production budget

Obj. 4

✔ Bath scale total units to be produced, 144,500 units

 SHOW ME HOW

Weightless Inc. produces a Bath and Gym version of its popular electronic scale. The anticipated unit sales for the scales by sales region are as follows:

	Bath Scale	Gym Scale
East Region unit sales	55,000	30,000
West Region unit sales	95,000	60,000
Total	150,000	90,000

The finished goods inventory estimated for October 1, for the Bath and Gym scale models is 18,000 and 10,000 units, respectively. The desired finished goods inventory for October 31 for the Bath and Gym scale models is 12,500 and 8,000 units, respectively.

Prepare a production budget for the Bath and Gym scales for the month ended October 31.

EX 7-6 Sales and production budgets

Obj. 4

✔ B. Model Rumble total production, 25,750 units

 SHOW ME HOW

 EXCEL TEMPLATE

Sonic Inc. manufactures two models of speakers, Rumble and Thunder. Based on the following production and sales data for June, prepare (A) a sales budget and (B) a production budget:

	Rumble	Thunder
Estimated inventory (units), June 1	750	300
Desired inventory (units), June 30	500	250
Expected sales volume (units):		
Midwest Region.	12,000	3,500
South Region	14,000	4,000
Unit sales price.	$60	$90

EX 7-7 Professional fees earned budget for a service company

Obj. 4

✔ Total professional fees earned, $10,270,000

Rollins and Cohen, CPAs, offer three types of services to clients: auditing, tax, and small business accounting. Based on experience and projected growth, the following billable hours have been estimated for the year ending December 31, 20Y8:

	Billable Hours
Audit Department:	
Staff..	22,400
Partners...	7,900
Tax Department:	
Staff..	13,200
Partners...	5,500
Small Business Accounting Department:	
Staff..	3,000
Partners...	600

The average billing rate for staff is $150 per hour, and the average billing rate for partners is $320 per hour. Prepare a professional fees earned budget for Rollins and Cohen, CPAs, for the year ending December 31, 20Y8, using the following column headings and showing the estimated professional fees by type of service rendered:

Billable Hours	Hourly Rate	Total Revenue

EX 7-8   Professional labor cost budget for a service company   Obj. 4

✔ Staff total labor cost, $1,737,000

Based on the data in Exercise 7 and assuming that the average compensation per hour for staff is $45 and for partners is $140, prepare a professional labor cost budget for each department for Rollins and Cohen, CPAs, for the year ending December 31, 20Y8. Use the following column headings:

Staff	Partners

EX 7-9   Direct materials purchases budget   Obj. 4

✔ Total cheese purchases, $35,448

Romano's Frozen Pizza Inc. has determined from its production budget the following estimated production volumes for 12" and 16" frozen pizzas for September:

SHOW ME HOW   EXCEL TEMPLATE

	Units	
	12" Pizza	16" Pizza
Budgeted production volume	5,300	8,900

There are three direct materials used in producing the two types of pizza. The quantities of direct materials expected to be used for each pizza are as follows:

	12" Pizza	16" Pizza
Direct materials:		
Dough	0.70 lb. per unit	1.50 lbs. per unit
Tomato	0.40	0.70
Cheese	0.60	1.30

In addition, Romano's has determined the following information about each material:

	Dough	Tomato	Cheese
Estimated inventory, September 1	520 lbs.	200 lbs.	295 lbs.
Desired inventory, September 30	580 lbs.	185 lbs.	315 lbs.
Price per pound	$0.80	$1.60	$2.40

Prepare September's direct materials purchases budget for Romano's Frozen Pizza Inc.

EX 7-10   Direct materials purchases budget   Obj. 4

✔ Concentrate budgeted purchases, $47,400

REAL WORLD

Coca-Cola Enterprises is the largest bottler of Coca-Cola® in Western Europe. The company purchases Coke® and Sprite® concentrate from **The Coca-Cola Company**, dilutes and mixes the concentrate with carbonated water, and then fills the blended beverage into cans or plastic

(Continued)

two-liter bottles. Assume that the estimated production for Coke and Sprite two-liter bottles at the Wakefield, UK, bottling plant is as follows for the month of May:

Coke	153,000 two-liter bottles
Sprite	86,500 two-liter bottles

In addition, assume that the concentrate costs $75 per pound for both Coke and Sprite and is used at a rate of 0.15 pound per 100 liters of carbonated water in blending Coke and 0.10 pound per 100 liters of carbonated water in blending Sprite. Assume that two liters of carbonated water are used for each two-liter bottle of finished product. Assume further that two-liter bottles cost $0.08 per bottle and carbonated water costs $0.06 per liter.

Prepare a direct materials purchases budget for May, assuming inventories are ignored, because there are no changes between beginning and ending inventories for concentrate, bottles, and carbonated water.

EX 7-11 Direct materials purchases budget Obj. 4

✔ Total steel belt purchases, $291,200

EXCEL TEMPLATE

Anticipated sales for Safety Grip Company were 42,000 passenger car tires and 19,000 truck tires. Rubber and steel belts are used in producing passenger car and truck tires as follows:

	Passenger Car	Truck
Rubber	35 lbs. per unit	78 lbs. per unit
Steel belts	5 lbs. per unit	8 lbs. per unit

The purchase prices of rubber and steel are $1.20 and $0.80 per pound, respectively. The desired ending inventories of rubber and steel belts are 40,000 and 10,000 pounds, respectively. The estimated beginning inventories for rubber and steel belts are 46,000 and 8,000 pounds, respectively.

Prepare a direct materials purchases budget for Safety Grip Company for the year ended December 31, 20Y9.

EX 7-12 Direct labor cost budget Obj. 4

✔ Total direct labor cost, Assembly, $31,080

Ace Racket Company manufactures two types of tennis rackets, the Junior and Pro Striker models. The production budget for July for the two rackets is as follows:

	Junior	Pro Striker
Production budget	1,500 units	6,200 units

Both rackets are produced in two departments, Forming and Assembly. The direct labor hours required for each racket are estimated as follows:

	Forming Department	Assembly Department
Junior	0.16 hr. per unit	0.24 hr. per unit
Pro Striker	0.20 hr. per unit	0.30 hr. per unit

The direct labor rate for each department is as follows:

Forming Department	$18 per hour
Assembly Department	$14 per hour

Prepare the direct labor cost budget for July.

EX 7-13 Production and direct labor cost budgets Obj. 4

✔ A. Total production of 501 Jeans, 53,300

EXCEL TEMPLATE   REAL WORLD

Levi Strauss & Co. manufactures slacks and jeans under a variety of brand names, such as Dockers® and 501 Jeans®. Slacks and jeans are assembled by a variety of different sewing operations. Assume that the sales budget for Dockers and 501 Jeans shows estimated sales of

23,600 and 53,100 pairs, respectively, for May. The finished goods inventory is assumed as follows:

	Dockers	501 Jeans
May 1 estimated inventory	670	1,660
May 31 desired inventory	420	1,860

Assume the following direct labor data per 10 pairs of Dockers and 501 Jeans for four different sewing operations:

	Direct Labor per 10 Pairs	
	Dockers	501 Jeans
Inseam	18 minutes	9 minutes
Outerseam	20	14
Pockets	6	9
Zipper	12	6
Total	56 minutes	38 minutes

A. Prepare a production budget for May. Prepare the budget in two columns: Dockers® and 501 Jeans®.

B. Prepare the May direct labor cost budget for the four sewing operations, assuming a $13 wage per hour for the inseam and outerseam sewing operations and a $15 wage per hour for the pocket and zipper sewing operations. Prepare the direct labor cost budget in four columns: inseam, outerseam, pockets, and zipper.

EX 7-14 Factory overhead cost budget
Obj. 4

✔ Total variable factory overhead costs, $268,000

EXCEL TEMPLATE

Sweet Tooth Candy Company budgeted the following costs for anticipated production for August:

Advertising expenses	$232,000	Production supervisor wages	$135,000
Manufacturing supplies	14,000	Production control wages	32,000
Power and light	48,000	Executive officer salaries	310,000
Sales commissions	298,000	Materials management wages	39,000
Factory insurance	30,000	Factory depreciation	22,000

Prepare a factory overhead cost budget, separating variable and fixed costs. Assume that factory insurance and depreciation are the only fixed factory costs.

EX 7-15 Cost of goods sold budget
Obj. 4

✔ Cost of goods sold, $3,788,100

EXCEL TEMPLATE

Delaware Chemical Company uses oil to produce two types of plastic products, P1 and P2. Delaware budgeted 35,000 barrels of oil for purchase in June for $90 per barrel. Direct labor budgeted in the chemical process was $240,000 for June. Factory overhead was budgeted at $400,000 during June. The inventories on June 1 were estimated to be:

Oil	$15,200
P1	8,300
P2	8,600
Work in process	12,900

The desired inventories on June 30 were:

Oil	$16,100
P1	9,400
P2	7,900
Work in process	13,500

Use the preceding information to prepare a cost of goods sold budget for June.

EX 7-16　Cost of goods sold budget

Obj. 4

✔ Cost of goods sold, $488,360

The controller of MingWare Ceramics Inc. wishes to prepare a cost of goods sold budget for September. The controller assembled the following information for constructing the cost of goods sold budget:

Direct materials:	Enamel	Paint	Porcelain	Total
Total direct materials purchases budgeted for September	$36,780	$6,130	$145,500	$188,410
Estimated inventory, September 1	1,240	950	4,250	6,440
Desired inventory, September 30	1,890	1,070	5,870	8,830

Direct labor cost:	Kiln Department	Decorating Department	Total
Total direct labor cost budgeted for September	$47,900	$145,700	$193,600

Finished goods inventories:	Dish	Bowl	Figurine	Total
Estimated inventory, September 1	$5,780	$3,080	$2,640	$11,500
Desired inventory, September 30	3,710	2,670	3,290	9,670

Work in process inventories:	
Estimated inventory, September 1	$3,400
Desired inventory, September 30	1,990

Budgeted factory overhead costs for September:	
Indirect factory wages	$ 81,900
Depreciation of plant and equipment	14,300
Power and light	5,200
Indirect materials	4,100
Total	$105,500

Use the preceding information to prepare a cost of goods sold budget for September.

EX 7-17　Schedule of cash collections of accounts receivable

Obj. 5

✔ Total cash collected in July, $163,050

Pet Place Supplies Inc., a pet wholesale supplier, was organized on May 1. Projected sales for each of the first three months of operations are as follows:

May	$134,000
June	155,000
July	169,000

SHOW ME HOW

EXCEL TEMPLATE

All sales are on account. Sixty-five percent of sales are expected to be collected in the month of the sale, 30% in the month following the sale, and the remainder in the second month following the sale.

Prepare a schedule indicating cash collections from sales for May, June, and July.

EX 7-18　Schedule of cash collections of accounts receivable

Obj. 5

✔ Total cash collected in October, $62,550

OfficeMart Inc. has "cash and carry" customers and credit customers. OfficeMart estimates that 25% of monthly sales are to cash customers, while the remaining sales are to credit customers. Of the credit customers, 30% pay their accounts in the month of sale, while the remaining 70% pay their accounts in the month following the month of sale. Projected sales for the next three months are as follows:

October	$58,000
November	65,000
December	72,000

The Accounts Receivable balance on September 30 was $35,000.

Prepare a schedule of cash collections from sales for October, November, and December.

EX 7-19 Schedule of cash payments for a service company

Obj. 5

✔ Total cash payments in May, $58,490

Horizon Financial Inc. was organized on February 28. Projected selling and administrative expenses for each of the first three months of operations are as follows:

March	$52,400
April	64,200
May	68,900

Depreciation, insurance, and property taxes represent $9,000 of the estimated monthly expenses. The annual insurance premium was paid on February 28, and property taxes for the year will be paid in June. Seventy percent of the remainder of the expenses are expected to be paid in the month in which they are incurred, with the balance to be paid in the following month.

Prepare a schedule of cash payments for selling and administrative expenses for March, April, and May.

EX 7-20 Schedule of cash payments for a service company

Obj. 5

✔ Total cash payments in March, $113,740

EXCEL TEMPLATE

EastGate Physical Therapy Inc. is planning its cash payments for operations for the first quarter (January–March). The Accrued Expenses Payable balance on January 1 is $15,000. The budgeted expenses for the next three months are as follows:

	January	February	March
Salaries	$56,900	$ 68,100	$ 72,200
Utilities	2,400	2,600	2,500
Other operating expenses	32,300	41,500	44,700
Total	$91,600	$112,200	$119,400

Other operating expenses include $3,000 of monthly depreciation expense and $500 of monthly insurance expense that was prepaid for the year on May 1 of the previous year. Of the remaining expenses, 70% are paid in the month in which they are incurred, with the remainder paid in the following month. The Accrued Expenses Payable balance on January 1 relates to the expenses incurred in December.

Prepare a schedule of cash payments for operations for January, February, and March.

EX 7-21 Capital expenditures budget

Obj. 5

✔ Total capital expenditures in 20Y6, $4,000,000

EXCEL TEMPLATE

On January 1, 20Y6, the controller of Omicron Inc. is planning capital expenditures for the years 20Y6–20Y9. The following interviews helped the controller collect the necessary information for the capital expenditures budget:

Director of Facilities: A construction contract was signed in late 20Y5 for the construction of a new factory building at a contract cost of $10,000,000. The construction is scheduled to begin in 20Y6 and be completed in 20Y9.

Vice President of Manufacturing: Once the new factory building is finished, we plan to purchase $1.5 million in equipment in late 20Y7. I expect that an additional $200,000 will be needed early in the following year (20Y8) to test and install the equipment before we can begin production. If sales continue to grow, I expect we'll need to invest another $1,000,000 in equipment in 20Y9.

Chief Operating Officer: We have really been growing lately. I wouldn't be surprised if we need to expand the size of our new factory building in 20Y9 by at least 35%. Fortunately, we expect inflation to have minimal impact on construction costs over the next four years. Additionally, I would expect the cost of the expansion to be proportional to the size of the expansion.

Director of Information Systems: We need to upgrade our information systems to wireless network technology. It doesn't make sense to do this until after the new factory building is completed and producing product. During 20Y8, once the factory is up and running, we should equip the whole facility with wireless technology. I think it would cost us $800,000 today to install the technology. However, prices have been dropping by 25% per year, so it should be less expensive at a later date.

Chief Financial Officer: I am excited about our long-term prospects. My only short-term concern is managing our cash flow while we expend the $4,000,000 of construction costs in 20Y6 and $6,000,000 in 20Y7 on the portion of the new factory building scheduled to be completed in 20Y9.

Use this interview information to prepare a capital expenditures budget for Omicron Inc. for the years 20Y6–20Y9.

Problems: Series A

✔ 3. Total revenue from
sales, $878,403

EXCEL TEMPLATE

PR 7-1A   Forecast sales volume and sales budget   Obj. 4

For 20Y8, Raphael Frame Company prepared the sales budget that follows.

At the end of December 20Y8, the following unit sales data were reported for the year:

	Unit Sales	
	8" × 10" Frame	12" × 16" Frame
East	8,755	3,686
Central	6,510	3,090
West	12,348	5,616

Raphael Frame Company
Sales Budget
For the Year Ending December 31, 20Y8

Product and Area	Unit Sales Volume	Unit Selling Price	Total Sales
8" × 10" Frame:			
East	8,500	$16	$136,000
Central	6,200	16	99,200
West	12,600	16	201,600
Total	27,300		$436,800
12" × 16" Frame:			
East	3,800	$30	$114,000
Central	3,000	30	90,000
West	5,400	30	162,000
Total	12,200		$366,000
Total revenue from sales			$802,800

For the year ending December 31, 20Y9, unit sales are expected to follow the patterns established during the year ending December 31, 20Y8. The unit selling price for the 8" × 10" frame is expected to increase to $17 and the unit selling price for the 12" × 16" frame is expected to increase to $32, effective January 1, 20Y9.

Instructions

1. Compute the increase or decrease of actual unit sales for the year ended December 31, 20Y8, over budget. Place your answers in a columnar table with the following format:

	Unit Sales, Year Ended 20Y8		Increase (Decrease) Actual Over Budget	
	Budget	Actual Sales	Amount	Percent
8" × 10" Frame:				
East				
Central				
West				
12" × 16" Frame:				
East				
Central				
West				

2. Assuming that the increase or decrease in actual sales to budget indicated in part (1) is to continue in 20Y9, compute the unit sales volume to be used for preparing the sales budget for the year ending December 31, 20Y9. Place your answers in a columnar table similar to that in part (1) but with the following column heads. Round budgeted units to the nearest unit.

20Y8 Actual Units	Percentage Increase (Decrease)	20Y9 Budgeted Units (rounded)

3. Prepare a sales budget for the year ending December 31, 20Y9.

PR 7-2A Sales, production, direct materials purchases, and direct labor cost budgets Obj. 4

✔ 3. Total direct
materials purchases,
$771,490

EXCEL TEMPLATE

The budget director of Gourmet Grill Company requests estimates of sales, production, and other operating data from the various administrative units every month. Selected information concerning sales and production for July is summarized as follows:

A. Estimated sales for July by sales territory:

Maine:

Backyard Chef...	310 units at $700 per unit
Master Chef	150 units at $1,200 per unit

Vermont:

Backyard Chef...	240 units at $750 per unit
Master Chef	110 units at $1,300 per unit

New Hampshire:

Backyard Chef...	360 units at $750 per unit
Master Chef	180 units at $1,400 per unit

B. Estimated inventories at July 1:

Direct materials:		Finished products:	
Grates.........................	290 units	Backyard Chef	30 units
Stainless steel.................	1,500 lbs.	Master Chef..............	32 units
Burner subassemblies	170 units		
Shelves......................	340 units		

C. Desired Inventories at July 31:

Direct materials:		Finished products:	
Grates.........................	340 units	Backyard Chef	40 units
Stainless steel.................	1,800 lbs.	Master Chef..............	22 units
Burner subassemblies	155 units		
Shelves......................	315 units		

D. Direct materials used in production:

In manufacture of Backyard Chef:

Grates..	3 units per unit of product
Stainless steel..	24 lbs. per unit of product
Burner subassemblies	2 units per unit of product
Shelves...	4 units per unit of product

In manufacture of Master Chef:

Grates..	6 units per unit of product
Stainless steel..	42 lbs. per unit of product
Burner subassemblies	4 units per unit of product
Shelves...	5 units per unit of product

E. Anticipated purchase price for direct materials:

Grates.....................	$15 per unit	Burner subassemblies	$110 per unit
Stainless steel..............	$6 per lb.	Shelves......................	$10 per unit

F. Direct labor requirements:

Backyard Chef:

Stamping Department..	0.50 hr. at $17 per hr.
Forming Department...	0.60 hr. at $15 per hr.
Assembly Department..	1.00 hr. at $14 per hr.

Master Chef:

Stamping Department..	0.60 hr. at $17 per hr.
Forming Department...	0.80 hr. at $15 per hr.
Assembly Department..	1.50 hrs. at $14 per hr.

(Continued)

Instructions
1. Prepare a sales budget for July.
2. Prepare a production budget for July.
3. Prepare a direct materials purchases budget for July.
4. Prepare a direct labor cost budget for July.

PR 7-3A   Budgeted income statement and supporting budgets   Obj. 4

✔ 4. Total direct labor cost in Fabrication Dept., $29,216

EXCEL TEMPLATE

The budget director of Feathered Friends Inc., with the assistance of the controller, treasurer, production manager, and sales manager, has gathered the following data for use in developing the budgeted income statement for December:

A. Estimated sales for December:

Bird house	3,200 units at $50 per unit
Bird feeder	3,000 units at $70 per unit

B. Estimated inventories at December 1:

Direct materials:		Finished products:	
Wood	200 ft.	Bird house	320 units at $27 per unit
Plastic........	240 lbs.	Bird feeder.......	270 units at $40 per unit

C. Desired inventories at December 31:

Direct materials:		Finished products:	
Wood	220 ft.	Bird house	290 units at $27 per unit
Plastic........	200 lbs.	Bird feeder.......	250 units at $41 per unit

D. Direct materials used in production:

In manufacture of Bird House:		In manufacture of Bird Feeder:	
Wood	0.80 ft. per unit of product	Wood	1.20 ft. per unit of product
Plastic............	0.50 lb. per unit of product	Plastic...........	0.75 lb. per unit of product

E. Anticipated cost of purchases and beginning and ending inventory of direct materials:

Wood	$7.00 per ft.	Plastic...........	$1.00 per lb.

F. Direct labor requirements:

Bird House:

Fabrication Department	0.20 hr. at $16 per hr.
Assembly Department..	0.30 hr. at $12 per hr.

Bird Feeder:

Fabrication Department	0.40 hr. at $16 per hr.
Assembly Department..	0.35 hr. at $12 per hr.

G. Estimated factory overhead costs for December:

Indirect factory wages	$75,000	Power and light	$6,000
Depreciation of plant and equipment	23,000	Insurance and property tax	5,000

H. Estimated operating expenses for December:

Sales salaries expense	$70,000
Advertising expense	18,000
Office salaries expense	21,000
Depreciation expense—office equipment	600
Telephone expense—selling	550
Telephone expense—administrative	250
Travel expense—selling	4,000
Office supplies expense	200
Miscellaneous administrative expense	400

I. Estimated other income and expense for December:

| Interest revenue | $200 |
| Interest expense | 122 |

J. Estimated tax rate: 30%

Instructions

1. Prepare a sales budget for December.

2. Prepare a production budget for December.

3. Prepare a direct materials purchases budget for December.

4. Prepare a direct labor cost budget for December.

5. Prepare a factory overhead cost budget for December.

6. Prepare a cost of goods sold budget for December. Work in process at the beginning of December is estimated to be $29,000, and work in process at the end of December is estimated to be $35,400.

7. Prepare a selling and administrative expenses budget for December.

8. Prepare a budgeted income statement for December.

PR 7-4A   Cash budget   **Obj. 5**

✔ 1. November
deficiency, $8,500

The controller of Bridgeport Housewares Inc. instructs you to prepare a monthly cash budget for the next three months. You are presented with the following budget information:

SHOW ME HOW   EXCEL TEMPLATE

	September	October	November
Sales	$250,000	$300,000	$315,000
Manufacturing costs.	150,000	180,000	185,000
Selling and administrative expenses	42,000	48,000	51,000
Capital expenditures			200,000

The company expects to sell about 10% of its merchandise for cash. Of sales on account, 70% are expected to be collected in the month following the sale and the remainder the following month (second month following sale). Depreciation, insurance, and property tax expense represent $50,000 of the estimated monthly manufacturing costs. The annual insurance premium is paid in January, and the annual property taxes are paid in December. Of the remainder of the manufacturing costs, 80% are expected to be paid in the month in which they are incurred and the balance in the following month.

Current assets as of September 1 include cash of $40,000, marketable securities of $75,000, and accounts receivable of $300,000 ($60,000 from July sales and $240,000 from August sales). Sales on account for July and August were $200,000 and $240,000, respectively. Current liabilities as of September 1 include $40,000 of accounts payable incurred in August for manufacturing costs. All selling and administrative expenses are paid in cash in the period they are incurred. An estimated income tax payment of $55,000 will be made in October. Bridgeport's regular quarterly dividend of $25,000 is expected to be declared in October and paid in November. Management desires to maintain a minimum cash balance of $50,000.

Instructions

1. Prepare a monthly cash budget and supporting schedules for September, October, and November.

2. ━━━▶ On the basis of the cash budget prepared in part (1), what recommendation should be made to the controller?

PR 7-5A Budgeted income statement and balance sheet

Obj. 4, 5

✔ 1. Budgeted net income, $96,600

EXCEL TEMPLATE

As a preliminary to requesting budget estimates of sales, costs, and expenses for the fiscal year beginning January 1, 20Y9, the following tentative trial balance as of December 31, 20Y8, is prepared by the Accounting Department of Regina Soap Co.:

Cash	$ 85,000	
Accounts Receivable	125,600	
Finished Goods	69,300	
Work in Process	32,500	
Materials	48,900	
Prepaid Expenses	2,600	
Plant and Equipment	325,000	
Accumulated Depreciation—Plant and Equipment		$156,200
Accounts Payable		62,000
Common Stock, $10 par		180,000
Retained Earnings		290,700
	$688,900	$688,900

Factory output and sales for 20Y9 are expected to total 200,000 units of product, which are to be sold at $5.00 per unit. The quantities and costs of the inventories at December 31, 20Y9, are expected to remain unchanged from the balances at the beginning of the year.

Budget estimates of manufacturing costs and operating expenses for the year are summarized as follows:

	Estimated Costs and Expenses	
	Fixed (Total for Year)	Variable (Per Unit Sold)
Cost of goods manufactured and sold:		
Direct materials	—	$1.10
Direct labor	—	0.65
Factory overhead:		
Depreciation of plant and equipment	$40,000	—
Other factory overhead	12,000	0.40
Selling expenses:		
Sales salaries and commissions	46,000	0.45
Advertising	64,000	—
Miscellaneous selling expense	6,000	0.25
Administrative expenses:		
Office and officers salaries	72,400	0.12
Supplies	5,000	0.10
Miscellaneous administrative expense	4,000	0.05

Balances of accounts receivable, prepaid expenses, and accounts payable at the end of the year are not expected to differ significantly from the beginning balances. Federal income tax of $30,000 on 20Y9 taxable income will be paid during 20Y9. Regular quarterly cash dividends of $0.15 per share are expected to be declared and paid in March, June, September, and December on 18,000 shares of common stock outstanding. It is anticipated that fixed assets will be purchased for $75,000 cash in May.

Instructions

1. Prepare a budgeted income statement for 20Y9.

2. Prepare a budgeted balance sheet as of December 31, 20Y9, with supporting calculations.

Problems: Series B

✔ 3. Total revenue from
sales, $2,148,950

EXCEL TEMPLATE

PR 7-1B   Forecast sales volume and sales budget

Obj. 4

Sentinel Systems Inc. prepared the following sales budget for 20Y8:

Sentinel Systems Inc.
Sales Budget
For the Year Ending December 31, 20Y8

Product and Area	Unit Sales Volume	Unit Selling Price	Total Sales
Home Alert System:			
United States	1,700	$200	$ 340,000
Europe	580	200	116,000
Asia	450	200	90,000
Total	2,730		$ 546,000
Business Alert System:			
United States	980	$750	$ 735,000
Europe	350	750	262,500
Asia	240	750	180,000
Total	1,570		$1,177,500
Total revenue from sales			$1,723,500

At the end of December 20Y8, the following unit sales data were reported for the year:

	Unit Sales	
	Home Alert System	Business Alert System
United States	1,734	1,078
Europe	609	329
Asia	432	252

For the year ending December 31, 20Y9, unit sales are expected to follow the patterns established during the year ending December 31, 20Y8. The unit selling price for the Home Alert System is expected to increase to $250, and the unit selling price for the Business Alert System is expected to be increased to $820, effective January 1, 20Y9.

Instructions

1. Compute the increase or decrease of actual unit sales for the year ended December 31, 20Y8, over budget. Place your answers in a columnar table with the following format:

	Unit Sales, Year Ended 20Y8		Increase (Decrease) Actual Over Budget	
	Budget	Actual Sales	Amount	Percent
Home Alert System:				
United States				
Europe				
Asia				
Business Alert System:				
United States				
Europe				
Asia				

(Continued)

2. Assuming that the increase or decrease in actual sales to budget indicated in part (1) is to continue in 20Y9, compute the unit sales volume to be used for preparing the sales budget for the year ending December 31, 20Y9. Place your answers in a columnar table similar to that in part (1) but with the following column heads. Round budgeted units to the nearest unit.

20Y8 Actual Units	Percentage Increase (Decrease)	20Y9 Budgeted Units (rounded)

3. Prepare a sales budget for the year ending December 31, 20Y9.

PR 7-2B   Sales, production, direct materials purchases, and direct labor cost budgets   Obj. 4

✔ 3. Total direct materials purchases, $987,478

EXCEL TEMPLATE

The budget director of Royal Furniture Company requests estimates of sales, production, and other operating data from the various administrative units every month. Selected information concerning sales and production for February is summarized as follows:

A. Estimated sales of King and Prince chairs for February by sales territory:

Northern Domestic:

King...	610 units at $780 per unit
Prince..	750 units at $550 per unit

Southern Domestic:

King...	340 units at $780 per unit
Prince..	440 units at $550 per unit

International:

King...	360 units at $850 per unit
Prince..	290 units at $600 per unit

B. Estimated inventories at February 1:

Direct materials:		Finished products:	
Fabric.....................	420 sq. yds.	King....................	90 units
Wood	580 linear ft.	Prince	25 units
Filler	250 cu. ft.		
Springs....................	660 units		

C. Desired inventories at February 28:

Direct materials:		Finished products:	
Fabric.....................	390 sq. yds.	King....................	80 units
Wood	650 linear ft.	Prince	35 units
Filler	300 cu. ft.		
Springs....................	540 units		

D. Direct materials used in production:

In manufacture of King:

Fabric	6.0 sq. yds. per unit of product
Wood	38 linear ft. per unit of product
Filler	4.2 cu. ft. per unit of product
Springs.....................................	16 units per unit of product

In manufacture of Prince:

Fabric	4.0 sq. yds. per unit of product
Wood	26 linear ft. per unit of product
Filler	3.4 cu. ft. per unit of product
Springs.....................................	12 units per unit of product

E. Anticipated purchase price for direct materials:

Fabric	$12.00 per sq. yd.	Filler	$3.00 per cu. ft.
Wood	7.00 per linear ft.	Springs................	4.50 per unit

F. Direct labor requirements:

King:

Framing Department...	1.2 hrs. at $12 per hr.
Cutting Department...	0.5 hr. at $14 per hr.
Upholstery Department..	0.8 hr. at $15 per hr.

Prince:

Framing Department...	1.0 hr. at $12 per hr.
Cutting Department...	0.4 hr. at $14 per hr.
Upholstery Department..	0.6 hr. at $15 per hr.

Instructions

1. Prepare a sales budget for February.

2. Prepare a production budget for February.

3. Prepare a direct materials purchases budget for February.

4. Prepare a direct labor cost budget for February.

PR 7-3B   Budgeted income statement and supporting budgets   Obj. 4

✔ 4. Total direct labor cost in Assembly Dept., $171,766

EXCEL TEMPLATE

The budget director of Gold Medal Athletic Co., with the assistance of the controller, treasurer, production manager, and sales manager, has gathered the following data for use in developing the budgeted income statement for March:

A. Estimated sales for March:

Batting helmet............................	1,200 units at $40 per unit
Football helmet	6,500 units at $160 per unit

B. Estimated inventories at March 1:

Direct materials:		Finished products:	
Plastic.............	90 lbs.	Batting helmet........	40 units at $25 per unit
Foam lining........	80 lbs.	Football helmet	240 units at $77 per unit

C. Desired inventories at March 31:

Direct materials:		Finished products:	
Plastic.............	50 lbs.	Batting helmet........	50 units at $25 per unit
Foam lining........	65 lbs.	Football helmet	220 units at $78 per unit

D. Direct materials used in production:

In manufacture of batting helmet:

Plastic....................................	1.2 lbs. per unit of product
Foam lining...............................	0.5 lb. per unit of product

In manufacture of football helmet:

Plastic....................................	3.5 lbs. per unit of product
Foam lining...............................	1.5 lbs. per unit of product

E. Anticipated cost of purchases and beginning and ending inventory of direct materials:

Plastic....................................	$6 per lb.
Foam lining...............................	$4 per lb.

F. Direct labor requirements:

Batting helmet:

Molding Department.....................	0.2 hr. at $20 per hr.
Assembly Department....................	0.5 hr. at $14 per hr.

Football helmet:

Molding Department.....................	0.5 hr. at $20 per hr.
Assembly Department....................	1.8 hrs. at $14 per hr.

(Continued)

G. Estimated factory overhead costs for March:

Indirect factory wages	$86,000	Power and light	$4,000
Depreciation of plant and equipment	12,000	Insurance and property tax	2,300

H. Estimated operating expenses for March:

Sales salaries expense	$184,300
Advertising expense	87,200
Office salaries expense	32,400
Depreciation expense—office equipment	3,800
Telephone expense—selling	5,800
Telephone expense—administrative	1,200
Travel expense—selling	9,000
Office supplies expense	1,100
Miscellaneous administrative expense	1,000

I. Estimated other income and expense for March:

Interest revenue	$940
Interest expense	872

J. Estimated tax rate: 30%

Instructions

1. Prepare a sales budget for March.

2. Prepare a production budget for March.

3. Prepare a direct materials purchases budget for March.

4. Prepare a direct labor cost budget for March.

5. Prepare a factory overhead cost budget for March.

6. Prepare a cost of goods sold budget for March. Work in process at the beginning of March is estimated to be $15,300, and work in process at the end of March is desired to be $14,800.

7. Prepare a selling and administrative expenses budget for March.

8. Prepare a budgeted income statement for March.

PR 7-4B   Cash budget   Obj. 5

✔ 1. August
deficiency, $9,000

SHOW ME HOW

EXCEL TEMPLATE

The controller of Mercury Shoes Inc. instructs you to prepare a monthly cash budget for the next three months. You are presented with the following budget information:

	June	July	August
Sales	$160,000	$185,000	$200,000
Manufacturing costs	66,000	82,000	105,000
Selling and administrative expenses	40,000	46,000	51,000
Capital expenditures	—	—	120,000

The company expects to sell about 10% of its merchandise for cash. Of sales on account, 60% are expected to be collected in the month following the sale and the remainder the following month (second month after sale). Depreciation, insurance, and property tax expense represent $12,000 of the estimated monthly manufacturing costs. The annual insurance premium is paid in February, and the annual property taxes are paid in November. Of the remainder of the manufacturing costs, 80% are expected to be paid in the month in which they are incurred and the balance in the following month.

Current assets as of June 1 include cash of $42,000, marketable securities of $25,000, and accounts receivable of $198,000 ($150,000 from May sales and $48,000 from April sales). Sales on account in April and May were $120,000 and $150,000, respectively. Current liabilities as of June 1 include $13,000 of accounts payable incurred in May for manufacturing costs. All selling and administrative expenses are paid in cash in the period they are incurred. An estimated income tax payment of $24,000 will be made in July. Mercury Shoes' regular quarterly dividend of $15,000 is expected to be declared in July and paid in August. Management desires to maintain a minimum cash balance of $40,000.

Instructions

1. Prepare a monthly cash budget and supporting schedules for June, July, and August.

2. ➤ On the basis of the cash budget prepared in part (1), what recommendation should be made to the controller?

PR 7-5B   Budgeted income statement and balance sheet   Obj. 4, 5

✔ 1. Budgeted net
income, $114,660

EXCEL TEMPLATE

As a preliminary to requesting budget estimates of sales, costs, and expenses for the fiscal year beginning January 1, 20Y9, the following tentative trial balance as of December 31, 20Y8, is prepared by the Accounting Department of Mesa Publishing Co.:

Cash	$ 26,000	
Accounts Receivable.......................................	23,800	
Finished Goods	16,900	
Work In Process	4,200	
Materials	6,400	
Prepaid Expenses	600	
Plant and Equipment	82,000	
Accumulated Depreciation—Plant and Equipment.................		$ 32,000
Accounts Payable		14,800
Common Stock, $1.50 par....................................		30,000
Retained Earnings...		83,100
	$159,900	$159,900

Factory output and sales for 20Y9 are expected to total 3,800 units of product, which are to be sold at $120 per unit. The quantities and costs of the inventories at December 31, 20Y9, are expected to remain unchanged from the balances at the beginning of the year.

Budget estimates of manufacturing costs and operating expenses for the year are summarized as follows:

	Estimated Costs and Expenses	
	Fixed **(Total for Year)**	**Variable** **(Per Unit Sold)**
Cost of goods manufactured and sold:		
Direct materials...	—	$30.00
Direct labor..	—	8.40
Factory overhead:		
Depreciation of plant and equipment..................	$ 4,000	—
Other factory overhead..............................	1,400	4.80
Selling expenses:		
Sales salaries and commissions...........................	12,800	13.50
Advertising...	13,200	—
Miscellaneous selling expense	1,000	2.50
Administrative expenses:		
Office and officers salaries	7,800	7.00
Supplies..	500	1.20
Miscellaneous administrative expense	400	2.40

Balances of accounts receivable, prepaid expenses, and accounts payable at the end of the year are not expected to differ significantly from the beginning balances. Federal income tax of $35,000 on 20Y9 taxable income will be paid during 20Y9. Regular quarterly cash dividends of $0.20 per share are expected to be declared and paid in March, June, September, and December on 20,000 shares of common stock outstanding. It is anticipated that fixed assets will be purchased for $22,000 cash in May.

Instructions

1. Prepare a budgeted income statement for 20Y9.

2. Prepare a budgeted balance sheet as of December 31, 20Y9, with supporting calculations.

Analysis for Decision Making

ADM-1 Nursing staff budget

Mercy Hospital staffs its medical/surgical floors with nurses depending on the number of patients assigned to the floor and the severity of their condition. The index used to capture nurse effort is termed a relative value unit, or RVU. For example, taking vital signs for a single patient may be equal to one RVU. RVU's are then summed to estimate the total RVU requirements for the floor. From this, the nursing staff budget is determined.

The medical/surgical floor is scheduled to have 25 patients for each day of the coming seven-day week. Some patients will require more nursing effort than others, depending on the severity of their conditions or their ages. The following table summarizes the expected RVU requirements for the patients:

Number of Patients	RVUs per Day
5	20
8	25
10	30
2	40

A nurse earns $180 per day and is able to perform 40 RVUs per day.

A. Determine the total number of RVUs expected per day for the coming week.

B. Determine the total weekly nurse budget for the coming week.

ADM-2 Parking lot staff budget

Adventure Park is a large theme park. Staffing for the theme park involves many different labor classifications, one of which is the parking lot staff. The parking lot staff collects parking fees, provides directions, and operates trams. The staff size is a function of the number of daily vehicles. Adventure Park has determined from historical experience that a staff member is needed for every 200 vehicles.

Adventure Park estimates staff for both school days and nonschool days. Nonschool days are higher attendance days than school days. The number of expected vehicles for each day is as follows:

	School Days	Nonschool Days
Number of vehicles per day	3,000	8,000
Number of days per year	165	200

Parking fees are $10 per vehicle. Each parking lot employee is paid $110 per day.

A. Determine the annual parking lot staff budget for school days, nonschool days, and total.

B. Determine the parking revenue for school days, nonschool days, and total.

C. If depreciation expense and other expenses for running the parking lot were estimated to be $2 million per year, determine the parking lot's budgeted profit.

ADM-3 Housekeeping staff budget

Ambassador Suites Inc. operates a downtown hotel property that has 300 rooms. On average, 80% of Ambassador Suites' rooms are occupied on weekdays, and 40% are occupied during the weekend. The manager has asked you to develop a budget for the housekeeping and restaurant staff for weekdays and weekends. You have determined that the housekeeping staff requires 30 minutes to clean each occupied room. The housekeeping staff is paid $14 per hour. The house-keeping labor cost is fully variable to the number of occupied rooms. The restaurant has six full-time staff on duty to staff the restaurant for breakfast and lunch (eight hours), regardless of occupancy. However, for every 60 occupied rooms, an additional person is brought in to work in the restaurant for breakfast and lunch (eight hours). The restaurant staff is paid $12 per hour.

Prepare two columns, labeled as weekday and weekend day.

A. Determine the number of rooms occupied for an average weekday and weekend day.

B. Determine the housekeeping staff budget for an average weekday and weekend day.

C. Determine the restaurant staff budget for an average weekday and weekend day.

D. Determine the total staff budget for an average weekday and weekend day.

Take It Further

TIF 7-1   Ethics in Action

The director of marketing for Starr Computer Co., Megan Hewitt, had the following discussion with the company controller, Cam Morley, on July 26 of the current year:

Megan: Cam, it looks like I'm going to spend much less than indicated on my July budget.

Cam: I'm glad to hear it.

Megan: Well, I'm not so sure it's good news. I'm concerned that the president will see that I'm under budget and reduce my budget in the future. The only reason that I look good is that we've delayed an advertising campaign. Once the campaign hits in September, I'm sure my actual expenditures will go up. You see, we are also having our sales convention in September. Having the advertising campaign and the convention at the same time is going to kill my September numbers.

Cam: I don't think that's anything to worry about. We all expect some variation in actual spending month to month. What's really important is staying within the budgeted targets for the year. Does that look as if it's going to be a problem?

Megan: I don't think so, but just the same, I'd like to be on the safe side.

Cam: What do you mean?

Megan: Well, this is what I'd like to do. I want to pay the convention-related costs in advance this month. I'll pay the hotel for room and convention space and purchase the airline tickets in advance. In this way, I can charge all these expenditures to July's budget. This would cause my actual expenses to come close to budget for July. Moreover, when the big advertising campaign hits in September, I won't have to worry about expenditures for the convention on my September budget as well. The convention costs will already be paid. Thus, my September expenses should be pretty close to budget.

Cam: I can't tell you when to make your convention purchases, but I'm not too sure that September items should be expensed in July's budget.

Megan: What's the problem? It looks like "no harm, no foul" to me. I can't see that there's anything wrong with this—it's just smart management.

⸺► How should Cam Morley respond to Megan Hewitt's request to expense the advanced payments for convention-related costs against July's budget?

REAL WORLD

TIF 7-2 Team Activity

In teams, find the home page of a state that interests you. The home page will be of the form *www.statename.gov*. For example, the state of Tennessee can be found at www.tennessee.gov. At the home page site, search for annual budget information.

1. What are the budgeted sources of revenue and their percentage breakdown?
2. What are the major categories of budgeted expenditures (or appropriations) and their percentage breakdown?
3. Is the projected budget in balance?

TIF 7-3 Communication

The city of Milton has an annual budget cycle that begins on July 1 and ends on June 30. At the beginning of each budget year, an annual budget is established for each department. The annual budget is divided equally among the 12 months to provide a constant monthly static budget. On June 30, all unspent budgeted monies for the budget year from the various city departments must be "returned" to the General Fund. Thus, if department heads fail to use their budget by year-end, they will lose it. A budget analyst prepared a chart of the difference between the monthly actual and budgeted amounts for all departments in a recent fiscal year. The chart was as follows:

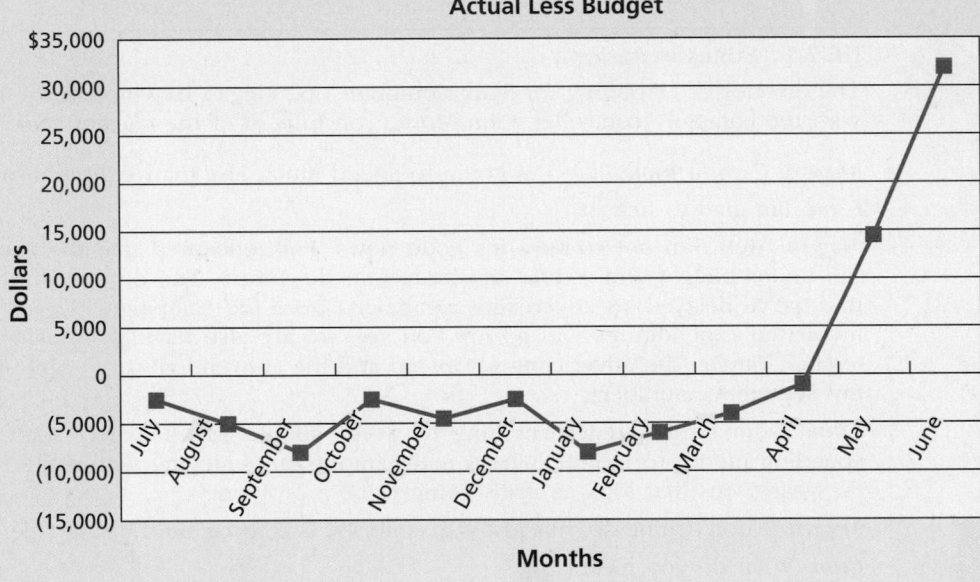

Write a memo to Stacy Poindexter, the city manager, interpreting the chart and suggesting improvements to the budgeting system.

Concepts and Principles

Chapter 1 *Introduction to Managerial Accounting*

Developing Information

COST SYSTEMS	COST BEHAVIOR

Chapter 2 *Job Order Costing*   **Chapter 5** *Cost-Volume-Profit Analysis*

Chapter 3 *Process Cost Systems*

Chapter 4 *Activity-Based Costing*

Decision Making

EVALUATING PERFORMANCE	COMPARING ALTERNATIVES

Chapter 6 *Variable Costing for Management Analysis*

Chapter 9 *Evaluating Decentralized Operations*

Chapter 7 *Budgeting*

Chapter 10 *Differential Analysis and Product Pricing*

Chapter 8 ***Evaluating Variances from Standard Costs***

Chapter 11 *Capital Investment Analysis*

Chapter 12 *Lean Manufacturing*

AP IMAGES/ALASTAIR GRANT

1959-2000

BMW Group

When you play a sport, you are evaluated with respect to how well you perform compared to a standard or to a competitor. In bowling, for example, your score is compared to a perfect score of 300 or to the scores of your competitors. In this class, you are compared to performance standards. These standards are often described in terms of letter grades, which provide a measure of how well you achieved the class objectives. In your job, you are also evaluated according to performance standards.

Just as your class performance is evaluated, managers are evaluated according to goals and plans. For example, **BMW Group** uses manufacturing standards at its automobile assembly plants to guide performance. The Mini Cooper, a BMW Group car, is manufactured in a modern facility in Oxford, England. There are a number of performance targets used in this plant.

For example, the bodyshell is welded by more than 250 robots so as to be two to three times stiffer than rival cars. In addition, the bodyshell dimensions are tested to the accuracy of the width of a human hair. Such performance standards are not surprising given the automotive racing background of John W. Cooper, the designer of the original Mini Cooper.

If you want to get a view of the BMW manufacturing process, go to the BMW Web site, search the phrase "How an automobile is born," and click on the Production link.

Performance is often measured as the difference between actual results and planned results. In this chapter, we will discuss and illustrate the ways in which business performance is evaluated.

Source: www.bmwgroup.com

Evaluating Variances from Standard Costs

Standards
- Setting Standards (Obj. 1)
- Types of Standards (Obj. 1)
- Reviewing and Revising Standards (Obj. 1)

Variance Analysis
- Budget Performance Report (Obj. 2)
- Direct Materials Variances (Obj. 3)
- Direct Labor Variances (Obj. 3)
- Factory Overhead Variances (Obj. 4)

Recording Variances
- Journalizing Variances (Obj. 5)
- Variances in the Income Statement (Obj. 5)
- Nonfinancial Performance Measures (Obj. 6)

Learning Objectives

Obj. 1 Describe the types of standards and how they are established.

Obj. 2 Describe and illustrate how standards are used in budgeting.

Obj. 3 Compute and interpret direct materials and direct labor variances.

Obj. 4 Compute and interpret factory overhead controllable and volume variances.

Obj. 5 Describe and illustrate the recording and reporting of standards and variances.

Obj. 6 Describe and illustrate nonfinancial performance measures.

Analysis for Decision Making

Describe and Illustrate the use of the direct labor time variance in evaluating staff performance in a service setting.

Objective 1
Describe the types of standards and how they are established.

Standards

Standards are performance goals. Manufacturing companies normally use **standard cost** for each of the three following product costs:

- Direct materials
- Direct labor
- Factory overhead

Accounting systems that use standards for product costs are called **standard cost systems**. Standard cost systems enable management to determine the following:

- How much a product *should* cost (standard cost)
- How much it does cost (actual cost)

When actual costs are compared with standard costs, the exceptions or cost variances are reported. This reporting by the *principle of exceptions* allows management to focus on correcting the cost variances.

BMW began in Germany in the early 1900s as a manufacturer of airplane engines. The BMW emblem, which was first used in 1917, represents a rotating airplane propeller with the white and blue state colors of Bavaria.

Setting Standards

The standard-setting process normally requires the joint efforts of accountants, engineers, and other management personnel. The accountant converts the results of judgments and process studies into dollars and cents. Engineers with the aid of operation managers identify the materials, labor, and machine requirements needed to produce the product. For example, engineers estimate direct materials by studying the product specifications and estimating normal spoilage. Time and motion studies may be used to determine the direct labor required for each manufacturing operation. Engineering studies may also be used to determine standards for factory overhead, such as the amount of power needed to operate machinery.

Types of Standards

Standards imply an acceptable level of production efficiency. One of the major objectives in setting standards is to motivate employees to achieve efficient operations.

Ideal standards, or *theoretical standards*, are standards that can be achieved only under perfect operating conditions, such as no idle time, no machine breakdowns, and no materials spoilage. Such standards may have a negative impact on performance because they may be viewed by employees as unrealistic.

Currently attainable standards, sometimes called *normal standards*, are standards that can be attained with reasonable effort. Such standards, which are used by most companies, allow for normal production difficulties and mistakes. When reasonable standards are used, employees focus more on cost and are more likely to put forth their best efforts.

An example from the game of golf illustrates the distinction between ideal and normal standards. In golf, *par* is an ideal standard for most players. Each player's USGA (United States Golf Association) handicap is the player's normal standard. The motivation of average players is to beat their handicaps because beating par is unrealistic for most players.

Reviewing and Revising Standards

Standard costs should be periodically reviewed to ensure that they reflect current operating conditions. Standards should not be revised, however, just because they differ from actual costs. For example, the direct labor standard would not be revised just because employees are unable to meet properly set standards. On the other hand, standards should be revised when prices, product designs, labor rates, or manufacturing methods change.

 Ethics: Do It!

Company Reputation: The Best of the Best

Harris Interactive annually ranks American corporations in terms of reputation. The ranking is based on how respondents rate corporations on 20 attributes in six major areas. The six areas are emotional appeal, products and services, financial performance, workplace environment, social responsibility, and vision and leadership. The five highest (best) ranked companies in a recent survey were **Amazon.com**, **Apple Inc.**, **The Walt Disney Company**, **Google**, and **Johnson & Johnson**.

Criticisms of Standard Costs

Some criticisms of using standard costs for performance evaluation include the following:

- Standards limit operating improvements by discouraging improvement beyond the standard.
- Standards are too difficult to maintain in a dynamic manufacturing environment, resulting in "stale standards."
- Standards can cause employees to lose sight of the larger objectives of the organization by focusing only on efficiency improvement.
- Standards can cause employees to unduly focus on their own operations to the possible harm of other operations that rely on them.

Regardless of these criticisms, standards are used widely. In addition, standard costs are only one part of the performance evaluation system used by most companies. As discussed in this chapter, other nonfinancial performance measures are often used to supplement standard costs, with the result that many of the preceding criticisms are overcome.

In addition to BMW, Mini Cooper, and Rolls-Royce automobiles, **BMW Group** manufactures motorcycles.

Link to BMW Group

Budgetary Performance Evaluation

As discussed in Chapter 7, the master budget assists a company in planning, directing, and controlling performance. The control function, or budgetary performance evaluation, compares the actual performance against the budget.

To illustrate, **Western Rider Inc.**, a manufacturer of blue jeans, uses standard costs in its budgets. The standards for direct materials, direct labor, and factory overhead are separated into the following two components:

- Standard price
- Standard quantity

The standard cost per unit for direct materials, direct labor, and factory overhead is computed as follows:

$$\text{Standard Cost per Unit} = \text{Standard Price} \times \text{Standard Quantity}$$

Western Rider's standard costs per unit for its XL jeans are shown in Exhibit 1.

Exhibit 1 Standard Cost for XL Jeans	**Manufacturing Costs**	**Standard Price**	×	**Standard Quantity per Pair**	=	**Standard Cost per Pair of XL Jeans**
	Direct materials	$5.00 per sq. yd.		1.5 sq. yds.		$ 7.50
	Direct labor	$9.00 per hr.		0.80 hr. per pair		7.20
	Factory overhead	$6.00 per hr.		0.80 hr. per pair		4.80
	Total standard cost per pair					$19.50

As shown in Exhibit 1, the standard cost per pair of XL jeans is $19.50, which consists of $7.50 for direct materials, $7.20 for direct labor, and $4.80 for factory overhead.

The standard price and standard quantity are separated for each product cost. For example, Exhibit 1 indicates that for each pair of XL jeans, the standard price for direct materials is $5.00 per square yard and the standard quantity is 1.5 square yards. The standard price and quantity are separated because the department responsible for their control is normally different. For example, the direct materials price per square yard is controlled by the Purchasing Department, and the direct materials quantity per pair is controlled by the Production Department.

As illustrated in Chapter 7, the master budget is prepared based on planned sales and production. The budgeted costs for materials purchases, direct labor, and factory overhead are determined by multiplying their standard costs per unit by the planned level of production. Budgeted (standard) costs are then compared to actual costs during the year for control purposes.

Budget Performance Report

The differences between actual and standard costs are called **cost variances**. A **favorable cost variance** occurs when the actual cost is less than the standard cost. An **unfavorable cost variance** occurs when the actual cost exceeds the standard cost. These cost variances are illustrated in Exhibit 2.

Exhibit 2 Cost Variances	**Favorable Cost Variance**	**Unfavorable Cost Variance**
	Actual cost < Standard cost at actual volumes	Actual cost > Standard cost at actual volumes

The report that summarizes actual costs, standard costs, and the differences for the units produced is called a **budget performance report**. To illustrate, assume that **Western Rider Inc.** produced the following pairs of jeans during June:

XL jeans produced and sold	5,000 pairs
Actual costs incurred in June:	
Direct materials	$ 40,150
Direct labor	38,500
Factory overhead	22,400
Total costs incurred	$101,050

Exhibit 3 illustrates the budget performance report for June for Western Rider.

Exhibit 3
Budget
Performance
Report

Western Rider Inc.
Budget Performance Report
For the Month Ended June 30

Manufacturing Costs	Actual Costs	Standard Cost at Actual Volume (5,000 pairs of XL Jeans)*	Cost Variance— (Favorable) Unfavorable
Direct materials.....................................	$ 40,150	$37,500	$ 2,650
Direct labor	38,500	36,000	2,500
Factory overhead.................................	22,400	24,000	(1,600)
Total manufacturing costs......................	$101,050	$97,500	$ 3,550

*5,000 pairs × $7.50 per pair = $37,500
5,000 pairs × $7.20 per pair = $36,000
5,000 pairs × $4.80 per pair − $24,000

The budget performance report shown in Exhibit 3 is based on the actual units produced in June of 5,000 XL jeans. Even though 6,000 XL jeans might have been *planned* for production, the budget performance report is based on *actual* production.

Manufacturing Cost Variances

The **total manufacturing cost variance** is the difference between total standard costs and total actual cost for the units produced. As shown in Exhibit 3, the total manufacturing cost unfavorable variance is $3,550, which consists of an unfavorable direct materials cost variance of $2,650, an unfavorable direct labor cost variance of $2,500, and a favorable factory overhead cost variance of $1,600.

For control purposes, each product cost variance is separated into two additional variances as shown in Exhibit 4.

Exhibit 4   Manufacturing Cost Variances

The total direct materials variance is separated into a *price* variance and a *quantity* variance. This is because standard and actual direct materials costs are computed as follows:

Actual Direct Materials Cost	=	Actual Price	× Actual Quantity
Standard Direct Materials Cost	=	Standard Price	× Standard Quantity
Direct Materials Cost Variance	=	Price Difference	+ Quantity Difference

Thus, the actual and standard direct materials costs may differ because of a price difference (variance), a quantity difference (variance), or both.

Likewise, the total direct labor variance is separated into a *rate* variance and a *time* variance. This is because standard and actual direct labor costs are computed as follows:

Actual Direct Labor Cost	=	Actual Rate	× Actual Time
Standard Direct Labor Cost	=	Standard Rate	× Standard Time
Direct Labor Cost Variance	=	Rate Difference	+ Time Difference

Therefore, the actual and standard direct labor costs may differ because of a rate difference (variance), a time difference (variance), or both.

The total factory overhead variance is separated into a *controllable* variance and a *volume* variance. Because factory overhead has fixed and variable cost elements, it uses different variances than direct materials and direct labor, which are variable costs.

In the next sections, the price and quantity variances for direct materials, the rate and time variances for direct labor, and the controllable and volume variances for factory overhead are further described and illustrated.

Link to
BMW Group

BMW's Spartanburg, South Carolina plant employs 8,000 workers in its 6 million-square-foot facility where it manufactures X3 and X5 SUVs. Visitors may tour the manufacturing plant and company museum.

Objective 3
Compute and interpret direct materials and direct labor variances.

Direct Materials and Direct Labor Variances

As indicated in the prior section, the total direct materials and direct labor variances are separated into the direct materials cost and direct labor cost variances for analysis and control purposes. These variances are illustrated in Exhibit 5.

Exhibit 5
Direct Materials and Direct Labor Cost Variances

Total Direct Materials Cost Variance ⟶ { Direct Materials Price Variance / Direct Materials Quantity Variance

Total Direct Labor Cost Variance ⟶ { Direct Labor Rate Variance / Direct Labor Time Variance

As a basis for illustration, the variances for Western Rider's June operations shown in Exhibit 3 are used.

Direct Materials Variances

During June, **Western Rider Inc.** reported an unfavorable total direct materials cost variance of $2,650 for the production of 5,000 XL style jeans, as shown in Exhibit 3. This variance was based on the following actual and standard costs:

Actual costs	$40,150
Standard costs	37,500
Total direct materials cost variance	$ 2,650

The actual costs incurred of $40,150 consist of the following:

Actual Direct Materials Cost = Actual Price × Actual Quantity
= ($5.50 per sq. yd.) × (7,300 sq. yds.)
= $40,150

The standard costs of $37,500 consist of the following:

Standard Direct Materials Cost = Standard Price × Standard Quantity
= $5.00 per sq. yd. × 7,500 sq. yds.
= $37,500

The standard price of $5.00 per square yard is taken from Exhibit 1. In addition, Exhibit 1 indicates that 1.5 square yards is the standard quantity of materials for producing one pair of XL jeans. Thus, 7,500 (5,000 × 1.5) square yards is the standard quantity of materials for producing 5,000 pairs of XL jeans.

Comparing the actual and standard cost computations indicates that the total direct materials unfavorable cost variance of $2,650 is caused by the following:

- A price per square yard of $0.50 ($5.50 – $5.00) more than standard
- A quantity usage of 200 square yards (7,300 sq. yds. – 7,500 sq. yds.) less than standard

The impact of these differences from standard is reported and analyzed as a direct materials *price* variance and direct materials *quantity* variance.

Direct Materials Price Variance The **direct materials price variance** is computed as follows:

Direct Materials Price Variance = (Actual Price – Standard Price) × Actual Quantity

If the actual price per unit exceeds the standard price per unit, the variance is unfavorable. This positive amount (unfavorable variance) can be thought of as increasing costs (a debit). If the actual price per unit is less than the standard price per unit, the variance is favorable. This negative amount (favorable variance) can be thought of as decreasing costs (a credit).

To illustrate, the direct materials price variance for **Western Rider Inc.** for June is $3,650 (unfavorable), computed as follows:[1]

Direct Materials Price Variance = (Actual Price – Standard Price) × Actual Quantity
= ($5.50 – $5.00) × 7,300 sq. yds.
= $3,650 Unfavorable Variance

Direct Materials Quantity Variance The **direct materials quantity variance** is computed as follows:

Direct Materials Quantity Variance = (Actual Quantity – Standard Quantity) × Standard Price

If the actual quantity for the units produced exceeds the standard quantity, the variance is unfavorable. This positive amount (unfavorable variance) can be thought of as increasing costs (a debit). If the actual quantity for the units produced is less than the standard quantity, the variance is favorable. This negative amount (favorable variance) can be thought of as decreasing costs (a credit).

To illustrate, the direct materials quantity variance for **Western Rider Inc.** for June is $1,000 (favorable), computed as follows:

Direct Materials Quantity Variance = (Actual Quantity – Standard Quantity) × Standard Price
= (7,300 sq. yds. – 7,500 sq. yds.) × $5.00
= $(1,000) Favorable Variance

Steel and aluminium are pressed into doors and side panels in **BMW**'s stamping facility.

Link to BMW Group

[1] To simplify, it is assumed that there is no change in the beginning and ending materials inventories. Thus, the amount of materials budgeted for production equals the amount purchased.

Direct Materials Variance Relationships The relationship among the *total* direct materials cost variance, the direct materials *price* variance, and the direct materials *quantity* variance is shown in Exhibit 6.

Reporting Direct Materials Variances The direct materials quantity variances should be reported to the manager responsible for the variance. For example, an unfavorable quantity variance might be caused by either of the following:

- Equipment that has not been properly maintained
- Low-quality (inferior) direct materials

Exhibit 6
Direct Materials
Variance
Relationships

DYNAMIC
EXHIBIT

In the first case, the Operating Department responsible for maintaining the equipment should be held responsible for the variance. In the second case, the Purchasing Department should be held responsible.

Not all variances are controllable. For example, an unfavorable materials price variance might be due to market-wide price increases. In this case, there is nothing the Purchasing Department might have done to avoid the unfavorable variance. On the other hand, if materials of the same quality could have been purchased from another supplier at the standard price, the variance was controllable.

Direct Labor Variances

During June, **Western Rider Inc.** reported an unfavorable total direct labor cost variance of $2,500 for the production of 5,000 XL style jeans, as shown in Exhibit 3. This variance was based on the following actual and standard costs:

Actual costs	$38,500
Standard costs	36,000
Total direct labor cost variance	$ 2,500

The actual costs incurred of $38,500 consist of the following:

Actual Direct Labor Cost = Actual Rate per Hour × Actual Time
= $10.00 per hr. × 3,850 hrs.
= $38,500

The standard costs of $36,000 consist of the following:

Standard Direct Labor Cost = Standard Rate per Hour × Standard Time
= $9.00 per hr. × 4,000 hrs.
= $36,000

The standard rate of $9.00 per direct labor hour is taken from Exhibit 1. In addition, Exhibit 1 indicates that 0.80 hour is the standard time required for producing one pair of XL jeans. Thus, 4,000 (5,000 units × 0.80 hr.) direct labor hours is the standard for producing 5,000 pairs of XL jeans.

Comparing the actual and standard cost computations indicates that the total direct labor unfavorable cost variance of $2,500 is caused by the following:

- A rate of $1.00 per hour ($10.00 – $9.00) more than standard
- A quantity of 150 hours (4,000 hrs. – 3,850 hrs.) less than standard

The impact of these differences from standard is reported and analyzed as a direct labor *rate* variance and a direct labor *time* variance.

The camshafts of **BMW**'s engines are manufactured using computer-controlled machine tools to a precision of one hundredth of a human hair. Workers are primarily used to adjust the machine tools.

Link to BMW Group

Direct Labor Rate Variance The **direct labor rate variance** is computed as follows:

Direct Labor Rate Variance = (Actual Rate per Hour – Standard Rate per Hour) × Actual Hours

If the actual rate per hour exceeds the standard rate per hour, the variance is unfavorable. This positive amount (unfavorable variance) can be thought of as increasing costs (a debit). If the actual rate per hour is less than the standard rate per hour, the variance is favorable. This negative amount (favorable variance) can be thought of as decreasing costs (a credit).

To illustrate, the direct labor rate variance for **Western Rider Inc.** in June is $3,850 (unfavorable), computed as follows:

Direct Labor Rate Variance = (Actual Rate per Hour – Standard Rate per Hour) × Actual Hours
= ($10.00 – $9.00) × 3,850 hours
= $3,850 Unfavorable Variance

Direct Labor Time Variance The **direct labor time variance** is computed as follows:

Direct Labor Time Variance = (Actual Direct Labor Hours – Standard Direct Labor Hours)
× Standard Rate per Hour

If the actual direct labor hours for the units produced exceed the standard direct labor hours, the variance is unfavorable. This positive amount (unfavorable variance) can be thought of as increasing costs (a debit). If the actual direct labor hours for the units produced are less than the standard direct labor hours, the variance is favorable. This negative amount (favorable variance) can be thought of as decreasing costs (a credit).

To illustrate, the direct labor time variance for **Western Rider Inc.** for June is $1,350 (favorable) computed as follows:

Direct Labor Time Variance = (Actual Direct Labor Hours – Standard Direct Labor Hours)
× Standard Rate per Hour
= (3,850 hours – 4,000 direct labor hours) × $9.00
= $(1,350) Favorable Variance

Direct Labor Variance Relationships The relationship among the *total* direct labor cost variance, the direct labor *rate* variance, and the direct labor *time* variance is shown in Exhibit 7.

Exhibit 7
Direct Labor
Variance
Relationships

DYNAMIC
EXHIBIT

Reporting Direct Labor Variances Production supervisors are normally responsible for controlling direct labor cost. For example, an investigation could reveal the following causes for unfavorable rate and time variances:

- An unfavorable rate variance may be caused by the improper scheduling and use of employees. In such cases, skilled, highly paid employees may be used in jobs that are normally performed by unskilled, lower-paid employees. In this case, the unfavorable rate variance should be reported to the managers who schedule work assignments.
- An unfavorable time variance may be caused by a shortage of skilled employees. In such cases, there may be an abnormally high turnover rate among skilled employees. In this case, production supervisors with high turnover rates should be questioned as to why their employees are quitting.

Direct Labor Standards for Nonmanufacturing Activities Direct labor time standards can also be developed for use in administrative, selling, and service activities. This is most appropriate when the activity involves a repetitive task that produces a common output. In these cases, the use of standards is similar to that for a manufactured product.

To illustrate, standards could be developed for customer service personnel who process sales orders. A standard time for processing a sales order (the output) could be developed and used to control sales order processing costs. Similar standards could be developed for computer help desk operators, nurses, and insurance application processors.

When labor-related activities are not repetitive, direct labor time standards are less commonly used. For example, the time spent by a senior executive or the work of a research and development scientist would not normally be controlled using time standards.

Check Up Corner 8-1	Direct Materials and Direct Labor Cost Variances

Menounos Manufacturing Co. uses standard costs in its budgets. Standard costs and actual costs for direct materials and direct labor for the manufacture of 3,000 units during 20Y6 were as follows:

	Standard Costs	Actual Costs
Direct materials	18,000 lbs. at $4.50 per lb.	18,500 lbs. at $4.35 per lb.
Direct labor	7,500 hours at $12.00 per hr.	7,420 hours at $12.30 per hr.

Each unit requires 2.5 hours of direct labor.

Determine:
A. The direct materials price variance, direct materials quantity variance, and total direct materials cost variance. Present your answer using the format shown in Exhibit 6.
B. The direct labor rate variance, direct labor time variance, and total direct labor cost variance. Present your answer using the format shown in Exhibit 7.

Solution:

A. Direct Materials Variances

Direct Materials Price Variance = (Actual Price − Standard Price) × Actual Quantity
= ($4.35 − $4.50) × 18,500 lbs.
= $(2,775) Favorable Variance

Direct Materials Quantity Variance = (Actual Quantity − Standard Quantity) × Standard Price
= (18,500 lbs. − 18,000 lbs.) × $4.50
= $2,250 Unfavorable Variance

Actual cost:
Actual Quantity ×
Actual Price
18,500 × $4.35 =
$80,475

Actual Quantity ×
Standard Price
18,500 × $4.50 =
$83,250

Standard cost:
Standard Quantity ×
Standard Price
18,000 × $4.50 =
$81,000

Direct materials
price variance

Direct materials
quantity variance

$80,475 − $83,250 =
$(2,775) F

$83,250 − $81,000 =
$2,250 U

Total direct materials cost variance

$80,475 − $81,000 = **($525)F**

The variance is **favorable** because the actual price is less than the standard price.

The variance is **unfavorable** because the actual quantity is greater than the standard quantity.

B. Direct Labor Variances

Direct Labor Rate Variance = (Actual Rate per Hour − Standard Rate per Hour) × Actual Hours
= ($12.30 − $12.00) × 7,420 hours
= $2,226 Unfavorable Variance

Direct Labor Time Variance = (Actual Direct Labor Hours − Standard Direct Labor Hours) × Standard Rate per Hour
= (7,420 hours − 7,500 direct labor hours) × $12.00
= $(960) Favorable Variance

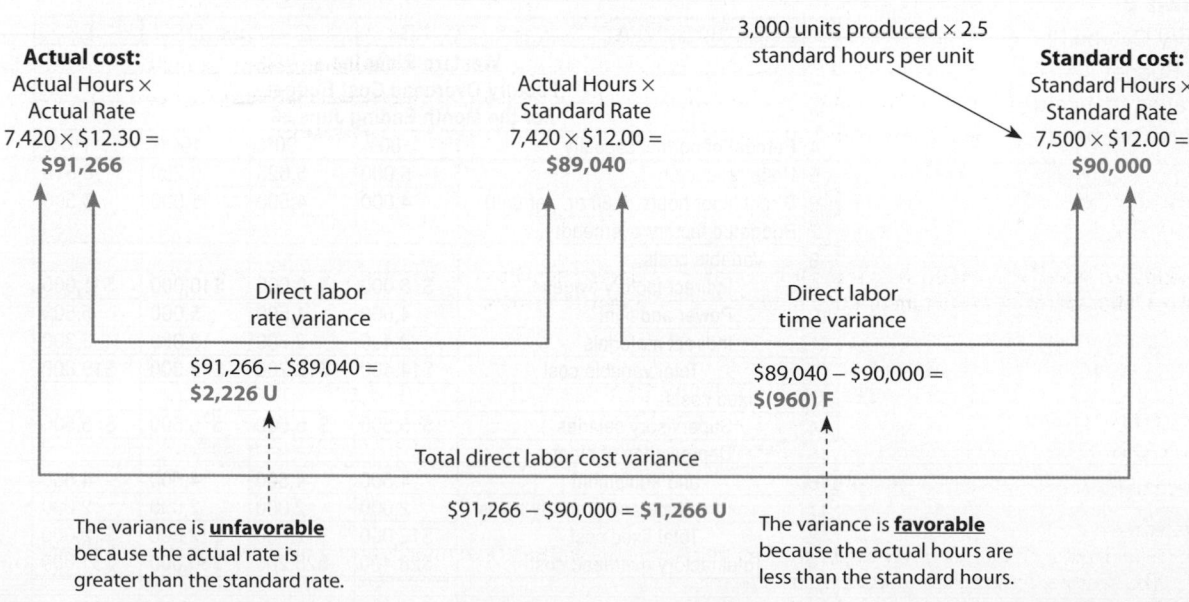

3,000 units produced × 2.5
standard hours per unit

Actual cost:
Actual Hours ×
Actual Rate
7,420 × $12.30 =
$91,266

Actual Hours ×
Standard Rate
7,420 × $12.00 =
$89,040

Standard cost:
Standard Hours ×
Standard Rate
7,500 × $12.00 =
$90,000

Direct labor
rate variance

Direct labor
time variance

$91,266 − $89,040 =
$2,226 U

$89,040 − $90,000 =
$(960) F

Total direct labor cost variance

$91,266 − $90,000 = **$1,266 U**

The variance is **unfavorable** because the actual rate is greater than the standard rate.

The variance is **favorable** because the actual hours are less than the standard hours.

Check Up Corner

Why It Matters

Standard Costing in the Restaurant Industry

Many restaurants use standard costs to manage their business. Food costs are typically the largest expense for a restaurant. As a result, many restaurants use food quantity standards to control food costs by establishing the amount of food that is served to a customer. For example, Red Lobster restaurants, a division of **Darden Restuarants, Inc.**, establishes food quantity standards for the number of shrimp, scallops, or clams on a seafood plate.

The second-largest cost to most restaurants is labor cost. Many restaurants base their labor cost standards on the labor cost percentage, which is the ratio of total labor cost to total sales. This ratio helps the restaurants of Darden Restaurants, Inc., including Olive Garden and Red Lobster, control and monitor labor costs. Focusing on this metric has paid off recently, as labor cost has dropped and earnings have increased as a percent of sales.

Source: N. Irwin, "What Olive Garden and Red Lobster tell us about the economy," *The Washington Post*, September 21, 2012.

Objective 4

Compute and interpret factory overhead controllable and volume variances.

Factory Overhead Variances

Factory overhead costs are analyzed differently than direct labor and direct materials costs. This is because factory overhead costs have fixed and variable cost elements. For example, indirect materials and factory supplies normally behave as a variable cost as units produced change. In contrast, straight-line plant depreciation on factory machinery is a fixed cost.

The **BMW Group** has significant overhead costs due to its investment in robotic and other state-of-the art technology, machinery, and facilities.

Factory overhead costs are budgeted and controlled by separating factory overhead into fixed and variable components. Doing so allows the preparation of flexible budgets and the analysis of factory overhead controllable and volume variances.

The Factory Overhead Flexible Budget

The preparation of a flexible budget was described and illustrated in Chapter 7. Exhibit 8 illustrates a flexible factory overhead budget for **Western Rider Inc.** for June.

Exhibit 8

Factory Overhead Cost Budget Indicating Standard Factory Overhead Rate

	A	B	C	D	E
1	Western Rider Inc.				
2	Factory Overhead Cost Budget				
3	For the Month Ending June 30				
4	Percent of normal capacity	80%	90%	100%	110%
5	Units produced	5,000	5,625	6,250	6,875
6	Direct labor hours (0.80 hr. per unit)	4,000	4,500	5,000	5,500
7	Budgeted factory overhead:				
8	Variable costs:				
9	Indirect factory wages	$ 8,000	$ 9,000	$10,000	$11,000
10	Power and light	4,000	4,500	5,000	5,500
11	Indirect materials	2,400	2,700	3,000	3,300
12	Total variable cost	$14,400	$16,200	$18,000	$19,800
13	Fixed costs:				
14	Supervisory salaries	$ 5,500	$ 5,500	$ 5,500	$ 5,500
15	Depreciation of plant				
16	and equipment	4,500	4,500	4,500	4,500
17	Insurance and property taxes	2,000	2,000	2,000	2,000
18	Total fixed cost	$12,000	$12,000	$12,000	$12,000
19	Total factory overhead cost	$26,400	$28,200	$30,000	$31,800
20					
21	Factory overhead rate per direct labor hour, $30,000 ÷ 5,000 hours = $6.00				
22					

Exhibit 8 indicates that the budgeted factory overhead rate for Western Rider is $6.00, computed as follows:

$$\text{Factory Overhead Rate} = \frac{\text{Budgeted Factory Overhead at Normal Capacity}}{\text{Normal Productive Capacity}}$$

$$= \frac{\$30,000}{5,000 \text{ direct labor hrs.}} = \$6.00 \text{ per direct labor hr.}$$

The normal productive capacity is expressed in terms of an activity base such as direct labor hours, direct labor cost, or machine hours. For Western Rider, 100% of normal capacity is 5,000 direct labor hours. The budgeted factory overhead cost at 100% of normal capacity is $30,000, which consists of variable overhead of $18,000 and fixed overhead of $12,000.

For analysis purposes, the budgeted factory overhead rate is subdivided into a variable factory overhead rate and a fixed factory overhead rate. For Western Rider, the variable overhead rate is $3.60 per direct labor hour, and the fixed overhead rate is $2.40 per direct labor hour, computed as follows:

$$\text{Variable Factory Overhead Rate} = \frac{\text{Budgeted Variable Overhead at Normal Capacity}}{\text{Normal Productive Capacity}}$$

$$= \frac{\$18,000}{5,000 \text{ direct labor hrs.}} = \$3.60 \text{ per direct labor hr.}$$

$$\text{Fixed Factory Overhead Rate} = \frac{\text{Budgeted Fixed Overhead at Normal Capacity}}{\text{Normal Productive Capacity}}$$

$$= \frac{\$12,000}{5,000 \text{ direct labor hrs.}} = \$2.40 \text{ per direct labor hr.}$$

To summarize, the budgeted factory overhead rates for Western Rider Inc. are as follows:

Variable factory overhead rate	$3.60
Fixed factory overhead rate	2.40
Total factory overhead rate	$6.00

As mentioned previously, factory overhead variances can be separated into a controllable variance and a volume variance as discussed in the next sections.

Variable Factory Overhead Controllable Variance

The variable factory overhead **controllable variance** is the difference between the actual variable overhead costs and the budgeted variable overhead for actual production. It is computed as follows:

$$\begin{array}{ccc} \text{Variable Factory Overhead} \\ \text{Controllable Variance} \end{array} = \begin{array}{c} \text{Actual} \\ \text{Variable Factory Overhead} \end{array} - \begin{array}{c} \text{Budgeted} \\ \text{Variable Factory Overhead} \end{array}$$

If the actual variable overhead is less than the budgeted variable overhead, the variance is favorable. If the actual variable overhead exceeds the budgeted variable overhead, the variance is unfavorable.

The **budgeted variable factory overhead** is the standard variable overhead for the *actual* units produced. It is computed as follows:

$$\text{Budgeted Variable Factory Overhead} = \text{Standard Hours for Actual Units Produced} \times \text{Variable Factory Overhead Rate}$$

To illustrate, the budgeted variable overhead for **Western Rider Inc.** for June, when 5,000 units of XL jeans were produced, is $14,400, computed as follows:

$$\begin{aligned} \text{Budgeted Variable Factory Overhead} &= \text{Standard Hours for Actual Units Produced} \\ &\quad \times \text{Variable Factory Overhead Rate} \\ &= 4,000 \text{ direct labor hrs.} \times \$3.60 \\ &= \$14,400 \end{aligned}$$

The preceding computation is based on the fact that Western Rider produced 5,000 XL jeans, which requires a standard of 4,000 (5,000 units × 0.8 hr.) direct labor hours. The variable factory overhead rate of $3.60 was computed earlier. Thus, the budgeted variable factory overhead is $14,400 (4,000 direct labor hrs. × $3.60).

During June, assume that Western Rider incurred the following actual factory overhead costs:

	Actual Costs in June
Variable factory overhead	$10,400
Fixed factory overhead	12,000
Total actual factory overhead	$22,400

Based on the actual variable factory overhead incurred in June, the variable factory overhead controllable variance is a $4,000 favorable variance, computed as follows:

$$\begin{matrix} \text{Variable Factory Overhead} \\ \text{Controllable Variance} \end{matrix} = \begin{matrix} \text{Actual} \\ \text{Variable Factory Overhead} \end{matrix} - \begin{matrix} \text{Budgeted} \\ \text{Variable Factory Overhead} \end{matrix}$$

$$= \$10,400 - \$14,400$$

$$= \$(4,000) \text{ Favorable Variance}$$

The variable factory overhead controllable variance indicates the ability to keep the factory overhead costs within the budget limits. Because variable factory overhead costs are normally controllable at the department level, responsibility for controlling this variance usually rests with department supervisors.

Fixed Factory Overhead Volume Variance

Western Rider's budgeted factory overhead is based on a 100% normal capacity of 5,000 direct labor hours, as shown in Exhibit 8. This is the expected capacity that management believes will be used under normal business conditions. Exhibit 8 indicates that the 5,000 direct labor hours is less than the total available capacity of 110%, which is 5,500 direct labor hours.

The fixed factory overhead **volume variance** is the difference between the budgeted fixed overhead at 100% of normal capacity and the standard fixed overhead for the actual units produced. It is computed as follows:

$$\begin{matrix} \text{Fixed Factory} \\ \text{Overhead} \\ \text{Volume Variance} \end{matrix} = \left(\begin{matrix} \text{Standard Hours} \\ \text{for 100\% of} \\ \text{Normal Capacity} \end{matrix} - \begin{matrix} \text{Standard Hours for} \\ \text{Actual Units} \\ \text{Produced} \end{matrix} \right) \times \begin{matrix} \text{Fixed Factory} \\ \text{Overhead Rate} \end{matrix}$$

The volume variance measures the use of fixed overhead resources (plant and equipment). The interpretation of an unfavorable and a favorable fixed factory overhead volume variance is as follows:

- *Unfavorable* fixed factory overhead volume variance. The actual units produced is *less than* 100% of normal capacity; thus, the company used its fixed overhead resources (plant and equipment) less than would be expected under normal operating conditions.
- *Favorable* fixed factory overhead volume variance. The actual units produced is *more than* 100% of normal capacity; thus, the company used its fixed overhead resources (plant and equipment) more than would be expected under normal operating conditions.

To illustrate, the fixed factory overhead volume variance for **Western Rider Inc.** is a $2,400 unfavorable variance, computed as follows:

$$\begin{matrix} \text{Fixed Factory} \\ \text{Overhead} \\ \text{Volume Variance} \end{matrix} = \left(\begin{matrix} \text{Standard Hours} \\ \text{for 100\% of} \\ \text{Normal Capacity} \end{matrix} - \begin{matrix} \text{Standard Hours for} \\ \text{Actual Units} \\ \text{Produced} \end{matrix} \right) \times \begin{matrix} \text{Fixed Factory} \\ \text{Overhead Rate} \end{matrix}$$

$$= \left(\begin{matrix} 5,000 \text{ direct} \\ \text{labor hrs.} \end{matrix} - \begin{matrix} 4,000 \text{ direct} \\ \text{labor hrs.} \end{matrix} \right) \times \$2.40$$

$$= \$2,400 \text{ Unfavorable Variance}$$

Because Western Rider produced 5,000 XL jeans during June, the standard for the actual units produced is 4,000 (5,000 units × 0.80) direct labor hours. This is 1,000 hours less than the 5,000 standard hours of normal capacity. The fixed overhead rate of $2.40 was computed earlier. Thus, the unfavorable fixed factory overhead volume variance is $2,400 (1,000 direct labor hrs. × $2.40).

Exhibit 9 illustrates graphically the fixed factory overhead volume variance for **Western Rider Inc.** The budgeted fixed overhead does not change and is $12,000 at all levels of production. At 100% of normal capacity (5,000 direct labor hours), the standard fixed overhead line intersects the budgeted fixed costs line. For production levels *more than* 100% of normal capacity (5,000 direct labor hours), the volume variance is *favorable*. For production levels *less than* 100% of normal capacity (5,000 direct labor hours), the volume variance is *unfavorable*.

Exhibit 9 indicates that Western Rider's fixed factory overhead volume variance is unfavorable in June because the actual production is 4,000 direct labor hours, or 80% of normal volume. The unfavorable volume variance of $2,400 can be viewed as the cost of the unused capacity (1,000 direct labor hours).

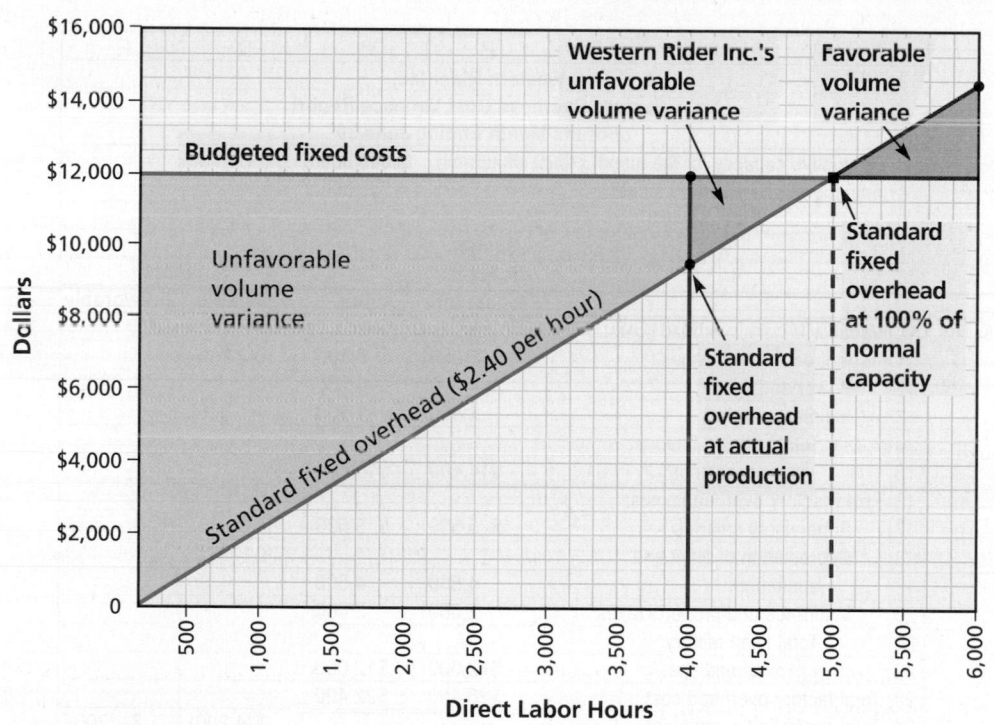

Exhibit 9
Graph of Fixed Overhead Volume Variance

An unfavorable volume variance may be due to factors such as the following:

- Failure to maintain an even flow of work
- Machine breakdowns
- Work stoppages caused by lack of materials or skilled labor
- Lack of enough sales orders to keep the factory operating at normal capacity

Management should determine the causes of the unfavorable variance and consider taking corrective action. For example, a volume variance caused by an uneven flow of work could be remedied by changing operating procedures. Lack of sales orders may be corrected through increased advertising.

Favorable volume variances may not always be desirable. For example, in an attempt to create a favorable volume variance, manufacturing managers might run the factory above the normal capacity. However, if the additional production cannot be sold, it must be stored as inventory, which would incur storage costs.

Reporting Factory Overhead Variances

The total factory overhead cost variance can also be determined as the sum of the variable factory overhead controllable and fixed factory overhead volume variances, computed as follows for **Western Rider Inc.**:

Variable factory overhead controllable variance	$(4,000) Favorable Variance
Fixed factory overhead volume variance	2,400 Unfavorable Variance
Total factory overhead cost variance	$(1,600) Favorable Variance

A **factory overhead cost variance report** is useful to management in controlling factory overhead costs. Budgeted and actual costs for variable and fixed factory overhead along with the related controllable and volume variances are reported by each cost element.

Exhibit 10 illustrates a factory overhead cost variance report for Western Rider Inc. for June.

Exhibit 10

Factory Overhead Cost Variance Report

	A	B	C	D	E
1	Western Rider Inc.				
2	Factory Overhead Cost Variance Report				
3	For the Month Ending June 30				
4	Productive capacity for the month (100% of normal)	5,000 hours			
5	Actual production for the month	4,000 hours			
6					
7		Budget			
8		(at Actual		Variances	
9		Production)	Actual	Favorable	Unfavorable
10	Variable factory overhead costs:				
11	Indirect factory wages	$ 8,000	$ 5,100	$(2,900)	
12	Power and light	4,000	4,200		$ 200
13	Indirect materials	2,400	1,100	(1,300)	
14	Total variable factory				
15	overhead cost	$14,400	$10,400		
16	Fixed factory overhead costs:				
17	Supervisory salaries	$ 5,500	$ 5,500		
18	Depreciation of plant and				
19	equipment	4,500	4,500		
20	Insurance and property taxes	2,000	2,000		
21	Total fixed factory				
22	overhead cost	$12,000	$12,000		
23	Total factory overhead cost	$26,400	$22,400		
24	Total controllable variances			$(4,200)	$ 200
25					
26					
27	Net controllable variance—favorable [$(4,200) favorable + $200] unfavorable				$(4,000)
28	Volume variance—unfavorable:				
29	Capacity not used at the standard rate for fixed				
30	factory overhead—1,000 × $2.40				2,400
31	Total factory overhead cost variance—favorable				$(1,600)
32					

Why It Matters

Standard Costing in Action: Expanding Brewing Operations

U.S. west coast craft brewers Sierra Nevada (CA) and New Belgium (CO) recently announced plans to expand their brewing operations to the Asheville, North Carolina, area. Both companies considered the standard cost of their product when making the decision to expand, and in selecting Asheville as their east coast location. The standard price of direct materials includes the cost of shipping direct materials to the manufacturers' place of business. The Asheville location was desirable when considering these costs.

In addition, New Belgium projected that its Fort Collins, Colorado, brewery would reach maximum capacity in three to five years. While operating at 100% capacity creates a favorable overhead volume variance, any demand in excess of 100% capacity will result in lost sales. Thus, New Belgium felt that adding a new brewery prior to reaching 100% capacity at Fort Collins was supported. In both cases, standard costing was used to support the expansion and location decisions.

Sources: H. Dornbusch, "The Case for Low Mileage Beer," *Brewers Association.org*; J. McCurry, "Hops City: Beer Culture Comes to a Head in the Asheville Region," *Site Selection*, July 2012; J. Shikes, "New Belgium, Maker of Fat Tire, Plans a Second Brewery on the East Coast," *Denver Westward*, May 19, 2011.

Factory Overhead Account

The applied factory overhead for **Western Rider Inc.** for the 5,000 XL jeans produced in June is $24,000, computed as follows:

Applied Factory Overhead = Standard Hours for Actual Units Produced × Total Factory Overhead Rate
= (5,000 jeans × 0.80 direct labor hr. per pair of Jeans) × $6.00
= 4,000 direct labor hrs. × $6.00 = $24,000

The total actual factory overhead for Western Rider, as shown in Exhibit 10, was $22,400. Thus, the total factory overhead cost variance for Western Rider for June is a $1,600 favorable variance, computed as follows:

Total Factory Overhead Cost Variance = Actual Factory Overhead − Applied Factory Overhead

= $22,400 − $24,000 = $(1,600) Favorable Variance

At the end of the period, the factory overhead account normally has a balance. A debit balance in Factory Overhead represents underapplied overhead. Underapplied overhead occurs when actual factory overhead costs exceed the applied factory overhead. A credit balance in Factory Overhead represents overapplied overhead. Overapplied overhead occurs when actual factory overhead costs are less than the applied factory overhead.

The difference between the actual factory overhead and the applied factory overhead is the total factory overhead cost variance. Thus, underapplied and overapplied factory overhead account balances represent the following total factory overhead cost variances:

- *Underapplied* Factory Overhead = *Unfavorable* Total Factory Overhead Cost Variance
- *Overapplied* Factory Overhead = *Favorable* Total Factory Overhead Cost Variance

The factory overhead account for **Western Rider Inc.** for the month ending June 30 is as follows:

Factory Overhead

Actual factory overhead ($10,400 + $12,000)	22,400	24,000	Applied factory overhead (4,000 hrs. × $6.00 per hr.)
		Bal., June 30 1,600	Overapplied factory overhead

The $1,600 overapplied factory overhead account balance and the favorable total factory overhead cost variance shown in Exhibit 10 are the same.

The variable factory overhead controllable variance and the volume variance can be computed by comparing the factory overhead account with the budgeted total overhead for the actual level produced, as shown in Exhibit 11.

The controllable and volume variances are determined as follows:

- The difference between the actual overhead incurred and the budgeted overhead is the *controllable* variance.
- The difference between the applied overhead and the budgeted overhead is the *volume* variance.

If the actual factory overhead exceeds (is less than) the budgeted factory overhead, the controllable variance is unfavorable (favorable). In contrast, if the applied factory overhead is less than (exceeds) the budgeted factory overhead, the volume variance is unfavorable (favorable).

Exhibit 11   Factory Overhead Variances

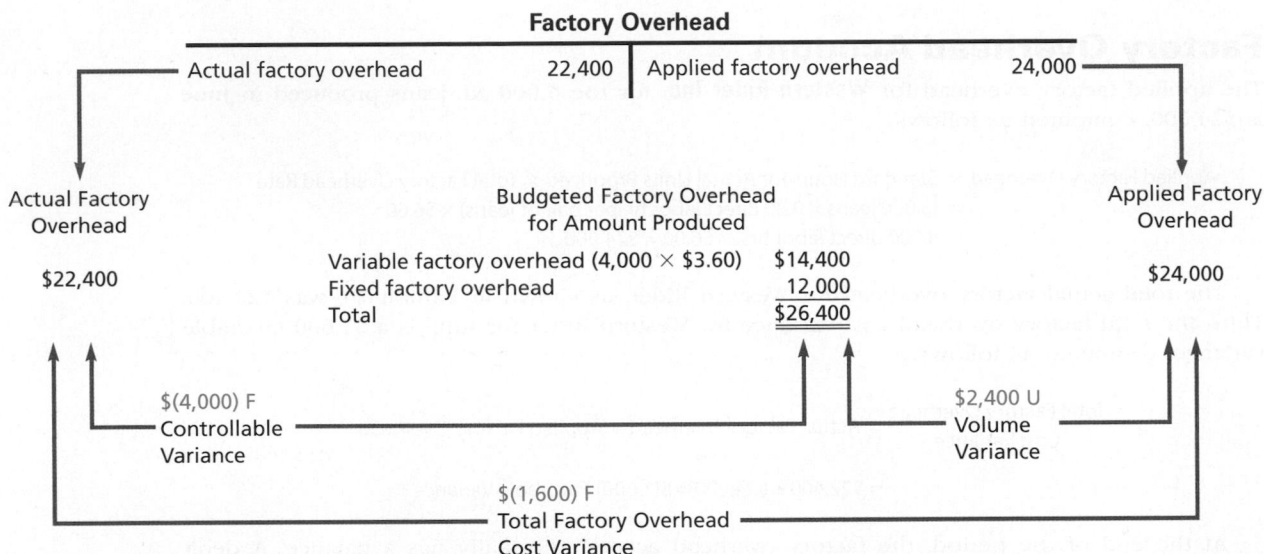

Check Up Corner 8-2   Factory Overhead Cost Variances

Menounos Manufacturing Co. uses standard costs in its budgets. Standard costs and actual costs for direct labor and factory overhead for the manufacture of 3,000 units during 20Y6 were as follows:

	Standard Costs	Actual Costs
Direct labor	7,500 hours at $12.00 per hour	7,420 hours at $12.30 per hour
Factory overhead	Rates per direct labor hr., based on 100% of normal capacity of 8,000 direct labor hrs.:	
	Variable cost, $2.20	$16,850 variable cost
	Fixed cost, $0.90	$7,200 fixed cost

Each unit requires 2.5 hours of direct labor.

Determine the:

A.   Variable factory overhead controllable variance,

B.   Fixed factory overhead volume variance, and

C.   Total factory overhead cost variance.

Solution:

A.

$$\begin{array}{ccc} \text{Variable Factory Overhead} \\ \text{Controllable Variance} \end{array} = \begin{array}{c} \text{Actual} \\ \text{Variable Factory Overhead} \end{array} - \begin{array}{c} \text{Budgeted} \\ \text{Variable Factory Overhead} \end{array}$$

= \$16,850 – \$16,500 ←

= \$350 Unfavorable Variance

Budgeted Variable Factory Overhead = Standard Hours for Actual Units Produced
× Variable Factory Overhead Rate

= 7,500 direct labor hrs. × \$2.20

= \$16,500 ————

B.

$$\begin{array}{c} \text{Fixed Factory} \\ \text{Overhead} \\ \text{Volume Variance} \end{array} = \left(\begin{array}{c} \text{Standard Hours} \\ \text{for 100\% of} \\ \text{Normal Capacity} \end{array} - \begin{array}{c} \text{Standard Hours for} \\ \text{Actual Units} \\ \text{Produced} \end{array} \right) \times \begin{array}{c} \text{Fixed Factory} \\ \text{Overhead Rate} \end{array}$$

$$= \left(\begin{array}{c} \text{8,000 direct} \\ \text{labor hrs.} \end{array} - \begin{array}{c} \text{7,500 direct} \\ \text{labor hrs.} \end{array} \right) \times \$0.90$$

= \$450 Unfavorable Variance

C.

Applied Factory Overhead = Standard Hours for Actual Units Produced × Total Factory Overhead Rate

= (3,000 units × 2.5 direct labor hrs. per unit) × (\$2.20 variable cost per hour
+ \$0.90 fixed cost per hour)

= 7,500 direct labor hrs. × \$3.10

$$\begin{array}{c} \text{Total Factory Overhead} \\ \text{Cost Variance} \end{array} = \begin{array}{l} \$23,250 \text{————} \\ = \text{Actual Factory Overhead – Applied Factory Overhead} \end{array}$$

= \$24,050 – \$23,250

= 800 Unfavorable Variance

Alternative Computation of Overhead Variances

(8,000 direct labor hours
@ 100%) × \$0.90 fixed
factory overhead rate

3,000 units produced × 2.5
standard hours per unit

Factory Overhead

| Actual factory overhead ($16,850 + $7,200) | 24,050 | Applied factory overhead [7,500 × ($2.20 + $0.90)] | 23,250 |

Actual Factory Overhead $24,050

Budgeted Factory Overhead for Amount Produced

Variable factory overhead (7,500 hrs. × \$2.20)   \$16,500
Fixed factory overhead   7,200 ←
Total   \$23,700

Applied Factory Overhead $23,250

\$350 U
Controllable
Variance

\$450 U
Volume
Variance

\$800 U
Total Factory Overhead
Cost Variance

The variance is
unfavorable because the
actual factory overhead is
greater than the budgeted
factory overhead.

The variance is **unfavorable**
because the applied factory
overhead is less than the
budgeted factory
overhead.

Check Up Corner

Objective 5

Describe and illustrate the recording and reporting of standards and variances.

Recording and Reporting Variances from Standards

Standard costs may be used as a management tool to control costs separately from the accounts in the general ledger. However, many companies include standard costs in their accounts. One method for doing so records standard costs and variances at the same time the actual product costs are recorded.

To illustrate, assume that **Western Rider Inc.** purchased, on account, the 7,300 square yards of blue denim used at $5.50 per square yard. The standard price for direct materials is $5.00 per square yard. The entry to record the purchase and the unfavorable direct materials price variance is as follows:

Materials (7,300 sq. yds. × $5.00)	36,500	
Direct Materials Price Variance	3,650	
Accounts Payable (7,300 sq. yds. × $5.50)		40,150

The materials account is debited for the *actual quantity* purchased at the *standard price*, $36,500 (7,300 square yards × $5.00). Accounts Payable is credited for the $40,150 actual cost and the amount due the supplier. The difference of $3,650 is the unfavorable direct materials price variance [($5.50 − $5.00) × 7,300 sq. yds.]. It is recorded by debiting Direct Materials Price Variance. If the variance had been favorable, Direct Materials Price Variance would have been credited for the variance.

A debit balance in the direct materials price variance account represents an unfavorable variance. Likewise, a credit balance in the direct materials price variance account represents a favorable variance.

The direct materials quantity variance is recorded in a similar manner. For example, **Western Rider Inc.** used 7,300 square yards of blue denim to produce 5,000 pairs of XL jeans. The standard quantity of denim for the 5,000 jeans produced is 7,500 square yards. The entry to record the materials used is as follows:

Work in Process (7,500 sq. yds. × $5.00)	37,500	
Direct Materials Quantity Variance		1,000
Materials (7,300 sq. yds. × $5.00)		36,500

Work in Process is debited for $37,500, which is the standard cost of the direct materials required to produce 5,000 XL jeans (7,500 sq. yds. × $5.00). Materials is credited for $36,500, which is the actual quantity of materials used at the standard price (7,300 sq. yds. × $5.00). The difference of $1,000 is the favorable direct materials quantity variance [(7,300 sq. yds. − 7,500 sq. yds.) × $5.00]. It is recorded by crediting Direct Materials Quantity Variance. If the variance had been unfavorable, Direct Materials Quantity Variance would have been debited for the variance.

A debit balance in the direct materials quantity variance account represents an unfavorable variance. Likewise, a credit balance in the direct materials quantity variance account represents a favorable variance.

The journal entries to record the standard costs and variances for *direct labor* are similar to those for direct materials. These entries are summarized as follows:

- Work in Process is debited for the standard cost of direct labor.
- Wages Payable is credited for the actual direct labor cost incurred.

- Direct Labor Rate Variance is debited for an unfavorable variance and credited for a favorable variance.
- Direct Labor Time Variance is debited for an unfavorable variance and credited for a favorable variance.

As illustrated in the prior section, the factory overhead account already incorporates standard costs and variances into its journal entries. That is, Factory Overhead is debited for actual factory overhead and credited for applied (standard) factory overhead. The ending balance of factory overhead (overapplied or underapplied) is the total factory overhead cost variance. By comparing the actual factory overhead with the budgeted factory overhead, the controllable variance can be determined. By comparing the budgeted factory overhead with the applied factory overhead, the volume variance can be determined.

When goods are completed, Finished Goods is debited and Work in Process is credited for the standard cost of the product transferred.

At the end of the period, the balances of each of the variance accounts indicate the net favorable or unfavorable variance for the period. These variances may be reported in an income statement prepared for management's use.

Exhibit 12 is an example of an income statement for **Western Rider Inc.** that includes variances. In Exhibit 12, a sales price of $28 per pair of jeans, selling expenses of $14,500, and administrative expenses of $11,225 are assumed.

Exhibit 12
Variance from Standards in Income Statement

Western Rider Inc. Income Statement For the Month Ended June 30	Favorable	Unfavorable	
Sales			$140,000[1]
Cost of goods sold—at standard..................................			97,500[2]
Gross profit—at standard			$ 42,500
Variances from standard cost:			
Direct materials price		$ 3,650	
Direct materials quantity	$(1,000)		
Direct labor rate		3,850	
Direct labor time...	(1,350)		
Factory overhead controllable	(4,000)		
Factory overhead volume..		2,400	
Net variance from standard cost—unfavorable			3,550
Gross profit			$ 38,950
Operating expenses:			
Selling expenses		$14,500	
Administrative expenses...		11,225	
Total operating expenses			25,725
Income before income tax			$ 13,225

[1]5,000 × $28
[2]$37,500 + $36,000 + $24,000 (from Exhibit 3), or 5,000 × $19.50 (from Exhibit 1)

The income statement shown in Exhibit 12 is for internal use by management. That is, variances are not reported to external users. Thus, the variances shown in Exhibit 12 must be transferred to other accounts in preparing an income statement for external users.

In preparing an income statement for external users, the balances of the variance accounts are normally transferred to Cost of Goods Sold. However, if the variances are significant or if many of the products manufactured are still in inventory, the variances should be allocated to Work in Process, Finished Goods, and Cost of Goods Sold. Such an allocation, in effect, converts these account balances from standard cost to actual cost.

Check Up Corner 8-3 | Income Statement with Variances

Using the variance data for Menounos Manufacturing Co. in Check Up Corners 8-1 (pp. 378–379) and 8-2 (pp. 386–387), prepare an income statement through gross profit for the year ended December 31, 20Y6. Assume the company sold 3,000 units at $100 per unit.

Solution:

Menounos Manufacturing Co.
Income Statement Through Gross Profit
For the Year Ended December 31, 20Y6

Sales..			$300,000	← 3,000 units sold × $100 selling price per unit
Cost of goods sold—at standard			194,250
Gross profit—at standard.........................			$105,750

	Favorable	**Unfavorable**	
Variances from standard cost:			
Direct materials price	$(2,775)		
Direct materials quantity.........................		$2,250	From Check Up
Direct labor rate		2,226	Corner 8-1
Direct labor time	(960)		
Factory overhead controllable		350	From Check Up
Factory overhead volume.......................		450	Corner 8-2
Net variance from standard cost—unfavorable		1,541	
Gross profit....................................		$104,209	

Direct materials at standard	$ 81,000
Direct labor cost at standard (3,000 units × 2.5 standard hours per unit × $12 standard rate per hour)	90,000
Factory overhead at standard (3,000 units × 2.5 standard hours per unit × $3.10 standard rate per hour)	23,250
Cost of goods sold at standard	$194,250

Check Up Corner

Nonfinancial Performance Measures

Objective 6

Describe and illustrate nonfinancial performance measures.

Many companies supplement standard costs and variances from standards with nonfinancial performance measures. A **nonfinancial performance measure** expresses performance in a measure other than dollars. For example, airlines use on-time performance, percent of bags lost, and number of customer complaints as nonfinancial performance measures. Such measures are often used to evaluate the time, quality, or quantity of a business activity.

Link to BMW Group

The **BMW Group** uses a variety of nonfinancial performance measures for its vehicles and its manufacturing operations, including energy consumption, water consumption, carbon dioxide emissions, percent of women in its workforce, average days of training per employee, and accident frequency.

Using financial and nonfinancial performance measures aids managers and employees in considering multiple performance objectives. Such measures often bring additional perspectives, such as quality of work, to evaluating performance. Some examples of nonfinancial performance measures are shown in Exhibit 13.

- Inventory turnover
- Percent on-time delivery
- Elapsed time between a customer order and product delivery
- Customer preference rankings compared to competitors
- Response time to a service call
- Time to develop new products
- Employee satisfaction
- Number of customer complaints

Exhibit 13
Nonfinancial
Performance
Measures

Nonfinancial measures are often linked to either the inputs or outputs of an activity or process. A **process** is a sequence of activities for performing a task. The relationship between an activity or a process and its inputs and outputs is shown in Exhibit 14.

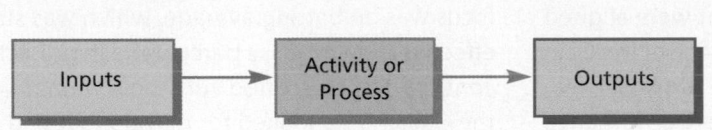

Exhibit 14
Relationship
Between a
Process and
Its Inputs and
Outputs

To illustrate, the counter service activity of a fast-food restaurant is used. The inputs/outputs for providing counter service at a fast-food restaurant are shown in Exhibit 15.

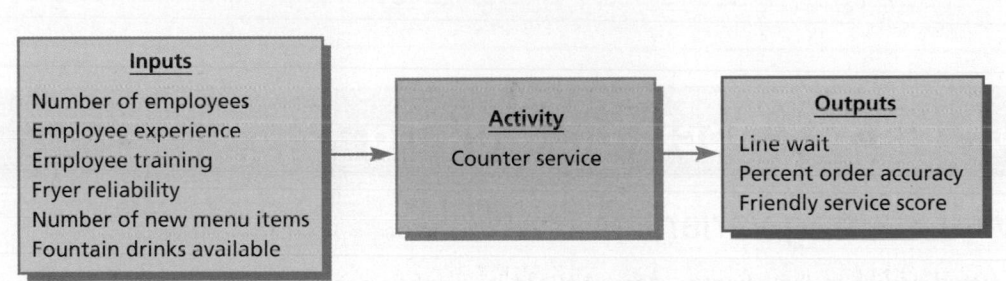

Exhibit 15
Inputs/Outputs
for a Fast-Food
Restaurant

The customer service outputs of the counter service activity include the following:

- Line wait for the customer
- Percent order accuracy in serving the customer
- Friendly service experience for the customer

Some of the inputs that impact the customer service outputs include the following:

- Number of employees
- Employee experience
- Employee training
- Fryer (and other cooking equipment) reliability
- Number of new menu items
- Fountain drink availability

A fast-food restaurant can develop a set of linked nonfinancial performance measures across inputs and outputs. The output measures tell management how the activity is performing, such as keeping the line wait to a minimum. The input measures are used to improve the output measures. For example, if the customer line wait is too long, then improving employee training or hiring more employees could improve the output (decrease customer line wait).

Link to BMW Group

The **BMW Group** assesses its suppliers using a BMW sustainablity standard that measures compliance with human rights, labor, and social issues.

Why It Matters

The Lesson of Moneyball

The book and movie, *Moneyball*, showed how the **Oakland A's** baseball organization built a winning team by using player performance measures that were aligned to winning games. At that time, the front office of the Oakland A's baseball organization analyzed the statistical relationship between various measures of player performance and scoring runs. It discovered "on-base percentage," an unlikely and underutilized measure, as the dominant predictor of scoring runs. The on-base percentage is the number of times a player gets on base as a percentage of total at-bats. Prior to this, baseball organizations relied on the manager's intuitive assessment of a player's performance. Oftentimes, this intuition poorly predicted a player's contribution to team success. In addition, the focus was on batting average, which was statistically less effective than on-base percentage in predicting a player's contribution to scoring runs and winning games. Thus, the Oakland A's looked for players that had high on-base percentages and built a winning team out of players the rest of the league overlooked. The lesson for business is that performance measures should be highly aligned to strategic objectives so that high performance on the measure will lead to high performance toward the organization's larger goals.

Analysis for Decision Making

Objective

Describe and illustrate the use of the direct labor time variance in evaluating staff performance in a service setting.

Service Staffing Variances

As we stated earlier in this chapter, standards can be used in nonmanufacturing settings where the tasks are repetitive in nature. Standards are used in hotels, hospitals, restaurants, transportation services, banks, retail stores, professional services, software development, automotive services, and many other service settings.

To illustrate, Marion Hotel uses labor standards to control the costs of the housekeeping staff. From historical information, the hotel expects a housekeeping employee to clean a room in 42 minutes. An occupied room for one night is termed a "guest room night." In addition, housekeeping employees are paid $13 per hour. Information for a recent week follows:

Number of guest room nights	1,050
Number of housekeeping staff hours	840

The guest room nights can be translated into standard staff hours as follows:

Number of guest room nights	1,050
Multiplied by standard hours per room (42 min. ÷ 60 min.)	× 0.70
Standard housekeeping staff hours	735

The direct labor time variance can be calculated as:

Direct Labor Time Variance = (Actual Staff Hours – Standard Staff Hours) × Standard Rate per Hour
= (840 hrs. – 735 hrs.) × $13 per hour
= $1,365 Unfavorable

The actual staff hours were greater than the standard hours, causing an unfavorable staff time variance. Management can investigate the causes of the variance, which may include overscheduling staff, insufficient staff training, difficult room cleaning situations, and staff inefficiency.

Make a Decision   Service Staffing Variances

Advent Software uses standards to manage the cost of the programming staff. There are two programmer levels, Level 1 and Level 2. Level 1 programmers normally work on the easier projects. Level 1 and Level 2 programmers are paid $25 and $35 per hour, respectively. It has been determined from experience that Level 2 programmers can complete 50 lines of code per hour. If a Level 1 programmer is assigned to a Level 2 task, the programming work will be slower than the Level 2 time standard, but will be accomplished at a lower labor rate.

   During a recent week, a Level 2 project was assigned to a Level 1 programmer. The programmer worked 40 hours and completed 1,400 lines of code.

A.   Determine the direct labor time variance for this worker.

B.   Determine the direct labor rate variance for this worker.

C.   Using the information in (A) and (B), is it more cost effective to use a Level 1 worker or a Level 2 worker on a Level 2 project?

Solution:

A.   Standard hours for coding:

Lines of code	1,400
Level 2 standard lines per hour	÷ 50
Standard hours at Level 2 coding standard	28

Direct Labor Time Variance = (Actual Staff Hours – Standard Staff Hours) × Standard Rate per Hour
= (40 hrs. – 28 hrs.) × $35 per hour
= $420 Unfavorable

Note that the standard rate per hour is set at the Level 2 rate for this Level 2 project. We are comparing the Level 1 performance to the Level 2 standard.

The Level 1 programmer is not as efficient as a Level 2 programmer on a Level 2 project. Therefore, there is an unfavorable labor time variance.

B.   Direct Labor Rate Variance = (Actual Rate per Hour – Standard Rate per Hour) × Actual Hours
= ($25 – $35) × 40 hrs.
= $(400) Favorable

The Level 1 programmer has a lower labor rate than the Level 2 programmer. Thus, there is a favorable direct labor rate variance.

C.   The amount of the unfavorable time variance is greater than the amount of the favorable rate variance. Thus, this analysis suggests that it is not cost effective to use a Level 1 programmer on a Level 2 project. The Level 1 programmer's lower cost per hour does not make up for the slower coding performance.

Make a Decision

Let's Review

Chapter Summary

1. Standards represent performance goals that can be compared to actual results in evaluating performance. Standards should be established so that they are neither too high nor too low, but are attainable.

2. Budgets are prepared by multiplying the standard cost per unit by the planned production. To measure performance, the standard cost per unit is multiplied by the actual number of units produced, and the actual results are compared with the standard cost at actual volumes (cost variance).

3. The direct materials cost variance can be separated into direct materials price and quantity variances. The direct labor cost variance can be separated into direct labor rate and time variances.

4. The factory overhead cost variance can be separated into a variable factory overhead controllable variance and a fixed factory overhead volume variance.

5. Standard costs and variances can be recorded in the accounts at the same time the manufacturing costs are recorded in the accounts. Work in Process is debited at standard. Under a standard cost system, the cost of goods sold will be reported at standard cost. Manufacturing variances can be disclosed on the income statement to adjust the gross profit at standard to the actual gross profit.

6. Many companies use a combination of financial and nonfinancial measures in order for multiple perspectives to be incorporated in evaluating performance. Nonfinancial measures are often used in conjunction with the inputs or outputs of a process or an activity.

Key Terms

budget performance report (372)
budgeted variable factory
  overhead (381)
controllable variance (381)
cost variances (372)
currently attainable standards (371)
direct labor rate variance (377)
direct labor time variance (377)
direct materials price variance (375)

direct materials quantity
  variance (375)
factory overhead cost
  variance report (384)
favorable cost variance (372)
ideal standards (371)
nonfinancial performance
  measure (390)
process (391)

standard cost (370)
standard cost systems (370)
standards (370)
total manufacturing cost
  variance (373)
unfavorable cost variance (372)
volume variance (382)

Practice

Multiple-Choice Questions

1. The actual and standard direct materials costs for producing a specified quantity of product are as follows:

Actual:	51,000 lbs. at $5.05	$257,550
Standard:	50,000 lbs. at $5.00	$250,000

   The direct materials price variance is:

   A. $50 unfavorable.
   B. $2,500 unfavorable.

   C. $2,550 unfavorable.
   D. $7,550 unfavorable.

2. Bower Company produced 4,000 units of product. Each unit requires 0.5 standard hour. The standard labor rate is $12 per hour. Actual direct labor for the period was $22,000 (2,200 hrs. × $10 per hr.). The direct labor time variance is:
   A. 200 hours unfavorable.
   B. $2,000 unfavorable.
   C. $4,000 favorable.
   D. $2,400 unfavorable.

3. The actual and standard factory overhead costs for producing a specified quantity of product are as follows:

Actual: Variable factory overhead	$72,500	
Fixed factory overhead	40,000	$112,500
Standard: 19,000 hrs. at $6		
($4 variable and $2 fixed)		114,000

   If 1,000 hours were unused, the fixed factory overhead volume variance would be:
   A. $1,500 favorable.
   B. $2,000 unfavorable.
   C. $4,000 unfavorable.
   D. $6,000 unfavorable.

4. Ramathan Company produced 6,000 units of Product Y, which is 80% of capacity. Each unit required 0.25 standard machine hour for production. The standard variable factory overhead rate is $5 per machine hour. The actual variable factory overhead incurred during the period was $8,000. The variable factory overhead controllable variance is:
   A. $500 favorable.
   B. $500 unfavorable.
   C. $1,875 favorable.
   D. $1,875 unfavorable.

5. Applegate Company has a normal budgeted capacity of 200 machine hours. Applegate produced 600 units. Each unit requires a standard 0.2 machine hour to complete. The standard fixed factory overhead is $12 per hour, determined at normal capacity. The fixed factory overhead volume variance is:
   A. $4,800 unfavorable.
   B. $4,800 favorable.
   C. $960 favorable.
   D. $960 unfavorable.

Answers provided after Problem. Need more practice? Find additional multiple-choice questions, exercises, and problems in CengageNOWv2.

Exercises

SHOW ME HOW

1. Direct materials variances   Obj. 3

Lo-bed Company produces a product that requires 2 standard gallons per unit. The standard price is $20.00 per gallon. If 4,000 units required 8,200 gallons, which were purchased at $19.75 per gallon, what is the direct materials (A) price variance, (B) quantity variance, and (C) total cost variance.

SHOW ME HOW

2. Direct labor variances   Obj. 3

Lo-bed Company produces a product that requires 4 standard direct labor hours per unit at a standard hourly rate of $28.00 per hour. If 4,000 units required 16,750 direct labor hours at an hourly rate of $28.40 per hour, what is the direct labor (A) rate variance, (B) time variance, and (C) total cost variance.

SHOW ME HOW

3. Factory overhead controllable variance   Obj. 4

Lo-bed Company produced 4,000 units of product that required 4 standard hours per unit. The standard variable overhead cost per unit is $3.00 per hour. The actual variable factory overhead was $51,240. Determine the variable factory overhead controllable variance.

SHOW ME HOW

4. Factory overhead volume variance   Obj. 4

Lo-bed Company produced 4,000 units of product that required 4 standard hours per unit. The standard fixed overhead cost per unit is $1.20 per hour at 16,400 hours, which is 100% of normal capacity. Determine the fixed factory overhead volume variance.

SHOW ME HOW

5. Standard cost journal entries
Obj. 5

Lo-bed Company produced 4,000 units that require 2 standard gallons per unit at $20.00 standard price per gallon. The company actually used 8,200 gallons in production. Journalize the entry to record the standard direct materials used in production.

SHOW ME HOW

6. Income statement with variances
Obj. 5

Prepare an income statement for Lo-bed Company for the month ending March 31. Prepare the income statement through gross profit using the variance data from Exercises 1, 2, 3, and 4. Assume Lo-bed sold 4,000 units at $250 per unit.

SHOW ME HOW

7. Activity inputs and outputs
Obj. 6

The following are inputs and outputs to the copying process of a copy shop:

Number of employee errors

Number of times paper supply runs out

Copy machine downtime (broken)

Number of pages copied per hour

Number of customer complaints

Percent jobs done on time

Identify whether each is an input or output to the copying process.

Answers provided after Problem. Need more practice? Find additional multiple-choice questions, exercises, and problems in CengageNOWv2.

Problem

Hawley Inc. manufactures designer iPod cases for national distribution. The standard costs for the manufacture of designer iPod cases were as follows:

	Standard Costs	**Actual Costs**
Direct materials	1,500 lbs. at $35	1,600 lbs. at $32
Direct labor	4,800 hrs. at $11	4,500 hrs. at $11.80
Factory overhead	Rates per labor hour, based on 100% of normal capacity of 5,500 labor hrs.:	
	Variable cost, $2.40	$12,300 variable cost
	Fixed cost, $3.50	$19,250 fixed cost

Instructions

1. Determine the direct materials price variance, direct materials quantity variance, and total direct materials cost variance for the designer iPod cases.

2. Determine the direct labor rate variance, direct labor time variance, and total direct labor cost variance for the designer iPod cases.

3. Determine the variable factory overhead controllable variance, fixed factory overhead volume variance, and total factory overhead cost variance for the designer iPod cases.

Need more practice? Find additional multiple-choice questions, exercises, and problems in CengageNOWv2.

Answers

Multiple-Choice Questions

1. **C** The unfavorable direct materials price variance of $2,550 is determined as follows:

Actual price	$ 5.05 per lb.
Standard price	5.00
Price variance	$0.05 per lb.
Actual lbs.	× 51,000 lbs.
Price variance—unfavorable	$ 2,550

2. **D** The unfavorable direct labor time variance of $2,400 is determined as follows:

Actual direct labor time	2,200 hrs.
Standard direct labor time	2,000 hrs.*
Direct labor time variance	200 hrs.
Standard direct labor rate	× $12
Direct labor time variance—unfavorable	$2,400

*4,000 units × 0.5 hr.

3. **B** The unfavorable factory overhead volume variance of $2,000 is determined as follows:

Productive capacity not used	1,000 hrs.
Standard fixed factory overhead cost rate	× $2
Factory overhead volume variance—unfavorable	$2,000

4. **B** The controllable variable factory overhead variance is determined as follows:

Actual variable overhead	$ 8,000
Budgeted variable overhead at actual volume	(7,500)*
Controllable variance—unfavorable	$ 500

*6,000 units × 0.25 hr. = 1,500 hours;
1,500 hrs. × $5 per hr. = $7,500

5. **D** The fixed factory overhead volume variance can be determined as follows:

Practical capacity	200 machine hrs.
Actual production in standard hours	120 machine hrs.*
Idle capacity	80 machine hrs.
Standard fixed factory overhead rate	×$12
Volume variance—unfavorable	$960

*600 units × 0.2 machine hr. = 120 machine hrs.

Exercises

1. A. Direct materials price variance (favorable) $(2,050)   [($19.75 – $20.00) × 8,200 gal.]

   B. Direct materials quantity variance (unfavorable) $4,000   [(8,200 gal. – 8,000 gal.) × $20.00]

   C. Direct materials total cost variance (unfavorable) $1,950   [$(2,050) + $4,000] or
     [($19.75 × 8,200 gal.) – ($20.00 × 8,000 gal.)]
     = $161,950 – $160,000

2. A. Direct labor rate variance (unfavorable) $6,700   [($28.40 – $28.00) × 16,750 hrs.]

   B. Direct labor time variance (unfavorable) $21,000   [(16,750 hrs. – 16,000 hrs.) × $28.00]

   C. Direct labor total cost variance (unfavorable) $27,700   ($6,700 + $21,000) or
     [($28.40 × 16,750 hrs.) – ($28.00 × 16,000 hrs.)]
     = $475,700 – $448,000

3. Variable Factory Overhead Controllable Variance = $51,240 – [$3.00 × (4,000 units × 4 hrs.)]

           = $51,240 – $48,000

           = $3,240 Unfavorable

4. $480 Unfavorable = $1.20 × [16,400 hrs. – (4,000 units × 4 hrs.)]

5.

Work in Process (8,000* gal. × $20.00)	160,000	
Direct Materials Quantity Variance**	4,000	
Materials (8,200 gal. × $20.00)		164,000

*4,000 units × 2 standard gal. per unit
**[(8,200 gal. – 8,000 gal.) × $20.00]

6.

Lo-bed Company
Income Statement Through Gross Profit
For the Month Ended March 31

Sales (4,000 units × $250)		$ 1,000,000
Cost of goods sold—at standard*		675,200
Gross profit—at standard		$ 324,800

	Favorable	Unfavorable
Variances from standard cost:		
Direct materials price (Exercise 1)	$(2,050)	
Direct materials quantity (Exercise 1)		$ 4,000
Direct labor rate (Exercise 2)		6,700
Direct labor time (Exercise 2)		21,000
Factory overhead controllable (Exercise 3)		3,240
Factory overhead volume (Exercise 4)		480
Net variance from standard cost—unfavorable		33,370
Gross profit		$ 291,430
*Direct materials (4,000 units × 2 gal. × $20.00)		$160,000
Direct labor (4,000 units × 4 hrs. × $28.00)		448,000
Factory overhead [4,000 units × 4 hrs. × ($3.00 + $1.20)]		67,200
Cost of goods sold at standard		$675,200

7.

Number of employee errors	Input
Number of times paper supply runs out	Input
Copy machine downtime (broken)	Input
Number of pages copied per hour	Output
Number of customer complaints	Output
Percent jobs done on time	Output

Need more help? Watch step-by-step videos of how to compute answers to these Exercises in CengageNOWv2.

Problem

1.
Direct Materials Cost Variance

Price variance:

Direct Materials Price Variance = (Actual Price – Standard Price) × Actual Quantity
= ($32 per lb. – $35 per lb.) × 1,600 lbs.
= $(4,800) Favorable Variance

Quantity variance:

Direct Materials Quantity Variance = (Actual Quantity – Standard Quantity) × Standard Price
= (1,600 lbs. – 1,500 lbs.) × $35 per lb.
= $3,500 Unfavorable Variance

Total direct materials cost variance:

Direct Materials Cost Variance = Direct Materials Quantity Variance + Direct Materials Price Variance
= $3,500 + $(4,800)
= $(1,300) Favorable Variance

2.   **Direct Labor Cost Variance**

Rate variance:

Direct Labor Rate Variance = (Actual Rate per Hour – Standard Rate per Hour) × Actual Hours

= ($11.80 – $11.00) × 4,500 hrs.

= $3,600 Unfavorable Variance

Time variance:

Direct Labor Time Variance = (Actual Direct Labor Hours – Standard Direct Labor Hours) ×

Standard Rate per Hour

= (4,500 hrs. – 4,800 hrs.) × $11.00 per hour

= $(3,300) Favorable Variance

Total direct labor cost variance:

Direct Labor Cost Variance = Direct Labor Time Variance + Direct Labor Rate Variance

= $(3,300) + $3,600

= $300 Unfavorable Variance

3.   **Factory Overhead Cost Variance**

Variable factory overhead controllable variance:

Variable Factory Overhead
Controllable Variance = Actual Variable Factory Overhead – Budgeted Variable Factory Overhead

= $12,300 – $11,520*

= $780 Unfavorable Variance

*4,800 hrs. × $2.40 per hour

Fixed factory overhead volume variance:

Fixed Factory
Overhead Volume = $\left(\begin{array}{c} \text{Standard Hours for 100\%} \\ \text{of Normal Capacity} \end{array} - \begin{array}{c} \text{Standard Hours for} \\ \text{Actual Units Produced} \end{array}\right) \times \begin{array}{c} \text{Fixed Factory} \\ \text{Overhead Rate} \end{array}$
Variance

= (5,500 hrs. – 4,800 hrs.) × $3.50 per hr.

= $2,450 Unfavorable Variance

Total factory overhead cost variance:

Factory Overhead   Variable Factory Overhead   Fixed Factory Overhead
Cost Variance   =   Controllable Variance   +   Volume Variance

= $780 + $2,450

= $3,230 Unfavorable Variance

Alternative Computation of Overhead Variances

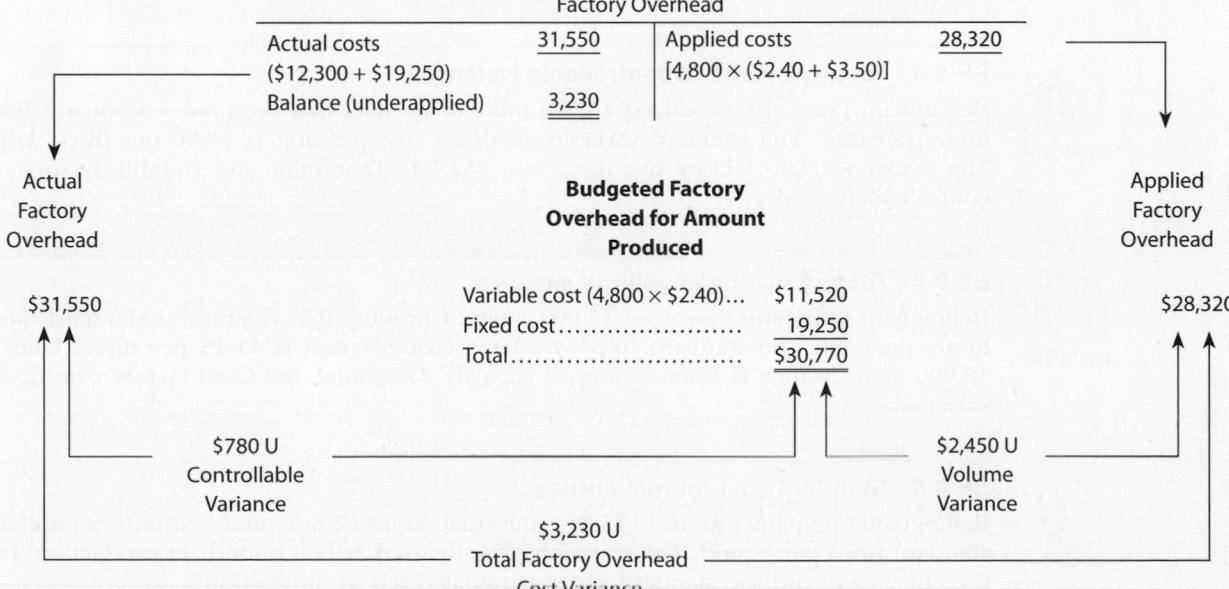

Discussion Questions

1. What are the basic objectives in the use of standard costs?

2. What is meant by reporting by the "principle of exceptions," as the term is used in reference to cost control?

3. What are the two variances between the actual cost and the standard cost for direct materials?

4. The materials cost variance report for Nickols Inc. indicates a large favorable materials price variance and a significant unfavorable materials quantity variance. What might have caused these offsetting variances?

5. A. What are the two variances between the actual cost and the standard cost for direct labor?

   B. Who generally has control over the direct labor cost variances?

6. A new assistant controller recently was heard to remark: "All the assembly workers in this plant are covered by union contracts, so there should be no labor variances." Was the controller's remark correct? Discuss.

7. Would the use of standards be appropriate in a nonmanufacturing setting, such as a fast-food restaurant?

8. A. Describe the two variances between the actual costs and the standard costs for factory overhead.

   B. What is a factory overhead cost variance report?

9. If variances are recorded in the accounts at the time the manufacturing costs are incurred, what does a debit balance in Direct Materials Price Variance represent?

10. Briefly explain why firms might use nonfinancial performance measures.

Basic Exercises

SHOW ME HOW

BE 8-1   Direct materials variances   Obj. 3

Bellingham Company produces a product that requires 2.5 standard pounds per unit. The standard price is $3.75 per pound. If 15,000 units used 36,000 pounds, which were purchased at $4.00 per pound, what is the direct materials (A) price variance, (B) quantity variance, and (C) cost variance?

SHOW ME HOW

BE 8-2   Direct labor variances   Obj. 3

Bellingham Company produces a product that requires 4 standard direct labor hours per unit at a standard hourly rate of $20 per hour. If 15,000 units used 61,800 hours at an hourly rate of $19.85 per hour, what is the direct labor (A) rate variance, (B) time variance, and (C) cost variance?

SHOW ME HOW

BE 8-3   Factory overhead controllable variance   Obj. 4

Bellingham Company produced 15,000 units of product that required 4 standard direct labor hours per unit. The standard variable overhead cost per unit is $0.90 per direct labor hour. The actual variable factory overhead was $52,770. Determine the variable factory overhead controllable variance.

SHOW ME HOW

BE 8-4   Factory overhead volume variance   Obj. 4

Bellingham Company produced 15,000 units of product that required 4 standard direct labor hours per unit. The standard fixed overhead cost per unit is $1.15 per direct labor hour at 58,000 hours, which is 100% of normal capacity. Determine the fixed factory overhead volume variance.

SHOW ME HOW

BE 8-5   Standard cost journal entries   Obj. 5

Bellingham Company produced 15,000 units that require 2.5 standard pounds per unit at a $3.75 standard price per pound. The company actually used 36,000 pounds in production. Journalize the entry to record the standard direct materials used in production.

SHOW ME HOW

BE 8-6 Income statement with variances   Obj. 5

Prepare an income statement through gross profit for Bellingham Company for the month ending March 31 using the variance data from Brief Exercises 1, 2, 3, and 4. Assume Bellingham sold 15,000 units at $172 per unit.

SHOW ME HOW

BE 8-7 Activity inputs and outputs   Obj. 6

The following are inputs and outputs to the cooking process of a restaurant:

Number of times ingredients are missing
Number of customer complaints
Number of hours kitchen equipment is down for repairs
Number of server order mistakes
Percent of meals prepared on time
Number of unexpected cook absences

Identify whether each is an input or output to the cooking process.

Exercises

SHOW ME HOW

EX 8-1 Standard direct materials cost per unit   Obj. 2

Roanoke Company produces chocolate bars. The primary materials used in producing chocolate bars are cocoa, sugar, and milk. The standard costs for a batch of chocolate (5,200 bars) are as follows:

Ingredient	Quantity	Price
Cocoa	400 lbs.	$1.25 per lb.
Sugar	80 lbs.	$0.40 per lb.
Milk	120 gal.	$2.50 per gal.

Determine the standard direct materials cost per bar of chocolate.

SHOW ME HOW

EX 8-2 Standard product cost   Obj. 2

Sana Rosa Furniture Company manufactures designer home furniture. Sana Rosa uses a standard cost system. The direct labor, direct materials, and factory overhead standards for an unfinished dining room table are as follows:

Direct labor:	standard rate	$18.00 per hr.
	standard time per unit	3.5 hrs.
Direct materials (oak):	standard price	$15.00 per bd. ft.
	standard quantity	26 bd. ft.
Variable factory overhead:	standard rate	$4.20 per direct labor hr.
Fixed factory overhead:	standard rate	$1.80 per direct labor hr.

A. Determine the standard cost per dining room table.

B. ➤ Why would Sana Rosa Furniture Company use a standard cost system?

✔ B. Direct labor cost
variance, $(580) F

SHOW ME HOW

EXCEL TEMPLATE

EX 8-3 Budget performance report   Obj. 2

Genie in a Bottle Company (GBC) manufactures plastic two-liter bottles for the beverage industry. The cost standards per 100 two-liter bottles are as follows:

Cost Category	Standard Cost per 100 Two-Liter Bottles
Direct labor	$ 2.00
Direct materials	9.10
Factory overhead	0.55
Total	$11.65

(Continued)

At the beginning of July, GBC management planned to produce 400,000 bottles. The actual number of bottles produced for July was 406,000 bottles. The actual costs for July of the current year were as follows:

Cost Category	Actual Cost for the Month Ended July 31
Direct labor	$ 7,540
Direct materials	35,750
Factory overhead	2,680
Total	$45,970

A. Prepare the July manufacturing standard cost budget (direct labor, direct materials, and factory overhead) for GBC, assuming planned production.

B. Prepare a budget performance report for manufacturing costs, showing the total cost variances for direct materials, direct labor, and factory overhead for July.

C. ━━━▶ Interpret the budget performance report.

EX 8-4 Direct materials variances

✔ A. Price variance, $7,250 U

SHOW ME HOW

Obj. 3

The following data relate to the direct materials cost for the production of 10,000 automobile tires:

Actual:	145,000 lbs. at $2.80 per lb.
Standard:	150,000 lbs. at $2.75 per lb.

A. Determine the direct materials price variance, direct materials quantity variance, and total direct materials cost variance.

B. ━━━▶ To whom should the variances be reported for analysis and control?

EX 8-5 Direct materials variances

✔ Quantity variance, $300 U

SHOW ME HOW

Obj. 3

Silicone Engine Inc. produces wrist-worn tablet computers. The company uses Thin Film Crystal (TFC) LCD displays for its products. Each tablet uses one display. The company produced 580 tablets during December. However, due to LCD defects, the company actually used 600 LCD displays during December. Each display has a standard cost of $15.00. Six hundred LCD displays were purchased for December production at a cost of $8,550.

Determine the price variance, quantity variance, and total direct materials cost variance for December.

SHOW ME HOW

EX 8-6 Standard direct materials cost per unit from variance data

Obj. 2, 3

The following data relating to direct materials cost for October of the current year are taken from the records of Good Clean Fun Inc., a manufacturer of organic toys:

Quantity of direct materials used	3,000 lbs.
Actual unit price of direct materials	$5.50 per lb.
Units of finished product manufactured	1,400 units
Standard direct materials per unit of finished product	2 lbs.
Direct materials quantity variance—unfavorable	$1,000
Direct materials price variance—unfavorable	$1,500

Determine the standard direct materials cost per unit of finished product, assuming that there was no inventory of work in process at either the beginning or the end of the month.

EX 8-7 Standard product cost, direct materials variance

Obj. 2, 3

✔ A. $1.25 per lb.

SHOW ME HOW

REAL WORLD

H.J. Heinz Company uses standards to control its materials costs. Assume that a batch of ketchup (3,128 pounds) has the following standards:

	Standard Quantity	Standard Price
Whole tomatoes	4,000 lbs.	$ 0.60 per lb.
Vinegar	260 gal.	2.25 per gal.
Corn syrup	25 gal.	28.00 per gal.
Salt	100 lbs.	2.25 per lb.

The actual materials in a batch may vary from the standard due to tomato characteristics. Assume that the actual quantities of materials for batch K-111 were as follows:

4,250 lbs. of tomatoes
275 gal. of vinegar
22 gal. of corn syrup
90 lbs. of salt

A. Determine the standard unit materials cost per pound for a standard batch.

B. Determine the direct materials quantity variance for batch K-111. Round your answer to the nearest cent.

EX 8-8 Direct labor variances

Obj. 3

✔ A. Rate variance, $(4,225) F

SHOW ME HOW

The following data relate to labor cost for production of 20,000 cellular telephones:

Actual:	8,450 hrs. at $22.50
Standard:	8,400 hrs. at $23.00

A. Determine the direct labor rate variance, direct labor time variance, and total direct labor cost variance.

B. ➤ Discuss what might have caused these variances.

EX 8-9 Direct labor variances

Obj. 3, 5

✔ A. Time variance, $(5,600) F

SHOW ME HOW

La Batre Bicycle Company manufactures commuter bicycles from recycled materials. The following data for July of the current year are available:

Quantity of direct labor used	5,050 hrs.
Actual rate for direct labor	$16.80 per hr.
Bicycles completed in April	1,000 bicycles
Standard direct labor per bicycle	5.4 hrs.
Standard rate for direct labor	$16.00 per hr.

A. Determine the direct labor rate variance, direct labor time variance, and total direct labor cost variance.

B. How much direct labor should be debited to Work in Process?

EX 8-10 Direct labor variances

Obj. 3

✔ A. Cutting Department rate variance, $(638) F

Greeson Clothes Company produced 25,000 units during June of the current year. The Cutting Department used 6,380 direct labor hours at an actual rate of $10.90 per hour. The Sewing Department used 9,875 direct labor hours at an actual rate of $11.12 per hour. Assume there were no work in process inventories in either department at the beginning or end of the month. The standard labor rate is $11.00. The standard labor time for the Cutting and Sewing departments is 0.25 hour and 0.4 hour per unit, respectively.

A. Determine the direct labor rate, direct labor time, and total direct labor cost variance for the (1) Cutting Department and (2) Sewing Department.

B. ➤ Interpret your results.

EX 8-11 Direct labor variances for a service company   Obj. 3

✔ A. Direct labor
rate variance, $(12) F

SHOW ME HOW

Hit-n-Run Food Trucks, Inc. owns and operates food trucks (mobile kitchens) throughout the west coast. The company's employees have varying wage levels depending on their experience and length of time with the company. Employees work 8-hour shifts and are assigned to a truck each day based on labor needs to support the daily menu. One of its trucks, Jose O'Brien's Mobile Fiesta, specializes in Irish-Mexican fusion cuisine. The truck offers a single menu item that changes daily. On November 11, the truck prepared 200 of its most popular item, the Irish Breakfast Enchilada. The following data are available for that day:

Quantity of direct labor used (3 employees, working 8-hour shifts)	24 hrs.
Actual rate for direct labor	$15.00 per hr.
Standard direct labor per meal	0.1 hr.
Standard rate for direct labor	$15.50 per hr.

A. Determine the direct labor rate variance, direct labor time variance, and total direct labor cost variance.

B. Discuss what might have caused these variances.

EX 8-12 Direct materials and direct labor variances   Obj. 3

✔ Direct materials
quantity variance,
$1,100 U

SHOW ME HOW

At the beginning of June, Bezco Toy Company budgeted 5,000 toy action figures to be manufactured in June at standard direct materials and direct labor costs as follows:

Direct materials	$50,000
Direct labor	36,000
Total	$86,000

The standard materials price is $4.00 per pound. The standard direct labor rate is $18.00 per hour. At the end of June, the actual direct materials and direct labor costs were as follows:

Actual direct materials	$49,600
Actual direct labor	34,020
Total	$83,620

There were no direct materials price or direct labor rate variances for June. In addition, assume no changes in the direct materials inventory balances in June. Bezco Toy Company actually produced 4,850 units during June.

Determine the direct materials quantity and direct labor time variances.

EX 8-13 Flexible overhead budget   Obj. 4

✔ Total factory
overhead, 22,000
hrs., $443,600

Leno Manufacturing Company prepared the following factory overhead cost budget for the Press Department for October of the current year, during which it expected to require 20,000 hours of productive capacity in the department:

Variable overhead costs:		
Indirect factory labor	$180,000	
Power and light	12,000	
Indirect materials	64,000	
Total variable overhead cost		$256,000
Fixed overhead costs:		
Supervisory salaries	$ 80,000	
Depreciation of plant and equipment	50,000	
Insurance and property taxes	32,000	
Total fixed overhead cost		162,000
Total factory overhead cost		$418,000

Assuming that the estimated costs for November are the same as for October, prepare a flexible factory overhead cost budget for the Press Department for November for 18,000, 20,000, and 22,000 hours of production.

EX 8-14 Flexible overhead budget
Obj. 4

✔ B. $94,500

Wiki Wiki Company has determined that the variable overhead rate is $4.50 per direct labor hour in the Fabrication Department. The normal production capacity for the Fabrication Department is 10,000 hours for the month. Fixed costs are budgeted at $60,000 for the month.

A. Prepare a monthly factory overhead flexible budget for 9,000, 10,000, and 11,000 hours of production.

B. How much overhead would be applied to production if 9,000 hours were used in the department during the month?

EX 8-15 Factory overhead cost variances
Obj. 4

✔ Volume variance, $6,000 U

The following data relate to factory overhead cost for the production of 10,000 computers:

Actual:	Variable factory overhead	$262,000
	Fixed factory overhead	90,000
Standard:	14,000 hrs. at $25	350,000

If productive capacity of 100% was 15,000 hours and the total factory overhead cost budgeted at the level of 14,000 standard hours was $356,000, determine the variable factory overhead controllable variance, fixed factory overhead volume variance, and total factory overhead cost variance. The fixed factory overhead rate was $6.00 per hour.

EX 8-16 Factory overhead cost variances
Obj. 4

✔ A. $(13,000) F

EXCEL TEMPLATE

Blumen Textiles Corporation began April with a budget for 90,000 hours of production in the Weaving Department. The department has a full capacity of 100,000 hours under normal business conditions. The budgeted overhead at the planned volumes at the beginning of April was as follows:

Variable overhead	$540,000
Fixed overhead	240,000
Total	$780,000

The actual factory overhead was $782,000 for April. The actual fixed factory overhead was as budgeted. During April, the Weaving Department had standard hours at actual production volume of 92,500 hours.

A. Determine the variable factory overhead controllable variance.

B. Determine the fixed factory overhead volume variance.

EX 8-17 Factory overhead variance corrections
Obj. 4

The data related to Shunda Enterprises Inc.'s factory overhead cost for the production of 100,000 units of product are as follows:

Actual:	Variable factory overhead	$458,000
	Fixed factory overhead	494,000
Standard:	132,000 hrs. at $7.30 ($3.50 for variable factory overhead)	963,600

Productive capacity at 100% of normal was 130,000 hours, and the factory overhead cost budgeted at the level of 132,000 standard hours was $956,000. Based on these data, the chief cost accountant prepared the following variance analysis:

Variable factory overhead controllable variance:		
Actual variable factory overhead cost incurred	$458,000	
Budgeted variable factory overhead for 132,000 hours	462,000	
Variance—favorable		$ (4,000)
Fixed factory overhead volume variance:		
Normal productive capacity at 100%	130,000 hrs.	
Standard for amount produced	132,000	

(Continued)

Productive capacity not used	2,000 hrs.	
Standard variable factory overhead rate	× $7.30	
Variance—unfavorable		14,600
Total factory overhead cost variance—unfavorable		$10,600

Identify the errors in the factory overhead cost variance analysis.

EX 8-18 Factory overhead cost variance report   Obj. 4

✔ Net controllable
variance, $900 U

EXCEL TEMPLATE

Tannin Products Inc. prepared the following factory overhead cost budget for the Trim Department for July of the current year, during which it expected to use 20,000 hours for production:

Variable overhead costs:		
Indirect factory labor	$46,000	
Power and light	12,000	
Indirect materials	20,000	
Total variable overhead cost		$ 78,000
Fixed overhead costs:		
Supervisory salaries	$54,500	
Depreciation of plant and equipment	40,000	
Insurance and property taxes	35,500	
Total fixed overhead cost		130,000
Total factory overhead cost		$208,000

Tannin has available 25,000 hours of monthly productive capacity in the Trim Department under normal business conditions. During July, the Trim Department actually used 22,000 hours for production. The actual fixed costs were as budgeted. The actual variable overhead for July was as follows:

Actual variable factory overhead costs:	
Indirect factory labor	$49,700
Power and light	13,000
Indirect materials	24,000
Total variable cost	$86,700

Construct a factory overhead cost variance report for the Trim Department for July.

EX 8-19 Recording standards in accounts   Obj. 5

Cioffi Manufacturing Company incorporates standards in its accounts and identifies variances at the time the manufacturing costs are incurred. Journalize the entries to record the following transactions:

A. Purchased 2,450 units of copper tubing on account at $52.00 per unit. The standard price is $48.50 per unit.

B. Used 1,900 units of copper tubing in the process of manufacturing 200 air conditioners. Ten units of copper tubing are required, at standard, to produce one air conditioner.

EX 8-20 Recording standards in accounts   Obj. 5

The Assembly Department produced 5,000 units of product during March. Each unit required 2.20 standard direct labor hours. There were 11,500 actual hours used in the Assembly Department during March at an actual rate of $17.60 per hour. The standard direct labor rate is $18.00 per hour. Assuming direct labor for a month is paid on the fifth day of the following month, journalize the direct labor in the Assembly Department on March 31.

EX 8-21 Income statement indicating standard cost variances   Obj. 5

✔ Income before
income tax, $85,900

The following data were taken from the records of Griggs Company for December:

Administrative expenses	$100,800
Cost of goods sold (at standard)	550,000
Direct materials price variance—unfavorable	1,680
Direct materials quantity variance—favorable	(560)

Direct labor rate variance—favorable	(1,120)
Direct labor time variance—unfavorable	490
Variable factory overhead controllable variance—favorable	(210)
Fixed factory overhead volume variance—unfavorable	3,080
Interest expense	2,940
Sales	868,000
Selling expenses	125,000

Prepare an income statement for presentation to management.

EX 8-22   Nonfinancial performance measures   Obj. 6

Diamond Inc. is an Internet retailer of woodworking equipment. Customers order woodworking equipment from the company, using an online catalog. The company processes these orders and delivers the requested product from its warehouse. The company wants to provide customers with an excellent purchase experience in order to expand the business through favorable word-of-mouth advertising and to drive repeat business. To help monitor performance, the company developed a set of performance measures for its order placement and delivery process:

> Average computer response time to customer "clicks"
> Dollar amount of returned goods
> Elapsed time between customer order and product delivery
> Maintenance dollars divided by hardware investment
> Number of customer complaints divided by the number of orders
> Number of misfilled orders divided by the number of orders
> Number of orders per warehouse employee
> Number of page faults or errors due to software programming errors
> Number of software fixes per week
> Server (computer) downtime
> Training dollars per programmer

A. For each performance measure, identify it as either an input or output measure related to the "order placement and delivery" process.

B. ➤ Provide an explanation for each performance measure.

EX 8-23   Nonfinancial performance measures   Obj. 6

Alpha University wishes to monitor the efficiency and quality of its course registration process.

A. Identify three input and three output measures for this process.

B. ➤ Why would Alpha University use nonfinancial measures for monitoring this process?

Problems: Series A

PR 8-1A   Direct materials and direct labor variance analysis   Obj. 2, 3

✔ C. Direct labor time
variance, $600 U

SHOW ME HOW

Abbeville Fixture Company manufactures faucets in a small manufacturing facility. The faucets are made from brass. Manufacturing has 90 employees. Each employee presently provides 36 hours of labor per week. Information about a production week is as follows:

Standard wage per hr.	$15.00
Standard labor time per faucet	40 min.
Standard number of lbs. of brass	3 lbs.
Standard price per lb. of brass	$2.40
Actual price per lb. of brass	$2.50
Actual lbs. of brass used during the week	14,350 lbs.
Number of faucets produced during the week	4,800
Actual wage per hr.	$14.40
Actual hrs. for the week (90 employees × 36 hours)	3,240

(Continued)

Instructions

Determine (A) the standard cost per unit for direct materials and direct labor; (B) the direct materials price variance, direct materials quantity variance, and total direct materials cost variance; and (C) the direct labor rate variance, direct labor time variance, and total direct labor cost variance.

PR 8-2A Flexible budgeting and variance analysis   Obj. 1, 2, 3

✔ 1. A. Direct
materials quantity
variance, $(625) F

EXCEL TEMPLATE

I Love My Chocolate Company makes dark chocolate and light chocolate. Both products require cocoa and sugar. The following planning information has been made available:

	Standard Amount per Case		
	Dark Chocolate	Light Chocolate	Standard Price per Pound
Cocoa	12 lbs.	8 lbs.	$7.25
Sugar	10 lbs.	14 lbs.	1.40
Standard labor time	0.50 hr.	0.60 hr.	

	Dark Chocolate	Light Chocolate
Planned production	4,700 cases	11,000 cases
Standard labor rate	$15.50 per hr.	$15.50 per hr.

I Love My Chocolate Company does not expect there to be any beginning or ending inventories of cocoa or sugar. At the end of the budget year, I Love My Chocolate Company had the following actual results:

	Dark Chocolate	Light Chocolate
Actual production (cases)	5,000	10,000

	Actual Price per Pound	Actual Pounds Purchased and Used
Cocoa	$7.33	140,300
Sugar	1.35	188,000

	Actual Labor Rate	Actual Labor Hours Used
Dark chocolate	$15.25 per hr.	2,360
Light chocolate	15.80 per hr.	6,120

Instructions

1. Prepare the following variance analyses for both chocolates and the total, based on the actual results and production levels at the end of the budget year:

   A. Direct materials price, quantity, and total variance.

   B. Direct labor rate, time, and total variance.

2. ➤ Why are the standard amounts in part (1) based on the actual production for the year instead of the planned production for the year?

PR 8-3A Direct materials, direct labor, and factory overhead   Obj. 3, 4
cost variance analysis

✔ C. Controllable
variance, $(4,800) F

EXCEL TEMPLATE

Mackinaw Inc. processes a base chemical into plastic. Standard costs and actual costs for direct materials, direct labor, and factory overhead incurred for the manufacture of 40,000 units of product were as follows:

	Standard Costs	Actual Costs
Direct materials	120,000 lbs. at $3.20 per lb.	118,500 lbs. at $3.25 per lb.
Direct labor	12,000 hrs. at $24.40 per hr.	11,700 hrs. at $25.00 per hr.
Factory overhead	Rates per direct labor hr.,	
	based on 100% of normal	
	capacity of 15,000 direct	
	labor hrs.:	
	Variable cost, $8.00	$91,200 variable cost
	Fixed cost, $10.00	$150,000 fixed cost

Each unit requires 0.3 hour of direct labor.

Instructions

Determine (A) the direct materials price variance, direct materials quantity variance, and total direct materials cost variance; (B) the direct labor rate variance, direct labor time variance, and total direct labor cost variance; and (C) the variable factory overhead controllable variance, fixed factory overhead volume variance, and total factory overhead cost variance.

PR 8-4A Factory overhead cost variance report

Obj. 4

✔ Controllable variance, $770 U

EXCEL TEMPLATE GENERAL LEDGER

Tiger Equipment Inc., a manufacturer of construction equipment, prepared the following factory overhead cost budget for the Welding Department for May of the current year. The company expected to operate the department at 100% of normal capacity of 8,400 hours.

Variable costs:		
Indirect factory wages	$30,240	
Power and light	20,160	
Indirect materials	16,800	
Total variable cost		$ 67,200
Fixed costs:		
Supervisory salaries	$20,000	
Depreciation of plant and equipment	36,200	
Insurance and property taxes	15,200	
Total fixed cost		71,400
Total factory overhead cost		$138,600

During May, the department operated at 8,860 hours, and the factory overhead costs incurred were indirect factory wages, $32,400; power and light, $21,000; indirect materials, $18,250; supervisory salaries, $20,000; depreciation of plant and equipment, $36,200; and insurance and property taxes, $15,200.

Instructions

Prepare a factory overhead cost variance report for May. To be useful for cost control, the budgeted amounts should be based on 8,860 hours.

PR 8-5A Standards for nonmanufacturing expenses

Obj. 3, 6

✔ 3. $1,600 U

CodeHead Software Inc. does software development. One important activity in software development is writing software code. The manager of the WordPro Development Team determined that the average software programmer could write 25 lines of code in an hour. The plan for the first week in May called for 4,650 lines of code to be written on the WordPro product. The WordPro Team has five programmers. Each programmer is hired from an employment firm that requires temporary employees to be hired for a minimum of a 40-hour week. Programmers are paid $32.00 per hour. The manager offered a bonus if the team could generate more lines for the week, without overtime. Due to a project emergency, the programmers wrote more code in the first week of May than planned. The actual amount of code written in the first week of May was 5,650 lines, without overtime. As a result, the bonus caused the average programmer's hourly rate to increase to $40.00 per hour during the first week in May.

Instructions

1. If the team generated 4,650 lines of code according to the original plan, what would have been the labor time variance?

2. What was the actual labor time variance as a result of generating 5,650 lines of code?

3. What was the labor rate variance as a result of the bonus?

4. ▬▬▶ Are there any performance-related issues that the labor time and rate variances fail to consider? Explain.

5. The manager is trying to determine if a better decision would have been to hire a temporary programmer to meet the higher programming demand in the first week of May, rather than paying out the bonus. If another employee was hired from the employment firm, what would have been the labor time variance in the first week?

6. ▬▬▶ Which decision is better, paying the bonus or hiring another programmer?

Problems: Series B

✔ C. Rate variance,
$(200) F

SHOW ME HOW

PR 8-1B Direct materials and direct labor variance analysis   Obj. 2, 3

Lenni Clothing Co. manufactures clothing in a small manufacturing facility. Manufacturing has 25 employees. Each employee presently provides 40 hours of productive labor per week. Information about a production week is as follows:

Standard wage per hr.	$12.00
Standard labor time per unit	12 min.
Standard number of yds. of fabric per unit	5.0 yds.
Standard price per yd. of fabric	$5.00
Actual price per yd. of fabric	$5.10
Actual yds. of fabric used during the week	26,200 yds.
Number of units produced during the week	5,220
Actual wage per hr.	$11.80
Actual hrs. for the week	1,000 hrs.

Instructions

Determine (A) the standard cost per unit for direct materials and direct labor; (B) the price variance, quantity variance, and total direct materials cost variance; and (C) the rate variance, time variance, and total direct labor cost variance.

PR 8-2B Flexible budgeting and variance analysis   Obj. 1, 2, 3

✔ 1. A. Direct
materials price
variance, $12,220 U

EXCEL TEMPLATE

I'm Really Cold Coat Company makes women's and men's coats. Both products require filler and lining material. The following planning information has been made available:

	Standard Amount per Unit		
	Women's Coats	Men's Coats	Standard Price per Unit
Filler	4.0 lbs.	5.20 lbs.	$2.00 per lb.
Liner	7.00 yds.	9.40 yds.	8.00 per yd.
Standard labor time	0.40 hr.	0.50 hr.	

	Women's Coats	Men's Coats
Planned production	5,000 units	6,200 units
Standard labor rate	$14.00 per hr.	$13.00 per hr.

I'm Really Cold Coat Company does not expect there to be any beginning or ending inventories of filler and lining material. At the end of the budget year, I'm Really Cold Coat Company experienced the following actual results:

	Women's Coats	Men's Coats
Actual production	4,400	5,800

	Actual Price per Unit	Actual Quantity Purchased and Used
Filler	$1.90 per lb.	48,000
Liner	8.20 per yd.	85,100

	Actual Labor Rate	Actual Labor Hours Used
Women's coats	$14.10 per hr.	1,825
Men's coats	13.30 per hr.	2,800

The expected beginning inventory and desired ending inventory were realized.

Instructions

1. Prepare the following variance analyses for both coats and the total, based on the actual results and production levels at the end of the budget year:

   A. Direct materials price, quantity, and total variance.

   B. Direct labor rate, time, and total variance.

2. ━━━➤ Why are the standard amounts in part (1) based on the actual production at the end of the year instead of the planned production at the beginning of the year?

PR 8-3B Direct materials, direct labor, and factory overhead   **Obj. 3, 4**
cost variance analysis

✔ A. Direct materials price variance, $10,100 U

EXCEL TEMPLATE

Road Gripper Tire Co. manufactures automobile tires. Standard costs and actual costs for direct materials, direct labor, and factory overhead incurred for the manufacture of 4,160 tires were as follows:

	Standard Costs	Actual Costs
Direct materials	100,000 lbs. at $6.40	101,000 lbs. at $6.50
Direct labor	2,080 hrs. at $15.75	2,000 hrs. at $15.40
Factory overhead	Rates per direct labor hr., based on 100% of normal capacity of 2,000 direct labor hrs.:	
	Variable cost, $4.00	$8,200 variable cost
	Fixed cost, $6.00	$12,000 fixed cost

Each tire requires 0.5 hour of direct labor.

Instructions

Determine (A) the direct materials price variance, direct materials quantity variance, and total direct materials cost variance; (B) the direct labor rate variance, direct labor time variance, and total direct labor cost variance; and (C) the variable factory overhead controllable variance, fixed factory overhead volume variance, and total factory overhead cost variance.

PR 8-4B Factory overhead cost variance report   **Obj. 4**

✔ Controllable variance, $(1,450) F

EXCEL TEMPLATE   GENERAL LEDGER

Feeling Better Medical Inc., a manufacturer of disposable medical supplies, prepared the following factory overhead cost budget for the Assembly Department for October of the current year. The company expected to operate the department at 100% of normal capacity of 30,000 hours.

Variable costs:		
Indirect factory wages	$247,500	
Power and light	189,000	
Indirect materials	52,500	
Total variable cost		$489,000
Fixed costs:		
Supervisory salaries	$126,000	
Depreciation of plant and equipment	70,000	
Insurance and property taxes	44,000	
Total fixed cost		240,000
Total factory overhead cost		$729,000

During October, the department operated at 28,500 hours, and the factory overhead costs incurred were indirect factory wages, $234,000; power and light, $178,500; indirect materials, $50,600; supervisory salaries, $126,000; depreciation of plant and equipment, $70,000; and insurance and property taxes, $44,000.

Instructions

Prepare a factory overhead cost variance report for October. To be useful for cost control, the budgeted amounts should be based on 28,500 hours.

PR 8-5B Standards for nonmanufacturing expenses for a service company Obj. 3, 6

✔ 2. $(161) F

The Radiology Department provides imaging services for Emergency Medical Center. One important activity in the Radiology Department is transcribing digitally recorded analyses of images into a written report. The manager of the Radiology Department determined that the average transcriptionist could type 700 lines of a report in an hour. The plan for the first week in May called for 81,900 typed lines to be written. The Radiology Department has three transcriptionists. Each transcriptionist is hired from an employment firm that requires temporary employees to be hired for a minimum of a 40-hour week. Transcriptionists are paid $23.00 per hour. The manager offered a bonus if the department could type more lines for the week, without overtime. Due to high service demands, the transcriptionists typed more lines in the first week of May than planned. The actual amount of lines typed in the first week of May was 88,900 lines, without overtime. As a result, the bonus caused the average transcriptionist hourly rate to increase to $30.00 per hour during the first week in May.

Instructions

1. If the department typed 81,900 lines according to the original plan, what would have been the labor time variance?

2. What was the labor time variance as a result of typing 88,900 lines?

3. What was the labor rate variance as a result of the bonus?

4. The manager is trying to determine if a better decision would have been to hire a temporary transcriptionist to meet the higher typing demands in the first week of May, rather than paying out the bonus. If another employee was hired from the employment firm, what would have been the labor time variance in the first week?

5. ▬▬▶ Which decision is better, paying the bonus or hiring another transcriptionist?

6. ▬▬▶ Are there any performance-related issues that the labor time and rate variances fail to consider? Explain.

Comprehensive Problem 5

Genuine Spice Inc. began operations on January 1 of the current year. The company produces 8-ounce bottles of hand and body lotion called *Eternal Beauty*. The lotion is sold wholesale in 12-bottle cases for $100 per case. There is a selling commission of $20 per case. The January direct materials, direct labor, and factory overhead costs are as follows:

DIRECT MATERIALS

	Cost Behavior	Units per Case	Cost per Unit	Direct Materials Cost per Case
Cream base	Variable	100 ozs.	$0.02	$ 2.00
Natural oils	Variable	30 ozs.	0.30	9.00
Bottle (8-oz.)	Variable	12 bottles	0.50	6.00
				$17.00

DIRECT LABOR

Department	Cost Behavior	Time per Case	Labor Rate per Hour	Direct Labor Cost per Case
Mixing	Variable	20 min.	$18.00	$6.00
Filling	Variable	5	14.40	1.20
		25 min.		$7.20

FACTORY OVERHEAD

	Cost Behavior	Total Cost
Utilities	Mixed	$ 600
Facility lease	Fixed	14,000
Equipment depreciation	Fixed	4,300
Supplies	Fixed	660
		$19,560

Part A—Break-Even Analysis

✔ 2. $55.60 The management of Genuine Spice Inc. wishes to determine the number of cases required to break even per month. The utilities cost, which is part of factory overhead, is a mixed cost. The following information was gathered from the first six months of operation regarding this cost:

Month	Case Production	Utility Total Cost
January	500	$600
February	800	660
March	1,200	740
April	1,100	720
May	950	690
June	1,025	705

Instructions

1. Determine the fixed and variable portions of the utility cost using the high-low method.

2. Determine the contribution margin per case.

3. Determine the fixed costs per month, including the utility fixed cost from part (1).

4. Determine the break-even number of cases per month.

Part B—August Budgets

✔ 6. Bottles During July of the current year, the management of Genuine Spice Inc. asked the controller
purchased, $8,070 to prepare August manufacturing and income statement budgets. Demand was expected to be 1,500 cases at $100 per case for August. Inventory planning information is provided as follows:

Finished Goods Inventory:

	Cases	Cost
Estimated finished goods inventory, August 1	300	$12,000
Desired finished goods inventory, August 31	175	7,000

Materials Inventory:

	Cream Base (ozs.)	Oils (ozs.)	Bottles (bottles)
Estimated materials inventory, August 1	250	290	600
Desired materials inventory, August 31	1,000	360	240

There was negligible work in process inventory assumed for either the beginning or end of the month; thus, none was assumed. In addition, there was no change in the cost per unit or estimated units per case operating data from January.

Instructions

5. Prepare the August production budget.

6. Prepare the August direct materials purchases budget.

7. Prepare the August direct labor budget. Round the hours required for production to the nearest hour.

8. Prepare the August factory overhead budget.

9. Prepare the August budgeted income statement, including selling expenses.

Part C—August Variance Analysis

✔ 11. Filling Dept. During September of the current year, the controller was asked to perform variance analyses
direct labor time for August. The January operating data provided the standard prices, rates, times, and quantities
variance, $216 U
✔ 12. $5 U

(Continued)

per case. There were 1,500 actual cases produced during August, which was 250 more cases than planned at the beginning of the month. Actual data for August were as follows:

	Actual Direct Materials Price per Unit	Actual Direct Materials Quantity per Case
Cream base	$0.016 per oz.	102 ozs.
Natural oils	$0.32 per oz.	31 ozs.
Bottle (8-oz.)	$0.42 per bottle	12.5 bottles

	Actual Direct Labor Rate	Actual Direct Labor Time per Case
Mixing	$18.20	19.50 min.
Filling	14.00	5.60 min.

Actual variable overhead	$305.00
Normal volume	1,600 cases

The prices of the materials were different than standard due to fluctuations in market prices. The standard quantity of materials used per case was an ideal standard. The Mixing Department used a higher grade labor classification during the month, thus causing the actual labor rate to exceed standard. The Filling Department used a lower grade labor classification during the month, thus causing the actual labor rate to be less than standard.

Instructions

10. Determine and interpret the direct materials price and quantity variances for the three materials.
11. Determine and interpret the direct labor rate and time variances for the two departments. Round hours to the nearest hour.
12. Determine and interpret the factory overhead controllable variance.
13. Determine and interpret the factory overhead volume variance.
14. Why are the standard direct labor and direct materials costs in the calculations for parts (10) and (11) based on the actual 1,500-case production volume rather than the planned 1,250 cases of production used in the budgets for parts (6) and (7)?

Analysis for Decision Making

ADM-1 Admissions time variance

Valley Hospital began using standards to evaluate its Admissions Department. The standard was broken into two types of admissions as follows:

Type of Admission	Standard Time to Complete Admission Record
Unscheduled	30 min.
Scheduled	15 min.

The unscheduled admission took longer because name, address, and insurance information needed to be determined and verified at the time of admission. Information was collected on scheduled admissions prior to admitting the patient, thus requiring less time in admissions.

The Admissions Department employs four full-time people for 40 hours per week at $15 per hour. For the most recent week, the department handled 140 unscheduled and 340 scheduled admissions.

A. How much was actually spent on labor for the week?

B. What are the standard hours for the actual volume of work for the week?

C. Compute the direct labor time variance, and report how well the department performed for the week.

D. ━━━▶ What are some factors that may cause an unfavorable direct labor time variance for the Admissions Department?

REAL WORLD

ADM-2 United States Postal Service: Mail sorting time variance

One of the operations in the **United States Postal Service** is a mechanical mail sorting operation. In this operation, handwritten letter mail is sorted at a rate of 1.5 letters per second. An operator sitting at a keyboard mechanically sorts the letter from a three-digit code. The manager of the mechanical sorting operation wishes to determine the number of temporary employees to hire for December. The manager estimates that there will be an additional 24,192,000 pieces of mail in December, due to the upcoming holiday season.

Assume that the sorting operators are temporary employees. The union contract requires that temporary employees be hired for one month at a time. Each temporary employee is hired to work 160 hours in the month.

A. How many temporary employees should the manager hire for December?

B. If each temporary employee earns a standard $17 per hour, what would be the direct labor time variance if the actual number of additional letters sorted in December was 23,895,000?

ADM-3 Direct labor time variance

Maywood City Police uses variance analysis to monitor police staffing. The following table identifies three common police activities, the standard time to perform each activity, and their actual frequency to establish the expected cost to serve these activities.

Police Activity	Standard Hours per Activity	Actual Activities for Year	Total Employee Hours
Theft	0.60	7,000	4,200
Arrest	1.50	18,000	27,000
Patrol activities	0.30	9,000	2,700
			33,900

The police are paid $25 per hour.

The actual amount of hours per activity for the year were as follows:

Police Activity	Actual Hours per Activity
Theft	0.75
Arrest	2.00
Patrol activities	0.40

A. Determine the total budgeted cost to perform the three police activities.

B. Determine the total actual cost to perform the three police activities.

C. Determine the direct labor time variance.

D. ━━━▶ What does the time variance suggest?

Take It Further

ETHICS

TIF 8-1 Ethics in Action

Dash Riprock is a cost analyst with Safe Insurance Company. Safe is applying standards to its claims payment operations. Claims payment is a repetitive operation that could be evaluated with standards. Dash used time and motion studies to identify an ideal standard of 36 claims processed per hour. The Claims Processing Department manager, Henry Tudor, has rejected this standard and has argued that the standard should be 30 claims processed per hour. Henry and Dash were unable to agree, so they decided to discuss this matter openly at a joint meeting with the Vice President of Operations, who would arbitrate a final decision. Prior to the meeting, Dash wrote the following memo to the Vice President:

To: Anne Boleyn, Vice President of Operations

From: Dash Riprock

Re: Standards in the Claims Processing Department

  As you know, Henry and I are scheduled to meet with you to discuss our disagreement about the appropriate standards for the Claims Processing Department. I have conducted time and motion studies and have determined that the ideal standard is 36 claims processed per hour. Henry argues that 30 claims processed per hour would be more appropriate. I believe he is trying to "pad" the budget with some slack. I'm not sure what he is trying to get away with, but I believe a tight standard will drive efficiency up in his area. I hope you will agree when we meet with you next week.

▶ Discuss the ethical and professional issues in this situation.

REAL WORLD

TIF 8-2 Team Activity

Many city and county governments realize that an entity can only control what it measures. As a result, many municipal governments are introducing nonfinancial performance measures to help improve municipal services. In a group, use the Google search engine to perform a search for "municipal government performance measurement." Google will provide a list of Internet sites that outline various city efforts in using nonfinancial performance measures.

▶ As a group, report on the types of measures used by one of the cities from the search.

TIF 8-3 Communication

The senior management of Tungston Company has proposed the following three performance measures for the company:

1. Net income as a percent of stockholders' equity
2. Revenue growth
3. Employee satisfaction

  Management believes these three measures combine both financial and nonfinancial measures and are thus superior to using only financial measures.

▶ Write a brief memo to David Tungston, the company president, providing suggestions on how to improve the company's performance measurement system.

Concepts and Principles

Chapter 1 *Introduction to Managerial Accounting*

Developing Information

Decision Making

Caterpillar Inc.

Have you ever wondered why large retail stores like **Macy's**, **JCPenney**, and **Sears** are divided into departments? Organizing into departments allows retailers to provide products and expertise in specialized areas while offering a wide range of products. Departments also allow companies to assign responsibility for financial performance. This information can be used to make product decisions, evaluate operations, and guide company strategy. Strong departmental performance might be attributable to a good department manager, while weak departmental performance may be the result of a product mix that has low customer appeal. By tracking departmental performance, companies can identify and reward excellent performance and take corrective action in departments that are performing poorly.

Like retailers, most businesses organize into operational units, such as divisions and departments. For example, **Caterpillar Inc.** manufactures a variety of equipment and machinery and is organized into a number of different segments, including Construction Industries, Resource Industries, Energy & Transportation, and Financial Products. The Construction Industries segment manufactures construction equipment such as tractors, dump trucks, and loaders. The Resource Industries segment makes equipment for the mining industry, such as off-highway and mining trucks. The Energy & Transportation segment manufactures equipment that is used to generate power, such as engines and turbines for power plants and railroads. The Financial Products segment provides financing for Caterpillar products to customers and dealers.

Managers at Caterpillar Inc. are responsible for running their business segment. Each segment is evaluated on segment profit, which excludes certain expense items from the calculation of profit that are not within the control of the business segment. The company uses segment profit to determine how to allocate resources between business segments and to plan and control the company's operations.

In this chapter, the role of accounting in assisting managers in planning and controlling organizational units, such as departments, divisions, and stores, is described and illustrated.

Source: www.caterpillar.com

Evaluating Decentralized Operations

Decentralized Operations
- Advantages (Obj. 1)
- Disadvantages (Obj. 1)

Responsibilty Accounting
- Cost Centers (Obj. 2)
- Profit Centers (Obj. 3)
- Investment Centers (Obj. 4)
- Balanced Scorecard (Obj. 4)

Transfer Pricing
- Market Price Approach (Obj. 5)
- Negotiated Price Approach (Obj. 5)
- Cost Price Approach (Obj. 5)

Learning Objectives

Obj. 1 Describe the advantages and disadvantages of decentralized operations.

Obj. 2 Prepare a responsibility accounting report for a cost center.

Obj. 3 Prepare responsibility accounting reports for a profit center.

Obj. 4 Compute and interpret the return on investment, the residual income, and the balanced scorecard for an investment center.

Obj. 5 Describe and illustrate how the market price, negotiated price, and cost price approaches to transfer pricing may be used by decentralized segments of a business.

Analysis for Decision Making

Describe and Illustrate the use of profit margin, investment turnover, and ROI in evaluating whether a company should expand through franchised or owner-operated stores.

Objective 1

Describe the advantages and disadvantages of decentralized operations.

Centralized and Decentralized Operations

In a *centralized* company, all major planning and operating decisions are made by top management. For example, a one-person, owner–manager-operated company is centralized because all plans and decisions are made by one person. In a small owner–manager-operated business, centralization may be desirable. This is because the owner–manager's close supervision ensures that the business will be operated in the way the owner–manager wishes.

In a *decentralized* company, managers of separate divisions or units are delegated operating responsibility. The division (unit) managers are responsible for planning and controlling the operations of their divisions. Divisions are often structured around products, customers, or regions.

The proper amount of decentralization for a company depends on the company's unique circumstances. For example, in some companies, division managers have authority over all operations, including fixed asset purchases. In other companies, division managers have authority over profits but not fixed asset purchases.

Advantages of Decentralization

For large companies, it is difficult for top management to:

- Maintain daily contact with all operations, and
- Maintain operating expertise in all product lines and services

In such cases, delegating authority to managers closest to the operations usually results in better decisions. These managers often anticipate and react to operating data more quickly than could top management. These managers can also focus their attention on becoming "experts" in their area of operation.

Decentralized operations provide excellent training for managers. Delegating responsibility allows managers to develop managerial experience early in their careers. This helps a company retain managers, some of whom may be later promoted to top management positions.

Managers of decentralized operations often work closely with customers. As a result, they tend to identify with customers and, thus, are often more creative in suggesting operating and product improvements. This helps create good customer relations.

Caterpillar uses a decentralized network of over a thousand dealers to sell its products.

Link to Caterpillar

Disadvantages of Decentralization

A primary disadvantage of decentralized operations is that decisions made by one manager may negatively affect the profits of the company. For example, managers of divisions whose products compete with one another might start a price war that decreases the profits of both divisions and, thus, the overall company.

Another disadvantage of decentralized operations is that assets and expenses may be duplicated across divisions. For example, each manager of a product line might have a separate sales force and office support staff.

The advantages and disadvantages of decentralization are summarized in Exhibit 1.

Advantages of Decentralization

- Allows managers closest to the operations to make decisions
- Provides excellent training for managers
- Allows managers to become experts in their area of operation
- Helps retain managers
- Improves creativity and customer relations

Disadvantages of Decentralization

- Decisions made by managers may negatively affect the profits of the company
- Duplicates assets and expenses

Exhibit 1

Advantages and Disadvantages of Decentralized Operations

Responsibility Accounting

In a decentralized business, accounting assists managers in evaluating and controlling their areas of responsibility, called *responsibility centers*. **Responsibility accounting** is the process of measuring and reporting operating data by responsibility center.

Why It Matters

Dover Corporation: Many Pieces, One Picture

Dover Corporation has grown over 45 years by acquiring more than 100 different manufacturing companies within a variety of industries. Dover uses a highly decentralized operating strategy. For example, of Dover's 30,000 employees, only about 50 employees staff the headquarters. Thus, almost all of the employees work within the 100 operating companies. The primary benefit of this approach is giving the operating companies room to respond to threats and opportunities without the bureaucratic hindrance of a centralized structure. As a result, the operating company presidents have unusual levels of autonomy. As stated by the company, "Dover company presidents set the direction of their own companies, make their own decisions, and nurture and grow their own organizations." The presidents are evaluated using metrics similar to those discussed in this chapter to keep the businesses aligned to the performance objectives of the overall organization.

Source: Dover Corporation Web Site, Dover's Culture and Operating Philosophy.

Three types of responsibility centers are as follows:

■ *Cost centers,* which have responsibility over costs
■ *Profit centers,* which have responsibility over revenues and costs
■ *Investment centers,* which have responsibility over revenues, costs, and investment in assets

Link to Caterpillar   **Caterpillar**'s corporate headquarters are located in Peoria, Illinois.

Objective 2
Prepare a responsibility accounting report for a cost center.

Responsibility Accounting for Cost Centers

A **cost center** manager has responsibility for controlling costs. For example, the supervisor of the Power Department has responsibility for the costs of providing power. A cost center manager does not make decisions concerning sales or the amount of fixed assets invested in the center.

Cost centers may vary in size from a small department to an entire manufacturing plant. In addition, cost centers may exist within other cost centers. For example, an entire university or college could be viewed as a cost center, and each college and department within the university could also be a cost center, as shown in Exhibit 2.

Exhibit 2
Cost Centers in a University

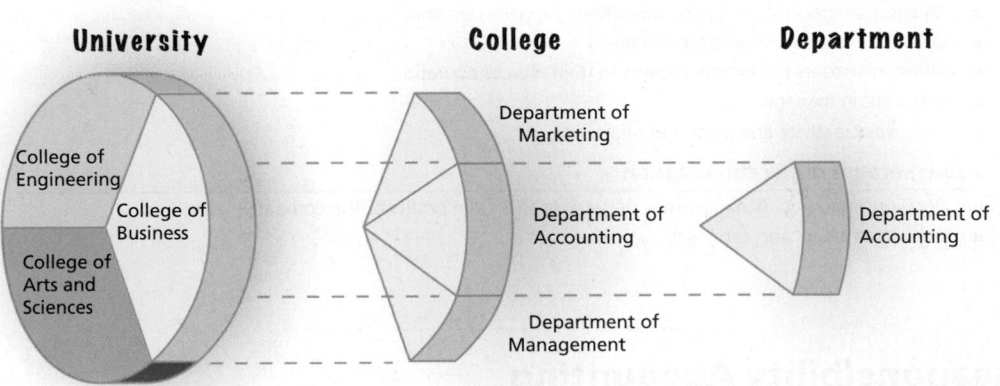

Responsibility accounting for cost centers focuses on the controlling and reporting of costs. Budget performance reports that report budgeted and actual costs are normally prepared for each cost center.

Link to Caterpillar   **Caterpillar**'s "Corporate Services" group performs support services for its operating segments and is organized as a cost center.

Exhibit 3 illustrates budget performance reports for the following cost centers:

■ Vice President, Production
■ Manager, Plant A
■ Supervisor, Department 1—Plant A

Exhibit 3 shows how cost centers are often linked together within a company. For example, the budget performance report for Department 1—Plant A supports the report for Plant A, which supports the report for the vice president of production.

Exhibit 3   Responsibility Accounting Reports for Cost Centers

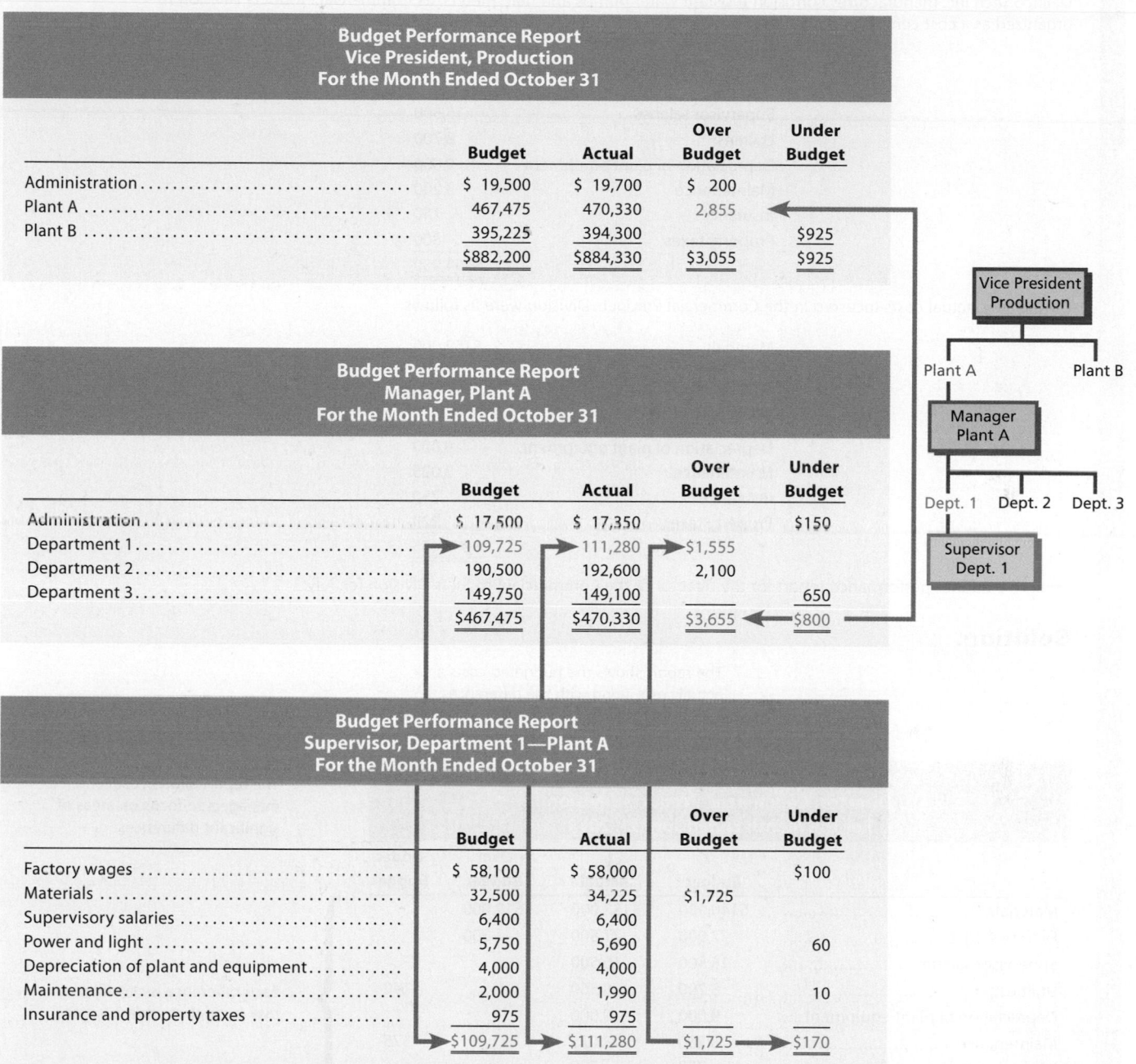

Budget Performance Report
Vice President, Production
For the Month Ended October 31

	Budget	Actual	Over Budget	Under Budget
Administration....................................	$ 19,500	$ 19,700	$ 200	
Plant A	467,475	470,330	2,855	
Plant B	395,225	394,300		$925
	$882,200	$884,330	$3,055	$925

Budget Performance Report
Manager, Plant A
For the Month Ended October 31

	Budget	Actual	Over Budget	Under Budget
Administration....................................	$ 17,500	$ 17,350		$150
Department 1....................................	109,725	111,280	$1,555	
Department 2....................................	190,500	192,600	2,100	
Department 3....................................	149,750	149,100		650
	$467,475	$470,330	$3,655	$800

Budget Performance Report
Supervisor, Department 1—Plant A
For the Month Ended October 31

	Budget	Actual	Over Budget	Under Budget
Factory wages	$ 58,100	$ 58,000		$100
Materials	32,500	34,225	$1,725	
Supervisory salaries	6,400	6,400		
Power and light	5,750	5,690		60
Depreciation of plant and equipment...........	4,000	4,000		
Maintenance....................................	2,000	1,990		10
Insurance and property taxes	975	975		
	$109,725	$111,280	$1,725	$170

The reports in Exhibit 3 show the budgeted costs and actual costs along with the differences. Each difference is classified as either *over* budget or *under* budget. Such reports allow cost center managers to focus on areas of significant differences.

For example, the supervisor for Department 1 of Plant A can focus on why the materials cost was over budget. The supervisor might discover that excess materials were scrapped. This could be due to such factors as machine malfunctions, improperly trained employees, or low-quality materials.

As shown in Exhibit 3, responsibility accounting reports are usually more summarized for higher levels of management. For example, the budget performance report for the manager of Plant A shows only administration and departmental data. This report enables the plant manager to identify the departments responsible for major differences. Likewise, the report for the vice president of production summarizes the cost data for each plant.

Delinco Tech Inc. manufactures corrosion-resistant water pumps and fluid meters. Its Commercial Products Division is organized as a cost center. The division's budget for the month ended July 31, 20Y1, is as follows (in thousands):

Materials	$140,000
Factory wages	77,000
Supervisor salaries	15,500
Utilities	8,700
Depreciation of plant equipment	9,000
Maintenance	3,200
Insurance	750
Property taxes	800
	$254,950

During July, actual costs incurred in the Commercial Products Division were as follows:

Materials	$152,000
Factory wages	77,800
Supervisor salaries	15,500
Utilities	8,560
Depreciation of plant equipment	9,000
Maintenance	3,025
Insurance	750
Property taxes	820
	$267,455

Prepare a budget performance report for the director of the Commercial Products Division for July.

Solution:

The report shows the budgeted costs and actual costs along with the differences.

The report allows cost center managers to focus on areas of significant differences.

Budget Performance Report
Director, Commercial Products Division
For the Month Ended July 31, 20Y1

	Budget	Actual	Over Budget	Under Budget
Materials	$140,000	$152,000	$12,000	
Factory wages	77,000	77,800	800	
Supervisor salaries	15,500	15,500		
Utilities	8,700	8,560		$140
Depreciation of plant equipment	9,000	9,000		
Maintenance	3,200	3,025		175
Insurance	750	750		
Property taxes	800	820	20	
	$254,950	$267,455	$12,820	$315

Each difference is classified as *over* budget or *under* budget.

Check Up Corner

Responsibility Accounting for Profit Centers

Objective 3
Prepare responsibility accounting reports for a profit center.

A **profit center** manager has the responsibility and authority for making decisions that affect revenues and costs and, thus, profits. Profit centers may be divisions, departments, or products.

The manager of a profit center does not make decisions concerning the fixed assets invested in the center. However, profit centers are an excellent training assignment for new managers.

Responsibility accounting for profit centers focuses on reporting revenues, expenses, and income from operations. Thus, responsibility accounting reports for profit centers take the form of income statements.

The profit center income statement should include only revenues and expenses that are controlled by the manager. **Controllable revenues** are revenues earned by the profit center. **Controllable expenses** are costs that can be influenced (controlled) by the decisions of profit center managers.

Service Department Charges

The controllable expenses of profit centers include *direct operating expenses* such as sales salaries and utility expenses. In addition, a profit center may incur expenses provided by internal centralized *service departments*. Examples of such service departments include the following:

- Research and Development
- Legal
- Telecommunications
- Information and Computer Systems
- Facilities Management
- Purchasing
- Advertising
- Payroll Accounting
- Transportation
- Human Resources

Caterpillar's research and development is conducted at its Tech Center in Mossville, Illinois.

Link to Caterpillar

Service department charges are *indirect* expenses to a profit center. They are similar to the expenses that would be incurred if the profit center purchased the services from outside the company. A profit center manager has control over service department expenses if the manager is free to choose how much service is used. In such cases, **service department charges** are allocated to profit centers based on the usage of the service by each profit center.

To illustrate, Nova Entertainment Group (NEG), a diversified entertainment company, is used. NEG has the following two operating divisions organized as profit centers:

- Theme Park Division
- Movie Production Division

The revenues and direct operating expenses for the two divisions follow. The operating expenses consist of direct expenses, such as the wages and salaries of a division's employees.

	Theme Park Division	Movie Production Division
Revenues	$6,000,000	$2,500,000
Operating expenses	2,495,000	405,000

NEG's service departments and the expenses they incurred for the year ended December 31, 20Y8, are as follows:

Purchasing	$400,000
Payroll Accounting	255,000
Legal	250,000
Total	$905,000

An activity base for each service department is used to charge service department expenses to the Theme Park and Movie Production divisions. The activity base for each service department is a measure of the services performed. For NEG, the service department activity bases are as follows:

Department	Activity Base
Purchasing	Number of purchase requisitions
Payroll Accounting	Number of payroll checks
Legal	Number of billed hours

The use of services by the Theme Park and Movie Production divisions is as follows:

	Service Usage		
Division	Purchasing	Payroll Accounting	Legal
Theme Park	25,000 purchase requisitions	12,000 payroll checks	100 billed hrs.
Movie Production	15,000	3,000	900
Total	40,000 purchase requisitions	15,000 payroll checks	1,000 billed hrs.

The rates at which services are charged to each division are called *service department charge rates*. These rates are computed as follows:

$$\text{Service Department Charge Rate} = \frac{\text{Service Department Expense}}{\text{Total Service Department Usage}}$$

NEG's service department charge rates are computed as follows:

$$\text{Purchasing Charge Rate} = \frac{\$400,000}{40,000 \text{ purchase requisitions}} = \$10 \text{ per purchase requisition}$$

$$\text{Payroll Charge Rate} = \frac{\$255,000}{15,000 \text{ payroll checks}} = \$17 \text{ per payroll check}$$

$$\text{Legal Charge Rate} = \frac{\$250,000}{1,000 \text{ billed hrs.}} = \$250 \text{ per hr.}$$

The services used by each division are multiplied by the service department charge rates to determine the service charges for each division, computed as follows:

$$\text{Service Department Charge} = \text{Service Usage} \times \text{Service Department Charge Rate}$$

Exhibit 4 illustrates the service department charges and related computations for NEG's Theme Park and Movie Production divisions.

The differences in the service department charges between the two divisions can be explained by the nature of their operations and, thus, usage of services. For example, the Theme Park Division employs many part-time employees who are paid weekly. As a result, the Theme Park Division requires 12,000 payroll checks and incurs a $204,000 payroll service department charge (12,000 × $17). In contrast, the Movie Production Division has more permanent employees who are paid monthly. Thus, the Movie Production Division requires only 3,000 payroll checks and incurs a payroll service department charge of $51,000 (3,000 × $17).

Nova Entertainment Group Service Department Charges to NEG Divisions For the Year Ended December 31, 20Y8		
Service Department	**Theme Park Division**	**Movie Production Division**
Purchasing (Note A)	$250,000	$150,000
Payroll Accounting (Note B)	204,000	51,000
Legal (Note C)...	25,000	225,000
Total service department charges	$479,000	$426,000

Note A:
25,000 purchase requisitions × $10 per purchase requisition = $250,000
15,000 purchase requisitions × $10 per purchase requisition = $150,000
Note B:
12,000 payroll checks × $17 per check = $204,000
3,000 payroll checks × $17 per check = $51,000
Note C:
100 hours × $250 per hour = $25,000
900 hours × $250 per hour = $225,000

Exhibit 4
Service Department Charges to NEG Divisions

Profit Center Reporting

The divisional income statements for NEG are shown in Exhibit 5.

Nova Entertainment Group Divisional Income Statements For the Year Ended December 31, 20Y8		
	Theme Park Division	**Movie Production Division**
Revenues*...	$6,000,000	$2,500,000
Operating expenses	2,495,000	405,000
Income from operations before service department charges.................................	$3,505,000	$2,095,000
Service department charges:		
Purchasing...	$ 250,000	$ 150,000
Payroll Accounting	204,000	51,000
Legal	25,000	225,000
Total service department charges	$ 479,000	$ 426,000
Income from operations	$3,026,000	$1,669,000

*For a profit center that sells products, the income statement would show: Sales – Cost of goods sold = Gross profit. The operating expenses would be deducted from the gross profit to get the income from operations before service department charges.

Exhibit 5
Divisional Income Statements—NEG

In evaluating the profit center manager, the income from operations should be compared over time to a budget. However, it should not be compared across profit centers because the profit centers are usually different in terms of size, products, and customers.

Check Up Corner 9-2 | Profit Center Responsibility Reporting

Johnson Company has two divisions, East and West, that operate as profit centers. Sales, cost of goods sold, and selling expenses for the two divisions for the year ended December 31 are as follows:

	East Division	West Division
Sales	$3,000,000	$8,000,000
Cost of goods sold	1,650,000	4,200,000
Selling expenses	850,000	1,850,000

In addition, the company has two service departments, Legal and Tech Support.

The service department expenses for the year ended December 31 are as follows:

Legal Department	Tech Support Department
$350,000	$250,000

The Legal Department costs are charged to user divisions based on the number of hours of service, and the Tech Support Department costs are charged to user divisions based on the number of computers. The usage of service by the two divisions is as follows:

	Legal	Tech Support
East Division	500 hours	80 computers
West Division	1,500	120
Total	2,000 hours	200 computers

Prepare income statements for the year ended December 31, showing income from operations for the two divisions. Use two column headings: East and West.

Solution:

Johnson Company
Divisional Income Statements
For the Year Ended December 31

	East	West
Sales	$3,000,000	$8,000,000
Cost of goods sold	1,650,000	4,200,000
Gross profit	$1,350,000	$3,800,000
Selling expenses	850,000	1,850,000
Income from operations before service departments charges	$ 500,000	$1,950,000
Service department charges:		
Legal	$ 87,500	$ 262,500
Tech Support	100,000	150,000
Total service department charges	$ 187,500	$ 412,500
Income from operations	$ 312,500	$1,537,500

500 hours × $175 per hour*
1,500 hours × $175 per hour*
120 computers × $1,250 per computer**
80 computers × $1,250 per computer**

*Legal Department Rate = $\frac{\$350,000}{2,000 \text{ hours}}$ = $175 per hour of service

**Tech Support Department Rate = $\frac{\$250,000}{200 \text{ computers}}$ = $1,250 per computer

Check Up Corner

Responsibility Accounting for Investment Centers

Objective 4
Compute and interpret the return on investment, the residual income, and the balanced scorecard for an investment center.

An **investment center** manager has the responsibility and the authority to make decisions that affect not only costs and revenues but also the assets invested in the center. Investment centers are often used in diversified companies organized by divisions. In such cases, the divisional manager has authority similar to that of a chief operating officer or president of a company.

Caterpillar has four group presidents that are responsible for the operations of each of its four major segments: Construction, Resource, Energy & Transportation, and Financial Products. A fifth group president is responsible for three smaller operating segments.

Link to Caterpillar

Because investment center managers have responsibility for revenues and expenses, *income from operations* is part of investment center reporting. In addition, because the manager has responsibility for the assets invested in the center, the following two additional measures of performance are used:

- Return on investment
- Residual income

To illustrate, DataLink Inc., a cellular phone company with three regional divisions, is used. Condensed divisional income statements for the Northern, Central, and Southern divisions of DataLink are shown in Exhibit 6.

DataLink Inc. Divisional Income Statements For the Year Ended December 31, 20Y8			
	Northern Division	**Central Division**	**Southern Division**
Revenues	$560,000	$672,000	$750,000
Operating expenses..................................	336,000	470,400	562,500
Income from operations before service department charges	$224,000	$201,600	$187,500
Service department charges..........................	154,000	117,600	112,500
Income from operations.............................	$ 70,000	$ 84,000	$ 75,000

Exhibit 6
Divisional Income Statements— DataLink Inc.

Using only income from operations, the Central Division is the most profitable division. However, income from operations does not reflect the amount of assets invested in each center. For example, the Central Division could have twice as many assets as the Northern Division. For this reason, performance measures that consider the amount of invested assets, such as the return on investment and residual income, are used.

Return on Investment

Because investment center managers control the amount of assets invested in their centers, they should be evaluated based on the use of these assets. One measure that considers the amount of assets invested is the **return on investment (ROI)** or *return on assets*. It is computed as follows:

$$\text{Return on Investment (ROI)} = \frac{\text{Income from Operations}}{\text{Invested Assets}}$$

The return on investment is useful because the three factors subject to control by divisional managers (revenues, expenses, and invested assets) are considered. The higher the return on investment, the better the division is using its assets to generate income. In effect, the return on investment measures the income (return) on each dollar invested. As a result, the return on investment can be used as a common basis for comparing divisions with each other.

To illustrate, the invested assets of DataLink's three divisions are as follows:

	Invested Assets
Northern Division	$350,000
Central Division	700,000
Southern Division	500,000

Using the income from operations for each division shown in Exhibit 6, the return on investment for each division is computed as follows:

Northern Division:

$$\text{Return on Investment} = \frac{\text{Income from Operations}}{\text{Invested Assets}} = \frac{\$70,000}{\$350,000} = 20\%$$

Central Division:

$$\text{Return on Investment} = \frac{\text{Income from Operations}}{\text{Invested Assets}} = \frac{\$84,000}{\$700,000} = 12\%$$

Southern Division:

$$\text{Return on Investment} = \frac{\text{Income from Operations}}{\text{Invested Assets}} = \frac{\$75,000}{\$500,000} = 15\%$$

Although the Central Division generated the largest income from operations, its return on investment (12%) is the lowest. Hence, relative to the assets invested, the Central Division is the least profitable division. In comparison, the return on investment of the Northern Division is 20%, and the Southern Division is 15%.

Link to Caterpillar

Based upon recent financial statements, the return on investment for each of **Caterpillar**'s four segments was as follows:

Construction	Resource	Energy & Transportation	Financial Products
35.2%	(1.0)%	37.9%	2.4%

To analyze differences in the return on investment across divisions, the **DuPont formula** for the return on investment is often used.[1] The DuPont formula views the return on investment as the product of the following two factors:

- **Profit margin**, which is the ratio of income from operations to sales.
- **Investment turnover**, which is the ratio of sales to invested assets.

---

[1] The DuPont formula was created by a financial executive of **E. I. du Pont de Nemours and Company** in 1919.

Using the DuPont formula, the return on investment is expressed as follows:

$$\text{Return on Investment} = \text{Profit Margin} \times \text{Investment Turnover}$$

$$\text{Return on Investment} = \frac{\text{Income from Operations}}{\text{Sales}} \times \frac{\text{Sales}}{\text{Invested Assets}}$$

The DuPont formula is useful in evaluating divisions. This is because the profit margin and the investment turnover reflect the following underlying operating relationships of each division:

- Profit margin indicates *operating profitability* by computing the profit earned on each sales dollar.
- Investment turnover indicates *operating efficiency* by computing the number of sales dollars generated by each dollar of invested assets.

If a division's profit margin increases, and all other factors remain the same, the division's return on investment will increase. For example, a division might add more profitable products to its sales mix and, thus, increase its operating profit, profit margin, and return on investment.

If a division's investment turnover increases, and all other factors remain the same, the division's return on investment will increase. For example, a division might attempt to increase sales through special sales promotions and thus increase operating efficiency, investment turnover, and return on investment.

The return on investment, profit margin, and investment turnover operate in relationship to one another. Specifically, more income can be earned by either increasing the investment turnover, increasing the profit margin, or both.

Using the DuPont formula yields the same return on investment for each of DataLink's divisions, computed as follows:

$$\text{Return on Investment} = \frac{\text{Income from Operations}}{\text{Sales}} \times \frac{\text{Sales}}{\text{Invested Assets}}$$

Northern Division:

$$\text{Return on Investment} = \frac{\$70,000}{\$560,000} \times \frac{\$560,000}{\$350,000} = 12.5\% \times 1.6 = 20\%$$

Central Division:

$$\text{Return on Investment} = \frac{\$84,000}{\$672,000} \times \frac{\$672,000}{\$700,000} = 12.5\% \times 0.96 = 12\%$$

Southern Division:

$$\text{Return on Investment} = \frac{\$75,000}{\$750,000} \times \frac{\$750,000}{\$500,000} = 10\% \times 1.5 = 15\%$$

The Northern and Central divisions have the same profit margins of 12.5%. However, the Northern Division's investment turnover of 1.6 is larger than that of the Central Division's turnover of 0.96. By using its invested assets more efficiently, the Northern Division's return on investment of 20% is 8 percentage points higher than the Central Division's return on investment of 12%.

The Southern Division's profit margin of 10% and investment turnover of 1.5 are lower than those of the Northern Division. The product of these factors results in a return on investment of 15% for the Southern Division, compared to 20% for the Northern Division.

Even though the Southern Division's profit margin is lower than the Central Division's, its higher turnover of 1.5 results in a return on investment of 15%, which is greater than the Central Division's return on investment of 12%.

Link to
Caterpillar

Based upon recent financial statements, the profit margin, investment turnover, and return on investment (ROI) for each of **Caterpillar**'s four segments were as follows:

	Construction	Resource	Energy & Transportation	Financial Products
Profit margin	11.5%	(1.1)%	16.4%	26.3%
Investment turnover	3.06	0.92	2.31	0.09
ROI	35.2%	(1.0)%	37.9%	2.4%

To increase the return on investment, the profit margin and investment turnover for a division may be analyzed. For example, assume that the Northern Division is in a highly competitive industry in which the profit margin cannot be easily increased. As a result, the division manager might focus on increasing the investment turnover.

To illustrate, assume that the revenues of the Northern Division could be increased by $56,000 through increasing operating expenses, such as advertising, to $385,000. The Northern Division's income from operations will increase from $70,000 to $77,000, computed as follows:

Revenues ($560,000 + $56,000)	$616,000
Operating expenses	385,000
Income from operations before service department charges	$231,000
Service department charges	154,000
Income from operations	$ 77,000

The return on investment for the Northern Division, using the DuPont formula, is recomputed as follows:

$$\text{Return on Investment} = \frac{\$77,000}{\$616,000} \times \frac{\$616,000}{\$350,000} = 12.5\% \times 1.76 = 22\%$$

Although the Northern Division's profit margin remains the same (12.5%), the investment turnover has increased from 1.6 to 1.76, an increase of 10% (0.16 ÷ 1.6). The 10% increase in investment turnover increases the return on investment by 10% (from 20% to 22%).

The return on investment is also useful in deciding where to invest additional assets or expand operations. For example, DataLink should give priority to expanding operations in the Northern Division because it earns the highest return on investment. In other words, an investment in the Northern Division will return 20 cents (20%) on each dollar invested. In contrast, investments in the Central and Southern divisions will earn only 12 cents and 15 cents, respectively, per dollar invested.

A disadvantage of the return on investment as a performance measure is that it may lead divisional managers to reject new investments that could be profitable for the company as a whole. To illustrate, assume the following returns on investment for the Northern Division of DataLink:

Current return on investment	20%
Minimum acceptable return on investment set by top management	10%
Expected return on investment for new project	14%

If the manager of the Northern Division invests in the new project, the Northern Division's overall return on investment will decrease from 20% due to averaging. Thus, the division manager might decide to reject the project, even though the new project's expected return on investment of 14% exceeds DataLink's minimum acceptable return on investment of 10%.

Why It Matters

Coca-Cola Company: Go West Young Man

A major decision early in the history of Coca-Cola was to expand outside of the United States to the rest of the world. As a result, Coca-Cola is known today the world over. What is revealing is how this decision has impacted the revenues and profitability of Coca-Cola across its international and North American segments. The following table shows the percent of revenues and percent of income from operations from the international and North American geographic segments.

	Revenues	Income from Operations
International segments	35.4%	94.3%
North American segment	49.2	28.5
Other (bottling companies, headquarters)	15.4	(22.8)
Total	100%	100%

The first column shows that the international segments provide over 35% of the revenues, while North America provides over 49% of the revenues, as the United States is a large market for Coca-Cola products. However, the income from operations tells a different story. More than 94% of Coca-Cola's profitability comes from international segments. Given the revenue segmentation, this suggests that the international profit margins must be much higher than the North American profit margin. Indeed this is the case, as can be seen in the following table:

	Profit Margin
International average	52.5%
North America	11.4%
Overall average	19.7%

The average profit margin for all the international segments is over four times as large as the North American segment. These results speak to the heart of the Coca-Cola marketing strategy. In international markets, Coca-Cola is able to charge relatively higher prices due to high demand and less competition as compared to the North American market.

Source: The Coca-Cola Company, Form 10-K for the Fiscal Year ended December 31, 2015

Residual Income

Residual income is useful in overcoming some of the disadvantages of the return on investment. **Residual income** is the excess of income from operations over a minimum acceptable income from operations, as shown in Exhibit 7.

Income from operations	$XXX
Minimum acceptable income from operations as a percent of invested assets	XXX
Residual income	$XXX

Exhibit 7
Residual Income

The minimum acceptable income from operations is computed by multiplying the company minimum return on investment by the invested assets. The minimum rate is set by top management, based on such factors as the cost of financing.

To illustrate, assume that DataLink Inc. has established 10% as the minimum acceptable return on investment for divisional assets. The residual incomes for the three divisions are shown in Exhibit 8.

	Northern Division	Central Division	Southern Division
Income from operations	$70,000	$84,000	$75,000
Minimum acceptable income from operations as a percent of invested assets:			
$350,000 × 10%	35,000		
$700,000 × 10%		70,000	
$500,000 × 10%			50,000
Residual income	$35,000	$14,000	$25,000

Exhibit 8
Residual Income—DataLink, Inc.

As shown in Exhibit 8, the Northern Division has more residual income ($35,000) than the other divisions, even though it has the least amount of income from operations ($70,000). This is because the invested assets are less for the Northern Division than for the other divisions.

The major advantage of residual income as a performance measure is that it considers the minimum acceptable return on investment, invested assets, and the income from operations for each division. In doing so, residual income encourages division managers to maximize income from operations in excess of the minimum. This provides an incentive to accept any project that is expected to have a return on investment in excess of the minimum.

To illustrate, assume the following returns on investment for the Northern Division of DataLink:

Current return on investment	20%
Minimum acceptable return on investment	
set by top management	10%
Expected return on investment for new project	14%

If the manager of the Northern Division is evaluated on new projects using only the return on investment, the division manager might decide to reject the new project. This is because investing in the new project will decrease Northern's current return on investment of 20%. While this helps the division maintain its high ROI, it hurts the company as a whole because the expected return on investment of 14% exceeds DataLink's minimum acceptable return on investment of 10%.

In contrast, if the manager of the Northern Division is evaluated using residual income, the new project would probably be accepted because it will increase the Northern Division's residual income. In this way, residual income supports both divisional and overall company objectives.

Check Up Corner 9-3   Investment Center Performance Measures

Yummy Foods Company is a diversified company with three divisions organized as investment centers. Condensed data taken from the records of the three divisions for the year ended December 31 are as follows:

	Snack Goods	Canned Foods	Frozen Foods
Revenues	$784,000	$940,800	$1,050,000
Operating expenses	470,400	700,000	562,500
Income from operations before service			
department charges	$313,600	$240,800	$ 487,500
Service department charges	219,520	99,680	382,500
Income from operations	$ 94,080	$141,120	$ 105,000
Invested assets	$448,000	$940,800	$ 750,000

A. Using the DuPont formula, for return on investment compute the profit margin, investment turnover, and return on investment for each division.
B. Determine the residual income for each division, assuming a minimum acceptable return on investment is 14%.

Solution:

A.

	Return on Investment	=	Profit Margin	×	Investment Turnover
Snack Goods Division	21.0%	=	12.0%	×	1.75
Canned Foods Division	15.0%	=	15.0%	×	1.00
Frozen Foods Division	14.0%	=	10.0%	×	1.40

The Snack Goods Division has the highest return on investment.

Profit Margin

	Snack Goods	Canned Foods	Frozen Foods
Income from operations	$ 94,080	$141,120	$ 105,000
Sales	÷784,000	÷940,800	÷1,050,000
Profit margin	12.0%	15.0%	10.0%

The Canned Foods Division has the highest income from operations.

Investment Turnover

	Snack Goods	Canned Foods	Frozen Foods
Sales	$784,000	$940,800	$1,050,000
Invested assets	÷448,000	÷940,800	÷750,000
Investment turnover	1.75	1.00	1.40

B.

	Residual Income	=	Income from Operations	−	Minimum Acceptable Income from Operations
Snack Goods Division	$31,360	=	$94,080	−	$62,720
Canned Foods Division	$9,408	=	$141,120	−	$131,712
Frozen Foods Division	$0	=	$105,000	−	$105,000

The Snack Goods Division has the highest residual income.

	Snack Goods	Canned Foods	Frozen Foods
Invested assets	$448,000	$940,800	$750,000
Minimum acceptable return	× 14%	× 14%	× 14%
Minimum acceptable income from operations	$ 62,720	$131,712	$105,000

Check Up Corner

The Balanced Scorecard[2]

The **balanced scorecard** is a set of multiple performance measures for a company. In addition to financial performance, a balanced scorecard normally includes performance measures for customer service, innovation and learning, and internal processes, as shown in Exhibit 9.

Exhibit 9
The Balanced
Scorecard

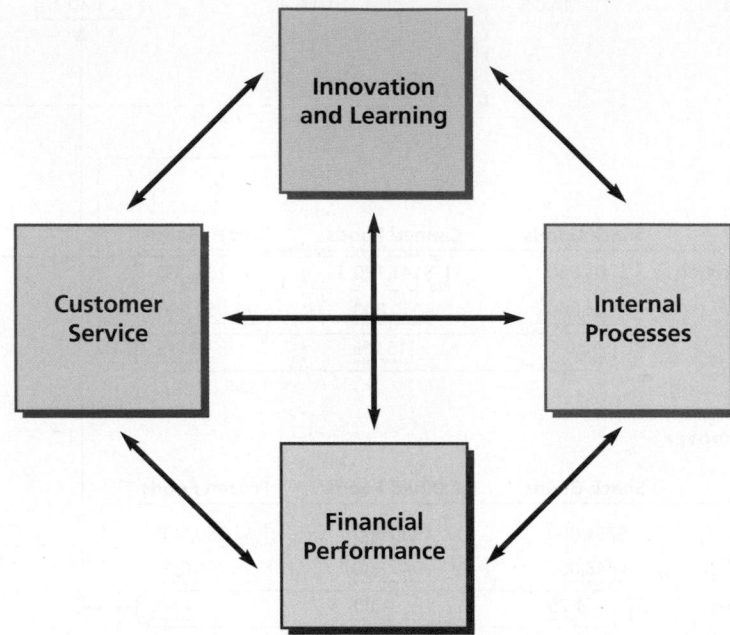

Performance measures for learning and innovation often revolve around a company's research and development efforts. For example, the number of new products developed during a year and the time it takes to bring new products to the market are performance measures for innovation. Performance measures for learning could include the number of employee training sessions and the number of employees who are cross-trained in several skills.

Performance measures for customer service include the number of customer complaints and the number of repeat customers. Customer surveys can also be used to gather measures of customer satisfaction with the company as compared to competitors.

Performance measures for internal processes include the length of time it takes to manufacture a product. The amount of scrap and waste is a measure of the efficiency of a company's manufacturing processes. The number of customer returns is a performance measure of both the manufacturing and sales ordering processes.

All companies will use financial performance measures. Some financial performance measures have been discussed earlier in this chapter and include income from operations, return on investment, and residual income.

The balanced scorecard attempts to identify the underlying nonfinancial drivers, or causes, of financial performance related to innovation and learning, customer service, and internal processes. In this way, the financial performance may be improved. For example, customer satisfaction is often measured by the number of repeat customers. By increasing the number of repeat customers, sales and income from operations can be increased.

Link to
Caterpillar   **Caterpillar**'s Financial Products segment's performance is measured by interest coverage and leverage ratios as well as its credit rating and timeliness of financial reporting.

[2] The balanced scorecard was developed by R. S. Kaplan and D. P. Norton and explained in *The Balanced Scorecard: Translating Strategy into Action* (Cambridge: Harvard Business School Press, 1996).

Some common performance measures used in the balanced scorecard approach are shown in Exhibit 10.

Innovation and Learning	Internal Processes
■ Number of new products	■ Waste and scrap
■ Number of new patents	■ Time to manufacture products
■ Number of cross-trained employees	■ Number of defects
■ Number of training hours	■ Number of rejected sales orders
■ Number of ethics violations	■ Number of stockouts
■ Employee turnover	■ Labor utilization

Customer Service	Financial Performance
■ Number of repeat customers	■ Sales
■ Customer brand recognition	■ Income from operations
■ Delivery time to customer	■ Return on investment
■ Customer satisfaction	■ Profit margin and investment turnover
■ Number of sales returns	■ Residual income
■ Customer complaints	■ Actual versus budgeted (standard) costs

Exhibit 10
Balanced Scorecard Performance Measures

Why It Matters

Turning Around Charles Schwab

Customer service is a key component to any balanced scorecard, and it is a particularly critical component in service industries. Since 2003, **Bain & Company** consulting has helped companies improve customer service by focusing on a customer loyalty metric called the *Net Promoter Score*. This metric, when used as part of a balanced scorecard, evaluates customer service by assessing how likely a customer is to recommend the company to others.

Charles Schwab Corporation is a full-service financial advisory firm that was founded in 1973. In 2004, the company was struggling. Although Schwab had been built on delivering exceptional customer service, the company had lost its way. When customers were surveyed, they gave Schwab a negative

35% Net Promoter Score, indicating that more customers wanted to see the company fail than would be willing to promote the company to others.

In response, Schwab enlisted Bain to help improve its customer experience and customer loyalty. Bain helped Schwab develop and implement a Client Promoter System that focused on embedding the Client Promoter Score deep within the company's values and core strategy. As Schwab CEO Walt Bettinger describes, "If you serve clients in the way that you would like to be served, they are going to want to do more business with you." The results were significant. By 2008, the company's stock price had more than doubled, and in 2010, Schwab received a Net Promoter Score of 46%, the highest in its sector.

Source: "Schwab Earns Highest Customer Loyalty Ranking Among Brokerage & Investment Firms in Satmetrix Net Promoter's 2010 Industry Report," *BusinessWire*, March 25, 2010. "Seeing the world through the client's eyes," Bain & Company, *www.netpromotersystem.com/videos/trailblazer-video/charles-schwab.aspx*

Transfer Pricing

When divisions transfer products or render services to each other, a **transfer price** is used to charge for the products or services.[3] Because transfer prices will affect a division's financial performance, setting a transfer price is a sensitive matter for the managers of both the selling and buying divisions.

Three common approaches to setting transfer prices are as follows:

■ Market price approach
■ Negotiated price approach
■ Cost price approach

Objective 5
Describe and illustrate how the market price, negotiated price, and cost price approaches to transfer pricing may be used by decentralized segments of a business.

Transfer prices may be used for cost, profit, or investment centers. The objective of setting a transfer price is to motivate managers to behave in a manner that will increase the overall company income. As will be illustrated, however, transfer prices may be misused in such a way that overall company income suffers.

Link to Caterpillar

In recent financial statements, Caterpillar reported $2,346 million of revenues among its four segments.

Transfer prices can be set as low as the variable cost per unit or as high as the market price. Often, transfer prices are negotiated at some point between variable cost per unit and market price. Exhibit 11 shows the possible range of transfer prices.

Exhibit 11
Commonly Used
Transfer Prices

To illustrate, Wilson Company, a packaged snack food company with no service departments, is used. Wilson has two operating divisions (Eastern and Western) that are organized as investment centers. Condensed income statements for Wilson, assuming no transfers between divisions, are shown in Exhibit 12.

Exhibit 12
Income
Statements—No
Transfers Between
Divisions

	Wilson Company Income Statements For the Year Ended December 31, 20Y1		
	Eastern Division	**Western Division**	**Total Company**
Sales:			
50,000 units × $20 per unit..................	$1,000,000		$1,000,000
20,000 units × $40 per unit..................		$800,000	800,000
Total sales			$1,800,000
Expenses:			
Variable:			
50,000 units × $10 per unit...............	$ 500,000		$ 500,000
20,000 units × $30* per unit..............		$600,000	600,000
Fixed	300,000	100,000	400,000
Total expenses	$ 800,000	$700,000	$1,500,000
Income from operations......................	$ 200,000	$100,000	$ 300,000

*$20 of the $30 per unit represents materials costs, and the remaining $10 per unit represents other variable conversion expenses incurred within the Western Division.

[3] The discussion in this chapter highlights the essential concepts of transfer pricing. In-depth discussion of transfer pricing can be found in advanced texts.

Market Price Approach

Using the **market price approach**, the transfer price is the price at which the product or service transferred could be sold to outside buyers. If an outside market exists for the product or service transferred, the current market price may be a proper transfer price.

Transfer Price = Market Price

To illustrate, assume that materials used by Wilson in producing snack food in the Western Division are currently purchased from an outside supplier at $20 per unit. The same materials are produced by the Eastern Division. The Eastern Division is operating at full capacity of 50,000 units and can sell all it produces to either the Western Division or to outside buyers.

A transfer price of $20 per unit (the market price) has no effect on the Eastern Division's income or total company income. The Eastern Division will earn revenues of $20 per unit on all its production and sales, regardless of who buys its product.

Likewise, the Western Division will pay $20 per unit for materials (the market price). Thus, the use of the market price as the transfer price has no effect on the Western Division's income or total company income.

In this situation, the use of the market price as the transfer price is proper. The condensed divisional income statements for Wilson would be the same as shown in Exhibit 12.

Negotiated Price Approach

If unused or excess capacity exists in the supplying division (the Eastern Division), and the transfer price is equal to the market price, total company profit may not be maximized. This is because the manager of the Western Division will be indifferent toward purchasing materials from the Eastern Division or from outside suppliers. That is, in both cases the Western Division manager pays $20 per unit (the market price). As a result, the Western Division may purchase the materials from outside suppliers.

If, however, the Western Division purchases the materials from the Eastern Division, the difference between the market price of $20 and the variable costs of the Eastern Division of $10 per unit (from Exhibit 12) can cover fixed costs and contribute to overall company profits. Thus, the Western Division manager should be encouraged to purchase the materials from the Eastern Division.

The **negotiated price approach** allows the managers to agree (negotiate) among themselves on a transfer price. The only constraint is that the transfer price be less than the market price but greater than the supplying division's variable costs per unit, as follows:

Variable Costs per Unit < Transfer Price < Market Price

To illustrate, assume that instead of a capacity of 50,000 units, the Eastern Division's capacity is 70,000 units. In addition, assume that the Eastern Division can continue to sell only 50,000 units to outside buyers.

A transfer price less than $20 would encourage the manager of the Western Division to purchase from the Eastern Division. This is because the Western Division is currently purchasing its materials from outside suppliers at a cost of $20 per unit. Thus, its materials cost would decrease, and its income from operations would increase.

At the same time, a transfer price above the Eastern Division's variable costs per unit of $10 would encourage the manager of the Eastern Division to supply materials to the Western Division. In doing so, the Eastern Division's income from operations would also increase.

Exhibit 13 illustrates the divisional and company income statements, assuming that the Eastern and Western division managers agree to a transfer price of $15.

The Eastern Division increases its sales by $300,000 (20,000 units × $15 per unit) to $1,300,000. As a result, the Eastern Division's income from operations increases by $100,000 ($300,000 sales − $200,000 variable costs) to $300,000, as shown in Exhibit 13.

Exhibit 13
Income Statements—Negotiated Transfer Price

DYNAMIC
EXHIBIT

	Eastern Division	Western Division	Total Company
Wilson Company Income Statements For the Year Ended December 31, 20Y1			
Sales:			
50,000 units × $20 per unit....................	$1,000,000		$1,000,000
20,000 units × $15 per unit....................	300,000		300,000
20,000 units × $40 per unit....................		$800,000	800,000
Total sales	$1,300,000	$800,000	$2,100,000
Expenses:			
Variable:			
70,000 units × $10 per unit.................	$ 700,000		$ 700,000
20,000 units × $25* per unit................		$500,000	500,000
Fixed	300,000	100,000	400,000
Total expenses	$1,000,000	$600,000	$1,600,000
Income from operations.......................	$ 300,000	$200,000	$ 500,000

*$10 of the $25 represents variable conversion expenses incurred solely within the Western Division, and $15 per unit represents the transfer price per unit from the Eastern Division.

The increase of $100,000 in the Eastern Division's income can also be computed as follows:

$$\text{Increase in Eastern (Supplying) Division's Income from Operations} = (\text{Transfer Price} - \text{Variable Cost per Unit}) \times \text{Units Transferred}$$

$$= (\$15 - \$10) \times 20{,}000 \text{ units} = \$100{,}000$$

The Western Division's materials cost decreases by $5 per unit ($20 − $15) for a total of $100,000 (20,000 units × $5 per unit). Thus, the Western Division's income from operations increases by $100,000 to $200,000, as shown in Exhibit 13.

The increase of $100,000 in the Western Division's income can also be computed as follows:

$$\text{Increase in Western (Purchasing) Division's Income from Operations} = (\text{Market Price} - \text{Transfer Price}) \times \text{Units Transferred}$$

$$= (\$20 - \$15) \times 20{,}000 \text{ units} = \$100{,}000$$

Comparing Exhibits 12 and 13 shows that Wilson's income from operations increased by $200,000, computed as follows:

	Income from Operations		
	No Units Transferred (Exhibit 12)	20,000 Units Transferred at $15 per Unit (Exhibit 13)	Increase (Decrease)
Eastern Division	$200,000	$300,000	$100,000
Western Division	100,000	200,000	100,000
Wilson Company	$300,000	$500,000	$200,000

In the preceding illustration, any negotiated transfer price between $10 and $20 is acceptable, as shown in the following formula:

$$\text{Variable Costs per Unit} < \text{Transfer Price} < \text{Market Price}$$
$$\$10 < \text{Transfer Price} < \$20$$

Any transfer price within this range will increase the overall income from operations for Wilson by $200,000. However, the increases in the Eastern and Western divisions' income from operations will vary depending on the transfer price.

To illustrate, a transfer price of $16 would increase the Eastern Division's income from operations by $120,000, computed as follows:

$$\text{Increase in Eastern (Supplying) Division's Income from Operations} = (\text{Transfer Price} - \text{Variable Cost per Unit}) \times \text{Units Transferred}$$

$$= (\$16 - \$10) \times 20{,}000 \text{ units} = \$120{,}000$$

A transfer price of $16 would increase the Western Division's income from operations by $80,000, computed as follows:

$$\text{Increase in Western (Purchasing) Division's Income from Operations} = (\text{Market Price} - \text{Transfer Price}) \times \text{Units Transferred}$$

$$= (\$20 - \$16) \times 20{,}000 \text{ units} = \$80{,}000$$

With a transfer price of $16, Wilson Company's income from operations still increases by $200,000, which consists of the Eastern Division's increase of $120,000 plus the Western Division's increase of $80,000.

As shown, a negotiated price provides each division manager with an incentive to negotiate the transfer of materials. At the same time, the overall company's income from operations will also increase. However, the negotiated approach only applies when the supplying division has excess capacity. In other words, the supplying division cannot sell all its production to outside buyers at the market price.

Check Up Corner 9-4 Transfer Pricing

The materials used by the South Division of Eagle Company are currently purchased from outside suppliers at $30 per unit. These same materials are produced by Eagle's North Division. Income from operations assuming no transfers between divisions is $1,200,000 for the North Division and $1,360,000 for the South Division.

The North Division has unused capacity and can produce the materials needed by the South Division at a variable cost of $15 per unit. The two divisions have recently negotiated a transfer price of $22 per unit for 30,000 units.

Based on the agreed upon transfer price, with no reduction in the North Division's current sales:
A. How much would the North Division's income from operations increase?
B. How much would the South Division's income from operations increase?
C. How much would Eagle Company's income from operations increase?

Solution:

A.

$$\text{Increase in North (Supplying) Division's Income from Operations} = (\text{Transfer Price} - \text{Variable Cost per Unit}) \times \text{Units Transferred}$$

$$= (\$22 - \$15) \times 30{,}000 \text{ units} = \$210{,}000$$

B.

$$\text{Increase in South (Purchasing) Division's Income from Operations} = (\text{Market Price} - \text{Transfer Price}) \times \text{Units Transferred}$$

$$= (\$30 - \$22) \times 30{,}000 \text{ units} = \$240{,}000$$

C.

	Income from Operations		
	No Units Transferred	30,000 Units Transferred	Increase (Decrease)
North Division	$1,200,000	$1,410,000	$210,000
South Division	1,360,000	1,600,000	240,000
Eagle Company	$2,560,000	$3,010,000	$450,000

Eagle company's income from operations will increase by $450,000; the sum of the income increases for the North Division ($210,000) and the South Division ($240,000).

Check Up Corner

Cost Price Approach

Under the **cost price approach**, cost is used to set transfer prices. A variety of costs may be used in this approach, including the following:

- Total product cost per unit
- Variable product cost per unit

If total product cost per unit is used, direct materials, direct labor, and factory overhead are included in the transfer price. If variable product cost per unit is used, the fixed factory overhead cost is excluded from the transfer price.

Actual costs or standard (budgeted) costs may be used in applying the cost price approach. If actual costs are used, inefficiencies of the producing (supplying) division are transferred to the purchasing division. Thus, there is little incentive for the producing (supplying) division to control costs. For this reason, most companies use standard costs in the cost price approach. In this way, differences between actual and standard costs remain with the producing (supplying) division for cost control purposes.

The cost price approach is most often used when the responsibility centers are organized as cost centers. When the responsibility centers are organized as profit or investment centers, the cost price approach is normally not used.

For example, using the cost price approach when the supplying division is organized as a profit center ignores the supplying division manager's responsibility for earning profits. In this case, using the cost price approach prevents the supplying division from reporting any profit (revenues – costs) on the units transferred. As a result, the division manager has little incentive to transfer units to another division, even though it may be in the best interests of the company.

 Ethics: Do It!

The Ethics of Transfer Prices

Transfer prices allow large multinational companies to minimize taxes by shifting taxable income from countries with high tax rates to countries with low taxes. For example, a British company will pay U.S. taxes on income from its U.S. division, and British taxes on income from its British division. Because this company can set its own transfer price, it can minimize its overall tax bill by setting a high transfer price when transferring goods to the United States. This increases cost of goods sold for the highly taxed U.S. division and increases sales for the lesser taxed British division. The overall result is a lower tax bill for the multinational company as a whole. In recent years, government tax authorities like the Internal Revenue Service (IRS) have become concerned with tax avoidance through transfer price manipulation. In response, many countries now have guidelines for setting transfer prices that assure that transfer prices are not subject to manipulation for tax purposes.

Source: L. Eden and L. M. Smith, "The Ethics of Transfer Pricing," unpublished working paper, Texas A&M University, 2011.

Analysis for Decision Making

Franchise Operations

Objective
Describe and illustrate the use of profit margin, investment turnover, and ROI in evaluating whether a company should expand through franchised or owner-operated stores.

Franchising is a popular method of expanding a brand, concept, product, or service offering. The franchisor is the entity that provides the franchise, while the franchisee is the entity that pays for the franchise. Under a franchise agreement, the franchisee pays a fee for the right to sell the franchised product or service. The franchise fee is often expressed as a percent of revenues earned by the franchisee. In addition, the franchisee invests in the property and equipment to deliver the franchised product or service. The franchisor often provides support in start-up, advertising, management development, business systems, and supplier relationships.

The benefits to a franchisee are instant access to a recognized brand, established customer base, and working business systems. The main benefit to the franchisor is an ability to expand the brand without investing significantly in property and equipment.

From the franchisor's perspective, the return on investment for franchised operations should be increased by the low investment. Thus, the DuPont formula should show a healthy profit margin combined with a high investment turnover. To illustrate, **Hilton Worldwide Holdings, Inc.** has both company-operated and franchised hotel operations. In a recent year, Hilton had 144 company-operated hotels and 4,178 franchised hotels around the world. Clearly, Hilton emphasizes franchised operations. Segment disclosures with some assumptions regarding owned and franchised operations are as follows (in millions):

	Company-Operated	Franchised
Revenues	$4,239	$1,401
Operating expenses	3,252	0
General and administrative expenses*		491
Property, plant, and equipment**	8,123	903

*Assume all the general and administrative expenses support franchised operations, since less than 3% of hotel properties are company-operated.
** Total property, plant, and equipment is $9,026. Assume 10% of total property, plant, and equipment support administrative (franchised) operations, while the remaining 90% consist of owned hotel properties.

The return on investment (ROI) using the DuPont formula for both segments is as follows:

$$\text{Return on Investment} = \text{Profit Margin} \times \text{Investment Turnover}$$

$$\text{Return on Investment} = \frac{\text{Income from Operations}}{\text{Revenues}} \times \frac{\text{Revenues}}{\text{Invested Assets}}$$

Company-Operated Hotels:

$$\text{Return on Investment} = \frac{\$987^*}{\$4,239} \times \frac{\$4,239}{\$8,123}$$

$$= 23\% \times 0.52$$
$$= 12\% \text{ (rounded)}$$

Franchised Hotels:

$$\text{Return on Investment} = \frac{\$910^{**}}{\$1,401} \times \frac{\$1,401}{\$903}$$

$$= 65\% \times 1.55$$
$$= 101\% \text{ (rounded)}$$

*$4,239 − $3,252
**$1,401 − $491

Under these assumptions, franchised hotels provide a superior ROI compared to company-operated hotels. The superior performance is caused by both a stronger profit margin and a higher investment turnover. The ROI will often favor franchised operations in this way. This is likely the reason for Hilton's decision to emphasize franchised operations.

Make a Decision — Franchise Operations

Kelly Kitchens operates both franchised and company-operated restaurants under the brand name Kelly Kitchens. Income from operations, sales, and invested assets for both segments are provided as follows:

	Company-Operated	Franchised
Income from operations	$ 180,000	$192,000
Sales	600,000	240,000
Invested assets	1,500,000	150,000

A. Determine the profit margin for company-operated and franchised restaurants. (Round to the nearest whole percent.)
B. Determine the investment turnover for company-operated and franchised restaurants. (Round to two decimal places.)
C. Use the DuPont formula to determine the return on investment for company-operated and franchised restaurants.
D. Kelly Kitchens is expanding to the Midwest. How would you advise management regarding the use of company-operated versus franchised restaurants in the expansion?

Solution:

A. $\text{Profit Margin} = \dfrac{\text{Income from Operations}}{\text{Sales}}$

Company-Operated: $\dfrac{\$180,000}{\$600,000} = 30\%$

Franchised: $\dfrac{\$192,000}{\$240,000} = 80\%$

B. $\text{Investment Turnover} = \dfrac{\text{Sales}}{\text{Invested Assets}}$

Company-Operated: $\dfrac{\$600,000}{\$1,500,000} = 0.40$

Franchised: $\dfrac{\$240,000}{\$150,000} = 1.60$

C. Return on Investment (ROI) = Profit Margin × Investment Turnover
Company-Operated: 30% × 0.40 = 12%
Franchised: 80% × 1.60 = 128%

D. The profit margin, investment turnover, and ROI favor franchised over company-operated restaurants. Thus, from a financial perspective, franchising appears to be a more favorable route for expanding into the Midwest. In addition, Kelly may be able to expand faster using franchisees rather than using its own funds for constructing restaurants. Kelly Kitchens may view company-operated restaurants as a way to protect the brand and control the customer experience. However, franchise agreements can be designed to provide for quality control and consistency of customer experience. Thus, Kelly can still protect the brand while expanding through franchisees.

Make a Decision

Let's Review

Chapter Summary

1. In a centralized business, all major planning and operating decisions are made by top management. In a decentralized business, these responsibilities are delegated to unit managers. Decentralization may be more effective because operational decisions are made by the managers closest to the operations.

2. Cost centers limit the responsibility and authority of managers to decisions related to the costs of their unit. The primary tools for planning and controlling are budgets and budget performance reports.

3. In a profit center, managers have the responsibility and authority to make decisions that affect both revenues and costs. Responsibility reports for a profit center usually show income from operations for the unit.

4. In an investment center, the unit manager has the responsibility and authority to make decisions that affect the unit's revenues, expenses, and assets invested in the center. Three measures are commonly used to assess investment center performance: return on investment (ROI), residual income, and the balanced scorecard. These measures are often used to compare investment center performance.

5. When divisions within a company transfer products or provide services to each other, a transfer price is used to charge for the products or services. Transfer prices should be set so that the overall company income is increased when goods are transferred between divisions. One of three approaches is typically used to establish transfer prices: market price, negotiated price, or cost price.

Key Terms

balanced scorecard (436)	investment center (429)	residual income (433)
controllable expenses (425)	investment turnover (430)	responsibility accounting (421)
controllable revenues (425)	market price approach (439)	return on investment (ROI) (430)
cost center (422)	negotiated price approach (439)	service department charges (425)
cost price approach (442)	profit center (425)	transfer price (437)
DuPont formula (430)	profit margin (430)	

Practice

Multiple-Choice Questions

1. When the manager has the responsibility and authority to make decisions that affect costs and revenues but no responsibility for or authority over assets invested in the department, the department is called a(n):

    A. cost center.
    B. profit center.
    C. investment center.
    D. service department.

2. The Accounts Payable Department has expenses of $600,000 and makes 150,000 payments to the various vendors who provide products and services to the divisions. Division A has income from operations of $900,000 before service department charges and requires 60,000 payments to vendors. If the Accounts Payable Department is treated as a service department, what is Division A's income from operations?
   A. $300,000   C. $660,000
   B. $900,000   D. $540,000

3. Division A of Kern Co. has sales of $350,000, cost of goods sold of $200,000, operating expenses of $30,000, and invested assets of $600,000. What is the return on investment for Division A?
   A. 20%   C. 33%
   B. 25%   D. 40%

4. Division L of Liddy Co. has a return on investment of 24% and an investment turnover of 1.6. What is the profit margin?
   A. 6%   C. 24%
   B. 15%   D. 38%

5. Which approach to transfer pricing uses the price at which the product or service transferred could be sold to outside buyers?
   A. Cost price approach   C. Market price approach
   B. Negotiated price approach   D. Standard cost approach

Answers provided after Problem. Need more practice? Find additional multiple-choice questions, exercises, and problems in CengageNOWv2.

Exercises

SHOW ME HOW

1. Budgetary performance for cost center   Obj. 2

Caroline Company's costs were over budget by $319,000. The company is divided into West and East regions. The East Region's costs were under budget by $47,500. Determine the amount that the West Region's costs were over or under budget.

SHOW ME HOW

2. Service department charges   Obj. 3

The centralized employee travel department of Camtro Company has expenses of $528,000. The department has serviced a total of 6,000 travel reservations for the period. The Southeast Division has made 2,400 reservations during the period, and the Pacific Northwest Division has made 3,600 reservations. How much should each division be charged for travel services?

SHOW ME HOW

3. Income from operations for profit center   Obj. 3

Using the data for Camtro Company from Exercise 2 along with the following data, determine the divisional income from operations for the Southeast and Pacific Northwest divisions:

	Southeast Division	Pacific Northwest Division
Sales	$1,155,000	$1,204,000
Cost of goods sold	590,800	658,000
Selling expenses	231,000	252,000

SHOW ME HOW

4. Profit margin, investment turnover, and ROI   Obj. 4

Cash Company has income from operations of $112,500, invested assets of $750,000, and sales of $1,875,000. Use the DuPont formula to compute the return on investment and show (A) the profit margin, (B) the investment turnover, and (C) the return on investment.

SHOW ME HOW

5. Residual income Obj. 4

The Consumer Division of Hernandez Company has income from operations of $90,000 and assets of $450,000. The minimum acceptable return on assets is 10%. What is the residual income for the division?

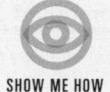

SHOW ME HOW

6. Transfer pricing Obj. 5

The materials used by the North Division of Horton Company are currently purchased from outside suppliers at $60 per unit. These same materials are produced by Horton's South Division. The South Division can produce the materials needed by the North Division at a variable cost of $42 per unit. The division is currently producing 200,000 units and has capacity of 250,000 units. The two divisions have recently negotiated a transfer price of $52 per unit for 30,000 units. By how much will each division's income increase as a result of this transfer?

Answers provided after Problem. Need more practice? Find additional multiple-choice questions, exercises, and problems in CengageNOWv2.

Problem

Quinn Company has two divisions, Domestic and International. Invested assets and condensed income statement data for each division for the year ended December 31, 20Y9, are as follows:

	Domestic Division	**International Division**
Revenues	$675,000	$480,000
Operating expenses	450,000	372,400
Service department charges	90,000	50,000
Invested assets	600,000	384,000

Instructions

1. Prepare condensed income statements for the past year for each division.

2. Using the DuPont formula, determine the profit margin, investment turnover, and return on investment for each division.

3. If management's minimum acceptable return on investment is 10%, determine the residual income for each division.

Need more practice? Find additional multiple-choice questions, exercises, and problems in CengageNOWv2.

Answers

Multiple-Choice Questions

1. **B** The manager of a profit center (answer B) has responsibility for and authority over costs and revenues. If the manager has responsibility for only costs, the department is called a cost center (answer A). If the responsibility and authority extend to the investment in assets as well as costs and revenues, it is called an investment center (answer C). A service department (answer D) provides services to other departments. A service department could be a cost center, a profit center, or an investment center.

2. **C** $600,000 ÷ 150,000 = $4 per payment. Division A anticipates 60,000 payments or $240,000 (60,000 × $4) in service department charges from the Accounts Payable Department. Income from operations is thus $900,000 − $240,000, or $660,000. Answer A assumes that all service department overhead is assigned to Division A, which would be incorrect, since Division A does not use all of the Accounts Payable service. Answer B incorrectly assumes that there are no service department charges from Accounts Payable. Answer D incorrectly determines the Accounts Payable transfer rate from Division A's income from operations.

3. **A** The return on investment for Division A is 20% (answer A), computed as follows:

$$\text{Return on Investment} = \frac{\text{Income from Operations}}{\text{Invested Assets}}$$

$$= \frac{\$350{,}000 - \$200{,}000 - \$30{,}000}{\$600{,}000} = 20\%$$

4. **B** The profit margin for Division L of Liddy Co. is 15% (answer B), computed as follows:

Return on Investment = Profit Margin × Investment Turnover
24% = Profit Margin × 1.6
15% = Profit Margin

5. **C** The market price approach (answer C) to transfer pricing uses the price at which the product or service transferred could be sold to outside buyers. The cost price approach (answer A) uses cost as the basis for setting transfer prices. The negotiated price approach (answer B) allows managers of decentralized units to agree (negotiate) among themselves as to the proper transfer price. The standard cost approach (answer D) is a version of the cost price approach that uses standard costs in setting transfer prices.

Exercises

1. $366,500 over budget ($319,000 + $47,500)

2. <u>Southeast Division Service Charge for Travel Department:</u>
$211,200 = 2,400 billed reservations × ($528,000 ÷ 6,000 reservations)

<u>Pacific Northwest Division Service Charge for Travel Department:</u>
$316,800 = 3,600 billed reservations × ($528,000 ÷ 6,000 reservations)

3.

	Southeast Division	Pacific Northwest Division
Sales	$1,155,000	$1,204,000
Cost of goods sold	590,800	658,000
Gross profit	$ 564,200	$ 546,000
Selling expenses	231,000	252,000
Income from operations before service department charges	$ 333,200	$ 294,000
Service department charges	211,200	316,800
Income from operations	$ 122,000	$ (22,800)

4. A. Profit Margin = $112,500 ÷ $1,875,000 = 6.0%
   B. Investment Turnover = $1,875,000 ÷ $750,000 = 2.5
   C. Return on Investment = 6.0% × 2.5 = 15.0%

5.
Income from operations	$90,000
Minimum acceptable income from operations as a percent of assets ($450,000 × 10%)	45,000
Residual income	$45,000

6. Increase in South (Supplying) Division's Income from Operations = (Transfer Price – Variable Cost per Unit) × Units Transferred
= ($52 – $42) × 30,000 units = $300,000

Increase in North (Purchasing) Division's Income from Operations = (Market Price – Transfer Price) × Units Transferred
= ($60 – $52) × 30,000 units = $240,000

Need more help? Watch step-by-step videos of how to compute answers to these Exercises in CengageNOWv2.

Problem

1.

	Quinn Company Divisional Income Statements For the Year Ended December 31, 20Y9	
	Domestic Division	**International Division**
Revenues	$675,000	$480,000
Operating expenses	450,000	372,400
Income from operations before service department charges	$225,000	$107,600
Service department charges	90,000	50,000
Income from operations	$135,000	$ 57,600

2. Return on Investment = Profit Margin × Investment Turnover

$$\text{Return on Investment} = \frac{\text{Income from Operations}}{\text{Sales}} \times \frac{\text{Sales}}{\text{Invested Assets}}$$

$$\text{Domestic Division: ROI} = \frac{\$135,000}{\$675,000} \times \frac{\$675,000}{\$600,000}$$

$$= 20\% \times 1.125$$

$$= 22.5\%$$

$$\text{International Division: ROI} = \frac{\$57,600}{\$480,000} \times \frac{\$480,000}{\$384,000}$$

$$= 12\% \times 1.25$$

$$= 15\%$$

3. Domestic Division: $75,000 [$135,000 − (10% × $600,000)]
   International Division: $19,200 [$57,600 − (10% × $384,000)]

Discussion Questions

1. Differentiate between centralized and decentralized operations.

2. Differentiate between a profit center and an investment center.

3. **Weyerhaeuser** developed a system that assigns service department expenses to user divisions on the basis of actual services consumed by the division. Here are a number of Weyerhaeuser's activities in its central Financial Services Department:

   REAL WORLD

   - Payroll
   - Accounts payable
   - Accounts receivable
   - Database administration—report preparation

   For each activity, identify an activity base that could be used to charge user divisions for service.

4. What is the major shortcoming of using income from operations as a performance measure for investment centers?

5. In a decentralized company in which the divisions are organized as investment centers, how could a division be considered the least profitable even though it earned the largest amount of income from operations?

6. How does using the return on investment facilitate comparability between divisions of decentralized companies?

7. Why would a firm use a balanced scorecard in evaluating divisional performance?

8. What is the objective of transfer pricing?

9. When is the negotiated price approach preferred over the market price approach in setting transfer prices?

10. When using the negotiated price approach to transfer pricing, within what range should the transfer price be established?

Basic Exercises

SHOW ME HOW

BE 9-1   Budgetary performance for cost center   Obj. 2

Vinton Company's costs were under budget by $36,000. The company is divided into North and South regions. The North Region's costs were over budget by $45,000. Determine the amount that the South Region's costs were over or under budget.

SHOW ME HOW

BE 9-2   Service department charges   Obj. 3

The centralized computer technology department of Hardy Company has expenses of $320,000. The department has provided a total of 4,000 hours of service for the period. The Retail Division has used 2,750 hours of computer technology service during the period, and the Commercial Division has used 1,250 hours of computer technology service. How much should each division be charged for computer technology department services?

SHOW ME HOW

BE 9-3   Income from operations for profit center   Obj. 3

Using the data for Hardy Company from Brief Exercise 2 along with the following data, determine the divisional income from operations for the Retail Division and the Commercial Division:

	Retail Division	Commercial Division
Sales	$2,150,000	$1,200,000
Cost of goods sold	1,300,000	800,000
Selling expenses	150,000	175,000

SHOW ME HOW

BE 9-4   Profit margin, investment turnover, and ROI   Obj. 4

Briggs Company has income from operations of $36,000, invested assets of $180,000, and sales of $720,000. Use the DuPont formula to compute the return on investment and show (A) the profit margin, (B) the investment turnover, and (C) the return on investment.

SHOW ME HOW

BE 9-5   Residual income   Obj. 4

The Commercial Division of Galena Company has income from operations of $12,680,000 and assets of $74,500,000. The minimum acceptable return on assets is 12%. What is the residual income for the division?

SHOW ME HOW

BE 9-6   Transfer pricing   Obj. 5

The materials used by the Multinomah Division of Isbister Company are currently purchased from outside suppliers at $90 per unit. These same materials are produced by the Pembroke Division. The Pembroke Division can produce the materials needed by the Multinomah Division at a variable cost of $75 per unit. The division is currently producing 120,000 units and has capacity of 150,000 units. The two divisions have recently negotiated a transfer price of $82 per unit for 15,000 units. By how much will each division's income increase as a result of this transfer?

Exercises

SHOW ME HOW

✔ A. (C) $22,950

EX 9-1   Budget performance reports for cost centers   Obj. 2

Partially completed budget performance reports for Garland Company, a manufacturer of light duty motors, follow:

Garland Company
Budget Performance Report—Vice President, Production
For the Month Ended November 30

Plant	Budget	Actual	Over Budget	Under Budget
Eastern Region	$2,300,000	$2,287,900		$ (12,100)
Central Region	3,000,000	2,988,400		(11,600)
Western Region	(G)	(H)	$ (I)	
	$ (J)	$ (K)	$ (L)	$ (23,700)

Garland Company
Budget Performance Report—Manager, Western Region Plant
For the Month Ended November 30

Department	Budget	Actual	Over Budget	Under Budget
Chip Fabrication	$ (A)	$ (B)	$ (C)	
Electronic Assembly	700,000	703,200	3,200	
Final Assembly	525,000	516,600		$(8,400)
	$ (D)	$ (E)	$ (F)	$(8,400)

Garland Company
Budget Performance Report—Supervisor, Chip Fabrication
For the Month Ended November 30

Cost	Budget	Actual	Over Budget	Under Budget
Factory wages	$ 82,000	$ 95,500	$13,500	
Materials	120,000	115,300		$(4,700)
Power and light	45,000	49,950	4,950	
Maintenance	28,000	37,200	9,200	
	$275,000	$297,950	$27,650	$(4,700)

A. Complete the budget performance reports by determining the correct amounts for the lettered spaces.

B. ▬▬▬▬▶ Compose a memo to Cassandra Reid, vice president of production for Garland Company, explaining the performance of the production division for November.

EX 9-2   Divisional income statements   Obj. 3

✔ Commercial Division income from operations, $179,890

The following data were summarized from the accounting records for Jersey Coast Construction Company for the year ended June 30, 20Y8:

Cost of goods sold:		Service department charges:	
Commercial Division	$912,250	Commercial Division	$112,560
Residential Division	423,675	Residential Division	67,830
Administrative expenses:		Sales:	
Commercial Division	$149,800	Commercial Division	$1,354,500
Residential Division	128,625	Residential Division	743,780

Prepare divisional income statements for Jersey Coast Construction Company.

EX 9-3 Service department charges and activity bases

Obj. 3

For each of the following service departments, identify an activity base that could be used for charging the expense to the profit center:

A. Legal
B. Duplication services
C. Electronic data processing
D. Central purchasing
E. Telecommunications
F. Accounts receivable

EX 9-4 Activity bases for service department charges

Obj. 3

✔ C. 2

For each of the following service departments, select the activity base listed that is most appropriate for charging service expenses to responsible units:

Service Department	Activity Base
A. Accounts Receivable	1. Number of conference attendees
B. Central Purchasing	2. Number of computers
C. Computer Support	3. Number of employees trained
D. Conferences	4. Number of cell phone minutes used
E. Employee Travel	5. Number of purchase requisitions
F. Payroll Accounting	6. Number of sales invoices
G. Telecommunications	7. Number of payroll checks
H. Training	8. Number of travel claims

EX 9-5 Service department charges

Obj. 3

✔ B. Residential payroll, $32,640

SHOW ME HOW

In divisional income statements prepared for Demopolis Company, the Payroll Department costs are charged back to user divisions on the basis of the number of payroll distributions, and the Purchasing Department costs are charged back on the basis of the number of purchase requisitions. The Payroll Department had expenses of $64,560, and the Purchasing Department had expenses of $40,000 for the year. The following annual data for Residential, Commercial, and Government Contract divisions were obtained from corporate records:

	Residential	Commercial	Government Contract
Sales	$2,000,000	$3,250,000	$2,900,000
Number of employees:			
Weekly payroll (52 weeks per year)	400	250	150
Monthly payroll	80	30	10
Number of purchase requisitions per year	7,500	3,000	2,000

A. Determine the total amount of payroll checks and purchase requisitions processed per year by the company and each division.

B. Using the activity base information in (A), determine the annual amount of payroll and purchasing costs charged back to the Residential, Commercial, and Government Contract divisions from payroll and purchasing services.

C. ▬▬▶ Why does the Residential Division have a larger service department charge than the other two divisions, even though its sales are lower?

EX 9-6 Service department charges and activity bases

Obj. 3

✔ B. Help desk, $93,600

Middler Corporation, a manufacturer of electronics and communications systems, uses a service department charge system to charge profit centers with Computing and Communications Services (CCS) service department costs. The following table identifies an abbreviated list of service categories and activity bases used by the CCS department. The table also includes some assumed cost and activity base quantity information for each service for October.

CCS Service Category	Activity Base	Budgeted Cost	Budgeted Activity Base Quantity
Help desk	Number of calls	$160,000	3,200
Network center	Number of devices monitored	735,000	9,800
Electronic mail	Number of user accounts	100,000	10,000
Smartphone support	Number of smartphones issued	124,600	8,900

One of the profit centers for Middler Corporation is the Communication Systems (COMM) sector. Assume the following information for the COMM sector:

- The sector has 5,200 employees, of whom 25% are office employees.
- All the office employees have been issued a smartphone, and 96% of them have a computer on the network.
- One hundred percent of the employees with a computer also have an e-mail account.
- The average number of help desk calls for October was 1.5 calls per individual with a computer.
- There are 600 additional printers, servers, and peripherals on the network beyond the personal computers.

A. Determine the service charge rate for the four CCS service categories for October.

B. Determine the charges to the COMM sector for the four CCS service categories for October.

EX 9-7 Divisional income statements with service department charges   Obj. 3

✔ Commercial income from operations, $1,261,260

SHOW ME HOW   EXCEL TEMPLATE

Yozamba Technology has two divisions, Consumer and Commercial, and two corporate service departments, Tech Support and Purchasing. The corporate expenses for the year ended December 31, 20Y7, are as follows:

Tech Support Department	$ 516,000
Purchasing Department	89,600
Other corporate administrative expenses	560,000
Total corporate expense	$1,165,600

The other corporate administrative expenses include officers' salaries and other expenses required by the corporation. The Tech Support Department charges the divisions for services rendered, based on the number of computers in the department, and the Purchasing Department charges divisions for services, based on the number of purchase orders for each department. The usage of service by the two divisions is as follows:

	Tech Support	Purchasing
Consumer Division	375 computers	1,960 purchase orders
Commercial Division	225	3,640
Total	600 computers	5,600 purchase orders

The service department charges of the Tech Support Department and the Purchasing Department are considered controllable by the divisions. Corporate administrative expenses are not considered controllable by the divisions. The revenues, cost of goods sold, and operating expenses for the two divisions are as follows:

	Consumer	Commercial
Revenues	$7,430,000	$6,184,000
Cost of goods sold	4,123,000	3,125,000
Operating expenses	1,465,000	1,546,000

Prepare the divisional income statements for the two divisions.

EX 9-8   Corrections to service department charges for a service company   Obj. 3

✔ B. Income from operations, Cargo Division, $84,400

Wild Sun Airlines Inc. has two divisions organized as profit centers, the Passenger Division and the Cargo Division. The following divisional income statements were prepared:

Wild Sun Airlines Inc.
Divisional Income Statements
For the Year Ended December 31, 20Y9

	Passenger Division	Cargo Division
Revenues	$3,025,000	$3,025,000
Operating expenses	2,450,000	2,736,000
Income from operations before service department charges	$ 575,000	$ 289,000
Service department charges:		
Training	$ 125,000	$ 125,000
Flight scheduling	108,000	108,000
Reservations	151,200	151,200
Total service department charges	384,200	384,200
Income from operations	$ 190,800	$ (95,200)

The service department charge rate for the service department costs was based on revenues. Because the revenues of the two divisions were the same, the service department charges to each division were also the same.

The following additional information is available:

	Passenger Division	Cargo Division	Total
Number of personnel trained	350	150	500
Number of flights	800	1,200	2,000
Number of reservations requested	20,000	0	20,000

A. ▬▬▬▶ Does the income from operations for the two divisions accurately measure performance? Explain.

B. Correct the divisional income statements, using the activity bases provided in revising the service department charges.

EX 9-9   Profit center responsibility reporting   Obj. 3

✔ Income from operations, Summer Sports Division, $1,499,400

SHOW ME HOW   EXCEL TEMPLATE

XSport Sporting Goods Co. operates two divisions—the Winter Sports Division and the Summer Sports Division. The following income and expense accounts were provided from the trial balance as of December 31, 20Y9, the end of the fiscal year, after all adjustments, including those for inventories, were recorded and posted:

Sales—Winter Sports Division	$10,500,000
Sales—Summer Sports Division	13,600,000
Cost of Goods Sold—Winter Sports Division	6,300,000
Cost of Goods Sold—Summer Sports Division	7,888,000
Sales Expense—Winter Sports Division	1,680,000
Sales Expense—Summer Sports Division	1,904,000
Administrative Expense—Winter Sports Division	1,050,000
Administrative Expense—Summer Sports Division	1,210,400
Advertising Expense	482,000
Transportation Expense	240,000
Accounts Receivable Collection Expense	120,500
Warehouse Expense	1,200,000

The bases to be used in allocating expenses, together with other essential information, are as follows:

A. Advertising expense—incurred at headquarters, charged back to divisions on the basis of usage: Winter Sports Division, $216,900; Summer Sports Division, $265,100.

B. Transportation expense—charged back to divisions at a charge rate of $8.00 per bill of lading: Winter Sports Division, 14,400 bills of lading; Summer Sports Division, 15,600 bills of lading.

C. Accounts receivable collection expense—incurred at headquarters, charged back to divisions at a charge rate of $5.00 per invoice: Winter Sports Division, 9,640 sales invoices; Summer Sports Division, 14,460 sales invoices.

D. Warehouse expense—charged back to divisions on the basis of floor space used in storing division products: Winter Sports Division, 94,000 square feet; Summer Sports Division, 106,000 square feet.

Prepare a divisional income statement with two column headings: Winter Sports Division and Summer Sports Division. Provide supporting calculations for service department charges.

EX 9-10   Return on investment   Obj. 4

✔ A. Retail, 18%

SHOW ME HOW

The income from operations and the amount of invested assets in each division of Beck Industries are as follows:

	Income from Operations	Invested Assets
Retail Division	$5,400,000	$30,000,000
Commercial Division	6,250,000	25,000,000
Internet Division	1,800,000	12,000,000

A. Compute the return on investment for each division.

B. Which division is the most profitable per dollar invested?

EX 9-11   Residual income   Obj. 4

✔ A. Retail Division, $2,700,000

SHOW ME HOW

Based on the data in Exercise 10 assume that management has established a 9% minimum acceptable return for invested assets.

A. Determine the residual income for each division.

B. Which division has the most residual income?

EX 9-12   Determining missing items in return on investment computation   Obj. 4

✔ D. 3.00

One item is omitted from each of the following computations of the return on investment:

Return on Investment	=	Profit Margin	×	Investment Turnover
13.2%	=	6%	×	(A)
(B)	=	10%	×	1.80
10.5%	=	(C)	×	1.50
15%	=	5%	×	(D)
(E)	=	12%	×	1.10

Determine the missing items, identifying each by the appropriate letter.

EX 9-13   Profit margin, investment turnover, and return on investment   Obj. 4

✔ A. ROI, 24%

SHOW ME HOW

The condensed income statement for the Consumer Products Division of Fargo Industries Inc. is as follows (assuming no service department charges):

Sales	$82,500,000
Cost of goods sold	53,625,000
Gross profit	$28,875,000
Administrative expenses	15,675,000
Income from operations	$13,200,000

(*Continued*)

The manager of the Consumer Products Division is considering ways to increase the return on investment.

A. Using the DuPont formula for return on investment, determine the profit margin, investment turnover, and return on investment of the Consumer Products Division, assuming that $55,000,000 of assets have been invested in the Consumer Products Division.

B. If expenses could be reduced by $1,650,000 without decreasing sales, what would be the impact on the profit margin, investment turnover, and return on investment for the Consumer Products Division?

EX 9-14 Return on investment   Obj. 4

✔ A. Media Networks ROI, 24.6%

The Walt Disney Company has four profitable business segments, described as follows:

REAL WORLD

- **Media Networks:** Television and radio
- **Parks and Resorts:** Resorts, including Disneyland
- **Studio Entertainment:** Motion pictures, musical recordings, and stage plays
- **Consumer Products:** Character merchandising, Disney stores, books, and magazines

Disney recently reported sector income from operations, revenue, and invested assets (in millions) as follows:

	Income from Operations	Revenue	Invested Assets
Media Networks	$7,321	$21,152	$29,887
Parks and Resorts	2,663	15,099	23,335
Studio Entertainment	1,549	6,988	15,155
Consumer Products	1,356	4,274	7,526

A. Use the DuPont formula to determine the return on investment for the four Disney sectors. (Round percentages to one decimal place and investment turnover to two decimal places.)

B. ➤ How do the four sectors differ in their profit margin, investment turnover, and return on investment?

EX 9-15 Determining missing items in return and residual income computations   Obj. 4

✔ C. $46,250

Data for Uberto Company are presented in the following table of returns on investment and residual incomes:

Invested Assets	Income from Operations	Return on Investment	Minimum Return on Investment	Minimum Acceptable Income from Operations	Residual Income
$925,000	$185,000	(A)	15%	(B)	(C)
$775,000	(D)	(E)	(F)	$93,000	$23,250
$450,000	(G)	18%	(H)	$58,500	(I)
$610,000	$97,600	(J)	12%	(K)	(L)

Determine the missing items, identifying each item by the appropriate letter.

EX 9-16 Determining missing items from computations   Obj. 4

✔ A. (E) $300,000

Data for the North, South, East, and West divisions of Free Bird Company are as follows:

	Sales	Income from Operations	Invested Assets	Return on Investment	Profit Margin	Investment Turnover
North	$860,000	(A)	(B)	17.5%	7.0%	(C)
South	(D)	$51,300	(E)	(F)	4.5%	3.8
East	$1,020,000	(G)	$680,000	15.0%	(H)	(I)
West	$1,120,000	$89,600	$560,000	(J)	(K)	(L)

A. Determine the missing items, identifying each by the letters (A) through (L). (Round percentages and investment turnover to one decimal place.)

B. Determine the residual income for each division, assuming that the minimum acceptable return on investment established by management is 12%.

C. Which division is the most profitable in terms of (1) return on investment and (2) residual income?

REAL WORLD

EX 9-17   Balanced scorecard for a service company   Obj. 4

American Express Company is a major financial services company, noted for its American Express® card. Some of the performance measures used by the company in its balanced scorecard follow:

Average card member spending	Number of Internet features
Cards in force	Number of merchant signings
Earnings growth	Number of new card launches
Hours of credit consultant training	Return on equity
Investment in information technology	Revenue growth
Number of card choices	

For each measure, identify whether the measure best fits the innovation, customer, internal process, or financial dimension of the balanced scorecard.

EX 9-18   Building a balanced scorecard   Obj. 4

Hit-n-Run Inc. owns and operates 10 food trucks (mobile kitchens) throughout metropolitan Los Angeles. Each food truck has a different food theme, such as Irish-Mexican fusion, traditional Mexican street food, Ethiopian cuisine, and Lebanese-Italian fusion. The company was founded three years ago by Juanita O'Brien when she opened a single food truck with a unique menu. As her business has grown, she has become concerned about her ability to manage and control the business. O'Brien describes how the company was built, its key success factors, and its recent growth.

"I built the company from the ground up. In the beginning it was just me. I drove the truck, set the menu, bought the ingredients, prepared the meals, served the meals, cleaned the kitchen, and maintained the equipment. I made unique meals from quality ingredients, and didn't serve anything that wasn't perfect. I changed my location daily and notified customers of my location via Twitter.

As my customer base grew, I hired employees to help me in the truck. Then one day I realized that I had a formula that could be expanded to multiple trucks. Before I knew it, I had 10 trucks and was hiring people to do everything that I used to do by myself. Now, I work with my team to build the menu, set daily locations for the trucks, and manage the operations of the business.

My business model is based on providing the highest quality street food and charging more for it than other trucks. You won't get the cheapest meal at one of my trucks, but you will get the best. The superior quality allows me to price my meals a little bit higher than the other trucks. My employees are critical to my success. I pay them a better wage than they could make on other food trucks, and I expect more from them. I rely on them to maintain the quality that I established when I opened my first truck.

Things are going great, but I'm feeling overwhelmed. So far, the growth in sales has led to a growth in profitability—but I'm getting nervous. If quality starts to fall off, my brand value erodes, and that could affect the prices that I charge for my meals and the success of my business."

Create balanced scorecard measures for Hit-n-Run Inc. Identify whether these measures best fit the innovation, customer, internal process, or financial dimension of the balanced scorecard.

EX 9-19 Decision on transfer pricing
Obj. 5

✔ A. $3,000,000

Materials used by the Instrument Division of XPort Industries are currently purchased from outside suppliers at a cost of $210 per unit. However, the same materials are available from the Components Division. The Components Division has unused capacity and can produce the materials needed by the Instrument Division at a variable cost of $160 per unit.

A. If a transfer price of $180 per unit is established and 60,000 units of materials are transferred, with no reduction in the Components Division's current sales, how much would XPort Industries' total income from operations increase?

B. How much would the Instrument Division's income from operations increase?

C. How much would the Components Division's income from operations increase?

EX 9-20 Decision on transfer pricing
Obj. 5

✔ B. $1,200,000

Based on XPort Industries' data in Exercise 19, assume that a transfer price of $190 has been established and that 60,000 units of materials are transferred, with no reduction in the Components Division's current sales.

A. How much would XPort Industries' total income from operations increase?

B. How much would the Instrument Division's income from operations increase?

C. How much would the Components Division's income from operations increase?

D. ➤ If the negotiated price approach is used, what would be the range of acceptable transfer prices and why?

Problems: Series A

EXCEL TEMPLATE

PR 9-1A Budget performance report for a cost center
Obj. 2

Valotic Tech Inc. sells electronics over the Internet. The Consumer Products Division is organized as a cost center. The budget for the Consumer Products Division for the month ended January 31 is as follows:

Customer service salaries	$ 546,840
Insurance and property taxes	114,660
Distribution salaries	872,340
Marketing salaries	1,028,370
Engineer salaries	836,850
Warehouse wages	586,110
Equipment depreciation	183,792
Total	$4,168,962

During January, the costs incurred in the Consumer Products Division were as follows:

Customer service salaries	$ 602,350
Insurance and property taxes	110,240
Distribution salaries	861,200
Marketing salaries	1,085,230
Engineer salaries	820,008
Warehouse wages	562,632
Equipment depreciation	183,610
Total	$4,225,270

Instructions

1. Prepare a budget performance report for the director of the Consumer Products Division for the month of January.

2. ➤ For which costs might the director be expected to request supplemental reports?

PR 9-2A Profit center responsibility reporting for a service company   Obj. 3

✔ 1. Income from
operations, West
Division, $341,650

SHOW ME HOW   EXCEL TEMPLATE

Red Line Railroad Inc. has three regional divisions organized as profit centers. The chief executive officer (CEO) evaluates divisional performance, using income from operations as a percent of revenues. The following quarterly income and expense accounts were provided from the trial balance as of December 31:

Revenues—East	$1,400,000
Revenues—West	2,000,000
Revenues—Central	3,200,000
Operating Expenses—East	800,000
Operating Expenses—West	1,350,000
Operating Expenses—Central	1,900,000
Corporate Expenses—Shareholder Relations	300,000
Corporate Expenses—Customer Support	320,000
Corporate Expenses—Legal	500,000
General Corporate Officers' Salaries	1,200,000

The company operates three service departments: Shareholder Relations, Customer Support, and Legal. The Shareholder Relations Department conducts a variety of services for shareholders of the company. The Customer Support Department is the company's point of contact for new service, complaints, and requests for repair. The department believes that the number of customer contacts is an activity base for this work. The Legal Department provides legal services for division management. The department believes that the number of hours billed is an activity base for this work. The following additional information has been gathered:

	East	West	Central
Number of customer contacts	1,500	2,800	5,700
Number of hours billed	750	1,750	1,500

Instructions

1. Prepare quarterly income statements showing income from operations for the three divisions. Use three column headings: East, West, and Central.

2. Identify the most successful division according to the profit margin. (Round to the nearest whole percent.)

3. ▬▬▶ Provide a recommendation to the CEO for a better method for evaluating the performance of the divisions. In your recommendation, identify the major weakness of the present method.

PR 9-3A Divisional income statements and return on investment analysis   Obj. 4

✔ 2. Cereal Division
ROI, 10.0%

EXCEL TEMPLATE

The Crunchy Granola Company is a diversified food company that specializes in all natural foods. The company has three operating divisions organized as investment centers. Condensed data taken from the records of the three divisions for the year ended June 30, 20Y7, are as follows:

	Cereal Division	Snack Cake Division	Retail Bakeries Division
Sales	$25,000,000	$8,000,000	$9,750,000
Cost of goods sold	16,670,000	5,575,000	6,795,000
Operating expenses	7,330,000	1,945,000	2,272,500
Invested assets	10,000,000	4,000,000	6,500,000

The management of The Crunchy Granola Company is evaluating each division as a basis for planning a future expansion of operations.

Instructions

1. Prepare condensed divisional income statements for the three divisions, assuming that there were no service department charges.

2. Using the DuPont formula for return on investment, compute the profit margin, investment turnover, and return on investment for each division. (Round percentages and the investment turnover to one decimal place.)

3. ▬▬▶ If available funds permit the expansion of operations of only one division, which of the divisions would you recommend for expansion, based on parts (1) and (2)? Explain.

PR 9-4A   Effect of proposals on divisional performance

Obj. 4

✔ 1. ROI, 16.8%

EXCEL TEMPLATE

A condensed income statement for the Commercial Division of Maxell Manufacturing Inc. for the year ended December 31, 20Y9, is as follows:

Sales	$3,500,000
Cost of goods sold	2,480,000
Gross profit	$1,020,000
Operating expenses	600,000
Income from operations	$ 420,000
Invested assets	$2,500,000

Assume that the Commercial Division received no charges from service departments. The president of Maxell Manufacturing has indicated that the division's return on a $2,500,000 investment must be increased to at least 21% by the end of the next year if operations are to continue. The division manager is considering the following three proposals:

Proposal 1: Transfer equipment with a book value of $312,500 to other divisions at no gain or loss and lease similar equipment. The annual lease payments would exceed the amount of depreciation expense on the old equipment by $105,000. This increase in expense would be included as part of the cost of goods sold. Sales would remain unchanged.

Proposal 2: Purchase new and more efficient machining equipment and thereby reduce the cost of goods sold by $560,000 after considering the effects of depreciation expense on the new equipment. Sales would remain unchanged, and the old equipment, which has no remaining book value, would be scrapped at no gain or loss. The new equipment would increase invested assets by an additional $1,875,000 for the year.

Proposal 3: Reduce invested assets by discontinuing a product line. This action would eliminate sales of $595,000, reduce cost of goods sold by $406,700, and reduce operating expenses by $175,000. Assets of $1,338,000 would be transferred to other divisions at no gain or loss.

Instructions

1. Using the DuPont formula for return on investment, determine the profit margin, investment turnover, and return on investment for the Commercial Division for the past year.

2. Prepare condensed estimated income statements and compute the invested assets for each proposal.

3. Using the DuPont formula for return on investment, determine the profit margin, investment turnover, and return on investment for each proposal. (Round the investment turnover and return on investment to one decimal place.)

4. Which of the three proposals would meet the required 21% return on investment?

5. If the Commercial Division were in an industry where the profit margin could not be increased, how much would the investment turnover have to increase to meet the president's required 21% return on investment?

PR 9-5A   Divisional performance analysis and evaluation

Obj. 4

✔ 2. Business Division ROI, 23.0%

SHOW ME HOW   EXCEL TEMPLATE

The vice president of operations of Recycling Industries is evaluating the performance of two divisions organized as investment centers. Invested assets and condensed income statement data for the past year for each division are as follows:

	Business Division	Consumer Division
Sales	$42,800,000	$56,000,000
Cost of goods sold	23,500,000	30,500,000
Operating expenses	11,424,800	14,300,000
Invested assets	34,240,000	70,000,000

Instructions

1. Prepare condensed divisional income statements for the year ended December 31, 20Y8, assuming that there were no service department charges.

2. Using the DuPont formula for return on investment, determine the profit margin, investment turnover, and return on investment for each division. (Round percentages to one decimal place and the investment turnover to two decimal places.)

3. If management desires a minimum acceptable return on investment of 10%, determine the residual income for each division.

4. ━━━► Discuss the evaluation of the two divisions, using the performance measures determined in parts (1), (2), and (3).

PR 9-6A   Transfer pricing   Obj. 5

✔ 3. Total income from operations, $1,759,680

EXCEL TEMPLATE

Garcon Inc. manufactures electronic products, with two operating divisions, Consumer and Commercial. Condensed divisional income statements, which involve no intracompany transfers and which include a breakdown of expenses into variable and fixed components, are as follows:

Garcon Inc.
Divisional Income Statements
For the Year Ended December 31, 20Y2

	Consumer Division	Commercial Division	Total
Sales:			
14,400 units × $144 per unit	$2,073,600		$2,073,600
21,600 units × $275 per unit		$5,940,000	5,940,000
Total sales	$2,073,600	$5,940,000	$8,013,600
Expenses:			
Variable:			
14,400 units × $104 per unit	$1,497,600		$1,497,600
21,600 units × $193* per unit		$4,168,800	4,168,800
Fixed	200,000	520,000	720,000
Total expenses	$1,697,600	$4,688,800	$6,386,400
Income from operations	$ 376,000	$1,251,200	$1,627,200

*$150 of the $193 per unit represents materials costs, and the remaining $43 per unit represents other variable conversion expenses incurred within the Commercial Division.

The Consumer Division is presently producing 14,400 units out of a total capacity of 17,280 units. Materials used in producing the Commercial Division's product are currently purchased from outside suppliers at a price of $150 per unit. The Consumer Division is able to produce the materials used by the Commercial Division. Except for the possible transfer of materials between divisions, no changes are expected in sales and expenses.

Instructions

1. ━━━► Would the market price of $150 per unit be an appropriate transfer price for Garcon Inc.? Explain.

2. ━━━► If the Commercial Division purchases 2,880 units from the Consumer Division, rather than externally, at a negotiated transfer price of $115 per unit, how much would the income from operations of each division and the total company income from operations increase?

3. Prepare condensed divisional income statements for Garcon Inc. based on the data in part (2).

4. ━━━► If a transfer price of $126 per unit is negotiated, how much would the income from operations of each division and the total company income from operations increase?

5. A. ━━━► What is the range of possible negotiated transfer prices that would be acceptable for Garcon Inc.?

   B. Assuming that the managers of the two divisions cannot agree on a transfer price, what price would you suggest as the transfer price?

Problems: Series B

EXCEL TEMPLATE

PR 9-1B Budget performance report for a cost center   Obj. 2

The Eastern District of Adelson Inc. is organized as a cost center. The budget for the Eastern District of Adelson Inc. for the month ended December 31 is as follows:

Sales salaries	$ 819,840
System administration salaries	448,152
Customer service salaries	152,600
Billing salaries	98,760
Maintenance	271,104
Depreciation of plant and equipment	92,232
Insurance and property taxes	41,280
Total	$1,923,968

During December, the costs incurred in the Eastern District were as follows:

Sales salaries	$ 818,880
System administration salaries	447,720
Customer service salaries	183,120
Billing salaries	98,100
Maintenance	273,000
Depreciation of plant and equipment	92,232
Insurance and property taxes	41,400
Total	$1,954,452

Instructions

1. Prepare a budget performance report for the manager of the Eastern District of Adelson for the month of December.

2. ⬛➤ For which costs might the manager be expected to request supplemental reports?

✔ 1. Income from operations, West Region, $820,800

SHOW ME HOW   EXCEL TEMPLATE

PR 9-2B Profit center responsibility reporting for a service company   Obj. 3

Thomas Railroad Company organizes its three divisions, the North (N), South (S), and West (W) regions, as profit centers. The chief executive officer (CEO) evaluates divisional performance, using income from operations as a percent of revenues. The following quarterly income and expense accounts were provided from the trial balance as of December 31:

Revenues—N Region	$3,780,000
Revenues—S Region	5,673,000
Revenues—W Region	5,130,000
Operating Expenses—N Region	2,678,500
Operating Expenses—S Region	4,494,890
Operating Expenses—W Region	3,770,050
Corporate Expenses—Dispatching	182,000
Corporate Expenses—Equipment Management	1,200,000
Corporate Expenses—Treasurer's	734,000
General Corporate Officers' Salaries	1,380,000

The company operates three service departments: the Dispatching Department, the Equipment Management Department, and the Treasurer's Department. The Dispatching Department manages the scheduling and releasing of completed trains. The Equipment Management Department manages the railroad cars inventories. It makes sure the right freight cars are at the right place at the right time. The Treasurer's Department conducts a variety of services for the company as a whole. The following additional information has been gathered:

	North	South	West
Number of scheduled trains	650	1,105	845
Number of railroad cars in inventory	6,000	8,400	9,600

Instructions

1. Prepare quarterly income statements showing income from operations for the three regions. Use three column headings: North, South, and West.

2. Identify the most successful region according to the profit margin.

3. ➤ Provide a recommendation to the CEO for a better method for evaluating the performance of the regions. In your recommendation, identify the major weakness of the present method.

✔ 2. Mutual Fund Division, ROI, 22.4%

EXCEL TEMPLATE

PR 9-3B   Divisional income statements and return on investment analysis   Obj. 4

E.F. Lynch Company is a diversified investment company with three operating divisions organized as investment centers. Condensed data taken from the records of the three divisions for the year ended June 30, 20Y8, are as follows:

	Mutual Fund Division	Electronic Brokerage Division	Investment Banking Division
Fee revenue	$4,140,000	$3,360,000	$4,560,000
Operating expenses	2,980,800	3,091,200	3,739,200
Invested assets	5,175,000	1,120,000	3,800,000

The management of E.F. Lynch Company is evaluating each division as a basis for planning a future expansion of operations.

Instructions

1. Prepare condensed divisional income statements for the three divisions, assuming that there were no service department charges.

2. Using the DuPont formula for return on investment, compute the profit margin, investment turnover, and return on investment for each division. (Round percentages and the investment turnover to one decimal place.)

3. ➤ If available funds permit the expansion of operations of only one division, which of the divisions would you recommend for expansion, based on parts (1) and (2)? Explain.

✔ 3. Proposal 3 ROI, 16.0%

EXCEL TEMPLATE

PR 9-4B   Effect of proposals on divisional performance   Obj. 4

A condensed income statement for the Electronics Division of Gihbli Industries Inc. for the year ended December 31, 20Y9, is as follows:

Sales	$1,575,000
Cost of goods sold	891,000
Gross profit	$ 684,000
Operating expenses	558,000
Income from operations	$ 126,000
Invested assets	$1,050,000

Assume that the Electronics Division received no charges from service departments.

The president of Gihbli Industries Inc. has indicated that the division's return on a $1,050,000 investment must be increased to at least 20% by the end of the next year if operations are to continue. The division manager is considering the following three proposals:

Proposal 1: Transfer equipment with a book value of $300,000 to other divisions at no gain or loss and lease similar equipment. The annual lease payments would be less than the amount of depreciation expense on the old equipment by $31,400. This decrease in expense would be included as part of the cost of goods sold. Sales would remain unchanged.

Proposal 2: Reduce invested assets by discontinuing a product line. This action would eliminate sales of $180,000, reduce cost of goods sold by $119,550, and reduce operating expenses by $60,000. Assets of $112,500 would be transferred to other divisions at no gain or loss.

(Continued)

Proposal 3: Purchase new and more efficient machinery and thereby reduce the cost of goods sold by $189,000 after considering the effects of depreciation expense on the new equipment. Sales would remain unchanged, and the old machinery, which has no remaining book value, would be scrapped at no gain or loss. The new machinery would increase invested assets by $918,750 for the year.

Instructions

1. Using the DuPont formula for return on investment, determine the profit margin, investment turnover, and return on investment for the Electronics Division for the past year. (Round percentages and investment turnover to one decimal place.)

2. Prepare condensed estimated income statements and compute the invested assets for each proposal.

3. Using the DuPont formula for return on investment, determine the profit margin, investment turnover, and return on investment for each proposal. (Round percentages and investment turnover to one decimal place.)

4. Which of the three proposals would meet the required 20% return on investment?

5. If the Electronics Division were in an industry where the profit margin could not be increased, how much would the investment turnover have to increase to meet the president's required 20% return on investment? (Round to one decimal place.)

PR 9-5B Divisional performance analysis and evaluation   Obj. 4

✔ 2. Road Bike Division ROI, 12.0%

SHOW ME HOW   EXCEL TEMPLATE

The vice president of operations of Free Ride Bike Company is evaluating the performance of two divisions organized as investment centers. Invested assets and condensed income statement data for the past year for each division are as follows:

	Road Bike Division	Mountain Bike Division
Sales	$1,728,000	$1,760,000
Cost of goods sold	1,380,000	1,400,000
Operating expenses	175,200	236,800
Invested assets	1,440,000	800,000

Instructions

1. Prepare condensed divisional income statements for the year ended December 31, 20Y7, assuming that there were no service department charges.

2. Using the DuPont formula for return on investment, determine the profit margin, investment turnover, and return on investment for each division. (Round percentages and the investment turnover to one decimal place.)

3. If management's minimum acceptable return on investment is 10%, determine the residual income for each division.

4. ➤ Discuss the evaluation of the two divisions, using the performance measures determined in parts (1), (2), and (3).

PR 9-6B Transfer pricing   Obj. 5

✔ 3. Navigational Systems Division, $179,410

EXCEL TEMPLATE

Exoplex Industries Inc. is a diversified aerospace company, including two operating divisions, Semiconductors and Navigational Systems. Condensed divisional income statements, which involve no intracompany transfers and include a breakdown of expenses into variable and fixed components, are as follows:

Exoplex Industries Inc.
Divisional Income Statements
For the Year Ended December 31, 20Y8

	Semiconductors Division	Navigational Systems Division	Total
Sales:			
2,240 units × $396 per unit	$887,040		$ 887,040
3,675 units × $590 per unit		$2,168,250	2,168,250
Total sales	$887,040	$2,168,250	$3,055,290
Expenses:			
Variable:			
2,240 units × $232 per unit	$519,680		$ 519,680
3,675 units × $472* per unit		$1,734,600	1,734,600
Fixed	220,000	325,000	545,000
Total expenses	$739,680	$2,059,600	$2,799,280
Income from operations	$147,360	$ 108,650	$ 256,010

*$432 of the $472 per unit represents materials costs, and the remaining $40 per unit represents other variable conversion expenses incurred within the Navigational Systems Division.

The Semiconductors Division is presently producing 2,240 units out of a total capacity of 2,820 units. Materials used in producing the Navigational Systems Division's product are currently purchased from outside suppliers at a price of $432 per unit. The Semiconductors Division is able to produce the components used by the Navigational Systems Division. Except for the possible transfer of materials between divisions, no changes are expected in sales and expenses.

Instructions

1. ▬▬▶ Would the market price of $432 per unit be an appropriate transfer price for Exoplex Industries Inc.? Explain.

2. ▬▬▶ If the Navigational Systems Division purchases 580 units from the Semiconductors Division, rather than externally, at a negotiated transfer price of $310 per unit, how much would the income from operations of each division and total company income from operations increase?

3. Prepare condensed divisional income statements for Exoplex Industries Inc. based on the data in part (2).

4. ▬▬▶ If a transfer price of $340 per unit is negotiated, how much would the income from operations of each division and total company income from operations increase?

5. A. ▬▬▶ What is the range of possible negotiated transfer prices that would be acceptable for Exoplex Industries Inc.?

   B. Assuming that the managers of the two divisions cannot agree on a transfer price, what price would you suggest as the transfer price?

Analysis for Decision Making

REAL WORLD

ADM-1 GNC: Franchise segment return on investment

GNC Holdings Inc. is a leading retailer of health and nutrition products, which are sold through both company-operated (3,500 outlets) and franchised retail (3,200 outlets) stores. In addition, GNC manufactures many of the products that it sells through its company-operated and franchised channels. As such, GNC's operating segments are Retail, Franchise, and Manufacturing. The Retail segment is made up of company-operated stores, and the Franchise segment is made up of franchised stores. Recent financial information from these segments is as follows (in millions):

	Retail	Franchise	Manufacturing
Sales	$1,939	$433	$486
Income from operations	349	157	90
Invested assets	1,573	512	407

A. Determine the profit margin for each segment. (Round percentages to one decimal place.)

B. ➡ Why might the profit margin of the Franchise segment be larger than the other two segments?

C. Determine the investment turnover for each segment. (Round to one decimal place.)

D. Use the DuPont formula to determine the return on investment for each segment. (Round percentages to one decimal place.)

E. What is the source of revenues for the Manufacturing segment? What are the revenue reporting considerations for sales to company-operated stores?

REAL WORLD

ADM-2 Domino's Pizza: Franchise segment return on investment

Domino's Pizza, Inc. is the second-largest pizza chain in the world. In the United States, Domino's has 377 company-owned restaurants and 4,690 franchised restaurants. In addition, Domino's has a supply chain that manufactures and delivers dough and other food products to all the domestic restaurants. Franchisees are required to purchase food products from the Domino's supply chain as part of their franchise agreement. Thus, in the United States, Domino's has three segments: Company-Owned Restaurants, Franchised Restaurants, and Supply Chain. Operating data for these three segments in the United States are as follows (in millions):

	Company-Owned Restaurants	Franchised Restaurants	Supply Chain
Sales	$348	$230	$1,262
Cost of sales	267		1,132
General and administrative expenses*	25	125	100
Invested assets**	32	30	146

*Allocation to segments assumed
**Allocation between Company-Owned and Franchised assumed

A. Determine the income from operations for each segment.

B. Determine the profit margin for each segment. (Round percentages to one decimal place.)

C. Determine the investment turnover for each segment. (Round to one decimal place.)

D. Use the DuPont formula to determine the return on investment for each segment. (Round to nearest whole percent.)

E. ➡ Explain Domino's business model and how it is related to ROI in each segment.

REAL WORLD

ADM-3 H&R Block: Franchise segment return on investment

H&R Block Inc. provides tax preparation services throughout the United States and other parts of the world. These services are provided through company-owned and franchised operations. The total number of U.S. offices that are company-owned and franchised for a recent year is as follows:

	Company-Owned	Franchised	Total
H&R Block Offices (U.S.)	6,365	3,921	10,286

Recent financial information provided by H&R Block for its company-owned and franchised operations is as follows (in millions):

	Company-Owned	Franchised
Revenues	$2,651	
Franchise fees		$335
Cost of services	1,630	
Property, plant, and equipment	2,979	

In addition, H&R Block had $653 million in selling, general, and administrative expenses. These expenses support both company-owned and franchised operations. For example, H&R Block advertising supports both segments. H&R Block had an additional $1,537 million in unallocated property, plant, and equipment. These fixed assets are not associated with its tax service offices, but represent other assets, such as those used at its general headquarters.

A. Allocate the selling, general, and administrative expenses to the company-owned and franchised operations based on the relative number of offices in each segment. (Round to the nearest million.)

B. Allocate the unallocated property, plant, and equipment to the company-owned and franchised operations based on the relative number of offices in each segment. (Round to the nearest million.)

C. Determine the income from operations for each segment, including the allocated selling, general, and administrative expenses from (A).

D. Determine the profit margin for each segment. (Round percentages to one decimal place.)

E. Determine the investment turnover for each segment, including the allocated property, plant, and equipment from (B). (Round to two decimal places.)

F. Use the DuPont formula to determine the return on investment for each segment. (Round percentages to one decimal place.)

G. ➤ What financial variables would impact an H&R Block franchisee's ROI as compared to variables impacting a non-franchised independent tax preparation business?

Take It Further

ETHICS

TIF 9-1   Ethics in Action

Sembotix Company has several divisions including a Semiconductor Division that sells semiconductors to both internal and external customers. The company's X-ray Division uses semiconductors as a component in its final product and is evaluating whether to purchase them from the Semiconductor Division or from an external supplier. The market price for semiconductors is $100 per 100 semiconductors. Dave Bryant is the controller of the X-ray Division, and Howard Hillman is the controller of the Semiconductor Division. The following conversation took place between Dave and Howard:

Dave: I hear you are having problems selling semiconductors out of your division. Maybe I can help.

Howard: You've got that right. We're producing and selling at about 90% of our capacity to outsiders. Last year, we were selling 100% of capacity. Would it be possible for your division to pick up some of our excess capacity? After all, we are part of the same company.

Dave: What kind of price could you give me?

Howard: Well, you know as well as I that we are under strict profit responsibility in our divisions, so I would expect to get market price, $100 for 100 semiconductors.

Dave: I'm not so sure we can swing that. I was expecting a price break from a "sister" division.

Howard: Hey, I can only take this "sister" stuff so far. If I give you a price break, our profits will fall from last year's levels. I don't think I could explain that. I'm sorry, but I must remain firm—market price. After all, it's only fair—that's what you would have to pay from an external supplier.

Dave: Fair or not, I think we'll pass. Sorry we couldn't have helped.

➤ Is Dave behaving unethically by trying to force the Semiconductor Division into a price break? Comment on Howard's reactions.

REAL WORLD

TIF 9-2   Team Activity

In teams, visit the Web site of a company that uses the balanced scorecard to evaluate the company's performance. Identify the performance measures used by the company on its balanced scorecard. For each measure, identify whether the measure best fits the innovation, customer, internal process, or financial dimension of the balanced scorecard.

TIF 9-3   Communication

The Norse Division of Gridiron Concepts Inc. experienced significant revenue and profit growth from 20Y4 to 20Y6 as shown in the following divisional income statements:

Gridiron Concepts Inc.
Divisional Income Statements, Norse Division
For the Three Years Ended December 31, 20Y6

	20Y4	20Y5	20Y6
Sales	$1,470,000	$2,100,000	$2,450,000
Cost of goods sold	1,064,000	1,498,000	1,680,000
Gross profit	$ 406,000	$ 602,000	$ 770,000
Operating expenses	185,500	224,000	231,000
Income from operations	$ 220,500	$ 378,000	$ 539,000
Invested assets	$ 735,000	$ 1,500,000	$3,500,000

There are no service department charges, and the division operates as an investment center that must maintain a 15% return on invested assets.

➤ Determine the profit margin, investment turnover, and return on investment for the Norse Division for 20Y4–20Y6. Based on your calculations, write a brief memo to the president of Gridiron Concepts Inc., Knute Holz, evaluating the division's performance.

Concepts and Principles

Chapter 1 *Introduction to Managerial Accounting*

Developing Information

COST SYSTEMS	COST BEHAVIOR
Chapter 2 *Job Order Costing*	**Chapter 5** *Cost-Volume-Profit Analysis*
Chapter 3 *Process Cost Systems*	
Chapter 4 *Activity-Based Costing*	

Decision Making

EVALUATING PERFORMANCE	COMPARING ALTERNATIVES
Chapter 6 *Variable Costing for Management Analysis*	**Chapter 9** *Evaluating Decentralized Operations*
Chapter 7 *Budgeting*	**Chapter 10** *Differential Analysis and Product Pricing*
Chapter 8 *Evaluating Variances from Standard Costs*	**Chapter 11** *Capital Investment Analysis*
	Chapter 12 *Lean Manufacturing*

PETER DASILVA/EPA/NEWSCOM

Facebook, Inc.

Many of the decisions that you make depend on comparing the estimated costs of alternatives. The payoff from such comparisons is described in the following report from a University of Michigan study:

Richard Nisbett and two colleagues quizzed Michigan faculty members and university seniors on such questions as how often they walk out on a bad movie, refuse to finish a bad meal, start over on a weak term paper, or abandon a research project that no longer looks promising. They believe that people who cut their losses this way are following sound economic rules: calculating the net benefits of alternative courses of action, writing off past costs that can't be recovered, and weighing the opportunity to use future time and effort more profitably elsewhere.

Among students, those who have learned to use cost-benefit analysis frequently are apt to have far better grades than their Scholastic Aptitude Test scores would have predicted. Again, the more economics courses the students have, the more likely they are to apply cost-benefit analysis outside the classroom.

Dr. Nisbett concedes that for many Americans, cost-benefit rules often appear to conflict with such traditional principles as "never give up" and "waste not, want not."

Managers must also evaluate the costs and benefits of alternative actions. **Facebook**, the largest social networking site in the world, was cofounded by Mark Zuckerberg in 2004. Since then, it has grown to more than 1 billion users and made Zuckerberg a multibillionaire. Such growth involves decisions about where to expand. For example, expanding the site to new languages and countries involves software programming, marketing, and computer hardware costs. The benefits include adding new users to Facebook.

Analysis of the benefits and costs might lead Facebook to expand in some languages before others. For example, such an analysis might lead Facebook to expand in Swedish before it expands in Tok Pisin (the language of Papua New Guinea).

In this chapter, differential analysis, which reports the effects of decisions on total revenues and costs, is discussed. Practical approaches to setting product prices are also described and illustrated. Finally, how production bottlenecks influence pricing and other decisions is also discussed.

Source: Alan L. Otten, "Economic Perspective Produces Steady Yields," from People Patterns, *The Wall Street Journal*, March 31, 1992, p. B1.

What's Covered

Differential Analysis and Product Pricing

Differential Analysis
- Lease or Sell (Obj. 1)
- Discontinue a Segment or Product (Obj. 1)
- Make or Buy (Obj. 1)
- Replace Equipment (Obj. 1)
- Process or Sell (Obj. 1)
- Accept Business at a Special Price (Obj. 1)

Normal Product Pricing
- Product Cost Method (Obj. 2)
- Target Costing (Obj. 2)

Managing Production Bottlenecks
- Contribution Margin Analysis (Obj. 3)
- Pricing Implications (Obj. 3)

Learning Objectives

Obj. 1 Prepare differential analysis reports for a variety of managerial decisions.

Obj. 2 Determine the selling price of a product, using the product cost method.

Obj. 3 Describe and illustrate the managing of manufacturing bottlenecks.

Analysis for Decision Making

Describe and illustrate the use of yield pricing for a service business.

Objective 1

Prepare differential analysis reports for a variety of managerial decisions.

Differential Analysis

Managerial decision making involves choosing between alternative courses of action. A commonly used decision-making process used in business is differential analysis. **Differential analysis**, sometimes called *incremental analysis*, analyzes differential revenues and costs in order to determine the differential impact on income of two alternative courses of action.

Differential revenue is the amount of increase or decrease in revenue that is expected from a course of action compared to an alternative. **Differential cost** is the amount of increase or decrease in cost that is expected from a course of action as compared to an alternative. **Differential income (loss)** is the difference between the differential revenue and differential costs. Differential income indicates that a decision is expected to increase income, while a differential loss indicates the decision is expected to decrease income.

Link to Facebook   **Facebook**'s purchase of **WhatsApp** in 2014 was estimated to yield differential income.

To illustrate, assume that on July 11 Bryant Restaurants is deciding whether to replace some of its customer seating (tables) with a salad bar. Exhibit 1 illustrates differential analysis for this decision.

Exhibit 1
Differential
Analysis—Bryant
Restaurants

Differential Analysis
Tables (Alternative 1) or Salad Bar (Alternative 2)
July 11

	Tables (Alternative 1)	Salad Bar (Alternative 2)	Differential Effect on Income (Alternative 2)
Revenues............................	$100,000	$120,000	$20,000
Costs.................................	–60,000	–65,000	–5,000
Income (loss)	$ 40,000	$ 55,000	$15,000

The differential analysis is prepared in three columns, where positive amounts indicate the effect is to increase income and negative amounts indicate the effect is to decrease income. The first column is the revenues, costs, and income for maintaining floor space for tables (Alternative 1). The second column is the revenues, costs, and income for using that floor space for a salad bar (Alternative 2). The third column is the difference between the revenues, costs, and income of one alternative over the other.

In Exhibit 1, the salad bar is being considered over retaining the existing tables. Thus, Column 3 in Exhibit 1 is expressed in terms of Alternative 2 (salad bar) over Alternative 1 (tables).

In Exhibit 1, the differential revenue of a salad bar over tables is $20,000 ($120,000 – $100,000). Because the increased revenue would increase income, it is entered as a positive $20,000 in the Differential Effect on Income column. The differential cost of a salad bar over tables is $5,000 ($65,000 – $60,000). Because the increased costs will decrease income, it is entered as a negative $5,000 in the Differential Effect on Income column.

The differential income (loss) of a salad bar over tables of $15,000 is determined by subtracting the differential costs from the differential revenues in the Differential Effect on Income column. Thus, installing a salad bar increases income by $15,000.

The preceding differential revenue, costs, and income can also be determined using the following formulas:

Differential Revenue = Revenue (Alt. 2) – Revenue (Alt. 1)
= $120,000 – $100,000 = $20,000

Differential Costs = Costs (Alt. 2) – Costs (Alt. 1)
= –$65,000 – (–$60,000) = –$5,000

Differential Income (Loss) = Income (Alt. 2) – Income (Alt. 1)
= $55,000 – $40,000 = $15,000

Based upon the differential analysis shown in Exhibit 1, Bryant Restaurants should decide to replace some of its tables with a salad bar. Doing so will increase its income by $15,000.

Over time, Bryant Restaurants should review its decision based upon actual revenues and costs. If the actual revenues and costs differ significantly from those shown in Exhibit 2, another differential analysis should be performed.

In this chapter, differential analysis is illustrated for the following common decisions:

- Leasing or selling equipment
- Discontinuing an unprofitable segment
- Manufacturing or purchasing a needed part
- Replacing fixed assets
- Selling a product or processing further
- Accepting additional business at a special price

Link to Facebook

Facebook used differential analyses in deciding to own data centers in Iowa, North Carolina, Oregon, and Lulea, Sweden, but to lease (rent) data centers in California and Virginia.

Lease or Sell

Management may lease or sell a piece of equipment that is no longer needed. This may occur when a company changes its manufacturing process and can no longer use the equipment in the manufacturing process. In making a decision, differential analysis can be used.

To illustrate, assume that on June 22 of the current year, Marcus Company is considering leasing or disposing of the following equipment:

Cost of equipment	$ 200,000
Accumulated depreciation	(120,000)
Book value	$ 80,000
Lease (Alternative 1):	
Total revenue for five-year lease	$ 160,000
Total estimated repair, insurance, and property tax expenses during life of lease	35,000
Residual value at end of fifth year of lease	0
Sell (Alternative 2):	
Sales price	$ 100,000
Commission on sales	6%

Exhibit 2 shows the differential analysis of whether to lease (Alternative 1) or sell (Alternative 2) the equipment.

Exhibit 2

Differential Analysis—Lease or Sell Equipment

Differential Analysis
Lease Equipment (Alternative 1) or Sell Equipment (Alternative 2)
June 22

	Lease Equipment (Alternative 1)	Sell Equipment (Alternative 2)	Differential Effect on Income (Alternative 2)
Revenues......................	$160,000	$100,000	–$60,000
Costs.........................	–35,000	–6,000	29,000
Income (loss)	$125,000	$ 94,000	–$31,000

If the equipment is sold, differential revenues will decrease by $60,000, differential costs will decrease by $29,000, and the differential effect on income is a decrease of $31,000. Thus, the decision should be to lease the equipment.

Exhibit 2 includes only the differential revenues and differential costs associated with the lease-or-sell decision. The $80,000 book value ($200,000 – $120,000) of the equipment is a *sunk cost* and is not considered in the differential analysis. **Sunk costs** are costs that have been incurred in the past, cannot be recouped, and are not relevant to future decisions. That is, the $80,000 is not affected regardless of which decision is made. For example, if the $80,000 were included in Exhibit 2, the costs for each alternative would both increase by $80,000, but the differential effect on income of –$31,000 would remain unchanged.

To simplify, the following factors were not considered in Exhibit 2:

- Differential revenue from investing funds
- Differential income tax

Differential revenue, such as interest revenue, could arise from investing the cash created by the two alternatives. Differential income tax could also arise from differences in income. These factors are discussed in Chapter 11.

Discontinue a Segment or Product

A product, department, branch, territory, or other segment of a business may be generating losses. As a result, management may consider discontinuing (eliminating) the product or segment. In such cases, it may be erroneously assumed that the total company income will increase by eliminating the operating loss.

Discontinuing the product or segment usually eliminates all of the product's or segment's variable costs. Such costs include direct materials, direct labor, variable factory overhead, and sales commissions. However, fixed costs such as depreciation, insurance, and property taxes may not be eliminated. Thus, it is possible for total company income to decrease rather than increase if the unprofitable product or segment is discontinued.

To illustrate, the income statement for Battle Creek Cereal Co. is shown in Exhibit 3. As shown in Exhibit 3, Bran Flakes incurred an operating loss of $11,000. Because Bran Flakes has incurred annual losses for several years, management is considering discontinuing it.

Exhibit 3

Income (Loss) by Product

Battle Creek Cereal Co. Condensed Income Statement For the Year Ended August 31, 20Y8	Corn Flakes	Toasted Oats	Bran Flakes	Total Company
Sales	$500,000	$400,000	$100,000	$1,000,000
Cost of goods sold:				
Variable costs	$220,000	$200,000	$ 60,000	$ 480,000
Fixed costs	120,000	80,000	20,000	220,000
Total cost of goods sold	$340,000	$280,000	$ 80,000	$ 700,000
Gross profit	$160,000	$120,000	$ 20,000	$ 300,000
Operating expenses:				
Variable expenses	$ 95,000	$ 60,000	$ 25,000	$ 180,000
Fixed expenses	25,000	20,000	6,000	51,000
Total operating expenses	$120,000	$ 80,000	$ 31,000	$ 231,000
Income (loss) from operations	$ 40,000	$ 40,000	$ (11,000)	$ 69,000

However, the differential analysis dated September 29, 20Y8, in Exhibit 4 indicates that discontinuing Bran Flakes (Alternative 2) actually decreases operating income by $15,000, even though it incurs a net loss of $11,000. This is because discontinuing Bran Flakes has no effect on fixed costs and expenses.

Exhibit 4 only considers the short-term (one-year) effects of discontinuing Bran Flakes. When discontinuing a product or segment, long-term effects should also be considered. For example, employee morale and productivity might suffer if employees have to be laid off or relocated.

Exhibit 4

Differential
Analysis—Continue
or Discontinue
Bran Flakes

Differential Analysis
Continue Bran Flakes (Alternative 1) or Discontinue Bran Flakes (Alternative 2)
September 29, 20Y8

	Continue Bran Flakes (Alternative 1)	Discontinue Bran Flakes (Alternative 2)	Differential Effect on Income (Alternative 2)
Revenues.............................	$100,000	$ 0	–$100,000
Costs:			
Variable	–$ 85,000	$ 0	$ 85,000
Fixed.............................	–26,000	–26,000	0
Income (loss).........................	–$ 11,000	–$26,000	–$ 15,000

> **Link to Facebook**   **Facebook** reports its financial results by geographic area (United States and Rest of the World), but does not have separate business segments.

Make or Buy

Companies often manufacture products made up of components that are assembled into a final product. For example, an automobile manufacturer assembles tires, radios, motors, interior seats, transmissions, and other parts into a finished automobile. In such cases, the manufacturer must decide whether to make a part or purchase it from a supplier.

Differential analysis can be used to decide whether to make or buy a part. The analysis is similar whether management is considering making a part that is currently being purchased or purchasing a part that is currently being made.

To illustrate, assume that an automobile manufacturer has been purchasing instrument panels for $240 a unit. The factory is currently operating at 80% of capacity, and no major increase in production is expected in the near future. The cost per unit of manufacturing an instrument panel internally is estimated on February 15 as follows:

Direct materials	$ 80
Direct labor	80
Variable factory overhead	52
Fixed factory overhead	68
Total cost per unit	$280

If the make price of $280 is simply compared with the buy price of $240, the decision is to buy the instrument panel. However, if unused capacity could be used in manufacturing the part, only the variable factory overhead costs would increase.

The differential analysis for this make (Alternative 1) or buy (Alternative 2) decision is shown in Exhibit 5. The first line shows that there is no revenue earned in this decision, since the component is not sold but used in production. The remaining lines show the cost per unit under each alternative. The fixed factory overhead cannot be eliminated by purchasing the panels. Thus, both alternatives include the fixed factory overhead. The differential analysis indicates there is a loss of $28 per unit from buying the instrument panels. Thus, the instrument panels should be manufactured.

Exhibit 5
Differential
Analysis—Make
or Buy Instrument
Panels

Differential Analysis
Make (Alternative 1) or Buy (Alternative 2) Panels
February 15

	Make Panels (Alternative 1)	Buy Panels (Alternative 2)	Differential Effect on Income (Alternative 2)
Sales price	$ 0	$ 0	$ 0
Unit costs:			
Purchase price	0	−240	−240
Direct materials	−80	0	80
Direct labor	−80	0	80
Variable factory overhead	−52	0	52
Fixed factory overhead	−68	−68	0
Income (loss)	−$280	−$308	−$ 28

Other factors should also be considered in the analysis. For example, productive capacity used to make the instrument panel would not be available for other production. The decision may also affect the future business relationship with the instrument panel supplier. For example, if the supplier provides other parts, the company's decision to make instrument panels might jeopardize the timely delivery of other parts.

Rather than develop its own virtual reality technology, **Facebook** purchased **Oculus VR, LLC**, a privately held company, in 2014.

Link to Facebook

Replace Equipment

The usefulness of a fixed asset may decrease before it is worn out. For example, old equipment may no longer be as efficient as new equipment.

Differential analysis can be used for decisions to replace fixed assets such as equipment and machinery. The analysis normally focuses on the costs of continuing to use the old equipment versus replacing the equipment. The book value of the old equipment is a sunk cost and, thus, is irrelevant.

To illustrate, assume that on November 28 of the current year, a business is considering replacing an old machine with a new machine:

Old Machine:	
Book value	$100,000
Estimated annual variable manufacturing costs	225,000
Estimated selling price	25,000
Estimated remaining useful life	5 years
New Machine:	
Purchase price of new machine	$250,000
Estimated annual variable manufacturing costs	150,000
Estimated residual value	0
Estimated useful life	5 years

The differential analysis for whether to continue with the old machine (Alternative 1) or replace the old machine with a new machine (Alternative 2) is shown in Exhibit 6.

Exhibit 6

Differential
Analysis—Continue
with or Replace
Old Equipment

	Continue with Old Machine (Alternative 1)	**Replace Old Machine (Alternative 2)**	**Differential Effect on Income (Alternative 2)**
Differential Analysis			
Continue with (Alternative 1) or Replace (Alternative 2) Machine			
November 28			
Revenues:			
Proceeds from sale of old machine	$ 0	$ 25,000	$ 25,000
Costs:			
Purchase price.............................	$ 0	–$ 250,000	–$250,000
Variable manufacturing costs (5 years)	–1,125,000	–750,000	375,000
Income (loss)	–$1,125,000	–$ 975,000	$150,000

As shown in Exhibit 6, there is five-year differential effect on income of $150,000 (or $30,000 per year) from replacing the machine. Thus, the decision should be to purchase the new machine and sell the old machine.

Link to Facebook

Facebook used cash to purchase $1,812 million of property and equipment in 2014.

Other factors are often important in equipment replacement decisions. For example, differences between the remaining useful life of the old equipment and the estimated life of the new equipment could exist. In addition, the new equipment might improve the overall quality of the product and, thus, increase sales.

The time value of money and other uses for the cash needed to purchase the new equipment could also affect the decision to replace equipment.[1] The revenue that is forgone from an alternative use of an asset, such as cash, is called an **opportunity cost**. Although the opportunity cost is not recorded in the accounting records, it is useful in analyzing alternative courses of action.

Process or Sell

During manufacturing, a product normally progresses through various stages or processes. In some cases, a product can be sold at an intermediate stage of production, or it can be processed further and then sold.

Differential analysis can be used to decide whether to sell a product at an intermediate stage or to process it further. In doing so, the differential revenues and costs from further processing are compared. The costs of producing the intermediate product do not change, regardless of whether the intermediate product is sold or processed further.

To illustrate, assume that a business produces kerosene as an intermediate product as follows:

Kerosene:
- Batch size — 4,000 gallons
- Cost of producing kerosene — $2,400 per batch
- Selling price — $2.50 per gallon

[1] The time value of money in purchasing equipment (capital assets) is discussed in Chapter 11.

The kerosene can be processed further to yield gasoline as follows:

Gasoline:	
Input batch size	4,000 gallons
Less evaporation (20%)	(800) (4,000 × 20%)
Output batch size	3,200 gallons
Cost of producing gasoline	$3,050 per batch
Selling price	$3.50 per gallon

Exhibit 7 shows the differential analysis dated October 1 for whether to sell kerosene (Alternative 1) or process it further into gasoline (Alternative 2).

As shown in Exhibit 7, there is additional income of $550 per batch from further processing the kerosene into gasoline. Therefore, the decision should be to process the kerosene further into gasoline.

Differential Analysis
Sell Kerosene (Alternative 1) or Process into Gasoline (Alternative 2)
October 1

	Sell Kerosene (Alternative 1)	Process into Gasoline (Alternative 2)	Differential Effect on Income (Alternative 2)
Revenues	$10,000*	$11,200**	$1,200
Costs	−2,400	−3,050	−650
Income (loss)	$ 7,600	$ 8,150	$ 550

*4,000 gallons × $2.50
**(4,000 gallons − 800 gallons) × $3.50

Exhibit 7
Differential Analysis—Sell Kerosene or Process into Gasoline

Facebook provides advertising and other services to its customers and does not manufacture a product.

Link to Facebook

Accept Business at a Special Price

A company may be offered the opportunity to sell its products at prices other than normal prices. For example, an exporter may offer to sell a company's products overseas at special discount prices.

Differential analysis can be used to decide whether to accept additional business at a special price. The differential revenue from accepting the additional business is compared to the differential costs of producing and delivering the product to the customer.

The differential costs of accepting additional business depend on whether the company is operating at less than capacity. If the company is operating at less than full capacity, then the additional production does not increase fixed manufacturing costs. However, selling and administrative expenses may change because of the additional business.

To illustrate, assume that B-Ball Inc. manufactures basketballs as follows:

Monthly productive capacity	12,500 basketballs
Current monthly sales	10,000 basketballs
Normal (domestic) selling price	$30.00 per basketball
Manufacturing costs:	
Variable costs	$12.50 per basketball
Fixed costs	7.50
Total manufacturing costs	$20.00 per basketball

On March 10 of the current year, B-Ball Inc. received an offer from an exporter for 5,000 basketballs at $18 each. Production can be spread over three months without interfering with normal production or incurring overtime costs. Pricing policies in the domestic market will not be affected.

As shown in Exhibit 8, a differential analysis on whether to reject the order (Alternative 1) or accept the order (Alternative 2) shows that the special order should be accepted. The special business is accepted even though the sales price of $18 per unit is less than the manufacturing cost of $20 per unit because the fixed costs are not affected by the decision and are, thus, omitted from the analysis.

Exhibit 8

Differential Analysis—Accept Business at a Special Price

Differential Analysis			
Reject Order (Alternative 1) or Accept Order (Alternative 2)			
March 10			
	Reject Order (Alternative 1)	**Accept Order (Alternative 2)**	**Differential Effect on Income (Alternative 2)**
Revenues	$0	$90,000*	$90,000
Costs:			
Variable manufacturing costs	0	−62,500**	−62,500
Income (loss)	$0	$27,500	$27,500

*5,000 units × $18
**5,000 units × $12.50 variable cost per unit

Proposals to sell products at special prices often require additional considerations. For example, special prices in one geographic area may result in price reductions in other areas, with the result that total company sales revenues decrease. Manufacturers must also conform to the Robinson-Patman Act, which prohibits price discrimination within the United States unless price differences can be justified by different costs.

Why It Matters

60% Off!

Priceline.com was founded in the late 1990s and has become a successful survivor of the Internet revolution. Priceline offers deep discounts of up to 60% for travel services, such as hotels and flights. How does it work? For hotel services, Priceline has arrangements with hotels to provide deeply discounted rooms. These rooms are resold to customers on Priceline's Web site. Why do hotels provide rooms at such a large discount? If the hotel has unused rooms, the variable cost of an incremental guest is low relative to the fixed cost of the room. During low occupancy times, any price greater than the variable cost of providing the room can add to the profitability of the hotel. Thus, hotels view Priceline as an additional source of profit from filling unused rooms during low demand periods.

Check Up Corner 10-1 | Differential Analysis

For the three cases below, prepare a differential analysis.

Case A (Discontinue a Segment): Product K has revenue of $65,000, variable cost of goods sold of $50,000, variable selling expenses of $12,000, and fixed costs of $25,000, creating a loss from operations of $22,000.

Required: Prepare a differential analysis dated February 22 to determine whether Product K should be continued (Alternative 1) or discontinued (Alternative 2), assuming fixed costs are unaffected by the decision.

Case B (Make vs. Buy): A company manufactures a subcomponent of a product for $80 per unit, including fixed costs of $25 per unit. The subcomponent could be purchased from an outside supplier for $60 per unit, plus $5 per unit freight.

Required: Prepare a differential analysis dated November 2 to determine whether the company should make (Alternative 1) or buy (Alternative 2) the subcomponent, assuming fixed costs are unaffected by the decision.

Case C (Sell or Process Further): Product T is produced for $2.50 per gallon. Product T can be sold without additional processing for $3.50 per gallon, or processed further into Product V at an additional total cost of $0.70 per gallon. Product V can be sold for $4.00 per gallon.

Required: Prepare a differential analysis dated April 8 to determine whether to sell Product T (Alternative 1) or process it further into Product V (Alternative 2).

Solution:

Case A (Discontinue a Segment):

Differential Analysis
Continue K (Alternative 1) or Discontinue K (Alternative 2)
February 22

	Continue Product K (Alternative 1)	Discontinue Product K (Alternative 2)	Differential Effect on Income (Alternative 2)
Revenues	$65,000	$ 0	–$65,000
Costs:			
Variable	–$62,000*	$ 0	$62,000
Fixed	– 25,000	– 25,000	0
Total costs	–$87,000	–$25,000	$62,000
Income (loss)	–$22,000	–$25,000	–$ 3,000

*$50,000 Variable cost of goods sold + $12,000 Variable selling expenses

If Product K is discontinued, revenues and variable costs will be zero.

If Product K is discontinued, fixed costs remain at $25,000.

The effect on income of discontinuing Product K is the difference between the income from discontinuing Product K and the income from continuing Product K.

Discontinuing Product K (Alternative 2) decreases operating income by $3,000. As a result, Product K should **not** be discontinued.

Case B (Make vs. Buy):

Differential Analysis
Make Subcomponent (Alternative 1) or Buy Subcomponent (Alternative 2)
November 2

	Make Subcomponent (Alternative 1)	Buy Subcomponent (Alternative 2)	Differential Effect on Income (Alternative 2)
Sales price	$ 0	$ 0	$ 0
Unit costs:			
Purchase price	0	–60	–60
Freight	0	–5	–5
Variable costs ($80 – $25)	–55	0	55
Fixed factory overhead	–25	–25	0
Income (loss)	–$80	–$90	–$10

There are no differential revenues in this case.

Variable costs to purchase, which are the differential costs of Alternative 2.

Differential income is the difference between the variable costs to purchase (differential cost of Alternative 2) and the variable costs to manufacture (differential cost of Alternative 1).

Variable cost to manufacture, which is the differential cost of Alternative 1.

Fixed factory overhead costs cannot be eliminated if the subcomponent is purchased.

The differential cost of buying the component ($65 per unit) is $10 per unit more than the differential cost of making the subcomponent ($55 per unit). Therefore, the subcomponent should be manufactured.

Case C (Sell or Process Further):

Differential Analysis
Sell Product T (Alternative 1) or Process Further into Product V (Alternative 2)
April 8

	Sell Product T (Alternative 1)	Process Further into Product V (Alternative 2)	Differential Effect on Income (Alternative 2)
Revenues, per unit	$3.50	$4.00	$0.50
Costs, per unit	–2.50	–3.20*	–0.70
Income (loss), per unit	$1.00	$0.80	–$0.20

*$2.50 + $0.70

Differential revenue from processing Product T (Alternative 1) into Product V (Alternative 2).

Differential costs from processing Product T (Alternative 1) further into Product V (Alternative 2).

Product V can be sold for $4.00 ($0.50 more than Product T).

It costs a total of $3.20 to make Product V ($2.50 to produce Product T and an additional $0.70 to process Product T into Product V).

Processing Product T further into Product V reduces income by $0.20 per unit. Therefore, Product T should **not** be processed further into Product V.

Check Up Corner

Setting Normal Product Selling Prices

The *normal* selling price is the target selling price to be achieved in the long term. The normal selling price must be set high enough to cover all costs and expenses (fixed and variable) and provide a reasonable profit. Otherwise, the business will not survive.

In contrast, in deciding whether to accept additional business at a special price, only differential costs are considered. Any price greater than the differential costs will increase profits in the short term. However, in the long term, products are sold at normal prices rather than special prices.

Managers can use one of two market methods to determine selling price:

- Demand-based method
- Competition-based method

The **demand-based method** sets the price according to the demand for the product. If there is high demand for the product, then the price is set high. Likewise, if there is a low demand for the product, then the price is set low.

The **competition-based method** sets the price according to the price offered by competitors. For example, if a competitor reduces the price, then management adjusts the price to meet the competition. The market-based pricing approaches are discussed in greater detail in marketing courses.

Facebook's prices are affected by its competitors such as *Google*.

Link to Facebook

Managers can use one of three cost-plus methods to determine the selling price:

- Product cost method
- Total cost method
- Variable cost method

The product cost method is illustrated in this section. The total cost and variable cost methods are illustrated in the appendix to this chapter.

Facebook generates advertising revenue based upon the number of clicks, impressions displayed, or number of actions taken by people. Facebook establishes prices for its customers for each of these options.

Link to Facebook

Why It Matters

Dynamic Pricing

Hotels and airlines were the first to dynamically adjust prices based on real-time demand. Thus, hotel rates and airfares were less expensive on the weekend than on busier weekdays. Dynamic pricing has since migrated into many other areas of product and service delivery. **Uber**'s cab fares adjust dynamically to ride demand. A ride during rush hour is more expensive than one in the middle of the day. The **Indianapolis Zoo** began dynamic pricing admission tickets so that cold, rainy days had an admission price as low as $8, while pleasant summer days had an admission price as high as $30. Prior to dynamic pricing, the zoo charged $18 for every admission. Since introducing dynamic pricing, revenues have increased by 12%. A seven-mile stretch of highway around Dallas can vary tolls from $0.90 to $4.50 depending on traffic patterns. **SeaWorld Entertainment** dynamically prices admissions based on daily demand. **Kohl's** now employs electronic price tags that can remotely adjust prices for hours, rather than days, depending upon real-time foot traffic and demand. Most **Major League Baseball** teams dynamically price admission tickets. It would seem dynamic pricing is here to stay, as information technology allows companies greater visibility to demand.

Source: Nicas, Jack, "The Price You Pay Depends on the Time and Day," *The Wall Street Journal*, December 14, 2015, p. B1.

Cost-Plus Methods

Cost-plus methods determine the normal selling price by estimating a cost amount per unit and adding a markup, computed as follows:

Normal Selling Price = Cost Amount per Unit + Markup

Management determines the markup based on the desired profit for the product. The markup must be sufficient to earn the desired profit plus cover any costs and expenses that are not included in the cost amount.

Product Cost Method

Under the **product cost method**, the costs of manufacturing the product, termed the *product costs*, are included in the cost amount per unit to which the markup is added. Estimated selling expenses, administrative expenses, and desired profit are included in the markup. The markup per unit is added to the product cost per unit to determine the normal selling price as shown in Exhibit 9.

Exhibit 9
Product Cost Method

MARKUP:

Administrative Expense

+

Selling Expense

+

Desired Profit

PRODUCT COST:
Manufacturing Cost

DESIRED SELLING PRICE

The product cost method is applied using the following steps:

- Step 1.   Estimate the total product cost as follows:

Product costs:	
Direct materials	$XXX
Direct labor	XXX
Factory overhead	XXX
Total product cost	$XXX

- Step 2.   Estimate the total selling and administrative expenses.
- Step 3.   Divide the total product cost by the number of units expected to be produced and sold to determine the total product cost per unit, computed as follows:

$$\text{Product Cost per Unit} = \frac{\text{Total Product Cost}}{\text{Estimated Units Produced and Sold}}$$

- Step 4. Compute the markup percentage as follows:

$$\text{Markup Percentage} = \frac{\text{Desired Profit} + \text{Total Selling and Administrative Expenses}}{\text{Total Product Cost}}$$

The numerator of the markup percentage is the desired profit plus the total selling and administrative expenses. These expenses must be included in the markup percentage because they are not included in the cost amount to which the markup is added.

The desired profit is normally computed based on a return on assets as follows:

$$\text{Desired Profit} = \text{Desired Return} \times \text{Total Assets}$$

- Step 5. Determine the markup per unit by multiplying the markup percentage times the product cost per unit as follows:

$$\text{Markup per Unit} = \text{Markup Percentage} \times \text{Product Cost per Unit}$$

- Step 6. Determine the normal selling price by adding the markup per unit to the product cost per unit as follows:

Product cost per unit	$XXX
Markup per unit	XXX
Normal selling price per unit	$XXX

Illustration

The product cost method is illustrated for determining the price of calculators produced by **Digital Solutions Inc.** Assume the following data for 100,000 calculators that Digital Solutions Inc. expects to produce and sell during the current year:

Manufacturing costs:	
Direct materials ($3.00 × 100,000)	$ 300,000
Direct labor ($10.00 × 100,000)	1,000,000
Factory overhead	200,000
Total product (manufacturing) costs	$1,500,000
Selling and administrative expenses	170,000
Total cost	$1,670,000
Total assets	$ 800,000
Desired return	20%

The normal selling price of $18.30 is determined under the product cost method as follows:

- Step 1. Total product cost: $1,500,000
- Step 2. Total selling and administrative expenses: $170,000
- Step 3. Total product cost per unit: $15.00

$$\text{Total Cost per Unit} = \frac{\text{Total Product Cost}}{\text{Estimated Units Produced and Sold}} = \frac{\$1,500,000}{100,000 \text{ units}} = \$15.00 \text{ per unit}$$

- Step 4. Markup percentage: 22%

$$\text{Desired Profit} = \text{Desired Return} \times \text{Total Assets} = 20\% \times \$800,000 = \$160,000$$

$$\text{Markup Percentage} = \frac{\text{Desired Profit} + \text{Total Selling and Administrative Expenses}}{\text{Total Product (Manufacturing) Costs}}$$

$$= \frac{\$160,000 + \$170,000}{\$1,500,000} = \frac{\$330,000}{\$1,500,000} = 22\%$$

- Step 5. Markup per unit: $3.30

$$\text{Markup per Unit} = \text{Markup Percentage} \times \text{Product Cost per Unit}$$

$$= 22\% \times \$15.00 = \$3.30 \text{ per unit}$$

■ Step 6.   Normal selling price: $18.30

Total product cost per unit	$15.00
Markup per unit	3.30
Normal selling price per unit	$18.30

Product cost estimates, rather than actual costs, may be used in computing the markup. Management should be careful, however, when using estimated or standard costs in applying the cost-plus approach. Specifically, estimates should be based on normal (attainable) operating levels and not theoretical (ideal) levels of performance. In product pricing, the use of estimates based on ideal operating performance could lead to setting product prices too low.

Target Costing Method

Target costing is a method of setting prices that combines market-based pricing with a cost-reduction emphasis. Under target costing, a future selling price is anticipated, using the demand or competition-based methods. The target cost is then determined by subtracting a desired profit from the expected selling price, computed as follows:

Target Cost = Expected Selling Price – Desired Profit

 Ethics: Don't Do It!

Price Fixing

Federal law prevents companies competing in similar markets from sharing cost and price information, or what is commonly termed "price fixing." For example, the Federal Trade Commission (FTC) brought a suit against **U-Haul** for releasing company-wide memorandums to its managers telling them to encourage competitors to match U-Haul price increases. Commenting on the case, the chairman of the FTC stated, "It's a bedrock principle that you can't conspire with your competitors to fix prices, and shouldn't even try."

Source: Edward Wyatt, "U-Haul to Settle with Trade Agency in Case on Truck Rental Price-Fixing," *The New York Times*, June 10, 2010, p. B3.

Target costing tries to reduce costs as shown in Exhibit 10. The bar at the left in Exhibit 10 shows the actual cost and profit that can be earned during the current period. The bar at the right shows that the market price is expected to decline in the future. The target cost is estimated as the difference between the expected market price and the desired profit.

The target cost is normally less than the current cost. Thus, managers must try to reduce costs from the design and manufacture of the product. The planned cost reduction is sometimes referred to as the cost drift. Costs can be reduced in a variety of ways such as the following:

■ Simplifying the design
■ Reducing the cost of direct materials
■ Reducing the direct labor costs
■ Eliminating waste

Target costing is especially useful in highly competitive markets such as the market for personal computers. Such markets require continual product cost reductions to remain competitive.

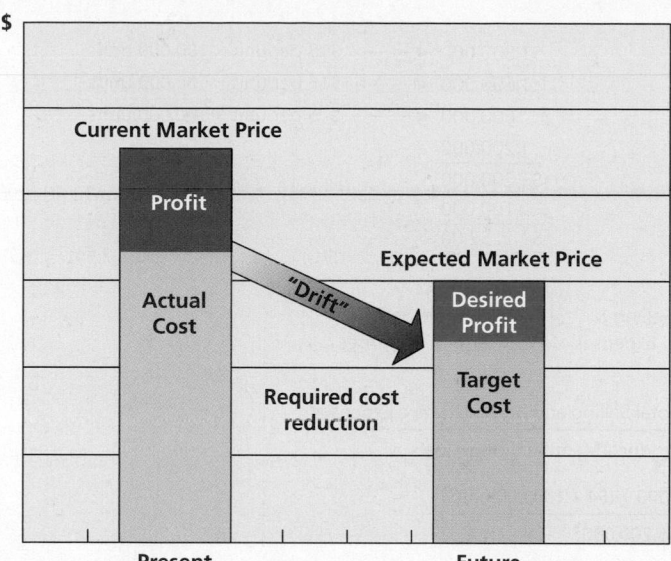

Exhibit 10
Target Cost
Method

Check Up Corner 10-2   Setting Product Selling Prices

SMB Company recently began production of a new product, Q, which required an investment of $2,500,000 in assets. The costs of producing and selling 100,000 units of Product Q are estimated as follows:

Variable costs:	
Direct materials	$18 per unit
Direct labor	16
Factory overhead	6
Selling and administrative expenses	4
Total variable costs	$44 per unit
Fixed costs:	
Factory overhead	$1,200,000
Selling and administrative expenses	600,000

Using the cost-plus approach to product pricing, a 12% return on invested assets is required.

A. Determine the amount of desired profit from the production and sale of Product Q.

B. Using the product cost method, determine (1) the cost per unit, (2) the markup percentage, and (3) the selling price.

C. If the market price for a similar product is estimated at $61, compute the reduction in manufacturing cost per unit needed to maintain (1) the desired profit [from part (A)] and (2) the existing selling and administrative expenses under target costing.

Solution:

A.		
Invested assets	$2,500,000	
Required return	× 12%	
Desired profit	$ 300,000	

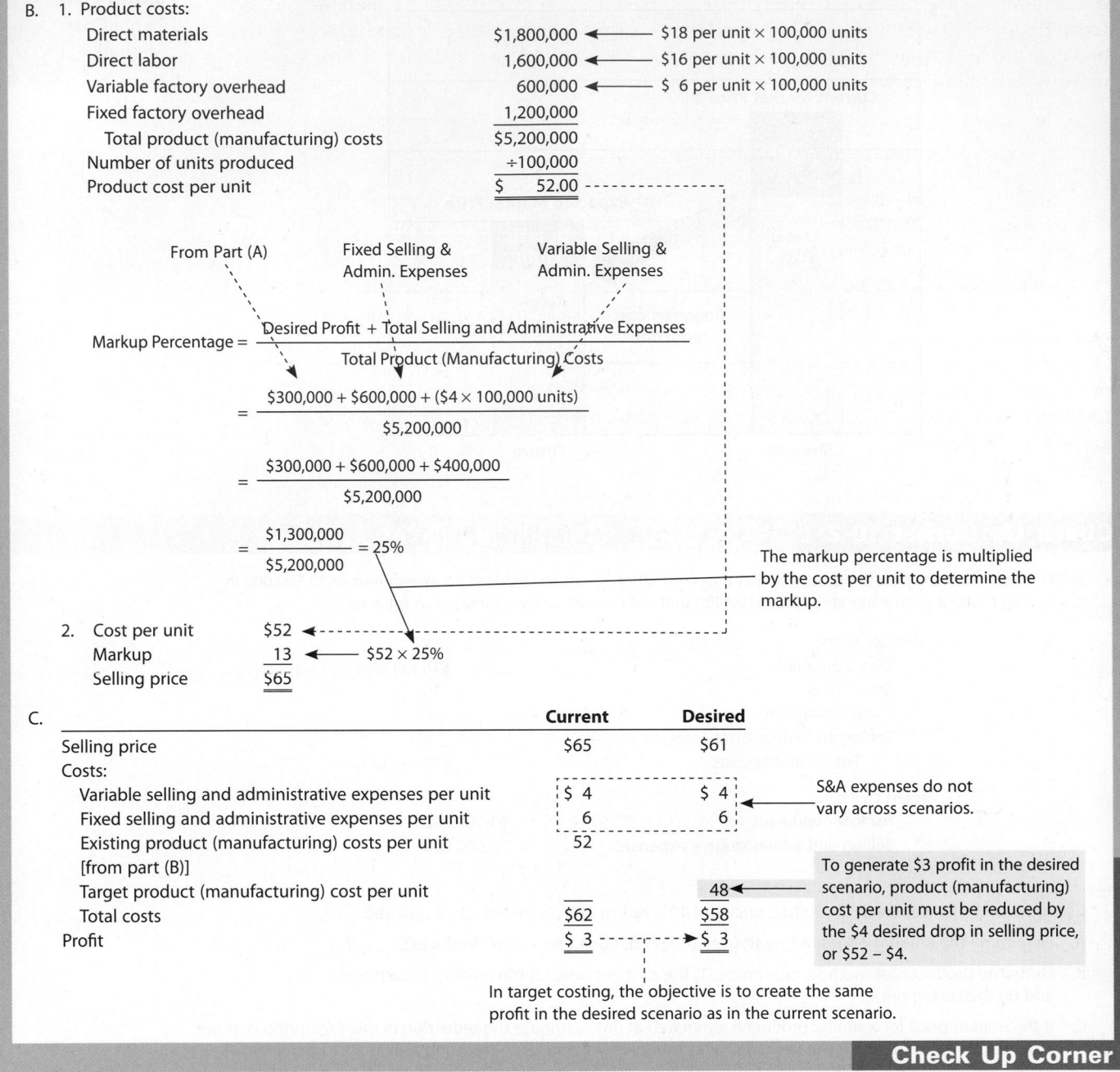

B. 1. Product costs:

Direct materials	$1,800,000 ◄───	$18 per unit × 100,000 units
Direct labor	1,600,000 ◄───	$16 per unit × 100,000 units
Variable factory overhead	600,000 ◄───	$ 6 per unit × 100,000 units
Fixed factory overhead	1,200,000	
Total product (manufacturing) costs	$5,200,000	
Number of units produced	÷100,000	
Product cost per unit	$ 52.00	

From Part (A) Fixed Selling & Admin. Expenses Variable Selling & Admin. Expenses

$$\text{Markup Percentage} = \frac{\text{Desired Profit} + \text{Total Selling and Administrative Expenses}}{\text{Total Product (Manufacturing) Costs}}$$

$$= \frac{\$300,000 + \$600,000 + (\$4 \times 100,000 \text{ units})}{\$5,200,000}$$

$$= \frac{\$300,000 + \$600,000 + \$400,000}{\$5,200,000}$$

$$= \frac{\$1,300,000}{\$5,200,000} = 25\%$$

The markup percentage is multiplied by the cost per unit to determine the markup.

2.
Cost per unit	$52 ◄───
Markup	13 ◄─── $52 × 25%
Selling price	$65

C.

	Current	Desired
Selling price	$65	$61
Costs:		
Variable selling and administrative expenses per unit	$ 4	$ 4
Fixed selling and administrative expenses per unit	6	6
Existing product (manufacturing) costs per unit [from part (B)]	52	
Target product (manufacturing) cost per unit		48 ◄───
Total costs	$62	$58
Profit	$ 3	$ 3

S&A expenses do not vary across scenarios.

To generate $3 profit in the desired scenario, product (manufacturing) cost per unit must be reduced by the $4 desired drop in selling price, or $52 − $4.

In target costing, the objective is to create the same profit in the desired scenario as in the current scenario.

Check Up Corner

Objective 3

Describe and illustrate the managing of manufacturing bottlenecks.

Production Bottlenecks

A **production bottleneck** (or *constraint*) is a point in the manufacturing process where the demand for the company's product exceeds the ability to produce the product. The **theory of constraints (TOC)** is a manufacturing strategy that focuses on reducing the influence of bottlenecks on production processes.

Managing Bottlenecks

When a company has a production bottleneck in its production process, it should attempt to maximize its profits, subject to the production bottleneck. In doing so, the unit contribution margin of each product per production bottleneck constraint is used.

To illustrate, assume that PrideCraft Tool Company makes three products: A, B, and C. All three products are processed through a heat treatment operation, which hardens the steel tools. PrideCraft Tool's heat treatment process is operating at full capacity and is a production bottleneck. The product unit contribution margin and the number of hours of heat treatment used by each type of tool are as follows:

	Product A	Product B	Product C
Unit selling price	$130	$140	$160
Unit variable cost	40	40	40
Unit contribution margin	$ 90	$100	$120
Heat treatment hours per unit	1 hr.	4 hrs.	8 hrs.

Product C appears to be the most profitable product because its unit contribution margin of $120 is the greatest. However, the unit contribution margin can be misleading in a production bottleneck operation.

In a production bottleneck operation, the best measure of profitability is the unit contribution margin per bottleneck constraint. For PrideCraft Tool, the bottleneck constraint is heat treatment process hours. Therefore, the unit contribution margin per bottleneck constraint is expressed as follows:

$$\text{Unit Contribution Margin per Production Bottleneck Hour} = \frac{\text{Unit Contribution Margin}}{\text{Heat Treatment Hours per Unit}}$$

The unit contribution per bottleneck hour for each of the products produced by PrideCraft Tool is computed as follows:

Product A
$$\text{Unit Contribution Margin per Bottleneck Hour} = \frac{\$90}{1 \text{ hr.}} = \$90 \text{ per hr.}$$

Product B
$$\text{Unit Contribution Margin per Bottleneck Hour} = \frac{\$100}{4 \text{ hrs.}} = \$25 \text{ per hr.}$$

Product C
$$\text{Unit Contribution Margin per Bottleneck Hour} = \frac{\$120}{8 \text{ hrs.}} = \$15 \text{ per hr.}$$

Product A produces the highest unit contribution margin per bottleneck hour (heat treatment) of $90 per hour. In contrast, Product C has the largest contribution margin per unit of $120 but has the smallest unit contribution margin per bottleneck hour of $15 per hour. Thus, Product A is the most profitable product per bottleneck hour and is the one that should be emphasized in the market.

Pricing Bottleneck Products

In the preceding illustration, Product A is the most profitable product per bottleneck hour. As a result, if one product is to be produced, it should be Product A. But, what about Products B and C?

Customers may expect a combination of products from a company. For example, even though Product A is the most profitable, PrideCraft Tool's customers may also want Products B and C. In these situations, Products B and C should be comparably priced to Product A or the production process for the other products should be adjusted so that they consume less of the bottleneck.

To illustrate, if the price of Product C were increased to $720 ($90 × 8 hrs.), Product C would produce a unit contribution margin of $90 per hour. Alternatively, the manufacturing process for Product C could be adjusted to reduce its consumption of the bottleneck.

Analysis for Decision Making

Yield Pricing in Service Businesses

Service businesses, compared to manufacturing or retail businesses, often have larger fixed costs because they require significant property, plant, and equipment to deliver the service. Examples include airlines, railroads, hotels, universities, and utility companies. Due to the large fixed costs, many service companies have a low variable cost per unit. For example, the additional variable cost of an additional guest in a hotel is small relative to the total cost of the service. High-fixed-cost service businesses often charge different prices to different customers, depending upon their utilization of fixed capacity. During periods when the demand on fixed capacity is high, prices are higher. During periods when the demand for fixed capacity is low, prices are lower. For example, a hotel with frequent business guests will charge lower prices during the weekend, when demand for rooms is lower, than on weekdays when demand for rooms is higher.

In addition, high-capacity-cost service businesses will offer attractive prices to customers who reserve a portion of fixed capacity early and will penalize customers for reserving a portion of fixed capacity late. It is more difficult for a business to manage scheduled capacity if everyone tries to schedule at the last minute. This is why booking a flight early provides better pricing than booking late. These practices are termed "yield pricing" and are common in many high-fixed-cost service businesses.

Yield pricing is a type of "accepting business at a special price" differential analysis. To illustrate, Alpine Airline provides flight services between Atlanta and Dallas. Assume an analysis reveals the following fixed and variable costs for a flight:

	Fixed Costs per Flight	**Variable Costs per Passenger**
Plane depreciation	$10,400	
Crew salaries	1,000	
Fuel	3,000	$12
Ground salaries	2,000	8
Airport fees	2,000	
Passenger services		15
Total	$18,400	$35

Alpine's the variable cost per passenger is not large. This is because many of the costs do not vary by changing the number of seats sold on a flight. For example, the number of crewmembers per flight is fixed and does not vary to the seats sold on a flight.

Assume the plane has a capacity of 200 seats, of which 170 have been sold at an average ticket price of $150. The contribution margin for each passenger is as follows:

$$\text{Contribution Margin per Passenger} = \text{Ticket Price} - \text{Variable Cost per Passenger}$$
$$= \$150 - \$35$$
$$= \$115$$

The break-even number of seats per flight is:

$$\text{Break-Even Seats per Flight} = \frac{\text{Fixed Costs per Flight}}{\text{Contribution Margin per Passenger}}$$

$$= \frac{\$18,400}{\$115}$$

$$= 160 \text{ seats}$$

Thus, each flight is earning a profit, since the actual seats sold (170) exceed the break-even number of seats (160).

To attract customers to its 30 unsold seats, Alpine offers a 50% discounted ticket for standby passengers. Assuming 10 standby passengers purchase the discounted ticket, Alpine will have additional income based on the contribution margin of these seats, determined as follows:

Discounted ticket price (50% × $150)	$ 75
Variable cost per passenger	35
Contribution margin per standby passenger	$ 40
Number of standby passengers per flight	× 10
Income from standby passengers per flight	$400

Make a Decision   Yield Pricing in Service Businesses

Pacific Airways provides air travel services between Los Angeles and Seattle. Cost information per flight is as follows:

	Fixed Costs per Flight	Variable Costs per Passenger
Plane depreciation	$ 9,500	
Crew salaries	900	
Fuel	2,500	$18
Ground salaries	1,100	12
Airport fees	2,100	
Passenger services		10
Total	$16,100	$40

Each flight has a capacity of 150 seats, with an average of 125 seats sold per flight at an average ticket price of $180. Assume Pacific Airways is considering a new service that would provide tickets at half price. Passengers would need to fly standby to receive the discount, but would be provided a flight for a given day of travel. An analysis revealed that an average of 8 existing passengers would use the new discounted tickets for travel. In addition, 15 new passengers would be attracted to the offer.

A. Determine the contribution margin per passenger for the full-priced ticket.

B. Determine the break-even number of seats sold per flight.

C. Determine the contribution margin per passenger for discounted tickets.

D. Should Pacific Airways offer the discounted ticket plan? Answer the question by computing the incremental contribution margin per flight for the plan.

Solution:

A. Contribution Margin per Passenger = Ticket Price – Variable Costs per Passenger

$$= \$180 - \$40$$

$$= \$140$$

B. Break-Even Seats per Flight $= \dfrac{\text{Fixed Costs per Flight}}{\text{Contribution Margin per Passenger}}$

$$= \dfrac{\$16,100}{\$140}$$

$$= 115 \text{ seats}$$

C. Contribution Margin per Passenger = Discounted Ticket Price – Variable Costs per Passenger

$$= \$90 - \$40$$

$$= \$50$$

D. Lost contribution margin from customers who switch tickets: 8 × $140 = $1,120

Gained contribution margin from discount customers: (8 + 15) × $50 = $1,150

Incremental contribution per flight from the discounted ticket plan: $1,150 − $1,120 = $30

The new ticket plan will produce a positive contribution margin per flight and should be implemented based on these assumptions.

The same answer can be determined from a differential analysis table, as follows:

Differential Analysis
Continue with No Change (Alternative A) or Execute the Discount Plan (Alternative B)

	No Change (Alternative 1)	Discount Plan (Alternative 2)	Differential Effect on Income (Alternative 2)
Revenues per flight[1]	$22,500	$23,130	$630
Costs per flight:			
Plane depreciation	−$ 9,500	−$ 9,500	0
Crew salaries	−900	−900	0
Fuel[2]	−4,750	−5,020	−$270
Ground salaries[3]	−2,600	−2,780	−180
Airport fees	−2,100	−2,100	0
Passenger services[4]	−1,250	−1,400	−150
Income per flight	$ 1,400	$ 1,430	$ 30

[1]Revenues:
  No change revenues: $180 × 125 seats

Discount plan revenues:

	Ticket Price	No. of Tickets	Revenue
Full price	$180	117*	$21,060
Discount price	90	23**	2,070
Total		140	$23,130

*125 − 8
**15 + 8

[2] Fuel:
  No change: $2,500 + ($18 × 125 seats)
  Discount Plan: $2,500 + ($18 × 140 seats)

[3] Ground salaries:
  No change: $1,100 + ($12 × 125 seats)
  Discount Plan: $1,100 + ($12 × 140 seats)

[4] Passenger services:
  No change: $10 × 125 seats
  Discount plan: $10 × 140 seats

Make a Decision

Appendix Total and Variable Cost Methods to Setting Normal Price

Recall from the chapter that cost-plus methods determine the normal selling price by estimating a cost amount per unit and adding a markup, as follows:

$$\text{Normal Selling Price} = \text{Cost Amount per Unit} + \text{Markup}$$

Management determines the markup based on the desired profit for the product. The markup should be sufficient to earn the desired profit plus cover any cost and expenses that are not included in the cost amount. The product cost method was discussed in the chapter, and the total and variable cost methods are discussed in this appendix.

Total Cost Method

As shown in Exhibit 11, under the **total cost method**, manufacturing cost plus the selling and administrative expenses are included in the total cost per unit. The markup per unit is then computed and added to the total cost per unit to determine the normal selling price.

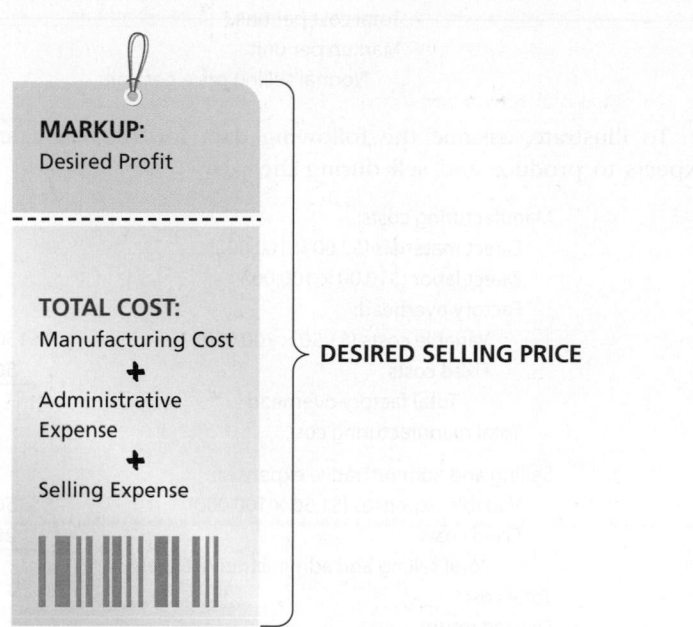

MARKUP:
Desired Profit

TOTAL COST:
Manufacturing Cost
+
Administrative
Expense
+
Selling Expense

DESIRED SELLING PRICE

Exhibit 11
Total Cost Method

The total cost method is applied using the following steps:

- Step 1.   Estimate the total manufacturing cost as follows:

Manufacturing costs:	
Direct materials	$XXX
Direct labor	XXX
Factory overhead	XXX
Total manufacturing cost	$XXX

- Step 2.   Estimate the total selling and administrative expenses.
- Step 3.   Estimate the total cost as follows:

Total manufacturing costs	$XXX
Selling and administrative expenses	XXX
Total cost	$XXX

- Step 4.   Divide the total cost by the number of units expected to be produced and sold to determine the total cost per unit, as follows:

$$\text{Total Cost per Unit} = \frac{\text{Total Cost}}{\text{Estimated Units Produced and Sold}}$$

- Step 5.   Compute the markup percentage as follows:

$$\text{Markup Percentage} = \frac{\text{Desired Profit}}{\text{Total Cost}}$$

The desired profit is normally computed based on a return on assets as follows:

$$\text{Desired Profit} = \text{Desired Return} \times \text{Total Assets}$$

- Step 6. Determine the markup per unit by multiplying the markup percentage times the total cost per unit as follows:

Markup per Unit = Markup Percentage × Total Cost per Unit

- Step 7. Determine the normal selling price by adding the markup per unit to the total cost per unit as follows:

Total cost per unit	$XXX
Markup per unit	XXX
Normal selling price per unit	$XXX

To illustrate, assume the following data for 100,000 calculators that **Digital Solutions Inc.** expects to produce and sell during the year:

Manufacturing costs:		
Direct materials ($3.00 × 100,000)		$ 300,000
Direct labor ($10.00 × 100,000)		1,000,000
Factory overhead:		
Variable costs ($1.50 × 100,000)	$150,000	
Fixed costs	50,000	
Total factory overhead		200,000
Total manufacturing cost		$1,500,000
Selling and administrative expenses:		
Variable expenses ($1.50 × 100,000)	$150,000	
Fixed costs	20,000	
Total selling and administrative expenses		170,000
Total cost		$1,670,000
Desired return		20%
Total assets		$ 800,000

Using the total cost method, the normal selling price of $18.30 is determined as follows:

- Step 1. Total manufacturing cost: $1,500,000
- Step 2. Total selling and administrative expenses: $170,000
- Step 3. Total cost: $1,670,000
- Step 4. Total cost per unit: $16.70

$$\text{Total Cost per Unit} = \frac{\text{Total Cost}}{\text{Estimated Units Produced and Sold}} = \frac{\$1,670,000}{100,000 \text{ units}} = \$16.70 \text{ per unit}$$

- Step 5. Markup percentage: 9.6% (rounded)

Desired Profit = Desired Return × Total Assets = 20% × $800,000 = $160,000

$$\text{Markup Percentage} = \frac{\text{Desired Profit}}{\text{Total Cost}} = \frac{\$160,000}{\$1,670,000} = 9.6\% \text{ (rounded)}$$

- Step 6. Markup per unit: $1.60

Markup per Unit = Markup Percentage × Total Cost per Unit
= 9.6% × $16.70 = $1.60 per unit (rounded)

- Step 7. Normal selling price: $18.30

Total cost per unit	$16.70
Markup per unit	1.60
Normal selling price per unit	$18.30

The ability of the selling price of $18.30 to generate the desired profit of $160,000 is illustrated by the income statement that follows:

Digital Solutions Inc.
Income Statement
For the Year Ended December 31, 20Y8

Sales (100,000 units × $18.30)....................................		$1,830,000
Expenses:		
Variable (100,000 units × $16.00)	$1,600,000	
Fixed ($50,000 + $20,000)	70,000	
Total expenses...		1,670,000
Income from operations		$ 160,000

The total cost method is often used by contractors who sell products to government agencies. This is because in many cases government contractors are required by law to be reimbursed for their products on a total-cost-plus-profit basis.

Variable Cost Method

As shown in Exhibit 12, under the **variable cost method**, only variable costs are included in the cost amount per unit to which the markup is added. All variable manufacturing costs, as well as variable selling and administrative expenses, are included in the cost amount. Fixed manufacturing costs, fixed selling and administrative expenses, and desired profit are included in the markup. The markup per unit is then added to the variable cost per unit to determine the normal selling price.

The variable cost method is applied using the following steps:

- Step 1. Estimate the total variable product cost as follows:

Variable product costs:	
Direct materials	$XXX
Direct labor	XXX
Variable factory overhead	XXX
Total variable product cost	$XXX

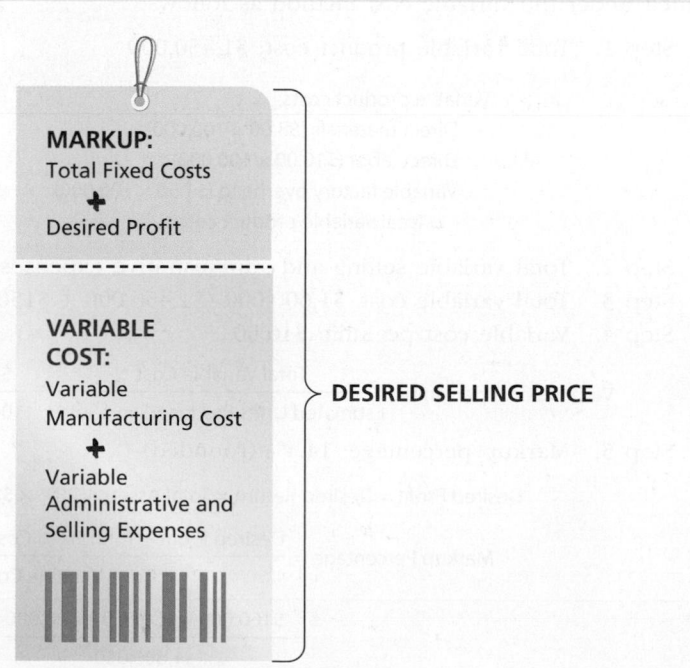

Exhibit 12
Variable Cost
Method

MARKUP:
Total Fixed Costs
+
Desired Profit

VARIABLE
COST:
Variable
Manufacturing Cost
+
Variable
Administrative and
Selling Expenses

DESIRED SELLING PRICE

- Step 2. Estimate the total variable selling and administrative expenses.
- Step 3. Determine the total variable cost as follows:

Total variable product cost	$XXX
Total variable selling and administrative expenses	XXX
Total variable cost	$XXX

- Step 4. Compute the variable cost per unit as follows:

$$\text{Variable Cost per Unit} = \frac{\text{Total Variable Cost}}{\text{Estimated Units Produced and Sold}}$$

- Step 5. Compute the markup percentage as follows:

$$\text{Markup Percentage} = \frac{\text{Desired Profit} + \text{Total Fixed Costs and Expenses}}{\text{Total Variable Cost}}$$

The numerator of the markup percentage is the desired profit plus the total fixed costs (fixed factory overhead) and expenses (selling and administrative). These fixed costs and expenses must be included in the markup percentage because they are not included in the cost amount to which the markup is added.

As illustrated for the total and product cost methods, the desired profit is normally computed based on a return on assets as follows:

$$\text{Desired Profit} = \text{Desired Return} \times \text{Total Assets}$$

- Step 6. Determine the markup per unit by multiplying the markup percentage times the variable cost per unit as follows:

$$\text{Markup per Unit} = \text{Markup Percentage} \times \text{Variable Cost per Unit}$$

- Step 7. Determine the normal selling price by adding the markup per unit to the variable cost per unit as follows:

Variable cost per unit	$XXX
Markup per unit	XXX
Normal selling price per unit	$XXX

To illustrate, assume the same data for the production and sale of 100,000 calculators by **Digital Solutions Inc.** as in the preceding example. The normal selling price of $18.30 is determined under the variable cost method as follows:

- Step 1. Total variable product cost: $1,450,000

Variable product costs:	
Direct materials ($3.00 × 100,000)	$ 300,000
Direct labor ($10.00 × 100,000)	1,000,000
Variable factory overhead ($1.50 × 100,000)	150,000
Total variable product cost	$1,450,000

- Step 2. Total variable selling and administrative expenses: $150,000 ($1.50 × 100,000)
- Step 3. Total variable cost: $1,600,000 ($1,450,000 + $150,000)
- Step 4. Variable cost per unit: $16.00

$$\text{Variable Cost per Unit} = \frac{\text{Total Variable Cost}}{\text{Estimated Units Produced and Sold}} = \frac{\$1,600,000}{100,000 \text{ units}} = \$16.00 \text{ per unit}$$

- Step 5. Markup percentage: 14.4% (rounded)

$$\text{Desired Profit} = \text{Desired Return} \times \text{Total Assets} = 20\% \times \$800,000 = \$160,000$$

$$\text{Markup Percentage} = \frac{\text{Desired Profit} + \text{Total Fixed Costs and Expenses}}{\text{Total Variable Cost}}$$

$$= \frac{\$160,000 + \$50,000 + \$20,000}{\$1,600,000} = \frac{\$230,000}{\$1,600,000}$$

$$= 14.4\% \text{ (rounded)}$$

- Step 6. Markup per unit: $2.30

$$\text{Markup per Unit} = \text{Markup Percentage} \times \text{Variable Cost per Unit}$$
$$= 14.4\% \times \$16.00 = \$2.30 \text{ per unit (rounded)}$$

- Step 7. Normal selling price: $18.30

Variable cost per unit	$16.00
Markup per unit	2.30
Normal selling price per unit	$18.30

Let's Review

Chapter Summary

1. Differential analyses for various decisions are illustrated in the chapter. Each analysis focuses on the differential effects of revenues and expenses on income (loss) for alternative courses of action.

2. The three cost methods commonly used in applying the cost-plus approach to product pricing are the product cost, total cost (appendix), and variable cost (appendix) methods. Target costing combines market-based methods with a cost-reduction emphasis.

3. Managing a production bottleneck focuses on the relative profitability of a product given the bottleneck. This profitability is measured by dividing the product's unit contribution margin by the bottleneck hours per unit.

Key Terms

competition-based method (483)
cost-plus methods (484)
demand-based method (483)
differential analysis (472)
differential cost (472)

differential income (loss) (472)
differential revenue (472)
opportunity cost (478)
product cost method (484)
production bottleneck (488)

sunk costs (474)
target costing (486)
theory of constraints (TOC) (488)
total cost method (493)
variable cost method (495)

Practice

Multiple-Choice Questions

1. Johnston Company is considering discontinuing a product. The costs of the product consist of $20,000 fixed costs and $15,000 variable costs. The variable operating expenses related to the product total $4,000. What is the differential cost of discontinuing the product?
   A. $19,000
   B. $15,000
   C. $35,000
   D. $39,000

2. Madden Company is considering disposing of equipment that was originally purchased for $200,000 and has $150,000 accumulated depreciation to date. The same equipment would cost $310,000 to replace. What is the sunk cost?
   A. $50,000
   B. $150,000
   C. $200,000
   D. $310,000

3. Hancock Inc. is considering spending $100,000 for a new grinding machine. This amount could be invested to yield a 12% return. What is the opportunity cost?
   A. $112,000
   B. $88,000
   C. $12,000
   D. $100,000

4. Which method of setting normal product selling prices includes administrative and selling expenses in the markup that is added to the cost amount?
   A. Target costing method
   B. Demand-based method
   C. Product cost method
   D. Competition-based method

5. Twitchell Industries produces three products. All of the products use a furnace operation, which is a production bottleneck. The following data are available:

	Product 1	Product 2	Product 3
Unit volume—May	1,000	1,500	1,000
Per-unit data:			
Sales price	$35	$33	$29
Variable cost	15	15	15
Contribution margin	$20	$18	$14
Furnace hours	4 hrs.	3 hrs.	2 hrs.

Which product is most profitable and should be emphasized in June's advertising campaign?
   A. Product 1
   B. Product 2
   C. Product 3
   D. The products are equally profitable.

Answers provided after Problem. Need more practice? Find additional multiple-choice questions, exercises, and problems in CengageNOWv2.

Exercises

1. Lease or sell
Obj. 1

Claxon Company owns a machine with a cost of $305,000 and accumulated depreciation of $65,000 that can be sold for $262,000, less a 5% sales commission. Alternatively, the machine can be leased by Claxon Company for three years for a total of $272,000, at the end of which there is no residual value. In addition, the repair, insurance, and property tax expense that would be incurred by Claxon Company on the machine would total $21,600 over the three years. Prepare a differential analysis on January 12 as to whether Claxon Company should lease (Alternative 1) or sell (Alternative 2) the machine.

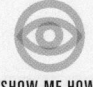

2. Discontinue a segment
Obj. 1

Product TS-20 has revenue of $102,000, variable cost of goods sold of $52,500, variable selling expenses of $21,500, and fixed costs of $35,000, creating a loss from operations of $7,000. Prepare a differential analysis as of September 12 to determine if Product TS-20 should be continued (Alternative 1) or discontinued (Alternative 2), assuming fixed costs are unaffected by the decision.

3. Make or buy
Obj. 1

A restaurant bakes its own bread for a cost of $165 per unit (100 loaves), including fixed costs of $43 per unit. A proposal is offered to purchase bread from an outside source for $110 per unit, plus $15 per unit for delivery. Prepare a differential analysis dated August 16 to determine whether the company should make (Alternative 1) or buy (Alternative 2) the bread, assuming fixed costs are unaffected by the decision.

SHOW ME HOW

4. Replace equipment
Obj. 1

A machine with a book value of $126,000 has an estimated six-year life. A proposal is offered to sell the old machine for $84,000 and replace it with a new machine at a cost of $145,000. The new machine has a six-year life with no residual value. The new machine would reduce annual direct labor costs from $55,000 to $43,000. Prepare a differential analysis dated February 18 on whether to continue with the old machine (Alternative 1) or replace the machine (Alternative 2).

SHOW ME HOW

5. Process or sell
Obj. 1

Product T is produced for $5.90 per pound. Product T can be sold without additional processing for $7.10 per pound, or processed further into Product U at an additional cost of $0.74 per pound. Product U can be sold for $8.00 per pound. Prepare a differential analysis dated August 2 on whether to sell Product T (Alternative 1) or process further into Product U (Alternative 2).

SHOW ME HOW

6. Accept business at special price
Obj. 1

Product R is normally sold for $52 per unit. A special price of $42 is offered for the export market. The variable production cost is $30 per unit. An additional export tariff of 30% of revenue must be paid for all export products. Assume there is sufficient capacity for the special order. Prepare a differential analysis dated October 23 on whether to reject (Alternative 1) or accept (Alternative 2) the special order.

SHOW ME HOW

7. Product cost markup percentage
Obj. 2

Magna Lighting Inc. produces and sells lighting fixtures. An entry light has a total cost of $125 per unit, of which $80 is product cost and $45 is selling and administrative expenses. In addition, the total cost of $125 is made up of $90 variable cost and $35 fixed cost. The desired profit is $55 per unit. Determine the markup percentage on product cost.

SHOW ME HOW

8. Bottleneck profit
Obj. 3

Product A has a unit contribution margin of $24. Product B has a unit contribution margin of $30. Product A requires four testing hours, while Product B requires six testing hours. Determine the most profitable product, assuming the testing is a bottleneck constraint.

Answers provided after Problem. Need more practice? Find additional multiple-choice questions, exercises, and problems in CengageNOWv2.

Problem

Inez Company recently began production of a new product, a digital clock, which required the investment of $1,600,000 in assets. The costs of producing and selling 80,000 units of the digital clock are estimated as follows:

Variable costs:	
Direct materials	$10.00 per unit
Direct labor	6.00
Factory overhead	4.00
Selling and administrative expenses	5.00
Total variable costs	$25.00 per unit
Fixed costs:	
Factory overhead	$800,000
Selling and administrative expenses	400,000

Inez Company is currently considering establishing a selling price for the digital clock. The president of Inez Company has decided to use the cost-plus approach to product pricing and has indicated that the digital clock must earn a 10% return on invested assets.

Instructions

1. Determine the amount of desired profit from the production and sale of the digital clock.

2. Assuming that the product cost method is used, determine (A) the cost amount per unit, (B) the markup percentage, and (C) the selling price of the digital clock.

3. Under what conditions should Inez Company consider using activity-based costing rather than a single factory overhead allocation rate in allocating factory overhead to the digital clock?

4. Assume the market price for similar digital clocks was estimated at $38. Compute the reduction in manufacturing cost per unit needed to maintain the desired profit and existing selling and administrative expenses under target costing.

5. Assume that for the current year, the selling price of the digital clock was $42 per unit. To date, 60,000 units have been produced and sold, and analysis of the domestic market indicates that 15,000 additional units are expected to be sold during the remainder of the year. On August 7, Inez Company received an offer from Wong Inc. for 4,000 units of the digital clock at $28 each. Wong Inc. will market the units in Korea under its own brand name, and no selling and administrative expenses associated with the sale will be incurred by Inez Company. The additional business is not expected to affect the domestic sales of the digital clock, and the additional units could be produced during the current year, using existing capacity. Prepare a differential analysis dated August 7 to determine whether to reject (Alternative 1) or accept (Alternative 2) the special order from Wong.

Need more practice? Find additional multiple-choice questions, exercises, and problems in CengageNOWv2.

Answers

Multiple-Choice Questions

1. **A** Differential cost is the amount of increase or decrease in cost that is expected from a particular course of action compared with an alternative. For Johnston Company, the differential cost is $19,000 (answer A). This is the total of the variable product cost ($15,000) and the variable operating expenses ($4,000), which would not be incurred if the product is discontinued.

2. **A** A sunk cost is not affected by later decisions. For Madden Company, the sunk cost is the $50,000 (answer A) book value of the equipment, which is equal to the original cost of $200,000 (answer C) less the accumulated depreciation of $150,000 (answer B). The original cost of the equipment of $200,000 (answer C) is the sunk cost immediately after the equipment was purchased. However, the sunk cost as of the date of the decision is the remaining book value of the equipment. The replacement cost of $310,000 (answer D) is not a sunk cost since it would be incurred in the future.

3. **C** The amount of income that could have been earned from the best available alternative to a proposed use of cash is the opportunity cost. For Hancock Inc., the opportunity cost is 12% times $100,000, or $12,000 (answer C).

4. **C** The product cost method (answer C) includes administrative and selling expenses in the markup that is added to the product cost amount. The target costing method (answer A) anticipates a future selling price and then determines the target cost by subtracting the desired markup (profit). The demand-based method (answer B) sets the price based upon the demand for the product. The competition-based method (answer D) sets the price based upon that offered by competitors.

5. **C** Product 3 has the highest unit contribution margin per bottleneck hour of $7 ($14 ÷ 2 hrs.). Product 1 (answer A) has the largest contribution margin per unit of $20, but the lowest unit contribution margin per bottleneck hour of $5 ($20 ÷ 4 hrs.) so it is the least profitable product in the constrained environment. Product 2 (answer B) has the highest total profitability in May of $27,000 (1,500 units × $18), but this does not suggest that it has the highest profit potential. Product 2's unit contribution margin per bottleneck hour of $6 ($18 ÷ 3 hrs.) is between Products 1 and 3. Answer D is not true since the products have different profit potential in terms of their unit contribution margin per bottleneck hour.

Exercises

1.

Differential Analysis
Lease (Alt. 1) or Sell (Alt. 2) Machine
January 12

	Lease Machine (Alternative 1)	Sell Machine (Alternative 2)	Differential Effect on Income (Alternative 2)
Revenues	$272,000	$262,000	–$10,000
Costs	–21,600	–13,100*	8,500
Income (loss)	$250,400	$248,900	–$ 1,500

*$262,000 × 5%

Claxon Company should lease the machine.

2.

Differential Analysis
Continue (Alt. 1) or Discontinue (Alt. 2) Product TS-20
September 12

	Continue Product TS-20 (Alternative 1)	Discontinue Product TS-20 (Alternative 2)	Differential Effect on Income (Alternative 2)
Revenue	$102,000	$ 0	–$102,000
Costs:			
Variable cost of goods sold	–52,500	0	52,500
Variable selling and admin. expenses	–21,500	0	21,500
Fixed costs	35,000	–35,000	0
Income (loss)	–$ 7,000	–$35,000	–$ 28,000

Product TS-20 should be continued.

3.

Differential Analysis
Make (Alt. 1) or Buy (Alt. 2) Bread
August 16

	Make Bread (Alternative 1)	Buy Bread (Alternative 2)	Differential Effect on Income (Alternative 2)
Sales price	$ 0	$ 0	$ 0
Unit costs:			
Purchase price	0	–110	–110
Delivery	0	–15	–15
Variable costs ($165 – $43)	–122	0	122
Fixed factory overhead	–43	–43	0
Income (loss)	–$165	–$168	–$ 3

The company should make the bread.

4.

Differential Analysis
Continue with (Alt. 1) or Replace (Alt. 2) Old Machine
February 18

	Continue with Old Machine (Alternative 1)	Replace Old Machine (Alternative 2)	Differential Effect on Income (Alternative 2)
Revenues:			
Proceeds from sale of old machine	$ 0	$ 84,000	$ 84,000
Costs:			
Purchase price	0	–145,000	–145,000
Direct labor (6 years)	–330,000[1]	–258,000[2]	72,000
Income (loss)	–$330,000	–$319,000	$ 11,000

[1]$55,000 × 6 years
[2]$43,000 × 6 years

The company should replace the old machine.

5.

Differential Analysis
Sell Product T (Alt. 1) or Process Further into Product U (Alt. 2)
August 2

	Sell Product T (Alternative 1)	Process Further into Product U (Alternative 2)	Differential Effect on Income (Alternative 2)
Revenues, per unit	$7.10	$8.00	$0.90
Costs, per unit	−5.90	−6.64*	−0.74
Income (loss), per unit	$1.20	$1.36	$0.16

*$5.90 + $0.74

The company should process further into Product U.

6.

Differential Analysis
Reject Order (Alt. 1) or Accept Order (Alt. 2)
October 23

	Reject Order (Alternative 1)	Accept Order (Alternative 2)	Differential Effect on Income (Alternative 2)
Revenues, per unit	$0.00	$42.00	$42.00
Costs:			
Variable manufacturing costs, per unit	0.00	−30.00	−30.00
Export tariff, per unit	0.00	−12.60*	−12.60
Income (loss), per unit	$0.00	−$ 0.60	−$ 0.60

*$42.00 ×30%

The company should not accept the special order.

7. $\text{Markup Percentage on Product Cost} = \dfrac{\text{Desired Profit} + \text{Total Selling and Administrative Expenses}}{\text{Total Product Cost}}$

$$= \frac{\$55 + \$45}{\$80*} = 125\%$$

*$125 − $45

8.

	Product A	Product B
Unit contribution margin	$24	$30
Testing hours per unit	÷ 4	÷ 6
Unit contribution margin per production bottleneck hour	$ 6	$ 5

Product A is the most profitable in using bottleneck resources.

Need more help? Watch step-by-step videos of how to compute answers to these Exercises in CengageNOWv2.

Problem

1. $160,000 ($1,600,000 × 10%)

2. A. Total manufacturing costs:

Variable ($20 × 80,000 units)	$1,600,000
Fixed factory overhead	800,000
Total	$2,400,000

Cost amount per unit: $2,400,000 ÷ 80,000 units = $30.00

B. Markup Percentage $= \dfrac{\text{Desired Profit} + \text{Total Selling and Administrative Expenses}}{\text{Total Product Cost}}$

$= \dfrac{\$160,000 + \$400,000 + (\$5 \times 80,000 \text{ units})}{\$2,400,000}$

$= \dfrac{\$160,000 + \$400,000 + \$400,000}{\$2,400,000}$

$= \dfrac{\$960,000}{\$2,400,000} = 40\%$

C.	
Cost amount per unit	$30.00
Markup ($30 × 40%)	12.00
Selling price	$42.00

3. Inez should consider using activity-based costing for factory overhead allocation when the product and manufacturing operations are complex. For example, if the digital clock was introduced as one among many different consumer digital products, then it is likely these products will consume factory activities in different ways. If this is combined with complex manufacturing and manufacturing support processes, then it is likely a single overhead allocation rate will lead to distorted factory overhead allocation. Specifically, the digital clock is a new product. Thus, it is likely that it will consume more factory overhead than existing stable and mature products. In this case, a single rate would result in the digital clock being undercosted compared to results using activity-based rates for factory overhead allocation.

4.
Current selling price	$42
Expected selling price	−38
Required reduction in manufacturing cost to maintain same profit	$ 4

Revised revenue and cost figures:

	Current	Desired
Selling price	$42	$38
Costs:		
Variable selling and administrative expenses per unit	$ 5	$ 5
Fixed selling and administrative expenses per unit		
($400,000 ÷ 80,000 units)	5	5
Existing manufacturing cost per unit [part (2)]	30	
Target manufacturing cost per unit ($30 – $4)		26
Total costs	$40	$36
Profit	$ 2	$ 2

5.

Differential Analysis—Wong Inc. Special Order
Reject (Alternative 1) or Accept (Alternative 2) Order
August 7

	Reject Order (Alternative 1)	Accept Order (Alternative 2)	Differential Effect on Income (Alternative 2)
Revenues	$0	$112,000*	$112,000
Costs:			
Variable manufacturing costs	0	−80,000**	−80,000
Income (loss)	$0	$ 32,000	$ 32,000

*4,000 units × $28 per unit
**4,000 units × $20 per unit

The proposal should be accepted.

Discussion Questions

1. Explain the meaning of (A) differential revenue, (B) differential cost, and (C) differential income.

2. A company could sell a building for $250,000 or lease it for $2,500 per month. What would need to be considered in determining if the lease option would be preferred?

3. A chemical company has a commodity-grade and premium-grade product. Why might the company elect to process the commodity-grade product further to the premium-grade product?

4. A company accepts incremental business at a special price that exceeds the variable cost. What other issues must the company consider in deciding whether to accept the business?

5. A company fabricates a component at a cost of $6.00. A supplier offers to supply the same component for $5.50. Under what circumstances is it reasonable to purchase from the supplier?

6. Many fast-food restaurant chains, such as **McDonald's**, will occasionally discontinue restaurants in their system. What are some financial considerations in deciding to eliminate a store?

REAL WORLD

7. In the long run, the normal selling price must be set high enough to cover what factors?

8. Although the cost-plus approach to product pricing may be used by management as a general guideline, what are some examples of other factors that managers should also consider in setting product prices?

9. How does the target cost method differ from cost-plus approaches?

10. What is the appropriate measure of a product's value when a firm is operating under production bottlenecks?

Basic Exercises

SHOW ME HOW

BE 10-1   Lease or sell   Obj. 1

McFadden Company owns equipment with a cost of $475,000 and accumulated depreciation of $280,000 that can be sold for $175,000, less a 7% sales commission. Alternatively, McFadden Company can lease the equipment for four years for a total of $180,000, at the end of which there is no residual value. In addition, the repair, insurance, and property tax expense that would be incurred by McFadden Company on the equipment would total $35,500 over the four-year lease. Prepare a differential analysis on February 18 as to whether McFadden Company should lease (Alternative 1) or sell (Alternative 2) the equipment.

SHOW ME HOW

BE 10-2   Discontinue a segment   Obj. 1

Product AG52 has revenue of $748,000, variable cost of goods sold of $640,000, variable selling expenses of $90,000, and fixed costs of $50,000, creating a loss from operations of $32,000. Prepare a differential analysis as of October 7 to determine if Product AG52 should be continued (Alternative 1) or discontinued (Alternative 2), assuming fixed costs are unaffected by the decision.

SHOW ME HOW

BE 10-3   Make or buy   Obj. 1

A company manufactures various-sized plastic bottles for its medicinal product. The manufacturing cost for small bottles is $75 per unit (100 bottles), including fixed costs of $28 per unit. A proposal is offered to purchase small bottles from an outside source for $40 per unit, plus $4 per unit for freight. Prepare a differential analysis dated July 31 to determine whether the company should make (Alternative 1) or buy (Alternative 2) the bottles, assuming fixed costs are unaffected by the decision.

SHOW ME HOW

BE 10-4 Replace equipment

Obj. 1

A machine with a book value of $80,000 has an estimated five-year life. A proposal is offered to sell the old machine for $50,500 and replace it with a new machine at a cost of $75,000. The new machine has a five-year life with no residual value. The new machine would reduce annual direct labor costs from $11,200 to $7,400. Prepare a differential analysis dated April 11 on whether to continue with the old machine (Alternative 1) or replace the old machine (Alternative 2).

SHOW ME HOW

BE 10-5 Process or sell

Obj. 1

Product J19 is produced for $11 per gallon. Product J19 can be sold without additional processing for $18 per gallon, or processed further into Product R33 at an additional cost of $7 per gallon. Product R33 can be sold for $24 per gallon. Prepare a differential analysis dated April 30 on whether to sell Product J19 (Alternative 1) or process further into Product R33 (Alternative 2).

SHOW ME HOW

BE 10-6 Accept business at special price

Obj. 1

Product A is normally sold for $9.60 per unit. A special price of $7.20 is offered for the export market. The variable production cost is $5.00 per unit. An additional export tariff of 15% of revenue must be paid for all export products. Assume there is sufficient capacity for the special order. Prepare a differential analysis dated March 16 on whether to reject (Alternative 1) or accept (Alternative 2) the special order.

SHOW ME HOW

BE 10-7 Product cost markup percentage

Obj. 2

Green Thumb Garden Tools Inc. produces and sells home and garden tools and equipment. A lawnmower has a total cost of $230 per unit, of which $160 is product cost and $70 is selling and administrative expenses. In addition, the total cost of $230 is made up of $120 variable cost and $110 fixed cost. The desired profit is $58 per unit. Determine the markup percentage on product cost.

SHOW ME HOW

BE 10-8 Bottleneck profit

Obj. 3

Product K has a unit contribution margin of $120. Product L has a unit contribution margin of $100. Product K requires five furnace hours, while Product L requires four furnace hours. Determine the most profitable product, assuming the furnace is a bottleneck constraint.

Exercises

✔ A. Differential
income from selling,
$5,400

SHOW ME HOW

EX 10-1 Differential analysis for a lease or sell decision

Obj. 1

Granite Construction Company is considering selling excess machinery with a book value of $175,000 (original cost of $315,000 less accumulated depreciation of $140,000) for $180,000, less a 5% brokerage commission. Alternatively, the machinery can be leased for a total of $200,000 for four years, after which it is expected to have no residual value. During the period of the lease, Granite Construction Company's costs of repairs, insurance, and property tax expenses are expected to be $34,400.

A. Prepare a differential analysis, dated November 7 to determine whether Granite should lease (Alternative 1) or sell (Alternative 2) the machinery.

B. ━━━▶ On the basis of the data presented, would it be advisable to lease or sell the machinery? Explain.

SHOW ME HOW

EX 10-2 Differential analysis for a lease or buy decision Obj. 1

Sloan Corporation is considering new equipment. The equipment can be purchased from an overseas supplier for $125,500. The freight and installation costs for the equipment are $1,600. If purchased, annual repairs and maintenance are estimated to be $2,500 per year over the five-year useful life of the equipment. Alternatively, Sloan can lease the equipment from a domestic supplier for $30,000 per year for five years, with no additional costs. Prepare a differential analysis dated December 3 to determine whether Sloan should lease (Alternative 1) or purchase (Alternative 2) the equipment. *Hint:* This is a "lease or *buy*" decision, which must be analyzed from the perspective of the equipment user, as opposed to the equipment owner.

✔ A. Differential loss, −$1,275,000

SHOW ME HOW

EX 10-3 Differential analysis for a discontinued product Obj. 1

A condensed income statement by product line for Healthy Beverage Inc. indicated the following for Fruit Cola for the past year:

Sales	$12,750,000
Cost of goods sold	8,500,000
Gross profit	$ 4,250,000
Operating expenses	6,000,000
Loss from operations	$ (1,750,000)

It is estimated that 25% of the cost of goods sold represents fixed factory overhead costs and that 15% of the operating expenses are fixed. Because Fruit Cola is only one of many products, the fixed costs will not be materially affected if the product is discontinued.

A. Prepare a differential analysis dated January 5 to determine whether Fruit Cola should be continued (Alternative 1) or discontinued (Alternative 2).

B. ▬▬▶ Should Fruit Cola be retained? Explain.

EX 10-4 Differential analysis for a discontinued product Obj. 1

The condensed product-line income statement for Dish N' Dat Company for the month of March is as follows:

✔ A. Alternative 1 loss, $2,200

EXCEL TEMPLATE

Dish N' Dat Company
Product-Line Income Statement
For the Month Ended March 31

	Bowls	Plates	Cups
Sales	$71,000	$105,700	$31,300
Cost of goods sold	32,600	42,300	16,800
Gross profit	$38,400	$ 63,400	$14,500
Selling and administrative expenses	27,400	42,800	16,700
Income from operations	$11,000	$ 20,600	$ (2,200)

Fixed costs are 15% of the cost of goods sold and 40% of the selling and administrative expenses. Dish N' Dat assumes that fixed costs would not be materially affected if the Cups line were discontinued.

A. Prepare a differential analysis dated March 31 to determine if Cups should be continued (Alternative 1) or discontinued (Alternative 2).

B. ▬▬▶ Should the Cups line be retained? Explain.

EX 10-5 Segment analysis for a service company Obj. 1

REAL WORLD

Charles Schwab Corporation is one of the more innovative brokerage and financial service companies in the United States. The company recently provided information about its major business segments as follows (in millions):

	Investor Services	Advisor Services
Revenues	$4,647	$1,360
Income from operations	1,673	459
Depreciation	154	45

A. ━━━► How does a brokerage company like Schwab define the Investor Services and Advisor Services segments? Use the Internet to develop your answer.

B. Provide a specific example of a variable and fixed cost in the Investor Services segment.

C. Estimate the contribution margin for each segment, assuming depreciation represents the majority of fixed costs.

D. If Schwab decided to sell its Advisor Services accounts to another company, estimate how much operating income would decline.

EX 10-6   Decision to discontinue a product   Obj. 1

━━━► On the basis of the following data, the general manager of Featherweight Shoes Inc. decided to discontinue Children's Shoes because it reduced income from operations by $17,000. What is the flaw in this decision, if it is assumed fixed costs would not be materially affected by the discontinuance?

Featherweight Shoes Inc.
Product-Line Income Statement
For the Year Ended April 30, 20Y8

	Children's Shoes	Men's Shoes	Women's Shoes	Total
Sales	$235,000	$300,000	$500,000	$1,035,000
Costs of goods sold:				
Variable costs	$130,000	$150,000	$220,000	$ 500,000
Fixed costs	41,000	60,000	120,000	221,000
Total cost of goods sold	$171,000	$210,000	$340,000	$ 721,000
Gross profit	$ 64,000	$ 90,000	$160,000	$ 314,000
Selling and adminstrative expenses:				
Variable selling and admin. expenses	$ 46,000	$ 45,000	$ 95,000	$ 186,000
Fixed selling and admin. expenses	35,000	20,000	25,000	80,000
Total selling and admin. expenses	$ 81,000	$ 65,000	$120,000	$ 266,000
Income (loss) from operations	$ (17,000)	$ 25,000	$ 40,000	$ 48,000

EX 10-7   Make-or-buy decision   Obj. 1

✔ A. Differential loss from buying, –$3.00 per case

SHOW ME HOW   EXCEL TEMPLATE

Fremont Computer Company has been purchasing carrying cases for its portable computers at a purchase price of $40 per unit. The company, which is currently operating below full capacity, charges factory overhead to production at the rate of 25% of direct labor cost. The unit costs to produce comparable carrying cases are expected to be as follows:

Direct materials	$16
Direct labor	20
Factory overhead (25% of direct labor)	5
Total cost per unit	$41

If Fremont Computer Company manufactures the carrying cases, fixed factory overhead costs will not increase and variable factory overhead costs associated with the cases are expected to be 5% of the direct labor costs.

A. Prepare a differential analysis dated September 30 to determine whether the company should make (Alternative 1) or buy (Alternative 2) the carrying case.

B. ━━━► On the basis of the data presented, would it be advisable to make the carrying cases or to continue buying them? Explain.

EX 10-8   Make-or-buy decision for a service company   Obj. 1

EXCEL TEMPLATE

The Theater Arts Guild of Dallas (TAG-D) employs five people in its Publication Department. These people lay out pages for pamphlets, brochures, magazines, and other publications for the TAG-D productions. The pages are delivered to an outside company for printing. The company is considering an outside publication service for the layout work. The outside service

(Continued)

is quoting a price of $13 per layout page. The budget for the Publication Department for the current year is as follows:

Salaries	$224,000
Benefits	36,000
Supplies	21,000
Office expenses	39,000
Office depreciation	28,000
Computer depreciation	24,000
Total	$372,000

The department expects to lay out 24,000 pages for the current year. The Publication Department office space and equipment would be used for future administrative needs, if the department's function were purchased from the outside.

A. Prepare a differential analysis dated February 22 to determine whether TAG-D should lay out pages internally (Alternative 1) or purchase layout services from the outside (Alternative 2).

B. ▬▬▶ On the basis of your analysis in part (A), should the page layout work be purchased from an outside company? Explain.

C. ▬▬▶ What additional considerations might factor into the decision making?

SHOW ME HOW

EX 10-9 Machine replacement decision
Obj. 1

A company is considering replacing an old piece of machinery, which cost $600,000 and has $350,000 of accumulated depreciation to date, with a new machine that has a purchase price of $545,000. The old machine could be sold for $231,000. The annual variable production costs associated with the old machine are estimated to be $61,000 per year for eight years. The annual variable production costs for the new machine are estimated to be $19,000 per year for eight years.

A. Prepare a differential analysis dated September 13 to determine whether to continue with (Alternative 1) or replace (Alternative 2) the old machine.

B. What is the sunk cost in this situation?

✔ A. Differential loss, −$2,500

EXCEL TEMPLATE

EX 10-10 Differential analysis for machine replacement
Obj. 1

Kim Kwon Digital Components Company assembles circuit boards by using a manually operated machine to insert electronic components. The original cost of the machine is $60,000, the accumulated depreciation is $24,000, its remaining useful life is five years, and its residual value is negligible. On May 4 of the current year, a proposal was made to replace the present manufacturing procedure with a fully automatic machine that has a purchase price of $180,000. The automatic machine has an estimated useful life of five years and no significant residual value. For use in evaluating the proposal, the accountant accumulated the following annual data on present and proposed operations:

	Present Operations	Proposed Operations
Sales	$205,000	$205,000
Direct materials	$ 72,000	$ 72,000
Direct labor	51,000	—
Power and maintenance	5,000	18,000
Taxes, insurance, etc.	1,500	4,000
Selling and administrative expenses	45,000	45,000
Total expenses	$174,500	$139,000

A. Prepare a differential analysis dated May 4 to determine whether to continue with (Alternative 1) or replace (Alternative 2) the old machine. Prepare the analysis over the useful life of the new machine.

B. Based only on the data presented, should the proposal be accepted?

C. ▬▬▶ What are some of the other factors that should be considered before a final decision is made?

SHOW ME HOW

EX 10-11 Sell or process further

Obj. 1

Calgary Lumber Company incurs a cost of $315 per hundred board feet (hbf) in processing certain "rough-cut" lumber, which it sells for $440 per hbf. An alternative is to produce a "finished cut" at a total processing cost of $465 per hbf, which can be sold for $600 per hbf. Prepare a differential analysis dated March 15 on whether to sell rough-cut lumber (Alternative 1) or process further into finished-cut lumber (Alternative 2).

EXCEL TEMPLATE

EX 10-12 Sell or process further

Obj. 1

Rise N' Shine Coffee Company produces Columbian coffee in batches of 6,000 pounds. The standard quantity of materials required in the process is 6,000 pounds, which cost $5.50 per pound. Columbian coffee can be sold without further processing for $9.22 per pound. Columbian coffee can also be processed further to yield Decaf Columbian, which can be sold for $11.88 per pound. The processing into Decaf Columbian requires additional processing costs of $10,230 per batch. The additional processing will also cause a 5% loss of product due to evaporation.

A. Prepare a differential analysis dated October 6 on whether to sell regular Columbian (Alternative 1) or process further into Decaf Columbian (Alternative 2).

B. ➤ Should Rise N' Shine sell Columbian coffee or process further and sell Decaf Columbian? Explain.

C. Determine the price of Decaf Columbian that would cause neither an advantage nor a disadvantage for processing further and selling Decaf Columbian.

EX 10-13 Decision on accepting additional business

Obj. 1

✔ A. Differential income, $54,000

Homestead Jeans Co. has an annual plant capacity of 65,000 units, and current production is 45,000 units. Monthly fixed costs are $54,000, and variable costs are $29 per unit. The present selling price is $42 per unit. On November 12 of the current year, the company received an offer from Dawkins Company for 18,000 units of the product at $32 each. Dawkins Company will market the units in a foreign country under its own brand name. The additional business is not expected to affect the domestic selling price or quantity of sales of Homestead Jeans Co.

A. Prepare a differential analysis dated November 12 on whether to reject (Alternative 1) or accept (Alternative 2) the Dawkins order.

B. ➤ Briefly explain the reason why accepting this additional business will increase operating income.

C. What is the minimum price per unit that would produce a positive contribution margin?

EX 10-14 Accepting business at a special price

Obj. 1

Portable Power Company expects to operate at 80% of productive capacity during July. The total manufacturing costs for July for the production of 25,000 batteries are budgeted as follows:

Direct materials	$162,500
Direct labor	70,000
Variable factory overhead	30,000
Fixed factory overhead	112,500
Total manufacturing costs	$375,000

The company has an opportunity to submit a bid for 2,500 batteries to be delivered by July 31 to a government agency. If the contract is obtained, it is anticipated that the additional activity will not interfere with normal production during July or increase the selling or administrative expenses. What is the unit cost below which Portable Power Company should not go in bidding on the government contract?

✔ A. Differential
revenues, $15,000,000

SHOW ME HOW   EXCEL TEMPLATE

EX 10-15   Decision on accepting additional business   Obj. 1

Talladega Tire and Rubber Company has capacity to produce 500,000 tires. Talladega presently produces and sells 400,000 tires for the North American market at a price of $200 per tire. Talladega is evaluating a special order from a European automobile company, Autobahn Motors. Autobahn is offering to buy 100,000 tires for $150 per tire. Talladega's accounting system indicates that the total cost per tire is as follows:

Direct materials	$ 75
Direct labor	20
Factory overhead (70% variable)	30
Selling and administrative expenses (60% variable)	18
Total	$143

Talladega pays a selling commission equal to 3% of the selling price on North American orders, which is included in the variable portion of the selling and administrative expenses. However, this special order would not have a sales commission. If the order was accepted, the tires would be shipped overseas for an additional shipping cost of $3 per tire. In addition, Autobahn has made the order conditional on receiving European safety certification. Talladega estimates that this certification would cost $400,000.

A. Prepare a differential analysis dated July 31 on whether to reject (Alternative 1) or accept (Alternative 2) the special order from Autobahn Motors.

B. What is the minimum price per unit that would be financially acceptable to Talladega?

EX 10-16   Product cost method of product pricing   Obj. 2

✔ B. $40.00

SHOW ME HOW

La Femme Accessories Inc. produces women's handbags. The cost of producing 800 handbags is as follows:

Direct materials	$18,000
Direct labor	8,500
Factory overhead	5,500
Total manufacturing cost	$32,000

The selling and administrative expenses are $17,000. The management desires a profit equal to 22% of invested assets of $250,000.

A. Determine the amount of desired profit from the production and sale of 800 handbags.

B. Determine the product cost per unit for the production of 800 handbags.

C. Determine the product cost markup percentage for handbags.

D. Determine the selling price of handbags.

EX 10-17   Product cost method of product costing   Obj. 2

✔ D. $325

Smart Stream Inc. uses the product cost method of applying the cost-plus approach to product pricing. The costs of producing and selling 10,000 cell phones are as follows:

Variable costs per unit:		Fixed costs:	
Direct materials	$150	Factory overhead	$350,000
Direct labor	25	Selling and admin. exp.	140,000
Factory overhead	40		
Selling and administrative expenses	25		
Total variable cost per unit	$240		

Smart Stream desires a profit equal to a 30% return on invested assets of $1,200,000.

A. Determine the amount of desired profit from the production and sale of 10,000 cell phones.

B. Determine the product cost per unit for the production of 10,000 cell phones.

C. Determine the product cost markup percentage for cell phones.

D. Determine the selling price of cell phones.

REAL WORLD

EX 10-18 Target costing   Obj. 2

Toyota Motor Corporation uses target costing. Assume that Toyota marketing personnel estimate that the competitive selling price for the Camry in the upcoming model year will need to be $27,000. Assume further that the Camry's total unit cost for the upcoming model year is estimated to be $22,500 and that Toyota requires a 20% profit margin on selling price (which is equivalent to a 25% markup on total cost).

A. What price will Toyota establish for the Camry for the upcoming model year?

B. ━━━▶ What impact will target costing have on Toyota, given the assumed information?

EX 10-19 Target costing   Obj. 2

✔ B. $30   Instant Image Inc. manufactures color laser printers. Model J20 presently sells for $460 and has a product cost of $230, as follows:

Direct materials	$175
Direct labor	40
Factory overhead	15
Total	$230

It is estimated that the competitive selling price for color laser printers of this type will drop to $400 next year. Instant Image has established a target cost to maintain its historical markup percentage on product cost. Engineers have provided the following cost-reduction ideas:

1. Purchase a plastic printer cover with snap-on assembly, rather than with screws. This will reduce the amount of direct labor by 15 minutes per unit.

2. Add an inspection step that will add six minutes per unit of direct labor but reduce the materials cost by $20 per unit.

3. Decrease the cycle time of the injection molding machine from four minutes to three minutes per part. Forty percent of the direct labor and 48% of the factory overhead are related to running injection molding machines.

The direct labor rate is $30 per hour.

A. Determine the target cost for Model J20, assuming that the historical markup on product cost and selling price are maintained.

B. Determine the required cost reduction.

C. Evaluate the three engineering improvements together to determine if the required cost reduction (drift) can be achieved.

EX 10-20 Product decisions under bottlenecked operations   Obj. 3

Mill Metals Inc. has three grades of metal product, Type 5, Type 10, and Type 20. Financial data for the three grades are as follows:

	Type 5	Type 10	Type 20
Revenues	$43,000	$49,000	$56,500
Variable cost	$34,000	$28,000	$26,500
Fixed cost	8,000	8,000	8,000
Total cost	$42,000	$36,000	$34,500
Income from operations	$ 1,000	$13,000	$22,000
Number of units	÷ 5,000	÷ 5,000	÷ 5,000
Income from operations per unit	$ 0.20	$ 2.60	$ 4.40

(Continued)

Mill's operations require all three grades to be melted in a furnace before being formed. The furnace runs 24 hours a day, 7 days a week, and is a production bottleneck. The furnace hours required per unit of each product are as follows:

Type 5:	6 hours
Type 10:	6 hours
Type 20:	12 hours

The Marketing Department is considering a new marketing and sales campaign.

Which product should be emphasized in the marketing and sales campaign in order to maximize profitability?

EX 10-21   Product decisions under bottlenecked operations   Obj. 3

✔ A. Total income from operations, $269,000

Youngstown Glass Company manufactures three types of safety plate glass: large, medium, and small. All three products have high demand. Thus, Youngstown Glass is able to sell all the safety glass that it can make. The production process includes an autoclave operation, which is a pressurized heat treatment. The autoclave is a production bottleneck. Total fixed costs are $85,000 for the company as a whole. In addition, the following information is available about the three products:

	Large	Medium	Small
Unit selling price	$184	$160	$100
Unit variable cost	130	120	76
Unit contribution margin	$ 54	$ 40	$ 24
Autoclave hours per unit	3	2	1
Total process hours per unit	5	4	2
Budgeted units of production	3,000	3,000	3,000

A. Determine the contribution margin by glass type and the total company income from operations for the budgeted units of production.

B. Prepare an analysis showing which product is the most profitable per bottleneck hour.

Appendix
EX 10-22   Total cost method of product pricing

✔ B. 12.46%

Based on the data presented in Exercise 17, assume that Smart Stream Inc. uses the total cost method of applying the cost-plus approach to product pricing.

A. Determine the total costs and the total cost amount per unit for the production and sale of 10,000 cellular phones.

B. Determine the total cost markup percentage (rounded to two decimal places) for cellular phones.

C. Determine the selling price of cellular phones. (Round markup to the nearest dollar.)

Appendix
EX 10-23   Variable cost method of product pricing

✔ B. 35.42%

Based on the data presented in Exercise 17, assume that Smart Stream Inc. uses the variable cost method of applying the cost-plus approach to product pricing.

A. Determine the variable costs and the variable cost amount per unit for the production and sale of 10,000 cellular phones.

B. Determine the variable cost markup percentage (rounded to two decimal places) for cellular phones.

C. Determine the selling price of cellular phones. (Round markup to the nearest dollar.)

Problems: Series A

PR 10-1A　Differential analysis involving opportunity costs　　Obj. 1

✔ 3. $1,450,000

On August 1, Rantoul Stores Inc. is considering leasing a building and purchasing the necessary equipment to operate a retail store. Alternatively, the company could use the funds to invest in $1,000,000 of 4% U.S. Treasury bonds that mature in 15 years. The bonds could be purchased at face value. The following data have been assembled:

Cost of store equipment	$1,000,000
Life of store equipment	15 years
Estimated residual value of store equipment	$50,000
Yearly costs to operate the store, excluding depreciation of store equipment	$200,000
Yearly expected revenues—years 1–6	$300,000
Yearly expected revenues—years 7–15	$400,000

Instructions

1. Prepare a differential analysis as of August 1 presenting the proposed operation of the store for the 15 years (Alternative 1) as compared with investing in U.S. Treasury bonds (Alternative 2).

2. Based on the results disclosed by the differential analysis, should the proposal be accepted?

3. If the proposal is accepted, what would be the total estimated income from operations of the store for the 15 years?

PR 10-2A　Differential analysis for machine replacement proposal　　Obj. 1

Lexigraphic Printing Company is considering replacing a machine that has been used in its factory for four years. Relevant data associated with the operations of the old machine and the new machine, neither of which has any estimated residual value, are as follows:

Old Machine	
Cost of machine, 10-year life	$89,000
Annual depreciation (straight-line)	8,900
Annual manufacturing costs, excluding depreciation	23,600
Annual nonmanufacturing operating expenses	6,100
Annual revenue	74,200
Current estimated selling price of machine	29,700

New Machine	
Purchase price of machine, six-year life	$119,700
Annual depreciation (straight-line)	19,950
Estimated annual manufacturing costs, excluding depreciation	6,900

Annual nonmanufacturing operating expenses and revenue are not expected to be affected by purchase of the new machine.

Instructions

1. Prepare a differential analysis as of April 30 comparing operations using the present machine (Alternative 1) with operations using the new machine (Alternative 2). The analysis should indicate the total differential income that would result over the six-year period if the new machine is acquired.

2. ▬▬▶ List other factors that should be considered before a final decision is reached.

✔ **1. Moisturizer differential revenue, $250,000**

SHOW ME HOW   EXCEL TEMPLATE

PR 10-3A   Differential analysis for sales promotion proposal   Obj. 1

Kankakee Cosmetics Company is planning a one-month campaign for December to promote sales of one of its two cosmetics products. A total of $150,000 has been budgeted for advertising, contests, redeemable coupons, and other promotional activities. The following data have been assembled for their possible usefulness in deciding which of the products to select for the campaign:

	Moisturizer	Perfume
Unit selling price	$35	$55
Unit production costs:		
Direct materials	$12	$20
Direct labor	8	10
Variable factory overhead	3	6
Fixed factory overhead	2	6
Total unit production costs	$25	$42
Unit variable selling expenses	2	3
Unit fixed selling expenses	2	8
Total unit costs	$29	$53
Operating income per unit	$ 6	$ 2

No increase in facilities would be necessary to produce and sell the increased output. It is anticipated that 40,000 additional units of moisturizer or 30,000 additional units of perfume could be sold from the campaign without changing the unit selling price of either product.

Instructions

1. Prepare a differential analysis as of November 2 to determine whether to promote moisturizer (Alternative 1) or perfume (Alternative 2).

2. ▬▬▶ The sales manager had tentatively decided to promote moisturizer estimating that operating income would be increased by $50,000 ($5 operating income per unit for 40,000 units, less promotion expenses of $150,000). The manager also believed that the selection of perfume would reduce operating income by $90,000 ($2 operating income per unit for 30,000 units, less promotion expenses of $150,000). State briefly your reasons for supporting or opposing the tentative decision.

PR 10-4A   Differential analysis for further processing   Obj. 1

✔ **1. Raw sugar income, $23,800**

The management of Dominican Sugar Company is considering whether to process further raw sugar into refined sugar. Refined sugar can be sold for $2.20 per pound, and raw sugar can be sold without further processing for $1.40 per pound. Raw sugar is produced in batches of 42,000 pounds by processing 100,000 pounds of sugar cane, which costs $0.35 per pound of cane. Refined sugar will require additional processing costs of $0.50 per pound of raw sugar, and 1.25 pounds of raw sugar will produce 1 pound of refined sugar.

Instructions

1. Prepare a differential analysis as of March 24 to determine whether to sell raw sugar (Alternative 1) or process further into refined sugar (Alternative 2).

2. ▬▬▶ Briefly report your recommendations.

Appendix

PR 10-5A Product pricing using the cost-plus approach methods; differential analysis for accepting additional business

Obj. 1, 2

✔ 2. B. Markup percentage, 44%

Crystal Displays Inc. recently began production of a new product, flat panel displays, which required the investment of $1,500,000 in assets. The costs of producing and selling 5,000 units of flat panel displays are estimated as follows:

Variable costs per unit:		Fixed costs:	
Direct materials	$120	Factory overhead	$250,000
Direct labor	30	Selling and administrative expenses	150,000
Factory overhead	50		
Selling and administrative expenses	35		
Total variable cost per unit	$235		

Crystal Displays Inc. is currently considering establishing a selling price for flat panel displays. The president of Crystal Displays has decided to use the cost-plus approach to product pricing and has indicated that the displays must earn a 15% return on invested assets.

Instructions

1. Determine the amount of desired profit from the production and sale of flat panel displays.

2. Assuming that the product cost method is used, determine (A) the cost amount per unit, (B) the markup percentage, and (C) the selling price of flat panel displays.

3. (*Appendix*) Assuming that the total cost method is used, determine (A) the cost amount per unit, (B) the markup percentage (rounded to two decimal places), and (C) the selling price of flat panel displays. (Round markup to nearest whole dollar.)

4. (*Appendix*) Assuming that the variable cost method is used, determine (A) the cost amount per unit, (B) the markup percentage (rounded to two decimal places), and (C) the selling price of flat panel displays. (Round markup to nearest whole dollar.)

5. ➤ Comment on any additional considerations that could influence establishing the selling price for flat panel displays.

6. Assume that as of August 1, 3,000 units of flat panel displays have been produced and sold during the current year. Analysis of the domestic market indicates that 2,000 additional units are expected to be sold during the remainder of the year at the normal product price determined under the product cost method. On August 3, Crystal Displays Inc. received an offer from Maple Leaf Visual Inc. for 800 units of flat panel displays at $225 each. Maple Leaf Visual Inc. will market the units in Canada under its own brand name, and no variable selling and administrative expenses associated with the sale will be incurred by Crystal Displays Inc. The additional business is not expected to affect the domestic sales of flat panel displays, and the additional units could be produced using existing factory, selling, and administrative capacity.

A. Prepare a differential analysis of the proposed sale to Maple Leaf Visual Inc.

B. Based on the differential analysis in part (A), should the proposal be accepted?

PR 10-6A Product pricing and profit analysis with bottleneck operations

Obj. 3

✔ 1. High Grade, $10

EXCEL TEMPLATE

Hercules Steel Company produces three grades of steel: high, good, and regular grade. Each of these products (grades) has high demand in the market, and Hercules is able to sell as much as it can produce of all three. The furnace operation is a bottleneck in the process and is running at 100% of capacity. Hercules wants to improve steel operation profitability. The variable conversion cost is $15 per process hour. The fixed cost is $200,000. In addition, the cost analyst was able to determine the following information about the three products:

	High Grade	Good Grade	Regular Grade
Budgeted units produced	5,000	5,000	5,000
Total process hours per unit	12	11	10
Furnace hours per unit	4	3	2.5
Unit selling price	$280	$270	$250
Direct materials cost per unit	$90	$84	$80

(Continued)

The furnace operation is part of the total process for each of these three products. Thus, for example, 4.0 of the 12.0 hours required to process High Grade steel are associated with the furnace.

Instructions

1. Determine the unit contribution margin for each product.

2. Provide an analysis to determine the relative product profitability, assuming that the furnace is a bottleneck.

Problems: Series B

EXCEL TEMPLATE

✔ 3. $525,000

PR 10-1B   Differential analysis involving opportunity costs   Obj. 1

On July 1, Coastal Distribution Company is considering leasing a building and buying the necessary equipment to operate a public warehouse. Alternatively, the company could use the funds to invest in $740,000 of 5% U.S. Treasury bonds that mature in 14 years. The bonds could be purchased at face value. The following data have been assembled:

Cost of equipment	$740,000
Life of equipment	14 years
Estimated residual value of equipment	$75,000
Yearly costs to operate the warehouse, excluding depreciation of equipment	$175,000
Yearly expected revenues—years 1–7	$280,000
Yearly expected revenues—years 8–14	$240,000

Instructions

1. Prepare a differential analysis as of July 1 presenting the proposed operation of the warehouse for the 14 years (Alternative 1) as compared with investing in U.S. Treasury bonds (Alternative 2).

2. Based on the results disclosed by the differential analysis, should the proposal be accepted?

3. If the proposal is accepted, what is the total estimated income from operations of the warehouse for the 14 years?

EXCEL TEMPLATE

PR 10-2B   Differential analysis for machine replacement proposal   Obj. 1

Flint Tooling Company is considering replacing a machine that has been used in its factory for two years. Relevant data associated with the operations of the old machine and the new machine, neither of which has any estimated residual value, are as follows:

Old Machine	
Cost of machine, eight-year life	$38,000
Annual depreciation (straight-line)	4,750
Annual manufacturing costs, excluding depreciation	12,400
Annual nonmanufacturing operating expenses	2,700
Annual revenue	32,400
Current estimated selling price of the machine	12,900

New Machine	
Cost of machine, six-year life	$57,000
Annual depreciation (straight-line)	9,500
Estimated annual manufacturing costs, exclusive of depreciation	3,400

Annual nonmanufacturing operating expenses and revenue are not expected to be affected by purchase of the new machine.

Instructions

1. Prepare a differential analysis as of November 8 comparing operations using the present machine (Alternative 1) with operations using the new machine (Alternative 2). The analysis should indicate the differential income that would result over the six-year period if the new machine is acquired.

2. ━━━▶ List other factors that should be considered before a final decision is reached.

PR 10-3B   Differential analysis for sales promotion proposal   **Obj. 1**

✔ 1. Differential revenues, $105,000

SHOW ME HOW   EXCEL TEMPLATE

Sole Mates Inc. is planning a one-month campaign for July to promote sales of one of its two shoe products. A total of $100,000 has been budgeted for advertising, contests, redeemable coupons, and other promotional activities. The following data have been assembled for their possible usefulness in deciding which of the products to select for the campaign:

	Tennis Shoes	Walking Shoes
Unit selling price	$85	$100
Unit production costs:		
Direct materials	$19	$ 32
Direct labor	8	12
Variable factory overhead	7	5
Fixed factory overhead	16	11
Total unit production costs	$50	$ 60
Unit variable selling expenses	6	10
Unit fixed selling expenses	20	15
Total unit costs	$76	$ 85
Operating income per unit	$ 9	$ 15

No increase in facilities would be necessary to produce and sell the increased output. It is anticipated that 7,000 additional units of tennis shoes or 7,000 additional units of walking shoes could be sold without changing the unit selling price of either product.

Instructions

1. Prepare a differential analysis as of June 19 to determine whether to promote tennis shoes (Alternative 1) or walking shoes (Alternative 2).

2. ━━━▶ The sales manager had tentatively decided to promote walking shoes, estimating that operating income would be increased by $5,000 ($15 operating income per unit for 7,000 units, less promotion expenses of $100,000). The manager also believed that the selection of tennis shoes would reduce operating income by $37,000 ($9 operating income per unit for 7,000 units, less promotion expenses of $100,000). State briefly your reasons for supporting or opposing the tentative decision.

PR 10-4B   Differential analysis for further processing   **Obj. 1**

✔ 1. Ingot income, $35,500

The management of International Aluminum Co. is considering whether to process aluminum ingot further into rolled aluminum. Rolled aluminum can be sold for $2,200 per ton, and ingot can be sold without further processing for $1,100 per ton. Ingot is produced in batches of 80 tons by smelting 500 tons of bauxite, which costs $105 per ton of bauxite. Rolled aluminum will require additional processing costs of $620 per ton of ingot, and 1.25 tons of ingot will produce 1 ton of rolled aluminum (due to trim losses).

Instructions

1. Prepare a differential analysis as of February 5 to determine whether to sell aluminum ingot (Alternative 1) or process further into rolled aluminum (Alternative 2).

2. ━━━▶ Briefly report your recommendations.

Appendix

PR 10-5B   **Product pricing using the cost-plus approach methods;**   **Obj. 1, 2**
differential analysis for accepting additional business

✔ **2. B. Markup**
percentage, 30%

Night Glow Inc. recently began production of a new product, the halogen light, which required the investment of $600,000 in assets. The costs of producing and selling 10,000 halogen lights are estimated as follows:

Variable costs per unit:		Fixed costs:	
Direct materials	$32	Factory overhead	$180,000
Direct labor	12	Selling and administrative expenses	80,000
Factory overhead	8		
Selling and administrative expenses	7		
Total variable cost per unit	$59		

Night Glow Inc. is currently considering establishing a selling price for the halogen light. The president of Night Glow Inc. has decided to use the cost-plus approach to product pricing and has indicated that the halogen light must earn a 10% return on invested assets.

Instructions

1. Determine the amount of desired profit from the production and sale of the halogen light.

2. Assuming that the product cost method is used, determine (A) the cost amount per unit, (B) the markup percentage, and (C) the selling price of the halogen light.

3. (*Appendix*) Assuming that the total cost method is used, determine (A) the cost amount per unit, (B) the markup percentage (rounded to two decimal places), and (C) the selling price of the halogen light. (Round markup to the nearest whole dollar.)

4. (*Appendix*) Assuming that the variable cost method is used, determine (A) the cost amount per unit, (B) the markup percentage (rounded to two decimal places), and (C) the selling price of the halogen light. (Round markup to nearest whole dollar.)

5. ➡ Comment on any additional considerations that could influence establishing the selling price for the halogen light.

6. Assume that as of September 1, 7,000 units of halogen light have been produced and sold during the current year. Analysis of the domestic market indicates that 3,000 additional units of the halogen light are expected to be sold during the remainder of the year at the normal product price determined under the product cost method. On September 5, Night Glow Inc. received an offer from Tokyo Lighting Inc. for 1,600 units of the halogen light at $57 each. Tokyo Lighting Inc. will market the units in Japan under its own brand name, and no variable selling and administrative expenses associated with the sale will be incurred by Night Glow Inc. The additional business is not expected to affect the domestic sales of the halogen light, and the additional units could be produced using existing productive, selling, and administrative capacity.

   A. Prepare a differential analysis of the proposed sale to Tokyo Lighting Inc.

   B. Based on the differential analysis in part (A), should the proposal be accepted?

PR 10-6B   **Product pricing and profit analysis with bottleneck operations**   **Obj. 3**

✔ **1. Ethylene, $15**

EXCEL TEMPLATE

Wilmington Chemical Company produces three products: ethylene, butane, and ester. Each of these products has high demand in the market, and Wilmington Chemical is able to sell as much as it can produce of all three. The reaction operation is a bottleneck in the process and is running at 100% of capacity. Wilmington wants to improve chemical operation profitability. The variable conversion cost is $10 per process hour. The fixed cost is $400,000. In addition, the cost analyst was able to determine the following information about the three products:

	Ethylene	Butane	Ester
Budgeted units produced	9,000	9,000	9,000
Total process hours per unit	4.0	4.0	3.0
Reactor hours per unit	1.5	1.0	0.5
Unit selling price	$170	$155	$130
Direct materials cost per unit	$115	$88	$85

The reaction operation is part of the total process for each of these three products. Thus, for example, 1.5 of the 4.0 hours required to process ethylene is associated with the reactor.

Instructions

1. Determine the unit contribution margin for each product.
2. Provide an analysis to determine the relative product profitabilities, assuming that the reactor is a bottleneck.

Analysis for Decision Making

ADM-1 Service yield pricing and differential analysis

Cityscape Hotels has 200 rooms available in a major metropolitan city. The hotel is able to attract business customers during the weekdays and leisure customers during the weekend. However, the leisure customers on weekends occupy fewer rooms than do business customers on weekdays. Thus, Cityscape plans to provide special weekend pricing to attract additional leisure customers. A hotel room is priced at $180 per room night. The cost of a hotel room night includes the following:

	Cost Per Room Night (at normal occupancy)
Housekeeping service	$ 23
Utilities	7
Amenities	3
Hotel depreciation	55
Hotel staff (excluding housekeeping)	42
Total	$130

The special weekend price is proposed for $120 per room night. At this price, it is anticipated that average occupancy for the weekend (Friday, Saturday, and Sunday) will increase from 30% to 50% of available rooms.

A. What is the contribution margin for a room night under the normal pricing if only the hotel depreciation and hotel staff (excluding housekeeping) are assumed fixed for all occupancy levels?

B. Determine the contribution margin for a room night under the proposed weekend pricing.

C. Prepare a differential analysis showing the differential income for an average weekend between the existing (Alternative 1) and discount (Alternative 2) price plan.

D. ➡ Should management accept the proposed weekend pricing plan? Explain.

ADM-2 Service yield pricing

Valley Power Company uses natural gas to create steam to spin turbines to generate electricity. The costs of the power plant, including depreciation, taxes, and insurance, are fixed to generating electricity. The costs of operating personnel, maintenance, and fuel are variable to generating electricity. The fixed and variable costs are expressed in terms of costs per megawatt hour. A megawatt is 1 million watts generated per hour. A kilowatt is one thousand watts generated per hour. The fixed and variable costs per megawatt hour for Valley Power Company are:

Fixed cost per megawatt hour	$ 50
Variable cost per megawatt hour	80
Total cost per megawatt hour	$130

Valley Power Company runs gas turbines at 85% of capacity during the day and at 40% of capacity during the night. Daytime is considered peak demand time, while night is considered off-peak time. Industrial customers are charged $0.15 per kilowatt-hour, regardless of time of use. A new industrial customer is contracting for service from Valley Power. The new customer has

(Continued)

the ability to move production to the night shift, and thereby shift electricity demand to the night hours. However, to accomplish this, the new customer expects a discounted price per kilowatt-hour.

A.   Determine the operating income per megawatt hour for industrial customers.

B.   Determine the contribution margin per megawatt hour for industrial customers.

C.   What is the lowest price per kilowatt-hour that Valley Power could offer for off-peak power and maintain a positive contribution margin?

D.   ━━━▶ What are some other implications in offering a discounted off-peak price to the new customer?

ADM-3   Service yield pricing and differential analysis

Atlantis Cruise Lines offers luxury, one-week cruise packages in the Greek Aegean Sea. The ship has a capacity for 1,200 people. Atlantis averages 1,000 passengers per cruise. The price per passenger is $6,000. Costs associated with a cruise are as follows:

Variable costs per cruise:	
Crew to serve passengers	$1,200,000
Food	1,500,000
Amenity and excursion	400,000
Total variable cost per cruise	$3,100,000
Fixed costs per cruise:	
Crew to run ship	$1,500,000
Depreciation expense	120,000
Fuel	50,000
Total fixed cost per cruise	$1,670,000

Atlantis proposes an early booking program to help increase the number of passengers per cruise. Under the proposed early booking program, the first 300 passengers to book a cruise will receive a $1,500 discount off the normal price for the cruise. Atlantis expects this program to increase the number of passengers from 1,000 to 1,180 per cruise. The proposed booking program will be launched with $15,000 of advertising per cruise.

A.   Determine the income from operations for a cruise.

B.   Determine the variable cost per passenger for each variable cost item.

C.   Determine the contribution margin per passenger.

D.   Prepare a differential analysis showing the differential income per cruise between the existing plan (Alternative 1) and the proposed early booking program (Alternative 2). Is the new booking program financially acceptable?

Take It Further

ETHICS

TIF 10-1   Ethics in Action

Aaron McKinney is a cost accountant for Majik Systems Inc. Martin Dodd, Vice President of Marketing, has asked Aaron to meet with representatives of Majik Systems' major competitor to discuss product cost data. Martin indicates that the sharing of these data will enable Majik Systems to determine a fair and equitable price for its products.

➤ Would it be ethical for Aaron to attend the meeting and share the relevant cost data? Explain your answer.

REAL WORLD

TIF 10-2   Team Activity

Product pricing and product costs vary significantly depending on company and industry. Three such companies, their industries, and an associated product are:

Company	Industry	Product
Delta Air Lines	Air travel	Airline tickets
Amazon	Internet retailing	Various consumer products
Dell Inc.	Computer manufacturer	Computers

In teams of three, assign each person in your group to one of the companies listed above. Go to the company's Web site and determine the following:

1. A product (or service) description
2. Based on your responses to part (1) along with the description of the company's business, identify the potential costs that are required to sell the product selected in part (1), and categorize them as fixed or variable.

TIF 10-3   Communication

The following conversation took place between Juanita Jackson, Vice President of Marketing, and Les Miles, Controller of Diamond Computer Company:

Juanita: I am really excited about our new computer coming out. I think it will be a real market success.

Les: I'm really glad you think so. I know that our success will be determined by our price. If our price is too high, our competitors will be the ones with the market success.

Juanita: Don't worry about it. We'll just mark our product cost up by 25%, and it will all work out. I know we'll make money at those markups. By the way, what does the estimated product cost look like?

Les: Well, there's the rub. The product cost looks as if it's going to come in at around $1,200. With a 25% markup, that will give us a selling price of $1,500.

Juanita: I see your concern. That's a little high. Our research indicates that computer prices are dropping and that this type of computer should be selling for around $1,250 when we release it to the market.

Les: I'm not sure what to do.

Juanita: Let me see if I can help. How much of the $1,200 is fixed cost?

Les: About $200.

Juanita: There you go. The fixed cost is sunk. We don't need to consider it in our pricing decision. If we reduce the product cost by $200, the new price with a 25% markup would be right at $1,250. Boy, I was really worried for a minute there. I knew something wasn't right.

➤ Write a brief memo from Les Miles to Juanita Jackson (1) responding to her solution to the pricing problem, and (2) explaining how target costing could be used to solve the problem.

Concepts and Principles

Chapter 1 *Introduction to Managerial Accounting*

Developing Information

COST SYSTEMS

Chapter 2 *Job Order Costing*
Chapter 3 *Process Cost Systems*
Chapter 4 *Activity-Based Costing*

COST BEHAVIOR

Chapter 5 *Cost-Volume-Profit Analysis*

Decision Making

EVALUATING PERFORMANCE

Chapter 6 *Variable Costing for Management Analysis*
Chapter 7 *Budgeting*
Chapter 8 *Evaluating Variances from Standard Costs*

COMPARING ALTERNATIVES

Chapter 9 *Evaluating Decentralized Operations*
Chapter 10 *Differential Analysis and Product Pricing*
Chapter 11 *Capital Investment Analysis*
Chapter 12 *Lean Manufacturing*

Vail Resorts, Inc.

Why are you paying tuition, studying this text, and spending time and money on a higher education? Most people believe that the money and time spent now will return them more earnings in the future. That is, the cost of higher education is an investment in your future earning ability. How would you know if this investment is worth it?

One method would be for you to compare the cost of a higher education against the estimated increase in your future earning power. The bigger the difference between your expected future earnings and the cost of your education, the better the investment. A business also evaluates its investments in fixed assets by comparing the initial cost of the investment to its future earnings and cash flows.

For example, **Vail Resorts, Inc.**, is one of the largest ski resort owner-operators in the world. It is known for its Vail, Breckenridge, and Keystone ski resorts, among others. A ski resort requires significant investments in property and equipment. Thus, Vail Resorts routinely makes major investments in new or improved amenities, lodging, retail, lifts, snowmaking and grooming equipment, and technology infrastructure. These investments are evaluated by their ability to enhance cash flows.

In this chapter, the methods used to make investment decisions, which may involve thousands, millions, or even billions of dollars, are described and illustrated. The similarities and differences among the most commonly used methods of evaluating investment proposals, as well as the benefits of each method, are emphasized. Factors that can complicate the analysis are also discussed.

What's Covered

Capital Investment Analysis

Capital Investments	**Methods Not Using Present Values**	**Methods Using Present Values**	**Additional Considerations**
■ Nature (Obj. 1)	■ Average Rate of Return Method (Obj. 2)	■ Present Value Concepts (Obj. 3)	■ Complicating Factors (Obj. 4)
■ Importance (Obj. 1)	■ Cash Payback Method (Obj. 2)	■ Net Present Value Method (Obj. 3)	■ Capital Rationing (Obj. 5)
■ Evaluation Methods (Obj. 1)		■ Internal Rate of Return Method (Obj. 3)	

Learning Objectives

Obj. 1   Describe the nature and importance of capital investment analysis.

Obj. 2   Evaluate capital investment proposals, using the average rate of return and cash payback methods.

Obj. 3   Evaluate capital investment proposals, using the net present value and internal rate of return methods.

Obj. 4   Describe factors that complicate capital investment analysis.

Obj. 5   Describe and diagram the capital rationing process.

Analysis for Decision Making

Describe and illustrate the use of capital investment analysis in evaluating a sustainability investment.

Objective 1

Describe the nature and importance of capital investment analysis.

Nature of Capital Investment Analysis

Companies use capital investment analysis to evaluate long-term investments. **Capital investment analysis** (or *capital budgeting*) is the process by which management plans, evaluates, and controls investments in fixed assets. Capital investments use funds and affect operations for many years and must earn a reasonable rate of return. Thus, capital investment decisions are some of the most important decisions that management makes.

Capital investment evaluation methods can be grouped into the following categories:

Methods That Do Not Use Present Values

- Average rate of return method
- Cash payback method

Methods That Use Present Values

- Net present value method
- Internal rate of return method

The two methods that use present values consider the time value of money. The **time value of money concept** recognizes that a dollar today is worth more than a dollar tomorrow because today's dollar can earn interest.

Link to Vail Resorts

In 2014, **Vail Resorts, Inc.**, purchased the Park City Mountain Resort and ski area in Park City, Utah, for $182.5 million.

Why It Matters

Business Use of Investment Analysis Methods

A survey of chief financial officers of large U.S. companies reported their use of the four investment methods as follows:

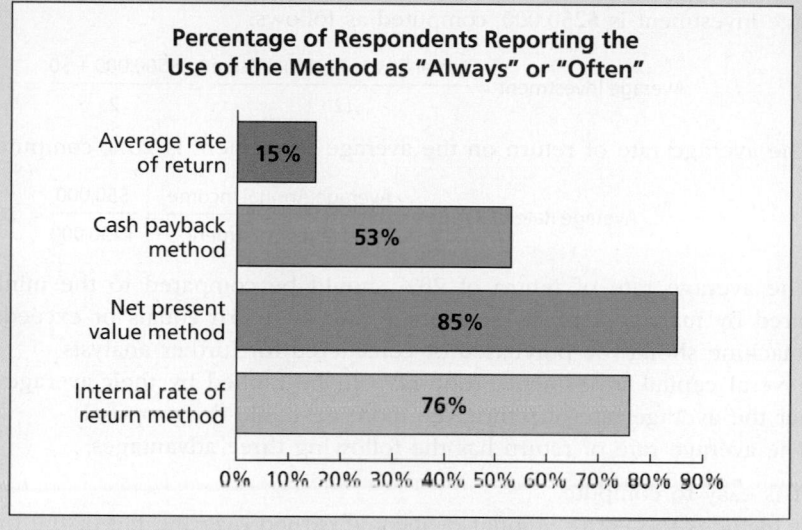

Source: Patricia A. Ryan and Glenn P. Ryan, "Capital Budgeting Practice of the Fortune 1000: How Have Things Changed?" *Journal of Business and Management* (Winter 2002).

Methods Not Using Present Values

Objective 2

Evaluate capital investment proposals, using the average rate of return and cash payback methods.

The methods not using present values are often useful in evaluating capital investment proposals that have relatively short useful lives. In such cases, the timing of the cash flows (the time value of money) is less important.

Because the methods not using present values are easy to use, they are often used to screen proposals. Minimum standards for accepting proposals are set, and proposals not meeting these standards are dropped. If a proposal meets the minimum standards, it may be subject to further analysis using the present value methods.

Average Rate of Return Method

The **average rate of return**, sometimes called the *accounting rate of return*, measures the average income as a percent of the average investment. The average rate of return is computed as follows:

$$\text{Average Rate of Return} = \frac{\text{Average Annual Income}}{\text{Average Investment}}$$

In the preceding equation, the numerator is the average of the annual income expected to be earned from the investment over its life, after deducting depreciation. The denominator is the average investment (book value) over the life of the investment. Assuming straight-line depreciation, the average investment is computed as follows:

$$\text{Average Investment} = \frac{\text{Initial Cost} + \text{Residual Value}}{2}$$

To illustrate, assume that management is evaluating the purchase of a new machine as follows:

Cost of new machine	$500,000
Residual value	0
Expected total income from machine	200,000
Expected useful life	4 years

The average annual income expected from the machine is $50,000 ($200,000 ÷ 4 years). The average investment is $250,000, computed as follows:

$$\text{Average Investment} = \frac{\text{Initial Cost} + \text{Residual Value}}{2} = \frac{\$500,000 + \$0}{2} = \$250,000$$

The average rate of return on the average investment is 20%, computed as follows:

$$\text{Average Rate of Return} = \frac{\text{Average Annual Income}}{\text{Average Investment}} = \frac{\$50,000}{\$250,000} = 20\%$$

The average rate of return of 20% should be compared to the minimum rate of return required by management. If the average rate of return equals or exceeds the minimum rate, the machine should be purchased or considered for further analysis.

Several capital investment proposals can be ranked by their average rates of return. The higher the average rate of return, the more desirable the proposal.

The average rate of return has the following three advantages:

note:
The average rate of return method considers the amount of income earned over the life of a proposal.

- It is easy to compute.
- It includes the entire amount of income earned over the life of the proposal.
- It emphasizes accounting income, which is often used by investors and creditors in evaluating management performance.

The average rate of return has the following two disadvantages:

- It does not directly consider the expected cash flows from the proposal.
- It does not directly consider the timing of the expected cash flows.

Link to Vail Resorts

Vail Resorts' average rate of return on its property, plant, and equipment is slightly more than 10%.

Cash Payback Method

A capital investment uses cash and must return cash in the future to be successful. The expected period of time between the date of an investment and the recovery in cash of the amount invested is the **cash payback period**.

When annual net cash inflows are equal, the cash payback period is computed as follows:

$$\text{Cash Payback Period} = \frac{\text{Initial Cost}}{\text{Annual Net Cash Inflow}}$$

To illustrate, assume that management is evaluating the purchase of the following new machine:

Cost of new machine	$200,000
Cash revenues from machine per year	50,000
Expenses of machine per year, including depreciation	30,000
Depreciation per year	20,000

To simplify, the revenues and expenses other than depreciation are assumed to be in cash. Hence, the net cash inflow per year from use of the machine is as follows:

Net cash flow per year:

Cash revenues from machine	$ 50,000
Cash expenses of machine	(10,000)*
Net cash inflow per year	$ 40,000

*Expenses of machine, including depreciation	$ 30,000
Depreciation expense	(20,000)
Cash expenses of machine	$ 10,000

The time required for the net cash flow to equal the cost of the new machine is the payback period. Thus, the cash payback period for the investment is five years, computed as follows:

$$\text{Cash Payback Period} = \frac{\text{Initial Cost}}{\text{Annual Net Cash Inflow}} = \frac{\$200,000}{\$40,000} = 5 \text{ years}$$

In the preceding illustration, the annual net cash inflows are equal ($40,000 per year). When the annual net cash inflows are not equal, the cash payback period is determined by adding the annual net cash inflows until the cumulative total equals the initial cost of the proposed investment.

To illustrate, assume that a proposed investment has an initial cost of $400,000. The annual and cumulative net cash inflows over the proposal's six-year life are as follows:

Year	Net Cash Flow	Cumulative Net Cash Flow
1	$ 60,000	$ 60,000
2	80,000	140,000
3	105,000	245,000
4	155,000	400,000
5	100,000	500,000
6	90,000	590,000

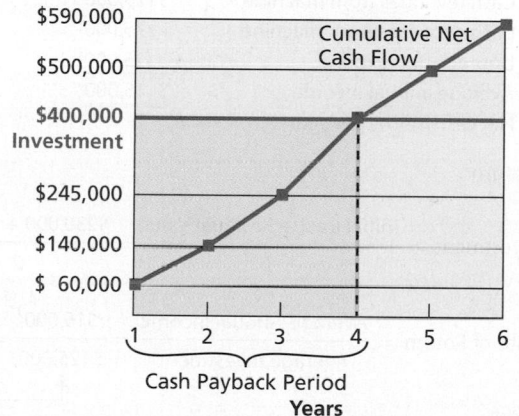

The cumulative net cash flow at the end of Year 4 equals the initial cost of the investment, $400,000. Thus, the payback period is four years.

If the initial cost of the proposed investment had been $450,000, the cash payback period would occur during Year 5. Because $100,000 of net cash flow is expected during Year 5, the additional $50,000 to increase the cumulative total to $450,000 occurs halfway through the year ($50,000 ÷ $100,000). Thus, the cash payback period would be 4½ years.[1]

A short cash payback period is desirable. This is because the sooner cash is recovered, the sooner it can be reinvested in other projects. In addition, there is less chance of losses from changing economic or business conditions. A short cash payback period is also desirable for quickly repaying any debt used to purchase the investment.

The cash payback method has the following two advantages:

- It is simple to use and understand.
- It analyzes cash flows.

The cash payback method has the following two disadvantages:

- It ignores cash flows occurring after the payback period.
- It does not use present value concepts in valuing cash flows occurring in different periods.

[1] Unless otherwise stated, net cash inflows are received uniformly throughout the year.

Link to Vail Resorts   The ski operations are seasonal in nature and typically run from mid-November to mid-April. To increase cash flows, **Vail Resorts** promotes nonski activities in the summer months, including sightseeing, mountain biking, and zip tours.

Check Up Corner 11-1   Capital Investment Analysis Not Using Present Value

Tyme Manufacturing Inc. is evaluating a capital investment proposal for a new machine. The new machine has a cost of $230,000, an expected useful life of six years, and a residual value of $20,000. Information on expected annual revenues and expenses associated with the machine is as follows:

Revenue from machine	$125,000
Expenses of machine, other than depreciation	75,000
Depreciation expense	35,000

All revenues and expenses are in cash, except for depreciation expense. Determine the following:

A.   The average rate of return, and

B.   The cash payback period.

Solution:

	Average Annual Income	Average Annual Cash Flow	
Cash revenues from machine	$125,000	$125,000	
Cash expenses from machine	(75,000)	(75,000)	Depreciation is not included in
Depreciation expense	(35,000)	⌐ ‑ ‑ ‑ ‑ ⌐	← determining cash flow because it is a
Average annual income	$ 15,000		noncash expense.
Net cash inflow per year		$ 50,000	

A.   Average Rate of Return:

$$\text{Average Investment} = \frac{\text{Initial Cost} + \text{Residual Value}}{2} = \frac{\$230,000 + \$20,000}{2} = \$125,000$$

$$\text{Average Rate of Return} = \frac{\text{Average Annual Income}}{\text{Average Investment}} = \frac{\$15,000}{\$125,000} = 12\%$$

B.   Cash Payback Period:

$$\text{Cash Payback Period} = \frac{\text{Initial Cost}}{\text{Annual Net Cash Inflow}} = \frac{\$230,000}{\$50,000} = 4.6 \text{ years}$$

Check Up Corner

Objective 3

Evaluate capital investment proposals, using the net present value and internal rate of return methods.

Methods Using Present Values

An investment in fixed assets may be viewed as purchasing a series of net cash flows over a period of time. The timing of when the net cash flows will be received is important in determining the value of a proposed investment.

Present value methods use the amount and timing of the net cash flows in evaluating an investment. The two methods of evaluating capital investments using present values are as follows:

- Net present value method
- Internal rate of return method

Present Value Concepts

Both the net present value and the internal rate of return methods use the following two **present value concepts**:

- Present value of an amount
- Present value of an annuity

Present Value of an Amount If you were given the choice, would you prefer to receive $1 now or $1 three years from now? You should prefer to receive $1 now, because you could invest the $1 and earn interest for three years. As a result, the amount you would have after three years would be greater than $1.

To illustrate, assume that you have $1 to invest as follows:

Amount to be invested	$1
Period to be Invested	3 years
Interest rate	12%

After one year, the $1 earns interest of $0.12 ($1 × 12%) and, thus, will grow to $1.12 ($1 × 1.12). In the second year, the $1.12 earns 12% interest of $0.134 ($1.12 × 12%) and, thus, will grow to $1.254 ($1.12 × 1.12) by the end of the second year. This process of interest earning interest is called *compounding*. By the end of the third year, your $1 investment will grow to $1.404 as shown in Exhibit 1.

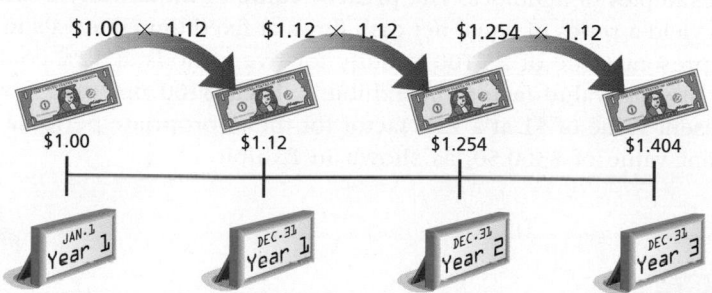

Exhibit 1
Compound Amount of $1 for Three Periods at 12%

On January 1, Year 1, what is the present value of $1.404 to be received on December 31, Year 3? This is a present value question. The answer can be determined with the aid of a present value of $1 table. For example, the partial table in Exhibit 2 indicates that the present value of $1 to be received in three years with earnings compounded at the rate of 12% per year is 0.712.[2]

Exhibit 2
Partial Present Value of $1 Table

		Present Value of $1 at Compound Interest			
Year	**6%**	**10%**	**12%**	**15%**	**20%**
1	0.943	0.909	0.893	0.870	0.833
2	0.890	0.826	0.797	0.756	0.694
3	0.840	0.751	0.712	0.658	0.579
4	0.792	0.683	0.636	0.572	0.482
5	0.747	0.621	0.567	0.497	0.402
6	0.705	0.564	0.507	0.432	0.335
7	0.665	0.513	0.452	0.376	0.279
8	0.627	0.467	0.404	0.327	0.233
9	0.592	0.424	0.361	0.284	0.194
10	0.558	0.386	0.322	0.247	0.162

[2] The present value factors in the table are rounded to three decimal places. More complete tables of present values are in Appendix A.

Multiplying 0.712 by $1.404 yields $1 as follows:

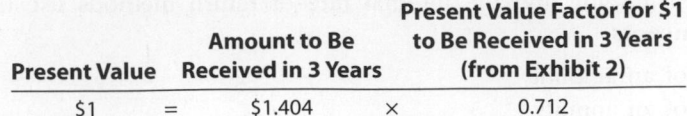

		Amount to Be Received in 3 Years		Present Value Factor for $1 to Be Received in 3 Years (from Exhibit 2)
Present Value				
$1	=	$1.404	×	0.712

That is, the present value of $1.404 to be received in three years using a compound interest rate of 12% is $1, as shown in Exhibit 3.

Exhibit 3

Present Value of an Amount of $1.404

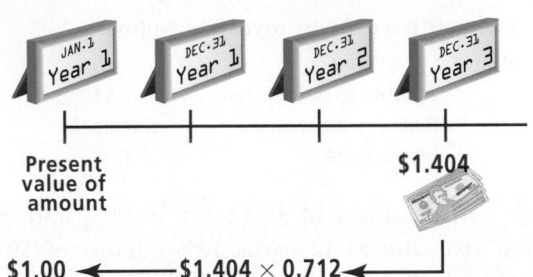

Present Value of an Annuity An **annuity** is a series of equal net cash flows at fixed time intervals. Annuities are very common in business. Cash payments for monthly rent, salaries, and bond interest are all examples of annuities. The **present value of an annuity** is the amount of cash needed today to yield a series of equal net cash flows at fixed time intervals in the future.

To illustrate, the present value of a $100 annuity for five periods at 12% could be determined by using the present value factors in Exhibit 2. Each $100 net cash flow could be multiplied by the present value of $1 at a 12% factor for the appropriate period and summed to determine a present value of $360.50, as shown in Exhibit 4.

Exhibit 4

Present Value of a $100 Amount for Five Consecutive Periods

Using a present value of an annuity table is a simpler approach. Exhibit 5 is a partial table of present value annuity factors.[3]

---

[3] The present value factors in the table are rounded to three decimal places. More complete tables of present values are in Appendix A.

		Present Value of an Annuity of $1 at Compound Interest			
Year	6%	10%	12%	15%	20%
1	0.943	0.909	0.893	0.870	0.833
2	1.833	1.736	1.690	1.626	1.528
3	2.673	2.487	2.402	2.283	2.106
4	3.465	3.170	3.037	2.855	2.589
5	4.212	3.791	3.605	3.353	2.991
6	4.917	4.355	4.111	3.785	3.326
7	5.582	4.868	4.564	4.160	3.605
8	6.210	5.335	4.968	4.487	3.837
9	6.802	5.759	5.328	4.772	4.031
10	7.360	6.145	5.650	5.019	4.192

Exhibit 5
Partial Present Value of an Annuity Table

The present value factors in the table shown in Exhibit 5 are the sum of the present value of $1 factors in Exhibit 2 for the number of annuity periods. Thus, 3.605 in the annuity table (Exhibit 5) is the sum of the five present value of $1 factors at 12% from Exhibit 2, computed as follows:

	Present Value Factor for $1 (Exhibit 2)
Present value factor for $1 for 1 year @12%	0.893
Present value factor for $1 for 2 years @12%	0.797
Present value factor for $1 for 3 years @12%	0.712
Present value factor for $1 for 4 years @12%	0.636
Present value factor for $1 for 5 years @12%	0.567
Present value factor for an annuity of $1 for 5 years (from Exhibit 5)	3.605

Multiplying $100 by 3.605 yields $360.50 as follows:

Present Value		Amount to Be Received Annually for 5 Years		Present Value Factor for an Annuity of $1 to Be Received for 5 Years (Exhibit 5)
$360.50	=	$100	×	3.605

Thus, $360.50 is the same amount that was determined in the preceding illustration by five successive multiplications.

Net Present Value Method and Index

The net present value method and present value index are often used in combination, as we illustrate in this section.

Net Present Value Method The **net present value method** compares the amount to be invested with the present value of the net cash inflows. It is sometimes called the *discounted cash flow method*.

The interest rate (return) used in net present value analysis is the company's minimum desired rate of return. This rate, sometimes termed the *hurdle rate*, is based on such factors as the purpose of the investment and the cost of obtaining funds for the investment. If the present value of the cash inflows equals or exceeds the amount to be invested, the proposal is desirable.

note:
The net present value method compares an investment's initial cash outflow with the present value of its cash inflows.

To illustrate, assume the following data for a proposed investment in new equipment:

Cost of new equipment	$200,000
Expected useful life	5 years
Minimum desired rate of return	10%
Expected cash flows to be received each year:	
Year 1	$ 70,000
Year 2	60,000
Year 3	50,000
Year 4	40,000
Year 5	40,000
Total expected cash flows	$260,000

The present value of the net cash flow for each year is computed by multiplying the net cash flow for the year by the present value factor of $1 for that year, as follows:

Year	Present Value of $1 at 10%	×	Net Cash Flow	=	Present Value of Net Cash Flow
1	0.909		$ 70,000		$ 63,630
2	0.826		60,000		49,560
3	0.751		50,000		37,550
4	0.683		40,000		27,320
5	0.621		40,000		24,840
Total			$260,000		$ 202,900
Amount to be invested					(200,000)
Net present value					$ 2,900

The preceding computations are also graphically illustrated in Exhibit 6.

Exhibit 6
Present Value of Equipment Cash Flows

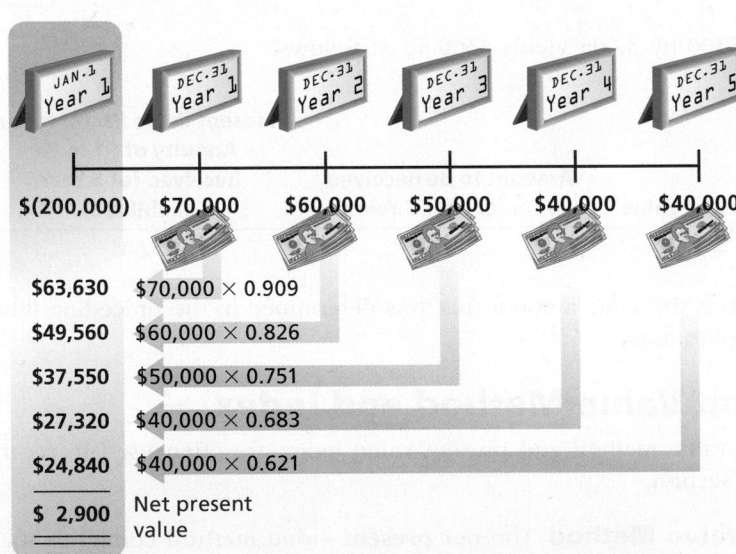

The net present value of $2,900 indicates that the purchase of the new equipment is expected to recover the investment and provide more than the minimum rate of return of 10%. Thus, the purchase of the new equipment is desirable.

The net present value method has the following three advantages:

- It considers the cash flows of the investment.
- It considers the time value of money.
- It can rank projects with equal lives, using the present value index.

The net present value method has the following two disadvantages:

- It has more complex computations than methods that don't use present value.
- It assumes the cash flows can be reinvested at the minimum desired rate of return, which may not be valid.

Vail Resorts uses present values in determining the value of assets and liabilities acquired in business acquisitions.

Source: Vail Resorts, Inc., *Form 10-K for the Fiscal Year Ended July 31, 2015.*

Link to Vail Resorts

Present Value Index When capital investment funds are limited and the proposals involve different investments, a ranking of the proposals can be prepared by using a present value index. The **present value index** is computed as follows:

$$\text{Present Value Index} = \frac{\text{Total Present Value of Net Cash Flow}}{\text{Amount to Be Invested}}$$

The present value index for the investment in the preceding illustration is 1.0145, computed as follows:

$$\text{Present Value Index} = \frac{\$202,900}{\$200,000} = 1.0145$$

Assume that a company is considering three proposals. The net present value and the present value index for each proposal are as follows:

	Proposal A	Proposal B	Proposal C
Total present value of net cash flow	$ 107,000	$ 86,400	$ 86,400
Amount to be invested	(100,000)	(80,000)	(90,000)
Net present value	$ 7,000	$ 6,400	$ (3,600)
Present value index:			
Proposal A ($107,000 ÷ $100,000)	1.07		
Proposal B ($86,400 ÷ $80,000)		1.08	
Proposal C ($86,400 ÷ $90,000)			0.96

A project will have a present value index greater than 1 when the net present value is positive. This is the case for Proposals A and B. When the net present value is negative, the present value index will be less than 1, as is the case for Proposal C.

Although Proposal A has the largest net present value, the present value indices indicate that it is not as desirable as Proposal B. That is, Proposal B returns $1.08 present value per dollar invested, whereas Proposal A returns only $1.07. Proposal B requires an investment of $80,000, compared to an investment of $100,000 for Proposal A. The possible use of the $20,000 difference between Proposals A and B investments should also be considered before making a final decision.

Internal Rate of Return Method

The **internal rate of return (IRR) method** uses present value concepts to compute the rate of return from a capital investment proposal based on its expected net cash flows. This method, sometimes called the *time-adjusted rate of return method*, starts with the proposal's net cash flows and works backward to estimate the proposal's expected rate of return.

To illustrate, assume that management is evaluating the following proposal to purchase new equipment:

Cost of new equipment	$33,530
Yearly expected cash flows to be received	$10,000
Expected life	5 years
Minimum desired rate of return	12%

The present value of the net cash flows, using the present value of an annuity table in Exhibit 5, is $2,520, as shown in Exhibit 7.

Exhibit 7

Net Present Value Analysis at 12%

Annual net cash flow (at the end of each of five years)	$10,000
Present value factor for an annuity of $1 at 12% for five years (Exhibit 5)	× 3.605
Present value of annual net cash flows	$36,050
Amount to be invested	(33,530)
Net present value	$ 2,520

In Exhibit 7, the $36,050 present value of the cash inflows, based on a 12% rate of return, is greater than the $33,530 to be invested. Thus, the internal rate of return must be greater than 12%. Through trial and error, the rate of return equating the $33,530 cost of the investment with the present value of the net cash flows can be determined to be 15%, as shown in Exhibit 8.

Exhibit 8

Present Value of an Annuity at the Internal Rate of Return Rate

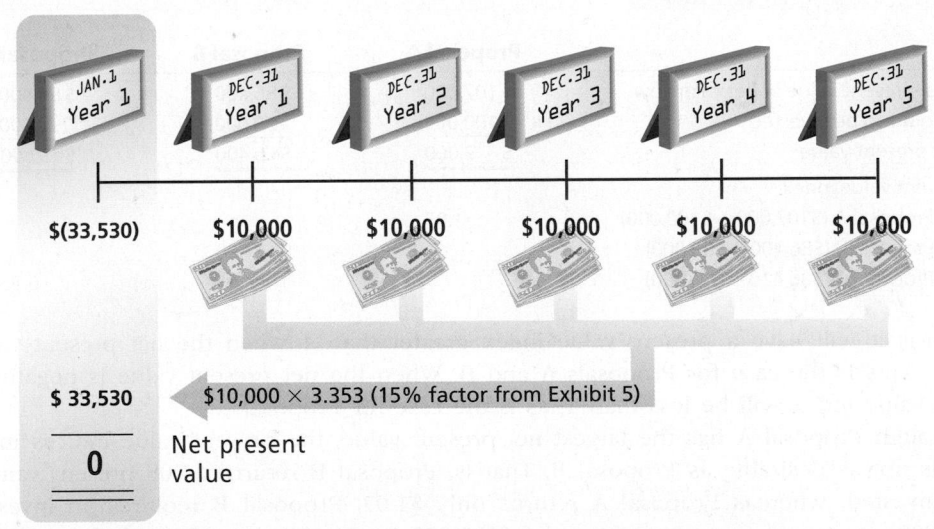

When equal annual net cash flows are expected from a proposal, as in the preceding example, the internal rate of return can be determined as follows:[4]

- Step 1. Determine a present value factor for an annuity of $1 as follows:

$$\text{Present Value Factor for an Annuity of \$1} = \frac{\text{Amount to Be Invested}}{\text{Equal Annual Net Cash Flows}}$$

---

[4] To simplify, equal annual net cash flows are assumed. If the net cash flows are not equal, spreadsheet software can be used to determine the rate of return.

- Step 2. Locate the present value factor determined in Step 1 in the present value of an annuity of $1 table (Exhibit 5) as follows:

    A. Locate the number of years of expected useful life of the investment in the Year column.

    B. Proceed horizontally across the table until you find the present value factor computed in Step 1.

- Step 3. Identify the internal rate of return by the heading of the column in which the present value factor in Step 2 is located.

To illustrate, assume that management is evaluating the following proposal to purchase new equipment:

Cost of new equipment	$97,360
Yearly expected cash flows to be received	$20,000
Expected useful life	7 years

The present value factor for an annuity of $1 is 4.868, computed as follows:

$$\text{Present Value Factor for an Annuity of \$1} = \frac{\text{Amount to Be Invested}}{\text{Equal Annual Net Cash Flows}}$$

$$= \frac{\$97,360}{\$20,000} = 4.868$$

Using the partial present value of an annuity of $1 table shown in Exhibit 9 and a period of seven years, the factor 4.868 is related to 10%. Thus, the internal rate of return for this proposal is 10%.

Present Value of an Annuity of $1 at Compound Interest

		Step 3	
Year	6%	10%	12%
1	0.943	0.909	0.893
2	1.833	1.736	1.690
3	2.673	2.487	2.402
4	3.465	3.170	3.037
5	4.212	3.791	3.605
6	4.917	Step 2(b) 4.355	4.111
Step 2(a) 7	5.582 →	4.868	4.564
8	6.210	5.335	4.968
9	6.802	5.759	5.328
10	7.360	6.145	5.650

Step 1: Determine present value factor for an annuity of $1 $= \dfrac{\$97,360}{\$20,000} = 4.868$

Exhibit 9

Partial Present Value of an Annuity Table

If the minimum acceptable rate of return is 10%, then the proposal is considered acceptable. Several proposals can be ranked by their internal rates of return. The proposal with the highest rate is the most desirable.

The internal rate of return method has the following three advantages:

- It considers the cash flows of the investment.
- It considers the time value of money.
- It ranks proposals based upon the cash flows over their complete useful life, even if the project lives are not the same.

The internal rate of return method has the following two disadvantages:

- It has complex computations, requiring a computer if the periodic cash flows are not equal.
- It assumes the cash received from a proposal can be reinvested at the internal rate of return, which may not be valid.

Check Up Corner 11-2 | **Net Present Value and Internal Rate of Return Analyses**

The management of Broncial Industries Inc. is considering a capital investment project. The net cash flows expected from the project are $50,000 a year for seven years. The project requires an investment of $243,400, and no residual value is expected.

Determine:

A. The net present value for the project, using a minimum rate of return of 6% and the present value of an annuity table appearing in this chapter (Exhibit 5).

B. The present value index. (Round to two decimal places.)

C. The internal rate of return for the project by (1) computing a present value factor for an annuity of $1 and (2) using the present value of an annuity table appearing in this chapter (Exhibit 5).

Solution:

A. & B.

	Net Present Value	Present Value Index
Annual net cash flows	$ 50,000	$ 50,000
Present value factor for an annuity of		
$1 at 6% for 7 periods	× 5.582	× 5.582
Total present value of net cash flows	$ 279,100	$279,100
Amount to be invested	(243,400)	÷243,400
A. Net present value	$ 35,700	
B. Present value index		1.15 (rounded)

The project has a positive net present value, which is also indicated by the present value index, which is greater than 1.00.

C.

$$\text{Present Value Factor for an Annuity of } \$1 = \frac{\text{Amount to Be Invested}}{\text{Equal Annual Net Cash Flows}}$$

$$= \frac{\$243,400}{\$50,000} = 4.868$$

Internal rate of return = 10%

The internal rate of return is the rate of return that equates the present value of equal annual net cash flows to the amount to be invested.

Present Value of an Annuity of $1 at Compound Interest					
Year	6%	10%	12%	15%	20%
1	0.943	0.909	0.893	0.870	0.833
2	1.833	1.736	1.690	1.626	1.528
3	2.673	2.487	2.402	2.283	2.106
4	3.465	3.170	3.037	2.855	2.589
5	4.212	3.791	3.605	3.353	2.991
6	4.917	4.355	4.111	3.785	3.326
7	5.582	4.868	4.564	4.160	3.605
8	6.210	5.335	4.968	4.487	3.837
9	6.802	5.759	5.328	4.772	4.031
10	7.360	6.145	5.650	5.019	4.192

Check Up Corner

Why It Matters

Panera Bread Store Rate of Return

Panera Bread owns, operates, and franchises bakery-cafes throughout the United States. A recent annual report to the Securities and Exchange Commission (SEC Form 10-K) allowed the following information to be determined about an average company-owned store:

Operating profit	$ 405,000
Depreciation	115,000
Investment book value	1,500,000

Assume that the operating profit and depreciation will remain unchanged for the next 15 years. Assume operating profit plus depreciation approximates annual net cash flows and that the investment residual value will be zero. The average rate of return on a company-owned store is:

$$\frac{\$405,000}{\$1,500,000 \div 2} = 54\%$$

The internal rate of return is calculated by first determining the present value of an annuity of $1:

$$\text{Present Value of an Annuity of \$1} = \frac{\$1,500,000}{\$405,000 + \$115,000} = 2.88$$

For a period of five years, this factor implies an internal rate of return of more than 20% (from Exhibit 5). However, if we more realistically assumed these cash flows for 15 years, Panera's company-owned stores generate an estimated internal rate of return of approximately 34% (from a spreadsheet calculation). Clearly, both investment evaluation methods indicate a highly successful business.

Source: Panera Bread, *Form 10-K for the Fiscal Year Ended December 25, 2015.*

Factors That Complicate Capital Investment Analysis

Objective 4
Describe factors that complicate capital investment analysis.

Four widely used methods of evaluating capital investment proposals have been described and illustrated in this chapter. In practice, additional factors such as the following may impact capital investment decisions:

- Income tax
- Proposals with unequal lives
- Leasing versus purchasing
- Uncertainty
- Changes in price levels
- Qualitative factors

Income Tax

The impact of income taxes on capital investment decisions can be material. For example, in determining depreciation for federal income tax purposes, useful lives that are much shorter than the actual useful lives are often used. Also, depreciation for tax purposes often differs from depreciation for financial statement purposes. As a result, the timing of the cash flows for income taxes can have a significant impact on capital investment analysis.[5]

Unequal Proposal Lives

The prior capital investment illustrations assumed that the alternative proposals had the same useful lives. In practice, however, proposals often have different lives.

To illustrate, assume that a company is considering purchasing a new truck or a new computer network. The data for each proposal follow:

	Truck	Computer Network
Cost	$100,000	$100,000
Minimum desired rate of return	10%	10%
Expected useful life	8 years	5 years

---

[5] The impact of taxes on capital investment analysis is covered in advanced accounting textbooks.

Yearly expected cash flows to be received:

Year 1	$ 30,000	$ 30,000
Year 2	30,000	30,000
Year 3	25,000	30,000
Year 4	20,000	30,000
Year 5	15,000	35,000
Year 6	15,000	0
Year 7	10,000	0
Year 8	10,000	0
Total	$155,000	$155,000

The expected cash flows and net present value for each proposal are shown in Exhibit 10. Because of the unequal useful lives, however, the net present values in Exhibit 10 are not comparable.

To make the proposals comparable, the useful lives are adjusted to end at the same time. In this illustration, this is done by assuming that the truck will be sold at the end of five years. The selling price (residual value) of the truck at the end of five years is estimated and included in the cash inflows. Both proposals will then cover five years; thus, the net present value analyses will be comparable.

Exhibit 10 Net Present Value Analysis—Unequal Lives of Proposals

	A	B	C	D
1			Truck	
2		Present	Net	Present
3		Value of	Cash	Value of
4	Year	$1 at 10%	Flow	Net Cash Flow
5	1	0.909	$ 30,000	$ 27,270
6	2	0.826	30,000	24,780
7	3	0.751	25,000	18,775
8	4	0.683	20,000	13,660
9	5	0.621	15,000	9,315
10	6	0.564	15,000	8,460
11	7	0.513	10,000	5,130
12	8	0.467	10,000	4,670
13	Total		$155,000	$112,060
14				
15	Amount to be invested			(100,000)
16	Net present value			$ 12,060
17				

	A	B	C	D
1			Computer Network	
2		Present	Net	Present
3		Value of	Cash	Value of
4	Year	$1 at 10%	Flow	Net Cash Flow
5	1	0.909	$ 30,000	$ 27,270
6	2	0.826	30,000	24,780
7	3	0.751	30,000	22,530
8	4	0.683	30,000	20,490
9	5	0.621	35,000	21,735
10	Total		$155,000	$116,805
11				
12	Amount to be invested			(100,000)
13	Net present value			$ 16,805
14				

Cannot be compared (unequal lives)

Exhibit 11

Net Present Value Analysis— Equalized Lives of Proposals

	A	B	C	D
1		Truck—Revised to 5-Year Life		
2		Present	Net	Present
3		Value of	Cash	Value of
4	Year	$1 at 10%	Flow	Net Cash Flow
5	1	0.909	$ 30,000	$ 27,270
6	2	0.826	30,000	24,780
7	3	0.751	25,000	18,775
8	4	0.683	20,000	13,660
9	5	0.621	15,000	9,315
10	5 (Residual value)	0.621	40,000	24,840
11	Total		$160,000	$118,640
12				
13	Amount to be invested			(100,000)
14	Net present value			$ 18,640
15				

Truck Net Present Value Greater than Computer Network Net Present Value by $1,835

Compared (equal lives)

To illustrate, assume that the truck's estimated selling price (residual value) at the end of Year 5 is $40,000. Exhibit 11 shows the truck's revised present value analysis assuming a five-year life.

As shown in Exhibit 11, the net present value for the truck exceeds the net present value for the computer network by $1,835 ($18,640 – $16,805). Thus, the truck is the more attractive of the two proposals.

Check Up Corner 11-3   Net Present Value—Unequal Lives

Acme Company is evaluating two projects with unequal lives. Project 1 requires an original investment of $50,000. The project will yield cash flows of $12,000 per year for five years. Project 1 could be sold at the end of five years for a price of $30,000. Project 2 has a net present value of $8,900 over a five-year life.

A. Determine the net present value of Project 1 over a five-year life, with residual value, assuming a minimum rate of return of 12%.

B. Which project provides the greater net present value?

Solution:

A.

Present value of $12,000 per year at 12% for 5 years	$ 43,260 ◄	[$12,000 × 3.605 (Exhibit 5, 12%, 5 years)]
Present value of $30,000 at 12% at the end of 5 years	17,010 ◄	[$30,000 × 0.567 (Exhibit 2, 12%, 5 years)]
Total present value of Project 1	$ 60,270	
Total cost of Project 1	(50,000)	
Net present value of Project 1	$ 10,270	

B. **Project 1.** Project 1 has a net present value of $10,270, which is greater than the net present value of Project 2, $8,900.

Check Up Corner

Lease Versus Capital Investment

Leasing fixed assets is common in many industries. For example, hospitals often lease medical equipment. Some advantages of leasing a fixed asset include the following:

■ The company has use of the fixed asset without spending large amounts of cash to purchase the asset.

■ The company eliminates the risk of owning an obsolete asset.

■ The company may deduct the annual lease payments for income tax purposes.

A disadvantage of leasing a fixed asset is that it is normally more costly than purchasing the asset. This is because the lessor (owner of the asset) includes in the rental price not only the costs of owning the asset, but also a profit.

The methods of evaluating capital investment proposals illustrated in this chapter can also be used to decide whether to lease or purchase a fixed asset.

Uncertainty

All capital investment analyses rely on factors that are uncertain. For example, estimates of revenues, expenses, and cash flows are uncertain. This is especially true for long-term capital investments. Errors in one or more of the estimates could lead to incorrect decisions. Methods that consider the impact of uncertainty on capital investment analysis are discussed in advanced accounting and finance textbooks.

Link to
Vail Resorts   A variety of factors add uncertainty to **Vail Resorts**' operations, including the effects of weather, gas and oil prices, economic conditions, and natural disasters such as forest fires and earthquakes.

Why It Matters

If You Build It, They Will Come

A business model describes how an organization delivers products or services to make a profit. Many service companies use what is termed a *network business model*. A network business model connects people and businesses with each other or to a centralized service. Examples of network service businesses include telecommunication, transportation, power and natural gas distribution, cable, satellite, and Internet companies. Network businesses often require significant investment in physical assets in order to create the network. Often, this is described as a *Field of Dreams strategy* (from the movie of that name) because the network can only generate revenue once it is largely built. For example, a cell phone company draws value from having many cell towers linking many callers together. A critical mass of cell towers must be pre-built in order to establish the business. This is risky. As a result, network businesses carefully evaluate capital investments prior to building networks.

Changes in Price Levels

Price levels normally change as the economy improves or deteriorates. General price levels often increase in a rapidly growing economy, which is called **inflation**. During such periods, the rate of return on an investment should exceed the rising price level. If this is not the case, the cash returned on the investment will be less than expected.

Link to
Vail Resorts   Some of **Vail Resorts**' rental (lease) agreements include increases for inflation that are linked to the Consumer Price Index (CPI).

Price levels may also change for foreign investments. This occurs as currency exchange rates change. **Currency exchange rates** are the rates at which currency in another country can be exchanged for U.S. dollars.

If the amount of local dollars that can be exchanged for one U.S. dollar increases, then the local currency is said to be weakening to the dollar. When a company has an investment in another country where the local currency is weakening, the return on the investment, as expressed in U.S. dollars, is adversely impacted. This is because the expected amount of local currency returned on the investment would purchase fewer U.S. dollars.[6]

Link to
Vail Resorts   In a recent financial statement, **Vail Resorts** reported a negative foreign currency adjustment of $(132) million.

---

[6] Further discussion on accounting for foreign currency transactions is available on the companion Web site at www.cengagebrain.com.

Qualitative Considerations

Some benefits of capital investments are qualitative in nature and cannot be estimated in dollar terms. However, if a company does not consider qualitative considerations, an acceptable investment proposal could be rejected.

Some examples of qualitative considerations that may influence capital investment analysis include the investment proposal's impact on the following:

- Product quality
- Manufacturing flexibility
- Employee morale
- Manufacturing productivity
- Market (strategic) opportunities

Many qualitative factors may be as important as, if not more important than, quantitative factors.

The mission of **Vail Resorts** is to provide exceptional guest experiences at each of its resorts.

Source: Vail Resorts, Inc., *Form 10-K for the Fiscal Year Ended July 31, 2015.*

Link to
Vail Resorts

 Ethics: Don't Do It!

Assumption Fudging

The results of any capital budgeting analysis depend on many subjective estimates, such as the cash flows, discount rate, time period, and total investment amount. The results of the analysis should be used to either support or reject a project. Capital budgeting should not be used to justify an assumed net present value. That is, the analyst should not work backwards, filling in assumed numbers that will produce the desired net present value. Such a reverse approach reduces the credibility of the entire process.

Capital Rationing

Capital rationing is the process by which management allocates funds among competing capital investment proposals. In this process, management often uses a combination of the methods described in this chapter.

Exhibit 12 illustrates the capital rationing decision process. Alternative proposals are initially screened by establishing minimum standards, using the cash payback and the average rate of return methods. The proposals that survive this screening are further analyzed, using the net present value and internal rate of return methods.

Qualitative factors related to each proposal should also be considered throughout the capital rationing process. For example, new equipment might improve the quality of the product and, thus, increase consumer satisfaction and sales.

At the end of the capital rationing process, accepted proposals are ranked and compared with the funds available. Proposals that are selected for funding are included in the capital expenditures budget. Unfunded proposals may be reconsidered if funds later become available.

Objective 5
Describe and diagram the capital rationing process.

Exhibit 12
Capital Rationing
Decision Process

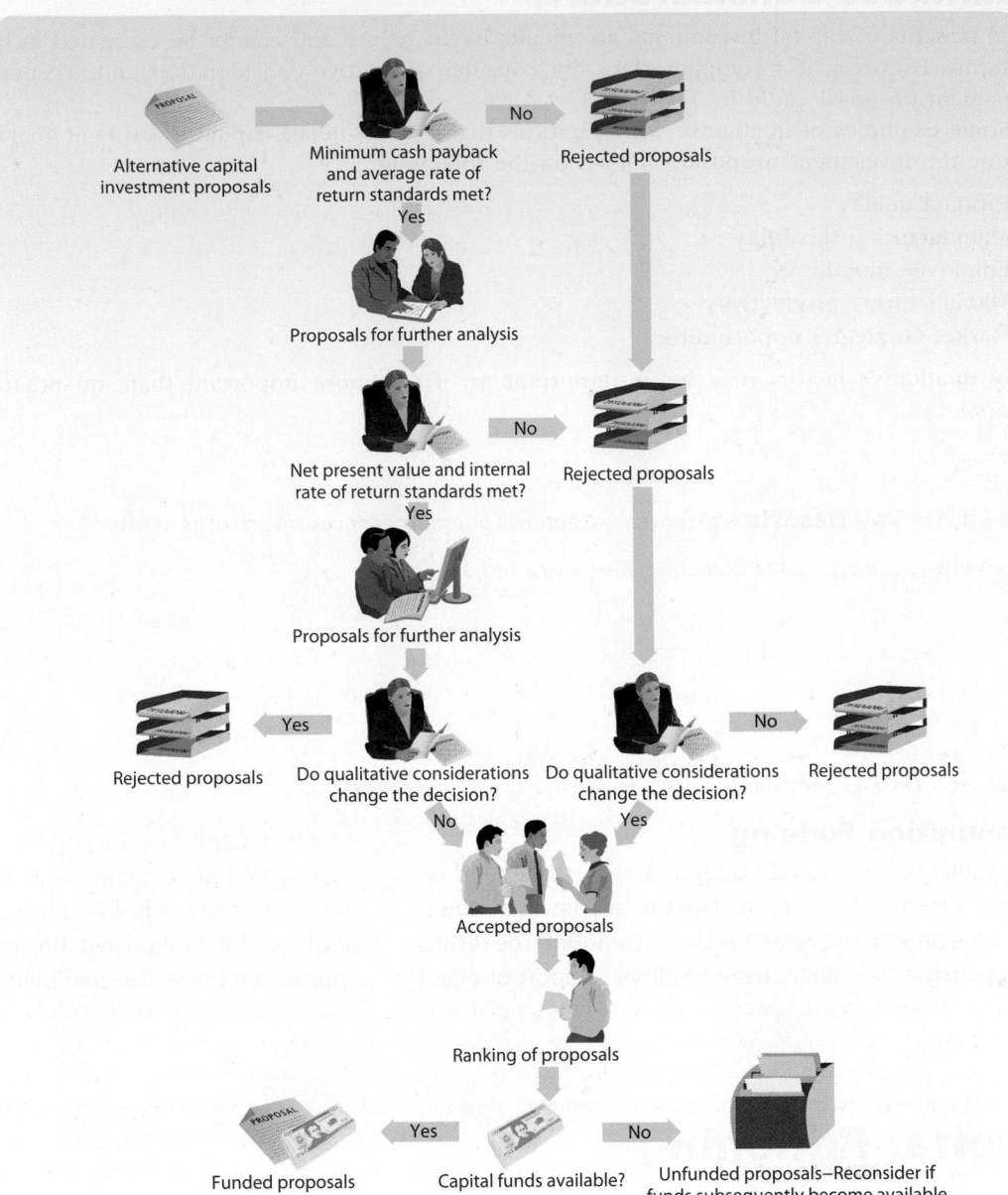

Alternative capital investment proposals

Minimum cash payback and average rate of return standards met?

No → Rejected proposals

Yes

Proposals for further analysis

Net present value and internal rate of return standards met?

No → Rejected proposals

Yes

Proposals for further analysis

Yes ← Rejected proposals

Do qualitative considerations change the decision?

No

Do qualitative considerations change the decision?

No → Rejected proposals

Yes

Accepted proposals

Ranking of proposals

Yes

Funded proposals

Capital funds available?

No

Unfunded proposals—Reconsider if funds subsequently become available

Analysis for Decision Making

Capital Investment for Sustainability

In Chapter 1, we defined sustainability as the practice of operating a business to maximize profits while attempting to preserve the environment, economy, and needs of future generations. Sustainability practices often require capital investments in order to establish these priorities. Some examples are listed in Exhibit 13.

Objective

Describe and illustrate the use of capital investment analysis in evaluating a sustainability investment.

Sustainability Objective	Capital Investment Example
Minimize resource waste and environmental degradation	Invest in land, soil, and water reclamation projects for a mining company.
Develop new sustainable markets	Invest in equipment to produce an environmentally safe cleaning product for a consumer products company.
Reduce litigation risks	Invest in wastewater recycling to avoid river contamination and potential legal liability for a papermaking company.
Maintain an attractive and safe working environment	Invest in an employee wellness and fitness center to attract and retain high-performance employees for a software company.

Exhibit 13

Examples of Sustainability Capital Investments

Often, sustainability investments can be analyzed using methods described in this chapter. An example would be manufacturing equipment for the new environmentally safe cleaning product listed in Exhibit 13. In contrast, the benefits of some sustainability investments may be difficult to measure and, thus, must be evaluated qualitatively. An example might be the wellness and fitness center for employees listed in Exhibit 13. In addition, sustainability investments may be legally mandated and, thus, are justified more by the requirements of the law than by their immediate economic benefits. Examples might be the land, soil, and water reclamation projects and the wastewater recycling project listed in Exhibit 13.

To illustrate a capital investment analysis, Carpenter Company proposes to install solar panels to satisfy a portion of its power requirements for its manufacturing plant. The solar panels investment cost is $150,000. The solar panels operating and maintenance cost is expected to be $20,000 per year. The plant uses an average of 3,000 kilowatt-hours (kwh) per day for 250 sunny days per year. A kilowatt-hour is the use of 1,000 watts per hour and is a standard measure of electricity consumption. The solar panels replace metered electricity from the power company that costs Carpenter $0.12 per kwh. The solar panels are expected to last 10 years with no salvage value.

Annual cost savings:

Kilowatt-hours per day	3,000	kwh
Number of sunny operating days	× 250	days
Kilowatt-hours per year	750,000	kwh
Metered electricity cost per kwh	× $0.12	per kwh
Total metered cost savings	$ 90,000	
Annual solar panel operating cost	(20,000)	
Net annual savings	$ 70,000	

The net present value of the project, assuming a minimum rate of return of 10%, is (use Exhibit 5):

Annual net cash flow savings from installing solar panels	$ 70,000
Present value factor for an annuity of $1 at 10% for 10 periods	× 6.145
Present value of annual savings (rounded)	$ 430,150
Amount to be invested	(150,000)
Net present value	$ 280,150

The net present value is positive; thus, the proposal is supported by the analysis.

Make a Decision — Capital Investment for Sustainability

Den-Tex Company is evaluating a proposal to replace its HID (high intensity discharge) lighting with LED (light emitting diode) lighting throughout its warehouse. LED lighting consumes less power and lasts longer than HID lighting for similar performance. The following information was developed:

HID watt hour consumption per fixture	500 watts per hr.
LED watt hour consumption per fixture	300 watts per hr.
Number of fixtures	700
Lifetime investment cost (in present value terms) to replace each HID fixture with LED	$500
Operating hours per day	10
Operating days per year	300
Metered utility rate per kilowatt-hour (kwh)*	$0.11

*Note a kilowatt-hour equals 1,000 watts per hour.

A. Determine the investment cost for replacing the 700 fixtures.

B. Determine the annual utility cost savings from employing the new energy solution.

C. Should the proposal be accepted? Evaluate the proposal using net present value, assuming a 15-year life and 8% minimum rate of return.

Solution:

A.
Lifetime cost to replace each HID fixture with LED	$ 500
Number of fixtures	× 700
Investment cost	$350,000

B.
HID kilowatt-hour consumption per fixture	0.5*
LED kilowatt-hour consumption per fixture	(0.3)
Kilowatt-hour savings per fixture	0.2
Number of operating hours per day	× 10
Number of operating days per year	× 300
Number of fixtures	× 700
Kilowatt-hour savings per year	420,000
Metered utility rate per kwh	× $0.11
Annual utility cost savings	$ 46,200

* 500 watts ÷ 1,000 watts = 0.5 kilowatts

C.
Annual net cash flow savings from installing LED	$ 46,200
Present value factor for an annuity of $1 at 8% for 15 periods (Appendix A)	× 8.55948
Present value of annual savings (rounded)	$ 395,448
Amount to be invested	(350,000)
Net present value	$ 45,448

The net present value is positive; thus, the proposal should be accepted.

Make a Decision

Let's Review

Chapter Summary

1. Capital investment analysis is the process by which management plans, evaluates, and controls investments involving fixed assets. Capital investment analysis is important to a business because such investments affect profitability for a long period of time.

2. The average rate of return method measures the expected profitability of an investment in fixed assets. The expected period of time that will pass between the date of an investment and the complete recovery in cash (or equivalent) of the amount invested is the cash payback period.

3. The net present value method computes the net present value of the cash inflows expected from a proposal and compares the result to the amount to be invested. The internal rate of return method uses present values to compute the rate of return from the net cash flows expected from capital investment proposals.

4. Factors that may complicate capital investment analysis include the impact of income tax, unequal lives of alternative proposals, leasing, uncertainty, changes in price levels, and qualitative considerations.

5. Capital rationing refers to the process by which management allocates available investment funds among competing capital investment proposals. A diagram of the capital rationing process appears in Exhibit 12.

Key Terms

annuity (530)
average rate of return (525)
capital investment analysis (524)
capital rationing (541)
cash payback period (526)

currency exchange rate (540)
inflation (540)
internal rate of return
  (IRR) method (533)
net present value method (531)

present value concepts (529)
present value index (533)
present value of an annuity (530)
time value of money concept (524)

Practice

Multiple-Choice Questions

1. Methods of evaluating capital investment proposals that ignore present value include:
   A. average rate of return.
   B. cash payback.
   C. both A and B.
   D. neither A nor B.

2. Management is considering a $100,000 investment in a project with a five-year life and no residual value. If the total income from the project is expected to be $60,000 and straight-line depreciation is used, the average rate of return is:
   A. 12%.
   B. 24%.
   C. 60%.
   D. 75%.

3. The expected period of time that will elapse between the date of a capital investment and the complete recovery of the amount of cash invested is called the:

    A. average rate of return period.   C. net present value period.

    B. cash payback period.   D. internal rate of return period.

4. A project that will cost $120,000 is estimated to generate cash flows of $25,000 per year for eight years. What is the net present value of the project, assuming an 11% required rate of return? (Use the present value tables in Appendix A.)

    A. $(38,214)   C. $55,180

    B. $8,653   D. $75,000

5. A project is estimated to generate cash flows of $40,000 per year for 10 years. The cost of the project is $226,009. What is the internal rate of return for this project?

    A. 8%   C. 12%

    B. 10%   D. 14%

Answers provided after Problem. Need more practice? Find additional multiple-choice questions, exercises, and problems in CengageNOWv2.

Exercises

SHOW ME HOW

1. Average rate of return
Obj. 2

Determine the average rate of return for a project that is estimated to yield total income of $170,000 over five years, has a cost of $320,000, and has a $20,000 residual value.

SHOW ME HOW

2. Cash payback period
Obj. 2

A project has estimated annual net cash flows of $118,600. It is estimated to cost $616,720. Determine the cash payback period. (Round to one decimal place.)

SHOW ME HOW

3. Net present value
Obj. 3

A project has estimated annual net cash flows of $6,800 for five years and is estimated to cost $23,125. Assume a minimum acceptable rate of return of 12%. Using Exhibit 5, determine (1) the net present value of the project and (2) the present value index, rounded to two decimal places.

SHOW ME HOW

4. Internal rate of return
Obj. 3

A project is estimated to cost $104,328 and provide annual net cash flows of $21,000 for eight years. Determine the internal rate of return for this project, using Exhibit 5.

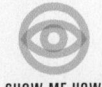
SHOW ME HOW

5. Net present value—unequal lives
Obj. 4

Project A requires an original investment of $32,600. The project will yield cash flows of $7,000 per year for nine years. Project B has a calculated net present value of $3,500 over a six-year life. Project A could be sold at the end of six years for a price of $15,000. (A) Determine the net present value of Project A over a six-year life, with residual value, assuming a minimum rate of return of 12%. (B) Which project provides the greatest net present value?

Answers provided after Problem. Need more practice? Find additional multiple-choice questions, exercises, and problems in CengageNOWv2.

Problem

The capital investment committee of Hopewell Company is currently considering two investments. The estimated income from operations and net cash flows expected from each investment are as follows:

	Truck		Equipment	
Year	Income from Operations	Net Cash Flow	Income from Operations	Net Cash Flow
1	$ 6,000	$ 22,000	$13,000	$ 29,000
2	9,000	25,000	10,000	26,000
3	10,000	26,000	8,000	24,000
4	8,000	24,000	8,000	24,000
5	11,000	27,000	3,000	19,000
	$44,000	$124,000	$42,000	$122,000

Each investment requires $80,000. Straight-line depreciation will be used, and no residual value is expected. The committee has selected a rate of 15% for purposes of the net present value analysis.

Instructions

1. Compute the following:

   A. The average rate of return for each investment.

   B. The net present value for each investment. Use the present value of $1 table appearing in this chapter (Exhibit 2).

2. Why is the net present value of the equipment greater than the truck, even though its average rate of return is less?

3. Prepare a summary for the capital investment committee, advising it on the relative merits of the two investments.

Need more practice? Find additional multiple-choice questions, exercises, and problems in CengageNOWv2.

Answers

Multiple-Choice Questions

1. **C** Methods of evaluating capital investment proposals that ignore the time value of money include the average rate of return method (answer A) and the cash payback method (answer B).

2. **B** The average rate of return is 24% (answer B), determined by dividing the expected average annual earnings by the average investment, as follows:

$$\frac{\$60,000 \div 5}{(\$100,000 + \$0) \div 2} = 24\%$$

3. **B** Of the four methods of analyzing proposals for capital investments, the cash payback period (answer B) refers to the expected period of time required to recover the amount of cash to be invested. The average rate of return (answer A) is a measure of the anticipated profitability of a proposal. The net present value method (answer C) reduces the expected future net cash flows originating from a proposal to their present values. The internal rate of return method (answer D) uses present value concepts to compute the rate of return from the net cash flows expected from the investment.

4. **B** The net present value is determined as follows:

Present value of $25,000 for 8 years at 11% ($25,000 × 5.14612)	$ 128,653
Project cost	(120,000)
Net present value	$ 8,653

5. **C** The internal rate of return for this project is determined by solving for the present value of an annuity factor that when multiplied by $40,000 will equal $226,009. By division, the factor is:

$$\frac{\$226,009}{\$40,000} = 5.65022$$

In Appendix A on pp. A-4 and A-5, scan along the n = 10 years row until finding the 5.65022 factor. The column for this factor is 12%.

Exercises

1. Estimate average annual income $34,000 ($170,000 ÷ 5 years)
   Average investment $170,000 [($320,000 + $20,000) ÷ 2]
   Average rate of return   20% ($34,000 ÷ $170,000)

2. 5.2 years ($616,720 ÷ $118,600)

3. A. $1,389   [($6,800 × 3.605) − $23,125]

   B. 1.06   ($24,514 ÷ $23,125)

4. 12%   [($104,328 ÷ $21,000) = 4.968, the present value of an annuity factor for eight periods at 12%, from Exhibit 5]

5. A.

Present value of $7,000 per year at 12% for 6 years*	$ 28,777
Present value of $15,000 at 12% at the end of 6 years**	7,605
Total present value of Project A	$ 36,382
Total cost of Project A	(32,600)
Net present value of Project A	$ 3,782

   *[$7,000 × 4.111 (Exhibit 5, 12%, 6 years)]
   **[$15,000 × 0.507 (Exhibit 2, 12%, 6 years)]

   B. Project A. Project A's net present value of $3,782 is more than the net present value of Project B, $3,500.

Need more help? Watch step-by-step videos of how to compute answers to these Exercises in CengageNOWv2.

Problem

1. A. Average rate of return for the truck:

$$\frac{\$44,000 \div 5}{(\$80,000 + \$0) \div 2} = 22\%$$

   Average rate of return for the equipment:

$$\frac{\$42,000 \div 5}{(\$80,000 + \$0) \div 2} = 21\%$$

B. Net present value analysis:

Year	Present Value Factor for $1 at 15%	Net Cash Flow		Present Value of Net Cash Flow	
		Truck	Equipment	Truck	Equipment
1	0.870	$ 22,000	$ 29,000	$ 19,140	$ 25,230
2	0.756	25,000	26,000	18,900	19,656
3	0.658	26,000	24,000	17,108	15,792
4	0.572	24,000	24,000	13,728	13,728
5	0.497	27,000	19,000	13,419	9,443
Total		$124,000	$122,000	$ 82,295	$ 83,849
Amount to be invested				(80,000)	(80,000)
Net present value				$ 2,295	$ 3,849

2. The equipment has a lower average rate of return than the truck because the equipment's total income from operations for the five years is $42,000, which is $2,000 less than the truck's. Even so, the net present value of the equipment is greater than that of the truck because the equipment has higher cash flows in the early years.

3. Both investments exceed the selected rate established for the net present value analysis. The truck has a higher average rate of return, but the equipment offers a larger net present value. Thus, if only one of the two investments can be accepted, the equipment would be the more attractive.

Discussion Questions

1. What are the principal objections to the use of the average rate of return method in evaluating capital investment proposals?

2. Discuss the principal limitations of the cash payback method for evaluating capital investment proposals.

3. Why would the average rate of return differ from the internal rate of return on the same project?

4. Your boss has suggested that a one-year payback period is the same as a 100% average rate of return. Do you agree?

5. Why would the cash payback method understate the attractiveness of a project with a large residual value?

6. Why would the use of the cash payback period for analyzing the financial performance of theatrical releases from a motion picture production studio be supported over the net present value method?

7. A net present value analysis used to evaluate a proposed equipment acquisition indicated a $7,900 net present value. What is the meaning of the $7,900 as it relates to the desirability of the proposal?

8. Two projects have an identical net present value of $9,000. Are both projects equal in desirability?

9. What are the major disadvantages of the use of the net present value method of analyzing capital investment proposals?

10. What are the major disadvantages of the use of the internal rate of return method of analyzing capital investment proposals?

11. What are the major advantages of leasing a fixed asset rather than purchasing it?

12. Give an example of a qualitative factor that should be considered in a capital investment analysis related to acquiring automated factory equipment.

Basic Exercises

SHOW ME HOW

BE 11-1 Average rate of return
Obj. 2

Determine the average rate of return for a project that is estimated to yield total income of $170,000 over five years, has a cost of $320,000, and has a $20,000 residual value.

SHOW ME HOW

BE 11-2 Cash payback period
Obj. 2

A project has estimated annual net cash flows of $36,500. It is estimated to cost $222,650. Determine the cash payback period. (Round to one decimal place.)

SHOW ME HOW

BE 11-3 Net present value
Obj. 3

A project has estimated annual net cash flows of $70,000 for four years and is estimated to cost $190,000. Assume a minimum acceptable rate of return of 10%. Using Exhibit 5, determine (A) the net present value of the project and (B) the present value index, rounded to two decimal places.

SHOW ME HOW

BE 11-4 Internal rate of return
Obj. 3

A project is estimated to cost $463,565 and provide annual net cash flows of $115,000 for nine years. Determine the internal rate of return for this project, using Exhibit 5.

SHOW ME HOW

BE 11-5 Net present value—unequal lives
Obj. 4

Project 1 requires an original investment of $125,000. The project will yield cash flows of $50,000 per year for 10 years. Project 2 has a calculated net present value of $135,000 over an eight-year life. Project 1 could be sold at the end of eight years for a price of $8,000. (A) Determine the net present value of Project 1 over an eight-year life, with residual value, assuming a minimum rate of return of 12%. (B) Which project provides the greatest net present value?

Exercises

✔ 3D Printer, 16%

SHOW ME HOW

EX 11-1 Average rate of return
Obj. 2

The following data are accumulated by Lone Peak Inc. in evaluating two competing capital investment proposals:

	3D Printer	Truck
Amount of investment	$40,000	$50,000
Useful life	7 years	10 years
Estimated residual value	$3,000	$6,000
Estimated total income over the useful life	$24,080	$36,400

Determine the expected average rate of return for each proposal.

EX 11-2 Average rate of return—cost savings
Obj. 2

Midwest Fabricators Inc. is considering an investment in equipment that will replace direct labor. The equipment has a cost of $132,000 with a $16,000 residual value and a 10-year life. The equipment will replace one employee who has an average wage of $34,000 per year. In addition, the equipment will have operating and energy costs of $5,380 per year.

Determine the average rate of return on the equipment, giving effect to straight-line depreciation on the investment.

EX 11-3 Average rate of return—new product

Obj. 2

✔ Average annual income, $405,000

SHOW ME HOW

Galactic Inc. is considering an investment in new equipment that will be used to manufacture a smartphone. The phone is expected to generate additional annual sales of 6,000 units at $250 per unit. The equipment has a cost of $850,000, residual value of $50,000, and an eight-year life. The equipment can only be used to manufacture the phone. The cost to manufacture the phone follows:

Cost per unit:	
Direct labor	$ 15.00
Direct materials	134.00
Factory overhead (including depreciation)	33.50
Total cost per unit	$182.50

Determine the average rate of return on the equipment.

EX 11-4 Calculate cash flows

Obj. 2

✔ Year 1: $(168,500)

SHOW ME HOW

Nature's Way Inc. is planning to invest in new manufacturing equipment to make a new garden tool. The new garden tool is expected to generate additional annual sales of 2,500 units at $60 each. The new manufacturing equipment will cost $227,000 and is expected to have a 10-year life and $17,000 residual value. Selling expenses related to the new product are expected to be 5% of sales revenue. The cost to manufacture the product includes the following on a per-unit basis:

Direct labor	$ 8.00
Direct materials	22.00
Fixed factory overhead—depreciation	8.40
Variable factory overhead	3.60
Total	$42.00

Determine the net cash flows for the first year of the project, Years 2–9, and for the last year of the project.

EX 11-5 Cash payback period for a service company

Obj. 2

✔ Location 1: 4.5 years

SHOW ME HOW

Chinook Industries Inc. is evaluating two capital investment proposals for a retail outlet, each requiring an investment of $900,000 and each with an eight-year life and expected total net cash flows of $1,000,000. Location 1 is expected to provide equal annual net cash flows of $200,000, and Location 2 is expected to have the following unequal annual net cash flows:

Year 1	$300,000	Year 5	$50,000
Year 2	220,000	Year 6	50,000
Year 3	180,000	Year 7	30,000
Year 4	150,000	Year 8	20,000

Determine the cash payback period for both location proposals.

EX 11-6 Cash payback method

Obj. 2

EXCEL TEMPLATE

Lily Products Company is considering an investment in one of two new product lines. The investment required for either product line is $540,000. The net cash flows associated with each product are as follows:

Year	Liquid Soap	Body Lotion
1	$170,000	$ 90,000
2	150,000	90,000
3	120,000	90,000
4	100,000	90,000
5	70,000	90,000
6	40,000	90,000
7	40,000	90,000
8	30,000	90,000
Total	$720,000	$720,000

(Continued)

A. Recommend a product offering to Lily Products Company, based on the cash payback period for each product line.

B. ━━━▸ Why is one product line preferred over the other, even though they both have the same total net cash flows through eight periods?

EX 11-7 Net present value method   Obj. 3

✔ A. NPV, $24,520

SHOW ME HOW

The following data are accumulated by Geddes Company in evaluating the purchase of $150,000 of equipment, having a four-year useful life:

	Net Income	Net Cash Flow
Year 1	$42,500	$80,000
Year 2	27,500	65,000
Year 3	12,500	50,000
Year 4	2,500	40,000

A. Assuming that the desired rate of return is 15%, determine the net present value for the proposal. Use the table of the present value of $1 appearing in Exhibit 2 of this chapter.

B. ━━━▸ Would management be likely to look with favor on the proposal? Explain.

EX 11-8 Net present value method for a service company   Obj. 3

✔ A. 20Y1, $13,000

AM Express Inc. is considering the purchase of an additional delivery vehicle for $55,000 on January 1, 20Y1. The truck is expected to have a five-year life with an expected residual value of $15,000 at the end of five years. The expected additional revenues from the added delivery capacity are anticipated to be $58,000 per year for each of the next five years. A driver will cost $42,000 in 20Y1, with an expected annual salary increase of $1,000 for each year thereafter. The annual operating costs for the truck are estimated to be $3,000 per year.

A. Determine the expected annual net cash flows from the delivery truck investment for 20Y1–20Y5.

B. Calculate the net present value of the investment, assuming that the minimum desired rate of return is 12%. Use the present value of $1 table appearing in Exhibit 2 of this chapter.

C. ━━━▸ Is the additional truck a good investment based on your analysis? Explain.

EX 11-9 Net present value method—annuity for a service company   Obj. 3

✔ B. $8 million

SHOW ME HOW

Welcome Inn Hotels is considering the construction of a new hotel for $90 million. The expected life of the hotel is 30 years, with no residual value. The hotel is expected to earn revenues of $26 million per year. Total expenses, including depreciation, are expected to be $15 million per year. Welcome Inn management has set a minimum acceptable rate of return of 14%.

A. Determine the equal annual net cash flows from operating the hotel.

B. Calculate the net present value of the new hotel, using the present value of an annuity of $1 table found in Appendix A. (Round to the nearest million dollars.)

C. ━━━▸ Does your analysis support construction of the new hotel? Explain.

EX 11-10 Net present value method—annuity   Obj. 3

✔ A. $46,000

Briggs Excavation Company is planning an investment of $132,000 for a bulldozer. The bulldozer is expected to operate for 1,500 hours per year for five years. Customers will be charged $110 per hour for bulldozer work. The bulldozer operator costs $28 per hour in wages and benefits. The bulldozer is expected to require annual maintenance costing $8,000. The bulldozer uses fuel that is expected to cost $46 per hour of bulldozer operation.

A. Determine the equal annual net cash flows from operating the bulldozer.

B. Determine the net present value of the investment, assuming that the desired rate of return is 10%. Use the present value of an annuity of $1 table in the chapter (Exhibit 5). (Round to the nearest dollar.)

C. ━━━▸ Should Briggs invest in the bulldozer, based on this analysis? Explain.

D. Determine the number of operating hours such that the present value of cash flows equals the amount to be invested. (Round all calculations to whole numbers.)

EX 11-11 Net present value method for a service company

Obj. 3

✔ A. $157,600,000

REAL WORLD

Carnival Corporation has recently placed into service some of the largest cruise ships in the world. One of these ships, the *Carnival Breeze*, can hold up to 3,600 passengers, and it can cost $750 million to build. Assume the following additional information:

- There will be 330 cruise days per year operated at a full capacity of 3,600 passengers.
- The variable expenses per passenger are estimated to be $140 per cruise day.
- The revenue per passenger is expected to be $340 per cruise day.
- The fixed expenses for running the ship, other than depreciation, are estimated to be $80,000,000 per year.
- The ship has a service life of 10 years, with a residual value of $140,000,000 at the end of 10 years.

A. Determine the annual net cash flow from operating the cruise ship.

B. Determine the net present value of this investment, assuming a 12% minimum rate of return. Use the present value tables (Exhibit 2 and Exhibit 5) provided in the chapter in determining your answer.

EX 11-12 Present value index

Obj. 3

✔ Ft. Collins, 0.98

Dip N' Dunk Doughnuts has computed the net present value for capital expenditure at two locations. Relevant data related to the computation are as follows:

	Ft. Collins	Boulder
Total present value of net cash flow	$ 607,600	$ 624,000
Amount to be invested	(620,000)	(600,000)
Net present value	$(12,400)	$ 24,000

A. Determine the present value index for each proposal.

B. ━━━▶ Which location does your analysis support? Explain.

EX 11-13 Net present value method and present value index

Obj. 3

✔ B. Packing machine, 1.55

Diamond & Turf Inc. is considering an investment in one of two machines. The sewing machine will increase productivity from sewing 150 baseballs per hour to sewing 290 per hour. The contribution margin per unit is $0.32 per baseball. Assume that any increased production of baseballs can be sold. The second machine is an automatic packing machine for the golf ball line. The packing machine will reduce packing labor cost. The labor cost saved is equivalent to $21 per hour. The sewing machine will cost $260,000, have an eight-year life, and will operate for 1,800 hours per year. The packing machine will cost $85,000, have an eight-year life, and will operate for 1,400 hours per year. Diamond & Turf seeks a minimum rate of return of 15% on its investments.

A. Determine the net present value for the two machines. Use the present value of an annuity of $1 table in the chapter (Exhibit 5). (Round to the nearest dollar.)

B. Determine the present value index for the two machines. (Round to two decimal places.)

C. ━━━▶ If Diamond & Turf has sufficient funds for only one of the machines and qualitative factors are equal between the two machines, in which machine should it invest? Explain.

EX 11-14 Average rate of return, cash payback period, net present value method for a service company

Obj. 2, 3

✔ B. 4 years

SHOW ME HOW

Spanish Peaks Railroad Inc. is considering acquiring equipment at a cost of $1,250,000. The equipment has an estimated life of eight years and no residual value. It is expected to provide yearly net cash flows of $312,500. The company's minimum desired rate of return for net present value analysis is 12%.

Compute the following:

A. The average rate of return, giving effect to straight-line depreciation on the investment.

B. The cash payback period.

C. The net present value. Use the present value of an annuity of $1 table appearing in this chapter (Exhibit 5).

EX 11-15 Cash payback period, net present value analysis, and qualitative considerations Obj. 2, 3, 4

✔ A. 4 years

The plant manager of Shenzhen Electronics Company is considering the purchase of new automated assembly equipment. The new equipment will cost $1,400,000. The manager believes that the new investment will result in direct labor savings of $350,000 per year for 10 years.

A. What is the payback period on this project?

B. What is the net present value, assuming a 10% rate of return? Use the present value of an annuity of $1 table in Exhibit 5.

C. ➤ What else should the manager consider in the analysis?

EX 11-16 Internal rate of return method Obj. 3

✔ A. 3.785

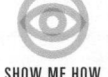

SHOW ME HOW

The internal rate of return method is used by Testerman Construction Co. in analyzing a capital expenditure proposal that involves an investment of $113,550 and annual net cash flows of $30,000 for each of the six years of its useful life.

A. Determine a present value factor for an annuity of $1, which can be used in determining the internal rate of return.

B. Using the factor determined in part (A) and the present value of an annuity of $1 table appearing in this chapter (Exhibit 5), determine the internal rate of return for the proposal.

EX 11-17 Internal rate of return method for a service company Obj. 3, 4

REAL WORLD

Park City Mountain Resort, a Utah ski resort, announced a $415 million expansion of lodging properties, lifts, and terrain. Assume that this investment is estimated to produce $99 million in equal annual cash flows for each of the first 10 years of the project life.

A. Determine the expected internal rate of return of this project for 10 years, using the present value of an annuity of $1 table found in Exhibit 5.

B. ➤ What are some uncertainties that could reduce the internal rate of return of this project?

EX 11-18 Internal rate of return method—two projects Obj. 3

✔ A. Delivery truck, 15%

Munch N' Crunch Snack Company is considering two possible investments: a delivery truck or a bagging machine. The delivery truck would cost $43,056 and could be used to deliver an additional 95,000 bags of pretzels per year. Each bag of pretzels can be sold for a contribution margin of $0.45. The delivery truck operating expenses, excluding depreciation, are $1.35 per mile for 24,000 miles per year. The bagging machine would replace an old bagging machine, and its net investment cost would be $61,614. The new machine would require three fewer hours of direct labor per day. Direct labor is $18 per hour. There are 250 operating days in the year. Both the truck and the bagging machine are estimated to have seven-year lives. The minimum rate of return is 13%. However, Munch N' Crunch has funds to invest in only one of the projects.

A. Compute the internal rate of return for each investment. Use the present value of an annuity of $1 table appearing in this chapter (Exhibit 5).

B. ➤ Provide a memo to management, with a recommendation.

EX 11-19 Net present value method and internal rate of return method for a service company

Obj. 3

✔ A. ($12,845)

Buckeye Healthcare Corp. is proposing to spend $186,725 on an eight-year project that has estimated net cash flows of $35,000 for each of the eight years.

A. Compute the net present value, using a rate of return of 12%. Use the present value of an annuity of $1 table in the chapter (Exhibit 5).

B. ━━━➤ Based on the analysis prepared in part (A), is the internal rate of return (1) more than 12%, (2) 12%, or (3) less than 12%? Explain.

C. Determine the internal rate of return by computing a present value factor for an annuity of $1 and using the present value of an annuity of $1 table presented in the text (Exhibit 5).

EX 11-20 Identify error in capital investment analysis calculations

Obj. 3

Artscape Inc. is considering the purchase of automated machinery that is expected to have a useful life of five years and no residual value. The average rate of return on the average investment has been computed to be 20%, and the cash payback period was computed to be 5.5 years.

━━━➤ Do you see any reason to question the validity of the data presented? Explain.

EX 11-21 Net present value—unequal lives

Obj. 3, 4

✔ Net present value, Processing mill, $196,220

Bunker Hill Mining Company has two competing proposals: a processing mill and an electric shovel. Both pieces of equipment have an initial investment of $750,000. The net cash flows estimated for the two proposals are as follows:

EXCEL TEMPLATE

	Net Cash Flow	
Year	Processing Mill	Electric Shovel
1	$310,000	$330,000
2	260,000	325,000
3	260,000	325,000
4	260,000	320,000
5	180,000	
6	130,000	
7	120,000	
8	120,000	

The estimated residual value of the processing mill at the end of Year 4 is $280,000.

Determine which equipment should be favored, comparing the net present values of the two proposals and assuming a minimum rate of return of 15%. Use the present value tables presented in this chapter (Exhibit 2).

EX 11-22 Net present value—unequal lives

Obj. 3, 4

✔ Net present value, blending equipment, $6,344

Daisy's Creamery Inc. is considering one of two investment options. Option 1 is a $75,000 investment in new blending equipment that is expected to produce equal annual cash flows of $19,000 for each of seven years. Option 2 is a $90,000 investment in a new computer system that is expected to produce equal annual cash flows of $27,000 for each of five years. The residual value of the blending equipment at the end of the fifth year is estimated to be $15,000. The computer system has no expected residual value at the end of the fifth year.

Assume there is sufficient capital to fund only one of the projects. Determine which project should be selected, computing the (A) net present values and (B) present value indices of the two projects. Assume a minimum rate of return of 10%. Round the present value index to two decimal places. Use the present value tables presented in this chapter (Exhibits 2 and 5).

Problems: Series A

PR 11-1A   Average rate of return method, net present value method, and analysis for a service company

Obj. 2, 3

✔ 1. A. 30.0%

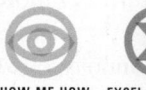

SHOW ME HOW   EXCEL TEMPLATE

The capital investment committee of Arches Landscaping Company is considering two capital investments. The estimated income from operations and net cash flows from each investment are as follows:

Year	Front-End Loader		Greenhouse	
	Income from Operations	Net Cash Flow	Income from Operations	Net Cash Flow
1	$25,000	$ 40,000	$11,250	$ 26,250
2	20,000	35,000	11,250	26,250
3	7,000	22,000	11,250	26,250
4	3,000	18,000	11,250	26,250
5	1,250	16,250	11,250	26,250
Total	$56,250	$131,250	$56,250	$131,250

Each project requires an investment of $75,000. Straight-line depreciation will be used, and no residual value is expected. The committee has selected a rate of 12% for purposes of the net present value analysis.

Instructions

1. Compute the following:

    A.   The average rate of return for each investment.

    B.   The net present value for each investment. Use the present value of $1 table appearing in this chapter (Exhibit 2). (Round present values to the nearest dollar.)

2.   ━━━▶   Prepare a brief report for the capital investment committee, advising it on the relative merits of the two investments.

PR 11-2A   Cash payback period, net present value method, and analysis

Obj. 2, 3

✔ 1. B. Plant expansion, $305,040

EXCEL TEMPLATE

Elite Apparel Inc. is considering two investment projects. The estimated net cash flows from each project are as follows:

Year	Plant Expansion	Retail Store Expansion
1	$ 450,000	$ 500,000
2	450,000	400,000
3	340,000	350,000
4	280,000	250,000
5	180,000	200,000
Total	$1,700,000	$1,700,000

Each project requires an investment of $900,000. A rate of 15% has been selected for the net present value analysis.

Instructions

1. Compute the following for each product:

    A.   Cash payback period.

    B.   The net present value. Use the present value of $1 table appearing in this chapter (Exhibit 2).

2.   ━━━▶   Prepare a brief report advising management on the relative merits of each project.

PR 11-3A Net present value method, present value index, and analysis for a service company   Obj. 3

✔ 2. Computer Network, 1.20

EXCEL TEMPLATE

Continental Railroad Company is evaluating three capital investment proposals by using the net present value method. Relevant data related to the proposals are summarized as follows:

	Maintenance Equipment	Ramp Facilities	Computer Network
Amount to be invested	$8,000,000	$20,000,000	$9,000,000
Annual net cash flows:			
Year 1	4,000,000	12,000,000	6,000,000
Year 2	3,500,000	10,000,000	5,000,000
Year 3	2,500,000	9,000,000	4,000,000

Instructions

1. Assuming that the desired rate of return is 20%, prepare a net present value analysis for each proposal. Use the present value of $1 table appearing in this chapter (Exhibit 2).

2. Determine a present value index for each proposal. (Round to two decimal places.)

3. ━━━━► Which proposal offers the largest amount of present value per dollar of investment? Explain.

PR 11-4A Net present value method, internal rate of return method, and analysis for a service company   Obj. 3

✔ 1. A. Wind turbines, $82,600

The management of Advanced Alternative Power Inc. is considering two capital investment projects. The estimated net cash flows from each project are as follows:

Year	Wind Turbines	Biofuel Equipment
1	$280,000	$300,000
2	280,000	300,000
3	280,000	300,000
4	280,000	300,000

The wind turbines require an investment of $887,600, while the biofuel equipment requires an investment of $911,100. No residual value is expected from either project.

Instructions

1. Compute the following for each project:

   A. The net present value. Use a rate of 6% and the present value of an annuity of $1 table appearing in this chapter (Exhibit 5).

   B. A present value index. (Round to two decimal places.)

2. Determine the internal rate of return for each project by (A) computing a present value factor for an annuity of $1 and (B) using the present value of an annuity of $1 table appearing in this chapter (Exhibit 5).

3. ━━━━► What advantage does the internal rate of return method have over the net present value method in comparing projects?

PR 11-5A Alternative capital investments   Obj. 3, 4

✔ 1. Servers, $11,105

EXCEL TEMPLATE

The investment committee of Sentry Insurance Co. is evaluating two projects, office expansion and upgrade to computer servers. The projects have different useful lives, but each requires an investment of $490,000. The estimated net cash flows from each project are as follows:

	Net Cash Flows	
Year	Office Expansion	Servers
1	$125,000	$165,000
2	125,000	165,000
3	125,000	165,000
4	125,000	165,000
5	125,000	
6	125,000	

(Continued)

The committee has selected a rate of 12% for purposes of net present value analysis. It also estimates that the residual value at the end of each project's useful life is $0, but at the end of the fourth year, the office expansion's residual value would be $180,000.

Instructions

1. For each project, compute the net present value. Use the present value of an annuity of $1 table appearing in this chapter (Exhibit 5). (Ignore the unequal lives of the projects.)

2. For each project, compute the net present value, assuming that the office expansion is adjusted to a four-year life for purposes of analysis. Use the present value of $1 table appearing in this chapter (Exhibit 2).

3. ➡ Prepare a report to the investment committee, providing your advice on the relative merits of the two projects.

PR 11-6A Capital rationing decision for a service company involving four proposals　　　　　　　　　　　　　　　**Obj. 2, 3, 5**

✔ 5. Proposal C, 1.57

EXCEL TEMPLATE

Renaissance Capital Group is considering allocating a limited amount of capital investment funds among four proposals. The amount of proposed investment, estimated income from operations, and net cash flow for each proposal are as follows:

	Investment	Year	Income from Operations	Net Cash Flow
Proposal A:	$680,000	1	$ 64,000	$ 200,000
		2	64,000	200,000
		3	64,000	200,000
		4	24,000	160,000
		5	24,000	160,000
			$240,000	$ 920,000
Proposal B:	$320,000	1	$ 26,000	$ 90,000
		2	26,000	90,000
		3	6,000	70,000
		4	6,000	70,000
		5	(44,000)	20,000
			$ 20,000	$340,000
Proposal C:	$108,000	1	$ 33,400	$ 55,000
		2	31,400	53,000
		3	28,400	50,000
		4	25,400	47,000
		5	23,400	45,000
			$142,000	$ 250,000
Proposal D:	$400,000	1	$100,000	$ 180,000
		2	100,000	180,000
		3	80,000	160,000
		4	20,000	100,000
		5	0	80,000
			$300,000	$700,000

The company's capital rationing policy requires a maximum cash payback period of three years. In addition, a minimum average rate of return of 12% is required on all projects. If the preceding standards are met, the net present value method and present value indexes are used to rank the remaining proposals.

Instructions

1. Compute the cash payback period for each of the four proposals.

2. Giving effect to straight-line depreciation on the investments and assuming no estimated residual value, compute the average rate of return for each of the four proposals. (Round to one decimal place.)

3. Using the following format, summarize the results of your computations in parts (1) and (2). By placing the calculated amounts in the first two columns on the left and by placing a check mark in the appropriate column to the right, indicate which proposals should be accepted for further analysis and which should be rejected.

Proposal	Cash Payback Period	Average Rate of Return	Accept for Further Analysis	Reject
A				
B				
C				
D				

4. For the proposals accepted for further analysis in part (3), compute the net present value. Use a rate of 15% and the present value of $1 table appearing in this chapter (Exhibit 2).

5. Compute the present value index for each of the proposals in part (4). (Round to two decimal places.)

6. Rank the proposals from most attractive to least attractive, based on the present values of net cash flows computed in part (4).

7. Rank the proposals from most attractive to least attractive, based on the present value indexes computed in part (5).

8. ━━━━━▶ Based on the analyses, comment on the relative attractiveness of the proposals ranked in parts (6) and (7).

Problems: Series B

PR 11-1B   Average rate of return method, net present value method, and analysis for a service company   Obj. 2, 3

✔ 1. A. 18.7%

SHOW ME HOW   EXCEL TEMPLATE

The capital investment committee of Ellis Transport and Storage Inc. is considering two investment projects. The estimated income from operations and net cash flows from each investment are as follows:

	Warehouse		Tracking Technology	
Year	Income from Operations	Net Cash Flow	Income from Operations	Net Cash Flow
1	$ 61,400	$135,000	$ 34,400	$108,000
2	51,400	125,000	34,400	108,000
3	36,400	110,000	34,400	108,000
4	26,400	100,000	34,400	108,000
5	(3,600)	70,000	34,400	108,000
Total	$172,000	$540,000	$172,000	$540,000

Each project requires an investment of $368,000. Straight-line depreciation will be used, and no residual value is expected. The committee has selected a rate of 15% for purposes of the net present value analysis.

Instructions

1. Compute the following:

   A.   The average rate of return for each investment. (Round to one decimal place.)

   B.   The net present value for each investment. Use the present value of $1 table appearing in this chapter (Exhibit 2). (Round present values to the nearest dollar.)

2. ━━━━━▶ Prepare a brief report for the capital investment committee, advising it on the relative merits of the two projects.

PR 11-2B Cash payback period, net present value method, and analysis for a service company

Obj. 2, 3

✔ 1. B. *Pro Gamer,* $49,465

EXCEL TEMPLATE

Social Circle Publications Inc. is considering two new magazine products. The estimated net cash flows from each product are as follows:

Year	Sound Cellar	Pro Gamer
1	$ 65,000	$ 70,000
2	60,000	55,000
3	25,000	35,000
4	25,000	30,000
5	45,000	30,000
Total	$220,000	$220,000

Each product requires an investment of $125,000. A rate of 10% has been selected for the net present value analysis.

Instructions

1. Compute the following for each product:

   A. Cash payback period.

   B. The net present value. Use the present value of $1 table appearing in this chapter (Exhibit 2).

2. ➡ Prepare a brief report advising management on the relative merits of each of the two products.

PR 11-3B Net present value method, present value index, and analysis for a service company

Obj. 3

✔ 2. Branch office expansion, 0.95

EXCEL TEMPLATE

First United Bank Inc. is evaluating three capital investment projects by using the net present value method. Relevant data related to the projects are summarized as follows:

	Branch Office Expansion	Computer System Upgrade	ATM Kiosk Expansion
Amount to be invested	$420,000	$350,000	$520,000
Annual net cash flows:			
Year 1	200,000	190,000	275,000
Year 2	160,000	180,000	250,000
Year 3	160,000	170,000	250,000

Instructions

1. Assuming that the desired rate of return is 15%, prepare a net present value analysis for each project. Use the present value of $1 table appearing in this chapter (Exhibit 2).

2. Determine a present value index for each project. (Round to two decimal places.)

3. ➡ Which project offers the largest amount of present value per dollar of investment? Explain.

PR 11-4B Net present value method, internal rate of return method, and analysis for a service company

Obj. 3

✔ 1. A. *After Hours* $100,800

The management of Style Networks Inc. is considering two TV show projects. The estimated net cash flows from each project are as follows:

Year	After Hours	Sun Fun
1	$320,000	$290,000
2	320,000	290,000
3	320,000	290,000
4	320,000	290,000

After Hours requires an investment of $913,600, while *Sun Fun* requires an investment of $880,730. No residual value is expected from either project.

Instructions

1. Compute the following for each project:

    A. The net present value. Use a rate of 10% and the present value of an annuity of $1 table appearing in this chapter (Exhibit 5).

    B. A present value index. (Round to two decimal places.)

2. Determine the internal rate of return for each project by (A) computing a present value factor for an annuity of $1 and (B) using the present value of an annuity of $1 table appearing in this chapter (Exhibit 5).

3. ━━━▶ What advantage does the internal rate of return method have over the net present value method in comparing projects?

PR 11-5B Alternative capital investments

Obj. 3, 4

✔ 1. Topeka,
$135,600

EXCEL TEMPLATE

The investment committee of Auntie M's Restaurants Inc. is evaluating two restaurant sites. The sites have different useful lives, but each requires an investment of $900,000. The estimated net cash flows from each site are as follows:

| | **Net Cash Flows** | |
Year	Wichita	Topeka
1	$310,000	$400,000
2	310,000	400,000
3	310,000	400,000
4	310,000	400,000
5	310,000	
6	310,000	

The committee has selected a rate of 20% for purposes of net present value analysis. It also estimates that the residual value at the end of each restaurant's useful life is $0, but at the end of the fourth year, Wichita's residual value would be $500,000.

Instructions

1. For each site, compute the net present value. Use the present value of an annuity of $1 table appearing in this chapter (Exhibit 5). (Ignore the unequal lives of the projects.)

2. For each site, compute the net present value, assuming that Wichita is adjusted to a four-year life for purposes of analysis. Use the present value of $1 table appearing in this chapter (Exhibit 2).

3. ━━━▶ Prepare a report to the investment committee, providing your advice on the relative merits of the two sites.

PR 11-6B Capital rationing decision for a service company involving four proposals

Obj. 2, 3, 5

✔ 5. Proposal B, 1.13

EXCEL TEMPLATE

Clearcast Communications Inc. is considering allocating a limited amount of capital investment funds among four proposals. The amount of proposed investment, estimated income from operations, and net cash flow for each proposal are as follows:

	Investment	Year	Income from Operations	Net Cash Flow
Proposal A:	$450,000	1	$ 30,000	$120,000
		2	30,000	120,000
		3	20,000	110,000
		4	10,000	100,000
		5	(30,000)	60,000
			$ 60,000	$510,000
Proposal B:	$200,000	1	$ 60,000	$100,000
		2	40,000	80,000
		3	20,000	60,000
		4	(10,000)	30,000
		5	(20,000)	20,000
			$ 90,000	$290,000

(Continued)

	Investment	Year	Income from Operations	Net Cash Flow
Proposal C:	$320,000	1	$ 36,000	$100,000
		2	26,000	90,000
		3	26,000	90,000
		4	16,000	80,000
		5	16,000	80,000
			$120,000	$440,000
Proposal D:	$540,000	1	$ 92,000	$200,000
		2	72,000	180,000
		3	52,000	160,000
		4	12,000	120,000
		5	(8,000)	100,000
			$220,000	$760,000

The company's capital rationing policy requires a maximum cash payback period of three years. In addition, a minimum average rate of return of 12% is required on all projects. If the preceding standards are met, the net present value method and present value indexes are used to rank the remaining proposals.

Instructions

1. Compute the cash payback period for each of the four proposals.

2. Giving effect to straight-line depreciation on the investments and assuming no estimated residual value, compute the average rate of return for each of the four proposals. (Round to one decimal place.)

3. Using the following format, summarize the results of your computations in parts (1) and (2). By placing the calculated amounts in the first two columns on the left and by placing a check mark in the appropriate column to the right, indicate which proposals should be accepted for further analysis and which should be rejected.

Proposal	Cash Payback Period	Average Rate of Return	Accept for Further Analysis	Reject
A				
B				
C				
D				

4. For the proposals accepted for further analysis in part (3), compute the net present value. Use a rate of 12% and the present value of $1 table appearing in this chapter (Exhibit 2).

5. Compute the present value index for each of the proposals in part (4). (Round to two decimal places.)

6. Rank the proposals from most attractive to least attractive, based on the present values of net cash flows computed in part (4).

7. Rank the proposals from most attractive to least attractive, based on the present value indexes computed in part (5).

8. Based on the analyses, comment on the relative attractiveness of the proposals ranked in parts (6) and (7).

Analysis for Decision Making

ADM-1 Wind turbine capital investment analysis

Central Plains Power Company is considering an investment in wind farm technology to reduce its use of natural gas. Initial installation costs are expected to be $1,200 per kilowatt-hour of capacity. The wind turbine has a capacity of generating 2 megawatts per hour. A kilowatt-hour is 1,000 watts generated per hour and a megawatt hour is 1,000 kilowatts generated per hour.

Annual operating information related to the wind turbine project was developed as follows:

Wind capacity factor	25%*
Operating cost per wind turbine megawatt hour	$10
Variable operating, fuel, and maintenance costs per natural gas megawatt hour	$95
Days per year	365

*A factor that measures the reduction from full capacity due to the variability of wind

A. Determine the initial investment cost of the wind turbine.

B. Determine the annual cost savings from the wind turbine in replacing natural gas generation. (Round to the nearest dollar.)

C. Determine the net present value of the project assuming a 15-year life and 12% minimum rate of return. (Use the present value tables in Appendix A.)

ADM-2 Paper reclaim capital investment analysis

The Victor Paper Company manufactures paper products from pulp. The process creates paper scrap from paper trim, off-grade, and machine errors. Presently, the scrap paper is discarded in a landfill. Management is considering a proposal for a scrap paper reclamation system. The system is designed so that paper is discarded in vacuum collection points located throughout the plant. The vacuum system would be attached to a reclaim process that would digest the scrap paper, turning it back into pulp, and then blending the reclaimed product back into the papermaking process with virgin (new) pulp. The blended stream is termed "blended pulp." It has been determined that the quality of the final product is not adversely impacted by using blended pulp versus using 100% virgin pulp. In addition, the cost of the reclaimed pulp is considered "free" to the blended stream, and causes the amount of virgin pulp used in the blended stream to be less than would be otherwise. These factors reduce the cost of the blended stream. Some information involving this proposal is as follows:

Reclaim system investment cost	$40,000,000
Annual operating cost of reclaim system	$500,000
Cost of virgin pulp	$600 per ton
Cost of blended pulp	$560 per ton
Finished processing volume	1,200 tons per day
Operating days per year	360

A. Determine the annual cost savings from using blended pulp.

B. Prepare a capital investment analysis using net present value to determine if the reclamation system is justified. Assume a 10-year life and 8% minimum rate of return. (Use the present value tables in Appendix A. Round present value calculations to the nearest dollar.)

ADM-3 Tire design capital investment analysis

AutoSource, Inc. designs and manufactures tires for automobiles. The company's strategy is to design products that incorporate the full environmental impact of the product over its life cycle. This includes designing tires for ease of recycling and fuel efficiency.

The technical team has determined that the tires manufactured with a silica blend will reduce road resistance. Thus, silica-blended tires will be significantly more fuel-efficient for the consumer without compromising tire life. To produce the silica-blended tires, AutoSource will need to invest $5,000,000 in new equipment. It is expected that the new tire will be attractive

(Continued)

to consumers and will result in increased tire sales. However, sales of conventional tires will be reduced as a result of the new silica-blended tires. To evaluate the project, the sales prices and costs of silica-blended and conventional tires are given as follows:

	Silica-Blended Tires	Conventional Tires
Sales price per tire	$160	$140
Material cost per tire	80	70
Variable manufacturing cost per tire	15	12

It is anticipated that there will be 80,000 silica-blended tires sold annually, while the sales of conventional tires will be reduced by 70,000 tires annually.

A. Determine the annual contribution margin for manufacturing and selling the silica-blended tires.

B. Determine the annual cash flows of manufacturing and selling silica-blended tires, incorporating the impact of lost sales from conventional tires.

C. Prepare a net present value analysis of the silica equipment investment assuming an eight-year life and 12% minimum rate of return. (Use the present value tables in Appendix A. Round to the nearest dollar.)

D. ━━━▶ AutoSource is also concerned with the cost of recycling tires. What questions must the company consider for recycling silica-blended tires?

Take It Further

ETHICS

TIF 11-1   Ethics in Action

Danielle Hastings was recently hired as a cost analyst by CareNet Medical Supplies Inc. One of Danielle's first assignments was to perform a net present value analysis for a new warehouse. Danielle performed the analysis and calculated a present value index of 0.75. The plant manager, Jerrod Moore, is very intent on purchasing the warehouse because he believes that more storage space is needed. Jerrod asks Danielle into his office and the following conversation takes place:

Jerrod: Danielle, you're new here, aren't you?

Danielle: Yes, I am.

Jerrod: Well, Danielle, I'm not at all pleased with the capital investment analysis that you performed on this new warehouse. I need that warehouse for my production. If I don't get it, where am I going to place our output?

Danielle: Well, we need to get product into our customers' hands.

Jerrod: I agree, and we need a warehouse to do that.

Danielle: My analysis does not support constructing a new warehouse. The numbers don't lie; the warehouse does not meet our investment return targets. In fact, it seems to me that purchasing a warehouse does not add much value to the business. We need to be producing product to satisfy customer orders, not to fill a warehouse.

Jerrod: The headquarters people will not allow me to build the warehouse if the numbers don't add up. You know as well as I that many assumptions go into your net present value analysis. Why don't you relax some of your assumptions so that the financial savings will offset the cost?

Danielle: I'm willing to discuss my assumptions with you. Maybe I overlooked something.

Jerrod: Good. Here's what I want you to do. I see in your analysis that you don't project greater sales as a result of the warehouse. It seems to me that if we can store more goods, then we will have more to sell. Thus, logically, a larger warehouse translates into more sales. If you incorporate this into your analysis, I think you'll see that the numbers will work out. Why don't you work it through and come back with a new analysis. I'm really counting on you on this one. Let's get off to a good start together and see if we can get this project accepted.

━━━▶ What is your advice to Danielle?

REAL WORLD

TIF 11-2 Team Activity

Divide your team into two groups. In one group, find a local business, such as a copy shop that rents time on desktop computers for an hourly rate. Determine the hourly rate. In the other group, determine the price of a mid-range desktop computer at www.dell.com. Combine this information from the two groups and perform a capital budgeting analysis. Assume that one student will use the computer for 40 hours per semester for the next three years. Also assume that the minimum rate of return is 10%. Use the interest tables in Appendix A in performing your analysis. [*Hint:* Use the appropriate present value of an annuity of $1 factor for 5% compounded for six semiannual periods (periods = 6).]

> Does your analysis support the student purchasing the computer?

TIF 11-3 Communication

Global Electronics Inc. invested $1,000,000 to build a plant in a foreign country. The labor and materials used in production are purchased locally. The plant expansion was estimated to produce an internal rate of return of 20% in U.S. dollar terms. Due to a currency crisis, the currency exchange rate between the local currency and the U.S. dollar doubled from two local units per U.S. dollar to four local units per U.S. dollar.

> Write a brief memo to the Chief Financial Officer, Tom Greene, explaining the impact that the currency exchange rate change would have on the project's internal rate of return if (1) the plant produced and sold product in the local economy only, and (2) the plant produced all product locally and exported all product to the United States for sale.

Concepts and Principles

Chapter 1 *Introduction to Managerial Accounting*

Developing Information

COST SYSTEMS	COST BEHAVIOR
Chapter 2 *Job Order Costing* **Chapter 3** *Process Cost Systems* **Chapter 4** *Activity-Based Costing*	**Chapter 5** *Cost-Volume-Profit Analysis*

Decision Making

EVALUATING PERFORMANCE	COMPARING ALTERNATIVES
Chapter 6 *Variable Costing for Management Analysis* **Chapter 7** *Budgeting* **Chapter 8** *Evaluating Variances from Standard Costs*	**Chapter 9** *Evaluating Decentralized Operations* **Chapter 10** *Differential Analysis and Product Pricing* **Chapter 11** *Capital Investment Analysis* **Chapter 12** ***Lean Manufacturing and Activity Analysis***

Precor Incorporated

When you order the salad bar at the local restaurant, you are able to serve yourself at your own pace. There is no waiting for the waitress to take the order or for the cook to prepare the meal. You are able to move directly to the salad bar and select from various offerings. You might wish to have salad with lettuce, cole slaw, bacon bits, croutons, and salad dressing. The offerings are arranged in a row so that you can build your salad as you move down the salad bar.

Many manufacturers are producing products in much the same way that the salad bar is designed to satisfy each customer's needs. Like customers at the salad bar, products move through a production process as they are built for each customer. Such a process eliminates many sources of waste, which is why it is called *lean*.

Using lean practices can improve performance. For example, when **Precor**, a manufacturer of fitness equipment, used lean principles, it improved its manufacturing operations and achieved the following results:

- Increased on-time shipments from near 40% to above 90%.
- Decreased direct labor costs by 30%.
- Reduced the number of suppliers from 3,000 to under 250.
- Reduced inventory by 40%.
- Reduced warranty claims by almost 60%.

In this chapter, lean practices are described and illustrated. The chapter concludes by describing and illustrating the accounting for quality costs and activity analysis.

What's Covered

Lean Manufacturing and Activity Analysis

Principles of Lean Manufacturing
- Reducing Inventory (Obj. 1)
- Reducing Lead Times (Obj. 1)
- Reducing Setup Time (Obj. 1)
- Product-Oriented Layout (Obj. 1)
- Employee Involvement (Obj. 1)
- Pull Manufacturing (Obj. 1)
- Zero Defects (Obj. 1)
- Supply Chain Management (Obj. 1)

Accounting for Lean Manufacturing
- Fewer Transactions (Obj. 2)
- Combined Accounts (Obj. 2)
- Nonfinancial Performance Measures (Obj. 2)
- Direct Tracing of Overhead (Obj. 2)

Activity Analysis
- Costs of Quality (Obj. 3)
- Quality Activity Analysis (Obj. 3)
- Value-Added Activity Analysis (Obj. 3)
- Process Activity Analysis (Obj. 3)

Learning Objectives

Obj. 1 Describe lean manufacturing practices.

Obj. 2 Describe the implications of lean manufacturing on the accounting system.

Obj. 3 Describe and illustrate activity analysis for improving operations.

Analysis for Decision Making

Describe and illustrate the use of lean principles and activity analysis in a service or administrative setting.

Objective 1
Describe lean manufacturing practices.

Lean Principles

The **lean enterprise** is a business that produces products or services with high quality, low cost, fast response, and immediate availability. **Lean manufacturing**, sometimes called *just-in-time processing (JIT)*, accomplishes these objectives in a manufacturing setting. Both manufacturing and nonmanufacturing businesses use **lean principles** to accomplish these service and cost objectives. However, these principles will be discussed within the context of lean manufacturing. Lean manufacturing principles are listed and contrasted with traditional manufacturing principles in Exhibit 1.

Exhibit 1 Lean versus Traditional Manufacturing Principles

Issue	Lean Manufacturing	Traditional Manufacturing
Inventory	Reduces inventory.	Increases inventory to protect against process problems.
Lead time	Reduces lead time.	Increases lead time to protect against uncertainty.
Setup time	Reduces setup time.	Disregards setup time as an improvement priority.
Production layout	Emphasizes product-oriented layout.	Emphasizes process-oriented layout.
Role of the employee	Emphasizes team-oriented employee involvement.	Emphasizes work of individuals, following manager instructions.
Production scheduling policy	Emphasizes pull manufacturing.	Emphasizes push manufacturing.
Quality	Emphasizes zero defects.	Tolerates defects.
Suppliers and customers	Emphasizes supply chain management.	Treats suppliers and customers as "arm's-length," independent entities.

Link to Precor

Precor was established in 1980 when the company began selling a rowing machine that supported the natural movement of the human body. Precor is currently owned by Amer Sports Corporation.

Reducing Inventory

Lean manufacturing views inventory as wasteful and unnecessary, and thus emphasizes reducing or eliminating inventory.

Under traditional manufacturing, inventory often hides underlying production problems. For example, if machine breakdowns occur, work in process inventories can be used to keep production running in other departments while the machines are being repaired. Likewise, inventories can be used to hide problems caused by a shortage of trained employees, unreliable suppliers, or poor product quality.

In contrast, lean manufacturing solves and removes production problems. In this way, raw materials, work in process, and finished goods inventories are reduced or eliminated.

The role of inventory in manufacturing can be illustrated using a river, as shown in Exhibit 2. Inventory is the water in a river. The rocks at the bottom of the river are production problems. When the water level (inventory) is high, the rocks (production problems) at the bottom of the river are hidden. As the water level (inventory) drops, the rocks (production problems) become visible, one by one. Lean manufacturing reduces the water level (inventory), exposes the rocks (production problems), and removes the rocks so that the river can flow smoothly.

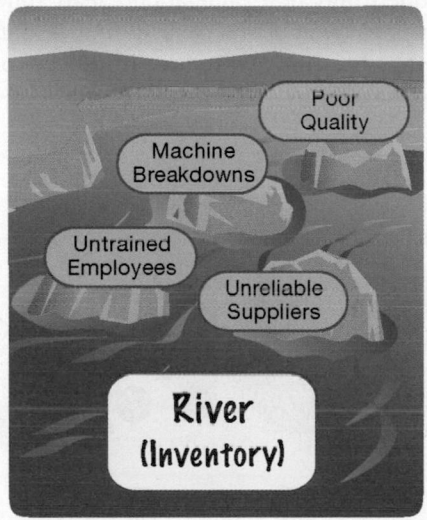

Exhibit 2

Inventory's Role in Manufacturing

Ethics: Don't Do It

The Inventory Shift

Some managers take a shortcut to reducing inventory by shifting inventory to their suppliers. With this tactic, the hard work of improving processes is avoided. Enlightened managers realize that such tactics often have short-lived savings. Suppliers will eventually increase their prices to compensate for the additional inventory holding costs, thus resulting in no savings. Therefore, shifting a problem doesn't eliminate a problem.

Reducing Lead Times

Lead time, sometimes called *throughput time*, measures the time interval between when a product enters production (started) and when it is completed (finished). That is, lead time measures how long it takes to manufacture a product. To illustrate, in Exhibit 3, if a product enters production at 1:00 P.M. and is completed at 5:00 P.M., the lead time is four hours.

Exhibit 3
Lead Time

Lead Time = 4 Hours

Raw Materials   **Work Centers**   Product

One   Two   Three

Production Process

The lead time can be classified as one of the following:

■ **Value-added lead time**, which is the time spent in converting raw materials into a finished unit of product

■ **Non-value-added lead time**, which is the time spent while the unit of product is waiting to enter the next production process or is moved from one process to another

Exhibit 4 illustrates value-added and non-value-added lead time. The time spent drilling and packing the unit of product is value-added time. The time spent waiting to enter the next process or the time spent moving the unit of product from one process to another is non-value-added time.

Exhibit 4   Components of Lead Time

Raw Materials   **Drill**   **Pack**   **Customer**

Non-Value-Added Time   Non-Value-Added Time   Value-Added Time   Non-Value-Added Time   Non-Value-Added Time   Value-Added Time

Start of Production   End of Production

The **value-added ratio** is computed as follows:

$$\text{Value-Added Ratio} = \frac{\text{Value-Added Lead Time}}{\text{Total Lead Time}}$$

To illustrate, assume that the lead time to manufacture a unit of product is as follows (value-added times are highlighted):

Move raw materials to machining	5 minutes
Machining	35
Move time to assembly	10
Assembly	20
Move time to packing	15
Wait time for packing	30
Packing	10
Total lead time	125 minutes

The value-added ratio for the preceding product is 52%, computed as follows:

$$\text{Value-Added Ratio} = \frac{\text{Value-Added Lead Time}}{\text{Total Lead Time}}$$

$$= \frac{(35 + 20 + 10) \text{ minutes}}{125 \text{ minutes}} = \frac{65 \text{ minutes}}{125 \text{ minutes}} = 52\%$$

A low value-added ratio indicates a poor manufacturing process. A good manufacturing process will reduce non-value-added lead time to a minimum and thus have a high value-added ratio.

Lean manufacturing reduces or eliminates non-value-added time. In contrast, traditional manufacturing processes may have a value-added ratio as small as 5%.

Reducing Setup Time

A *setup* is the effort spent preparing an operation or process for production. A **batch size** is the amount of production in units of product that is produced after a setup. If setups are long and costly, the batch size for the related production run is normally large. Large batch sizes allow setup costs to be spread over more units and, thus, reduce the cost per unit. However, large batch sizes increase inventory and lead time.

Exhibit 5 shows the relationship between setup times and lead time.

Exhibit 5   Relationship between Setup Times and Lead Time

To help understand the relationship of batch sizes to lead time, consider a group of 10 friends purchasing a ticket at a single-window ticket counter as shown in Exhibit 6.

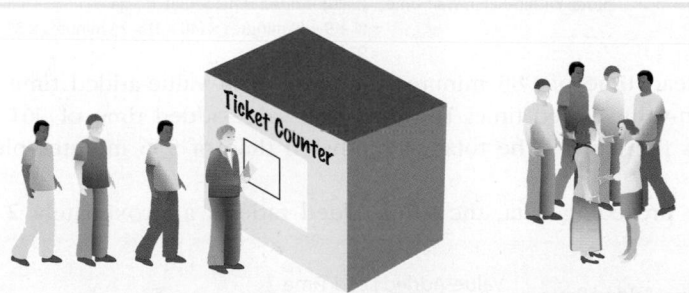

Exhibit 6
Batch Size and
Lead Time

The friends are traveling together, so they are like a "batch" of production. If each friend takes one minute to purchase a ticket, the other nine friends are either waiting in line, or waiting for the remaining friends to finish. Thus, it takes 10 minutes for all of the friends to receive tickets as a group, but it took only one minute for any one friend to actually buy a ticket.

The amount of time each friend is waiting is called within-batch wait time. The total within-batch wait time is computed as follows:

Total Within-Batch Wait Time = (Value-Added Time) × (Batch Size – 1)

In this example, the value-added time is the 1 minute to purchase a ticket. So the total within-batch wait time is 9 minutes, computed as follows:

$$\text{Total Within-Batch Wait Time} = 1 \text{ minute} \times (10 - 1) = 9 \text{ minutes}$$

The value added ratio is 10%, computed as follows:

$$\text{Value-Added Ratio} = \frac{\text{Value-Added Lead Time}}{\text{Total Lead Time}}$$

$$= \frac{1 \text{ minute}}{10 \text{ minutes}} = 10\%$$

Now consider someone buying a ticket without a group of friends present. A single person would only take one minute to buy the ticket, with no waiting for friends. In this case, the lead-time drops down to one minute, or simply the time to purchase the ticket, and the value-added ratio is 100%.

Lean manufacturing emphasizes decreasing setup times in order to reduce the batch size, whereas traditional manufacturing does not treat setup improvement as an important priority. By reducing batch sizes, work in process inventory and within-batch wait time decrease, thus reducing total lead-time and increasing the value-added ratio.

To illustrate in a manufacturing setting, assume that Automotive Components Inc. manufactures engine starters as follows (value-added times are highlighted):

	Processing Time per Unit
Move raw materials to Machining	5 minutes
Machining	7
Move time to Assembly	10
Assembly	9
Move time to Testing	10
Testing	8
Total	49 minutes
Batch size	40 units

The total lead time is 985 minutes, computed as follows:

Value-added time (7 + 9 + 8)	24 minutes
Move time (5 + 10 + 10)	25
Total within-batch wait time	936*
Total time	985 minutes

*Total Within-Batch Wait Time = (Value-Added Time) × (Batch Size – 1)
= (7 + 9 + 8) minutes × (40 – 1) = 24 minutes × 39
= 936 minutes

Of the total lead time of 985 minutes, 24 minutes is value-added time and 961 minutes (985 – 24) is non-value-added time. The total non-value-added time of 961 minutes can also be determined as the sum of the total within-batch time of 936 minutes plus the move time of 25 minutes.

Based on the preceding data, the value-added ratio is approximately 2.4%, computed as follows:

$$\text{Value-Added Ratio} = \frac{\text{Value-Added Lead Time}}{\text{Total Lead Time}}$$

$$= \frac{(7+9+8) \text{ minutes}}{985 \text{ minutes}} = \frac{24 \text{ minutes}}{985 \text{ minutes}} = 2.4\% \text{ (rounded)}$$

Thus, the non-value-added time for Automotive Components Inc. is approximately 97.6% (100% – 2.4%).

Automotive Components can increase its value-added ratio by reducing setups so that the batch size is one unit, called *one-piece flow*. Automotive Components could also move the Machining, Assembly, and Testing activities closer to each other so that the move time could be reduced. With these changes, Automotive Components' value-added ratio would increase.

Why It Matters

P&G's "Pit Stops"

What do **Procter & Gamble (P&G)** and **Formula One** racing have in common? P&G answered this question by realizing that Formula One racing pit stops could teach the company how to more quickly change over from one sized package to another on its packing lines. As a result, P&G videotaped actual Formula One pit stops to identify the principles for conducting a fast setup, as follows:

- Position the tools near their point of use on the line prior to stopping the line, to reduce time going back and forth to the tool room.

- Arrange the tools in the exact order of work, so that no time is wasted looking for a tool.
- Have each employee perform a very specific task during the setup.
- Design the workflow so that employees don't interfere with each other.
- Have each employee in position at the moment the line is stopped.
- Train each employee, and practice, practice, practice.
- Put a stop watch on the setup process.
- Plot improvements over time on a visible chart.

As a result of these changes, P&G was able to reduce pack-line setup time from several hours to 20 minutes. This decrease allowed the company to reduce lead time and to improve the cost performance of the Packing Department.

Emphasizing Product-Oriented Layout

Manufacturing processes can be organized around a product, which is called a **product-oriented layout** (or *product cells*). Alternatively, manufacturing processes can be organized around a process, which is called a **process-oriented layout**.

Lean manufacturing normally organizes manufacturing around products rather than processes. Organizing work around products reduces:

- Moving materials and products between processes
- Work in process inventory
- Lead time
- Production costs

In addition, a product-oriented layout improves coordination among the various work activities, or operations, of the facility.

Emphasizing Employee Involvement

Traditional manufacturing often values direct labor employees only for their manual labor, whereas lean manufacturing values labor for contributions beyond labor tasks, using employee involvement. **Employee involvement** is a management approach that grants employees the responsibility and authority to make decisions about operations. Employee involvement is often applied in lean manufacturing by organizing employees into *product cells*. Within each product cell, employees are organized as teams where the employees are cross-trained to perform any operation within the product cell.

To illustrate, employees learn how to operate several different machines within their product cell. In addition, team members are trained to perform functions traditionally performed by centralized service departments. For example, product cell employees may perform their own equipment maintenance, quality control, housekeeping, and improvement studies.

Precor encourages a collaborative, innovative environment for its employees. Precor believes that its employees are its #1 asset.

Link to Precor

Emphasizing Pull Manufacturing

Pull manufacturing (or *make to order*) is an important lean practice. In pull manufacturing, products are manufactured only as they are needed by the customer. Products can be thought of as being pulled through the manufacturing process. In other words, the status of the next operation determines when products are moved or produced. If the next operation is busy, production stops so that work in process does not pile up in front of the busy operation. When the next operation is ready, the product is moved to that operation.

A system used in pull manufacturing is *kanban*, which is Japanese for "cards." Electronic cards or containers signal production quantities to be filled by the preceding operation. The cards link the customer's order for a product back through each stage of production. In other words, when a consumer orders a product, a kanban card triggers the manufacture of the product.

In contrast, the traditional approach to manufacturing is based on estimated customer demand. This principle is called **push manufacturing** (or make to stock). In push manufacturing, products are manufactured according to a production schedule that is based upon estimated sales. The schedule "pushes" product into inventory before customer orders are received. As a result, push manufacturers normally have more inventory than pull manufacturers.

Emphasizing Zero Defects

Lean manufacturing attempts to eliminate poor quality. Poor quality creates:

- Scrap
- Rework, which is fixing product made wrong the first time
- Disruption in the production process
- Dissatisfied customers
- Warranty costs and expenses

One way to improve product quality and manufacturing processes is Six Sigma. **Six Sigma** was developed by **Motorola Corporation** and consists of five steps: define, measure, analyze, improve, and control (DMAIC).[1] Since its development, Six Sigma has been adopted by thousands of organizations worldwide.

Emphasizing Supply Chain Management

Supply chain management coordinates and controls the flow of materials, services, information, and finances with suppliers, manufacturers, and customers. Supply chain management partners with suppliers using long-term agreements. These agreements ensure that products are delivered with the right quality, at the right cost, at the right time.

To enhance the interchange of information between suppliers and customers, supply chain management often uses:

- **Electronic data interchange (EDI)**, which uses computers to electronically communicate orders, relay information, and make or receive payments from one organization to another
- **Radio frequency identification devices (RFID)**, which are electronic tags (chips) placed on or embedded within products that can be read by radio waves that allow instant monitoring of product location
- **Enterprise resource planning (ERP)** systems, which are used to plan and control internal and supply chain operations

Lean Manufacturing in Action

- **Yamaha** manufactures musical instruments such as trumpets, horns, saxophones, clarinets, and flutes using **product-oriented layouts**.
- **Sony** uses **employee involvement** to organize employees into small, four-person teams to completely assemble a camcorder, doing everything from soldering to testing. This team-based approach reduces assembly time from 70 minutes to 15 minutes per camcorder.

- **Kenney Manufacturing Company**, a manufacturer of window shades, estimated that 50% of its window shade process was non-value-added. By using **pull manufacturing** and changing the line layout, it was able to reduce inventory by 82% and lead time by 84%.
- **Motorola** has claimed over $17 billion in savings from **Six Sigma**.
- **Hyundia/Kia Motors Group** will use 20 million RFID tags annually to track automotive parts from its suppliers, providing greater **supply chain** transparency and flexibility.

---

[1] The term "Six Sigma" refers to a statistical property where a process has less than 3.4 defects per one million items.

| **Check Up Corner 12-1** | Lean Concepts and Lead Time Analysis |

I. Lean Concepts

Match the following lean concepts with the appropriate description.

Concept	Description
1. Batch	A. Measures the time interval between when a product enters production and when it is completed.
2. Lead time	
3. Product-oriented layout	B. Manufacturing process that reduces (1) moving materials and products between processes, (2) work-in process inventory, (3) lead time, and (4) production costs.
4. Pull manufacturing	
5. Setup time	C. The effort spent preparing an operation or process for production.
	D. Products are manufactured only as they are needed by the customer.
	E. The amount of production in units of product that is produced after setup.

II. Lead Time Analysis

The Helping Hands Company manufactures designer gloves. Gloves are manufactured in 50-glove batch sizes, and cut and assembled by the company's workforce. The cutting time is 4 minutes per glove. The assembly time is 6 minutes per glove. It takes 12 minutes to move a batch of gloves from cutting to assembly.

A. For this process, compute (1) the value-added lead time, (2) the non-value-added lead time, and (3) total lead time.
B. Compute the value-added ratio. (Round to one decimal place.)

Solution:

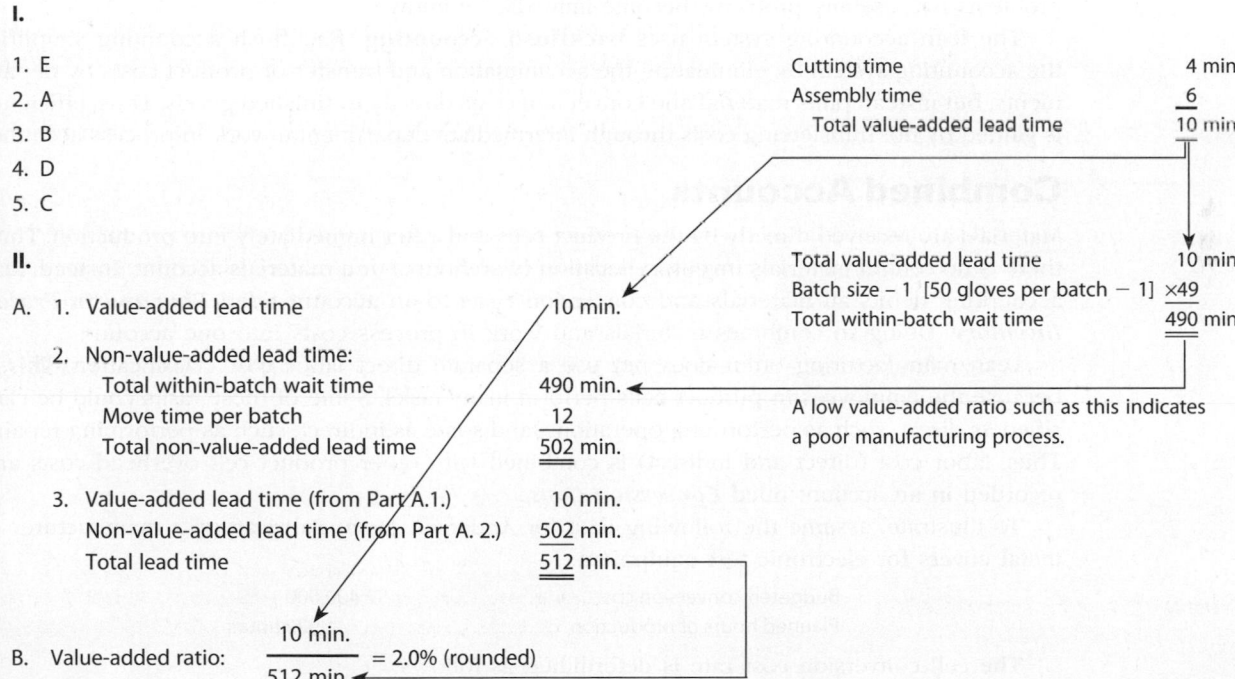

I.

1. E
2. A
3. B
4. D
5. C

Cutting time	4 min.
Assembly time	6
Total value-added lead time	10 min.

II.

A. 1. Value-added lead time   10 min.

Total value-added lead time	10 min.
Batch size − 1 [50 gloves per batch − 1]	×49
Total within-batch wait time	490 min.

2. Non-value-added lead time:

Total within-batch wait time	490 min.
Move time per batch	12
Total non-value-added lead time	502 min.

A low value-added ratio such as this indicates a poor manufacturing process.

3.
Value-added lead time (from Part A.1.)	10 min.
Non-value-added lead time (from Part A. 2.)	502 min.
Total lead time	512 min.

B. Value-added ratio: $\dfrac{10 \text{ min.}}{512 \text{ min.}}$ = 2.0% (rounded)

Objective 2

Describe the implications of lean manufacturing on the accounting system.

Lean Accounting

In lean manufacturing, the accounting system reflects the lean philosophy. Such systems are called **lean accounting**, and have the following characteristics:

- *Fewer transactions.* There are fewer transactions to record, thus simplifying the accounting system.
- *Combined accounts.* All in-process work is combined with raw materials to form a new account, **Raw and In Process (RIP) Inventory**. Direct labor is also combined with other costs to form a new account titled **Conversion Costs**.
- *Nonfinancial performance measures.* Nonfinancial performance measures are emphasized.
- *Direct tracing of overhead.* Indirect labor is directly assigned to product cells; thus, less factory overhead is allocated to products.

Fewer Transactions

The traditional process cost accounting system accumulates product costs by department. These costs are transferred from department to department as the product is manufactured. Thus, materials are recorded into and out of work in process inventories as the product moves through the factory.

The recording of product costs by departments facilitates the control of costs. However, this requires that many transactions and costs be recorded and reported. This adds cost and complexity to the cost accounting system.

In lean manufacturing, there is less need for cost control. This is because lower inventory levels make problems more visible. That is, managers don't need accounting reports to indicate problems because any problems become immediately known.

The lean accounting system uses **backflush accounting**. Backflush accounting simplifies the accounting system by eliminating the accumulation and transfer of product costs by departments, but instead pulls material and conversion costs directly to finished goods. Thus, efficiency is gained by not transferring costs through intermediate departmental work in process accounts.

Combined Accounts

Materials are received directly by the product cells and enter immediately into production. Thus, there is no central materials inventory location (warehouse) or a materials account. Instead, lean accounting debits all materials and conversion costs to an account titled *Raw and In Process Inventory*. Doing so combines materials and work in process costs into one account.

Lean manufacturing often does not use a separate direct labor cost classification. This is because the employees in product cells perform many tasks. Some of these tasks could be classified as direct, such as performing operations, and some as indirect, such as performing repairs. Thus, labor cost (direct and indirect) is combined with other product cell overhead costs and recorded in an account titled *Conversion Costs*.

To illustrate, assume the following data for Anderson Metal Fabricators, a manufacturer of metal covers for electronic test equipment:

Budgeted conversion cost $2,400,000
Planned hours of production .... 1,920 hours

The cell conversion cost rate is determined as follows:

$$\text{Cell Conversion Cost Rate} = \frac{\text{Budgeted Conversion Cost}}{\text{Planned Hours of Production}}$$

$$= \frac{\$2,400,000}{1,920 \text{ hours}} = \$1,250 \text{ per hour}$$

The cell conversion rate is similar to a predetermined factory overhead rate, except that it includes all conversion costs in the numerator.

Assume that Anderson Metal's cover product cell is expected to require 0.02 hour of manufacturing time per unit. Thus, the conversion cost for the cover is $25 per unit, computed as follows:

Conversion Cost for Cover = Manufacturing Time × Cell Conversion Cost Rate

= 0.02 hour × $1,250 – $25 per unit

The recording of selected lean accounting transactions for Anderson Metal Fabricators for April is illustrated in Exhibit 7.

Exhibit 7 Transactions Using Lean Accounting—Anderson Metal Fabricators

Transaction	Journal Entry	Comment

	Raw and In Process Inventory 120,000
	  Accounts Payable 120,000
	   To record materials purchases.
		Note that the materials purchased are debited to the combined account, Raw and In Process Inventory. A separate materials account is not used, because materials are received directly in the product cells, rather than in an inventory location.

Conversion costs are applied to 8,000 covers at a rate of $25 per cover.	Raw and In Process Inventory 200,000
	  Conversion Costs. 200,000
	   To record applied conversion
	   costs of the medium-cover line.
		The raw and in process inventory account is used to accumulate the applied cell conversion costs during the period. The credit to Conversion Costs is similar to the treatment of applied factory overhead.

All 8,000 covers were completed in the cell. The raw and in process inventory account is reduced by the $15 per unit materials cost and the $25 per unit conversion cost.	Finished Goods Inventory. 320,000
	  Raw and In Process Inventory 320,000
	   To transfer the cost of completed
	   units to finished goods.
		Materials ($15 × 8,000 units) $120,000
		Conversion ($25 × 8,000 units) 200,000
		  Total $320,000
		
		After the cost of the completed units is transferred from the raw and in process inventory account, the account's balance is zero. There are no units left in process within the cell.[2] This is a backflush transaction.

Of the 8,000 units completed, 7,800 were sold and shipped to customers at $70 per unit, leaving 200 finished units in stock. Thus, the finished goods inventory account has a balance of $8,000 (200 × $40).	Accounts Receivable. 546,000
	  Sales. 546,000
	   To record sales.
	
	Cost of Goods Sold 312,000
	  Finished Goods Inventory 312,000
	   To record cost of goods sold.
		Units sold 7,800
		Conversion and materials
		  cost per unit . . . . × $40
		Transferred to Cost of Goods Sold $312,000

[2] The actual conversion cost per unit may be different from the budgeted conversion cost per unit due to cell inefficiency, improvements in processing methods, or excess scrap. These deviations from the budgeted cost can be accounted for as cost variances, as illustrated in more advanced texts.

Check Up Corner 12-2 Lean Accounting

The budgeted conversion costs for a lean cell are $142,500 for 1,900 production hours. Each unit produced by the cell requires 10 minutes of cell process time. During the month, 1,050 units are manufactured in the cell. The estimated materials cost is $46 per unit. Journalize entries for the following:

A. Materials are purchased to produce 1,100 units.
B. Conversion costs are applied to 1,050 units of production.
C. The cell completes 1,030 units, which are placed into finished goods.

Solution:

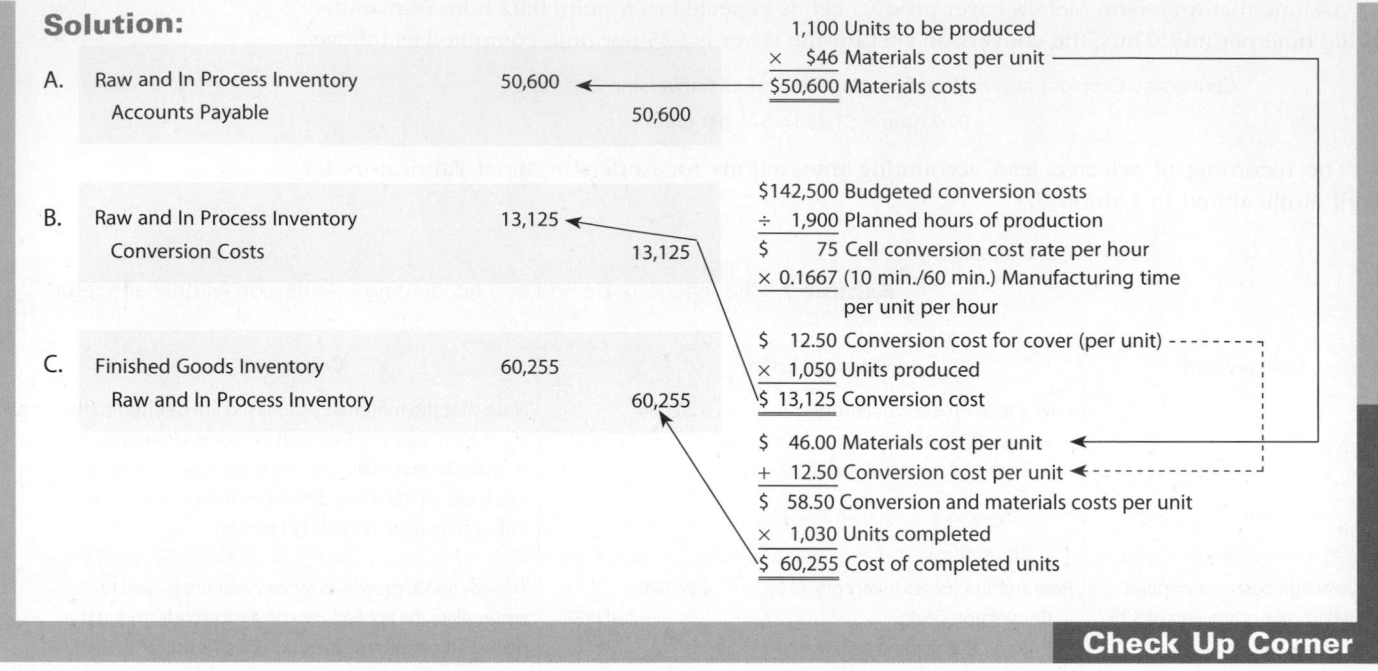

A. Raw and In Process Inventory 50,600
    Accounts Payable 50,600

B. Raw and In Process Inventory 13,125
    Conversion Costs 13,125

C. Finished Goods Inventory 60,255
    Raw and In Process Inventory 60,255

1,100	Units to be produced
× $46	Materials cost per unit
$50,600	Materials costs

$142,500	Budgeted conversion costs
÷ 1,900	Planned hours of production
$ 75	Cell conversion cost rate per hour
× 0.1667	(10 min./60 min.) Manufacturing time per unit per hour
$ 12.50	Conversion cost for cover (per unit)
× 1,050	Units produced
$ 13,125	Conversion cost

$ 46.00	Materials cost per unit
+ 12.50	Conversion cost per unit
$ 58.50	Conversion and materials costs per unit
× 1,030	Units completed
$ 60,255	Cost of completed units

Check Up Corner

Nonfinancial Performance Measures

Lean manufacturing normally uses nonfinancial measures to help guide short-term operating performance. A **nonfinancial measure** is operating information not stated in dollar terms. Examples of nonfinancial measures of performance include:

- Lead time
- Value-added ratio
- Setup time
- Number of production line stops
- Number of units scrapped
- Deviations from scheduled production
- Number of failed inspections

Most companies use a combination of financial and nonfinancial operating measures, which are often referred to as *key performance indicators* (or *KPIs*). Nonfinancial measures are often available more quickly than financial measures. Thus, nonfinancial measures are often used for day-to-day operating decisions that require quick feedback. In contrast, traditional financial accounting measures are often used for longer-term operating decisions.

Direct Tracing of Overhead

In lean manufacturing, many indirect tasks are assigned to a product cell. For example, maintenance department personnel may be assigned to a product cell and cross-trained to perform other operations. Thus, the salary of maintenance personnel can be traced directly to the product cell and, thus, to the product.

In traditional manufacturing, maintenance personnel are part of the maintenance department. The cost of the maintenance department is then allocated to products based on predetermined factory overhead rates. Such allocations are not necessary when maintenance personnel are assigned directly to a product cell.

Activity Analysis

Objective 3
Describe and
illustrate
activity analysis
for improving
operations.

In Chapter 4, we discussed activity-based costing for product costing. Activities can also be used to support operational improvement in the lean enterprise using activity analysis. **Activity analysis** determines the cost of activities for the purpose of determining the cost of the following:

- Quality
- Value-added activities
- Processes

Costs of Quality

Competition encourages businesses to emphasize high-quality products, services, and processes. In doing so, businesses incur **costs of quality**, as illustrated in Exhibit 8. These costs of quality can be classified as follows:

- **Prevention costs**, which are costs of preventing defects before or during the manufacture of the product or delivery of services

    Examples: Costs of engineering good product design, controlling vendor quality, training equipment operators, maintaining equipment

- **Appraisal costs**, which are costs of activities that detect, measure, evaluate, and inspect products and processes to ensure that they meet customer needs

    Examples: Costs of inspecting and testing products

- **Internal failure costs**, which are costs associated with defects discovered before the product is delivered to the consumer

    Examples: Cost of scrap and rework

- **External failure costs**, which are costs incurred after defective products have been delivered to consumers

    Examples: Cost of recalls and warranty work

Exhibit 8 Costs of Quality

Costs of Controlling Quality		Costs of Failing to Control Quality	
Prevention Costs	Appraisal Costs	Internal Failure Costs	External Failure Costs

Prevention and appraisal costs can be thought of as costs of controlling quality *before* any products are known to be defective. Internal and external failure costs can be thought of as the cost of controlling quality *after* products have become defective. Internal and external failure costs also can be thought of as the costs of "failing to control quality" through prevention and appraisal efforts.

Prevention and appraisal costs are incurred *before* the product is manufactured or delivered to the customer. Prevention costs are incurred in an attempt to permanently improve product quality. In contrast, appraisal costs are incurred in an attempt to limit the amount of defective products that "slip out the door."

Internal and external failure costs are incurred *after* the defective products have been discovered. In addition to costs of scrap and rework, internal failure costs may be incurred for lost equipment time because of rework and the costs of carrying additional inventory used for reworking. In addition to costs of recall and warranty work, external failure costs include the loss of customer goodwill. Although the loss of customer goodwill is difficult to measure, it may be the largest and most important quality control cost.

Link to Precor   **Precor** provides training and workout videos on how to use its equipment.

The relationship between the costs of quality is shown in Exhibit 9. The graph in Exhibit 9 indicates that as prevention and appraisal costs (blue line) increase, the percent of good units increases. In contrast, as internal and external failure costs (green line) decrease, the percent of good units increases. Total quality costs (red line) is the sum of the prevention/appraisal costs and internal/external failure costs.

Exhibit 9

The Relationship between the Costs of Quality

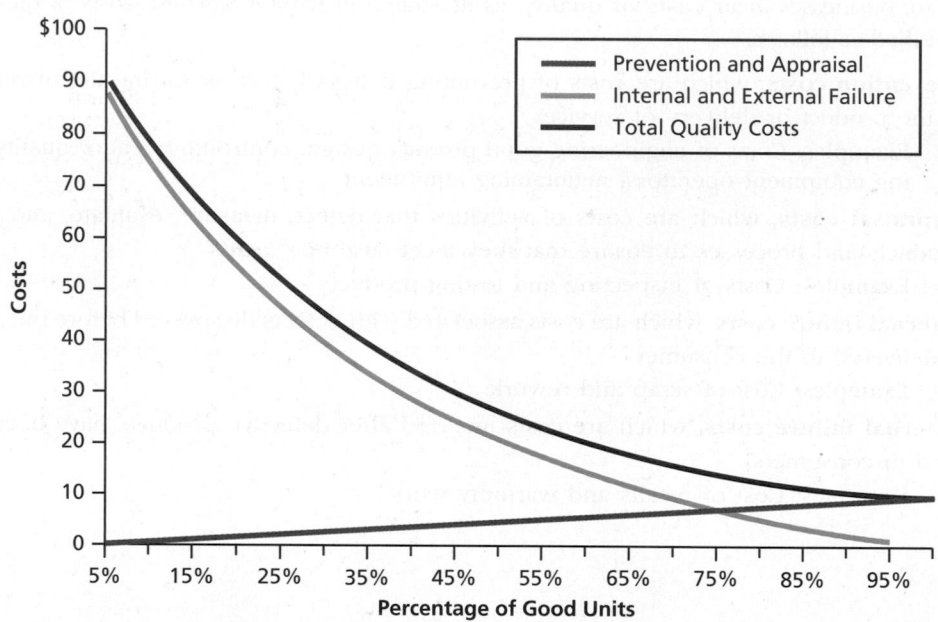

The optimal level of quality (percent of good units) is the one that minimizes the total quality costs. At this point, prevention and appraisal costs are balanced against internal and external failure costs. Exhibit 9 indicates that the optimal level of quality occurs at (or near) 100% quality. This is because prevention and appraisal costs grow moderately as quality increases. However, the costs of internal and external failure drop dramatically as quality increases.

Why It Matters

External Failure Costs: Lululemon Stretched Thin

Lululemon Athletica Inc. experienced a significant product recall in 2013 because its women's black luon pants produced

a visible level of "sheerness," which was deemed unacceptable to its customers. It was discovered that the material purchased for the product failed to meet its technical specifications. As a result, 17% of the pants were recalled and returned to the manufacturer, resulting in rework, allowances, and nearly $60 million in lost revenues.

Source: E. Tovar, "Cost of Quality: Case Study of Lululemon Recall 2013," *Prezi.com*, February 14, 2014.

Quality Activity Analysis

An activity analysis of quality quantifies the costs of quality in dollar terms. To illustrate, the quality control activities, activity costs, and quality cost classifications for Gifford Company, a consumer electronics company, are shown in Exhibit 10.

Quality Control Activities	Activity Cost	Quality Cost Classification
Design engineering	$ 55,000	Prevention
Disposing of rejected materials	160,000	Internal Failure
Finished goods inspection	140,000	Appraisal
Materials inspection	70,000	Appraisal
Preventive maintenance	80,000	Prevention
Processing returned materials	150,000	External Failure
Disposing of scrap	195,000	Internal Failure
Assessing vendor quality	45,000	Prevention
Rework	380,000	Internal Failure
Warranty work	225,000	External Failure
Total activity cost	$1,500,000	

Exhibit 10
Quality Control
Activity Analysis—
Gifford Company

Pareto Chart of Quality Costs One method of reporting quality cost information is using a Pareto chart. A **Pareto chart** is a bar chart that shows the totals of an attribute for a number of categories. The categories are ranked and shown left to right, so that the largest total attribute is on the left and the smallest total is on the right.

To illustrate, Exhibit 11 is a Pareto chart for the quality control activities in Exhibit 10. In Exhibit 11, the vertical axis is dollars, which represents quality control costs. The horizontal axis represents activity categories, which are the 10 quality control cost activities. The 10 quality control cost categories are ranked from the one with the largest total on the left to the one with the smallest total on the right. Thus, the largest bar on the left is rework costs ($380,000), the second bar is warranty work ($225,000), and so on.

The Pareto chart gives managers a quick visual tool for identifying the most important quality control cost categories. Exhibit 11 indicates that Gifford Company should focus efforts on reducing rework and warranty costs.

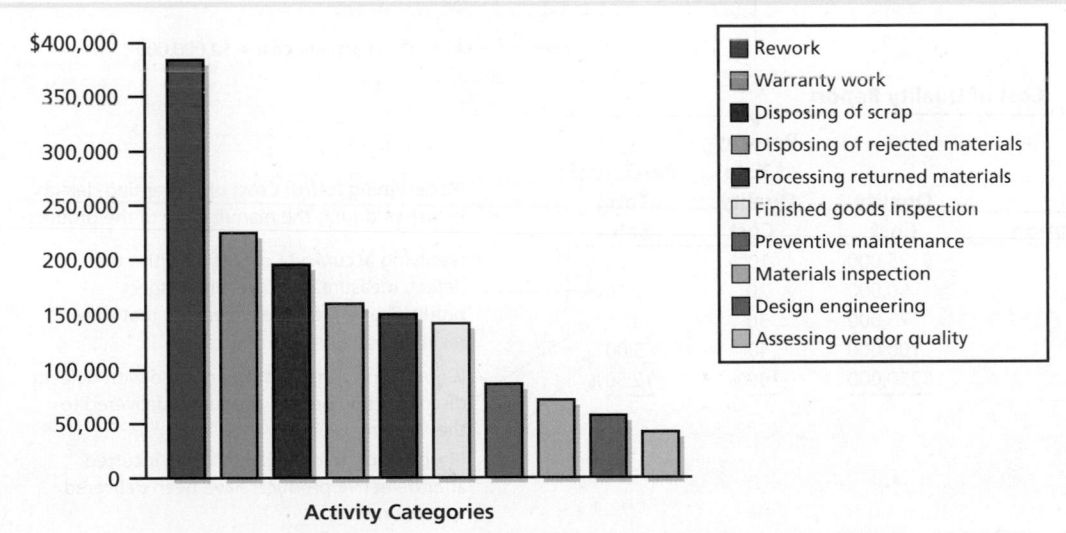

Exhibit 11
Pareto Chart of
Quality Costs

Cost of Quality Report The costs of quality also can be summarized in a cost of quality report. A **cost of quality report** normally reports the following:

- Total activity cost for each quality cost classification
- Percent of total quality costs associated with each classification
- Percent of each quality cost classification to sales

Exhibit 12 is a cost of quality report for Gifford Company, based on assumed sales of $5,000,000. Exhibit 12 indicates that only 12% of the total quality cost is the cost of preventing quality problems, while 14% is the cost of appraisal activities. Thus, prevention and appraisal costs make up only 26% of the total quality control costs. In contrast, 74% (49% + 25%) of the quality control costs are incurred for internal (49%) and external failure (25%) costs. In addition, internal and external failure costs are 22.2% (14.7% + 7.5%) of sales.

Exhibit 12 implies that Gifford Company is not spending enough on prevention and appraisal activities. By spending more on prevention and appraisal, internal and external failure costs will decrease, as was shown in Exhibit 9.

Exhibit 12

Cost of Quality Report—Gifford Company

Gifford Company
Cost of Quality Report

Quality Cost Classification	Quality Cost	Percent of Total Quality Cost	Percent of Total Sales
Prevention	$ 180,000	12%	3.6%
Appraisal	210,000	14	4.2
Internal failure	735,000	49	14.7
External failure	375,000	25	7.5
Total	$1,500,000	100%	30.0%

Check Up Corner 12-3   Cost of Quality Report

A quality control activity analysis indicated the following four activity costs of an administrative department:

Verifying the accuracy of a form	$ 50,000
Responding to customer complaints	100,000
Correcting errors in forms	75,000
Redesigning forms to reduce errors	25,000
Total	$250,000

Sales are $2,000,000. Prepare a cost of quality report.

Solution:

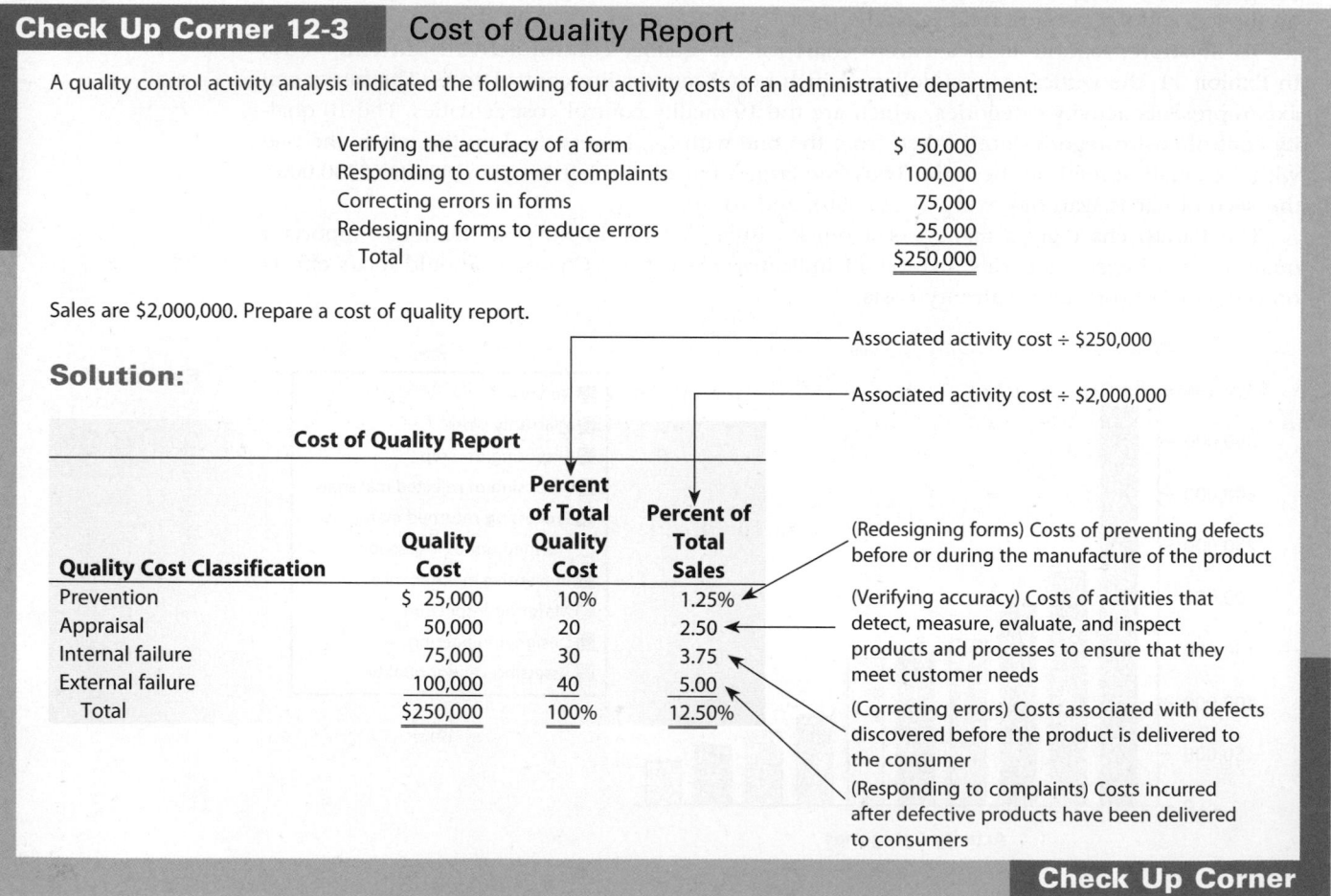

Associated activity cost ÷ $250,000

Associated activity cost ÷ $2,000,000

Cost of Quality Report

Quality Cost Classification	Quality Cost	Percent of Total Quality Cost	Percent of Total Sales
Prevention	$ 25,000	10%	1.25%
Appraisal	50,000	20	2.50
Internal failure	75,000	30	3.75
External failure	100,000	40	5.00
Total	$250,000	100%	12.50%

(Redesigning forms) Costs of preventing defects before or during the manufacture of the product

(Verifying accuracy) Costs of activities that detect, measure, evaluate, and inspect products and processes to ensure that they meet customer needs

(Correcting errors) Costs associated with defects discovered before the product is delivered to the consumer

(Responding to complaints) Costs incurred after defective products have been delivered to consumers

Check Up Corner

Value-Added Activity Analysis

In the preceding section, the quality control activities of Gifford Company were classified as prevention, appraisal, internal failure, and external failure activities. Activities also may be classified as follows:

- Value-added
- Non-value-added

A **value-added activity** is one that is necessary to meet customer requirements. A **non-value-added activity** is *not* required by the customer but occurs because of mistakes, errors, omissions, and process failures.

To illustrate, Exhibit 13 shows the value-added and non-value-added classification for the quality control activities for Gifford Company.[3] This exhibit also reveals that internal and external failure costs are classified as non-value-added. In contrast, prevention and appraisal costs are classified as value-added.[4]

A summary of the value-added and non-value-added activities follows. The summary expresses value-added and non-value-added costs as a percent of total costs.

Quality Control Activities	Activity Cost	Classification
Design engineering	$ 55,000	Value-added
Disposing of rejected materials	160,000	Non-value-added
Finished goods inspection	140,000	Value-added
Materials inspection	70,000	Value-added
Preventive maintenance	80,000	Value-added
Processing returned materials	150,000	Non-value-added
Disposing of scrap	195,000	Non-value-added
Assessing vendor quality	45,000	Value-added
Rework	380,000	Non-value-added
Warranty work	225,000	Non-value-added
Total activity cost	$1,500,000	

Exhibit 13
Value-Added/ Non-Value-Added Quality Control Activities

Classification	Amount	Percent
Value-added	$ 390,000	26%
Non-value-added	1,110,000	74
Total	$1,500,000	100%

The preceding summary indicates that 74% of Gifford Company's quality control activities are non-value-added. This should motivate Gifford Company to make improvements to reduce non-value-added activities.

Innovation and product improvement are value-added activities. **Precor** holds numerous patents for treadmills, bikes, and elliptical products.

Link to Precor

Process Activity Analysis

Activity analysis can be used to evaluate business processes. A **process** is a series of activities that converts an input into an output. In other words, a process is a set of activities linked together by inputs and outputs. Common business processes include the following:

- Procurement
- Product development
- Manufacturing
- Distribution
- Sales order fulfillment

Exhibit 14 shows a sales order fulfillment process for Masters Company. This process converts a customer order (the input) into a product received by the customer (the output).

---

[3] We use the quality control activities for illustrating the value-added and non-value-added activities in this section. However, a value-added/non-value-added activity analysis can be done for any activity in a business, not just quality control activities.

[4] Some believe that appraisal costs are non-value-added. They argue that if the product had been made correctly, then no inspection would be required. We take a less strict view and assume that appraisal costs are value-added.

Exhibit 14 Sales Order Fulfillment Process

*Operators driving forklifts receive a list of orders, drive to stacking locations within the warehouse, pick the orders, and then transport them back to an area to prepare for shipment.

Exhibit 14 indicates that Masters Company's sales order fulfillment process has the following four activities:

- Customer credit check
- Order entered into computer system
- Order picked from warehouse
- Order shipped

A process activity analysis can be used to determine the cost of the preceding activities. To illustrate, assume that a process activity analysis determines that the cost of the four activities is as follows:

Sales Order Fulfillment Activities	Activity Cost	Percent of Total Process Cost
Customer credit check	$14,400	18%
Order entered into computer system	9,600	12
Order picked from warehouse	36,000	45
Order shipped	20,000	25
Total sales order fulfillment process cost	$80,000	100%

If 10,000 sales orders are filled during the current period, the per-unit process cost is $8 per order ($80,000 ÷ 10,000 orders).

Management can use process activity analysis to improve a process. To illustrate, assume that Masters Company sets a cost improvement target of $6 per order. A $2 reduction per order ($8 – $6) requires improving efficiency or eliminating unnecessary activities.

Masters Company determines that only *new* customers need to have a credit check. If this change is made, it is estimated that only 25% of sales orders would require credit checks. In addition, by revising the warehouse product layout, it is estimated that the cost of picking orders can be reduced by 35%.

Assuming that 10,000 orders will be filled, the cost savings from these two improvements are as follows:

Sales Order Fulfillment Activities	Activity Cost Prior to Improvement	Activity Cost After Improvement	Activity Cost Savings
Customer credit check	$14,400	$ 3,600*	$10,800
Order entered in computer system	9,600	9,600	0
Order picked from warehouse	36,000	23,400**	12,600
Order shipped	20,000	20,000	0
Total sales order fulfillment process cost...............	$80,000	$56,600	$23,400
Cost per order (total cost divided by 10,000 orders)	$8.00	$5.66	

* $14,400 × 25%

** $36,000 – ($36,000 × 35%)

As illustrated, the activity changes generate a savings of $23,400.[5] In addition, the cost per order is reduced to $5.66, which is less than the $6.00 per order targeted cost.[6]

---

[5] This analysis assumes that the activity costs are variable to the inputs and outputs of the process. While this is likely true for processes primarily using labor, such as a sales order fulfillment process, other types of processes may have significant fixed costs that would not change with changes of inputs and outputs.

[6] Process activity analysis also can be integrated into a company's budgeting system using flexible budgets. Process activity analysis used in this way is discussed in advanced texts.

Analysis for Decision Making

Lean Performance for Nonmanufacturing

Objective

Describe and illustrate the use of lean principles and activity analysis in a service or administrative setting.

All of the lean principles and activity analyses discussed for a manufacturer can be adapted to service businesses or administrative processes. Examples of service businesses that use lean principles include hospitals, banks, insurance companies, and hotels. For service businesses, the "product" is normally the customer. Thus, for example, a hospital would measure the length of time to admit a patient in evaluating its admissions process.

Examples of administrative processes that use lean principles include processing insurance applications, product designs, and sales orders. For administrative processes, the "product" is often information. Thus, for example, a product design department would measure how long it takes to process a product design modification.

To illustrate, the customer service department of Municipal Water Services, Inc. resolves residential water problems. To determine how to improve its customer service, the department would measure its resolution response time. Resolution response time data are as follows:

	Average Response Time
First contact	0.5 hour
Service scheduling	0.5 hour
Wait for service	17.0 hours
Service	2.0 hours
Total resolution time	20.0 hours

The total lead time from the customer's first contact to final resolution is 20 hours. Of this time, 17 hours represent the customer waiting for the service. This represents 85% (17 hrs. ÷ 20 hrs.) non-value-added lead time in this process, or a 15% value-added ratio. Process improvement should focus on reducing the amount of time a customer waits for service. Improving scheduling or adding resources to the process could reduce wait time.

Make a Decision   Lean Performance for Nonmanufacturing

Northern Highlands Hospital is evaluating its admissions process by measuring the time elapsed between patient check-in and arrival in the clinical area. The present process involves a patient checking in at a centralized area and providing information to an admissions specialist. After being admitted, the patient is escorted from the admissions area to the appropriate clinical area in the hospital. Average lead time information is as follows:

	Average Lead Time
Wait in line at check-in window	15 min.
Check in (one check-in service line)	5
Wait in check-in area for admissions desk	30
Give information at admissions desk (one desk)	10
Wait for escort in check-in area	15
Go with escort to clinical area	5
Total lead time to arrive at clinical area	80 min.

The hospital staffs one person at check-in and one person at the admissions desk. There is one dedicated escort.

A. Determine the non-value-added lead time in this process.
B. Determine the value-added ratio of this process.
C. Identify some areas where the hospital could make improvements to increase the value-added ratio of this process.

Solution:

A.

	Average Lead Time
Wait in line at check-in desk	15 min.
Wait in check-in area for admissions desk	30
Wait for escort in check-in area	15
Total non-value-added lead time to arrive at clinical area	60 min.

B. Value-Added Ratio $= \dfrac{\text{Value–Added Lead Time}}{\text{Total Lead Time}}$

$= \dfrac{20 \text{ min.*}}{80 \text{ min.}} = 25\%$

*20 min. = 80 min. – 60 min.

C. The non-value-added lead time is related to waiting between each process element. Adding resources to the process during the busier times of the day can reduce the waiting. The check-in window could be expanded to multiple service lines, and the admissions desk could be expanded to multiple desks. This would reduce the waiting time between these activities. Adding more escorts could reduce the amount of time waiting to be escorted to a clinical area. A more radical approach would be to provide patients access to an admissions Web site prior to arriving at the hospital. In this way, admissions information could be input by the patient prior to coming to the hospital. In this scenario, the patient would check in and be escorted directly to a clinical area, because admissions information would have been captured previously. A complete redesign could decentralize the check-in process and make it part of the clinical areas. In this way, the patient could just go directly to the appropriate clinical area to check in. Combining preadmission with decentralized check-in at the clinical areas would virtually eliminate the existing process.

Let's Review

Chapter Summary

1. Lean manufacturing emphasizes reduced lead time, a product-oriented production layout, a team-oriented work environment, setup time reduction, pull manufacturing, high quality, and supplier and customer partnering in order to improve the supply chain.

2. Under lean manufacturing, the lean accounting system will have fewer transactions, will combine the materials and work in process accounts, and will account for direct labor as a part of cell conversion cost. Lean accounting will use nonfinancial reporting measures and result in more direct tracing of factory overhead to product cells.

3. Companies use activity analysis to identify the costs of quality, which include prevention, appraisal, internal failure, and external failure costs. The quality cost activities may be reported on a Pareto chart or quality cost report. An alternative method for categorizing activities is by value-added and non-value-added classifications. An activity analysis also can be used to improve the cost of processes.

Key Terms

activity analysis (579)
appraisal costs (579)
backflush accounting (576)
batch size (571)
Conversion Costs (576)
cost of quality report (581)
costs of quality (579)
electronic data interchange (EDI) (574)
employee involvement (573)
enterprise resource planning (ERP) (574)
external failure costs (579)

internal failure costs (579)
lead time (569)
lean accounting (576)
lean enterprise (568)
lean manufacturing (568)
lean principles (568)
nonfinancial measure (578)
non-value-added activity (583)
non-value-added lead time (570)
Pareto chart (581)
prevention costs (579)
process (583)

process-oriented layout (573)
product-oriented layout (573)
pull manufacturing (573)
push manufacturing (574)
radio frequency identification devices (RFID) (574)
Raw and In Process (RIP) Inventory (576)
Six Sigma (574)
supply chain management (574)
value-added activity (583)
value-added lead time (570)
value-added ratio (570)

Practice

Multiple-Choice Questions

1. Which of the following is **not** a characteristic of the lean manufacturing philosophy?
   A. Product-oriented layout
   B. Push manufacturing (make to stock)
   C. Short lead times
   D. Reducing setup time as a critical improvement priority

2. Accounting for lean manufacturing is best described as:
   A. more complex.
   B. focused on direct labor.
   C. providing detailed variance reports.
   D. providing less transaction control.

3. A product cell for Dynah Company has budgeted conversion costs of $420,000 for the year. The cell is planned to be available 2,100 hours for production. Each unit requires $12.50 of materials cost. The cell started and completed 700 units. The cell process time for the product is 15 minutes per unit. What is the cost to be debited to Finished Goods for the period?
   A. $8,750
   B. $35,000
   C. $43,750
   D. $140,000

4. In-process inspection activities are an example of what type of quality cost?
   A. Prevention
   B. Appraisal
   C. Internal failure
   D. External failure

5. A Pareto chart is used to display:
   A. a ranking of attribute totals, by category, in the form of a bar chart.
   B. important trends in the form of a line chart.
   C. percentage information in the form of a pie chart.
   D. a listing of attribute totals, by category, in a table.

Answers provided after Problem. Need more practice? Find additional multiple-choice questions, exercises, and problems in CengageNOWv2.

Exercises

SHOW ME HOW

1. Lead time   Obj. 1

The Swift Mountain Ski Company manufactures skis in the finishing and assembly process. Skis are manufactured in 30-ski batch sizes. The finishing time is 14 minutes per ski. The assembly time is 10 minutes per ski. It takes 8 minutes to move a batch of skis from finishing to assembly.

A. Compute the value-added, non-value-added, and total lead time of this process.

B. Compute the value-added ratio. (Round to one decimal place.)

SHOW ME HOW

2. Lean features   Obj. 1

Which of the following are features of a lean manufacturing system?

A. Production pace matches demand

B. Centralized work in process inventory locations

C. Push scheduling

D. Receive raw materials directly to manufacturing cells

SHOW ME HOW

3. Lean accounting   Obj. 2

The annual budgeted conversion costs for a lean cell are $663,000 for 1,950 production hours. Each unit produced by the cell requires 15 minutes of cell process time. During the month, 665 units are manufactured in the cell. The estimated materials costs are $160 per unit. Journalize entries for the following:

A. Materials are purchased to produce 700 units.

B. Conversion costs are applied to 665 units of production.

C. The cell completes 650 units, which are placed into finished goods.

SHOW ME HOW

4. Cost of quality report   Obj. 3

A quality control activity analysis indicated the following four activity costs of a manufacturing department:

Rework	$ 39,000
Inspecting incoming raw materials	51,000
Warranty work	27,000
Process improvement effort	183,000
Total	$300,000

Sales are $1,000,000. Prepare a cost of quality report. (Round percentages to one decimal place.)

SHOW ME HOW

5. Process activity analysis   Obj. 3

Lexter Company incurred an activity cost of $180,000 for inspecting 25,000 units of production. Management determined that the inspecting objectives could be met without inspecting every unit. Therefore, rather than inspecting 25,000 units of production, the inspection activity was limited to 40% of the production. Determine the inspection activity cost per unit on 25,000 units of total production both before and after the improvement.

Answers provided after Problem. Need more practice? Find additional multiple-choice questions, exercises, and problems in CengageNOWv2.

Problem

Krisco Company operates under the lean philosophy. As such, it has a production cell for its microwave ovens. The conversion cost for 2,400 hours of production is budgeted for the year at $4,800,000.

During January, 2,000 microwave ovens were started and completed. Each oven requires 6 minutes of cell processing time. The materials cost for each oven is $100.

Instructions
Use lean accounting to:
1. Determine the budgeted cell conversion cost per hour.
2. Determine the manufacturing cost per unit.
3. Journalize the entry to record the costs charged to the production cell in January.
4. Journalize the entry to record the costs transferred to finished goods.

Need more practice? Find additional multiple-choice questions, exercises, and problems in CengageNOWv2.

Answers

Multiple-Choice Questions

1. **B** The lean manufacturing philosophy embraces a product-oriented layout (answer A), making lead times short (answer C), and reducing setup times (answer D). Pull manufacturing, the opposite of push manufacturing (answer B), is also a lean manufacturing principle.

2. **D** Accounting in a lean manufacturing environment should not be complex (answer A), should not focus on direct labor (answer B) because it is combined with other conversion costs, and should not provide detailed variance reporting (answer C) because of higher reliance on nonfinancial performance measures. However, the lean manufacturing environment will have fewer transaction control features than the traditional system (answer D).

3. **C** $420,000 ÷ 2,100$ hours = $200 per hour

    $200 per hour × 0.25 per hour = $50 per unit

    700 units × ($50 + $12.50) = $43,750

4. **B** Appraisal costs (answer B) are the cost of inspecting and testing activities, which include detecting, measuring, evaluating, and auditing products and processes. Prevention (answer A) activities are incurred to prevent defects from occurring during the design and delivery of products or services. Internal failure costs (answer C) are associated with defects that are discovered by the organization before the product or service is delivered to the customer. External failure costs (answer D) are costs incurred after defective units or services have been delivered to customers.

5. **A** A Pareto chart is a bar chart that ranks attribute totals by category (answer A). A line chart (answer B), a pie chart (answer C), and a table listing (answer D) are other ways of displaying information, but they are not Pareto charts.

Exercises

1. A. Value-added lead time ....   24 min. (14 min. + 10 min.)
    Non-value-added lead time:
         Total within-batch wait time.................   696 (14 min. + 10 min.) × (30 − 1)
         Move time   8
    Total lead time...................................   <u>728</u> min.

    B. Value-added ratio: $\dfrac{24 \text{ min}}{728 \text{ min.}} = 3.3\%$

2. A. Production pace matches demand

    D. Receive raw materials directly to manufacturing cells

3. A. Raw and In Process Inventory*   112,000
        Accounts Payable   112,000

    *$160 per unit × 700 units

    B. Raw and In Process Inventory*   56,525
        Conversion Costs   56,525

    *[($663,000 ÷ 1,950 hours) × (15 min. ÷ 60 min.)]
    = $85 per unit; $85 × 665 units = $56,525

    C. Finished Goods Inventory*   159,250
        Raw and In Process Inventory   159,250

    *($160 + $85) × 650 units

4.

Cost of Quality Report

Quality Cost Classification	Quality Cost	Percent of Total Quality Cost	Percent of Total Sales
Prevention	$183,000	61%	18.3%
Appraisal...................................	51,000	17	5.1
Internal failure.............................	39,000	13	3.9
External failure	27,000	9	2.7
Total...................................	$300,000	100%	30.0%

5. Inspection activity before improvement .... $180,000 ÷ 25,000 units = $7.20 per unit
    Inspection activity after improvement:
        Revised inspection cost.....................   (40% × 25,000 units) × $7.20 per unit = $72,000
        Revised inspection cost per unit .... $72,000 ÷ 25,000 units = $2.88 per unit

***Need more help? Watch step-by-step videos of how to compute answers to these
Exercises in CengageNOWv2.***

Problem

1. Budgeted Cell Conversion Cost Rate = $\dfrac{\$4,800,000}{2,400 \text{ hours}}$ = $2,000 per cell hour

2. Materials $100 per unit
    Conversion cost [($2,000 per hour ÷ 60 min.) × 6 min.]   200
        Total $300 per unit

3.
    Raw and In Process Inventory   200,000
        Accounts Payable   200,000
            To record materials costs.
                (2,000 units × $100 per unit)

    Raw and In Process Inventory   400,000
        Conversion Costs   400,000
            To record conversion costs.
                (2,000 units × $200 per unit)

4.
    Finished Goods (2,000 × $300 per unit)   600,000
        Raw and In Process Inventory   600,000
            To record finished production.

Discussion Questions

1. What is the benefit of the lean philosophy?

2. What are some examples of non-value-added lead time?

3. Why is a product-oriented layout preferred by lean manufacturers over a process-oriented layout?

4. How is setup time related to lead time?

5. Why do lean manufacturers favor pull or "make to order" manufacturing?

6. Why would a lean manufacturer strive to produce zero defects?

7. How is supply chain management different from traditional supplier and customer relationships?

8. Why does lean accounting result in fewer transactions?

9. Why do lean manufacturers use a "raw and in process inventory" account, rather than separately reporting materials and work in process?

10. Why is the direct labor cost category eliminated in many lean manufacturing environments?

11. How does a Pareto chart assist management?

12. What is the benefit of identifying non-value-added activities?

13. In what ways can the cost of a process be improved?

Basic Exercises

SHOW ME HOW

BE 12-1 Lead time   Obj. 1

Rough Riders Inc. manufactures jeans in the cutting and sewing process. Jeans are manufactured in 50-jean batch sizes. The cutting time is 6 minutes per jean. The sewing time is 15 minutes per jean. It takes 5 minutes to move a batch of jeans from cutting to sewing.

A. Compute the value-added, non-value-added, and total lead time of this process.

B. Compute the value-added ratio. (Round to one decimal place.)

SHOW ME HOW

BE 12-2 Lean features   Obj. 1

Which of the following are features of a lean manufacturing system?

A. Centralized maintenance areas

B. Smaller batch sizes

C. Employee involvement

D. Less wasted movement of material and people

SHOW ME HOW

BE 12-3 Lean accounting   Obj. 2

The annual budgeted conversion costs for a lean cell are $180,000 for 2,000 production hours. Each unit produced by the cell requires 18 minutes of cell process time. During the month, 550 units are manufactured in the cell. The estimated materials costs are $32 per unit. Journalize the following entries for the month:

A. Materials are purchased to produce 600 units.

B. Conversion costs are applied to 550 units of production.

C. The cell completes 500 units, which are placed into finished goods.

SHOW ME HOW

BE 12-4 Cost of quality report   Obj. 3

A quality control activity analysis indicated the following four activity costs of a hotel:

Inspecting cleanliness of rooms	$175,000
Processing lost customer reservations	40,000
Rework incorrectly prepared room service meal	20,000
Employee training	265,000
Total	$500,000

Sales are $4,000,000. Prepare a cost of quality report. (Round percentage to one decimal.)

SHOW ME HOW

BE 12-5   Process activity analysis   Obj. 3

Roen Company incurred an activity cost of $105,600 for inspecting 40,000 units of production. Management determined that the inspecting objectives could be met without inspecting every unit. Therefore, rather than inspecting 40,000 units of production, the inspection activity was limited to a random selection of 5,000 units out of the 40,000 units of production. Determine the inspection activity cost per unit on 40,000 units of total production both before and after the improvement.

Exercises

EX 12-1   Lean principles   Obj. 1

The chief executive officer (CEO) of Platnum Inc. has just returned from a management seminar describing the benefits of the lean philosophy. The CEO issued the following statement after returning from the conference:

This company will become a lean manufacturing company. Presently, we have too much inventory. To become lean, we need to eliminate the excess inventory. Therefore, I want all employees to begin reducing inventories until we make products "just in time." Thank you for your cooperation.

➤ How would you respond to the CEO's statement?

EX 12-2   Lean as a strategy   Obj. 1

The American textile industry has moved much of its operations offshore in the pursuit of lower labor costs. Textile imports have risen from 2% of all textile production in the early 1960s to over 70%. Offshore manufacturers make long runs of standard mass-market apparel items. These are then brought to the United States in container ships, requiring significant time between original order and delivery. As a result, retail customers must accurately forecast market demands for imported apparel items.

➤ Assuming that you work for a U.S.-based textile company, how would you recommend responding to the low-cost imports?

EX 12-3   Lean principles   Obj. 1

Active Apparel Company manufactures various styles of men's casual wear. Shirts are cut and assembled by a workforce that is paid by piece rate. This means that they are paid according to the amount of work completed during a period of time. To illustrate, if the piece rate is $0.15 per sleeve assembled, and the worker assembles 700 sleeves during the day, then the worker would be paid $105 (700 × $0.15) for the day's work.

The company is considering adopting a lean manufacturing philosophy by organizing work cells around various types of products and employing pull manufacturing. However, no change is expected in the compensation policy. On this point, the manufacturing manager stated the following:

"Piecework compensation provides an incentive to work fast. Without it, the workers will just goof off and expect a full day's pay. We can't pay straight hourly wages—at least not in this industry."

➤ How would you respond to the manufacturing manager's comments?

EX 12-4   Lead time analysis   Obj. 1

Palm Pals Inc. manufactures toy stuffed animals. The direct labor time required to cut, sew, and stuff a toy is 12 minutes per unit. The company makes two types of stuffed toys—a lion and a bear. The lion is assembled in lot sizes of 40 units per batch, while the bear is assembled in lot sizes of 5 units per batch. Since each product has direct labor time of 12 minutes per unit, management has determined that the lead time for each product is 12 minutes.

➤ Is management correct? What are the lead times for each product?

EX 12-5 Reduce setup time

Obj. 1

Hammond Inc. has analyzed the setup time on its computer-controlled lathe. The setup requires changing the type of fixture that holds a part. The average setup time has been 135 minutes, consisting of the following steps:

Turn off machine and remove fixture from lathe	10 minutes
Go to tool room with fixture	15
Record replacement of fixture to tool room	18
Return to lathe	20
Clean lathe	15
Return to tool room	20
Record withdrawal of new fixture from tool room	12
Return to lathe	15
Install new fixture and turn on machine	10
Total setup time	135 minutes

A. ✏️ Why should management be concerned about improving setup time?

B. ✏️ What do you recommend to Hammond Inc. for improving setup time?

C. How much time would be required for a setup, using your suggestion in (B)?

EX 12-6 Calculate lead time

Obj. 1

Value-added, 12 minutes

EXCEL TEMPLATE

Flint Fabricators Inc. machines metal parts for the automotive industry. Under the traditional manufacturing approach, the parts are machined through two processes: milling and finishing. Parts are produced in batch sizes of 30 parts. A part requires 5 minutes in milling and 7 minutes in finishing. The move time between the two operations for a complete batch is 5 minutes.

Under the lean philosophy, the part is produced in a cell that includes both the milling and finishing operations. The operating time is unchanged; however, the batch size is reduced to 4 parts and the move time is eliminated.

Determine the value-added, non-value-added, and total lead times, and the value-added ratio under the traditional and lean manufacturing methods. (Round percentages to one decimal place.)

EX 12-7 Calculate lead time

Obj. 1

✔ B. Non-value-added, 50 minutes

EXCEL TEMPLATE

Williams Optical Inc. is considering a new lean product cell. The present manufacturing approach produces a product in four separate steps. The production batch sizes are 45 units. The process time for each step is as follows:

Process Step 1	5 minutes
Process Step 2	8 minutes
Process Step 3	4 minutes
Process Step 4	3 minutes

The time required to move each batch between steps is 5 minutes. In addition, the time to move raw materials to Process Step 1 is also 5 minutes, and the time to move completed units from Process Step 4 to finished goods inventory is 5 minutes.

The new lean layout will allow the company to reduce the batch sizes from 45 units to 3 units. The time required to move each batch between steps and the inventory locations will be reduced to 2 minutes. The processing time in each step will stay the same.

Determine the value-added, non-value-added, and total lead times, and the value-added ratio under the (A) present and (B) proposed production approaches. (Round percentages to one decimal place.)

REAL WORLD

EX 12-8 Supply chain management   Obj. 1

The following is an excerpt from an article discussing supplier relationships with the Big Three North American automakers.

"The Big Three select suppliers on the basis of lowest price and annual price reductions," said Neil De Koker, president of the Original Equipment Suppliers Association. "They look globally for the lowest parts prices from the lowest cost countries," De Koker said. "There is little trust and respect. Collaboration is missing." Japanese auto makers want long-term supplier relationships. They select suppliers as a person would a mate. The Big Three are quick to beat down prices with methods such as electronic auctions or rebidding work to a competitor. The Japanese are equally tough on price but are committed to maintaining supplier continuity. "They work with you to arrive at a competitive price, and they are willing to pay because they want long-term partnering," said Carl Code, a vice president at **Ernie Green Industries**. "They [**Honda** and **Toyota**] want suppliers to make enough money to stay in business, grow, and bring them innovation." The Big Three's supply chain model is not much different from the one set by Henry Ford. In 1913, he set up the system of independent supplier firms operating at arm's length on short-term contracts. One consequence of the Big Three's low-price-at-all-costs mentality is that suppliers are reluctant to offer them their cutting-edge technology out of fear the contract will be resourced before the research and development costs are recouped.

Source: Robert Sherefkin and Amy Wilson, "Suppliers Prefer Japanese Business Model," *Rubber & Plastics News*, March 17, 2003, Vol. 24, No. 11.

A. Contrast the Japanese supply chain model with that of the Big Three.

B. Why might a supplier prefer the Japanese model?

C. What benefits might accrue to the Big Three by adopting the Japanese supply chain practices?

REAL WORLD

EX 12-9 Employee involvement   Obj. 1

Quickie Designs Inc. uses teams in the manufacture of lightweight wheelchairs. Two features of its team approach are team hiring and peer reviews. Under team hiring, the team recruits, interviews, and hires new team members from within the organization. Using peer reviews, the team evaluates each member of the team with regard to quality, knowledge, teamwork, goal performance, attendance, and safety. These reviews provide feedback to the team member for improvement.

How do these two team approaches differ from using managers to hire and evaluate employees?

EX 12-10 Lean principles for a restaurant   Obj. 1

The management of Grill Rite Burger fast-food franchise wants to provide hamburgers quickly to customers. It has been using a process by which precooked hamburgers are prepared and placed under hot lamps. These hamburgers are then sold to customers. In this process, every customer receives the same type of hamburger and dressing (ketchup, onions, mustard). If a customer wants something different, then a "special order" must be cooked to the customer's requirements. This requires the customer to wait several minutes, which often slows down the service line. Grill Rite has been receiving more and more special orders from customers, which has been slowing service down considerably.

A. Is the Grill Rite service delivery system best described as a push or pull system? Explain.

B. How might you use lean principles to provide customers quick service, yet still allow them to custom order their burgers?

EX 12-11 Accounting issues in a lean environment   Obj. 2

Pinnacle Technologies has recently implemented a lean manufacturing approach. A production manager has approached the controller with the following comments:

I am very upset with our accounting system now that we have implemented our new lean manufacturing methods. It seems as if all I'm doing is paperwork. Our product is moving so fast through the manufacturing process that the paperwork can hardly keep up. For example, it just doesn't make sense to me to fill out daily labor reports. The employees are assigned to complete cells, performing many different tasks. I can't keep up with direct labor reports on each individual task. I thought we were trying to eliminate waste. Yet the information requirements of the accounting system are slowing us down and adding to overall lead time. Moreover, I'm still getting my monthly variance reports. I don't think that these are necessary. I have nonfinancial performance measures that are more timely than these reports. Besides, the employees don't really understand accounting variances. How about giving some information that I can really use?

What accounting system changes would you suggest in light of the production department manager's criticisms?

EX 12-12 Lean accounting
Obj. 2

✔ B. $105

SHOW ME HOW

Westgate Inc. uses a lean manufacturing strategy to manufacture DVR (digital video recorder) players. The company manufactures DVR players through a single product cell. The budgeted conversion cost for the year is $600,000 for 2,000 production hours. Each unit requires 21 minutes of cell process time. During March, 500 DVR players were manufactured in the cell. The materials cost per unit is $60. The following summary transactions took place during March:

1. Materials were purchased for March production.
2. Conversion costs were applied to production.
3. 500 DVR players were assembled and placed in finished goods.
4. 480 DVR players were sold for $240 per unit.

A. Determine the budgeted cell conversion cost per hour.
B. Determine the budgeted cell conversion cost per unit.
C. Journalize the summary transactions (1)–(4) for March.

EX 12-13 Lean accounting
Obj. 2

✔ A. $140

SHOW ME HOW

Modern Lighting Inc. manufactures lighting fixtures, using lean manufacturing methods. Style Omega has a materials cost per unit of $16. The budgeted conversion cost for the year is $308,000 for 2,200 production hours. A unit of Style Omega requires 18 minutes of cell production time. The following transactions took place during June:

1. Materials were acquired to assemble 620 Style Omega units for June.
2. Conversion costs were applied to 620 Style Omega units of production.
3. 600 units of Style Omega were completed in June.
4. 580 units of Style Omega were sold in June for $100 per unit.

A. Determine the budgeted cell conversion cost per hour.
B. Determine the budgeted cell conversion cost per unit.
C. Journalize the summary transactions (1)–(4) for June.

EX 12-14 Lean accounting
Obj. 2

✔ B. Finished goods, $7,300

SHOW ME HOW

Vintage Audio Inc. manufactures audio speakers. Each speaker requires $48 per unit of direct materials. The speaker manufacturing assembly cell includes the following estimated costs for the period:

Speaker assembly cell, estimated costs:	
Labor	$30,000
Depreciation	12,000
Supplies	6,000
Power	2,000
Total cell costs for the period	$50,000

The operating plan calls for 800 operating hours for the period. Each speaker requires 24 minutes of cell process time. The unit selling price for each speaker is $90. During the period, the following transactions occurred:

1. Purchased materials to produce 2,000 speaker units.
2. Applied conversion costs to production of 1,800 speaker units.

(Continued)

3. Completed and transferred 1,700 speaker units to finished goods.

4. Sold 1,600 speaker units.

There were no inventories at the beginning of the period.

A. Journalize the summary transactions (1)–(4) for the period.

B. Determine the ending balance of Raw and In Process Inventory and Finished Goods Inventory.

EX 12-15   Pareto chart   **Obj. 3**

Meagher Solutions Inc. manufactures memory chips for personal computers. An activity analysis was conducted, and the following activity costs were identified with the manufacture and sale of memory chips:

Activities	Activity Cost
Correct shipment errors	$ 150,000
Disposing of scrap	95,000
Emergency equipment maintenance	125,000
Employee training	50,000
Final inspection	80,000
Inspecting incoming materials	60,000
Preventive equipment maintenance	40,000
Processing customer returns	90,000
Scrap reporting	45,000
Supplier development	15,000
Warranty claims	250,000
Total	$1,000,000

Prepare a Pareto chart of these activities.

EX 12-16   Cost of quality report   **Obj. 3**

✔ B. Appraisal, 14.0% of total quality cost

A. Using the information in Exercise 15, identify the cost of quality classification for each activity.

B. Prepare of cost of quality report. Assume sales for the period were $4,000,000. (Round percentages to one decimal place.)

SHOW ME HOW

C. ━━━━━▶ Interpret the cost of quality report.

EX 12-17   Pareto chart for a service company   **Obj. 1, 3**

Three Rivers Inc. provides cable TV and Internet service to the local community. The activities and activity costs of Three Rivers are identified as follows:

Activities	Activity Cost
Billing error correction	$ 60,000
Cable signal testing	140,000
Reinstalling service (installed incorrectly the first time)	40,000
Repairing satellite equipment	50,000
Repairing underground cable connections to the customer	25,000
Replacing old technology cable with higher quality cable	175,000
Replacing old technology signal switches with higher quality switches	150,000
Responding to customer home repair requests	30,000
Training employees	80,000
Total	$750,000

Prepare a Pareto chart of these activities.

EX 12-18   Cost of quality and value-added/non-value-added reports for a service company

Obj. 1, 3

✔ **B. External failure, 20.7% of total cost**

SHOW ME HOW   EXCEL TEMPLATE

A. Using the information in Exercise 17, identify the cost of quality classification for each activity and whether the activity is value-added or non-value-added.

B. Prepare a cost of quality report. Assume that sales are $3,000,000. (Round percentages to one decimal place.)

C. Prepare a value-added/non-value-added analysis.

D. ━━━━▸ Interpret the information in (B) and (C).

EX 12-19   Process activity analysis

Obj. 3

✔ **A. $0.08 per can**

The Brite Beverage Company bottles soft drinks into aluminum cans. The manufacturing process consists of three activities:

1. **Mixing:** water, sugar, and beverage concentrate are mixed.
2. **Filling:** mixed beverage is filled into 12-oz. cans.
3. **Packaging:** properly filled cans are boxed into cardboard "fridge packs."

The activity costs associated with these activities for the period are as follows:

Mixing	$216,000
Filling	168,000
Packaging	96,000
Total	$480,000

The activity costs do not include materials costs, which are ignored for this analysis. Each can is expected to contain 12 ounces of beverage. Thus, after being filled, each can is automatically weighed. If a can is too light, it is rejected, or "kicked," from the filling line prior to being packaged. The primary cause of kicks is heat expansion. With heat expansion, the beverage overflows during filling, resulting in underweight cans.

This process begins by mixing and filling 6,300,000 cans during the period, of which only 6,000,000 cans are actually packaged. Three hundred thousand cans are rejected due to underweight kicks.

A process improvement team has determined that cooling the cans prior to filling them will reduce the amount of overflows due to expansion. After this improvement, the number of kicks is expected to decline from 300,000 cans to 63,000 cans, thus increasing the number of filled cans to 6,237,000 [6,000,000 + (300,000 − 63,000)].

A. Determine the total activity cost per packaged can under present operations.

B. Determine the amount of increased packaging activity costs from the expected improvements.

C. Determine the expected total activity cost per packaged can after improvements. (Round to three decimal places.)

EX 12-20   Process activity analysis for a service company

Obj. 1, 3

✔ **B. $250 per paid claim**

SHOW ME HOW   EXCEL TEMPLATE

Statewide Insurance Company has a process for making payments on insurance claims as follows:

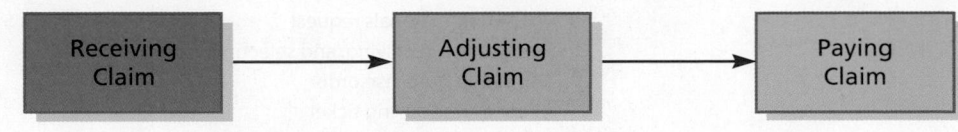

An activity analysis revealed that the cost of these activities was as follows:

Receiving claim	$ 120,000
Adjusting claim	260,000
Paying claim	120,000
Total	$ 500,000

(Continued)

This process includes only the cost of processing the claim payments, not the actual amount of the claim payments. The adjusting activity involves verifying and estimating the amount of the claim and is variable to the number of claims adjusted.

The process received, adjusted, and paid 2,000 claims during the period. All claims were treated identically in this process.

To improve the cost of this process, management has determined that claims should be segregated into two categories. Claims under $1,000 and claims greater than $1,000: claims under $1,000 would not be adjusted but would be accepted upon the insured's evidence of claim. Claims above $1,000 would be adjusted. It is estimated that 80% of the claims are under $1,000 and would thus be paid without adjustment. It is also estimated that the additional effort to segregate claims would add 10% to the "receiving claim" activity cost.

A. Develop a table showing the percent of individual activity cost to the total process cost.

B. Determine the average total process cost per claim payment, assuming 2,000 total claims.

C. Prepare a table showing the changes in the activity costs as a result of the changes proposed by management. Show columns of activity cost prior to improvement, after improvement, and savings.

D. Estimate the average cost per claim payment, assuming that the changes proposed by management are enacted for 2,000 total claims.

EX 12-21 Process activity analysis   Obj. 1, 3

✔ B. $20 per payment

EXCEL TEMPLATE

The procurement process for Omni Wholesale Company includes a series of activities that transforms a materials requisition into a vendor check. The process begins with a request for materials. The requesting department prepares and sends a materials request form to the Purchasing Department. The Purchasing Department then places a request for a quote to vendors. Vendors prepare bids in response to the request for a quote. A vendor is selected based on the lowest bid. A purchase order to the low-bid vendor is prepared. The vendor delivers the materials to the company, whereupon a receiving ticket is prepared. Payment to the vendor is authorized if the materials request form, receiving ticket, and vendor invoice are in agreement. These three documents fail to agree 40% of the time, initiating effort to reconcile the differences. Once the three documents agree, a check is issued. The process can be diagrammed as follows:

Correcting Reconciliation Differences

An activity analysis indicated the following activity costs with this process:

Preparing materials request	$ 36,000
Requesting, receiving, and selecting vendor bids	100,000
Preparing purchase order	20,000
Preparing receiving ticket	24,000
Matching M/R, R/T, and invoice	48,000
Correcting reconciliation differences	140,000
Preparing and delivering vendor payment	32,000
Total process activity cost	$400,000

On average, the process handles 20,000 individual requests for materials that result in 20,000 individual payments to vendors.

Management proposes to improve this process in two ways. First, the Purchasing Department will develop a preapproved vendor list for which orders can be placed without a request for quote. It is expected that this will reduce the cost of requesting and receiving vendor bids by 75%. Second, additional training and standardization will be provided to reduce errors introduced into the materials requisition form and receiving tickets. It is expected that this will reduce the number of reconciliation differences from 40% to 10%, over an average of 20,000 payments.

A. Develop a table showing the percent of individual activity cost to the total process cost.

B. Determine the average total process cost per vendor payment, assuming 20,000 payments.

C. Prepare a table showing the improvements in the activity costs as a result of the changes proposed by management. Show columns of activity cost prior to improvement, after improvement, and savings.

D. Estimate the average cost per vendor payment, assuming that the changes proposed by management are enacted for 20,000 total payments.

Problems: Series A

PR 12-1A   Lean principles

Obj. 1

3. Average inventory for quarter, 22,500 lbs.

Soft Glow, Inc. manufactures light bulbs. Its purchasing policy requires that the purchasing agents place each quarter's purchasing requirements out for bid. This is because the Purchasing Department is evaluated solely by its ability to get the lowest purchase prices. The lowest bidder receives the order for the next quarter (90 working days).

To make its bulb products, Soft Glow requires 45,000 pounds of glass per quarter. Soft Glow received two glass bids for the third quarter, as follows:

- *Mid-States Glass Company*: $28.00 per pound of glass. Delivery schedule: 45,000 (500 lbs. × 90 days) pounds at the beginning of July to last for 3 months.
- *Cleveland Glass Company*: $28.20 per pound of glass. Delivery schedule: 500 pounds per working day (90 days in the quarter).

Soft Glow accepted Mid-States Glass Company's bid because it was the low-cost bid.

Instructions

1. ▬▬▬► Comment on Soft Glow's purchasing policy.

2. ▬▬▬► What are the additional (hidden) costs, beyond price, of Mid-States Glass Company's bid? Why weren't these costs considered?

3. Considering only inventory financing costs, what is the additional cost per pound of Mid-States Glass Company's bid if the annual cost of money is 10%? (*Hint:* Determine the average value of glass inventory held for the quarter and multiply by the quarterly interest charge, then divide by the number of pounds.)

PR 12-2A   Lead time

Obj. 1

✔ 1. Total wait time, 1,741 minutes

EXCEL TEMPLATE

Sound Tek Inc. manufactures electronic stereo equipment. The manufacturing process includes printed circuit (PC) board assembly, final assembly, testing, and shipping. In the PC board assembly operation, a number of individuals are responsible for assembling electronic components into printed circuit boards. Each operator is responsible for soldering components according to a given set of instructions. Operators work on batches of 45 printed circuit boards. Each board requires 5 minutes of board assembly time. After each batch is completed, the operator moves the assembled boards to the final assembly area. This move takes 10 minutes to complete.

The final assembly for each stereo unit requires 15 minutes and is also done in batches of 45 units. A batch of 45 stereos is moved into the test building, which is across the street. The move takes 20 minutes. Before conducting the test, the test equipment must be set up for the particular stereo model. The test setup requires 25 minutes. The units wait while the setup is performed. In the final test, the 45-unit batch is tested one at a time. Each test requires 9 minutes. The completed batch, after all testing, is sent to shipping for packaging and final shipment to customers. A complete batch of 45 units is sent from testing to shipping. The Shipping Department

(Continued)

is located next to testing. Thus, there is no move time between these two operations. Packaging and labeling requires 10 minutes per unit.

Instructions

1. Determine the amount of value-added and non-value-added lead time and the value-added ratio in this process for an average stereo unit in a batch of 45 units. (Round percentages to one decimal place.) Categorize the non-value-added time into wait and move time.

2. ━━━━▶ How could this process be improved so as to reduce the amount of waste?

PR 12-3A   Lean accounting   **Obj. 2**

✔ 4. Raw and In Process Inventory, $22,400

SHOW ME HOW   EXCEL TEMPLATE

Dashboard Inc. manufactures and assembles automobile instrument panels for both eCar Motors and Greenville Motors. The process consists of a lean product cell for each customer's instrument assembly. The data that follow concern only the eCar lean cell.

For the year, Dashboard Inc. budgeted the following costs for the eCar production cell:

Conversion Cost Categories	Budget
Labor	$ 800,000
Supplies	275,000
Utilities	325,000
Total	$1,400,000

Dashboard Inc. plans 2,000 hours of production for the eCar cell for the year. The materials cost is $240 per instrument assembly. Each assembly requires 24 minutes of cell assembly time. There was no April 1 inventory for either Raw and In Process Inventory or Finished Goods Inventory.

The following summary events took place in the eCar cell during April:

A. Electronic parts and wiring were purchased to produce 450 instrument assemblies in April.

B. Conversion costs were applied for the production of 400 units in April.

C. 380 units were started, completed, and transferred to finished goods in April.

D. 350 units were shipped to customers at a price of $800 per unit.

Instructions

1. Determine the budgeted cell conversion cost per hour.

2. Determine the budgeted cell conversion cost per unit.

3. Journalize the summary transactions (A) through (D).

4. Determine the ending balance in Raw and In Process Inventory and Finished Goods Inventory.

5. ━━━━▶ How does the accounting in a lean environment differ from traditional accounting?

PR 12-4A   Pareto chart and cost of quality report for a service company   **Obj. 1, 3**

✔ 4. Non-value-added, 61%

EXCEL TEMPLATE

The administrator of Hope Hospital has been asked to perform an activity analysis of the emergency room (ER). The ER activities include cost of quality and other patient care activities. The lab tests and transportation are hospital services external to the ER for determining external failure costs. The result of the activity analysis is summarized as follows:

Activities	Activity Cost
Patient registration	$ 6,400
Verifying patient information	9,600
Assigning patients	12,800
Searching/waiting for doctor	8,000
Doctor exam	4,800
Waiting for transport	17,600
Transporting patients	16,000
Verifying lab orders	14,400
Searching for equipment	8,000
Incorrect labs	12,800
Lab tests	17,600
Counting supplies	19,200

Looking for supplies	8,000
Staff training	4,800
Total	$160,000

Instructions

1. Prepare a Pareto chart of the ER activities.

2. Classify the activities into prevention, appraisal, internal failure, external failure, and other patient care activities. Classify the activities into value-added and non-value-added activities.

3. Use the activity cost information to determine the percentages of total ER costs that are prevention, appraisal, internal failure, external failure, and other patient care activities.

4. Determine the percentages of the total ER costs that are value-added and non-value-added.

5. ➤ Interpret the information.

Problems: Series B

PR 12-1B   Lean principles   **Obj. 1**

3. Average frames in inventory, 2,250

HD Hogg Motorcycle Company manufactures a variety of motorcycles. Hogg's purchasing policy requires that the purchasing agents place each quarter's purchasing requirements out for bid. This is because the Purchasing Department is evaluated solely by its ability to get the lowest purchase prices. The lowest cost bidder receives the order for the next quarter (90 days). To make its motorcycles, Hogg requires 4,500 frames per quarter. Hogg received two frame bids for the third quarter, as follows:

- *Famous Frames, Inc.*: $301 per frame. Delivery schedule: 50 frames per working day (90 days in the quarter).
- *Iron Horse Frames Inc.*: $300 per frame. Delivery schedule: 4,500 (50 frames × 90 days) frames at the beginning of July to last for three months.

Hogg accepted Iron Horse Frames Inc.'s bid because it was the low-cost bid.

Instructions

1. ➤ Comment on Hogg's purchasing policy.

2. ➤ What are the additional (hidden) costs, beyond price, of Iron Horse Frames Inc.'s bid? Why weren't these costs considered?

3. Considering only inventory financing costs, what is the additional cost per frame of Iron Horse Frames Inc.'s bid if the annual cost of money is 12%? (*Hint:* Determine the average value of frame inventory held for the quarter and multiply by the quarterly interest charge, then divide by the number of frames.)

PR 12-2B   Lead time   **Obj. 1**

✔ 1. Total wait time, 2,010 minutes

EXCEL TEMPLATE

Master Chef Appliance Company manufactures home kitchen appliances. The manufacturing process includes stamping, final assembly, testing, and shipping. In the stamping operation, a number of individuals are responsible for stamping the steel outer surface of the appliance. The stamping operation is set up prior to each run. A run of 40 stampings is completed after each setup. A setup requires 60 minutes. The parts wait for the setup to be completed before stamping begins. Each stamping requires 5 minutes of operating time. After each batch is completed, the operator moves the stamped covers to the final assembly area. This move takes 10 minutes to complete.

The final assembly for each appliance unit requires 22 minutes and is also done in batches of 40 appliance units. The batch of 40 appliance units is moved into the test building, which is across the street. The move takes 25 minutes. In the final test, the 40-unit batch is tested one at a time. Each test requires 8 minutes. The completed units are sent to shipping for packaging and final shipment to customers. A complete batch of 40 units is sent from testing to shipping. The Shipping Department is located next to testing. Thus, there is no move time between these two operations. Packaging and shipment labeling requires 15 minutes per unit.

(Continued)

Instructions

1. Determine the amount of value-added and non-value-added lead time and the value-added ratio in this process for an average kitchen appliance in a batch of 40 units. (Round percentages to one decimal place.) Categorize the non-value-added time into wait and move time.

2. ━━━➤ How could this process be improved so as to reduce the amount of waste?

PR 12-3B   Lean accounting   Obj. 2

✔ 4. Raw and In Process Inventory, $9,700

SHOW ME HOW   EXCEL TEMPLATE

Com-Tel Inc. manufactures and assembles two models of smartphones—the Tiger Model and the Lion Model. The process consists of a lean cell for each product. The data that follow concern only the Lion Model lean cell.

For the year, Com-Tel Inc. budgeted these costs for the Lion Model production cell:

Conversion Cost Categories	Budget
Labor	$122,000
Supplies	49,000
Utilities	18,000
Total	$189,000

Com-Tel plans 2,100 hours of production for the Lion Model cell for the year. The materials cost is $185 per unit. Each assembly requires 12 minutes of cell assembly time. There was no May 1 inventory for either Raw and In Process Inventory or Finished Goods Inventory.

The following summary events took place in the Lion Model cell during May:

A. Electronic parts were purchased to produce 900 Lion Model assemblies in May.

B. Conversion costs were applied for 875 units of production in May.

C. 850 units were completed and transferred to finished goods in May.

D. 800 units were shipped to customers at a price of $500 per unit.

Instructions

1. Determine the budgeted cell conversion cost per hour.

2. Determine the budgeted cell conversion cost per unit.

3. Journalize the summary transactions (A) through (D).

4. Determine the ending balance in Raw and In Process Inventory and Finished Goods Inventory.

5. ━━━➤ How does the accounting in a lean environment differ from traditional accounting?

PR 12-4B   Pareto chart and cost of quality report for a manufacturing   Obj. 3
company

✔ 4. Non-value-added, 35%

The president of Mission Inc. has been concerned about the growth in costs over the last several years. The president asked the controller to perform an activity analysis to gain a better insight into these costs. The activity analysis revealed the following:

Activities	Activity Cost
Correcting invoice errors	$ 7,500
Disposing of incoming materials with poor quality	15,000
Disposing of scrap	27,500
Expediting late production	22,500
Final inspection	20,000
Inspecting incoming materials	5,000
Inspecting work in process	25,000
Preventive machine maintenance	15,000
Producing product	97,500
Responding to customer quality complaints	15,000
Total	$250,000

The production process is complicated by quality problems, requiring the production manager to expedite production and dispose of scrap.

Instructions

1. Prepare a Pareto chart of the company activities.

2. Classify the activities into prevention, appraisal, internal failure, external failure, and not costs of quality (producing product). Classify the activities into value-added and non-value-added activities.

3. Use the activity cost information to determine the percentages of total costs that are prevention, appraisal, internal failure, external failure, and not costs of quality.

4. Determine the percentages of total costs that are value-added and non-value-added.

5. ━━━━➤ Interpret the information.

Analysis for Decision Making

ADM-1 Lead time reduction for an insurance company

Shield Insurance Company takes 10 days to make payments on insurance claims. Claims are processed through three departments: Data Input, Claims Audit, and Claims Adjustment. The three departments are located in different buildings, approximately one hour apart from each other. Claims are processed in batches of 100. Each batch of 100 claims moves through the three departments on a wheeled cart. Management is concerned about customer dissatisfaction caused by the long lead time for claim payments.

━━━━➤ How might this process be changed so that the lead time is reduced significantly?

ADM-2 Turn around time in an operating room of a hospital

Turn around time (TAT) is a measure of the length of time from the end of one surgery in an operating room to the beginning of the next surgery. Improving TAT improves the operating room efficiency by allowing more surgeries to be performed per day. TAT involves:

- sterilizing the operating room.
- setting up equipment and supplies for the next patient.
- preparing the next patient for surgery.

The average times associated with TAT activities were determined as follows:

Sterilization	15 min.
Equipment and supply setup	10
Patient preparation	15
Total TAT	40 min.

Each activity is performed in the operating room sequentially so that the total TAT averages 40 minutes. A process improvement team determined that the TAT could be improved by moving some of this activity outside of the operating room, thus allowing these activities to be done simultaneously. Sterilization must be done in the operating room, so this activity was not changed. However, equipment and supplies were prepared in a room outside of the operating room while sterilization was proceeding. The equipment and supplies were placed on a rolling cart, and then rolled into the operating room and staged for the next surgery. In addition, the improvement team determined the patient could be prepared outside of the operating room by using a small room for patient preparation. When the operating room was ready, the patient could be rolled in on a rolling bed and staged for the procedure. As a result of these changes, the total equipment and supply setup only consumed 2 minutes in the operating room, while the total patient preparation only consumed 3 minutes in the operating room.

(Continued)

A. Determine the revised TAT of the new process.

B. What is the ratio of TAT improvement between the old and new processes?

C. If the average surgical time took 40 minutes, how many additional surgeries could be performed in an eight-hour day as a result of the new process?

ADM-3   Lead time in a doctor's office

Marcus Simmons caught the flu and needed to see the doctor. Simmons called to set up an appointment and was told to come in at 1:00 P.M. Simmons arrived at the doctor's office promptly at 1:00 P.M. The waiting room had five other people in it. Patients were admitted from the waiting room in FIFO (first-in, first-out) order at a rate of 5 minutes per patient. After waiting until his turn, a nurse finally invited Simmons to an examining room. Once in the examining room, Simmons waited another 5 minutes before a nurse arrived to take some basic readings (temperature, blood pressure). The nurse needed 10 minutes to collect this clinical information. After the nurse left, Simmons waited 30 additional minutes before the doctor arrived. The doctor diagnosed the flu and provided a prescription for antibiotics, which took 5 minutes. Before leaving the doctor's office, Simmons waited 10 minutes at the business office to pay for the office visit.

Simmons spent 5 minutes walking next door to fill the prescription at the pharmacy. There were four people in front of Simmons, each person requiring 5 minutes to fill and purchase a prescription. Simmons arrived home 15 minutes after paying for his prescription.

A. What time does Simmons arrive home?

B. How much of the total elapsed time from 1:00 P.M. until when Simmons arrived home was non-value-added time?

C. What is the value-added ratio? (Round percentage to one decimal place.)

D. ➤ Why does the doctor require patients to wait so long for service?

Take It Further

ETHICS

TIF 12-1   Ethics in Action

In August, Lannister Company introduced a new performance measurement system in manufacturing operations. One of the new performance measures is lead time, which is determined by tagging a random sample of items with a log sheet throughout the month. The log sheets recorded the time that the sample items started production and the time that they ended production, as well as all steps in between. At the end of the month, the controller collected the log sheets and calculated the average lead time of the tagged products. This number was reported to central management and was used to evaluate the performance of the plant manager. Because of the poor lead time results reported for August, the plant was under extreme pressure to reduce lead time in September.

The following memo was intercepted by the controller.

Date: September 3

To: Hourly Employees

From: Plant Manager

During last month, you may have noticed that some of the products were tagged with a log sheet. This sheet records the time that a product enters production and the time that it leaves production. The difference between these two times is termed the "lead time." Our plant is evaluated on improving lead time. From now on, I ask all of you to keep an eye out for the tagged items. When you see a tagged item, it is to receive special attention. Work on that item first, and then immediately move it to the next operation. Under no circumstances should tagged items wait on any other work that you have. Naturally, report accurate information. I insist that you record the correct times on the log sheet as the product goes through your operations.

━━━► How should the controller respond to this discovery?

REAL WORLD

TIF 12-2   Team Activity

In groups of two to four people, visit a sit-down restaurant and do a lead time study. If more than one group chooses to visit the same restaurant, choose different times for your visits. Note the time when you walk in the door of the restaurant and the time when you walk out the door after you have eaten. The difference between these two times is the total lead time of your restaurant experience. While in the restaurant, determine the time spent on non-value-added time, such as wait time, and the time spent on value-added eating time. Note the various activities and the time required to perform each activity during your visit to the restaurant.

━━━► Compare your analyses, identifying possible reasons for differences in the times recorded by teams that visited the same restaurant.

TIF 12-3   Communication

Ethan Fromme, the Chief Financial Officer of Maximal Inc., has asked for your help in interpreting the company's operating performance. He has provided you with the following three performance graphs for the most recent fiscal year.

━━━► Based on the information in these graphs, write a brief memo to Mr. Fromme, evaluating the company's ability to produce high-quality products at a low cost with a fast response time and immediate availability.

13 Statement of Cash Flows

Concepts and Principles

Chapter 1 *Introduction to Managerial Accounting*

Developing Information

COST SYSTEMS	COST BEHAVIOR
Chapter 2 *Job Order Costing* Chapter 3 *Process Cost Systems* Chapter 4 *Activity-Based Costing*	Chapter 5 *Cost-Volume-Profit Analysis*

Decision Making

EVALUATING PERFORMANCE	COMPARING ALTERNATIVES
Chapter 6 *Variable Costing for Management Analysis* Chapter 7 *Budgeting* Chapter 8 *Evaluating Variances from Standard Costs* Chapter 9 *Evaluating Decentralized Operations*	Chapter 10 *Differential Analysis and Product Pricing* Chapter 11 *Capital Investment Analysis* Chapter 12 *Lean Manufacturing*

Financial Accounting

Chapter 13

Statement of Cash Flows

Chapter 14

Financial Statement Analysis

Managerial Accounting

©AREK. MALANG/SHUTTERSTOCK.COM

National Beverage Corp.

Suppose you were to receive $100 from an event. Would it make a difference what the event was? Yes, it would! If you received $100 for your birthday, then it's a gift. If you received $100 as a result of working part time for a week, then it's the result of your effort. If you received $100 as a loan, then it's money that you will have to pay back in the future. If you received $100 as a result of selling your iPod, then it's the result of selling an asset. Thus, $100 received can be associated with different types of events, and these events have different meanings to you, and different implications for your future. You would much rather receive a $100 gift than take out a $100 loan. Likewise, company stakeholders view inflows and outflows of cash differently, depending on their source.

Companies are required to report information about the events causing a change in cash over a period of time. This information is reported on the statement of cash flows. One such company is **National Beverage**, which is an alternative beverage company, known for its innovative soft drinks, enhanced juices and waters, and fortified powders and supplements. You have probably seen the company's **Shasta** and **Faygo** soft drinks, or **LaCroix**, **Everfresh**, and **Crystal Bay** drinks at your local grocery or convenience store. As with any company, cash is important to National Beverage. Without cash, National Beverage would be unable to expand its brands, distribute its products, support extreme sports, or provide a return for its owners. Thus, its managers are concerned about the sources and uses of cash.

In this chapter, we focus on the events causing a change in cash by presenting the preparation and use of the statement of cash flows.

Statement of Cash Flows

Cash Flows	Operating Activities — Indirect Method	Investing Activities	Financing Activities	Reporting Cash Flows
▪ Types of Cash Flows (Obj. 1)	▪ Net Income (Obj. 2)	▪ Land (Obj. 3)	▪ Bonds Payable (Obj. 4)	▪ Preparing the Statement of Cash Flows (Obj. 5)
▪ Direct Method (Obj. 1)	▪ Noncash Expenses (Obj. 2)	▪ Buildings (Obj. 3)	▪ Common Stock (Obj. 4)	
▪ Indirect Method (Obj. 1)	▪ Gains and Losses (Obj. 2)		▪ Dividends and Dividends Payable (Obj. 4)	
▪ Noncash Transactions (Obj. 1)	▪ Current Assets and Liabilities (Obj. 2)			

Learning Objectives

Obj. 1 Describe the cash flow activities reported on the statement of cash flows.

Obj. 2 Prepare the cash flows from operating activities section of the statement of cash flows using the indirect method.

Obj. 3 Prepare the cash flows from investing activities section of the statement of cash flows.

Obj. 4 Prepare the cash flows from financing activities section of the statement of cash flows.

Obj. 5 Prepare a statement of cash flows.

Analysis for Decision Making

Describe and illustrate the use of free cash flow in evaluating a company's cash flow.

Objective 1

Describe the cash flow activities reported on the statement of cash flows.

Reporting Cash Flows

The **statement of cash flows** reports a company's cash inflows and outflows for a period.[1] The statement of cash flows provides useful information about a company's ability to do the following:

- Generate cash from operations
- Maintain and expand its operating capacity
- Meet its financial obligations
- Pay dividends

The statement of cash flows is used by managers in evaluating past operations and in planning future investing and financing activities. It is also used by external users such as investors and creditors to assess a company's profit potential and ability to pay its debt and pay dividends.

The statement of cash flows reports three types of cash flow activities, as follows:

1. **Cash flows from operating activities** are the cash flows from transactions that affect the net income of the company.

     Example: Purchase and sale of merchandise by a retailer.

2. **Cash flows from investing activities** are the cash flows from transactions that affect investments in the noncurrent assets of the company.

     Example: Purchase and sale of fixed assets, such as equipment and buildings.

3. **Cash flows from financing activities** are the cash flows from transactions that affect the debt and equity of the company.

     Example: Issuing or retiring equity and debt securities.

note:

The statement of cash flows reports cash flows from operating, investing, and financing activities.

---

[1] As used in this chapter, *cash* refers to cash and cash equivalents. Examples of cash equivalents include short-term, highly liquid investments, such as money market accounts, bank certificates of deposit, and U.S. Treasury bills.

The cash flows are reported on the statement of cash flows as follows:

Cash flows from operating activities	$XXX
Cash flows from investing activities	XXX
Cash flows from financing activities	XXX
Change in cash	$XXX
Cash at the beginning of the period	XXX
Cash at the end of the period	$XXX

The ending cash on the statement of cash flows equals the cash reported on the company's balance sheet at the end of the year.

Exhibit 1 illustrates the sources (increases) and uses (decreases) of cash by each of the three cash flow activities. A *source* of cash causes the cash flow to increase and is called a *cash inflow*. A *use* of cash causes cash flow to decrease and is called *cash outflow*.

Exhibit 1

Sources and Uses of Cash

Cash Flows from Operating Activities

Cash flows from operating activities reports the cash inflows and outflows from a company's day-to-day operations. Companies may select one of two alternative methods for reporting cash flows from operating activities on the statement of cash flows:

- The direct method
- The indirect method

Both methods result in the same amount of cash flows from operating activities. They differ in the way they report cash flows from operating activities.

The Direct Method The **direct method** reports operating cash inflows (receipts) and cash outflows (payments) as follows:

Cash flows from operating activities:	
Cash received from customers	$ XXX
Cash payments for merchandise	(XXX)
Cash payments for operating expenses	(XXX)
Cash payments for interest	(XXX)
Cash payments for income taxes	(XXX)
Net cash flow from operating activities	$XXX

The primary operating cash inflow is cash received from customers. The primary operating cash outflows are cash payments for merchandise, operating expenses, interest, and income tax payments. The cash received from operating activities less the cash payments for operating activities is the net cash flow from operating activities.

The primary advantage of the direct method is that it *directly* reports cash receipts and cash payments on the statement of cash flows. Its primary disadvantage is that these data may not be readily available in the accounting records. Thus, the direct method is normally more costly to prepare and, as a result, is used infrequently in practice. For this reason, the direct method is described and illustrated in an appendix to this chapter.

The Indirect Method The **indirect method** reports cash flows from operating activities by beginning with net income and adjusting it for revenues and expenses that do not involve the receipt or payment of cash, as follows:

Cash flows from operating activities:
Net income $XXX
Adjustments to reconcile net income to net
  cash flow from operating activities   XXX
        Net cash flow from operating activities $XXX

The adjustments to reconcile net income to net cash flow from operating activities include such items as depreciation and gains or losses on fixed assets. Changes in current operating assets and liabilities such as accounts receivable or accounts payable are also added or deducted, depending on their effect on cash flows. In effect, these additions and deductions adjust net income, which is reported on an accrual accounting basis, to cash flows from operating activities, which is a cash basis.

A primary advantage of the indirect method is that it reconciles the differences between net income and net cash flow from operations. In doing so, it shows how net income is related to the ending cash balance that is reported on the balance sheet.

Because the data are readily available, the indirect method is less costly to prepare than the direct method. As a result, the indirect method of reporting cash flows from operations is most commonly used in practice.

Link to National Beverage

National Beverage Corp. uses the indirect method of reporting the cash flows from operating activities in its statement of cash flows.

Comparing the Direct and Indirect Methods Exhibit 2 illustrates the Cash Flows from Operating Activities section of the statement of cash flows for **NetSolutions**, and shows the direct and indirect methods. As Exhibit 2 illustrates, both methods report the same amount of net cash flow from operating activities of $2,900.

Exhibit 2   Cash Flow from Operations: Direct and Indirect Methods—NetSolutions

Direct Method
Cash flows from operating activities:
  Cash received from customers.................... $ 7,500
  Cash payments for expenses
    and payments to creditors .... (4,600)
      Net cash flow from operating activities .... $ 2,900

Indirect Method
Cash flows from operating activities:
  Net income $3,050
  Increase in accounts payable 400
  Increase in supplies .... (550)
      Net cash flow from operating activities $2,900

the same

Why It Matters

Cash Crunch!

	Year 3	Year 2	Year 1
Cash provided (used in) operating activities	$(17,589)	$(26,191)	$61,900

The Wet Seal, Inc., a young women's clothing retailer, recently filed for bankruptcy protection. The cash flows from operating activities for the three years prior to bankruptcy (in thousands) follow:

As can be seen, cash flows from operating activities trended into negative territory during the two years prior to the firm's bankruptcy. Thus, when cash flows from operating activities are negative, it can lead to financial distress.

Cash Flows from Investing Activities

Cash flows from investing activities show the cash inflows and outflows related to changes in a company's long-term assets. Cash flows from investing activities are reported on the statement of cash flows as follows:

Cash flows from investing activities:	
Cash inflows from investing activities	$ XXX
Cash used for investing activities	(XXX)
Net cash flow from investing activities	$XXX

Cash inflows from investing activities normally arise from selling fixed assets, investments, and intangible assets. Cash outflows normally include payments to purchase fixed assets, investments, and intangible assets.

For a recent year, **National Beverage** reported net cash used in investing activities of $9,725,000.

Link to National Beverage

Cash Flows from Financing Activities

Cash flows from financing activities show the cash inflows and outflows related to changes in a company's long-term liabilities and stockholders' equity. Cash flows from financing activities are reported on the statement of cash flows as follows:

Cash flows from financing activities:	
Cash inflows from financing activities	$ XXX
Cash used for financing activities	(XXX)
Net cash flow from financing activities	$XXX

Cash inflows from financing activities normally arise from issuing long-term debt or equity securities. For example, issuing bonds, notes payable, preferred stock, and common stock creates cash inflows from financing activities. Cash outflows from financing activities include paying cash dividends, repaying long-term debt, and acquiring treasury stock.

For a recent year, **National Beverage** reported net cash used in financing activities of $25,771,000.

Link to National Beverage

Why It Matters

Growing Pains

Twitter, Inc. is a global social media platform used for real-time self-expression and conversation within the limits of 140 character tweets. Twitter is a new, fast-growing company. The cash flows from operating, investing, and financing activities are summarized for its first three years as a public company (in thousands):

	Cash provided from (used in)			
	Operating activities	**Investing activities**	**Financing activities**	**Net change for year**
Year 1	$(27,935)	$ 49,443	$ (37,124)	$ (15,616)
Year 2	1,398	(1,306,066)	1,942,176	637,508
Year 3	81,796	(1,097,272)	1,691,722	676,246

One can see the significant improvement in Twitter's cash flows from operations from Year 1 to Year 3. This indicates that Twitter is succeeding as a new company and is able to provide cash from operations after only three years of operating as a public company. However, as a new company, Twitter must make significant investments in order to expand. This is clear in the trend in cash flows used in investing activities. Since the cash flows from operations are insufficient to fund this growth, the company must obtain cash from financing activities. We see significant sources of cash from stockholders in Year 2 and Year 3, which was used to expand and provide future flexibility.

Noncash Investing and Financing Activities

A company may enter into transactions involving investing and financing activities that do not *directly* affect cash. For example, a company may issue common stock to retire long-term debt. Although this transaction does not directly affect cash, it does eliminate future cash payments for interest and for paying the bonds when they mature. Because such transactions *indirectly* affect cash flows, they are reported in a separate section of the statement of cash flows. This section usually appears at the bottom of the statement of cash flows.

Format of the Statement of Cash Flows

The statement of cash flows presents the cash flows generated by, or used for, the three activities previously discussed: operating, investing, and financing. These three activities are always reported in the same order, as shown in Exhibit 3.

Exhibit 3

Order of Reporting Statement of Cash Flows

Rundell Inc. Statement of Cash Flows For the Year Ended 20Y8		
Cash flows from operating activities		
(List of individual items, as illustrated in Exhibit 1)	$XXX	
Net cash flow from operating activities		$XXX
Cash flows from investing activities		
(List of individual items, as illustrated in Exhibit 1)	$XXX	
Net cash flow from (used for) investing activities		XXX
Cash flows from financing activities		
(List of individual items, as illustrated in Exhibit 1)	$XXX	
Net cash flow from (used for) financing activities		XXX
Change in cash		$XXX
Cash at the beginning of the period		XXX
Cash at the end of the period		$XXX
Noncash investing and financing activities		$XXX

No Cash Flow per Share

Cash flow per share is sometimes reported in the financial press. As reported, cash flow per share is normally computed as *cash flow from operations divided by the number of common shares outstanding*. However, such reporting may be misleading because of the following:

- Users may misinterpret cash flow per share as the per-share amount available for dividends. This would not be the case if the cash generated by operations is required for repaying loans or for reinvesting in the business.
- Users may misinterpret cash flow per share as equivalent to (or better than) earnings per share.

For these reasons, the financial statements, including the statement of cash flows, should not report cash flow per share.

Check Up Corner 13-1 Classifications of Cash Flows

During its first month of operations, Templeton Company had the following cash transactions:

A. Issued 30,000 shares of common stock.
B. Purchased a new piece of equipment.
C. Sold merchandise to customers.
D. Paid employees' wages.
E. Paid a dividend.

Identify whether each of these transactions would be reported as an operating, investing, or financing activity on the statement of cash flows.

Solution:

A. Financing   Issued 30,000 shares of common stock.
B. Investing   Purchased a new piece of equipment.
C. Operating   Sold merchandise to customers.
D. Operating   Paid employees' wages.
E. Financing   Paid a dividend.

Operating activities show the cash inflows and outflows from a company's day-to-day operations.

Investing activities show the cash inflows and outflows related to changes in a company's long-term assets.

Financing activities show the cash inflows and outflows related to changes in a company's long-term liabilities and stockholders' equity.

Check Up Corner

Cash Flows from Operating Activities— The Indirect Method

Objective 2
Prepare the cash flows from operating activities section of the statement of cash flows using the indirect method.

The indirect method of reporting cash flows from operating activities uses the logic that a change in any balance sheet account (including cash) can be analyzed in terms of changes in the other balance sheet accounts. Thus, by analyzing changes in noncash balance sheet accounts, any change in the cash account can be *indirectly* determined.

To illustrate, the accounting equation can be solved for cash as follows:

$$\text{Assets} = \text{Liabilities} + \text{Stockholders' Equity}$$
$$\text{Cash} + \text{Noncash Assets} = \text{Liabilities} + \text{Stockholders' Equity}$$
$$\text{Cash} = \text{Liabilities} + \text{Stockholders' Equity} - \text{Noncash Assets}$$

Therefore, any change in the cash account can be determined by analyzing changes in the liability, stockholders' equity, and noncash asset accounts as follows:

Change in Cash = *Change* in Liabilities + *Change* in Stockholders' Equity − *Change* in Noncash Assets

Under the indirect method, there is no order in which the balance sheet accounts must be analyzed. However, net income (or net loss) is the first amount reported on the statement of cash flows. Because net income (or net loss) is a component of any change in Retained Earnings, the first account normally analyzed is Retained Earnings.

To illustrate the indirect method, the income statement and comparative balance sheets for **Rundell Inc.**, shown in Exhibit 4, are used. Ledger accounts and other data supporting the income statement and balance sheet are presented as needed.[2]

Exhibit 4

Income Statement and Comparative Balance Sheet

Rundell Inc.
Income Statement
For the Year Ended December 31, 20Y8

Sales		$1,180,000
Cost of goods sold..		790,000
Gross profit		$ 390,000
Operating expenses:		
Depreciation expense	$ 7,000	
Other operating expenses	196,000	
Total operating expenses.......................................		203,000
Income from operations		$ 187,000
Other revenue and expense:		
Gain on sale of land	$ 12,000	
Interest expense	(8,000)	4,000
Income before income tax		$ 191,000
Income tax expense		83,000
Net income		$ 108,000

Rundell Inc.
Comparative Balance Sheet
December 31, 20Y8 and 20Y7

	20Y8	20Y7	Increase (Decrease)
Assets			
Cash	$ 97,500	$ 26,000	$ 71,500
Accounts receivable (net)	74,000	65,000	9,000
Inventories	172,000	180,000	(8,000)
Land	80,000	125,000	(45,000)
Building	260,000	200,000	60,000
Accumulated depreciation—building............	(65,300)	(58,300)	(7,000)*
Total assets	$618,200	$537,700	$ 80,500
Liabilities			
Accounts payable (merchandise creditors)	$ 43,500	$ 46,700	$ (3,200)
Accrued expenses payable (operating expenses)	26,500	24,300	2,200
Income taxes payable	7,900	8,400	(500)
Dividends payable	14,000	10,000	4,000
Bonds payable	100,000	150,000	(50,000)
Total liabilities	$191,900	$239,400	$(47,000)
Stockholders' Equity			
Common stock, $2 par.................................	$ 24,000	$ 16,000	$ 8,000
Paid-in capital in excess of par.....................	120,000	80,000	40,000
Retained earnings......................................	282,300	202,300	80,000
Total stockholders' equity...........................	$426,300	$298,300	$128,000
Total liabilities and stockholders' equity.........	$618,200	$537,700	$ 80,500

*There is a $7,000 increase to Accumulated Depreciation—Building, which is a contra asset account. As a result, the $7,000 increase in this account must be subtracted in summing to the increase in total assets of $80,500.

[2] An appendix that discusses using a spreadsheet (work sheet) as an aid in assembling data for the statement of cash flows is presented at the end of this chapter. This appendix illustrates the use of this spreadsheet in reporting cash flows from operating activities using the indirect method.

Net Income

Rundell Inc.'s net income for 20Y8 is $108,000 as shown in the income statement in Exhibit 4. Since net income is closed to Retained Earnings, net income also helps explain the change in retained earnings during the year. The retained earnings account for Rundell is as follows:

Account Retained Earnings				Account No.	
				Balance	
Date	**Item**	**Debit**	**Credit**	**Debit**	**Credit**
20Y8					
Jan. 1	Balance				202,300
June 30	Dividends declared	14,000			188,300
Dec. 31	Net income		108,000		296,300
31	Dividends declared	14,000			282,300

The retained earnings account indicates that the $80,000 ($108,000 − $28,000) change resulted from net income of $108,000 and cash dividends of $28,000. The net income of $108,000 is the first amount reported in the Cash Flows from Operating Activities section. The impact of the dividends of $28,000 on cash flows will be included as part of financing activities.

Adjustments to Net Income

The net income of $108,000 reported by **Rundell Inc.** does not equal the cash flows from operating activities for the period. This is because net income is determined using the accrual method of accounting.

Under the accrual method of accounting, revenues and expenses are recorded at different times from when cash is received or paid. For example, merchandise may be sold on account and the cash received at a later date. Likewise, insurance premiums may be paid in the current period but expensed in a following period.

Thus, under the indirect method, adjustments to net income must be made to determine cash flows from operating activities. The typical adjustments to net income are shown in Exhibit 5.[3]

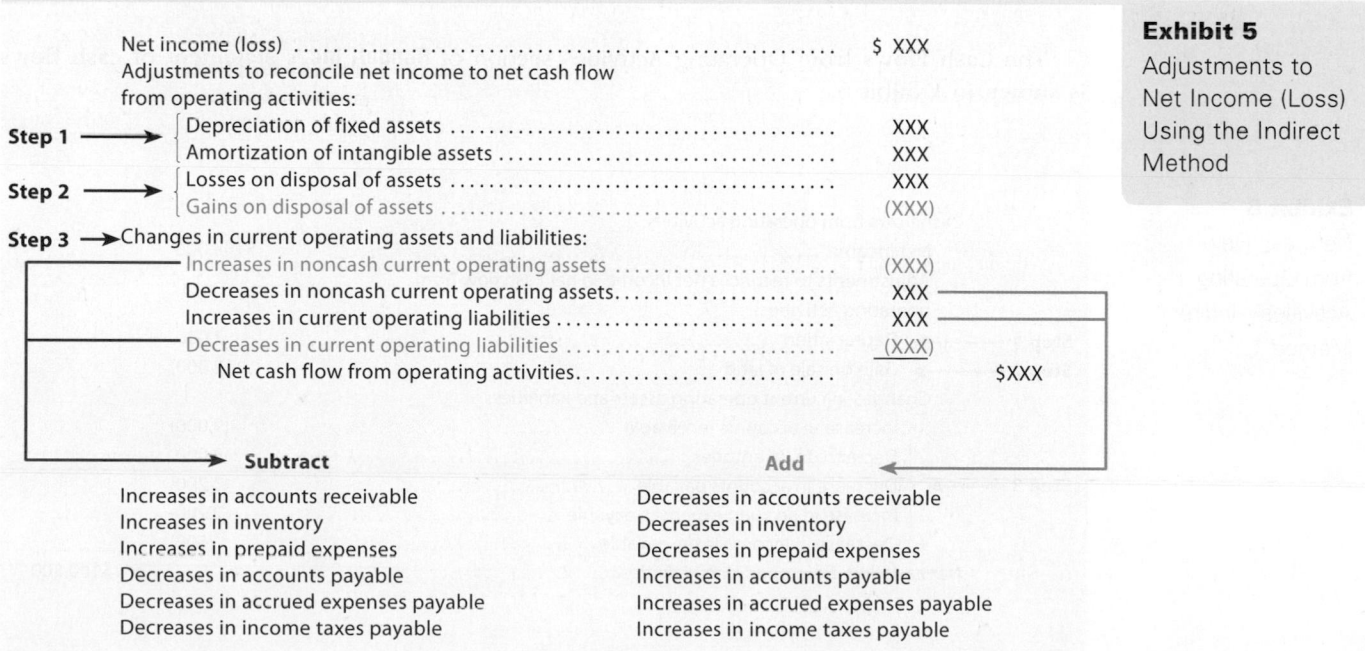

Exhibit 5
Adjustments to Net Income (Loss) Using the Indirect Method

[3] Other items that also require adjustments to net income to obtain cash flows from operating activities include amortization of bonds payable discounts (add), losses on debt retirement (add), amortization of bonds payable premiums (deduct), and gains on retirement of debt (deduct). These topics are covered in advanced accounting courses.

Net income is normally adjusted to cash flows from operating activities, using the following steps:

- Step 1. Expenses that do not affect cash are added. Such expenses decrease net income but do not involve cash payments.

  Example: Depreciation of fixed assets and amortization of intangible assets are added to net income.

- Step 2. Losses on the disposal of assets are added and gains on the disposal of assets are deducted. The disposal (sale) of assets is an investing activity rather than an operating activity. However, such losses and gains are reported as part of net income. As a result, any *losses* on disposal of assets are *added* back to net income. Likewise, any *gains* on disposal of assets are *deducted* from net income.

  Example: Land costing $100,000 is sold for $90,000. The loss of $10,000 is added back to net income.

- Step 3. Changes in current operating assets and liabilities are added or deducted as follows:

  - Increases in noncash current operating assets are deducted.
  - Decreases in noncash current operating assets are added.
  - Increases in current operating liabilities are added.
  - Decreases in current operating liabilities are deducted.

  Example: A sale of $10,000 on account increases sales, accounts receivable, and net income by $10,000. However, cash is not affected. Thus, the $10,000 increase in accounts receivable is deducted. Similar adjustments are required for the changes in the other current asset and liability accounts, such as inventory, prepaid expenses, accounts payable, accrued expenses payable, and income taxes payable, as shown in Exhibit 5.

Link to National Beverage

In a recent statement of cash flows, **National Beverage** reported changes in current asset and liability accounts for accounts receivable, inventories, prepaid assets, accounts payable, and accrued liabilities.

The Cash Flows from Operating Activities section of **Rundell Inc.**'s statement of cash flows is shown in Exhibit 6.

Exhibit 6
Net Cash Flow from Operating Activities—Indirect Method

Cash flows from operating activities:	
Net income	$108,000
Adjustments to reconcile net income to net cash flow from operating activities:	
Step 1 → Depreciation	7,000
Step 2 → Gain on sale of land	(12,000)
Changes in current operating assets and liabilities:	
Increase in accounts receivable	(9,000)
Decrease in inventories	8,000
Step 3 → Decrease in accounts payable	(3,200)
Increase in accrued expenses payable	2,200
Decrease in income taxes payable	(500)
Net cash flow from operating activities	$100,500

Rundell's net income of $108,000 is converted to cash flows from operating activities of $100,500 as follows:

- Step 1. Add depreciation of $7,000.

  Analysis: The comparative balance sheet in Exhibit 4 indicates that Accumulated Depreciation—Building increased by $7,000. The following account indicates that depreciation for the year was $7,000 for the building:

Account Accumulated Depreciation—Building   Account No.

Date	Item	Debit	Credit	Balance Debit	Balance Credit
20Y8					
Jan. 1	Balance				58,300
Dec. 31	Depreciation for year		7,000		65,300

- Step 2. Deduct the gain on the sale of land of $12,000.

  Analysis: The income statement in Exhibit 4 reports a gain of $12,000 from the sale of land. The proceeds, which include the gain, are reported in the Investing section of the statement of cash flows.[4] Thus, the gain of $12,000 is deducted from net income in determining cash flows from operating activities.

- Step 3. Add and deduct changes in current operating assets and liabilities excluding cash.

  Analysis: The increases and decreases in the current operating asset and current liability accounts excluding cash are as follows:

Accounts	December 31 20Y8	20Y7	Increase (Decrease)
Accounts Receivable (net)	$ 74,000	$ 65,000	$ 9,000
Inventories	172,000	180,000	(8,000)
Accounts Payable (merchandise creditors)	43,500	46,700	(3,200)
Accrued Expenses Payable (operating expenses)	26,500	24,300	2,200
Income Taxes Payable	7,900	8,400	(500)

Accounts receivable (net): The $9,000 increase is deducted from net income. This is because the $9,000 increase in accounts receivable indicates that sales on account were $9,000 more than the cash received from customers. Thus, sales (and net income) includes $9,000 that was not received in cash during the year.

Inventories: The $8,000 decrease is added to net income. This is because the $8,000 decrease in inventories indicates that the cost of goods *sold* exceeds the cost of the merchandise *purchased* during the year by $8,000. In other words, the cost of goods sold includes $8,000 of merchandise from inventory that were not purchased (used cash) during the year.

Accounts payable (merchandise creditors): The $3,200 decrease is deducted from net income. This is because a decrease in accounts payable indicates that the cash *payments* to merchandise creditors exceed the merchandise *purchased on account* by $3,200. Therefore, the cost of goods sold is $3,200 less than the cash paid to merchandise creditors during the year.

Accrued expenses payable (operating expenses): The $2,200 increase is added to net income. This is because an increase in accrued expenses payable indicates that operating expenses exceed the cash payments for operating expenses by $2,200. In other words, operating expenses reported on the income statement include $2,200 that did not require a cash outflow during the year.

Income taxes payable: The $500 decrease is deducted from net income. This is because a decrease in income taxes payable indicates that taxes paid exceed the amount of taxes incurred during the year by $500. In other words, the amount reported on the income statement for income tax expense is less than the amount paid by $500.

[4] The reporting of the proceeds (cash flows) from the sale of land as part of investing activities is discussed later in this chapter.

Check Up Corner 13-2   Cash Flows from Operating Activities

Omicron Inc. reported net income of $120,000 for 20Y2. In addition, the income statement reported $12,000 of depreciation expense and a $15,000 loss on the disposal of equipment. The current operating assets and liabilities from the company's comparative balance sheet are as follows:

	12/31/20Y2	12/31/20Y1	Increase (Decrease)
Accounts receivable	$18,240	$13,240	$ 5,000
Accounts payable	11,200	13,200	(2,000)

Prepare the Cash Flows from Operating Activities section of the statement of cash flows, using the indirect method.

Solution:

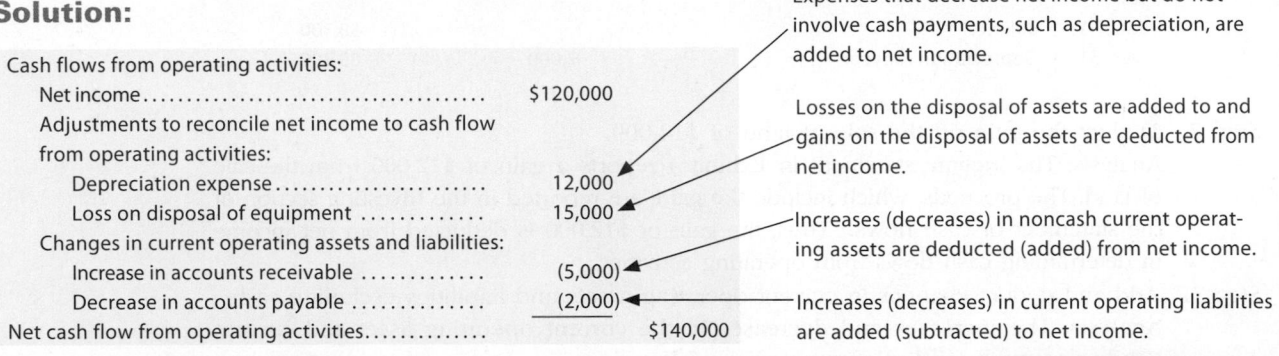

Cash flows from operating activities:		
Net income......................................		$120,000
Adjustments to reconcile net income to cash flow from operating activities:		
Depreciation expense........................	12,000	
Loss on disposal of equipment	15,000	
Changes in current operating assets and liabilities:		
Increase in accounts receivable	(5,000)	
Decrease in accounts payable	(2,000)	
Net cash flow from operating activities..............		$140,000

Expenses that decrease net income but do not involve cash payments, such as depreciation, are added to net income.

Losses on the disposal of assets are added to and gains on the disposal of assets are deducted from net income.

Increases (decreases) in noncash current operating assets are deducted (added) from net income.

Increases (decreases) in current operating liabilities are added (subtracted) to net income.

Check Up Corner

Objective 3

Prepare the cash flows from investing activities section of the statement of cash flows.

Cash Flows from Investing Activities

Cash flows from investing activities reports the cash inflows and outflows related to changes in a company's long-term assets. **Rundell Inc.**'s comparative balance sheet in Exhibit 4 lists land, building, and accumulated depreciation—building as long-term assets. Similar to preparing the cash flows from operating section, each change in each long-term asset account is analyzed for its effect on cash flows from investing activities.

Land

The $45,000 decline in the land account of **Rundell Inc.** was from two transactions, as follows:

Account *Land*				Account No.	
				Balance	
Date	**Item**	**Debit**	**Credit**	**Debit**	**Credit**
20Y8					
Jan. 1	Balance			125,000	
June 8	Sold for $72,000 cash		60,000	65,000	
Oct. 12	Purchased for $15,000 cash	15,000		80,000	

The June 8 transaction is the sale of land with a cost of $60,000 for $72,000 in cash. The $72,000 proceeds from the sale are reported in the Investing Activities section as follows:

Cash flows from investing activities:

Cash received from sale of land $72,000

The proceeds of $72,000 include the $12,000 gain on the sale of land and the $60,000 cost (book value) of the land. As shown in Exhibit 6, the $12,000 gain in deducted from net income in the Cash Flows from Operating Activities section. This is so that the $12,000 cash inflow related to the gain is not included twice as a cash inflow.

The October 12 transaction is the purchase of land for cash of $15,000. This transaction is reported as an outflow of cash in the Investing Activities section as follows:

Cash flows from investing activities:

Cash paid for purchase of land .... $(15,000)

Building and Accumulated Depreciation—Building

The building account of **Rundell Inc.** increased by $60,000, and the accumulated depreciation—building account increased by $7,000, as follows:

Account Building				**Account No.**	
				Balance	
Date	**Item**	**Debit**	**Credit**	**Debit**	**Credit**
20Y8					
Jan. 1	Balance			200,000	
Dec. 27	Purchased for cash	60,000		260,000	

Account Accumulated Depreciation—Building				**Account No.**	
				Balance	
Date	**Item**	**Debit**	**Credit**	**Debit**	**Credit**
20Y8					
Jan. 1	Balance				58,300
Dec. 31	Depreciation for the year		7,000		65,300

The purchase of a building for cash of $60,000 is reported as an outflow of cash in the Investing Activities section as follows:

Cash flows from investing activities:

Cash paid for purchase of building .... $(60,000)

The credit in the accumulated depreciation—building account represents depreciation expense for the year. This depreciation expense of $7,000 on the building was added to net income in determining cash flows from operating activities, as reported in Exhibit 6.

In a recent statement of cash flows, **National Beverage** reported cash used for purchases of property, plant, and equipment of $11,630,000 and cash received for selling property, plant, and equipment of $1,905,000 resulting in net cash used for investing activities of $9,725,000.

Link to National Beverage

Check Up Corner 13-3	Cash Flows from Investing Activities

Mercury Inc. reported net income of $100,000 for 20Y2. In addition, the income statement reported $20,000 of depreciation expense and a $10,000 gain on the sale of land. The noncurrent assets from the company's comparative balance sheet are as follows:

			Increase
	12/31/20Y2	**12/31/20Y1**	**(Decrease)**
Land	$ 125,000	$ 225,000	$(100,000)
Equipment	500,000	400,000	100,000
Accumulated depreciation—equipment	(120,000)	(100,000)	20,000

There were no disposals of equipment, and all purchases of equipment were for cash. Prepare the Cash Flows from Investing Activities section of the statement of cash flows.

Solution:

Cash flows from investing activities:	
Cash received from sale of land...................	$ 110,000
Cash paid for purchase of equipment	(100,000)
Net cash flow from investing activities	$10,000

Land was sold for $110,000 ($100,000 decrease in land account + $10,000 gain on the sale). This is the amount of cash received from the sale of land.

The increase in the balance of the equipment account comes from the purchase of equipment for cash.

Note: The increase in Accumulated Depreciation—Equipment is from 20Y2 depreciation expense, which is included in cash flows from operating activities.

Check Up Corner

Objective 4
Prepare the cash flows from financing activities section of the statement of cash flows.

Cash Flows from Financing Activities

Cash flows from financing activities reports the cash inflows and outflows related to changes in a company's long-term liabilities and stockholders' equity. **Rundell Inc.**'s comparative balance sheet in Exhibit 4 reports changes in bonds payable, common stock, and paid-in capital in excess of par. In addition, dividends payable has changed, which impacts retained earnings. Each change must be analyzed to determine its effect on cash flows from financing activities.

Bonds Payable

The bonds payable account of **Rundell Inc.** decreased by $50,000, as follows:

Account Bonds Payable				Account No.	
				Balance	
Date	Item	Debit	Credit	Debit	Credit
20Y8					
Jan. 1	Balance				150,000
June 1	Retired by payment of cash at face amount	50,000			100,000

This decrease is from retiring the bonds by a cash payment for their face amount. This cash outflow is reported in the Financing Activities section as follows:

Cash flows from financing activities:
Cash paid to retire bonds payable................. $(50,000)

Common Stock

The common stock account of **Rundell Inc.** increased by $8,000, and the paid-in capital in excess of par—common stock account increased by $40,000, as follows:

Account Common Stock				Account No.	
				Balance	
Date	Item	Debit	Credit	Debit	Credit
20Y8					
Jan. 1	Balance				16,000
Nov. 1	4,000 shares issued for cash		8,000		24,000

Account Paid-In Capital in Excess of Par—Common Stock				Account No.	
				Balance	
Date	Item	Debit	Credit	Debit	Credit
20Y8					
Jan. 1	Balance				80,000
Nov. 1	4,000 shares issued for cash		40,000		120,000

These increases were from issuing 4,000 shares of common stock for $12 per share. This cash inflow is reported in the Financing Activities section as follows:

Cash flows from financing activities:

Cash received from sale of common stock $48,000

Dividends and Dividends Payable

The retained earnings account of **Rundell Inc.** indicates cash dividends of $28,000 were declared during the year. However, the following dividends payable account indicates that only $24,000 ($10,000 + $14,000) of dividends were paid during the year:

Account Dividends Payable				Account No.	
				Balance	
Date	Item	Debit	Credit	Debit	Credit
20Y8					
Jan. 1	Balance				10,000
10	Cash paid	10,000		—	—
June 30	Dividends declared		14,000		14,000
July 10	Cash paid	14,000		—	—
Dec. 31	Dividends declared		14,000		14,000

Cash dividends paid during the year can also be computed by adjusting the dividends declared during the year for the change in the dividends payable account as follows:

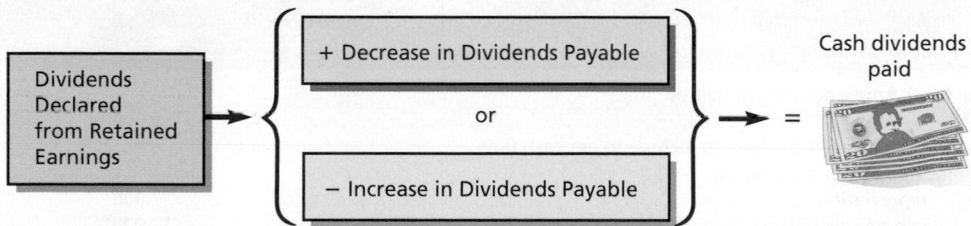

The cash dividends paid by Rundell Inc. during 20Y8 are $24,000, computed as follows:

Dividends declared ($14,000 + $14,000) $28,000
Increase in Dividends Payable   (4,000)
Cash dividends paid $24,000

Because dividend payments are a financing activity, the cash dividends paid of $24,000 are reported in the Financing Activities section of the statement of cash flows, as follows:

Cash flows from financing activities:

Cash paid for dividends . . . . $(24,000)

In a recent statement of cash flows, **National Beverage** reported cash used for dividends of $239,000; cash used for payment of debt of $20,000,000; and cash used for redeeming preferred stock of $6,000,000.

Link to National Beverage

Check Up Corner 13-4 Cash Flows from Financing Activities

Mohroman Inc. reported net income of $80,000 for 20Y2. The liability and equity accounts from the company's comparative balance sheet are as follows:

	12/31/20Y2	12/31/20Y1	Increase (Decrease)
Accounts payable	$ 42,680	$ 41,500	$ 1,180
Dividends payable	10,000	8,000	2,000
Bonds payable	210,000	300,000	(90,000)
Common stock, $10 par value	120,000	100,000	20,000
Excess of issue price over par value—common stock	300,000	200,000	100,000
Retained earnings	240,000	180,000	60,000

During the year, the company retired bonds payable at their face amount, declared dividends of $20,000, and issued 2,000 shares of common stock for $60 per share. Prepare the Cash Flows from Financing Activities section of the statement of cash flows.

Solution:

		Bonds payable with a $90,000 face amount were retired. This is a cash outflow from financing activities.
Cash flows from financing activities:		
Cash paid to retire bonds...........................	$(90,000)	$120,000 in cash was received from the issuance of common stock (2,000 shares × $60 per share).
Cash received from issuing common stock........	120,000	
Cash paid for dividends...........................	(18,000)	$20,000 in dividends declared less the $2,000 increase in dividends payable
Net cash flow from financing activities	$12,000	

Check Up Corner

Objective 5

Prepare a statement of cash flows.

Preparing the Statement of Cash Flows

The statement of cash flows for **Rundell Inc.**, using the indirect method, is shown in Exhibit 7. The statement of cash flows indicates that cash increased by $71,500 during the year. The most significant increase in net cash flows ($100,500) was from operating activities.

Exhibit 7

Statement of Cash Flows—Indirect Method

Rundell Inc. Statement of Cash Flows For the Year Ended December 31, 20Y8		
Cash flows from operating activities:		
Net income	$108,000	
Adjustments to reconcile net income to net cash flow from operating activities:		
Depreciation...	7,000	
Gain on sale of land	(12,000)	
Changes in current operating assets and liabilities:		
Increase in accounts receivable.........................	(9,000)	
Decrease in inventories..................................	8,000	
Decrease in accounts payable	(3,200)	
Increase in accrued expenses payable...................	2,200	
Decrease in income taxes payable	(500)	
Net cash flow from operating activities		$100,500
Cash flows from investing activities:		
Cash received from sale of land.........................	$ 72,000	
Cash paid for purchase of land..........................	(15,000)	
Cash paid for purchase of building.......................	(60,000)	
Net cash flow used for investing activities.............		(3,000)
Cash flows from financing activities:		
Cash received from sale of common stock	$ 48,000	
Cash paid to retire bonds payable	(50,000)	
Cash paid for dividends	(24,000)	
Net cash flow used for financing activities.............		(26,000)
Change in cash		$ 71,500
Cash at the beginning of the year		26,000
Cash at the end of the year		$ 97,500

The most significant use of cash ($26,000) was for financing activities. The ending balance of cash on December 31, 20Y8, is $97,500. This ending cash balance is also reported on the December 31, 20Y8, balance sheet shown in Exhibit 4.

In a recent statement of cash flows, **National Beverage** reported net cash provided by operating activities of $58,020,000; net cash used for investing activities of $9,725,000; net cash used for financing activities of $25,771,000 for a net increase in cash of $22,524,000 for the year.

Link to National Beverage

International Connection

IFRS

IFRS for Statement of Cash Flows

The statement of cash flows is required under International Financial Reporting Standards (IFRS). The statement of cash flows under IFRS is similar to that reported under U.S. GAAP in that the statement has separate sections for operating, investing, and financing activities. Like U.S. GAAP, IFRS also allow the use of either the indirect or direct method of reporting cash flows from operating activities. IFRS differ from U.S. GAAP in some minor areas, including:

- Interest paid can be reported as either an operating or a financing activity, while interest received can be reported as either an operating or an investing activity. In contrast, U.S. GAAP reports interest paid or received as an operating activity.
- Dividends paid can be reported as either an operating or a financing activity, while dividends received can be reported as either an operating or an investing activity. In contrast, U.S. GAAP reports dividends paid as a financing activity and dividends received as an operating activity.
- Cash flows to pay taxes are reported as a separate line in the operating activities, in contrast to U.S. GAAP, which does not require a separate line disclosure.

Analysis for Decision Making

Free Cash Flow

A valuable tool for evaluating the profitability of a business is free cash flow. **Free cash flow** measures the operating cash flow available to a company after it purchases the property, plant, and equipment (PP&E) necessary to maintain its current operations. Since the investments in PP&E necessary to maintain current operations cannot often be determined from financial statements, analysts estimate this amount using the cash used to purchase PP&E, as shown in the statement of cash flows. Thus, free cash flow is computed as follows:

Objective
Describe and illustrate the use of free cash flow in evaluating a company's cash flow.

Cash flows from operating activities	XXX
Cash used to purchase property, plant, and equipment	(XXX)
Free cash flow	XXX

The free cash flow can be expressed as a percentage of sales in order to provide a relative measure that can be compared over time or to other companies. This ratio is computed as follows:

$$\text{Ratio of Free Cash Flow to Sales} = \frac{\text{Free Cash Flow}}{\text{Sales}}$$

Positive free cash flow is considered favorable. A company that has free cash flow is able to fund growth and acquisitions, retire debt, purchase treasury stock, and pay dividends. A company with no free cash flow may have limited financial flexibility, potentially leading to liquidity problems. As one analyst notes, "Free cash flow gives the company firepower to reduce debt and ultimately generate consistent, actual income."

To illustrate, information from the annual reports of **National Beverage** for three recent years is as follows (in thousands):

	Year 3	Year 2	Year 1
Cash flows from operating activities............................	$ 58,020	$ 52,383	$ 40,264
Cash used to purchase property, plant, and equipment..........	11,630	12,124	9,693
Sales..	645,825	641,135	662,007

The free cash flow is computed for the three years as follows:

	Year 3	Year 2	Year 1
Cash flows from operating activities............................	$ 58,020	$ 52,383	$40,264
Cash used to purchase property, plant, and equipment..........	(11,630)	(12,124)	(9,693)
Free cash flow	$ 46,390	$ 40,259	$30,571

As can be seen, free cash flow has increased across the three years. In Year 3, it is nearly 52% higher than in Year 1 [($46,390 − $30,571) ÷ $30,571]. The ratio of free cash flow to sales is as follows (rounded to one decimal place):

	Year 3	Year 2	Year 1
Ratio of free cash flow to sales	7.2%	6.3%	4.6%
	($46,390 ÷	($40,259 ÷	($30,571 ÷
	$645,825)	$641,135)	$662,007)

The ratio of free cash flow to sales has also increased across these three years, from 4.6% in Year 1 to 7.2% in Year 3, which is a 57% increase [(7.2% − 4.6%) ÷ 4.6%].

Make a Decision   Free Cash Flow

Financial information for **Apple Inc.** (a consumer electronics company), **The Coca-Cola Company** (a beverage company), and **Verizon Communications** (a telecommunications company) follows (in millions):

	Apple	Coca-Cola	Verizon
Sales...	$182,795	$45,998	$127,079
Cash flows from operating activities...........................	59,713	10,615	30,631
Cash used to purchase property, plant, and equipment..........	9,571	2,406	17,191

A. Compute the free cash flow for each company.

B. Compute the ratio of free cash flow to sales for each company. (Round to one decimal place.)

C. Which company has the greatest free cash flow?

D. How does Verizon differ from the other two companies?

Solution:

	Apple	Coca-Cola	Verizon
A. Cash flows from operating activities	$59,713	$10,615	$ 30,631
Cash used to purchase property, plant, and equipment	(9,571)	(2,406)	(17,191)
Free cash flow...	$50,142	$ 8,209	$13,440

B.

	Apple	Coca-Cola	Verizon
Ratio of free cash flow to sales...............................	27.4%	17.8%	10.6%
	($50,142 ÷	($8,209 ÷	($13,440 ÷
	$182,795)	$45,998)	$127,079)

C.   Apple has the largest free cash flow. The ratio of free cash flow to sales is the best metric for comparing the three companies. In this comparison, the three companies, ranking from largest to smallest, are Apple, Coca-Cola, and Verizon. However, all three ratios would be considered acceptable.

D.   Over 56% of Verizon's cash flows from operations are used to purchase PP&E ($17,191 ÷ $30,631), an amount much greater than the other two companies. Industries such as airlines, railroads, and telecommunications companies must invest heavily in new equipment to remain competitive. Such investments can significantly reduce free cash flow.

Make a Decision

Why It Matters

Twenty Years After

The S&P 500 is made of the 500 largest publicly traded companies in the United States. **Deutsche Bank**, one of the world's largest financial institutions, aggregated the free cash flow performance of today's S&P 500 companies and the S&P 500 companies from 20 years ago, as follows:

S&P 500 in aggregate (in billions, except ratio)	20 Years Ago	Currently
Free cash flow...	$148	$958
Ratio of free cash flow to sales...........................	6%	8%
Cash paid for dividends...................................	$58	$426
Cash paid for treasury stock purchases...................	30	475
Total...	$88	$901

As can be seen, the free cash flow has grown over six-fold while the ratio of free cash flow to sales has improved from 6% 20 years ago to 8% currently. Twenty years ago, $88 billion of free cash flow, or nearly 60% of free cash flow ($88 ÷ $148), was used to pay dividends and treasury stock. Currently, $901 billion of free cash flow, or 94% of free cash flow ($901 ÷ $958), is used to pay dividends and treasury stock. Compared to twenty years ago, companies are using a much greater portion of their free cash flow to return cash to stockholders. This suggests companies are seeing fewer opportunities for internal investment than 20 years ago.

Appendix 1 Spreadsheet (Work Sheet) for Statement of Cash Flows—The Indirect Method

A spreadsheet (work sheet) may be used in preparing the statement of cash flows. However, whether or not a spreadsheet (work sheet) is used, the concepts presented in this chapter are not affected.

The data for **Rundell Inc.**, presented in Exhibit 4, are used as a basis for illustrating the spreadsheet (work sheet) for the indirect method. The steps in preparing this spreadsheet (work sheet), shown in Exhibit 8, are as follows:

- Step 1.   List the title of each balance sheet account in the Accounts column.
- Step 2.   For each balance sheet account, enter its balance as of December 31, 20Y7, in the first column and its balance as of December 31, 20Y8, in the last column. Place the credit balances in parentheses.
- Step 3.   Add the December 31, 20Y7 and 20Y8 column totals, which should total to zero.
- Step 4.   Analyze the change during the year in each noncash account to determine its net increase (decrease) and classify the change as affecting cash flows from operating activities, investing activities, financing activities, or noncash investing and financing activities.

Exhibit 8   End-of-Period Spreadsheet (Work Sheet) for Statement of Cash Flows—Indirect Method

Step 2

	A	B	C	D	E	F	G
1	Rundell Inc.						
2	End-of-Period Spreadsheet (Work Sheet) for Statement of Cash Flows						
3	For the Year Ended December 31, 20Y8						
4	Accounts	Balance,	Transactions				Balance,
5		Dec. 31, 20Y7	Debit		Credit		Dec. 31, 20Y8
6	Cash	26,000	(O)	71,500			97,500
7	Accounts receivable (net)	65,000	(N)	9,000			74,000
8	Inventories	180,000			(M)	8,000	172,000
9	Land	125,000	(K)	15,000	(L)	60,000	80,000
10	Building	200,000	(J)	60,000			260,000
11	Accumulated depreciation—building	(58,300)			(I)	7,000	(65,300)
12	Accounts payable (merchandise creditors)	(46,700)	(H)	3,200			(43,500)
13	Accrued expenses payable (operating expenses)	(24,300)			(G)	2,200	(26,500)
14	Income taxes payable	(8,400)	(F)	500			(7,900)
15	Dividends payable	(10,000)			(E)	4,000	(14,000)
16	Bonds payable	(150,000)	(D)	50,000			(100,000)
17	Common stock	(16,000)			(C)	8,000	(24,000)
18	Paid-in capital in excess of par	(80,000)			(C)	40,000	(120,000)
19	Retained earnings	(202,300)	(B)	28,000	(A)	108,000	(282,300)
20	Totals Step 3 →	0		237,200		237,200	0 ← Step 3
21	Operating activities:						
22	Net income		(A)	108,000			
23	Depreciation of building		(I)	7,000			
24	Gain on sale of land				(L)	12,000	
25	Increase in accounts receivable				(N)	9,000	
26	Decrease in inventories		(M)	8,000			
27	Decrease in accounts payable				(H)	3,200	
28	Increase in accrued expenses payable		(G)	2,200			
29	Decrease in income taxes payable				(F)	500	
30	Investing activities:						
31	Sale of land		(L)	72,000			
32	Purchase of land				(K)	15,000	
33	Purchase of building				(J)	60,000	
34	Financing activities:						
35	Issued common stock		(C)	48,000			
36	Retired bonds payable				(D)	50,000	
37	Declared cash dividends				(B)	28,000	
38	Increase in dividends payable		(E)	4,000			
39	Net increase in cash				(O)	71,500	
40	Totals			249,200		249,200	
41							

Step 1

Steps 4–7

- Step 5. Indicate the effect of the change on cash flows by making entries in the Transactions columns.
- Step 6. After all noncash accounts have been analyzed, enter the net increase (decrease) in cash during the period.
- Step 7. Add the Debit and Credit Transactions columns. The totals should be equal.

Analyzing Accounts

In analyzing the noncash accounts (Step 4), try to determine the type of cash flow activity (operating, investing, or financing) that led to the change in the account. As each noncash account is analyzed, an entry (Step 5) is made on the spreadsheet (work sheet) for the type of cash flow activity that caused the change. After all noncash accounts have been analyzed, an entry (Step 6) is made for the increase (decrease) in cash during the period.

The entries made on the spreadsheet are not posted to the ledger. They are only used in preparing and summarizing the data on the spreadsheet.

The order in which the accounts are analyzed is not important. However, it is more efficient to begin with Retained Earnings and proceed upward in the account listing.

Retained Earnings

The spreadsheet (work sheet) shows a Retained Earnings balance of $202,300 at December 31, 20Y7, and $282,300 at December 31, 20Y8. Thus, Retained Earnings increased $80,000 during the year. This increase is from the following:

- Net income of $108,000
- Declaring cash dividends of $28,000

To identify the cash flows from these activities, two entries are made on the spreadsheet.

The $108,000 is reported on the statement of cash flows as part of cash flows from operating activities. Thus, an entry is made in the Transactions columns on the spreadsheet, as follows:

(A)	Operating Activities—Net Income.	108,000	
	Retained Earnings		108,000

The preceding entry accounts for the net income portion of the change to Retained Earnings. It also identifies the cash flow in the bottom portion of the spreadsheet as related to operating activities.

The $28,000 of dividends is reported as a financing activity on the statement of cash flows. Thus, an entry is made in the Transactions columns on the spreadsheet, as follows:

(B)	Retained Earnings	28,000	
	Financing Activities—Declared Cash Dividends		28,000

The preceding entry accounts for the dividends portion of the change to Retained Earnings. It also identifies the cash flow in the bottom portion of the spreadsheet as related to financing activities. The $28,000 of declared dividends will be adjusted later for the actual amount of cash dividends paid during the year.

Other Accounts

The entries for the other noncash accounts are made in the spreadsheet in a manner similar to entries (A) and (B). A summary of these entries follows:

(C)	Financing Activities—Issued Common Stock	48,000	
	Common Stock		8,000
	Paid-In Capital in Excess of Par—Common Stock		40,000
(D)	Bonds Payable	50,000	
	Financing Activities—Retired Bonds Payable		50,000
(E)	Financing Activities—Increase in Dividends Payable	4,000	
	Dividends Payable		4,000
(F)	Income Taxes Payable	500	
	Operating Activities—Decrease in Income Taxes Payable		500
(G)	Operating Activities—Increase in Accrued Expenses Payable	2,200	
	Accrued Expenses Payable		2,200
(H)	Accounts Payable	3,200	
	Operating Activities—Decrease in Accounts Payable		3,200
(I)	Operating Activities—Depreciation of Building	7,000	
	Accumulated Depreciation—Building		7,000
(J)	Building	60,000	
	Investing Activities—Purchase of Building		60,000

(K)	Land	15,000	
	Investing Activities—Purchase of Land.		15,000
(L)	Investing Activities—Sale of Land	72,000	
	Operating Activities—Gain on Sale of Land.		12,000
	Land		60,000
(M)	Operating Activities—Decrease in Inventories	8,000	
	Inventories		8,000
(N)	Accounts Receivable.	9,000	
	Operating Activities—Increase in Accounts Receivable		9,000
(O)	Cash	71,500	
	Net Increase in Cash.		71,500

After all the balance sheet accounts are analyzed and the entries made on the spreadsheet (work sheet), all the operating, investing, and financing activities are identified in the bottom portion of the spreadsheet. The accuracy of the entries is verified by totaling the Debit and Credit Transactions columns. The totals of the columns should be equal.

Preparing the Statement of Cash Flows

The statement of cash flows prepared from the spreadsheet is identical to the statement in Exhibit 7. The data for the three sections of the statement are obtained from the bottom portion of the spreadsheet.

Appendix 2 Preparing the Statement of Cash Flows—The Direct Method

The direct method reports cash flows from operating activities as follows:

Cash flows from operating activities:	
Cash received from customers	$ XXX
Cash payments for merchandise	(XXX)
Cash payments for operating expenses	XXX
Cash payments for interest	XXX)
Cash payments for income taxes	(XXX)
Net cash flow from operating activities	$XXX

The Cash Flows from Investing and Financing Activities sections of the statement of cash flows are exactly the same under both the direct and indirect methods. The amount of net cash flow from operating activities is also the same, but the manner in which it is reported is different.

Under the direct method, the income statement is adjusted to cash flows from operating activities as shown in Exhibit 9.

Exhibit 9

Converting Income Statement to Cash Flows from Operating Activities Using the Direct Method

Income Statement	Adjusted to	Cash Flows from Operating Activities
Sales	→	Cash received from customers
Cost of goods sold	→	Cash payments for merchandise
Operating expenses:		
Depreciation expense*	n/a	n/a
Other operating expenses	→	Cash payments for operating expenses
Gain (loss) on sale of land**	n/a	n/a
Interest expense	→	Cash payments for interest
Income tax expense	→	Cash payments for income taxes
Net income	→	Net cash flow from operating activities

* Depreciation does not affect cash, thus, is not considered in the direct method.
** Gains (Losses) on sales of property, plant, and equipment are reported as part of investing activities.

As shown in Exhibit 9, depreciation expense is not adjusted or reported as part of cash flows from operating activities. This is because deprecation expense does not involve a cash outflow. The gain on the sale of the land is also not adjusted and is not reported as part of cash flows from operating activities. This is because the cash flow from operating activities is determined directly, rather than by reconciling net income. The cash proceeds from the sale of the land are reported as an investing activity.

To illustrate the direct method, the income statement and comparative balance sheet for **Rundell Inc.**, shown in Exhibit 4, are used.

Cash Received from Customers

The income statement (shown in Exhibit 4) of **Rundell Inc.** reports sales of $1,180,000. To determine the cash received from customers, the $1,180,000 is adjusted for any increase or decrease in accounts receivable. The adjustment is summarized in Exhibit 10.

Exhibit 10
Determining the
Cash Received
from Customers

The cash received from customers is $1,171,000, computed as follows:

Sales	$1,180,000
Increase in accounts receivable	(9,000)
Cash received from customers	$1,171,000

The increase of $9,000 in accounts receivable (shown in Exhibit 4) during 20Y8 indicates that sales on account exceeded cash received from customers by $9,000. In other words, sales include $9,000 that did not result in a cash inflow during the year. Thus, $9,000 is deducted from sales to determine the cash received from customers.

Cash Payments for Merchandise

The income statement (shown in Exhibit 4) for **Rundell Inc.** reports cost of goods sold of $790,000. To determine the cash payments for merchandise, the $790,000 is adjusted for any increases or decreases in inventories and accounts payable. Assuming the accounts payable are owed to merchandise suppliers, the adjustment is summarized in Exhibit 11.

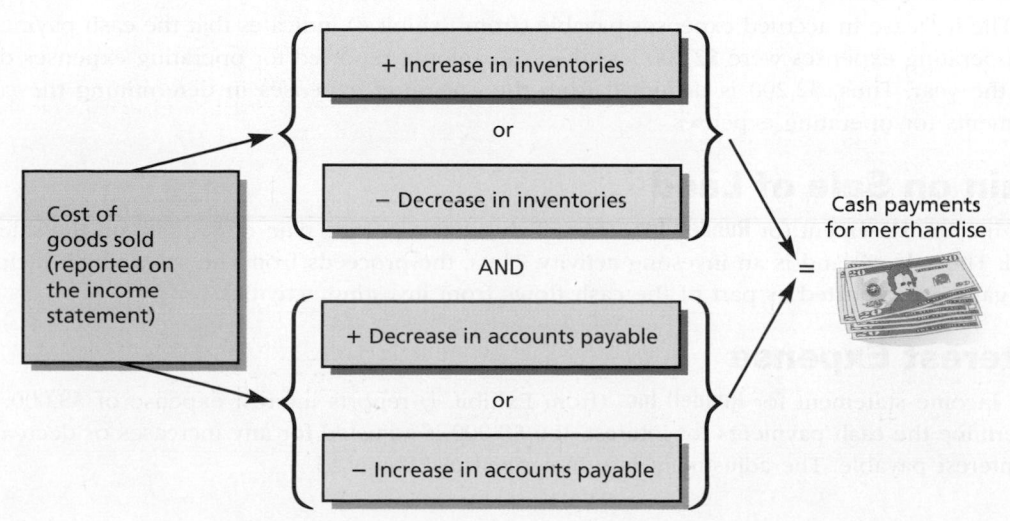

Exhibit 11
Determining the
Cash Payments for
Merchandise

The cash payments for merchandise are $785,200, computed as follows:

Cost of goods sold	$790,000
Decrease in inventories	(8,000)
Decrease in accounts payable	3,200
Cash payments for merchandise	$785,200

The $8,000 decrease in inventories (from Exhibit 4) indicates that the merchandise sold exceeded the cost of the merchandise purchased by $8,000. In other words, the cost of goods sold includes $8,000 of merchandise sold from inventory that did not require a cash outflow during the year. Thus, $8,000 is deducted from the cost of goods sold in determining the cash payments for merchandise.

The $3,200 decrease in accounts payable (from Exhibit 4) indicates that cash payments for merchandise were $3,200 more than the purchases on account during 20Y8. Therefore, $3,200 is added to the cost of goods sold in determining the cash payments for merchandise.

Cash Payments for Operating Expenses

The income statement for **Rundell Inc.** (from Exhibit 4) reports total operating expenses of $203,000, which includes depreciation expense of $7,000. Because depreciation expense does not require a cash outflow, it is omitted from cash payments for operating expenses.

To determine the cash payments for operating expenses, the other operating expenses (excluding depreciation) of $196,000 ($203,000 − $7,000) are adjusted for any increase or decrease in accrued expenses payable. Assuming that the accrued expenses payable are all operating expenses, this adjustment is summarized in Exhibit 12.

Exhibit 12

Determining the Cash Payments for Operating Expenses

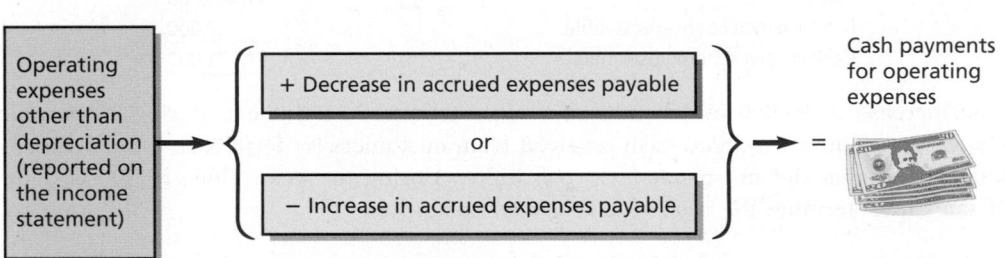

The cash payments for operating expenses are $193,800, computed as follows:

Operating expenses other than depreciation	$196,000
Increase in accrued expenses payable	(2,200)
Cash payments for operating expenses	$193,800

The increase in accrued expenses payable (from Exhibit 4) indicates that the cash payments for operating expenses were $2,200 less than the amount reported for operating expenses during the year. Thus, $2,200 is deducted from the operating expenses in determining the cash payments for operating expenses.

Gain on Sale of Land

The income statement for **Rundell Inc.** (from Exhibit 4) reports a gain of $12,000 on the sale of land. The sale of land is an investing activity. Thus, the proceeds from the sale, which include the gain, are reported as part of the cash flows from investing activities.

Interest Expense

The income statement for **Rundell Inc.** (from Exhibit 4) reports interest expense of $8,000. To determine the cash payments for interest, the $8,000 is adjusted for any increases or decreases in interest payable. The adjustment is summarized in Exhibit 13.

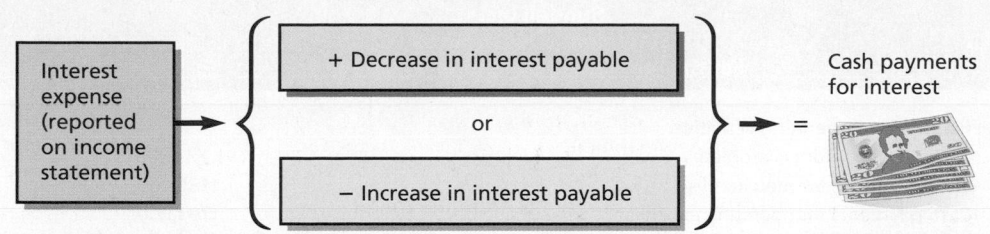

Exhibit 13
Determining the
Cash Payments for
Interest

The comparative balance sheet of Rundell in Exhibit 4 indicates no interest payable. This is because the interest expense on the bonds payable is paid on June 1 and December 31. Because there is no interest payable, no adjustment of the interest expense of $8,000 is necessary.

Cash Payments for Income Taxes

The income statement for **Rundell Inc.** (from Exhibit 4) reports income tax expense of $83,000. To determine the cash payments for income taxes, the $83,000 is adjusted for any increases or decreases in income taxes payable. The adjustment is summarized in Exhibit 14.

Exhibit 14
Determining the
Cash Payments for
Income Taxes

The cash payments for income taxes are $83,500, computed as follows:

Income tax expense	$83,000
Decrease in income taxes payable	500
Cash payments for income taxes	$83,500

The $500 decrease in income taxes payable (from Exhibit 4) indicates that the cash payments for income taxes were $500 more than the amount reported for income tax expense during 20Y8. Thus, $500 is added to the income tax expense in determining the cash payments for income taxes.

Reporting Cash Flows from Operating Activities—Direct Method

The statement of cash flows for **Rundell Inc.**, using the direct method for reporting cash flows from operating activities, is shown in Exhibit 15. The portions of the statement that differ from those prepared under the indirect method are highlighted.

Exhibit 15 also includes the separate schedule reconciling net income and net cash flow from operating activities. This schedule is included as part of the statement of cash flows when the direct method is used. This schedule is similar to the Cash Flows from Operating Activities section prepared under the indirect method.

Exhibit 15

Statement of Cash Flows—Direct Method

Rundell Inc. Statement of Cash Flows For the Year Ended December 31, 20Y8		
Cash flows from operating activities:		
Cash received from customers	$1,171,000	
Cash payments for merchandise	(785,200)	
Cash payments for operating expenses	(193,800)	
Cash payments for interest	(8,000)	
Cash payments for income taxes	(83,500)	
Net cash flow from operating activities		$100,500
Cash flows from investing activities:		
Cash received from sale of land	$ 72,000	
Cash paid for purchase of land	(15,000)	
Cash paid for purchase of building	(60,000)	
Net cash flow used for investing activities		(3,000)
Cash flows from financing activities:		
Cash received from sale of common stock....................	$ 48,000	
Cash paid to retire bonds payable	(50,000)	
Cash paid for dividends.....................................	(24,000)	
Net cash flow used for financing activities		(26,000)
Change in cash...		$ 71,500
Cash at the beginning of the year...........................		26,000
Cash at the end of the year.................................		$ 97,500
Schedule Reconciling Net Income with Cash		
Flows from Operating Activities:		
Cash flows from operating activities:		
Net income...		$108,000
Adjustments to reconcile net income to net cash		
flow from operating activities:		
Depreciation		7,000
Gain on sale of land...................................		(12,000)
Changes in current operating assets and liabilities:		
Increase in accounts receivable..............................		(9,000)
Decrease in inventory..		8,000
Decrease in accounts payable		(3,200)
Increase in accrued expenses payable........................		2,200
Decrease in income taxes payable		(500)
Net cash flow from operating activities....................		$100,500

Let's Review

Chapter Summary

1. The statement of cash flows reports cash receipts and cash payments by three types of activities: operating activities, investing activities, and financing activities. Cash flows from operating activities reports the cash inflows and outflows from a company's day-to-day operations. Cash flows from investing activities reports the cash inflows and outflows related to changes in a company's long-term assets. Cash flows from financing activities reports the cash inflows and outflows related to changes in a company's long-term liabilities and stockholders' equity. Investing and financing for a business may be affected by transactions that do not involve cash. The effect of such transactions should be reported in a separate schedule accompanying the statement of cash flows.

2. The indirect method reports cash flows from operating activities by adjusting net income for revenues and expenses that do not involve the receipt or payment of cash. Noncash expenses such as depreciation are added back to net income. Gains and losses on the disposal of assets are added to or deducted from net income. Changes in current operating assets and liabilities are added to or subtracted from net income, depending on their effect on cash.

3. Cash flows from investing activities are reported below cash flows from operating activities on the statement of cash flows. Cash flows from investing activities reports the cash inflows and outflows related to changes in a company's long-term assets.

4. Cash flows from financing activities are reported below cash flows from operating activities on the statement of cash flows. Cash flows from financing activities reports the cash inflows and outflows related to changes in a company's long-term liabilities and stockholders' equity.

5. The statement of cash flows reports cash flows from operating activities followed by cash flows from investing and financing activities. The result of adding the net cash flows from operating, investing, and financing activities is the net increase or decrease in cash for the period. Cash at the beginning of the year is added to determine the cash at the end of the period. This ending cash amount must agree with cash reported on the end-of-period balance sheet.

Key Terms

cash flow per share (613)
cash flows from financing
   activities (608)
cash flows from investing
   activities (608)

cash flows from operating
   activities (608)
direct method (609)
free cash flow (623)

indirect method (610)
statement of cash flows (608)

Practice

Multiple-Choice Questions

1. An example of a cash flow from an operating activity is:
   A. receipt of cash from the sale of stock.
   B. receipt of cash from the sale of bonds.
   C. payment of cash for dividends.
   D. receipt of cash from customers on account.

2. An example of a cash flow from an investing activity is:
   A. receipt of cash from the sale of equipment.
   B. receipt of cash from the sale of stock.
   C. payment of cash for dividends.
   D. payment of cash to acquire treasury stock.

3. An example of a cash flow from a financing activity is:
   A. receipt of cash from customers on account.
   B. receipt of cash from the sale of equipment.
   C. payment of cash for dividends.
   D. payment of cash to acquire land.

4. Which of the following methods of reporting cash flows from operating activities adjusts net income for revenues and expenses not involving the receipt or payment of cash?
   A. Direct method
   B. Purchase method
   C. Reciprocal method
   D. Indirect method

5. The net income reported on the income statement for the year was $55,000, and depreciation of fixed assets for the year was $22,000. The balances of the current asset and current liability accounts at the beginning and end of the year are as follows:

	End of Year	Beginning of Year
Cash	$ 65,000	$ 70,000
Accounts receivable	100,000	90,000
Inventories	145,000	150,000
Prepaid expenses	7,500	8,000
Accounts payable (merchandise creditors)	51,000	58,000

The total amount reported for cash flows from operating activities on the statement of cash flows using the indirect method is:
   A. $33,000.
   B. $55,000.
   C. $65,500.
   D. $77,000.

Answers provided after Problem. Need more practice? Find additional multiple-choice questions, exercises, and problems in CengageNOWv2.

Exercises

SHOW ME HOW

1. Classifying cash flows   Obj. 1

Identify whether each of the following would be reported as an operating, investing, or financing activity on the statement of cash flows:

A. Repurchase of common stock

B. Cash received from customers

C. Payment of accounts payable

D. Retirement of bonds payable

E. Purchase of equipment

F. Purchase of inventory for cash

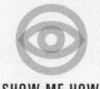

2. Adjustments to net income—indirect method Obj. 2

Pearl Corporation's accumulated depreciation—furniture account increased by $8,400, while $3,080 of patent amortization was recognized between balance sheet dates. There were no purchases or sales of depreciable or intangible assets during the year. In addition, the income statement showed a loss of $4,480 from the sale of land. Reconcile a net income of $120,400 to net cash flow from operating activities.

3. Changes in current operating assets and liabilities—indirect method Obj. 2

Alpenrose Corporation's comparative balance sheet for current assets and liabilities was as follows:

	Dec. 31, Year 2	Dec. 31, Year 1
Accounts receivable	$27,000	$32,400
Inventory	18,000	15,480
Accounts payable	16,200	14,220
Dividends payable	49,500	53,100

Adjust net income of $207,000 for changes in operating assets and liabilities to arrive at net cash flow from operating activities.

4. Cash flows from operating activities—indirect method Obj. 2

Pettygrove Inc. reported the following data:

Net income	$405,000
Depreciation expense	45,000
Gain on disposal of equipment	36,900
Decrease in accounts receivable	25,200
Decrease in accounts payable	6,480

Prepare the Cash Flows from Operating Activities section of the statement of cash flows, using the indirect method.

5. Land transactions on the statement of cash flows Obj. 3

Milo Corporation purchased land for $540,000. Later in the year, the company sold a different piece of land with a book value of $270,000 for $180,000. How are the effects of these transactions reported on the statement of cash flows?

6. Common stock transactions on the statement of cash flows Obj. 4

Wright Inc. received $1,200,000 from issuing shares of its common stock. During the year, Wright Inc. paid $500,000 to retire bonds and paid dividends of $250,000. How are the effects of these transactions reported on the statement of cash flows?

Answers provided after Problem. Need more practice? Find additional multiple-choice questions, exercises, and problems in CengageNOWv2.

Problem

The comparative balance sheet of Dowling Company for December 31, 20Y5 and 20Y4, is as follows:

Dowling Company Comparative Balance Sheet December 31, 20Y5 and 20Y4		
	20Y5	**20Y4**
Assets		
Cash	$ 140,350	$ 95,900
Accounts receivable (net)	95,300	102,300
Inventories	165,200	157,900
Prepaid expenses	6,240	5,860
Investments (long-term)	35,700	84,700
Land	75,000	90,000
Buildings	375,000	260,000
Accumulated depreciation—buildings	(71,300)	(58,300)
Machinery and equipment	428,300	428,300
Accumulated depreciation—machinery and equipment.........	(148,500)	(138,000)
Patents	58,000	65,000
Total assets	$1,159,290	$1,093,660
Liabilities and Stockholders' Equity		
Accounts payable (merchandise creditors)	$ 43,500	$ 46,700
Accrued expenses payable (operating expenses)	14,000	12,500
Income taxes payable...	7,900	8,400
Dividends payable..	14,000	10,000
Mortgage note payable, due in 10 years.......................	40,000	0
Bonds payable	150,000	250,000
Common stock, $30 par...	450,000	375,000
Excess of issue price over par—common stock	66,250	41,250
Retained earnings...	373,640	349,810
Total liabilities and stockholders' equity......................	$1,159,290	$1,093,660

The income statement for Dowling Company follows:

Dowling Company Income Statement For the Year Ended December 31, 20Y5		
Sales		$1,100,000
Cost of goods sold		710,000
Gross profit		$ 390,000
Operating expenses:		
Depreciation expense	$ 23,500	
Patent amortization	7,000	
Other operating expenses	196,000	
Total operating expenses............................		226,500
Income from operations		$ 163,500
Other revenue and expense:		
Gain on sale of investments.............................	$ 11,000	
Interest expense	(26,000)	(15,000)
Income before income tax		$ 148,500
Income tax expense		50,000
Net income		$ 98,500

An examination of the accounting records revealed the following additional information applicable to 20Y5:

A. Land costing $15,000 was sold for $15,000.

B. A mortgage note was issued for $40,000.

C. A building costing $115,000 was constructed.

D. 2,500 shares of common stock were issued at $40 in exchange for the bonds payable.

E. Cash dividends declared were $74,670.

Instructions

1. Prepare a statement of cash flows, using the indirect method of reporting cash flows from operating activities.

2. (*Appendix 2*) Prepare a statement of cash flows, using the direct method of reporting cash flows from operating activities.

Need more practice? Find additional multiple-choice questions, exercises, and problems in CengageNOWv2.

Answers

Multiple-Choice Questions

1. **D** Cash flows from operating activities affect transactions that enter into the determination of net income, such as the receipt of cash from customers on account (answer D). Receipts of cash from the sale of stock (answer A) and the sale of bonds (answer B) and payments of cash for dividends (answer C) are cash flows from financing activities.

2. **A** Cash flows from investing activities include receipts from the sale of noncurrent assets, such as equipment (answer A), and payments to acquire noncurrent assets. Receipts of cash from the sale of stock (answer B) and payments of cash for dividends (answer C) and to acquire treasury stock (answer D) are cash flows from financing activities.

3. **C** Payment of cash for dividends (answer C) is an example of a financing activity. The receipt of cash from customers on account (answer A) is an operating activity. The receipt of cash from the sale of equipment (answer B) and the payment of cash to acquire land (answer D) are examples of investing activities.

4. **D** The indirect method (answer D) reports cash flows from operating activities by beginning with net income and adjusting it for revenues and expenses not involving the receipt or payment of cash.

5. **C** The Cash Flows from Operating Activities section of the statement of cash flows would report net cash flow from operating activities of $65,500, determined as follows:

Cash flows from operating activities:		
Net income	$ 55,000	
Adjustments to reconcile net income to net cash flow from operating activities:		
Depreciation expense	22,000	
Changes in current operating assets and liabilities:		
Increase in accounts receivable	(10,000)	
Decrease in inventories	5,000	
Decrease in prepaid expenses	500	
Decrease in accounts payable	(7,000)	
Net cash flow from operating activities		$65,500

Exercises

1.

A. Financing

B. Operating

C. Operating

D. Financing

E. Investing

F. Operating

2.

Net income	$120,400
Adjustments to reconcile net income to net cash flow from operating activities:	
Depreciation	8,400
Amortization of patents..	3,080
Loss from sale of land	4,480
Net cash flow from operating activities.....................................	$136,360

3.

Net income	$207,000
Changes in current operating assets and liabilities:	
Decrease in accounts receivable	5,400
Increase in inventory..	(2,520)
Increase in accounts payable	1,980
Net cash flow from operating activities	$211,860

Note: The change in dividends payable impacts the cash paid for dividends, which is disclosed under financing activities.

4.

Cash flows from operating activities:	
Net income	$405,000
Adjustments to reconcile net income to net cash flow from operating activities:	
Depreciation	45,000
Gain on disposal of equipment	(36,900)
Changes in current operating assets and liabilities:	
Decrease in accounts receivable...	25,200
Decrease in accounts payable...	(6,480)
Net cash flow from operating activities...........................	$431,820

5. The loss on the sale of land is added to net income in the Operating Activities section.

Loss on sale of land	$ 90,000

The purchase and sale of land is reported as part of cash flows from investing activities as follows:

Cash received from sale of land	$ 180,000
Cash paid for purchase of land	(540,000)

6.

Cash flows from financing activities:	
Cash received from issuing common stock	$1,200,000
Cash paid to retire bonds..	(500,000)
Cash paid for dividends	(250,000)
Net cash flows used for financing activities...........................	$ 450,000

Need more help? Watch step-by-step videos of how to compute answers to these Exercises in CengageNOWv2.

Problem

1.

Dowling Company
Statement of Cash Flows—Indirect Method
For the Year Ended December 31, 20Y5

Cash flows from operating activities:

Net income...	$ 98,500	
Adjustments to reconcile net income to net cash flow		
from operating activities:		
Depreciation.....................................	23,500	
Amortization of patents........................	7,000	
Gain on sale of investments	(11,000)	
Changes in current operating assets and liabilities:		
Decrease in accounts receivable	7,000	
Increase in inventories.........................	(7,300)	
Increase in prepaid expenses	(380)	
Decrease in accounts payable	(3,200)	
Increase in accrued expenses payable..........	1,500	
Decrease in income taxes payable	(500)	
Net cash flow from operating activities		$115,120
Cash flows from investing activities:		
Cash received from sale of investments................	$60,000[1]	
Cash received from sale of land	15,000	
Cash paid for construction of building................	(115,000)	
Net cash flow used for investing activities		(40,000)
Cash flows from financing activities:		
Cash received from issuing mortgage note payable.....	$ 40,000	
Cash paid for dividends................................	(70,670)[2]	
Net cash flow used for financing activities		(30,670)
Change in cash.......................................		$ 44,450
Cash at the beginning of the year......................		95,900
Cash at the end of the year............................		$140,350

Schedule of Noncash Investing and Financing Activities:

Issued common stock to retire bonds payable..........	$100,000

[1]$60,000 = $11,000 gain + $49,000 (decrease in investments)
[2]$70,670 = $74,670 − $4,000 (increase in dividends)

2.

Dowling Company
Statement of Cash Flows—Direct Method
For the Year Ended December 31, 20Y5

Cash flows from operating activities:

Cash received from customers[1].......................	$1,107,000	
Cash paid for merchandise[2]..........................	(720,500)	
Cash paid for operating expenses[3]....................	(194,880)	
Cash paid for interest expense	(26,000)	
Cash paid for income tax[4]............................	(50,500)	
Net cash flow from operating activities		$115,120
Cash flows from investing activities:		
Cash received from sale of investments................	$ 60,000[5]	
Cash received from sale of land	15,000	
Cash paid for construction of building................	(115,000)	
Net cash flow used for investing activities		(40,000)

(Continued)

Cash flows from financing activities:
    Cash received from issuing mortgage note payable............. $ 40,000
    Cash paid for dividends[6].......................................   (70,670)
    Net cash flow used for financing activities ....   (30,670)
Change in cash.. $ 44,450
Cash at the beginning of the year..............................   95,900
Cash at the end of the year...................................... $140,350

Schedule of Noncash Investing and Financing Activities:
    Issued common stock to retire bonds payable................. $100,000
Schedule Reconciling Net Income with Cash Flows from
    Operating Activities[7]

Computations:

[1]$1,100,000 + $7,000 = $1,107,000
[2]$710,000 + $3,200 + $7,300 = $720,500
[3]$196,000 + $380 – $1,500 = $194,880
[4]$50,000 + $500 = $50,500
[5]$60,000 = $11,000 gain + $49,000 (decrease in investments)
[6]$74,670 + $10,000 – $14,000 = $70,670
[7]The content of this schedule is the same as the Operating Activities section of part (1) of this solution and is not reproduced here for the sake of brevity.

Discussion Questions

1. What is the principal disadvantage of the direct method of reporting cash flows from operating activities?

2. What are the major advantages of the indirect method of reporting cash flows from operating activities?

3. A corporation issued $2,000,000 of common stock in exchange for $2,000,000 of fixed assets. Where would this transaction be reported on the statement of cash flows?

4. A retail business, using the accrual method of accounting, owed merchandise creditors (accounts payable) $320,000 at the beginning of the year and $350,000 at the end of the year. How would the $30,000 increase be used to adjust net income in determining the amount of cash flows from operating activities by the indirect method? Explain.

5. If salaries payable was $100,000 at the beginning of the year and $75,000 at the end of the year, should the $25,000 decrease be added to or deducted from income to determine the amount of cash flows from operating activities by the indirect method? Explain.

6. A long-term investment in bonds with a cost of $500,000 was sold for $600,000 cash. (A) What was the gain or loss on the sale? (B) What was the effect of the transaction on cash flows? (C) How should the transaction be reported on the statement of cash flows if cash flows from operating activities are reported by the indirect method?

7. A corporation issued $2,000,000 of 20-year bonds for cash at 98. How would the transaction be reported on the statement of cash flows?

8. Fully depreciated equipment costing $50,000 was discarded. What was the effect of the transaction on cash flows if (A) $15,000 cash is received for the equipment, and (B) no cash is received for the equipment?

9. For the current year, Packers Company decided to switch from the indirect method to the direct method for reporting cash flows from operating activities on the statement of cash flows. Will the change cause the amount of net cash flow from operating activities to be larger, smaller, or the same as if the indirect method had been used? Explain.

10. Name five common major classes of operating cash receipts or operating cash payments presented on the statement of cash flows when the cash flows from operating activities are reported by the direct method.

Basic Exercises

SHOW ME HOW

BE 13-1   Classifying cash flows   Obj. 1

Identify whether each of the following would be reported as an operating, investing, or financing activity on the statement of cash flows:

A.   Purchase of investments   D.   Collection of accounts receivable

B.   Disposal of equipment   E.   Cash sales

C.   Payment for selling expenses   F.   Issuance of bonds payable

SHOW ME HOW

BE 13-2   Adjustments to net income—indirect method   Obj. 2

Ripley Corporation's accumulated depreciation—equipment account increased by $11,575 while $2,500 of patent amortization was recognized between balance sheet dates. There were no purchases or sales of depreciable or intangible assets during the year. In addition, the income statement showed a gain of $33,190 from the sale of investments. Reconcile a net income of $224,500 to net cash flow from operating activities.

SHOW ME HOW

BE 13-3   Changes in current operating assets and liabilities—indirect method   Obj. 2

Huluduey Corporation's comparative balance sheet for current assets and liabilities was as follows:

	Dec. 31, Year 2	Dec. 31, Year 1
Accounts receivable	$17,500	$12,500
Inventory	51,650	44,200
Accounts payable	8,480	5,100
Dividends payable	9,480	6,100

Adjust net income of $75,800 for changes in operating assets and liabilities to arrive at net cash flow from operating activities.

SHOW ME HOW

BE 13-4   Cash flows from operating activities—indirect method   Obj. 2

Staley Inc. reported the following data:

Net income	$396,200
Depreciation expense	61,250
Loss on disposal of equipment	27,600
Increase in accounts receivable	9,000
Increase in accounts payable	3,350

Prepare the Cash Flows from Operating Activities section of the statement of cash flows, using the indirect method.

SHOW ME HOW

BE 13-5   Land transactions on the statement of cash flows   Obj. 3

IZ Corporation purchased land for $400,000. Later in the year, the company sold a different piece of land with a book value of $200,000 for $240,000. How are the effects of these transactions reported on the statement of cash flows?

SHOW ME HOW

BE 13-6   Common stock transactions on the statement of cash flows   Obj. 4

Jones Industries received $800,000 from issuing shares of its common stock and $700,000 from issuing bonds. During the year, Jones Industries also paid dividends of $90,000. How are the effects of these transactions reported on the statement of cash flows?

SHOW ME HOW

Appendix 2

BE 13-7   Cash received from customers—direct method

Sales reported on the income statement were $112,000. The accounts receivable balance decreased $10,500 over the year. Determine the amount of cash received from customers.

SHOW ME HOW

Appendix 2

BE 13-8   Cash payments for merchandise—direct method

The cost of goods sold reported on the income statement was $240,000. The accounts payable balance increased $12,000, and the inventory balance increased by $19,200 over the year. Determine the amount of cash paid for merchandise.

Exercises

REAL WORLD

EX 13-1   Cash flows from operating activities—net loss   **Obj. 1**

United Continental Holdings, Inc., the parent company of **United Airlines**, reported a net *loss* of $723 million from operations. However, on its statement of cash flows, it reported $935 million of cash flows from operating activities.

➡ Explain this apparent contradiction between the loss and the positive cash flows.

EX 13-2   Effect of transactions on cash flows   **Obj. 1**

✔ A. Cash payment, $411,000

State the effect (cash receipt or cash payment and amount) of each of the following transactions, considered individually, on cash flows:

A. Retired $400,000 of bonds, on which there was $3,000 of unamortized discount, for $411,000.

B. Sold 20,000 shares of $5 par common stock for $22 per share.

C. Sold equipment with a book value of $55,800 for $60,000.

D. Purchased land for $650,000 cash.

E. Purchased a building by paying $50,000 cash and issuing a $450,000 mortgage note payable.

F. Sold a new issue of $500,000 of bonds at 98.

G. Purchased 10,000 shares of $10 par common stock as treasury stock at $33.25 per share.

H. Paid dividends of $1.50 per share. There were 1,000,000 shares issued and 120,000 shares of treasury stock.

EX 13-3   Classifying cash flows   **Obj. 1**

Identify the type of cash flow activity for each of the following events (operating, investing, or financing):

A. Net income

B. Paid cash dividends

C. Issued common stock

D. Issued bonds

E. Redeemed bonds

F. Sold long-term investments

G. Purchased treasury stock

H. Sold equipment

I. Issued preferred stock

J. Purchased buildings

K. Purchased patents

EX 13-4 Cash flows from operating activities—indirect method

Obj. 2

Indicate whether each of the following would be added to or deducted from net income in determining net cash flow from operating activities by the indirect method:

A. Decrease in inventory

B. Increase in accounts receivable

C. Increase in accounts payable

D. Loss on retirement of long-term debt

E. Depreciation of fixed assets

F. Decrease in notes receivable due in 60 days from customers

G. Increase in salaries payable

H. Decrease in prepaid expenses

I. Amortization of patent

J. Increase in notes payable due in 120 days to vendors

K. Gain on disposal of fixed assets

EX 13-5 Cash flows from operating activities—indirect method

Obj. 1, 2

✔ Net cash flow from operating activities, $103,850

SHOW ME HOW

The net income reported on the income statement for the current year was $73,600. Depreciation recorded on store equipment for the year amounted to $27,400. Balances of the current asset and current liability accounts at the beginning and end of the year are as follows:

	End of Year	Beginning of Year
Cash	$23,500	$18,700
Accounts receivable (net)	56,000	48,000
Inventories	35,500	40,000
Prepaid expenses	4,750	7,000
Accounts payable (merchandise creditors)	21,000	16,800
Wages payable	4,900	5,800

A. Prepare the Cash Flows from Operating Activities section of the statement of cash flows, using the indirect method.

B. ▬▬▶ Briefly explain why net cash flow from operating activities is different than net income.

EX 13-6 Cash flows from operating activities—indirect method

Obj. 1, 2

✔ Net cash flow from operating activities, $260,850

SHOW ME HOW

The net income reported on the income statement for the current year was $185,000. Depreciation recorded on equipment and a building amounted to $96,000 for the year. Balances of the current asset and current liability accounts at the beginning and end of the year are as follows:

	End of Year	Beginning of Year
Cash	$ 75,900	$ 86,150
Accounts receivable (net)	84,550	90,000
Inventories	186,200	175,000
Prepaid expenses	3,600	4,500
Accounts payable (merchandise creditors)	91,500	110,000
Salaries payable	7,200	4,000

A. Prepare the Cash Flows from Operating Activities section of the statement of cash flows, using the indirect method.

B. ▬▬▶ If the direct method had been used, would the net cash flow from operating activities have been the same? Explain.

EX 13-7 Cash flows from operating activities—indirect method

Obj. 1, 2

✔ Net cash flow from operating activities, $525,410

SHOW ME HOW

The income statement disclosed the following items for the year:

Depreciation expense	$ 57,600
Gain on disposal of equipment	33,600
Net income	508,000

(Continued)

The changes in the current asset and liability accounts for the year are as follows:

	Increase (Decrease)
Accounts receivable	$ 8,960
Inventory	(5,120)
Prepaid insurance	(1,920)
Accounts payable	(6,080)
Income taxes payable	1,410
Dividends payable	2,200

A. Prepare the Cash Flows from Operating Activities section of the statement of cash flows, using the indirect method.

B. ➤ Briefly explain why net cash flow from operating activities is different than net income.

EX 13-8 Reporting changes in equipment on statement of cash flows   Obj. 3

An analysis of the general ledger accounts indicates that office equipment, which cost $202,500 and on which accumulated depreciation totaled $84,375 on the date of sale, was sold for $101,250 during the year. Using this information, indicate the items to be reported on the statement of cash flows.

EX 13-9 Reporting changes in equipment on statement of cash flows   Obj. 3

An analysis of the general ledger accounts indicates that delivery equipment, which cost $80,000 and on which accumulated depreciation totaled $36,000 on the date of sale, was sold for $37,200 during the year. Using this information, indicate the items to be reported on the statement of cash flows.

EX 13-10 Reporting land transactions on statement of cash flows   Obj. 3

On the basis of the details of the following fixed asset account, indicate the items to be reported on the statement of cash flows:

ACCOUNT *Land*   **ACCOUNT NO.**

Date		Item	Debit	Credit	Balance Debit	Balance Credit
Jan.	1	Balance			868,000	
Mar.	12	Purchased for cash	104,300		972,300	
Oct.	4	Sold for $95,550		63,840	908,460	

EX 13-11 Determining cash payments to stockholders   Obj. 4

The board of directors declared cash dividends totaling $1,200,000 during the current year. The comparative balance sheet indicates dividends payable of $250,000 at the beginning of the year and $100,000 at the end of the year. What was the amount of cash payments to stockholders during the year?

SHOW ME HOW

EX 13-12 Reporting stockholders' equity items on statement of cash flows   Obj. 4

On the basis of the following stockholders' equity accounts, indicate the items, exclusive of net income, to be reported on the statement of cash flows. There were no unpaid dividends at either the beginning or the end of the year.

ACCOUNT *Common Stock, $40 par*   ACCOUNT NO.

Date		Item	Debit	Credit	Balance Debit	Balance Credit
Jan.	1	Balance, 120,000 shares				4,800,000
Apr.	2	30,000 shares issued for cash		1,200,000		6,000,000
June	30	5% stock dividend		300,000		6,300,000

ACCOUNT *Paid-In Capital in Excess of Par—Common Stock*   ACCOUNT NO.

Date		Item	Debit	Credit	Balance Debit	Balance Credit
Jan.	1	Balance				360,000
Apr.	2	30,000 shares issued for cash		720,000		1,080,000
June	30	Stock dividend		150,000		1,230,000

ACCOUNT *Retained Earnings*   ACCOUNT NO.

Date		Item	Debit	Credit	Balance Debit	Balance Credit
Jan.	1	Balance				2,000,000
June	30	Stock dividend	450,000			1,550,000
Dec.	30	Cash dividend	315,000			1,235,000
	31	Net income		1,000,000		2,235,000

EX 13-13   Reporting land acquisition for cash and mortgage note on statement of   Obj. 3, 4
cash flows

On the basis of the details of the following fixed asset account, indicate the items to be reported on the statement of cash flows:

ACCOUNT *Land*   ACCOUNT NO.

Date		Item	Debit	Credit	Balance Debit	Balance Credit
Jan.	1	Balance			156,000	
Feb.	10	Purchased for cash	246,000		402,000	
Nov.	20	Purchased with long-term mortgage note	324,000		726,000	

EX 13-14   Reporting issuance and retirement of long-term debt   Obj. 4

On the basis of the details of the following bonds payable and related discount accounts, indicate the items to be reported in the Financing Activities section of the statement of cash flows, assuming no gain or loss on retiring the bonds:

ACCOUNT *Bonds Payable*   ACCOUNT NO.

Date		Item	Debit	Credit	Balance Debit	Balance Credit
Jan.	1	Balance				750,000
	2	Retire bonds	150,000			600,000
June	30	Issue bonds		450,000		1,050,000

(Continued)

ACCOUNT *Discount on Bonds Payable*   **ACCOUNT NO.**

Date		Item	Debit	Credit	Balance Debit	Balance Credit
Jan.	1	Balance			33,750	
	2	Retire bonds		12,000	21,750	
June	30	Issue bonds	30,000		51,750	
Dec.	31	Amortize discount		2,625	49,125	

EX 13-15   **Determining net income from net cash flow from**   **Obj. 2, 3, 4**
operating activities

✔ Net income,
$341,770

SHOW ME HOW

Curwen Inc. reported net cash flow from operating activities of $357,500 on its statement of cash flows for the year ended December 31. The following information was reported in the Cash Flows from Operating Activities section of the statement of cash flows, using the indirect method:

Decrease in income taxes payable	$ 7,700
Decrease in inventories	19,140
Depreciation	29,480
Gain on sale of investments	13,200
Increase in accounts payable	5,280
Increase in prepaid expenses	2,970
Increase in accounts receivable	14,300

A. Determine the net income reported by Curwen Inc. for the year ended December 31.

B. ➤ Briefly explain why Curwen's net income is different than net cash flow from operating activities.

EX 13-16   **Cash flows from operating activities—indirect method**   **Obj. 2**

✔ Net cash flow
from operating
activities, $58,020

EXCEL TEMPLATE   REAL WORLD

Selected data (in thousands) derived from the income statement and balance sheet of **National Beverage Corp.** for a recent year are as follows:

Income statement data:	
Net income	$49,311
Gain on disposal of property	1,188
Depreciation expense	11,580
Other items involving noncash expenses	1,383
Balance sheet data:	
Increase in accounts receivable	1,746
Decrease in inventory	990
Increase in prepaid expenses	605
Decrease in accounts payable	710
Decrease in accrued and other current liabilities	995

A. Prepare the Cash Flows from Operating Activities section of the statement of cash flows, using the indirect method for National Beverage Corp.

B. ➤ Interpret your results in part (A).

EX 13-17 Statement of cash flows—indirect method

Obj. 2, 3, 4, 5

✔ Net cash flow from operating activities, $38

SHOW ME HOW   EXCEL TEMPLATE

The comparative balance sheet of Olson-Jones Industries Inc. for December 31, 20Y2 and 20Y1, is as follows:

	Dec. 31, 20Y2	Dec. 31, 20Y1
Assets		
Cash	$183	$ 14
Accounts receivable (net)	55	49
Inventories	117	99
Land	250	330
Equipment...	205	175
Accumulated depreciation—equipment	(68)	(42)
Total assets	$742	$625
Liabilities and Stockholders' Equity		
Accounts payable (merchandise creditors)	$ 51	$ 37
Dividends payable...	5	—
Common stock, $1 par.......................................	125	80
Paid-in capital: Excess of issue price over par—common stock	85	70
Retained earnings...	476	438
Total liabilities and stockholders' equity........................	$742	$625

The following additional information is taken from the records:

A. Land was sold for $120.

B. Equipment was acquired for cash.

C. There were no disposals of equipment during the year.

D. The common stock was issued for cash.

E. There was a $62 credit to Retained Earnings for net income.

F. There was a $24 debit to Retained Earnings for cash dividends declared.

A. Prepare a statement of cash flows, using the indirect method of presenting cash flows from operating activities.

B. ━━━▶ Was Olson-Jones's net cash flow from operations more or less than net income? What is the source of this difference?

EX 13-18 Statement of cash flows—indirect method

Obj. 2, 3, 4, 5

List the errors you find in the following statement of cash flows. The cash balance at the beginning of the year was $240,000. All other amounts are correct, except the cash balance at the end of the year.

Shasta Inc.
Statement of Cash Flows
For the Year Ended December 31, 20Y9

Cash flows from operating activities:		
Net income	$ 360,000	
Adjustments to reconcile net income to net cash flow from operating activities:		
Depreciation...	100,800	
Gain on sale of investments...........................	17,280	
Changes in current operating assets and liabilities:		
Increase in accounts receivable.........................	27,360	
Increase in inventories................................	(36,000)	
Increase in accounts payable	(3,600)	
Decrease in accrued expenses payable..................	(2,400)	
Net cash flow from operating activities		$ 463,440
Cash flows from investing activities:		
Cash received from sale of investments	$ 240,000	
Cash paid for purchase of land	(259,200)	
Cash paid for purchase of equipment.....................	(432,000)	
Net cash flow used for investing activities.............		(415,200)

(Continued)

Cash flows from financing activities:

Cash received from sale of common stock.................	$312,000	
Cash paid for dividends..................................	(132,000)	
Net cash flow from financing activities.................		180,000
Change in cash...		$ 47,760
Cash at the end of the year..............................		192,240
Cash at the beginning of the year........................		$240,000

Appendix 2

EX 13-19   Cash flows from operating activities—direct method

✔ A. $801,900

The cash flows from operating activities are reported by the direct method on the statement of cash flows. Determine the following:

A. If sales for the current year were $753,500 and accounts receivable decreased by $48,400 during the year, what was the amount of cash received from customers?

B. If income tax expense for the current year was $50,600 and income tax payable decreased by $5,500 during the year, what was the amount of cash payments for income taxes?

C. ▬▬▬▶ Briefly explain why the cash received from customers in (A) is different than sales.

Appendix 2

EX 13-20   Determining selected amounts for cash flows from operating activities—direct method

✔ A. $1,025,800

Selected data taken from the accounting records of Ginis Inc. for the current year ended December 31 are as follows:

	Balance, December 31	Balance, January 1
Accrued expenses payable (operating expenses)	$ 12,650	$ 14,030
Accounts payable (merchandise creditors)	96,140	105,800
Inventories	178,020	193,430
Prepaid expenses	7,360	8,970

During the current year, the cost of goods sold was $1,031,550, and the operating expenses other than depreciation were $179,400. The direct method is used for presenting the cash flows from operating activities on the statement of cash flows.

Determine the amount reported on the statement of cash flows for (A) cash payments for merchandise and (B) cash payments for operating expenses.

Appendix 2

EX 13-21   Cash flows from operating activities—direct method

✔ Net cash flow from operating activities, $96,040

The income statement of Booker T Industries Inc. for the current year ended June 30 is as follows:

Sales		$511,000
Cost of goods sold.......................................		290,500
Gross profit		$220,500
Operating expenses:		
Depreciation expense	$ 39,200	
Other operating expenses	105,000	
Total operating expenses		144,200
Income before income tax		$ 76,300
Income tax expense		21,700
Net income		$ 54,600

Changes in the balances of selected accounts from the beginning to the end of the current year are as follows:

	Increase (Decrease)
Accounts receivable (net)	$(11,760)
Inventories	3,920
Prepaid expenses	(3,780)
Accounts payable (merchandise creditors)	(7,980)
Accrued expenses payable (operating expenses)	1,260
Income tax payable...	(2,660)

A. Prepare the Cash Flows from Operating Activities section of the statement of cash flows, using the direct method.

B. ━━━▶ What does the direct method show about a company's cash flows from operating activities that is not shown using the indirect method?

Appendix 2

EX 13-22 Cash flows from operating activities—direct method

✔ Net cash flow from operating activities, $123,860

The income statement for Rhino Company for the current year ended June 30 and balances of selected accounts at the beginning and the end of the year are as follows:

Sales	$445,500
Cost of goods sold.......................................	154,000
Gross profit	$291,500
Operating expenses:	
Depreciation expense .... $ 38,500	
Other operating expenses 115,280	
Total operating expenses	153,780
Income before income tax	$137,720
Income tax expense	39,600
Net income	$ 98,120

	End of Year	Beginning of Year
Accounts receivable (net)	$36,300	$31,240
Inventories	92,400	80,300
Prepaid expenses	14,520	15,840
Accounts payable (merchandise creditors)	67,540	62,700
Accrued expenses payable (operating expenses)	19,140	20,900
Income tax payable.......................................	4,400	4,400

Prepare the Cash Flows from Operating Activities section of the statement of cash flows, using the direct method.

Problems: Series A

PR 13-1A Statement of cash flows—indirect method   Obj. 2, 3, 4, 5

✔ Net cash flow from operating activities, $490,000

SHOW ME HOW   EXCEL TEMPLATE

The comparative balance sheet of Livers Inc. for December 31, 20Y3 and 20Y2, is shown as follows:

	Dec. 31, 20Y3	Dec. 31, 20Y2
Assets		
Cash	$ 155,000	$ 150,000
Accounts receivable (net)	450,000	400,000
Inventories	770,000	750,000
Investments	0	100,000
Land	500,000	0
Equipment	1,400,000	1,200,000
Accumulated depreciation—equipment	(600,000)	(500,000)
Total assets	$2,675,000	$2,100,000
Liabilities and Stockholders' Equity		
Accounts payable (merchandise creditors)	$ 340,000	$ 300,000
Accrued expenses payable (operating expenses)	45,000	50,000
Dividends payable	30,000	25,000
Common stock, $4 par	700,000	600,000
Paid-in capital: Excess of issue price over par—common stock	200,000	175,000
Retained earnings	1,360,000	950,000
Total liabilities and stockholders' equity	$2,675,000	$2,100,000

Additional data obtained from an examination of the accounts in the ledger for 20Y3 are as follows:

A. The investments were sold for $175,000 cash.

B. Equipment and land were acquired for cash.

C. There were no disposals of equipment during the year.

D. The common stock was issued for cash.

E. There was a $500,000 credit to Retained Earnings for net income.

F. There was a $90,000 debit to Retained Earnings for cash dividends declared.

Instructions

Prepare a statement of cash flows, using the indirect method of presenting cash flows from operating activities.

PR 13-2A Statement of cash flows—indirect method   Obj. 2, 3, 4, 5

✔ Net cash flow from operating activities, $225,000

SHOW ME HOW   EXCEL TEMPLATE

The comparative balance sheet of Yellow Dog Enterprises Inc. at December 31, 20Y8 and 20Y7, is as follows:

	Dec. 31, 20Y8	Dec. 31, 20Y7
Assets		
Cash	$ 80,000	$ 100,000
Accounts receivable (net)	275,000	300,000
Inventories	510,000	400,000
Prepaid expenses	15,000	10,000
Equipment	1,070,000	750,000
Accumulated depreciation—equipment	(200,000)	(160,000)
Total assets	$1,750,000	$1,400,000
Liabilities and Stockholders' Equity		
Accounts payable (merchandise creditors)	$ 100,000	$ 90,000
Mortgage note payable	0	400,000
Common stock, $10 par	600,000	200,000
Paid-in capital: Excess of issue price over par—common stock	300,000	100,000
Retained earnings	750,000	610,000
Total liabilities and stockholders' equity	$1,750,000	$1,400,000

Additional data obtained from the income statement and from an examination of the accounts in the ledger for 20Y8 are as follows:

A. Net income, $190,000.

B. Depreciation reported on the income statement, $115,000.

C. Equipment was purchased at a cost of $395,000 and fully depreciated equipment costing $75,000 was discarded, with no salvage realized.

D. The mortgage note payable was not due for six years, but the terms permitted earlier payment without penalty.

E. 40,000 shares of common stock were issued at $15 for cash.

F. Cash dividends declared and paid, $50,000.

Instructions

Prepare a statement of cash flows, using the indirect method of presenting cash flows from operating activities.

PR 13-3A   Statement of cash flows—indirect method   Obj. 2, 3, 4, 5

✔ Net cash flow used for operating activities, $(169,600)

EXCEL TEMPLATE

The comparative balance sheet of Whitman Co. at December 31, 20Y2 and 20Y1, is as follows:

	Dec. 31, 20Y2	Dec. 31, 20Y1
Assets		
Cash	$ 918,000	$ 964,800
Accounts receivable (net)	828,900	761,940
Inventories	1,268,460	1,162,980
Prepaid expenses	29,340	35,100
Land	315,900	479,700
Buildings	1,462,500	900,900
Accumulated depreciation—buildings...........................	(408,600)	(382,320)
Equipment...	512,280	454,680
Accumulated depreciation—equipment	(141,300)	(158,760)
Total assets	$4,785,480	$4,219,020
Liabilities and Stockholders' Equity		
Accounts payable (merchandise creditors)	$ 922,500	$ 958,320
Bonds payable	270,000	0
Common stock, $25 par..	317,000	117,000
Paid-in capital: Excess of issue price over par—common stock	758,000	558,000
Retained earnings...	2,517,980	2,585,700
Total liabilities and stockholders' equity........................	$4,785,480	$4,219,020

The noncurrent asset, noncurrent liability, and stockholders' equity accounts for 20Y2 are as follows:

ACCOUNT *Land*   **ACCOUNT NO.**

					Balance	
Date		Item	Debit	Credit	Debit	Credit
20Y2						
Jan.	1	Balance			479,700	
Apr.	20	Realized $151,200 cash				
		from sale		163,800	315,900	

ACCOUNT *Buildings*   **ACCOUNT NO.**

					Balance	
Date		Item	Debit	Credit	Debit	Credit
20Y2						
Jan.	1	Balance			900,900	
Apr.	20	Acquired for cash	561,600		1,462,500	

(Continued)

ACCOUNT *Accumulated Depreciation—Buildings* **ACCOUNT NO.**

Date		Item	Debit	Credit	Balance Debit	Balance Credit
20Y2						
Jan.	1	Balance				382,320
Dec.	31	Depreciation for year		26,280		408,600

ACCOUNT *Equipment* **ACCOUNT NO.**

Date		Item	Debit	Credit	Balance Debit	Balance Credit
20Y2						
Jan.	1	Balance			454,680	
	26	Discarded, no salvage		46,800	407,880	
Aug.	11	Purchased for cash	104,400		512,280	

ACCOUNT *Accumulated Depreciation—Equipment* **ACCOUNT NO.**

Date		Item	Debit	Credit	Balance Debit	Balance Credit
20Y2						
Jan.	1	Balance				158,760
	26	Equipment discarded	46,800			111,960
Dec.	31	Depreciation for year		29,340		141,300

ACCOUNT *Bonds Payable* **ACCOUNT NO.**

Date		Item	Debit	Credit	Balance Debit	Balance Credit
20Y2						
May	1	Issued 20-year bonds		270,000		270,000

ACCOUNT *Common Stock, $25 par* **ACCOUNT NO.**

Date		Item	Debit	Credit	Balance Debit	Balance Credit
20Y2						
Jan.	1	Balance				117,000
Dec.	7	Issued 8,000 shares of common stock for $50 per share		200,000		317,000

ACCOUNT *Paid-In Capital in Excess of Par—Common Stock* **ACCOUNT NO.**

Date		Item	Debit	Credit	Balance Debit	Balance Credit
20Y2						
Jan.	1	Balance				558,000
Dec.	7	Issued 8,000 shares of common stock for $50 per share		200,000		758,000

ACCOUNT *Retained Earnings*					ACCOUNT NO.	
					Balance	
Date		**Item**	**Debit**	**Credit**	**Debit**	**Credit**
20Y2						
Jan.	1	Balance				2,585,700
Dec.	31	Net loss	35,320			2,550,380
	31	Cash dividends	32,400			2,517,980

Instructions

Prepare a statement of cash flows, using the indirect method of presenting cash flows from operating activities.

Appendix 2

PR 13-4A   Statement of cash flows—direct method

✔ Net cash flow from operating activities, $293,600

SHOW ME HOW   EXCEL TEMPLATE

GENERAL LEDGER

The comparative balance sheet of Canace Products Inc. for December 31, 20Y6 and 20Y5, is as follows:

	Dec. 31, 20Y6	Dec. 31, 20Y5
Assets		
Cash	$ 643,400	$ 679,400
Accounts receivable (net)	566,800	547,400
Inventories	1,011,000	982,800
Investments	0	240,000
Land	520,000	0
Equipment...	880,000	680,000
Accumulated depreciation	(244,400)	(200,400)
Total assets	$3,376,800	$2,929,200
Liabilities and Stockholders' Equity		
Accounts payable (merchandise creditors)	$ 771,800	$ 748,400
Accrued expenses payable (operating expenses)	63,400	70,800
Dividends payable..	8,800	6,400
Common stock, $2 par......................................	56,000	32,000
Paid-in capital: Excess of issue price over par—common stock	408,000	192,000
Retained earnings...	2,068,800	1,879,600
Total liabilities and stockholders' equity..............	$3,376,800	$2,929,200

The income statement for the year ended December 31, 20Y6, is as follows:

Sales		$5,980,000
Cost of goods sold...		2,452,000
Gross profit		$3,528,000
Operating expenses:		
Depreciation expense	$ 44,000	
Other operating expenses	3,100,000	
Total operating expenses		3,144,000
Operating income...		$ 384,000
Other expense:		
Loss on sale of investments		(64,000)
Income before income tax		$ 320,000
Income tax expense		102,800
Net income		$ 217,200

Additional data obtained from an examination of the accounts in the ledger for 20Y6 are as follows:

A. Equipment and land were acquired for cash.

B. There were no disposals of equipment during the year.

(Continued)

C. The investments were sold for $176,000 cash.

D. The common stock was issued for cash.

E. There was a $28,000 debit to Retained Earnings for cash dividends declared.

Instructions

Prepare a statement of cash flows, using the direct method of presenting cash flows from operating activities.

Appendix 2

PR 13-5A   Statement of cash flows—direct method applied to PR 13-1A

✔ Net cash flow from operating activities, $490,000

EXCEL TEMPLATE

The comparative balance sheet of Livers Inc. for December 31, 20Y3 and 20Y2, is as follows:

	Dec. 31, 20Y3	Dec. 31, 20Y2
Assets		
Cash	$ 155,000	$ 150,000
Accounts receivable (net)	450,000	400,000
Inventories	770,000	750,000
Investments	0	100,000
Land	500,000	0
Equipment	1,400,000	1,200,000
Accumulated depreciation—equipment	(600,000)	(500,000)
Total assets	$2,675,000	$2,100,000
Liabilities and Stockholders' Equity		
Accounts payable (merchandise creditors)	$ 340,000	$ 300,000
Accrued expenses payable (operating expenses)	45,000	50,000
Dividends payable	30,000	25,000
Common stock, $4 par	700,000	600,000
Paid-in capital: Excess of issue price over par—common stock	200,000	175,000
Retained earnings	1,360,000	950,000
Total liabilities and stockholders' equity	$2,675,000	$2,100,000

The income statement for the year ended December 31, 20Y3, is as follows:

Sales		$3,000,000
Cost of goods sold		1,400,000
Gross profit		$1,600,000
Operating expenses:		
Depreciation expense	$100,000	
Other operating expenses	950,000	
Total operating expenses		1,050,000
Operating income		$ 550,000
Other income:		
Gain on sale of investments		75,000
Income before income tax		$ 625,000
Income tax expense		125,000
Net income		$ 500,000

Additional data obtained from an examination of the accounts in the ledger for 20Y3 are as follows:

A. The investments were sold for $175,000 cash.

B. Equipment and land were acquired for cash.

C. There were no disposals of equipment during the year.

D. The common stock was issued for cash.

E. There was a $90,000 debit to Retained Earnings for cash dividends declared.

Instructions

Prepare a statement of cash flows, using the direct method of presenting cash flows from operating activities.

Problems: Series B

PR 13-1B Statement of cash flows—indirect method

Obj. 2, 3, 4, 5

✔ Net cash flow from operating activities, $154,260

SHOW ME HOW   EXCEL TEMPLATE

The comparative balance sheet of Merrick Equipment Co. for December 31, 20Y9 and 20Y8, is as follows:

	Dec. 31, 20Y9	Dec. 31, 20Y8
Assets		
Cash	$ 70,720	$ 47,940
Accounts receivable (net)	207,230	188,190
Inventories	298,520	289,850
Investments	0	102,000
Land	295,800	0
Equipment	438,600	358,020
Accumulated depreciation—equipment	(99,110)	(84,320)
Total assets	$1,211,760	$901,680
Liabilities and Stockholders' Equity		
Accounts payable (merchandise creditors)	$ 205,700	$194,140
Accrued expenses payable (operating expenses)	30,600	26,860
Dividends payable	25,500	20,400
Common stock, $1 par	202,000	102,000
Paid-in capital: Excess of issue price over par—common stock	354,000	204,000
Retained earnings	393,960	354,280
Total liabilities and stockholders' equity	$1,211,760	$901,680

Additional data obtained from an examination of the accounts in the ledger for 20Y9 are as follows:

A. Equipment and land were acquired for cash.

B. There were no disposals of equipment during the year.

C. The investments were sold for $91,800 cash.

D. The common stock was issued for cash.

E. There was a $141,680 credit to Retained Earnings for net income.

F. There was a $102,000 debit to Retained Earnings for cash dividends declared.

Instructions

Prepare a statement of cash flows, using the indirect method of presenting cash flows from operating activities.

PR 13-2B Statement of cash flows—indirect method

Obj. 2, 3, 4, 5

✔ Net cash flow from operating activities, $561,400

SHOW ME HOW   EXCEL TEMPLATE

The comparative balance sheet of Harris Industries Inc. at December 31, 20Y4 and 20Y3, is as follows:

	Dec. 31, 20Y4	Dec. 31, 20Y3
Assets		
Cash	$ 443,240	$ 360,920
Accounts receivable (net)	665,280	592,200
Inventories	887,880	1,022,560
Prepaid expenses	31,640	25,200
Land	302,400	302,400
Buildings	1,713,600	1,134,000
Accumulated depreciation—buildings	(466,200)	(414,540)
Machinery and equipment	781,200	781,200
Accumulated depreciation—machinery and equipment	(214,200)	(191,520)
Patents	106,960	112,000
Total assets	$4,251,800	$3,724,420

(Continued)

Liabilities and Stockholders' Equity

Accounts payable (merchandise creditors)	$ 837,480	$ 927,080
Dividends payable..	32,760	25,200
Salaries payable..	78,960	87,080
Mortgage note payable, due in nine years..................	224,000	0
Bonds payable	0	390,000
Common stock, $5 par.....................................	200,400	50,400
Paid-in capital: Excess of issue price over par—common stock.......	366,000	126,000
Retained earnings..	2,512,200	2,118,660
Total liabilities and stockholders' equity....................	$4,251,800	$3,724,420

An examination of the income statement and the accounting records revealed the following additional information applicable to 20Y4:

A. Net income, $524,580.

B. Depreciation expense reported on the income statement: buildings, $51,660; machinery and equipment, $22,680.

C. Patent amortization reported on the income statement, $5,040.

D. A building was constructed for $579,600.

E. A mortgage note for $224,000 was issued for cash.

F. 30,000 shares of common stock were issued at $13 in exchange for the bonds payable.

G. Cash dividends declared, $131,040.

Instructions

Prepare a statement of cash flows, using the indirect method of presenting cash flows from operating activities.

PR 13-3B Statement of cash flows—indirect method

Obj. 2, 3, 4, 5

✔ Net cash flow from operating activities, $162,800

EXCEL TEMPLATE

The comparative balance sheet of Coulson, Inc. at December 31, 20Y2 and 20Y1, is as follows:

	Dec. 31, 20Y2	Dec. 31, 20Y1
Assets		
Cash	$ 300,600	$ 337,800
Accounts receivable (net)	704,400	609,600
Inventories	918,600	865,800
Prepaid expenses	18,600	26,400
Land	990,000	1,386,000
Buildings	1,980,000	990,000
Accumulated depreciation—buildings.....................	(397,200)	(366,000)
Equipment	660,600	529,800
Accumulated depreciation—equipment	(133,200)	(162,000)
Total assets	$5,042,400	$4,217,400
Liabilities and Stockholders' Equity		
Accounts payable (merchandise creditors)	$ 594,000	$ 631,200
Income taxes payable	26,400	21,600
Bonds payable	330,000	0
Common stock, $20 par...................................	320,000	180,000
Paid-in capital: Excess of issue price over par—common stock	950,000	810,000
Retained earnings.......................................	2,822,000	2,574,600
Total liabilities and stockholders' equity....................	$5,042,400	$4,217,400

The noncurrent asset, noncurrent liability, and stockholders' equity accounts for 20Y2 are as follows:

ACCOUNT *Land*   ACCOUNT NO.

					Balance	
Date		Item	Debit	Credit	Debit	Credit
20Y2						
Jan.	1	Balance			1,386,000	
Apr.	20	Realized $456,000 cash from sale		396,000	990,000	

ACCOUNT *Buildings*   ACCOUNT NO.

					Balance	
Date		Item	Debit	Credit	Debit	Credit
20Y2						
Jan.	1	Balance			990,000	
Apr.	20	Acquired for cash	990,000		1,980,000	

ACCOUNT *Accumulated Depreciation—Buildings*   ACCOUNT NO.

					Balance	
Date		Item	Debit	Credit	Debit	Credit
20Y2						
Jan.	1	Balance				366,000
Dec.	31	Depreciation for year		31,200		397,200

ACCOUNT *Equipment*   ACCOUNT NO.

					Balance	
Date		Item	Debit	Credit	Debit	Credit
20Y2						
Jan.	1	Balance			529,800	
	26	Discarded, no salvage		66,000	463,800	
Aug.	11	Purchased for cash	196,800		660,600	

ACCOUNT *Accumulated Depreciation—Equipment*   ACCOUNT NO.

					Balance	
Date		Item	Debit	Credit	Debit	Credit
20Y2						
Jan.	1	Balance				162,000
	26	Equipment discarded	66,000			96,000
Dec.	31	Depreciation for year		37,200		133,200

ACCOUNT *Bonds Payable*   ACCOUNT NO.

					Balance	
Date		Item	Debit	Credit	Debit	Credit
20Y2						
May	1	Issued 20-year bonds		330,000		330,000

(Continued)

ACCOUNT *Common Stock, $20 par*   **ACCOUNT NO.**

Date		Item	Debit	Credit	Balance Debit	Balance Credit
20Y2						
Jan.	1	Balance				180,000
Dec.	7	Issued 7,000 shares of common stock for $40 per share		140,000		320,000

ACCOUNT *Paid-In Capital in Excess of Par—Common Stock*   **ACCOUNT NO.**

Date		Item	Debit	Credit	Balance Debit	Balance Credit
20Y2						
Jan.	1	Balance				810,000
Dec.	7	Issued 7,000 shares of common stock for $40 per share		140,000		950,000

ACCOUNT *Retained Earnings*   **ACCOUNT NO.**

Date		Item	Debit	Credit	Balance Debit	Balance Credit
20Y2						
Jan.	1	Balance				2,574,600
Dec.	31	Net income		326,600		2,901,200
	31	Cash dividends	79,200			2,822,000

Instructions

Prepare a statement of cash flows, using the indirect method of presenting cash flows from operating activities.

Appendix 2

PR 13-4B   Statement of cash flows—direct method

✔ Net cash flow from operating activities, $509,220

The comparative balance sheet of Martinez Inc. for December 31, 20Y4 and 20Y3, is as follows:

SHOW ME HOW

EXCEL TEMPLATE

GENERAL LEDGER

	Dec. 31, 20Y4	Dec. 31, 20Y3
Assets		
Cash	$ 661,920	$ 683,100
Accounts receivable (net)	992,640	914,400
Inventories	1,394,400	1,363,800
Investments	0	432,000
Land	960,000	0
Equipment...	1,224,000	984,000
Accumulated depreciation—equipment	(481,500)	(368,400)
Total assets	$4,751,460	$4,008,900
Liabilities and Stockholders' Equity		
Accounts payable (merchandise creditors)	$1,080,000	$ 966,600
Accrued expenses payable (operating expenses)	67,800	79,200
Dividends payable..	100,800	91,200
Common stock, $5 par	130,000	30,000
Paid-in capital: Excess of issue price over par—common stock......	950,000	450,000
Retained earnings.......................................	2,422,860	2,391,900
Total liabilities and stockholders' equity...................	$4,751,460	$4,008,900

The income statement for the year ended December 31, 20Y3, is as follows:

Sales		$4,512,000
Cost of goods sold..		2,352,000
Gross profit		$2,160,000
Operating expenses:		
Depreciation expense	$ 113,100	
Other operating expenses	1,344,840	
Total operating expenses		1,457,940
Operating income...		$ 702,060
Other income:		
Gain on sale of investments............................		156,000
Income before income tax		$ 858,060
Income tax expense		299,100
Net income		$ 558,960

Additional data obtained from an examination of the accounts in the ledger for 20Y3 are as follows:

A. Equipment and land were acquired for cash.

B. There were no disposals of equipment during the year.

C. The investments were sold for $588,000 cash.

D. The common stock was issued for cash.

E. There was a $528,000 debit to Retained Earnings for cash dividends declared.

Instructions

Prepare a statement of cash flows, using the direct method of presenting cash flows from operating activities.

Appendix 2

PR 13-5B Statement of cash flows—direct method applied to PR 13-1B

✔ Net cash flow from operating activities, $154,260

EXCEL TEMPLATE

The comparative balance sheet of Merrick Equipment Co. for Dec. 31, 20Y9 and 20Y8, is:

	Dec. 31, 20Y9	Dec. 31, 20Y8
Assets		
Cash	$ 70,720	$ 47,940
Accounts receivable (net)	207,230	188,190
Inventories	298,520	289,850
Investments	0	102,000
Land	295,800	0
Equipment...	438,600	358,020
Accumulated depreciation—equipment	(99,110)	(84,320)
Total assets	$1,211,760	$ 901,680
Liabilities and Stockholders' Equity		
Accounts payable (merchandise creditors)	$ 205,700	$ 194,140
Accrued expenses payable (operating expenses)	30,600	26,860
Dividends payable..	25,500	20,400
Common stock, $1 par....................................	202,000	102,000
Paid-in capital: Excess of issue price over par—common stock	354,000	204,000
Retained earnings..	393,960	354,280
Total liabilities and stockholders' equity....................	$1,211,760	$ 901,680

(Continued)

The income statement for the year ended December 31, 20Y9, is as follows:

Sales		$2,023,898
Cost of goods sold		1,245,476
Gross profit		$ 778,422
Operating expenses:		
Depreciation expense	$ 14,790	
Other operating expenses	517,299	
Total operating expenses		532,089
Operating income		$ 246,333
Other expenses:		
Loss on sale of investments		(10,200)
Income before income tax		$ 236,133
Income tax expense		94,453
Net income		$ 141,680

Additional data obtained from an examination of the accounts in the ledger for 20Y9 are as follows:

A. Equipment and land were acquired for cash.

B. There were no disposals of equipment during the year.

C. The investments were sold for $91,800 cash.

D. The common stock was issued for cash.

E. There was a $102,000 debit to Retained Earnings for cash dividends declared.

Instructions

Prepare a statement of cash flows, using the direct method of presenting cash flows from operating activities.

Analysis for Decision Making

REAL WORLD

ADM-1   Continuing Company Analysis—Amazon, Best Buy, and Walmart: Free cash flow

Amazon.com, Inc. is one of the largest Internet retailers in the world. **Best Buy, Inc.** is a leading retailer of consumer electronics and media products in the United States, while **Walmart Stores, Inc.** is the leading retailer in the United States. Amazon, Best Buy, and Walmart compete in similar markets. Best Buy and Walmart sell through both traditional retail stores and the Internet, while Amazon sells only through the Internet. Sales and cash flow information from recent annual reports for all three companies is as follows (in millions):

	Amazon	Best Buy	Walmart
Sales	$88,988	$40,339	$485,651
Cash flows from operating activities	6,842	1,935	28,564
Purchases of property, plant, and equipment	4,893	561	12,174

A. Determine the free cash flow for all three companies.

B. Compute the ratio of free cash flow to sales for all three companies. (Round percentages to one decimal place.)

C. ━━━▶ How does Amazon compare to the other two companies with respect to generating free cash flow?

REAL WORLD

ADM-2   RadioShack: Free cash flow

RadioShack Corporation is a consumer electronics retailer. Recently, the company declared bankruptcy to provide financial protection while attempting to reorganize its operations. Annual report information for the three most recent years prior to the bankruptcy are as follows (in millions):

	Year 3	Year 2	Year 1
Cash flows from operating activities	$ 36	$ (43)	$ 218
Cash used to purchase property, plant, and equipment	(42)	(68)	(82)
Sales	3,434	3,831	4,032

A. Determine the free cash flow.

B. Determine the ratio of free cash flow to sales. (Round percentages to one decimal place.)

C. ⬛▬▶ Did the free cash flow information indicate financial stress? Explain.

REAL WORLD

ADM-3   AT&T and Facebook: Free cash flow

AT&T Inc. is a leading global provider of telecommunication services. **Facebook, Inc.** is a major worldwide social media company. AT&T has a lengthy history and was founded by Alexander Graham Bell. Facebook has a short history and was founded by Mark Zuckerberg. Facebook uses telecommunication networks, like those of AT&T, to deliver social content to its users. Free cash flow and revenue information for both companies for three recent years is as follows (in millions):

AT&T
Information from the statement of cash flows:

	Year 3	Year 2	Year 1
Cash flows from operating activities	$ 31,338	$ 34,796	$ 39,176
Cash used to purchase property, plant, and equipment	(21,433)	(21,228)	(19,728)

Information from the income statement:

	Year 3	Year 2	Year 1
Revenue	$132,447	$128,752	$127,434

Facebook
Information from the statement of cash flows:

	Year 3	Year 2	Year 1
Cash flows from operating activities	$ 5,457	$ 4,222	$ 1,612
Cash used to purchase property, plant, and equipment	(1,831)	(1,362)	(1,235)

Information from the income statement:

	Year 3	Year 2	Year 1
Revenue	$12,466	$7,872	$5,089

A. Using total revenue, which company appears to be the larger at the end of Year 3?

B. Using total revenue, which company appears to be growing faster across the three years?

C. Compute the cash used to purchase property, plant, and equipment (PP&E) as a percent of the cash flows from operating activities for all three years for each company. (Round to nearest whole percent.)

D. ⬛▬▶ Using the computations in (C), which company appears to require more cash to purchase PP&E, and what impact does this have on free cash flow?

(Continued)

E. Compute the ratio of free cash flow to revenue for all three years for each company, and plot the data on a line chart with the years on the horizontal axis.

F. ▬▬▬▶ Interpret the chart.

REAL WORLD

ADM-4   Priceline: Free cash flow

Priceline Group, Inc. is a leading provider of online travel reservation services, including brand names Priceline, KAYAK, and OpenTable. Selected cash flow information from the statement of cash flows for three recent years is as follows (in millions):

	Year 3	Year 2	Year 1
Net cash provided by operating activities	$ 2,914	$ 2,301	$ 1,786
Net cash used in investing activities	(2,349)	(2,162)	(1,563)
Net cash provided by (used in) financing activities	1,429	(404)	669
Additions to property, plant, and equipment	(132)	(84)	(55)
Repurchase common stock	(750)	(884)	(257)
Acquisitions and investments	(2,146)	(1,997)	(1,587)

A. Determine the net change in cash for each year.

B. Determine the free cash flow for each year.

C. ▬▬▬▶ How is the free cash flow being used based on the data provided?

D. ▬▬▬▶ Which is better for measuring the cash flow available for investment, dividends, debt repayments, and stock repurchases: the change in cash for the period or the free cash flow? Explain.

Take It Further

ETHICS

TIF 13-1   Ethics in Action

Head Donuts Inc. is a retailer of designer headphones, earphones, and hands-free audio devices. Polly Ester, the company president, is reviewing the company's financial statements after the close of the fiscal year and is troubled that earnings decreased by 10%. She shares her concerns with the company's chief accountant, Lucas Simmons, who points out that the drop in earnings was balanced by a 20% increase in cash flows, from operating activities. Polly is encouraged by the increase in cash flows from operating activities, but is worried that investors might miss this information because it is "buried" in the statement of cash flows. To make it easier for investors to find this information, she instructs Lucas to include an operating cash flow per share number on the face of the income statement, directly below earnings per share. While Lucas is concerned about using such an unconventional financial reporting tactic, he agrees to include the information on the income statement.

▬▬▬▶ Is Lucas behaving in an ethical and professional manner? Explain your answer.

REAL WORLD

TIF 13-2   Team Activity

In teams, select a public company that interests you. Obtain the company's most recent annual report on Form 10-K. The Form 10-K is a company's annually required filing with the Securities and Exchange Commission (SEC). It includes the company's financial statements and accompanying notes. The Form 10-K can be obtained either (A) from the investor relations section of the company's Web site or (B) by using the company search feature of the SEC's EDGAR database service found at www.sec.gov/edgar/searchedgar/companysearch.html.

1. Based on the information in the company's most recent annual report, answer the following questions:

    A. What is the net cash flows from operating activities reported by the company at the end of the most recent year?

    B. What is the net cash flows from investing activities reported by the company at the end of the most recent year?

    C. What is the net cash flows from financing activities reported by the company at the end of the most recent year?

    D. What was the net increase (or decrease) in cash during the year?

2. ➤ Evaluate the company's cash inflows and outflows.

TIF 13-3   Communication

Tidewater Inc., a retailer, provided the following financial information for its most recent fiscal year:

Net income	$ 945,000
Return on invested capital	8%
Cash flows from operating activities	(1,428,000)
Cash flows from investing activities	600,000
Cash flows from financing activities	900,000

The company's Cash Flows from Operating Activities Section is as follows:

Net income	$ 945,000
Depreciation	210,000
Increase in accounts receivable	(1,134,000)
Increase in inventory	(1,260,000)
Decrease in accounts payable	(189,000)
Net cash flow from operating activities	$(1,428,000)

An examination of the financial statements revealed the following additional information:

■ Revenues increased during the year as a result of an aggressive marketing campaign aimed at increasing the number of new "Tidewater Card" credit card customers. This is the company's branded credit card, which can only be used at Tidewater stores. The credit card balances are accounts receivable on Tidewater's balance sheet.

■ Some suppliers have made their merchandise available at a deep discount. As a result, the company purchased large quantities of these goods in an attempt to improve the company's profitability.

■ In recent years, the company has struggled to pay its accounts payable on time. The company has improved on this during the past year and is nearly caught up on overdue payables balances.

■ The company reported net losses in each of the two prior years.

➤ Write a brief memo to your instructor evaluating the financial condition of Tidewater Inc.

Concepts and Principles

Chapter 1 *Introduction to Managerial Accounting*

Developing Information

COST SYSTEMS	COST BEHAVIOR

Chapter 2 *Job Order Costing*
Chapter 3 *Process Cost Systems*
Chapter 4 *Activity-Based Costing*

Chapter 5 *Cost-Volume-Profit Analysis*

Decision Making

EVALUATING PERFORMANCE	COMPARING ALTERNATIVES

Chapter 6 *Variable Costing for Management Analysis*
Chapter 7 *Budgeting*
Chapter 8 *Evaluating Variances from Standard Costs*
Chapter 9 *Evaluating Decentralized Operations*

Chapter 10 *Differential Analysis and Product Pricing*
Chapter 11 *Capital Investment Analysis*
Chapter 12 *Lean Manufacturing*

Chapter 13
Statement of Cash Flows

Chapter 14
Financial Statement Analysis

Financial Accounting

Managerial Accounting

Nike, Inc.

"**J**ust do it." These three words identify one of the most recognizable brands in the world, **Nike**. While this phrase inspires athletes to "compete and achieve their potential," it also defines the company.

Nike began in 1964 as a partnership between University of Oregon track coach Bill Bowerman and one of his former student-athletes, Phil Knight. The two began by selling shoes imported from Japan out of the back of Knight's car to athletes at track-and-field events. As sales grew, the company opened retail outlets, calling itself **Blue Ribbon Sports**. The company also began to develop its own shoes. In 1971, the company commissioned a graphic design student at Portland State University to develop the swoosh logo for a fee of $35. In 1978, the company changed its name to Nike, and in 1980, it sold its first shares of stock to the public.

Nike would have been a great company to invest in at the time. If you had invested in Nike's common stock back in 1990,

you would have paid $5 per share. As of November 2015, Nike's stock was worth over $130 per share. Unfortunately, you can't invest using hindsight.

How can you select companies in which to invest? Like any significant purchase, you should do some research to guide your investment decision. If you were buying a car, for example, you might go to **Edmunds.com** to obtain reviews, ratings, prices, specifications, options, and fuel economies to evaluate different vehicles. In selecting companies in which to invest, you can use financial analysis to gain insight into a company's past performance and future prospects. This chapter describes and illustrates common financial data that can be analyzed to assist you in making investment decisions such as whether or not to invest in Nike's stock.

Source: www.nikebiz.com/.

Financial Statement Analysis

Analyzing and Interpreting Financial Statements	Analytical Methods	Analyzing			Understanding Corpoate Annual Reports
		Liquidity	**Solvency**	**Profitability**	
■ Value of Financial Statement Information (Obj. 1)	■ Horizontal Analysis (Obj. 2)	■ Current Position (Obj. 3)	■ Fixed Assets to Long-Term Liabilities (Obj. 4)	■ Asset Turnover (Obj. 5)	■ Management Discussion (Obj. 6)
■ Techniques (Obj. 1)	■ Vertical Analysis (Obj. 2)	■ Accounts Receivable (Obj. 3)	■ Liabilities to Stockholders' Equity (Obj. 4)	■ Rates of Return (Obj. 5)	■ Internal Control (Obj. 6)
	■ Common-Sized Statements (Obj. 2)	■ Inventory (Obj. 3)	■ Times Interest Earned (Obj. 4)	■ Earnings per Share (Obj. 5)	■ Audit Report (Obj. 6)
				■ Price to Earnings (Obj. 5)	
				■ Dividend Measures (Obj. 5)	

Learning Objectives

Obj. 1 Describe the techniques and tools used to analyze financial statement information.

Obj. 2 Describe and illustrate basic financial statement analytical methods.

Obj. 3 Describe and illustrate how to use financial statement analysis to assess liquidity.

Obj. 4 Describe and illustrate how to use financial statement analysis to assess solvency.

Obj. 5 Describe and illustrate how to use financial statement analysis to assess profitability.

Obj. 6 Describe the contents of corporate annual reports.

Analysis for Decision Making

Describe and illustrate the use of financial statement analysis in evaluating potential stock price appreciation.

Objective 1

Describe the techniques and tools used to analyze financial statement information.

Analyzing and Interpreting Financial Statements

The objective of accounting is to provide relevant and timely information to support the decision-making needs of financial statement users. Bankers, creditors, and investors all rely on financial statements to provide insight into a company's financial condition and performance. This chapter discusses the value of financial statement information, techniques used to evaluate financial statements, and the impact of that information on decision making.

The Value of Financial Statement Information

General-purpose financial statements are distributed to a wide range of potential users, providing each group with valuable information about a company's economic performance and financial condition. Users typically evaluate this information along three dimensions: liquidity, solvency, and profitability.

Liquidity Short-term creditors such as banks and financial institutions are primarily concerned with whether a company will be able to repay short-term borrowings such as loans and notes. As such, they are most interested in evaluating a company's ability to convert assets into cash, which is called **liquidity**.

Solvency Long-term creditors, such as bondholders, loan money for long periods of time. Thus, they are interested in evaluating a company's ability to make its periodic interest payments and repay the face amount of debt at maturity, which is called **solvency**.

Profitability Investors, such as stockholders, are the owners of the company. They benefit from increases in the price of a company's shares and are interested in evaluating the potential for the price of the company's stock to increase. The price of a company's stock depends on a variety of factors, including the company's current and potential future earnings. As such, investors focus on evaluating a company's ability to generate earnings, which is called **profitability**.

Techniques for Analyzing Financial Statements

Financial statement users rely on the following techniques to analyze and interpret a company's financial performance and condition:

- **Analytical methods** examine changes in the amount and percentage of financial statement items within and across periods.
- **Ratios** express a financial statement item or set of financial statement items as a percentage of another financial statement item, in order to measure an important economic relationship as a single number.

Both analytical methods and ratios can be used to compare a company's financial performance over time or to another company.

- *Comparisons Over Time:* The comparison of a financial statement item or ratio with the same item or ratio from a prior period often helps the user identify trends in a company's economic performance, financial condition, liquidity, solvency, and profitability.
- *Comparisons Between Companies:* The comparison of a financial statement item or ratio to another company in the same industry can provide insight into a company's economic performance and financial condition relative to its competitors.

Analytical Methods

Objective 2
Describe and illustrate basic financial statement analytical methods.

Users analyze a company's financial statements using a variety of analytical methods. Three such methods are:

- Horizontal analysis
- Vertical analysis
- Common-sized statements

Horizontal Analysis

The analysis of increases and decreases in the amount and percentage of comparative financial statement items is called **horizontal analysis**. Each item on the most recent statement is compared with the same item on one or more earlier statements in terms of the following:

- *Amount* of increase or decrease
- *Percent* of increase or decrease

When comparing statements, the earlier statement is normally used as the base year for computing increases and decreases.

Exhibit 1 illustrates horizontal analysis for the December 31, 20Y6 and 20Y5 balance sheets of **Lincoln Company**. In Exhibit 1, the December 31, 20Y5, balance sheet (the earliest year presented) is used as the base year.

Exhibit 1 indicates that total assets decreased by $91,000 (7.4%), liabilities decreased by $133,000 (30.0%), and stockholders' equity increased by $42,000 (5.3%). Since the long-term investments account decreased by $82,500, it appears that most of the decrease in long-term liabilities of $100,000 was achieved through the sale of long-term investments.

Exhibit 1
Comparative
Balance Sheet—
Horizontal
Analysis

Lincoln Company
Comparative Balance Sheet
December 31, 20Y6 and 20Y5

	Dec. 31, 20Y6	Dec. 31, 20Y5	Increase (Decrease) Amount	Percent
Assets				
Current assets	$ 550,000	$ 533,000	$ 17,000	3.2%
Long-term investments	95,000	177,500	(82,500)	(46.5%)
Property, plant, and equipment (net)	444,500	470,000	(25,500)	(5.4%)
Intangible assets	50,000	50,000	—	—
Total assets	$1,139,500	$1,230,500	$ (91,000)	(7.4%)
Liabilities				
Current liabilities	$ 210,000	$ 243,000	$ (33,000)	(13.6%)
Long-term liabilities	100,000	200,000	(100,000)	(50.0%)
Total liabilities	$ 310,000	$ 443,000	$(133,000)	(30.0%)
Stockholders' Equity				
Preferred 6% stock, $100 par	$ 150,000	$ 150,000	—	—
Common stock, $10 par	500,000	500,000	—	—
Retained earnings	179,500	137,500	$ 42,000	30.5%
Total stockholders' equity	$ 829,500	$ 787,500	$ 42,000	5.3%
Total liabilities and stockholders' equity	$1,139,500	$1,230,500	$ (91,000)	(7.4%)

The balance sheets in Exhibit 1 may be expanded or supported by a separate schedule that includes the individual asset and liability accounts. For example, Exhibit 2 is a supporting schedule of Lincoln Company's current asset accounts.

Exhibit 2
Comparative
Schedule of
Current Assets—
Horizontal Analysis

Lincoln Company
Comparative Schedule of Current Assets
December 31, 20Y6 and 20Y5

	Dec. 31, 20Y6	Dec. 31, 20Y5	Increase (Decrease) Amount	Percent
Cash	$ 90,500	$ 64,700	$ 25,800	39.9%
Temporary investments	75,000	60,000	15,000	25.0%
Accounts receivable, net	115,000	120,000	(5,000)	(4.2%)
Inventories	264,000	283,000	(19,000)	(6.7%)
Prepaid expenses	5,500	5,300	200	3.8%
Total current assets	$550,000	$533,000	$ 17,000	3.2%

Exhibit 2 indicates that while cash and temporary investments increased, accounts receivable and inventories decreased. The decrease in accounts receivable could be caused by improved collection policies, which would increase cash. The decrease in inventories could be caused by increased sales.

Exhibit 3 illustrates horizontal analysis for the 20Y6 and 20Y5 income statements of Lincoln Company. Exhibit 3 indicates an increase in sales of $298,000, or 24.8%. However, the percentage increase in sales of 24.8% was accompanied by an even greater percentage increase in the cost of goods sold of 27.2%. Thus, gross profit increased by only 19.7% rather than by the 24.8% increase in sales.

Exhibit 3 also indicates that selling expenses increased by 29.9%. Thus, the 24.8% increases in sales could have been caused by an advertising campaign, which increased selling expenses. Administrative expenses increased by only 6.8%, total operating expenses increased by 20.7%, and income from operations increased by 18.0%. Interest expense decreased by 50.0%. This decrease was probably caused by the 50.0% decrease in long-term liabilities (Exhibit 1). Overall, net income increased by 19.0%, a favorable result.

Lincoln Company Comparative Income Statement For the Years Ended December 31, 20Y6 and 20Y5					Exhibit 3
			Increase (Decrease)		Comparative Income Statement— Horizontal Analysis
	20Y6	**20Y5**	**Amount**	**Percent**	
Sales	$1,498,000	$1,200,000	$298,000	24.8%	
Cost of goods sold..	1,043,000	820,000	223,000	27.2%	
Gross profit...	$ 455,000	$ 380,000	$ 75,000	19.7%	
Selling expenses	$ 191,000	$ 147,000	$ 44,000	29.9%	
Administrative expenses...................................	104,000	97,400	6,600	6.8%	
Total operating expenses	$ 295,000	$ 244,400	$ 50,600	20.7%	
Income from operations	$ 160,000	$ 135,600	$ 24,400	18.0%	
Other income...	8,500	11,000	(2,500)	(22.7%)	
	$ 168,500	$ 146,600	$ 21,900	14.9%	
Other expense (interest)	6,000	12,000	(6,000)	(50.0%)	
Income before income tax	$ 162,500	$ 134,600	$ 27,900	20.7%	
Income tax expense	71,500	58,100	13,400	23.1%	
Net income	$ 91,000	$ 76,500	$ 14,500	19.0%	

Exhibit 4 illustrates horizontal analysis for the 20Y6 and 20Y5 retained earnings statements of **Lincoln Company**. Exhibit 4 indicates that retained earnings increased by 30.5% for the year. The increase is due to net income of $91,000 for the year, less dividends of $49,000.

Lincoln Company Comparative Retained Earnings Statement For the Years Ended December 31, 20Y6 and 20Y5					Exhibit 4
			Increase (Decrease)		Comparative Retained Earnings Statement— Horizontal Analysis
	20Y6	**20Y5**	**Amount**	**Percent**	
Retained earnings, January 1...........................	$137,500	$100,000	$37,500	37.5%	
Net income	91,000	76,500	14,500	19.0%	
Total	$228,500	$176,500	$52,000	29.5%	
Dividends:					
On preferred stock	$ 9,000	$ 9,000	—	—	
On common stock.................................	40,000	30,000	$10,000	33.3%	
Total dividends	$ 49,000	$ 39,000	$10,000	25.6%	
Retained earnings, December 31	$179,500	$137,500	$42,000	30.5%	

For a recent year, **Nike**'s net income increased by 21.5%.

Link to Nike

Vertical Analysis

The percentage analysis of the relationship of each component in a financial statement to a total within the statement is called **vertical analysis**. Although vertical analysis is applied to a single statement, it may be applied on the same statement over time. This enhances the analysis by showing how the percentages of each item have changed over time.

In vertical analysis of the balance sheet, the percentages are computed as follows:

- Each asset item is stated as a percent of the total assets.
- Each liability and stockholders' equity item is stated as a percent of the total liabilities and stockholders' equity.

Exhibit 5 illustrates the vertical analysis of the December 31, 20Y6 and 20Y5 balance sheets of **Lincoln Company**. Exhibit 5 indicates that current assets have increased from 43.3% to 48.3% of total assets. Long-term investments decreased from 14.4% to 8.3% of total assets. Stockholders' equity increased from 64.0% to 72.8%, with a comparable decrease in liabilities.

Exhibit 5

Comparative Balance Sheet— Vertical Analysis

Lincoln Company
Comparative Balance Sheet
December 31, 20Y6 and 20Y5

	Dec. 31, 20Y6		Dec. 31, 20Y5	
	Amount	Percent	Amount	Percent
Assets				
Current assets......................................	$ 550,000	48.3%	$ 533,000	43.3%
Long-term investments...............................	95,000	8.3	177,500	14.4
Property, plant, and equipment (net)	444,500	39.0	470,000	38.2
Intangible assets	50,000	4.4	50,000	4.1
Total assets	$1,139,500	100.0%	$1,230,500	100.0%
Liabilities				
Current liabilities....................................	$ 210,000	18.4%	$ 243,000	19.7%
Long-term liabilities.................................	100,000	8.8	200,000	16.3
Total liabilities	$ 310,000	27.2%	$ 443,000	36.0%
Stockholders' Equity				
Preferred 6% stock, $100 par	$ 150,000	13.2%	$ 150,000	12.2%
Common stock, $10 par..............................	500,000	43.9	500,000	40.6
Retained earnings....................................	179,500	15.7	137,500	11.2
Total stockholders' equity............................	$ 829,500	72.8%	$ 787,500	64.0%
Total liabilities and stockholders' equity...............	$1,139,500	100.0%	$1,230,500	100.0%

Link to Nike   For a recent year, **Nike**'s current assets were 73.6% of total assets.

In a vertical analysis of the income statement, each item is stated as a percent of sales. Exhibit 6 illustrates the vertical analysis of the 20Y6 and 20Y5 income statements of **Lincoln Company**.

Exhibit 6

Comparative Income Statement—Vertical Analysis

Lincoln Company
Comparative Income Statement
For the Years Ended December 31, 20Y6 and 20Y5

	20Y6		20Y5	
	Amount	Percent	Amount	Percent
Sales	$1,498,000	100.0%	$1,200,000	100.0%
Cost of goods sold..................................	1,043,000	69.6	820,000	68.3
Gross profit	$ 455,000	30.4%	$ 380,000	31.7%
Selling expenses	$ 191,000	12.8%	$ 147,000	12.3%
Administrative expenses..............................	104,000	6.9	97,400	8.1
Total operating expenses	$ 295,000	19.7%	$ 244,400	20.4%
Income from operations	$ 160,000	10.7%	$ 135,600	11.3%
Other income.......................................	8,500	0.6	11,000	0.9
	$ 168,500	11.3%	$ 146,600	12.2%
Other expense (interest)	6,000	0.4	12,000	1.0
Income before income tax	$ 162,500	10.9%	$ 134,600	11.2%
Income tax expense	71,500	4.8	58,100	4.8
Net income	$ 91,000	6.1%	$ 76,500	6.4%

Exhibit 6 indicates a decrease in the gross profit rate from 31.7% in 20Y5 to 30.4% in 20Y6. Although this is only a 1.3 percentage point (31.7% – 30.4%) decrease, in dollars of potential gross profit, it represents a decrease of $19,474 (1.3% × $1,498,000) based on 20Y6 sales. Thus, a small percentage decrease can have a large dollar effect.

Common-Sized Statements

In a **common-sized statement**, all items are expressed as percentages, with no dollar amounts shown. Common-sized statements are often useful for comparing one company with another or for comparing a company with industry averages.

Exhibit 7 illustrates common-sized income statements for **Lincoln Company** and Madison Corporation. Exhibit 7 indicates that Lincoln has a slightly higher gross profit percentage (30.4%) than Madison (30.0%). However, Lincoln has a higher percentage of selling expenses (12.8%) and administrative expenses (6.9%) than does Madison (11.5% and 4.1%). As a result, the income from operations as a percentage of sales of Lincoln (10.7%) is less than that of Madison (14.4%).

	Lincoln Company	Madison Corporation
Sales	100.0%	100.0%
Cost of goods sold	69.6	70.0
Gross profit	30.4%	30.0%
Selling expenses	12.8%	11.5%
Administrative expenses	6.9	4.1
Total operating expenses	19.7%	15.6%
Income from operations	10.7%	14.4%
Other income	0.6	0.6
	11.3%	15.0%
Other expense (interest)	0.4	0.5
Income before income tax	10.9%	14.5%
Income tax expense	4.8	5.5
Net income	6.1%	9.0%

Exhibit 7
Common-Sized Income Statements

For a recent year, **Nike**'s net income was 9.7% of sales.

Link to Nike

The unfavorable difference of 3.7 (14.4% – 10.7%) percentage points in income from operations would concern the managers and other stakeholders of Lincoln. The underlying causes of the difference should be investigated and possibly corrected. For example, Lincoln may decide to outsource some of its administrative duties so that its administrative expenses are more comparative to that of Madison.

Check Up Corner 14-1 | Horizontal and Vertical Analyses

Select income statement data for Bukasy Company for two recent years ended December 31 are as follows:

	20Y2	20Y1
Sales	$2,200,000	$2,000,000
Cost of goods sold	1,337,500	1,250,000
Gross profit	$ 862,500	$ 750,000
Selling, general, and administrative expenses	440,000	400,000
Income from operations	$ 422,500	$ 350,000

Prepare horizontal and vertical analyses of Bukasy's income statement. (Round percentages to one decimal place.)

Solution:

Horizontal Analysis

	20Y2	20Y1	Increase (Decrease) Amount	Percent
Sales	$2,200,000	$2,000,000	$200,000	10.0%
Cost of goods sold	1,337,500	1,250,000	87,500	7.0%
Gross profit	$ 862,500	$ 750,000	$112,500	15.0%
Selling, general, and administrative expenses	440,000	400,000	40,000	10.0%
Income from operations	$ 422,500	$ 350,000	$ 72,500	20.7%

Horizontal analysis shows increases and decreases in the amount and percentage of comparative financial statement items. The amount and percentage of each item on the most recent statement is compared with the same item on one or more earlier statements.

Vertical Analysis

	20Y2 Amount	Percent	20Y1 Amount	Percent
Sales	$2,200,000	100.0%	$2,000,000	100.0%
Cost of goods sold	1,337,500	60.8	1,250,000	62.5
Gross profit	$ 862,500	39.2%	$ 750,000	37.5%
Selling, general, and administrative expenses	440,000	20.0	400,000	20.0
Income from operations	$ 422,500	19.2%	$ 350,000	17.5%

Vertical analysis compares each component in a financial statement to a total within the statement. It can be applied to a single statement or to the same statement over time.

Check Up Corner

Objective 3
Describe and illustrate how to use financial statement analysis to assess liquidity.

Analyzing Liquidity

Liquidity analysis evaluates the ability of a company to convert current assets into cash. Banks and other short-term creditors rely heavily on liquidity analysis, because they are interested in evaluating a company's ability to repay loans and short-term notes. Exhibit 8 shows three categories of measures used to evaluate a company's liquidity. These ratios and measures focus upon a company's current position (current assets and liabilities), accounts receivable, and inventory.

Exhibit 8
Liquidity Ratios and Measures

Current Position Analysis	Accounts Receivable Analysis	Inventory Analysis
Working Capital	Accounts Receivable Turnover	Inventory Turnover
Current Ratio	Number of Days' Sales in Receivables	Number of Days' Sales in Inventory
Quick Ratio		

Current Position Analysis

Current position analysis evaluates a company's ability to pay its current liabilities. This information helps short-term creditors determine how quickly they will be repaid. This analysis includes:

- Working capital
- Current ratio
- Quick ratio

Working Capital A company's **working capital** is computed as follows:

$$\text{Working Capital} = \text{Current Assets} - \text{Current Liabilities}$$

To illustrate, the working capital for **Lincoln Company** for 20Y6 and 20Y5 is computed as follows:

	20Y6	20Y5
Current assets	$ 550,000	$ 533,000
Current liabilities	(210,000)	(243,000)
Working capital	$ 340,000	$ 290,000

The working capital is used to evaluate a company's ability to pay current liabilities. A company's working capital is often monitored monthly, quarterly, or yearly by creditors and other debtors. However, it is difficult to use working capital to compare companies of different sizes. For example, working capital of $250,000 may be adequate for a local sporting goods store, but it would be inadequate for **Nike**.

Current Ratio The **current ratio**, sometimes called the *working capital ratio*, is computed as follows:

$$\text{Current Ratio} = \frac{\text{Current Assets}}{\text{Current Liabilities}}$$

To illustrate, the current ratio for **Lincoln Company** is computed as follows:

	20Y6	20Y5
Current assets	$550,000	$533,000
Current liabilities	$210,000	$243,000
Current ratio	2.6 ($550,000 ÷ $210,000)	2.2 ($533,000 ÷ $243,000)

The current ratio is a more reliable indicator of a company's ability to pay its current liabilities than is working capital, and it is much easier to compare across companies. To illustrate, assume that as of December 31, 20Y6, the working capital of a competitor is much greater than Lincoln's $340,000, but its current ratio is only 1.3. Considering these facts alone, Lincoln is in a more favorable position to obtain short-term credit than the competitor because it has a higher current ratio.

For a recent five-year period, **Nike**'s average current ratio was 2.9.

Link to Nike

Quick Ratio One limitation of working capital and the current ratio is that they do not consider the types of current assets a company has and how easily they can be turned into cash. Because of this, two companies may have the same working capital and current ratios but differ significantly in their ability to pay their current liabilities.

To illustrate, the current assets and liabilities for **Lincoln Company** and Jefferson Company as of December 31, 20Y6, are as follows:

	Lincoln Company	**Jefferson Company**
Current assets:		
Cash	$ 90,500	$ 45,500
Temporary investments	75,000	25,000
Accounts receivable (net)	115,000	90,000
Inventories	264,000	380,000
Prepaid expenses	5,500	9,500
Total current assets	$ 550,000	$ 550,000
Current assets	$ 550,000	$ 550,000
Current liabilities	(210,000)	(210,000)
Working capital	$ 340,000	$ 340,000
Current ratio (Current assets ÷ Current liabilities)	2.6	2.6

Lincoln and Jefferson both have a working capital of $340,000 and current ratios of 2.6. Jefferson, however, has more of its current assets in inventories. These inventories must be sold and the receivables collected before all the current liabilities can be paid. This takes time. In addition, if the market for its product declines, Jefferson may have difficulty selling its inventory. This, in turn, could impair its ability to pay its current liabilities.

In contrast, Lincoln's current assets contain more cash, temporary investments, and accounts receivable, which can easily be converted to cash. Thus, Lincoln is in a stronger current position than Jefferson to pay its current liabilities.

A ratio that captures this difference and measures the "instant" debt-paying ability of a company is the **quick ratio**, sometimes called the *acid-test ratio*. The quick ratio is computed as follows:

$$\text{Quick Ratio} = \frac{\text{Quick Assets}}{\text{Current Liabilities}}$$

Quick assets are cash and other current assets that can be easily converted to cash. Quick assets normally include cash, temporary investments, and receivables but exclude inventories and prepaid assets.

To illustrate, the quick ratios for **Lincoln Company** and Jefferson Company are computed as follows:

	Lincoln Company	**Jefferson Company**
Quick assets:		
Cash	$ 90,500	$ 45,500
Temporary investments	75,000	25,000
Accounts receivable (net)	115,000	90,000
Total quick assets	$280,500	$160,500
Current liabilities	$210,000	$210,000
Quick ratio	1.3 ($280,500 ÷ $210,000)	0.8 ($160,500 ÷ $210,000)

Accounts Receivable Analysis

A company's ability to collect its accounts receivable is called **accounts receivable analysis**. It includes the computation and analysis of the following:

- Accounts receivable turnover
- Number of days' sales in receivables

Collecting accounts receivable as quickly as possible improves a company's liquidity. In addition, the cash collected from receivables may be used to improve or expand operations. Quick collection of receivables also reduces the risk of uncollectible accounts.

Accounts Receivable Turnover The **accounts receivable turnover** is computed as follows:

$$\text{Accounts Receivable Turnover} = \frac{\text{Sales}^{[1]}}{\text{Average Accounts Receivable}}$$

[1] If known, *credit* sales should be used in the numerator. Because credit sales are not normally known by external users, we use sales in the numerator.

To illustrate, the accounts receivable turnover for **Lincoln Company** for 20Y6 and 20Y5 is computed as follows. Lincoln's accounts receivable balance at the beginning of 20Y5 is $140,000.

	20Y6	**20Y5**
Sales	$1,498,000	$1,200,000
Accounts receivable (net):		
Beginning of year	$ 120,000	$ 140,000
End of year	115,000	120,000
Total	$ 235,000	$ 260,000
Average accounts receivable	$117,500 ($235,000 ÷ 2)	$130,000 ($260,000 ÷ 2)
Accounts receivable turnover	12.7 ($1,498,000 ÷ $117,500)	9.2 ($1,200,000 ÷ $130,000)

The increase in Lincoln's accounts receivable turnover from 9.2 to 12.7 indicates that the collection of receivables has improved during 20Y6. This may be due to a change in how credit is granted, collection practices, or both.

For Lincoln, the average accounts receivable was computed using the accounts receivable balance at the beginning and the end of the year. When sales are seasonal and, thus, vary throughout the year, monthly balances of receivables are often used. Also, if sales on account include notes receivable as well as accounts receivable, notes and accounts receivable are normally combined for analysis.

Number of Days' Sales in Receivables The **number of days' sales in receivables** is computed as follows:

$$\text{Number of Days' Sales in Receivables} = \frac{\text{Average Accounts Receivable}}{\text{Average Daily Sales}}$$

where

$$\text{Average Daily Sales} = \frac{\text{Sales}}{365 \text{ days}}$$

To illustrate, the number of days' sales in receivables for **Lincoln Company** is computed as follows:

	20Y6	**20Y5**
Average accounts receivable	$117,500 ($235,000 ÷ 2)	$130,000 ($260,000 ÷ 2)
Average daily sales	$4,104 ($1,498,000 ÷ 365)	$3,288 ($1,200,000 ÷ 365)
Number of days' sales in receivables	28.6 ($117,500 ÷ $4,104)	39.5 ($130,000 ÷ $3,288)

The number of days' sales in receivables is an estimate of the time (in days) that the accounts receivable have been outstanding. The number of days' sales in receivables is often compared with a company's credit terms to evaluate the efficiency of the collection of receivables.

To illustrate, if Lincoln's credit terms are 2/10, n/30, then Lincoln was very *inefficient* in collecting receivables in 20Y5. In other words, receivables should have been collected in 30 days or less but were being collected in 39.5 days. Although collections improved during 20Y6 to 28.6 days, there is probably still room for improvement. On the other hand, if Lincoln's credit terms are n/45, then there is probably little room for improving collections.

Inventory Analysis

A company's ability to manage its inventory effectively is evaluated using **inventory analysis**. It includes the computation and analysis of the following:

- Inventory turnover
- Number of days' sales in inventory

Excess inventory decreases liquidity by tying up funds (cash) in inventory. In addition, excess inventory increases insurance expense, property taxes, storage costs, and other related expenses. These expenses further reduce funds that could be used elsewhere to improve or expand operations.

Why It Matters

Flying Off the Shelves

Two companies with a fast inventory turnover relative to their industries are **Apple Inc.** and **Costco Wholesale Corporation**:

	Inventory Turnover	Industry	Industry Average
Apple	53.2	Technology	15.6
Costco	11.5	Retail	7.7

Apple turns over its inventory approximately every week. There are two primary reasons for this performance. First, Apple does not manufacture its products, but contracts their manufacture by others. Thus, Apple has no inventory related to manufacturing. Second, the Apple Store inventory moves very quickly due to the popularity of its products. Costco is ranked number one in the retail industry for inventory turns. This is because Costco employs a club warehouse model that stocks a minimum variety of highly popular products. Products that don't sell quickly are removed from its offerings.

Excess inventory also increases the risk of losses because of price declines or obsolescence of the inventory. On the other hand, a company should keep enough inventory in stock so that it doesn't lose sales because of lack of inventory.

Inventory Turnover The **inventory turnover** is computed as follows:

$$\text{Inventory Turnover} = \frac{\text{Cost of Goods Sold}}{\text{Average Inventory}}$$

To illustrate, the inventory turnover for **Lincoln Company** for 20Y6 and 20Y5 is computed as follows. Lincoln's inventory balance at the beginning of 20Y5 is $311,000.

	20Y6	20Y5
Cost of goods sold	$1,043,000	$820,000
Inventories:		
Beginning of year	$ 283,000	$311,000
End of year	264,000	283,000
Total	$ 547,000	$594,000
Average inventory	$273,500 ($547,000 ÷ 2)	$297,000 ($594,000 ÷ 2)
Inventory turnover	3.8 ($1,043,000 ÷ $273,500)	2.8 ($820,000 ÷ $297,000)

The increase in Lincoln's inventory turnover from 2.8 to 3.8 indicates that the management of inventory has improved in 20Y6. The inventory turnover improved because of an increase in the cost of goods sold, which indicates more sales and a decrease in the average inventories.

What is considered a good inventory turnover varies by type of inventory, company, and industry. For example, grocery stores have a higher inventory turnover than jewelers or furniture stores. Likewise, within a grocery store, perishable foods have a higher turnover than the soaps and cleansers.

Link to Nike   For a recent five-year period, **Nike**'s average inventory turnover was 4.3.

Number of Days' Sales in Inventory The **number of days' sales in inventory** is computed as follows:

$$\text{Number of Days' Sales in Inventory} = \frac{\text{Average Inventory}}{\text{Average Daily Cost of Goods Sold}}$$

where

$$\text{Average Daily Cost of Goods Sold} = \frac{\text{Cost of Goods Sold}}{365 \text{ days}}$$

To illustrate, the number of days' sales in inventory for **Lincoln Company** is computed as follows:

	20Y6	20Y5
Average inventory	$273,500 ($547,000 ÷ 2)	$297,000 ($594,000 ÷ 2)
Average daily cost of goods sold	$2,858 ($1,043,000 ÷ 365)	$2,247 ($820,000 ÷ 365)
Number of days' sales in inventory	95.7 ($273,500 ÷ $2,858)	132.2 ($297,000 ÷ $2,247)

The number of days' sales in inventory is a rough measure of the length of time it takes to purchase, sell, and replace the inventory. Lincoln's number of days' sales in inventory improved from 132.2 days to 95.7 days during 20Y6. This is a major improvement in managing inventory.

Check Up Corner 14-2 Liquidity Analysis

Select financial statement data for OM&M Inc. for two recent years follows:

	20Y2	20Y1
Select income statement information:		
Sales	$1,800,000	$1,740,000
Cost of goods sold	1,200,000	1,120,000
Select balance sheet information:		
Cash	$ 300,000	$ 290,000
Temporary investments	100,000	100,000
Accounts receivable (net)	200,000	160,000
Inventory	160,000	140,000
Accounts payable	400,000	350,000

Based on these data, calculate the following liquidity measures for 20Y2:

A. Current ratio
B. Quick ratio
C. Accounts receivable turnover
D. Inventory turnover

Solution:

A.

$$\text{Current Ratio} = \frac{\text{Current Assets}}{\text{Current Liabilities}} = \frac{\$300,000 + \$100,000 + \$200,000 + \$160,000}{\$400,000} = \frac{\$760,000}{\$400,000} = 1.9$$

The current ratio is used to evaluate a company's ability to pay current liabilities.

B.

$$\text{Quick Ratio} = \frac{\text{Quick Assets}}{\text{Current Liabilities}} = \frac{\$300,000 + \$100,000 + \$200,000}{\$400,000} = \frac{\$600,000}{\$400,000} = 1.5$$

The quick ratio measures the "instant" debt-paying ability of a company. Quick assets are cash and other current assets that can be easily converted to cash.

C.

$$\text{Accounts Receivable Turnover} = \frac{\text{Sales}}{\text{Average Accounts Receivable}} = \frac{\$1,800,000}{(\$200,000 + \$160,000) \div 2} = \frac{\$1,800,000}{\$180,000} = 10.0$$

Accounts receivable turnover measures the speed with which a company collects its accounts receivable.

D.

$$\text{Inventory Turnover} = \frac{\text{Cost of Goods Sold}}{\text{Average Inventory}} = \frac{\$1,200,000}{(\$160,000 + \$140,000) \div 2} = \frac{\$1,200,000}{\$150,000} = 8.0$$

Inventory turnover measures the number of times each year that a company sells its inventory.

Check Up Corner

Objective 4

Describe and illustrate how to use financial statement analysis to assess solvency.

Analyzing Solvency

Solvency analysis evaluates a company's ability to pay its long-term debts. Bondholders and other long-term creditors use solvency analysis to evaluate a company's ability to (i) repay the face amount of debt at maturity and (ii) make periodic interest payments. Three common solvency ratios are shown in Exhibit 9.

Exhibit 9

Solvency Ratios

Solvency Ratios		
Ratio of Fixed Assets to Long-Term Liabilities	Ratio of Liabilities to Stockholders' Equity	Times Interest Earned

Ratio of Fixed Assets to Long-Term Liabilities

Fixed assets are often pledged as security for long-term notes and bonds. The **ratio of fixed assets to long-term liabilities** provides a measure of how much fixed assets a company has to support its long-term debt. This measures a company's ability to repay the face amount of debt at maturity and is computed as follows:

$$\text{Ratio of Fixed Assets to Long-Term Liabilities} = \frac{\text{Fixed Assets (net)}}{\text{Long-Term Liabilities}}$$

To illustrate, the ratio of fixed assets to long-term liabilities for **Lincoln Company** is computed as follows:

	20Y6	20Y5
Fixed assets (net)	$444,500	$470,000
Long-term liabilities	$100,000	$200,000
Ratio of fixed assets to long-term liabilities	4.4 ($444,500 ÷ $100,000)	2.4 ($470,000 ÷ $200,000)

During 20Y6, Lincoln's ratio of fixed assets to long-term liabilities increased from 2.4 to 4.4. This increase was due primarily to Lincoln paying off one-half of its long-term liabilities in 20Y6.

 Link to Nike   For a recent year, **Nike**'s ratio of fixed assets to long-term liabilities was 1.0.

Ratio of Liabilities to Stockholders' Equity

The **ratio of liabilities to stockholders' equity** measures how much of the company is financed by debt and equity. It is computed as follows:

$$\text{Ratio of Liabilities to Stockholders' Equity} = \frac{\text{Total Liabilities}}{\text{Total Stockholders' Equity}}$$

To illustrate, the ratio of liabilities to stockholders' equity for **Lincoln Company** is computed as follows:

	20Y6	20Y5
Total liabilities	$310,000	$443,000
Total stockholders' equity	$829,500	$787,500
Ratio of liabilities to stockholders' equity	0.4 ($310,000 ÷ $829,500)	0.6 ($443,000 ÷ $787,500)

Lincoln's ratio of liabilities to stockholders' equity decreased from 0.6 to 0.4 during 20Y6. The lower ratio indicates that the proportion of Lincoln's liabilities and equity that is made up of liabilities is decreasing. This is an improvement and indicates that the margin of safety for Lincoln's creditors is improving.

For a recent five-year period, **Nike**'s average ratio of liabilities to stockholders' equity was 0.6. *Link to Nike*

Times Interest Earned

The **times interest earned**, sometimes called the *coverage ratio*, measures the risk that interest payments will not be made if earnings decrease. It is computed as follows:

$$\text{Times Interest Earned} = \frac{\text{Income Before Income Tax} + \text{Interest Expense}}{\text{Interest Expense}}$$

Interest expense is paid before income taxes. In other words, interest expense is deducted in determining taxable income and, thus, income tax. For this reason, income *before taxes* is used in computing the times interest earned.

The *higher* the ratio, the more likely interest payments will be paid if earnings decrease. To illustrate, the times interest earned for **Lincoln Company** is computed as follows:

	20Y6	20Y5
Income before income tax	$162,500	$134,600
Interest expense	6,000	12,000
Amount available to pay interest	$168,500	$146,600
Times interest earned	28.1 ($168,500 ÷ $6,000)	12.2 ($146,600 ÷ $12,000)

The times interest earned improved from 12.2 to 28.1 during 20Y6. The higher ratio indicates that the relationship between the amount of income available to pay interest and the amount of interest expense has improved. Lincoln has more than enough earnings (28 times) to make its interest payments.

For a recent year, **Nike**'s times interest earned ratio was nine times higher than the industry average. *Link to Nike*

Why It Matters

Liquidity Crunch

RadioShack Corporation, an electronics retailer, filed for bankruptcy protection. Information on the company's liquidity and solvency for the three years prior to bankruptcy follow:

	20Y3	20Y2	20Y1
Liquidity measures:			
Working capital (in thousands)	$748,400	$1,003,700	$1,176,700
Current ratio	2.3	2.0	2.9
Quick ratio	0.7	1.0	1.5
Solvency measures:			
Ratio of liabilities to stockholders' equity	6.7	2.8	1.9
Ratio of fixed assets to long-term liabilities	0.2	0.3	0.3

The data shows that the company's liquidity and solvency measures deteriorated in the years prior to the firm's bankruptcy. All three of the company's liquidity measures declined significantly during the three-year period, indicating a growing risk that the company would not be able to repay its current liabilities. The ratio of liabilities to stockholder's equity also increased significantly during this period, indicating that the company might not be able to repay its long-term debts. Finally, the ratio of fixed assets to long-term liabilities began to deteriorate in 20Y3, indicating that fewer assets would be available to secure the company's long-term liabilities.

680 **Chapter 14** Financial Statement Analysis

Check Up Corner 14-3 — Solvency Analysis

The following are select balance sheet and income statement data for Wilton Strand Inc. for a recent year:

	Dec. 31, 20Y3
Assets	
Current assets	$ 560,000
Property, plant, and equipment (net)	1,400,000
Total assets	$1,960,000
Liabilities	
Current liabilities	$ 160,000
Long-term liabilities	400,000
Total liabilities	$ 560,000
Stockholders' Equity	
Common stock, $5 par	$ 200,000
Retained earnings	1,200,000
Total stockholders' equity	$1,400,000
Total liabilities and stockholders' equity	$1,960,000
Select income statement information:	
Interest expense	$ 100,000
Income before income tax	260,000

Based on these data, calculate the following solvency measures:

A. Ratio of fixed assets to long-term liabilities
B. Ratio of liabilities to stockholders' equity
C. Times interest earned

Solution:

A.

$$\text{Ratio of Fixed Assets to Long-Term Liabilities} = \frac{\text{Fixed Assets (net)}}{\text{Long-Term Liabilities}} = \frac{\$1,400,000}{\$400,000} = 3.5$$

Because fixed assets are often pledged as security for long-term notes and bonds, the ratio of fixed assets to long-term liabilities provides a measure of whether noteholders or bondholders will be paid.

B.

$$\text{Ratio of Liabilities to Stockholders' Equity} = \frac{\text{Total Liabilities}}{\text{Total Stockholders' Equity}} = \frac{\$560,000}{\$1,400,000} = 0.4$$

The ratio of liabilities to stockholders' equity measures how much of the company is financed by debt and equity.

C.

$$\text{Times Interest Earned} = \frac{\text{Income before Income Tax + Interest Expense}}{\text{Interest Expense}} = \frac{\$260,000 + \$100,000}{\$100,000} = \frac{\$360,000}{\$100,000} = 3.6$$

Times interest earned measures the risk that interest payments will not be made if earnings decrease.

Check Up Corner

Objective 5

Describe and illustrate how to use financial statement analysis to assess profitability.

Profitability

Profitability analysis evaluates the ability of a company to generate future earnings. This ability depends on the relationship between the company's operating results and the assets the company has available for use in its operations. Thus, the relationship between income statement and balance sheet items are used to evaluate profitability.

Common profitability ratios are shown in Exhibit 10:

Profitability Ratios		
Asset Turnover	Return on Stockholders' Equity	Price-Earnings Ratio
Return on Total Assets	Return on Common Stockholders' Equity	Dividends per Share
	Earnings per Share on Common Stock	Dividend Yield

Exhibit 10
Profitability Ratios

Asset Turnover

The **asset turnover** ratio measures how effectively a company uses its assets. It is computed as follows:

$$\text{Asset Turnover} = \frac{\text{Sales}}{\text{Average Total Assets (excluding long-term investments)}}$$

Note that long-term investments are excluded in computing asset turnover. This is because long-term investments are unrelated to normal operations and sales.

To illustrate, the asset turnover for **Lincoln Company** is computed as follows. Total assets (excluding long-term investments) are $1,010,000 at the beginning of 20Y5.

	20Y6	20Y5
Sales	$1,498,000	$1,200,000
Total assets (excluding long-term investments):		
Beginning of year	$1,053,000*	$1,010,000
End of year	1,044,500**	1,053,000*
Total	$2,097,500	$2,063,000
Average total assets	$1,048,750 ($2,097,500 ÷ 2)	$1,031,500 ($2,063,000 ÷ 2)
Asset turnover	1.4 ($1,498,000 ÷ $1,048,750)	1.2 ($1,200,000 ÷ $1,031,500)

*($1,230,500 total assets – $177,500 long-term investments)
**($1,139,500 total assets – $95,000 long-term investments)

For Lincoln, the average total assets was computed using total assets (excluding long-term investments) at the beginning and end of the year. The average total assets could also be based on monthly or quarterly averages.

The asset turnover ratio indicates that Lincoln's use of its operating assets has improved in 20Y6. This was primarily due to the increase in sales in 20Y6.

Return on Total Assets

The **return on total assets** measures the profitability of total assets, without considering how the assets are financed. In other words, this rate is not affected by the portion of assets financed by creditors or stockholders. It is computed as follows:

$$\text{Return on Total Assets} = \frac{\text{Income + Interest Expense}}{\text{Average Total Assets}}$$

The return on total assets is computed by adding interest expense to net income. By adding interest expense to net income, the effect of whether the assets are financed by creditors (debt) or stockholders (equity) is eliminated. Because net income includes any income earned from long-term investments, the average total assets includes long-term investments as well as the net operating assets.

To illustrate, the rate earned on total assets by **Lincoln Company** is computed as follows. Total assets are $1,187,500 at the beginning of 20Y5.

	20Y6	20Y5
Net income	$ 91,000	$ 76,500
Interest expense	6,000	12,000
	$ 97,000	$ 88,500
Total assets:		
Beginning of year	$1,230,500	$1,187,500
End of year	1,139,500	1,230,500
Total	$2,370,000	$2,418,000
Average total assets	$1,185,000 ($2,370,000 ÷ 2)	$1,209,000 ($2,418,000 ÷ 2)
Return on total assets	8.2% ($97,000 ÷ $1,185,000)	7.3% ($88,500 ÷ $1,209,000)

The return on total assets improved from 7.3% to 8.2% during 20Y6.

The *return on operating assets* is sometimes computed when there are large amounts of nonoperating income and expense. It is computed as follows:

$$\text{Return on Operating Assets} = \frac{\text{Income from Operations}}{\text{Average Operating Assets}}$$

Because Lincoln does not have a significant amount of nonoperating income and expense, the return on operating assets is not illustrated.

Return on Stockholders' Equity

The **return on stockholders' equity** measures the rate of income earned on the amount invested by the stockholders. It is computed as follows:

$$\text{Return on Stockholders' Equity} = \frac{\text{Net Income}}{\text{Average Total Stockholders' Equity}}$$

To illustrate, the return on stockholders' equity for **Lincoln Company** is computed as follows. Total stockholders' equity is $750,000 at the beginning of 20Y5.

	20Y6	20Y5
Net income	$ 91,000	$ 76,500
Total stockholders' equity:		
Beginning of year	$ 787,500	$ 750,000
End of year	829,500	787,500
Total	$1,617,000	$1,537,500
Average total stockholders' equity	$808,500 ($1,617,000 ÷ 2)	$768,750 ($1,537,500 ÷ 2)
Return on stockholders' equity	11.3% ($91,000 ÷ $808,500)	10.0% ($76,500 ÷ $768,750)

The return on stockholders' equity improved from 10.0% to 11.3% during 20Y6.

Leverage involves using debt to increase the return on an investment. The rate earned on stockholders' equity is normally higher than the rate earned on total assets. This is because of the effect of leverage.

For **Lincoln Company**, the effect of leverage for 20Y6 is 3.1% and for 20Y5 is 2.7% computed as follows:

	20Y6	20Y5
Return on stockholders' equity	11.3%	10.0%
Return on total assets	(8.2)	(7.3)
Effect of leverage	3.1%	2.7%

Exhibit 11 shows the 20Y6 and 20Y5 effects of leverage for Lincoln.

Link to Nike For a recent five-year period, **Nike**'s average return on stockholders' equity was 23.9%.

Why It Matters

Gearing for Profit

Another term for leverage is "financial gearing." **Exxon Mobil Corporation**, a worldwide-integrated energy company, is an example of a company that uses leverage for financial advantage. Exxon had a return on total assets of 9.35% for a recent year,

while its return on stockholders' equity was 18.7%. Thus, Exxon is "geared" 2:1 by using debt on its balance sheet. Exxon is very profitable, thus leverage is beneficial. In contrast, **Chesapeake Energy**, an oil and gas exploration company, had return on assets of –7.5% for a recent 12-month period, and return on stockholders' equity of –25%. In this case, the over 3:1 leverage (25% ÷ 7.5%) creates a financial disadvantage because the company is experiencing losses.

Exhibit 11

Effect of Leverage

Return on Common Stockholders' Equity

The **return on common stockholders' equity** measures the rate of profits earned on the amount invested by the common stockholders. It is computed as follows:

$$\frac{\text{Return on Common}}{\text{Stockholders' Equity}} = \frac{\text{Net Income} - \text{Preferred Dividends}}{\text{Average Common Stockholders' Equity}}$$

Because preferred stockholders rank ahead of the common stockholders in their claim on earnings, any preferred dividends are subtracted from net income in computing the return on common stockholders' equity.

Lincoln Company had $150,000 par value of 6% preferred stock outstanding on December 31, 20Y6 and 20Y5. Thus, preferred dividends of $9,000 ($150,000 × 6%) are deducted from net income. Lincoln's common stockholders' equity is determined as follows:

	December 31		
	20Y6	**20Y5**	**20Y4**
Common stock, $10 par	$500,000	$500,000	$500,000
Retained earnings	179,500	137,500	100,000
Common stockholders' equity	$679,500	$637,500	$600,000

The retained earnings on December 31, 20Y4, of $100,000 is the same as the retained earnings on January 1, 20Y5, as shown in Lincoln's retained earnings statement in Exhibit 4.

Using this information, the return on common stockholders' equity for Lincoln is computed as follows:

	20Y6	**20Y5**
Net income	$ 91,000	$ 76,500
Preferred dividends	(9,000)	(9,000)
Total	$ 82,000	$ 67,500
Common stockholders' equity:		
Beginning of year	$ 637,500	$ 600,000
End of year	679,500*	637,500**
Total	$1,317,000	$1,237,500
Average common stockholders' equity	$658,500 ($1,317,000 ÷ 2)	$618,750 ($1,237,500 ÷ 2)
Return on common stockholders' equity	12.5% ($82,000 ÷ $658,500)	10.9% ($67,500 ÷ $618,750)

*($829,500 total stockholders' equity – $150,000 preferred 6% stock)
**($787,500 total stockholders' equity – $150,000 preferred 6% stock)

Lincoln's return on common stockholders' equity improved from 10.9% to 12.5% in 20Y6. This return differs from Lincoln's returns on total assets and stockholders' equity, which follow:

	20Y6	20Y5
Return on total assets	8.2%	7.3%
Return on stockholders' equity	11.3%	10.0%
Return on common stockholders' equity	12.5%	10.9%

These returns differ because of leverage, as discussed in the preceding section.

Earnings per Share on Common Stock

Earnings per share (EPS) on common stock measures the share of profits that are earned by a share of common stock. Earnings per share must be reported on the income statement. As a result, earnings per share (EPS) is often reported in the financial press. It is computed as follows:

$$\text{Earnings per Share (EPS) on Common Stock} = \frac{\text{Net Income} - \text{Preferred Dividends}}{\text{Shares of Common Stock Outstanding}}$$

When preferred and common stock are outstanding, preferred dividends are subtracted from net income to determine the income related to the common shares.

To illustrate, the earnings per share (EPS) of common stock for **Lincoln Company** is computed as follows:

	20Y6	20Y5
Net income	$91,000	$76,500
Preferred dividends	(9,000)	(9,000)
Total	$82,000	$67,500
Shares of common stock outstanding	50,000	50,000
Earnings per share on common stock	$1.64 ($82,000 ÷ 50,000)	$1.35 ($67,500 ÷ 50,000)

Lincoln had $150,000 par value of 6% preferred stock outstanding on December 31, 20Y6 and 20Y5. Thus, preferred dividends of $9,000 ($150,000 × 6%) are deducted from net income in computing earnings per share on common stock.

Lincoln did not issue any additional shares of common stock in 20Y6. If Lincoln had issued additional shares in 20Y6, a weighted average of common shares outstanding during the year would have been used.

Lincoln's earnings per share (EPS) on common stock improved from $1.35 to $1.64 during 20Y6.

Lincoln has a simple capital structure with only common stock and preferred stock outstanding. Many corporations, however, have complex capital structures with various types of equity securities outstanding, such as convertible preferred stock, stock options, and stock warrants. In such cases, the possible effects of such securities on the shares of common stock outstanding are considered in reporting earnings per share. These possible effects are reported separately as *earnings per common share assuming dilution* or *diluted earnings per share*. This topic is described and illustrated in advanced accounting courses and textbooks.

Link to Nike   On a recent income statement, **Nike** reported net income of $2,693 million.

Price-Earnings Ratio

The **price-earnings (P/E) ratio** on common stock measures a company's future earnings prospects. It is often quoted in the financial press and is computed as follows:

$$\text{Price-Earnings (P/E) Ratio} = \frac{\text{Market Price per Share of Common Stock}}{\text{Earnings per Share on Common Stock}}$$

To illustrate, the price-earnings (P/E) ratio for **Lincoln Company** is computed as follows:

	20Y6	20Y5
Market price per share of common stock	$41.00	$27.00
Earnings per share on common stock	$1.64	$1.35
Price-earnings ratio on common stock	25 ($41 ÷ $1.64)	20 ($27 ÷ $1.35)

The price-earnings ratio improved from 20 to 25 during 20Y6. In other words, a share of common stock of Lincoln was selling for 20 times earnings per share at the end of 20Y5. At the end of 20Y6, the common stock was selling for 25 times earnings per share. This indicates that the market expects Lincoln to experience favorable earnings in the future.

Dividends per Share

Dividends per share measures the extent to which earnings are being distributed to common shareholders. It is computed as follows:

$$\text{Dividends per Share} = \frac{\text{Dividends on Common Stock}}{\text{Shares of Common Stock Outstanding}}$$

To illustrate, the dividends per share for **Lincoln Company** are computed as follows:

	20Y6	20Y5
Dividends on common stock	$40,000	$30,000
Shares of common stock outstanding	50,000	50,000
Dividends per share of common stock	$0.80 ($40,000 ÷ 50,000)	$0.60 ($30,000 ÷ 50,000)

The dividends per share of common stock increased from $0.60 to $0.80 during 20Y6.

Dividends per share are often reported with earnings per share. Comparing the two per-share amounts indicates the extent to which earnings are being retained for use in operations. To illustrate, the dividends and earnings per share for **Lincoln Company** are shown in Exhibit 12.

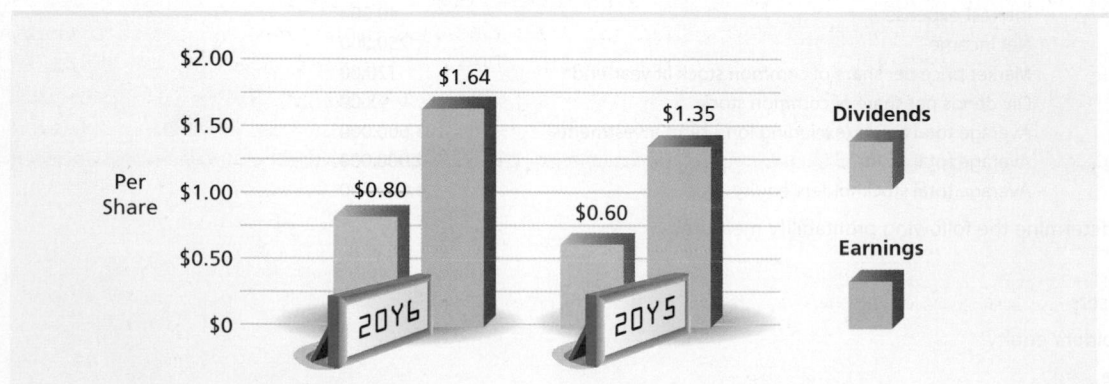

Exhibit 12
Dividends and Earnings per Share of Common Stock

Why It Matters

Investing for Yield

Companies that provide attractive dividend yields are often mature companies found in stable industries. Examples of such industries are public utilities and food. **Coca Cola**, **Procter & Gamble**, **Kellogg's**, **Consolidated Edison**, **Southern Company**, and **General Mills** all have attractive dividend yields in excess of 3%. Procter & Gamble has had 58 consecutive years of dividend payouts, and Kellogg's has not reduced its dividend for 56 years. The stability of the food industry has allowed these companies to maintain dividends for many years. Growth companies, such as **Google** or **Facebook**, do not pay dividends, because they use their cash to grow the business. Investors in such growth companies expect to make their return from stock price appreciation, rather than dividends. Mark Cuban, billionaire, Shark Tank® investor, and owner of the **Dallas Mavericks**, stated, "I believe non-dividend stocks aren't much more than baseball cards. They are worth what you can convince someone to pay for it."

Quote source: Parker, Tim, "The Top Ten Dividend Quotes," *Dividend.com*, August 29, 2012.

Dividend Yield

The **dividend yield** on common stock measures the rate of return to common stockholders from cash dividends. It is of special interest to investors whose objective is to earn revenue (dividends) from their investment. It is computed as follows:

$$\text{Dividend Yield} = \frac{\text{Dividends per Share of Common Stock}}{\text{Market Price per Share of Common Stock}}$$

To illustrate, the dividend yield for **Lincoln Company** is computed as follows:

	20Y6	20Y5
Dividends per share of common stock	$0.80	$0.60
Market price per share of common stock	$41.00	$27.00
Dividend yield on common stock	2.0% ($0.80 ÷ $41)	2.2% ($0.60 ÷ $27)

The dividend yield declined slightly from 2.2% to 2.0% in 20Y6. This decline was primarily due to the increase in the market price of Lincoln's common stock.

Link to Nike   For a recent five-year period, **Nike**'s average dividend yield was 1.24%.

Check Up Corner 14-4   Profitability Analysis

The following data were taken from the financial statements of French Broad Steel Works Inc. for a recent year:

Shares of common stock outstanding	20,000
Sales	$2,400,000
Interest expense	40,000
Net income	250,000
Market price per share of common stock at year-end	120.00
Dividends per share of common stock	3.00
Average total assets (excluding long-term investments)	1,600,000
Average total assets	2,000,000
Average total stockholders' equity	1,000,000

Based on these data, determine the following profitability measures:

A. Asset turnover
B. Return on total assets
C. Return on stockholders' equity
D. Earnings per share
E. Price-earnings ratio
F. Dividend yield

Solution:

A.

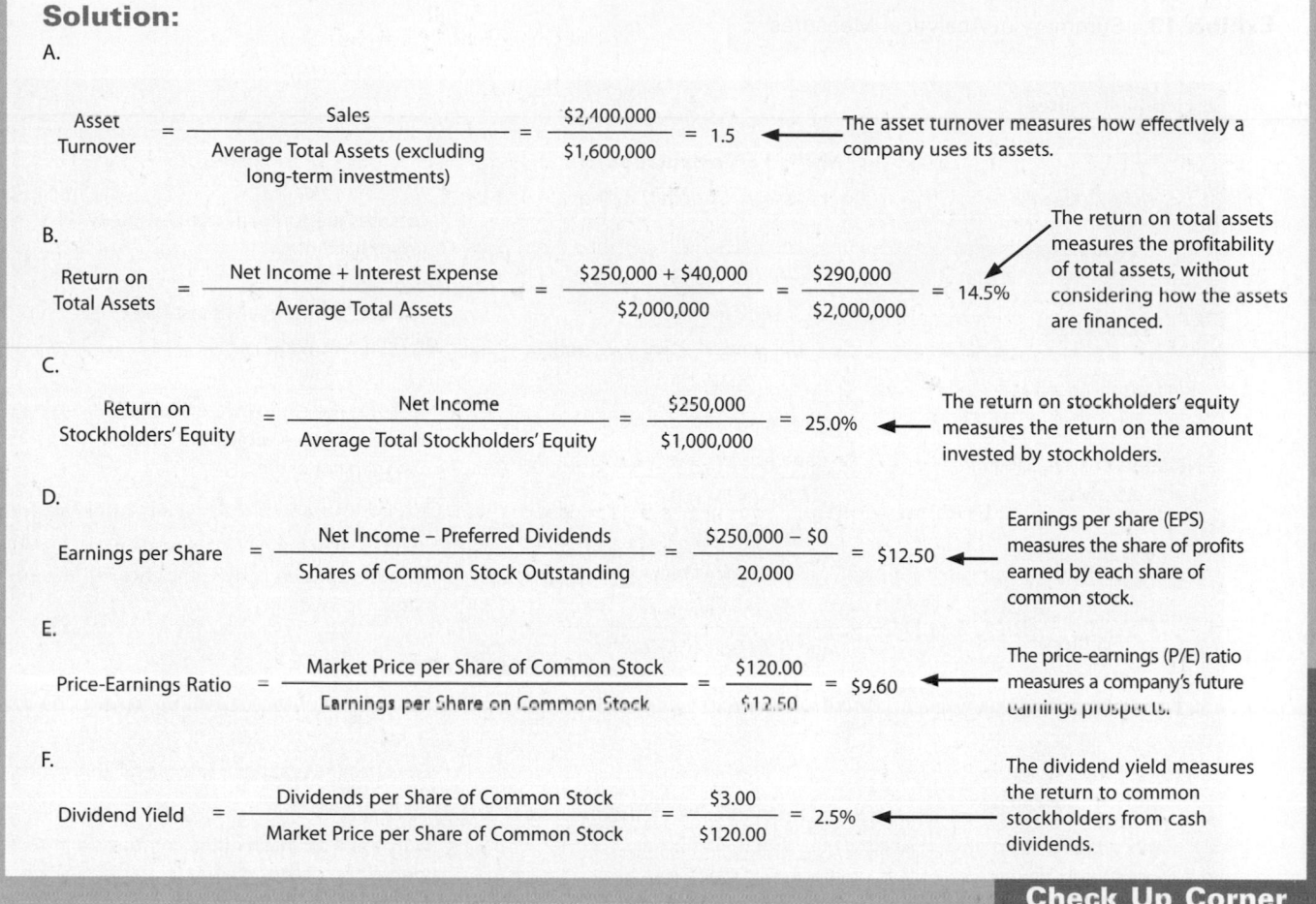

$$\text{Asset Turnover} = \frac{\text{Sales}}{\text{Average Total Assets (excluding long-term investments)}} = \frac{\$2{,}100{,}000}{\$1{,}600{,}000} = 1.5$$

The asset turnover measures how effectively a company uses its assets.

B.

$$\text{Return on Total Assets} = \frac{\text{Net Income} + \text{Interest Expense}}{\text{Average Total Assets}} = \frac{\$250{,}000 + \$40{,}000}{\$2{,}000{,}000} = \frac{\$290{,}000}{\$2{,}000{,}000} = 14.5\%$$

The return on total assets measures the profitability of total assets, without considering how the assets are financed.

C.

$$\text{Return on Stockholders' Equity} = \frac{\text{Net Income}}{\text{Average Total Stockholders' Equity}} = \frac{\$250{,}000}{\$1{,}000{,}000} = 25.0\%$$

The return on stockholders' equity measures the return on the amount invested by stockholders.

D.

$$\text{Earnings per Share} = \frac{\text{Net Income} - \text{Preferred Dividends}}{\text{Shares of Common Stock Outstanding}} = \frac{\$250{,}000 - \$0}{20{,}000} = \$12.50$$

Earnings per share (EPS) measures the share of profits earned by each share of common stock.

E.

$$\text{Price-Earnings Ratio} = \frac{\text{Market Price per Share of Common Stock}}{\text{Earnings per Share on Common Stock}} = \frac{\$120.00}{\$12.50} = \$9.60$$

The price-earnings (P/E) ratio measures a company's future earnings prospects.

F.

$$\text{Dividend Yield} = \frac{\text{Dividends per Share of Common Stock}}{\text{Market Price per Share of Common Stock}} = \frac{\$3.00}{\$120.00} = 2.5\%$$

The dividend yield measures the return to common stockholders from cash dividends.

Check Up Corner

Summary of Analytical Measures

Exhibit 13 shows a summary of the solvency and profitability measures discussed in this chapter. The type of industry and the company's operations usually affect which measures are used. In many cases, additional measures are used for a specific industry. For example, airlines use *revenue per passenger mile* and *cost per available seat* as profitability measures. Likewise, hotels use *occupancy rates* as a profitability measure.

The analytical measures shown in Exhibit 13 are a useful starting point for analyzing a company's liquidity, solvency and profitability. However, they are not a substitute for sound judgment. The general economic and business environment should always be considered in analyzing a company's future prospects. In addition, any trends and interrelationships among the measures should be carefully studied.

Exhibit 13 Summary of Analytical Measures

Liquidity Measures

	Method of Computation	Use
Working Capital	Current Assets – Current Liabilities	Measures the company's ability to pay current liabilities.
Current Ratio	$\dfrac{\text{Current Assets}}{\text{Current Liabilities}}$	
Quick Ratio	$\dfrac{\text{Quick Assets}}{\text{Current Liabilities}}$	Measures the company's instant debt-paying ability.
Accounts Receivable Turnover	$\dfrac{\text{Sales}}{\text{Average Accounts Receivable}}$	Measures the company's efficiency in collecting receivables and in the management of credit .
Numbers of Days' Sales in Receivables	$\dfrac{\text{Average Accounts Receivable}}{\text{Average Daily Sales}}$	
Inventory Turnover	$\dfrac{\text{Cost of Goods Sold}}{\text{Average Inventory}}$	Measures the company's efficiency in managing inventory.
Number of Days' Sales in Inventory	$\dfrac{\text{Average Inventory}}{\text{Average Daily Cost of Goods Sold}}$	

Solvency Measures

Ratio of Fixed Assets to Long-Term Liabilities	$\dfrac{\text{Fixed Assets (net)}}{\text{Long-Term Liabilities}}$	Measures the margin of safety available to long-term creditors.
Ratio of Liabilities to Stockholders' Equity	$\dfrac{\text{Total Liabilities}}{\text{Total Stockholders' Equity}}$	Measures how much of the company is financed by debt and equity.
Times Interest Earned	$\dfrac{\text{Income Before Income Tax + Interest Expense}}{\text{Interest Expense}}$	Measures the risk that interest payments will not be made if earnings decrease.

Profitability Measures

Asset Turnover	$\dfrac{\text{Sales}}{\text{Average Total Assets (excluding long-term investments)}}$	Measures how effectively a company uses its assets.
Return on Total Assets	$\dfrac{\text{Net Income + Interest Expense}}{\text{Average Total Assets}}$	Measures the profitability of a company's assets.
Return on Stockholders' Equity	$\dfrac{\text{Net Income}}{\text{Average Total Stockholders' Equity}}$	Measures the profitability of the investment by stockholders.
Return on Common Stockholders' Equity	$\dfrac{\text{Net Income – Preferred Dividends}}{\text{Average Common Stockholders' Equity}}$	Measures the profitability of the investment by common stockholders.
Earnings per Share (EPS) on Common Stock	$\dfrac{\text{Net Income – Preferred Dividends}}{\text{Shares of Common Stock Outstanding}}$	
Price-Earnings (P/E) Ratio	$\dfrac{\text{Market Price per Share of Common Stock}}{\text{Earnings per Share on Common Stock}}$	Measures future earnings prospects, based on the relationship between market value of common stock and earnings.
Dividends per Share	$\dfrac{\text{Dividends on Common Stock}}{\text{Shares of Common Stock Outstanding}}$	Measures the extent to which earnings are being distributed to common stockholders.
Dividend Yield	$\dfrac{\text{Dividends per Share of Common Stock}}{\text{Market Price per Share of Common Stock}}$	Measures the rate of return to common stockholders in terms of dividends.

Corporate Annual Reports

Objective 6
Describe the contents of corporate annual reports.

Public corporations issue annual reports summarizing their operating activities for the past year and plans for the future. Such annual reports include the financial statements and the accompanying notes. In addition, annual reports normally include the following sections:

- Management discussion and analysis
- Report on internal control
- Report on fairness of the financial statements

Management Discussion and Analysis

Management's Discussion and Analysis (MD&A) is required in annual reports filed with the Securities and Exchange Commission. It includes management's analysis of current operations and its plans for the future. Typical items included in the MD&A are as follows:

- Management's analysis and explanations of any significant changes between the current and prior years' financial statements.
- Important accounting principles or policies that could affect interpretation of the financial statements, including the effect of changes in accounting principles or the adoption of new accounting principles.
- Management's assessment of the company's liquidity and the availability of capital to the company.
- Significant risk exposures that might affect the company.
- Any "off-balance-sheet" arrangements such as leases not included in the financial statements. Such arrangements are discussed in advanced accounting courses and textbooks.

Report on Internal Control

The Sarbanes-Oxley Act of 2002 requires a report on internal control by management. The report states management's responsibility for establishing and maintaining internal control. In addition, management's assessment of the effectiveness of internal controls over financial reporting is included in the report.

Sarbanes-Oxley also requires a public accounting firm to verify management's conclusions on internal control. Thus, two reports on internal control, one by management and one by a public accounting firm, are included in the annual report. In some situations, these may be combined into a single report on internal control.

⭐ *Ethics: Don't Do It!*

Characteristics of Financial Statement Fraud

Each year the Association of Certified Fraud Examiners conducts a worldwide survey examining the characteristics of corporate fraud. The most recent study found that:

- 43.3% of frauds were detected by a tip from an employee or someone close to the company;
- Frauds committed by owners and executives tended to be much larger than those caused by employees;

- Most people who are caught committing fraud are first-time offenders with clean employment histories; and
- In 81% of the cases, the person committing the fraud displayed one or more behavioral red flags, such as living beyond their means, financial difficulties, and excessive control issues.

Fraud examiners can use these trends to help them narrow their focus when searching for fraud.

Source: *2012 Report to the Nations*, Association of Certified Fraud Examiners, 2012.

Report on Fairness of the Financial Statements

All publicly held corporations are required to have an independent audit (examination) of their financial statements. The Certified Public Accounting (CPA) firm that conducts the audit renders an opinion, called the *Report of Independent Registered Public Accounting Firm*, on the fairness of the statements.

An opinion stating that the financial statements present fairly the financial position, results of operations, and cash flows of the company is said to be an *unmodified opinion*, sometimes called a *clean opinion*. Any report other than an unmodified opinion raises a "red flag" for financial statement users and requires further investigation as to its cause. The types and nature of audit opinions are covered in more detail in advanced courses on auditing.

The annual report of **Nike Inc.** is shown in Appendix B. The Nike report includes the financial statements as well as the Management Discussion and Analysis, the Report on Internal Control, and the Report on Fairness of the Financial Statements.

Analysis for Decision Making

Make a Decision   Price-Earnings Ratio and Dividend Yield

Objective

Describe and illustrate the use of financial statement analysis in evaluating potential stock price appreciation.

The following table shows the stock price, earnings per share, and dividends per share for three companies for a recent year:

	Google	PepsiCo	Caterpillar
Market price of common stock at year-end	$526.40	$94.56	$91.53
Earnings per share	21.02	4.27	5.88
Dividends per share	0.00	2.53	2.70

A. For each company, determine the:
   • Price-earnings ratio (round to one decimal place)
   • Dividend yield (round to one decimal place)
B. Based on the information available, which company would you expect to have the best potential for future common stock price appreciation? Why?

Solution:

A.

	Google	PepsiCo	Caterpillar
Earnings per share	$ 21.02	$ 4.27	$ 5.88
Market price per share of common stock	$ 526.40	$94.56	$ 91.53
Earnings per share	÷ 21.02	÷ 4.27	÷ 5.88
Price-earnings ratio	25.0	22.1	15.6
Dividends per share	$ 0.00	$ 2.53	$ 2.70
Market price per share of common stock	÷526.40	÷94.56	÷91.53
Dividend yield	0.0%	2.7%	2.9%

B. Caterpillar has the largest dividend yield and strong earnings per share but has the lowest price-earnings ratio. Stock market participants seem to be skeptical about Caterpillar's future prospects and are discounting its stock price despite its relatively solid performance. Google pays no dividend and, thus, has no dividend yield. However, Google has the largest price-earnings ratio. Stock market participants are expecting a strong return on their investment from appreciation in Google's stock price. PepsiCo has the second highest price-earnings ratio, but has a lower dividend yield and earnings per share than Caterpillar. This suggests that the market expects PepsiCo's combination of earnings and dividends to improve in the coming years.

Make a Decision

Appendix 1 Unusual Items on the Income Statement

Generally accepted accounting principles require that unusual items be reported separately on the income statement. This is because such items do not occur frequently and are typically unrelated to current operations. Without separate reporting of these items, users of the financial statements might be misled about current and future operations.

Unusual items on the income statement are classified as one of the following:

- Affecting the *current period* income statement
- Affecting a *prior period* income statement

Unusual Items Affecting the Current Period's Income Statement

Discontinued operations are an unusual item that affects the current period's:

- Income statement presentation
- Earnings per share presentation

Discontinued operations are reported separately on the income statement for any period in which they occur.

Income Statement Presentation A company may discontinue a component of its operations by selling or abandoning the component's operations. For example, a retailer might decide to sell its product only online and, thus, discontinue selling its merchandise at its retail outlets (stores).

If the discontinued component is (1) the result of a strategic shift and (2) has a major effect on the entity's operations and financial results, any gain or loss on discontinued operations is reported on the income statement as a *Gain (or loss) from discontinued operations*. It is reported immediately following *Income from continuing operations*.

To illustrate, assume that Jones Corporation produces and sells electrical products, hardware supplies, and lawn equipment. Because of a lack of profits, Jones discontinues its electrical products operation and sells the remaining inventory and other assets at a loss of $100,000. Exhibit 14 illustrates the reporting of the loss on discontinued operations.[2]

Jones Corporation Income Statement For the Year Ended December 31, 20Y2	
Sales	$12,350,000
Cost of goods sold	5,800,000
Gross profit	$ 6,550,000
Selling and administrative expenses	5,240,000
Income from continuing operations before income tax	$ 1,310,000
Income tax expense	620,000
Income from continuing operations	$ 690,000
Loss on discontinued operations	100,000
Net income	$ 590,000

Exhibit 14

Unusual Items in the Income Statement

[2] The gain or loss on discontinued operations is reported net of any tax effects. To simplify, the tax effects are not specifically identified in Exhibit 14.

In addition, a note to the financial statements should describe the operations sold, including the date operations were discontinued, and details about the assets, liabilities, income, and expenses of the discontinued component.

Earnings per Share Earnings per common share should be reported separately for discontinued operations. To illustrate, a partial income statement for Jones Corporation is shown in Exhibit 15. The company has 200,000 shares of common stock outstanding.

Jones Corporation Income Statement For the Year Ended December 31, 20Y2	
Earnings per common share:	
Income from continuing operations..	$3.45
Loss on discontinued operations	0.50
Net income	$2.95

Exhibit 15 reports earnings per common share for income from continuing operations, discontinued operations. However, only earnings per share for income from continuing operations and net income are required by generally accepted accounting principles. The other per-share amounts may be presented in the notes to the financial statements.

Unusual Items Affecting the Prior Period's Income Statement

An unusual item may occur that affects a prior period's income statement. Two such items are as follows:

- Errors in applying generally accepted accounting principles
- Changes from one generally accepted accounting principle to another

If an error is discovered in a prior period's financial statement, the prior-period statement and all following statements are restated and thus corrected.

A company may change from one generally accepted accounting principle to another. In this case, the prior-period financial statements are restated as if the new accounting principle had always been used.[3]

For both of the preceding items, the current-period earnings are not affected. That is, only the earnings reported in prior periods are restated. However, because the prior earnings are restated, the beginning balance of Retained Earnings may also have to be restated. This, in turn, may cause the restatement of other balance sheet accounts. Illustrations of these types of adjustments and restatements are provided in advanced accounting courses.

Appendix 2 Fair Value and Comprehensive Income

Many companies acquire assets that are required by GAAP to be reported on the balance sheet at a different measurement basis called *fair value*. When a company reports assets at fair value, the financial reporting becomes complex. In the following sections, the concept of fair value and the financial statement effects of using fair value are introduced. A detailed discussion of these concepts is provided in intermediate and advanced accounting texts.

---

[3] Changes from one acceptable depreciation method to another acceptable depreciation method are an exception to this general rule and are to be treated prospectively as a change in estimate.

Fair Value

Fair value is the price that could be received for an asset if it were sold today. This differs from historical cost, in that the amount reported on the balance sheet changes each period to reflect the asset's fair (current) value at the balance sheet date. The change in an asset's fair value from one period to the next is recorded in the financial statements as either:

- a gain or loss on the income statement, or
- an increase or decrease in stockholders' equity reported as other comprehensive income.

Comprehensive Income

When a change in an asset's fair value is not recorded as a gain or loss on the income statement, it is recorded as an element of **other comprehensive income**.[4] These include changes in the fair value of certain investment securities, foreign currency exposures, and pension assets.

The elements of other comprehensive income are included in the computation of **comprehensive income**, which is defined as all changes in stockholders' equity during a period, except those resulting from dividends and stockholders' investments. Comprehensive income is determined by adding or subtracting *other comprehensive income* elements to (from) net income, as follows:

Net income	$XXX
Other comprehensive income	XXX
Comprehensive income	$XXX

Companies must report comprehensive income in the financial statements either:

- On the income statement, directly below net income, or
- In a separate statement of comprehensive income.

Reporting Comprehensive Income on the Income Statement Bart Company purchased investment securities during the year that had an increase of $2,600 in fair value. Because of the accounting methods selected by Bart, this increase in fair value is recorded as an element of other comprehensive income and is called an **unrealized gain**. If Bart elects to report other comprehensive income on the income statement, the elements of other comprehensive income are added to or subtracted from net income at the bottom of the income statement as follows:

Bart Company Income Statement For the Year Ended December 31, 20Y2	
Sales	$1,200,000
Cost of goods sold...	960,000
Gross profit	$ 240,000
Operating expenses	144,500
Income from operations	$ 95,500
Income tax expense	36,290
Net income	$ 59,210
Other comprehensive income......................................	2,600
Comprehensive income..	$ 61,810

Reporting Comprehensive Income in the Statement of Comprehensive Income
As an alternative to reporting comprehensive income on the income statement, companies may elect to report comprehensive income on a separate statement of comprehensive income.

---

[4] Fair value accounting is discussed in greater detail in intermediate and advanced accounting texts.

This statement should immediately follow the income statement. Using the Bart Company example, the income statement and statement of comprehensive income would be presented as follows:

Bart Company Income Statement For the Year Ended December 31, 20Y2	
Sales	$1,200,000
Cost of goods sold	960,000
Gross profit	$ 240,000
Operating expenses	144,500
Income from operations	$ 95,500
Income tax expense	36,290
Net income	$ 59,210

Bart Company Statement of Comprehensive Income For the Year Ended December 31, 20Y2	
Net income	$59,210
Other comprehensive income	2,600
Comprehensive income	$61,810

Reporting Accumulated Other Comprehensive Income on the Balance Sheet

The *cumulative* effect of the elements of other comprehensive income is reported on the balance sheet as **accumulated other comprehensive income**.

Continuing the Bart Company example, the unrealized gain of $2,600 would be reported as accumulated other comprehensive income in the Stockholders' Equity section of the balance sheet, as follows:

Bart Company Balance Sheet December 31, 20Y2	
Stockholders' Equity	
Common stock	$ 20,000
Paid-in capital in excess of par	300,000
Retained earnings	250,000
Accumulated other comprehensive income	2,600
Total stockholders' equity	$572,600

Let's Review

Chapter Summary

1. The basic financial statements provide important information that users rely on to make economic decisions. Financial statement users typically evaluate this information along three dimensions: liquidity, solvency, and profitability. Two common techniques are used to analyze a company's financial performance and condition: analytical methods and ratios. Both analytical methods and ratios can be used to compare a company's financial performance over time or to another company.

2. Analytical methods are used to compare items on a current financial statement with related items on earlier statements or to examine relationships within a financial statement. Horizontal analysis is the analysis of percentage increases and decreases in related items in comparative financial statements. The analysis of the relationship of each component in a financial statement to a significant total within the statement is called vertical analysis. In a common-sized statement, all items are expressed as percentages with no dollar amounts shown.

3. Liquidity analysis evaluates a company's ability to convert current assets into cash. Short-term creditors use liquidity analysis to evaluate a company's ability to repay short-term debts by focusing on a company's current position, accounts receivable, and inventory. The measures and ratios used to evaluate a company's liquidity include: (1) working capital, (2) current ratio, (3) quick ratio, (4) accounts receivable turnover, (5) number of days' sales in receivables, (6) inventory turnover, and (7) number of days' sales in inventory.

4. Solvency analysis evaluates the ability of a company to pay its long-term debts. Long-term creditors use solvency analysis to evaluate a company's ability to make its periodic interest payments and repay the face amount of bonds at maturity. Solvency is normally assessed by examining (1) the ratio of fixed assets to long-term liabilities, (2) the ratio of liabilities to stockholders' equity, and (3) the times interest earned ratio.

5. Profitability analysis focuses on the relationship between operating results (income statement) and assets (balance sheet). Profitability analyses include (1) the asset turnover ratio, (2) the return on total assets, (3) the return on stockholders' equity, (4) the return on common stockholders' equity, (5) earnings per share on common stock, (6) the price-earnings ratio, (7) dividends per share, and (8) dividend yield.

6. Public corporations issue annual reports summarizing their operating activities for the past year and plans for the future. In addition to the financial statements and accompanying notes, annual reports include management discussion and analysis (MD&A), a report on internal control, and a report on fairness of the financial statements. Management discussion and analysis includes management's analysis of current operations and its plans for the future. The report on internal control states management's responsibility for establishing and maintaining internal controls. The report on fairness of the financial statements provides the CPA firm's opinion on whether the financial statements fairly present the financial position, results of operations, and cash flows of the company.

Key Terms

accounts receivable
   analysis (674)
accounts receivable turnover (674)
accumulated other comprehensive
   income (694)
analytical methods (667)
asset turnover (681)
common-sized statement (671)
comprehensive income (693)
current position analysis (673)
current ratio (673)
dividend yield (686)
dividends per share (685)
earnings per share (EPS)
   on common stock (684)
fair value (693)

horizontal analysis (667)
inventory analysis (675)
inventory turnover (676)
leverage (682)
liquidity (666)
Management's Discussion and
   Analysis (MD&A) (689)
number of days' sales in
   inventory (676)
number of days' sales in
   receivables (675)
other comprehensive income (693)
price-earnings (P/E) ratio (685)
profitability (667)
quick assets (674)
quick ratio (674)

ratio of fixed assets to long-term
   liabilities (678)
ratio of liabilities to
   stockholders' equity (678)
ratios (667)
return on common stockholders'
   equity (683)
return on stockholders' equity (682)
return on total assets (681)
solvency (666)
times interest earned (679)
unrealized gain (693)
vertical analysis (669)
working capital (673)

Practice

Multiple-Choice Questions

1. What type of analysis is indicated by the following?

	Amount	Percent
Current assets	$100,000	20%
Property, plant, and equipment	400,000	80%
Total assets	$500,000	100%

   A. Vertical analysis
   B. Horizontal analysis
   C. Liquidity analysis
   D. Profitability analysis

2. The ability of a company to pay its debts is called:
   A. earnings per share.
   B. liquidity.
   C. profitability.
   D. solvency.

3. The ratio that measures how much of a company is financed by debt and equity is the:
   A. current ratio.
   B. ratio of fixed assets to long-term
        debt.
   C. ratio of liabilities to stockholders'
        equity.
   D. price-earnings ratio.

4. The ratio that measures the "instant" debt-paying ability of a firm, by focusing on current
   assets that can be easily converted to cash, is the:
   A. working capital.
   B. quick ratio.
   C. number of days' sales in inventory.
   D. ratio of fixed assets to long-term
        liabilities.

5. A measure useful in evaluating efficiency in the management of inventories is the:
   A. working capital.
   B. quick ratio.
   C. number of days' sales in inventory.
   D. ratio of fixed assets to long-term
        liabilities.

*Answers provided after Problem. Need more practice? Find additional multiple-choice
questions, exercises, and problems in CengageNOWv2.*

Exercises

SHOW ME HOW

1. Horizontal analysis

Obj. 2

The comparative temporary investments and inventory balances of a company follow.

	Current Year	Previous Year
Temporary investments	$59,280	$52,000
Inventory	70,680	76,000

Based on this information, what is the amount and percentage of increase or decrease that would be shown on a balance sheet with horizontal analysis?

SHOW ME HOW

2. Vertical analysis

Obj. 2

Income statement information for Axiom Corporation follows:

Sales	$725,000
Cost of goods sold	391,500
Gross profit	333,500

Prepare a vertical analysis of the income statement for Axiom Corporation.

SHOW ME HOW

3. Current position analysis

Obj. 3

The following items are reported on a company's balance sheet:

Cash	$160,000
Marketable securities	75,000
Accounts receivable (net)	65,000
Inventory	140,000
Accounts payable	200,000

Determine (A) the current ratio and (B) the quick ratio. (Round to one decimal place.)

SHOW ME HOW

4. Accounts receivable analysis

Obj. 3

A company reports the following:

Sales	$832,000
Average accounts receivable (net)	80,000

Determine (A) the accounts receivable turnover and (B) the number of days' sales in receivables. (Round to one decimal place.)

5. Inventory analysis

Obj. 3

SHOW ME HOW

A company reports the following:

Cost of goods sold	$630,000
Average inventory	90,000

Determine (A) the inventory turnover and (B) the number of days' sales in inventory. (Round to one decimal place.)

6. Long-term solvency analysis

Obj. 4

SHOW ME HOW

The following information was taken from Kellman Company's balance sheet:

Fixed assets (net)	$ 960,000
Long-term liabilities	800,000
Total liabilities	1,000,000
Total stockholders' equity	625,000

Determine the company's (A) ratio of fixed assets to long-term liabilities and (B) ratio of liabilities to stockholders' equity. (Round to one decimal place.)

SHOW ME HOW

7. Times interest earned

Obj. 4

A company reports the following:

Income before income tax	$4,000,000
Interest expense	400,000

Determine the times interest earned ratio. (Round to one decimal place.)

SHOW ME HOW

8. Asset turnover

Obj. 5

A company reports the following:

Sales	$1,800,000
Average total assets (excluding long-term investments)	1,125,000

Determine the asset turnover ratio. (Round to one decimal place.)

SHOW ME HOW

9. Return on total assets

Obj. 5

A company reports the following income statement and balance sheet information for the current year:

Net income	$ 250,000
Interest expense	100,000
Average total assets	2,500,000

Determine the return on total assets. (Round to one decimal place.)

SHOW ME HOW

10. Common stockholders' profitability analysis

Obj. 5

A company reports the following:

Net income	$ 375,000
Preferred dividends	75,000
Average stockholders' equity	2,500,000
Average common stockholders' equity	1,875,000

Determine (A) the return on stockholders' equity and (B) the return on common stockholders' equity. (Round to one decimal place.)

SHOW ME HOW

11. Earnings per share and price-earnings ratio

Obj. 5

A company reports the following:

Net income	$185,000
Preferred dividends	$25,000
Shares of common stock outstanding	100,000
Market price per share of common stock	$20

A. Determine the company's earnings per share on common stock.

B. Determine the company's price-earnings ratio. (Round to one decimal place.)

Answers provided after Problem. Need more practice? Find additional multiple-choice questions, exercises, and problems in CengageNOWv2.

Problem

Rainbow Paint Co.'s comparative financial statements for the years ending December 31, 20Y9 and 20Y8, are as follows. The market price of Rainbow Paint's common stock was $25 on December 31, 20Y9, and $30 on December 31, 20Y8.

Rainbow Paint Co. Comparative Income Statement For the Years Ended December 31, 20Y9 and 20Y8		
	20Y9	**20Y8**
Sales	$5,000,000	$3,200,000
Cost of goods sold...	3,400,000	2,080,000
Gross profit	$1,600,000	$1,120,000
Selling expenses	$ 650,000	$ 464,000
Administrative expenses.......................................	325,000	224,000
Total operating expenses	$ 975,000	$ 688,000
Income from operations	$ 625,000	$ 432,000
Other income...	25,000	19,200
	$ 650,000	$ 451,200
Other expense (interest)	105,000	64,000
Income before income tax	$ 545,000	$ 387,200
Income tax expense	300,000	176,000
Net income	$ 245,000	$ 211,200

Rainbow Paint Co. Comparative Retained Earnings Statement For the Years Ended December 31, 20Y9 and 20Y8		
	20Y9	**20Y8**
Retained earnings, January 1.......................................	$723,000	$581,800
Net income	245,000	211,200
Total	$968,000	$793,000
Dividends:		
On preferred stock..	$ 40,000	$ 40,000
On common stock...	45,000	30,000
Total dividends	$ 85,000	$ 70,000
Retained earnings, December 31	$883,000	$723,000

(Continued)

Rainbow Paint Co. Comparative Balance Sheet December 31, 20Y9 and 20Y8		
	20Y9	**20Y8**
Assets		
Current assets:		
Cash..	$ 175,000	$ 125,000
Temporary investments......................................	150,000	50,000
Accounts receivable (net)	425,000	325,000
Inventories...	720,000	480,000
Prepaid expenses...	30,000	20,000
Total current assets......................................	$1,500,000	$1,000,000
Long-term investments..	250,000	225,000
Property, plant, and equipment (net)	2,093,000	1,948,000
Total assets	$3,843,000	$3,173,000
Liabilities		
Current liabilities...	$ 750,000	$ 650,000
Long-term liabilities:		
Mortgage note payable, 10%, due in five years	$ 410,000	—
Bonds payable, 8%, due in fifteen years	800,000	$ 800,000
Total long-term liabilities	$1,210,000	$ 800,000
Total liabilities	$1,960,000	$1,450,000
Stockholders' Equity		
Preferred 8% stock, $100 par	$ 500,000	$ 500,000
Common stock, $10 par...	500,000	500,000
Retained earnings...	883,000	723,000
Total stockholders' equity......................................	$1,883,000	$1,723,000
Total liabilities and stockholders' equity.........................	$3,843,000	$3,173,000

Instructions

Determine the following measures for 20Y9 (round percentages and ratios other than per-share amounts to one decimal place):

1. Working capital
2. Current ratio
3. Quick ratio
4. Accounts receivable turnover
5. Number of days' sales in receivables
6. Inventory turnover
7. Number of days' sales in inventory
8. Ratio of fixed assets to long-term liabilities
9. Ratio of liabilities to stockholders' equity
10. Times interest earned
11. Asset turnover
12. Return on total assets
13. Return on stockholders' equity
14. Return on common stockholders' equity
15. Earnings per share on common stock
16. Price-earnings ratio
17. Dividends per share
18. Dividend yield

Need more practice? Find additional multiple-choice questions, exercises, and problems in CengageNOWv2.

Answers

Multiple-Choice Questions

1. **A** Vertical analysis compares each component in a financial statement to a total within the statement. Horizontal analysis (answer B) compares the amount and percentage of each item on the most recent statement to the same item on an earlier statement. Liquidity analysis (answer C) evaluates the ability of a company to convert current assets into cash. Profitability analysis (answer D) focuses on the ability of a company to earn profits by examining the relationship between operating results and the resources available.

2. **D** Solvency is a company's ability to pay its debts. Earnings per share (answer A) measures the share of profits that are earned by a share of common stock. Liquidity (answer B) is the ability of a company to convert current assets into cash. Profitability (answer C) focuses on the ability of a company to earn profits by examining the relationship between operating results and the resources available.

3. **C** The ratio of liabilities to stockholders' equity measures the relationship between debt and equity, which measures how much of the company is financed with debt and equity. The current ratio (answer A) measures a company's ability to pay its current liabilities. The ratio of fixed assets to long-term liabilities (answer B) provides a measure of whether noteholders or bondholders will be paid. The price-earnings ratio (answer D) measures a company's future earnings prospects.

4. **D** The quick ratio measures the "instant" debt-paying ability of a company. Working capital (answer A) is the difference between current assets and current liabilities. The number of days' sales in inventory (answer C) is a measure of the length of time it takes to purchase, sell, and replace the inventory. The ratio of fixed assets to long-term liabilities (answer D) provides a measure of whether noteholders or bondholders will be paid.

5. **C** The number of days' sales in inventory is a measure of the length of time it takes to purchase, sell, and replace the inventory. Working capital (answer A) is the difference between current assets and current liabilities. The quick ratio (answer B) measures the "instant" debt-paying ability of a company. The ratio of fixed assets to long-term liabilities (answer D) provides a measure of whether noteholders or bondholders will be paid.

Exercises

1. Temporary investments.................... $7,280 increase ($59,280 – $52,000), or 14%

   Inventory .... $5,320 decrease ($70,680 – $76,000), or –7%

2.

	Amount	Percentage	
Sales	$725,000	100%	($725,000 ÷ $725,000)
Cost of goods sold	391,500	54%	($391,500 ÷ $725,000)
Gross profit...................................	$333,500	46%	($333,500 ÷ $725,000)

3. A.   Current Ratio = Current Assets ÷ Current Liabilities

   = ($160,000 + $75,000 + $65,000 + $140,000) ÷ $200,000

   = 2.2

   B.   Quick Ratio = Quick Assets ÷ Current Liabilities

   = ($160,000 + $75,000 + $65,000) ÷ $200,000

   = 1.5

4. A.   Accounts Receivable Turnover = Sales ÷ Average Accounts Receivable

   = $832,000 ÷ $80,000

   = 10.4

(Continued)

B. Number of Days' Sales in Receivables $= \dfrac{\text{Average Accounts Receivable}}{\text{Average Daily Sales}}$

$$= \$80{,}000 \div (\$832{,}000 \div 365)$$

$$= \$80{,}000 \div \$2{,}279$$

$$= 35.1 \text{ days}$$

5. A. Inventory Turnover = Cost of Goods Sold ÷ Average Inventory

$$= \$630{,}000 \div \$90{,}000$$

$$= 7.0$$

B. Number of Days' Sales in Inventory $= \dfrac{\text{Average Inventory}}{\text{Average Daily Cost of Goods Sold}}$

$$= \$90{,}000 \div (\$630{,}000 \div 365)$$

$$= \$90{,}000 \div \$1{,}726$$

$$= 52.1 \text{ days}$$

6. A. Ratio of Fixed Assets to Long-Term Liabilities $= \dfrac{\text{Fixed Assets}}{\text{Long-Term Liabilities}}$

$$= \$960{,}000 \div \$800{,}000$$

$$= 1.2$$

B. Ratio of Liabilities to Stockholders' Equity $= \dfrac{\text{Total Liabilities}}{\text{Total Stockholders' Equity}}$

$$= \$1{,}000{,}000 \div \$625{,}000$$

$$= 1.6$$

7. Times Interest Earned $= \dfrac{\text{Income Before Income Tax + Interest Expense}}{\text{Interest Expense}}$

$$= \dfrac{\$4{,}000{,}000 + \$400{,}000}{\$400{,}000}$$

$$= 11.0$$

8. Asset Turnover = Sales ÷ Average Total Assets

$$= \$1{,}800{,}000 \div \$1{,}125{,}000$$

$$= 1.6$$

9. Return on Total Assets $= \dfrac{\text{Net Income + Interest Expense}}{\text{Average Total Assets}}$

$$= \dfrac{\$250{,}000 + \$100{,}000}{\$2{,}500{,}000}$$

$$= \dfrac{\$350{,}000}{\$2{,}500{,}000}$$

$$= 14.0\%$$

10. A. Return on Stockholders' Equity $= \dfrac{\text{Net Income}}{\text{Average Stockholders' Equity}}$

$$= \$375{,}000 \div \$2{,}500{,}000$$

$$= 15.0\%$$

B. Return on Common Stockholders' Equity $= \dfrac{\text{Net Income} - \text{Preferred Dividends}}{\text{Average Common Stockholders' Equity}}$

$$= \dfrac{\$375,000 - \$75,000}{\$1,875,000}$$

$$= 16.0\%$$

11. A. Earnings per Share on Common Stock $= \dfrac{\text{Net Income} - \text{Preferred Dividends}}{\text{Shares of Common Stock Outstanding}}$

$$= (\$185,000 - \$25,000) \div \$100,000$$

$$= \$1.60$$

B. Price-Earnings Ratio $= \dfrac{\text{Market Price per Share of Common Stock}}{\text{Earnings per Share on Common Stock}}$

$$= \$20.00 \div \$1.60$$

$$= 12.5$$

Need more help? Watch step-by-step videos of how to compute answers to these Exercises in CengageNOWv2.

Problem

(Ratios are rounded to one decimal place.)

1. Working capital: $750,000

    $1,500,000 − $750,000

2. Current ratio: 2.0

    $1,500,000 ÷ $750,000

3. Quick ratio: 1.0

    $750,000 ÷ $750,000

4. Accounts receivable turnover: 13.3

    $5,000,000 ÷ [($425,000 + $325,000) ÷ 2]

5. Number of days' sales in receivables: 27.4 days

    $5,000,000 ÷ 365 days = $13,699

    $375,000 ÷ $13,699

6. Inventory turnover: 5.7

    $3,400,000 ÷ [($720,000 + $480,000) ÷ 2]

7. Number of days' sales in inventory: 64.4 days

    $3,400,000 ÷ 365 days = $9,315

    $600,000 ÷ $9,315

8. Ratio of fixed assets to long-term liabilities: 1.7

    $2,093,000 ÷ $1,210,000

9. Ratio of liabilities to stockholders' equity: 1.0

    $1,960,000 ÷ $1,883,000

10. Times interest earned: 6.2

    ($545,000 + $105,000) ÷ $105,000

11. Asset turnover: 1.5

    $5,000,000 ÷ [($3,593,000 + $2,948,000) ÷ 2]

12. Return on total assets: 10.0%

    ($245,000 + $105,000) ÷ [($3,843,000 + $3,173,000) ÷ 2]

(Continued)

13. Return on stockholders' equity: 13.6%

    $245,000 ÷ [($1,883,000 + $1,723,000) ÷ 2]

14. Return on common stockholders' equity: 15.7%

    ($245,000 − $40,000) ÷ [($1,383,000 + $1,223,000) ÷ 2]

15. Earnings per share on common stock: $4.10

    ($245,000 − $40,000) ÷ 50,000 shares

16. Price-earnings ratio: 6.1

    $25 ÷ $4.10

17. Dividends per share: $0.90

    $45,000 ÷ 50,000 shares

18. Dividend yield: 3.6%

    $0.90 ÷ $25

Discussion Questions

1. Briefly explain the difference between liquidity, solvency, and profitability analysis.

2. What is the advantage of using comparative statements for financial analysis rather than statements for a single date or period?

3. A company's current year net income (after income tax) is 25% larger than that of the preceding year. Does this indicate improved operating performance? Why?

4. How would the current and quick ratios of a service business compare?

5. A. Why is a high inventory turnover considered to be a positive indicator?

   B. Is it possible to have a high inventory turnover and a high number of days' sales in inventory? Why?

6. What do the following data, taken from a comparative balance sheet, indicate about the company's ability to borrow additional long-term debt in the current year as compared to the preceding year?

	Current Year	Preceding Year
Fixed assets (net)	$1,260,000	$1,360,000
Total long-term liabilities	300,000	400,000

7. A. How does the rate earned on total assets differ from the rate earned on stockholders' equity?

   B. Which ratio is normally higher? Why?

8. **Kroger**, a grocery store, recently had a price-earnings ratio of 13.7, while the average price-earnings ratio in the grocery store industry was 22.5. What might explain this difference?

REAL WORLD

9. The dividend yield of **Suburban Propane** was 7.7% in a recent year, and the dividend yield of **Google** was 0% in the same year. What might explain the difference between these ratios?

REAL WORLD

10. Describe two reports provided by independent auditors in the annual report to shareholders.

Basic Exercises

SHOW ME HOW

BE 14-1 Horizontal analysis   Obj. 2

The comparative accounts payable and long-term debt balances for a company follow.

	Current Year	Previous Year
Accounts payable	$111,000	$100,000
Long-term debt	132,680	124,000

Based on this information, what is the amount and percentage of increase or decrease that would be shown on a balance sheet with horizontal analysis?

SHOW ME HOW

BE 14-2 Vertical analysis   Obj. 2

Income statement information for Einsworth Corporation follows:

Sales	$1,200,000
Cost of goods sold	780,000
Gross profit	420,000

Prepare a vertical analysis of the income statement for Einsworth Corporation. (Round percentages to one decimal place.)

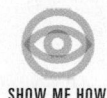
SHOW ME HOW

BE 14-3 Current position analysis   Obj. 3

The following items are reported on a company's balance sheet:

Cash	$210,000
Marketable securities	120,000
Accounts receivable (net)	110,000
Inventory	160,000
Accounts payable	200,000

Determine (A) the current ratio and (B) the quick ratio. (Round to one decimal place.)

SHOW ME HOW

BE 14-4 Accounts receivable analysis   Obj. 3

A company reports the following:

Sales	$3,150,000
Average accounts receivable (net)	210,000

Determine (A) the accounts receivable turnover and (B) the number of days' sales in receivables. (Round to one decimal place.)

SHOW ME HOW

BE 14-5 Inventory analysis   Obj. 3

A company reports the following:

Cost of goods sold	$435,000
Average inventory	72,500

Determine (A) the inventory turnover and (B) the number of days' sales in inventory. (Round to one decimal place.)

SHOW ME HOW

BE 14-6 Long-term solvency analysis   Obj. 4

The following information was taken from Charu Company's balance sheet:

Fixed assets (net)	$860,000
Long-term liabilities	200,000
Total liabilities	600,000
Total stockholders' equity	250,000

Determine the company's (A) ratio of fixed assets to long-term liabilities and (B) ratio of liabilities to stockholders' equity. (Round to one decimal place.)

SHOW ME HOW

BE 14-7 Times interest earned   Obj. 4

A company reports the following:

Income before income tax	$8,000,000
Interest expense	500,000

Determine the number of times interest charges are earned. (Round to one decimal place.)

SHOW ME HOW

BE 14-8   Asset turnover   Obj. 5

A company reports the following:

Sales	$4,400,000
Average total assets (excluding long-term investments)	2,000,000

Determine the asset turnover ratio. (Round percentages to one decimal place.)

SHOW ME HOW

BE 14-9   Return on total assets   Obj. 5

A company reports the following income statement and balance sheet information for the current year:

Net income	$ 410,000
Interest expense	90,000
Average total assets	5,000,000

Determine the return on total assets. (Round percentages to one decimal place.)

SHOW ME HOW

BE 14-10   Common stockholders' profitability analysis   Obj. 5

A company reports the following:

Net income	$1,000,000
Preferred dividends	50,000
Average stockholders' equity	6,250,000
Average common stockholders' equity	3,800,000

Determine (A) the return on stockholders' equity and (B) the return on common stockholders' equity. (Round percentages to one decimal place.)

SHOW ME HOW

BE 14-11   Earnings per share and price-earnings ratio   Obj. 5

A company reports the following:

Net income	$410,000
Preferred dividends	$60,000
Shares of common stock outstanding	50,000
Market price per share of common stock	$84

A. Determine the company's earnings per share on common stock.

B. Determine the company's price-earnings ratio. (Round to one decimal place.)

Exercises

✔ A. Current year net
income: $360,000; 9%
of sales

SHOW ME HOW

EX 14-1   Vertical analysis of income statement   Obj. 2

Revenue and expense data for Innovation Quarter Inc. for two recent years are as follows:

	Current Year	Previous Year
Sales	$4,000,000	$3,600,000
Cost of goods sold	2,280,000	1,872,000
Selling expenses	600,000	648,000
Administrative expenses	520,000	360,000
Income tax expense	240,000	216,000

A. Prepare an income statement in comparative form, stating each item for both years as a percent of sales. (Round to the nearest whole percentage.)

B. ▬▬▶ Comment on the significant changes disclosed by the comparative income statement.

✔ **A. Current fiscal year income from continuing operations, 13.0% of revenues**

EXCEL TEMPLATE   REAL WORLD

EX 14-2 Vertical analysis of income statement   Obj. 2

The following comparative income statement (in thousands of dollars) for two recent fiscal years was adapted from the annual report of **Speedway Motorsports, Inc.**, owner and operator of several major motor speedways, such as the Atlanta, Texas, and Las Vegas Motor Speedways.

	Current Year	Previous Year
Revenues:		
Admissions	$116,034	$130,239
Event-related revenue	151,562	163,621
NASCAR broadcasting revenue	192,662	185,394
Other operating revenue	29,902	26,951
Total revenues	$490,160	$506,205
Expenses and other:		
Direct expense of events	$101,402	$106,204
NASCAR purse and sanction fees	122,950	120,146
Other direct expenses	18,908	20,352
General and administrative	183,215	241,223
Total expenses and other	$426,475	$487,925
Income from continuing operations	$ 63,685	$ 18,280

A. Prepare a comparative income statement for these two years in vertical form, stating each item as a percent of revenues. (Round percentages to one decimal place.)

B. ➤ Comment on the significant changes.

EX 14-3 Common-sized income statement   Obj. 2

✔ **A. Tannenhill net income: $120,000; 3.0% of sales**

SHOW ME HOW

Revenue and expense data for the current calendar year for Tannenhill Company and for the electronics industry are as follows. Tannenhill's data are expressed in dollars. The electronics industry averages are expressed in percentages.

	Tannenhill Company	Electronics Industry Average
Sales	$4,000,000	100.0%
Cost of goods sold	2,120,000	60.0
Gross profit	$1,880,000	40.0%
Selling expenses	$1,080,000	24.0%
Administrative expenses	640,000	14.0
Total operating expenses	$1,720,000	38.0%
Operating income	$ 160,000	2.0%
Other income	120,000	3.0
	$ 280,000	5.0%
Other expense	80,000	2.0
Income before income tax	$ 200,000	3.0%
Income tax expense	80,000	2.0
Net income	$ 120,000	1.0%

A. Prepare a common-sized income statement comparing the results of operations for Tannenhill Company with the industry average. (Round to the nearest whole percentage.)

B. ➤ As far as the data permit, comment on significant relationships revealed by the comparisons.

✔ Retained earnings,
Current year, 36.8%

SHOW ME HOW   EXCEL TEMPLATE

EX 14-4 Vertical analysis of balance sheet
Obj. 2

Balance sheet data for Alvarez Company on December 31, the end of two recent fiscal years, follow:

	Current Year	Previous Year
Current assets	$2,500,000	$1,840,000
Property, plant, and equipment	5,600,000	6,072,000
Intangible assets	1,900,000	1,288,000
Current liabilities	2,000,000	1,380,000
Long-term liabilities	3,400,000	3,680,000
Common stock	920,000	920,000
Retained earnings	3,680,000	3,220,000

Prepare a comparative balance sheet for both years, stating each asset as a percent of total assets and each liability and stockholders' equity item as a percent of the total liabilities and stockholders' equity. (Round percentages to one decimal place.)

✔ A. Net income
increase, 66.0%

SHOW ME HOW   EXCEL TEMPLATE

EX 14-5 Horizontal analysis of the income statement
Obj. 2

Income statement data for Winthrop Company for two recent years ended December 31 are as follows:

	Current Year	Previous Year
Sales	$2,280,000	$2,000,000
Cost of goods sold	1,960,000	1,750,000
Gross profit	$ 320,000	$ 250,000
Selling expenses	$ 156,500	$ 125,000
Administrative expenses	122,000	100,000
Total operating expenses	$ 278,500	$ 225,000
Income before income tax	$ 41,500	$ 25,000
Income tax expense	16,600	10,000
Net income	$ 24,900	$ 15,000

A. Prepare a comparative income statement with horizontal analysis, indicating the increase (decrease) for the current year when compared with the previous year. (Round percentages to one decimal place.)

B. ➤ What conclusions can be drawn from the horizontal analysis?

✔ A. Current year
working capital,
$1,170,000

SHOW ME HOW

EX 14-6 Current position analysis
Obj. 3

The following data were taken from the balance sheet of Nilo Company at the end of two recent fiscal years:

	Current Year	Previous Year
Current assets:		
Cash	$ 414,000	$ 320,000
Marketable securities	496,800	336,000
Accounts and notes receivable (net)	619,200	464,000
Inventories	351,900	272,000
Prepaid expenses	188,100	208,000
Total current assets	$2,070,000	$1,600,000
Current liabilities:		
Accounts and notes payable (short-term)	$ 675,000	$ 600,000
Accrued liabilities	225,000	200,000
Total current liabilities	$ 900,000	$ 800,000

A. Determine for each year (1) the working capital, (2) the current ratio, and (3) the quick ratio. (Round ratios to one decimal place.)

B. ➤ What conclusions can be drawn from these data as to the company's ability to meet its currently maturing debts?

EX 14-7 Current position analysis   **Obj. 3**

✔ A. (1) Current year's current ratio, 1.1

REAL WORLD

PepsiCo, Inc., the parent company of Frito-Lay snack foods and Pepsi beverages, had the following current assets and current liabilities at the end of two recent years:

	Current Year (in millions)	Previous Year (in millions)
Cash and cash equivalents	$ 6,297	$ 4,067
Short-term investments, at cost	322	358
Accounts and notes receivable, net	7,041	6,912
Inventories	3,581	3,827
Prepaid expenses and other current assets	1,479	2,277
Short-term obligations	4,815	6,205
Accounts payable	12,274	11,949

A. Determine the (1) current ratio and (2) quick ratio for both years. (Round to one decimal place.)

B. ➤ What conclusions can you draw from these data about PepsiCo's liquidity?

EX 14-8 Current position analysis   **Obj. 3**

The bond indenture for the 10-year, 9% debenture bonds issued January 2, 20Y5, required working capital of $100,000, a current ratio of 1.5, and a quick ratio of 1.0 at the end of each calendar year until the bonds mature. At December 31, 20Y6, the three measures were computed as follows:

1.	Current assets:		
	Cash......................................	$102,000	
	Temporary investments	48,000	
	Accounts and notes receivable (net)...........	120,000	
	Inventories.................................	36,000	
	Prepaid expenses............................	24,000	
	Intangible assets	124,800	
	Property, plant, and equipment...............	55,200	
	Total current assets (net)		$510,000
	Current liabilities:		
	Accounts and short-term notes payable	$ 96,000	
	Accrued liabilities...........................	204,000	
	Total current liabilities		300,000
	Working capital		$210,000
2.	Current ratio	1.7	$510,000 ÷ $300,000
3.	Quick ratio..................................	1.2	$115,200 ÷ $ 96,000

A. List the errors in the determination of the three measures of current position analysis.

B. ➤ Is the company satisfying the terms of the bond indenture?

EX 14-9 Accounts receivable analysis   **Obj. 3**

✔ A. Accounts receivable turnover, 20Y3, 8.2

SHOW ME HOW

The following data are taken from the financial statements of Sigmon Inc. Terms of all sales are 2/10, n/45.

	20Y3	20Y2	20Y1
Accounts receivable, end of year	$ 725,000	$ 650,000	$600,000
Sales on account	5,637,500	4,687,500	

A. For 20Y2 and 20Y3, determine (1) the accounts receivable turnover and (2) the number of days' sales in receivables. (Round to the nearest dollar and one decimal place.)

B. ➤ What conclusions can be drawn from these data concerning accounts receivable and credit policies?

EX 14-10   Accounts receivable analysis   Obj. 3

✔ A. 1. Lestrade, 7.0

Xavier Stores Company and Lestrade Stores Inc. are large retail department stores. Both companies offer credit to their customers through their own credit card operations. Information from the financial statements for both companies for two recent years is as follows (in millions):

	Xavier	Lestrade
Sales	$8,500,000	$4,585,000
Credit card receivables—beginning	820,000	600,000
Credit card receivables—ending	880,000	710,000

A. Determine the (1) accounts receivable turnover and (2) the number of days' sales in receivables for both companies. (Round to one decimal place.)

B. ━━━➤ Compare the two companies with regard to their credit card policies.

EX 14-11   Inventory analysis   Obj. 3

✔ A. Inventory turnover, current year, 9.0

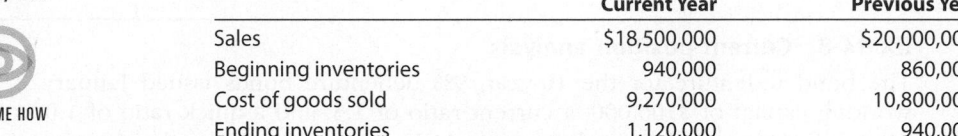

SHOW ME HOW

The following data were extracted from the income statement of Keever Inc.:

	Current Year	Previous Year
Sales	$18,500,000	$20,000,000
Beginning inventories	940,000	860,000
Cost of goods sold	9,270,000	10,800,000
Ending inventories	1,120,000	940,000

A. Determine for each year (1) the inventory turnover and (2) the number of days' sales in inventory. (Round to the nearest dollar and one decimal place.)

B. ━━━➤ What conclusions can be drawn from these data concerning the inventories?

EX 14-12   Inventory analysis   Obj. 3

✔ A. QT inventory turnover, 32.1

QT, Inc. and Elppa Computers, Inc. compete with each other in the personal computer market. QT assembles computers to customer orders, building and delivering a computer within four days of a customer entering an order online. Elppa, on the other hand, builds computers for inventory prior to receiving an order. These computers are sold from inventory once an order is received. Selected financial information for both companies from recent financial statements follows (in millions):

	QT	Elppa
Sales	$56,940	$120,357
Cost of goods sold	44,754	92,385
Inventory, beginning of period	1,382	6,317
Inventory, end of period	1,404	7,490

A. Determine for both companies (1) the inventory turnover and (2) the number of days' sales in inventory. (Round to one decimal place.)

B. ━━━➤ Interpret the inventory ratios in the context of both companies' operating strategies.

EX 14-13   Ratio of liabilities to stockholders' equity and number of times   Obj. 4
interest earned

✔ A. Ratio of liabilities to stockholders' equity, current year, 0.9

The following data were taken from the financial statements of Hunter Inc. for December 31 of two recent years:

	Current Year	Previous Year
Accounts payable	$ 924,000	$ 800,000
Current maturities of serial bonds payable	200,000	200,000
Serial bonds payable, 10%	1,000,000	1,200,000
Common stock, $10 par value	250,000	250,000
Paid-in capital in excess of par	1,250,000	1,250,000
Retained earnings	860,000	500,000

The income before income tax was $480,000 and $420,000 for the current and previous years, respectively.

A. Determine the ratio of liabilities to stockholders' equity at the end of each year. (Round to one decimal place.)

B. Determine the times interest earned ratio for both years. (Round to one decimal place.)

C. ➤ What conclusions can be drawn from these data as to the company's ability to meet its currently maturing debts?

EX 14-14 Ratio of liabilities to stockholders' equity and times interest earned   Obj. 4

✔ A. Hasbro, 1.9

REAL WORLD

Hasbro, Inc. and **Mattel, Inc.**, are the two largest toy companies in North America. Condensed liabilities and stockholders' equity from a recent balance sheet are shown for each company as follows (in thousands):

	Hasbro	Mattel
Liabilities:		
Current liabilities	$ 960,435	$ 1,716,012
Long-term debt	1,396,421	1,100,000
Deferred liabilities	461,152	643,729
Total liabilities	$ 2,818,008	$ 3,459,741
Shareholders' equity:		
Common stock	$ 104,847	$ 441,369
Additional paid in capital	655,943	1,727,682
Retained earnings	3,354,545	3,515,181
Accumulated other comprehensive loss and other equity items	(72,307)	(464,486)
Treasury stock, at cost	(2,535,649)	(2,152,702)
Total stockholders' equity	$ 1,507,379	$ 3,067,044
Total liabilities and stockholders' equity	$ 4,325,387	$ 6,526,785

The income from operations and interest expense from the income statement for each company were as follows (in thousands):

	Hasbro	Mattel
Income from operations (before income tax)	$453,402	$945,045
Interest expense	117,403	88,835

A. Determine the ratio of liabilities to stockholders' equity for both companies. (Round to one decimal place.)

B. Determine the times interest earned ratio for both companies. (Round to one decimal place.)

C. ➤ Interpret the ratio differences between the two companies.

EX 14-15 Ratio of liabilities to stockholders' equity and ratio of fixed assets to long-term liabilities   Obj. 4

✔ A. Mondelez International, Inc., 1.3

REAL WORLD

Recent balance sheet information for two companies in the food industry, **Mondelez International, Inc.** and **The Hershey Company**, is as follows (in thousands):

	Mondelez	Hershey
Net property, plant, and equipment	$10,010,000	$1,674,071
Current liabilities	14,873,000	1,471,110
Long-term debt	15,574,000	1,530,967
Other long-term liabilities	12,816,000	716,013
Stockholders' equity	32,215,000	1,036,749

A. Determine the ratio of liabilities to stockholders' equity for both companies. (Round to one decimal place.)

B. Determine the ratio of fixed assets to long-term liabilities for both companies. (Round to one decimal place.)

C. ➤ Interpret the ratio differences between the two companies.

EX 14-16 Asset turnover
Obj. 5

✔ A. YRC, 1.5

REAL WORLD

Three major segments of the transportation industry are motor carriers, such as **YRC Worldwide**; railroads, such as **Union Pacific**; and transportation logistics services, such as **C.H. Robinson Worldwide, Inc.** Recent financial statement information for these three companies follows (in thousands):

	YRC	Union Pacific	C.H. Robinson
Sales	$4,334,640	$16,965,000	$9,274,305
Average total assets	2,812,504	42,636,000	1,914,974

A. Determine the asset turnover for all three companies. (Round to one decimal place.)

B. ▬▬▶ Assume that the asset turnover for each company represents their respective industry segment. Interpret the differences in the asset turnover in terms of the operating characteristics of each of the respective segments.

EX 14-17 Profitability ratios
Obj. 5

✔ A. return on total assets, 20Y7, 12.0%
SHOW ME HOW

The following selected data were taken from the financial statements of Vidahill Inc. for December 31, 20Y7, 20Y6, and 20Y5:

	20Y7	20Y6	20Y5
Total assets	$4,800,000	$4,400,000	$4,000,000
Notes payable (8% interest)	2,250,000	2,250,000	2,250,000
Common stock	250,000	250,000	250,000
Preferred 4% stock, $100 par (no change during year)	500,000	500,000	500,000
Retained earnings	1,574,000	1,222,000	750,000

The 20Y7 net income was $372,000, and the 20Y6 net income was $492,000. No dividends on common stock were declared between 20Y5 and 20Y7. Preferred dividends were declared and paid in full in 20Y6 and 20Y7.

A. Determine the return on total assets, the rate earned on stockholders' equity, and the return on common stockholders' equity for the years 20Y6 and 20Y7. (Round percentages to one decimal place.)

B. ▬▬▶ What conclusions can be drawn from these data as to the company's profitability?

EX 14-18 Profitability ratios
Obj. 5

✔A. Year 3 return on total assets, 12.2%

REAL WORLD

Ralph Lauren Corporation sells apparel through company-owned retail stores. Recent financial information for Ralph Lauren follows (in thousands):

	Fiscal Year 3	Fiscal Year 2	
Net income	$567,600	$479,500	
Interest expense	18,300	22,200	

	Fiscal Year 3	Fiscal Year 2	Fiscal Year 1
Total assets (at end of fiscal year)	$4,981,100	$4,648,900	$4,356,500
Total stockholders' equity (at end of fiscal year)	3,304,700	3,116,600	2,735,100

Assume the apparel industry average return on total assets is 8.0%, and the average rate earned on stockholders' equity is 10.0% for the year ended April 2, Year 3.

A. Determine the return on total assets for Ralph Lauren for fiscal Years 2 and 3. (Round percentages to one decimal place.)

B. Determine the return on stockholders' equity for Ralph Lauren for fiscal Years 2 and 3. (Round percentages to one decimal place.)

C. ▬▬▶ Evaluate the two-year trend for the profitability ratios determined in (A) and (B).

D. ▬▬▶ Evaluate Ralph Lauren's profit performance relative to the industry.

EX 14-19 Six measures of solvency or profitability Obj. 4, 5

✔ C. Asset turnover, 4.2 The following data were taken from the financial statements of Gates Inc. for the current fiscal year.

Property, plant, and equipment (net)		$ 3,200,000
Liabilities:		
Current liabilities.......................................	$1,000,000	
Note payable, 6%, due in 15 years	2,000,000	
Total liabilities		$ 3,000,000
Stockholders' equity:		
Preferred $10 stock, $100 par (no change during year) ...		$ 1,000,000
Common stock, $10 par (no change during year)		2,000,000
Retained earnings:		
Balance, beginning of year............................	$1,570,000	
Net income	930,000 $2,500,000	
Preferred dividends	$ 100,000	
Common dividends	400,000 500,000	
Balance, end of year..................................		2,000,000
Total stockholders' equity...............................		$ 5,000,000
Sales		$18,900,000
Interest expense		$ 120,000

Assuming that long-term investments totaled $3,000,000 throughout the year and that total assets were $7,000,000 at the beginning of the current fiscal year, determine the following: (A) ratio of fixed assets to long-term liabilities, (B) ratio of liabilities to stockholders' equity, (C) asset turnover, (D) return on total assets, (E) return on stockholders' equity, and (F) return on common stockholders' equity. (Round ratios and percentages to one decimal place as appropriate.)

EX 14-20 Five measures of solvency or profitability Obj. 4, 5

✔ C. Price-earnings ratio, 10.0 The balance sheet for Garcon Inc. at the end of the current fiscal year indicated the following:

Bonds payable, 8%	$5,000,000
Preferred $4 stock, $50 par	2,500,000
Common stock, $10 par	5,000,000

Income before income tax was $3,000,000, and income taxes were $1,200,000 for the current year. Cash dividends paid on common stock during the current year totaled $1,200,000. The common stock was selling for $32 per share at the end of the year. Determine each of the following: (A) times interest earned ratio (B) earnings per share on common stock, (C) price-earnings ratio, (D) dividends per share of common stock, and (E) dividend yield. (Round ratios and percentages to one decimal place, except for per-share amounts.)

EX 14-21 Earnings per share, price-earnings ratio, dividend yield Obj. 5

✔ B. Price-earnings ratio, 15.0 The following information was taken from the financial statements of Tolbert Inc. for December 31 of the current fiscal year:

SHOW ME HOW

Common stock, $20 par (no change during the year)	$10,000,000
Preferred $4 stock, $40 par (no change during the year)	2,500,000

The net income was $1,750,000 and the declared dividends on the common stock were $1,125,000 for the current year. The market price of the common stock is $45 per share.

For the common stock, determine (A) the earnings per share, (B) the price-earnings ratio, (C) the dividends per share, and (D) the dividend yield. (Round ratios and percentages to one decimal place, except for per-share amounts.)

REAL WORLD

✔ A. Google, 23.8

EX 14-22   Price-earnings ratio; dividend yield   **Obj. 5**

The table that follows shows the stock price, earnings per share, and dividends per share for three companies for a recent year:

	Price	Earnings per Share	Dividends per Share
Deere & Company	$ 86.20	$ 8.71	$2.04
Google	873.32	36.75	0.00
The Coca-Cola Company	39.79	1.97	1.02

A. Determine the price-earnings ratio and dividend yield for the three companies. (Round ratios and percentages to one decimal place as appropriate.)

B. ➤ Explain the differences in these ratios across the three companies.

Appendix 1

EX 14-23   Earnings per share, discontinued operations

✔ B. Earnings per share on common stock, $7.60

The net income reported on the income statement of Cutler Co. was $4,000,000. There were 500,000 shares of $10 par common stock and 100,000 shares of $2 preferred stock outstanding throughout the current year. The income statement included a gain on discontinued operations of $400,000 after applicable income tax. Determine the per-share figures for common stock for (A) income before discontinued operations and (B) net income.

Appendix 1

EX 14-24   Income statement and earnings per share for discontinued operations

Apex Inc. reports the following for a recent year:

Income from continuing operations before income tax	$1,000,000
Loss from discontinued operations	$240,000*
Weighted average number of shares outstanding	20,000
Applicable tax rate	40%

*Net of any tax effect.

A. Prepare a partial income statement for Apex Inc., beginning with income from continuing operations before income tax.

B. Determine the earnings per common share for Apex Inc., including per-share amounts for unusual items.

Appendix 1

EX 14-25   Unusual items

➤ Explain whether Colston Company correctly reported the following items in the financial statements:

A. In a recent year, the company discovered a clerical error in the prior year's accounting records. As a result, the reported net income for the previous year was overstated by $45,000. The company corrected this error by restating the prior-year financial statements.

B. In a recent year, the company voluntarily changed its method of accounting for long-term construction contracts from the percentage of completion method to the completed contract method. Both methods are acceptable under generally acceptable accounting principles. The cumulative effect of this change was reported as a separate component of income in the current period income statement.

Appendix 2

EX 14-26   Comprehensive Income

Anson Industries, Inc. reported the following information on its 20Y1 income statement:

Sales	$4,000,000
Cost of goods sold	2,300,000
Operating expenses	1,000,000
Income tax expense	280,000
Other comprehensive income	450,000

Prepare the following for Anson Industries, Inc.:

A. Income statement, including comprehensive income.

B. Income statement and a separate statement of comprehensive income.

Problems: Series A

SHOW ME HOW   EXCEL TEMPLATE

GENERAL LEDGER

PR 14-1A Horizontal analysis of income statement

Obj. 2

✔ 1. Sales, 12% increase

For 20Y2, McDade Company reported a decline in net income. At the end of the year, T. Burrows, the president, is presented with the following condensed comparative income statement:

McDade Company
Comparative Income Statement
For the Years Ended December 31, 20Y2 and 20Y1

	20Y2	20Y1
Sales	$16,800,000	$ 15,000,000
Cost of goods sold......................................	11,500,000	10,000,000
Gross profit	$ 5,300,000	$ 5,000,000
Selling expenses	$ 1,770,000	$ 1,500,000
Administrative expenses................................	1,220,000	1,000,000
Total operating expenses	$ 2,990,000	$ 2,500,000
Income from operations	$ 2,310,000	$ 2,500,000
Other income	256,950	225,000
Income before income tax	$ 2,556,950	$ 2,725,000
Income tax expense	1,413,000	1,500,000
Net income	$ 1,153,950	$ 1,225,000

Instructions

1. Prepare a comparative income statement with horizontal analysis for the two-year period, using 20Y1 as the base year. (Round percentages to one decimal place.)

2. ➡ To the extent the data permit, comment on the significant relationships revealed by the horizontal analysis prepared in (1).

PR 14-2A Vertical analysis of income statement

Obj. 2

✔ 1. Net income, 20Y2, 10.0%

GENERAL LEDGER   EXCEL TEMPLATE

For 20Y2, Tri-Comic Company initiated a sales promotion campaign that included the expenditure of an additional $50,000 for advertising. At the end of the year, Lumi Neer, the president, is presented with the following condensed comparative income statement:

Tri-Comic Company
Comparative Income Statement
For the Years Ended December 31, 20Y2 and 20Y1

	20Y2	20Y1
Sales	$1,500,000	$1,250,000
Cost of goods sold......................................	510,000	475,000
Gross profit	$ 990,000	$ 775,000
Selling expenses	$ 270,000	$ 200,000
Administrative expenses................................	180,000	156,250
Total operating expenses	$ 450,000	$ 356,250
Income from operations	$ 540,000	$ 418,750
Other income	60,000	50,000
Income before income tax	$ 600,000	$ 468,750
Income tax expense	450,000	375,000
Net income	$ 150,000	$ 93,750

(Continued)

Instructions

1. Prepare a comparative income statement for the two-year period, presenting an analysis of each item in relationship to sales for each of the years. (Round percentages to one decimal place.)

2. ➤ To the extent the data permit, comment on the significant relationships revealed by the vertical analysis prepared in (1).

PR 14-3A Effect of transactions on current position analysis   Obj. 3

✔ 2. C. Current
ratio, 2.0

EXCEL TEMPLATE

Data pertaining to the current position of Forte Company follow:

Cash	$412,500
Marketable securities	187,500
Accounts and notes receivable (net)	300,000
Inventories	700,000
Prepaid expenses	50,000
Accounts payable	200,000
Notes payable (short-term)	250,000
Accrued expenses	300,000

Instructions

1. Compute (A) the working capital, (B) the current ratio, and (C) the quick ratio. (Round to one decimal place.)

2. List the following captions on a sheet of paper:

Transaction	Working Capital	Current Ratio	Quick Ratio

Compute the working capital, the current ratio, and the quick ratio after each of the following transactions, and record the results in the appropriate columns. *Consider each transaction separately* and assume that only that transaction affects the data given. (Round to one decimal place.)

A. Sold marketable securities at no gain or loss, $70,000.
B. Paid accounts payable, $125,000.
C. Purchased goods on account, $110,000.
D. Paid notes payable, $100,000.
E. Declared a cash dividend, $150,000.
F. Declared a common stock dividend on common stock, $50,000.
G. Borrowed cash from bank on a long-term note, $225,000.
H. Received cash on account, $125,000.
I. Issued additional shares of stock for cash, $600,000.
J. Paid cash for prepaid expenses, $10,000.

PR 14-4A Measures of liquidity, solvency, and profitability   Obj. 3, 4, 5

✔ 5. Number of days'
sales in receivables, 18.3

EXCEL TEMPLATE

The comparative financial statements of Marshall Inc. are as follows. The market price of Marshall common stock was $82.60 on December 31, 20Y2.

Marshall Inc.
Comparative Retained Earnings Statement
For the Years Ended December 31, 20Y2 and 20Y1

	20Y2	20Y1
Retained earnings, January 1	$3,704,000	$3,264,000
Net income	600,000	550,000
Total	$4,304,000	$3,814,000
Dividends:		
On preferred stock	$ 10,000	$ 10,000
On common stock	100,000	100,000
Total dividends	$ 110,000	$ 110,000
Retained earnings, December 31	$4,194,000	$3,704,000

Marshall Inc.
Comparative Income Statement
For the Years Ended December 31, 20Y2 and 20Y1

	20Y2	20Y1
Sales	$10,850,000	$10,000,000
Cost of goods sold	6,000,000	5,450,000
Gross profit	$ 4,850,000	$ 4,550,000
Selling expenses	$ 2,170,000	$ 2,000,000
Administrative expenses	1,627,500	1,500,000
Total operating expenses	$ 3,797,500	$ 3,500,000
Income from operations	$ 1,052,500	$ 1,050,000
Other income	99,500	20,000
	$ 1,152,000	$ 1,070,000
Other expense (interest)	132,000	120,000
Income before income tax	$ 1,020,000	$ 950,000
Income tax expense	420,000	400,000
Net income	$ 600,000	$ 550,000

Marshall Inc.
Comparative Balance Sheet
December 31, 20Y2 and 20Y1

	20Y2	20Y1
Assets		
Current assets:		
Cash	$1,050,000	$ 950,000
Marketable securities	301,000	420,000
Accounts receivable (net)	585,000	500,000
Inventories	420,000	380,000
Prepaid expenses	108,000	20,000
Total current assets	$ 2,464,000	$2,270,000
Long-term investments	800,000	800,000
Property, plant, and equipment (net)	5,760,000	5,184,000
Total assets	$ 9,024,000	$8,254,000
Liabilities		
Current liabilities	$ 880,000	$ 800,000
Long-term liabilities:		
Mortgage note payable, 6%,	$ 200,000	$ 0
Bonds payable, 4%,	3,000,000	3,000,000
Total long-term liabilities	$ 3,200,000	$3,000,000
Total liabilities	$ 4,080,000	$3,800,000
Stockholders' Equity		
Preferred 4% stock, $5 par	$ 250,000	$ 250,000
Common stock, $5 par	500,000	500,000
Retained earnings	4,194,000	3,704,000
Total stockholders' equity	$ 4,944,000	$4,454,000
Total liabilities and stockholders' equity	$ 9,024,000	$8,254,000

Instructions

Determine the following measures for 20Y2 (round to one decimal place, including percentages, except for per-share amounts):

1. Working capital
2. Current ratio
3. Quick ratio
4. Accounts receivable turnover
5. Number of days' sales in receivables
6. Inventory turnover
7. Number of days' sales in inventory
8. Ratio of fixed assets to long-term liabilities
9. Ratio of liabilities to stockholders' equity
10. Times interest earned

(Continued)

11. Asset turnover
12. Return on total assets
13. Return on stockholders' equity
14. Return on common stockholders' equity
15. Earnings per share on common stock
16. Price-earnings ratio
17. Dividends per share of common stock
18. Dividend yield

PR 14-5A   Solvency and profitability trend analysis   Obj. 4, 5

Addai Company has provided the following comparative information:

	20Y8	20Y7	20Y6	20Y5	20Y4
Net income	$ 273,406	$ 367,976	$ 631,176	$ 884,000	$ 800,000
Interest expense	616,047	572,003	528,165	495,000	440,000
Income tax expense	31,749	53,560	106,720	160,000	200,000
Total assets (ending balance)	4,417,178	4,124,350	3,732,443	3,338,500	2,750,000
Total stockholders' equity (ending balance)	3,706,557	3,433,152	3,065,176	2,434,000	1,550,000
Average total assets	4,270,764	3,928,396	3,535,472	3,044,250	2,475,000
Average total stockholders' equity	3,569,855	3,249,164	2,749,588	1,992,000	1,150,000

You have been asked to evaluate the historical performance of the company over the last five years.

Selected industry ratios have remained relatively steady at the following levels for the last five years:

	20Y4–20Y8
Return on total assets	28%
Return on stockholders' equity	18%
Times interest earned	2.7
Ratio of liabilities to stockholders' equity	0.4

Instructions

1. Prepare four line graphs with the ratio on the vertical axis and the years on the horizontal axis for the following four ratios (round to one decimal place):

   A. Return on total assets

   B. Return on stockholders' equity

   C. Times interest earned

   D. Ratio of liabilities to stockholders' equity

   Display both the company ratio and the industry benchmark on each graph. That is, each graph should have two lines.

2. ➤ Prepare an analysis of the graphs in (1).

Problems: Series B

PR 14-1B Horizontal analysis of Income statement

Obj. 2

✔ 1. Sales,
30.0% increase

SHOW ME HOW

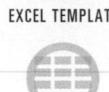

EXCEL TEMPLATE

GENERAL LEDGER

For 20Y2, Macklin Inc. reported a significant increase in net income. At the end of the year, John Mayer, the president, is presented with the following condensed comparative income statement:

Macklin Inc.
Comparative Income Statement
For the Years Ended December 31, 20Y2 and 20Y1

	20Y2	20Y1
Sales	$910,000	$700,000
Cost of goods sold.....................................	441,000	350,000
Gross profit	$469,000	$350,000
Selling expenses	$139,150	$115,000
Administrative expenses.............................	99,450	85,000
Total operating expenses	$238,600	$200,000
Income from operations	$230,400	$150,000
Other income..	65,000	50,000
Income before income tax	$295,400	$200,000
Income tax expense	65,000	50,000
Net income...	$230,400	$150,000

Instructions

1. Prepare a comparative income statement with horizontal analysis for the two-year period, using 20Y1 as the base year. (Round percentages to one decimal place.)

2. ➤ To the extent the data permit, comment on the significant relationships revealed by the horizontal analysis prepared in (1).

PR 14-2B Vertical analysis of income statement

Obj. 2

✔ 1. Net income, 20Y1,
14.0%

GENERAL LEDGER

EXCEL TEMPLATE

For 20Y2, Fielder Industries Inc. initiated a sales promotion campaign that included the expenditure of an additional $40,000 for advertising. At the end of the year, Leif Grando, the president, is presented with the following condensed comparative income statement:

Fielder Industries Inc.
Comparative Income Statement
For the Years Ended December 31, 20Y2 and 20Y1

	20Y2	20Y1
Sales	$1,300,000	$1,180,000
Cost of goods sold.....................................	682,500	613,600
Gross profit	$ 617,500	$ 566,400
Selling expenses	$ 260,000	$ 188,800
Adminstrative expenses	169,000	177,000
Total operating expenses	$ 429,000	$ 365,800
Income from operations	$ 188,500	$ 200,600
Other income..	78,000	70,800
Income before income tax	$ 266,500	$ 271,400
Income tax expense	117,000	106,200
Net income...	$ 149,500	$ 165,200

Instructions

1. Prepare a comparative income statement for the two-year period, presenting an analysis of each item in relationship to sales for each of the years. (Round percentages to one decimal place.)

2. ➤ To the extent the data permit, comment on the significant relationships revealed by the vertical analysis prepared in (1).

✔ 2. G. Quick
ratio, 1.6

EXCEL TEMPLATE

PR 14-3B   Effect of transactions on current position analysis   Obj. 3

Data pertaining to the current position of Lucroy Industries Inc. follows:

Cash	$ 800,000
Marketable securities	550,000
Accounts and notes receivable (net)	850,000
Inventories	700,000
Prepaid expenses	300,000
Accounts payable	1,200,000
Notes payable (short-term)	700,000
Accrued expenses	100,000

Instructions

1. Compute (A) the working capital, (B) the current ratio, and (C) the quick ratio. (Round to one decimal place.)

2. List the following captions on a sheet of paper:

Transaction	Working Capital	Current Ratio	Quick Ratio

Compute the working capital, the current ratio, and the quick ratio after each of the following transactions, and record the results in the appropriate columns. *Consider each transaction separately* and assume that only that transaction affects the data given. (Round to one decimal place.)

A. Sold marketable securities at no gain or loss, $500,000.
B. Paid accounts payable, $287,500.
C. Purchased goods on account, $400,000.
D. Paid notes payable, $125,000.
E. Declared a cash dividend, $325,000.
F. Declared a common stock dividend on common stock, $150,000.
G. Borrowed cash from bank on a long-term note, $1,000,000.
H. Received cash on account, $75,000.
I. Issued additional shares of stock for cash, $2,000,000.
J. Paid cash for prepaid expenses, $200,000.

PR 14-4B   Measures of liquidity, solvency and profitability   Obj. 3, 4, 5

✔ 9. Ratio of liabilities
to stockholders'
equity, 0.4

EXCEL TEMPLATE

The comparative financial statements of Stargel Inc. are as follows. The market price of Stargel common stock was $119.70 on December 31, 20Y2.

Stargel Inc.
Comparative Retained Earnings Statement
For the Years Ended December 31, 20Y2 and 20Y1

	20Y2	20Y1
Retained earnings, January 1	$5,375,000	$4,545,000
Net income	900,000	925,000
Total	$6,275,000	$5,470,000
Dividends:		
On preferred stock	$ 45,000	$ 45,000
On common stock	50,000	50,000
Total dividends	$ 95,000	$ 95,000
Retained earnings, December 31	$6,180,000	$5,375,000

Stargel Inc.
Comparative Income Statement
For the Years Ended December 31, 20Y2 and 20Y1

	20Y2	20Y1
Sales	$10,000,000	$9,400,000
Cost of goods sold	5,350,000	4,950,000
Gross profit	$ 4,650,000	$4,450,000
Selling expenses	$ 2,000,000	$1,880,000
Administrative expenses	1,500,000	1,410,000
Total operating expenses	$ 3,500,000	$3,290,000
Income from operations	$ 1,150,000	$1,160,000
Other income	150,000	140,000
	$ 1,300,000	$1,300,000
Other expense (interest)	170,000	150,000
Income before income tax	$ 1,130,000	$1,150,000
Income tax expense	230,000	225,000
Net income	$ 900,000	$ 925,000

Stargel Inc.
Comparative Balance Sheet
December 31, 20Y2 and 20Y1

	20Y2	20Y1
Assets		
Current assets:		
Cash	$ 500,000	$ 400,000
Marketable securities	1,010,000	1,000,000
Accounts receivable (net)	740,000	510,000
Inventories	1,190,000	950,000
Prepaid expenses	250,000	229,000
Total current assets	$3,690,000	$3,089,000
Long-term investments	2,350,000	2,300,000
Property, plant, and equipment (net)	3,740,000	3,366,000
Total assets	$9,780,000	$8,755,000
Liabilities		
Current liabilities	$ 900,000	$ 880,000
Long-term liabilities:		
Mortgage note payable, 10%	$ 200,000	$ 0
Bonds payable, 10%	1,500,000	1,500,000
Total long-term liabilities	$1,700,000	$1,500,000
Total liabilities	$2,600,000	$2,380,000
Stockholders' Equity		
Preferred $0.90 stock, $10 par	$ 500,000	$ 500,000
Common stock, $5 par	500,000	500,000
Retained earnings	6,180,000	5,375,000
Total stockholders' equity	$7,180,000	$6,375,000
Total liabilities and stockholders' equity	$9,780,000	$8,755,000

Instructions
Determine the following measures for 20Y2 (round to one decimal place including percentages, except for per-share amounts):

1. Working capital
2. Current ratio
3. Quick ratio
4. Accounts receivable turnover
5. Number of days' sales in receivables
6. Inventory turnover

(Continued)

7. Number of days' sales in inventory
8. Ratio of fixed assets to long-term liabilities
9. Ratio of liabilities to stockholders' equity
10. Times interest earned
11. Asset turnover
12. Return on total assets
13. Return on stockholders' equity
14. Return on common stockholders' equity
15. Earnings per share on common stock
16. Price-earnings ratio
17. Dividends per share of common stock
18. Dividend yield

PR 14-5B Solvency and profitability trend analysis   Obj. 4, 5

✔ 1.B. 20Y7, 32.9%   Crosby Company has provided the following comparative information:

	20Y8	20Y7	20Y6	20Y5	20Y4
Net income	$ 5,571,720	$ 3,714,480	$ 2,772,000	$ 1,848,000	$ 1,400,000
Interest expense	1,052,060	891,576	768,600	610,000	500,000
Income tax expense	1,225,572	845,222	640,320	441,600	320,000
Total assets (ending balance)	29,378,491	22,598,839	17,120,333	12,588,480	10,152,000
Total stockholders' equity (ending balance)	18,706,200	13,134,480	9,420,000	6,648,000	4,800,000
Average total assets	25,988,665	19,859,586	14,854,406	11,370,240	8,676,000
Average total stockholders' equity	15,920,340	11,277,240	8,034,000	5,724,000	4,100,000

You have been asked to evaluate the historical performance of the company over the last five years.

Selected industry ratios have remained relatively steady at the following levels for the last five years:

	20Y4–20Y8
Return on total assets	19%
Return on stockholders' equity	26%
Times interest earned	3.4
Ratio of liabilities to stockholders' equity	1.4

Instructions

1. Prepare four line graphs with the ratio on the vertical axis and the years on the horizontal axis for the following four ratios (round ratios and percentages to one decimal place):

   A. Return on total assets

   B. Return on stockholders' equity

   C. Times interest earned

   D. Ratio of liabilities to stockholders' equity

   Display both the company ratio and the industry benchmark on each graph. That is, each graph should have two lines.

2. ━━━▶ Prepare an analysis of the graphs in (1).

Nike, Inc., Problem

Financial Statement Analysis

The financial statements for **Nike, Inc.**, are presented in Appendix B at the end of the text. The following additional information is available (in thousands):

Accounts receivable at May 31, 2013	$ 3,117
Inventories at May 31, 2013	3,484
Total assets at May 31, 2013	17,545
Stockholders' equity at May 31, 2013	11,081

Instructions

1. Determine the following measures for the fiscal years ended May 31, 2015, and May 31, 2014. (Round ratios and percentages to one decimal place.)

   A. Working capital

   B. Current ratio

   C. Quick ratio

   D. Accounts receivable turnover

   E. Number of days' sales in receivables

   F. Inventory turnover

   G. Number of days' sales in inventory

   H. Ratio of liabilities to stockholders' equity

   I. Asset turnover

   J. Return on total assets, assuming interest expense is $28 million for the year ending May 31, 2015, and $24 million for the year ending May 31, 2014

   K. Return on common stockholders' equity

   L. Price-earnings ratio, assuming that the market price was $101.67 per share on May 29, 2015, and $76.91 per share on May 30, 2014

   M. Percentage relationship of net income to sales

2. ▬▬▶ What conclusions can be drawn from these analyses?

Analysis for Decision Making

REAL WORLD

ADM-1 Continuing Company Analysis—Amazon, Best Buy, and Walmart: Common-sized income statements

The condensed income statements through income from operations for **Amazon.com, Inc.**, **Best Buy, Inc.**, and **Walmart Stores, Inc.** for a recent fiscal year follow (in millions):

	Amazon	Best Buy	Walmart
Sales	$88,988	$40,339	$485,651
Cost of sales	62,752	31,292	365,086
Gross profit	$26,236	$ 9,047	$120,565
Selling, general, and administrative expenses	26,058	7,592	93,418
Operating expenses	0	5	0
Income from operations	$ 178	$ 1,450	$ 27,147

1. Prepare comparative common-sized income statements for each company. (Round percentages to one decimal place.)

2. ▬▬▶ Use the common-sized analysis to compare the financial performance of the three companies.

REAL WORLD

ADM-2   Deere: Profitability analysis

Deere & Company manufactures and distributes farm and construction machinery that it sells around the world. In addition to its manufacturing operations, Deere's credit division loans money to customers to finance the purchase of their farm and construction equipment.

The following information is available for three recent years (in millions except per-share amounts):

	Year 3	Year 2	Year 1
Net income (loss)	$3,064.7	$2,799.9	$1,865.0
Preferred dividends	$ 0.00	$ 0.00	$ 0.00
Interest expense	$ 782.8	$ 759.4	$ 811.4
Shares outstanding for computing earnings per share	397	417	424
Cash dividend per share	$ 1.79	$ 1.52	$ 1.16
Average total assets	$ 52,237	$ 45,737	$ 42,200
Average stockholders' equity	$ 6,821	$ 6,545	$ 5,555
Average stock price per share	$ 79.27	$ 80.48	$ 61.18

1. Calculate the following ratios for each year (round ratios and percentages to one decimal place, except for per-share amounts):
   A. Return on total assets
   B. Return on stockholders' equity
   C. Earnings per share
   D. Dividend yield
   E. Price-earnings ratio
2. ➤ Based on these data, evaluate Deere's profitability.

ADM-3   Marriott and Hyatt: Solvency and profitability analysis

Marriott International, Inc., and **Hyatt Hotels Corporation** are two major owners and managers of lodging and resort properties in the United States. Abstracted income statement information for the two companies is as follows for a recent year (in millions):

	Marriott	Hyatt
Operating profit before other expenses and interest	$ 677	$ 39
Other income (expenses)	54	118
Interest expense	(180)	(54)
Income before income taxes	$ 551	$103
Income tax expense	93	37
Net income	$ 458	$ 66

Balance sheet information is as follows:

	Marriott	Hyatt
Total liabilities	$7,398	$2,125
Total stockholders' equity	1,585	5,118
Total liabilities and stockholders' equity	$8,983	$7,243

The average liabilities, average stockholders' equity, and average total assets are as follows:

	Marriott	Hyatt
Average total liabilities	$7,095	$2,132
Average total stockholders' equity	1,364	5,067
Average total assets	8,458	7,199

1. Determine the following ratios for both companies (round ratios and percentages to one decimal place):
   A. Return on total assets
   B. Return on stockholders' equity
   C. Times interest earned
   D. Ratio of total liabilities to stockholders' equity
2. ➤ Based on the information in (1), analyze and compare the two companies' solvency and profitability.

Take It Further

ETHICS

TIF 14-1   Ethics in Action

Rodgers Industries Inc. completed its fiscal year on December 31. Near the end of the fiscal year, the company's internal audit department determined that an important internal control procedure had not been functioning properly. The head of internal audit, Dash Riprock, reported the internal control failure to the company's chief accountant, Todd Barleywine. Todd reported the failure to the company's chief financial officer, Josh McCoy. After discussing the issue, Josh instructed Todd not to inform the external auditors of the internal control failure and to fix the problem quietly after the end of the fiscal year. The external auditors did not discover the internal control failure during their audit. In March, after the audit was complete, the company released its annual report, including associated reports by management. As chief financial officer, Josh authorized the release of Management's Report on Internal Control, which stated that the management team believed that the company's internal controls were effective during the period covered by the annual report.

Did Josh behave ethically in this situation? Explain your answer.

REAL WORLD

TIF 14-2   Team Activity

In teams, select a public company that interests you. Obtain the company's most recent annual report on Form 10-K. The Form 10-K is a company's annually required filing with the Securities and Exchange Commission (SEC). It includes the company's financial statements and accompanying notes. The Form 10-K can be obtained either (A) from the investor relations section of the company's Web site or (B) by using the company search feature of the SEC's EDGAR database service found at www.sec.gov/edgar/searchedgar/companysearch.html.

1. Based on the information in the company's annual report, compute the following for the most recent year (round ratios and percentages to one decimal place, except for per-share amounts):
    A. Liquidity analysis:
        (1) Working capital
        (2) Current ratio
        (3) Quick ratio
        (4) Accounts receivable turnover
        (5) Number of days' sales in receivables
        (6) Inventory turnover
        (7) Number of days' sales in inventory
    B. Solvency analysis:
        (1) Ratio of liabilities to stockholders' equity
        (2) Times interest earned
    C. Profitability analysis:
        (1) Asset turnover
        (2) Return on total assets
        (3) Return on stockholders' equity
        (4) Earnings per share
        (5) Price-earnings ratio
2. Evaluate the company's liquidity, solvency, and profitability.

TIF 14-3 Communication

The president of Freeman Industries Inc. made the following statement in the annual report to shareholders: "The founding family and majority shareholders of the company do not believe in using debt to finance future growth. The founding family learned from hard experience during Prohibition and the Great Depression that debt can cause loss of flexibility and eventual loss of corporate control. The company will not place itself at such risk again. As such, all future growth will be financed either by stock sales to the public or by internally generated resources."

➤ Write a brief memo to the company's president, Boss Freeman, outlining the errors in his logic.

Appendices

Appendix A

Interest Tables

Present Value of $1 at Compound Interest Due in *n* Periods

Periods	4.0%	4.5%	5%	5.5%	6%	6.5%	7%
1	0.96154	0.95694	0.95238	0.94787	0.94340	0.93897	0.93458
2	0.92456	0.91573	0.90703	0.89845	0.89000	0.88166	0.87344
3	0.88900	0.87630	0.86384	0.85161	0.83962	0.82785	0.81630
4	0.85480	0.83856	0.82270	0.80722	0.79209	0.77732	0.76290
5	0.82193	0.80245	0.78353	0.76513	0.74726	0.72988	0.71299
6	0.79031	0.76790	0.74622	0.72525	0.70496	0.68533	0.66634
7	0.75992	0.73483	0.71068	0.68744	0.66506	0.64351	0.62275
8	0.73069	0.70319	0.67684	0.65160	0.62741	0.60423	0.58201
9	0.70259	0.67290	0.64461	0.61763	0.59190	0.56735	0.54393
10	0.67556	0.64393	0.61391	0.58543	0.55839	0.53273	0.50835
11	0.64958	0.61620	0.58468	0.55491	0.52679	0.50021	0.47509
12	0.62460	0.58966	0.55684	0.52598	0.49697	0.46968	0.44401
13	0.60057	0.56427	0.53032	0.49856	0.46884	0.44102	0.41496
14	0.57748	0.53997	0.50507	0.47257	0.44230	0.41410	0.38782
15	0.55526	0.51672	0.48102	0.44793	0.41727	0.38883	0.36245
16	0.53391	0.49447	0.45811	0.42458	0.39365	0.36510	0.33873
17	0.51337	0.47318	0.43630	0.40245	0.37136	0.34281	0.31657
18	0.49363	0.45280	0.41552	0.38147	0.35034	0.32189	0.29586
19	0.47464	0.43330	0.39573	0.36158	0.33051	0.30224	0.27651
20	0.45639	0.41464	0.37689	0.34273	0.31180	0.28380	0.25842
21	0.43883	0.39679	0.35894	0.32486	0.29416	0.26648	0.24151
22	0.42196	0.37970	0.34185	0.30793	0.27751	0.25021	0.22571
23	0.40573	0.36335	0.32557	0.29187	0.26180	0.23494	0.21095
24	0.39012	0.34770	0.31007	0.27666	0.24698	0.22060	0.19715
25	0.37512	0.33273	0.29530	0.26223	0.23300	0.20714	0.18425
26	0.36069	0.31840	0.28124	0.24856	0.21981	0.19450	0.17220
27	0.34682	0.30469	0.26785	0.23560	0.20737	0.18263	0.16093
28	0.33348	0.29157	0.25509	0.22332	0.19563	0.17148	0.15040
29	0.32065	0.27902	0.24295	0.21168	0.18456	0.16101	0.14056
30	0.30832	0.26700	0.23138	0.20064	0.17411	0.15119	0.13137
31	0.29646	0.25550	0.22036	0.19018	0.16425	0.14196	0.12277
32	0.28506	0.24450	0.20987	0.18027	0.15496	0.13329	0.11474
33	0.27409	0.23397	0.19987	0.17087	0.14619	0.12516	0.10723
34	0.26355	0.22390	0.19035	0.16196	0.13791	0.11752	0.10022
35	0.25342	0.21425	0.18129	0.15352	0.13011	0.11035	0.09366
40	0.20829	0.17193	0.14205	0.11746	0.09722	0.08054	0.06678
45	0.17120	0.13796	0.11130	0.08988	0.07265	0.05879	0.04761
50	0.14071	0.11071	0.08720	0.06877	0.05429	0.04291	0.03395

Present Value of $1 at Compound Interest Due in *n* Periods

Periods	8%	9%	10%	11%	12%	13%	14%
1	0.92593	0.91743	0.90909	0.90090	0.89286	0.88496	0.87719
2	0.85734	0.84168	0.82645	0.81162	0.79719	0.78315	0.76947
3	0.79383	0.77218	0.75131	0.73119	0.71178	0.69305	0.67497
4	0.73503	0.70843	0.68301	0.65873	0.63552	0.61332	0.59208
5	0.68058	0.64993	0.62092	0.59345	0.56743	0.54276	0.51937
6	0.63017	0.59627	0.56447	0.53464	0.50663	0.48032	0.45559
7	0.58349	0.54703	0.51316	0.48166	0.45235	0.42506	0.39964
8	0.54027	0.50187	0.46651	0.43393	0.40388	0.37616	0.35056
9	0.50025	0.46043	0.42410	0.39092	0.36061	0.33288	0.30751
10	0.46319	0.42241	0.38554	0.35218	0.32197	0.29459	0.26974
11	0.42888	0.38753	0.35049	0.31728	0.28748	0.26070	0.23662
12	0.39711	0.35553	0.31863	0.28584	0.25668	0.23071	0.20756
13	0.36770	0.32618	0.28966	0.25751	0.22917	0.20416	0.18207
14	0.34046	0.29925	0.26333	0.23199	0.20462	0.18068	0.15971
15	0.31524	0.27454	0.23939	0.20900	0.18270	0.15989	0.14010
16	0.29189	0.25187	0.21763	0.18829	0.16312	0.14150	0.12289
17	0.27027	0.23107	0.19784	0.16963	0.14564	0.12522	0.10780
18	0.25025	0.21199	0.17986	0.15282	0.13004	0.11081	0.09456
19	0.23171	0.19449	0.16351	0.13768	0.11611	0.09806	0.08295
20	0.21455	0.17843	0.14864	0.12403	0.10367	0.08678	0.07276
21	0.19866	0.16370	0.13513	0.11174	0.09256	0.07680	0.06383
22	0.18394	0.15018	0.12285	0.10067	0.08264	0.06796	0.05599
23	0.17032	0.13778	0.11168	0.09069	0.07379	0.06014	0.04911
24	0.15770	0.12640	0.10153	0.08170	0.06588	0.05323	0.04308
25	0.14602	0.11597	0.09230	0.07361	0.05882	0.04710	0.03779
26	0.13520	0.10639	0.08391	0.06631	0.05252	0.04168	0.03315
27	0.12519	0.09761	0.07628	0.05974	0.04689	0.03689	0.02908
28	0.11591	0.08955	0.06934	0.05382	0.04187	0.03264	0.02551
29	0.10733	0.08215	0.06304	0.04849	0.03738	0.02889	0.02237
30	0.09938	0.07537	0.05731	0.04368	0.03338	0.02557	0.01963
31	0.09202	0.06915	0.05210	0.03935	0.02980	0.02262	0.01722
32	0.08520	0.06344	0.04736	0.03545	0.02661	0.02002	0.01510
33	0.07889	0.05820	0.04306	0.03194	0.02376	0.01772	0.01325
34	0.07305	0.05339	0.03914	0.02878	0.02121	0.01568	0.01162
35	0.06763	0.04899	0.03558	0.02592	0.01894	0.01388	0.01019
40	0.04603	0.03184	0.02209	0.01538	0.01075	0.00753	0.00529
45	0.03133	0.02069	0.01372	0.00913	0.00610	0.00409	0.00275
50	0.02132	0.01345	0.00852	0.00542	0.00346	0.00222	0.00143

Present Value of Ordinary Annuity of $1 per Period

Periods	4.0%	4.5%	5%	5.5%	6%	6.5%	7%
1	0.96154	0.95694	0.95238	0.94787	0.94340	0.93897	0.93458
2	1.88609	1.87267	1.85941	1.84632	1.83339	1.82063	1.80802
3	2.77509	2.74896	2.72325	2.69793	2.67301	2.64848	2.62432
4	3.62990	3.58753	3.54595	3.50515	3.46511	3.42580	3.38721
5	4.45182	4.38998	4.32948	4.27028	4.21236	4.15568	4.10020
6	5.24214	5.15787	5.07569	4.99553	4.91732	4.84101	4.76654
7	6.00205	5.89270	5.78637	5.68297	5.58238	5.48452	5.38929
8	6.73274	6.59589	6.46321	6.33457	6.20979	6.08875	5.97130
9	7.43533	7.26879	7.10782	6.95220	6.80169	6.65610	6.51523
10	8.11090	7.91272	7.72173	7.53763	7.36009	7.18883	7.02358
11	8.76048	8.52892	8.30641	8.09254	7.88687	7.68904	7.49867
12	9.38507	9.11858	8.86325	8.61852	8.38384	8.15873	7.94269
13	9.98565	9.68285	9.39357	9.11708	8.85268	8.59974	8.35765
14	10.56312	10.22283	9.89864	9.58965	9.29498	9.01384	8.74547
15	11.11839	10.73955	10.37966	10.03758	9.71225	9.40267	9.10791
16	11.65230	11.23402	10.83777	10.46216	10.10590	9.76776	9.44665
17	12.16567	11.70719	11.27407	10.86461	10.47726	10.11058	9.76322
18	12.65930	12.15999	11.68959	11.24607	10.82760	10.43247	10.05909
19	13.13394	12.59329	12.08532	11.60765	11.15812	10.73471	10.33560
20	13.59033	13.00794	12.46221	11.95038	11.46992	11.01851	10.59401
21	14.02916	13.40472	12.82115	12.27524	11.76408	11.28498	10.83553
22	14.45112	13.78442	13.16300	12.58317	12.04158	11.53520	11.06124
23	14.85684	14.14777	13.48857	12.87504	12.30338	11.77014	11.27219
24	15.24696	14.49548	13.79864	13.15170	12.55036	11.99074	11.46933
25	15.62208	14.82821	14.09394	13.41393	12.78336	12.19788	11.65358
26	15.98277	15.14661	14.37519	13.66250	13.00317	12.39237	11.82578
27	16.32959	15.45130	14.64303	13.89810	13.21053	12.57500	11.98671
28	16.66306	15.74287	14.89813	14.12142	13.40616	12.74648	12.13711
29	16.98371	16.02189	15.14107	14.33310	13.59072	12.90749	12.27767
30	17.29203	16.28889	15.37245	14.53375	13.76483	13.05868	12.40904
31	17.58849	16.54439	15.59281	14.72393	13.92909	13.20063	12.53181
32	17.87355	16.78889	15.80268	14.90420	14.08404	13.33393	12.64656
33	18.14765	17.02286	16.00255	15.07507	14.23023	13.45909	12.75379
34	18.41120	17.24676	16.19290	15.23703	14.36814	13.57661	12.85401
35	18.66461	17.46101	16.37419	15.39055	14.49825	13.68696	12.94767
40	19.79277	18.40158	17.15909	16.04612	15.04630	14.14553	13.33171
45	20.72004	19.15635	17.77407	16.54773	15.45583	14.48023	13.60552
50	21.48218	19.76201	18.25593	16.93152	15.76186	14.72452	13.80075

Present Value of Ordinary Annuity of $1 per Period

Periods	8%	9%	10%	11%	12%	13%	14%
1	0.92593	0.91743	0.90909	0.90090	0.89286	0.88496	0.87719
2	1.78326	1.75911	1.73554	1.71252	1.69005	1.66810	1.64666
3	2.57710	2.53129	2.48685	2.44371	2.40183	2.36115	2.32163
4	3.31213	3.23972	3.16987	3.10245	3.03735	2.97447	2.91371
5	3.99271	3.88965	3.79079	3.69590	3.60478	3.51723	3.43308
6	4.62288	4.48592	4.35526	4.23054	4.11141	3.99755	3.88867
7	5.20637	5.03295	4.86842	4.71220	4.56376	4.42261	4.28830
8	5.74664	5.53482	5.33493	5.14612	4.96764	4.79677	4.63886
9	6.24689	5.99525	5.75902	5.53705	5.32825	5.13166	4.94637
10	6.71008	6.41766	6.14457	5.88923	5.65022	5.42624	5.21612
11	7.13896	6.80519	6.49506	6.20652	5.93770	5.68694	5.45273
12	7.53608	7.16073	6.81369	6.49236	6.19437	5.91765	5.66029
13	7.90378	7.48690	7.10336	6.74987	6.42355	6.12181	5.84236
14	8.22424	7.78615	7.36669	6.96187	6.62817	6.30249	6.00207
15	8.55948	8.06069	7.60608	7.19087	6.81086	6.46238	6.14217
16	8.85137	8.31256	7.82371	7.37916	6.97399	6.60388	6.26506
17	9.12164	8.54363	8.02155	7.54879	7.11963	6.72909	6.37286
18	9.37189	8.75563	8.20141	7.70162	7.24967	6.83991	6.46742
19	9.60360	8.95011	8.36492	7.83929	7.36578	6.93797	6.55037
20	9.81815	9.12855	8.51356	7.96333	7.46944	7.02475	6.62313
21	10.01680	9.29224	8.64869	8.07507	7.56200	7.10155	6.68696
22	10.20074	9.44243	8.77154	8.17574	7.64465	7.16951	6.74294
23	10.37106	9.58021	8.88322	8.26643	7.71843	7.22966	6.79206
24	10.52876	9.70661	8.98474	8.34814	7.78432	7.28288	6.83514
25	10.67478	9.82258	9.07704	8.42174	7.84314	7.32998	6.87293
26	10.80998	9.92897	9.16095	8.48806	7.89566	7.37167	6.90608
27	10.93516	10.02658	9.23722	8.54780	7.94255	7.40856	6.93515
28	11.05108	10.11613	9.30657	8.60162	7.98442	7.44120	6.96066
29	11.15841	10.19828	9.36961	8.65011	8.02181	7.47009	6.98304
30	11.25778	10.27365	9.42691	8.69379	8.05518	7.49565	7.00266
31	11.34980	10.34280	9.47901	8.73315	8.08499	7.51828	7.01988
32	11.43500	10.40624	9.52638	8.76860	8.11159	7.53830	7.03498
33	11.51389	10.46444	9.56943	8.80054	8.13535	7.55602	7.04823
34	11.58693	10.51784	9.60857	8.82932	8.15656	7.57170	7.05985
35	11.65457	10.56682	9.64416	8.85524	8.17550	7.58557	7.07005
40	11.92461	10.75736	9.77905	8.95105	8.24378	7.63438	7.10504
45	12.10840	10.88120	9.86281	9.00791	8.28252	7.66086	7.12322
50	12.23348	10.96168	9.91481	9.04165	8.30450	7.67524	7.13266

Nike Inc., Form 10-K for the Fiscal Year Ended May 31, 2015

UNITED STATES
SECURITIES AND EXCHANGE COMMISSION
Washington, D.C. 20549

FORM 10-K

(Mark One)

☑ ANNUAL REPORT PURSUANT TO SECTION 13 OR 15(D) OF THE SECURITIES EXCHANGE ACT OF 1934
FOR THE FISCAL YEAR ENDED MAY 31, 2015

OR

☐ TRANSITION REPORT PURSUANT TO SECTION 13 OR 15(D) OF THE SECURITIES EXCHANGE ACT OF 1934
FOR THE TRANSITION PERIOD FROM _____ TO _____ .

Commission File No. 1-10635

NIKE, Inc.

(Exact name of Registrant as specified in its charter)

OREGON	93-0584541
(State or other jurisdiction of incorporation)	*(IRS Employer Identification No.)*
One Bowerman Drive, Beaverton, Oregon	97005-6453
(Address of principal executive offices)	*(Zip Code)*

(503) 671-6453
(Registrant's Telephone Number, Including Area Code)

SECURITIES REGISTERED PURSUANT TO SECTION 12(B) OF THE ACT:	
Class B Common Stock	**New York Stock Exchange**
(Title of Each Class)	*(Name of Each Exchange on Which Registered)*

SECURITIES REGISTERED PURSUANT TO SECTION 12(G) OF THE ACT:
NONE

Indicate by check mark:	YES	NO
• if the registrant is a well-known seasoned issuer, as defined in Rule 405 of the Securities Act.	☑	☐
• if the registrant is not required to file reports pursuant to Section 13 or Section 15(d) of the Act.	☐	☑
• whether the Registrant (1) has filed all reports required to be filed by Section 13 or 15(d) of the Securities Exchange Act of 1934 during the preceding 12 months (or for such shorter period that the Registrant was required to file such reports), and (2) has been subject to such filing requirements for the past 90 days.	☑	☐
• whether the registrant has submitted electronically and posted on its corporate Website, if any, every Interactive Data File required to be submitted and posted pursuant to Rule 405 of Regulation S-T (§232.405 of this chapter) during the preceding 12 months (or for such shorter period that the registrant was required to submit and post such files).	☑	☐
• if disclosure of delinquent filers pursuant to Item 405 of Regulation S-K (§229.405 of this chapter) is not contained herein, and will not be contained, to the best of Registrant's knowledge, in definitive proxy or information statements incorporated by reference in Part III of this Form 10-K or any amendment to this Form 10-K.	☑	

• whether the Registrant is a large accelerated filer, an accelerated filer, a non-accelerated filer, or a smaller reporting company. See the definitions of "large accelerated filer," "accelerated filer" and "smaller reporting company" in Rule 12b-2 of the Exchange Act.

Large accelerated filer ☑   Accelerated filer ☐   Non-accelerated filer ☐   Smaller reporting company ☐

• whether the registrant is a shell company (as defined in Rule 12b-2 of the Act).	☐	☑

As of November 30, 2014, the aggregate market values of the Registrant's Common Stock held by non-affiliates were:

Class A	$ 4,394,312,083
Class B	67,997,995,244
	$72,392,307,327

As of July 17, 2015, the number of shares of the Registrant's Common Stock outstanding were:

Class A	177,457,876
Class B	677,893,713
	855,351,589

DOCUMENTS INCORPORATED BY REFERENCE:

Parts of Registrant's Proxy Statement for the Annual Meeting of Shareholders to be held on September 17, 2015 are incorporated by reference into Part III of this Report.

ITEM 8.   Financial Statements and Supplementary Data

Management of NIKE, Inc. is responsible for the information and representations contained in this report. The financial statements have been prepared in conformity with the generally accepted accounting principles we considered appropriate in the circumstances and include some amounts based on our best estimates and judgments. Other financial information in this report is consistent with these financial statements.

Our accounting systems include controls designed to reasonably assure assets are safeguarded from unauthorized use or disposition and provide for the preparation of financial statements in conformity with generally accepted accounting principles. These systems are supplemented by the selection and training of qualified financial personnel and an organizational structure providing for appropriate segregation of duties.

An internal Corporate Audit department reviews the results of its work with the Audit Committee of the Board of Directors, presently consisting of four outside directors. The Audit Committee is responsible for the appointment of the independent registered public accounting firm and reviews, with the independent registered public accounting firm, management and the internal audit staff, the scope and the results of the annual examination, the effectiveness of the accounting control system and other matters relating to the financial affairs of NIKE as the Audit Committee deems appropriate. The independent registered public accounting firm and the internal auditors have full access to the Committee, with and without the presence of management, to discuss any appropriate matters.

Management's Annual Report on Internal Control Over Financial Reporting

Management is responsible for establishing and maintaining adequate internal control over financial reporting, as such term is defined in Rule 13(a)-15(f) and Rule 15(d)-15(f) of the Securities Exchange Act of 1934, as amended. Internal control over financial reporting is a process designed to provide reasonable assurance regarding the reliability of financial reporting and the preparation of the financial statements for external purposes in accordance with generally accepted accounting principles in the United States of America. Internal control over financial reporting includes those policies and procedures that: (i) pertain to the maintenance of records that, in reasonable detail, accurately and fairly reflect the transactions and dispositions of assets of the Company; (ii) provide reasonable assurance that transactions are recorded as necessary to permit preparation of financial statements in accordance with generally accepted accounting principles, and that receipts and expenditures of the Company are being made only in accordance with authorizations of our management and directors; and (iii) provide reasonable assurance regarding prevention or timely detection of unauthorized acquisition, use or disposition of assets of the Company that could have a material effect on the financial statements.

While "reasonable assurance" is a high level of assurance, it does not mean absolute assurance. Because of its inherent limitations, internal control over financial reporting may not prevent or detect every misstatement and instance of fraud. Controls are susceptible to manipulation, especially in instances of fraud caused by the collusion of two or more people, including our senior management. Also, projections of any evaluation of effectiveness to future periods are subject to the risk that controls may become inadequate because of changes in conditions, or that the degree of compliance with the policies or procedures may deteriorate.

Under the supervision and with the participation of our Chief Executive Officer and Chief Financial Officer, our management conducted an evaluation of the effectiveness of our internal control over financial reporting based upon the framework in *Internal Control — Integrated Framework (2013)* issued by the Committee of Sponsoring Organizations of the Treadway Commission (COSO). Based on the results of our evaluation, our management concluded that our internal control over financial reporting was effective as of May 31, 2015.

PricewaterhouseCoopers LLP, an independent registered public accounting firm, has audited (1) the Consolidated Financial Statements and (2) the effectiveness of our internal control over financial reporting as of May 31, 2015, as stated in their report herein.

Mark G. Parker
President and Chief Executive Officer

Donald W. Blair
Chief Financial Officer

Report of Independent Registered Public Accounting Firm

To the Board of Directors and Shareholders of NIKE, Inc.:

In our opinion, the consolidated financial statements listed in the index appearing under Item 15(a)(1) present fairly, in all material respects, the financial position of NIKE, Inc. and its subsidiaries at May 31, 2015 and 2014, and the results of their operations and their cash flows for each of the three years in the period ended May 31, 2015 in conformity with accounting principles generally accepted in the United States of America. In addition, in our opinion, the financial statement schedule listed in the index appearing under Item 15(a)(2) presents fairly, in all material respects, the information set forth therein when read in conjunction with the related consolidated financial statements. Also in our opinion, the Company maintained, in all material respects, effective internal control over financial reporting as of May 31, 2015, based on criteria established in *Internal Control — Integrated Framework (2013)* issued by the Committee of Sponsoring Organizations of the Treadway Commission (COSO). The Company's management is responsible for these financial statements and financial statement schedule, for maintaining effective internal control over financial reporting and for its assessment of the effectiveness of internal control over financial reporting, included in Management's Annual Report on Internal Control Over Financial Reporting appearing under Item 8. Our responsibility is to express opinions on these financial statements, on the financial statement schedule and on the Company's internal control over financial reporting based on our integrated audits. We conducted our audits in accordance with the standards of the Public Company Accounting Oversight Board (United States). Those standards require that we plan and perform the audits to obtain reasonable assurance about whether the financial statements are free of material misstatement and whether effective internal control over financial reporting was maintained in all material respects. Our audits of the financial statements included examining, on a test basis, evidence supporting the amounts and disclosures in the financial statements, assessing the accounting principles used and significant estimates made by management and evaluating the overall financial statement presentation. Our audit of internal control over financial reporting included obtaining an understanding of internal control over financial reporting, assessing the risk that a material weakness exists and testing and evaluating the design and operating effectiveness of internal control based on the assessed risk. Our audits also included performing such other procedures as we considered necessary in the circumstances. We believe that our audits provide a reasonable basis for our opinions.

A company's internal control over financial reporting is a process designed to provide reasonable assurance regarding the reliability of financial reporting and the preparation of financial statements for external purposes in accordance with generally accepted accounting principles. A company's internal control over financial reporting includes those policies and procedures that (i) pertain to the maintenance of records that, in reasonable detail, accurately and fairly reflect the transactions and dispositions of the assets of the Company; (ii) provide reasonable assurance that transactions are recorded as necessary to permit preparation of financial statements in accordance with generally accepted accounting principles, and that receipts and expenditures of the Company are being made only in accordance with authorizations of management and directors of the Company; and (iii) provide reasonable assurance regarding prevention or timely detection of unauthorized acquisition, use, or disposition of the Company's assets that could have a material effect on the financial statements.

Because of its inherent limitations, internal control over financial reporting may not prevent or detect misstatements. Also, projections of any evaluation of effectiveness to future periods are subject to the risk that controls may become inadequate because of changes in conditions, or that the degree of compliance with the policies or procedures may deteriorate.

/s/ PRICEWATERHOUSECOOPERS LLP

Portland, Oregon
July 23, 2015

NIKE, Inc. Consolidated Statements of Income

(In millions, except per share data)		Year Ended May 31,				
		2015		2014		2013
Income from continuing operations:						
Revenues	$	30,601	$	27,799	$	25,313
Cost of sales		16,534		15,353		14,279
Gross profit		14,067		12,446		11,034
Demand creation expense		3,213		3,031		2,745
Operating overhead expense		6,679		5,735		5,051
Total selling and administrative expense		9,892		8,766		7,796
Interest expense (income), net (Notes 6, 7 and 8)		28		33		(3)
Other (income) expense, net (Note 17)		(58)		103		(15)
Income before income taxes		4,205		3,544		3,256
Income tax expense (Note 9)		932		851		805
NET INCOME FROM CONTINUING OPERATIONS		**3,273**		**2,693**		**2,451**
NET INCOME FROM DISCONTINUED OPERATIONS		**—**		**—**		**21**
NET INCOME	**$**	**3,273**	**$**	**2,693**	**$**	**2,472**
Earnings per common share from continuing operations:						
Basic (Notes 1 and 12)	$	3.80	$	3.05	$	2.74
Diluted (Notes 1 and 12)	$	3.70	$	2.97	$	2.68
Earnings per common share from discontinued operations:						
Basic (Notes 1 and 12)	$	—	$	—	$	0.02
Diluted (Notes 1 and 12)	$	—	$	—	$	0.02
Dividends declared per common share	$	1.08	$	0.93	$	0.81

The accompanying Notes to the Consolidated Financial Statements are an integral part of this statement.

NIKE, Inc. Consolidated Statements of Comprehensive Income

(In millions)	Year Ended May 31,		
	2015	2014	2013
Net income	$ 3,273	$ 2,693	$ 2,472
Other comprehensive income (loss), net of tax:			
Change in net foreign currency translation adjustment[1]	(20)	(32)	38
Change in net gains (losses) on cash flow hedges[2]	1,188	(161)	12
Change in net gains (losses) on other[3]	(7)	4	(8)
Change in release of cumulative translation loss related to Umbro[4]	—	—	83
Total other comprehensive income (loss), net of tax	1,161	(189)	125
TOTAL COMPREHENSIVE INCOME	$ 4,434	$ 2,504	$ 2,597

(1) Net of tax benefit (expense) of $0 million, $0 million and $(13) million, respectively.

(2) Net of tax benefit (expense) of $(31) million, $18 million and $(22) million, respectively.

(3) Net of tax benefit (expense) of $0 million, $0 million and $1 million, respectively.

(4) Net of tax benefit (expense) of $0 million, $0 million and $47 million, respectively.

The accompanying Notes to the Consolidated Financial Statements are an integral part of this statement.

NIKE, Inc. Consolidated Balance Sheets

(In millions)		May 31, 2015		May 31, 2014
ASSETS				
Current assets:				
Cash and equivalents (Note 6)	$	3,852	$	2,220
Short-term investments (Note 6)		2,072		2,922
Accounts receivable, net (Note 1)		3,358		3,434
Inventories (Notes 1 and 2)		4,337		3,947
Deferred income taxes (Note 9)		389		355
Prepaid expenses and other current assets (Notes 6 and 17)		1,968		818
Total current assets		15,976		13,696
Property, plant and equipment, net (Note 3)		3,011		2,834
Identifiable intangible assets, net (Note 4)		281		282
Goodwill (Note 4)		131		131
Deferred income taxes and other assets (Notes 6, 9 and 17)		2,201		1,651
TOTAL ASSETS	$	21,600	$	18,594
LIABILITIES AND SHAREHOLDERS' EQUITY				
Current liabilities:				
Current portion of long-term debt (Note 8)	$	107	$	7
Notes payable (Note 7)		74		167
Accounts payable (Note 7)		2,131		1,930
Accrued liabilities (Notes 5, 6 and 17)		3,951		2,491
Income taxes payable (Note 9)		71		432
Total current liabilities		6,334		5,027
Long-term debt (Note 8)		1,079		1,199
Deferred income taxes and other liabilities (Notes 6, 9, 13 and 17)		1,480		1,544
Commitments and contingencies (Note 16)				
Redeemable preferred stock (Note 10)		—		—
Shareholders' equity:				
Common stock at stated value (Note 11):				
Class A convertible — 178 and 178 shares outstanding		—		—
Class B — 679 and 692 shares outstanding		3		3
Capital in excess of stated value		6,773		5,865
Accumulated other comprehensive income (Note 14)		1,246		85
Retained earnings		4,685		4,871
Total shareholders' equity		12,707		10,824
TOTAL LIABILITIES AND SHAREHOLDERS' EQUITY	$	21,600	$	18,594

The accompanying Notes to the Consolidated Financial Statements are an integral part of this statement.

NIKE, Inc. Consolidated Statements of Cash Flows

(In millions)	Year Ended May 31,		
	2015	2014	2013
Cash provided by operations:			
Net income	$ 3,273	$ 2,693	$ 2,472
Income charges (credits) not affecting cash:			
Depreciation	606	518	438
Deferred income taxes	(113)	(11)	20
Stock-based compensation (Note 11)	191	177	174
Amortization and other	43	68	64
Net foreign currency adjustments	424	56	66
Net gain on divestitures	—	—	(124)
Changes in certain working capital components and other assets and liabilities:			
(Increase) decrease in accounts receivable	(216)	(298)	142
(Increase) in inventories	(621)	(505)	(219)
(Increase) in prepaid expenses and other current assets	(144)	(210)	(28)
Increase in accounts payable, accrued liabilities and income taxes payable	1,237	525	27
Cash provided by operations	4,680	3,013	3,032
Cash used by investing activities:			
Purchases of short-term investments	(4,936)	(5,386)	(4,133)
Maturities of short-term investments	3,655	3,932	1,663
Sales of short-term investments	2,216	1,126	1,330
Investments in reverse repurchase agreements	(150)	—	—
Additions to property, plant and equipment	(963)	(880)	(598)
Disposals of property, plant and equipment	3	3	14
Proceeds from divestitures	—	—	786
(Increase) in other assets, net of other liabilities	—	(2)	(2)
Cash used by investing activities	(175)	(1,207)	(940)
Cash used by financing activities:			
Net proceeds from long-term debt issuance	—	—	986
Long-term debt payments, including current portion	(7)	(60)	(49)
(Decrease) increase in notes payable	(63)	75	10
Payments on capital lease obligations	(19)	(17)	—
Proceeds from exercise of stock options and other stock issuances	514	383	313
Excess tax benefits from share-based payment arrangements	218	132	72
Repurchase of common stock	(2,534)	(2,628)	(1,674)
Dividends — common and preferred	(899)	(799)	(703)
Cash used by financing activities	(2,790)	(2,914)	(1,045)
Effect of exchange rate changes on cash and equivalents	(83)	(9)	36
Net increase (decrease) in cash and equivalents	1,632	(1,117)	1,083
Cash and equivalents, beginning of year	2,220	3,337	2,254
CASH AND EQUIVALENTS, END OF YEAR	$ 3,852	$ 2,220	$ 3,337
Supplemental disclosure of cash flow information:			
Cash paid during the year for:			
Interest, net of capitalized interest	$ 53	$ 53	$ 20
Income taxes	1,262	856	702
Non-cash additions to property, plant and equipment	206	167	137
Dividends declared and not paid	240	209	188

The accompanying Notes to the Consolidated Financial Statements are an integral part of this statement.

NIKE, Inc. Consolidated Statements of Shareholders' Equity

(In millions, except per share data)	Common Stock				Capital in Excess of Stated Value	Accumulated Other Comprehensive Income	Retained Earnings	Total
	Class A		Class B					
	Shares	Amount	Shares	Amount				
Balance at May 31, 2012	180	$ —	736	$ 3	$ 4,641	$ 149	$ 5,526	$ 10,319
Stock options exercised			10		322			322
Conversion to Class B Common Stock	(2)		2					—
Repurchase of Class B Common Stock			(34)		(10)		(1,647)	(1,657)
Dividends on common stock ($0.81 per share)							(727)	(727)
Issuance of shares to employees			2		65			65
Stock-based compensation (Note 11)					174			174
Forfeiture of shares from employees			—		(8)		(4)	(12)
Net income							2,472	2,472
Other comprehensive income (loss)						125		125
Balance at May 31, 2013	178	$ —	716	$ 3	$ 5,184	$ 274	$ 5,620	$ 11,081
Stock options exercised			11		445			445
Repurchase of Class B Common Stock			(37)		(11)		(2,617)	(2,628)
Dividends on common stock ($0.93 per share)							(821)	(821)
Issuance of shares to employees			2		78			78
Stock-based compensation (Note 11)					177			177
Forfeiture of shares from employees			—		(8)		(4)	(12)
Net income							2,693	2,693
Other comprehensive income (loss)						(189)		(189)
Balance at May 31, 2014	178	$ —	692	$ 3	$ 5,865	$ 85	$ 4,871	$ 10,824
Stock options exercised			14		639			639
Repurchase of Class B Common Stock			(29)		(9)		(2,525)	(2,534)
Dividends on common stock ($1.08 per share)							(931)	(931)
Issuance of shares to employees			2		92			92
Stock-based compensation (Note 11)					191			191
Forfeiture of shares from employees			—		(5)		(3)	(8)
Net income							3,273	3,273
Other comprehensive income (loss)						1,161		1,161
Balance at May 31, 2015	178	$ —	679	$ 3	$ 6,773	$ 1,246	$ 4,685	$ 12,707

The accompanying Notes to the Consolidated Financial Statements are an integral part of this statement.

Notes to Consolidated Financial Statements

NOTE 1 — Summary of Significant Accounting Policies

Description of Business

NIKE, Inc. is a worldwide leader in the design, development and worldwide marketing and selling of athletic footwear, apparel, equipment, accessories and services. NIKE, Inc. portfolio brands include the NIKE Brand, Jordan Brand, Hurley and Converse. The NIKE Brand is focused on performance athletic footwear, apparel, equipment, accessories and services across a wide range of sport categories, amplified with sport-inspired sportswear products carrying the Swoosh trademark as well as other NIKE Brand trademarks. The Jordan Brand is focused on athletic and casual footwear, apparel and accessories, using the Jumpman trademark. Sales of Jordan Brand products are included within the NIKE Brand Basketball category. The Hurley brand is focused on surf and action sports and youth lifestyle footwear, apparel and accessories, using the Hurley trademark. Sales of Hurley brand products are included within the NIKE Brand Action Sports category. Converse designs, distributes, markets and sells casual sneakers, apparel and accessories under the Converse, Chuck Taylor, All Star, One Star, Star Chevron and Jack Purcell trademarks. In some markets outside the U.S., these trademarks are licensed to third parties who design, distribute, market and sell similar products. Operating results of the Converse brand are reported on a stand-alone basis.

Basis of Consolidation

The Consolidated Financial Statements include the accounts of NIKE, Inc. and its subsidiaries (the "Company"). All significant intercompany transactions and balances have been eliminated.

The Company completed the sale of Cole Haan during the third quarter ended February 28, 2013 and completed the sale of Umbro during the second quarter ended November 30, 2012. As a result, the Company reports the operating results of Cole Haan and Umbro in the *Net income from discontinued operations* line in the Consolidated Statements of Income for all applicable periods presented. There were no assets or liabilities of discontinued operations as of May 31, 2015 and May 31, 2014 (refer to Note 15 — Discontinued Operations). Unless otherwise indicated, the disclosures accompanying the Consolidated Financial Statements reflect the Company's continuing operations.

On November 15, 2012, the Company announced a two-for-one split of both NIKE Class A and Class B Common shares. The stock split was a 100 percent stock dividend payable on December 24, 2012 to shareholders of record at the close of business on December 10, 2012. Common stock began trading at the split-adjusted price on December 26, 2012. All share numbers and per share amounts presented reflect the stock split.

Reclassifications

Certain prior year amounts have been reclassified to conform to fiscal 2015 presentation.

Revisions

During the third quarter of fiscal 2015, management determined it had incorrectly reflected unrealized gains and losses from re-measurement of non-functional currency intercompany balances between certain of its foreign wholly-owned subsidiaries in its Consolidated Statements of Cash Flows. These unrealized gains and losses should have been classified as non-cash reconciling items from *Net income* to *Cash provided by operations*, but were instead reported on the *Effect of exchange rate changes on cash and equivalents* line of the Consolidated Statements of Cash Flows. This resulted in an understatement of *Cash provided by operations* reported on the Consolidated Statements of Cash Flows for certain prior periods; there was no impact for any period to *Net increase (decrease) in cash and equivalents* reported on the Consolidated Statements of Cash Flows, or *Cash and equivalents* reported on the Consolidated Statements of Cash Flows and Balance Sheets. The Company assessed the materiality of the misclassifications on prior periods' financial statements in accordance with SEC Staff Accounting Bulletin ("SAB") No. 99, Materiality, codified in Accounting Standards Codification ("ASC") 250, Presentation of Financial Statements, and concluded that these misstatements were not material to any prior annual or interim periods. Accordingly, in accordance with ASC 250 (SAB No. 108, Considering the Effects of Prior Year Misstatements when Quantifying Misstatements in Current Year Financial Statements), the amounts have been revised in the applicable Consolidated Statements of Cash Flows. For the three and six months ended August 31, 2014 and November 30, 2014 of fiscal 2015, the revisions increased *Cash provided by operations* and decreased *Effect of exchange rate changes on cash and equivalents* by $95 million and $312 million, respectively. For the fiscal years ended May 31, 2014 and 2013, the revisions increased *Cash provided by operations* and decreased *Effect of exchange rate changes on cash and equivalents* by $10 million and $64 million, respectively. These amounts have been reflected in the applicable tables below. As part of the revision to the Consolidated Statements of Cash Flows, the Company has updated its presentation to separately report *Net foreign currency adjustments*, which was previously included within *Amortization and other*.

The following are selected line items from the Company's Unaudited Condensed Consolidated Statements of Cash Flows illustrating the effect of these corrections:

NIKE, Inc. Unaudited Condensed Consolidated Statements of Cash Flows

(In millions)	Three Months Ended August 31, 2014			Six Months Ended November 30, 2014		
	As Reported	Adjustment	As Revised	As Reported	Adjustment	As Revised
Cash provided by operations:						
Net income	$ 962	$ —	$ 962	$ 1,617	$ —	$ 1,617
Income charges (credits) not affecting cash:						
Amortization and other	(34)	42	8	(54)	69	15
Net foreign currency adjustments	—	53	53	—	243	243
Cash provided by operations	588	95	683	1,235	312	1,547
Effect of exchange rate changes on cash and equivalents	97	(95)	2	288	(312)	(24)
Net increase (decrease) in cash and equivalents	83	—	83	53	—	53
Cash and equivalents, beginning of period	2,220	—	2,220	2,220	—	2,220
CASH AND EQUIVALENTS, END OF PERIOD	$ 2,303	$ —	$ 2,303	$ 2,273	$ —	$ 2,273

The following are selected line items from the Company's Consolidated Statements of Cash Flows illustrating the effect of these corrections on the amounts previously reported in the Company's fiscal 2014 Annual Report on Form 10-K:

| | NIKE, Inc. Consolidated Statements of Cash Flows | | | | | |
| | Year Ended May 31, 2014 | | | Year Ended May 31, 2013 | | |
(In millions)	As Reported	Adjustment	As Revised	As Reported	Adjustment	As Revised
Cash provided by operations:						
Net income	$ 2,693	$ —	$ 2,693	$ 2,472	$ —	$ 2,472
Income charges (credits) not affecting cash:						
Amortization and other	114	(46)	68	66	(2)	64
Net foreign currency adjustments	—	56	56	—	66	66
Cash provided by operations	3,003	10	3,013	2,968	64	3,032
Effect of exchange rate changes on cash and equivalents	1	(10)	(9)	100	(64)	36
Net increase (decrease) in cash and equivalents	(1,117)	—	(1,117)	1,083	—	1,083
Cash and equivalents, beginning of year	3,337	—	3,337	2,254	—	2,254
CASH AND EQUIVALENTS, END OF YEAR	$ 2,220	$ —	$ 2,220	$ 3,337	$ —	$ 3,337

Recognition of Revenues

Wholesale revenues are recognized when title and the risks and rewards of ownership have passed to the customer, based on the terms of sale. This occurs upon shipment or upon receipt by the customer depending on the country of the sale and the agreement with the customer. Retail store revenues are recorded at the time of sale and online store revenues are recorded upon delivery to the customer. Provisions for post invoice sales discounts, returns and miscellaneous claims from customers are estimated and recorded as a reduction to revenue at the time of sale. Post-invoice sales discounts consist of contractual programs with certain customers or discretionary discounts that are expected to be granted to certain customers at a later date. Estimates of discretionary discounts, returns and claims are based on historical rates, specific identification of outstanding claims and outstanding returns not yet received from customers and estimated discounts, returns and claims expected, but not yet finalized with customers. As of May 31, 2015 and 2014, the Company's reserve balances for post-invoice sales discounts, returns and miscellaneous claims were $724 million and $610 million, respectively.

Cost of Sales

Cost of sales consists primarily of inventory costs, as well as warehousing costs (including the cost of warehouse labor), third-party royalties, certain foreign currency hedge gains and losses and research, design and development costs.

Shipping and Handling Costs

Outbound shipping and handling costs are expensed as incurred and included in Cost of sales.

Operating Overhead Expense

Operating overhead expense consists primarily of payroll and benefit related costs, rent, depreciation and amortization, professional services and meetings and travel.

Demand Creation Expense

Demand creation expense consists of advertising and promotion costs, including costs of endorsement contracts, television, digital and print advertising, brand events and retail brand presentation. Advertising production costs are expensed the first time an advertisement is run. Advertising communication costs are expensed when the advertisement appears. Costs related to brand events are expensed when the event occurs. Costs related to retail brand presentation are expensed when the presentation is completed and delivered.

A significant amount of the Company's promotional expenses result from payments under endorsement contracts. Accounting for endorsement payments is based upon specific contract provisions. Generally, endorsement payments are expensed on a straight-line basis over the term of the contract after giving recognition to periodic performance compliance provisions of the contracts. Prepayments made under contracts are included in Prepaid expenses and other current assets or Deferred income taxes and other assets depending on the period to which the prepayment applies.

Certain contracts provide for contingent payments to endorsers based upon specific achievements in their sports (e.g., winning a championship). The Company records demand creation expense for these amounts when the endorser achieves the specific goal.

Certain contracts provide for variable payments based upon endorsers maintaining a level of performance in their sport over an extended period of time (e.g., maintaining a specified ranking in a sport for a year). When the Company determines payments are probable, the amounts are reported in demand creation expense ratably over the contract period based on our best estimate of the endorser's performance. In these instances, to the extent that actual payments to the endorser differ from the Company's estimate due to changes in the endorser's performance, increased or decreased demand creation expense may be recorded in a future period.

Certain contracts provide for royalty payments to endorsers based upon a predetermined percent of sales of particular products. The Company expenses these payments in Cost of sales as the related sales occur. In certain contracts, the Company offers minimum guaranteed royalty payments. For contracts for which the Company estimates it will not meet the minimum guaranteed amount of royalty fees through sales of product, the Company records the amount of the guaranteed payment in excess of that earned through sales of product in Demand creation expense uniformly over the guarantee period.

Through cooperative advertising programs, the Company reimburses retail customers for certain costs of advertising the Company's products. The Company records these costs in Demand creation expense at the point in time when it is obligated to its customers for the costs. This obligation may arise prior to the related advertisement being run.

Total advertising and promotion expenses were $3,213 million, $3,031 million and $2,745 million for the years ended May 31, 2015, 2014 and 2013, respectively. Prepaid advertising and promotion expenses totaled $455 million and $516 million at May 31, 2015 and 2014, respectively, and were recorded in Prepaid expenses and other current assets and Deferred income taxes and other assets depending on the period to which the prepayment applies.

Cash and Equivalents

Cash and equivalents represent cash and short-term, highly liquid investments, including commercial paper, U.S. Treasury, U.S. Agency, money market funds, time deposits and corporate debt securities with maturities of 90 days or less at the date of purchase.

Short-Term Investments

Short-term investments consist of highly liquid investments, including commercial paper, U.S. Treasury, U.S. Agency and corporate debt securities, with maturities over 90 days at the date of purchase. Debt securities that the Company has the ability and positive intent to hold to maturity are carried at amortized cost. At May 31, 2015 and 2014, the Company did not hold any short-term investments that were classified as trading or held-to-maturity.

At May 31, 2015 and 2014, *Short-term investments* consisted of available-for-sale securities. Available-for-sale securities are recorded at fair value with unrealized gains and losses reported, net of tax, in *Other comprehensive income*, unless unrealized losses are determined to be other than temporary. Realized gains and losses on the sale of securities are determined by specific identification. The Company considers all available-for-sale securities, including those with maturity dates beyond 12 months, as available to support current operational liquidity needs and therefore classifies all securities with maturity dates beyond 90 days at the date of purchase as current assets within *Short-term investments* on the Consolidated Balance Sheets.

Refer to Note 6 — Fair Value Measurements for more information on the Company's short-term investments.

Allowance for Uncollectible Accounts Receivable

Accounts receivable consists primarily of amounts receivable from customers. The Company makes ongoing estimates relating to the collectability of its accounts receivable and maintains an allowance for estimated losses resulting from the inability of its customers to make required payments. In determining the amount of the allowance, the Company considers historical levels of credit losses and makes judgments about the creditworthiness of significant customers based on ongoing credit evaluations. Accounts receivable with anticipated collection dates greater than 12 months from the balance sheet date and related allowances are considered non-current and recorded in *Deferred income taxes and other assets*. The allowance for uncollectible accounts receivable was $78 million and $78 million at May 31, 2015 and 2014, respectively, of which $24 million and $37 million, respectively, was classified as long-term and recorded in *Deferred income taxes and other assets*.

Inventory Valuation

Inventories are stated at lower of cost or market and valued on either an average or specific identification cost basis. For inventories in transit that represent direct shipments to customers, the related inventory and cost of sales are recognized on a specific identification basis. Inventory costs primarily consist of product cost from the Company's suppliers, as well as inbound freight, import duties, taxes, insurance and logistics and other handling fees.

Property, Plant and Equipment and Depreciation

Property, plant and equipment are recorded at cost. Depreciation is determined on a straight-line basis for buildings and leasehold improvements over 2 to 40 years and for machinery and equipment over 2 to 15 years.

Depreciation and amortization of assets used in manufacturing, warehousing and product distribution are recorded in *Cost of sales*. Depreciation and amortization of other assets are recorded in *Total selling and administrative expense*.

Software Development Costs

Internal Use Software. Expenditures for major software purchases and software developed for internal use are capitalized and amortized over a 2 to 10 year period on a straight-line basis. The Company's policy provides for the capitalization of external direct costs of materials and services associated with developing or obtaining internal use computer software. In addition, the Company also capitalizes certain payroll and payroll-related costs for employees who are directly associated with internal use computer software projects. The amount of capitalizable payroll costs with respect to these employees is limited to the time directly spent on such projects. Costs associated with preliminary project stage activities, training, maintenance and all other post-implementation stage activities are expensed as incurred.

Computer Software to be Sold, Leased or Otherwise Marketed. Development costs of computer software to be sold, leased or otherwise marketed as an integral part of a product are subject to capitalization beginning when a product's technological feasibility has been established and ending when a product is available for general release to customers. In most instances, the Company's products are released soon after technological feasibility has been established. Therefore, software development costs incurred subsequent to achievement of technological feasibility are usually not significant, and generally most software development costs have been expensed as incurred.

Impairment of Long-Lived Assets

The Company reviews the carrying value of long-lived assets or asset groups to be used in operations whenever events or changes in circumstances indicate that the carrying amount of the assets might not be recoverable. Factors that would necessitate an impairment assessment include a significant adverse change in the extent or manner in which an asset is used, a significant adverse change in legal factors or the business climate that could affect the value of the asset or a significant decline in the observable market value of an asset, among others. If such facts indicate a potential impairment, the Company would assess the recoverability of an asset group by determining if the carrying value of the asset group exceeds the sum of the projected undiscounted cash flows expected to result from the use and eventual disposition of the assets over the remaining economic life of the primary asset in the asset group. If the recoverability test indicates that the carrying value of the asset group is not recoverable, the Company will estimate the fair value of the asset group using appropriate valuation methodologies, which would typically include an estimate of discounted cash flows. Any impairment would be measured as the difference between the asset group's carrying amount and its estimated fair value.

Goodwill and Indefinite-Lived Intangible Assets

The Company performs annual impairment tests on goodwill and intangible assets with indefinite lives in the fourth quarter of each fiscal year, or when events occur or circumstances change that would, more likely than not, reduce the fair value of a reporting unit or an intangible asset with an indefinite life below its carrying value. Events or changes in circumstances that may trigger interim impairment reviews include significant changes in business climate, operating results, planned investments in the reporting unit, planned divestitures or an expectation that the carrying amount may not be recoverable, among other factors. The Company may first assess qualitative factors to determine whether it is more likely than not that the fair value of a reporting unit is less than its carrying amount. If, after assessing the totality of events and circumstances, the Company determines that it is more likely than not that the fair value of the reporting unit is greater than its carrying amount, the two-step impairment test is unnecessary. The two-step impairment test first requires the Company to estimate the fair value of its reporting units. If the carrying value of a reporting unit exceeds its fair value, the goodwill of that reporting unit is potentially impaired and the Company proceeds to step two of the impairment analysis. In step two of the analysis, the Company measures and records an impairment loss equal to the excess of the carrying value of the reporting unit's goodwill over its implied fair value, if any.

The Company generally bases its measurement of the fair value of a reporting unit on a blended analysis of the present value of future discounted cash flows and the market valuation approach. The discounted cash flows model indicates the fair value of the reporting unit based on the present value of the cash flows that the Company expects the reporting unit to generate in the future. The Company's significant estimates in the discounted cash flows model include: its weighted average cost of capital; long-term rate of growth and profitability of the reporting unit's business; and working capital effects. The market valuation approach indicates the fair value of the business based on a comparison of the reporting unit to comparable publicly traded companies in similar lines of business. Significant estimates in the market valuation approach model include identifying similar companies with comparable business factors such as size, growth, profitability, risk and return on investment and assessing comparable revenue and operating income multiples in estimating the fair value of the reporting unit.

Indefinite-lived intangible assets primarily consist of acquired trade names and trademarks. The Company may first perform a qualitative assessment to determine whether it is more likely than not that an indefinite-lived intangible asset is impaired. If, after assessing the totality of events and circumstances, the Company determines that it is more likely than not that the indefinite-lived intangible asset is not impaired, no quantitative fair value measurement is necessary. If a quantitative fair value measurement calculation is required for these intangible assets, the Company utilizes the relief-from-royalty method. This method assumes that trade names and trademarks have value to the extent that their owner is relieved of the obligation to pay royalties for the benefits received from them. This method requires the Company to estimate the future revenue for the related brands, the appropriate royalty rate and the weighted average cost of capital.

Operating Leases

The Company leases retail store space, certain distribution and warehouse facilities, office space and other non-real estate assets under operating leases. Operating lease agreements may contain rent escalation clauses, rent holidays or certain landlord incentives, including tenant improvement allowances. Rent expense for non-cancelable operating leases with scheduled rent increases or landlord incentives are recognized on a straight-line basis over the lease term, beginning with the effective lease commencement date, which is generally the date in which the Company takes possession of or controls the physical use of the property. Certain leases also provide for contingent rents, which are determined as a percent of sales in excess of specified levels. A contingent rent liability is recognized together with the corresponding rent expense when specified levels have been achieved or when the Company determines that achieving the specified levels during the period is probable.

Fair Value Measurements

The Company measures certain financial assets and liabilities at fair value on a recurring basis, including derivatives and available-for-sale securities. Fair value is the price the Company would receive to sell an asset or pay to transfer a liability in an orderly transaction with a market participant at the measurement date. The Company uses a three-level hierarchy established by the Financial Accounting Standards Board ("FASB") that prioritizes fair value measurements based on the types of inputs used for the various valuation techniques (market approach, income approach and cost approach).

The levels of hierarchy are described below:

- Level 1: Quoted prices in active markets for identical assets or liabilities.

- Level 2: Inputs other than quoted prices that are observable for the asset or liability, either directly or indirectly; these include quoted prices for similar assets or liabilities in active markets and quoted prices for identical or similar assets or liabilities in markets that are not active.

- Level 3: Unobservable inputs for which there is little or no market data available, which require the reporting entity to develop its own assumptions.

The Company's assessment of the significance of a particular input to the fair value measurement in its entirety requires judgment and considers factors specific to the asset or liability. Financial assets and liabilities are classified in their entirety based on the most conservative level of input that is significant to the fair value measurement.

Pricing vendors are utilized for certain Level 1 and Level 2 investments. These vendors either provide a quoted market price in an active market or use observable inputs without applying significant adjustments in their pricing. Observable inputs include broker quotes, interest rates and yield curves observable at commonly quoted intervals, volatilities and credit risks. The fair value of derivative contracts is determined using observable market inputs such as the daily market foreign currency rates, forward pricing curves, currency volatilities, currency correlations and interest rates and considers nonperformance risk of the Company and that of its counterparties.

The Company's fair value processes include controls that are designed to ensure appropriate fair values are recorded. These controls include a comparison of fair values to another independent pricing vendor.

Refer to Note 6 — Fair Value Measurements for additional information.

Foreign Currency Translation and Foreign Currency Transactions

Adjustments resulting from translating foreign functional currency financial statements into U.S. Dollars are included in the foreign currency translation adjustment, a component of *Accumulated other comprehensive income* in *Total shareholders' equity*.

The Company's global subsidiaries have various assets and liabilities, primarily receivables and payables, which are denominated in currencies other than their functional currency. These balance sheet items are subject to re-measurement, the impact of which is recorded in *Other (income) expense, net,* within the Consolidated Statements of Income.

Accounting for Derivatives and Hedging Activities

The Company uses derivative financial instruments to reduce its exposure to changes in foreign currency exchange rates and interest rates. All derivatives are recorded at fair value on the Consolidated Balance Sheets and changes in the fair value of derivative financial instruments are either recognized in *Accumulated other comprehensive income* (a component of *Total shareholders' equity*), *Long-term debt* or *Net income* depending on the nature of the underlying exposure, whether the derivative is formally designated as a hedge and, if designated, the extent to which the hedge is effective. The Company classifies the cash flows at settlement from derivatives in the same category as the cash flows from the related hedged items. For undesignated hedges and designated cash flow hedges, this is primarily within the *Cash provided by operations* component of the Consolidated Statements of Cash Flows. For designated net investment hedges, this is within the *Cash used by investing activities* component of the Consolidated Statement of Cash Flows. For the Company's fair value hedges, which are interest rate swaps used to mitigate the change in fair value of its fixed-rate debt attributable to changes in interest rates, the related cash flows from periodic interest payments are reflected within the *Cash provided by operations* component of the Consolidated Statements of Cash Flows. Refer to Note 17 — Risk Management and Derivatives for more information on the Company's risk management program and derivatives.

Stock-Based Compensation

The Company estimates the fair value of options and stock appreciation rights granted under the NIKE, Inc. 1990 Stock Incentive Plan (the "1990 Plan") and employees' purchase rights under the Employee Stock Purchase Plans ("ESPPs") using the Black-Scholes option pricing model. The Company recognizes this fair value, net of estimated forfeitures, as *Operating overhead expense* in the Consolidated Statements of Income over the vesting period using the straight-line method.

Refer to Note 11 — Common Stock and Stock-Based Compensation for more information on the Company's stock programs.

Income Taxes

The Company accounts for income taxes using the asset and liability method. This approach requires the recognition of deferred tax assets and liabilities for the expected future tax consequences of temporary differences between the carrying amounts and the tax basis of assets and liabilities. The Company records a valuation allowance to reduce deferred tax assets to the amount management believes is more likely than not to be realized. United States income taxes are provided currently on financial statement earnings of non-U.S. subsidiaries that are expected to be repatriated. The Company determines annually the amount of undistributed non-U.S. earnings to invest indefinitely in its non-U.S. operations.

The Company recognizes a tax benefit from uncertain tax positions in the financial statements only when it is more likely than not that the position will be sustained upon examination by relevant tax authorities. The Company recognizes interest and penalties related to income tax matters in *Income tax expense*.

Refer to Note 9 — Income Taxes for further discussion.

Earnings Per Share

Basic earnings per common share is calculated by dividing *Net income* by the weighted average number of common shares outstanding during the year. Diluted earnings per common share is calculated by adjusting weighted average outstanding shares, assuming conversion of all potentially dilutive stock options and awards.

Refer to Note 12 — Earnings Per Share for further discussion.

Management Estimates

The preparation of financial statements in conformity with generally accepted accounting principles requires management to make estimates, including estimates relating to assumptions that affect the reported amounts of assets and liabilities and disclosure of contingent assets and liabilities at the date of financial statements and the reported amounts of revenues and expenses during the reporting period. Actual results could differ from these estimates.

Recently Adopted Accounting Standards

In July 2013, the FASB issued an accounting standards update intended to provide guidance on the presentation of unrecognized tax benefits, reflecting the manner in which an entity would settle, at the reporting date, any additional income taxes that would result from the disallowance of a tax position when net operating loss carryforwards, similar tax losses or tax credit carryforwards exist. This accounting standard was effective for the Company beginning June 1, 2014 and early adoption was permitted. Management early adopted this guidance and the adoption did not have a material impact on the Company's consolidated financial position or results of operations.

In July 2012, the FASB issued an accounting standards update intended to simplify how an entity tests indefinite-lived intangible assets other than goodwill for impairment by providing entities with an option to perform a qualitative assessment to determine whether further impairment testing is necessary. This accounting standards update was effective for the Company beginning June 1, 2013. The adoption of this standard did not have a material impact on the Company's consolidated financial position or results of operations.

In December 2011, the FASB issued guidance enhancing disclosure requirements surrounding the nature of an entity's right to offset and related arrangements associated with its financial instruments and derivative instruments. This new guidance requires companies to disclose both gross and net information about instruments and transactions eligible for offset in the statement of financial position and instruments and transactions subject to master netting arrangements. This new guidance was effective for the Company beginning June 1, 2013. As this guidance only requires expanded disclosures, the adoption had no impact on the Company's consolidated financial position or results of operations.

Recently Issued Accounting Standards

In May 2014, the FASB issued an accounting standards update that replaces existing revenue recognition guidance. The updated guidance requires companies to recognize revenue in a way that depicts the transfer of promised goods or services to customers in an amount that reflects the consideration to which the entity expects to be entitled in exchange for those goods or services. In addition, the new standard requires that reporting companies disclose the nature, amount, timing and uncertainty of revenue and cash flows arising from contracts with customers. Based on the FASB's decision in July 2015 to defer the effective date and to allow more flexibility with implementation, the Company anticipates the new standard will be effective for the Company beginning June 1, 2018. The new standard is required to be applied retrospectively to each prior reporting period presented or retrospectively with the cumulative effect of initially applying it recognized at the date of initial application. The Company has not yet selected a transition method and is currently evaluating the effect the guidance will have on the Consolidated Financial Statements.

NOTE 2 — Inventories

Inventory balances of $4,337 million and $3,947 million at May 31, 2015 and 2014, respectively, were substantially all finished goods.

NOTE 3 — Property, Plant and Equipment

Property, plant and equipment, net included the following:

(In millions)	As of May 31, 2015	As of May 31, 2014
Land	$ 273	$ 270
Buildings	1,250	1,261
Machinery, equipment and internal-use software	3,329	3,376
Leasehold improvements	1,150	1,066
Construction in process	350	247
Total property, plant and equipment, gross	6,352	6,220
Less accumulated depreciation	3,341	3,386
TOTAL PROPERTY, PLANT AND EQUIPMENT, NET	$ **3,011**	$ **2,834**

Capitalized interest was not material for the years ended May 31, 2015, 2014 and 2013. The Company had $5 million and $74 million in capital lease obligations as of May 31, 2015 and May 31, 2014, respectively, included in machinery, equipment and internal-use software. During the fiscal year ended May 31, 2015, the Company restructured the terms of certain capital leases, which now qualify as operating leases.

NOTE 4 — Identifiable Intangible Assets and Goodwill

Identifiable intangible assets, net consists of indefinite-lived trademarks, which are not subject to amortization, and acquired trademarks and other intangible assets, which are subject to amortization. At May 31, 2015 and 2014, indefinite-lived trademarks were $281 million and $282 million, respectively. Acquired trademarks and other intangible assets at May 31, 2015 and 2014 were $17 million and $39 million, respectively, and were fully amortized at the end of both periods. *Goodwill* was $131 million at May 31, 2015 and 2014 of which $65 million and $64 million were included in the Converse segment in the respective periods. The remaining amounts were included in Global Brand Divisions for segment reporting purposes. There were no accumulated impairment balances for goodwill as of either period end.

NOTE 5 — Accrued Liabilities

Accrued liabilities included the following:

(In millions)	As of May 31, 2015	As of May 31, 2014
Compensation and benefits, excluding taxes	$ 997	$ 782
Collateral received from counterparties to hedging instruments	968	—
Endorsement compensation	388	328
Dividends payable	240	209
Import and logistics costs	207	127
Taxes other than income taxes	174	204
Fair value of derivatives	162	85
Advertising and marketing	117	133
Other[1]	698	623
TOTAL ACCRUED LIABILITIES	$ **3,951**	$ **2,491**

(1) Other consists of various accrued expenses with no individual item accounting for more than 5% of the total Accrued liabilities balance at May 31, 2015 and 2014.

NOTE 6 — Fair Value Measurements

The following tables present information about the Company's financial assets and liabilities measured at fair value on a recurring basis as of May 31, 2015 and 2014 and indicate the fair value hierarchy of the valuation techniques utilized by the Company to determine such fair value. Refer to Note 1 — Summary of Significant Accounting Policies for additional detail regarding the Company's fair value measurement methodology.

	As of May 31, 2015			
(In millions)	Assets at Fair Value	Cash and Cash Equivalents	Short-term Investments	Other Long-term Assets
Cash	$ 615	$ 615	$ —	$ —
Level 1:				
U.S. Treasury securities	869	225	644	—
Level 2:				
Time deposits	684	684	—	—
U.S. Agency securities	976	110	866	—
Commercial paper and bonds	914	352	562	—
Money market funds	1,866	1,866	—	—
Total level 2	4,440	3,012	1,428	—
Level 3:				
Non-marketable preferred stock	8	—	—	8
TOTAL	$ **5,932**	$ **3,852**	$ **2,072**	$ **8**

	As of May 31, 2014			
(In millions)	Assets at Fair Value	Cash and Cash Equivalents	Short-term Investments	Other Long-term Assets
Cash	$ 780	$ 780	$ —	$ —
Level 1:				
U.S. Treasury securities	1,137	151	986	—
Level 2:				
Time deposits	227	227	—	—
U.S. Agency securities	1,027	25	1,002	—
Commercial paper and bonds	959	25	934	—
Money market funds	1,012	1,012	—	—
Total level 2	3,225	1,289	1,936	—
Level 3:				
Non-marketable preferred stock	7	—	—	7
TOTAL	$ **5,149**	$ **2,220**	$ **2,922**	$ **7**

The Company elects to record the gross assets and liabilities of its derivative financial instruments on the Consolidated Balance Sheets. The Company's derivative financial instruments are subject to master netting arrangements that allow for the offset of assets and liabilities in the event of default or early termination of the contract. Any amounts of cash collateral received related to these instruments associated with the Company's credit-related contingent features are recorded in *Cash and equivalents* and *Accrued liabilities*, the latter of which would further offset against the Company's derivative asset balance (refer to Note 17 — Risk Management and Derivatives). Cash collateral received related to the Company's credit related contingent features is presented in the *Cash provided by operations* component of the Consolidated Statement of Cash Flows. Any amounts of non-cash collateral received, such as securities, are not recorded on the Consolidated Balance Sheets pursuant to the accounting standards for non-cash collateral received.

The following tables present information about the Company's derivative assets and liabilities measured at fair value on a recurring basis as of May 31, 2015 and May 31, 2014, and indicate the level in the fair value hierarchy in which the Company classifies the fair value measurement.

	As of May 31, 2015					
	Derivative Assets			Derivative Liabilities		
(In millions)	Assets at Fair Value	Other Current Assets	Other Long-term Assets	Liabilities at Fair Value	Accrued Liabilities	Other Long-term Liabilities
Level 2:						
Foreign exchange forwards and options[1]	$ 1,554	$ 1,034	$ 520	$ 164	$ 160	$ 4
Embedded derivatives	7	2	5	11	2	9
Interest rate swaps[2]	78	78	—	—	—	—
TOTAL	$ **1,639**	$ **1,114**	$ **525**	$ **175**	$ **162**	$ **13**

(1) If the foreign exchange derivative instruments had been netted in the Consolidated Balance Sheets, the asset and liability positions each would have been reduced by $161 million as of May 31, 2015. As of that date, the Company had received $900 million of cash collateral and $74 million of securities from various counterparties related to these foreign exchange derivative instruments. No amount of collateral was posted on the Company's derivative liability balance as of May 31, 2015.

(2) As of May 31, 2015, the Company had received $68 million of cash collateral related to its interest rate swaps.

| | | As of May 31, 2014 | | | | | |
| | | Derivative Assets | | | Derivative Liabilities | | |
(In millions)		Assets at Fair Value	Other Current Assets	Other Long-term Assets	Liabilities at Fair Value	Accrued Liabilities	Other Long-term Liabilities
Level 2:							
Foreign exchange forwards and options[1]	$	127	$ 101	$ 26	$ 85	$ 84	$ 1
Interest rate swaps		6	—	6	—	—	—
TOTAL	$	133	$ 101	$ 32	$ 85	$ 84	$ 1

(1) If the foreign exchange derivative financial instruments had been netted in the Consolidated Balance Sheets, the asset and liability positions each would have been reduced by $63 million as of May 31, 2014. No amounts of collateral were received or posted on the Company's derivative assets and liabilities as of May 31, 2014.

Available-for-sale securities comprise investments in U.S. Treasury and Agency securities, money market funds, corporate commercial paper and bonds. These securities are valued using market prices on both active markets (Level 1) and less active markets (Level 2). The gross realized gains and losses on sales of available-for-sale securities were immaterial for the fiscal years ended May 31, 2015 and 2014. Unrealized gains and losses on available-for-sale securities included in *Other comprehensive income* were immaterial as of May 31, 2015 and 2014.

The Company regularly reviews its available-for-sale securities for other-than-temporary impairment. For the years ended May 31, 2015 and 2014, the Company did not consider its securities to be other-than-temporarily impaired and accordingly, did not recognize any impairment losses.

As of May 31, 2015, the Company held $1,808 million of available-for-sale securities with maturity dates within one year and $264 million with maturity dates over one year and less than five years within *Short-term investments* on the Consolidated Balance Sheets.

Included in *Interest expense (income), net* was interest income related to the Company's available-for-sale securities of $6 million, $5 million and $4 million for the years ended May 31, 2015, 2014 and 2013, respectively.

The Company's Level 3 assets comprise investments in certain non-marketable preferred stock. These Level 3 investments are an immaterial portion of the Company's portfolio. Changes in Level 3 investment assets were immaterial during the years ended May 31, 2015 and 2014.

Derivative financial instruments include foreign exchange forwards and options, embedded derivatives and interest rate swaps. Refer to Note 17 — Risk Management and Derivatives for additional detail.

No transfers among the levels within the fair value hierarchy occurred during the years ended May 31, 2015 or 2014.

As of May 31, 2015 and 2014, the Company had no assets or liabilities that were required to be measured at fair value on a non-recurring basis.

For fair value information regarding *Notes payable* and *Long-term debt*, refer to Note 7 — Short-Term Borrowings and Credit Lines and Note 8 — Long-Term Debt.

At May 31, 2015, the Company had $150 million of outstanding receivables related to its investments in reverse repurchase agreements recorded within *Prepaid expenses and other current assets* on the Consolidated Balance Sheet. The carrying amount of these agreements approximates their fair value based upon observable inputs other than quoted prices (Level 2). The reverse repurchase agreements are fully collateralized.

NOTE 7 — Short-Term Borrowings and Credit Lines

Notes payable and interest-bearing accounts payable to Sojitz Corporation of America ("Sojitz America") as of May 31, 2015 and 2014 are summarized below:

| | | As of May 31, | | | |
| | | 2015 | | 2014 | |
(Dollars in millions)		Borrowings	Interest Rate	Borrowings	Interest Rate
Notes payable:					
U.S. operations	$	—	0.00%[1]	$ —	0.00%[1]
Non-U.S. operations		74	12.39%[1]	167	10.04%[1]
TOTAL NOTES PAYABLE	$	74		$ 167	
Interest-bearing accounts payable:					
Sojitz America	$	78	0.98%	$ 60	0.94%

(1) Weighted average interest rate includes non-interest bearing overdrafts.

The carrying amounts reflected in the Consolidated Balance Sheets for *Notes payable* approximate fair value.

The Company purchases through Sojitz America certain NIKE Brand products it acquires from non-U.S. suppliers. These purchases are for products sold in certain countries in the Company's Emerging Markets geographic operating segment and Canada, excluding products produced and sold in the same country. Accounts payable to Sojitz America are generally due up to 60 days after shipment of goods from the foreign port. The interest rate on such accounts payable is the 60-day London Interbank Offered Rate ("LIBOR") as of the beginning of the month of the invoice date, plus 0.75%.

As of May 31, 2015 and 2014, the Company had no amounts outstanding under its commercial paper program.

On November 1, 2011, the Company entered into a committed credit facility agreement with a syndicate of banks which provides for up to $1 billion of borrowings with the option to increase borrowings to $1.5 billion with lender approval. Following an extension agreement on September 17, 2013 between the Company and the syndicate of banks, the facility matures November 1, 2017. Based on the Company's current long-term senior unsecured debt ratings of AA- and A1 from Standard and Poor's Corporation and Moody's Investor Services, respectively, the interest rate charged on any outstanding borrowings would be the prevailing LIBOR plus 0.445%. The facility fee is 0.055% of the total commitment. Under this committed credit facility, the Company must maintain, among other things, certain minimum specified financial ratios with which the Company was in compliance at May 31, 2015. No amounts were outstanding under this facility as of May 31, 2015 or 2014.

NOTE 8 — Long-Term Debt

Long-term debt, net of unamortized premiums and discounts and swap fair value adjustments, comprises the following:

Scheduled Maturity (Dollars and Yen in millions)	Original Principal	Interest Rate	Interest Payments	Book Value Outstanding As of May 31,	
				2015	2014
Corporate Bond Payables:(4)					
October 15, 2015(1)	$ 100	5.15%	Semi-Annually	$ 101	$ 108
May 1, 2023(5)	$ 500	2.25%	Semi-Annually	499	499
May 1, 2043(5)	$ 500	3.63%	Semi-Annually	499	499
Promissory Notes:					
April 1, 2017(2)	$ 40	6.20%	Monthly	39	39
January 1, 2018(2)	$ 19	6.79%	Monthly	19	19
Japanese Yen Notes:					
August 20, 2001 through November 20, 2020(3)	¥ 9,000	2.60%	Quarterly	20	29
August 20, 2001 through November 20, 2020(3)	¥ 4,000	2.00%	Quarterly	9	13
Total				1,186	1,206
Less current maturities				107	7
TOTAL LONG-TERM DEBT				$ **1,079**	$ **1,199**

(1) The Company has entered into interest rate swap agreements whereby the Company receives fixed interest payments at the same rate as the note and pays variable interest payments based on the six-month LIBOR plus a spread. The swaps have the same notional amount and maturity date as the corresponding note. At May 31, 2015, the interest rates payable on these swap agreements ranged from approximately 0.3% to 0.5%.

(2) The Company assumed a total of $59 million in bonds payable as part of its agreement to purchase certain Corporate properties; this was treated as a non-cash financing transaction. The property serves as collateral for the debt. The purchase of these properties was accounted for as a business combination where the total consideration of $85 million was allocated to the land and buildings acquired; no other tangible or intangible assets or liabilities resulted from the purchase. The bonds mature in 2017 and 2018 and the Company does not have the ability to re-negotiate the terms of the debt agreements and would incur significant financial penalties if the notes were paid-off prior to maturity.

(3) NIKE Logistics YK assumed a total of ¥13.0 billion in loans as part of its agreement to purchase a distribution center in Japan, which serves as collateral for the loans. These loans mature in equal quarterly installments during the period August 20, 2001 through November 20, 2020.

(4) These senior unsecured obligations rank equally with the Company's other unsecured and unsubordinated indebtedness.

(5) The bonds are redeemable at the Company's option prior to February 1, 2023 and November 1, 2042, respectively, at a price equal to the greater of (i) 100% of the aggregate principal amount of the notes to be redeemed, and (ii) the sum of the present values of the remaining scheduled payments, plus in each case, accrued and unpaid interest. Subsequent to February 1, 2023 and November 1, 2042, respectively, the bonds also feature a par call provision, which allows for the bonds to be redeemed at a price equal to 100% of the aggregate principal amount of the notes being redeemed, plus accrued and unpaid interest.

The scheduled maturity of *Long-term debt* in each of the years ending May 31, 2016 through 2020 are $106 million, $44 million, $24 million, $6 million and $6 million, respectively, at face value.

The fair value of the Company's *Long-term debt*, including the current portion, was approximately $1,160 million at May 31, 2015 and $1,154 million at May 31, 2014. The fair value of *Long-term debt* is estimated based upon quoted prices of similar instruments (level 2).

NOTE 9 — Income Taxes

Income before income taxes is as follows:

(In millions)	Year Ended May 31,		
	2015	2014	2013
Income before income taxes:			
United States	$ 1,967	$ 3,066	$ 1,231
Foreign	2,238	478	2,025
TOTAL INCOME BEFORE INCOME TAXES	$ **4,205**	$ **3,544**	$ **3,256**

The provision for income taxes is as follows:

(In millions)	2015	2014	2013
Current:			
United States			
Federal	$ 596	$ 259	$ 378
State	80	104	79
Foreign	369	499	442
Total	1,045	862	899
Deferred:			
United States			
Federal	(66)	19	(4)
State	(11)	(3)	(4)
Foreign	(36)	(27)	(86)
Total	(113)	(11)	(94)
TOTAL INCOME TAX EXPENSE	$ 932	$ 851	$ 805

A reconciliation from the U.S. statutory federal income tax rate to the effective income tax rate is as follows:

	2015	2014	2013
Federal income tax rate	35.0%	35.0%	35.0%
State taxes, net of federal benefit	0.9%	1.8%	1.4%
Foreign earnings	-15.7%	2.2%	-11.8%
Deferred charge	0.9%	-14.6%	0.0%
Other, net	1.1%	-0.4%	0.1%
EFFECTIVE INCOME TAX RATE	22.2%	24.0%	24.7%

The effective tax rate from continuing operations for the year ended May 31, 2015 was 180 basis points lower than the effective tax rate from continuing operations for the year ended May 31, 2014 primarily due to the favorable resolution of audits in several jurisdictions.

The effective tax rate from continuing operations for the year ended May 31, 2014 was 70 basis points lower than the effective tax rate from continuing operations for the year ended May 31, 2013 primarily due to an increase in the amount of earnings from lower tax rate jurisdictions.

During the fourth quarter of the fiscal year ended May 31, 2014, the Company reached a resolution with the IRS on a U.S. Unilateral Advanced Pricing Agreement that covers intercompany transfer pricing for fiscal years 2011 through 2020. This agreement resulted in an increase in the effective tax rate due to a reduction in the Company's permanently reinvested foreign earnings, which was partially offset by a reduction in previously unrecognized tax benefits. It also resulted in a decrease in the effective tax rate due to the recognition of a deferred tax charge. The net result of the agreement did not have a material impact on the Company's effective income tax rate in fiscal 2014.

Deferred tax assets and (liabilities) comprise the following:

(In millions)	2015	2014
Deferred tax assets:		
Allowance for doubtful accounts	$ 11	$ 11
Inventories	59	49
Sales return reserves	143	113
Deferred compensation	258	211
Stock-based compensation	179	162
Reserves and accrued liabilities	92	95
Net operating loss carry-forwards	10	16
Undistributed earnings of foreign subsidiaries	149	194
Other	76	51
Total deferred tax assets	977	902
Valuation allowance	(9)	(9)
Total deferred tax assets after valuation allowance	968	893
Deferred tax liabilities:		
Property, plant and equipment	(220)	(237)
Intangibles	(93)	(94)
Other	(38)	(2)
Total deferred tax liability	(351)	(333)
NET DEFERRED TAX ASSET	$ 617	$ 560

The following is a reconciliation of the changes in the gross balance of unrecognized tax benefits:

	As of May 31,		
(In millions)	2015	2014	2013
Unrecognized tax benefits, beginning of the period	$ 506	$ 447	$ 285
Gross increases related to prior period tax positions[1]	32	814	77
Gross decreases related to prior period tax positions[1]	(123)	(166)	(3)
Gross increases related to current period tax positions	82	125	130
Gross decreases related to current period tax positions	(9)	(30)	(9)
Settlements[1]	(27)	(676)	—
Lapse of statute of limitations	(10)	(4)	(21)
Changes due to currency translation	(13)	(4)	(12)
UNRECOGNIZED TAX BENEFITS, END OF THE PERIOD	$ 438	$ 506	$ 447

(1) *During the fourth quarter of the fiscal year ended May 31, 2014, the Company reached a resolution with the IRS on a U.S. Unilateral Advanced Pricing Agreement that covers intercompany transfer pricing for fiscal years 2011 through 2020. As a result, the Company recorded a gross increase in unrecognized tax benefits related to prior period tax positions, a gross decrease in unrecognized tax benefits related to prior period tax positions and a settlement. The net impact of these items resulted in a decrease to unrecognized tax benefits.*

As of May 31, 2015, total gross unrecognized tax benefits, excluding related interest and penalties, were $438 million, $260 million of which would affect the Company's effective tax rate if recognized in future periods.

The Company recognizes interest and penalties related to income tax matters in *Income tax expense*. The liability for payment of interest and penalties decreased $3 million during the year ended May 31, 2015, and increased $55 million and $4 million during the years ended May 31, 2014 and 2013, respectively. As of May 31, 2015 and 2014, accrued interest and penalties related to uncertain tax positions were $164 million and $167 million, respectively (excluding federal benefit).

The Company incurs tax liabilities primarily in the United States, China and the Netherlands, as well as various state and other foreign jurisdictions. The Company is currently under audit by the U.S. Internal Revenue Service (IRS) for the 2012 through 2014 tax years. The Company has closed all U.S. federal income tax matters through fiscal 2011, with the exception of the validation of foreign tax credits utilized. As previously disclosed, the Company received a statutory notice of deficiency for fiscal 2011 proposing an increase in tax of $31 million, subject to interest, related to the foreign tax credit matter. This notice also reported a decrease in foreign tax credit carryovers for fiscal 2010 and 2011. The Company has contested this deficiency notice by filing a petition with the U.S Tax Court in April 2015. The Company does not expect the outcome of this matter to have a material impact on the financial statements. No payments on the assessment would be required until the dispute is definitively resolved. Based on the information currently available, the Company does not anticipate a significant increase or decrease to its unrecognized tax benefits for this matter within the next 12 months.

The Company's major foreign jurisdictions, China, the Netherlands and Brazil, have concluded substantially all income tax matters through calendar 2005, fiscal 2009 and calendar 2008, respectively. Although the timing of resolution of audits is not certain, the Company evaluates all domestic and foreign audit issues in the aggregate, along with the expiration of applicable statutes of limitations, and estimates that it is reasonably possible the total gross unrecognized tax benefits could decrease by up to $63 million within the next 12 months.

The Company provides for U.S. income taxes on the undistributed earnings of foreign subsidiaries unless they are considered indefinitely reinvested outside the United States. At May 31, 2015, the indefinitely reinvested earnings in foreign subsidiaries upon which United States income taxes have not been provided were approximately $8.3 billion. If these undistributed earnings were repatriated to the United States, or if the shares of the relevant foreign subsidiaries were sold or otherwise transferred, they would generate foreign tax credits that would reduce the federal tax liability associated with the foreign dividend or the otherwise taxable transaction. Assuming a full utilization of the foreign tax credits, the potential net deferred tax liability associated with these temporary differences of undistributed earnings would be approximately $2.7 billion at May 31, 2015.

A portion of the Company's foreign operations are benefiting from a tax holiday, which is set to expire in 2021. This tax holiday may be extended when certain conditions are met or may be terminated early if certain conditions are not met. The impact of this tax holiday decreased foreign taxes by $174 million, $138 million and $108 million for the fiscal years ended May 31, 2015, 2014 and 2013, respectively. The benefit of the tax holiday on diluted earnings per common share was $0.20, $0.15 and $0.12 for the fiscal years ended May 31, 2015, 2014 and 2013, respectively.

Deferred tax assets at May 31, 2015 and 2014 were reduced by a valuation allowance relating to tax benefits of certain subsidiaries with operating losses. There was no net change in the valuation allowance for the year ended May 31, 2015 compared to a net increase of $4 million and a net decrease of $22 million for the years ended May 31, 2014 and 2013, respectively.

The Company has available domestic and foreign loss carry-forwards of $36 million at May 31, 2015. Such losses will expire as follows:

	Year Ending May 31,						
(In millions)	2016	2017	2018	2019	2020-2035	Indefinite	Total
Net operating losses	$ —	$ —	$ 4	$ 1	$ 17	$ 14	$ 36

During the years ended May 31, 2015, 2014 and 2013, income tax benefits attributable to employee stock-based compensation transactions of $224 million, $135 million and $76 million, respectively, were allocated to *Total shareholders' equity*.

NOTE 10 — Redeemable Preferred Stock

Sojitz America is the sole owner of the Company's authorized redeemable preferred stock, $1 par value, which is redeemable at the option of Sojitz America or the Company at par value aggregating $0.3 million. A cumulative dividend of $0.10 per share is payable annually on May 31 and no dividends may be declared or paid on the common stock of the Company unless dividends on the redeemable preferred stock have been declared and paid in full. There have been no changes in the redeemable preferred stock in the three years ended May 31, 2015, 2014 and 2013. As the holder of the redeemable preferred stock, Sojitz America does not have general voting rights, but does have the right to vote as a separate class on the sale of all or substantially all of the assets of the Company and its subsidiaries, on merger, consolidation, liquidation or dissolution of the Company or on the sale or assignment of the NIKE trademark for athletic footwear sold in the United States. The redeemable preferred stock has been fully issued to Sojitz America and is not blank check preferred stock. The Company's articles of incorporation do not permit the issuance of additional preferred stock.

NOTE 11 — Common Stock and Stock-Based Compensation

The authorized number of shares of Class A Common Stock, no par value, and Class B Common Stock, no par value, are 200 million and 1,200 million, respectively. Each share of Class A Common Stock is convertible into one share of Class B Common Stock. Voting rights of Class B Common Stock are limited in certain circumstances with respect to the election of directors. There are no differences in the dividend and liquidation preferences or participation rights of the Class A and Class B common shareholders.

In 1990, the Board of Directors adopted, and the shareholders approved, the NIKE, Inc. 1990 Stock Incentive Plan (the "1990 Plan"). The 1990 Plan, as amended, provides for the issuance of up to 326 million previously unissued shares of Class B Common Stock in connection with stock options and other awards granted under the plan. The 1990 Plan authorizes the grant of non-statutory stock options, incentive stock options, stock appreciation rights, restricted stock, restricted stock units and performance-based awards. The exercise price for stock options and stock appreciation rights may not be less than the fair market value of the underlying shares on the date of grant. A committee of the Board of Directors administers the 1990 Plan. The committee has the authority to determine the employees to whom awards will be made, the amount of the awards and the other terms and conditions of the awards. Substantially all stock option grants outstanding under the 1990 Plan were granted in the first quarter of each fiscal year, vest ratably over four years and expire 10 years from the date of grant.

The following table summarizes the Company's total stock-based compensation expense recognized in *Operating overhead expense*:

	Year Ended May 31,		
(In millions)	2015	2014	2013
Stock options[1]	$ 136	$ 125	$ 123
ESPPs	24	22	19
Restricted stock	31	30	32
TOTAL STOCK-BASED COMPENSATION EXPENSE	$ 191	$ 177	$ 174

(1) Expense for stock options includes the expense associated with stock appreciation rights. Accelerated stock option expense is recorded for employees eligible for accelerated stock option vesting upon retirement. Accelerated stock option expense for the years ended May 31, 2015, 2014 and 2013 was $19 million, $15 million and $22 million, respectively.

As of May 31, 2015, the Company had $180 million of unrecognized compensation costs from stock options, net of estimated forfeitures, to be recognized in *Operating overhead expense* over a weighted average period of 1.9 years.

The weighted average fair value per share of the options granted during the years ended May 31, 2015, 2014 and 2013, as computed using the Black-Scholes pricing model, was $16.95, $14.89 and $12.71, respectively. The weighted average assumptions used to estimate these fair values are as follows:

	Year Ended May 31,		
	2015	2014	2013
Dividend yield	1.2%	1.3%	1.5%
Expected volatility	23.0%	27.9%	35.0%
Weighted average expected life (in years)	5.8	5.3	5.3
Risk-free interest rate	1.7%	1.3%	0.6%

The Company estimates the expected volatility based on the implied volatility in market traded options on the Company's common stock with a term greater than one year, along with other factors. The weighted average expected life of options is based on an analysis of historical and expected future exercise patterns. The interest rate is based on the U.S. Treasury (constant maturity) risk-free rate in effect at the date of grant for periods corresponding with the expected term of the options.

The following summarizes the stock option transactions under the plan discussed above:

	Shares[1]	Weighted Average Option Price
	(In millions)	
Options outstanding May 31, 2012	64.3	$ 30.59
Exercised	(9.9)	24.70
Forfeited	(1.3)	40.14
Granted	14.6	46.55
Options outstanding May 31, 2013	67.7	$ 34.72
Exercised	(11.0)	28.29
Forfeited	(1.3)	48.33
Granted	8.1	63.54
Options outstanding May 31, 2014	63.5	$ 39.28
Exercised	(13.6)	30.78
Forfeited	(1.0)	59.02
Granted	9.2	77.68
Options outstanding May 31, 2015	58.1	$ 47.00
Options exercisable at May 31,		
2013	35.9	$ 27.70
2014	37.0	31.42
2015	34.3	36.53

(1) Includes stock appreciation rights transactions.

The weighted average contractual life remaining for options outstanding and options exercisable at May 31, 2015 was 6.0 years and 4.7 years, respectively. The aggregate intrinsic value for options outstanding and exercisable at May 31, 2015 was $3,178 million and $2,235 million, respectively. The aggregate intrinsic value was the amount by which the market value of the underlying stock exceeded the exercise price of the options. The total intrinsic value of the options exercised during the years ended May 31, 2015, 2014 and 2013 was $795 million, $474 million and $293 million, respectively.

In addition to the 1990 Plan, the Company gives employees the right to purchase shares at a discount to the market price under employee stock purchase plans ("ESPPs"). Employees are eligible to participate through payroll deductions of up to 10% of their compensation. At the end of each six-month offering period, shares are purchased by the participants at 85% of the lower of the fair market value at the beginning or the end of the offering period. Employees purchased 1.4 million, 1.4 million and 1.6 million shares during each of the three years ended May 31, 2015, 2014 and 2013, respectively.

From time to time, the Company grants restricted stock and restricted stock units to key employees under the 1990 Plan. The number of shares underlying such awards granted to employees during the years ended May 31, 2015, 2014 and 2013 were 0.3 million, 0.3 million and 1.6 million, respectively, with weighted average values per share of $79.38, $63.89 and $46.86, respectively. Recipients of restricted stock are entitled to cash dividends and to vote their respective shares throughout the period of restriction. Recipients of restricted stock units are entitled to dividend equivalent cash payments upon vesting. The value of all grants of restricted stock and restricted stock units was established by the market price on the date of grant. During the years ended May 31, 2015, 2014 and 2013, the aggregate fair value of restricted stock and restricted stock units vested was $20 million, $28 million and $25 million, respectively, determined as of the date of vesting. As of May 31, 2015, the Company had $48 million of unrecognized compensation costs from restricted stock units to be recognized in *Operating overhead expense* over a weighted average period of 1.5 years.

NOTE 12 — Earnings Per Share

The following is a reconciliation from Basic earnings per common share to Diluted earnings per common share. The computation of Diluted earnings per common share omitted options to purchase an additional 0.1 million, 0.1 million and 0.1 million shares of common stock outstanding for the years ended May 31, 2015, 2014 and 2013, respectively, because the options were anti-dilutive.

	Year Ended May 31,		
(In millions, except per share data)	**2015**	**2014**	**2013**
Determination of shares:			
Weighted average common shares outstanding	861.7	883.4	897.3
Assumed conversion of dilutive stock options and awards	22.7	22.4	19.1
DILUTED WEIGHTED AVERAGE COMMON SHARES OUTSTANDING	**884.4**	**905.8**	**916.4**
Earnings per common share from continuing operations:			
Basic	$ 3.80	$ 3.05	$ 2.74
Diluted	$ 3.70	$ 2.97	$ 2.68
Earnings per common share from discontinued operations:			
Basic	$ —	$ —	$ 0.02
Diluted	$ —	$ —	$ 0.02
Basic earnings per common share for NIKE, Inc.	$ 3.80	$ 3.05	$ 2.76
Diluted earnings per common share for NIKE, Inc.	$ 3.70	$ 2.97	$ 2.70

NOTE 13 — Benefit Plans

The Company has a qualified 401(k) Savings and Profit Sharing Plan to which all U.S. employees who work at least 1,000 hours in a year are able to participate. The Company matches a portion of employee contributions. Company contributions to the savings plan were $58 million, $51 million and $46 million for the years ended May 31, 2015, 2014 and 2013, respectively, and are included in *Operating overhead expense*. The terms of the plan also allow for annual discretionary profit sharing contributions to the accounts of eligible employees by the Company as determined by the Board of Directors. Contributions of $58 million, $49 million and $47 million were made to the plan and are included in *Operating overhead expense* for the years ended May 31, 2015, 2014 and 2013, respectively.

The Company also has a Long-Term Incentive Plan ("LTIP") that was adopted by the Board of Directors and approved by shareholders in September 1997 and later amended in fiscal 2007. The Company recognized $68 million, $46 million and $50 million of *Operating overhead expense* related to cash awards under the LTIP during the years ended May 31, 2015, 2014 and 2013, respectively.

The Company allows certain highly compensated employees and non-employee directors of the Company to defer compensation under a nonqualified deferred compensation plan. Deferred compensation plan liabilities were $443 million and $390 million at May 31, 2015 and 2014, respectively, and primarily classified as long-term in *Deferred income taxes and other liabilities*.

The Company has pension plans in various countries worldwide. The pension plans are only available to local employees and are generally government mandated. The liability related to the unfunded pension liabilities of the plans was $98 million and $100 million at May 31, 2015 and May 31, 2014, respectively, which was primarily classified as long-term in *Deferred income taxes and other liabilities*.

NOTE 14 — Accumulated Other Comprehensive Income

The changes in *Accumulated other comprehensive income*, net of tax, were as follows:

(In millions)	Foreign Currency Translation Adjustment[1]	Cash Flow Hedges	Net Investment Hedges[1]	Other	Total
Balance at May 31, 2014	$ 9	$ 32	$ 95	$ (51)	$ 85
Other comprehensive gains (losses) before reclassifications[2]	(20)	1,447	—	33	1,460
Reclassifications to net income of previously deferred (gains) losses[3]	—	(259)	—	(40)	(299)
Other comprehensive income (loss)	(20)	1,188	—	(7)	1,161
Balance at May 31, 2015	$ (11)	$ 1,220	$ 95	$ (58)	$ 1,246

(1) The accumulated foreign currency translation adjustment and net investment hedge gains/losses related to an investment in a foreign subsidiary are reclassified to Net income upon sale or upon complete or substantially complete liquidation of the respective entity.

(2) Net of tax benefit (expense) of $ 0 million, $ (33) million, $ 0 million, $ 0 million and $ (33) million, respectively.

(3) Net of tax (benefit) expense of $ 0 million, $ 2 million, $ 0 million, $ 0 million and $ 2 million, respectively.

(In millions)	Foreign Currency Translation Adjustment[1]	Cash Flow Hedges	Net Investment Hedges[1]	Other	Total
Balance at May 31, 2013	$ 41	$ 193	$ 95	$ (55)	$ 274
Other comprehensive gains (losses) before reclassifications[2]	(32)	(134)	—	—	(166)
Reclassifications to net income of previously deferred (gains) losses[3]	—	(27)	—	4	(23)
Other comprehensive income (loss)	(32)	(161)	—	4	(189)
Balance at May 31, 2014	$ 9	$ 32	$ 95	$ (51)	$ 85

(1) The accumulated foreign currency translation adjustment and net investment hedge gains/losses related to an investment in a foreign subsidiary are reclassified to Net income upon sale or upon complete or substantially complete liquidation of the respective entity.

(2) Net of tax benefit (expense) of $ 0 million, $ 9 million, $ 0 million, $ 0 million and $ 9 million, respectively.

(3) Net of tax (benefit) expense of $ 0 million, $ 9 million, $ 0 million, $ 0 million and $ 9 million respectively.

The following table summarizes the reclassifications from *Accumulated other comprehensive income* to the Consolidated Statements of Income:

(In millions)	Amount of Gain (Loss) Reclassified from Accumulated Other Comprehensive Income into Income — Year Ended May 31, 2015	2014	Location of Gain (Loss) Reclassified from Accumulated Other Comprehensive Income into Income
Gains (losses) on cash flow hedges:			
Foreign exchange forwards and options	$ (95)	$ 14	Revenues
Foreign exchange forwards and options	220	12	Cost of sales
Foreign exchange forwards and options	—	—	Total selling and administrative expense
Foreign exchange forwards and options	136	10	Other (income) expense, net
Total before tax	261	36	
Tax expense	(2)	(9)	
Gain, net of tax	259	27	
Gains (losses) on other	40	(4)	Other (income) expense, net
Total before tax	40	(4)	
Tax expense	—	—	
Gain (loss), net of tax	40	(4)	
Total net gain reclassified for the period	$ 299	$ 23	

Refer to Note 17 — Risk Management and Derivatives for more information on the Company's risk management program and derivatives.

NOTE 15 — Discontinued Operations

During the year ended May 31, 2013, the Company divested of Umbro and Cole Haan, allowing it to focus its resources on driving growth in the NIKE, Jordan, Converse and Hurley brands.

On February 1, 2013, the Company completed the sale of Cole Haan to Apax Partners for an agreed upon purchase price of $570 million and received at closing $561 million, net of $9 million of purchase price adjustments. The transaction resulted in a gain on sale of $231 million, net of $137 million in *Income tax expense*; this gain is included in the *Net income from discontinued operations* line item on the Consolidated Statements of Income. There were no adjustments to these recorded amounts as of May 31, 2015. Beginning November 30, 2012, the Company classified the Cole Haan disposal group as held-for-sale and presented the results of Cole Haan's operations in the *Net income from discontinued operations* line item on the Consolidated Statements of Income. From this date until the sale, the assets and liabilities of Cole Haan were recorded in the *Assets of discontinued operations* and

Liabilities of discontinued operations line items on the Consolidated Balance Sheets, respectively. Previously, these amounts were reported in the Company's operating segment presentation as "Other Businesses."

Under the sale agreement, the Company agreed to provide certain transition services to Cole Haan for an expected period of 3 to 9 months from the date of sale. These services were essentially complete as of May 31, 2013 and the Company has had no significant involvement with Cole Haan beyond the transition services. The Company has also licensed NIKE proprietary Air and Lunar technologies to Cole Haan for a transition period. The continuing cash flows related to these items are not significant to Cole Haan. Additionally, preexisting guarantees of certain Cole Haan lease payments remained in place after the sale; the maximum exposure under the guarantees is $23 million at May 31, 2015. The fair value of the guarantees is not material.

On November 30, 2012, the Company completed the sale of certain assets of Umbro to Iconix Brand Group ("Iconix") for $225 million. The Umbro disposal group was classified as held-for-sale as of November 30, 2012 and the results of Umbro's operations are presented in the *Net income from discontinued operations* line item on the Consolidated Statements of Income. The liabilities of Umbro were recorded in the *Liabilities of discontinued operations* line items on the Consolidated Balance Sheets. Previously, these amounts were reported in the Company's operating segment presentation as "Other Businesses." Upon meeting the held-for-sale criteria, the Company recorded a loss of $107 million, net of tax, on the sale of Umbro and the loss is included in the *Net income from discontinued operations* line item on the Consolidated Statements of Income. The loss on sale was calculated as the net sales price less Umbro assets of $248 million, including intangibles, goodwill and fixed assets, other miscellaneous charges of $22 million and the release of the associated cumulative translation adjustment of $129 million. The tax benefit on the loss was $67 million. There were no adjustments to these recorded amounts as of May 31, 2015.

Summarized results of the Company's discontinued operations are as follows:

(In millions)	Year Ended May 31,		
	2015	2014	2013
Revenues	$ —	$ —	$ 523
Income before income taxes	—	—	108
Income tax expense	—	—	87
NET INCOME FROM DISCONTINUED OPERATIONS	$ —	$ —	$ 21

There were no assets or liabilities of discontinued operations as of May 31, 2015 and May 31, 2014.

NOTE 16 — Commitments and Contingencies

The Company leases space for certain of its offices, warehouses and retail stores under leases expiring from 1 to 19 years after May 31, 2015. Rent expense was $594 million, $533 million and $482 million for the years ended May 31, 2015, 2014 and 2013, respectively. Amounts of minimum future annual commitments under non-cancelable operating and capital leases are as follows (in millions):

	2016	2017	2018	2019	2020	Thereafter	Total
Operating leases	$ 447	$ 423	$ 371	$ 311	$ 268	$ 1,154	$ 2,974
Capital leases	$ 2	$ 2	$ 1	$ —	$ —	$ —	$ 5

As of May 31, 2015 and 2014, the Company had letters of credit outstanding totaling $165 million and $135 million, respectively. These letters of credit were generally issued for the purchase of inventory and guarantees of the Company's performance under certain self-insurance and other programs.

In connection with various contracts and agreements, the Company provides routine indemnification relating to the enforceability of intellectual property rights, coverage for legal issues that arise and other items where the Company is acting as the guarantor. Currently, the Company has several such agreements in place. However, based on the Company's historical experience and the estimated probability of future loss, the Company has

determined that the fair value of such indemnification is not material to the Company's financial position or results of operations.

In the ordinary course of its business, the Company is involved in various legal proceedings involving contractual and employment relationships, product liability claims, trademark rights and a variety of other matters. While the Company cannot predict the outcome of its pending legal matters with certainty, the Company does not believe any currently identified claim, proceeding or litigation, either individually or in aggregate, will have a material impact on the Company's results of operations, financial position or cash flows.

NOTE 17 — Risk Management and Derivatives

The Company is exposed to global market risks, including the effect of changes in foreign currency exchange rates and interest rates, and uses derivatives to manage financial exposures that occur in the normal course of business. The Company does not hold or issue derivatives for trading or speculative purposes.

The Company may elect to designate certain derivatives as hedging instruments under the accounting standards for derivatives and hedging. The Company formally documents all relationships between designated hedging instruments and hedged items as well as its risk management objectives and

strategies for undertaking hedge transactions. This process includes linking all derivatives designated as hedges to either recognized assets or liabilities or forecasted transactions.

The majority of derivatives outstanding as of May 31, 2015 are designated as foreign currency cash flow hedges primarily for Euro/U.S. Dollar, British Pound/Euro and Japanese Yen/U.S. Dollar currency pairs. All derivatives are recognized on the Consolidated Balance Sheets at fair value and classified based on the instrument's maturity date.

The following table presents the fair values of derivative instruments included within the Consolidated Balance Sheets as of May 31, 2015 and 2014:

| (In millions) | Asset Derivatives | | | Liability Derivatives | | |
	Balance Sheet Location	2015	2014	Balance Sheet Location	2015	2014
Derivatives formally designated as hedging instruments:						
Foreign exchange forwards and options	Prepaid expenses and other current assets	$ 825	$ 76	Accrued liabilities	$ 140	$ 57
Interest rate swaps	Prepaid expenses and other current assets	78	—	Accrued liabilities	—	—
Foreign exchange forwards and options	Deferred income taxes and other assets	520	26	Deferred income taxes and other liabilities	4	1
Interest rate swaps	Deferred income taxes and other assets	—	6	Deferred income taxes and other liabilities	—	—
Total derivatives formally designated as hedging instruments		1,423	108		144	58
Derivatives not designated as hedging instruments:						
Foreign exchange forwards and options	Prepaid expenses and other current assets	209	25	Accrued liabilities	20	27
Embedded derivatives	Prepaid expenses and other current assets	2	—	Accrued liabilities	2	—
Embedded derivatives	Deferred income taxes and other assets	5	—	Deferred income taxes and other liabilities	9	—
Total derivatives not designated as hedging instruments		216	25		31	27
TOTAL DERIVATIVES		$ 1,639	$ 133		$ 175	$ 85

The following tables present the amounts affecting the Consolidated Statements of Income for years ended May 31, 2015, 2014 and 2013:

| (In millions) | Amount of Gain (Loss) Recognized in Other Comprehensive Income on Derivatives[1] Year Ended May 31, | | | Location of Gain (Loss) Reclassified From Accumulated Other Comprehensive Income Into Income[1] | Amount of Gain (Loss) Reclassified From Accumulated Other Comprehensive Income into Income[1] Year Ended May 31, | | |
	2015	2014	2013		2015	2014	2013
Derivatives designated as cash flow hedges:							
Foreign exchange forwards and options	$ (202)	$ (48)	$ 42	Revenues	$ (95)	$ 14	$ (19)
Foreign exchange forwards and options	1,109	(78)	67	Cost of sales	220	12	113
Foreign exchange forwards and options	—	4	(3)	Total selling and administrative expense	—	—	2
Foreign exchange forwards and options	497	(21)	33	Other (income) expense, net	136	10	9
Interest rate swaps	76	—	—	Interest expense (income), net	—	—	—
Total designated cash flow hedges	$1,480	$(143)	$ 139		$261	$ 36	$105
Derivatives designated as net investment hedges:							
Foreign exchange forwards and options	$ —	$ —	$ —	Other (income) expense, net	$ —	$ —	$ —

(1) For the years ended May 31, 2015, 2014 and 2013, the amounts recorded in Other (income) expense, net as a result of hedge ineffectiveness and the discontinuance of cash flow hedges because the forecasted transactions were no longer probable of occurring were immaterial.

| (In millions) | Amount of Gain (Loss) Recognized in Income on Derivatives Year Ended May 31, | | | Location of Gain (Loss) Recognized in Income on Derivatives |
	2015	2014	2013	
Derivatives designated as fair value hedges:				
Interest rate swaps[1]	$ 5	$ 5	$ 5	Interest expense (income), net
Derivatives not designated as hedging instruments:				
Foreign exchange forwards and options	$ 611	$ (75)	$ 51	Other (income) expense, net
Embedded derivatives	$ (1)	$ (1)	$ (4)	Other (Income) expense, net

(1) All interest rate swaps designated as fair value hedges meet the shortcut method requirements under the accounting standards for derivatives and hedging. Accordingly, changes in the fair values of the interest rate swaps are considered to exactly offset changes in the fair value of the underlying long-term debt. Refer to "Fair Value Hedges" in this note for additional detail.

Refer to Note 6 — Fair Value Measurements for a description of how the above financial instruments are valued and Note 14 — Accumulated Other Comprehensive Income and the Consolidated Statements of Shareholders' Equity for additional information on changes in Other comprehensive income for the years ended May 31, 2015, 2014 and 2013.

Cash Flow Hedges

The purpose of the Company's foreign exchange risk management program is to lessen both the positive and negative effects of currency fluctuations on the Company's consolidated results of operations, financial position and cash flows. Foreign currency exposures that the Company may elect to hedge in this manner include product cost exposures, non-functional currency denominated external and intercompany revenues, selling and administrative expenses, investments in U.S. Dollar-denominated available-for-sale debt securities and certain other intercompany transactions.

Product cost exposures are primarily generated through non-functional currency denominated product purchases and the foreign currency adjustment program described below. NIKE entities primarily purchase products in two ways: (1) Certain NIKE entities, including those supporting the Company's North America, Greater China, Japan and European geographies, purchase product from the NIKE Trading Company ("NTC"), a wholly owned sourcing hub that buys NIKE branded products from third party factories, predominantly in U.S. Dollars. The NTC, whose functional currency is the U.S. Dollar, then sells the products to NIKE entities in their respective functional currencies. When the NTC sells to a NIKE entity with a different functional currency, the result is a foreign currency exposure for the NTC. (2) Other NIKE entities purchase product directly from third party factories in U.S. Dollars. These purchases generate a foreign currency exposure for those NIKE entities with a functional currency other than the U.S. Dollar.

The Company operates a foreign currency adjustment program with certain factories. The program is designed to more effectively manage foreign currency risk by assuming certain of the factories' foreign currency exposures, some of which are natural offsets to the Company's existing foreign currency exposures. Under this program, the Company's payments to these factories are adjusted for rate fluctuations in the basket of currencies ("factory currency exposure index") in which the labor, materials and overhead costs incurred by the factories in the production of NIKE branded products ("factory input costs") are denominated. For the portion of the indices denominated in the local or functional currency of the factory, the Company may elect to place formally designated cash flow hedges. For all currencies within the indices, excluding the U.S. Dollar and the local or functional currency of the factory, an embedded derivative contract is created upon the factory's acceptance of NIKE's purchase order. Embedded derivative contracts are separated from the related purchase order, and their accounting treatment is described further below.

The Company's policy permits the utilization of derivatives to reduce its foreign currency exposures where internal netting or other strategies cannot be effectively employed. Typically the Company may enter into hedge contracts starting up to 12 to 24 months in advance of the forecasted transaction and may place incremental hedges up to 100% of the exposure by the time the forecasted transaction occurs. The total notional amount of outstanding foreign currency derivatives designated as cash flow hedges was $14.4 billion as of May 31, 2015.

During the year ended May 31, 2015, the Company entered into a series of forward-starting interest rate swap agreements with a total notional amount of $1 billion. These instruments were designated as cash flow hedges of the variability in the expected cash outflows of interest payments on future debt due to changes in benchmark interest rates.

All changes in fair value of derivatives designated as cash flow hedges, excluding any ineffective portion, are recorded in *Other comprehensive income* until *Net income* is affected by the variability of cash flows of the hedged transaction. In most cases, amounts recorded in *Other comprehensive income* will be released to *Net income* in periods following the maturity of the related derivative, rather than at maturity. Effective hedge results are classified within the Consolidated Statements of Income in the same manner as the underlying exposure, with the results of hedges of non-functional currency denominated revenues and product cost exposures, excluding embedded derivatives as described below, recorded in *Revenues* or *Cost of sales*, when the underlying hedged transaction affects consolidated *Net income*. Results of hedges of selling and administrative expense are recorded together with those costs when the related expense is recorded. Amounts recorded in *Other comprehensive income* related to forward-starting interest rate swaps will be released through *Interest expense (income), net* over the term of the issued debt. Results of hedges of anticipated purchases and sales of U.S. Dollar-denominated available-for-sale securities are recorded in *Other (income) expense, net* when the securities are sold. Results of hedges of certain anticipated intercompany transactions are recorded in *Other (income) expense, net* when the transaction occurs. The Company classifies the cash flows at settlement from these designated cash flow hedge derivatives in the same category as the cash flows from the related hedged items, primarily within the *Cash provided by operations* component of the Consolidated Statements of Cash Flows.

Premiums paid on options are initially recorded as deferred charges. The Company assesses the effectiveness of options based on the total cash flows method and records total changes in the options' fair value to *Other comprehensive income* to the degree they are effective.

The Company formally assesses, both at a hedge's inception and on an ongoing basis, whether the derivatives that are used in the hedging transaction have been highly effective in offsetting changes in the cash flows of hedged items and whether those derivatives may be expected to remain highly effective in future periods. Effectiveness for cash flow hedges is assessed based on changes in forward rates. Ineffectiveness was immaterial for the years ended May 31, 2015, 2014 and 2013.

The Company discontinues hedge accounting prospectively when: (1) it determines that the derivative is no longer highly effective in offsetting changes in the cash flows of a hedged item (including hedged items such as firm commitments or forecasted transactions); (2) the derivative expires or is sold, terminated or exercised; (3) it is no longer probable that the forecasted transaction will occur; or (4) management determines that designating the derivative as a hedging instrument is no longer appropriate.

When the Company discontinues hedge accounting because it is no longer probable that the forecasted transaction will occur in the originally expected period, but is expected to occur within an additional two-month period of time thereafter, the gain or loss on the derivative remains in *Accumulated other comprehensive income* and is reclassified to *Net income* when the forecasted transaction affects consolidated *Net income*. However, if it is probable that a forecasted transaction will not occur by the end of the originally specified time period or within an additional two-month period of time thereafter, the gains and losses that were accumulated in *Other comprehensive income* will be recognized immediately in *Other (income) expense, net*. In all situations in which hedge accounting is discontinued and the derivative remains outstanding, the Company will carry the derivative at its fair value on the Consolidated Balance Sheets, recognizing future changes in the fair value in *Other (income) expense, net*. For the years ended May 31, 2015, 2014 and 2013, the amounts recorded in *Other (income) expense, net* as a result of the discontinuance of cash flow hedging because the forecasted transaction was no longer probable of occurring were immaterial.

As of May 31, 2015, $685 million of deferred net gains (net of tax) on both outstanding and matured derivatives accumulated in *Other comprehensive income* are expected to be reclassified to *Net income* during the next 12 months concurrent with the underlying hedged transactions also being recorded in *Net income*. Actual amounts ultimately reclassified to *Net income* are dependent on the exchange rates in effect when derivative contracts that are currently outstanding mature. As of May 31, 2015, the maximum term over which the Company is hedging exposures to the variability of cash flows for its forecasted transactions was 36 months.

Fair Value Hedges

The Company is also exposed to the risk of changes in the fair value of certain fixed-rate debt attributable to changes in interest rates. Derivatives currently used by the Company to hedge this risk are receive-fixed, pay-variable interest rate swaps. All interest rate swaps designated as fair value hedges of the related long-term debt meet the shortcut method requirements under the accounting standards for derivatives and hedging. Accordingly, changes in the fair values of the interest rate swaps are considered to exactly offset changes in the fair value of the underlying long-term debt. The cash flows associated with the Company's fair value hedges are periodic interest payments while the swaps are outstanding, which are reflected within the *Cash provided by operations* component of the Consolidated Statements of Cash Flows. The Company recorded no ineffectiveness from its interest rate swaps designated as fair value hedges for the years ended May 31, 2015, 2014 or 2013. As of May 31, 2015, interest rate swaps designated as fair value hedges had a total notional amount of $100 million.

Net Investment Hedges

The Company has, in the past, hedged and may, in the future, hedge the risk of variability in foreign-currency-denominated net investments in wholly-owned international operations. All changes in fair value of the derivatives designated as net investment hedges, except ineffective portions, are reported as a component of *Other comprehensive income* along with the foreign currency translation adjustments on those investments. The Company classifies the cash flows at settlement of its net investment hedges within the *Cash used by investing activities* component of the Consolidated Statement of Cash Flows. The Company assesses hedge effectiveness based on changes in forward rates. The Company recorded no ineffectiveness from its net investment hedges for the years ended May 31, 2015, 2014 or 2013. The Company had no outstanding net investment hedges as of May 31, 2015.

Undesignated Derivative Instruments

The Company may elect to enter into foreign exchange forwards to mitigate the change in fair value of specific assets and liabilities on the balance sheet and/or the embedded derivative contracts explained below. These forwards are not designated as hedging instruments under the accounting standards for derivatives and hedging. Accordingly, these undesignated instruments are recorded at fair value as a derivative asset or liability on the Consolidated Balance Sheets with their corresponding change in fair value recognized in *Other (income) expense, net*, together with the re-measurement gain or loss from the hedged balance sheet position or embedded derivative contract. The Company classifies the cash flows at settlement from undesignated instruments within the *Cash provided by operations* component of the Consolidated Statements of Cash Flows. The total notional amount of outstanding undesignated derivative instruments was $4.4 billion as of May 31, 2015.

Embedded Derivatives

As part of the foreign currency adjustment program described above, an embedded derivative contract is created upon the factory's acceptance of NIKE's purchase order for currencies within the factory currency exposure indices that are neither the U.S. Dollar nor the local or functional currency of the factory. Embedded derivative contracts are treated as foreign currency forward contracts that are bifurcated from the related purchase order and recorded at fair value as a derivative asset or liability on the Consolidated Balance Sheets with their corresponding change in fair value recognized in *Other (income) expense, net*, from the date a purchase order is accepted by a factory through the date the purchase price is no longer subject to foreign currency fluctuations.

In addition, the Company has entered into certain other contractual agreements which have payments that are indexed to currencies that are not the functional currency of either substantial party to the contracts. These payment terms expose NIKE to variability in foreign exchange rates and create embedded derivative contracts that must be bifurcated from the related contract and recorded at fair value as derivative assets or liabilities on the Consolidated Balance Sheets with their corresponding changes in fair value recognized in *Other (income) expense, net* until each payment is settled.

At May 31, 2015, the notional amount of all embedded derivatives outstanding was approximately $205 million.

Credit Risk

The Company is exposed to credit-related losses in the event of nonperformance by counterparties to hedging instruments. The counterparties to all derivative transactions are major financial institutions with investment grade credit ratings. However, this does not eliminate the Company's exposure to credit risk with these institutions. This credit risk is limited to the unrealized gains in such contracts should any of these counterparties fail to perform as contracted. To manage this risk, the Company has established strict counterparty credit guidelines that are continually monitored.

The Company's derivative contracts contain credit risk related contingent features designed to protect against significant deterioration in counterparties' creditworthiness and their ultimate ability to settle outstanding derivative contracts in the normal course of business. The Company's bilateral credit related contingent features generally require the owing entity, either the Company or the derivative counterparty, to post collateral for the portion of the fair value in excess of $50 million should the fair value of outstanding derivatives per counterparty be greater than $50 million. Additionally, a certain level of decline in credit rating of either the Company or the counterparty could also trigger collateral requirements. As of May 31, 2015, the Company was in compliance with all credit risk related contingent features and had derivative instruments with credit risk related contingent features in a net liability position of $4 million. Accordingly, the Company was not required to post any collateral as a result of these contingent features. Further, as of May 31, 2015, the Company had received $968 million of cash collateral and $74 million of securities from various counterparties to its derivative contracts (refer to Note 6 — Fair Value Measurements). Given the considerations described above, the Company considers the impact of the risk of counterparty default to be immaterial.

NOTE 18 — Operating Segments and Related Information

The Company's operating segments are evidence of the structure of the Company's internal organization. The NIKE Brand segments are defined by geographic regions for operations participating in NIKE Brand sales activity.

Each NIKE Brand geographic segment operates predominantly in one industry: the design, development, marketing and selling of athletic footwear, apparel and equipment. The Company's reportable operating segments for the NIKE Brand are: North America, Western Europe, Central & Eastern Europe, Greater China, Japan and Emerging Markets, and include results for the NIKE, Jordan and Hurley brands. The Company's NIKE Brand Direct to Consumer operations are managed within each geographic operating segment. Converse is also a reportable segment for NIKE, Inc., and operates in one industry: the design, marketing, licensing and selling of casual sneakers, apparel and accessories.

Global Brand Divisions is included within the NIKE Brand for presentation purposes to align with the way management views the Company. Global Brand Divisions primarily represent NIKE Brand licensing businesses that are not part of a geographic operating segment, and demand creation, operating overhead and product creation and design expenses that are centrally managed for the NIKE Brand.

Corporate consists largely of unallocated general and administrative expenses, including expenses associated with centrally managed departments; depreciation and amortization related to the Company's headquarters; unallocated insurance, benefit and compensation programs, including stock-based compensation; and certain foreign currency gains and losses, including certain hedge gains and losses.

The primary financial measure used by the Company to evaluate performance of individual operating segments is earnings before interest and taxes (commonly referred to as "EBIT"), which represents *Net income* before *Interest expense (income), net* and *Income tax expense* in the Consolidated Statements of Income. Reconciling items for EBIT represent corporate expense items that are not allocated to the operating segments for management reporting.

As part of the Company's centrally managed foreign exchange risk management program, standard foreign currency rates are assigned twice per year to each NIKE Brand entity in the Company's geographic operating segments and to Converse. These rates are set approximately nine months in advance of the future selling season based on average market spot rates in the calendar month preceding the date they are established. *Inventories* and *Cost of sales* for geographic operating segments and Converse reflect use of these standard rates to record non-functional currency product purchases in the entity's functional currency. Differences between assigned standard

foreign currency rates and actual market rates are included in Corporate, together with foreign currency hedge gains and losses generated from the Company's centrally managed foreign exchange risk management program and other conversion gains and losses.

Accounts receivable, net, *Inventories* and *Property, plant and equipment, net* for operating segments are regularly reviewed by management and are therefore provided below. Additions to long-lived assets as presented in the following table represent capital expenditures.

Certain prior year amounts have been reclassified to conform to fiscal 2015 presentation.

		Year Ended May 31,				
(In millions)		2015		2014		2013
REVENUES						
North America	$	13,740	$	12,299	$	11,158
Western Europe		5,709		4,979		4,193
Central & Eastern Europe		1,417		1,387		1,229
Greater China		3,067		2,602		2,478
Japan		755		771		876
Emerging Markets		3,898		3,949		3,832
Global Brand Divisions		115		125		115
Total NIKE Brand		28,701		26,112		23,881
Converse		1,982		1,684		1,449
Corporate		(82)		3		(17)
TOTAL NIKE CONSOLIDATED REVENUES	$	30,601	$	27,799	$	25,313
EARNINGS BEFORE INTEREST AND TAXES						
North America	$	3,645	$	3,077	$	2,639
Western Europe		1,277		855		643
Central & Eastern Europe		247		279		234
Greater China		993		816		813
Japan		100		131		139
Emerging Markets		818		952		985
Global Brand Divisions		(2,263)		(1,993)		(1,716)
Total NIKE Brand		4,817		4,117		3,737
Converse		517		496		425
Corporate		(1,101)		(1,036)		(909)
Total NIKE Consolidated Earnings Before Interest and Taxes		4,233		3,577		3,253
Interest expense (income), net		28		33		(3)
TOTAL NIKE CONSOLIDATED EARNINGS BEFORE TAXES	$	4,205	$	3,544	$	3,256
ADDITIONS TO LONG-LIVED ASSETS						
North America	$	208	$	240	$	132
Western Europe		216		120		75
Central & Eastern Europe		20		19		22
Greater China		69		63		52
Japan		15		9		7
Emerging Markets		37		55		50
Global Brand Divisions		225		225		270
Total NIKE Brand		790		731		608
Converse		69		30		20
Corporate		144		161		153
TOTAL ADDITIONS TO LONG-LIVED ASSETS	$	1,003	$	922	$	781
DEPRECIATION						
North America	$	121	$	109	$	92
Western Europe		75		71		68
Central & Eastern Europe		12		11		9
Greater China		46		38		32
Japan		22		19		22
Emerging Markets		27		25		20
Global Brand Divisions		210		175		122
Total NIKE Brand		513		448		365
Converse		18		16		15
Corporate		75		54		38
TOTAL DEPRECIATION	$	606	$	518	$	418

(In millions)	As of May 31,			
	2015		2014	
ACCOUNTS RECEIVABLE, NET				
North America	$	1,737	$	1,505
Western Europe		344		341
Central & Eastern Europe		242		280
Greater China		84		68
Japan		134		162
Emerging Markets		461		819
Global Brand Divisions		88		71
Total NIKE Brand		3,090		3,246
Converse		258		171
Corporate		10		17
TOTAL ACCOUNTS RECEIVABLE, NET	$	3,358	$	3,434
INVENTORIES				
North America	$	2,207	$	1,758
Western Europe		699		711
Central & Eastern Europe		169		271
Greater China		249		221
Japan		94		94
Emerging Markets		528		633
Global Brand Divisions		32		18
Total NIKE Brand		3,978		3,706
Converse		237		261
Corporate		122		(20)
TOTAL INVENTORIES	$	4,337	$	3,947
PROPERTY, PLANT AND EQUIPMENT, NET				
North America	$	632	$	545
Western Europe		451		384
Central & Eastern Europe		47		51
Greater China		254		232
Japan		205		258
Emerging Markets		103		115
Global Brand Divisions		484		537
Total NIKE Brand		2,176		2,122
Converse		122		70
Corporate		713		642
TOTAL PROPERTY, PLANT AND EQUIPMENT, NET	$	3,011	$	2,834

Revenues by Major Product Lines

Revenues to external customers for NIKE Brand products are attributable to sales of footwear, apparel and equipment. Other revenues to external customers consist primarily of sales by Converse.

(In millions)	Year Ended May 31,					
	2015		2014		2013	
Footwear	$	18,318	$	16,208	$	14,635
Apparel		8,636		8,109		7,491
Equipment		1,632		1,670		1,640
Other		2,015		1,812		1,547
TOTAL NIKE CONSOLIDATED REVENUES	$	30,601	$	27,799	$	25,313

Revenues and Long-Lived Assets by Geographic Area

After allocation of revenues for Global Brand Divisions, Converse and Corporate to geographical areas based on the location where the sales originated, revenues by geographical area are essentially the same as reported above under operating segments with the exception of the United States. Revenues derived in the United States were $14,180 million, $12,711 million and $11,385 million for the years ended May 31, 2015, 2014 and 2013, respectively. The Company's largest concentrations of long-lived assets primarily consist of the Company's world headquarters and distribution facilities in the United States and distribution facilities in Japan, Belgium and China. Long-lived assets attributable to operations in the United States, which are primarily composed of net property, plant & equipment, were $1,877 million and $1,652 million at May 31, 2015 and 2014, respectively. Long-lived assets attributable to operations in Japan were $205 million and $258 million at May 31, 2015 and 2014, respectively. Long-lived assets attributable to operations in Belgium were $234 million and $175 million at May 31, 2015 and 2014, respectively. Long-lived assets attributable to operations in China were $267 million and $234 million at May 31, 2015 and 2014, respectively.

Major Customers

No customer accounted for 10% or more of the Company's net revenues during the years ended May 31, 2015, 2014 and 2013.

Glossary

A

absorption costing The reporting of the costs of manufactured products, normally direct materials, direct labor, and factory overhead, as product costs. (Ch. 6)

accounts receivable analysis A company's ability to collect its accounts receivable. (Ch. 14)

accounts receivable turnover The relationship between sales and accounts receivable, computed by dividing sales by the average accounts receivable; measures how frequently during the year the accounts receivable are being converted to cash. (Ch. 14)

accumulated other comprehensive income The cumulative effects of other comprehensive income items reported separately in the Stockholders' Equity section of the balance sheet. (Ch. 14)

activities The types of work, or actions, involved in a manufacturing or service process. (Ch. 4)

activity analysis The study of employee effort and other business records to determine the cost of activities. (Ch. 12)

activity base (driver) A measure of activity that is related to changes in cost. Used in analyzing and classifying cost behavior. Activity bases are also used in the denominator in calculating the predetermined factory overhead rate to assign overhead costs to cost objects. (Chs. 2, 4, 5)

activity rate The estimated activity cost divided by estimated activity-base usage. (Ch. 4)

activity-based costing (ABC) A cost allocation method that identifies activities causing the incurrence of costs and allocates these costs to products (or other cost objects), based on activity drivers (bases). (Chs. 2, 4)

analytical methods Methods that examine changes in the amount and percentage of financial statement items within and across periods. (Ch. 14)

annuity A series of equal cash flows at fixed intervals. (Ch. 11)

appraisal costs Costs to detect, measure, evaluate, and inspect products and processes to ensure that they conform to customer requirements and performance standards. (Ch. 12)

asset turnover A ratio that measures how effectively a business is using its assets to generate sales, computed as sales divided by average total assets. (Ch. 14)

average rate of return A method of evaluating capital investment proposals that focuses on the expected profitability of the investment. (Ch. 11)

B

backflush accounting Simplification of the accounting system by eliminating accumulation and transfer of costs as products move through production. (Ch. 12)

balanced scorecard A performance evaluation approach that incorporates multiple performance dimensions by combining financial and nonfinancial measures. (Ch. 9)

batch size The amount of production in units of product that is produced after a setup. (Ch. 12)

break-even point The level of business operations at which revenues and expired costs are equal. (Ch. 5)

budget An accounting device used to plan and control resources of operational departments and divisions. (Ch. 7)

budget performance report A report comparing actual results with budget figures. (Ch. 8)

budgetary slack Excess resources set within a budget to provide for uncertain events. (Ch. 7)

budgeted variable factory overhead The standard variable overhead for the actual units produced. (Ch. 8)

C

capital expenditures budget The budget summarizing future plans for acquiring plant facilities and equipment. (Ch. 7)

capital investment analysis The process by which management plans, evaluates, and controls long-term capital investments involving property, plant, and equipment. (Ch. 11)

capital rationing The process by which management plans, evaluates, and controls long-term capital investments involving fixed assets. (Ch. 11)

cash budget A budget of estimated cash receipts and payments. (Ch. 7)

cash flow per share Normally computed as cash flow from operations per share. (Ch. 13)

cash flows from financing activities The section of the statement of cash flows that reports cash flows from transactions affecting the equity and debt of the business. (Ch. 13)

cash flows from investing activities The section of the statement of cash flows that reports cash flows from transactions affecting investments in noncurrent assets. (Ch. 13)

cash flows from operating activities The section of the statement of cash flows that reports the cash transactions affecting the determination of net income. (Ch. 13)

cash payback period The expected period of time between the date of an investment and the recovery in cash of the amount invested. (Ch. 11)

common-sized statement A financial statement in which all items are expressed only in relative terms. (Ch. 14)

comprehensive income All changes in stockholders' equity during a period, except those resulting from dividends and stockholders' investments. (Ch. 14)

continuous budgeting A method of budgeting that provides for maintaining a 12-month projection into the future. (Ch. 7)

continuous process improvement A management approach that is part of the overall total quality management philosophy. The approach requires all employees to constantly improve processes of which they are a part or for which they have managerial responsibility. (Ch. 1)

contribution margin The excess of sales over variable costs. (Chs. 5, 6)

contribution margin analysis The systematic examination of the differences between planned and actual contribution margins. (Ch. 6)

contribution margin ratio The percentage of each sales dollar that is available to cover the fixed costs and provide an operating income. (Chs. 5, 6)

controllable costs Costs that can be influenced (increased, decreased, or eliminated) by someone such as a manager or factory worker. (Ch. 6)

controllable expenses Costs that can be influenced by the decisions of a manager. (Ch. 9)

controllable revenues Revenues earned by the profit center. (Ch. 9)

controllable variance The difference between the actual amount of variable factory overhead cost incurred and the amount of variable factory overhead budgeted for the standard product. (Ch. 8)

controller The chief management accountant of a division or other segment of a business. (Ch. 1)

controlling A phase in the management process that consists of monitoring the operating results of implemented plans and comparing the actual results with the expected results. (Ch. 1)

conversion costs The combination of direct labor and factory overhead costs. (Chs. 1, 12)

cost A payment of cash (or a commitment to pay cash in the future) for the purpose of generating revenues. (Ch. 1)

cost accounting systems Systems that measure, record, and report product costs. (Ch. 2)

cost allocation The process of assigning indirect cost to a cost object, such as a job. (Ch. 2)

cost behavior The manner in which a cost changes in relation to its activity base (driver). (Ch. 5)

cost center A decentralized unit in which the department or division manager has responsibility for the control of costs incurred and the authority to make decisions that affect these costs. (Ch. 9)

cost object The object or segment of operations to which costs are related for management's use, such as a product or department. (Ch. 1)

cost of goods manufactured The total cost of making and finishing a product. (Ch. 1)

cost of goods sold The cost of finished goods available for sale minus the ending finished goods inventory. (Ch. 1)

cost of goods sold budget A budget of the estimated direct materials, direct labor, and factory overhead consumed by sold products. (Ch. 7)

cost of production report A report prepared periodically by a processing department, summarizing (1) the units for which the department is accountable and the disposition of those units and (2) the costs incurred by the department and the allocation of those costs between completed and incomplete production. (Ch. 3)

cost of quality report A report summarizing the costs, percent of total, and percent of sales by appraisal, prevention, internal failure, and external failure cost of quality categories. (Ch. 12)

cost per equivalent unit The rate used to allocate costs between completed and partially completed production. (Ch. 3)

cost price approach An approach to transfer pricing that uses cost as the basis for setting the transfer price. (Ch. 9)

cost variance The difference between actual cost and the flexible budget at actual volumes. (Ch. 8)

costs of quality The cost associated with controlling quality (prevention and appraisal) and failing to control quality (internal and external failure). (Ch. 12)

cost-volume-profit analysis The systematic examination of the relationships among selling prices, volume of sales and production, costs, expenses, and profits. (Ch. 5)

cost-volume-profit chart A chart that graphically shows sales, costs, and the related profit or loss for various levels of units sold. (Ch. 5)

currency exchange rate The rate at which currency in another country can be exchanged for local currency. (Ch. 11)

current position analysis A company's ability to pay its current liabilities. (Ch. 14)

current ratio A financial ratio that is computed by dividing current assets by current liabilities. (Ch. 14)

currently attainable standards Standards that represent levels of operation that can be attained with reasonable effort. (Ch. 8)

D

decision making A component inherent in the other management processes of planning, directing, controlling, and improving. (Ch. 1)

differential analysis The area of accounting concerned with the effect of alternative courses of action on revenues and costs. (Ch. 10)

differential cost The amount of increase or decrease in cost expected from a particular course of action compared with an alternative. (Ch. 10)

differential income (loss) The difference between the differential revenue and the differential costs. (Ch. 10)

differential revenue The amount of increase or decrease in revenue expected from a particular course of action as compared with an alternative. (Ch. 10)

direct costs Costs that can be traced directly to a cost object. (Ch. 1)

direct labor cost The wages of factory workers who are directly involved in converting materials into a finished product. (Ch. 1)

direct labor cost budget Budget that estimates direct labor hours and related cost needed to support budgeted production. (Ch. 7)

direct labor rate variance The cost associated with the difference between the actual rate and the standard rate paid for direct labor multiplied by the actual direct labor hours used in producing a commodity. (Ch. 8)

direct labor time variance The cost associated with the difference between the actual hours and the standard hours of direct labor spent producing a commodity multiplied by the standard direct labor rate per hour. (Ch. 8)

direct materials cost The cost of materials that are an integral part of the finished product. (Ch. 1)

direct materials price variance The cost associated with the difference between the actual price and the standard price of direct materials multiplied by the actual quantity of direct materials used in producing a commodity. (Ch. 8)

direct materials purchases budget A budget that uses the production budget as a starting point to budget materials purchases. (Ch. 7)

direct materials quantity variance The cost associated with the difference between the actual quantity and the standard quantity of direct materials used in producing a commodity multiplied by the standard direct material price. (Ch. 8)

direct method A method of reporting the cash flows from operating activities as the difference between the operating cash receipts and the operating cash payments. (Ch. 13)

directing The process by which managers, given their assigned level of responsibilities, run day-to-day operations. (Ch. 1)

dividend yield A ratio, computed by dividing the annual dividends paid per share of common stock by the market price per share at a specific date, that indicates the rate of return to stockholders in terms of cash dividend distributions. (Ch. 14)

dividends per share Measures the extent to which earnings are being distributed to common shareholders. (Ch. 14)

DuPont formula An expanded expression of return on investment determined by multiplying the profit margin by the investment turnover. (Ch. 9)

E

earnings per share (EPS) on common stock The profitability ratio of net income available to common shareholders to the number of common shares outstanding. (Ch. 14)

EBITDA Term for earnings before interest, taxes, depreciation, and amortization; operating income expressed by adding back depreciation and amortization expense. (Ch. 6)

eco-efficiency measures Measures that help managers evaluate the savings generated by using fewer natural resources in a company's operations. (Ch. 1)

electronic data interchange (EDI) An information technology that allows different business organizations to use computers to communicate orders, relay information, and make or receive payments. (Ch. 12)

employee involvement A philosophy that grants employees the responsibility and authority to make their own decisions about their operations. (Ch. 12)

engineering change order (ECO) The document that initiates changing a product or process. (Ch. 4)

enterprise resource planning (ERP) An integrated business and information system used by companies to plan and control both internal and supply chain operations. (Ch. 12)

equivalent units of production The number of production units that could have been completed within a given accounting period, given the resources consumed. (Ch. 3)

external failure costs The costs incurred after defective units or services have been delivered to consumers. (Ch. 12)

F

factory burden Another term for manufacturing overhead or factory overhead. (Ch. 1)

factory overhead cost All of the costs of producing a product except for direct materials and direct labor. (Ch. 1)

factory overhead cost budget Budget that estimates the cost for each item of factory overhead needed to support budgeted production. (Ch. 7)

factory overhead cost variance report Reports budgeted and actual costs for variable and fixed factory overhead along with the related controllable and volume variances. (Ch. 8)

fair value The price that would be received for selling an asset or paying off a liability, often the market price for an equity or debt security. (Ch. 14)

favorable cost variance A variance that occurs when the actual cost is less than standard cost. (Ch. 8)

feedback Measures provided to operational employees or managers on the performance of subunits of the organization. These measures are used by employees to adjust a process or a behavior to achieve goals. See management by exception. (Ch. 1)

financial accounting The branch of accounting that is concerned with recording transactions using generally accepted accounting principles (GAAP) for a business or other economic unit and with a periodic preparation of various statements from such records. (Ch. 1)

finished goods inventory The direct materials costs, direct labor costs, and factory overhead costs of finished products that have not been sold. (Ch. 1)

finished goods ledger The subsidiary ledger that contains the individual accounts for each kind of commodity or product produced. (Ch. 2)

first-in, first-out (FIFO) inventory cost flow method The method of inventory costing based on the assumption that the costs of merchandise sold should be charged against revenue in the order in which the costs were incurred. (Ch. 3)

fixed costs Costs that tend to remain the same in amount, regardless of variations in the level of activity. (Ch. 5)

flexible budget A budget that adjusts for varying rates of activity. (Ch. 7)

free cash flow The amount of operating cash flow remaining after replacing current productive capacity and maintaining current dividends. (Ch. 13)

G

goal conflict A condition that occurs when individual objectives conflict with organizational objectives. (Ch. 7)

H

high-low method A technique that uses the highest and lowest total costs as a basis for estimating the variable cost per unit and the fixed cost component of a mixed cost. (Ch. 5)

horizontal analysis Financial analysis that compares an item in a current statement with the same item in prior statements. (Ch. 14)

I

ideal standards Standards that can be achieved only under perfect operating conditions, such as no idle time, no machine breakdowns, and no materials spoilage; also called theoretical standards. (Ch. 8)

indirect costs Costs that cannot be traced directly to a cost object. (Ch. 1)

indirect method A method of reporting the cash flows from operating activities as the net income from operations adjusted for all deferrals of past cash receipts and payments and all accruals of expected future cash receipts and payments. (Ch. 13)

inflation A period when prices in general are rising and the purchasing power of money is declining. (Ch. 11)

internal failure costs The costs associated with defects that are discovered by the organization before the product or service is delivered to the consumer. (Ch. 12)

internal rate of return (IRR) method A method of analysis of proposed capital investments that uses present value concepts to compute the rate of return from the net cash flows expected from the investment. (Ch. 11)

inventory analysis A company's ability to manage its inventory effectively. (Ch. 14)

inventory turnover The relationship between the volume of goods sold and inventory, computed by dividing the cost of goods sold by the average inventory. (Ch. 14)

investment center A decentralized unit in which the manager has the responsibility and authority to make decisions that affect not only costs and revenues but also the fixed assets available to the center. (Ch. 9)

investment turnover A component of the rate of return on investment, computed as the ratio of sales to invested assets. (Ch. 9)

J

job cost sheet An account in the work in process subsidiary ledger in which the costs charged to a particular job order are recorded. (Ch. 2)

job order cost system A type of cost accounting system that provides for a separate record of the cost of each particular quantity of product that passes through the factory. (Ch. 2)

L

lead time The elapsed time between starting a unit of product into the beginning of a process and its completion. (Ch. 12)

lean accounting An accounting system characterized by fewer transactions, combined accounts, nonfinancial performance measures, and direct tracing of overhead. (Ch. 12)

lean enterprise A business that produces products or services with high quality, low cost, fast response, and immediate availability using lean principles. (Ch. 12)

lean manufacturing (or just-in-time manufacturing) A manufacturing enterprise that uses lean principles. (Chs. 3, 12)

lean principles Principles associated with the lean enterprise that include reducing inventory, reducing lead time, reducing setup time, product-/customer-oriented layouts, employee involvement, pull scheduling, zero defects, and supply chain management. (Ch. 12)

leverage Using debt to increase the return on an investment. (Ch. 14)

line department A unit that is directly involved in the basic objectives of an organization. (Ch. 1)

liquidity The ability to convert assets into cash. (Ch. 14)

M

management (or managerial) accounting The branch of accounting that uses both historical and estimated data in providing information that management uses in conducting daily operations, in planning future operations, and in developing overall business strategies. (Ch. 1)

management by exception The philosophy of managing which involves monitoring the operating results of implemented plans and comparing the expected results with the actual results. This feedback allows management to isolate significant variations for further investigation and possible remedial action. (Ch. 1)

management process The five basic management functions of (1) planning, (2) directing, (3) controlling, (4) improving, and (5) decision making. (Ch. 1)

Management's Discussion and Analysis (MD&A) An annual report disclosure that provides management's analysis of the results of operations and financial condition. (Ch. 14)

manufacturing cells A grouping of processes where employees are cross-trained to perform more than one function. (Ch. 3)

manufacturing margin The variable cost of goods sold deducted from sales. (Ch. 6)

manufacturing overhead Costs, other than direct materials and direct labor costs, that are incurred in the manufacturing process. (Ch. 1)

margin of safety Indicates the possible decrease in sales that may occur before an operating loss results. (Ch. 5)

market price approach An approach to transfer pricing that uses the price at which the product or service transferred could be sold to outside buyers as the transfer price. (Ch. 9)

market segment A portion of business that can be assigned to a manager for profit responsibility. (Ch. 6)

master budget The comprehensive budget plan linking all the individual budgets related to sales, cost of goods sold, operating expenses, projects, capital expenditures, and cash. (Ch. 7)

materials inventory The cost of materials that have not yet entered into the manufacturing process. (Ch. 1)

materials ledger The subsidiary ledger containing the individual accounts for each type of material. (Ch. 2)

materials requisition The form or electronic transmission used by a manufacturing department to authorize materials issuances from the storeroom. (Ch. 2)

mixed costs Costs with both variable and fixed characteristics, sometimes called semivariable or semifixed costs. (Ch. 5)

multiple production department factory overhead rate method A method that allocated factory overhead to product by using factory overhead rates for each production department. (Ch. 4)

N

negotiated price approach An approach to transfer pricing that allows managers of decentralized units to agree (negotiate) among themselves as to the transfer price. (Ch. 9)

net present value method A method of analysis of proposed capital investments that focuses on the present value of the cash flows expected from the investments. (Ch. 11)

noncontrollable cost Cost that cannot be influenced (increased, decreased, or eliminated) by someone such as a manager or factory worker. (Ch. 6)

nonfinancial measure A performance measure that has not been stated in dollar terms. (Ch. 12)

nonfinancial performance measure A performance measure expressed in units rather than dollars. (Ch. 8)

non-value-added activity The cost of activities that are perceived as unnecessary from the customer's perspective and are thus candidates for elimination. (Ch. 12)

non-value-added lead time The time that units wait in inventories, move unnecessarily, and wait during machine breakdowns. (Ch. 12)

number of days' sales in inventory The relationship between the volume of sales and inventory, computed by dividing the average inventory by the average daily cost of goods sold. (Ch. 14)

number of days' sales in receivables The relationship between sales and accounts receivable, computed by dividing average accounts receivable by average daily sales. (Ch. 14)

O

objectives (goals) Developed in the planning stage, these reflect the direction and desired outcomes of certain courses of action. (Ch. 1)

operating leverage A measure of the relative mix of a business's variable costs and fixed costs, computed as contribution margin divided by income from operations. (Ch. 5)

operational planning The development of short-term plans to achieve goals identified in a business's strategic plan. Sometimes called tactical planning. (Ch. 1)

opportunity cost The amount of income forgone from an alternative to a proposed use of cash or its equivalent. (Ch. 10)

other comprehensive income Specified items that are reported separately from net income, including foreign currency items, pension liability adjustments, and unrealized gains and losses on investments. (Ch. 14)

overapplied factory overhead The amount of factory overhead applied in excess of the actual factory overhead costs incurred for production during a period. (Ch. 2)

P

Pareto chart A bar chart that shows the totals of a particular attribute for a number of categories, ranked left to right from the largest to smallest totals. (Ch. 12)

period costs Those costs that are used up in generating revenue during the current period and that are not involved in manufacturing a product, such as selling, general, and administrative expenses. (Ch. 1)

planning A phase of the management process whereby objectives are outlined and courses of action determined. (Ch. 1)

predetermined factory overhead rate The rate used to apply factory overhead costs to the goods manufactured. The rate is determined by dividing the budgeted overhead cost by the estimated activity usage at the beginning of the fiscal period. (Ch. 2)

present value concept Cash to be received (or paid) in the future is not the equivalent of the same amount of money received at an earlier date. (Ch. 11)

present value index An index computed by dividing the total present value of the net cash flow to be received from a proposed capital investment by the amount to be invested. (Ch. 11)

present value of an annuity The sum of the present values of a series of equal cash flows to be received at fixed intervals. (Ch. 11)

prevention costs Costs incurred to prevent defects from occurring during the design and delivery of products or services. (Ch. 12)

price-earnings (P/E) ratio The ratio of the market price per share of common stock, at a specific date, to the annual earnings per share. (Ch. 14)

prime costs The combination of direct materials and direct labor costs. (Ch. 1)

process A sequence of activities linked together for performing a particular task. (Chs. 8, 12)

process cost system A type of cost system that accumulates costs for each of the various departments within a manufacturing facility. (Chs. 2, 3)

process manufacturer A manufacturer that uses large machines to process a continuous flow of raw materials through various stages of completion into a finished state. (Ch. 3)

process-oriented layout Organizing work in a plant or administrative function around processes (tasks). (Ch. 12)

product cost method A concept used in applying the cost-plus approach to product pricing in which only the costs of manufacturing the product, termed the product cost, are included in the cost amount to which the markup is added. (Ch. 10)

product costing Determining the cost of a product. (Ch. 4)

product costs The three components of manufacturing cost: direct materials, direct labor, and factory overhead costs. (Ch. 1)

production bottleneck A condition that occurs when product demand exceeds production capacity. (Ch. 10)

production budget A budget of estimated unit production. (Ch. 7)

production department factory overhead rates Rates determined by dividing the budgeted production department factory overhead by the budgeted allocation base for each department. (Ch. 4)

product-oriented layout Organizing work in a plant or administrative function around products; sometimes referred to as product cells. (Ch. 12)

profit center A decentralized unit in which the manager has the responsibility and the authority to make decisions that affect both costs and revenues (and thus profits). (Ch. 9)

profit margin A component of the rate of return on investment, computed as the ratio of income from operations to sales. (Ch. 9)

profit-volume chart A chart used to assist management in understanding the relationship between profit and volume. (Ch. 5)

profitability The ability of a firm to earn income. (Ch. 14)

pull manufacturing A just-in-time method wherein customer orders trigger the release of finished goods, which triggers production, which triggers release of materials from suppliers. (Ch. 12)

push manufacturing Materials are released into production and work in process is released into finished goods in anticipation of future sales. (Ch. 12)

Q

quantity factor The effect of a difference in the number of units sold, assuming no change in unit sales price or unit cost. (Ch. 6)

quick assets Cash and other current assets that can be quickly converted to cash, such as marketable securities and receivables. (Ch. 14)

quick ratio A financial ratio that measures the ability to pay current liabilities with quick assets (cash, marketable securities, accounts receivable). (Ch. 14)

R

radio frequency identification devices (RFID) Electronic tags (chips) placed on or embedded within products that can be read by radio waves that allow instant monitoring of product location. (Ch. 12)

ratio of fixed assets to long-term liabilities A leverage ratio that measures the margin of safety of long-term creditors, calculated as the net fixed assets divided by the long-term liabilities. (Ch. 14)

ratio of liabilities to stockholders' equity A comprehensive leverage ratio that measures the relationship of the claims of creditors to stockholders' equity. (Ch. 14)

ratios A number that expresses a financial statement item or set of financial statement items as a percentage of another financial item, in order to measure an important economic relationship as a single number. (Ch. 14)

Raw and In Process (RIP) Inventory The capitalized cost of direct materials purchases, labor, and overhead charged to the production cell. (Ch. 12)

receiving report The form or electronic transmission used by the receiving personnel to indicate that materials have been received and inspected. (Ch. 2)

relevant range The range of activity over which changes in cost are of interest to management. (Ch. 5)

residual income The excess of divisional income from operations over a "minimum" acceptable income from operations. (Ch. 9)

responsibility accounting The process of measuring and reporting operating data by areas of responsibility. (Ch. 9)

responsibility center An organizational unit for which a manager is assigned responsibility over costs, revenues, or assets. (Ch. 7)

return on common stockholders' equity The rate of profits earned on the amount invested by the common stockholders. (Ch. 14)

return on investment (ROI) A measure of managerial efficiency in the use of investments in assets, computed as income from operations divided by invested assets. (Ch. 9)

return on stockholders' equity A measure of profitability computed by dividing net income by average total stockholders' equity. (Ch. 14)

return on total assets The profitability of total assets, without considering how the assets are financed. (Ch. 14)

S

sales budget One of the major elements of the income statement budget that indicates the quantity of estimated sales and the expected unit selling price. (Ch. 7)

sales mix The relative distribution of sales among the various products available for sale. (Chs. 5, 6)

service department charges The costs of services provided by an internal service department and transferred to a responsibility center. (Ch. 9)

setup An overhead activity that consists of changing tooling in machines in preparation for making a new product. (Ch. 4)

single plantwide factory overhead rate method A method that allocates all factory overhead to products by using a single factory overhead rate. (Ch. 4)

Six Sigma A quality improvement process developed by Motorola Corporation consisting of five steps: define, measure, analyze, improve, and control (DMAIC). (Ch. 12)

solvency The ability of a firm to pay its debts as they come due. (Ch. 14)

staff department A unit that provides services, assistance, and advice to the departments with line or other staff responsibilities. (Ch. 1)

standard cost A detailed estimate of what a product should cost. (Ch. 8)

standard cost systems Accounting systems that use standards for each element of manufacturing cost entering into the finished product. (Ch. 8)

standards Performance goals, often relating to how much a product should cost. (Ch. 8)

statement of cash flows A summary of the cash receipts and cash payments for a specific period of time, such as a month or a year. (Ch. 13)

statement of cost of goods manufactured The income statement of manufacturing companies. (Ch. 1)

static budget A budget that does not adjust to changes in activity levels. (Ch. 7)

strategic planning The development of a long-range course of action to achieve business goals. (Ch. 1)

strategies The means by which business goals and objectives will be achieved. (Ch. 1)

sunk cost A cost that is not affected by subsequent decisions. (Ch. 10)

supply chain management The coordination and control of materials, services, information, and finances as they move in a process from supplier, through the manufacturer, wholesaler, and retailer to the consumer. (Ch. 12)

sustainability The practice of operating a business to maximize profits while attempting to preserve the environment, economy, and needs of future generations. (Ch. 1)

Sustainability Accounting Standards Board (SASB) A board that was organized in 2011 to develop accounting standards that help companies report decision-useful sustainability information to external financial statement users. (Ch. 1)

T

target costing The target cost is determined by subtracting a desired profit from a market method determined price. The resulting target cost is used to motivate cost improvements in design and manufacture. (Ch. 10)

theory of constraints (TOC) A manufacturing strategy that attempts to remove the influence of bottlenecks (constraints) on a process. (Ch. 10)

time tickets The form on which the amount of time spent by each employee and the labor cost incurred for each individual job, or for factory overhead, are recorded. (Ch. 2)

time value of money concept The concept that an amount of money invested today will earn income. (Ch. 11)

times interest earned A ratio that computes the number of times interest payments could be paid out of current-period earnings. (Ch. 14)

total cost method A concept used in applying the cost-plus approach to product pricing in which all the costs of manufacturing the product plus the selling and administrative expenses are included in the cost amount to which the markup is added. (Ch. 10)

total manufacturing cost variance The difference between total standard costs and total actual costs for units produced. (Ch. 8)

transfer price The price charged one decentralized unit by another for the goods or services provided. (Ch. 9)

U

underapplied factory overhead The amount of actual factory overhead in excess of the factory overhead applied to production during a period. (Ch. 2)

unfavorable cost variance A variance that occurs when the actual cost exceeds the standard cost. (Ch. 8)

unit contribution margin The dollars available from each unit of sales to cover fixed costs and provide operating profits. (Ch. 5)

unit price (cost) factor The effect of a difference in unit sales price or unit cost on the number of units sold. (Ch. 6)

unrealized gain Changes in the fair value of equity or debt securities for a period. (Ch. 14)

utilization A measure of the use of a fixed asset in serving customers relative to the asset's capacity. (Ch. 1)

V

value-added activity The cost of activities that are needed to meet customer requirements. (Ch. 12)

value-added lead time The time required to manufacture a unit of product or other output. (Ch. 12)

value-added ratio The ratio of the value-added lead time to the total lead time. (Ch. 12)

variable cost method A concept used in applying the cost-plus approach to product pricing in which only the variable costs are included in the cost amount to which the markup is added. (Ch. 10)

variable cost of goods sold Consists of direct materials, direct labor, and variable factory overhead for the units sold. (Ch. 6)

variable costing The concept that considers the cost of products manufactured to be composed only of those manufacturing costs that increase or decrease as the volume of production rises or falls (direct materials, direct labor, and variable factory overhead). (Chs. 5, 6)

variable costs Costs that vary in total dollar amount as the level of activity changes. (Ch. 5)

vertical analysis An analysis that compares each item in a current statement with a total amount within the same statement. (Ch. 14)

volume variance The difference between the budgeted fixed overhead at 100% of normal capacity and the standard fixed overhead for the actual production achieved during the period. (Ch. 8)

W

whole units The number of units in production during a period, whether completed or not. (Ch. 3)

work in process inventory The direct materials costs, the direct labor costs, and the applied factory overhead costs that have entered into the manufacturing process but are associated with products that have not been finished. (Ch. 1)

working capital The excess of the current assets of a business over its current liabilities. (Ch. 14)

Z

zero-based budgeting A concept of budgeting that requires all levels of management to start from zero and estimate budget data as if there had been no previous activities in their units. (Ch. 7)

Index

The Basics

Accounting Equation:

Assets = Liabilities + Stockholders' Equity

T Account:

Account Title	
Left side	Right side
debit	credit

Rules of Debit and Credit:

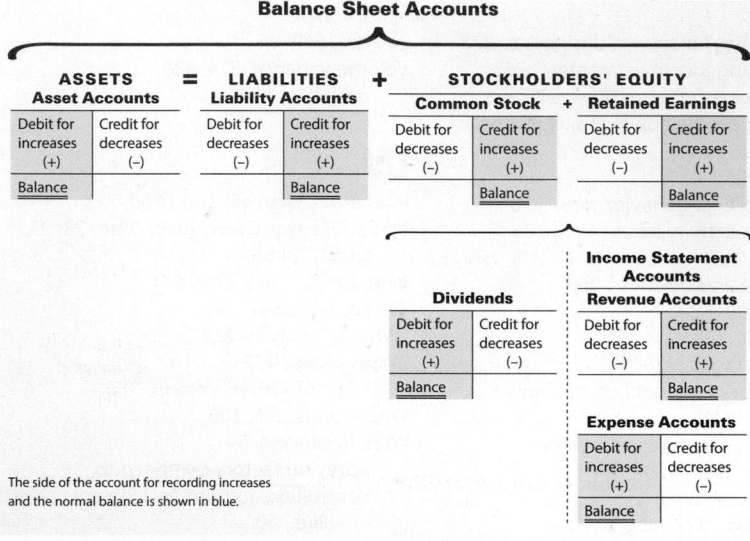

Balance Sheet Accounts

The side of the account for recording increases and the normal balance is shown in blue.

Accounting Cycle:

1. Transactions are analyzed and recorded in the journal.
2. Transactions are posted to the ledger.
3. An unadjusted trial balance is prepared.
4. Adjustment data are assembled and analyzed.
5. An optional end-of-period spreadsheet is prepared.
6. Adjusting entries are journalized and posted to the ledger.
7. An adjusted trial balance is prepared.
8. Financial statements are prepared.
9. Closing entries are journalized and posted to the ledger.
10. A post-closing trial balance is prepared.

Types of Adjusting Entries:

- Accrued revenue (accrued asset)
- Accrued expense (accrued liability)
- Unearned revenue (deferred revenue)
- Prepaid expense (deferred expense)
- Depreciation expense

Each entry will always affect both a balance sheet account and an income statement account.

Analyzing and Journalizing Transactions

1. Carefully read the description of the transaction to determine whether an asset, liability, common stock, retained earnings, revenue, expense, or dividends account is affected.
2. For each account affected by the transaction, determine whether the account increases or decreases.
3. Determine whether each increase or decrease should be recorded as a debit or a credit, following the rules of debit and credit.
4. Record the transaction using a journal entry.
5. Periodically post journal entries to the accounts in the ledger.
6. Prepare an unadjusted trial balance at the end of the period.

Financial Statements:

- **Income statement:** A summary of the revenue and expenses of a business entity for a specific period of time, such as a month or a year.
- **Retained earnings statement:** A summary of the changes in the retained earnings of a business entity that have occurred during a specific period of time, such as a month or a year.
- **Balance sheet:** A list of the assets, liabilities, and stockholders' equity of a business entity as of a specific date, usually at the close of the last day of a month or a year.
- **Statement of cash flows:** A summary of the cash receipts and cash payments of a business entity for a specific period of time, such as a month or a year.

Closing Entries:

1. Revenue account balances are transferred to an account called Income Summary.
2. Expense account balances are transferred to an account called Income Summary.
3. The balance of Income Summary (net income or net loss) is transferred to Retained Earnings.
4. The balance of the dividends account is transferred to Retained Earnings.

Shipping Terms:

	FOB Shipping Point	FOB Destination
Ownership (title) passes to buyer when merchandise is.................	delivered to freight carrier	delivered to buyer
Freight costs are paid by........................	buyer	seller

Format for Bank Reconciliation:

Cash balance according to bank statement		$XXX
Add: Additions by company not on bank		
statement	$XXX	
Bank errors	XXX	XXX
		$XXX
Deduct: Deductions by company not on bank		
statement	$XXX	
Bank errors	XXX	XXX
Adjusted balance		$XXX

Cash balance according to company's records		$XXX
Add: Additions by bank not recorded by company	$XXX	
Company errors	XXX	XXX
		$XXX
Deduct: Deductions by bank not recorded		
by company	$XXX	
Company errors	XXX	XXX
Adjusted balance		$XXX

Inventory Costing Methods:

- First-in, First-out (FIFO)
- Last-in, First-out (LIFO)
- Average Cost

Interest Computations:

$$\text{Interest} = \text{Face Amount (or Principal)} \times \text{Rate} \times \text{Time}$$

Methods of Determining Annual Depreciation:

Straight-Line: $\dfrac{\text{Cost} - \text{Estimated Residual Value}}{\text{Estimated Life}}$

Double-Declining-Balance: Rate* × Book Value at Beginning of Period

*Rate is commonly twice the straight-line rate (1 ÷ Estimated Life).

Adjustments to Net Income (Loss) Using the Indirect Method:

	Increase (Decrease)
Net income (loss)	$ XXX
Adjustments to reconcile net income to net cash flow from operating activities:	
Depreciation of fixed assets	XXX
Amortization of intangible assets	XXX
Losses on disposal of assets	XXX
Gains on disposal of assets	(XXX)
Changes in current operating assets and liabilities:	
Increases in noncash current operating assets	(XXX)
Decreases in noncash current operating assets	XXX
Increases in current operating liabilities	XXX
Decreases in current operating liabilities	(XXX)
Net cash flow from operating activities	$ XXX
	or
	$(XXX)

Contribution Margin Ratio $= \dfrac{\text{Sales} - \text{Variable Costs}}{\text{Sales}}$

Break-Even Sales (Units) $= \dfrac{\text{Fixed Costs}}{\text{Unit Contribution Margin}}$

Sales (Units) $= \dfrac{\text{Fixed Costs} + \text{Target Profit}}{\text{Unit Contribution Margin}}$

Margin of Safety $= \dfrac{\text{Sales} - \text{Sales at Break-Even Point}}{\text{Sales}}$

Operating Leverage $= \dfrac{\text{Contribution Margin}}{\text{Income from Operations}}$

Variances:

$\text{Direct Materials Price Variance} = \left(\begin{array}{c}\text{Actual Price} - \\ \text{Standard Price}\end{array}\right) \times \text{Actual Quantity}$

$\text{Direct Materials Quantity Variance} = \left(\begin{array}{c}\text{Actual Quantity} - \\ \text{Standard Quantity}\end{array}\right) \times \begin{array}{c}\text{Standard} \\ \text{Price}\end{array}$

$\text{Direct Labor Rate Variance} = \left(\begin{array}{c}\text{Actual Rate per Hour} - \\ \text{Standard Rate per Hour}\end{array}\right) \times \text{Actual Hours}$

$\text{Direct Labor Time Variance} = \left(\begin{array}{c}\text{Actual Direct Labor Hours} - \\ \text{Standard Direct Labor Hours}\end{array}\right) \times \begin{array}{c}\text{Standard Rate} \\ \text{per Hour}\end{array}$

$\begin{array}{c}\text{Variable Factory} \\ \text{Overhead Controllable} \\ \text{Variance}\end{array} = \begin{array}{c}\text{Actual Variable} \\ \text{Factory} \\ \text{Overhead}\end{array} - \begin{array}{c}\text{Budgeted Variable} \\ \text{Factory Overhead}\end{array}$

$\begin{array}{c}\text{Fixed Factory} \\ \text{Overhead} \\ \text{Volume} \\ \text{Variance}\end{array} = \left(\begin{array}{c}\text{Standard Hours for} \\ \text{100\% of Normal} \\ \text{Capacity}\end{array} - \begin{array}{c}\text{Standard} \\ \text{Hours for} \\ \text{Actual Units} \\ \text{Produced}\end{array}\right) \times \begin{array}{c}\text{Fixed Factory} \\ \text{Overhead} \\ \text{Rate}\end{array}$

Return on Investment (ROI) $= \dfrac{\text{Income from Operations}}{\text{Invested Assets}}$

Alternative ROI Computation:

$$\text{ROI} = \dfrac{\text{Income from Operations}}{\text{Sales}} \times \dfrac{\text{Sales}}{\text{Invested Assets}}$$

Capital Investment Analysis Methods:

Methods That Ignore Present Values:

- Average Rate of Return Method
- Cash Payback Method

Methods That Use Present Values:

- Net Present Value Method
- Internal Rate of Return Method

Average Rate of Return $= \dfrac{\text{Estimated Average Annual Income}}{\text{Average Investment}}$

Present Value Index $= \dfrac{\text{Total Present Value of Net Cash Flow}}{\text{Amount to Be Invested}}$

Present Value Factor for an Annuity of $1 $= \dfrac{\text{Amount to Be Invested}}{\text{Equal Annual Net Cash Flows}}$

Abbreviations and Acronyms Commonly Used in Business and Accounting

AAA	American Accounting Association
ABC	Activity-based costing
AICPA	American Institute of Certified Public Accountants
B2B	Business-to-business
B2C	Business-to-consumer
CFO	Chief Financial Officer
CMA	Certified Management Accountant
COGM	Cost of goods manufactured
COGS	Cost of goods sold
CPA	Certified Public Accountant
Cr.	Credit
CVP	Cost-volume-profit
Dr.	Debit
EFT	Electronic funds transfer
EPS	Earnings per share
ERP	Enterprise resource planning
FASB	Financial Accounting Standards Board
FICA tax	Federal Insurance Contributions Act tax
FIFO	First-in, first-out
FOB	Free on board
FUTA	Federal unemployment compensation tax
GAAP	Generally accepted accounting principles
IASB	International Accounting Standards Board
IFRS	International Financial Reporting Standards
IMA	Institute of Management Accountants
IRC	Internal Revenue Code
IRR	Internal rate of return
IRS	Internal Revenue Service
JIT	Just-in-time
LIFO	Last-in, first-out
LCM	Lower of cost or market
MACRS	Modified Accelerated Cost Recovery System
MD&A	Management's Discussion and Analysis
n/30	Net 30
n/eom	Net, end-of-month
NPV	Net present value
NSF	Not sufficient funds
P/E Ratio	Price-earnings ratio
POS	Point of sale
ROI	Return on investment
R&D	Research and development
SCM	Supply chain management
SEC	Securities and Exchange Commission
SOX	Sarbanes-Oxley Act
TQC	Total quality control
W-4	Employee's Withholding Allowance Certificate
WIP	Work in process

Classification of Accounts

Account Title	Account Classification	Normal Balance	Financial Statement
Accounts Payable	Current liability	Credit	Balance sheet
Accounts Receivable	Current asset	Debit	Balance sheet
Accumulated Depletion	Contra fixed asset	Credit	Balance sheet
Accumulated Depreciation	Contra fixed asset	Credit	Balance sheet
Advertising Expense	Operating expense	Debit	Income statement
Allowance for Doubtful Accounts	Contra current asset	Credit	Balance sheet
Amortization Expense	Operating expense	Debit	Income statement
Bonds Payable	Long-term liability	Credit	Balance sheet
Building	Fixed asset	Debit	Balance sheet
Cash	Current asset	Debit	Balance sheet
Cash Dividends	Stockholders' equity	Debit	Retained earnings statement
Cash Dividends Payable	Current liability	Credit	Balance sheet
Common Stock	Stockholders' equity	Credit	Balance sheet
Cost of Goods Sold	Cost of goods sold	Debit	Income statement
Customer Refunds Payable	Current liability	Credit	Balance sheet
Delivery Expense	Operating expense	Debit	Income statement
Depletion Expense	Operating expense	Debit	Income statement
Discount on Bonds Payable	Long-term liability	Debit	Balance sheet
Dividend Revenue	Other income	Credit	Income statement
Dividends	Stockholders' equity	Debit	Retained earnings statement
Employees Federal Income Tax Payable	Current liability	Credit	Balance sheet
Equipment	Fixed asset	Debit	Balance sheet
Estimated Returns Inventory	Current asset	Debit	Balance sheet
Factory Overhead (Overapplied)	Deferred credit	Credit	Balance sheet (interim)
Factory Overhead (Underapplied)	Deferred debit	Debit	Balance sheet (interim)
Federal Income Tax Payable	Current liability	Credit	Balance sheet
Federal Unemployment Tax Payable	Current liability	Credit	Balance sheet
Finished Goods	Current asset	Debit	Balance sheet
Freight In	Cost of goods sold	Debit	Income statement
Freight Out	Operating expense	Debit	Income statement
Gain on Disposal of Fixed Assets	Other income	Credit	Income statement
Gain on Redemption of Bonds	Other income	Credit	Income statement
Gain on Sale of Investments	Other income	Credit	Income statement
Goodwill	Intangible asset	Debit	Balance sheet
Income Tax Expense	Income tax	Debit	Income statement
Income Tax Payable	Current liability	Credit	Balance sheet
Insurance Expense	Operating expense	Debit	Income statement
Interest Expense	Other expense	Debit	Income statement
Interest Receivable	Current asset	Debit	Balance sheet
Interest Revenue	Other income	Credit	Income statement
Inventory	Current asset/Cost of goods sold	Debit	Balance sheet/Income statement
Investment in Bonds	Investment	Debit	Balance sheet
Investment in Stocks	Investment	Debit	Balance sheet
Investment in Subsidiary	Investment	Debit	Balance sheet
Land	Fixed asset	Debit	Balance sheet
Loss on Disposal of Fixed Assets	Other expense	Debit	Income statement
Loss on Redemption of Bonds	Other expense	Debit	Income statement

I-16

Account Title	Account Classification	Normal Balance	Financial Statement
Loss on Sale of Investments	Other expense	Debit	Income statement
Marketable Securities	Current asset	Debit	Balance sheet
Materials	Current asset	Debit	Balance sheet
Medicare Tax Payable	Current liability	Credit	Balance sheet
Notes Payable	Current liability/Long-term liability	Credit	Balance sheet
Notes Receivable	Current asset/Investment	Debit	Balance sheet
Patents	Intangible asset	Debit	Balance sheet
Paid-In Capital from Sale of Treasury Stock	Stockholders' equity	Credit	Balance sheet
Paid-In Capital in Excess of Par (Stated Value)	Stockholders' equity	Credit	Balance sheet
Payroll Tax Expense	Operating expense	Debit	Income statement
Pension Expense	Operating expense	Debit	Income statement
Petty Cash	Current asset	Debit	Balance sheet
Preferred Stock	Stockholders' equity	Credit	Balance sheet
Premium on Bonds Payable	Long-term liability	Credit	Balance sheet
Prepaid Insurance	Current asset	Debit	Balance sheet
Prepaid Rent	Current asset	Debit	Balance sheet
Purchases	Cost of goods sold	Debit	Income statement
Purchases Discounts	Cost of goods sold	Credit	Income statement
Purchases Returns and Allowances	Cost of goods sold	Credit	Income statement
Rent Expense	Operating expense	Debit	Income statement
Rent Revenue	Other income	Credit	Income statement
Retained Earnings	Stockholders' equity	Credit	Balance sheet/Retained earnings statement
Salaries Expense	Operating expense	Debit	Income statement
Salaries Payable	Current liability	Credit	Balance sheet
Sales Tax Payable	Current liability	Credit	Balance sheet
Social Security Tax Payable	Current liability	Credit	Balance sheet
State Unemployment Tax Payable	Current liability	Credit	Balance sheet
Stock Dividends	Stockholders' equity	Debit	Retained earnings statement
Stock Dividends Distributable	Stockholders' equity	Credit	Balance sheet
Supplies	Current asset	Debit	Balance sheet
Supplies Expense	Operating expense	Debit	Income statement
Treasury Stock	Stockholders' equity	Debit	Balance sheet
Uncollectible Accounts Expense	Operating expense	Debit	Income statement
Unearned Rent	Current liability	Credit	Balance sheet
Utilities Expense	Operating expense	Debit	Income statement
Vacation Pay Expense	Operating expense	Debit	Income statement
Vacation Pay Payable	Current liability/Long-term liability	Credit	Balance sheet
Work in Process	Current asset	Debit	Balance sheet

Abbreviations and Acronyms Commonly Used in Business and Accounting

AAA	American Accounting Association
ABC	Activity-based costing
AICPA	American Institute of Certified Public Accountants
B2B	Business-to-business
B2C	Business-to-consumer
CFO	Chief Financial Officer
CMA	Certified Management Accountant
COGM	Cost of goods manufactured
COGS	Cost of goods sold
CPA	Certified Public Accountant
Cr.	Credit
CVP	Cost-volume-profit
Dr.	Debit
EFT	Electronic funds transfer
EPS	Earnings per share
ERP	Enterprise resource planning
FASB	Financial Accounting Standards Board
FICA tax	Federal Insurance Contributions Act tax
FIFO	First-in, first-out
FOB	Free on board
FUTA	Federal unemployment compensation tax
GAAP	Generally accepted accounting principles
IASB	International Accounting Standards Board
IFRS	International Financial Reporting Standards
IMA	Institute of Management Accountants
IRC	Internal Revenue Code
IRR	Internal rate of return
IRS	Internal Revenue Service
JIT	Just-in-time
LIFO	Last-in, first-out
LCM	Lower of cost or market
MACRS	Modified Accelerated Cost Recovery System
MD&A	Management's Discussion and Analysis
n/30	Net 30
n/eom	Net, end-of-month
NPV	Net present value
NSF	Not sufficient funds
P/E Ratio	Price-earnings ratio
POS	Point of sale
ROI	Return on investment
R&D	Research and development
SCM	Supply chain management
SEC	Securities and Exchange Commission
SOX	Sarbanes-Oxley Act
TQC	Total quality control
W-4	Employee's Withholding Allowance Certificate
WIP	Work in process

Classification of Accounts

Account Title	Account Classification	Normal Balance	Financial Statement
Accounts Payable	Current liability	Credit	Balance sheet
Accounts Receivable	Current asset	Debit	Balance sheet
Accumulated Depletion	Contra fixed asset	Credit	Balance sheet
Accumulated Depreciation	Contra fixed asset	Credit	Balance sheet
Advertising Expense	Operating expense	Debit	Income statement
Allowance for Doubtful Accounts	Contra current asset	Credit	Balance sheet
Amortization Expense	Operating expense	Debit	Income statement
Bonds Payable	Long-term liability	Credit	Balance sheet
Building	Fixed asset	Debit	Balance sheet
Cash	Current asset	Debit	Balance sheet
Cash Dividends	Stockholders' equity	Debit	Retained earnings statement
Cash Dividends Payable	Current liability	Credit	Balance sheet
Common Stock	Stockholders' equity	Credit	Balance sheet
Cost of Goods Sold	Cost of goods sold	Debit	Income statement
Customer Refunds Payable	Current liability	Credit	Balance sheet
Delivery Expense	Operating expense	Debit	Income statement
Depletion Expense	Operating expense	Debit	Income statement
Discount on Bonds Payable	Long-term liability	Debit	Balance sheet
Dividend Revenue	Other income	Credit	Income statement
Dividends	Stockholders' equity	Debit	Retained earnings statement
Employees Federal Income Tax Payable	Current liability	Credit	Balance sheet
Equipment	Fixed asset	Debit	Balance sheet
Estimated Returns Inventory	Current asset	Debit	Balance sheet
Factory Overhead (Overapplied)	Deferred credit	Credit	Balance sheet (interim)
Factory Overhead (Underapplied)	Deferred debit	Debit	Balance sheet (interim)
Federal Income Tax Payable	Current liability	Credit	Balance sheet
Federal Unemployment Tax Payable	Current liability	Credit	Balance sheet
Finished Goods	Current asset	Debit	Balance sheet
Freight In	Cost of goods sold	Debit	Income statement
Freight Out	Operating expense	Debit	Income statement
Gain on Disposal of Fixed Assets	Other income	Credit	Income statement
Gain on Redemption of Bonds	Other income	Credit	Income statement
Gain on Sale of Investments	Other income	Credit	Income statement
Goodwill	Intangible asset	Debit	Balance sheet
Income Tax Expense	Income tax	Debit	Income statement
Income Tax Payable	Current liability	Credit	Balance sheet
Insurance Expense	Operating expense	Debit	Income statement
Interest Expense	Other expense	Debit	Income statement
Interest Receivable	Current asset	Debit	Balance sheet
Interest Revenue	Other income	Credit	Income statement
Inventory	Current asset/Cost of goods sold	Debit	Balance sheet/Income statement
Investment in Bonds	Investment	Debit	Balance sheet
Investment in Stocks	Investment	Debit	Balance sheet
Investment in Subsidiary	Investment	Debit	Balance sheet
Land	Fixed asset	Debit	Balance sheet
Loss on Disposal of Fixed Assets	Other expense	Debit	Income statement
Loss on Redemption of Bonds	Other expense	Debit	Income statement